2024
Big Easy Read
BRITAIN

T0318186

Scale 1:160,000
or 2.52 miles to 1 inch

19th edition June 2023 © AA Media Limited 2023
Original edition printed 1991.

All cartography in this atlas edited, designed and produced by the Mapping Services Department of AA Media Limited (A05839).

This atlas contains Ordnance Survey data © Crown copyright and database right 2023. Contains public sector information licensed under the Open Government Licence v3.0. Distances and journey times contains data available from openstreetmap.org © under the Open Database License found at opendatacommons.org

Published by AA Media Limited, whose registered office is Grove House, Lutyens Close, Basingstoke, Hampshire RG24 8AG, UK.
Registered number 06112600

ISBN: 978 0 7495 8332 3 (spiral bound)
ISBN: 978 0 7495 8331 6 (paperback)

A CIP catalogue record for this book is available from The British Library.

Disclaimer: The contents of this atlas are believed to be correct at the time of the latest revision, it will not contain any subsequent amended, new or temporary information including diversions and traffic control or enforcement systems. The publishers cannot be held responsible or liable for any loss or damage occasioned to any person acting or refraining from action as a result of any use or reliance on material in this atlas, nor for any errors, omissions or changes in such material. This does not affect your statutory rights.

The publishers would welcome information to correct any errors or omissions and to keep this atlas up to date. Please write to the Atlas Editor, AA Media Limited, Grove House, Lutyens Close, Basingstoke, Hampshire RG24 8AG, UK.
E-mail: roadatlasfeedback@aamediagroup.co.uk

Acknowledgements: AA Media Limited would like to thank the following for information used in the creation of this atlas:
Cadw, English Heritage, Forestry Commission, Historic Scotland, National Trust and National Trust for Scotland, RSPB, The Wildlife Trust, Scottish Natural Heritage, Natural England, The Countryside Council for Wales. Award winning beaches from 'Blue Flag' and 'Keep Scotland Beautiful' (summer 2022 data): for latest information visit www.blueflag.org and www.keepscotlandbeautiful.org. Road signs are © Crown Copyright 2023. Reproduced under the terms of the Open Government Licence.
Printed by 1010 Printing International Ltd, China

* The UK's most up-to-date atlases based on a comparison of 2023 UK Road Atlases available on the market in November 2022.

Contents

Map pages	inside front cover
Route planning	**II–XII**
Route planner	II–V
Caravan and camping sites in Britain	VI–VII
Traffic signs and road markings	VIII–IX
Ferries and port plans	X–XII
Motorways	**XIII–XVI**
Restricted junctions	XIII
M25 London Orbital motorway	XIV
M6 Toll motorway	XV
Smart motorways	XVI
Atlas symbols	**1**
Road maps 1:160,000 scale	**2–152**
Channel Islands 1:113,000 scale	12–13
Isle of Man 1:200,000 scale	102
Orkney and Shetland Islands 1:605,000 scale	147
Western Isles 1:528,000 scale	152

Ferry ports

Aberdeen Harbour..........XII	Harwich International	Liverpool Docks.............XII	Port of Tyne....................XII
Calais X	Port XII	Newhaven Harbour XI	Portsmouth Harbour........X
Channel Tunnel..............XI	Heysham Harbour XII	Pembroke Dock XII	Southampton, Port of......X
Dover, Port of XI	Holyhead Harbour XII	Plymouth, Port of X	
Fishguard Harbour........XII	Hull, Port of XII	Poole, Port of X	

Town plans

Aberdeen....................133	Durham 154	London.........................156	St Andrews..................125
Aberystwyth 48	Edinburgh...................154	Manchester 156	Salisbury.....................157
Bath 153	Exeter.............................9	Middlesbrough 93	Scarborough 93
Birmingham.................153	Glasgow 155	Milton Keynes..............156	Sheffield 157
Blackpool 82	Great Yarmouth 71	Newcastle upon	Shrewsbury 157
Bradford 153	Harrogate 155	Tyne............................101	Southampton 158
Bristol 153	Inverness....................155	Newquay 3	Southend-on-Sea.........35
Cambridge 153	Ipswich.........................47	Norwich 156	Stratford-upon-Avon....158
Canterbury 153	Kingston upon Hull......155	Nottingham 156	Sunderland..................101
Cardiff........................154	Leeds 155	Oxford 157	Swansea 26
Chester 154	Leicester....................155	Peterborough 157	Swindon 158
Coventry.....................154	Lincoln........................156	Plymouth 4	Wolverhampton 158
Derby 154	Liverpool.......................74	Portsmouth 157	Worcester....................158
Dundee 125	Llandudno 73	Ramsgate......................35	York.............................158

Tourist sites with satnav friendly postcodes	**159**
London district map	**160–161**
Index to place names	**162–192**
County, administrative area map	162
Place name index	162–192
Distances and journey times	**inside back cover**

Discover quality and friendly
B&Bs at RatedTrips.com

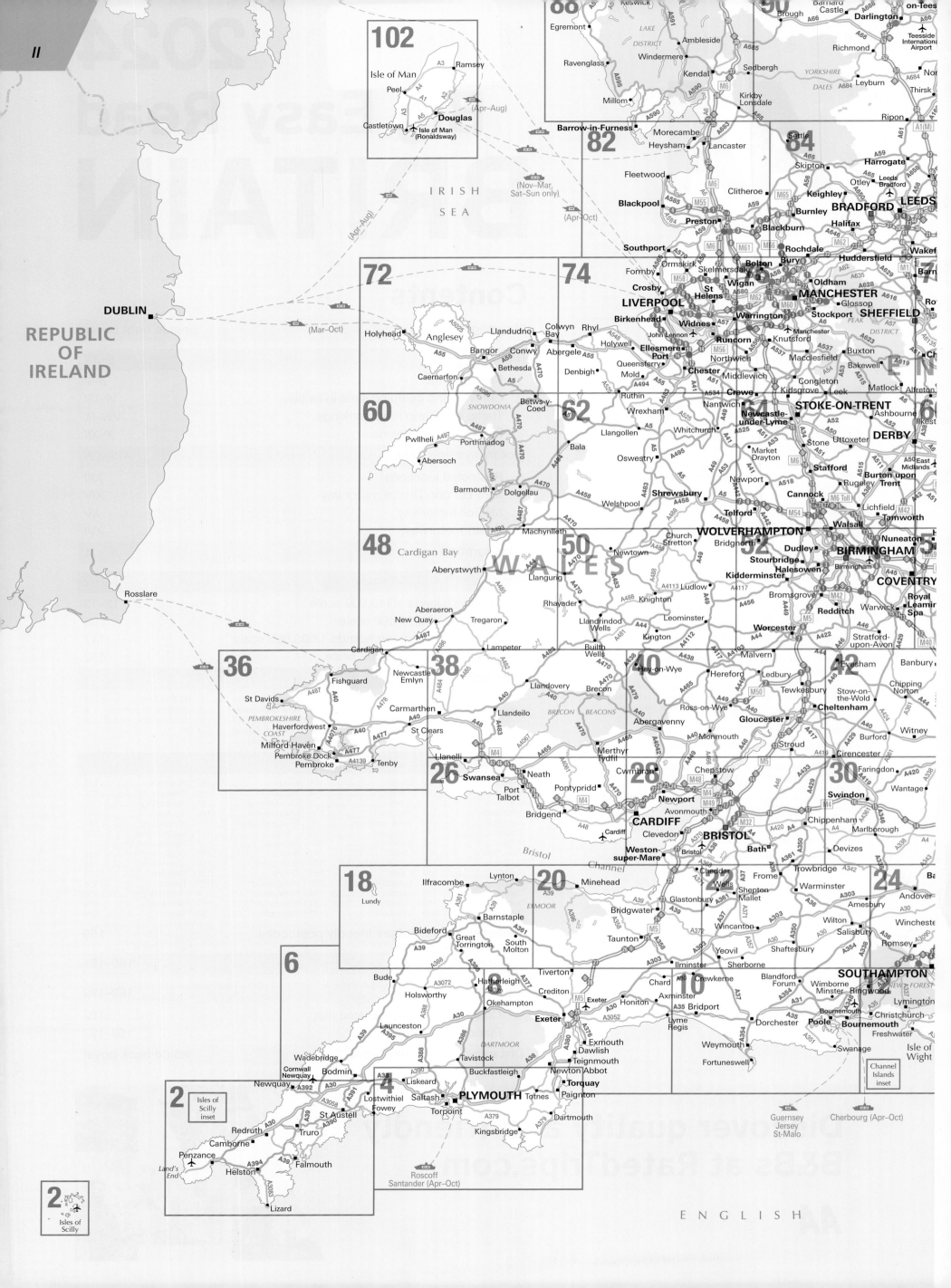

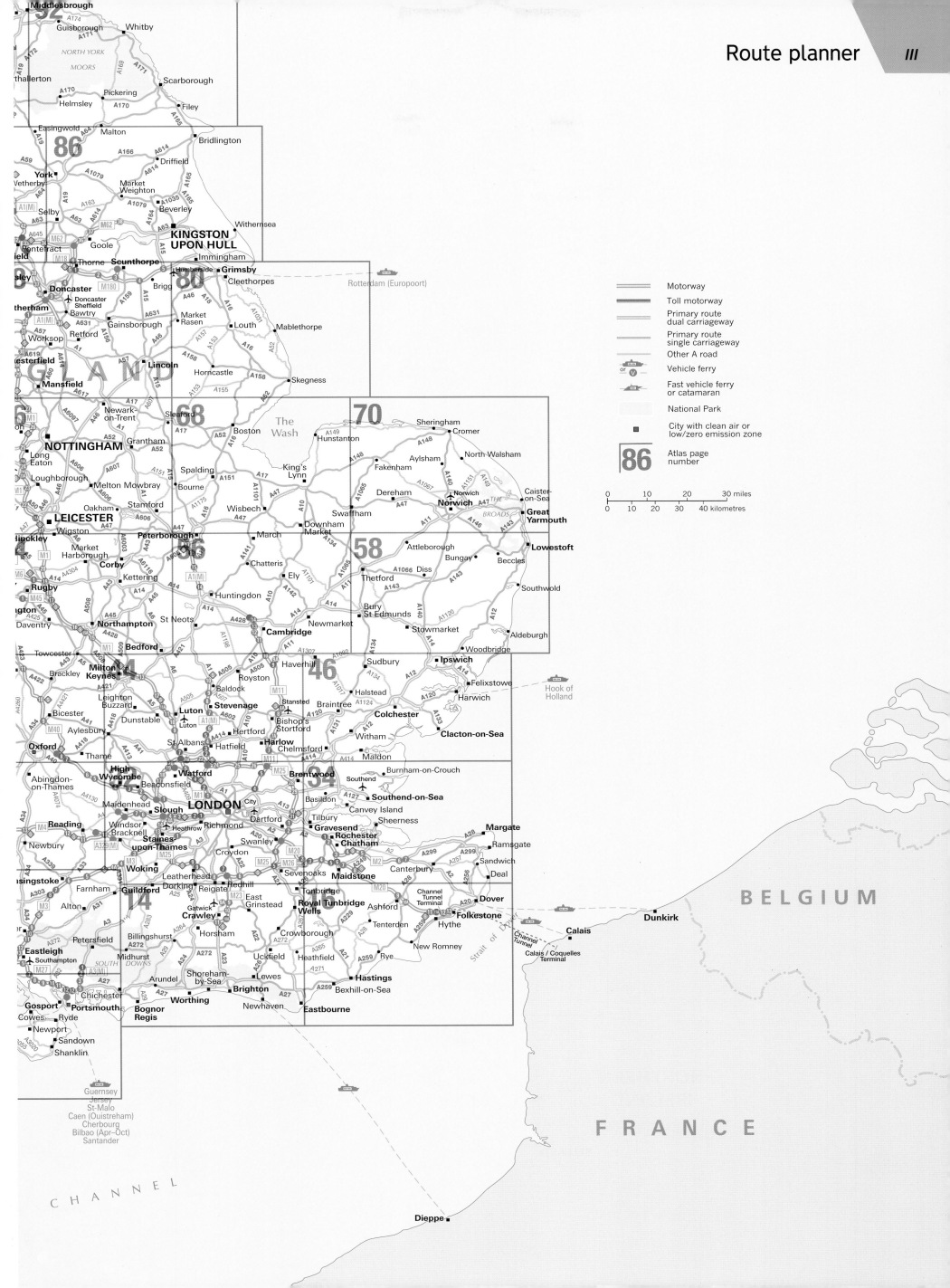

Legend

	Motorway
	Toll motorway
	Primary route dual carriageway
	Primary route single carriageway
	Other A road
or V	Vehicle ferry
	Fast vehicle ferry or catamaran
	National Park
■	City with clean air or low/zero emission zone
86	Atlas page number

0   10   20   30 miles
0   10   20   30   40 kilometres

BELGIUM

FRANCE

CHANNEL

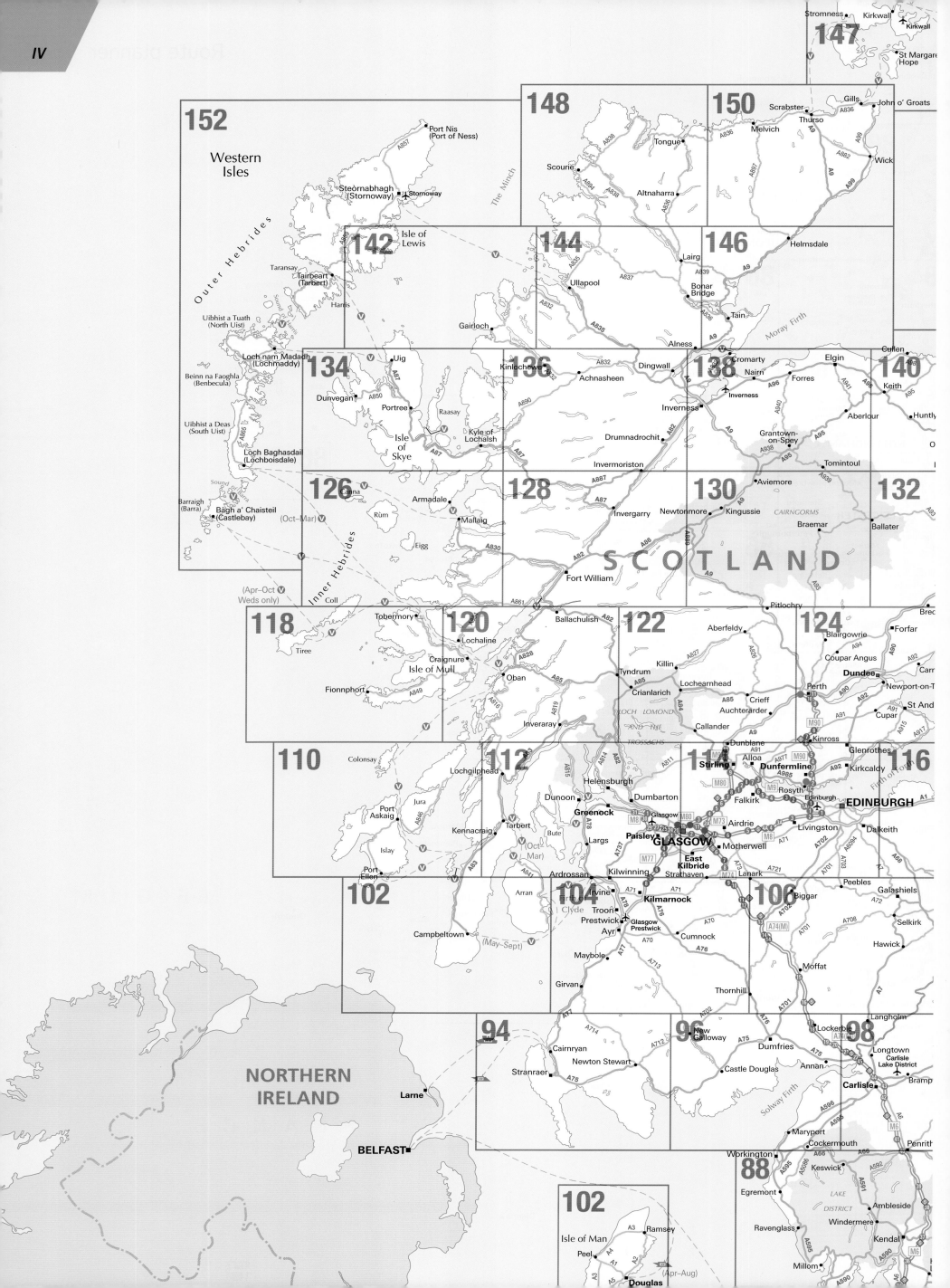

147
Orkney
Islands

147
Shetland
Islands

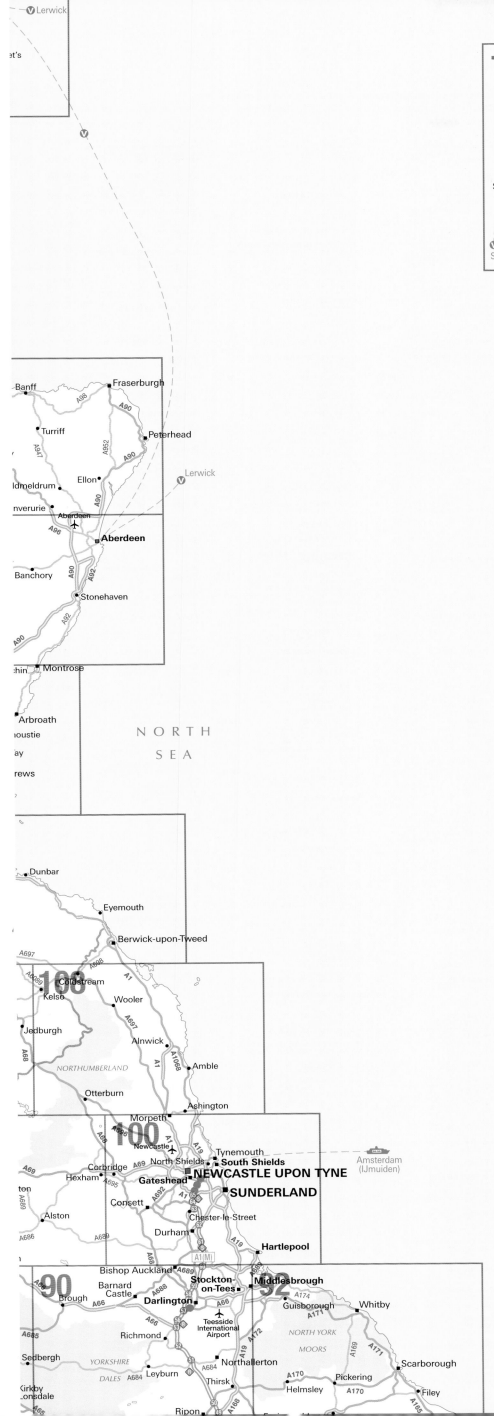

EMERGENCY DIVERSION ROUTES

In an emergency it may be necessary to close a section of motorway or other main road to traffic, so a temporary sign may advise drivers to follow a diversion route. To help drivers navigate the route, black symbols on yellow patches may be permanently displayed on existing direction signs, including motorway signs. Symbols may also be used on separate signs with yellow backgrounds.

FERRY INFORMATION

Information on ferry routes and operators can be found on pages X–XII.

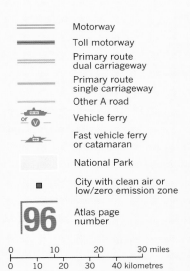

	Motorway
	Toll motorway
	Primary route dual carriageway
	Primary route single carriageway
	Other A road
	Vehicle ferry
	Fast vehicle ferry or catamaran
	National Park
	City with clean air or low/zero emission zone
96	Atlas page number

0   10   20   30 miles
0   10   20   30   40 kilometres

Caravan and camping sites in Britain

These pages list the top 300 AA-inspected Caravan and Camping (C & C) sites in the Pennant rating scheme. **Five Pennant Premier sites are shown in green,** Four Pennant sites are shown in blue.
Listings include addresses, telephone numbers and websites together with page and grid references to locate the sites in the atlas. The total number of touring pitches is also included for each site, together with the type of pitch available.
The following abbreviations are used: **C = Caravan CV = Campervan T = Tent**
To discover more AA-rated caravan and camping sites not included on these pages please visit **RatedTrips.com**

ENGLAND

Alders Caravan Park
Home Farm, Alne, York
YO61 1RY
Tel: 01347 838722 85 P2
alderscaravanpark.co.uk
Total Pitches: 87 (C, CV & T)

Andrewshayes Holiday Park
Dalwood, Axminster
EX13 7DY
Tel: 01404 831225 9 N5
andrewshayes.co.uk
Total Pitches: 150 (C, CV & T)

Atlantic Bays Holiday Park
Padstow, Cornwall
PL28 8PY
Tel: 01841 520855 6 C10
atlanticbaysholidaypark.co.uk
Total Pitches: 70 (C, CV & T)

Ayr Holiday Park
St Ives, Cornwall
TR26 1EJ
Tel: 01736 795855 2 E6
ayrholidaypark.co.uk
Total Pitches: 100 (C, CV & T)

Back of Beyond Touring Park
234 Ringwood Road,
St Leonards, Dorset
BH24 2SB
Tel: 01202 876968 11 Q4
backofbeyondtouringpark.co.uk
Total Pitches: 80 (C, CV & T)

Bagwell Farm Touring Park
Knights in the Bottom, Chickerell,
Weymouth
DT3 4EA
Tel: 01305 782575 10 G8
bagwellfarm.co.uk
Total Pitches: 320 (C, CV & T)

Bardsea Leisure Park
Priory Road, Ulverston
LA12 9QE
Tel: 01229 584712 89 J11
bardsealeisure.co.uk
Total Pitches: 83 (C & CV)

Bath Chew Valley Caravan Park
Ham Lane, Bishop Sutton
BS39 5TZ
Tel: 01275 332127 29 J10
bathchewvalley.co.uk
Total Pitches: 45 (C, CV & T)

Bay View Farm C & C Park
Croyde, Devon
EX33 1PN
Tel: 01271 890501 19 J6
bayviewfarm.co.uk
Total Pitches: 70 (C, CV & T)

Bay View Holiday Park
Bolton le Sands, Carnforth
LA5 9TN
Tel: 01524 732854 83 L1
holgates.co.uk
Total Pitches: 100 (C, CV & T)

Beacon Cottage Farm Touring Park
Beacon Drive, St Agnes
TR5 0NU
Tel: 01872 552347 2 H4
beaconcottagefarmholidays.co.uk
Total Pitches: 60 (C, CV & T)

Beaconsfield Holiday Park
Battlefield, Shrewsbury
SY4 4AA
Tel: 01939 210370 63 N8
beaconsfieldholidaypark.co.uk
Total Pitches: 60 (C & CV)

Beech Croft Farm C & C Park
Beech Croft, Blackwell in the Peak,
Buxton
SK17 9TQ
Tel: 01298 85330 77 L9
beechcroftfarm.co.uk
Total Pitches: 30 (C, CV & T)

Bellingham C & C Club Site
Brown Rigg, Bellingham
NE48 2JY
Tel: 01434 220175 99 N2
campingandcaravanningclub.co.uk/bellingham
Total Pitches: 64 (C, CV & T)

Beverley Park C & C Park
Goodrington Road, Paignton
TQ4 7JE
Tel: 01803 843887 5 Q5
beverley-holidays.co.uk
Total Pitches: 149 (C, CV & T)

Birchwood Tourist Park
Bere Road, Coldharbour, Wareham
BH20 7PA
Tel: 01929 554763 11 L6
birchwoodtouristpark.co.uk
Total Pitches: 175 (C, CV & T)

Blue Rose Caravan & Country Park
Star Carr Lane, Brandesburton
YO25 8RU
Tel: 01964 543366 87 L6
bluerosepark.com
Total Pitches: 58 (C & CV)

Briarfields Motel & Touring Park
Gloucester Road, Cheltenham
GL51 0SX
Tel: 01242 235324 41 P7
briarfields.net
Total Pitches: 72 (C, CV & T)

Bridge House Marina & Caravan Park
Nateby Crossing Lane, Nateby,
Garstang
PR3 0JJ
Tel: 01995 603207 83 L6
bridgehousemarina.co.uk
Total Pitches: 50 (C & CV)

Broadhembury C & C Park
Steeds Lane, Kingsnorth, Ashford
TN26 1NQ
Tel: 01233 620859 16 H3
broadhembury.co.uk
Total Pitches: 100 (C, CV & T)

Brook Lodge Farm C & C Park
Cowslip Green, Redhill, Bristol,
Somerset
BS40 5RB
Tel: 01934 862311 28 G10
brooklodgefarm.com
Total Pitches: 29 (C, CV & T)

Burnham-on-Sea Holiday Village
Marine Drive, Burnham-on-Sea
TA8 1LA
Tel: 01278 783391 21 M4
haven.com/burnhamonsea
Total Pitches: 75 (C, CV & T)

Burns Farm C & C
St Johns in the Vale, Keswick
CA12 4RR
Tel: 017687 79225 89 J2
burns-farm.co.uk
Total Pitches: 32 (C, CV & T)

Burrowhayes Farm C & C Site
& Riding Stables
West Luccombe, Porlock,
Minehead
TA24 8HT
Tel: 01643 862463 20 D4
burrowhayes.co.uk
Total Pitches: 120 (C, CV & T)

Burton Constable Holiday Park
& Arboretum
Old Lodges, Sproatley, Hull
HU11 4LJ
Tel: 01964 562508 87 M8
burtonconstableholidaypark.co.uk
Total Pitches: 105 (C, CV & T)

Caistor Lakes
99a Brigg Road, Caistor
LN7 6RX
Tel: 01472 859626 80 B3
caistorlakes.co.uk
Total Pitches: 28 (C & CV)

Cakes & Ale
Abbey Lane, Theberton, Leiston
IP16 4TE
Tel: 01728 831655 59 N8
cakesandale.co.uk
Total Pitches: 55 (C, CV & T)

Calloose C & C Park
Leedstown, Hayle
TR27 5ET
Tel: 01736 850431 2 F7
calloose.co.uk
Total Pitches: 109 (C, CV & T)

Camping Caradon Touring Park
Trelawne, Looe
PL13 2NA
Tel: 01503 272388 4 C6
campingcaradon.co.uk
Total Pitches: 75 (C, CV & T)

Capesthorne Hall
Congleton Road, Siddington,
Macclesfield
SK11 9JY
Tel: 01625 861221 76 F9
capesthorne.com/caravan-park
Total Pitches: 50 (C & CV)

Carlyon Bay C & C Park
Bethesda, Cypress Avenue,
Carlyon Bay
PL25 3RE
Tel: 01726 812735 3 P4
carlyonbay.net
Total Pitches: 180 (C, CV & T)

Carnevas Holiday Park
Carnevas Farm, St Merryn, Cornwall
PL28 8PN
Tel: 01841 520230 6 B10
carnevasholidaypark.com
Total Pitches: 195 (C, CV & T)

Cartref C & C
Cartref, Ford Heath, Shrewsbury,
Shropshire
SY5 9GD
Tel: 01743 821688 63 L10
cartrefcaravansite.co.uk
Total Pitches: 44 (C, CV & T)

Carvynick Holiday Park
Summercourt, Newquay
TR8 5AF
Tel: 01872 510716 3 L3
carvynick.co.uk
Total Pitches: 47 (C, CV & T)

Castlerigg Hall C & C Park
Castlerigg Hall, Keswick
CA12 4TE
Tel: 017687 74499 89 J2
castlerigg.co.uk
Total Pitches: 68 (C, CV & T)

Cheddar Mendip Heights
C & C Club Site
Townsend, Priddy, Wells
BA5 3BP
Tel: 01749 870241 22 C3
campingandcaravanningclub.co.uk/cheddar
Total Pitches: 90 (C, CV & T)

Chy Carne Holiday Park
Kuggar, Ruan Minor, Helston,
Cornwall
TR12 7LX
Tel: 01326 290200 2 H11
chycarne.co.uk
Total Pitches: 30 (C, CV & T)

Clippesby Hall
Hall Lane, Clippesby, Great Yarmouth
NR29 3BL
Tel: 01493 367800 71 N9
clippesbyhall.com
Total Pitches: 120 (C, CV & T)

Cofton Holidays
Starcross, Dawlish
EX6 8RP
Tel: 01626 890111 8 H8
coftonholidays.co.uk
Total Pitches: 450 (C, CV & T)

Concierge Camping
Ratham Estate, Ratham Lane,
West Ashling, Chichester
PO18 8DL
Tel: 01243 573118 13 P3
conciergecamping.co.uk
Total Pitches: 27 (C & CV)

Coombe Touring Park
Race Plain, Netherhampton,
Salisbury
SP2 8PN
Tel: 01722 328451 23 N7
coombecaravanpark.co.uk
Total Pitches: 50 (C, CV & T)

Cornish Farm Touring Park
Shoreditch, Taunton
TA3 7BS
Tel: 01823 327746 21 K9
cornishfarm.com
Total Pitches: 48 (C, CV & T)

Cosawes Park
Perranarworthal, Truro
TR3 7QS
Tel: 01872 863724 3 J7
cosawes.co.uk
Total Pitches: 59 (C, CV & T)

Cote Ghyll C & C Park
Osmotherley, Northallerton
DL6 3AH
Tel: 01609 883425 91 Q7
coteghyll.com
Total Pitches: 95 (C, CV & T)

Country View Holiday Park
Sand Road, Sand Bay,
Weston-super-Mare
BS22 9UJ
Tel: 01934 627595 28 D9
cvhp.co.uk
Total Pitches: 190 (C, CV & T)

Crealy Theme Park & Resort
Sidmouth Road, Clyst St Mary, Exeter
EX5 1DR
Tel: 01395 234888 9 J6
crealy.co.uk
Total Pitches: 120 (C, CV & T)

Crows Nest Caravan Park
Gristhorpe, Filey
YO14 9PS
Tel: 01723 582206 93 M10
crowsnestcaravanpark.com
Total Pitches: 43 (C, CV & T)

Deepdale Backpackers & Camping
Deepdale Farm,
Burnham Deepdale
PE31 8DD
Tel: 01485 210256 69 Q3
deepdalebackpackers.co.uk
Total Pitches: 80 (CV & T)

Dibles Park
Dibles Road, Warsash,
Southampton, Hampshire
SO31 9SA
Tel: 01489 575232 12 H3
diblespark.co.uk
Total Pitches: 11 (C, CV & T)

Dornafield
Dornafield Farm, Two Mile Oak,
Newton Abbot
TQ12 6DD
Tel: 01803 812732 5 P3
dornafield.com
Total Pitches: 135 (C, CV & T)

East Fleet Farm Touring Park
Chickerell, Weymouth
DT3 4DW
Tel: 01305 785768 10 G9
eastfleet.co.uk
Total Pitches: 400 (C, CV & T)

Eastham Hall Holiday Park
Saltcotes Road,
Lytham St Annes,
Lancashire
FY8 4LS
Tel: 01253 737907 83 J9
easthamhall.co.uk
Total Pitches: 113 (C & CV)

Eden Valley Holiday Park
Lanlivery, Nr Lostwithiel
PL30 5BU
Tel: 01208 872277 3 Q3
edenvalleyholidaypark.co.uk
Total Pitches: 56 (C, CV & T)

Exe Valley Caravan Site
Mill House, Bridgetown, Dulverton
TA22 9JR
Tel: 01643 851432 20 E7
exevalleycamping.co.uk
Total Pitches: 48 (C, CV & T)

Eye Kettleby Lakes
Eye Kettleby, Melton Mowbray
LE14 2TN
Tel: 01664 565900 67 J9
eyekettlebylakes.com
Total Pitches: 130 (C, CV & T)

Fernwood Caravan Park
Lyneal, Ellesmere, Shropshire
SY12 0QF
Tel: 01948 710221 63 M5
fernwoodpark.co.uk
Total Pitches: 60 (C & CV)

Fields End Water Caravan Park & Fishery
Benwick Road, Doddington,
March
PE15 0TY
Tel: 01354 740199 56 G2
fieldsendwater.co.uk
Total Pitches: 80 (C, CV & T)

Flaxton Meadows
York Lane, Flaxton, York
YO60 7QZ
Tel: 01904 393943 86 C3
flaxtonmeadows.co.uk
Total Pitches: 35 (C, CV & T)

Flower of May Holiday Park
Lebberston Cliff, Filey,
Scarborough
YO11 3NU
Tel: 01723 584311 93 M10
flowerofmay.com
Total Pitches: 300 (C, CV & T)

Forest Glade Holiday Park
Near Kentisbeare, Cullompton,
Devon
EX15 2DT
Tel: 01404 841381 9 L3
forest-glade.co.uk
Total Pitches: 80 (C, CV & T)

Freshwater Beach Holiday Park
Burton Bradstock, Bridport
DT6 4PT
Tel: 01308 897317 10 D7
freshwaterbeach.co.uk
Total Pitches: 500 (C, CV & T)

Glenfield Caravan Park
Blackmoor Lane, Bardsey,
Leeds
LS17 9DZ
Tel: 01937 574657 85 M7
glenfieldcaravanpark.co.uk
Total Pitches: 30 (C, CV & T)

Globe Vale Holiday Park
Radnor, Redruth
TR16 4BH
Tel: 01209 891183 2 H5
globevale.co.uk
Total Pitches: 138 (C, CV & T)

Glororum Caravan Park
Glororum Farm, Bamburgh
NE69 7AW
Tel: 01670 860256 109 K3
northumbrianleisure.co.uk
Total Pitches: 43 (C & CV)

Golden Cap Holiday Park
Seatown, Chideock, Bridport
DT6 6JX
Tel: 01308 422139 10 C6
wdlh.co.uk
Total Pitches: 108 (C, CV & T)

Golden Coast Holiday Park
Station Road, Woolacombe
EX34 7HW
Tel: 01271 872302 19 J5
woolacombe.com
Total Pitches: 89 (C, CV & T)

Golden Sands Holiday Park
Quebec Road, Mablethorpe
LN12 1QJ
Tel: 01507 477871 81 J6
haven.com/goldensands
Total Pitches: 172 (C, CV & T)

Golden Square C & C Park
Oswaldkirk, Helmsley
YO62 5YQ
Tel: 01439 788269 92 C10
goldensquarecaravanpark.com
Total Pitches: 129 (C, CV & T)

Golden Valley C & C Park
Coach Road, Ripley,
Derbyshire
DE55 4ES
Tel: 01773 513881 66 C2
goldenvalleycaravanpark.co.uk
Total Pitches: 45 (C, CV & T)

Goosewood Holiday Park
Sutton-on-the-Forest, York
YO61 1ET
Tel: 01347 810829 86 B3
flowerofmay.com
Total Pitches: 100 (C & CV)

Greenacre Place Touring Caravan Park
Bristol Road, Edithmead,
Highbridge
TA9 4HA
Tel: 01278 785227 21 M4
greenacreplace.com
Total Pitches: 10 (C & CV)

Green Acres Caravan Park
High Knells, Houghton, Carlisle
CA6 4JW
Tel: 01228 675418 98 E6
caravanpark-cumbria.com
Total Pitches: 35 (C, CV & T)

Greenhill Farm C & C Park
Greenhill Farm, New Road,
Landford, Salisbury
SP5 2AZ
Tel: 01794 324117 24 D9
greenhillfarm.co.uk
Total Pitches: 160 (C, CV & T)

Greenhills Holiday Park
Crowhill Lane, Bakewell, Derbyshire
DE45 1PX
Tel: 01629 813052 77 M10
greenhillsholidaypark.co.uk
Total Pitches: 172 (C, CV & T)

Grouse Hill Caravan Park
Flask Bungalow Farm, Fylingdales,
Robin Hood's Bay
YO22 4QH
Tel: 01947 880543 93 J7
grousehill.co.uk
Total Pitches: 175 (C, CV & T)

Gunvenna Holiday Park
St Minver, Wadebridge
PL27 6QN
Tel: 01208 862405 6 D9
gunvenna.com
Total Pitches: 75 (C, CV & T)

Haggerston Castle Holiday Park
Beal, Berwick-upon-Tweed
TD15 2PA
Tel: 01289 381333 108 G1
haven.com/haggerstoncastle
Total Pitches: 140 (C & CV)

Harbury Fields
Harbury Fields Farm, Harbury,
Nr Leamington Spa
CV33 9JN
Tel: 01926 612457 54 B8
harburyfields.co.uk
Total Pitches: 59 (C & CV)

Harford Bridge Holiday Park
Peter Tavy, Tavistock
PL19 9LS
Tel: 01822 810349 7 P9
harfordbridge.co.uk
Total Pitches: 125 (C, CV & T)

Haw Wood Farm Caravan Park
Hinton, Saxmundham
IP17 3QT
Tel: 01502 359550 59 N6
hawwoodfarm.co.uk
Total Pitches: 60 (C, CV & T)

Heathfield Farm Camping
Heathfield Road, Freshwater,
Isle of Wight
PO40 9SH
Tel: 01983 407822 12 E7
heathfieldcamping.co.uk
Total Pitches: 81 (C, CV & T)

Heathland Beach Holiday Park
London Road, Kessingland
NR33 7PJ
Tel: 01502 740337 59 Q3
heathlandbeach.co.uk
Total Pitches: 63 (C, CV & T)

Hendra Holiday Park
Newquay
TR8 4NY
Tel: 01637 875778 3 K2
hendra-holidays.com
Total Pitches: 548 (C, CV & T)

Herding Hill Farm Touring
& Camping Site
Shield Hill, Haltwhistle,
Northumberland
NE49 9NW
Tel: 01434 320175 99 K5
herdinghillfarm.co.uk
Total Pitches: 22 (C, CV & T)

Hidden Valley Park
West Down, Braunton,
Ilfracombe, Devon
EX34 8NU
Tel: 01271 813837 19 K5
hiddenvalleypark.com
Total Pitches: 114 (C, CV & T)

Highfield Farm Touring Park
Long Road, Comberton, Cambridge
CB23 7DG
Tel: 01223 262308 56 H9
highfieldfarmtouringpark.co.uk
Total Pitches: 120 (C, CV & T)

Highlands End Holiday Park
Eype, Bridport, Dorset
DT6 6AR
Tel: 01308 422139 10 C6
wdlh.co.uk
Total Pitches: 195 (C, CV & T)

Hill of Oaks & Blakeholme
Windermere
LA12 8NR
Tel: 015395 31578 89 K9
hillofoaks.co.uk
Total Pitches: 263 (C & CV)

Hillside Caravan Park
Canvas Farm, Moor Road,
Knayton, Thirsk
YO7 4BR
Tel: 01845 537349 91 Q9
hillsidecaravanpark.co.uk
Total Pitches: 60 (C & CV)

Holiday Resort Unity
Coast Road, Brean Sands,
Brean
TA8 2RB
Tel: 01278 751235 21 L3
hru.co.uk
Total Pitches: 453 (C, CV & T)

Hollins Farm C & C
Far Arnside, Carnforth
LA5 0SL
Tel: 01524 701767 89 M11
holgates.co.uk
Total Pitches: 12 (C, CV & T)

Hylton Caravan Park
Eden Street, Silloth
CA7 4AY
Tel: 016973 32666 97 M7
stanwix.com
Total Pitches: 90 (C, CV & T)

Island Lodge C & C Site
Stumpy Post Cross, Kingsbridge
TQ7 4BL
Tel: 01548 852956 5 M7
islandlodgesite.co.uk
Total Pitches: 30 (C, CV & T)

Isle of Avalon Touring Caravan Park
Godney Road, Glastonbury
BA6 9AF
Tel: 01458 833618 22 C5
avaloncaravanpark.co.uk
Total Pitches: 120 (C, CV & T)

Jasmine Caravan Park
Cross Lane, Snainton,
Scarborough
YO13 9BE
Tel: 01723 859240 93 J10
jasminepark.co.uk
Total Pitches: 68 (C, CV & T)

Kennford International Holiday Park
Kennford, Exeter
EX6 7YN
Tel: 01392 833046 8 G7
kennfordinternational.co.uk
Total Pitches: 22 (C, CV & T)

Killiwerris Touring Park
Penstraze, Chacewater, Truro, Cornwall
TR4 8PF
Tel: 01872 561356 3 J5
killiwerris.co.uk
Total Pitches: 17 (C & CV)

King's Lynn C & C Park
New Road, North Runcton, King's Lynn
PE33 0RA
Tel: 01553 840004 69 M9
kl-cc.co.uk
Total Pitches: 150 (C, CV & T)

Kneps Farm Holiday Caravan Park
River Road, Stanah, Thornton-Cleveleys,
Blackpool
FY5 5LR
Tel: 01253 823632 83 J6
knepsfarm.co.uk
Total Pitches: 40 (C & CV)

Knight Stainforth Hall
Caravan & Campsite
Stainforth, Settle
BD24 0DP
Tel: 01729 822200 84 B2
knightstainforth.co.uk
Total Pitches: 100 (C, CV & T)

Ladycross Plantation Caravan Park
Egton, Whitby
YO21 1UA
Tel: 01947 895502 92 G5
ladycrossplantation.co.uk
Total Pitches: 130 (C & CV)

Lady's Mile Holiday Park
Dawlish, Devon
EX7 0LX
Tel: 01626 863411 8 H9
ladysmile.co.uk
Total Pitches: 570 (C, CV & T)

Lakeland Leisure Park
Moor Lane, Flookburgh
LA11 7LT
Tel: 01539 558556 89 K12
haven.com/lakeland
Total Pitches: 177 (C, CV & T)

Lamb Cottage Caravan Park
Dalefords Lane, Whitegate, Northwich
CW8 2BN
Tel: 01606 882302 75 Q10
lambcottage.co.uk
Total Pitches: 45 (C & CV)

Langstone Manor C & C Park
Moortown, Tavistock
PL19 9JZ
Tel: 01822 613371 7 P10
langstonemanor.co.uk
Total Pitches: 40 (C, CV & T)

Lanyon Holiday Park
Loscombe Lane, Four Lanes, Redruth
TR16 6LP
Tel: 01209 313474 2 H7
lanyonholidaypark.co.uk
Total Pitches: 25 (C, CV & T)

Lickpenny Caravan Site
Lickpenny Lane, Tansley, Matlock
DE4 5GF
Tel: 01629 583040 77 Q11
lickpennycaravanpark.co.uk
Total Pitches: 80 (C & CV)

Lime Tree Park
Dukes Drive, Buxton
SK17 9RP
Tel: 01298 22988 77 K9
limetreeparkbuxton.com
Total Pitches: 106 (C, CV & T)

Lincoln Farm Park Oxfordshire
High Street, Standlake
OX29 7RH
Tel: 01865 300239 43 J11
lincolnfarmpark.co.uk
Total Pitches: 90 (C, CV & T)

Littlesea Holiday Park
Lynch Lane, Weymouth
DT4 9DT
Tel: 01305 774414 10 G9
haven.com/littlesea
Total Pitches: 141 (C, CV & T)

Little Trevothan C & C Park
Trevothan, Coverack, Helston, Cornwall
TR12 6SD
Tel: 01326 280260 3 J11
littletrevothan.co.uk
Total Pitches: 80 (C, CV & T)

Long Acres Touring Park
Station Road, Old Leake, Boston
PE22 9RF
Tel: 01205 871555 68 G2
long-acres.co.uk
Total Pitches: 40 (C, CV & T)

Long Hazel Park
High Street, Sparkford, Yeovil, Somerset
BA22 7JH
Tel: 01963 440002 22 E8
longhazelpark.co.uk
Total Pitches: 46 (C, CV & T)

Longnor Wood Holiday Park
Newtown, Longnor, Nr Buxton
SK17 0NG
Tel: 01298 83648 77 K11
longnorwood.co.uk
Total Pitches: 47 (C, CV & T)

Manor Wood Country Caravan Park
Manor Wood, Coddington, Chester
CH3 9EN
Tel: 01829 782990 63 M1
cheshire-caravan-sites.co.uk
Total Pitches: 45 (C, CV & T)

Marsh House Holiday Park
Marsh House Farm, Carnforth,
Lancashire
LA5 9JA
Tel: 01524 732854 83 L1
holgates.co.uk/our-parks/marsh-house
Total Pitches: 74 (C & CV)

Marton Mere Holiday Village
Mythop Road, Blackpool
FY4 4XN
Tel: 01253 767544 82 H8
haven.com/martonmere
Total Pitches: 82 (C & CV)

Mayfield Park
Cheltenham Road, Cirencester
GL7 7BH
Tel: 01285 831301 42 B10
mayfieldpark.co.uk
Total Pitches: 105 (C, CV & T)

Meadow Lakes Holiday Park
Hewas Water, St Austell, Cornwall
PL26 7JG
Tel: 01726 882540 3 N5
meadow-lakes.co.uk
Total Pitches: 190 (C, CV & T)

Meadowbank Holidays
Stour Way, Christchurch
BH23 2PQ
Tel: 01202 483597 12 B6
meadowbank-holidays.co.uk
Total Pitches: 41 (C & CV)

Mena Farm: Touring, Camping, Glamping
Bodmin, Lanivet
PL30 5HW
Tel: 01208 831845 3 P2
menafarm.co.uk
Total Pitches: 25 (C, CV & T)

Middlewood Farm Holiday Park
Middlewood Lane, Fylingthorpe,
Robin Hood's Bay, Whitby
YO22 4UF
Tel: 01947 880414 93 J6
middlewoodfarm.com
Total Pitches: 100 (C, CV & T)

Mill Farm C & C Park
Fiddington, Bridgwater, Somerset
TA5 1JQ
Tel: 01278 732286 21 K5
millfarm.biz
Total Pitches: 275 (C, CV & T)

Mill Park Touring C & C Park
Mill Lane, Berrynarbor,
Ilfracombe, Devon
EX34 9SH
Tel: 01271 882647 19 L4
millpark.com
Total Pitches: 125 (C, CV & T)

Minnows Touring Park
Holbrook Lane, Sampford Peverell
EX16 7EN
Tel: 01884 821770 20 G10
minnowstouringpark.co.uk
Total Pitches: 59 (C, CV & T)

Monkey Tree Holiday Park
Hendra Croft, Scotland Road,
Newquay
TR8 5QR
Tel: 01872 572032 3 K4
monkeytreeholidaypark.co.uk
Total Pitches: 700 (C, CV & T)

Monkton Wyld Holiday Park
Scott's Lane, Charmouth, Dorset
DT6 6DB
Tel: 01297 631131 9 Q5
monktonwyld.co.uk
Total Pitches: 155 (C, CV & T)

Moon & Sixpence
Newbourn Road, Waldringfield,
Woodbridge
IP12 4PP
Tel: 01473 736650 47 N3
moonandsixpence.co.uk
Total Pitches: 50 (C & CV)

Moss Wood Caravan Park
Crimbles Lane, Cockerham
LA2 0ES
Tel: 01524 791041 83 L5
mosswood.co.uk
Total Pitches: 25 (C, CV & T)

Naburn Lock Caravan Park
Naburn
YO19 4RU
Tel: 01904 728697 86 B6
naburnlock.co.uk
Total Pitches: 115 (C, CV & T)

New Lodge Farm C & C Site
New Lodge Farm, Bulwick, Corby
NN17 3DU
Tel: 01780 450493 55 N2
newlodgefarm.com
Total Pitches: 72 (C, CV & T)

Newberry Valley Park
Woodlands, Combe Martin
EX34 0AT
Tel: 01271 882334 19 L4
newberryvalleypark.co.uk
Total Pitches: 110 (C, CV & T)

Newlands Holidays
Charmouth, Bridport
DT6 6RB
Tel: 01297 560259 10 B6
newlandsholidays.co.uk
Total Pitches: 240 (C, CV & T)

Ninham Country Holidays
Ninham, Shanklin, Isle of Wight
PO37 7PL
Tel: 01983 864243 13 J8
ninham-holidays.co.uk
Total Pitches: 140 (C, CV & T)

Northam Farm Caravan & Touring Park
Brean, Burnham-on-Sea
TA8 2SE
Tel: 01278 751244 21 M2
northamfarm.co.uk
Total Pitches: 350 (C, CV & T)

North Morte Farm C & C Park
North Morte Road, Mortehoe,
Woolacombe
EX34 7EG
Tel: 01271 870381 19 J4
northmortefarm.co.uk
Total Pitches: 180 (C, CV & T)

Oakdown Country Holiday Park
Gatedown Lane, Weston, Sidmouth
EX10 0PT
Tel: 01297 680387 9 M7
oakdown.co.uk
Total Pitches: 150 (C, CV & T)

Old Hall Caravan Park
Capernwray, Carnforth
LA6 1AD
Tel: 01524 733276 83 M1
oldhallcaravanpark.co.uk
Total Pitches: 38 (C & CV)

Old Oaks Touring & Glamping
Wick Farm, Wick,
Glastonbury
BA6 8JS
Tel: 01458 831437 22 C5
theoldoaks.co.uk
Total Pitches: 88 (C, CV & T)

Orchard Farm Holiday Village
Stonegate, Hunmanby, Filey,
North Yorkshire
YO14 0PU
Tel: 01723 891582 93 M11
orchardfarmholidayvillage.co.uk
Total Pitches: 91 (C, CV & T)

Ord House Country Park
East Ord, Berwick-upon-Tweed
TD15 2NS
Tel: 01289 305288 117 L11
maguirescountryparks.co.uk
Total Pitches: 79 (C, CV & T)

Otterington Park
Station Farm, South Otterington,
Northallerton, North Yorkshire
DL7 9JB
Tel: 01609 780656 91 P9
otteringtonpark.com
Total Pitches: 62 (C, CV & T)

Oxon Hall Touring Park
Welshpool Road, Shrewsbury
SY3 5FB
Tel: 01743 340868 63 M9
morris-leisure.co.uk
Total Pitches: 105 (C, CV & T)

Park Cliffe C & C Estate
Birks Road, Tower Wood,
Windermere
LA23 3PG
Tel: 015395 31344 89 L8
parkcliffe.co.uk
Total Pitches: 60 (C, CV & T)

Parkers Farm Holiday Park
Higher Mead Farm, Ashburton,
Devon
TQ13 7LJ
Tel: 01364 654869 8 E10
parkersfarmholidays.co.uk
Total Pitches: 100 (C, CV & T)

Park Foot Holiday Park
Howtown Road, Pooley Bridge
CA10 2NA
Tel: 01768 486309 — 89 M2
parkfootullswater.co.uk
Total Pitches: 323 (C, CV & T)

Parkland C & C Site
Sorley Green Cross, Kingsbridge
TQ7 4AF
Tel: 01548 852723 — 5 M7
parklandsite.co.uk
Total Pitches: 50 (C, CV & T)

Pebble Bank Caravan Park
Camp Road, Wyke Regis, Weymouth
DT4 9HF
Tel: 01305 774844 — 10 G9
pebblebank.co.uk
Total Pitches: 40 (C, CV & T)

Perran Sands Holiday Park
Perranporth, Truro
TR6 0AQ
Tel: 01872 573551 — 3 J3
haven.com/perransands
Total Pitches: 341 (C, CV & T)

Petwood Caravan Park
Off Stixwould Road, Woodhall Spa
LN10 6QH
Tel: 01526 354799 — 80 D11
petwoodcaravanpark.com
Total Pitches: 98 (C, CV & T)

Plough Lane Touring Caravan Site
Plough Lane, Chippenham, Wiltshire
SN15 5PS
Tel: 01249 750146 — 29 Q7
ploughlane.co.uk
Total Pitches: 52 (C & CV)

Polladras Holiday Park
Carleen, Breage, Helston
TR13 9NX
Tel: 01736 762220 — 2 F8
polladrasholidaypark.co.uk
Total Pitches: 39 (C, CV & T)

Polmanter Touring Park
Halsetown, St Ives
TR26 3LX
Tel: 01736 795640 — 2 E7
polmanter.com
Total Pitches: 294 (C, CV & T)

Porthtowan Tourist Park
Mile Hill, Porthtowan, Truro
TR4 8TY
Tel: 01209 890256 — 2 H5
porthtowantouristpark.co.uk
Total Pitches: 80 (C, CV & T)

Primrose Valley Holiday Park
Filey
YO14 9RF
Tel: 01723 513771 — 93 M11
haven.com/primrosevalley
Total Pitches: 35 (C & CV)

Ranch Caravan Park
Station Road, Honeybourne, Evesham
WR11 7PR
Tel: 01386 830744 — 42 C3
ranch.co.uk
Total Pitches: 120 (C & CV)

Ripley Caravan Park
Knaresborough Road, Ripley, Harrogate
HG3 3AU
Tel: 01423 770050 — 85 L3
ripleycaravanpark.com
Total Pitches: 60 (C, CV & T)

River Dart Country Park
Holne Park, Ashburton
TQ13 7NP
Tel: 01364 652511 — 5 M3
riverdart.co.uk
Total Pitches: 170 (C, CV & T)

River Valley Holiday Park
London Apprentice, St Austell
PL26 7AP
Tel: 01726 73533 — 3 N4
rivervalleyholidaypark.co.uk
Total Pitches: 45 (C, CV & T)

Riverside C & C Park
Marsh Lane, North Molton Road, South Molton
EX36 3HQ
Tel: 01769 579269 — 19 P8
exmoorriverside.co.uk
Total Pitches: 58 (C, CV & T)

Riverside Caravan Park
High Bentham, Lancaster
LA2 7FJ
Tel: 015242 61272 — 83 P1
riversidecaravanpark.co.uk
Total Pitches: 61 (C & CV)

Riverside Meadows Country Caravan Park
Ure Bank Top, Ripon
HG4 1JD
Tel: 01765 602964 — 91 N12
flowerofmay.com
Total Pitches: 80 (C)

Robin Hood C & C Park
Green Dyke Lane, Slingsby
YO62 4AP
Tel: 01653 628391 — 92 E11
robinhoodcaravanpark.co.uk
Total Pitches: 32 (C, CV & T)

Rose Farm Touring & Camping Park
Stepshort, Belton, Nr Great Yarmouth
NR31 9JS
Tel: 01493 738292 — 71 P11
rosefarmtouringpark.co.uk
Total Pitches: 145 (C, CV & T)

Rosedale Abbey Caravan Park
Rosedale Abbey, Pickering
YO18 8SA
Tel: 01751 417272 — 92 E7
rosedaleabbeycaravanpark.co.uk
Total Pitches: 100 (C, CV & T)

Rudding Holiday Park
Follifoot, Harrogate
HG3 1JH
Tel: 01423 870439 — 85 L4
ruddingholidaypark.co.uk
Total Pitches: 86 (C, CV & T)

Run Cottage Touring Park
Alderton Road, Hollesley, Woodbridge
IP12 3RQ
Tel: 01394 411309 — 47 P3
runcottage.co.uk
Total Pitches: 45 (C, CV & T)

Rutland C & C
Park Lane, Greetham, Oakham
LE15 7FN
Tel: 01572 813520 — 67 M9
rutlandcaravanandcamping.co.uk
Total Pitches: 130 (C, CV & T)

St Helens in the Park
Wykeham, Scarborough
YO13 9QD
Tel: 01723 862771 — 93 K10
sthelenscaravanpark.co.uk
Total Pitches: 250 (C, CV & T)

St Ives Bay Beach Resort
73 Loggans Road, Upton Towans, Hayle
TR27 5BH
Tel: 01736 752274 — 2 F6
stivesbay.co.uk
Total Pitches: 240 (C, CV & T)

Salcombe Regis C & C Park
Salcombe Regis, Sidmouth
EX10 0JH
Tel: 01395 514303 — 9 M7
salcombe-regis.co.uk
Total Pitches: 100 (C, CV & T)

Sand le Mere Holiday Village
Southfield Lane, Tunstall
HU12 0JF
Tel: 01964 670403 — 87 P9
sand-le-mere.co.uk
Total Pitches: 72 (C & CV)

Searles Leisure Resort
South Beach Road, Hunstanton
PE36 5BB
Tel: 01485 534211 — 69 M4
searles.co.uk
Total Pitches: 255 (C, CV & T)

Seaview Holiday Park
Preston, Weymouth
DT3 6DZ
Tel: 01305 832271 — 10 H8
haven.com/parks/dorset/seaview
Total Pitches: 82 (C, CV & T)

Severn Gorge Park
Bridgnorth Road, Tweedale, Telford
TF7 4JB
Tel: 01952 684789 — 64 D11
severngorgepark.co.uk
Total Pitches: 12 (C & CV)

Shamba Holidays
East Moors Lane, St Leonards, Ringwood
BH24 2SB
Tel: 01202 873302 — 11 Q4
shambaholidays.co.uk
Total Pitches: 82 (C, CV & T)

Shrubbery Touring Park
Rousdon, Lyme Regis
DT7 3XW
Tel: 01297 442227 — 9 P6
shrubberypark.co.uk
Total Pitches: 120 (C, CV & T)

Silverdale Caravan Park
Middlebarrow Plain, Cove Road, Silverdale, Nr Carnforth
LA5 0SH
Tel: 01524 701508 — 89 M11
holgates.co.uk
Total Pitches: 80 (C, CV & T)

Skelwith Fold Caravan Park
Ambleside, Cumbria
LA22 0HX
Tel: 015394 32277 — 89 K6
skelwith.com
Total Pitches: 150 (C & CV)

Skirlington Leisure Park
Driffield, Skipsea
YO25 8SY
Tel: 01262 468213 — 87 M5
skirlington.com
Total Pitches: 280 (C & CV)

Sleningford Watermill Caravan Camping Park
North Stainley, Ripon
HG4 3HQ
Tel: 01765 635201 — 91 M11
sleningfordwatermill.co.uk
Total Pitches: 150 (C, CV & T)

Somers Wood Caravan Park
Somers Road, Meriden
CV7 7PL
Tel: 01676 522978 — 53 N4
somerswood.co.uk
Total Pitches: 48 (C & CV)

Southfork Caravan Park
Parrett Works, Martock, Somerset
TA12 6AE
Tel: 01935 825661 — 21 P9
southforkcaravans.co.uk
Total Pitches: 27 (C, CV & T)

South Lytchett Manor C & C Park
Dorchester Road, Lytchett Minster, Poole
BH16 6JB
Tel: 01202 622577 — 11 M6
southlytchettmanor.co.uk
Total Pitches: 150 (C, CV & T)

South Meadows Caravan Park
South Road, Belford
NE70 7DP
Tel: 01668 213326 — 109 J3
southmeadows.co.uk
Total Pitches: 169 (C, CV & T)

Stanmore Hall Touring Park
Stourbridge Road, Bridgnorth
WV15 6DT
Tel: 01746 761761 — 52 D2
morris-leisure.co.uk
Total Pitches: 129 (C, CV & T)

Stanwix Park Holiday Centre
Greenrow, Silloth
CA7 4HH
Tel: 016973 32666 — 97 M7
stanwix.com
Total Pitches: 121 (C, CV & T)

Stroud Hill Park
Fen Road, Pidley, St Ives
PE28 3DE
Tel: 01487 741333 — 56 G5
stroudhillpark.co.uk
Total Pitches: 60 (C, CV & T)

Summer Valley Touring Park
Shortlanesend, Truro, Cornwall
TR4 9DW
Tel: 07933 212643 — 3 K5
summervalley.co.uk
Total Pitches: 55 (C, CV & T)

Sumners Ponds Fishery & Campsite
Chapel Road, Barns Green, Horsham
RH13 0PR
Tel: 01403 732539 — 14 G5
sumnersponds.co.uk
Total Pitches: 86 (C, CV & T)

Swiss Farm Touring & Camping
Marlow Road, Henley-on-Thames
RG9 2HY
Tel: 01491 573419 — 31 Q6
swissfarmhenley.co.uk
Total Pitches: 140 (C, CV & T)

Tanner Farm Touring C & C Park
Tanner Farm, Goudhurst Road, Marden
TN12 9ND
Tel: 01622 832399 — 16 C3
tannerfarmpark.co.uk
Total Pitches: 120 (C, CV & T)

Tehidy Holiday Park
Harris Mill, Illogan, Portreath
TR16 4JQ
Tel: 01209 216489 — 2 H6
tehidy.co.uk
Total Pitches: 18 (C, CV & T)

Tencreek Holiday Park
Polperro Road, Looe
PL13 2JR
Tel: 01503 262447 — 4 C6
dolphinholidays.co.uk
Total Pitches: 254 (C, CV & T)

The Inside Park
Down House Estate, Blandford Forum, Dorset
DT11 9AD
Tel: 01258 453719 — 11 L4
theinsidepark.co.uk
Total Pitches: 125 (C, CV & T)

The Laurels Holiday Park
Padstow Road, Whitecross, Wadebridge
PL27 7JQ
Tel: 01208 813341 — 6 D10
thelaurelsholidaypark.co.uk
Total Pitches: 30 (C, CV & T)

The Old Brick Kilns
Little Barney Lane, Barney, Fakenham
NR21 0NL
Tel: 01328 878305 — 70 E5
old-brick-kilns.co.uk
Total Pitches: 65 (C, CV & T)

The Orchards Holiday Caravan Park
Main Road, Newbridge, Yarmouth, Isle of Wight
PO41 0TS
Tel: 01983 531331 — 12 G7
orchards-holiday-park.co.uk
Total Pitches: 120 (C, CV & T)

The Quiet Site
Ullswater, Watermillock
CA11 0LS
Tel: 07768 727016 — 89 L2
thequietsite.co.uk
Total Pitches: 100 (C, CV & T)

Thornton's Holt Camping Park
Stragglethorpe Road, Stragglethorpe, Radcliffe on Trent
NG12 2JZ
Tel: 0115 933 2125 — 66 G5
thorntons-holt.co.uk
Total Pitches: 155 (C, CV & T)

Thornwick Bay Holiday Village
North Marine Road, Flamborough
YO15 1AU
Tel: 01262 850569 — 93 P12
haven.com/parks/yorkshire/thornwick-bay
Total Pitches: 67 (C, CV & T)

Thorpe Park Holiday Centre
Cleethorpes
DN35 0PW
Tel: 01472 813395 — 80 F2
haven.com/thorpepark
Total Pitches: 134 (C, CV & T)

Treago Farm Caravan Site
Crantock, Newquay
TR8 5QS
Tel: 01637 830277 — 3 J2
treagofarm.co.uk
Total Pitches: 90 (C, CV & T)

Treloy Touring Park
Newquay
TR8 4JN
Tel: 01637 872063 — 3 L2
treloy.co.uk
Total Pitches: 223 (C, CV & T)

Trencreek Holiday Park
Hillcrest, Higher Trencreek, Newquay
TR8 4NS
Tel: 01637 874210 — 3 K2
trencreekholidaypark.co.uk
Total Pitches: 194 (C, CV & T)

Trethem Mill Touring Park
St Just-in-Roseland, Nr St Mawes, Truro
TR2 5JF
Tel: 01872 580504 — 3 L7
trethem.com
Total Pitches: 84 (C, CV & T)

Trevalgan Touring Park
Trevalgan, St Ives
TR26 3BJ
Tel: 01736 791892 — 2 D6
trevalgantouringpark.co.uk
Total Pitches: 135 (C, CV & T)

Trevarrian Holiday Park
Mawgan Porth, Newquay, Cornwall
TR8 4AQ
Tel: 01637 860381 — 6 B11
trevarrian.co.uk
Total Pitches: 185 (C, CV & T)

Trevarth Holiday Park
Blackwater, Truro
TR4 8HR
Tel: 01872 560266 — 3 J5
trevarth.co.uk
Total Pitches: 30 (C, CV & T)

Trevedra Farm C & C Site
Sennen, Penzance
TR19 7BE
Tel: 01736 871818 — 2 B9
trevedrafarm.co.uk
Total Pitches: 100 (C, CV & T)

Trevornick
Holywell Bay, Newquay
TR8 5PW
Tel: 01637 830531 — 3 J3
trevornick.co.uk
Total Pitches: 575 (C, CV & T)

Trewan Hall
St Columb Major, Cornwall
TR9 6DB
Tel: 01637 880261 — 3 M2
trewan-hall.co.uk
Total Pitches: 200 (C, CV & T)

Tudor C & C
Shepherds Patch, Slimbridge, Gloucester
GL2 7BP
Tel: 01453 890483 — 41 L11
tudorcaravanpark.com
Total Pitches: 75 (C, CV & T)

Twitchen House Holiday Park
Mortehoe Station Road, Mortehoe, Woolacombe
EX34 7ES
Tel: 01271 872302 — 19 J4
woolacombe.com
Total Pitches: 252 (C, CV & T)

Two Mills Touring Park
Yarmouth Road, North Walsham
NR28 9NA
Tel: 01692 405829 — 71 K6
twomills.co.uk
Total Pitches: 81 (C, CV & T)

Ulwell Cottage Caravan Park
Ulwell Cottage, Ulwell, Swanage
BH19 3DG
Tel: 01929 422823 — 11 N8
ulwellcottagepark.co.uk
Total Pitches: 77 (C, CV & T)

Upper Lynstone Caravan Park
Lynstone, Bude
EX23 0LP
Tel: 01288 352017 — 7 J4
upperlynstone.co.uk
Total Pitches: 65 (C, CV & T)

Vale of Pickering Caravan Park
Carr House Farm, Allerston, Pickering
YO18 7PQ
Tel: 01723 859280 — 92 H10
valeofpickering.co.uk
Total Pitches: 120 (C, CV & T)

Waldegraves Holiday Park
Mersea Island, Colchester
CO5 8SE
Tel: 01206 382898 — 47 J9
waldegraves.co.uk
Total Pitches: 126 (C, CV & T)

Waleswood C &C Park
Delves Lane, Waleswood, Wales Bar, Wales, South Yorkshire
S26 5RN
Tel: 07825 125328 — 78 D7
waleswood.co.uk
Total Pitches: 163 (C, CV & T)

Wareham Forest Tourist Park
North Trigon, Wareham
BH20 7NZ
Tel: 01929 551393 — 11 L6
warehamforest.co.uk
Total Pitches: 200 (C, CV & T)

Waren C & C Park
Waren Mill, Bamburgh
NE70 7EE
Tel: 01668 214366 — 109 J3
meadowhead.co.uk/parks/waren
Total Pitches: 150 (C, CV & T)

Warren Farm Holiday Centre
Brean Sands, Brean, Burnham-on-Sea
TA8 2RP
Tel: 01278 751227 — 28 D11
warrenfarm.co.uk
Total Pitches: 575 (C, CV & T)

Waterfoot Caravan Park
Pooley Bridge, Penrith, Cumbria
CA11 0JF
Tel: 017684 86302 — 89 M2
waterfootpark.co.uk
Total Pitches: 34 (C, CV & T)

Watergate Bay Touring Park
Watergate Bay, Tregurrian
TR8 4AD
Tel: 01637 860387 — 6 B11
watergatebaytouringpark.co.uk
Total Pitches: 171 (C, CV & T)

Waterrow Touring Park
Wiveliscombe, Taunton
TA4 2AZ
Tel: 01984 623464 — 20 G8
waterrowpark.co.uk
Total Pitches: 42 (C, CV & T)

Wayfarers C & C Park
Relubbus Lane, St Hilary, Penzance
TR20 9EF
Tel: 01736 763326 — 2 E8
wayfarerspark.co.uk
Total Pitches: 32 (C, CV & T)

Wells Touring Park
Haybridge, Wells
BA5 1AJ
Tel: 01749 676869 — 22 C4
wellstouringpark.co.uk
Total Pitches: 56 (C & CV)

Westbrook Park
Little Hereford, Herefordshire
SY8 4AU
Tel: 01584 711280 — 51 P7
westbrookpark.co.uk
Total Pitches: 53 (C, CV & T)

Wheathill Touring Park
Wheathill, Bridgnorth
WV16 6QT
Tel: 01584 823456 — 51 Q4
wheathillpark.co.uk
Total Pitches: 50 (C & CV)

Whitefield Forest Touring Park
Brading Road, Ryde, Isle of Wight
PO33 1QL
Tel: 01983 617069 — 13 K7
whitefieldforest.co.uk
Total Pitches: 90 (C, CV & T)

Whitehill Country Park
Stoke Road, Paignton, Devon
TQ4 7PF
Tel: 01803 782338 — 5 P5
whitehill-park.co.uk
Total Pitches: 260 (C, CV & T)

Whitemead Caravan Park
East Burton Road, Wool
BH20 6HG
Tel: 01929 462241 — 11 K7
whitemeadcaravanpark.co.uk
Total Pitches: 105 (C, CV & T)

Widdicombe Farm Touring Park
Marldon, Paignton, Devon
TQ3 1ST
Tel: 01803 558325 — 5 P4
widdicombefarm.co.uk
Total Pitches: 180 (C, CV & T)

Willowbank Holiday Home & Touring Park
Coastal Road, Ainsdale, Southport
PR8 3ST
Tel: 01704 571566 — 75 K2
willowbankcp.co.uk
Total Pitches: 87 (C & CV)

Willow Valley Holiday Park
Bush, Bude, Cornwall
EX23 9LB
Tel: 01288 353104 — 7 J3
willowvalley.co.uk
Total Pitches: 41 (C, CV & T)

Wilson House Holiday Park
Lancaster Road, Out Rawcliffe, Preston, Lancashire
PR3 6BN
Tel: 07807 560685 — 83 K6
whhp.co.uk
Total Pitches: 40 (C & CV)

Wolds View Country Park
115 Brigg Road, Caistor
LN7 6RX
Tel: 01472 851099 — 80 B3
woldsviewtouringpark.co.uk
Total Pitches: 60 (C, CV & T)

Wooda Farm Holiday Park
Poughill, Bude
EX23 9HJ
Tel: 01288 352069 — 7 J3
wooda.co.uk
Total Pitches: 200 (C, CV & T)

Woodclose Caravan Park
High Casterton, Kirkby Lonsdale
LA6 2SE
Tel: 01524 271597 — 89 Q11
woodclosepark.com
Total Pitches: 22 (C & CV)

Woodhall Country Park
Stixwold Road, Woodhall Spa
LN10 6UJ
Tel: 01526 353710 — 80 D10
woodhallcountrypark.co.uk
Total Pitches: 141 (C, CV & T)

Woodland Springs Adult Touring Park
Venton, Drewsteignton
EX6 6PG
Tel: 01647 231648 — 8 D6
woodlandsprings.co.uk
Total Pitches: 93 (C, CV & T)

Woodlands Grove C & C Park
Blackawton, Dartmouth
TQ9 7DQ
Tel: 01803 712598 — 5 N6
woodlandsgrove.com
Total Pitches: 350 (C, CV & T)

Woodovis Park
Gulworthy, Tavistock
PL19 8NY
Tel: 01822 832968 — 7 N10
woodovis.com
Total Pitches: 50 (C, CV & T)

Yeatheridge Farm Caravan Park
East Worlington, Crediton, Devon
EX17 4TN
Tel: 01884 860330 — 8 E3
yeatheridge.co.uk
Total Pitches: 103 (C, CV & T)

York Caravan Park
Stockton Lane, York, North Yorkshire
YO32 9UB
Tel: 01904 424222 — 86 B4
yorkcaravanpark.com
Total Pitches: 55 (C & CV)

York Meadows Caravan Park
York Road, Sheriff Hutton, York, North Yorkshire
YO60 6QP
Tel: 01347 878508 — 86 B2
yorkmeadowscaravanpark.com
Total Pitches: 45 (C, CV & T)

SCOTLAND

Auchenlarie Holiday Park
Gatehouse of Fleet
DG7 2EX
Tel: 01556 506200 — 95 P8
swalwellholidaygroup.co.uk
Total Pitches: 49 (C, CV & T)

Banff Links Caravan Park
Inverboyndie, Banff, Aberdeenshire
AB45 2JJ
Tel: 01261 812228 — 140 G3
banfflinkscaravanpark.co.uk
Total Pitches: 93 (C, CV & T)

Beecraigs C & C Site
Beecraigs Country Park, The Visitor Centre, Linlithgow
EH49 6PL
Tel: 01506 284516 — 115 J6
westlothian.gov.uk/stay-at-beecraigs
Total Pitches: 36 (C, CV & T)

Belhaven Bay C & C Park
Belhaven Bay, Dunbar, East Lothian
EH42 1TS
Tel: 01368 865956 — 116 F5
meadowhead.co.uk
Total Pitches: 52 (C, CV & T)

Blair Castle Caravan Park
Blair Atholl, Pitlochry
PH18 5SR
Tel: 01796 481263 — 130 F11
blaircastlecaravanpark.co.uk
Total Pitches: 184 (C, CV & T)

Brighouse Bay Holiday Park
Brighouse Bay, Borgue, Kirkcudbright
DG6 4TS
Tel: 01557 870267 — 96 D9
gillespie-leisure.co.uk
Total Pitches: 190 (C, CV & T)

Cairnsmill Holiday Park
Largo Road, St Andrews
KY16 8NN
Tel: 01334 473604 — 125 K10
cairnsmill.co.uk
Total Pitches: 62 (C, CV & T)

Craig Tara Holiday Park
Ayr
KA7 4LB
Tel: 0800 975 7579 — 104 E6
haven.com/craigtara
Total Pitches: 44 (C & CV)

Craigtoun Meadows Holiday Park
Mount Melville, St Andrews
KY16 8PQ
Tel: 01334 475959 — 125 J10
craigtounmeadows.co.uk
Total Pitches: 56 (C, CV & T)

Faskally Caravan Park
Pitlochry
PH16 5LA
Tel: 01796 472007 — 130 G12
faskally.co.uk
Total Pitches: 300 (C, CV & T)

Glenearly Caravan Park
Dalbeattie, Dumfries & Galloway
DG5 4NE
Tel: 01556 611393 — 96 G6
glenearlycaravanpark.co.uk
Total Pitches: 39 (C, CV & T)

Glen Nevis C & C Park
Glen Nevis, Fort William
PH33 6SX
Tel: 01397 702191 — 128 F10
glen-nevis.co.uk
Total Pitches: 380 (C, CV & T)

Hoddom Castle Caravan Park
Hoddom, Lockerbie
DG11 1AS
Tel: 01576 300251 — 97 N4
hoddomcastle.co.uk
Total Pitches: 200 (C, CV & T)

Huntly Castle Caravan Park
The Meadow, Huntly
AB54 4UJ
Tel: 01466 794999 — 140 E8
huntlycastle.co.uk
Total Pitches: 90 (C, CV & T)

Invercoe C & C Park
Ballachulish, Glencoe
PH49 4HP
Tel: 01855 811210 — 121 L1
invercoe.co.uk
Total Pitches: 60 (C, CV & T)

Linwater Caravan Park
West Clifton, East Calder
EH53 0HT
Tel: 0131 333 3326 — 115 K7
linwater.co.uk
Total Pitches: 60 (C, CV & T)

Milton of Fonab Caravan Park
Bridge Road, Pitlochry
PH16 5NA
Tel: 01796 472882 — 123 N1
fonab.co.uk
Total Pitches: 154 (C, CV & T)

Sands of Luce Holiday Park
Sands of Luce, Sandhead, Stranraer
DG9 9JN
Tel: 01776 830456 — 94 G8
sandsofluce.com
Total Pitches: 80 (C, CV & T)

Seal Shore Camping and Touring Site
Kildonan, Isle of Arran, North Ayrshire
KA27 8SE
Tel: 01770 820320 — 103 Q5
campingarran.com
Total Pitches: 43 (C, CV & T)

Seaward Holiday Park
Dhoon Bay, Kirkudbright
DG6 4TJ
Tel: 01557 870267 — 96 D8
gillespie-leisure.co.uk
Total Pitches: 25 (C, CV & T)

Seton Sands Holiday Village
Longniddry
EH32 0QF
Tel: 01875 813333 — 116 A6
haven.com/setonsands
Total Pitches: 40 (C & CV)

Shieling Holidays Mull
Craignure, Isle of Mull, Argyll & Bute
PA65 6AY
Tel: 01680 812496 — 120 D5
shielingholidays.co.uk
Total Pitches: 90 (C, CV & T)

Silver Sands Holiday Park
Covesea, West Beach, Lossiemouth
IV31 6SP
Tel: 01343 813262 — 147 M11
silver-sands.co.uk
Total Pitches: 111 (C, CV & T)

Thurston Manor Leisure Park
Innerwick, Dunbar
EH42 1SA
Tel: 01368 840643 — 116 G6
thurstonmanor.co.uk
Total Pitches: 120 (C & CV)

Witches Craig C & C Park
Blairlogie, Stirling
FK9 5PX
Tel: 01786 474947 — 114 E2
witchescraig.co.uk
Total Pitches: 60 (C, CV & T)

WALES

Bron Derw Touring Caravan Park
Llanrwst
LL26 0YT
Tel: 01492 640494 — 73 N11
bronderw-wales.co.uk
Total Pitches: 48 (C & CV)

Caerfai Bay Caravan & Tent Park
Caerfai Bay, St Davids, Haverfordwest
SA62 6QT
Tel: 01437 720274 — 36 E5
caerfaibay.co.uk
Total Pitches: 106 (C, CV & T)

Cenarth Falls Resort Limited
Cenarth, Newcastle Emlyn
SA38 9JS
Tel: 01239 710345 — 37 P2
cenarth-holipark.co.uk
Total Pitches: 30 (C, CV & T)

Commonwood Leisure
Buck Road, Holt, Wrexham
LL13 9TF
Tel: 01978 664547 — 63 L1
commonwoodleisure.com/cabins-tents
Total Pitches: 5 (C & CV)

Daisy Bank Caravan Park
Snead, Montgomery
SY15 6EB
Tel: 01588 620471 — 51 K2
daisy-bank.co.uk
Total Pitches: 64 (C, CV & T)

Dinlle Caravan Park
Dinas Dinlle, Caernarfon
LL54 5TW
Tel: 01286 830324 — 72 G12
thornleyleisure.co.uk
Total Pitches: 175 (C, CV & T)

Eisteddfa
Eisteddfa Lodge, Pentrefelin, Criccieth
LL52 0PT
Tel: 01766 522696 — 61 J4
eisteddfapark.co.uk
Total Pitches: 100 (C, CV & T)

Fforest Fields C & C Park
Hundred House, Builth Wells
LD1 5RT
Tel: 01982 570406 — 50 F10
fforestfields.co.uk
Total Pitches: 120 (C, CV & T)

Fishguard Bay Resort
Garn Gelli, Fishguard
SA65 9ET
Tel: 01348 811415 — 37 J3
fishguardbay.com
Total Pitches: 50 (C, CV & T)

Greenacres Holiday Park
Black Rock Sands, Morfa Bychan, Porthmadog
LL49 9YF
Tel: 01766 512781 — 61 J5
haven.com/greenacres
Total Pitches: 39 (C & CV)

Hafan y Môr Holiday Park
Pwllheli
LL53 6HJ
Tel: 01758 612112 — 60 G5
haven.com/hafanymor
Total Pitches: 75 (C & CV)

Hendre Mynach Touring C & C Park
Llanaber Road, Barmouth
LL42 1YR
Tel: 01341 280262 — 61 K8
hendremynach.co.uk
Total Pitches: 240 (C, CV & T)

Home Farm Caravan Park
Marian-glas, Isle of Anglesey
LL73 8PH
Tel: 01248 410614 — 72 H7
homefarm-anglesey.co.uk
Total Pitches: 102 (C, CV & T)

Islawrffordd Caravan Park
Talybont, Barmouth
LL43 2AQ
Tel: 01341 247269 — 61 K8
islawrffordd.co.uk
Total Pitches: 105 (C & CV)

Kiln Park Holiday Centre
Marsh Road, Tenby
SA70 8RB
Tel: 01834 844121 — 37 M10
haven.com/kilnpark
Total Pitches: 146 (C, CV & T)

Pencelli Castle C & C Park
Pencelli, Brecon
LD3 7LX
Tel: 01874 665451 — 39 P7
pencelli-castle.com
Total Pitches: 80 (C, CV & T)

Penisar Mynydd Caravan Park
Caerwys Road, Rhuallt, St Asaph
LL17 0TY
Tel: 01745 582227 — 74 F8
penisarmynydd.co.uk
Total Pitches: 71 (C, CV & T)

Plassey Holiday Park
The Plassey, Eyton, Wrexham
LL13 0SP
Tel: 01978 780277 — 63 K3
plassey.com
Total Pitches: 90 (C, CV & T)

Pont Kemys C & C Park
Chainbridge, Abergavenny
NP7 9DS
Tel: 01873 880688 — 40 D10
pontkemys.com
Total Pitches: 65 (C, CV & T)

Presthaven Beach Holiday Park
Gronant, Prestatyn
LL19 9TT
Tel: 01745 856471 — 74 F7
haven.com/presthaven
Total Pitches: 50 (C & CV)

Red Kite Touring Park
Van Road, Llanidloes
SY18 6NG
Tel: 01686 412122 — 50 C4
redkitetouringpark.co.uk
Total Pitches: 66 (C & CV)

Riverside Camping
Seiont Nurseries, Pont Rug, Caernarfon
LL55 2BB
Tel: 01286 678781 — 72 H11
riversidecamping.co.uk
Total Pitches: 73 (C, CV & T)

The Trotting Mare Caravan Park
Overton, Wrexham
LL13 0LE
Tel: 01978 711963 — 63 L4
thetrottingmare.co.uk
Total Pitches: 54 (C, CV & T)

Trawsdir Touring C & C Park
Llanaber, Barmouth
LL42 1RR
Tel: 01341 280999 — 61 K8
barmouthholidays.co.uk
Total Pitches: 70 (C, CV & T)

Tyddyn Isaf Caravan Park
Lligwy Bay, Dulas, Isle of Anglesey
LL70 9PQ
Tel: 01248 410203 — 72 H6
tyddynisaf.co.uk
Total Pitches: 80 (C, CV & T)

Wern Farm Caravan & Glamping Park
Ty'n-y-Groes, Conwy
LL32 8SY
Tel: 01492 650257 — 73 N9
wernfarmcaravanpark.co.uk
Total Pitches: 24 (C & CV)

White Tower Holiday Park
Llandwrog, Caernarfon
LL54 5UH
Tel: 01286 830649 — 72 G12
whitetowerpark.co.uk
Total Pitches: 52 (C & CV)

CHANNEL ISLANDS

La Bailloterie Camping
Bailloterie Lane, Vale, Guernsey
GY3 5HA
Tel: 01481 243636 — 12 c1
campinginguernsey.com
Total Pitches: 100 (C, CV & T)

Traffic signs

Signs giving orders

Signs with red circles are mostly prohibitive. Plates below signs qualify their message

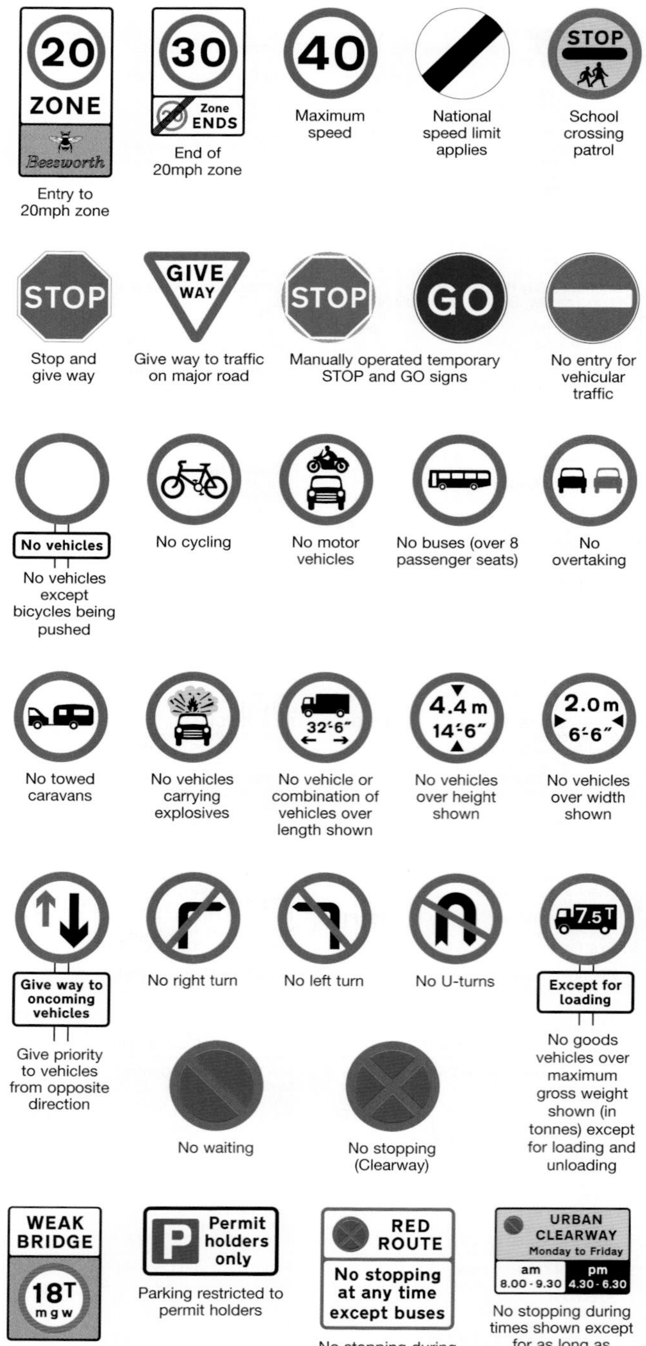
20 ZONE
Beesworth
30
Zone ENDS
40
STOP
STOP
GIVE WAY
STOP
GO
No vehicles
4.4 m
14'6"
2.0 m
6'6"
32'6"
7.5T
Give way to oncoming vehicles
Except for loading
WEAK BRIDGE
18T mgw
P Permit holders only
RED ROUTE
No stopping at any time except buses
URBAN CLEARWAY
Monday to Friday
am 8.00 - 9.30
pm 4.30 - 6.30

Entry to 20mph zone · End of 20mph zone · Maximum speed · National speed limit applies · School crossing patrol

Stop and give way · Give way to traffic on major road · Manually operated temporary STOP and GO signs · No entry for vehicular traffic

No vehicles except bicycles being pushed · No cycling · No motor vehicles · No buses (over 8 passenger seats) · No overtaking

No towed caravans · No vehicles carrying explosives · No vehicle or combination of vehicles over length shown · No vehicles over height shown · No vehicles over width shown

Give priority to vehicles from opposite direction · No right turn · No left turn · No U-turns · No goods vehicles over maximum gross weight shown (in tonnes) except for loading and unloading · No waiting · No stopping (Clearway)

No vehicles over maximum gross weight shown (in tonnes) · Parking restricted to permit holders · No stopping during period indicated except for buses · No stopping during times shown except for as long as necessary to set down or pick up passengers

Signs with blue circles but no red border mostly give positive instruction.

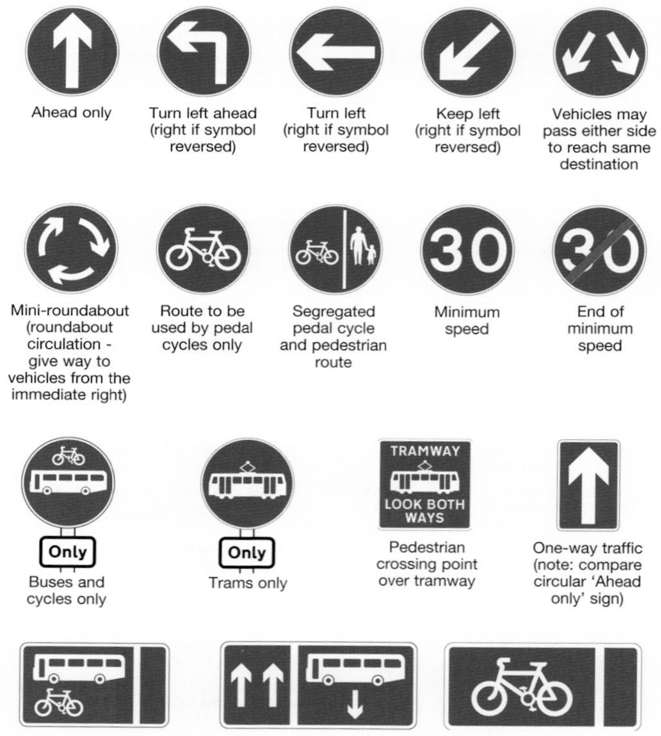
30
30
Only
Only
TRAMWAY
LOOK BOTH WAYS

Ahead only · Turn left ahead (right if symbol reversed) · Turn left (right if symbol reversed) · Keep left (right if symbol reversed) · Vehicles may pass either side to reach same destination

Mini-roundabout (roundabout circulation - give way to vehicles from the immediate right) · Route to be used by pedal cycles only · Segregated pedal cycle and pedestrian route · Minimum speed · End of minimum speed

Buses and cycles only · Trams only · Pedestrian crossing point over tramway · One-way traffic (note: compare circular 'Ahead only' sign)

With-flow bus and cycle lane · Contraflow bus lane · With-flow pedal cycle lane

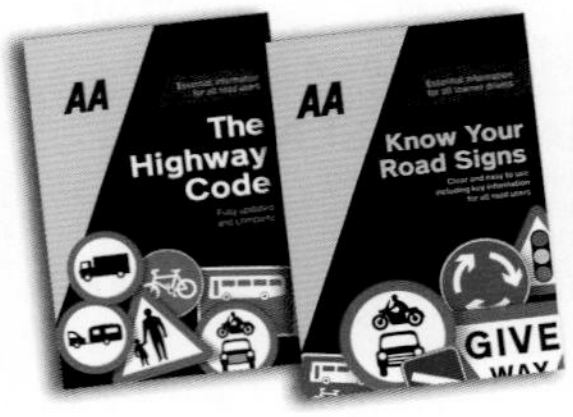
AA
The Highway Code
AA
Know Your Road Signs
GIVE WAY

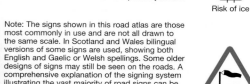

Note: The signs shown in this road atlas are those most commonly in use and are not all drawn to the same scale. In Scotland and Wales bilingual versions of some signs are used, showing both English and Gaelic or Welsh spellings. Some older designs of signs may still be seen on the roads. A comprehensive explanation of the signing system illustrating the vast majority of road signs can be found in the AA's handbook Know Your Road Signs. Where there is a reference to a rule number, this refers to The Highway Code.

Warning signs

Mostly triangular

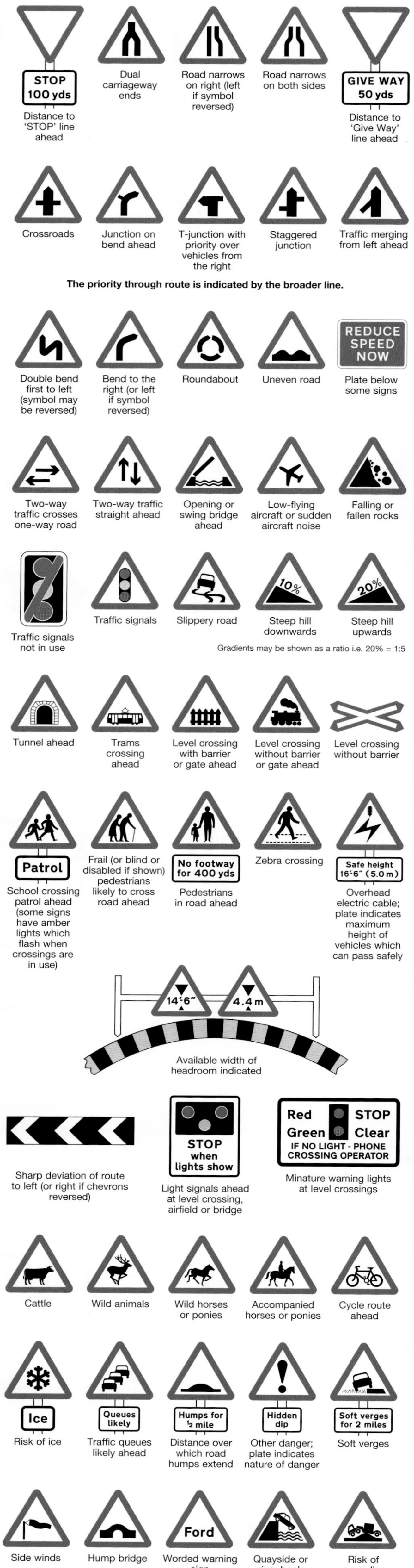
STOP 100 yds
GIVE WAY 50 yds
REDUCE SPEED NOW
10%
20%
Patrol
No footway for 400 yds
Safe height 16'-6" (5.0 m)
14'6"
4.4 m
STOP when lights show
Red
STOP
Green
Clear
IF NO LIGHT - PHONE CROSSING OPERATOR
Ice
Queues likely
Humps for ½ mile
Hidden dip
Soft verges for 2 miles
Ford

Distance to 'STOP' line ahead · Dual carriageway ends · Road narrows on right (left if symbol reversed) · Road narrows on both sides · Distance to 'Give Way' line ahead

Crossroads · Junction on bend ahead · T-junction with priority over vehicles from the right · Staggered junction · Traffic merging from left ahead

The priority through route is indicated by the broader line.

Double bend first to left (symbol may be reversed) · Bend to the right (or left if symbol reversed) · Roundabout · Uneven road · Plate below some signs

Two-way traffic crosses one-way road · Two-way traffic straight ahead · Opening or swing bridge ahead · Low-flying aircraft or sudden aircraft noise · Falling or fallen rocks

Traffic signals not in use · Traffic signals · Slippery road · Steep hill downwards · Steep hill upwards

Gradients may be shown as a ratio i.e. 20% = 1:5

Tunnel ahead · Trams crossing ahead · Level crossing with barrier or gate ahead · Level crossing without barrier or gate ahead · Level crossing without barrier

School crossing patrol ahead (some signs have amber lights which flash when crossings are in use) · Frail (or blind or disabled if shown) pedestrians likely to cross road ahead · Pedestrians in road ahead · Zebra crossing · Overhead electric cable; plate indicates maximum height of vehicles which can pass safely

Available width of headroom indicated

Sharp deviation of route to left (or right if chevrons reversed) · Light signals ahead at level crossing, airfield or bridge · Miniature warning lights at level crossings

Cattle · Wild animals · Wild horses or ponies · Accompanied horses or ponies · Cycle route ahead

Risk of ice · Traffic queues likely ahead · Distance over which road humps extend · Other danger; plate indicates nature of danger · Soft verges

Side winds · Hump bridge · Worded warning sign · Quayside or river bank · Risk of grounding

Direction signs

Mostly retangular

Signs on motorways - blue backgrounds

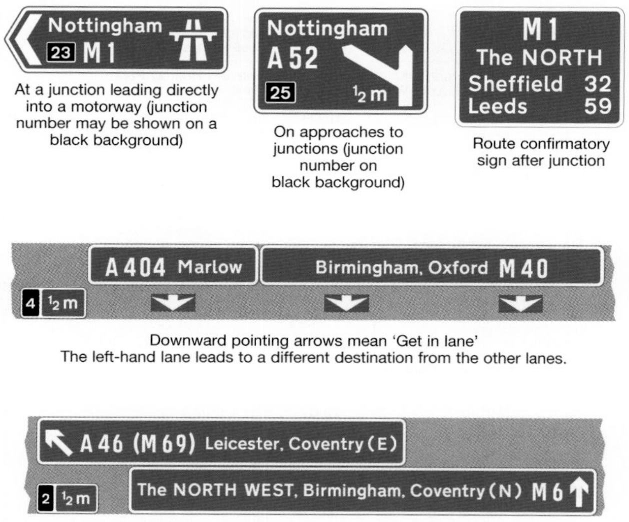
Nottingham
23 M1
Nottingham
A52
25
½ m
M1
The NORTH
Sheffield 32
Leeds 59
A404 Marlow
Birmingham, Oxford M40
4 ½ m
A46 (M69) Leicester, Coventry (E)
2 ½ m
The NORTH WEST, Birmingham, Coventry (N) M6

At a junction leading directly into a motorway (junction number may be shown on a black background) · On approaches to junctions (junction number on black background) · Route confirmatory sign after junction

Downward pointing arrows mean 'Get in lane'
The left-hand lane leads to a different destination from the other lanes.

The panel with the inclined arrow indicates the destinations which can be reached by leaving the motorway at the next junction.

Signs on primary routes - green backgrounds

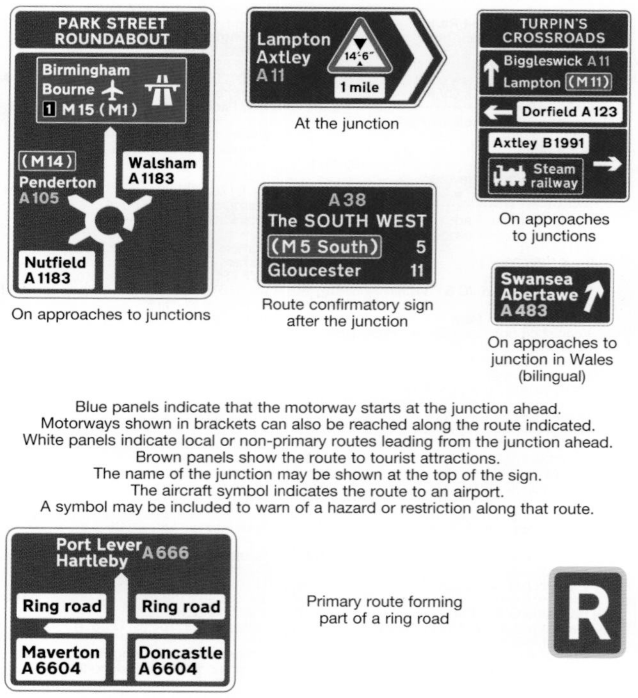
PARK STREET ROUNDABOUT
Birmingham
Bourne
1 M15 (M1)
(M14)
Penderton
A105
Walsham
A1183
Nutfield
A1183
Lampton
Axtley
A11
14'6"
1 mile
A38
The SOUTH WEST
(M5 South) 5
Gloucester 11
TURPIN'S CROSSROADS
Biggleswick A11
Lampton (M11)
Dorfield A123
Axtley B1991
Steam railway
Swansea
Abertawe
A483
Port Lever
Hartleby A666
Ring road
Ring road
Maverton A6604
Doncastle A6604
R

On approaches to junctions · At the junction · Route confirmatory sign after the junction · On approaches to junctions · On approaches to junction in Wales (bilingual)

Blue panels indicate that the motorway starts at the junction ahead.
Motorways shown in brackets can also be reached along the route indicated.
White panels indicate local or non-primary routes leading from the junction ahead.
Brown panels show the route to tourist attractions.
The name of the junction may be shown at the top of the sign.
The aircraft symbol indicates the route to an airport.
A symbol may be included to warn of a hazard or restriction along that route.

Primary route forming part of a ring road

Signs on non-primary and local routes - black borders

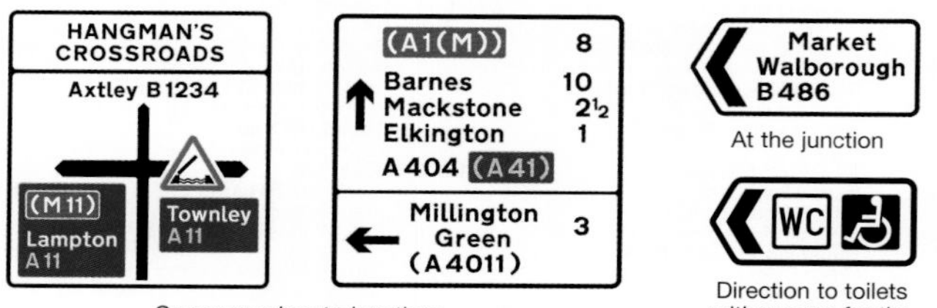
HANGMAN'S CROSSROADS
Axtley B1234
(M11)
Lampton
A11
Townley
A11
(A1(M)) 8
Barnes 10
Mackstone 2½
Elkington 1
A404 (A41)
Millington Green (A4011) 3
Market
Walborough
B486
WC

On approaches to junctions · At the junction · Direction to toilets with access for the disabled

Green panels indicate that the primary route starts at the junction ahead.
Route numbers on a blue background show the direction to a motorway.
Route numbers on a green background show the direction to a primary route.

Signs on non-primary and local routes - black borders

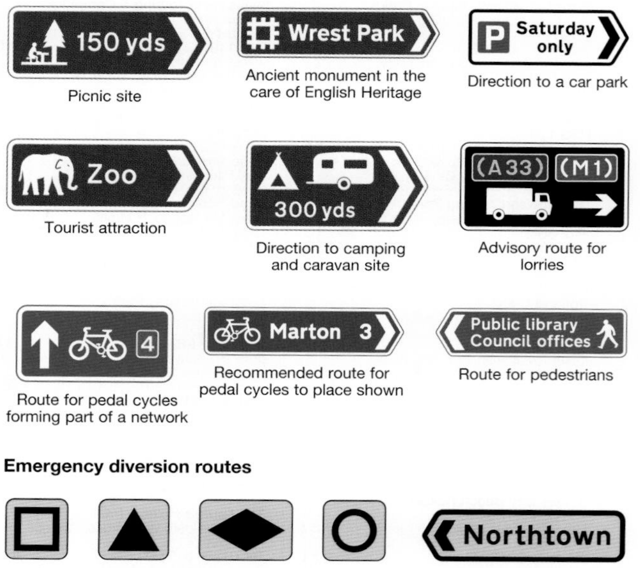
150 yds
Wrest Park
Saturday only
Zoo
300 yds
(A33) (M1)
4
Marton 3
Public library
Council offices
Northtown

Picnic site · Ancient monument in the care of English Heritage · Direction to a car park

Tourist attraction · Direction to camping and caravan site · Advisory route for lorries

Route for pedal cycles forming part of a network · Recommended route for pedal cycles to place shown · Route for pedestrians

Emergency diversion routes

Symbols showing emergency diversion route for motorway and other main road traffic · Diversion route

In an emergency it may be necessary to close a section of motorway or other main road to traffic, so a temporary sign may advise drivers to follow a diversion route. To help drivers navigate the route, black symbols on yellow patches may be permanently displayed on existing direction signs, including motorway signs. Symbols may also be used on separate signs with yellow backgrounds.

Information signs
All retangular

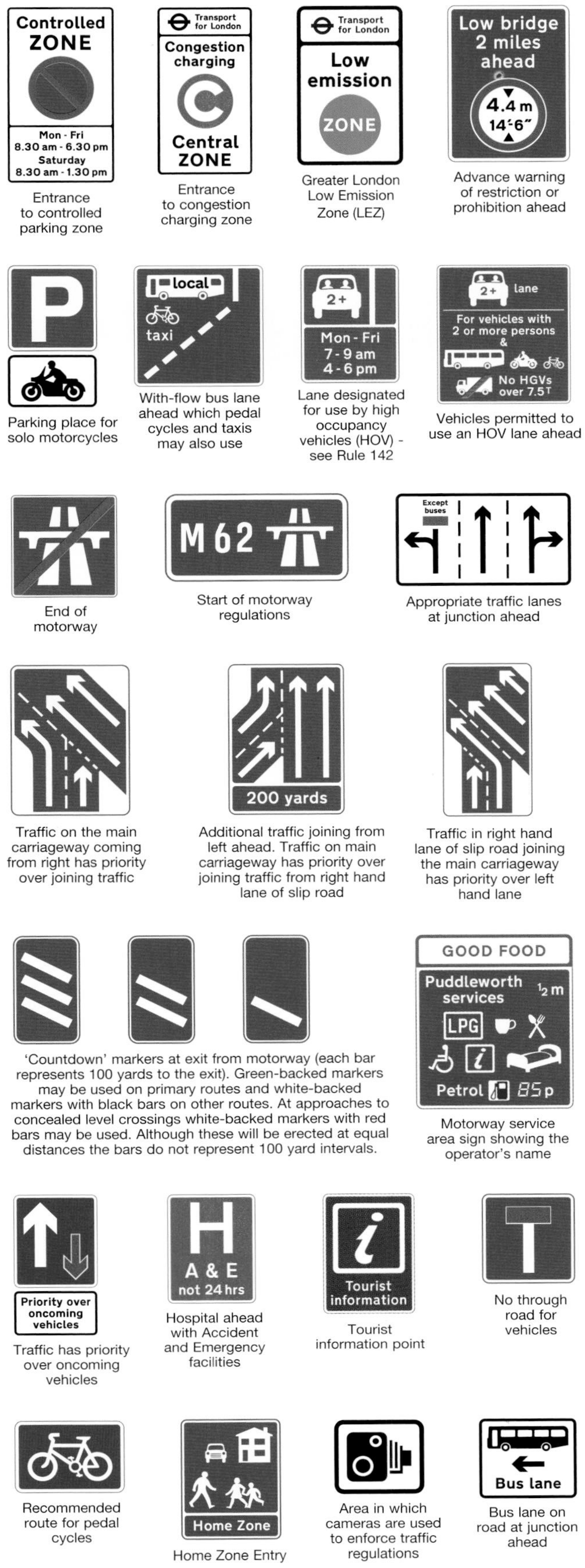

Entrance to controlled parking zone

Entrance to congestion charging zone

Greater London Low Emission Zone (LEZ)

Advance warning of restriction or prohibition ahead

Parking place for solo motorcycles

With-flow bus lane ahead which pedal cycles and taxis may also use

Lane designated for use by high occupancy vehicles (HOV) - see Rule 142

Vehicles permitted to use an HOV lane ahead

End of motorway

Start of motorway regulations

Appropriate traffic lanes at junction ahead

Traffic on the main carriageway coming from right has priority over joining traffic

Additional traffic joining from left ahead. Traffic on main carriageway has priority over joining traffic from right hand lane of slip road

Traffic in right hand lane of slip road joining the main carriageway has priority over left hand lane

'Countdown' markers at exit from motorway (each bar represents 100 yards to the exit). Green-backed markers may be used on primary routes and white-backed markers with black bars on other routes. At approaches to concealed level crossings white-backed markers with red bars may be used. Although these will be erected at equal distances the bars do not represent 100 yard intervals.

Motorway service area sign showing the operator's name

Traffic has priority over oncoming vehicles

Hospital ahead with Accident and Emergency facilities

Tourist information point

No through road for vehicles

Recommended route for pedal cycles

Home Zone Entry

Area in which cameras are used to enforce traffic regulations

Bus lane on road at junction ahead

*Home Zone Entry – You are entering an area where people could be using the whole street for a range of activities. You should drive slowly and carefully and be prepared to stop to allow people time to move out of the way.

Roadworks signs

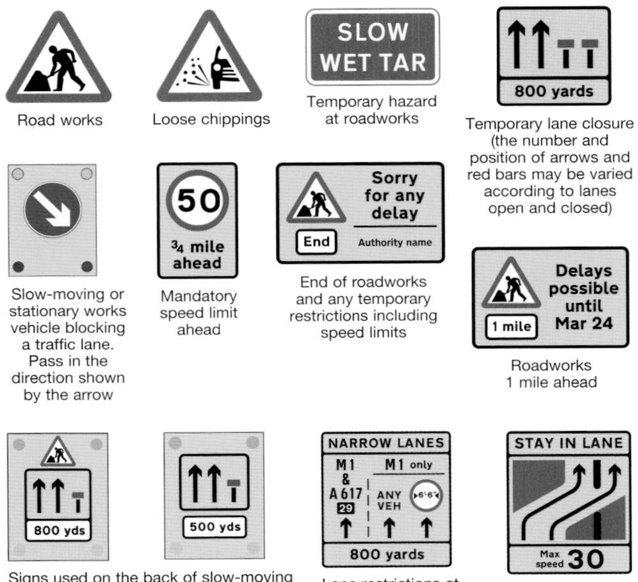

Road works

Loose chippings

Temporary hazard at roadworks

Temporary lane closure (the number and position of arrows and red bars may be varied according to lanes open and closed)

Slow-moving or stationary works vehicle blocking a traffic lane. Pass in the direction shown by the arrow

Mandatory speed limit ahead

End of roadworks and any temporary restrictions including speed limits

Roadworks 1 mile ahead

Signs used on the back of slow-moving or stationary vehicles warning of a lane closed ahead by a works vehicle. There are no cones on the road

Lane restrictions at roadworks ahead

One lane crossover at contraflow roadworks

Road markings
Across the carriageway

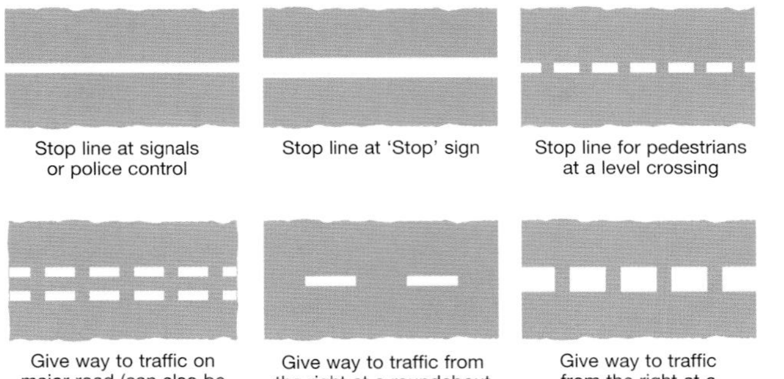

Stop line at signals or police control

Stop line at 'Stop' sign

Stop line for pedestrians at a level crossing

Give way to traffic on major road (can also be used at mini roundabouts)

Give way to traffic from the right at a roundabout

Give way to traffic from the right at a mini-roundabout

Along the carriageway

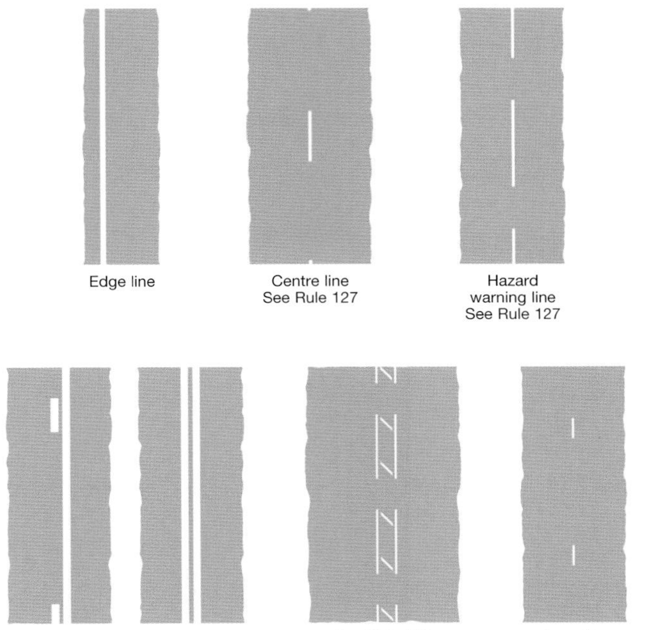

Edge line

Centre line See Rule 127

Hazard warning line See Rule 127

Double white lines See Rules 128 and 129

See Rule 130

Lane line See Rule 131

Along the edge of the carriageway
Waiting restrictions

Waiting restrictions indicated by yellow lines apply to the carriageway, pavement and verge. You may stop to load or unload (unless there are also loading restrictions as described below) or while passengers board or alight. Double yellow lines mean no waiting at any time, unless there are signs that specifically indicate seasonal restrictions. The times at which the restrictions apply for other road markings are shown on nearby plates or on entry signs to controlled parking zones. If no days are shown on the signs, the restrictions are in force every day including Sundays and Bank Holidays. White bay markings and upright signs (see below) indicate where parking is allowed.

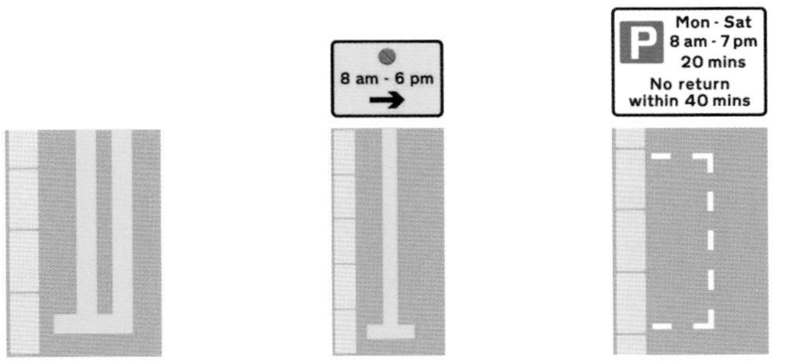

No waiting at any time

No waiting during times shown on sign

Waiting is limited to the duration specified during the days and times shown

Red Route stopping controls

Red lines are used on some roads instead of yellow lines. In London the double and single red lines used on Red Routes indicate that stopping to park, load/unload or to board and alight from a vehicle (except for a licensed taxi or if you hold a Blue Badge) is prohibited. The red lines apply to the carriageway, pavement and verge. The times that the red line prohibitions apply are shown on nearby signs, but the double red line ALWAYS means no stopping at any time. On Red Routes you may stop to park, load/unload in specially marked boxes and adjacent signs specify the times and purposes and duration allowed. A box MARKED IN RED indicates that it may only be available for the purpose specified for part of the day (e.g. between busy peak periods). A box MARKED IN WHITE means that it is available throughout the day.

RED AND SINGLE YELLOW LINES CAN ONLY GIVE A GUIDE TO THE RESTRICTIONS AND CONTROLS IN FORCE AND SIGNS, NEARBY OR AT A ZONE ENTRY, MUST BE CONSULTED.

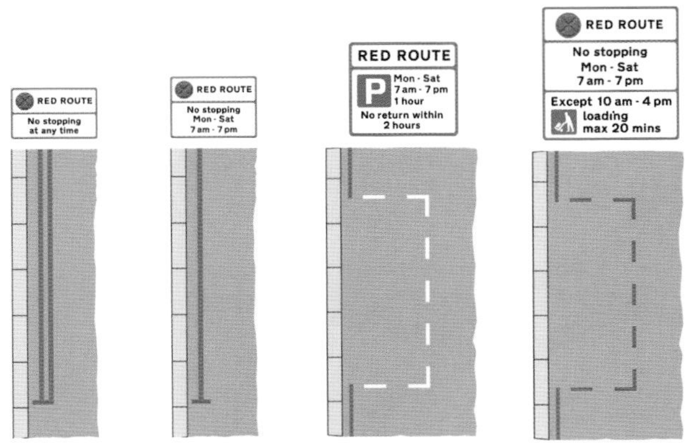

No stopping at any time

No stopping during times shown on sign

Parking is limited to the duration specified during the days and times shown

Only loading may take place at the times shown for up to a maximum duration of 20 mins

On the kerb or at the edge of the carriageway
Loading restrictions on roads other than Red Routes

Yellow marks on the kerb or at the edge of the carriageway indicate that loading or unloading is prohibited at the times shown on the nearby black and white plates. You may stop while passengers board or alight. If no days are indicated on the signs the restrictions are in force every day including Sundays and Bank Holidays.

ALWAYS CHECK THE TIMES SHOWN ON THE PLATES.

Lengths of road reserved for vehicles loading and unloading are indicated by a white 'bay' marking with the words 'Loading Only' and a sign with the white on blue 'trolley' symbol. This sign also shows whether loading and unloading is restricted to goods vehicles and the times at which the bay can be used. If no times or days are shown it may be used at any time. Vehicles may not park here if they are not loading or unloading.

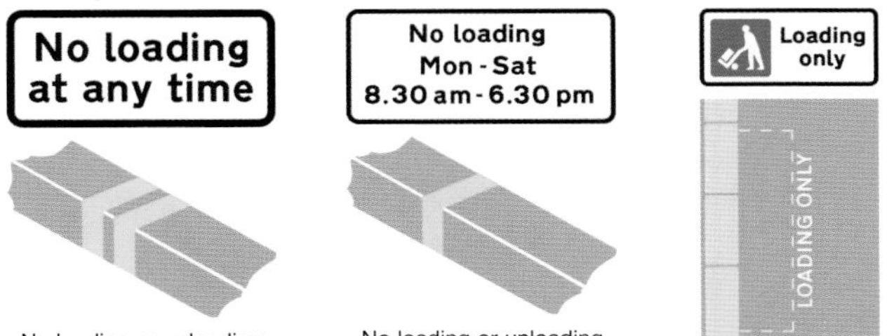

No loading or unloading at any time

No loading or unloading at the times shown

Loading bay

Other road markings

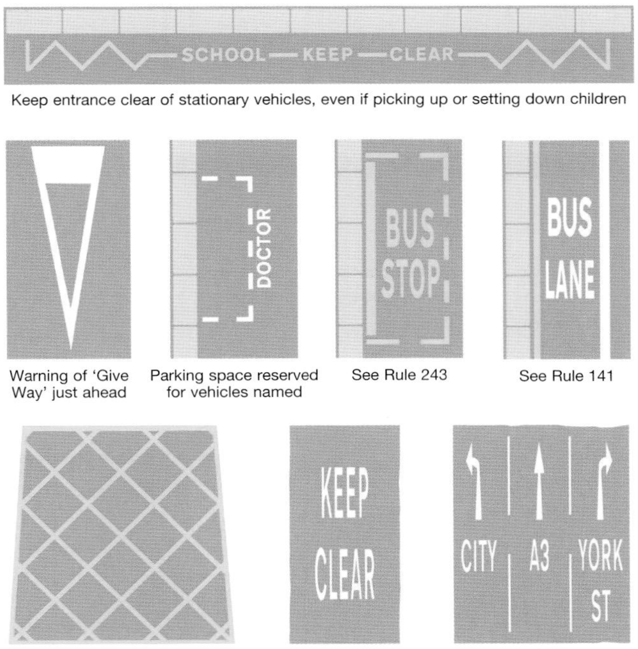

Keep entrance clear of stationary vehicles, even if picking up or setting down children

Warning of 'Give Way' just ahead

Parking space reserved for vehicles named

See Rule 243

See Rule 141

Box junction - See Rule 174

Do not block that part of the carriageway indicated

Indication of traffic lanes

Light signals controlling traffic
Traffic Light Signals

RED means 'Stop'. Wait behind the stop line on the carriageway

RED AND AMBER also means 'Stop'. Do not pass through or start until GREEN shows

GREEN means you may go on if the way is clear. Take special care if you intend to turn left or right and give way to pedestrians who are crossing

AMBER means 'Stop' at the stop line. You may go on only if the AMBER appears after you have crossed the stop line or are so close to it that to pull up might cause an accident

A GREEN ARROW may be provided in addition to the full green signal if movement in a certain direction is allowed before or after the full green phase. If the way is clear you may go but only in the direction shown by the arrow. You may do this whatever other lights may be showing. White light signals may be provided for trams

Flashing red lights
Alternately flashing red lights mean YOU MUST STOP

At level crossings, lifting bridges, airfields, fire stations, etc.

Motorway signals

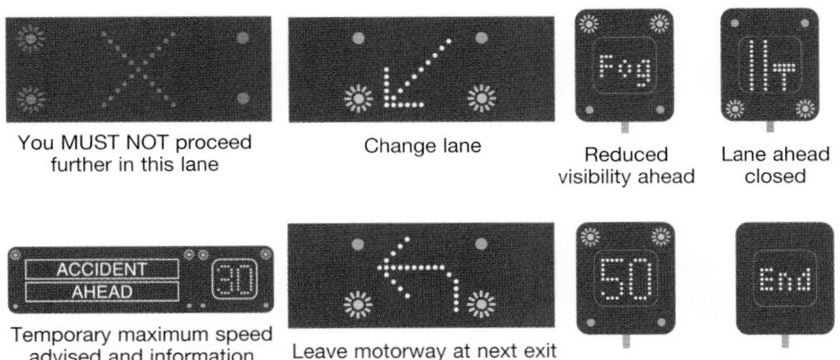

You MUST NOT proceed further in this lane

Change lane

Reduced visibility ahead

Lane ahead closed

Temporary maximum speed advised and information message

Leave motorway at next exit

Temporary maximum speed advised

End of restriction

Lane control signals

Green arrow - lane available to traffic facing the sign
Red crosses - lane closed to traffic facing the sign
White diagonal arrow - change lanes in direction shown

For business or pleasure, hopping on a ferry across to France, the Channel Islands or Isle of Wight has never been easier.

The vehicle ferry services listed in the table give you all the options, together with detailed port plans to help you navigate to and from the ferry terminals. Simply choose your preferred route, not forgetting the fast sailings (see ). Bon voyage!

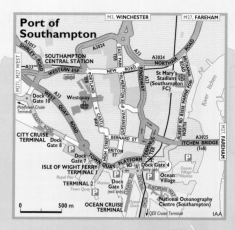

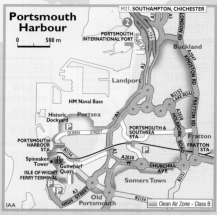

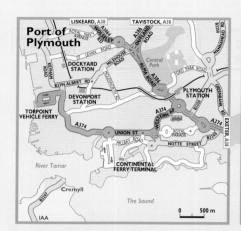

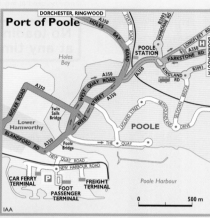

ENGLISH CHANNEL AND ISLE OF WIGHT FERRY CROSSINGS

From	To	Journey time	Operator website
Dover	Calais	1 hr 30 mins	dfdsseaways.co.uk
Dover	Calais	1 hr 30 mins	poferries.com
Dover	Dunkirk	2 hrs	dfdsseaways.co.uk
Folkestone	Calais (Coquelles)	35 mins	eurotunnel.com
Lymington	Yarmouth (IOW)	40 mins	wightlink.co.uk
Newhaven	Dieppe	4 hrs	dfdsseaways.co.uk
Plymouth	Roscoff	5 hrs 30 mins	brittany-ferries.co.uk
Poole	Cherbourg	4 hrs 30 mins (Apr–Oct)	brittany-ferries.co.uk
Poole	Guernsey	3 hrs 🚢	condorferries.co.uk
Poole	Jersey	4 hrs 🚢	condorferries.co.uk
Poole	St-Malo	6 hrs 20 mins–12 hrs (via Channel Is.) 🚢	condorferries.co.uk
Portsmouth	Caen (Ouistreham)	5 hrs 45 mins–7 hrs	brittany-ferries.co.uk
Portsmouth	Cherbourg	8 hrs	brittany-ferries.co.uk
Portsmouth	Fishbourne (IOW)	45 mins	wightlink.co.uk
Portsmouth	Guernsey	7 hrs	condorferries.co.uk
Portsmouth	Jersey	8–11 hrs	condorferries.co.uk
Portsmouth	St-Malo	11 hrs	brittany-ferries.co.uk
Southampton	East Cowes (IOW)	1 hr	redfunnel.co.uk

The information listed is provided as a guide only, as services are liable to change at short notice and are weather dependent. Services shown are for vehicle ferries only, operated by conventional ferry unless indicated as a fast ferry service (🚢). Please check sailings before planning your journey.

Travelling further afield? For ferry services to Northern Spain see *brittany-ferries.co.uk*.

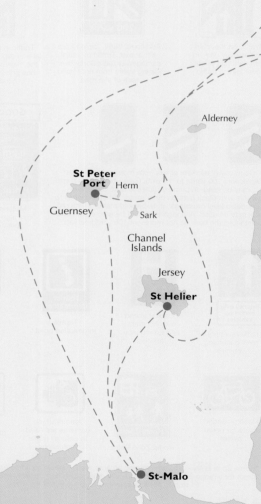

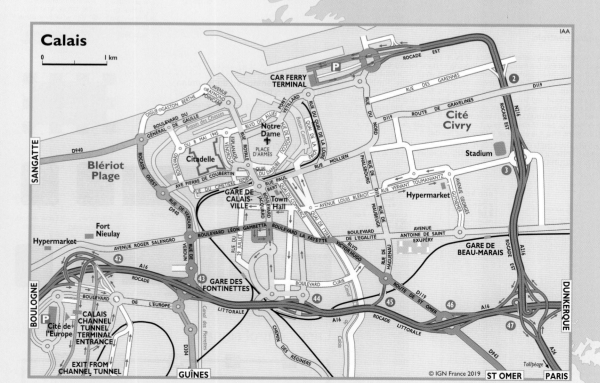

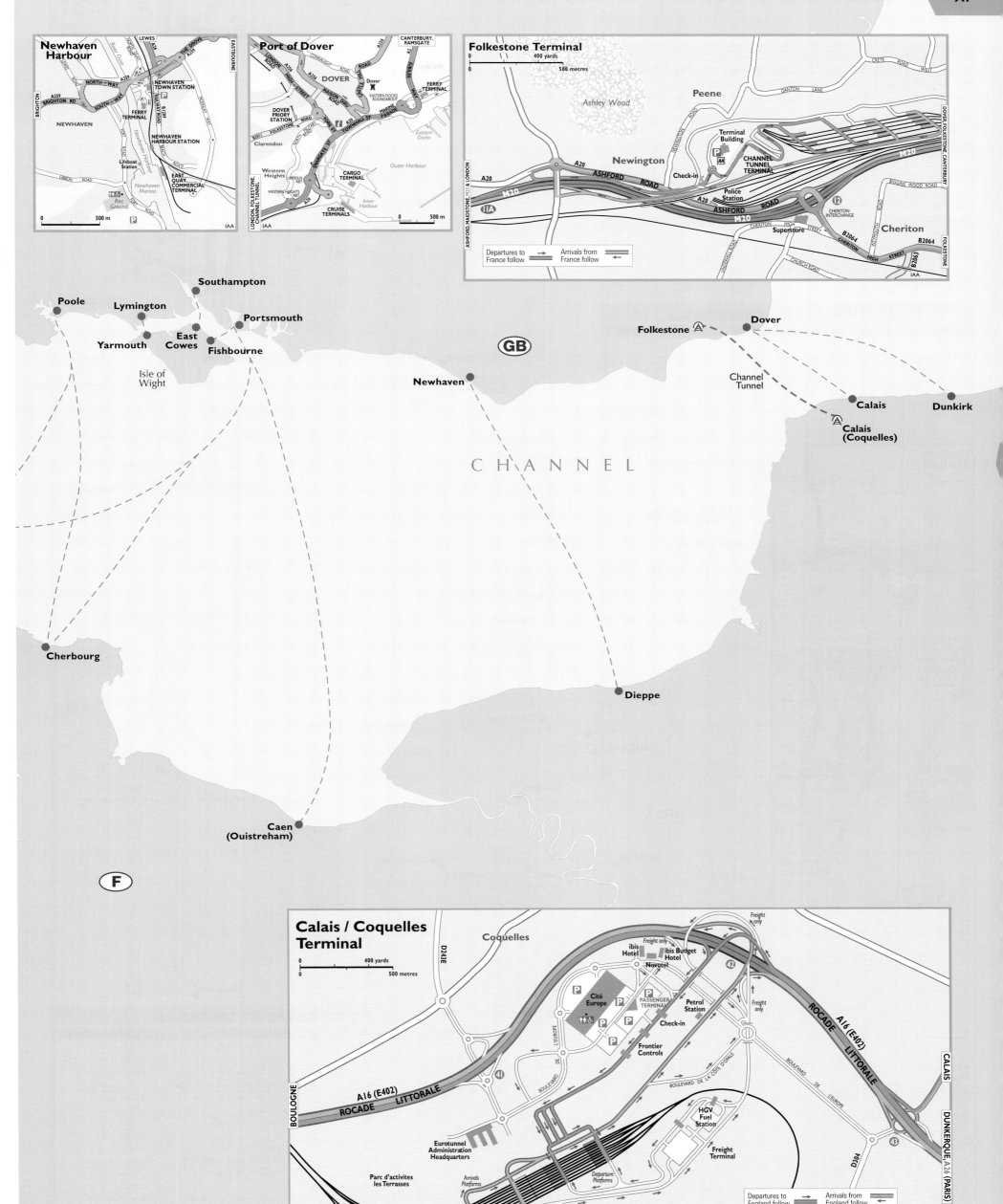

Newhaven Harbour

LEWES
EASTBOURNE
BRIGHTON
THE DROVE
NORTH WAY
SOUTH WAY
RAILWAY APPROACH
NEWHAVEN TOWN STATION
FERRY TERMINAL
NEWHAVEN HARBOUR STATION
NEWHAVEN
River Ouse
BRIGHTON RD
GIBBON ROAD
Lifeboat Station
Newhaven Marina
Rec Ground
EAST QUAY COMMERCIAL TERMINAL
0   500 m
IAA

Port of Dover

CANTERBURY, RAMSGATE
DOVER
Dover
COURT ROAD
MAISON DIEU
CASTLE STREET
FERRY TERMINAL
EASTERN DOCKS ROUNDABOUT
MARINE PARADE
TOWNWALL ST
DOVER PRIORY STATION
Clarendon
Western Heights
WESTERN HEIGHTS RBT
BREXLN RBT
SNARGATE ST
CARGO TERMINAL
Eastern Docks
Outer Harbour
Inner Harbour
CRUISE TERMINALS
LONDON, FOLKESTONE, CHANNEL TUNNEL
0   500 m
IAA

Folkestone Terminal

0   400 yards
0   500 metres
Ashley Wood
Peene
Newington
CRETE WAY WEST
DOVER FOLKESTONE, CANTERBURY
DANTON LANE
Terminal Building
P
AA
Check-in
CHANNEL TUNNEL TERMINAL
M20
Police Station
ASHFORD ROAD
A20
A20
M20
ASHFORD ROAD
ASHFORD, MAIDSTONE M15 & LONDON
11A
BIGGINS WOOD ROAD
12
CHERITON INTERCHANGE
Cheriton
Superstore
CHERITON HIGH STREET
B2064
B2063
FOLKESTONE
CHURCH ROAD
IAA

Departures to France follow →
Arrivals from France follow ←

Poole
Lymington
Southampton
Yarmouth
East Cowes
Fishbourne
Portsmouth
Isle of Wight
GB
Folkestone (A)
Dover
Newhaven
Channel Tunnel
Calais
Calais (Coquelles) (A)
Dunkirk

C H A N N E L

Cherbourg
Dieppe
Caen (Ouistreham)

F

Calais / Coquelles Terminal

0   400 yards
0   500 metres
Coquelles
D243E
ibis Hotel
ibis Budget Hotel
Novotel
Freight only
42
Cité Europe
P
P
P
P
P
PASSENGER TERMINAL
Petrol Station
Check-in
Frontier Controls
Freight only
ROCADE LITTORALE   A16 (E402)
A16 (E402) ROCADE LITTORALE
BOULOGNE
BOULEVARD DE L'EUROPE
BOULEVARD DE LA CÔTE D'ORALE
41
HGV Fuel Station
Eurotunnel Administration Headquarters
Freight Terminal
Parc d'activites les Terrasses
Arrivals Platforms
Departure Platforms
Freight only
Freight only
CALAIS
DUNKERQUE, A26 (PARIS)
D304
43
IAA

Departures to England follow →
Arrivals from England follow ←

SCOTLAND FERRIES

From	To	Journey time	Operator website
Scottish Islands/west coast of Scotland			
Gourock	Dunoon	20 mins	western-ferries.co.uk
Glenelg	Skye	20 mins (Easter–Oct)	skyeferry.co.uk
Numerous and varied sailings from the west coast of Scotland to Scottish islands are provided by Caledonian MacBrayne. Please visit calmac.co.uk for all ferry information, including those of other operators.			
Orkney Islands			
Aberdeen	Kirkwall	6 hrs–7 hrs 15 mins	northlinkferries.co.uk
Gills	St Margaret's Hope	1 hr	pentlandferries.co.uk
Scrabster	Stromness	1 hr 30 mins	northlinkferries.co.uk
Lerwick	Kirkwall	5 hrs 30 mins	northlinkferries.co.uk
Inter-island services are operated by Orkney Ferries. Please see orkneyferries.co.uk for details.			
Shetland Islands			
Aberdeen	Lerwick	12 hrs	northlinkferries.co.uk
Kirkwall	Lerwick	7 hrs 45 mins	northlinkferries.co.uk
Inter-island services are operated by Shetland Island Council Ferries. Please see shetland.gov.uk/ferries for details.			

Please note that some smaller island services are day and weather dependent. Reservations are required for some routes. Book and confirm sailing schedules by contacting the operator.

NORTH SEA FERRY CROSSINGS

From	To	Journey time	Operator website
Harwich	Hook of Holland	6 hrs 30 mins	stenaline.co.uk
Kingston upon Hull	Rotterdam (Europoort)	11 hrs	poferries.com
Newcastle upon Tyne	Amsterdam (IJmuiden)	15 hrs 30 mins	dfdsseaways.co.uk

Heysham Harbour

Liverpool Docks

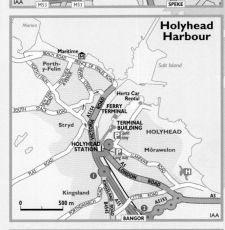

Holyhead Harbour

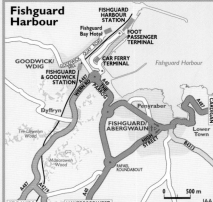

Fishguard Harbour

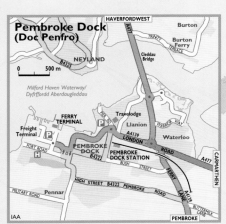

Pembroke Dock (Doc Penfro)

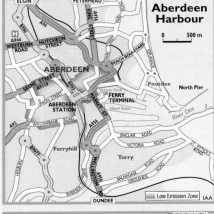

Aberdeen Harbour

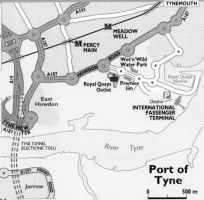

Port of Tyne

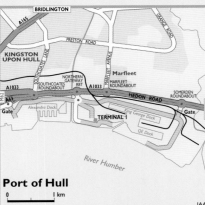

Port of Hull

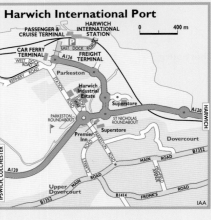

Harwich International Port

IRISH SEA FERRY CROSSINGS

From	To	Journey time	Operator website
Cairnryan	Belfast	2 hrs 15 mins	stenaline.co.uk
Cairnryan	Larne	2 hrs	poferries.com
Douglas	Belfast	2 hrs 45 mins (April–Aug)	steam-packet.com
Douglas	Dublin	2 hrs 55 mins (April–Aug)	steam-packet.com
Fishguard	Rosslare	3 hrs 15 mins	stenaline.co.uk
Heysham	Douglas	3 hrs 45 mins	steam-packet.com
Holyhead	Dublin	2 hrs (Mar–Oct)	irishferries.com
Holyhead	Dublin	3 hrs 15 mins	irishferries.com
Holyhead	Dublin	3 hrs 15 mins	stenaline.co.uk
Liverpool	Douglas	2 hrs 45 mins (Apr–Oct)	steam-packet.com
Liverpool	Dublin	8 hrs–8 hrs 30 mins	poferries.com
Liverpool (Birkenhead)	Belfast	8 hrs	stenaline.co.uk
Liverpool (Birkenhead)	Douglas	4 hrs (Nov–Mar, Sat–Sun only)	steam-packet.com
Pembroke Dock	Rosslare	4 hrs	irishferries.com

The information listed is provided as a guide only, as services are liable to change at short notice and are weather dependent. Services shown are for vehicle ferries only, operated by conventional ferry unless indicated as a fast ferry service. Please check sailings before planning your journey.

Restricted junctions

Motorway and primary route junctions which have access or exit restrictions are shown on the map pages thus:

M1 London - Leeds

Junction	Northbound	Southbound
2	Access only from A1 *(northbound)*	Exit only to A1 *(southbound)*
4	Access only from A41 *(northbound)*	Exit only to A41 *(southbound)*
6A	Access only from M25 (no link from A405)	Exit only to M25 (no link from A405)
7	Access only from A414	Exit only to A414
17	Exit only to M45	Access only from M45
19	Exit only to M6 *(northbound)*	Exit only to A14 *(southbound)*
21A	Exit only, no access	Access only, no exit
24A	Access only, no exit	Access only from A50 *(eastbound)*
35A	Exit only, no access	Access only, no exit
43	Exit only to M621	Access only from M621
48	Exit only to A1(M) *(northbound)*	Access only from A1(M) *(southbound)*

M2 Rochester - Faversham

Junction	Westbound	Eastbound
1	No exit to A2 *(eastbound)*	No access from A2 *(westbound)*

M3 Sunbury - Southampton

Junction	Northeastbound	Southwestbound
8	Access only from A303, no exit	Exit only to A303, no access
10	Exit only, no access	Access only, no exit
14	Access from M27 only, no exit	No access to M27 *(westbound)*

M4 London - South Wales

Junction	Westbound	Eastbound
1	Access only from A4 *(westbound)*	Exit only to A4 *(eastbound)*
2	Access only from A4 *(westbound)*	Access only from A4 *(eastbound)*
21	Exit only to M48	Access only from M48
23	Access only from M48	Exit only to M48
25	Exit only, no access	Access only, no exit
25A	Exit only, no access	Access only, no exit
29	Exit only to A48(M)	Access only from A48(M)
38	Exit only, no access	No restriction
39	Access only, no exit	No access or exit
42	Exit only to A483	Access only from A483

M5 Birmingham - Exeter

Junction	Northeastbound	Southwestbound
10	Access only, no exit	Exit only, no access
11A	Access only from A417 *(westbound)*	Exit only to A417 *(eastbound)*
18A	Exit only to M49	Access only from M49
18	Exit only, no access	Access only, no exit

M6 Toll Motorway

Junction	Northwestbound	Southeastbound
T1	Access only, no exit	No access or exit
T2	No access or exit	Exit only, no access
T5	Access only, no exit	Exit only to A5148 *(northbound)*, no access
T7	Exit only, no access	Access only, no exit
T8	Exit only, no access	Access only, no exit

M6 Rugby - Carlisle

Junction	Northbound	Southbound
3A	Exit only to M6 Toll	Access only from M6 Toll
4	Exit only to M42 *(southbound)* & A446	Exit only to A446
4A	Access only from M42 *(southbound)*	Exit only to M42
5	Exit only, no access	Access only, no exit
10A	Exit only to M54	Access only from M54
11A	Access only from M6 Toll	Exit only to M6 Toll
with M56 (jct 20A)	No restriction	Access only from M56 *(eastbound)*
20	Exit only to M56 *(westbound)*	Access only from M56 *(eastbound)*
24	Access only, no exit	Exit only, no access
25	Exit only, no access	Access only, no exit
30	Access only from M61	Exit only to M61
31A	Exit only, no access	Access only, no exit
45	Exit only, no access	Access only, no exit

M8 Edinburgh - Bishopton

Junction	Westbound	Eastbound
6	Exit only, no access	Access only, no exit
6A	Access only, no exit	Exit only, no access
7	Access only, no exit	Exit only, no access
7A	Exit only, no access	Access only from A725 *(northbound)*, no exit
8	No access from M73 *(southbound)* or from A8 *(eastbound)* & A89	No exit to M73 *(northbound)* or to A8 *(westbound)* & A89
9	Access only, no exit	Exit only, no access
13	Access only from M80 *(southbound)*	Exit only to M80 *(northbound)*
14	Access only, no exit	Exit only, no access
16	Exit only to A804	Access only from A879
17	Exit only to A82	No restriction
18	Access only from A82 *(eastbound)*	Exit only to A814
19	No access from A814 *(westbound)*	Exit only to A814 *(westbound)*
20	Exit only, no access	Access only, no exit
21	Access only, no exit	Exit only to A8
22	Exit only to M77 *(southbound)*	Access only from M77 *(northbound)*
23	Exit only to B768	Access only from B768
25	No access or exit from or to A8	No access or exit from or to A8
25A	Exit only, no access	Access only, no exit
28	Exit only, no access	Access only, no exit
28A	Exit only to A737	Access only from A737
29A	Exit only to A8	Access only, no exit

M9 Edinburgh - Dunblane

Junction	Northwestbound	Southeastbound
2	Access only, no exit	Exit only, no access
3	Exit only, no access	Access only, no exit
6	Access only, no exit	Exit only to A905
8	Exit only to M876 *(southwestbound)*	Access only from M876 *(northeastbound)*

M11 London - Cambridge

Junction	Northbound	Southbound
4	Access only from A406 *(eastbound)*	Exit only to A406
5	Exit only, no access	Access only, no exit
8A	Exit only, no access	No direct access, use jct 8
9	Exit only to A11	Access only from A11
13	Exit only, no access	Access only, no exit
14	Exit only, no access	Access only, no exit

M20 Swanley - Folkestone

Junction	Northwestbound	Southeastbound
2	Staggered junction; follow signs - access only	Staggered junction; follow signs - exit only
3	Exit only to M26 *(westbound)*	Access only from M26 *(eastbound)*
5	Access only from A20	For access follow signs - exit only to A20
6	No restriction	For exit follow signs
10	Access only, no exit	Exit only, no access
11A	Access only, no exit	Exit only, no access

M23 Hooley - Crawley

Junction	Northbound	Southbound
7	Exit only to A23 *(northbound)*	Access only from A23 *(southbound)*
10A	Access only, no exit	Exit only, no access

M25 London Orbital

Junction	Clockwise	Anticlockwise
1B	No direct access, use slip road to jct 2 Exit only	Access only, no exit
5	No exit to M26 *(eastbound)*	No access from M26
19	Exit only, no access	Access only, no exit
21	Access only from M1 *(southbound)* Exit only to M1 *(northbound)*	Access only from M1 *(southbound)* Exit only to M1 *(northbound)*
31	No exit (use slip road via jct 30), access only	No access (use slip road via jct 30), exit only

M26 Sevenoaks - Wrotham

Junction	Westbound	Eastbound
with M25 (jct 5)	Exit only to clockwise M25 *(westbound)*	Access only from anticlockwise M25 *(eastbound)*
with M20 (jct 3)	Access only from M20 *(northwestbound)*	Exit only to M20 *(southeastbound)*

M27 Cadnam - Portsmouth

Junction	Westbound	Eastbound
4	Staggered junction; follow signs - access only from M3 *(southbound)*. Exit only to M3 *(northbound)*	Staggered junction; follow signs - access only from M3 *(southbound)*. Exit only to M3 *(northbound)*
10	Exit only, no access	Access only, no exit
12	Staggered junction; follow signs - exit only to M275 *(southbound)*	Staggered junction; follow signs - access only from M275 *(northbound)*

M40 London - Birmingham

Junction	Northwestbound	Southeastbound
3	Exit only, no access	Access only, no exit
7	Exit only, no access	Access only, no exit
8	Exit only to M40/A40	Access only from M40/A40
13	Exit only, no access	Access only, no exit
14	Access only, no exit	Exit only, no access
16	Access only, no exit	Exit only, no access

M42 Bromsgrove - Measham

Junction	Northeastbound	Southwestbound
1	Access only, no exit	Exit only, no access
7	Exit only to M6 *(northwestbound)*	Access only from M6 *(northwestbound)*
7A	Exit only to M6 *(southeastbound)*	No access or exit
8	Access only from M6 *(southeastbound)*	Exit only to M6 *(northwestbound)*

M45 Coventry - M1

Junction	Westbound	Eastbound
Dunchurch (unnumbered)	Access only from A45	Exit only, no access
with M1 (jct 17)	Access only from M1 *(northbound)*	Exit only to M1 *(southbound)*

M48 Chepstow

Junction	Westbound	Eastbound
21	Access only from M4 *(westbound)*	Exit only to M4 *(eastbound)*
23	No exit to M4 *(eastbound)*	No access from M4 *(westbound)*

M53 Mersey Tunnel - Chester

Junction	Northbound	Southbound
11	Access only from M56 *(westbound)* Exit only to M56 *(eastbound)*	Access only from M56 *(westbound)* Exit only to M56 *(eastbound)*

M54 Telford - Birmingham

Junction	Westbound	Eastbound
with M6 (jct 10A)	Access only from M6 *(northbound)*	Exit only to M6 *(southbound)*

M56 Chester - Manchester

Junction	Westbound	Eastbound
1	Access only from M60 *(westbound)*	Exit only to M60 *(eastbound)* & A34 *(northbound)*
2	Exit only, no access	Access only, no exit
3	Access only, no exit	Exit only, no access
4	Exit only, no access	Access only, no exit
7	Exit only, no access	No restriction
8	Access only, no exit	No access or exit
9	No exit to M6 *(southbound)*	No access from M6 *(northbound)*
15	Exit only to M53	Access only from M53
16	No access or exit	No restriction

M57 Liverpool Outer Ring Road

Junction	Northwestbound	Southeastbound
3	Access only, no exit	Exit only, no access
5	Access only from A580 *(westbound)*	Exit only, no access

M60 Manchester Orbital

Junction	Clockwise	Anticlockwise
2	Access only, no exit	Exit only, no access
3	No access from M56	Access only from A34 *(northbound)*
4	Access only from A34 *(northbound)*. Exit only to M56	Access only from M56 *(eastbound)*. Exit only to A34 *(southbound)*
5	Access and exit only from and to A5103 *(northbound)*	Access and exit only from and to A5103 *(southbound)*
7	No direct access, use slip road to jct 8. Exit only to A56	Access only from A56. No exit, use jct 8
14	Access from A580 *(eastbound)*	Exit only to A580 *(westbound)*
16	Access only, no exit	Exit only, no access
20	Exit only, no access	Access only, no exit
22	No restriction	Exit only, no access
25	Exit only, no access	No restriction
26	No restriction	Exit only, no access
27	Access only, no exit	Exit only, no access

M61 Manchester - Preston

Junction	Northwestbound	Southeastbound
3	No access or exit	Exit only, no access
with M6 (jct 30)	Exit only to M6 *(northbound)*	Access only from M6 *(southbound)*

M62 Liverpool - Kingston upon Hull

Junction	Westbound	Eastbound
23	Access only, no exit	Exit only, no access
32A	No access to A1(M) *(southbound)*	No restriction

M65 Preston - Colne

Junction	Northeastbound	Southwestbound
9	Exit only, no access	Access only, no exit
11	Access only, no exit	Exit only, no access

M66 Bury

Junction	Northbound	Southbound
with A56	Exit only to A56 *(northbound)*	Access only from A56 *(southbound)*
1	Exit only, no access	Access only, no exit

M67 Hyde Bypass

Junction	Westbound	Eastbound
1A	Access only, no exit	Exit only, no access
2	Exit only, no access	Access only, no exit

M69 Coventry - Leicester

Junction	Northbound	Southbound
2	Access only, no exit	Exit only, no access

M73 East of Glasgow

Junction	Northbound	Southbound
1	No exit to A74 & A721	No exit to A74 & A721
2	No access from or exit to A89. No access from *(eastbound)*	No access from or exit to A89. No exit to M8 *(westbound)*

M74 and A74(M) Glasgow - Gretna

Junction	Northbound	Southbound
3	Exit only, no access	Access only, no exit
3A	Access only, no exit	Exit only, no access
4	No access from A74 & A721	Access only, no exit to A74 & A721
7	Access only, no exit	Exit only, no access
9	No access or exit	Exit only, no access
10	No restriction	Access only, no exit
11	Access only, no exit	Exit only, no access
12	Exit only, no access	Access only, no exit
18	Exit only, no access	Access only, no exit

M77 Glasgow - Kilmarnock

Junction	Northbound	Southbound
with M8 (jct 22)	No exit to M8 *(westbound)*	No access from M8 *(eastbound)*
4	Access only, no exit	Exit only, no access
6	Access only, no exit	Exit only, no access
7	Access only, no exit	No restriction
8	Exit only, no access	Exit only, no access

M80 Glasgow - Stirling

Junction	Northbound	Southbound
4A	Exit only, no access	Access only, no exit
6A	Access only, no exit	Exit only, no access
8	Exit only to M876 *(northeastbound)*	Access only from M876 *(southwestbound)*

M90 Edinburgh - Perth

Junction	Northbound	Southbound
1	No exit, access only	Exit only to A90 *(eastbound)*
2A	Exit only to A92 *(eastbound)*	Access only from A92 *(westbound)*
7	Access only, no exit	Exit only, no access
8	Exit only, no access	Access only, no exit
10	No access from A912. No exit to A912 *(southbound)*	No access from A912 *(northbound)* No exit to A912

M180 Doncaster - Grimsby

Junction	Westbound	Eastbound
1	Access only, no exit	Exit only, no access

M606 Bradford Spur

Junction	Northbound	Southbound
2	Exit only, no access	No restriction

M621 Leeds - M1

Junction	Clockwise	Anticlockwise
2A	Access only, no exit	Exit only, no access
4	No exit or access	No restriction
5	Access only, no exit	Exit only, no access
6	Exit only, no access	Access only, no exit
with M1 (jct 43)	Exit only to M1 *(southbound)*	Access only from M1 *(northbound)*

M876 Bonnybridge - Kincardine Bridge

Junction	Northeastbound	Southwestbound
with M80 (jct 5)	Access only from M80 *(northeastbound)*	Exit only to M80 *(southwestbound)*
with M9 (jct 8)	Exit only to M9 *(eastbound)*	Access only from M9 *(westbound)*

A1(M) South Mimms - Baldock

Junction	Northbound	Southbound
2	Exit only, no access	Access only, no exit
3	No restriction	Exit only, no access
5	Access only, no exit	No access or exit

A1(M) Pontefract - Bedale

Junction	Northbound	Southbound
41	No access to M62 *(eastbound)*	No restriction
43	Access only from M1 *(northbound)*	Exit only to M1 *(southbound)*

A1(M) Scotch Corner - Newcastle upon Tyne

Junction	Northbound	Southbound
57	Exit only to A66(M) *(eastbound)*	Access only from A66(M) *(westbound)*
65	No access Exit only to A194(M) & A1 *(northbound)*	No exit Access only from A194(M) & A1 *(southbound)*

A3(M) Horndean - Havant

Junction	Northbound	Southbound
1	Access only from A3	Exit only to A3
4	Exit only, no access	Access only, no exit

A38(M) Birmingham, Victoria Road (Park Circus)

Junction	Northbound	Southbound
with B4132	No exit	No access

A48(M) Cardiff Spur

Junction	Westbound	Eastbound
29	Access only from M4 *(westbound)*	Exit only to M4 *(eastbound)*
29A	Exit only to A48 *(westbound)*	Access only from A48 *(eastbound)*

A57(M) Manchester, Brook Street (A34)

Junction	Westbound	Eastbound
with A34	No exit	No access

A58(M) Leeds, Park Lane and Westgate

Junction	Northbound	Southbound
with A58	No restriction	No access

A64(M) Leeds, Clay Pit Lane (A58)

Junction	Westbound	Eastbound
with A58	No exit (to Clay Pit Lane)	No access (from Clay Pit Lane)

A66(M) Darlington Spur

Junction	Westbound	Eastbound
with A1(M) (jct 57)	Exit only to A1(M) *(southbound)*	Access only from A1(M) *(northbound)*

A74(M) Gretna - Abington

Junction	Northbound	Southbound
18	Exit only, no access	Access only, no exit

A194(M) Newcastle upon Tyne

Junction	Northbound	Southbound
with A1(M) (jct 65)	Access only from A1(M) *(northbound)*	Exit only to A1(M) *(southbound)*

A12 M25 - Ipswich

Junction	Northeastbound	Southwestbound
13	Access only, no exit	No restriction
14	Exit only, no access	Access only, no exit
20A	Exit only, no access	Access only, no exit
20B	Access only, no exit	Exit only, no access
21	No restriction	Access only, no exit
23	Exit only, no access	Access only, no exit
24	Access only, no exit	Exit only, no access
27	Exit only, no access	Access only, no exit
Dedham & Stratford St Mary (unnumbered)	Exit only	Access only

A14 M1 - Felixstowe

Junction	Westbound	Eastbound
with M1/M6 (jct19)	Exit only to M6 and M1 *(northbound)*	Access only from M6 and M1 *(southbound)*
4	Exit only, no access	Access only, no exit
21	Access only, no exit	Exit only, no access
22	Exit only, no access	Access only from A1 *(southbound)*
23	Access only, no exit	Exit only, no access
31	No restriction	Access only, no exit
34	Access only, no exit	Exit only, no access
36	Exit only to A11, access only from A1303	Access only from A11
38	Access only from A11	Exit only to A11
39	Exit only, no access	Access only, no exit
61	Access only, no exit	Exit only, no access

A55 Holyhead - Chester

Junction	Westbound	Eastbound
8A	Exit only, no access	Access only, no exit
23A	Access only, no exit	Exit only, no access
24A	Exit only, no access	No access or exit
27A	No restriction	No access or exit
33A	Exit only, no access	No access or exit
33B	Exit only, no access	Access only, no exit
36A	Exit only to A5104	Access only from A5104

Refer also to atlas pages 32–33. In August 2023 the Ultra Low Emission Zone is due to be extended.
For further information visit www.tfl.gov.uk/modes/driving/ultra-low-emission-zone

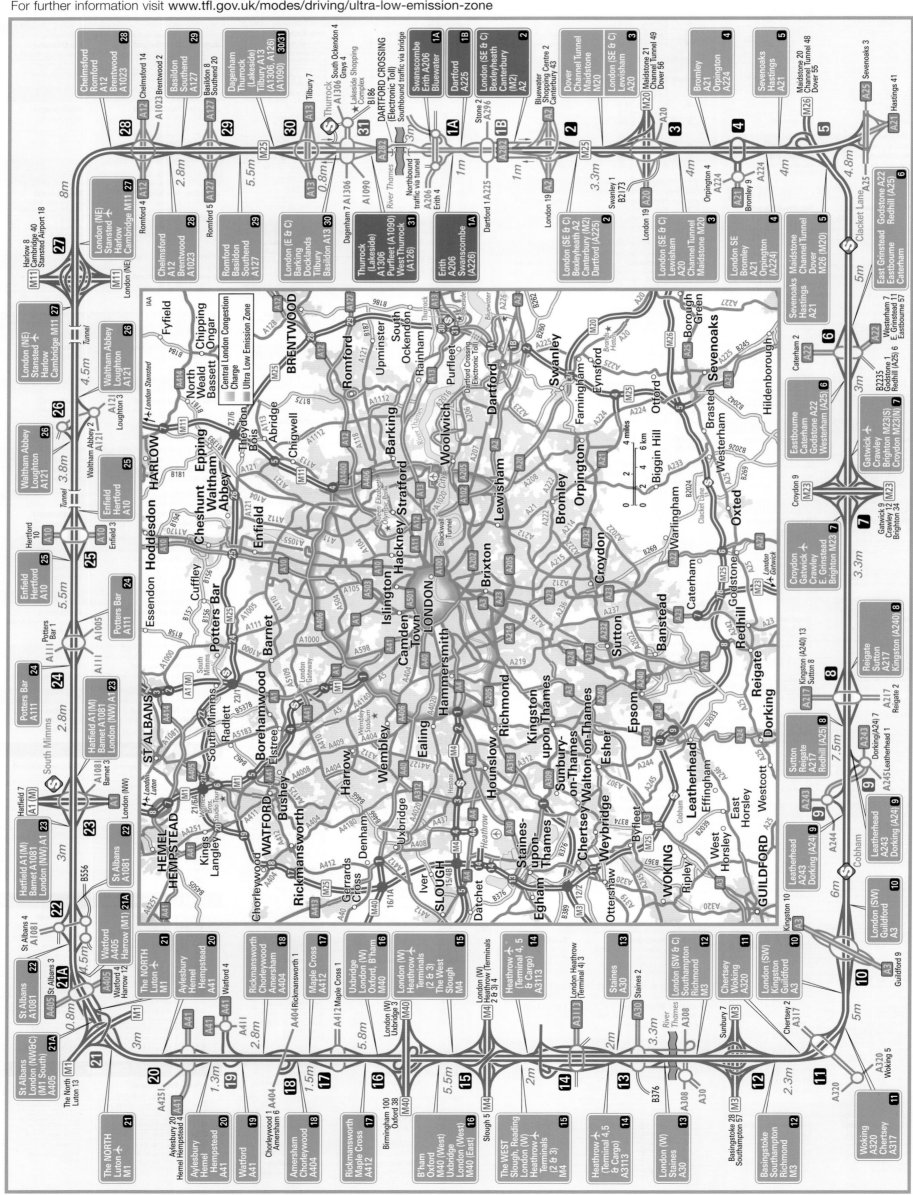

Refer also to atlas pages 53, 64–65

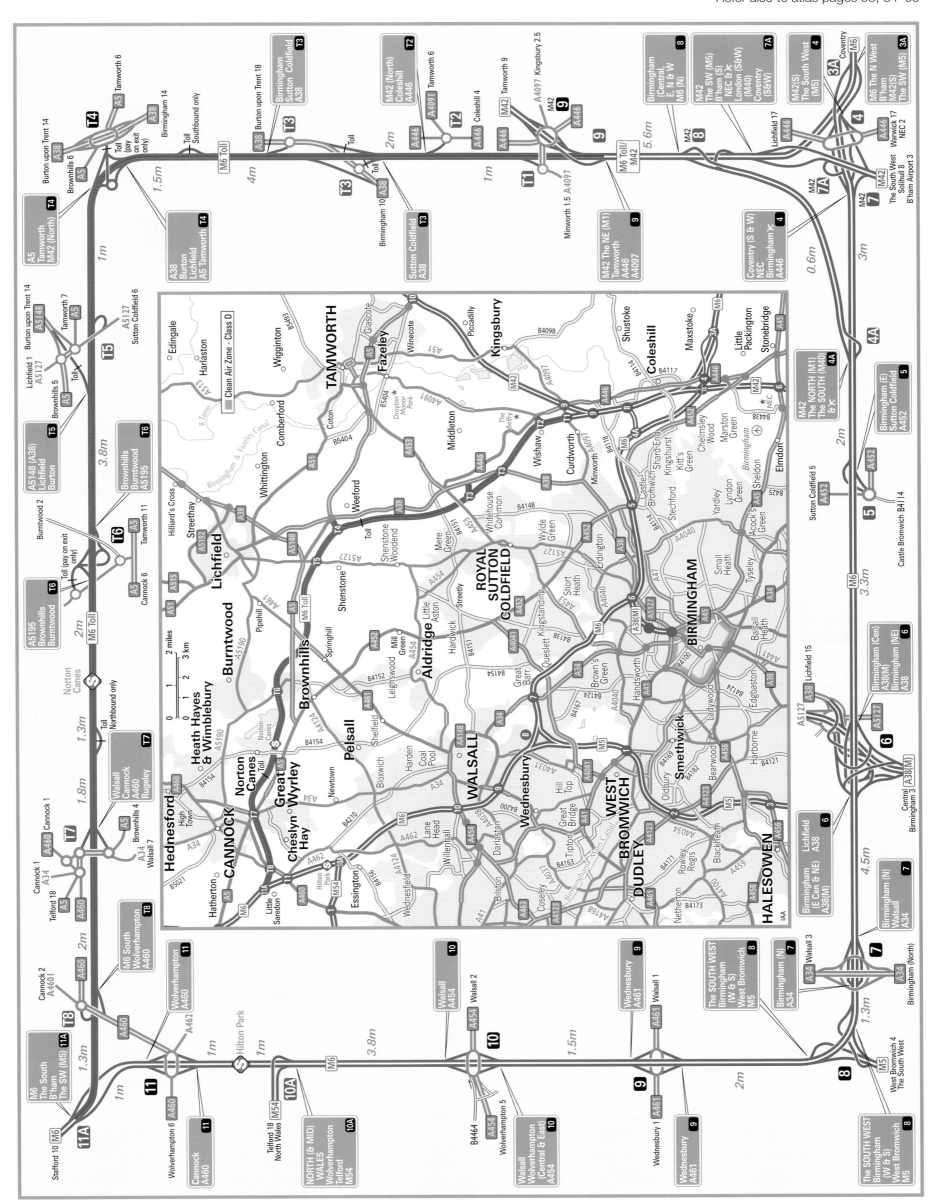

Smart motorways

Since Britain's first motorway (the Preston Bypass) opened in 1958, motorways have changed significantly. A vast increase in car journeys over the last 64 years has meant that motorways quickly filled to capacity. To combat this, the recent development of **smart motorways** uses technology to monitor and actively manage traffic flow and congestion.

How they work

Smart motorways utilise various active traffic management methods, monitored through a regional traffic control centre:

- Traffic flow is monitored using CCTV
- Speed limits are changed to smooth traffic flow and reduce stop-start driving
- Capacity of the motorway can be increased by either temporarily or permanently opening the hard shoulder to traffic
- Warning signs and messages alert drivers to hazards and traffic jams ahead
- Lanes can be closed in the case of an accident or emergency by displaying a red X sign

- Emergency refuge areas are located regularly along the motorway where there is no hard shoulder available

The map shows the main motorway network with the three different types of smart motorway in operation. Since January 2022, plans for the opening of further schemes have been put on hold to allow a review of safety data and the improvement of existing schemes.

—— **Controlled motorway**
Variable speed limits without hard shoulder (the hard shoulder is used in emergencies only)

—— **Hard shoulder running**
Variable speed limits with part-time hard shoulder (the hard shoulder is open to traffic at busy times when signs permit)

—— **All lane running**
Variable speed limits with hard shoulder as permanent running lane (there is no hard shoulder); this is standard for all new motorway schemes since 2013

—— **Standard motorway**

Quick tips

- Never drive in a lane closed by a red X

- Keep to the speed limit shown on the gantries
- A solid white line indicates the hard shoulder – do not drive in it unless directed or in the case of an emergency
- A broken white line indicates a normal running lane
- Exit the smart motorway where possible if your vehicle is in difficulty. In an emergency, move onto the hard shoulder where there is one, or the nearest emergency refuge area
- Put on your hazard lights if you break down

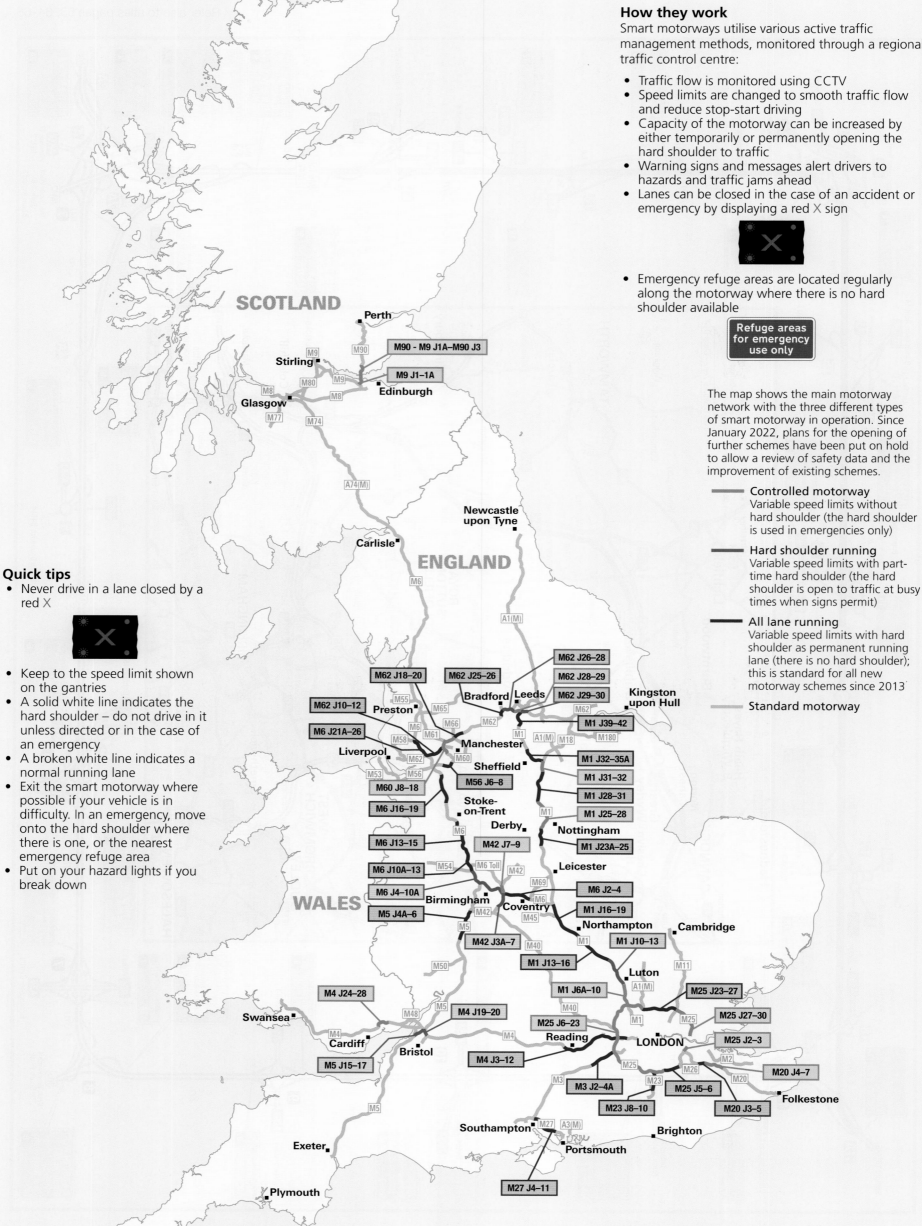

Motoring information

Motorway with number	Restricted primary route junctions	Narrow primary/other A/B road with passing places (Scotland)	Railway line, in tunnel
Toll motorway with toll station	Primary route service area	Road under construction	Railway station, tram stop, level crossing
Motorway junction with and without number	Primary route destination BATH	Road tunnel	Preserved or tourist railway
Restricted motorway junctions A1123	Other A road single/ dual carriageway	Road toll, steep gradient (arrows point downhill)	Airport (major/minor)
Motorway service area, rest area B2070	B road single/ dual carriageway	Distance in miles between symbols	Heliport
Motorway and junction under construction	Minor road more than 4 metres wide, less than 4 metres wide	Vehicle ferry (all year, seasonal)	International freight terminal
Primary route single/ dual carriageway	Roundabout	Fast vehicle ferry or catamaran	24-hour Accident & Emergency hospital
Primary route junction with and without number	Interchange/junction	Passenger ferry (all year, seasonal)	Crematorium

Park and Ride (at least 6 days per week)

City, town, village or other built-up area

628 Height in metres

637 Lecht Summit — Mountain pass

Snow gates (on main routes)

National boundary

County or administrative boundary

City with clean air zone, low/zero emission zone

Touring information   To avoid disappointment, check opening times before visiting

Scenic route	Industrial interest	RSPB site	Cave or cavern	National Trust site
Tourist Information Centre	Aqueduct or viaduct	National Nature Reserve (England, Scotland, Wales)	Windmill, monument or memorial	National Trust for Scotland site
Tourist Information Centre (seasonal)	Vineyard	Local nature reserve	Beach (award winning)	English Heritage site
Visitor or heritage centre	Brewery or distillery	Wildlife Trust reserve	Lighthouse	Historic Scotland site
Picnic site	Garden	Forest drive	Golf course	Cadw (Welsh heritage) site
Caravan site (AA inspected)	Arboretum	National trail	Football stadium	Other place of interest
Camping site (AA inspected)	Country park	Viewpoint	County cricket ground	Boxed symbols indicate attractions within urban area
Caravan & camping site (AA inspected)	Showground	Waterfall	Rugby Union national stadium	World Heritage Site (UNESCO)
Abbey, cathedral or priory	Theme park	Hill-fort	International athletics stadium	National Park and National Scenic Area (Scotland)
Ruined abbey, cathedral or priory	Farm or animal centre	Roman antiquity	Horse racing, show jumping	Forest Park
Castle	Zoological or wildlife collection	Prehistoric monument	Motor-racing circuit	Sandy beach
Historic house or building	Bird collection	Battle site with year 1066	Air show venue	Heritage coast
Museum or art gallery	Aquarium	Preserved or tourist railway	Ski slope (natural, artificial)	Major shopping centre

Town plans

Motorway and junction	Railway station	Toilet, with facilities for the less able	Tourist Information Centre	Abbey, chapel, church
Primary road single/ dual carriageway and numbered junction	Tramway	Building of interest	Visitor or heritage centre	Synagogue
A road single/ dual carriageway and numbered junction	London Underground station	Ruined building	Post Office	Mosque
B road single/ dual carriageway	London Overground station	City wall	Public library	Golf course
Local road single/ dual carriageway	Rail interchange	Cliff lift	Shopping centre	Racecourse
Other road single/dual carriageway, minor road	Docklands Light Railway (DLR) station	Escarpment	Shopmobility	Nature reserve
One-way, gated/ closed road	Light rapid transit system station	River/canal, lake	Theatre or performing arts centre	Aquarium
Restricted access road	Airport, heliport	Lock, weir	Cinema	World Heritage Site (UNESCO)
Pedestrian area	Railair terminal	Park/sports ground	Museum	English Heritage site
Footpath	Park and Ride (at least 6 days per week)	Cemetery	Castle	Historic Scotland site
Road under construction	Car park, with electric charging point	Woodland	Castle mound	Cadw (Welsh heritage) site
Road tunnel	Bus/coach station	Built-up area	Monument, memorial, statue	National Trust site
Level crossing	Hospital, 24-hour Accident & Emergency hospital	Beach	Viewpoint	National Trust for Scotland site

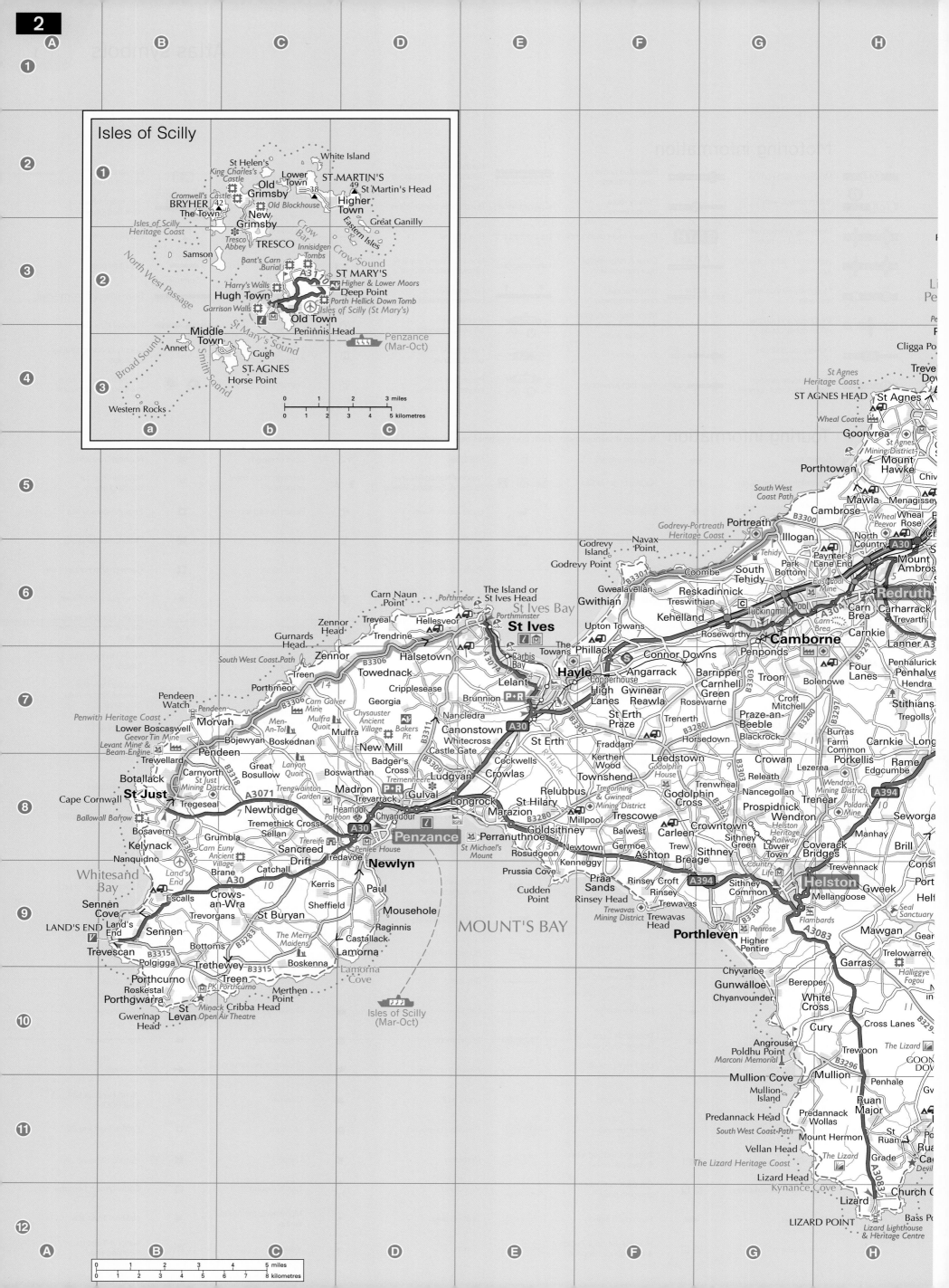

2

Isles of Scilly

White Island
St Helen's
King Charles's Castle
Cromwell's Castle
Old Grimsby
Lower Town
ST. MARTIN'S
38
49 St Martin's Head
Higher Town
BRYHER
The Town
42
Old Blockhouse
New Grimsby
Eastern Isles
Great Ganilly
Tresco Abbey
TRESCO
Innisidgen Tombs
Crow Bar
Crow Sound
Samson
Bant's Carn Burial
Isles of Scilly Heritage Coast
A3110
ST MARY'S
Higher & Lower Moors
Harry's Walls
Hugh Town
Deep Point
Garrison Walls
Porth Hellick Down Tomb
Old Town
Isles of Scilly (St Mary's)
North West Passage
Peninnis Head
Penzance (Mar-Oct)
Middle Town
St Mary's Sound
Broad Sound
Annet
Gugh
ST AGNES
Horse Point
Smith Sound
Western Rocks

0   1   2   3 miles
0 1 2 3 4 5 kilometres

a   **b**   **c**

St Agnes Heritage Coast
ST AGNES HEAD
St Agnes
Wheal Coates
Goonvrea
St Agnes Mining District
Porthtowan
Mount Hawke
Menagissey
Mawla
Cambrose
Wheal Peevor
Wheal Rose
South West Coast Path
Godrevy-Portreath Heritage Coast
Portreath
B3300
Illogan
North Country
A30
Mount Ambros
Redruth
Navax Point
Godrevy Island
Godrevy Point
Coombe
South Tehidy
Tehidy
Park Bottom
Paynter's Lane End
Eastpool Mine
Tuckingmill
Pool
Carn Brea
Carharrack
Gwealavellan
Reskadinnick
Treswithian
Carn Brea
Trevarth
The Island or St Ives Head
Porthmeor
Porthminster
St Ives Bay
Gwithian
Kehelland
Roseworthy
Camborne
Carnkie
Lanner
Carn Naun Point
Treveal
Hellesveor
St Ives
Upton Towans
Penponds
Four Lanes
Penhalurick Penhalve
Hendra
Zennor Head
Trendrine
Carbis Bay
The Towans
Phillack
High Gwinear
Barripper
Carnhell Green
Troon
Bolenowe
Gurnards Head
Zennor
B3306
Halsetown
Hayle
Copperhouse
Angarrack
Reawla
Rosewarne
Praze-an-Beeble
Burras
Farm Common
Stithians
Tregolls
South West Coast Path
Treen
Towednack
Cripplesease
Lelant
Connor Downs
High Lanes
St Erth Praze
Trenerth
Horsedown
Blackrock
Carnkie
Edgcumbe
Rame
Long
Pendeen Watch
Porthmeor
Carn Galver Mine
Georgia
Bakers Pit
Brunnion
P+R
A30
St Erth
Fraddam
Kerthen Wood
Leedstown
Crowan
Lezerea
Porkellis
Penwith Heritage Coast
Pendeen
Morvah
Men-An-Tol
Mulfra Quoit
Chysauster Ancient Village
Mulfra
Nancledra
Whitecross
Castle Gate
Cockwells
Crowlas
Townshend
Godolphin House
Tregonning & Gwinear Mining District
Godolphin Cross
Trenwheal
Nancegollan
Wendron
Trenear
A394
Levant Mine & Beam Engine
Geevor Tin Mine
Trewellard
Carnyorth
St Just Mining District
Great Bosullow
Lanyon Quoit
Boskednan
Boswarthan
Badger's Cross
Tremenheere
B3309
B3311
Ludgvan
Crowlas
St Hilary
Relubbus
Millpool
Trescowe
Balwest
Carleen
Prospidnick
Wendron
Trenear
Seworga
Botallack
St Just
Tregeseal
B3318
Newbridge
A3071
Trengwainton Garden
Madron
Heamoor
Trevarrack
P+R
Gulval
Longrock
Marazion
A30
Goldsithney
Newtown
Germoe
Ashton
Trew
Sithney
Crowntown
Sithney Green
Lower Town
Helston Heritage Railway
Coverack Bridges
Trewennack
Manhay
Brill
Cape Cornwall
Ballowall Barrow
Bosavern
Grumbla
Tremethick Cross
Sellan
Trereife
Polgoon
Chyandour
Penlee House
Penzance
Perranuthnoe
St Michael's Mount
Rosudgeon
Kenneggy
Praa Sands
Balwest
Germoe
Breage
Ashton
Sithney Common
Helston
Gweek
Port
Helf
Kelynack
Nanquidno
Carn Euny Ancient Village
Sancreed
Drift
Catchall
Brane
A30
Tredavoe
Newlyn
Goldsithney
Whitesand Bay
Land's End
Escalls
Crows-an-Wra
Trevorgans
Kerris
Paul
Mousehole
MOUNT'S BAY
Cudden Point
Prussia Cove
Rinsey Croft
Rinsey
Trewavas
A394
Sithney Common
Life
Country
Porthleven
Higher Pentire
Mawgan
Garras
Trelowarren
Sennen Cove
LAND'S END
Land's End
Sennen
Trevescan
Polgigga
Trethewey
Treen
Bottoms
B3315
B3283
Sheffield
The Merry Maidens
Boskenna
Castallack
Lamorna
Raginnis
Merthen Point
Lamorna Cove
Isles of Scilly (Mar-Oct)
Chyvarloe
Gunwalloe
Chyanvounder
White Cross
Berepper
Porthcurno
Roskestal
Porthgwarra
Gwennap Head
St Levan
Minack Open Air Theatre
PK Porthcurno
Cribba Head
Trewavas Head
Trewavas Mining District
Rinsey Head
Angrouse
Poldhu Point
Marconi Memorial
Cury
Cross Lanes
The Lizard
Trewoon
GOON DO
Mullion Cove
Mullion Island
Mullion
Penhale
Predannack Wollas
Ruan Major
Predannack Head
South West Coast Path
Mount Hermon
St Ruan
Ru
Vellan Head
The Lizard Heritage Coast
The Lizard
Grade
A3083
Lizard Head
Kynance Cove
Lizard
LIZARD POINT
Lizard Lighthouse & Heritage Centre
Bass Po
Church C
Devil

0   1   2   3   4   5 miles
0 1 2 3 4 5 6 7 8 kilometres

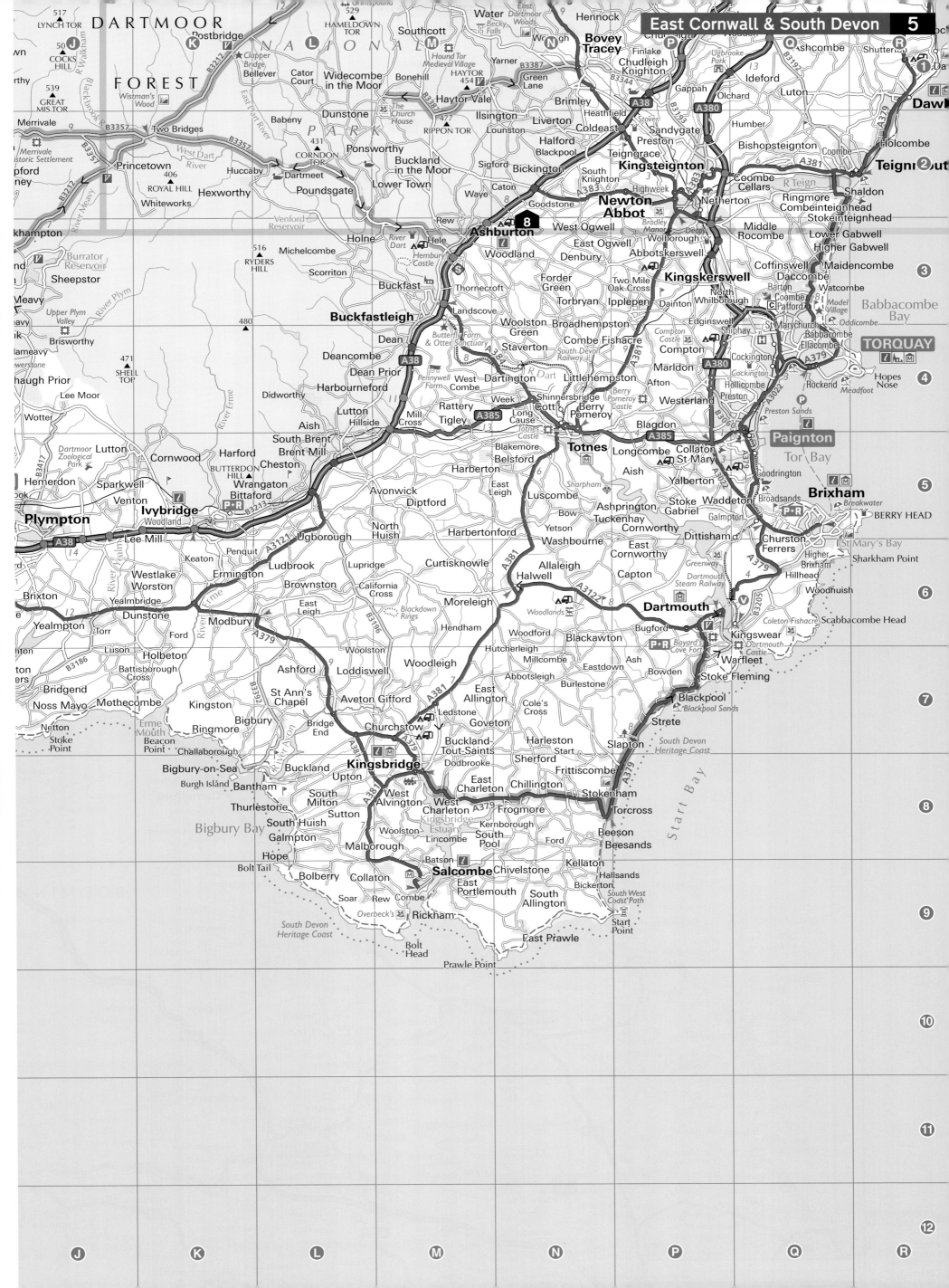

A B C D E F G H

① ② ③ ④ ⑤ ⑥ ⑦ ⑧ ⑨ ⑩ ⑪ ⑫

Morwenstow
Higher Sharpnose Point
South West Coast Path
Lower Sharpnose Point

Steeple Point

Sandy Mouth
Northcott Mouth
Crooklets
Bude Bay *i* **Bud**
Lynstone
Hele

Widemouth Bay
Box's Sh

Millook
Dizzard Point Poundstock
Dizzard
Penlean
St Gennys Tregole
Coxford
Crackington Haven
Cambeak Rosecare
Sweets Wainhouse Corner
15 B3263 *19* Treng

Witchcraft & Magic Beeny A39 Marshgate
Pentire Point - Widemouth Heritage Coast
Boscastle Treworld
Trevalga Tresparrett Otterham Trelash
14 B3263 Lesnewth Otterham Station
TINTAGEL HEAD Castle Trethevey B3266 Treneg
Tintagel Bossiney Hallworthy
Old Post Office Tregatta Davidstow
Penhallic Point Trewarmett Trewassa Cold
Treknow *Vale of Avalon* Trefrew B3266 Northcot
Trebarwith Penpethy *Cornwall at War*
Rockhead Tregoodwell St Clether
Treligga Delabole Pengelly Trevia Crowdy Reservoir
South West Coast Path Valley Truckle **Camelford**
Westdowns Trewalder Lanteglos Bowithick 346 347
Port Isaac Helstone Pencarrow *Wesley Co*
Bay B3314 Tresinney Watergate
Rumps Point Kellan Head Port-Gaverne Knightsmill 419
Port Quin Bay Varley Head Port Isaac Treveighan BROWN WILLY
Pentire Point Port Quin Trewetha Treburgett Michaelstow
New Polzeath Plain Street Trelights Pendoggett B O D M I N
Padstow Bay *Bee Centre* Treharrock A39 Trenewth
Hayle Bay Trebetherick B3314 St Endellion Trequite Churchtown
Stepper Point Polzeath St Minver Tregellist St Tudy Jamaica Inn Bolven
Trevanger Tregellist St Breward
Trevose Head Gunver Head Pityme Tredrizzick Trewethern St Kew Lank Row Bradford
Heritage Coast Crugmeer *Prideaux Place* Splatt St Kew Highway Wenfordbridge
TREVOSE HEAD Mother Ivey's Bay Harlyn Rock Stoptide Hendra Penpont
Dinas Head Trevone Bay Treator Chapel Amble *De Lank River*
Constantine Bay Harlyn Trevone Bodieve St Mabyn Blisland Colliford Lake
Constantine Bay Windmill **Padstow** *i* Tregunna Waterloo Temple
Treyarnon Towan Dinas Trevanson Tredethy *Colliford Lake Park*
St Merryn 8 Tregonce Croanford Hellandbridge A30 BROWN DOW
Trehemborne Shop Trevorrick Edmonton *Pencarrow House*
Porthcothan St Issey **Wadebridge** Egloshayle Helland Millpool
Whitecross *Royal Cornwall* St Breock Sladesbridge Warleggan
Park Head Treburrick Penrose Little Petherick Treneague Burlawn Washaway Cardinham Mount St Neot
Rumford Trenance Tredinnick Hay Polbrock Lane End Dunmere Pantersbridge
Engollan St Ervan Trelow St Jidgey *St Breock Downs Monolith* Brocton *R Camel* Boscarne Cooksland Lampe
Bedruthan Steps Downhill St Eval *Camel Creek Adventure Park* Ruthernbridge Nanstallon Fletchersbridge Tredinnick Ley Carnglaze
Carnewas 8 Nine Maidens Tregawne *Bodmin & Wenford Railway* A38 Doublebois
Trenance B3274 A39 Withielgoose St Lawrence **Bodmin** *i* A30 *13*
Berryl's Point Mawgan Porth *Cornish Birds of Prey Centre* Rutherbridge Tremore Tregullon Trebyan West Middle *12*
Griffin's Point St Mawgan Rosenannon Retire Lanivet Cutmadoc Taphouse Taphouse
Trevarrian Carloggas Talskiddy St Wenn Withiel Lamorick *Lanhydrock* Sweetshouse East
Watergate Bay Tregurrian Gluvian Reterth **3** Demelza Victoria Higher Lockengate *Restormel Castle* A390 Taphouse
Towan Head *Vale of* Cornwall Newquay St Columb Major Tregonetha Down A391 Bokiddick Braddock Herod
i **Newquay** St Columb Minor Trebudannon Tregaswith *Castle-an-Dinas* B3274 *11* Cornwall A38 Boconnoc
ral Bay Porth Trevithick Black Cross *Screech Owl Sanctuary* Belowda *Lan Tor* Bodwen Penhale Trebell **Lostwithiel**
West Pentire Colan Ruthvoes Roche Tregoss Lanivet Tregellast
Crantock Trenowah *Goss Moor* Criggan Carbis Penhale
Enniscaven Tredinnick

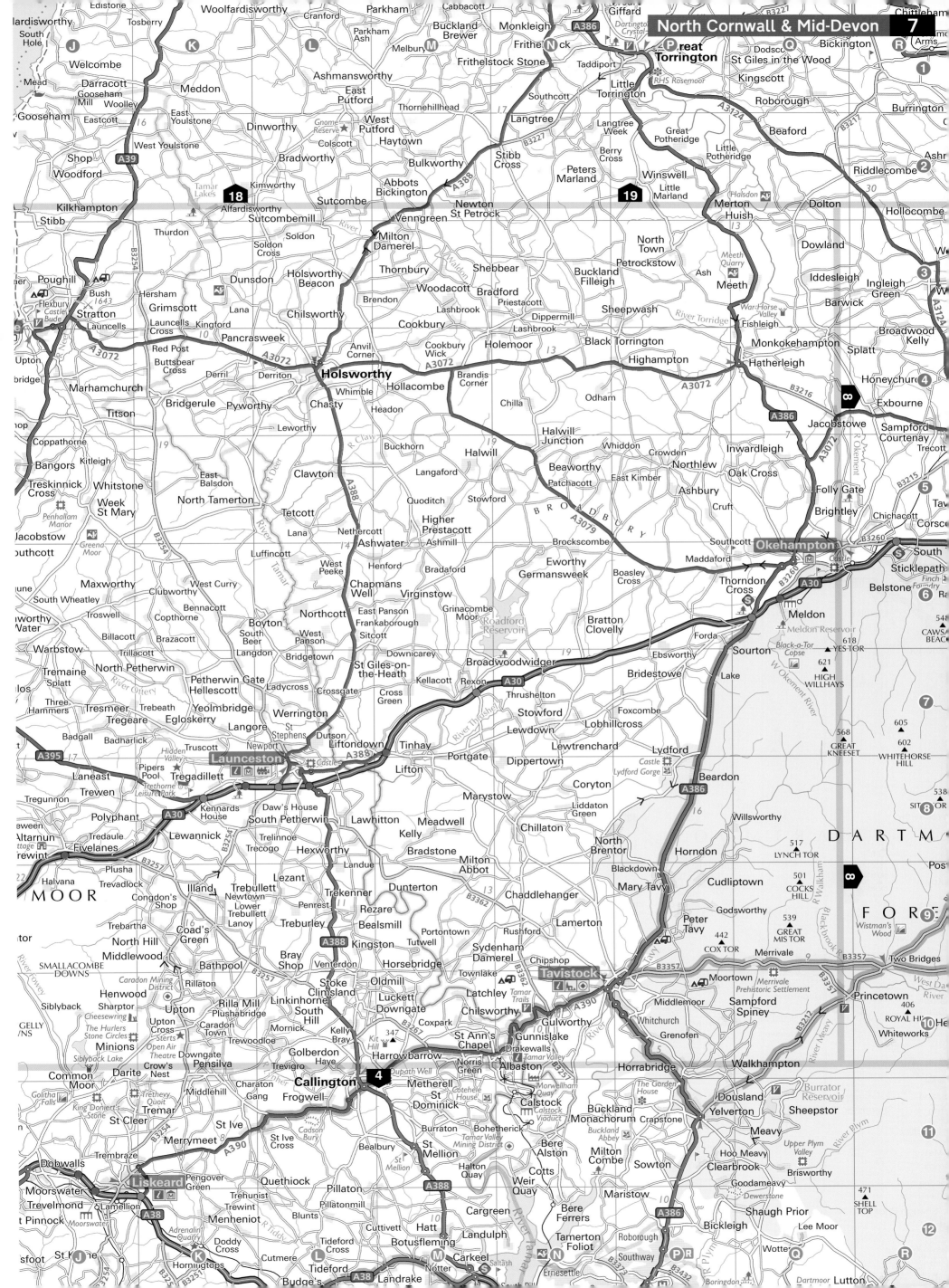

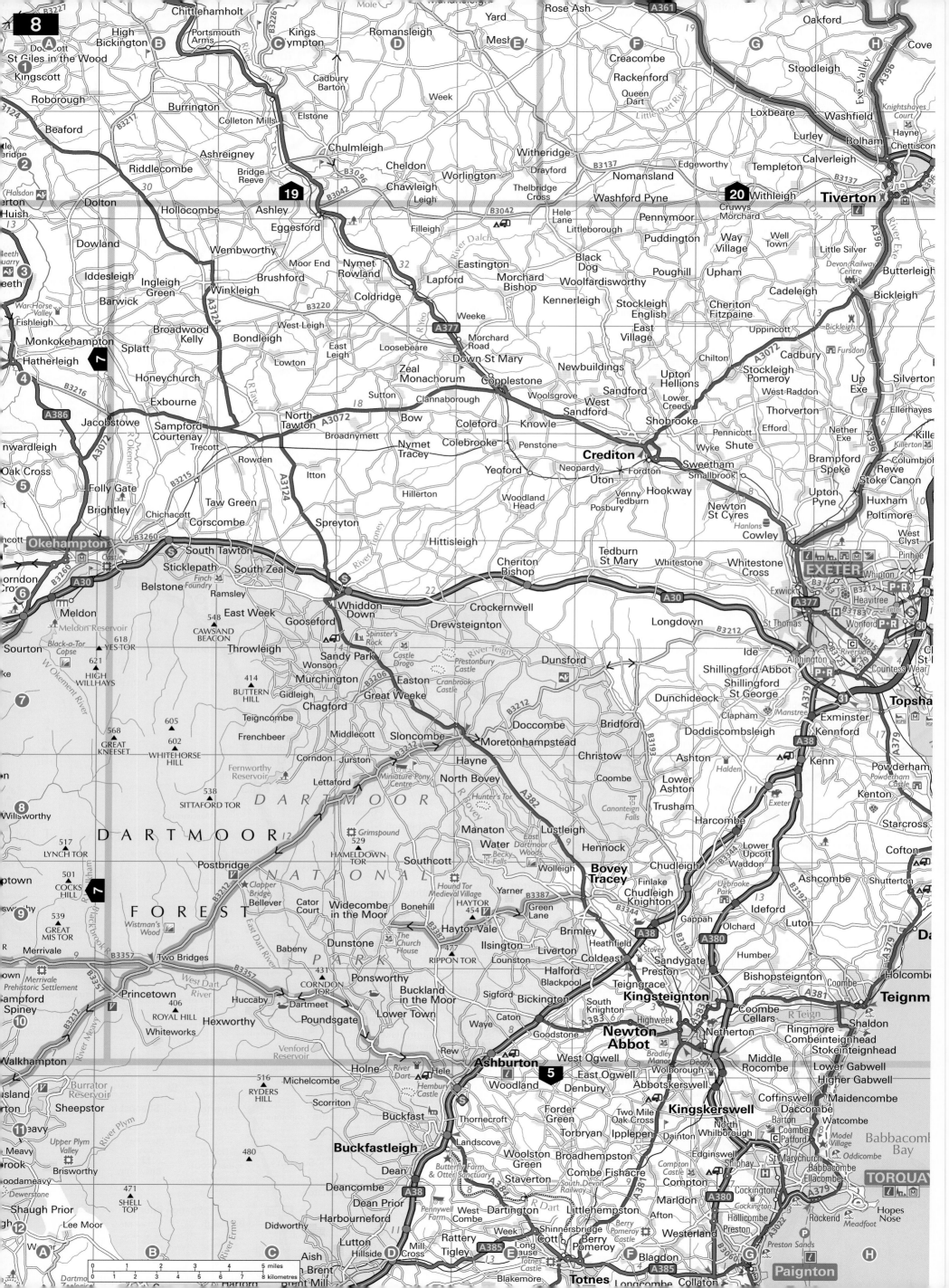

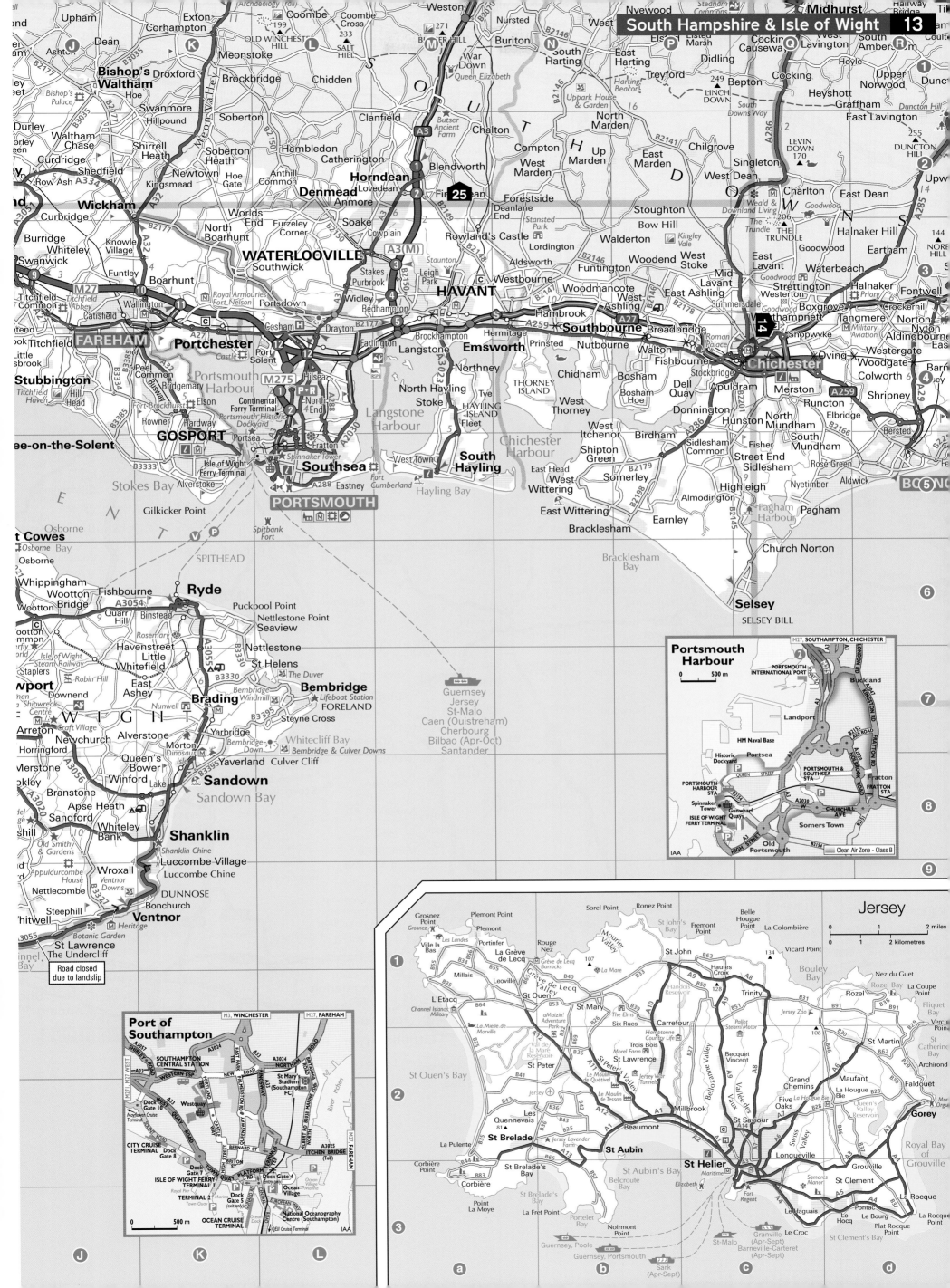

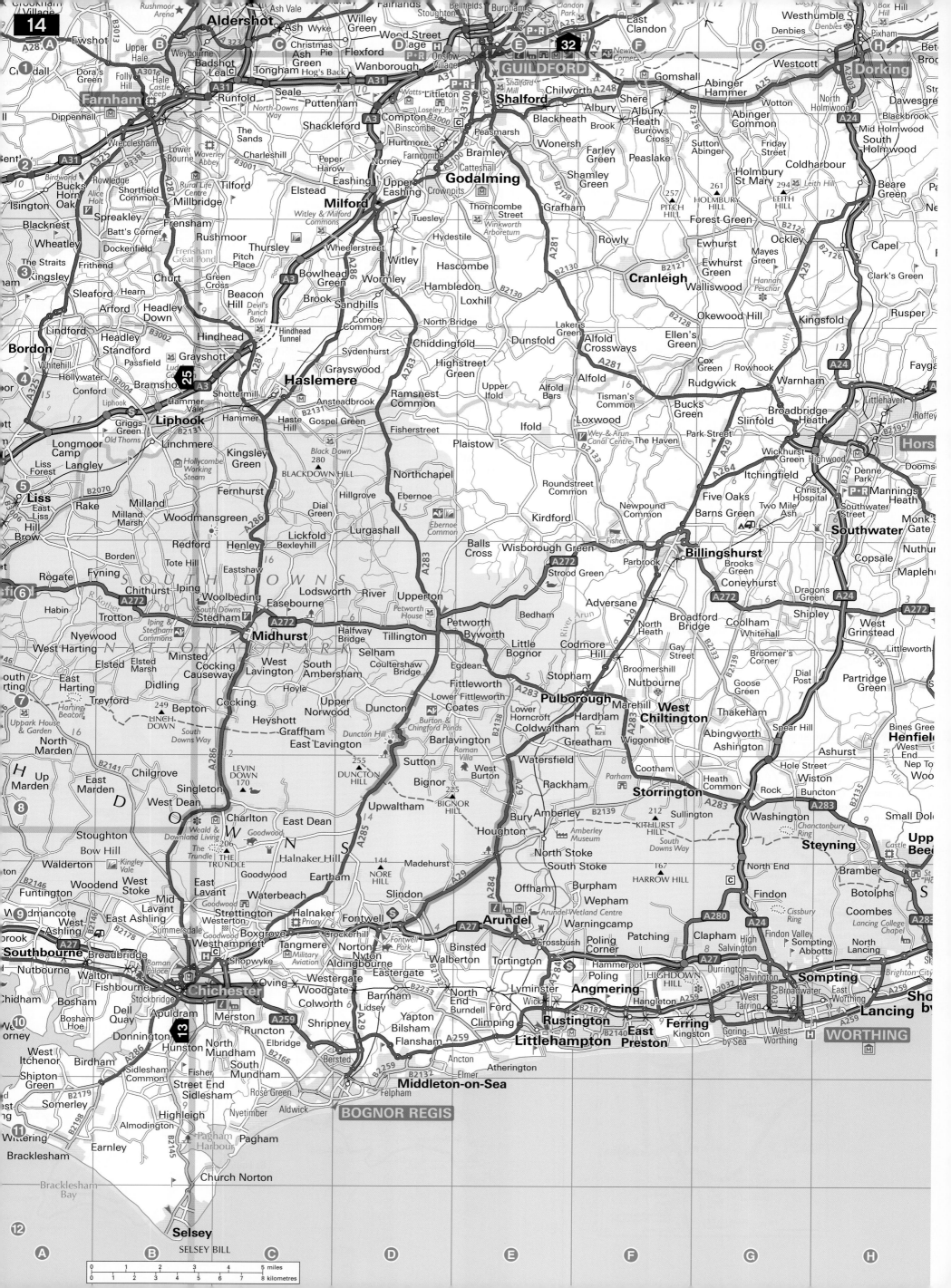

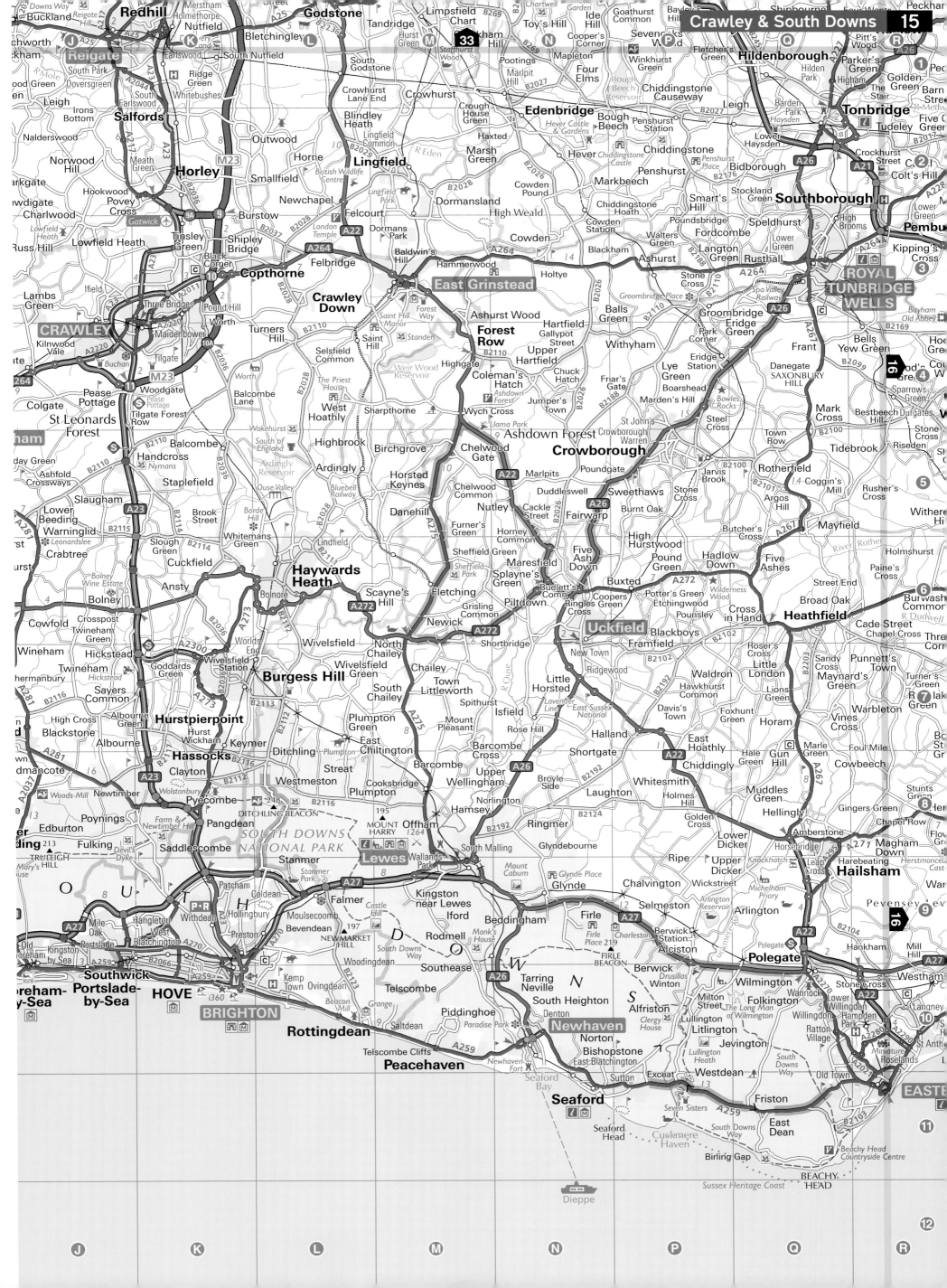

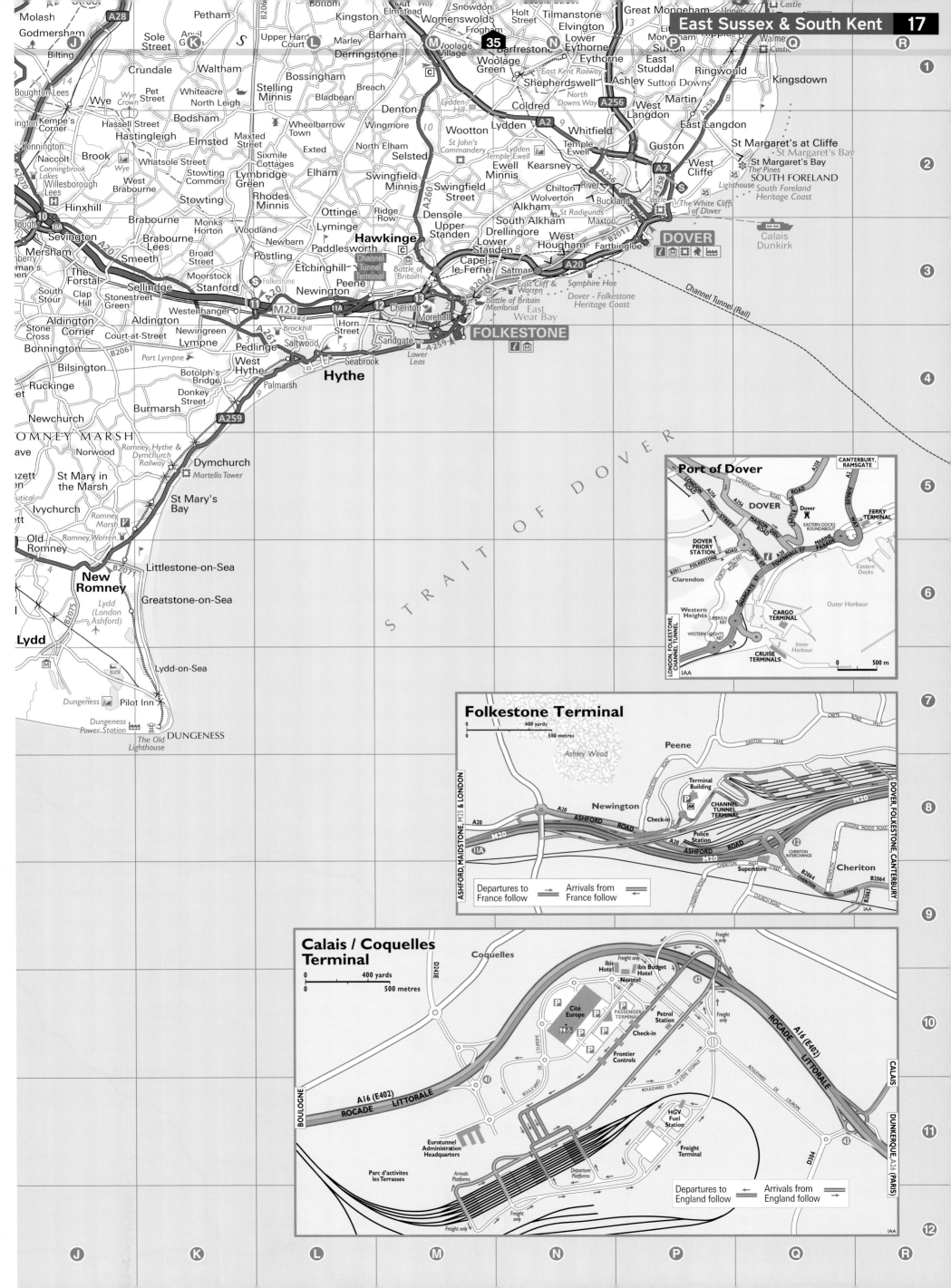

North West Point

Lundy Heritage Coast

LUNDY

▲142

Marine Reserve

Shutter Point

Surf Point

Ⓟ Bideford (Apr-Oct)
Ilfracombe (Apr-Oct)

Ro

Morte
Point

Wooda
Mo
Ba

Baggy
Point · Putsboro

Croyde Bay

Croyde Bay

North Devon Heritage Coast

Lundy Ⓟ
(Apr-Oct)

B A R N S T A P L E

O R

B I D E F O R D   B A Y

Northam
Burrows

App
N

Westward Ho!

Abbotsham

The Big
Sheep

Bid

HARTLAND POINT

Shipload Bay

Titchberry

Brownsham

Hartland Heritage Coast

Ford

Yeo
Vale

Littleha
Salt

Damehole
Point

Hartland Abbey & Gardens

Stoke

Velly

Clovelly

Higher
Clovelly

Buck's
Mills

Fairy Cross

Horns
Cross

Woodtown

Goldworthy

Cabbacott

Hartland Quay

Speke's Mill Mouth

Hartland

B3248

Buck's
Cross

Milky Way

A39

10

Milford

Docton Mill

Philham

Woolfardisworthy

Cranford

Parkham

Buckland
Brewer

Monk

Fri

Elmscott

Edistone

Tosberry

Parkham
Ash

Melbury

Frithelstock St

Hardisworthy

South
Hole

Ashmansworthy

Welcombe

Meddon

East
Putford

Thornehillhead

Lan

Mead

Darracott

Gooseham
Mill

Woolley

East
Youlstone

Dinworthy

Gnome Reserve ★

West
Putford

Haytown

Colscott

Stibb
Cross

Gooseham

Eastcott

16

Morwenstow

West Youlstone

Bradworthy

Bulkworthy

Abbots
Bickington

A388

Higher Sharpnose Point

Shop

A39

Kimworthy

Sutcombe

Newton
St Petrock

South West Coast Path

Woodford

Tamar Lakes

▲ **7**

Alfardisworthy

Sutcombemill

River

Venngreen

Lower Sharpnose Point

Kilkhampton

Thurdon

Soldon
Cross

Milton
Damerel

Thornbury

Shebbear

Steeple Point

Stibb

Soldon

B3254

Dunsdon

Holsworthy
Beacon

Woodacott

Bradford

Priesta

*Sandy
Mouth*

B3254

Brendon

Lashbrook

*Northcott
Mouth*

Maer

Poughill

Bush

Hersham

Lana

Grimscott

Chilsworthy

Cookbury

Crooklets

Flexbury

*Castle
Bude*

1643

Stratton

Launcells

Launcells
Cross

Kingford

Anvil
Corner

Cookbury
Wick

Holemoo

Ⓘ **Bude**

Bude
Bay

Lynstone

Upton

Helebridge

A3072

Widemouth

Marhamchurch

Red Post

Buttspear
Cross

E

Derri

Derriton

A3072

Holsworthy

Hollacombe

Brandis
Corner

Whimble

A3072

Pancrasweek

10

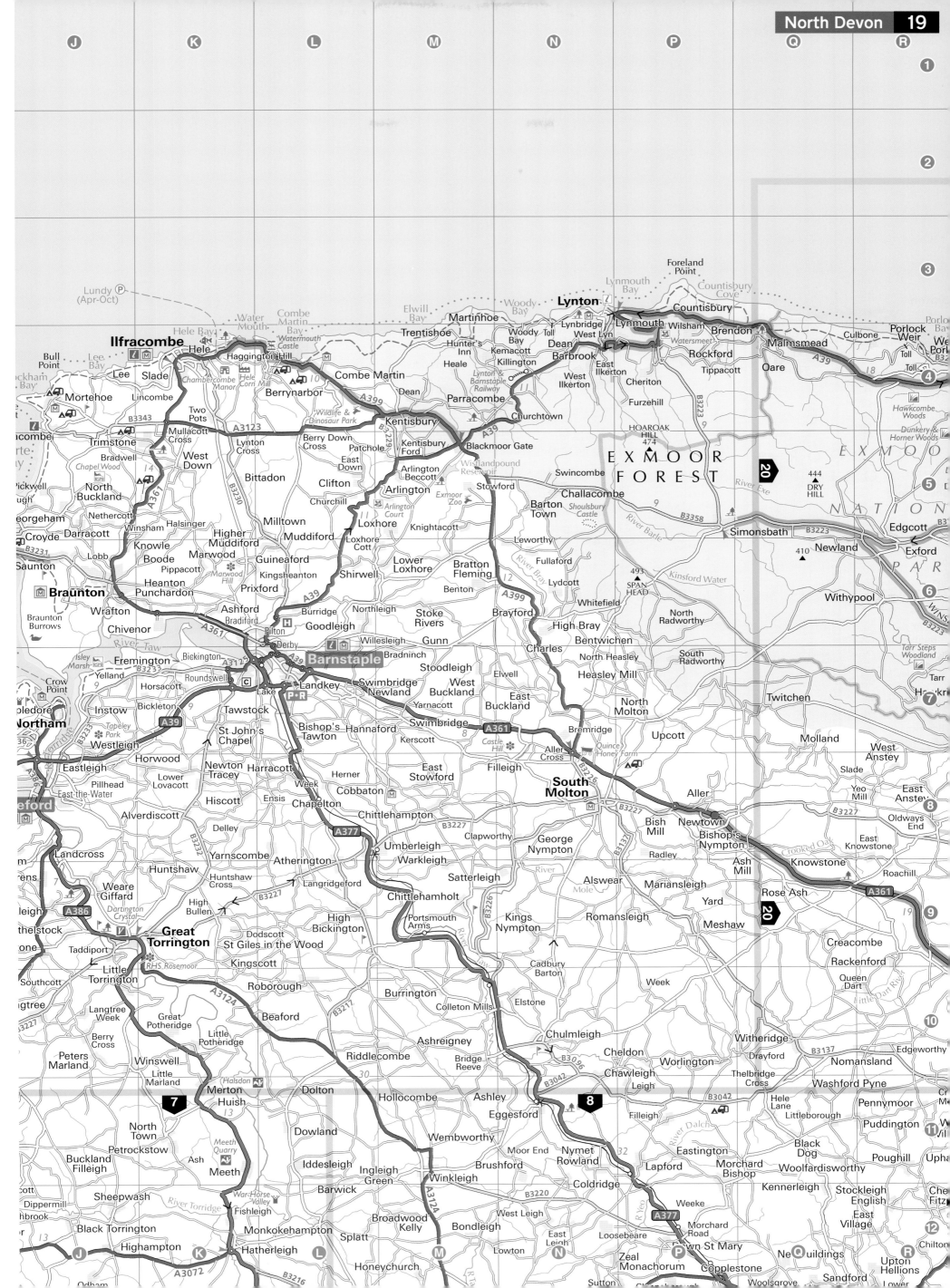

J K L M N P Q R

1 2 3 4 5 6 7 8 9 10 11 12

Foreland Point

Lundy (P) (Apr-Oct)

Lynmouth Bay

Countisbury Cove

Lynton
Lynbridge
West Lyn
Lynmouth
Wilsham
Brendon
Countisbury
Culbone
Porlock Weir
Porlo

Combe Martin Bay
Elwill Bay
Woody Bay
Martinhoe
Trentishoe
Hunter's Inn
Heale
Woody Bay
Toll
Kemacott
Killington

Ilfracombe
Hele Bay
Hele
Watermouth Castle
Haggington Hill
Hele Corn Mill
Combe Martin
Dean
Parracombe

West Ilkerton
Dean
Barbrook
East Ilkerton
Cheriton
Furzehill
Malmsmead
Oare
Toll
Toll

Bull Point
Lee Bay
Lee
Slade
Chambercombe Manor
Berrynarbor
Wildlife & Dinosaur Park

Rockford
Tippacott
Watersmeet

Mortehoe
Lincombe
Two Pots
Mullacott Cross
A3123
Lynton Cross
West Down
Berry Down Cross
Patchole
Kentisbury
Kentisbury Ford
Blackmoor Gate
Churchtown
HOAROAK HILL 474
Hawkcombe Woods
Dunkery & Horner Woods

Trimstone
Bradwell
Chapel Wood
West Down
B3343
Bittadon
Clifton
Churchill
East Down
Arlington Beccott
Arlington
Wistlandpound Reservoir
Stowford
Knightacott
Arlington Court
Exmoor Zoo
Swincombe
Challacombe
Shoulsbury Castle
Barton Town
EXMOOR FOREST
River Exe
DRY HILL 444
EXMOO

Pickwell
North Buckland
Nethercott
Winsham
Halsinger
Higher Muddiford
Milltown
Muddiford
Loxhore
Loxhore Cott
Lower Loxhore
Leworthy
Fullaford
Whitefield
SPAN HEAD 493
Kinsford Water
North Radworthy
NATION
Newland
Edgcott
Exford
PAR

Georgeham
Croyde
Darracott
Knowle
Boode
Pippacott
Marwood
Marwood Hill
Kingsheanton
Guineaford
Shirwell
Bratton Fleming
Benton
River Bray
Lydcott
High Bray
North Heasley
South Radworthy
Heasley Mill
Withypool
Tarr Steps Woodland

Lobb
Heanton Punchardon
Prixford
Ashford
A39
Northleigh
Stoke Rivers
Brayford
Charles
Bentwichen
Tarr

Braunton
Wrafton
Chivenor
Bradiford
Pilton
Derby
Burridge
Goodleigh
Willesleigh
Gunn
Bradninch
Elwell
North Molton
North Heasley
Twitchen

Braunton Burrows
River Taw
Fremington
Bickington
B3233
Roundswell
Barnstaple
Lake
Landkey
Swimbridge Newland
Stoodleigh
West Buckland
Yarnacott
East Buckland
Swimbridge
A361
Castle Hill
Bremridge
Upcott
Molland
West Anstey
Slade

Crow Point
Isley Marsh
Yelland
Instow
Horsacott
Bickleton
Tawstock
St John's Chapel
Bishop's Tawton
Hannaford
Kerscott
East Stowford
Filleigh
Aller Cross
Quince Honey Farm
South Molton
Aller
Yeo Mill
East Anste

Northam
Tapeley Park
Westleigh
Eastleigh
Horwood
Lower Lovacott
Newton Tracey
Harracott
Week
Herner
Cobbaton
East Stowford
Filleigh
Bish Mill
Newtown
Bishop's Nympton
Ash Mill
Knowstone
Oldways End
East Knowstone

ford
East-the-Water
Pillhead
Alverdiscott
Hiscott
Delley
Ensis
Chapelton
Chittlehampton
B3227
Clapworthy
George Nympton
Radley
Alswear
Marians leigh
Knowstone
Roachill
A361

Landcross
Huntshaw
Yarnscombe
Atherington
Umberleigh
Warkleigh
Satterleigh
River Mole
Kings Nympton
Romansleigh
Yard
Meshaw
Rose Ash
A361

leigh
A386
Weare Giffard
Huntshaw Cross
Langridgeford
High Bullen
Chittlehamholt
Portsmouth Arms
Kings Nympton
Cadbury Barton
Week
Creacombe
Rackenford

Great Torrington
Dartington Crystal
RHS Rosemoor
St Giles in the Wood
Dodscott
High Bickington
River Taw
Queen Dart

thelstock
one
Taddiport
Little Torrington
Kingscott
Roborough
Burrington
Colleton Mills
Elstone
Witheridge
B3137
Nomansland
Edgeworthy

Southcott
Langtree
Berry Cross
Beaford
Ashreigney
Bridge Reeve
Chulmleigh
Cheldon
Worlington
Chawleigh
Leigh
Thelbridge Cross
Washford Pyne

ngtree
B3227
Peters Marland
Langtree Week
Great Potheridge
Little Potheridge
Riddlecombe
Hollocombe
Ashley
Eggesford
B3042
Leigh
Filleigh
Hele Lane
Littleborough
Pennymoor

Winswell
Little Marland
Halsdon
Merton
Huish
Dolton
B3096
Nymet Rowland
Lapford
Morchard Bishop
Woolfardisworthy
Black Dog
Poughill
Upha

North Town
Petrockstowe
Buckland Filleigh
Meeth Quarry
Ash
Meeth
Dowland
War Horse Valley
Winkleigh
Brushford
Moor End
Eastington
Morchard Road
Kennerleigh
Stockleigh English
Che Fitz

Dippermill
hbrook
Black Torrington
Sheepwash
Fishleigh
Monkokehampton
Iddesleigh
Ingleigh Green
Barwick
Broadwood Kelly
Bondleigh
West Leigh
Coldridge
Weeke
B3220
East Leigh
Loosebeare
Morchard Road
Weeke
East Village

cott
Highampton
Hatherleigh
Honeychurch
Lowton
Zeal Monachorum
Copplestone
Woolsgrove
Sutton
Chu

A3072
Odh
A3216
wn St Mary
NeQuildings
Upton Hellions
Sandford
Lower

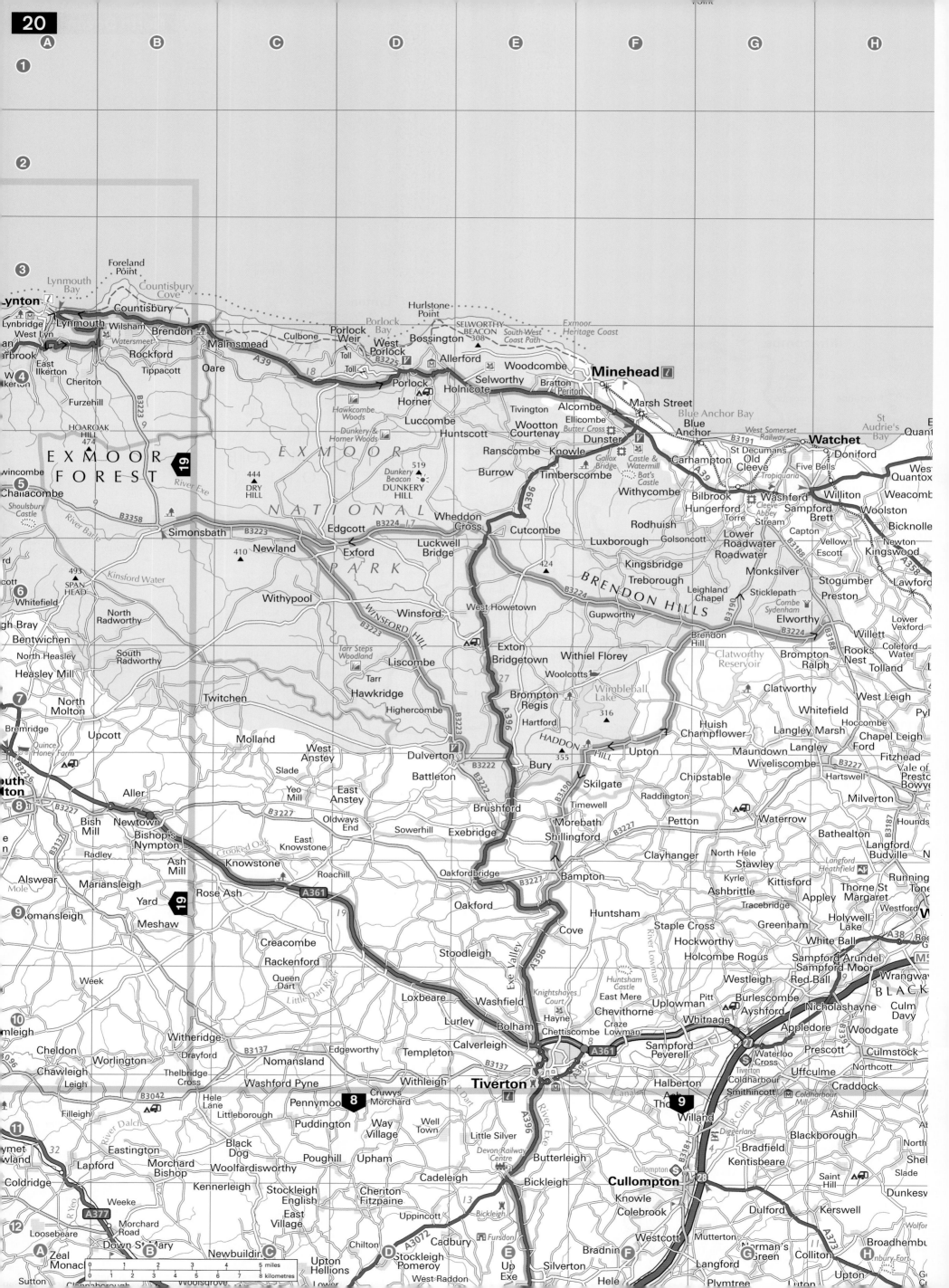

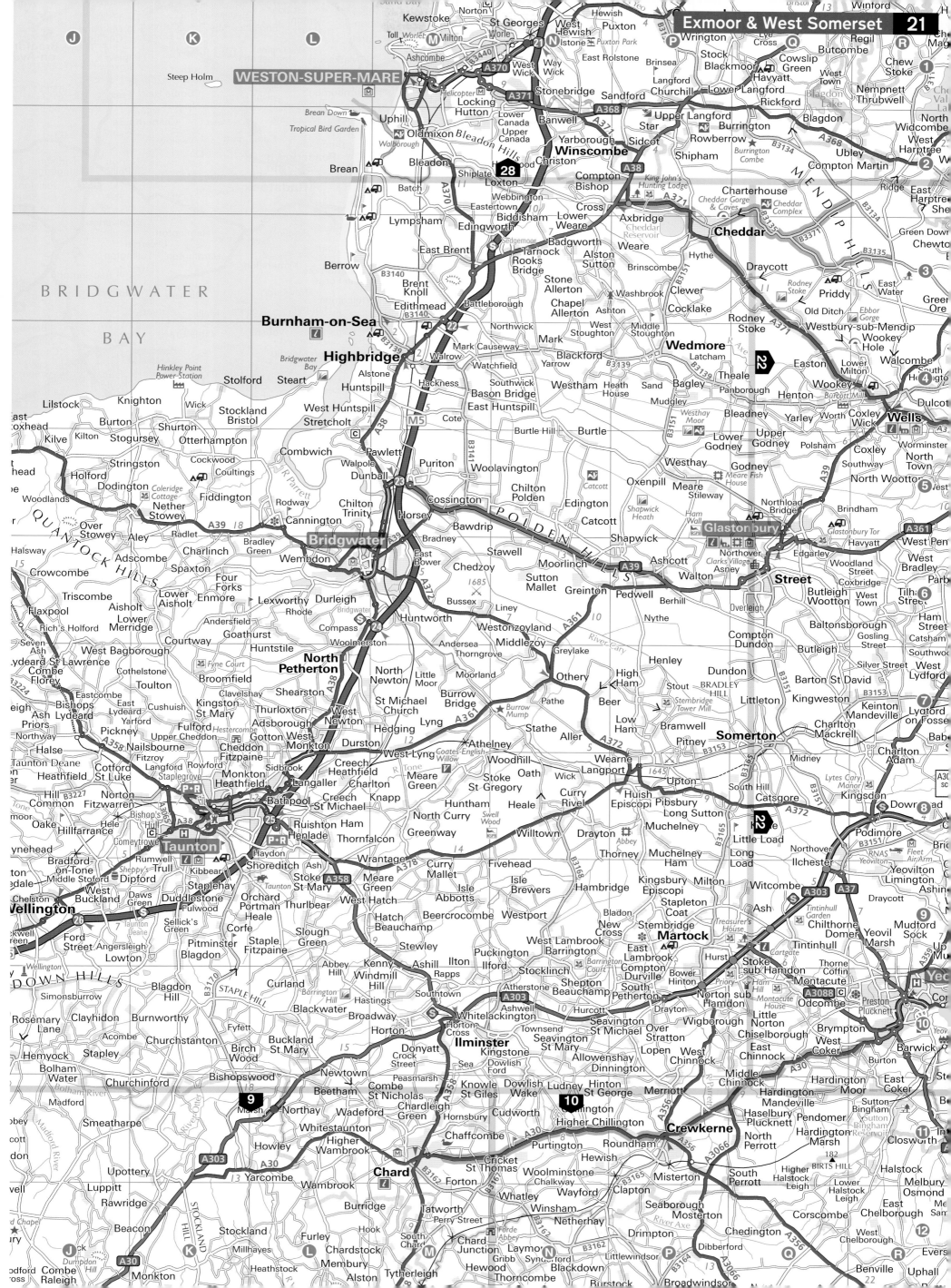

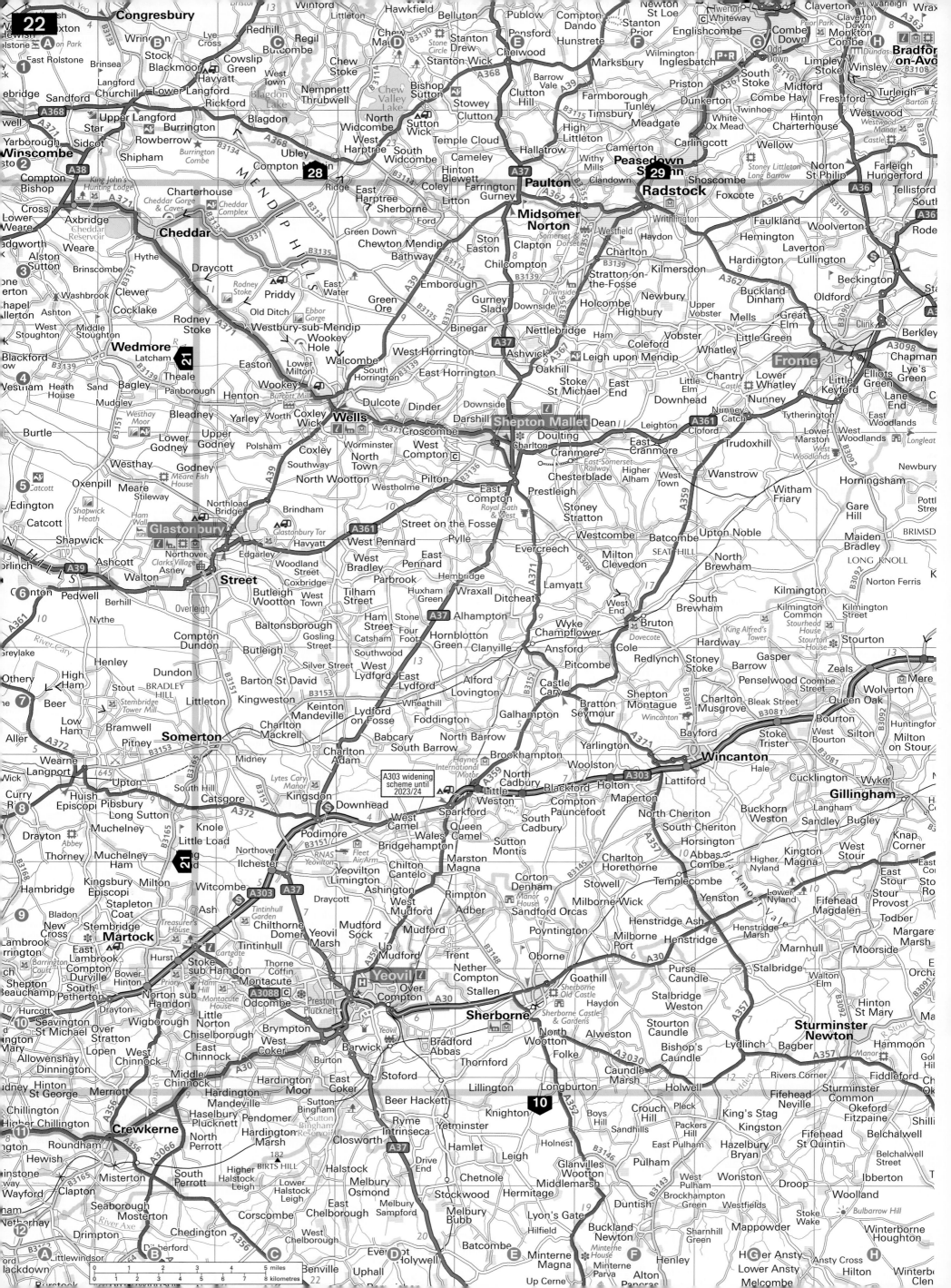

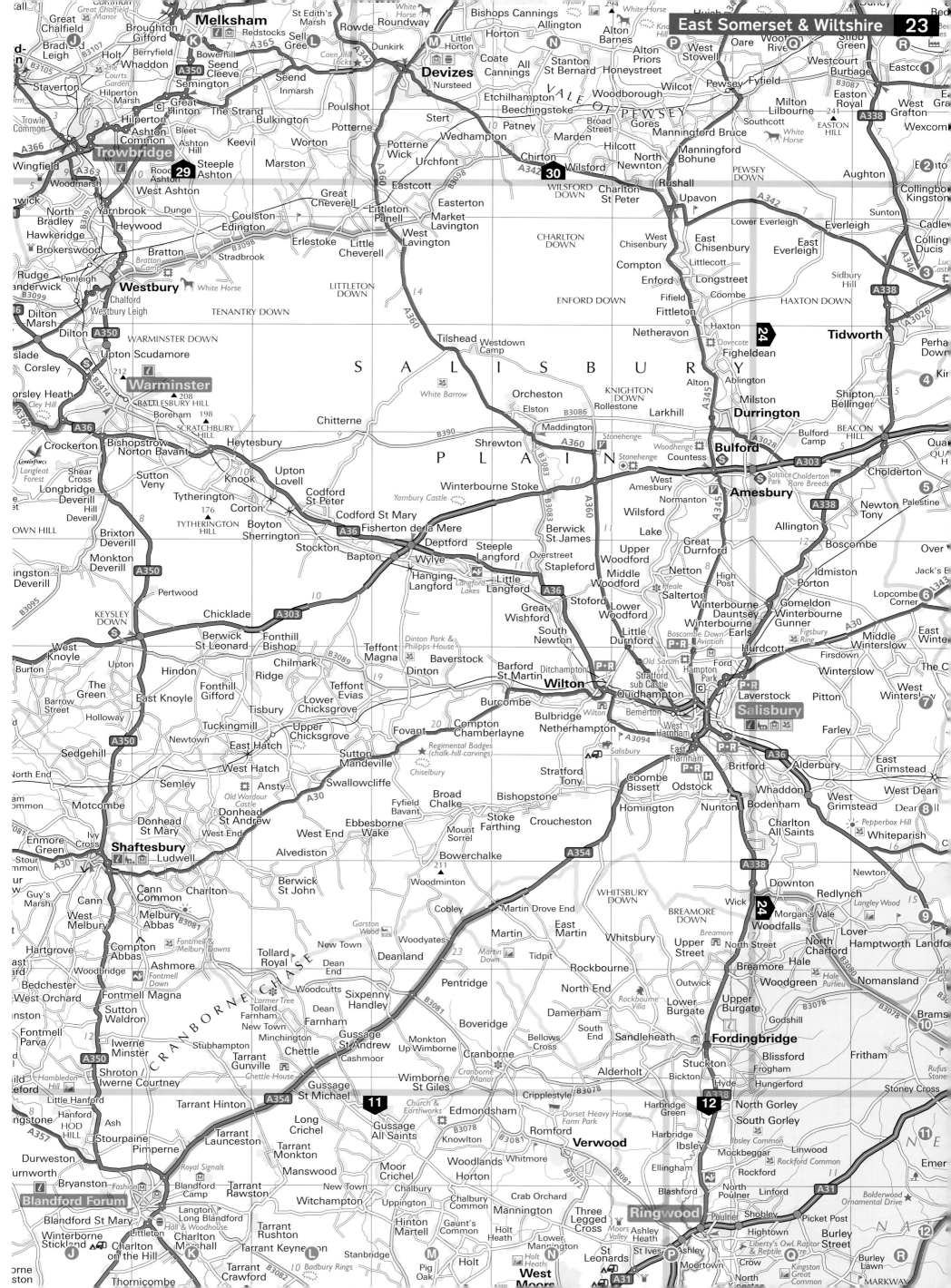

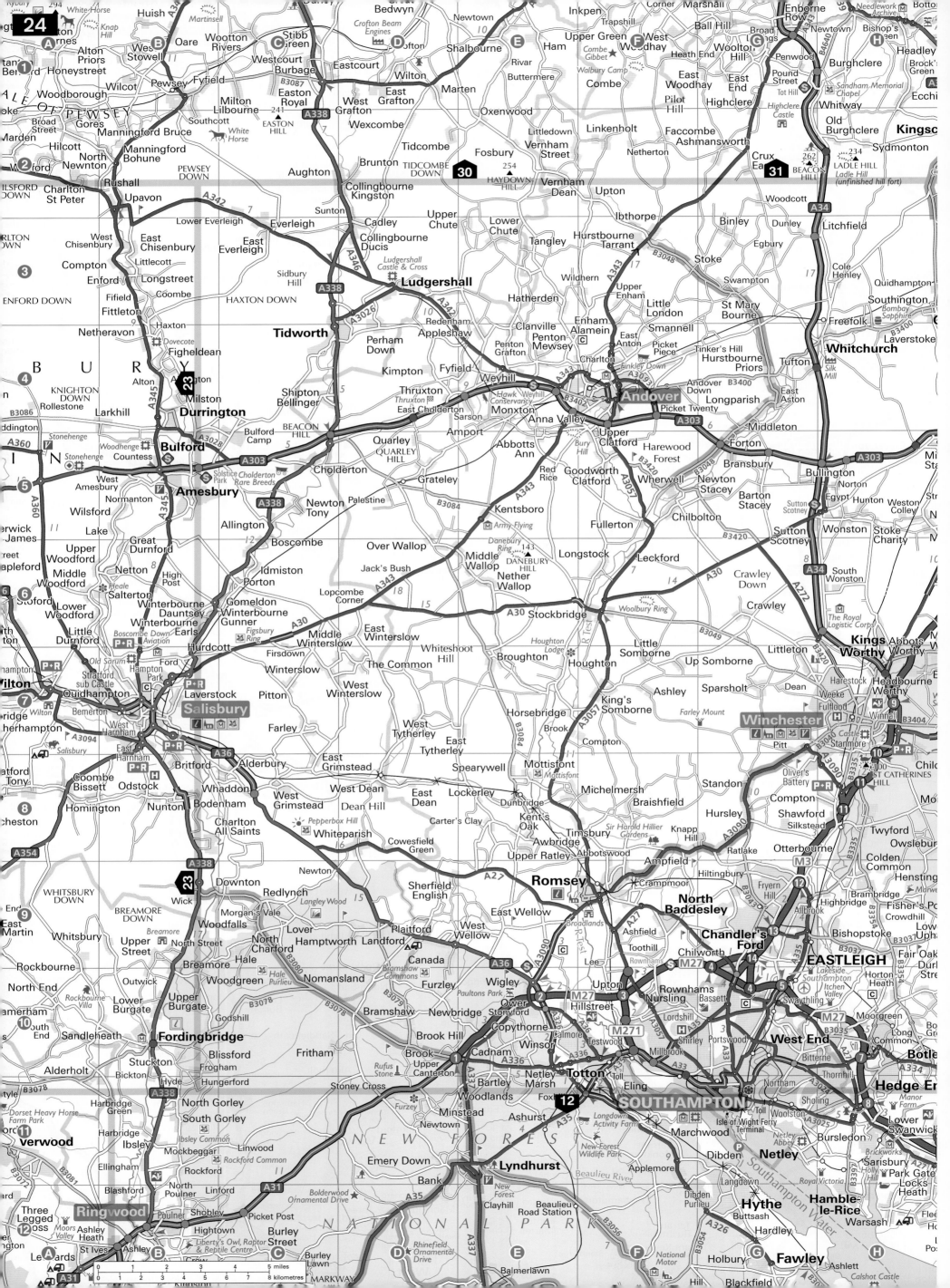

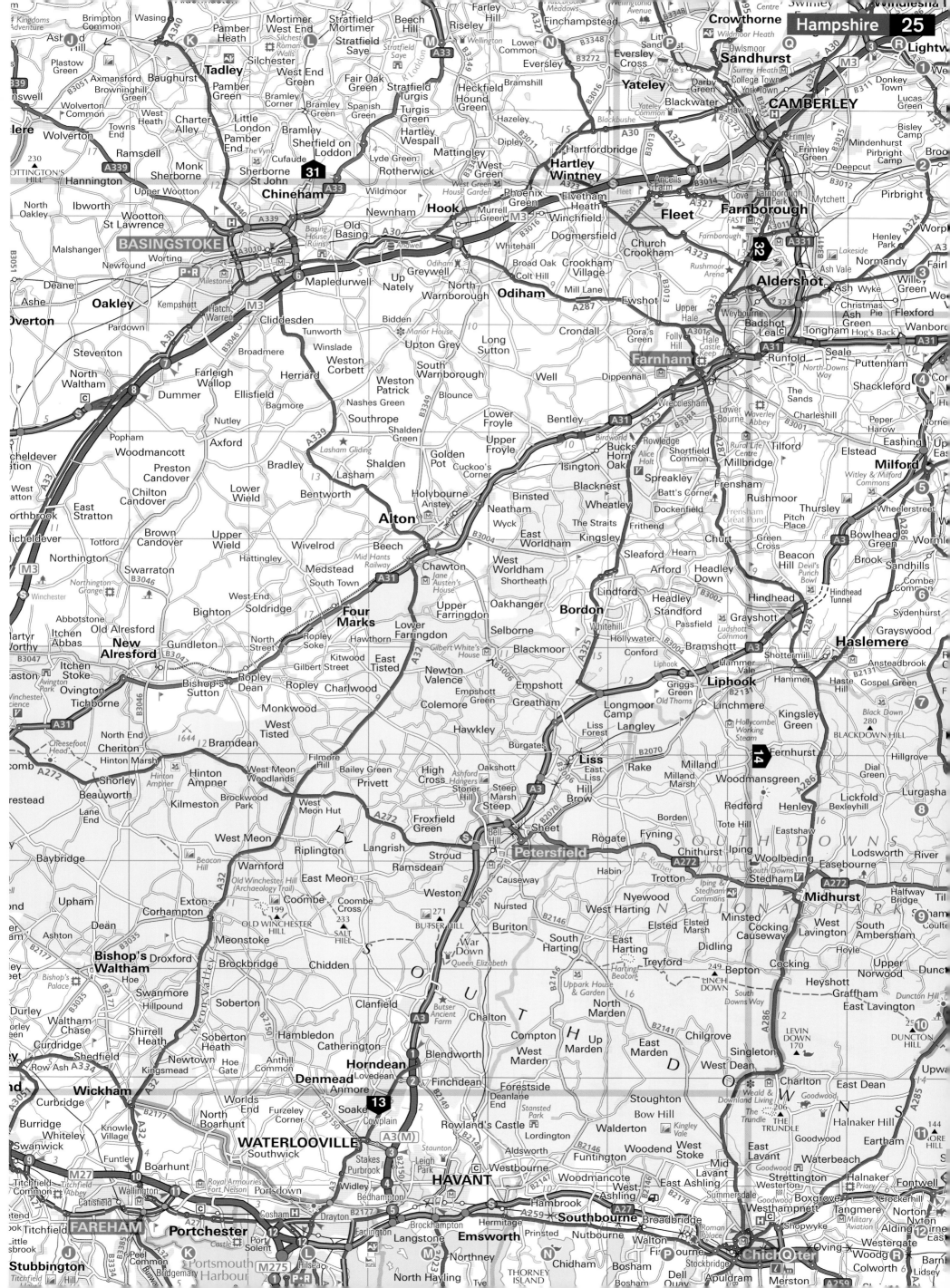

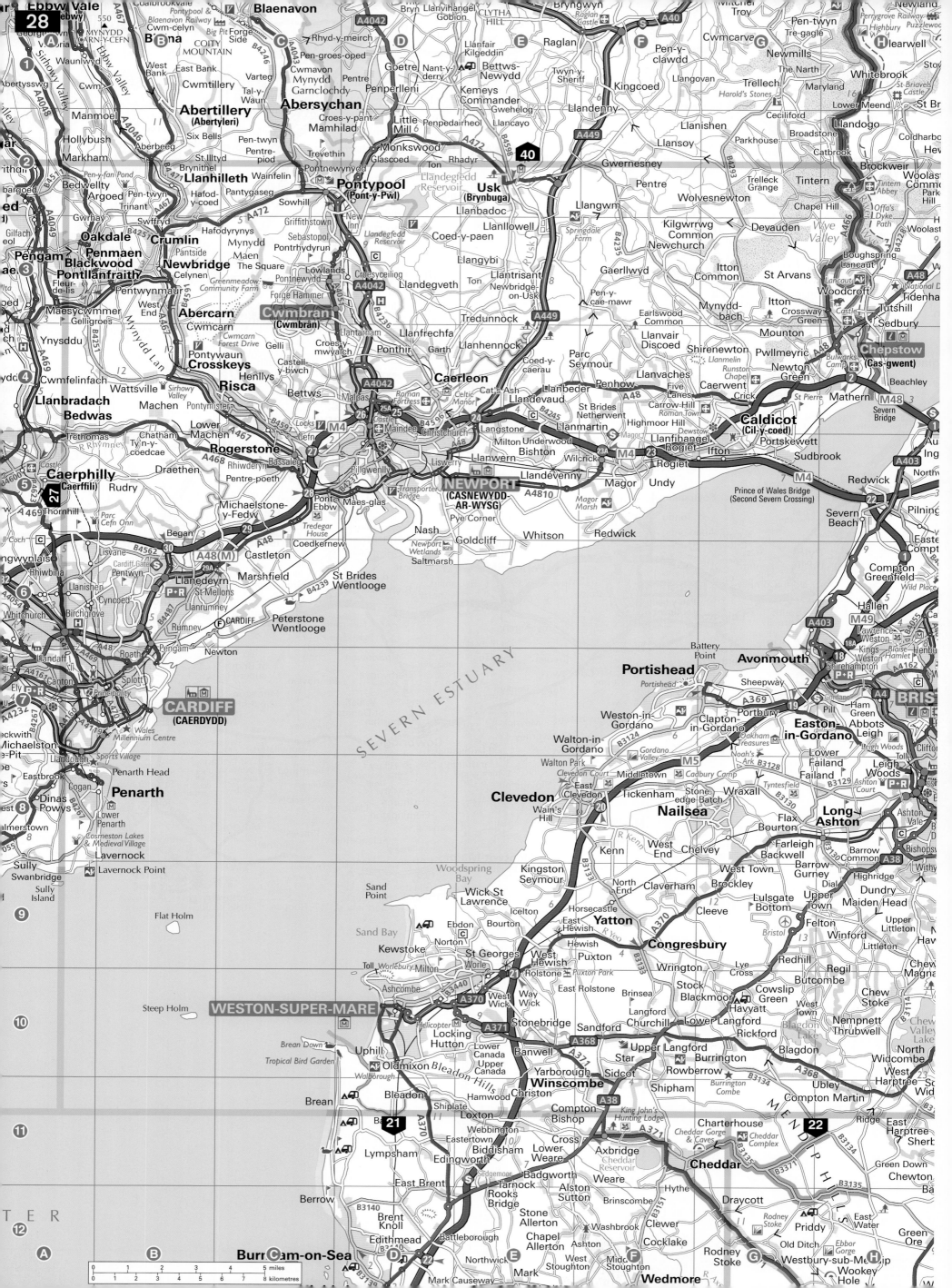

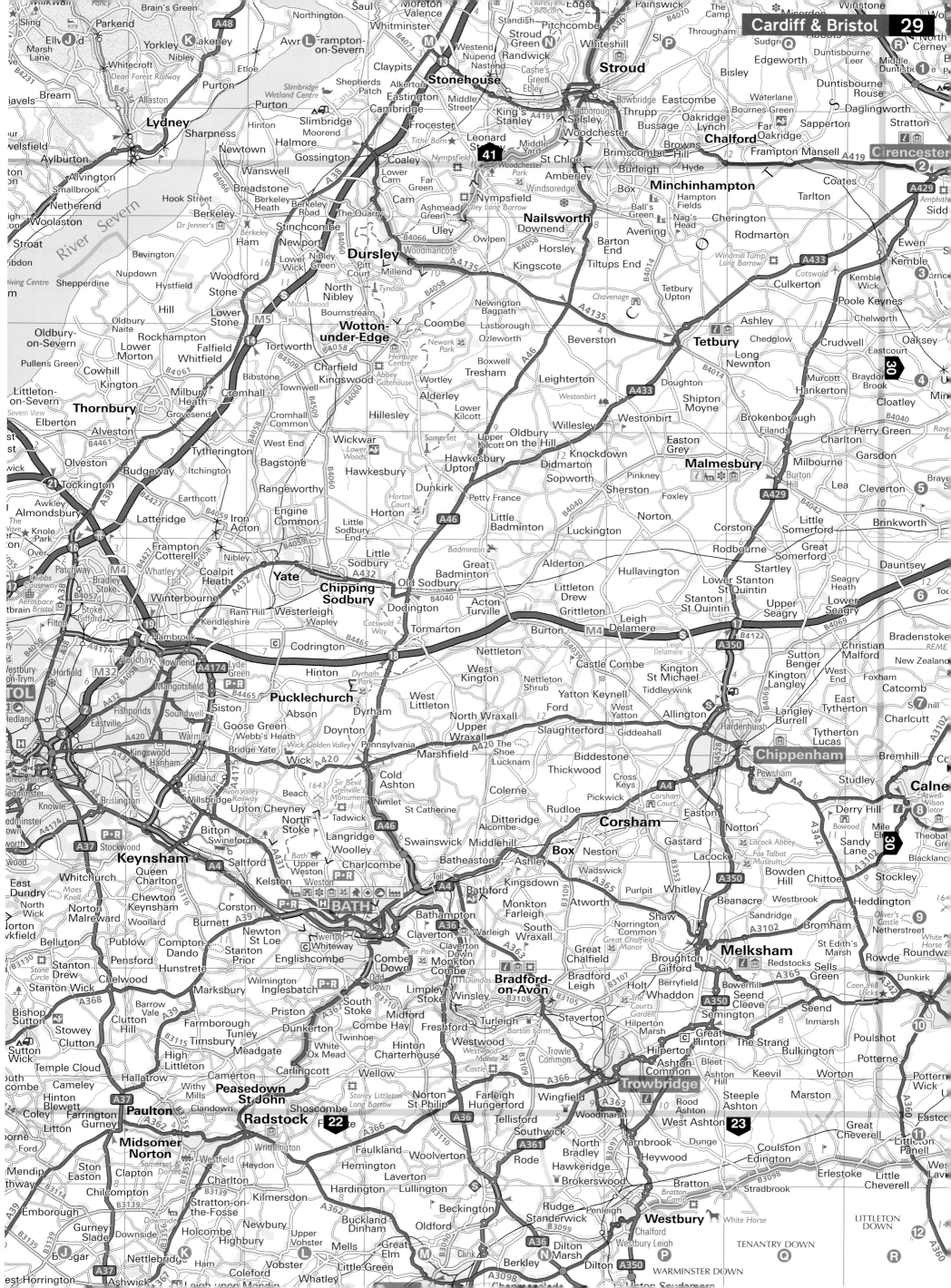

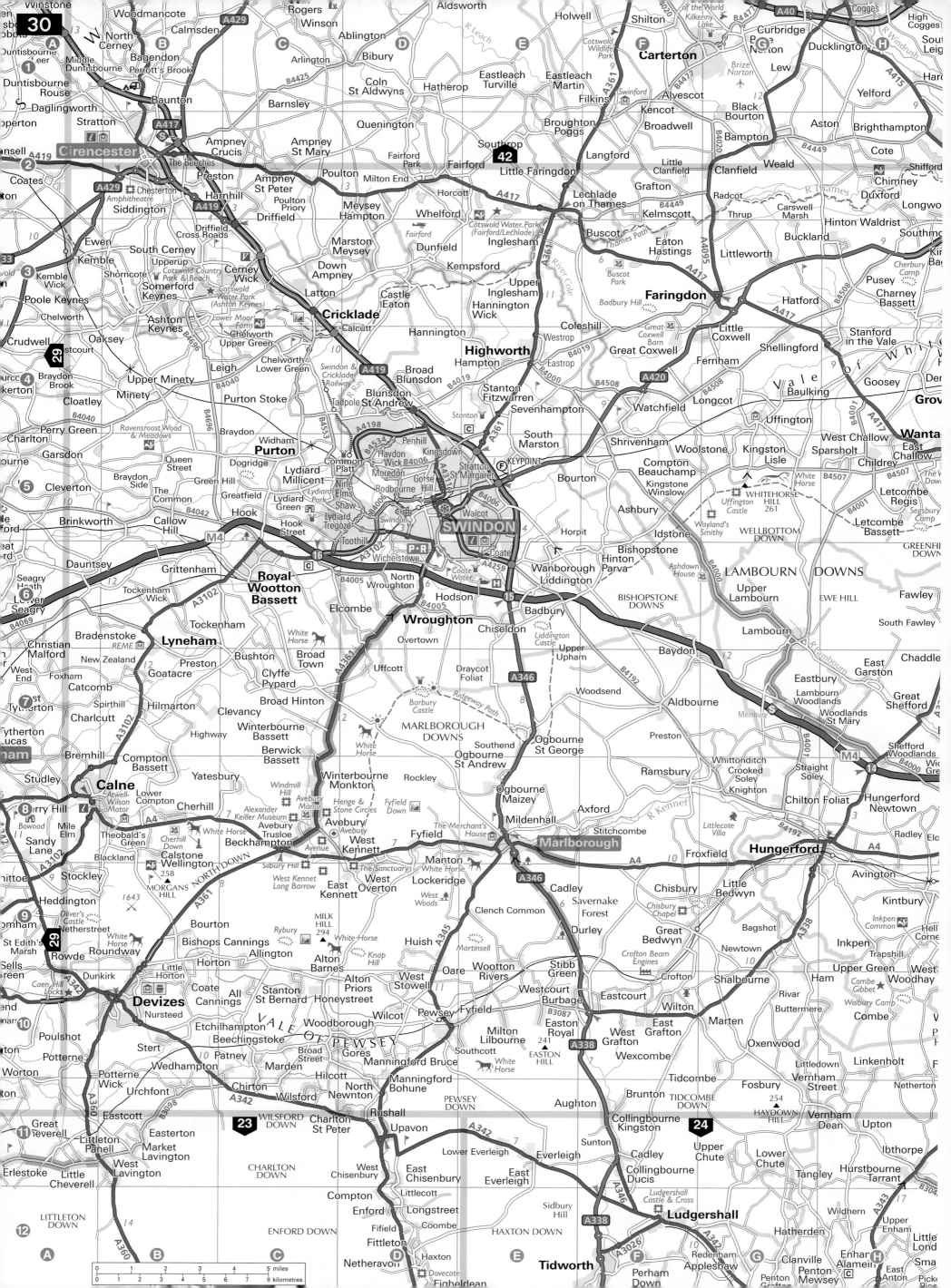

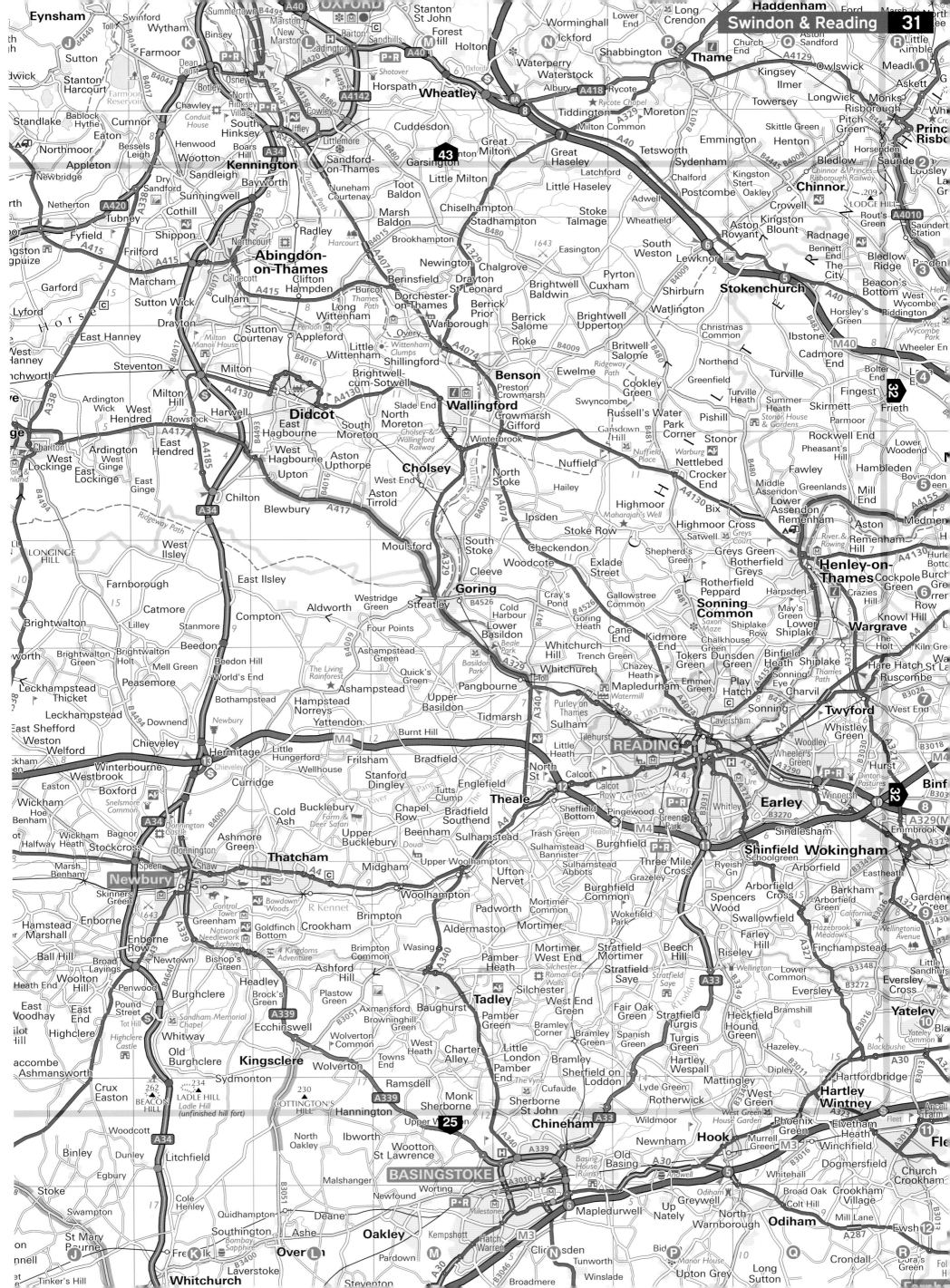

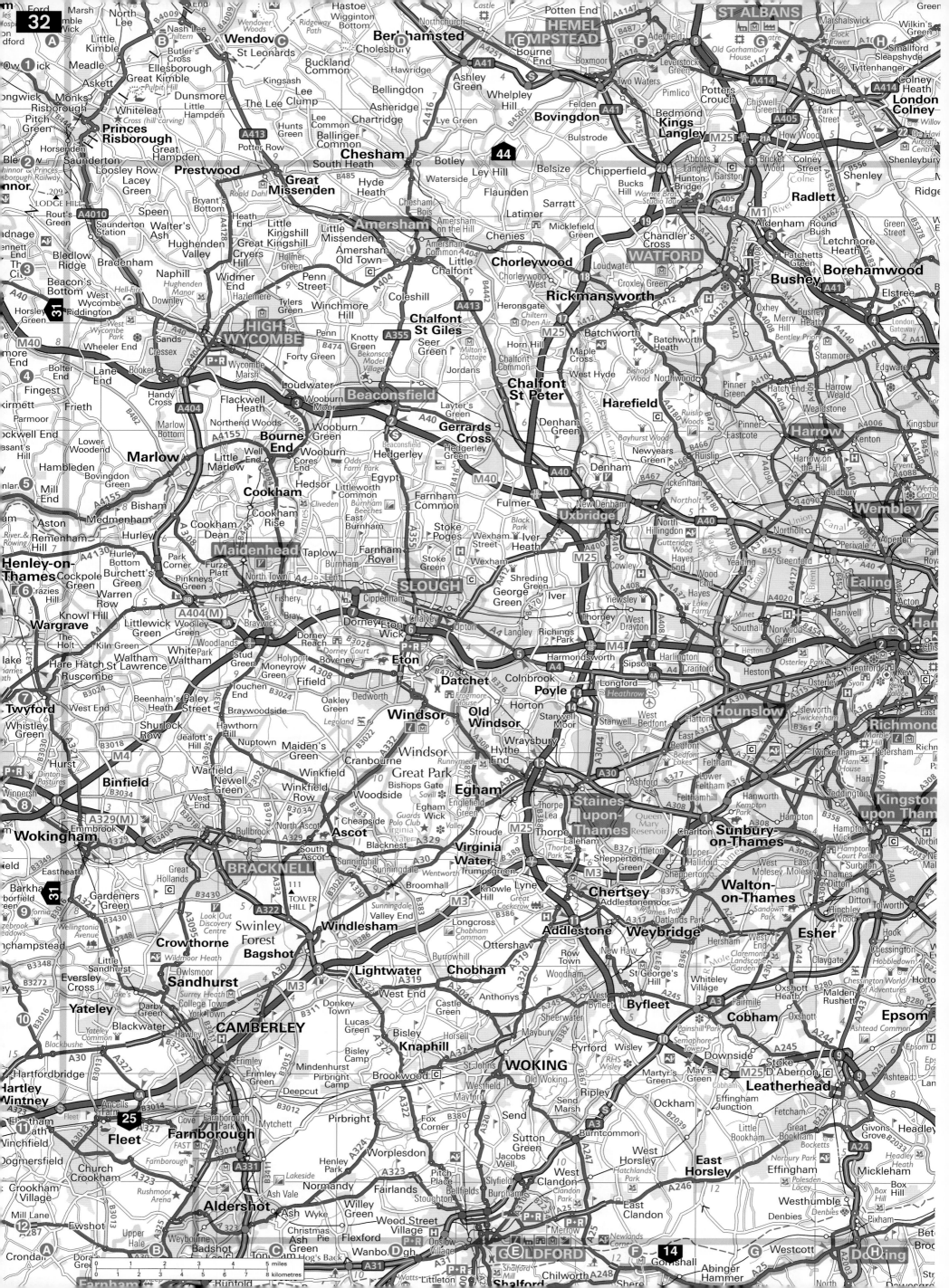

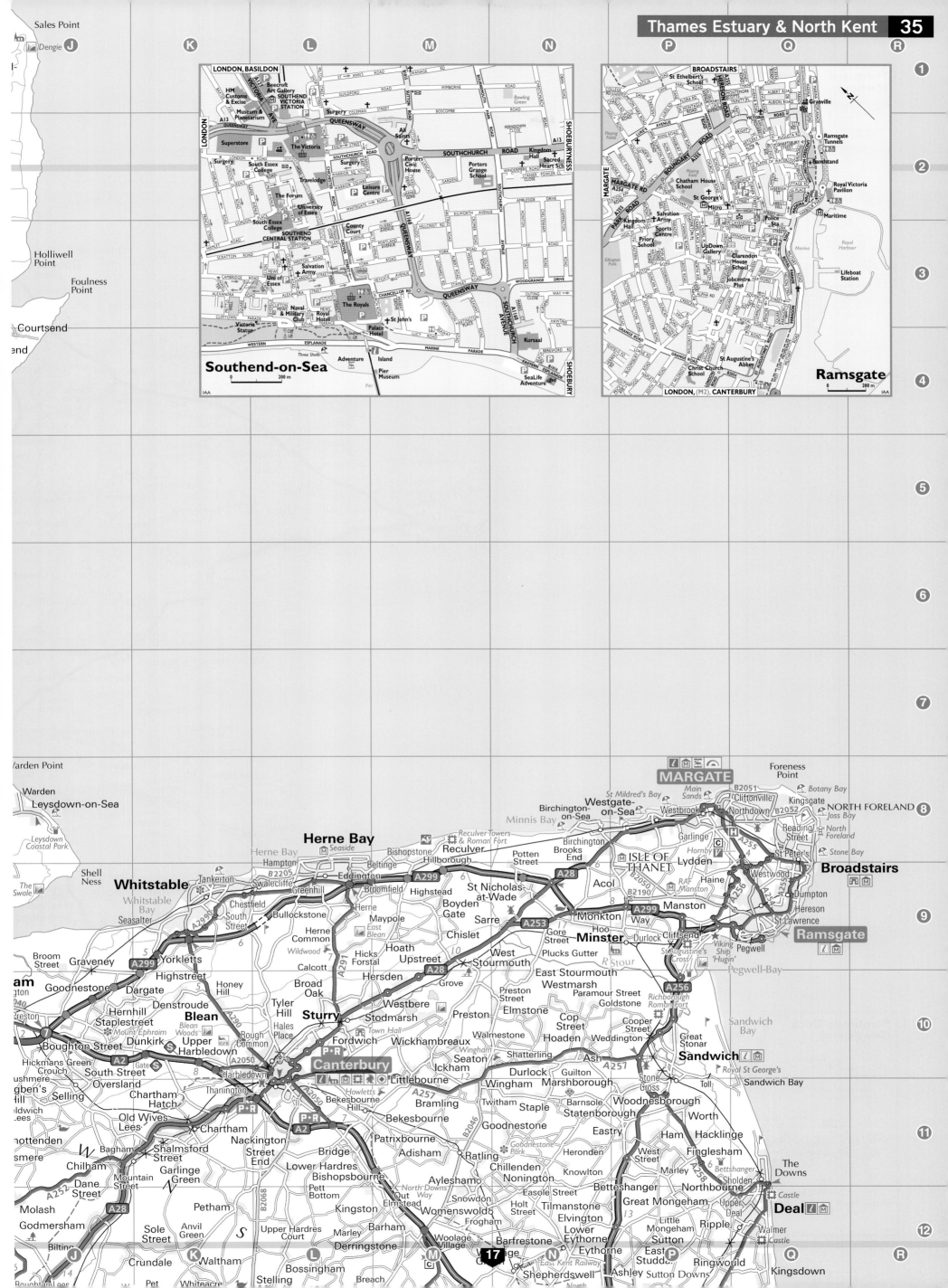

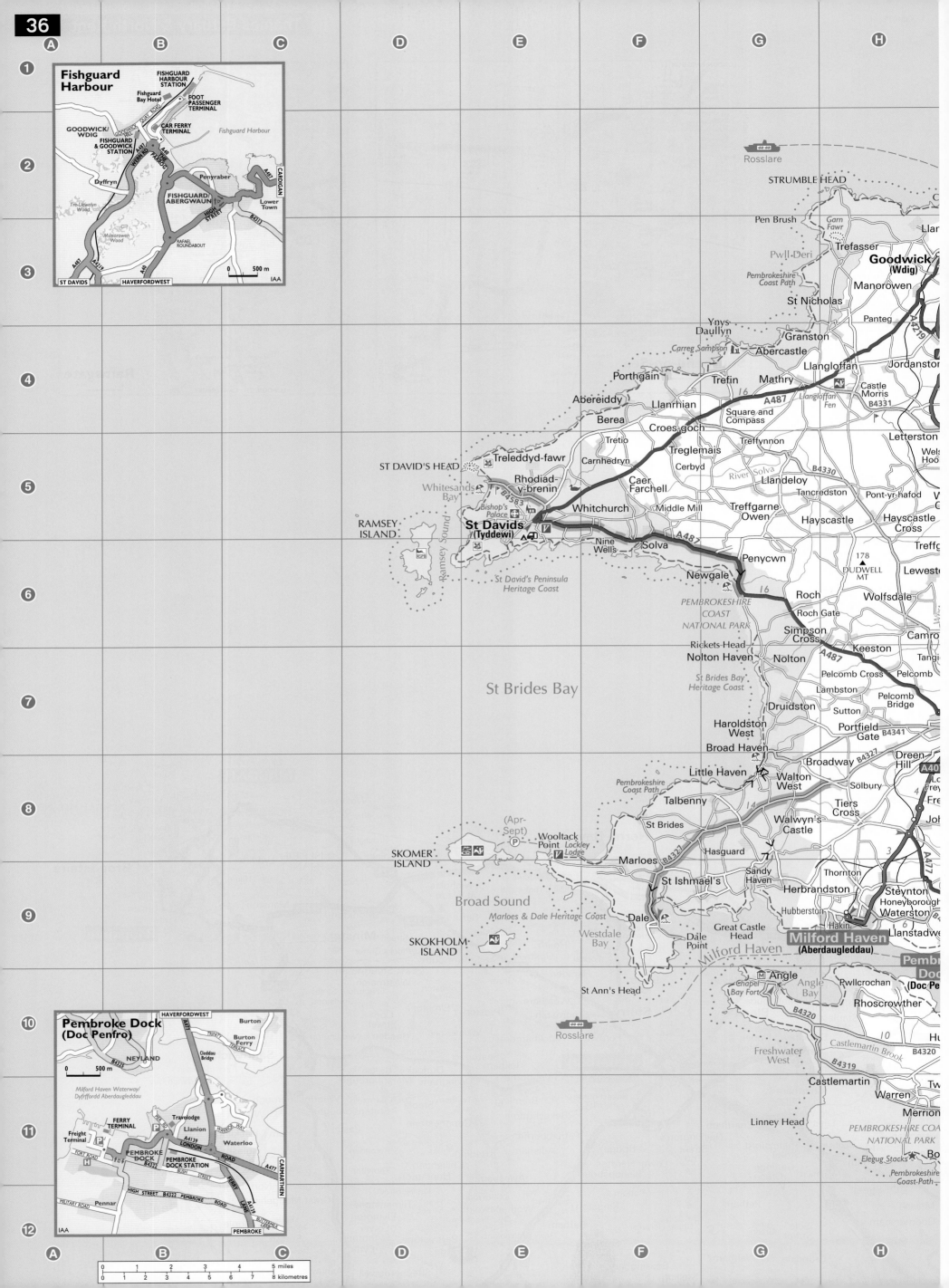

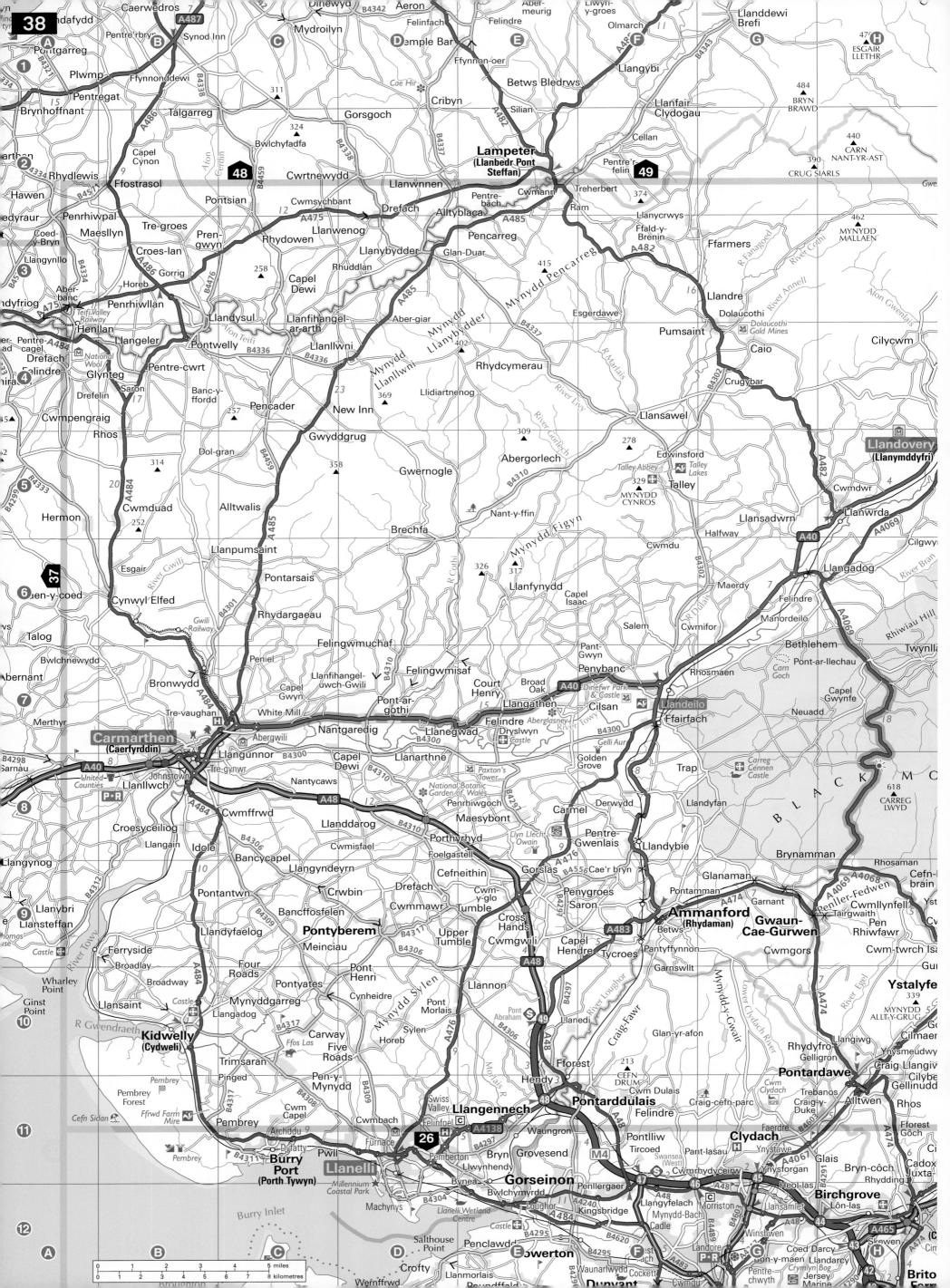

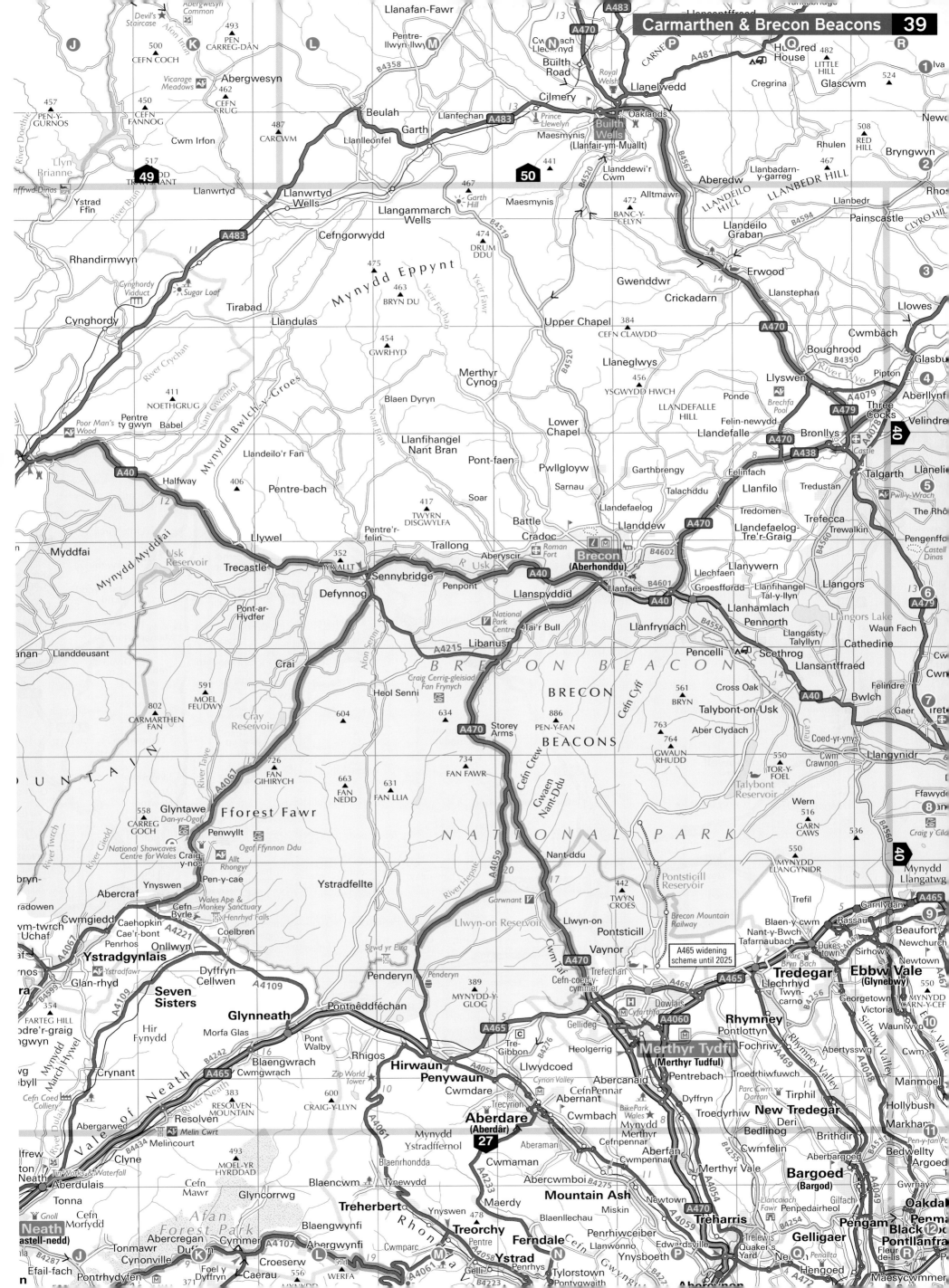

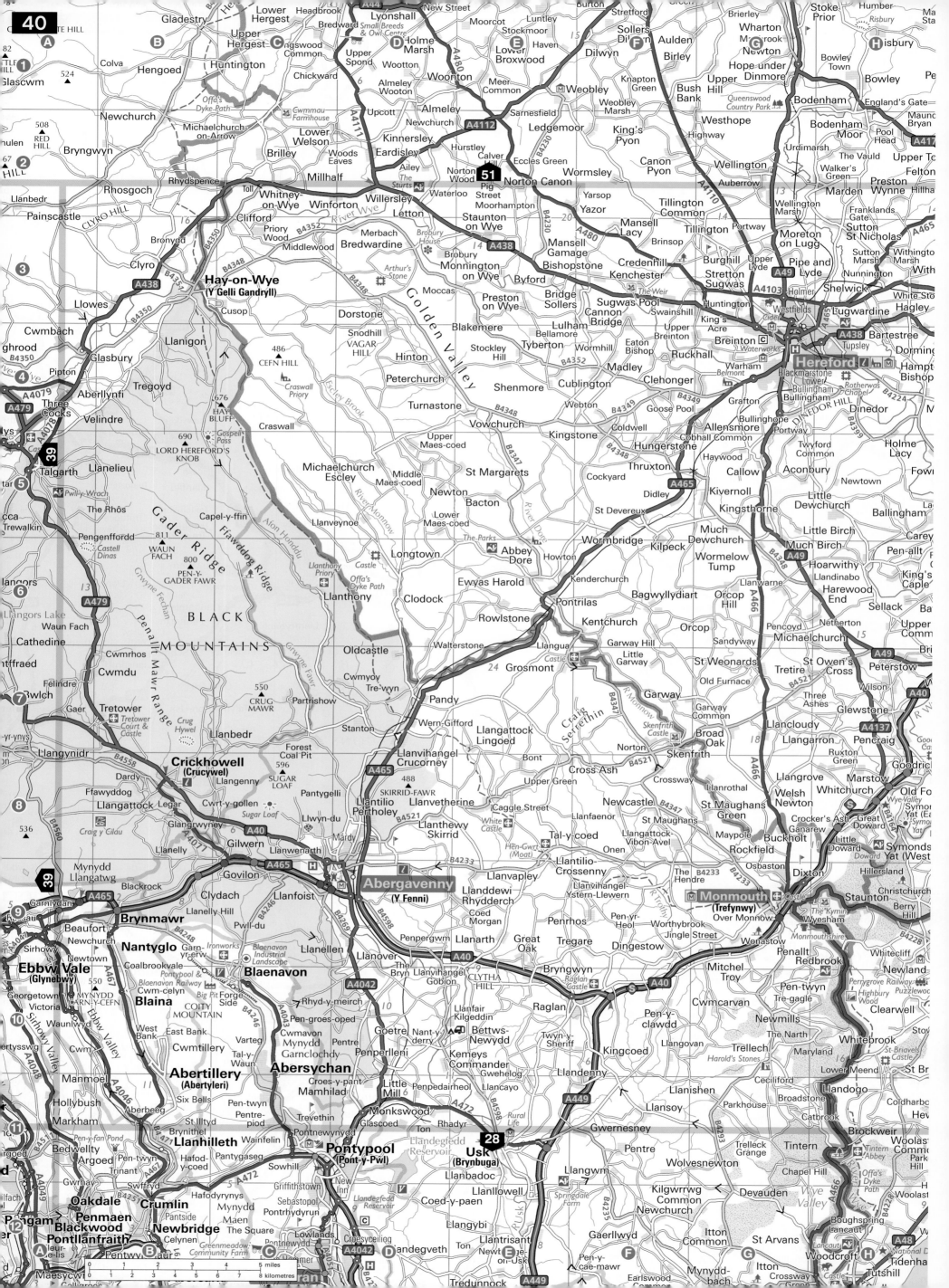

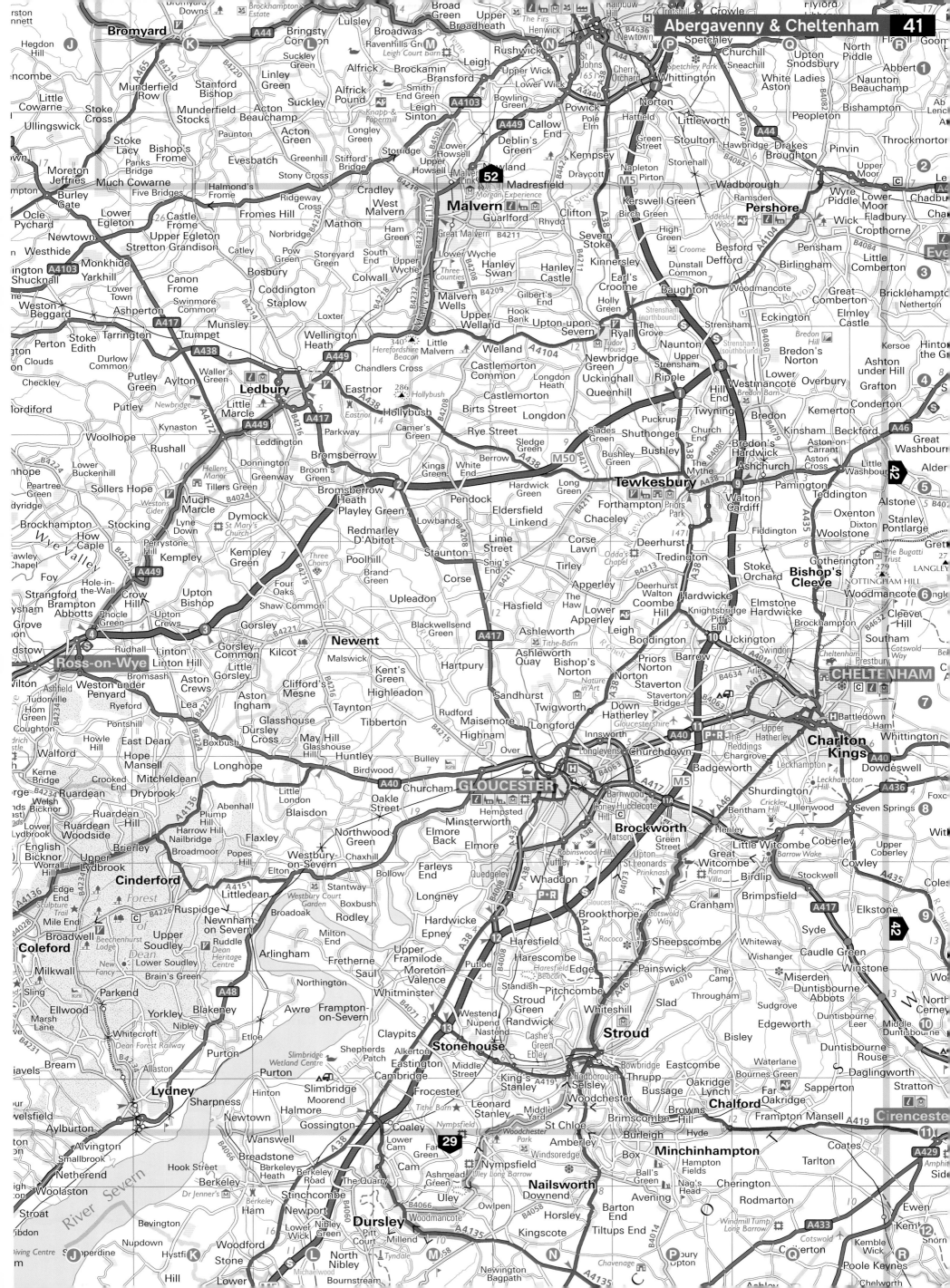

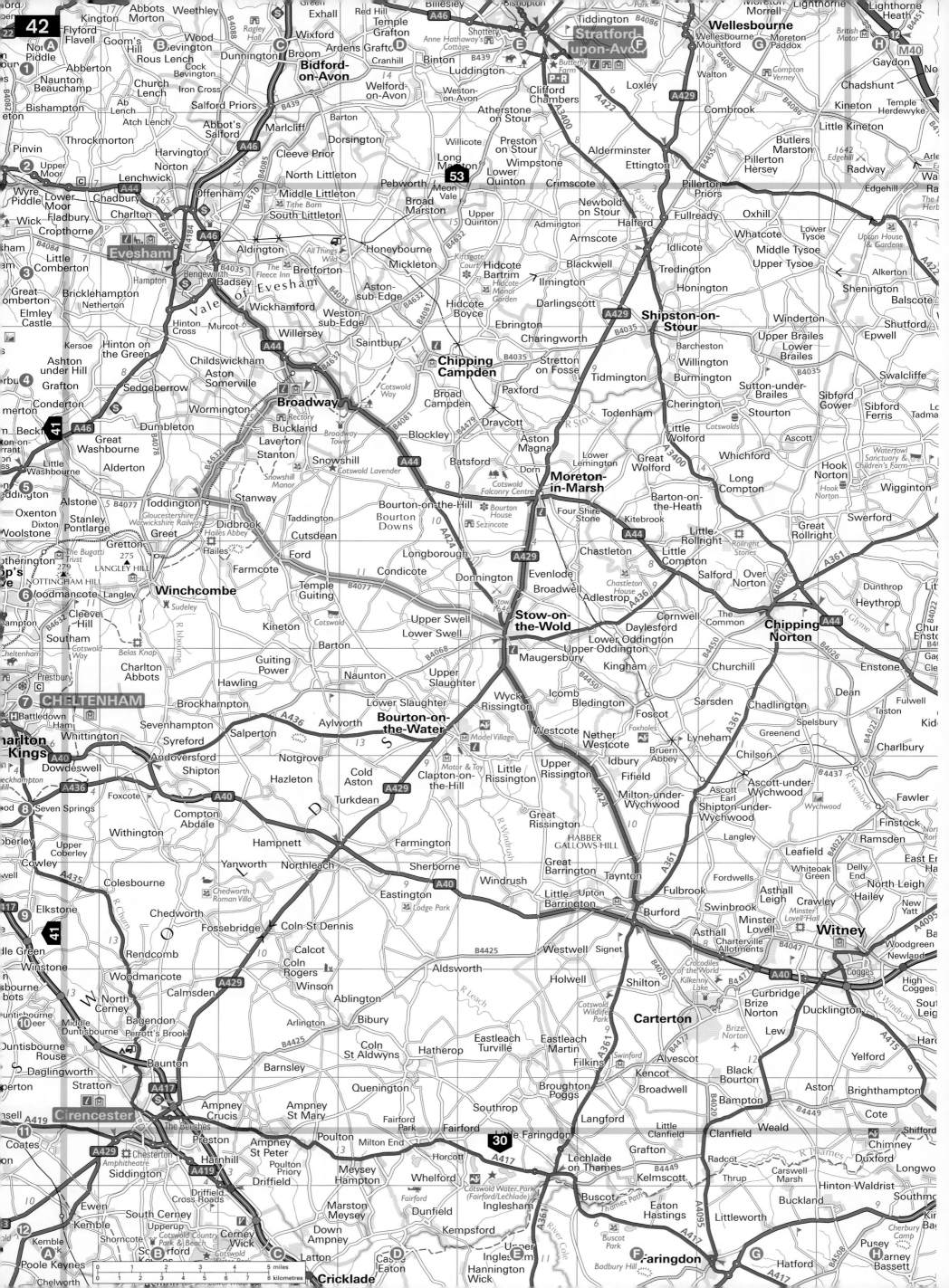

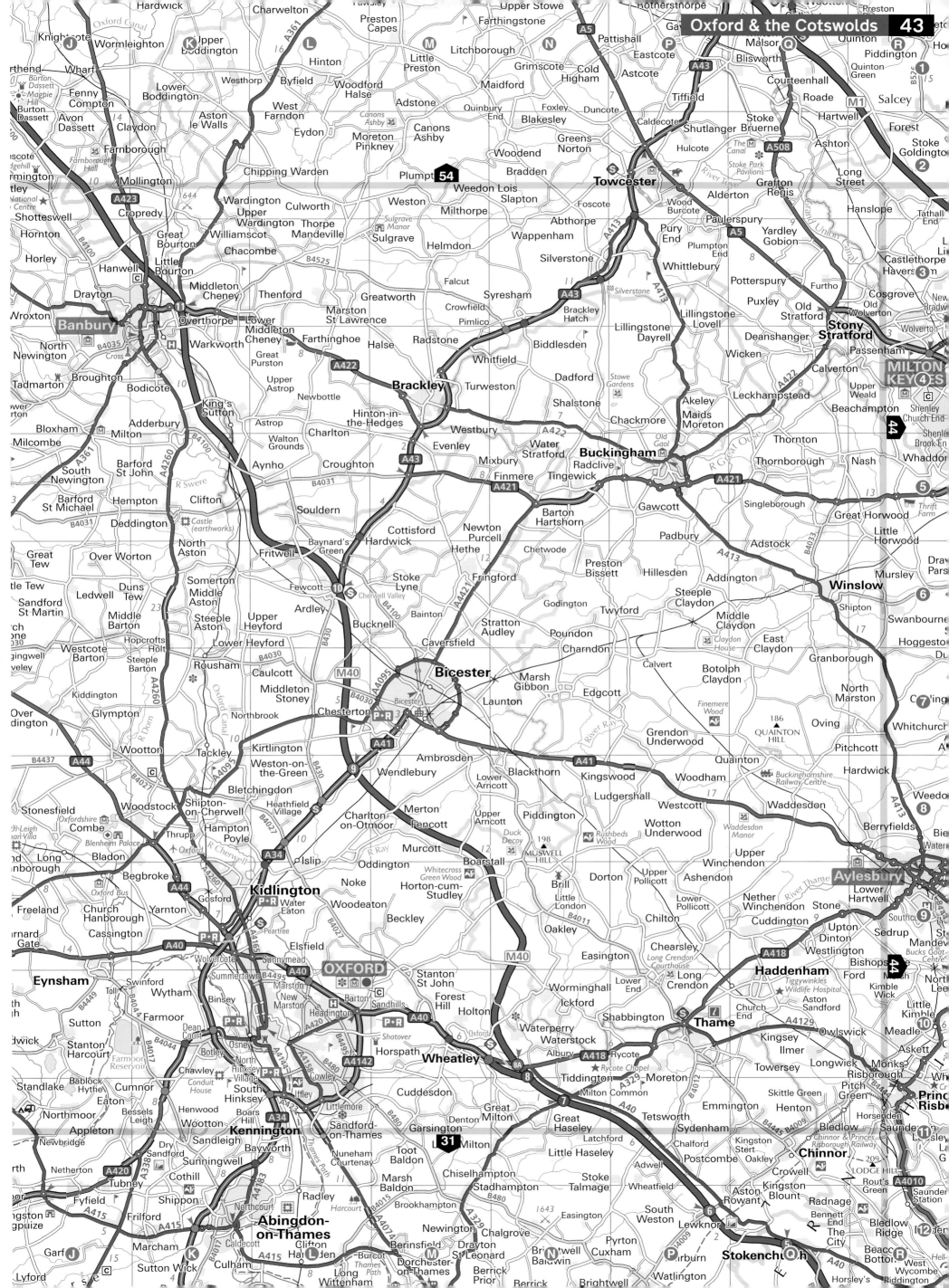

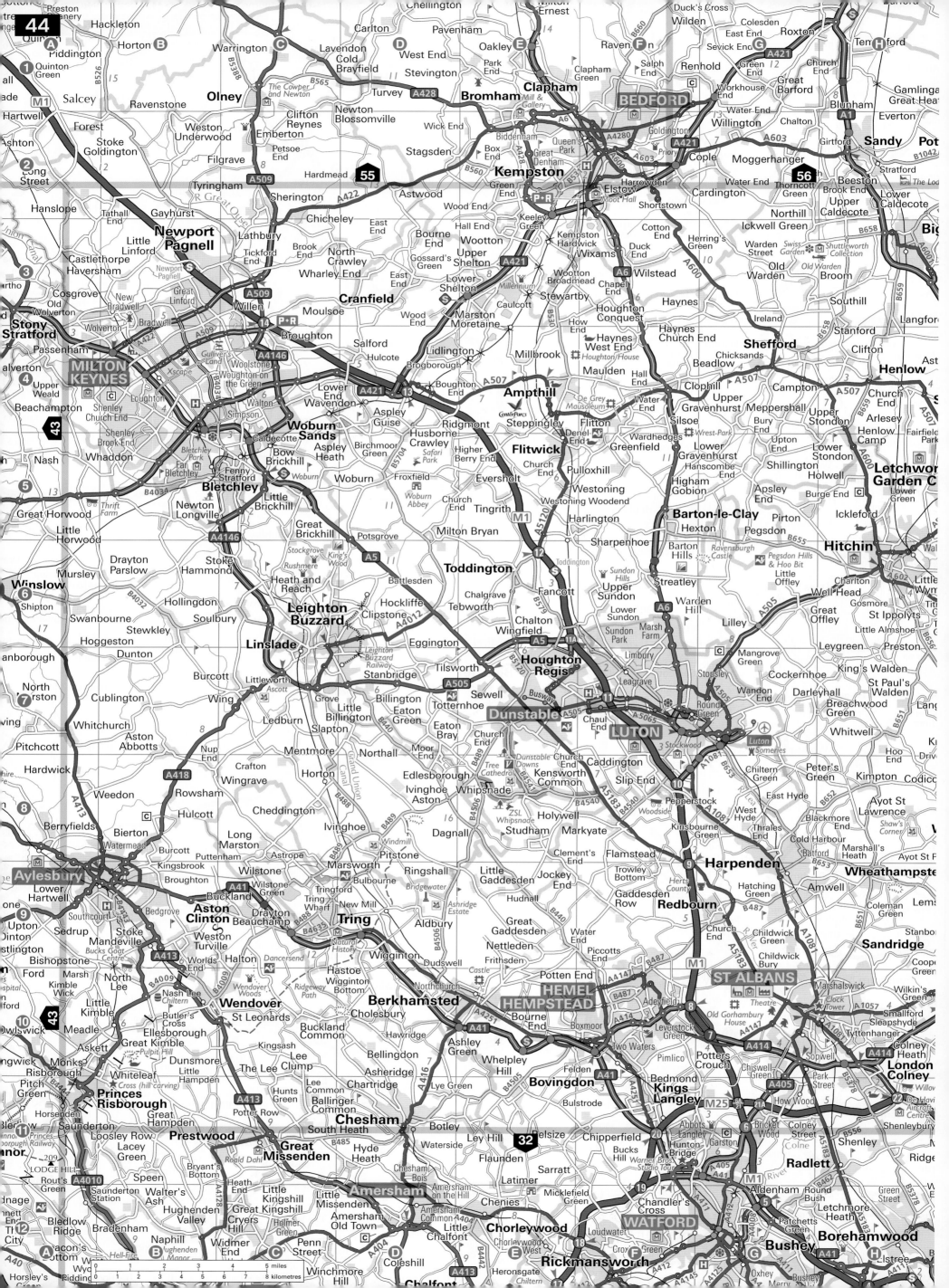

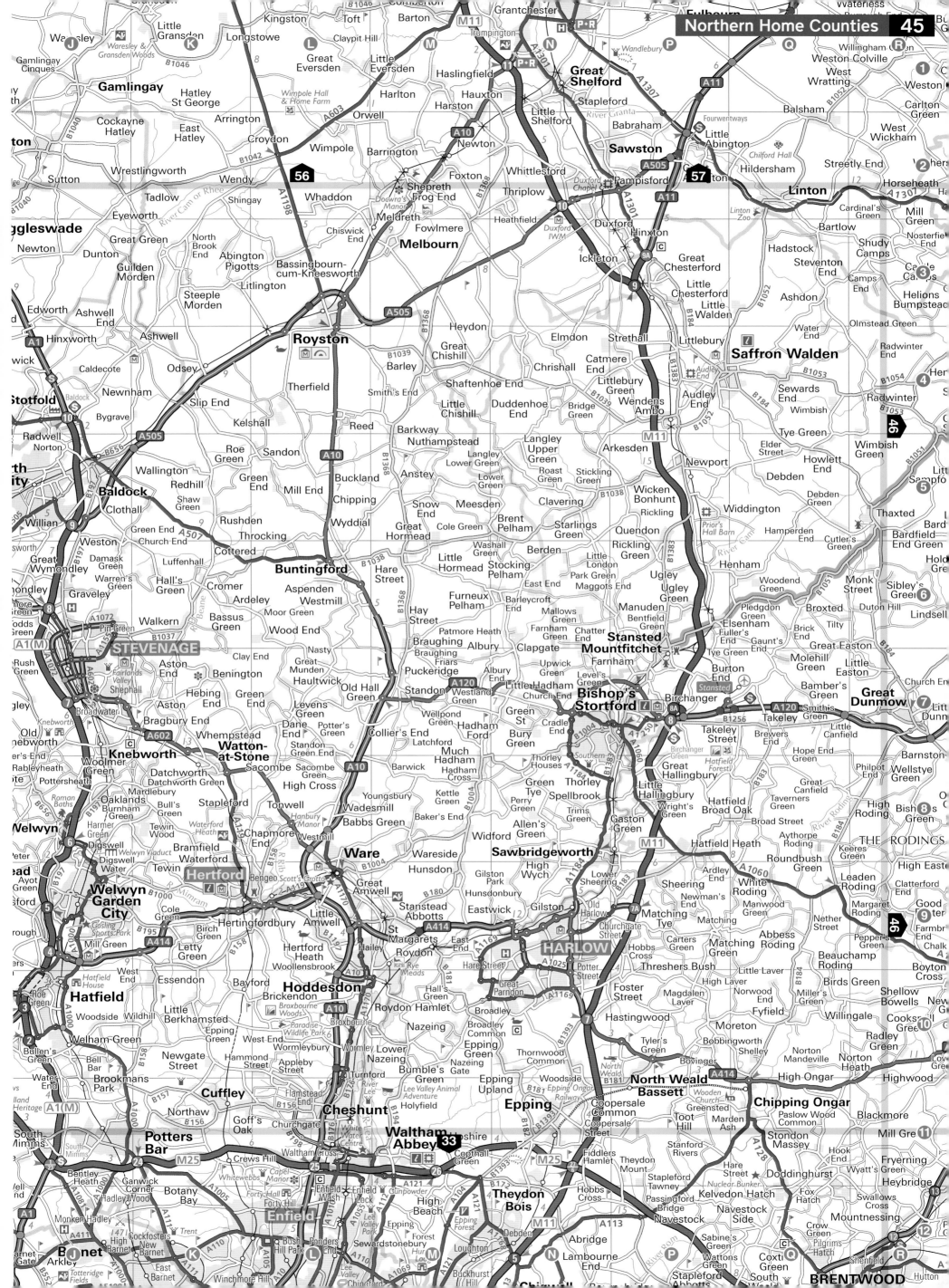

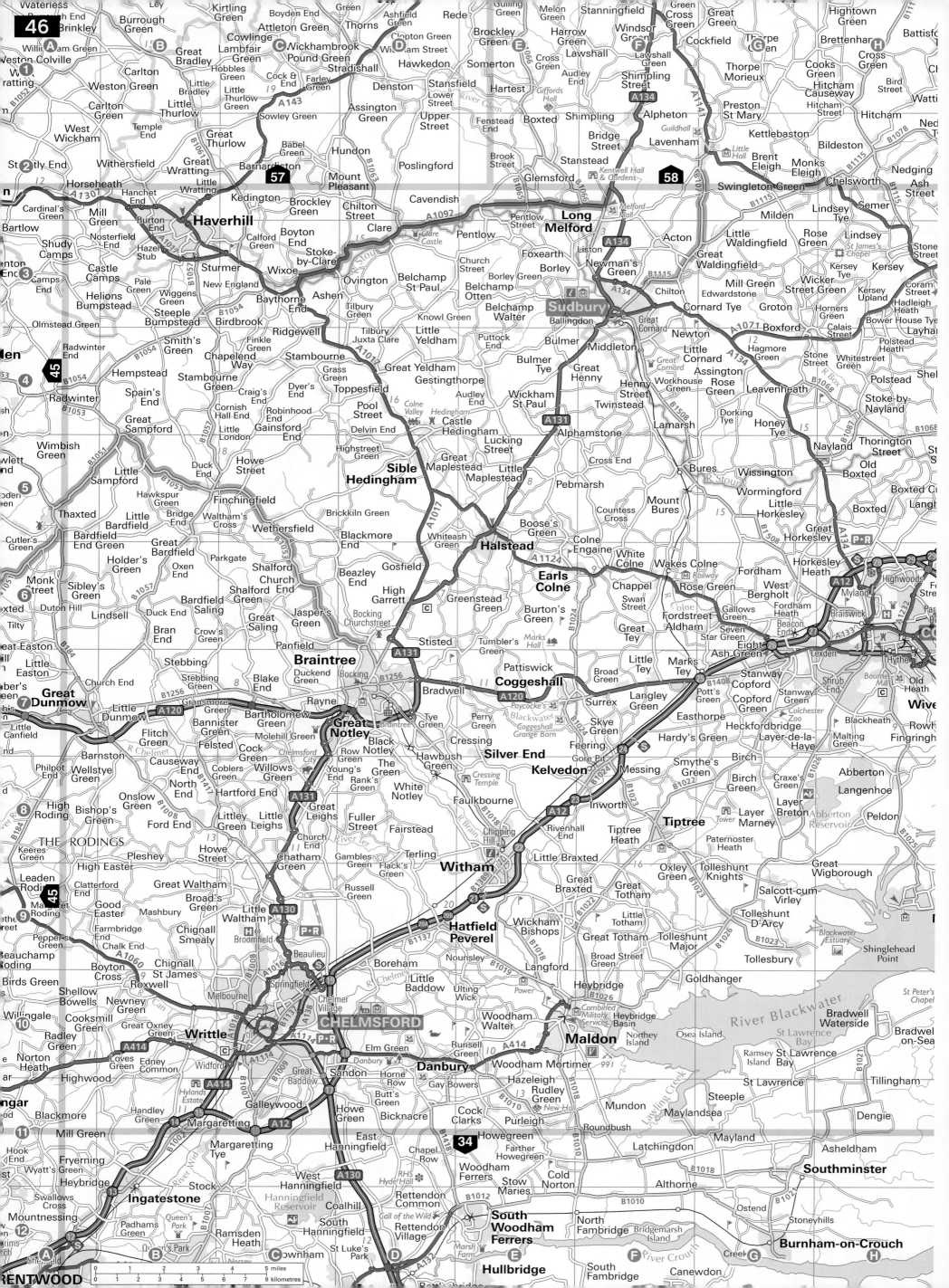

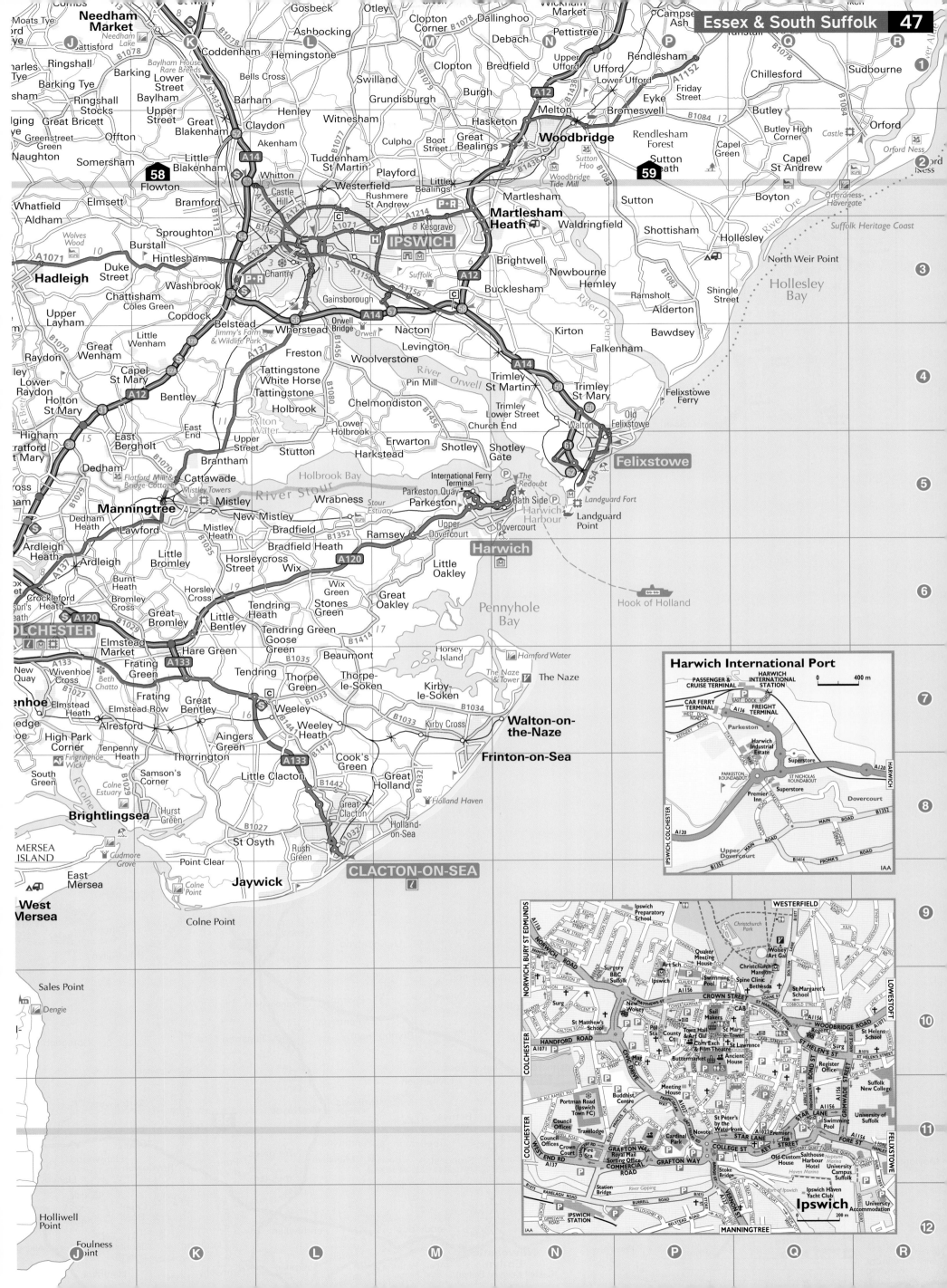

A B C D E F G H

1 2 3 4 5 6 7 8 9 10 11 12

Aberystwyth

0   200 m

Cardigan Bay

Bandstand
St Paul Methodist
St David's URC
Ceredigion
Royal Pier
The Morlan Centre
Surgery
Capel Morfa
Bethel
University (Old College)
Coastguard Station
Clock Tower
Market Hall
St Michael's
Castle
Aberystwyth Castle (ruins)
Monument
Eglwys y Santes Fair
Salvation Army
ABERYSTWYTH STATION
Holy Trinity
Superstores
Ystwyth Retail Park
Rheidol
University (School of Art)
St Padarn's Primary School
CAB
Aberystwyth South Beach
Ro-fawr
Trefechan Bridge
Slipway
Justice Centre
Marina
Fire Station
Park Avenue (Aberystwyth Town FC)
Police Station
TA Centre
Vale of Rheidol Steam Railway Station
Plascrug CP School
Recreation Ground
Lifeboat Station
IAA
Aqua Terra
CARDIGAN

NORTHGATE ST
A487
PENGLAIS ROAD
MACHYNLLETH, LLANGURIG
National Library of Wales
LLANBADARN ROAD
Penglais Woods
NORTH ROAD
NEWPORT ROAD
NORTH PARADE
GREAT DARKGATE ST
TERRACE ROAD
MARINE TERRACE
NEW PROMENADE
SOUTH ROAD
NEW STREET
VIEW
HIGH STREET
BRIDGE STREET
DAN DRE MILL ST
PENPARCAU ROAD
River Rheidol
Afon Rheidol
BOULEVARD ST BRIUC
CAMBRIAN STREET
ALEXANDRA ROAD
CAE MELYN
LLWYN AFALLON
ELYSIAN GROVE
TREFOR ROAD
BUARTH
TRINITY

C A R D I G A N

B A Y

Llan

Llansantffraid

Llanon

Aberarth
Pennant

Aberaeron
Henfynyw
Foss-y-ffin
Llyswen
Mona
Llanerchaeron
Llwyncelyn
A482
Newl

New Quay
(Ceinewydd)
Marine
Llanina
Gilfachrheda
Llanarth
Oakford
Ciliau-Aeron
B4339
Ystra
Aero
13

Ceredigion Heritage Coast
Maen-y-groes
Cross Inn
Cwmtydu
Nanternis
A486
Caerwedros
7
Dihewyd
B4342
Mydroilyn

Ynys-Lochtyn
Pendinas Lochtyn
Llwyndafydd
Pentre'rbryn
Synod Inn
A487
Fel
Tem

Llangrannog
Pontgarreg
Capel Cynon

Morfa
B4321
Plwmp
Ffynnonddewi
B4338
Cae Hir
Penbryn
Sarnau
Pentregat
311
Gorsgoch

Ceredigion Heritage Coast
Parcllyn
Brynhoffnant
Talgarreg
Bwlchyfadfa
B4459
Cwrtnewydd

Cardigan Island
Mwnt Beach
Tresaith
Aberporth
15
A486
324
B4338

Cardigan Island Coastal Farm
Gwbert on Sea
Y Ferwig
Tan-y-groes
Capel Cynon
Ffostrasol
Llanw
Poppit Sands
Blaenannerch
A487
Glynarthen
Rhydlewis
B4571
38
tsian
Cwmsychbant
12
A475
Drefach

Pembrokeshire Coast Path
Penparc
Tremain
Blaenporth
Bettws Ifan
Hawen
Penrhiwpal
Tre-groes
Prengwyn
Rhydowen
Llanwenog
Llanybydder

Cardigan
(Aberteifi)
St Dogmaels
Abbey & Coach House
Llangoedmor
Beulah
Troedyraur
Coed-y-Bryn
Maesllyn
Croes-lan
A486
Rhuddlan
258
Capel Dewi

Ceibwr Bay
Moylegrove
Bridgend
B4570
Ponthirwaun
Brongest
Gorrig
Horeb
Llanfihangel-ar-arth
Llanllwni

Nevern
Monington
Pen-y-bryn
Welsh Wildlife Centre
37
Llandygwydd
Llangynllo
Aber-banc
A475
Penrhiwllan
Pontwelly
A485

Glanrhyd
Llantood
Bridell
Cilgerran
Castle
Afon Teifi
TIVY SIDE
Cwm-cou
Llandyfriog
Teifi Valley Railway
Henllan
Llangeler

B4582
Pengelli Forest
Pontgarreg
Rhosl
Abercych
Cenarth
National Coracle Centre
Adpar
Newcastle Emlyn
(Castell Newydd Emlyn)
Aber-arad
Pentre-cagel
Drefach
B4336

Felindre Farchog

A B C D E F G H

0 1 2 3 4 5 miles
0 1 2 3 4 5 6 7 8 kilometres

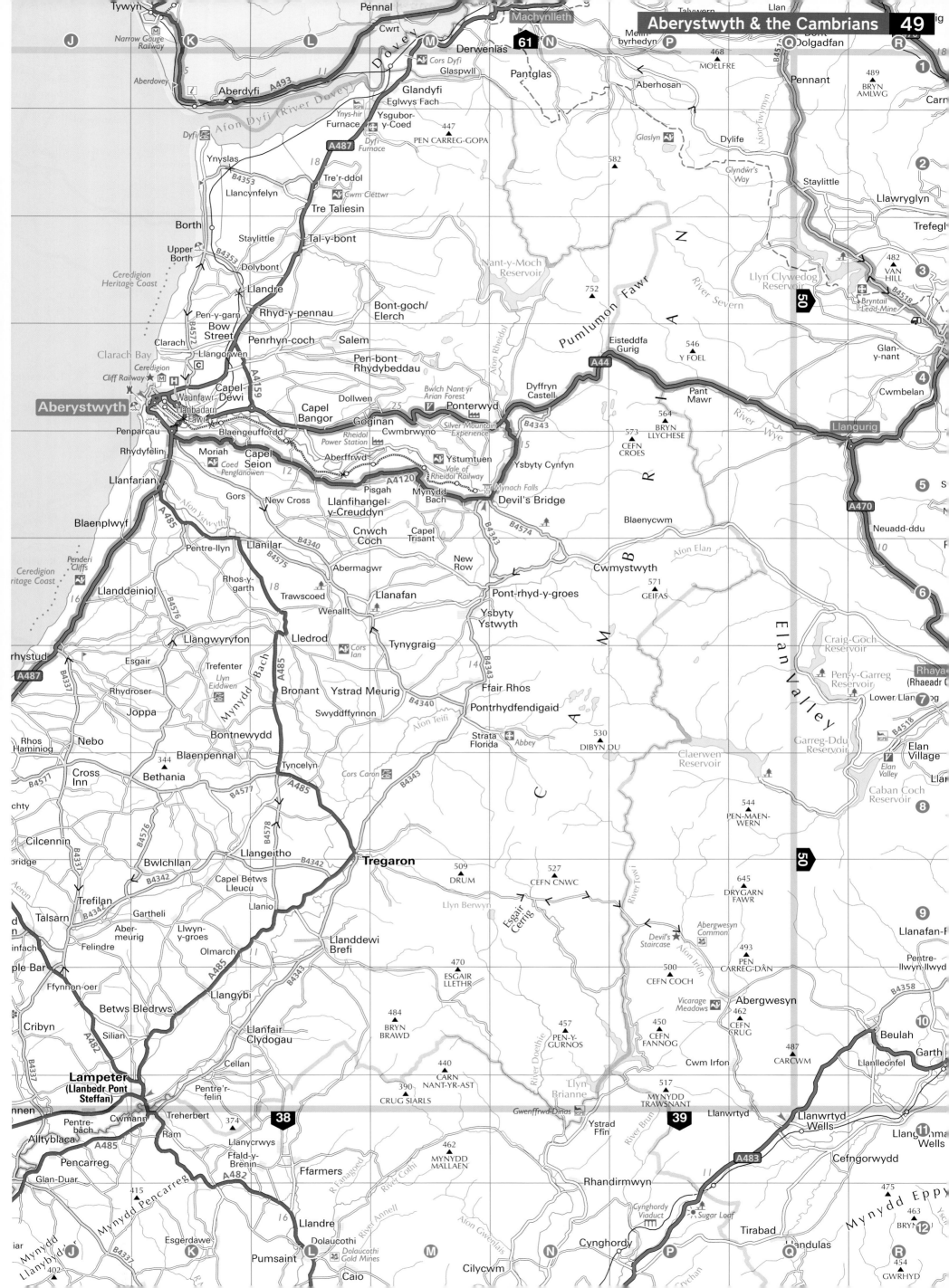

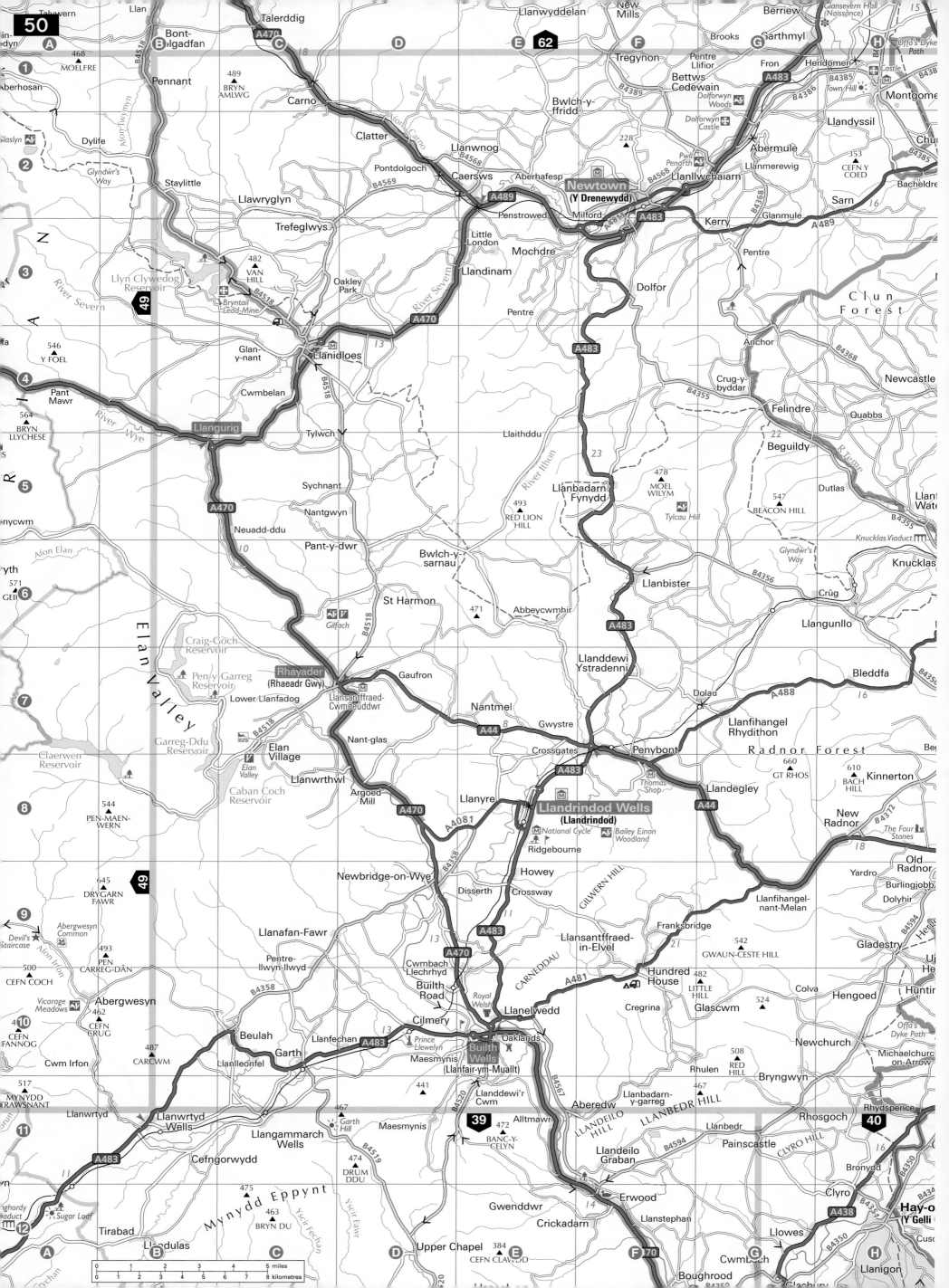

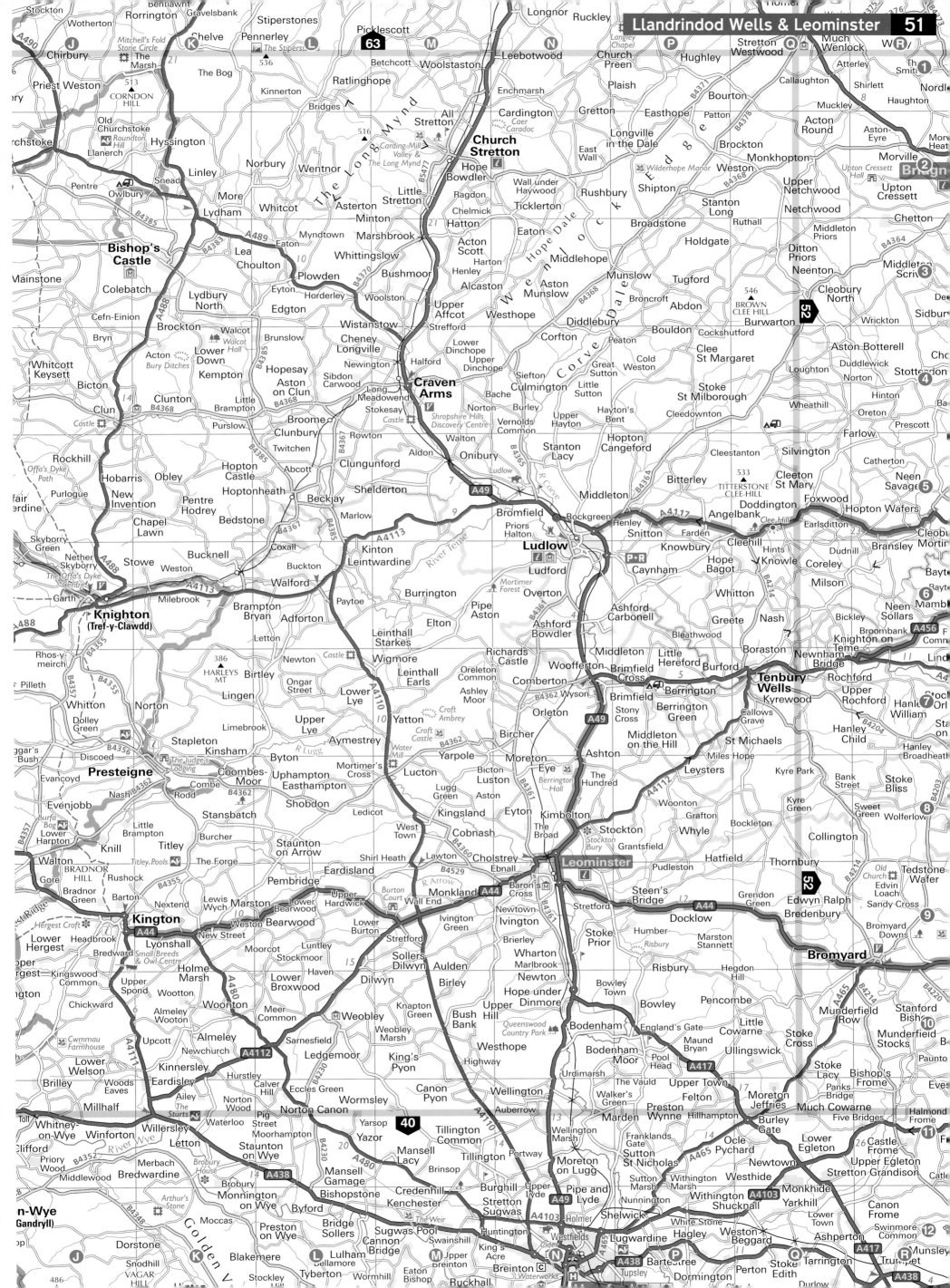

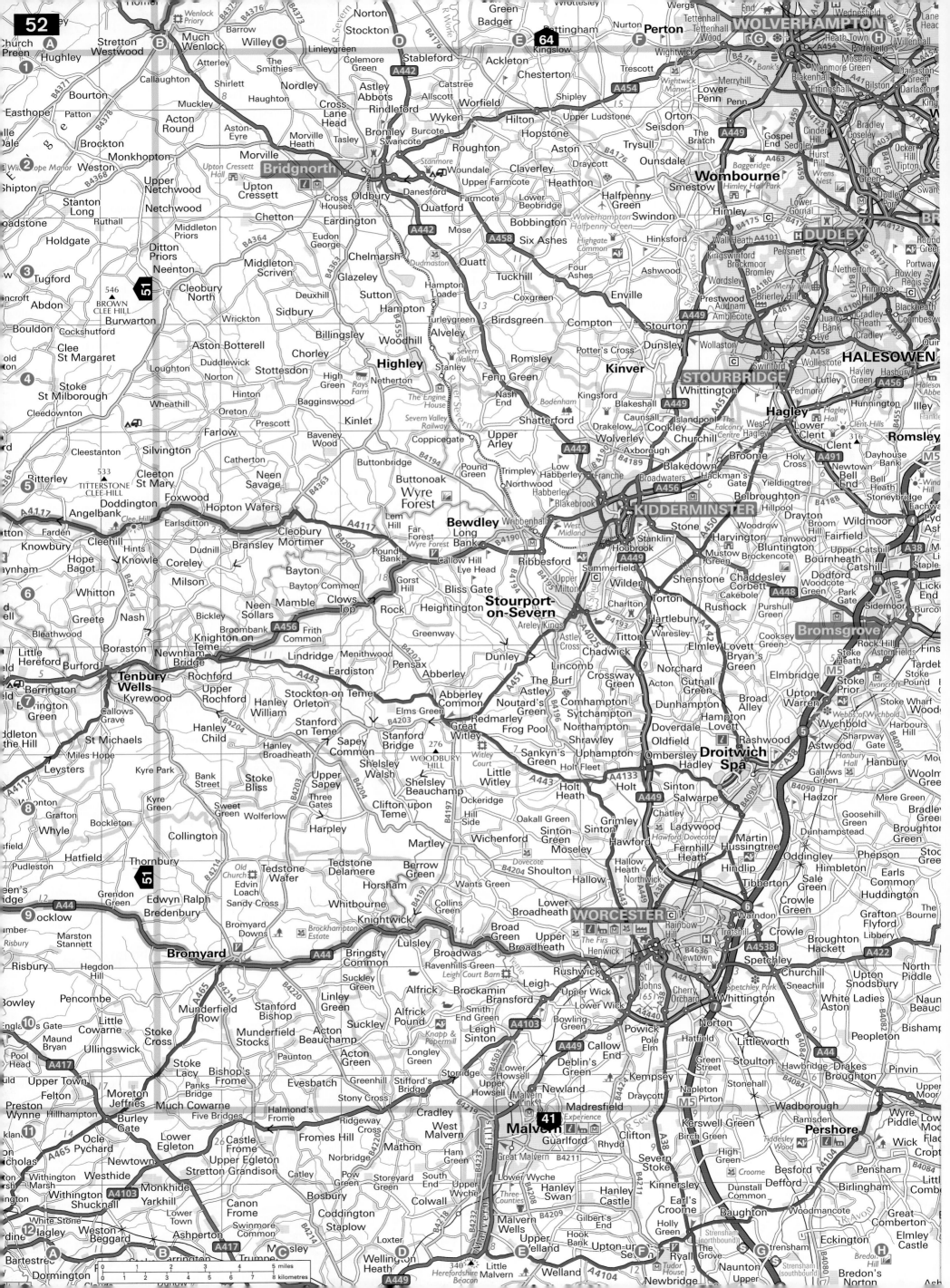

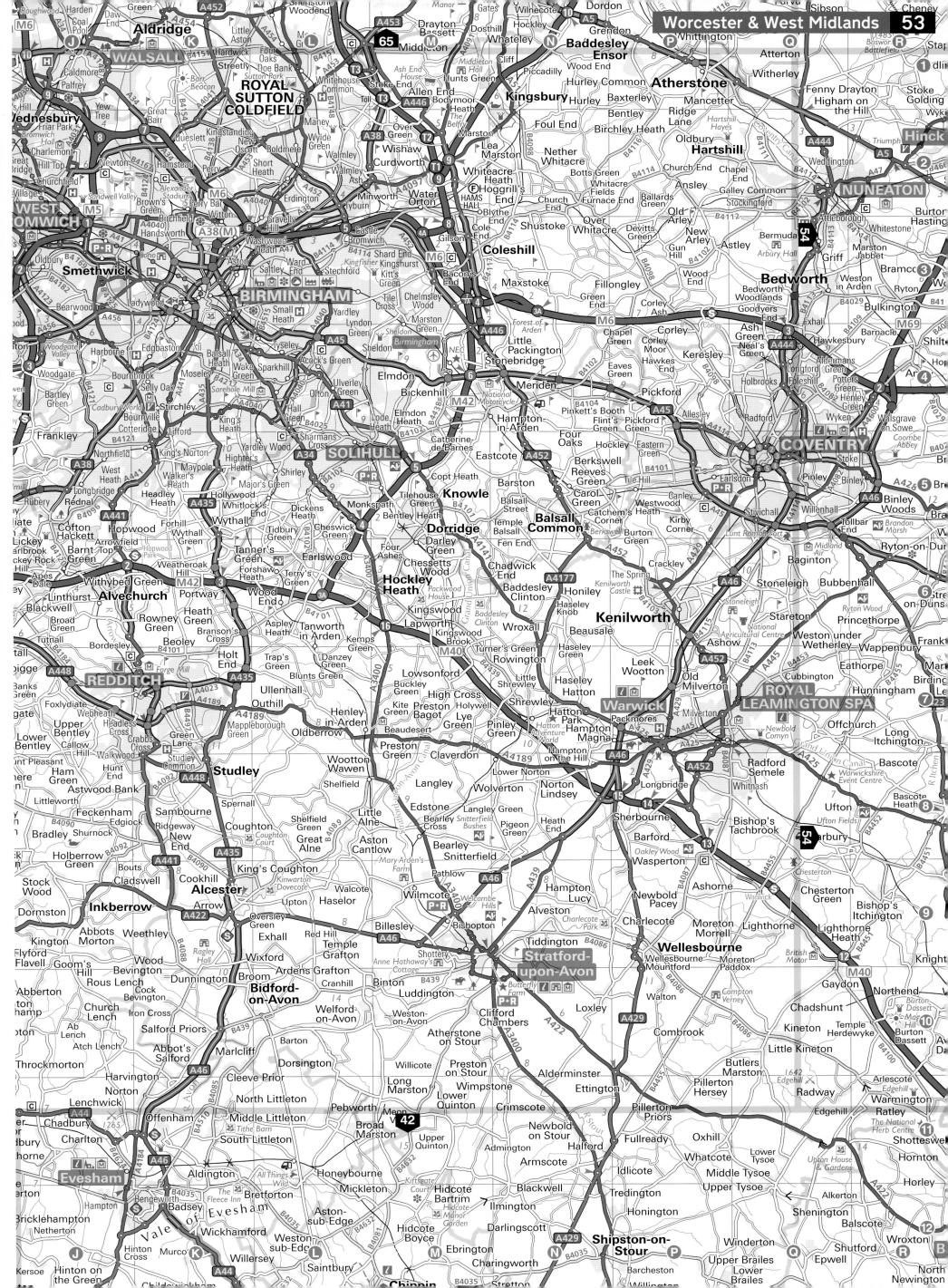

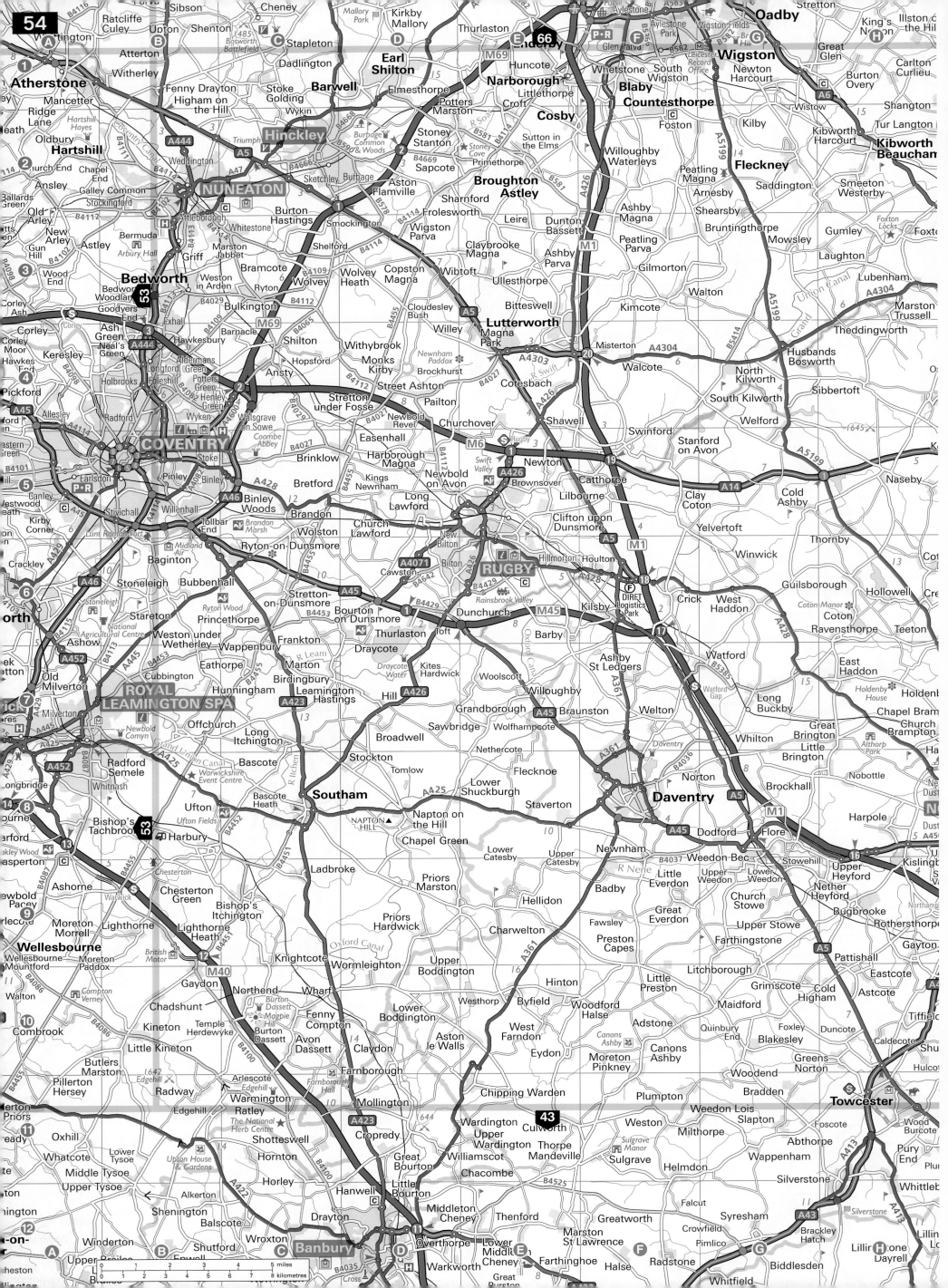

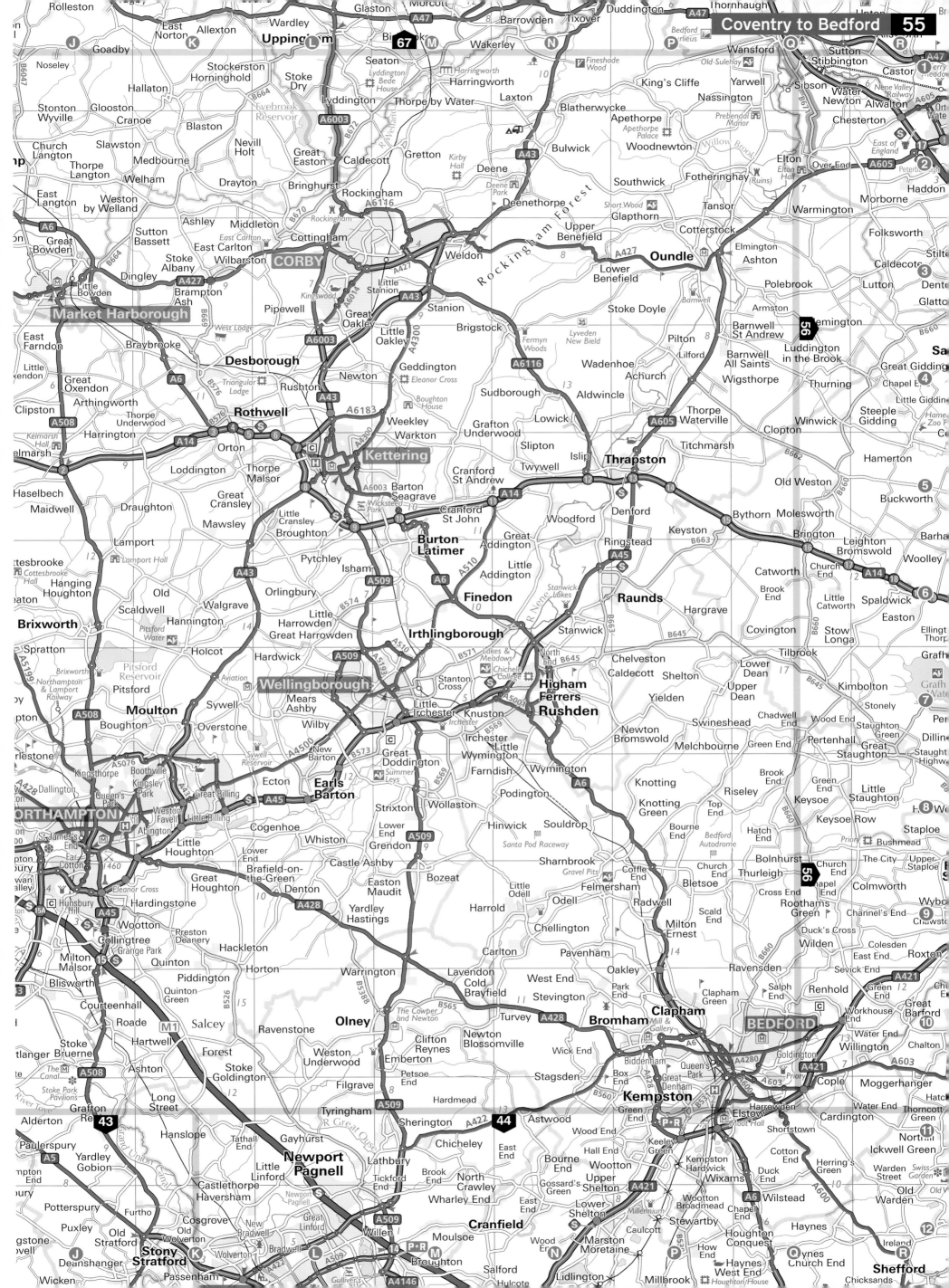

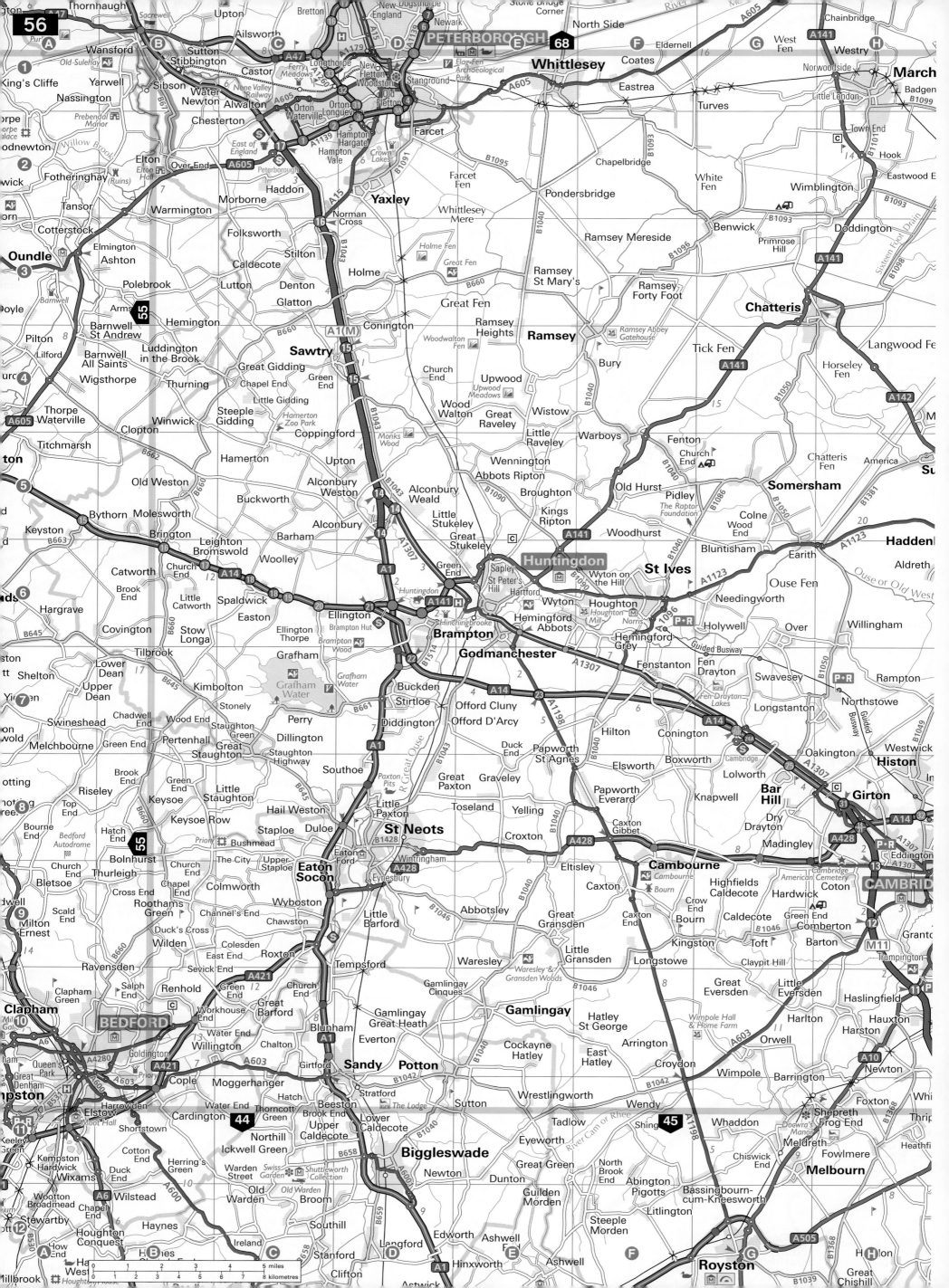

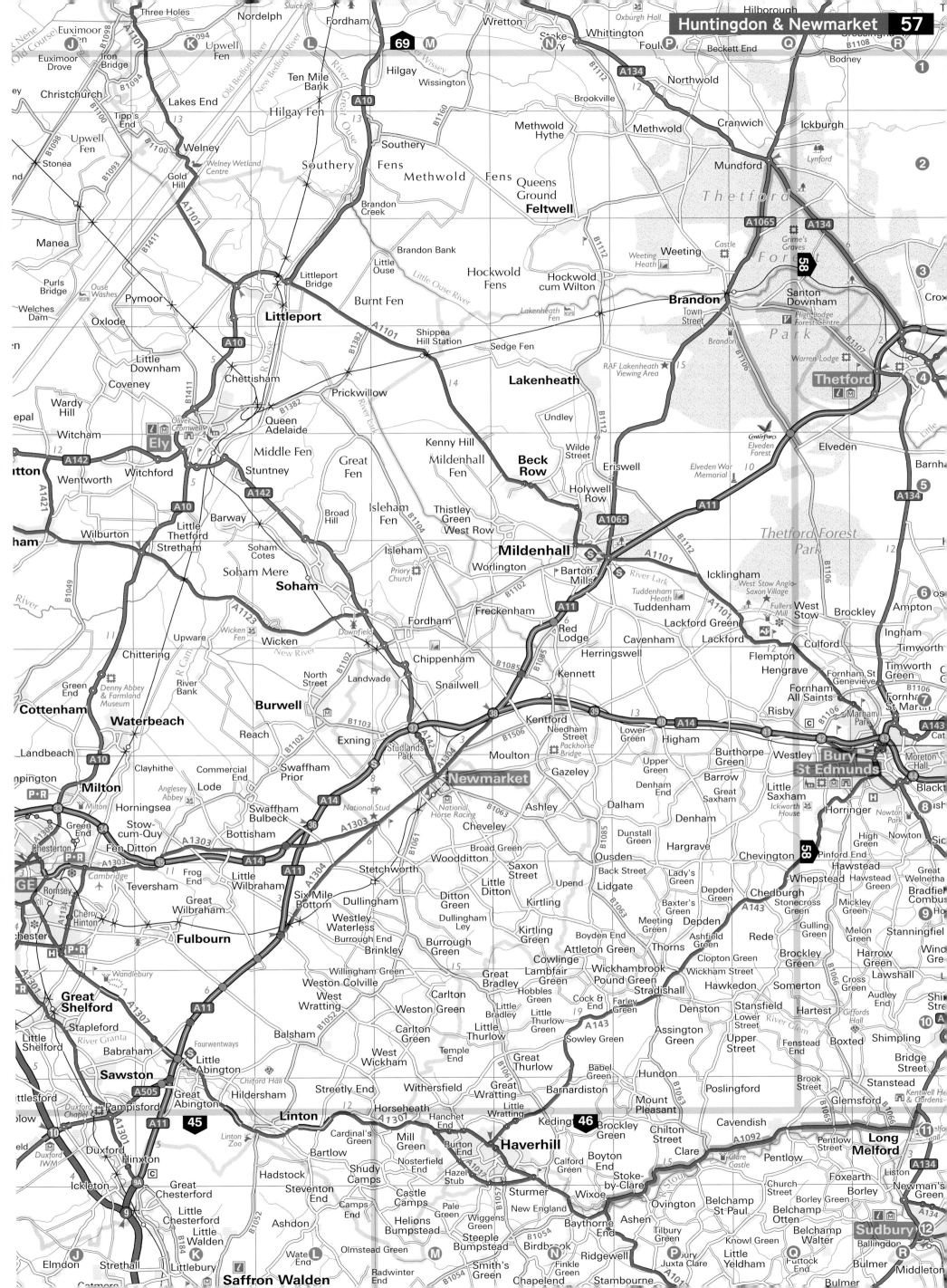

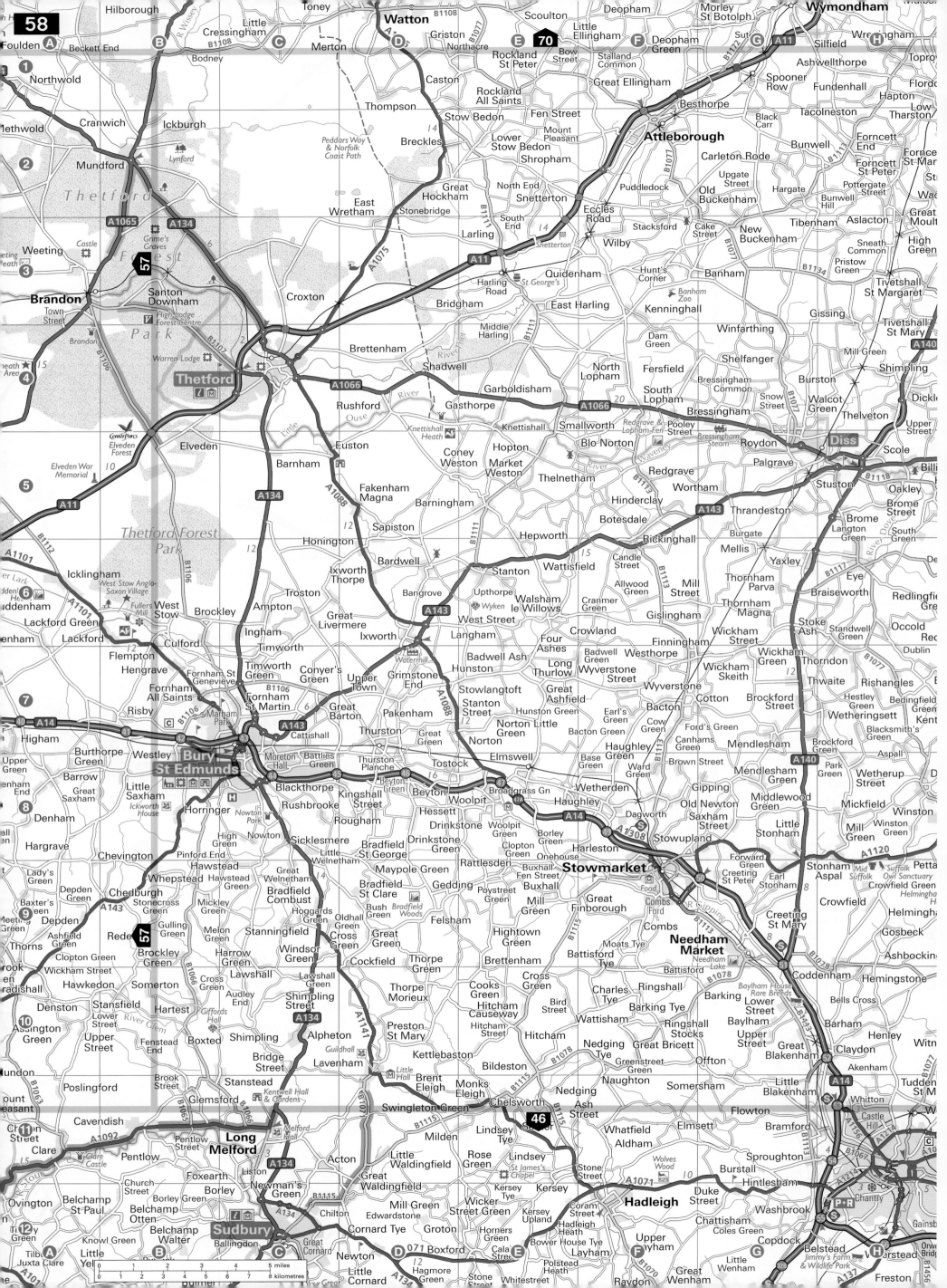

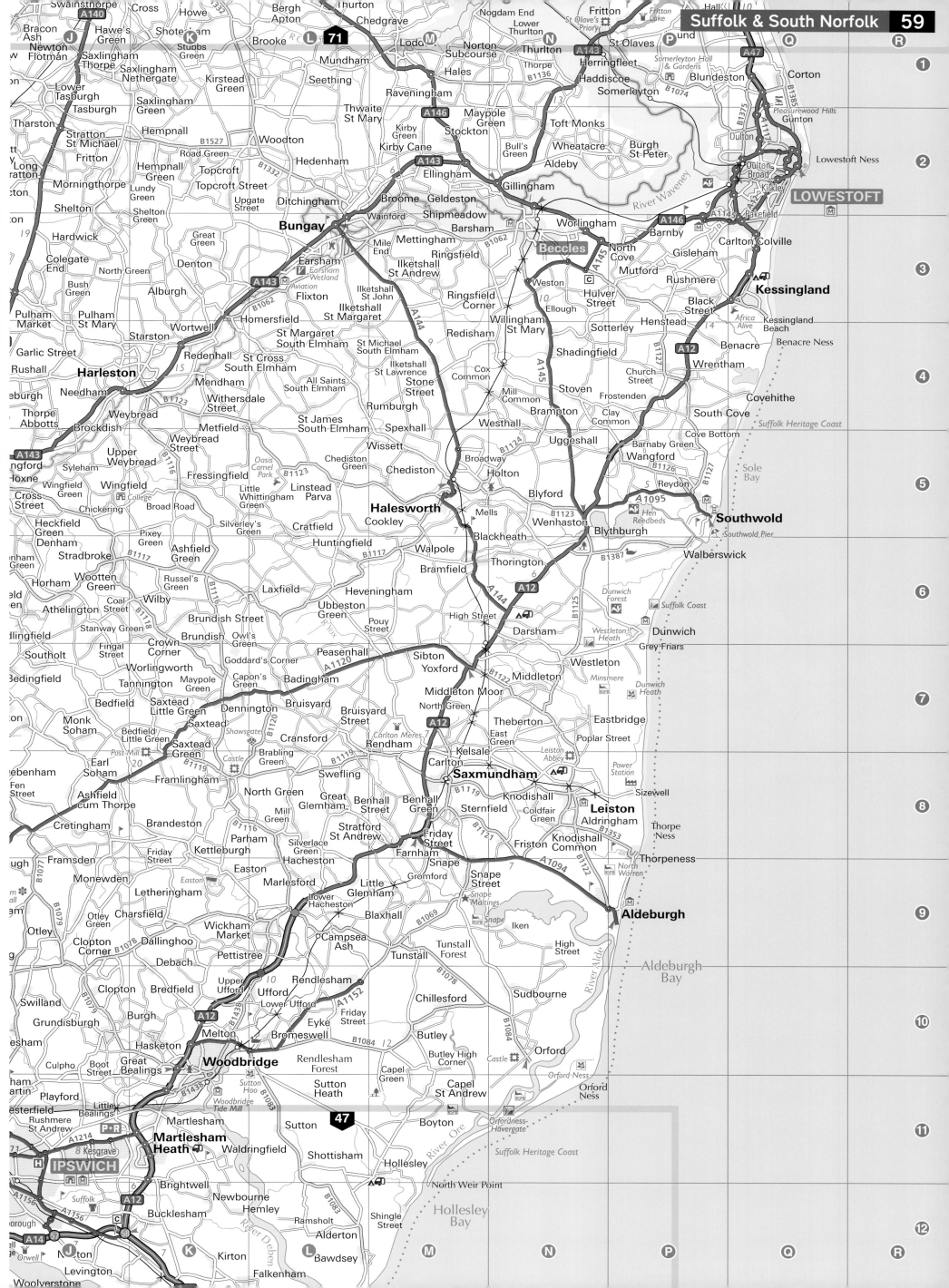

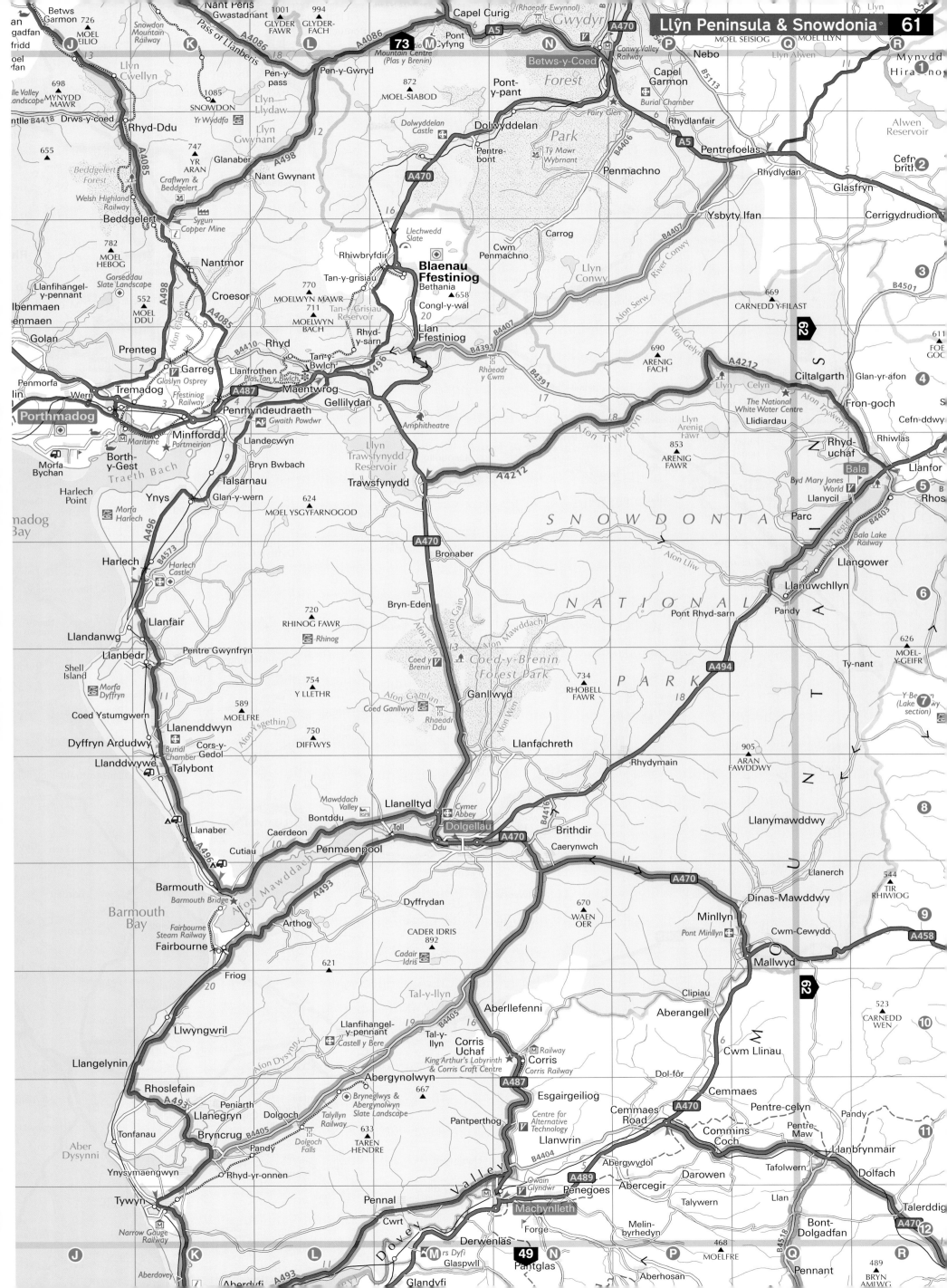

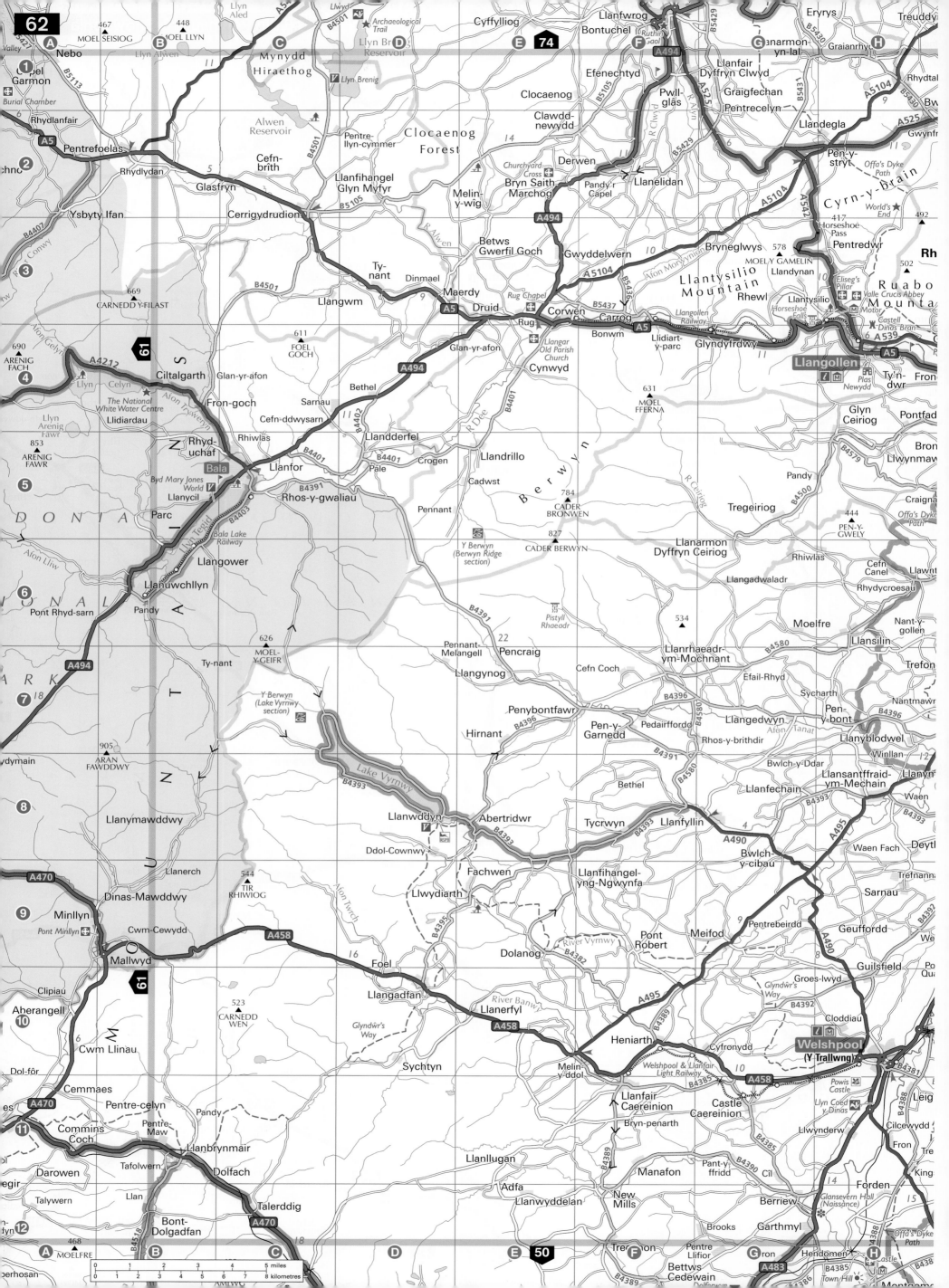

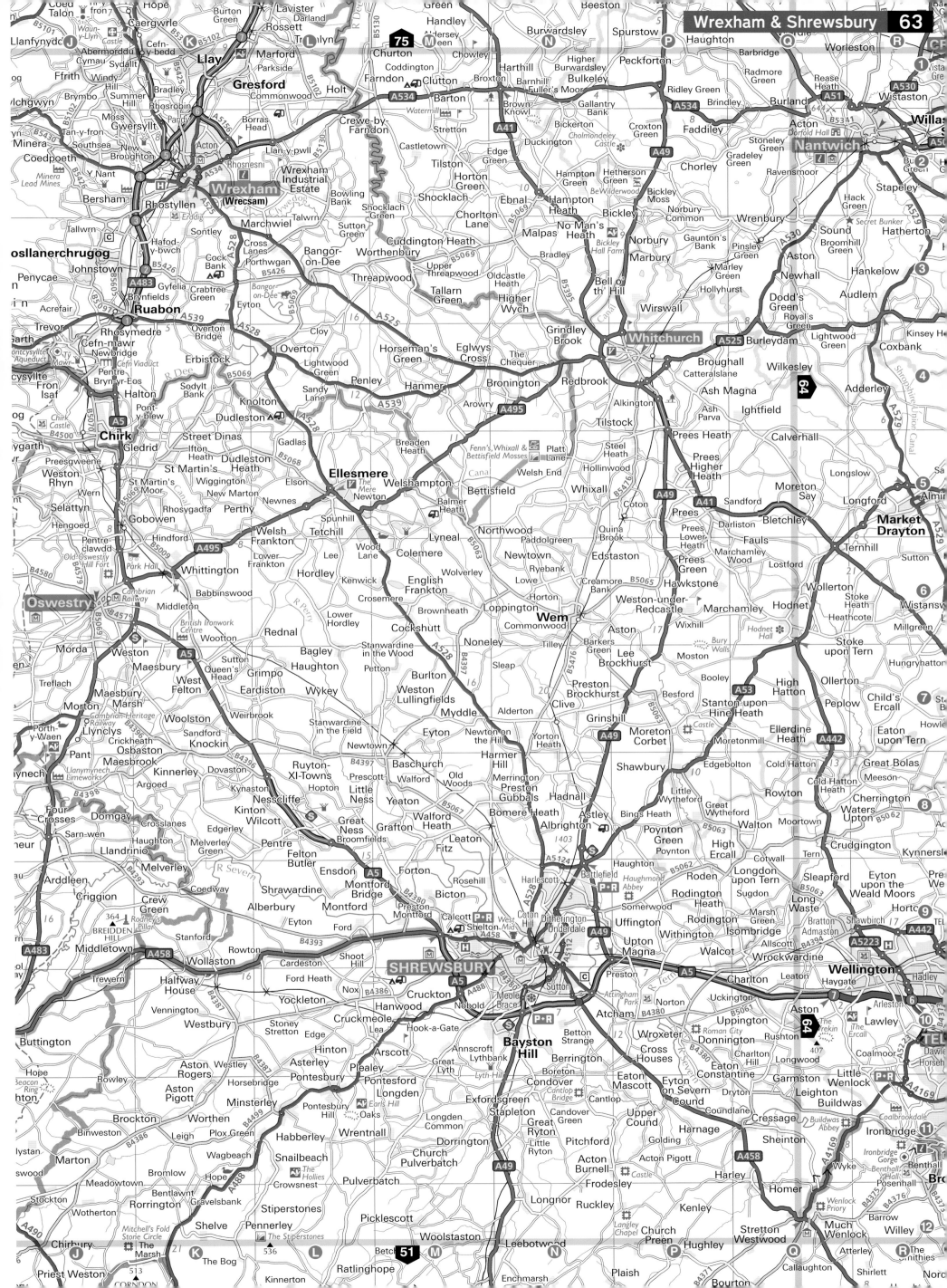

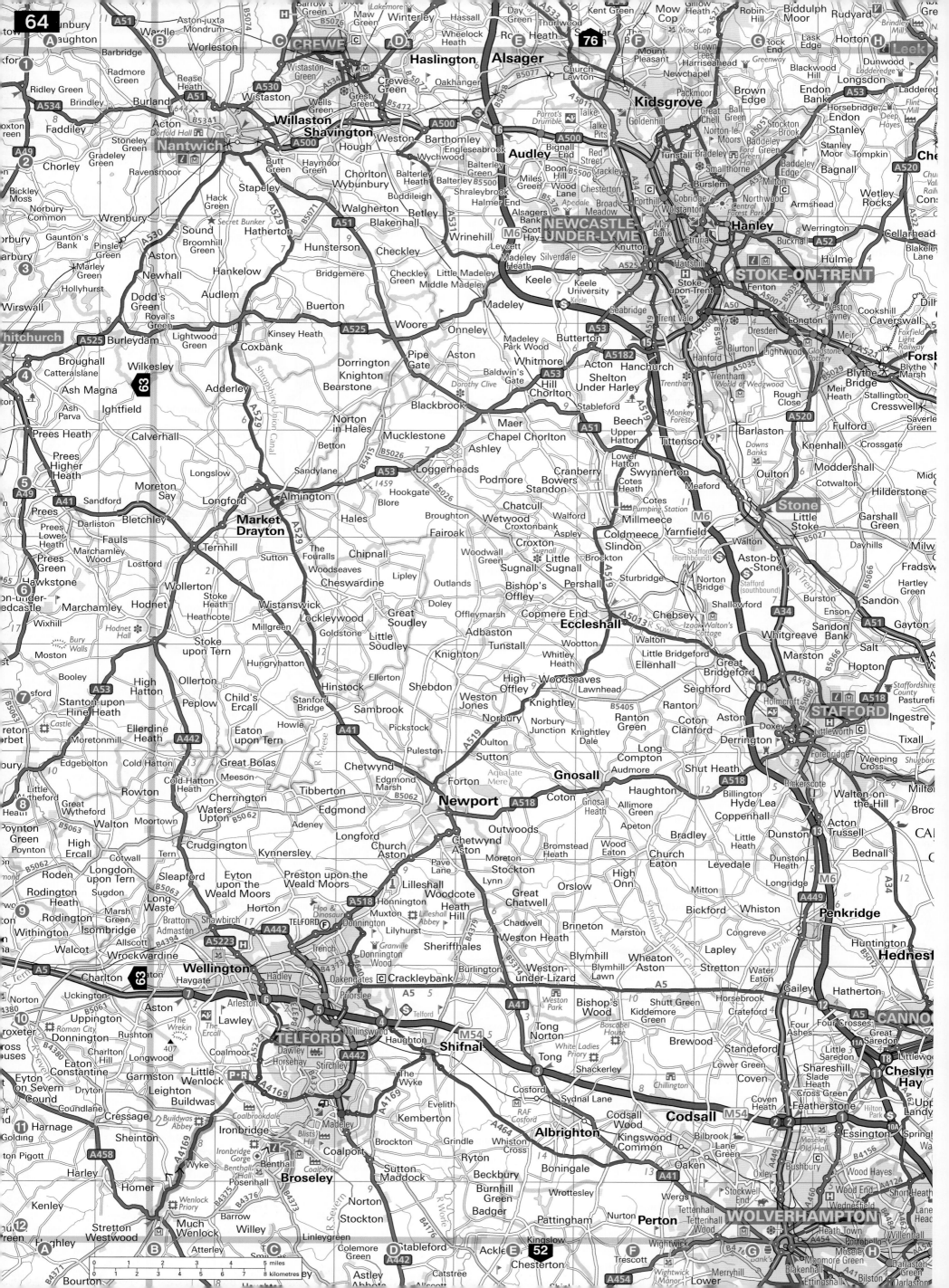

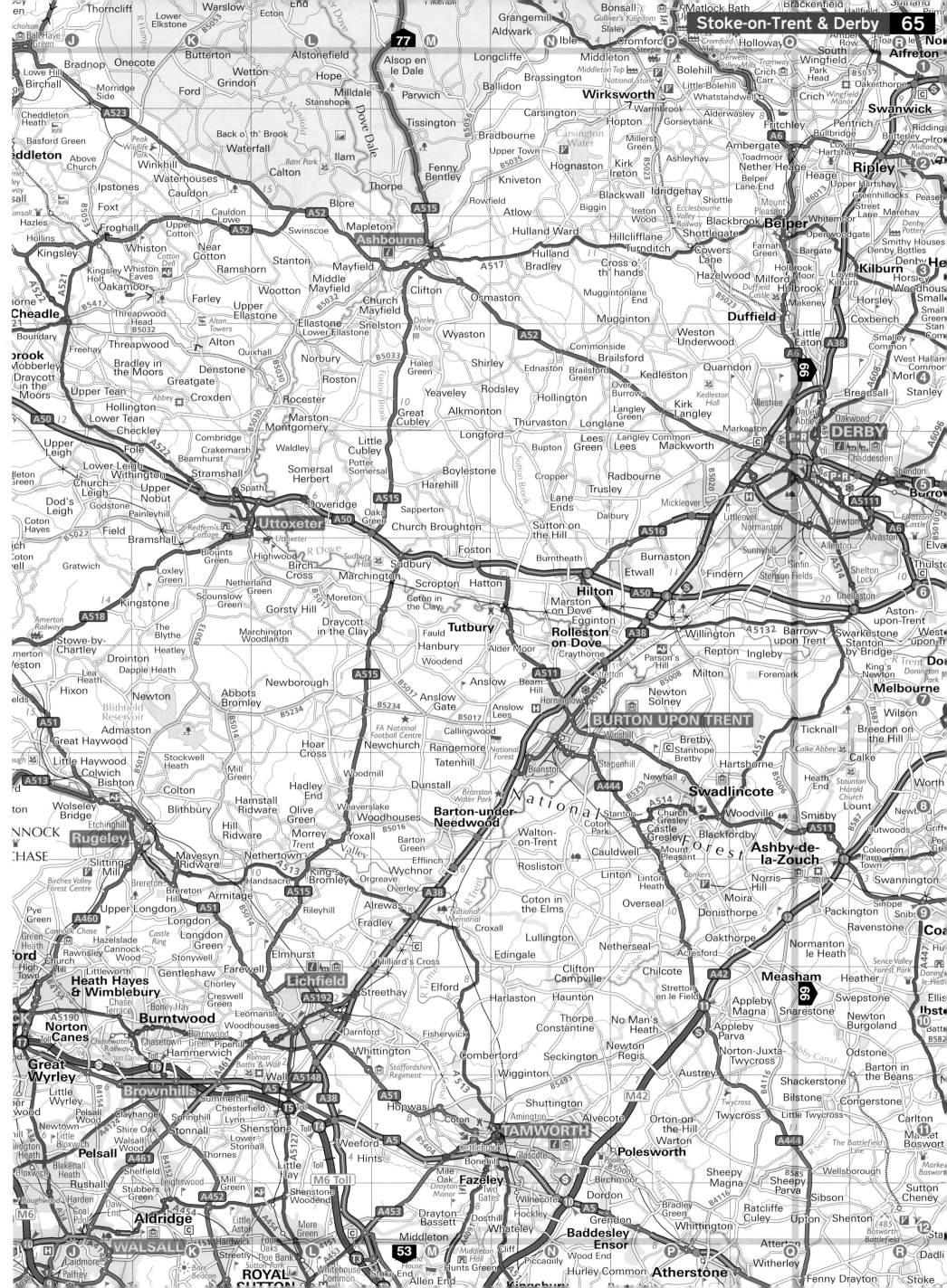

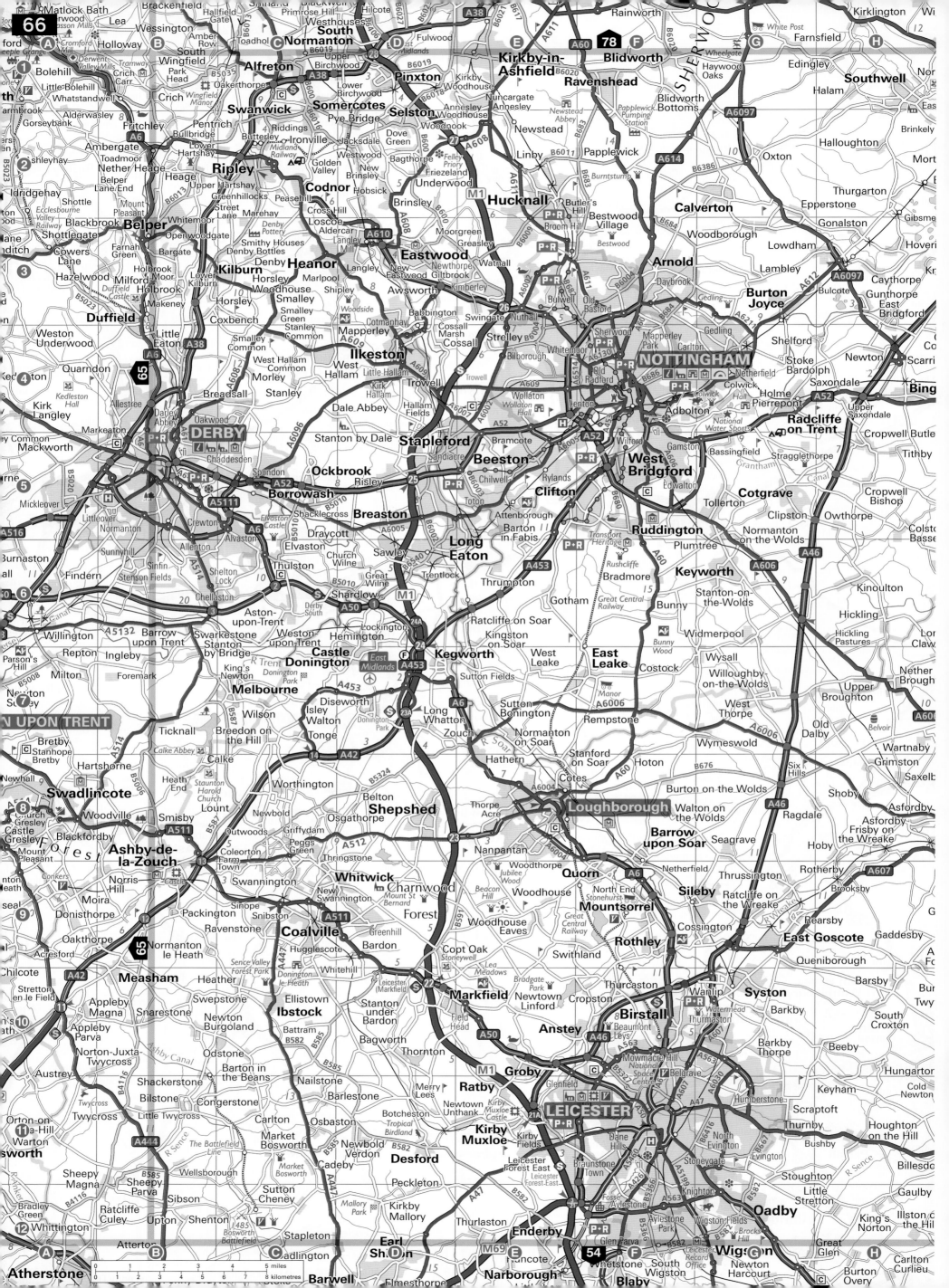

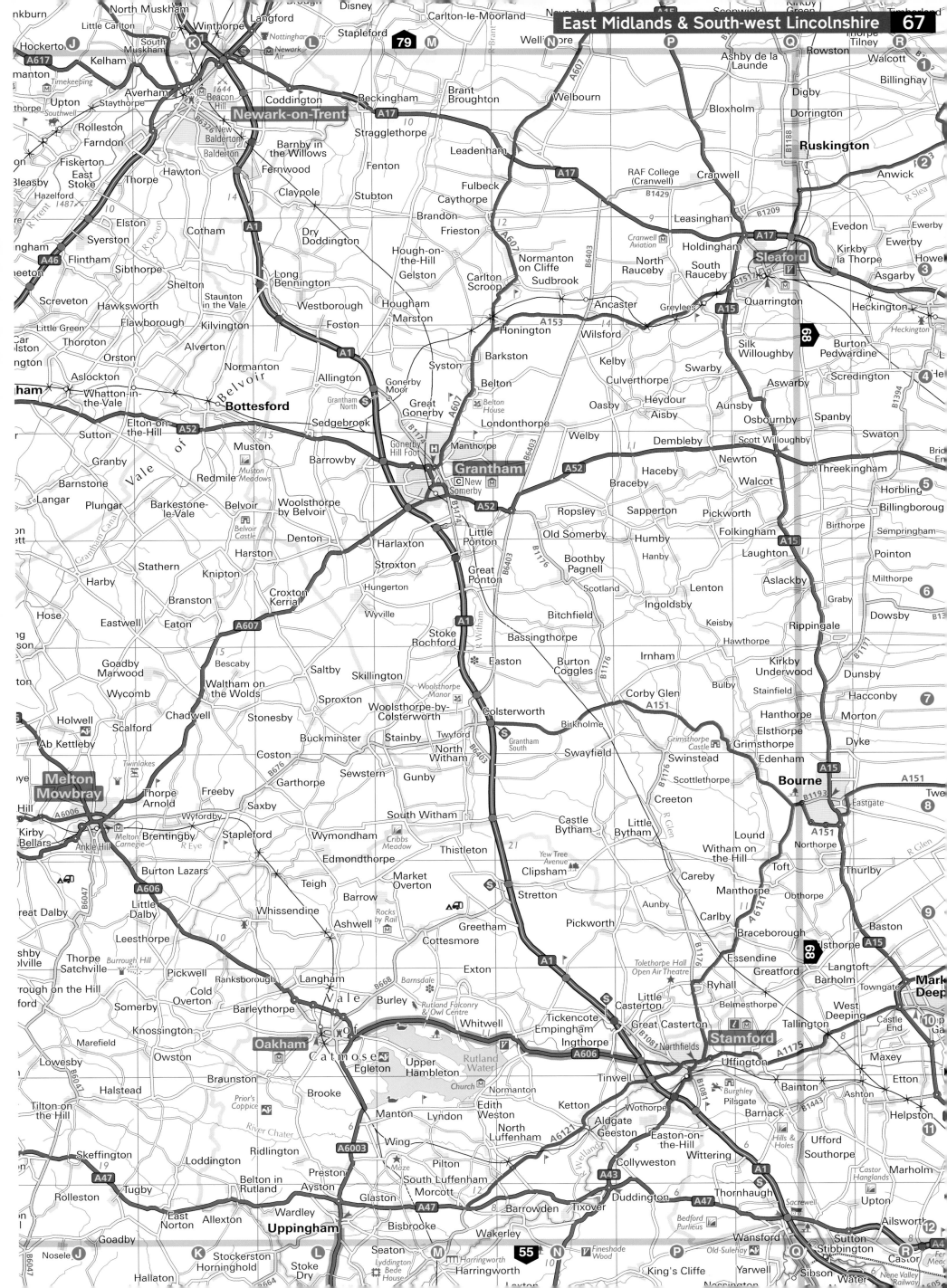

THE WASH

Gibraltar
Gibraltar Point

All Saints

Wainfleet
St Mary
J A52 K 81 L M N P Q R

Frangle
owgate

23

London

Dawsmere

Gedney
Drove End

Sutton
Sutton
Bridge

Walpole
Cross Keys

Tydd
Gote
Walpole
St Andrew

Walpole
St Peter
Four
Gotes
Ingleborough

West
Walton
Walton
Highway

Wisbech
New
Walsoken
Marshland
St James
Chequers Corner

Emneth
Gaultree
Emneth Hungate

Elm

Begdale

Friday
Bridge
Outwell

Laddus
Fen
Upwell

Euximoor
Fen
Iron
Bridge

Christchurch

Holme next
the Sea
Old
Hunstanton
Hunstanton
Ringstead

Heacham
Norfolk
Lavender

Snettisham
Snettisham Park
Southgate
Ingoldisthorpe
Shernborne

Dersingham
Doddshill

Wolferton
Dersingham Bog
Sandringham
West
Newton

Babingley River
Castle
Rising
B1439
Flitcham

The Wash
North
Wootton
Castle
Congham
Roydon

R Great Ouse
South Wootton
A148
A148

Little
London
Clenchwarton
West
Lynn
South
Lynn
Gaywood
Bawsey
B1145
Bawsey

Terrington
St Clement
Tilney
All Saints
King's Lynn
Leziate

Hay Green
A17
A47
Fair Green
Ashwicken

Tilney High End
Saddlebow
West
Winch
North
Runcton
East
Winch

St John's
Highway
A10
Middleton
Blackborough
End
West
Bilney

Tilney St
Lawrence
Wiggenhall
St Germans
Setchey
Pentney

Terrington
St John
Wiggenhall
St Peter
Watatunga
Wildlife Reserve
Watlington

Walpole
Highway
Wiggenhall
St Mary the Virgin
Wormegay
River Nar
Narborough

Lordsbridge

St John's
Fen End
Wiggenhall
St Mary Magdalen
Runcton
Holme
Tottenhill
Marham
Shouldham

Walsoken
Thorpland
South
Runcton
Shouldham
Thorpe
Upper
Marham

Stowbridge
West
Head
Fincham

Stow
Bardolph
Fen
Wimbotsham
Stow
Bardolph
A134
Stradsett
Barton
Bendish

**Downham
Market**
A1122
Bexwell
Crimplesham
Eastmoor
Boughton

Barroway
Drove
West
Dereham
Wereham
Oxborough

Denver
Denver
Sluice
Fordham
Stoke
Ferry
Whittington
Foulden

Nordelph
Wretton
Beckett End

Upwell
Fen
Ten Mile
Bank
Wissington
Northwold

Brancaster
Bay
Scolt Head
Island
Holkham
Peddars Way &
Norfolk Coast Path
Titchfield Marsh
Brancaster
Staithe
Burnham
Deepdale
Burnham
Overy
Staithe
Brancaster
Holme
Dunes
Thornham
Titchwell
Branodunum
Roman Fort
Burnham
Norton
Burnham
Market
Burnham Overy
Burnham
Thorpe
New
Holkham
North
Creake
Creake
Abbey
Summerfield
Peddars Way
& Norfolk
Coast Path
Docking
Stanhoe
South
Creake
Waterd

Sedgeford
B1454
Fring
Bircham
Newton
Barmer
Southgate

Great
Bircham
Bircham
Tofts
Syderstone
Wicken Green
Village
Sculth

Anmer
Houghton
Hall
West
Rudham
Tattersett
Dunt
Coxford
Shereford

New
Houghton
A148
East
Rudham
Broomsthorpe
Tatterf

Hillington
Little
Massingham
Helhoughton
Harpley
West
Raynham
Ea
Raynha

Grimston
Great
Massingham
West
Raynham
South
Raynham

Pott
Row
Gayton
Weasenham
St Peter

Gayton
Thorpe
Weasenham
All Saints
Rougham

East
Walton
West
Acre
Castle Acre
A1065
West
Lexham
East
Lexham

West
Bilney
B1153
South
Acre
Priory
Castle
Newton

Pentney
Great
Palgrave
South
Acre
Little
Dunham
Wood

Narborough
Great
Dunham
Frans

Sporle
70
A47

Shouldham
A1122
Swaffham
Necto

Marham
Barton
Bendish
Beachamwell
North
Pickenham
Holme
Hale

South
Pickenham

Cockley
Cley
A1065
Great
Cressingham

Gooderstone
Water
 Iceni
Village
Little
Cressingham

Oxburgh Hall
Hilborough
Gooderstone

57 A134
Northwold
Bodney

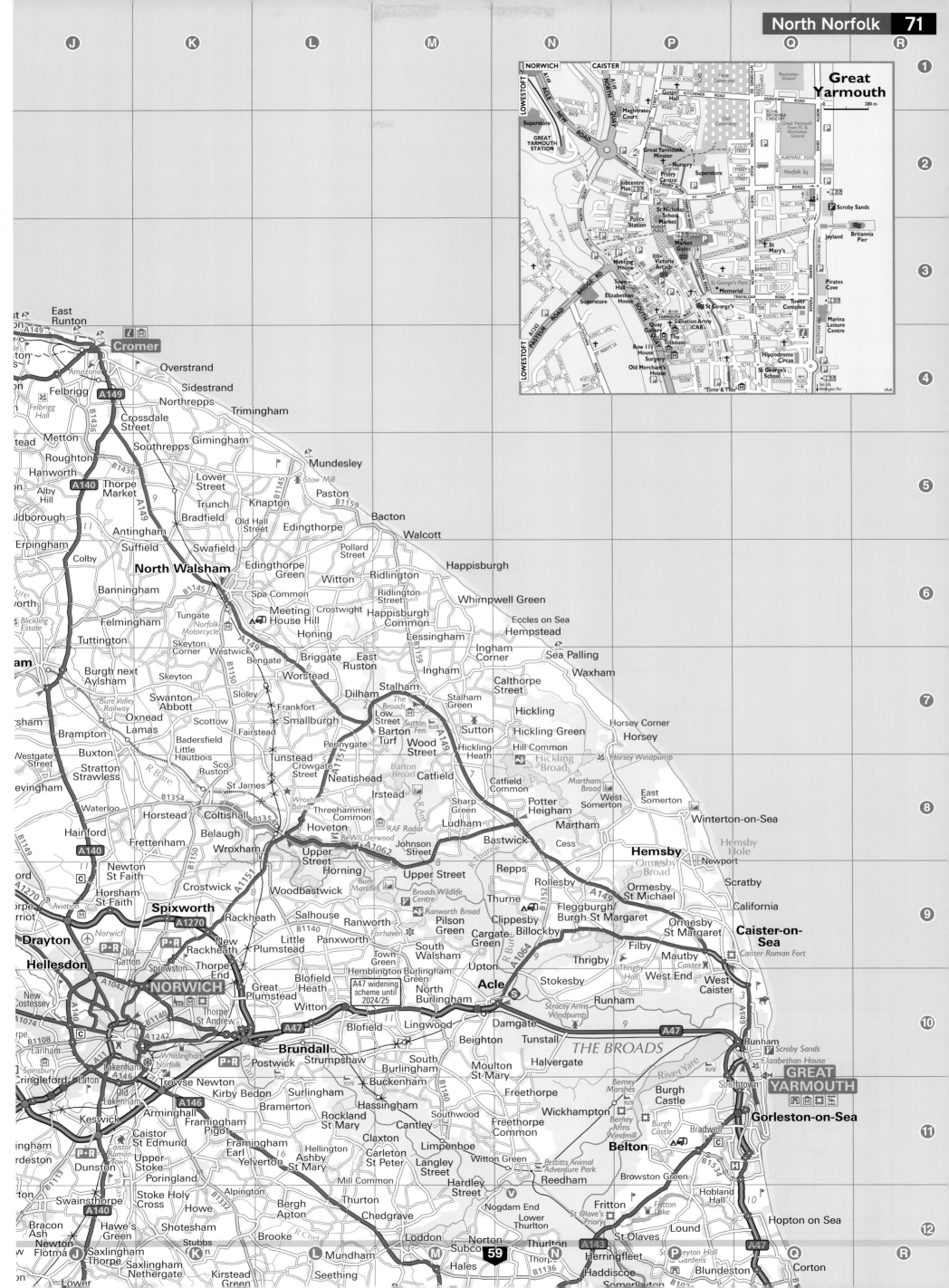

Great Yarmouth

A   B   C   D   E   F   G   H

The Skerries

North Anglesey
Heritage Coast

Wylfa
Head   Cemaes   Porth
Wen   Bull
Bay

Cemlyn
Bay   Llanbadrig   Bull Bay   **Amlwch**

Hen
Borth   Cemaes   Copper
Kingdom   Point Lynas

CARMEL HEAD   Tregele   A5025   Burwen   Llaneilian

Pentrefelin   Pengorffwysfa

Llanfairynghornwy   Mynydd
Mechell   Llanfechell   Bodewryd   Penysarn   Nebo

Swtan
Heritage   Rhosbeirio   A5025   Gadfa   Dulas

Church
Bay   Llanrhyddlad   Llanflewyn   Rhosgoch   Rhosybol   City
Dulas   Dulas
Bay

Llanfaethlu   Carreglefn   Capel
Parc   Brynrefail   Rhôs Lligwy

Dublin   Llanddeusant   Llanbabo   Llyn
Alaw   Din Lligwy

Dublin
(Mar-Oct)   Llynon
Mill   Gwredog   Llandyfrydog

Porth
Tywynmawr   Elim   B5111   Maenaddwyn

North Stack   Breakwater   Holyhead
Maritime   Llanfwrog   Llantrisant   Llanerchymedd   Hebron
Bachau   Capel
Coch   Brynteg   B5108

Gogarth
Bay   Llaingoch   Stryd-y-
Facsen   Pen-llyn   Cors
Erddreiniog   Tynygongl

Holyhead   B5112   A N G L E S E Y   Cors
Goch

South Stack   Holyhead Mountain
Hut Circles   **(Caergybi)**   Llyn
Llywenan   Llechcynfarwy   Tregaian   Llanbedrgoch

Holyhead Mountain
Heritage Coast   Ellins
Tower   Penrhos Feilw   Kingsland   Penrhos   Llanynghenedl   Presaddfed   B5109   Trefor   Llangwyllog   Rhosmeirch   Llanddyfnan   B5109

Penrhyn Mawr   Trefignath   Valley A5025   Llanfachraeth   Bodedern   Llynfaes   Rhoscefn

Trearddur Bay   A5   A55   Caergeiliog   Bodffordd   Oriel Môn   Rhoscefni

HOLY ISLAND   B4545   Four Mile
Bridge   Llanfihangel
yn Nhowyn   Bryngwran   Gwalchmai   Cefni
Reservoir   Talwrn

Llanfair-yn-Neubwll   Llechylched   Valley   A5   Heneglwys   Anglesey   Rhostrehwfa   **Llangefni**   B5420

Rhoscolyn   Capel Gwyn   Dothan   A55   A5114   Penmynydd

Rhoscolyn
Head   Plas
Cymyran   Ty Newydd   A4080   Cerrigceinwen   Din-Dryfol   Henblas   Langristiolus   Llanfairpw
Star

Cymyran
Bay   Pencarnisiog   Pentre Berw   Llanfairpw

Rhosneigr   Llanfaelog   Bryn Du   Bethel   Capel Mawr   Aton Cefni   Gaerwen   Bryn
Celli Ddu

A4080   Ty
Croes   Trefdraeth   Llanddaniel Fab

Barclodiad
y Gawres   Aberffraw   Llangadwaladr   Malltraeth   Llangaffo   Bodowyr
Burial Chamber   A4080   B4419   Caer Lêb

Porth Trecastell   Anglesey
Circuit   Hermon   Bodorgan   A4080   Brynsiencyn   Llanidan

Aberffraw
Bay   Newborough   Pen-lôn   Anglesey
Sea Zoo   Castell
Bryn Gwyn   Dwyran   Foel Farm
Park   Y Felin

Aberffraw Bay
Heritage Coast   Aberffraw
Bay   A4085

Malltraeth Bay   Newborough
Warren   **Caernarfon**   Waterloo
Port

Llanddwyn Island   Llanddwyn
Bay   Abermenai
Point   Caernarfon Castle   Segontium   Caeathro

C A E R N A R F O N   Welsh Highlands
Railway   Gypsy
Wood   A4085

B A Y   Foryd
Bay   A487   Bontnewydd

Airworld
Aviation   Saron   Dinas

Morfa Dinlle   Rhostryfan   Rhos

Dinas Dinlle   Llandwrog   Groeslon   Penyf

Parc
Glynllifon   Carmel   Try

Inigo-Jones
Slateworks   Cilgwyn   M

**Holyhead
Harbour**

Marina   Salt Island

Maritime   BEACH ROAD

Porth-
y-Felin   PRINCE OF WALES ROAD

Hertz Car
Rental

FERRY
TERMINAL

Stryd   TERMINAL
BUILDING   HOLYHEAD

HOLYHEAD
STATION   Môrawelon

Kingsland   LONDON
ROAD   A5

0   500 m   BANGOR   IAA

0   1   2   3   4   5 miles
0   1   2   3   4   5   6   7   8 kilometres

60

Llandudno (inset map)

0   200 m

Great Orme Tramway
TABOR HILL
Great Orme
OLD ROAD
Llandudno Pier
The Grand Hotel
North Shore Beach
Llandudno Bay
Tabernacle Welsh Baptist Chapel
War Memorial
The Promenade
Travelodge
Town Hall
Victoria
St John's
The Parade
GLODDAETH STREET
MOSTYN STREET
SOUTH PARADE
A546
Our Lady Star of the Sea
Mostyn Gallery
MOSTYN BROADWAY
Holy Trinity
Medical Centre
Swimming Pool
Venue Cymru
St Paul's
B5115
LLANDUDNO STATION
CONWAY ROAD
Parc Llandudno Retail Park
CYLCH TUDUR
Mostyn Champneys Retail Park
Police Station
Magistrates' Court
Fire & Ambulance Station
Ysgol Tudno
CLARENCE DRIVE
Superstore
Ysgol Craig Y Don
Ysgol Fford Dyffryn
Coach
Ysgol Morfa Rhianedd
Ysgol John Bright
Llandudno FC
A55, BETWS-Y-COED
DEGANWY

RNLI Moelfre Seawatch Centre
Moelfre
llgo
an-glas
Benllech
Red Wharf Bay
Red Wharf Bay
Pentraeth
Llanddona
Glan-yr-afon
Caim
Penmon Priory
Toll
Penmon
Puffin Island
Black Point
GREAT ORME'S HEAD
Great Orme Heritage Coast
Great Orme Tramway
Toll
Little Ormes Head
Penrhyn Bay
Conwy Bay
Llandudno
Penrhynside
Rhos-on-Sea
Abergele Roa
Llangoed
Llanfaes
B5109
Hafoty Medieval House
Gaol
Beaumaris Castle
Deganwy
Llanrhos
Llandrillo yn-Rhos
Colwyn Bay (Bae Colwyn)
A55
Pydew
Llandudno Junction
A470
Esgyryn
Tywyn
Welsh
Llanelian-yn-Rhos
Old Colwyn
A55
Llanddulas
Beaumaris
Llansadwrn
Courthouse
Llandegfan
Conwy
Conwy Castle
Capelulo
Penmaenan
Penmaenmawr
Llansanffraid Glan Conwy
Bryn-y-Maen
Llysfaen
Rhyd-y-foel
Abergele
A548
Menai Bridge (Porthaethwy)
Plas Cadnant
Bangor
Llanfairfechan
A55
Henryd
Dwygyfylchi
B5113
B5383
Dawn
Gwrych
A5025
B5109
Pili Palas
Plas Newydd
llgwyngyll
Anglesey Column
Britannia Bridge
Penrhos garnedd
Penrhyn Castle
Llandygai
Nant-y-pandy
Gorddinog
Abergwyngregyn
SNOWDONIA
TAL-Y-FAN
610
Rowen
Ty'n-y-Groes
Caerhun
Castell
Graig
Trofarth
Tal-y-Cafn
Eglwysbach
Bodnant
Pentre'r Felin
Betws-yn-Rhos
Llanfair Talhaiarn
A544
Capel-y-graig
Waen-wen
Glasinfryn
Rhyd-y-groes
Tal-y-bont
Coedydd Aber
Afon Anafon
Aber Falls
NATIONAL
Llanbedr-y-Cennin
Tal-y-Bont
Dolgarrog
Maenan
Llanddoged
River Elwy
Hafodunos
Llangernyw
74
GreenWood Family Park
B5547
Pentir
Seion
Llanddeiniolen
Saron
Penisarwaun
Llanrug
Sling
Waen-pentir
Mynydd Llandygai
Rachub
Gerlan
Bethesda
Y DROSGL
757
MOEL WINION
580
942
FOEL-FRAS
Afon Dulyn
Llyn Eigiau
PARK
Afon Ddu
Pont Dolgarrog
Llyn Cowlyd
Llanrhychwyn
Trefriw Woollen Mills
Trefriw
Llanddoged
Pandy Tudur
B5384
Pentre-tafarn-y-fedw
A548
B5382
Llansan
Rhiwlas
Rhiwen
Deiniolen
Clwt-y-bont
Gallt-y-foel
Penrhyn Slate Landscape
Zip World Penrhyn Quarry
Ogwen Bank
A5
CARNEDD LLEWELYN
1062
CARNEDD DAFYDD
1044
Afon Caseg
Llyn Ogwen
Gwyther in
Cwm-y-glo
Brynrefail
Dinorwig
923
Llanberis Lake Railway
National Slate Museum
Dolbadarn Castle
Padarn
ELIDIR FAWR
Pont Pen-y-benglog
946
Y GARN
947
Y TRYFAN
994
GLYDER FACH
Llyn Eigiau
Llyn Crafnant
Llyn Geirionydd
Gwydir
Gwydir Uchaf Chapel
Coed Bodgynydd
Melin-y-coed
Llanrwst
Gwytherin
Llyn Aled
Llyn Padarn
442
Groeslon
ro
nant
Llanberis
Waunfawr
Betws Garmon
726
MOEL EILIO
Nant Peris
Gwastadnant
1001
GLYDER FAWR
917
Snowdon Mountain Railway
Pass of Llanberis
A4086
Pen-y-pass
Pen-y-Gwryd
61
872
MOEL SIABOD
Pont-y-pant
Capel Curig
A5
Pont Cyfyng
National Mountain Centre (Plas y Brenin)
Gwydyr
Swallow Falls (Rhaeadr Ewynnol)
Conwy Valley Railway
Betws-y-Coed
Forest
467
MOEL SEISIOG
448
MOEL LLYN
A470
B5427
Nebo
Capel Garmon
Llyn Alwen
Llyn Aled
Mynydd Hiraethog
698
MOEL
fridd
MOEL EILIO
1085
le Valley
Llyn Cwellyn
Moel
fan
13
J   K   L   M   N   P   Q   R
1   2   3   4   5   6   7   8   9   10   11   12

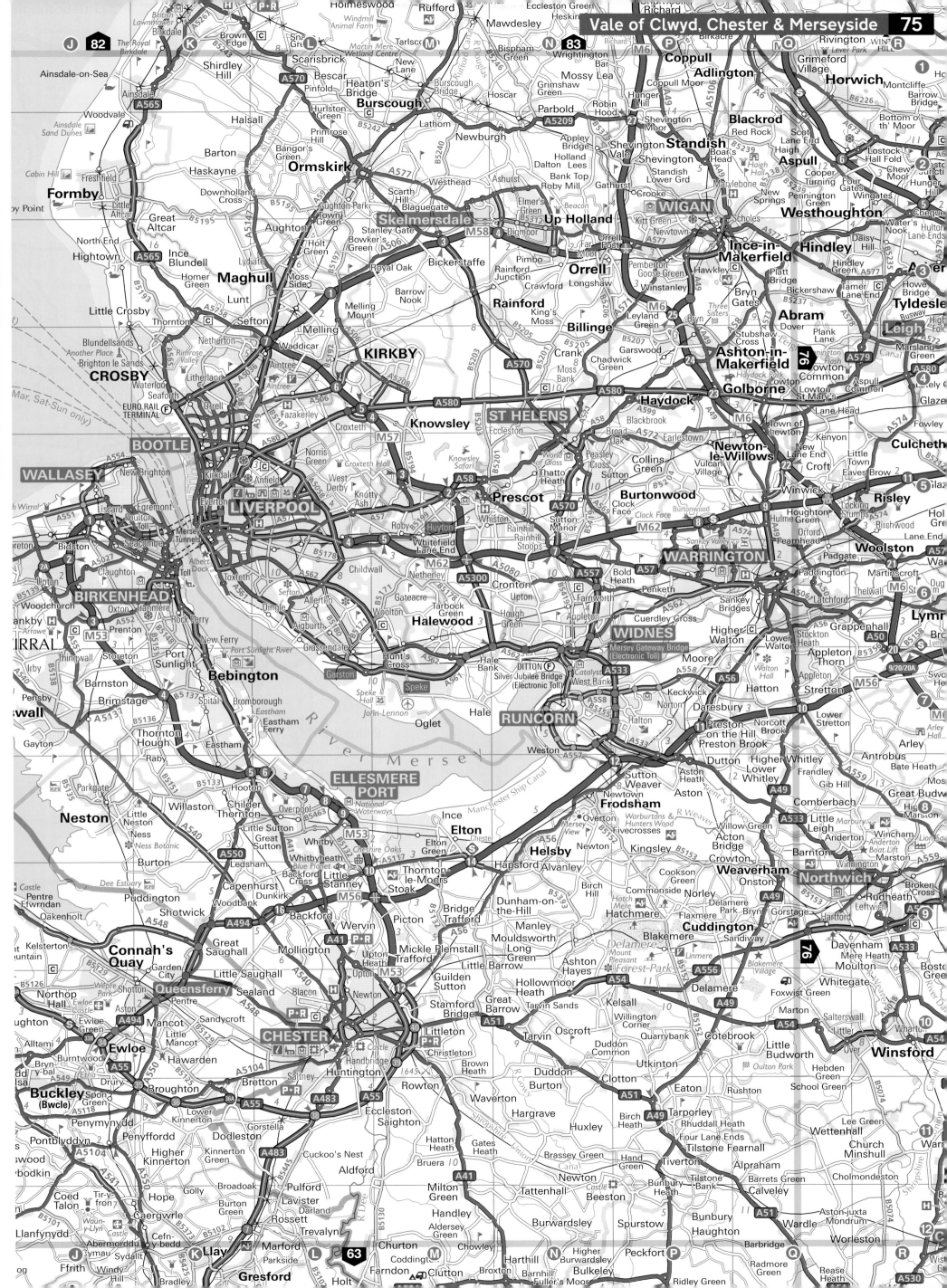

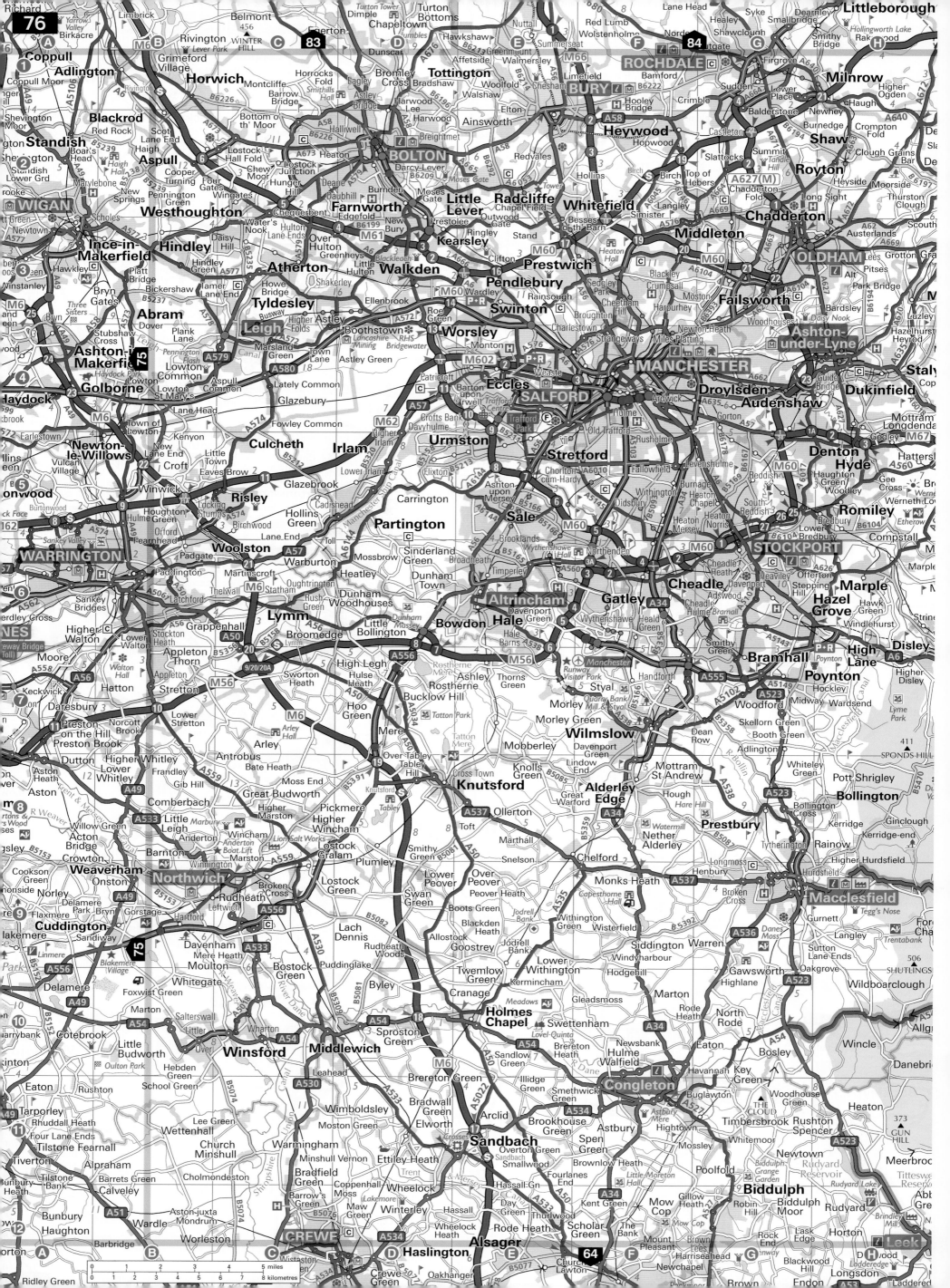

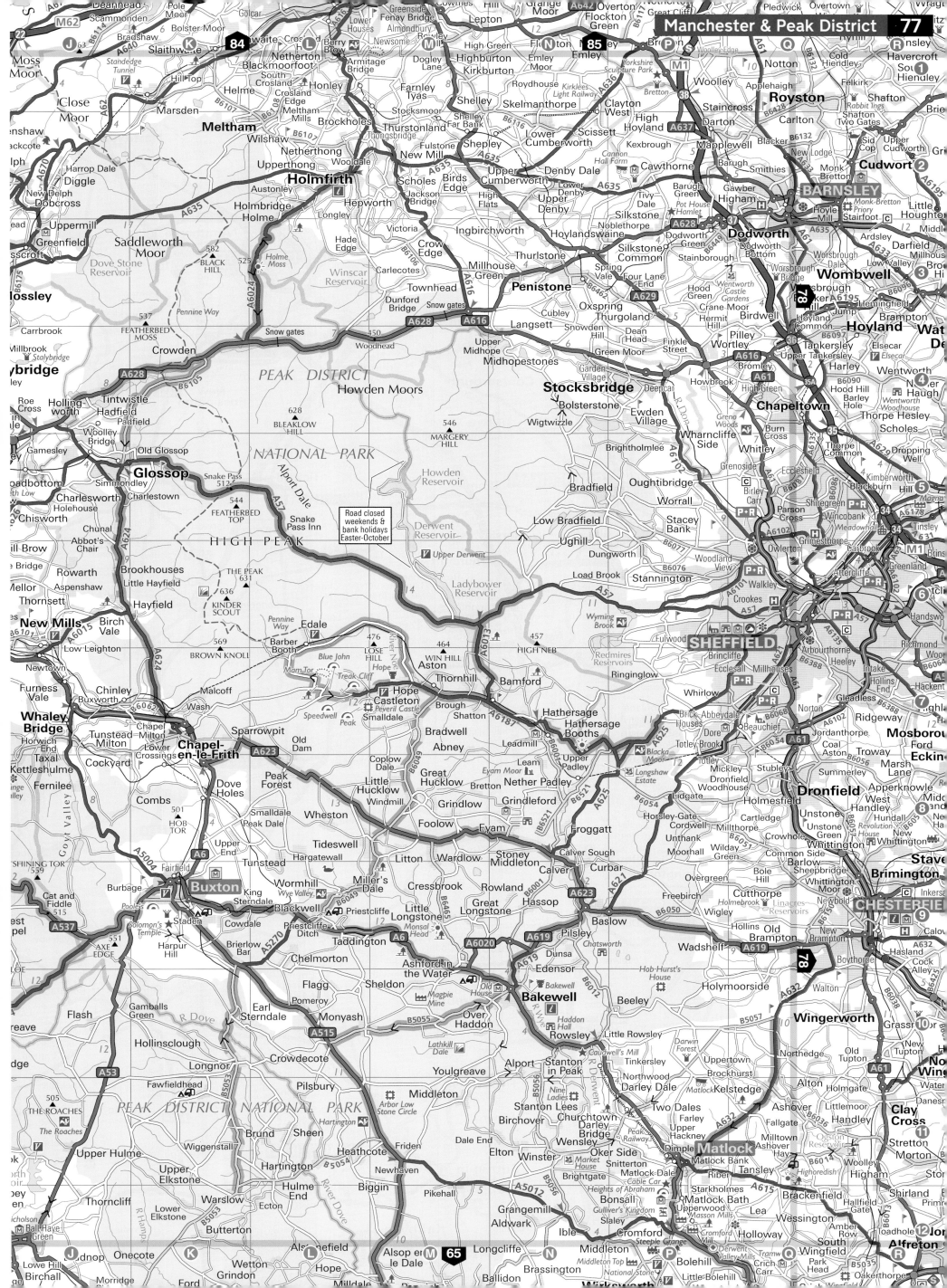

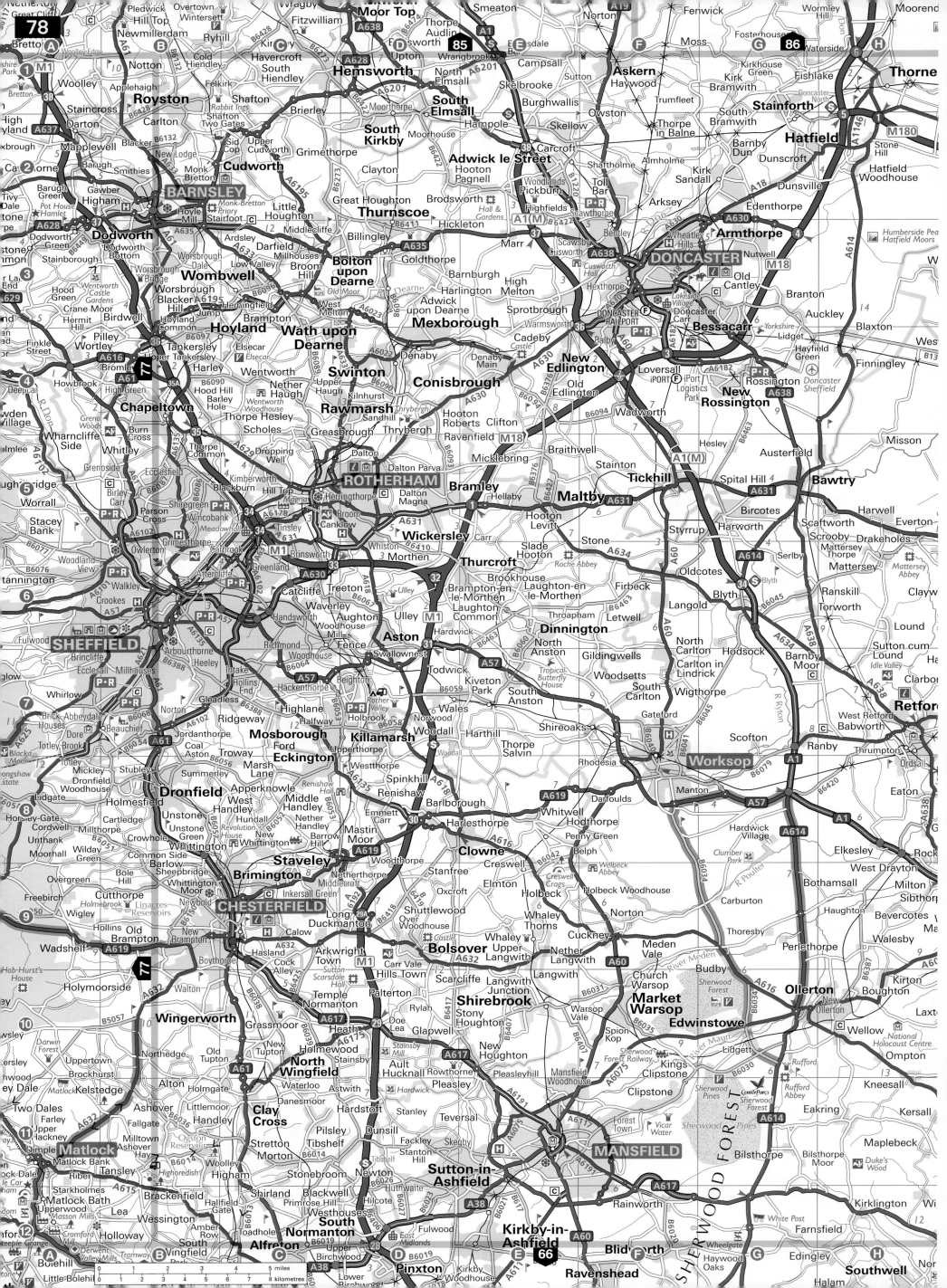

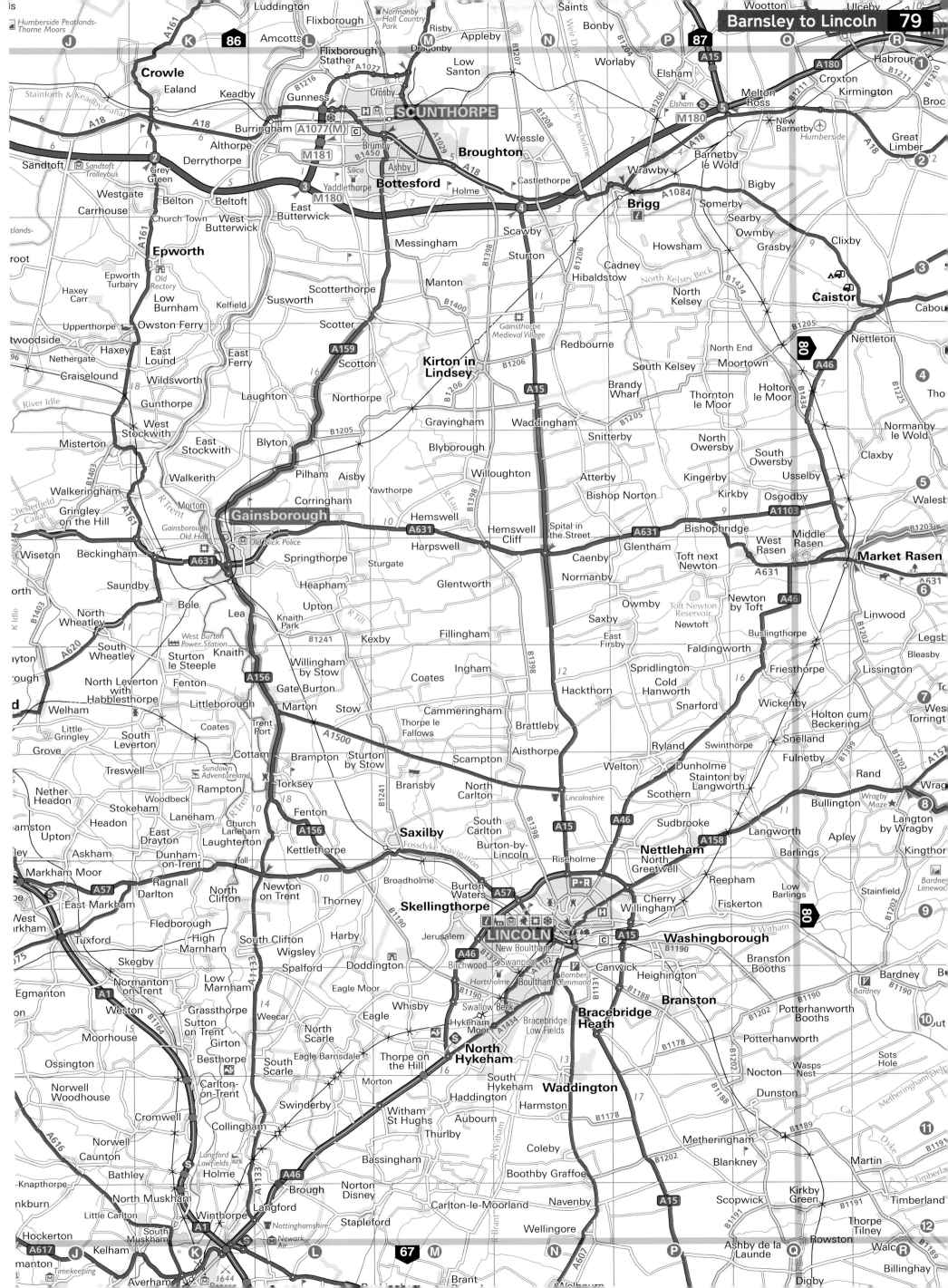

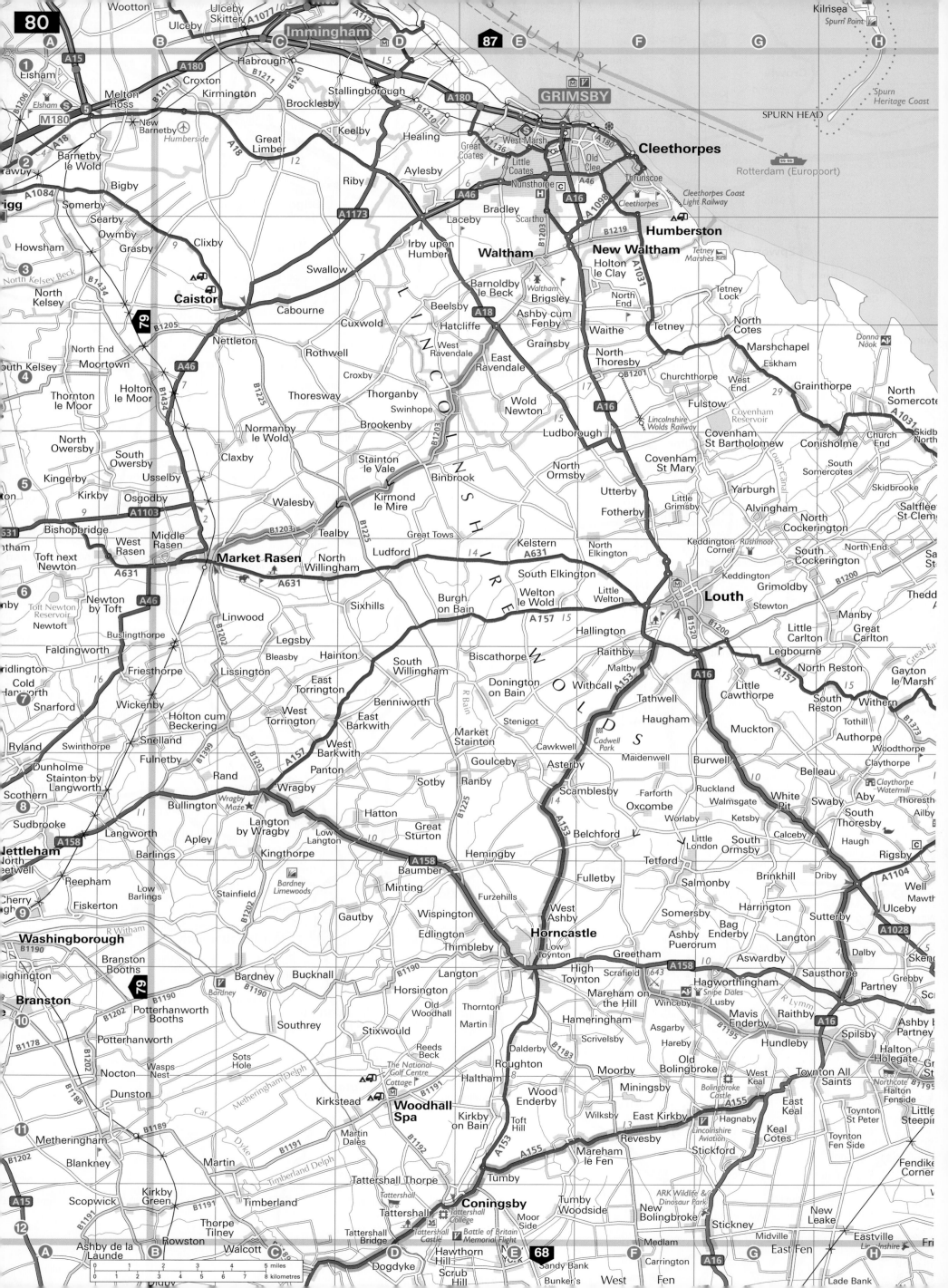

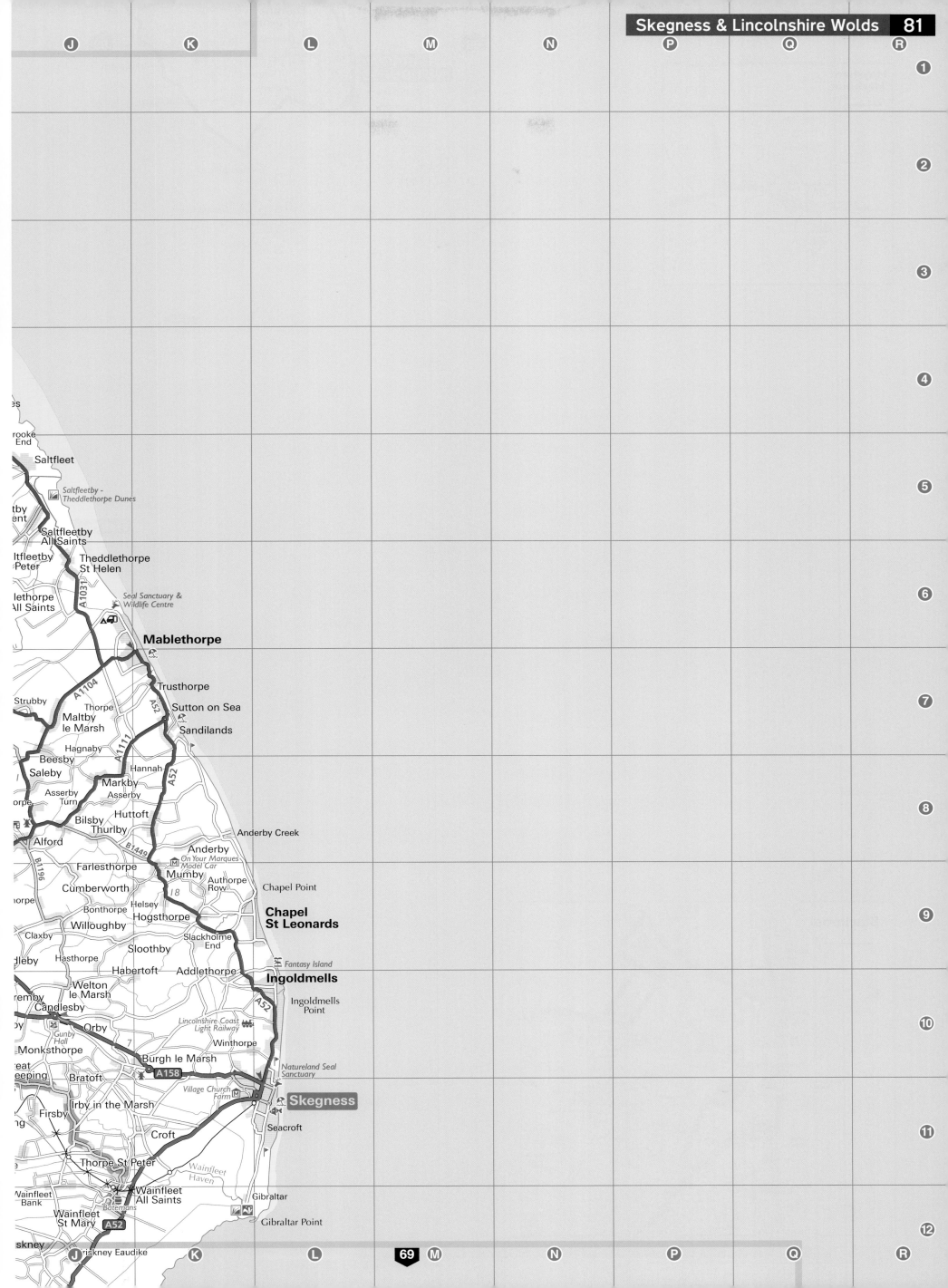

Saltfleet

Saltfleetby - Theddlethorpe Dunes

Saltfleetby All Saints

Theddlethorpe St Helen

Seal Sanctuary & Wildlife Centre

Mablethorpe

Trusthorpe

Strubby
Thorpe
Maltby le Marsh
Sutton on Sea
Sandilands

Hagnaby
Beesby
Saleby
Hannah
Markby
Asserby Turn
Asserby
Huttoft
Bilsby
Thurlby
Anderby Creek
Alford
Anderby
Farlesthorpe
On Your Marques Model Car
Cumberworth
Mumby
Authorpe Row
Chapel Point
Helsey
Hogsthorpe
Bonthorpe
Chapel St Leonards
Willoughby
Claxby
Sloothby
Slackholme End
Hasthorpe
Fantasy Island
Habertoft
Addlethorpe
Ingoldmells
Welton le Marsh
Ingoldmells Point
Candlesby
Orby
Lincolnshire Coast Light Railway
Winthorpe
Gunby Hall
Monksthorpe
Burgh le Marsh
Natureland Seal Sanctuary
Bratoft
Village Church Farm
Irby in the Marsh
Skegness
Firsby
Seacroft
Croft
Thorpe St Peter
Wainfleet Haven
Gibraltar
Wainfleet Bank
Wainfleet All Saints
Batemans
Wainfleet St Mary
Gibraltar Point
skney
riskney Eaudike

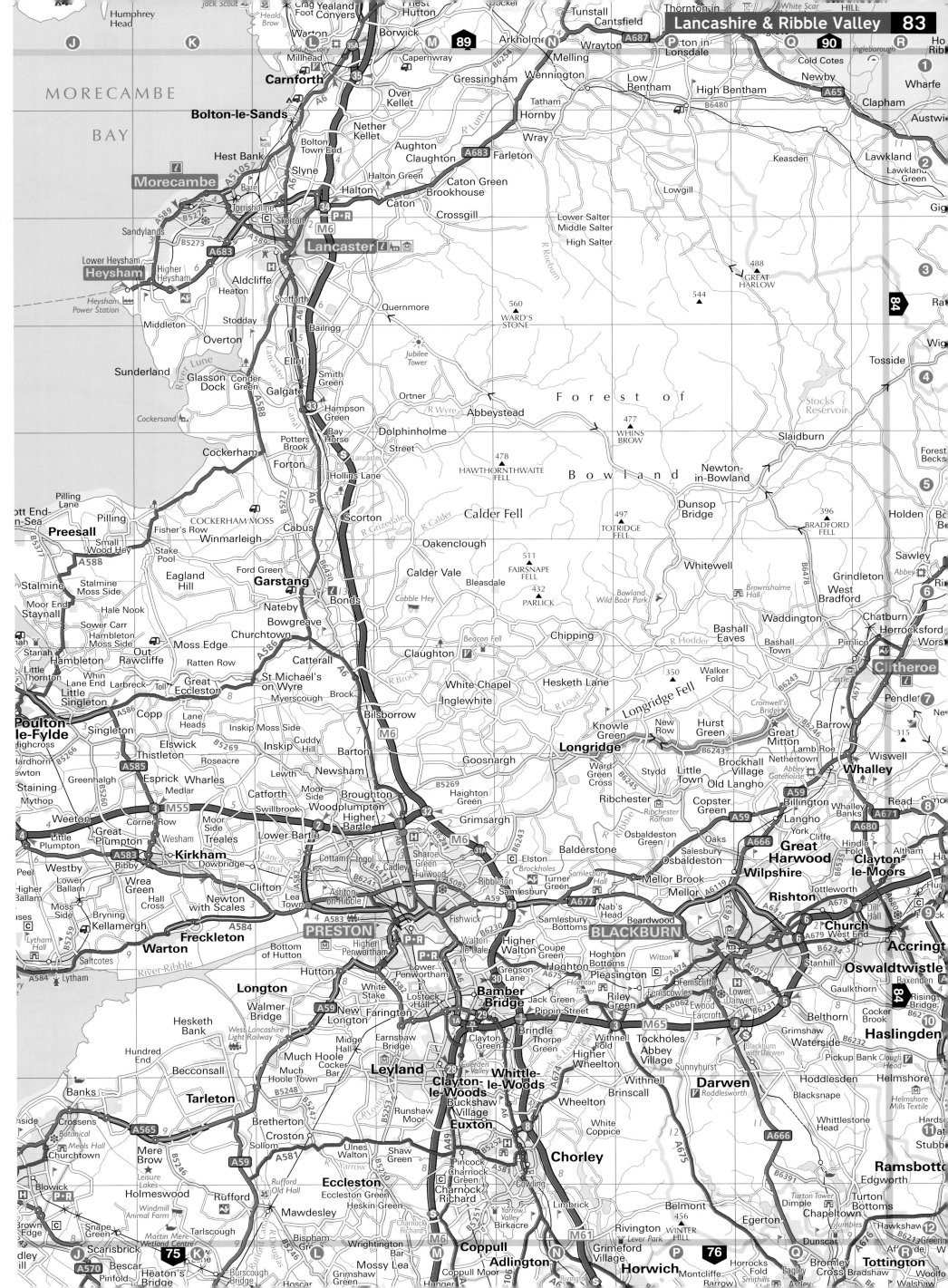

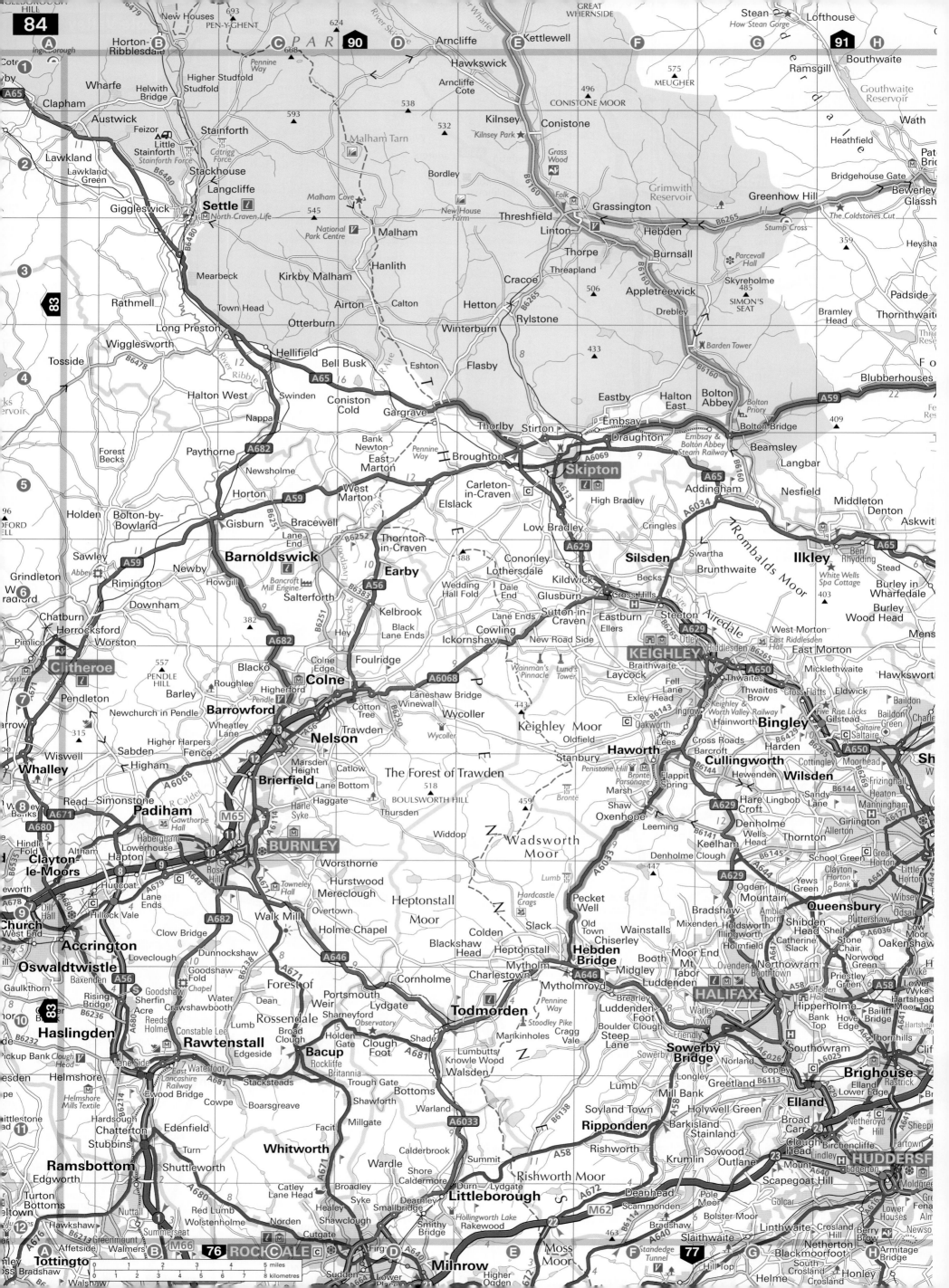

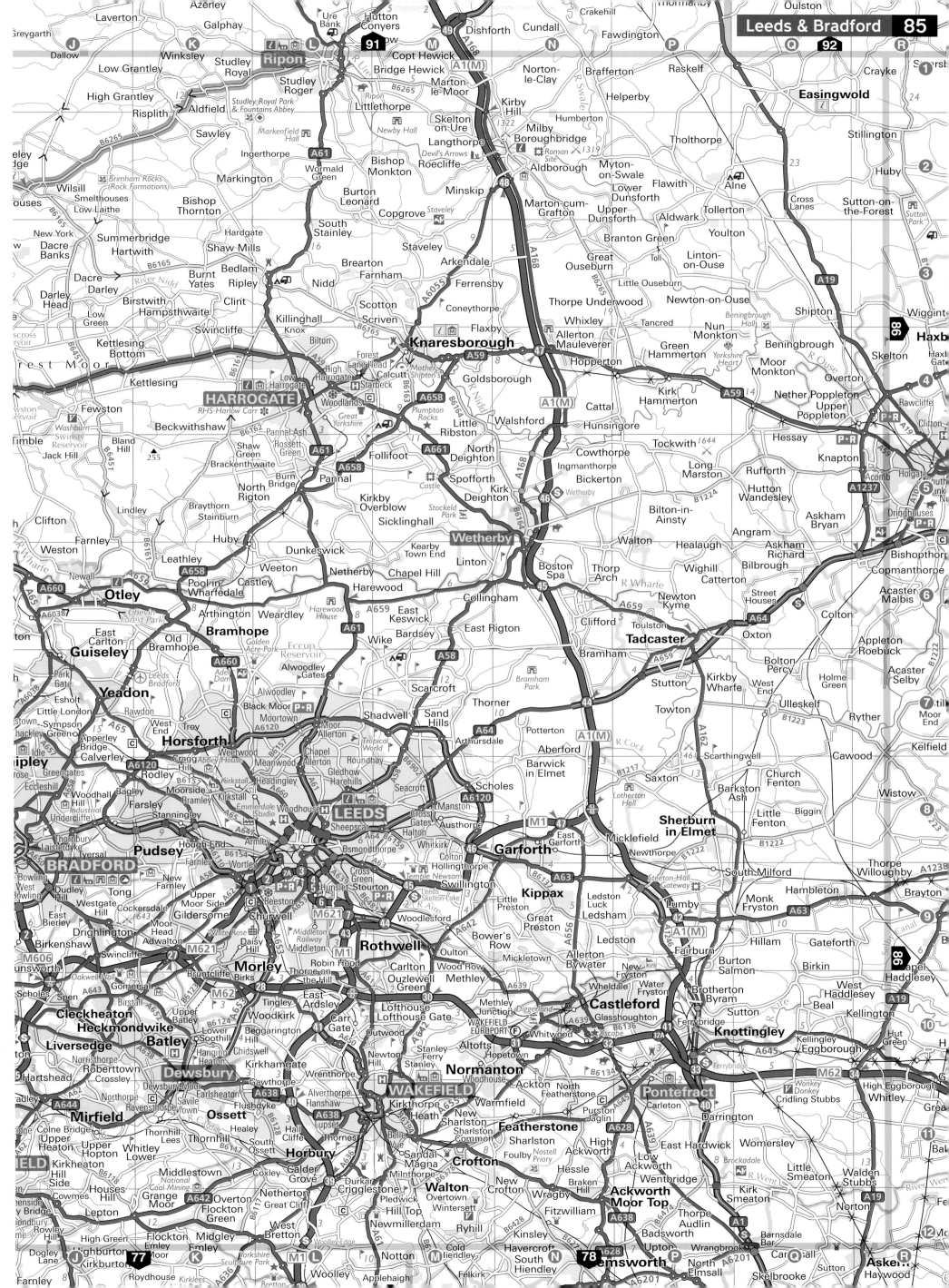

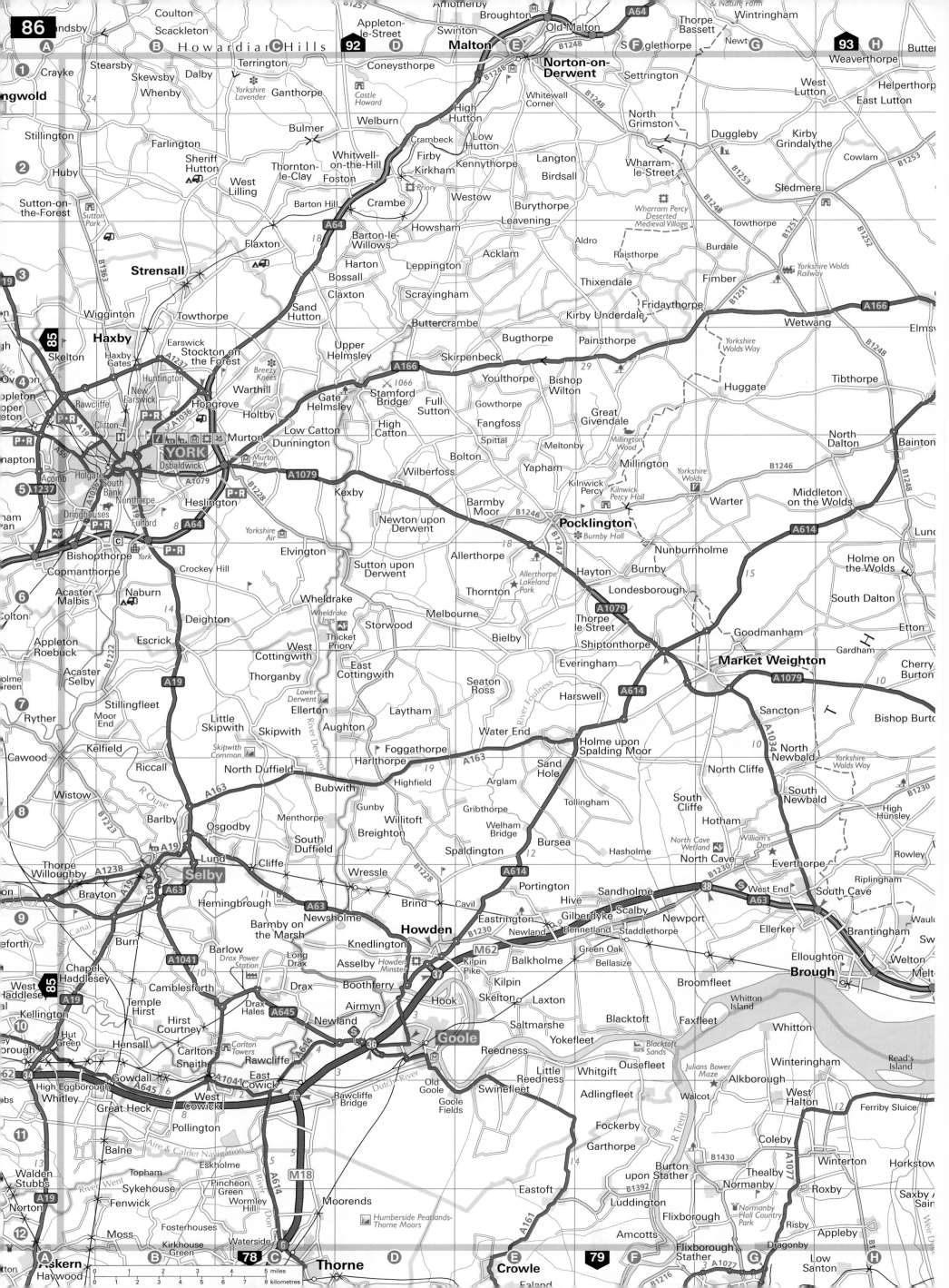

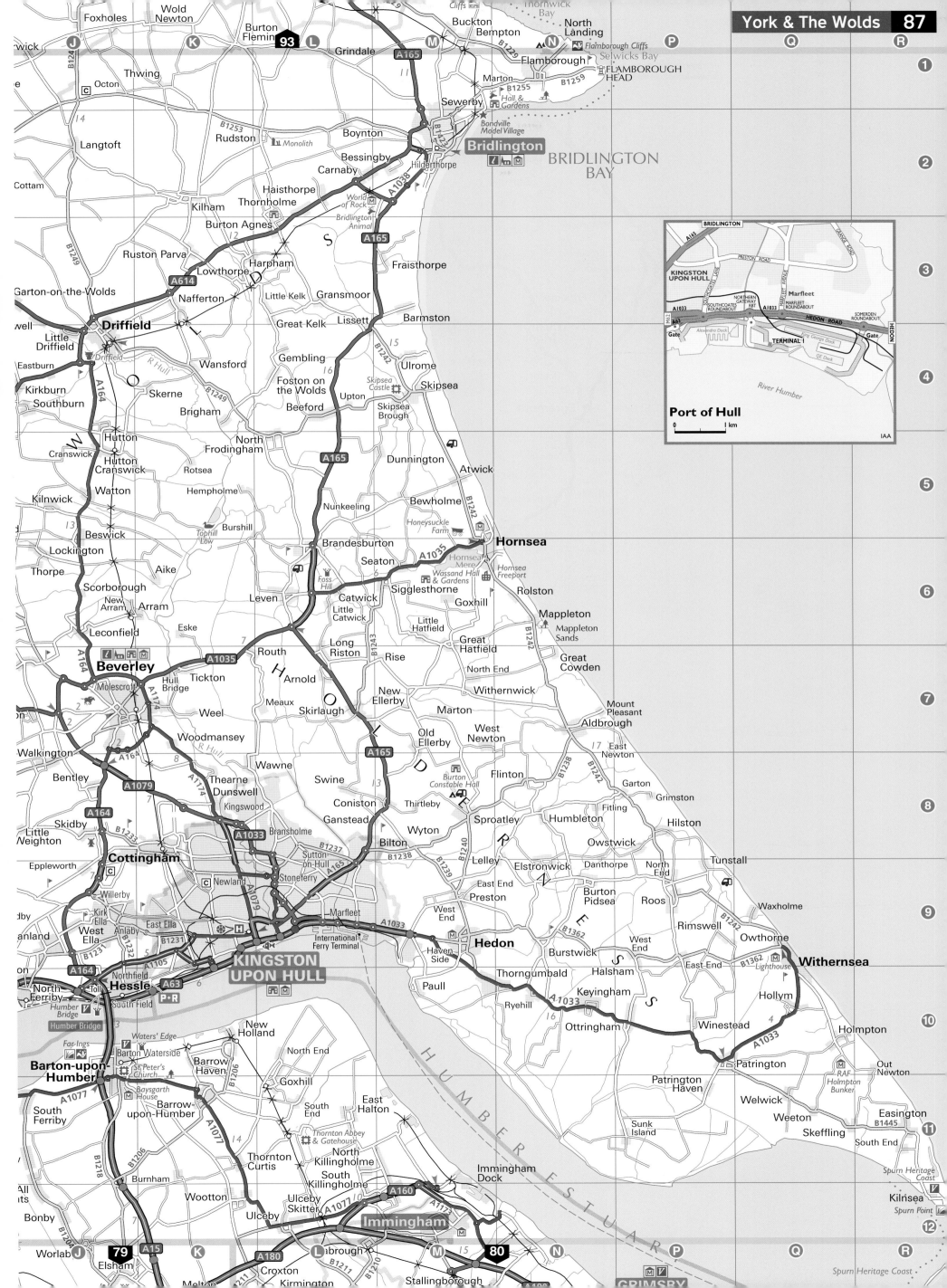

Port of Hull

0   1 km

IAA

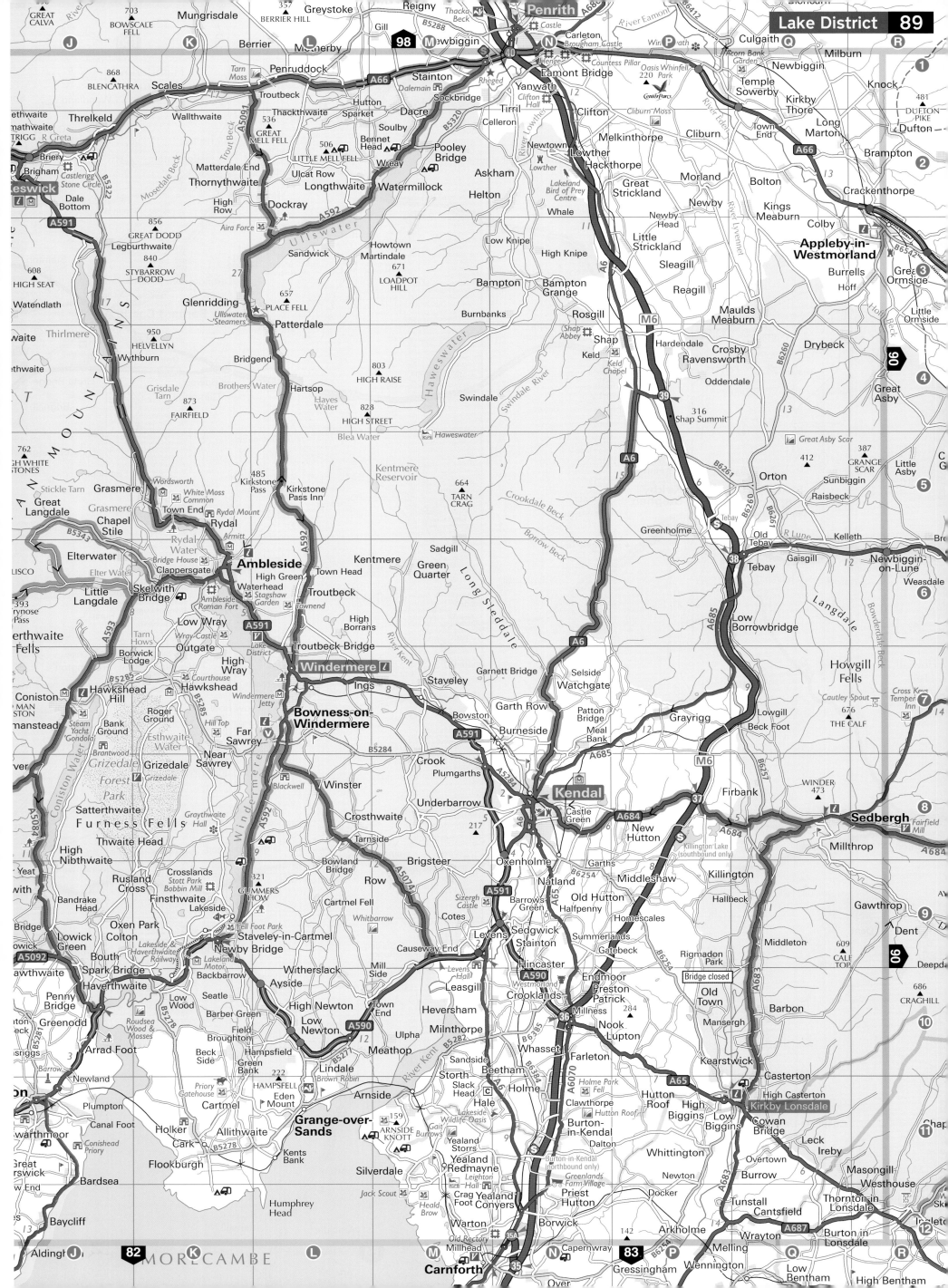

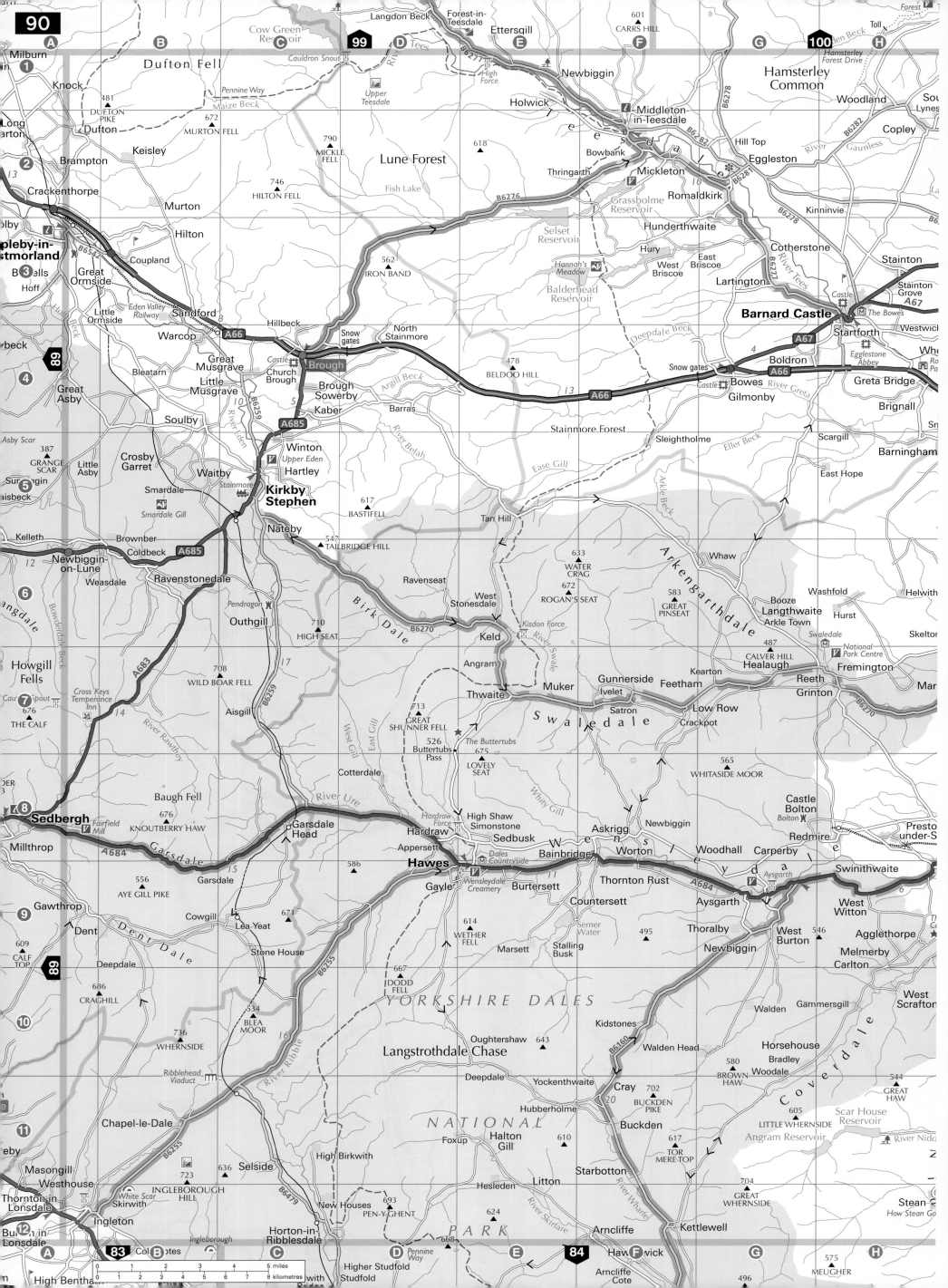

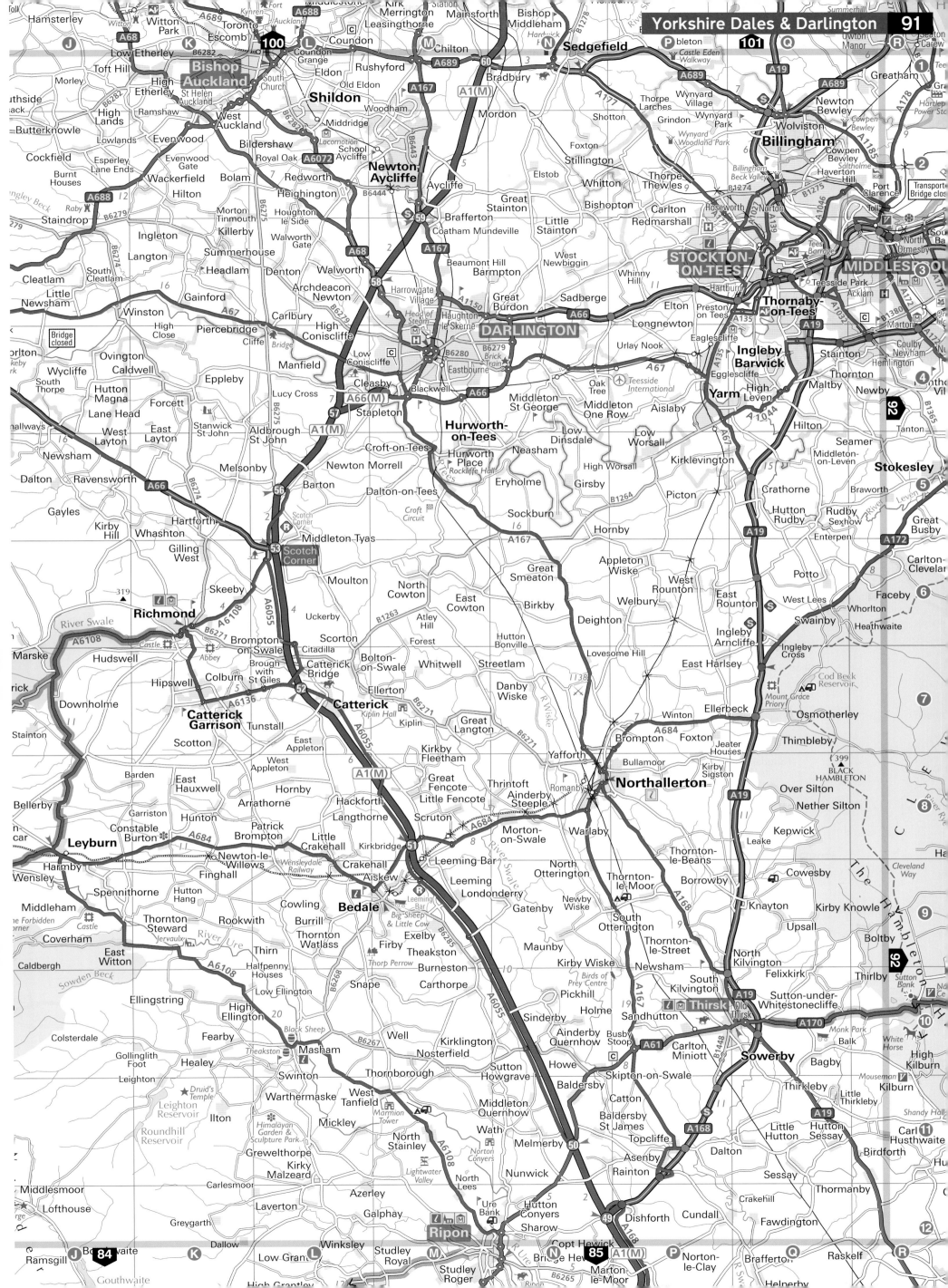

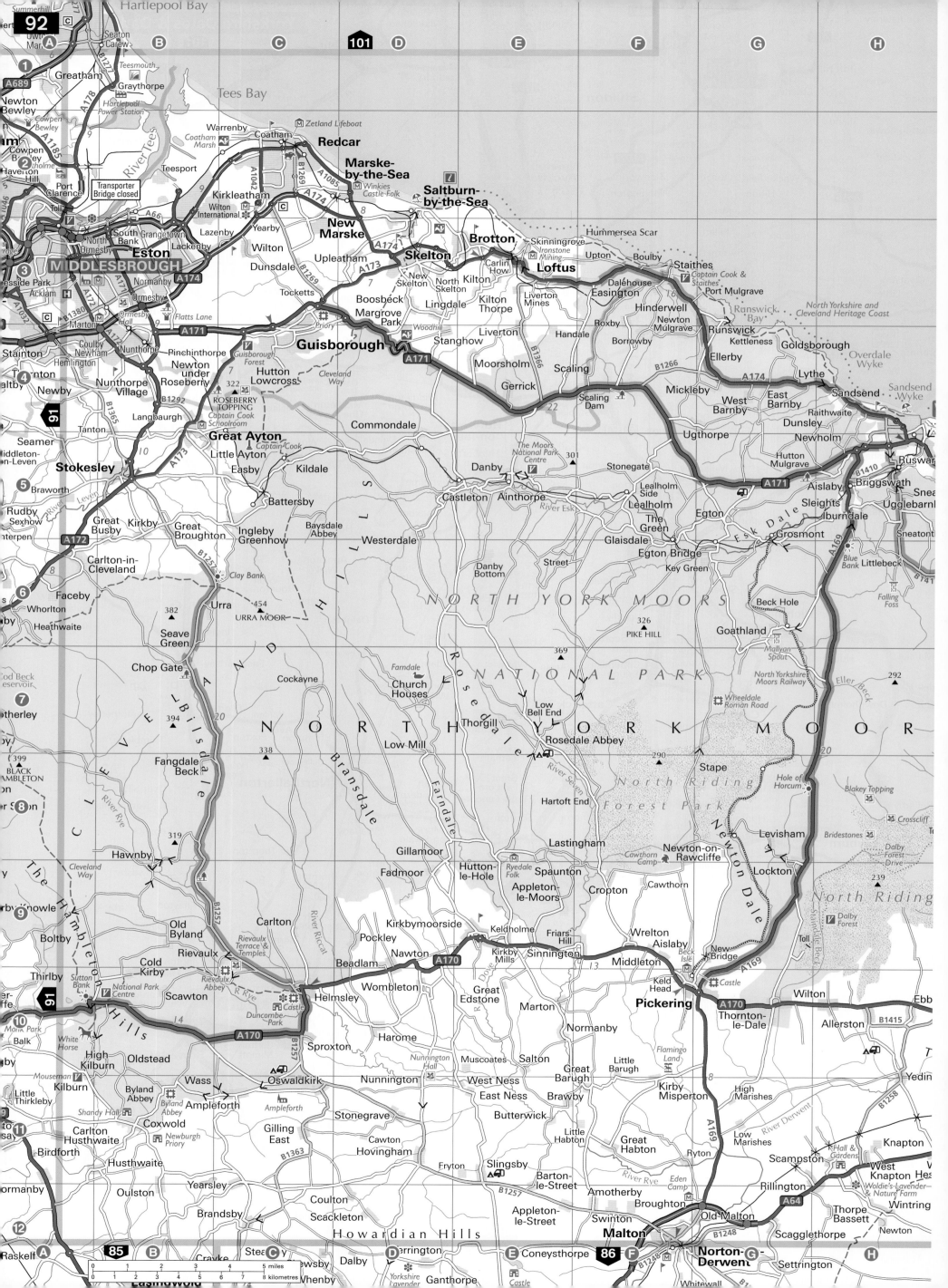

J   K   L   M   N   P   Q   R

Middlesbrough

TRANSPORTER BRIDGE

Scarborough

WHITBY

Whitby

Stainsacre
High Hawsker
Low Hawsker
Ness Point or North Cheek
Robin Hood's Bay
Old Coastguard
Fylingthorpe
Robin Hood's Bay
Old Peak or South Cheek
Ravenscar
A171
20
Staintondale
Hayburn Wyke
Harwood Dale
Cloughton Newlands
Cloughton Wyke
Cloughton
Cromer Point
Burniston
A165
Cleveland Way
Bickley
Broxa
Silpho
Suffield
Scalby
Langdale End
Hackness
Newby
North Bay Railway
Wrench Green
Everley
Forest Park
River Derwent
Sea Cut
Castle
Falsgrave
Scarborough
Bee Dale
A170
Oliver's Mount
Forge Valley Wood
East Ayton
West Ayton
Betton
P+R
A165
P+R
Osgodby
Cayton Bay
Sawdon
Hutton Buscel
Irton
Eastfield
The Wyke
Ruston
Wykeham
Seamer
Crossgates
High Killerby
Snainton
Cayton
Fair Collection
Brompton-by-Sawdon
B1261
Lebberston
A1039
Filey Brigg
A64
R Hertford
Gristhorpe
Bird Garden & Animal Park
Filey
Willerby
Folkton
Muston
Filey Bay
Flixton
West Flotmanby
Staxton
Sherburn
Ganton
Yorkshire Wolds Way
Hunmanby
East Heslerton
West Heslerton
Potter Brompton
Fordon
Reighton
Flamborough Head Heritage Coast
Jackson's Wold
Speeton
B1229
Bempton Cliffs
Thornwick Bay
Foxholes
Wold Newton
Butterwick
Burton Fleming
Buckton
Bempton
North Landing
Waxenthorpe
Grindale
A165
Flamborough
Flamborough Cliffs
Selwick Bay
West Lutton
Helperthorpe
Thwing
Octon
Marton
FLAMBOROUGH HEAD
B1255
B1259

86   87

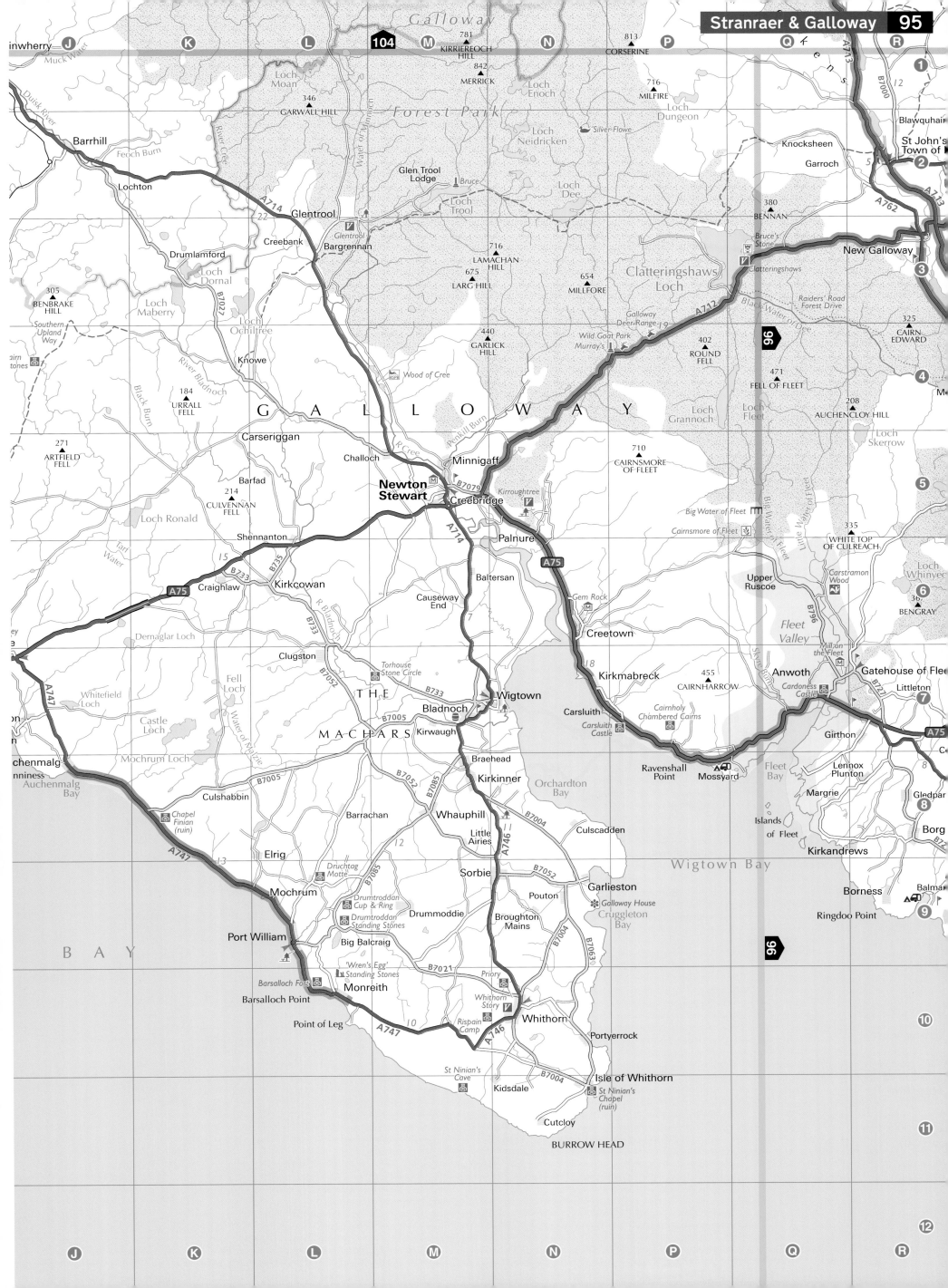

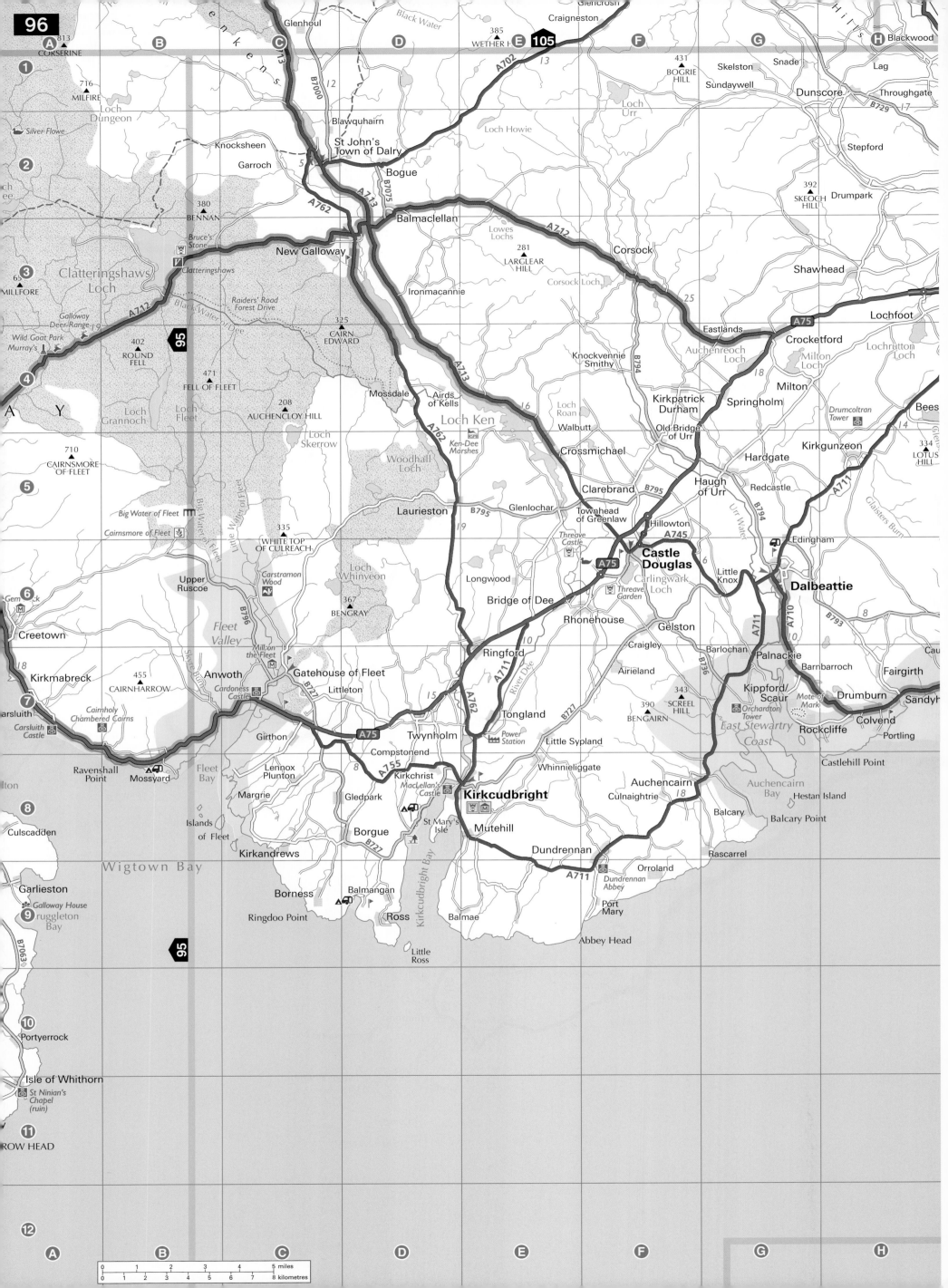

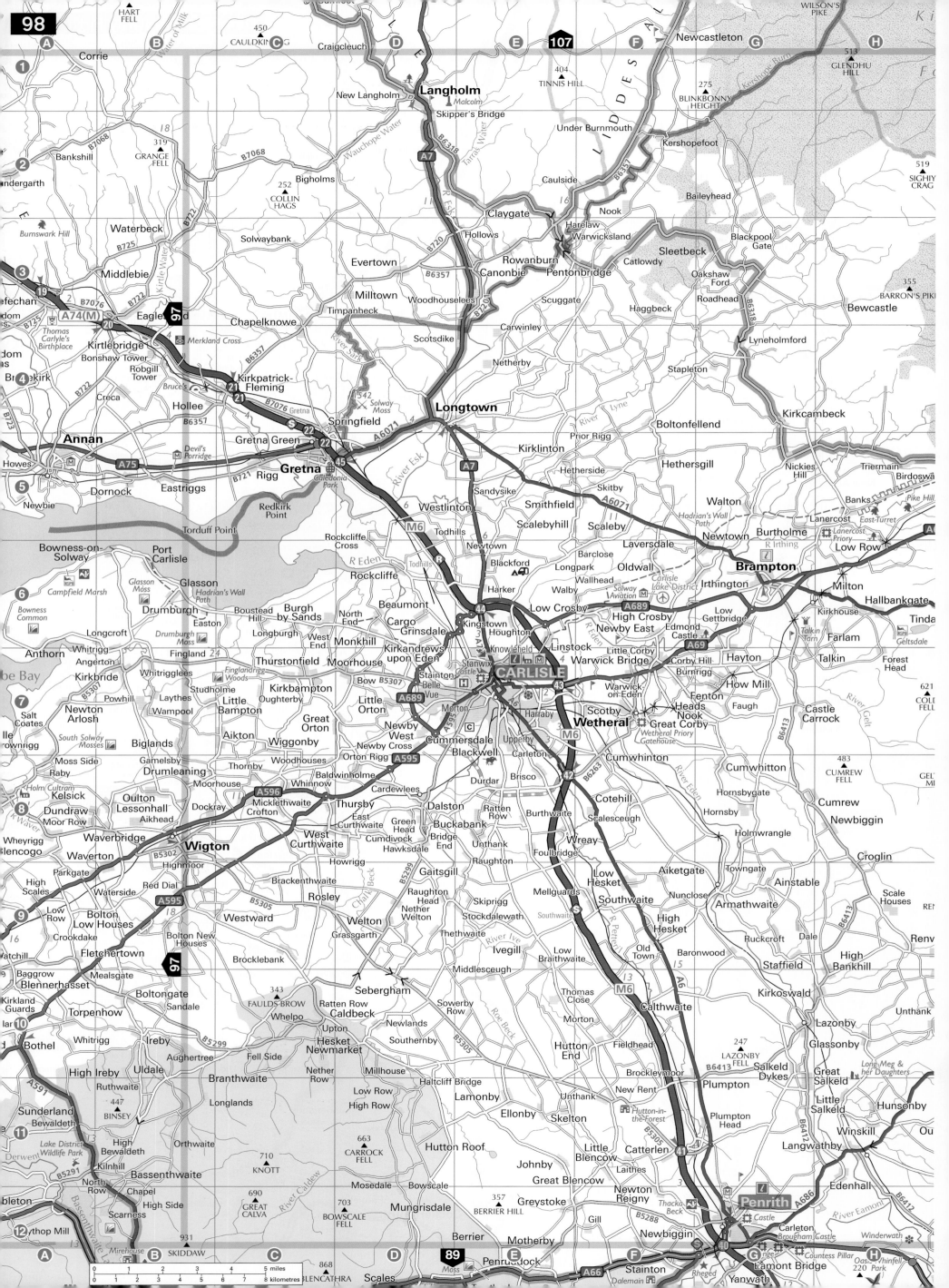

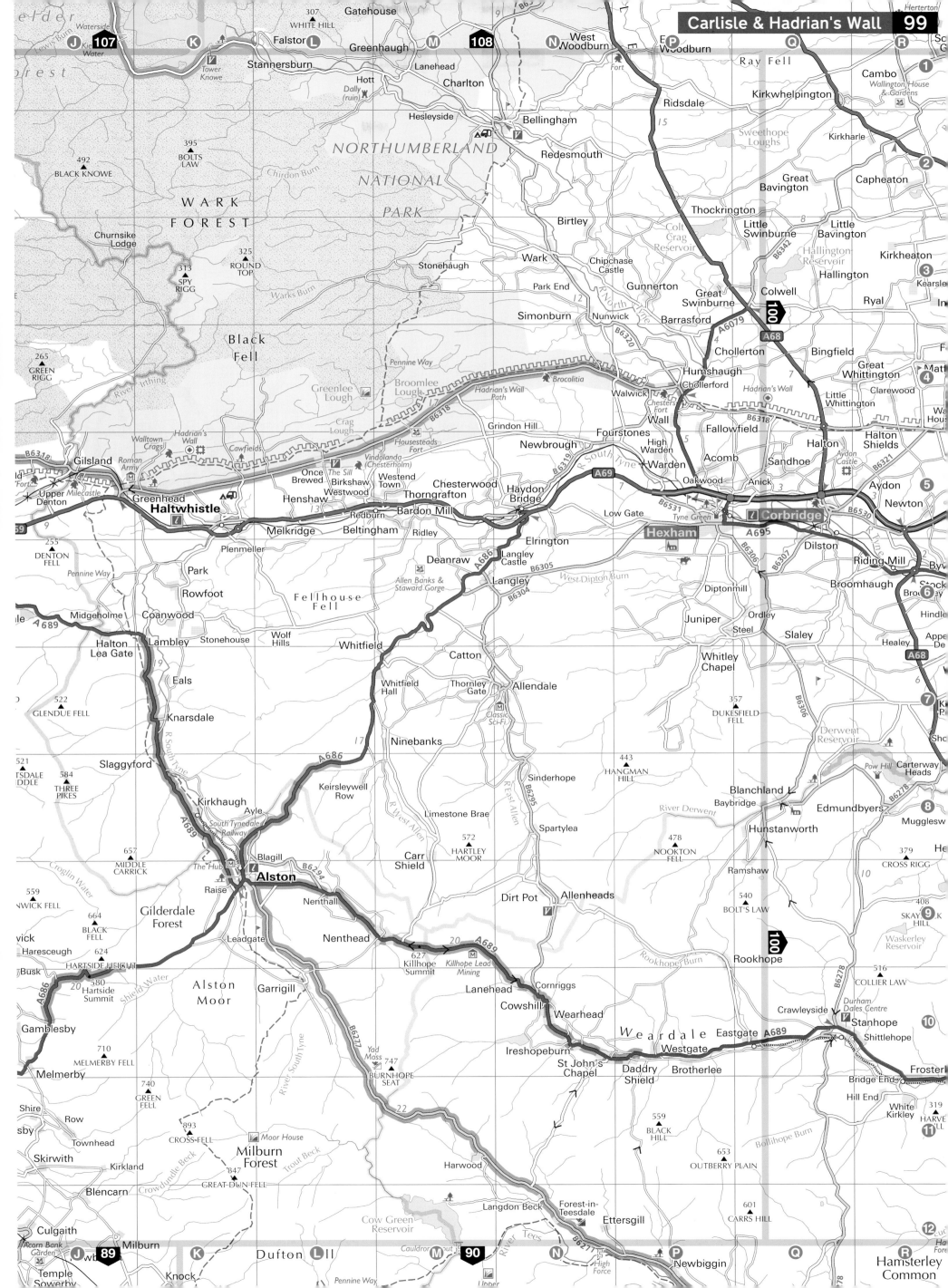

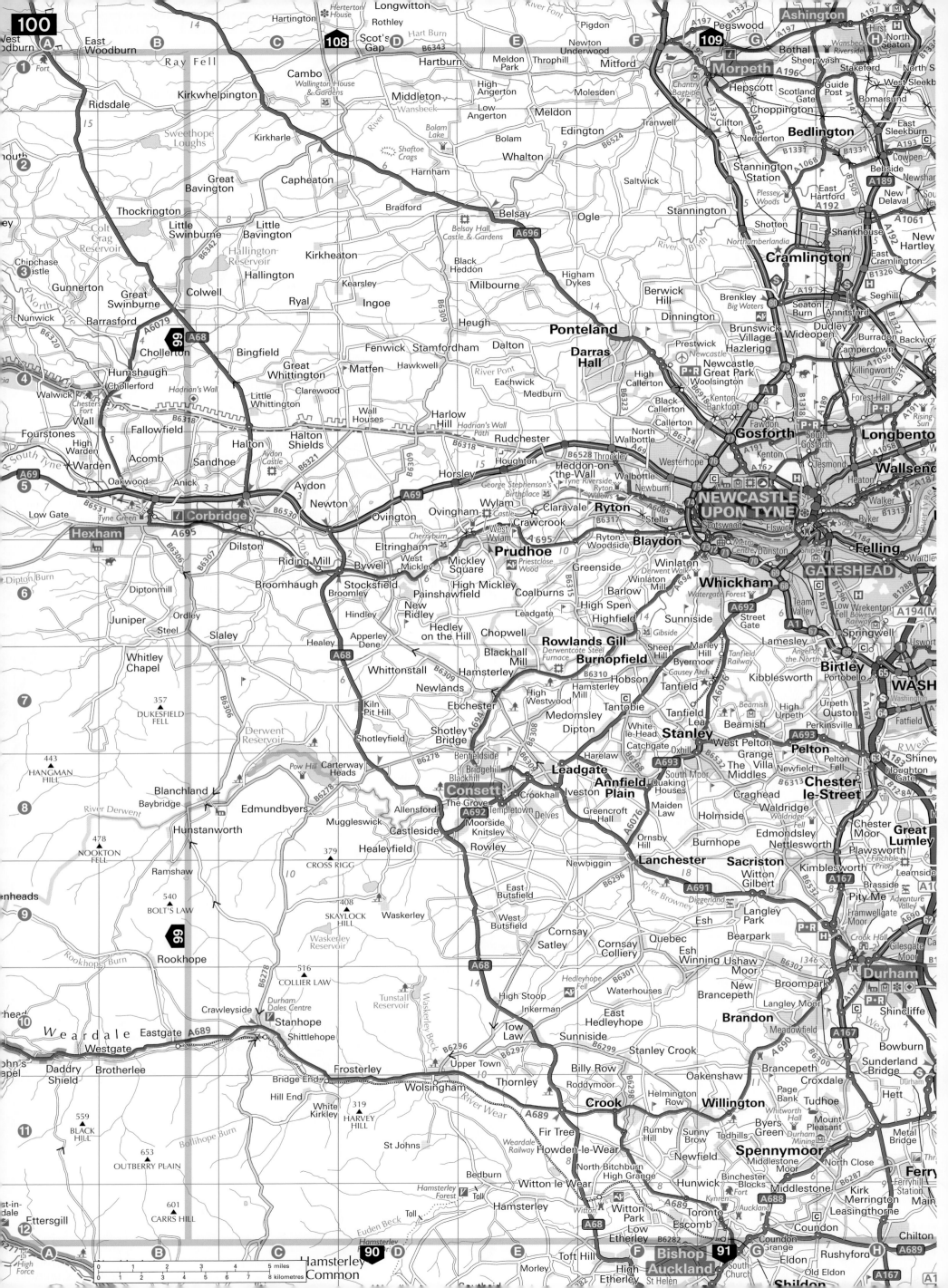

Port of Tyne

Newcastle upon Tyne

Sunderland

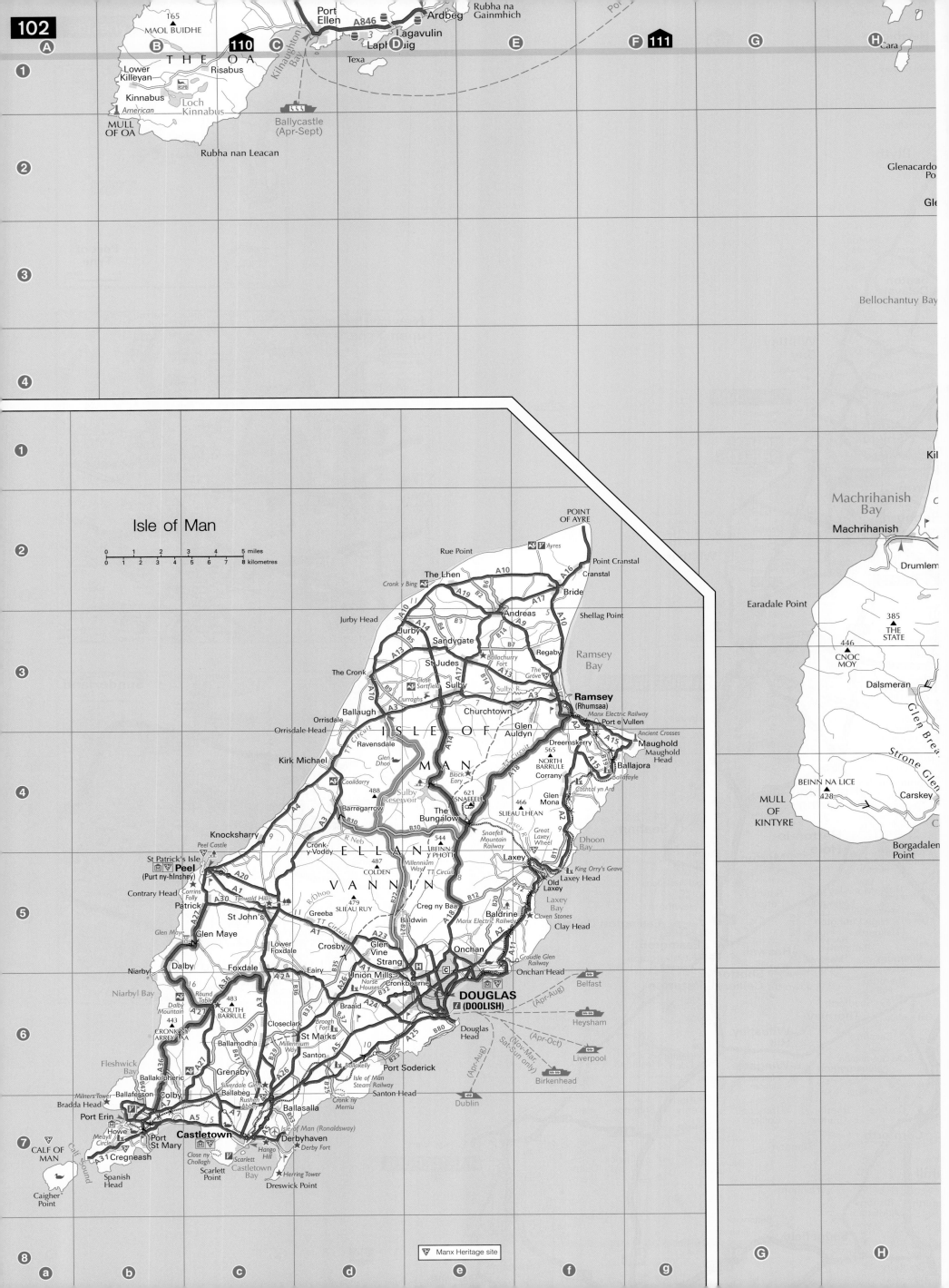

Isle of Man

0 1 2 3 4 5 miles
0 1 2 3 4 5 6 7 8 kilometres

Manx Heritage site

Tayinloan

J **111** **K** **L** Grogport **M** Pirnmill Penrioch **N** **112** th Arran **P** 34 **Q** **R**

1

CASTEAL ABHAIL Corrie

Barmollack Loch
Tanna

354 Whitefarland 715 874
CRUACH BEINN GOATFELL
NAN GABHAR BHARRAIN Glen Iorsa 6 Merkland Point
A83 Imachar 792 Glen Rosa Brodick Castle, Garden 2
Muasdale Balliekine BEINN & Country Park
842 NUIS Brodick Bay
Belloch Iorsa Water A R R A N M Strathwhillan
enbarr Carradale Brodick Corriegills
Carradale Village Auchagallon 512
Bridgend Port Righ Machrie Stone Circle A'CHRUACH 4 104 3
454 Dippen Machrie Machrie Moor H Clauchlands
BEINN AN TUIRC Waterfoot Bay Stone Circles Lamlash Point
319 Torrisdale Carradale Tormore 503 Margnaheglish
Point Moss Farm Road BEINN BHREAC Lamlash
408 Stone Circle Balmichael Lamlash Holy Island
BORD Saddell Water Torbeg Bay
MOR Saddell Shiskine Cordon
Bellochantuy Carradale Drumadoon Blackwaterfoot 4 104
Saddell Bay Point Kilpatrick Auchencairn
Lussa 396 Saddell Bay Drumadoon Kilpatrick Dun Glen Scorrodale Kingscross
Loch SGREADAN Bay Carn Ban Knockenkelly
Tangy Loch HILL Ugadale Brown Head Whiting Bay
Whiting
Glen Lussa Bay
Peninver Corriecravie Glenashdale
kenzie Ardnacross Torr a' Chaisteal Fort Sliddery Kilmory Water Largymore 5
A83 Kilmichael Bay Dippin Largybeg
Dippin Head
Lagg Torrylin Kilmory
Campbeltown Cairn Bennan
Campbeltown B842 Bennan Head Kildonan 6
B843 Loch Island Davaar Pladda
ble Stewarton (May-Sept, Sat only)
Kilkerran Campbeltown-Ardrossan (May-Sept)
352 Kildalloig V
BEINN GHUILEAN Achinhoan
6
Conie Glen Ballycastle
10 (Apr-Sept) 7
Ru Stafnish
Cattadale Glen Kerran
B842 Polliwilline Bay 8
Southend Macharioch
Dunaverty
arskey Bay Sound of Sanda Sheep Island
more Sanda Island 9
Ailsa
Craig
340 104
10

11

12

J **K** **L** **M** **N** **P** **Q** **R**

0 1 2 3 4 5 miles
0 1 2 3 4 5 6 7 8 kilometres

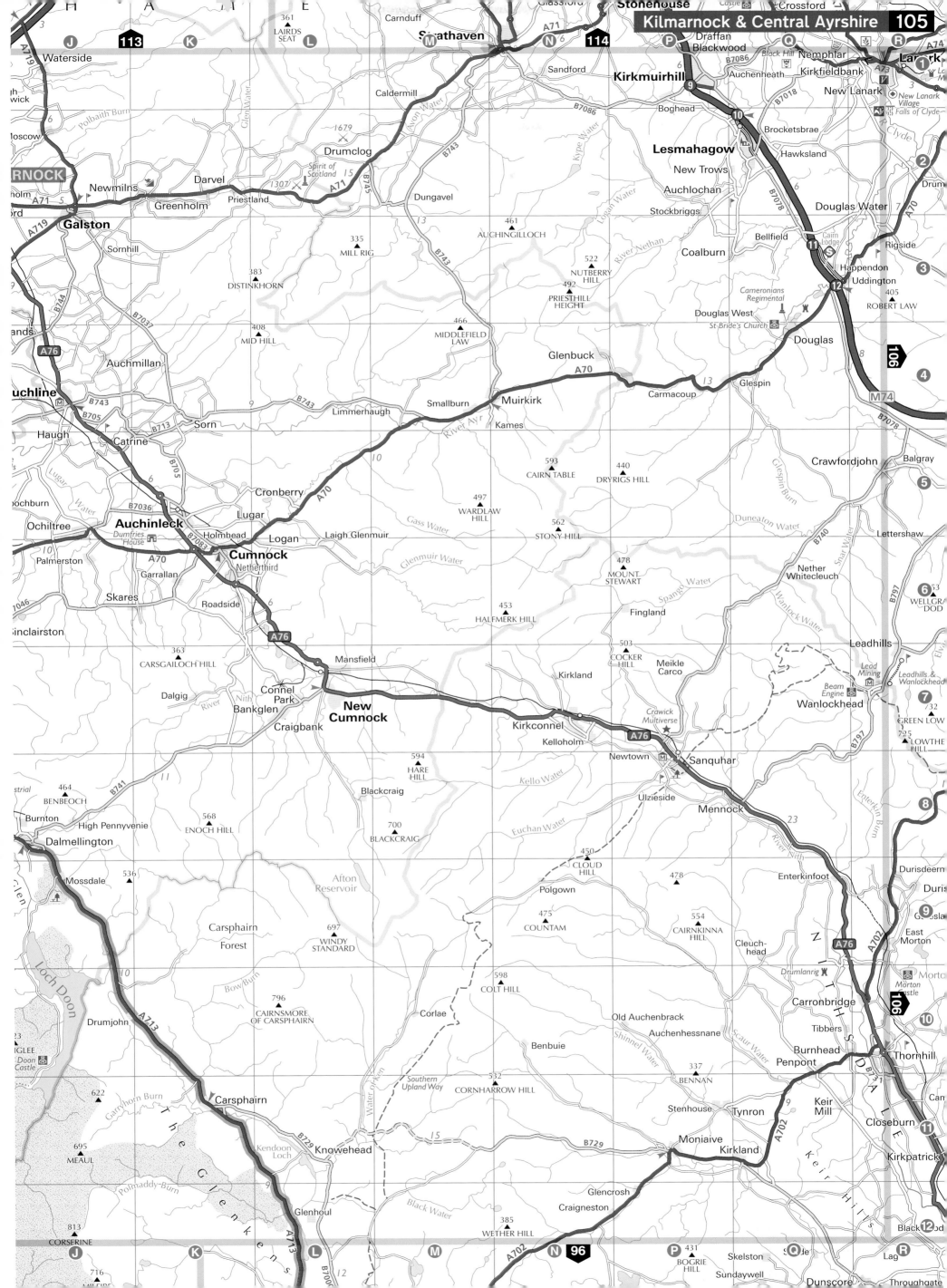

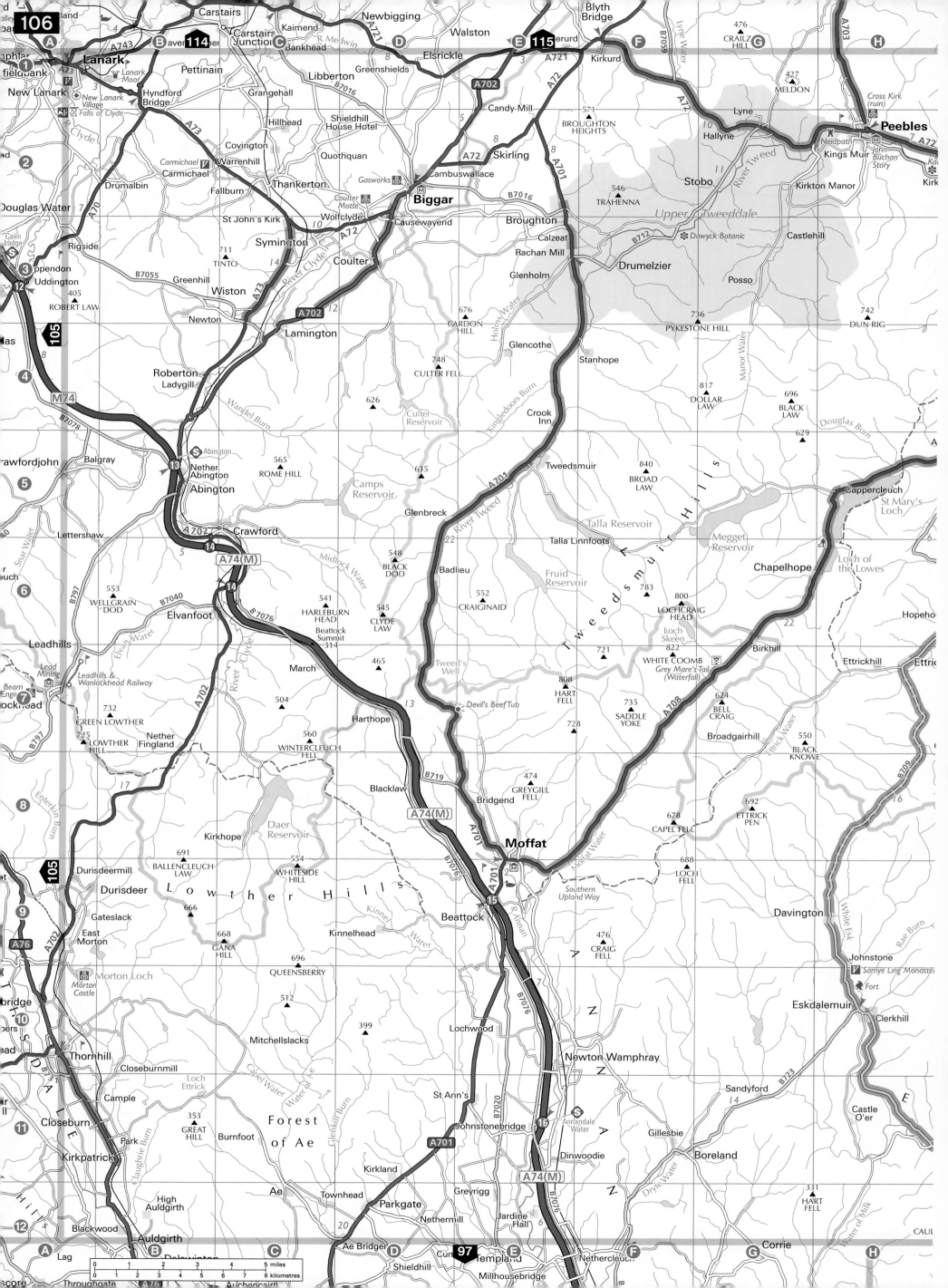

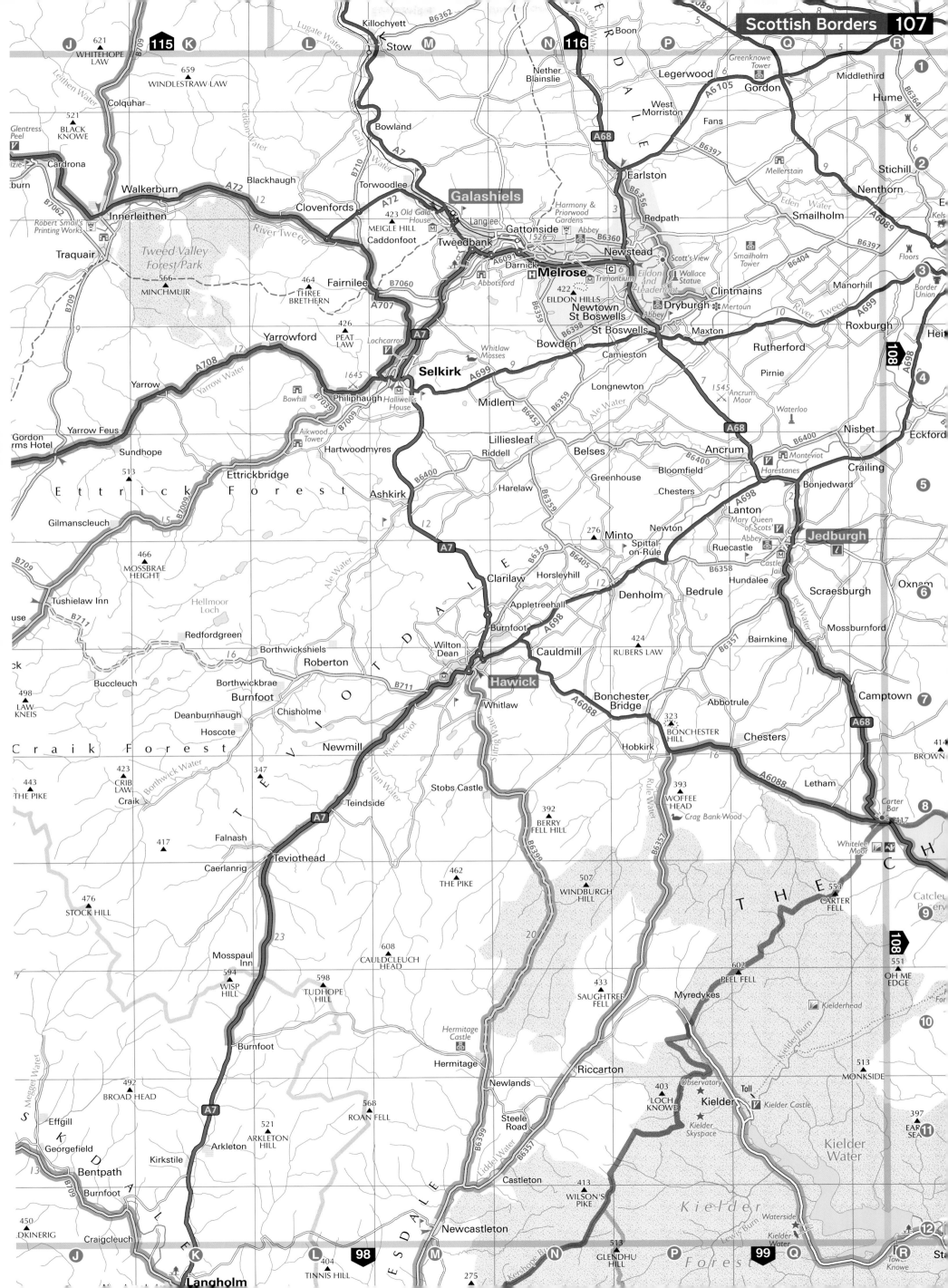

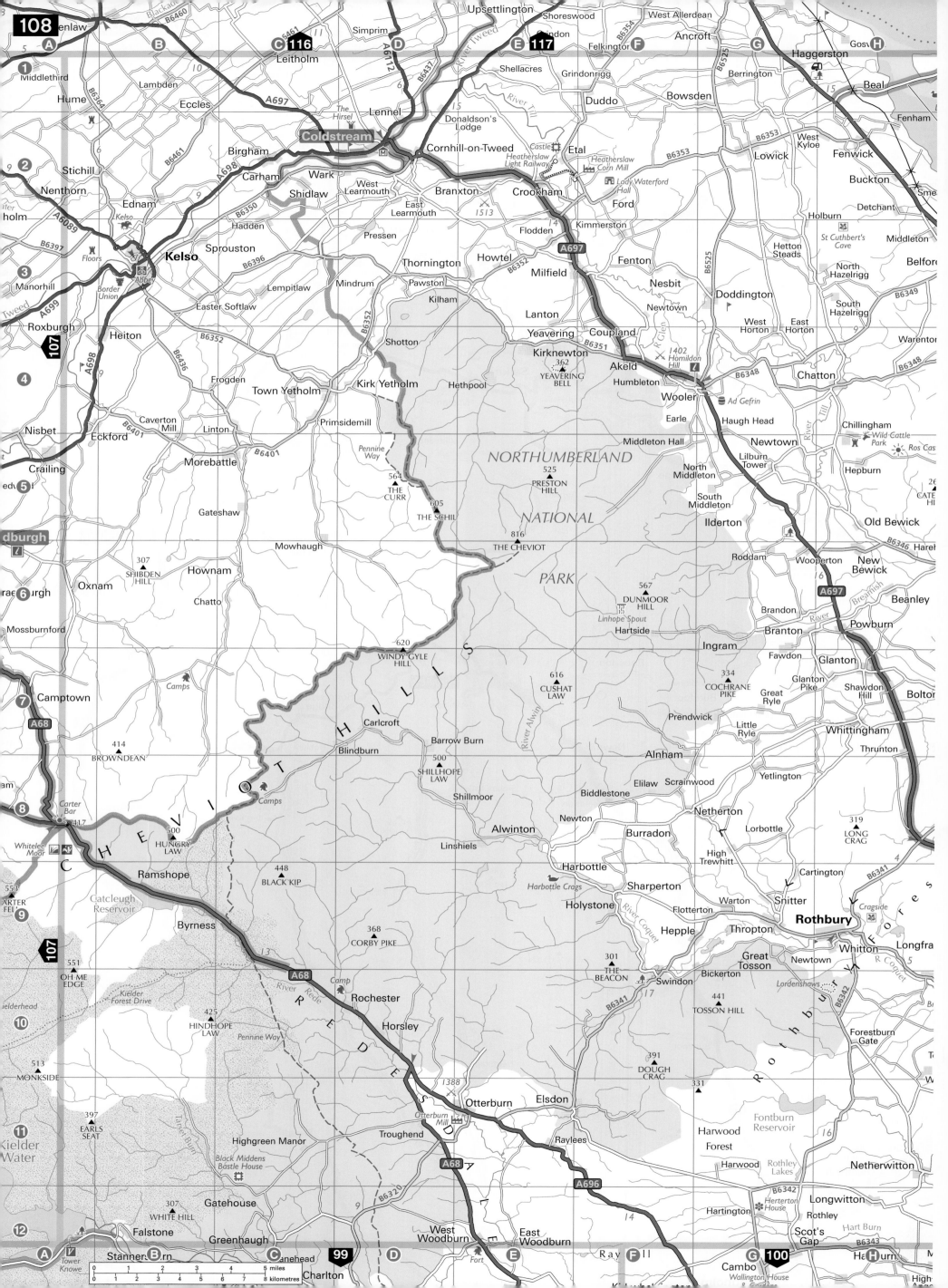

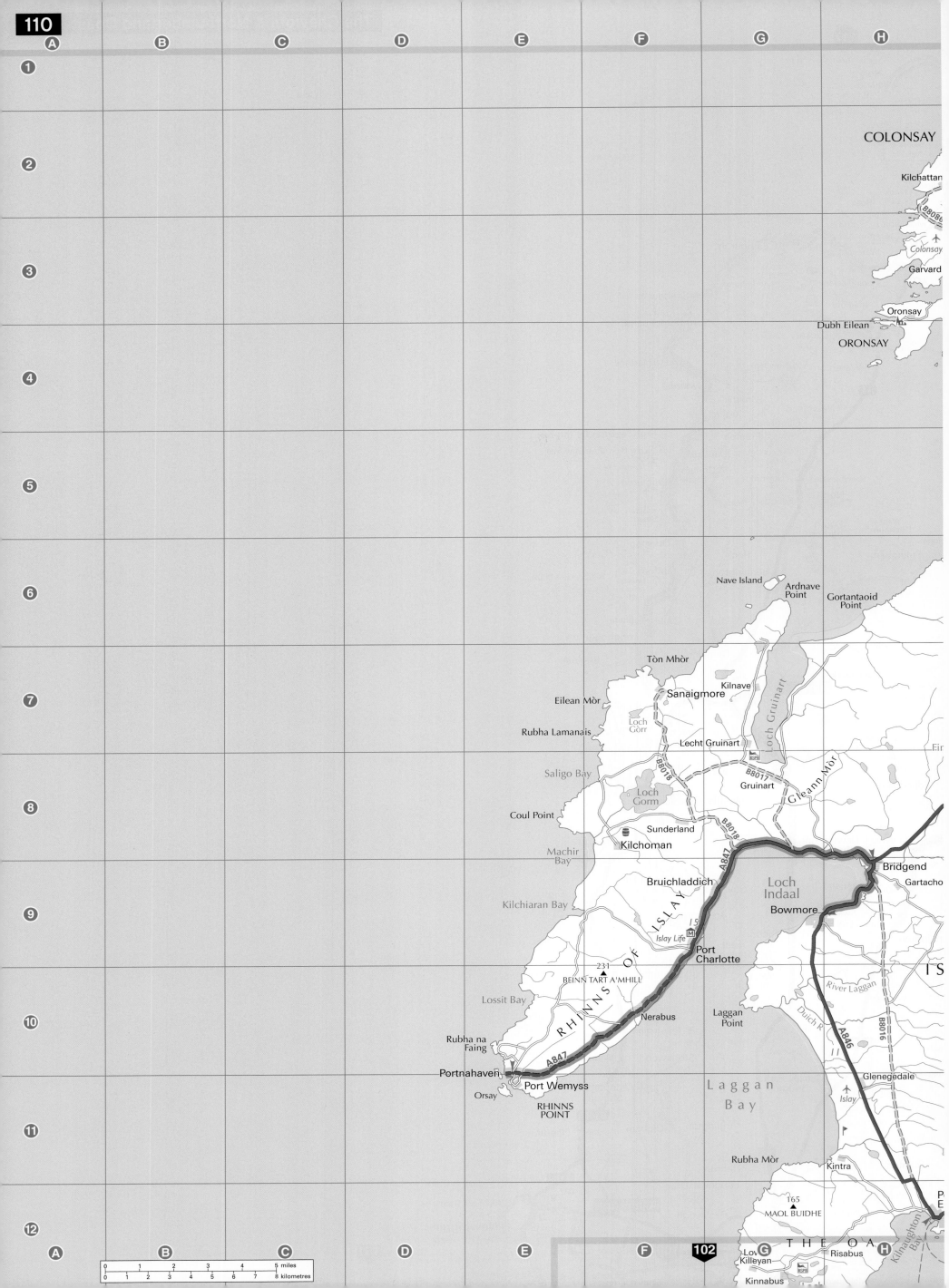

COLONSAY

Kilchattan

B8086

Colonsay

Garvard

Oronsay

Dubh Eilean

ORONSAY

Nave Island

Ardnave
Point

Gortantaoid
Point

Tòn Mhòr

Kilnave

Sanaigmore

Eilean Mòr

Loch
Gòrr

Loch Gruinart

Rubha Lamanais

Lecht Gruinart

Saligo Bay

B8018

B8017

Gruinart

Gleann Mòr

Eir

Loch
Gorm

B8018

Coul Point

Sunderland

A847

Kilchoman

Bridgend

Machir
Bay

Gartacho

Bruichladdich

Loch
Indaal

Kilchiaran Bay

Bowmore

3

Islay Life

R H I N N S   O F   I S L A Y

I S

Port
Charlotte

231
▲
BEINN TART A'MHILL

River Laggan

Lossit Bay

Dutch R

B8016

A846

Nerabus

Laggan
Point

Rubha na
Faing

A847

Glenegedale

Portnahaven

Islay

Port Wemyss

Orsay

Laggan
Bay

RHINNS
POINT

Rubha Mòr

Kintra

165
▲
MAOL BUIDHE

P
E

Kilnaughton
Bay

T H E   O A

Lov
Killeyan

Risabus

Kinnabus

0 1 2 3 4 5 miles
0 1 2 3 4 5 6 7 8 kilometres

J K 119 L M N 120 P Q R

CRUACH SCARBA
Ardfern

Gulf of Corryvreckan

1 Aird

Eilean
Dubh

Kiloran Bay
143
CARNAN
EOIN
Kiloran

Rubh' a' Geodha

Oban

Glengarrisdale
Bay

295
CRUACH NA
SEILCHEIG

Craignish Point

Island
Macaskin
Temple Wo
Stone Circl

2
Ri C
Po

Scalasaig

Glendebadel Bay

Loch Crinan

Crinan

Kilmahumaig

Bellanoch

Machrins

Corpach Bay

364
BEN
GARRISDALE

3
Argyll
Beaver

Rubha
Bàn

J U R A

466
BEINN
BHREAC

Glen Grundale

Knapdale

112

Eilean
Ghaoideamal

Shian
Bay

453
RAINBERG MÒR

Ardlussa

Carsaig Bay

Tayvallich

Achnamara

Lussa Point
Lussagiven

Loch Sween

Kilmicha f of Inv

4

Rubh' an t-Sàilein

A846

Taynish

466
CRUACH
LUSACH

Rubha a' Mhàil

Loch
Right Mòr

Loch Tarbert

Keills Chapel

Loch na Cille

5

Rubha
Bholsa

363
SGARBH
BREAC

506
SCRINADLE

398
BEINN
TARSUINN

Danna
Island

Kilbride
Castle
Sween

Lochead

Achahois

Jura Forest

784
BEINN
AN OIR

St Cormac's
Chapel

Kilmory Knap
Chapel

Kilmory

Ellary

6

Bunnahabhain

316
GUIR-
BHEINN

Loch a'
Chnuic Bhric

734

Paps of Jura

Jura

Knockrome
Ardfernal

24

Kilmory Bay

Point of Knap

Ormsary

Druimdrishaig

48 7
DUBH
CHREAG

Finlaggan

Port
Askaig

Keills

Feolin Ferry

560
GLAS BHEINN

529
DUBH
BHEINN Craighouse

Keils

Small
Isles

Loch-nan
Torran

Ballygrant
8
A846

Loch
Ballygrant

Loch/
Lossit

342
BRAT
BHEINN

Rubha na
Caillich

Cretshengan

Coulaghailtro

8

266
BEINNE
DUBH

Cabrach

Kilberry
Sculptured
Stones

Kilberry

Torinturk

Am Fraoch
Eilean

Brosdale
Island

Rubha na Tràille

Kilberry Head

Keppoch Point

Tiretigan

213
CRUACH AIRDE

ssan

429
SGÒRR NAM
FAOILEANN

McArthur's
Head

Loch Stornoway

Kilchan

Kilennan Burn

471

Ardpatrick

9

112

L A Y

490
BEINN BHEIGEIR

Port Askaig - Kennacraig

Portachoillan

Clachan

Ronachan Point

454
BEINN URARAIDH
Loch Uraraidh

Rubha Liath

Ardtalla

Claggain
Bay

Ronachan

10

Loch
Ciàran

Loch
Garasdale

Kintour

Ardmore
Point

Kinerarach

247
CRUACH MHIC
GOUGAIN

346
BEINN SHOLUM

Kildalton
Cross

Tarbert

GIGHA

Rhunahaorine
Point

11
CNOC AN T-
SAMHLAIDE

ort
llen
A846

Ardbeg

Rubha na
Gainmhich

Eilean
a' Chùirn

Port Ellen - Kennacraig

Ardminish

Achamore

Rhunahaorine

38

Lagavulin
Laphroaig

Texa

Cara

Tayinloan

12

J K 102 L M N P 103 Q R

354

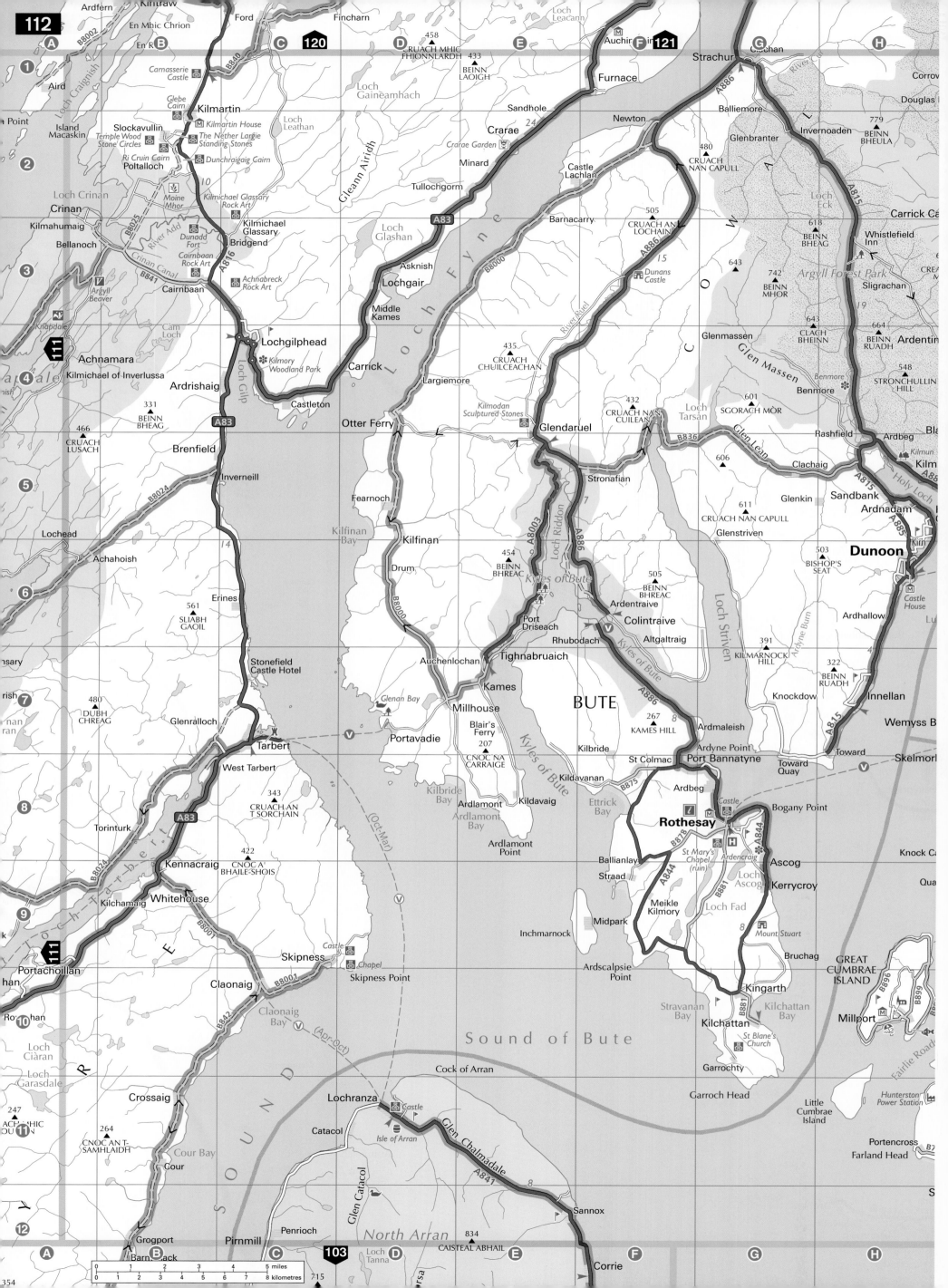

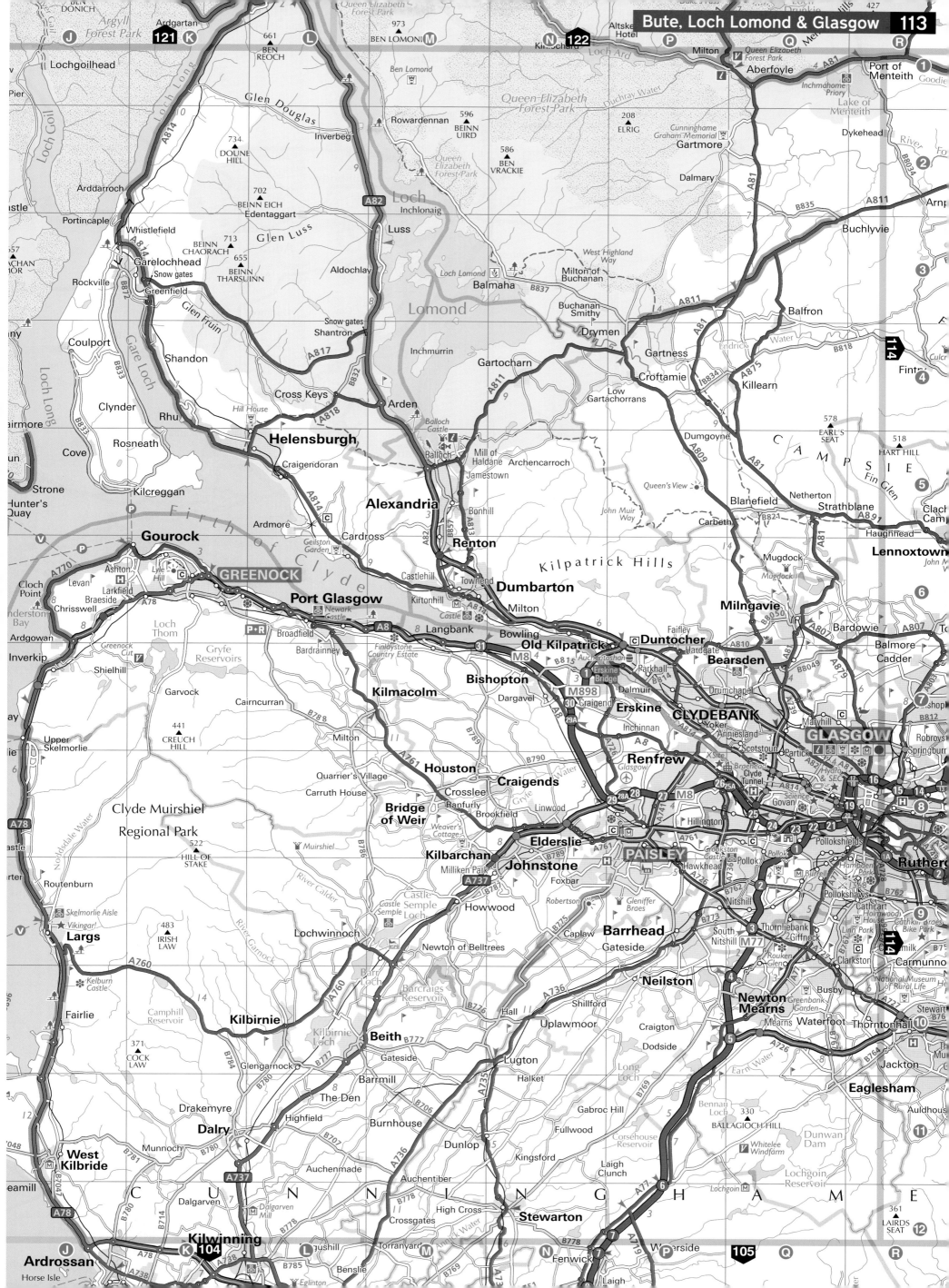

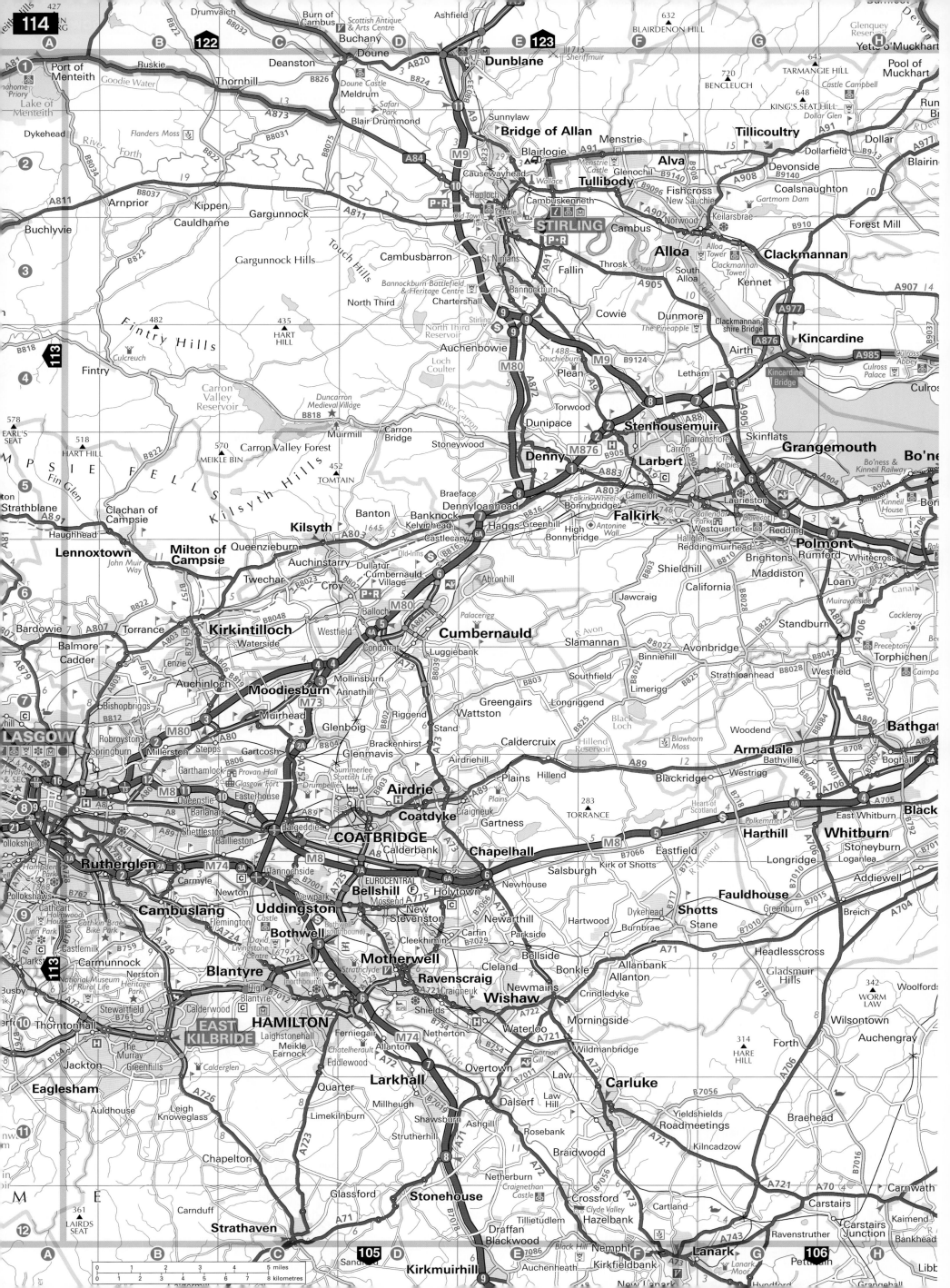

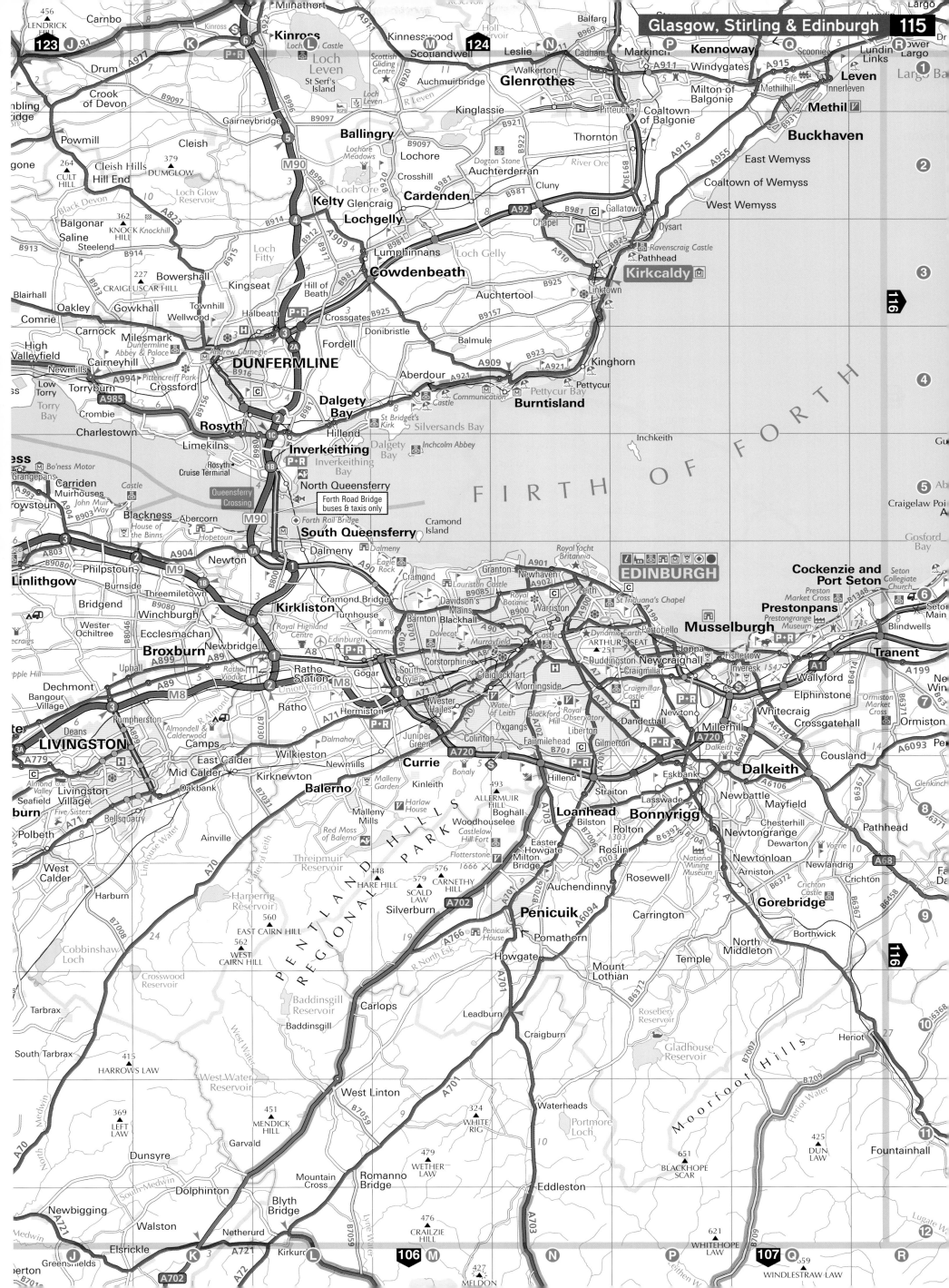

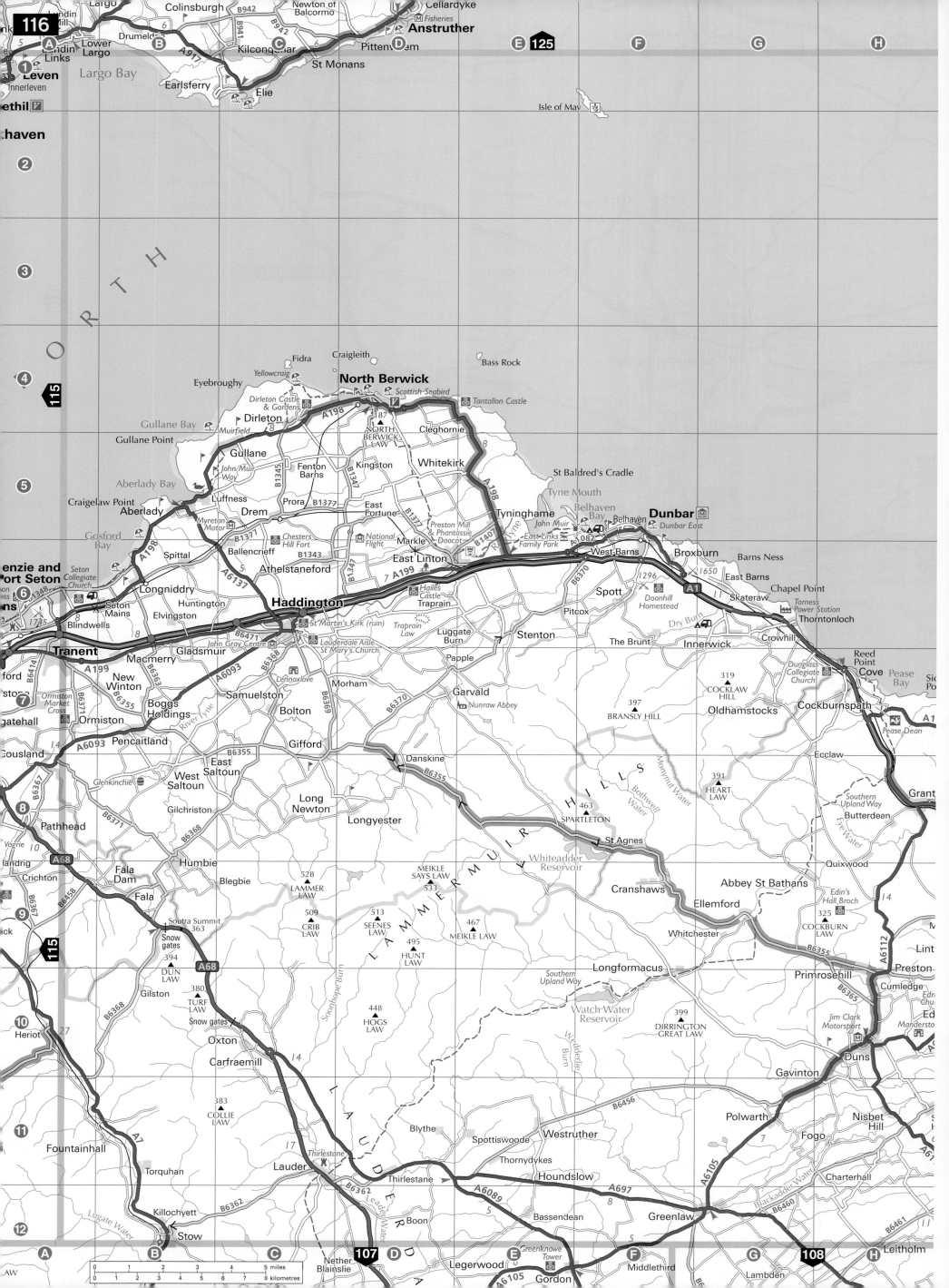

J   K   L   M   N   P   Q   R

1
2
3
4
5
6
7
8
9
10
11
12

Fast Castle Head

scar int

ST ABB'S HEAD

107

196
▲
BROWN
RIG

Coldingham
Loch

St Abbs

shouse

Coldingham

B6438

A1107

Coldingham
Bay

22

Eyemouth

Houndwood

Heugh
Head

Cairncross

P

M

262
▲
HORSELEY HILL

Reston

A1

Ayton

Burnmouth

B6438

Auchencrow

B6355

Marygold

B6437

Lamberton

law

Chirnside

B6437

B6355

Marshall Meadows Bay

Foulden

North Northumberland
Heritage Coast

Chirnsidebridge

15

Broadhaugh

Edington

Whiteadder Water

Foulden
Tithe Barn

1333

A6105

B6355

om
rch

rom

Allanton

Hutton

Berwick-upon-Tweed

B6460

Blackadder

Paxton

Barracks &
Main Guard

i

Castle

B6461

Town
Ramparts

Tweedmouth

A105

B6460

B6437

Whitsome

Hilton

Paxton

Loanend

East
Ord

Spittal

Huds
Head

Sinclair's
Hill

B6461

Horndean

Horncliffe

A1167

Scremerston

Ladykirk

13

Castle

Murton

Unthank

A1

2

Swinton

B6470

Norham

A698

Thornton

Cheswick

Upsettlington

Shoreswood

West Allerdean

Causeway
flooded at
high tide

Simprim

Grindon

Ancroft

A6

River Tweed

Felkington

Goswick

Haggerston

llacres

Grindonrigg

Berrington

Beal

Holy
Island

Bowsden

B6437

B635

B6525

15

HOLY ISLAND

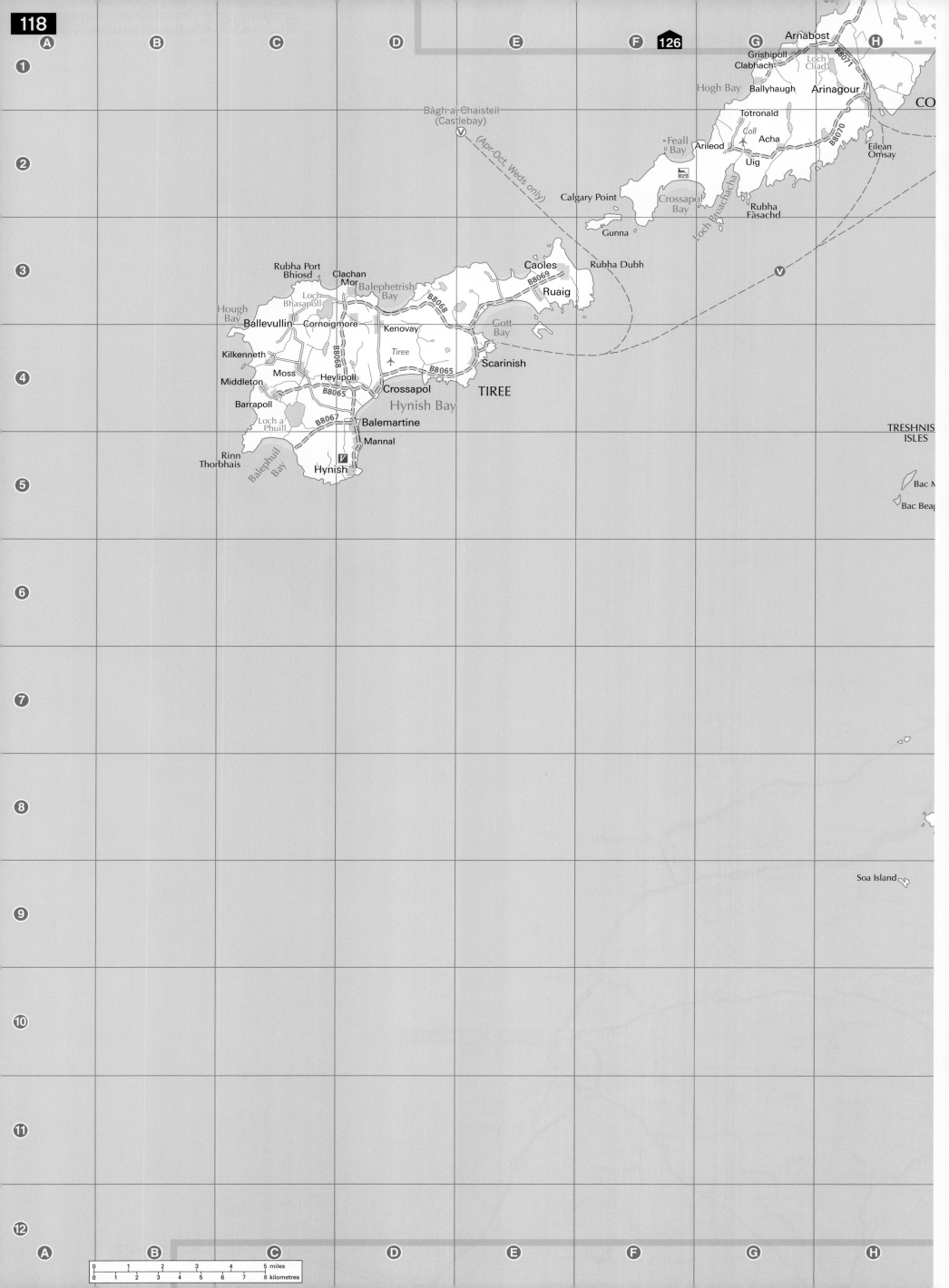

A B C D E F G H

1
2
3
4
5
6
7
8
9
10
11
12

A B C D E F G H

Arnabost
Grishipoll
Clabhach
Loch Cliad
Hogh Bay Ballyhaugh Arinagour
Totronald
CO
Feall Bay Coll Acha
Arileod Eilean Ornsay
Uig
Calgary Point Rubha Fàsachd
Crossapol Bay
Gunna Loch Breachacha

Bàgh a' Chaisteil
(Castlebay)
(Apr-Oct, Weds only)

Caoles
Rubha Dubh
B8069
Ruaig
Rubha Port Bhiosd
Clachan Mor Balephetrish Bay
Hough Bay B8068
Loch Bhasapoll Gott Bay
Ballevullin Cornoigmore Kenovay
Kilkenneth Tiree Scarinish
B8068
Moss Heylipoll TIREE
Middleton B8065
Crossapol
B8065
Barrapoll Hynish Bay
Loch a' Phuill B8067 Balemartine
TRESHNISH
Rinn Mannal ISLES
Thorbhais
Balephuil Bay Hynish
Bac M
Bac Beag

Soa Island

0 1 2 3 4 5 miles
0 1 2 3 4 5 6 7 8 kilometres

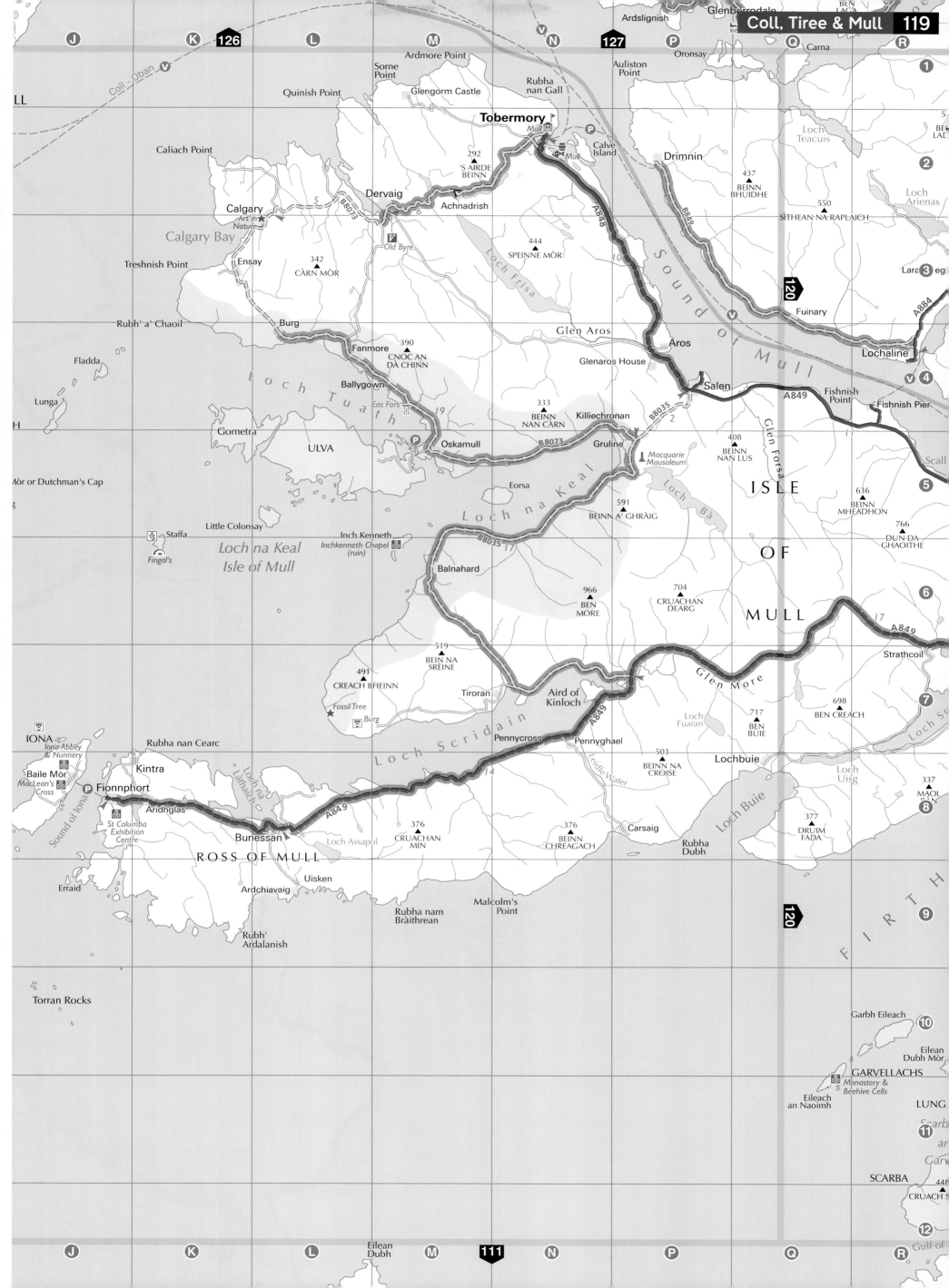

Glenberrodale
Ardslignish
Ardmore Point
Sorne Point
Quinish Point
Glengorm Castle
Rubha nan Gall
Auliston Point
Oronsay
Carna
Caliach Point
Tobermory
Mull
Calve Island
Drimnin
Loch Teacuis
292
'S AIRDE BEINN
Dervaig
Achnadrish
437
BEINN BHUIDHE
Loch Arienas
Calgary
Art in Nature
5
B8073
Old Byre
550
SÌTHEAN-NA-RAPLAICH
Calgary Bay
342
CÀRN MÒR
444
SPEINNE MÒR
Treshnish Point
Ensay
Loch Frisa
Lara eg
Rubh'a'Chaoil
Burg
Glen Aros
Aros
Fuinary
Fanmore
390
CNOC AN DÀ CHINN
Glenaros House
Sound of Mull
Lochaline
Ballygown
Salen
Fishnish Point
Fishnish Pier
Loch Tuath
Eas Fors
19
333
BEINN NAN CÀRN
Killiechronan
B8035
2
A849
Gometra
ULVA
Oskamull
B8073
Gruline
Macquarie Mausoleum
408
BEINN NAN LUS
Glen Forsa
Scall
Mòr or Dutchman's Cap
Eorsa
Loch Bà
591
BEINN A' GHRÀIG
636
BEINN MHEADHON
ISLE
Lunga
Little Colonsay
Loch na Keal
Isle of Mull
Staffa
Inch Kenneth
Inchkenneth Chapel (ruin)
B8035
17
766
DUN DA GHAOITHE
OF
Fingal's
Balnahard
966
BEN MORE
704
CRUACHAN DEARG
MULL
IONA
Iona Abbey & Nunnery
Rubha nan Cearc
519
BEIN NA SREINE
Strathcoil
Baile Mòr
MacLean's Cross
Kintra
Fionnphort
491
CREACH BHEINN
Fossil Tree
Burg
Tiroran
Aird of Kinloch
Glen More
17
A849
698
BEN CREACH
717
BEN BUIE
Aridhglas
St Columba Exhibition Centre
Pennycross
Pennyghael
Loch Fuaran
Loch Sc
Bunessan
Loch na Lathaich
Sound of Iona
Loch Scridain
A849
14
Leidle Water
503
BEINN NA CROISE
Lochbuie
Loch Uisg
337
MAOL
ROSS OF MULL
Loch Assapol
376
CRUACHAN MIN
376
BEINN CHREAGACH
Carsaig
Rubha Dubh
Loch Buie
377
DRUIM FADA
Uisken
Erraid
Ardchiavaig
Malcolm's Point
F
Rubh' Ardalanish
Rubha nam Bràithrean
I
R
T
H
Torran Rocks
Garbh Eileach
Eilean Dubh Mòr
GARVELLACHS
Monastery & Beehive Cells
Eileach an Naoimh
LUNG
Eilean Dubh
SCARBA
CRUACH

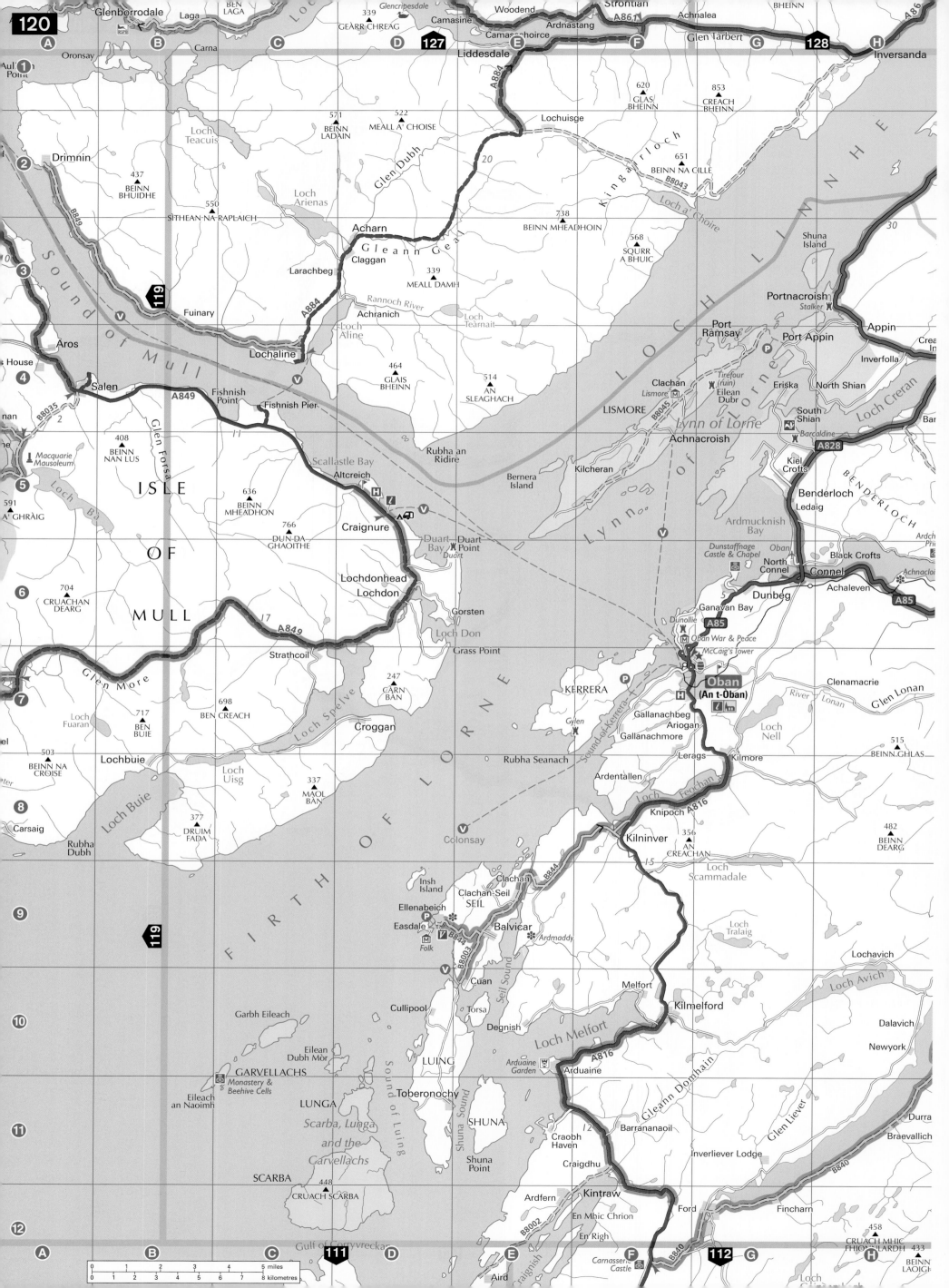

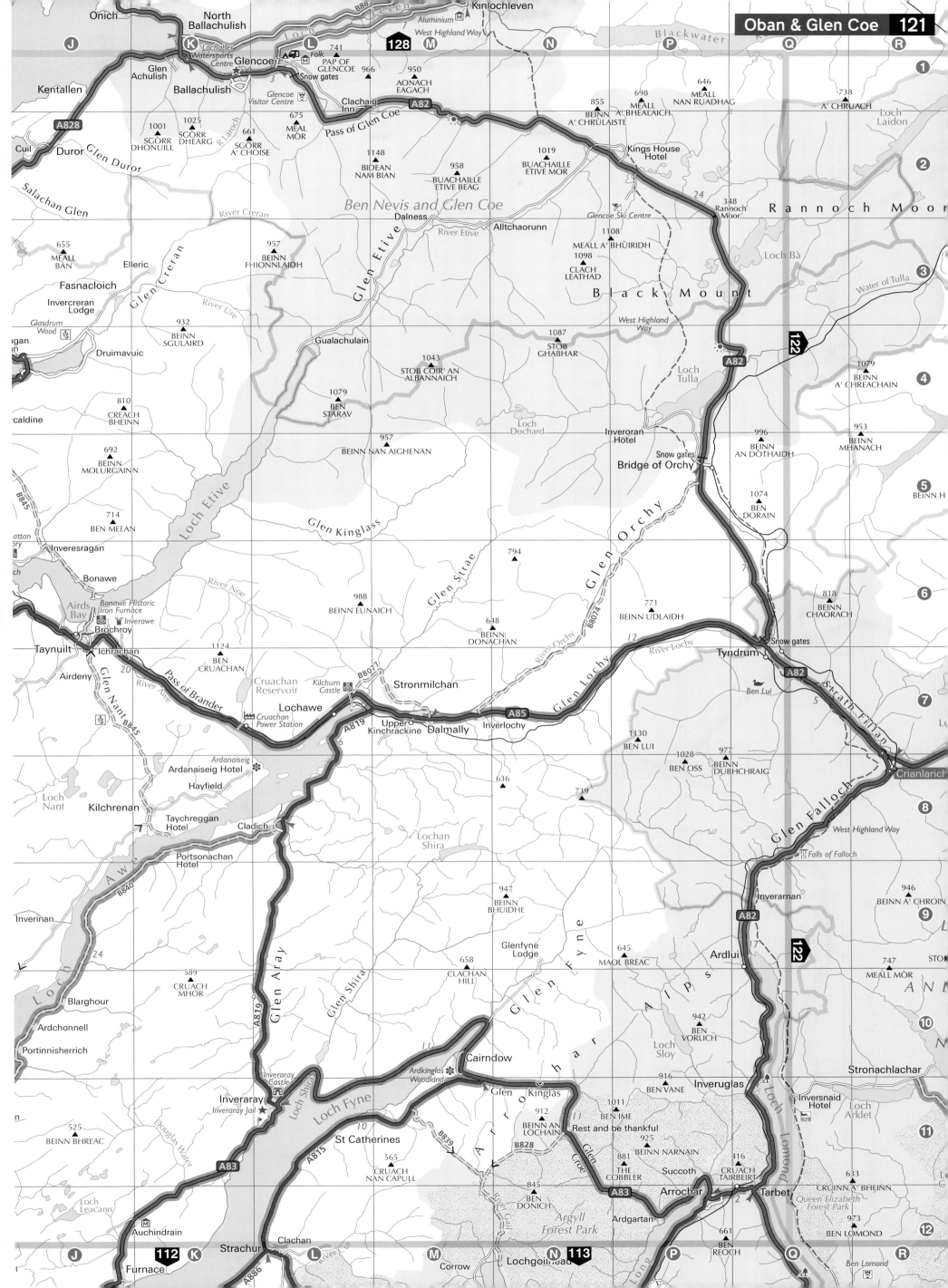

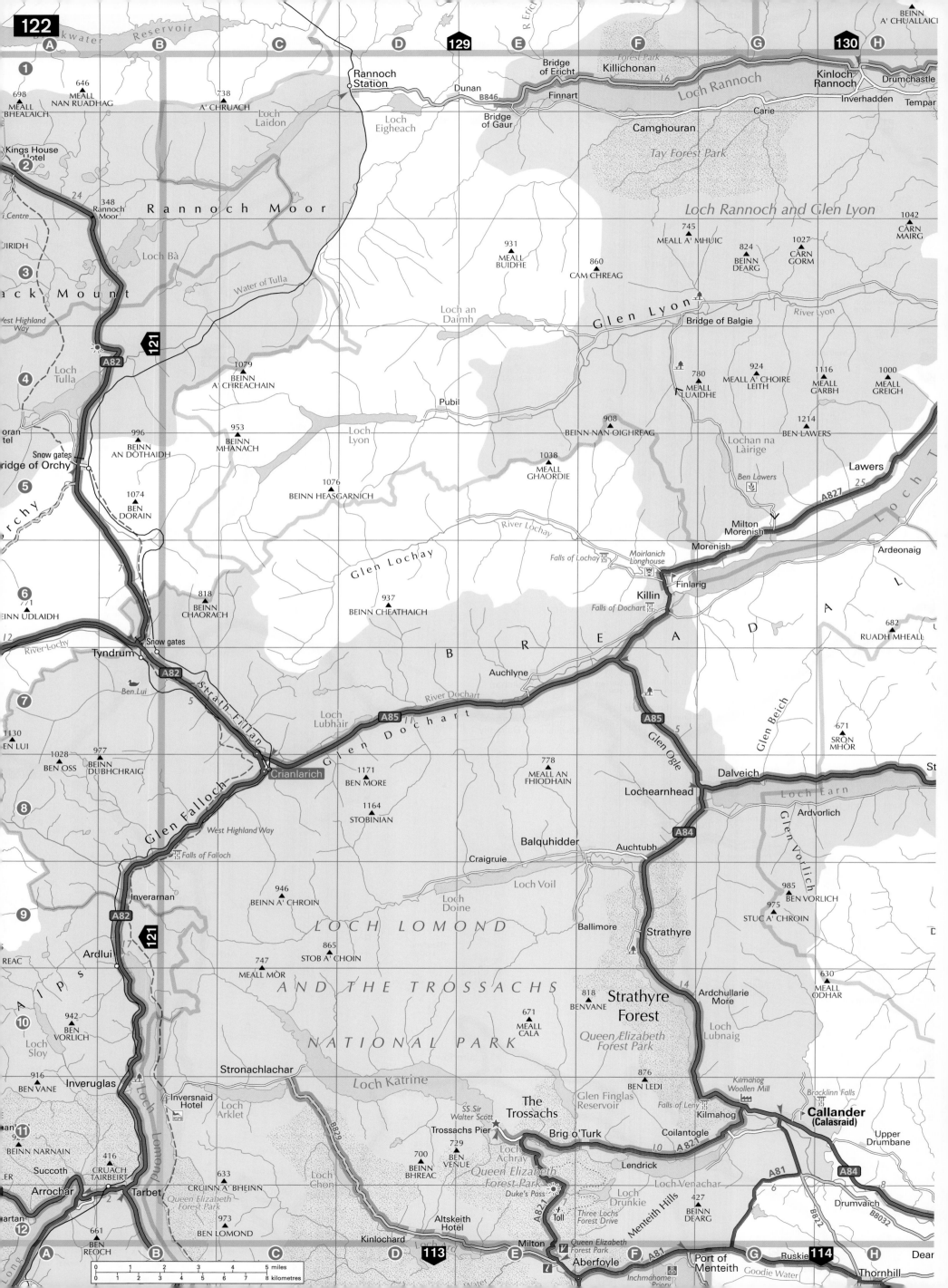

A   B   C   D   129   E   F   G   130   H

BEINN A' CHUALLAICH

1
698 ▲ MEALL BHEALAICH
646 ▲ MEALL NAN RUADHAG
738 ▲ A' CHRUACH
Blackwater Reservoir
Rannoch Station
Loch Laidon
Loch Eigheach
Dunan   B846
Bridge of Gaur
Bridge of Ericht   Killichonan   Forest Park   1.6   Loch Rannoch   Kinloch Rannoch   Drumchastle
Finnart   Inverhadden   Tempar
Camghouran   Carie

2
Kings House Hotel
i Centre
24
348 Rannoch Moor
Rannoch Moor
Tay Forest Park
Loch Rannoch and Glen Lyon

3
ack Mount
Loch Bà
Water of Tulla
931 ▲ MEALL BUIDHE
860 ▲ CAM CHREAG
745 ▲ MEALL A' MHUIC
824 ▲ BEINN DEARG
1027 ▲ CÀRN GORM
1042 ▲ CÀRN MAIRG
West Highland Way

4
A82   121
Loch Tulla
1079 ▲ BEINN A' CHREACHAIN
Loch an Daimh
Glen Lyon
Bridge of Balgie
River Lyon
780 ▲ MEALL LUAIDHE
924 ▲ MEALL A' CHOIRE LEITH
1116 ▲ MEALL GARBH
1000 ▲ MEALL GREIGH

oran tel
996 ▲ BEINN AN DOTHAIDH
953 ▲ BEINN MHANACH
Pubil
Loch Lyon
908 ▲ BEINN NAN OIGHREAG
1038 ▲ MEALL GHAORDIE
Lochan na Làirige
1214 ▲ BEN LAWERS

5
ridge of Orchy
Snow gates
1074 ▲ BEN DORAIN
1076 ▲ BEINN HEASGARNICH
Ben Lawers
Milton Morenish
Lawers
25
rchy
7
River Lochay
Morenish
A827
Ardeonaig

6
6 771
EINN UDLAIDH
818 ▲ BEINN CHAORACH
Glen Lochay
Falls of Lochay
Moirlanich Longhouse
Finlarig
Killin
Falls of Dochart
682 ▲ RUADH MHEALL

12
River Lochy
Snow gates
Tyndrum
937 ▲ BEINN CHEATHAICH
B   R   E   A   D   A   L

7
A82
Ben Lui
Strath Fillan
Loch Lubhair
A85   River Dochart
Auchlyne
Glen Ogle
5
Glen Beich
671 ▲ SRON MHOR

1130 EN LUI
1028 ▲ BEN OSS
977 ▲ BEINN DUBHCHRAIG
Crianlarich
1171 ▲ BEN MORE
778 ▲ MEALL AN FHIODHAIN
A85
Dalveich
Loch Earn
St

8
Glen Falloch
West Highland Way
1164 ▲ STOBINIAN
Lochearnhead
Ardvorlich
Glen Vorlich
Balquhidder
Auchtubh
A84

9
A82   121
Falls of Falloch
946 ▲ BEINN A' CHROIN
Craigruie
Loch Voil
Loch Doine
Ballimore
Strathyre
985 ▲ BEN VORLICH
975 ▲ STUC A' CHROIN

Ardlui
865 ▲ STOB A' CHOIN
LOCH LOMOND
747 ▲ MEALL MÒR
AND THE TROSSACHS
818 ▲ BENVANE
Strathyre Forest
14
Ardchullarie More
630 ▲ MEALL ODHAR

10
REAC
942 ▲ BEN VORLICH
Loch Sloy
Inveruglas
916 ▲ BEN VANE
NATIONAL PARK
671 ▲ MEALL CALA
Queen Elizabeth Forest Park
Loch Lubnaig

Inversnaid Hotel
Loch Arklet
Stronachlachar
Loch Katrine
Glen Finglas Reservoir
876 ▲ BEN LEDI
Kilmahog Woollen Mill
Bracklinn Falls

11
11
BEINN NARNAIN
Succoth
416 ▲ CRUACH TAIRBEIRT
B829
SS Sir Walter Scott
The Trossachs
Trossachs Pier
Brig o'Turk
Falls of Leny
Kilmahog
Coilantogle
A821
Callander (Calasraid)
Upper Drumbane

an
661 ▲ BEN REOCH
Arrochar
Tarbet
Queen Elizabeth Forest Park
Loch Lomond
Loch Chon
973 ▲ BEN LOMOND
633 ▲ CRUINN A' BHEINN
700 ▲ BEINN BHREAC
729 ▲ BEN VENUE
Loch Achray
Queen Elizabeth Forest Park
Duke's Pass
Altskeith Hotel
Toll
A821
Milton
Three Lochs Forest Drive
Loch Drunkie
Lendrick
427 ▲ BEINN DEARG
Menteith Hills
Loch Venachar
A81
A84
Drumvaich
B872

12
12
artan
Kinlochard
Loch A
113
Aberfoyle
A81
Port of Menteith
Inchmahome Priory
Goodie Water
Ruskie
114
Dear
Thornhill
B8032

A   B   C   D   113   E   F   G   114   H

0   1   2   3   4   5 miles
0   1   2   3   4   5   6   7   8 kilometres

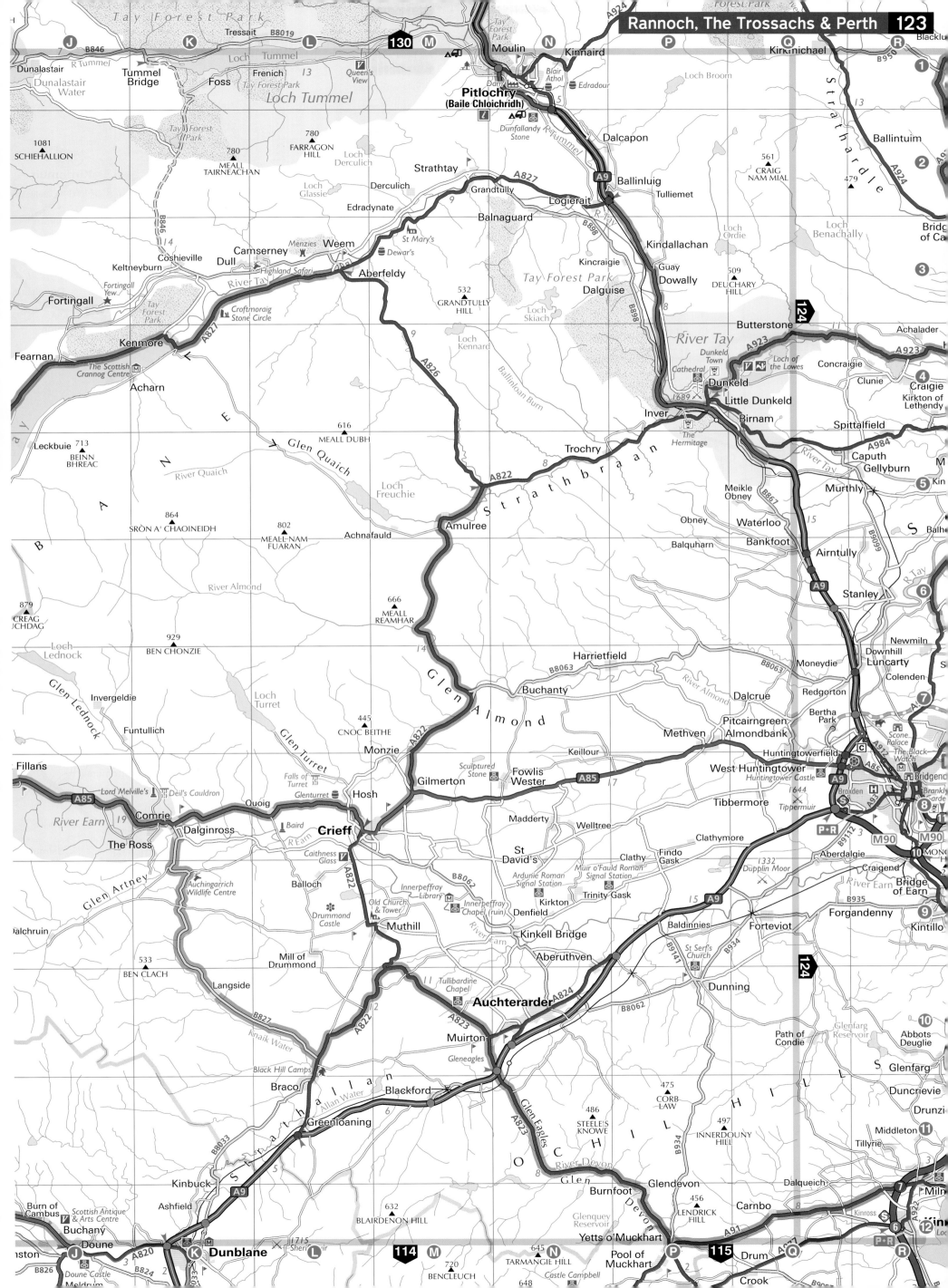

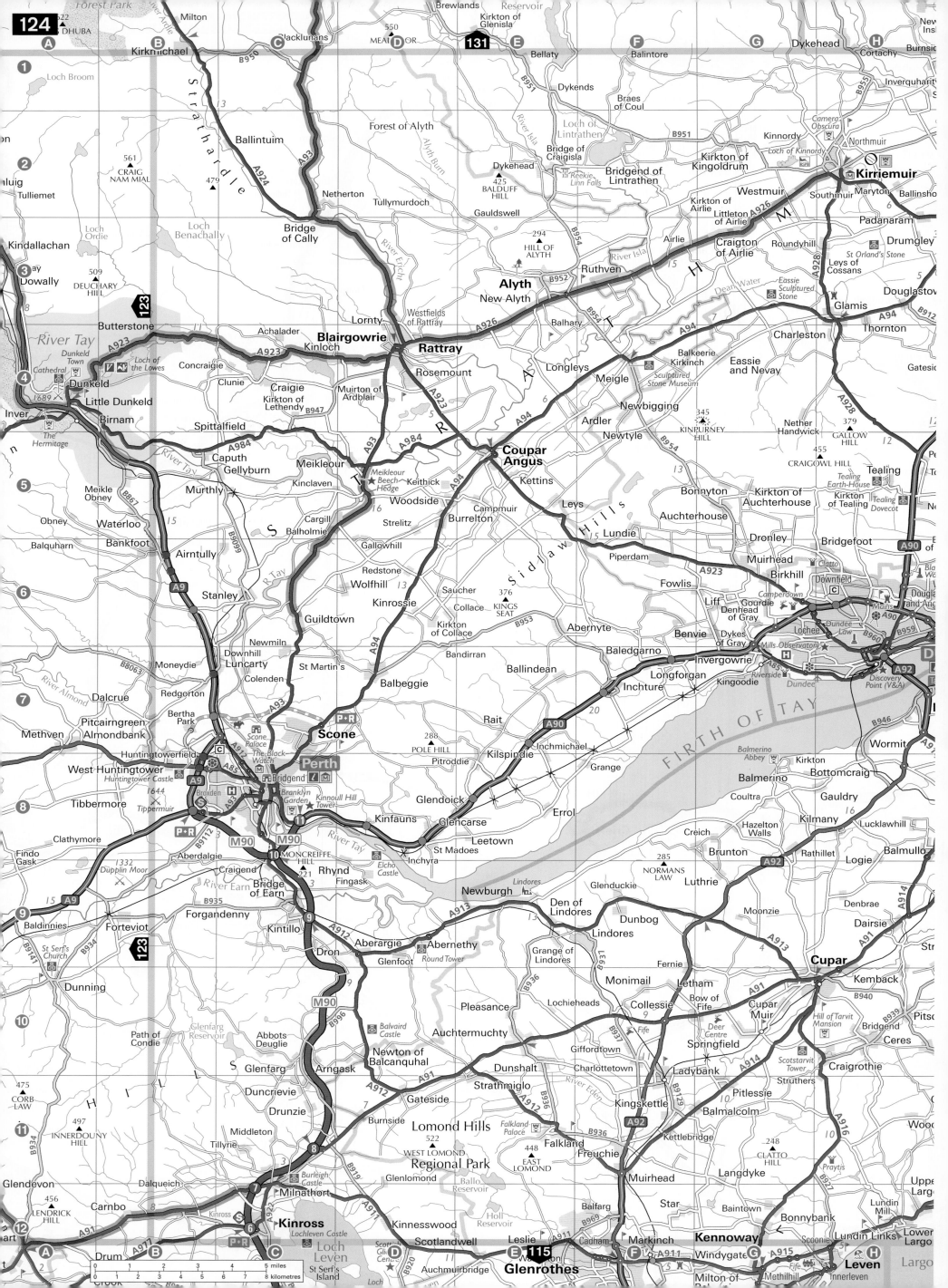

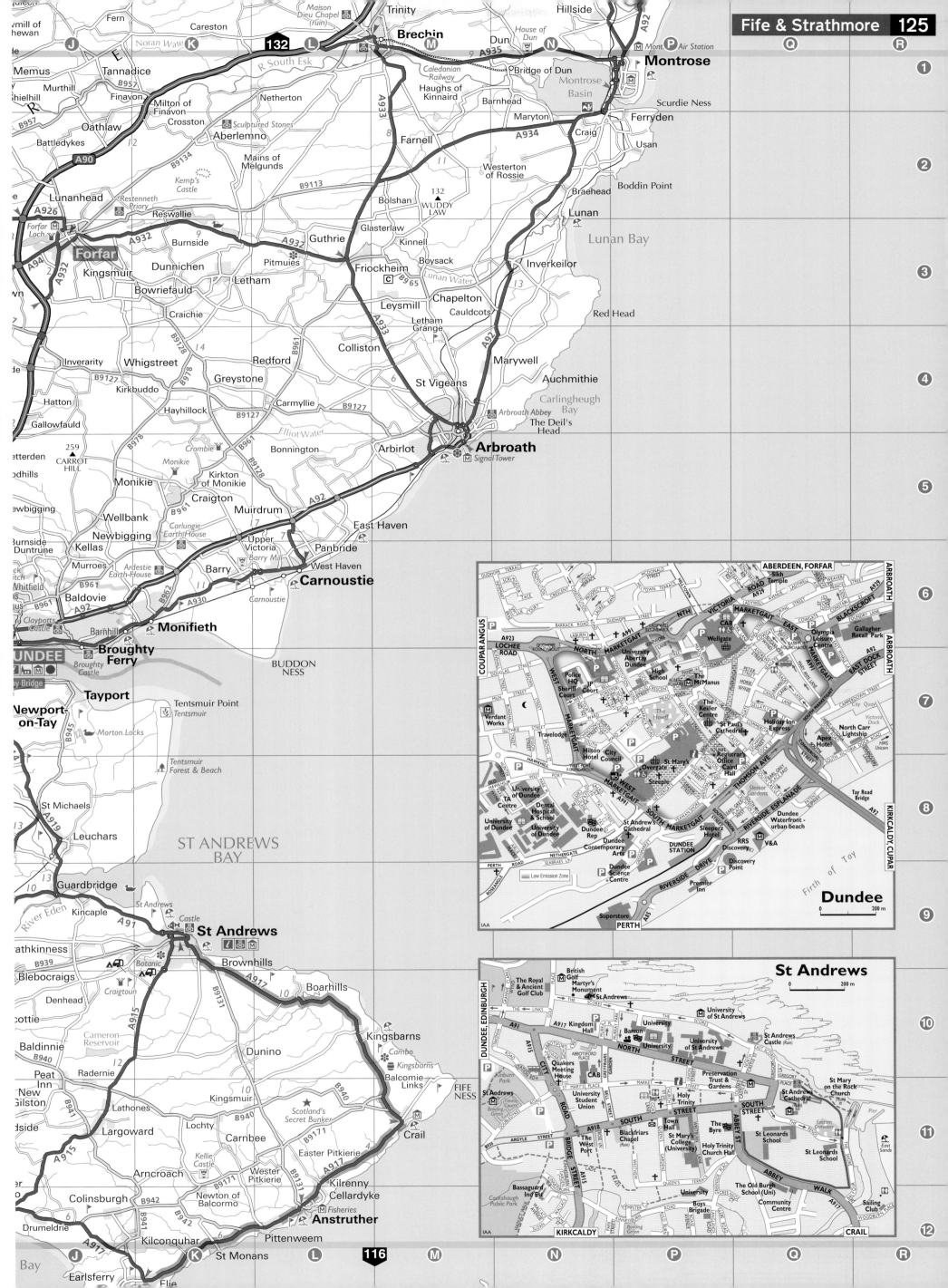

A B C D E F **134** G H

1 Rubha an Dùnain

894
GARS
BHEINN

225
CEANN NA BEINNE

Loch Britt

Soay Sound

139
BEINN
BHREAC

Mol-chlach

SOAY

2 ⓥ
Loch Baghasdail
(Lochboisdale)

Rubh'
Aonghais

3 CANNA
210
CÀRN A' GHAILL
Garrisdale Point
A'Chill
Canna
Harbour
Sanday

Kilmory
Bay
Rubha
Shamhnan
Insir

C U I L L I N   S O U N D

Sound of Canna

4 A' Bhrìdeanach
302
MULLACH
MÒR
Rubha
na Roinne
570
ORVAL
Kinloch
Loch Scresort

5 Oigh-sgeir
RÙM
810
ASKIVAL

Harris
Bay

All vehicles must have
the relevant island
permit prior to travel
to The Small Isles.
Services are seasonal,
day & weather dependent.

6 *The Small Isles*
763
SGÙRR NAN
GILLEAN
Rubha nam
Meirleach

Sound of Rùm

Bay of
Laig

7 Rubha an
Fhasaidh
Laig
EIGG
393
AN SGÙRR

Sound of Eigg

8 Eilean
nan Each
MUCK
Port Mòr

9

10 Sanna Point

Sanna
Bay
Sanna
Portuairk
Achnaha
Ardnamurchan
Point
Achosnich

11 ⓥ
Bàgh a' Chaisteil
(Castlebay)
Loch Baghasdail
(Lochboisdale)
(Oct-Mar)
Rubha
Mòr
Eilean Mòr
Rubha
Sgor-innis
342
BEINN
NA SEILG
Ormsaigmore

12 Bousd
Sorisdale
Cliad
Bay
Arnabost
Grishipoll
Clab...h
Arinagour

A B C **118** D E F **119** G H

Ardmore
Point
Sorne
Point
Coll - Oban
Quinish Point
Glengorm Castle

0 1 2 3 4 5 miles
0 1 2 3 4 5 6 7 8 kilometres

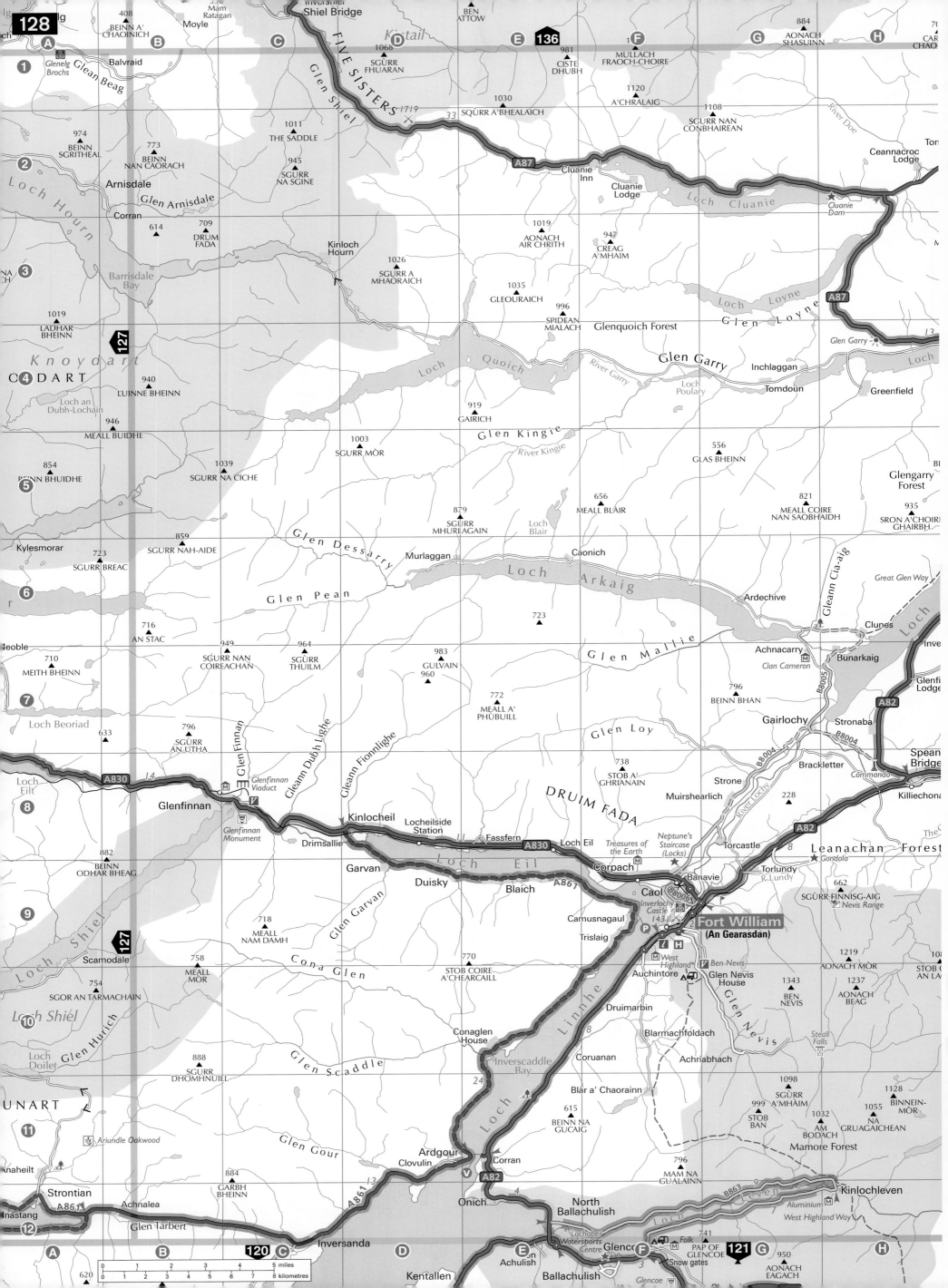

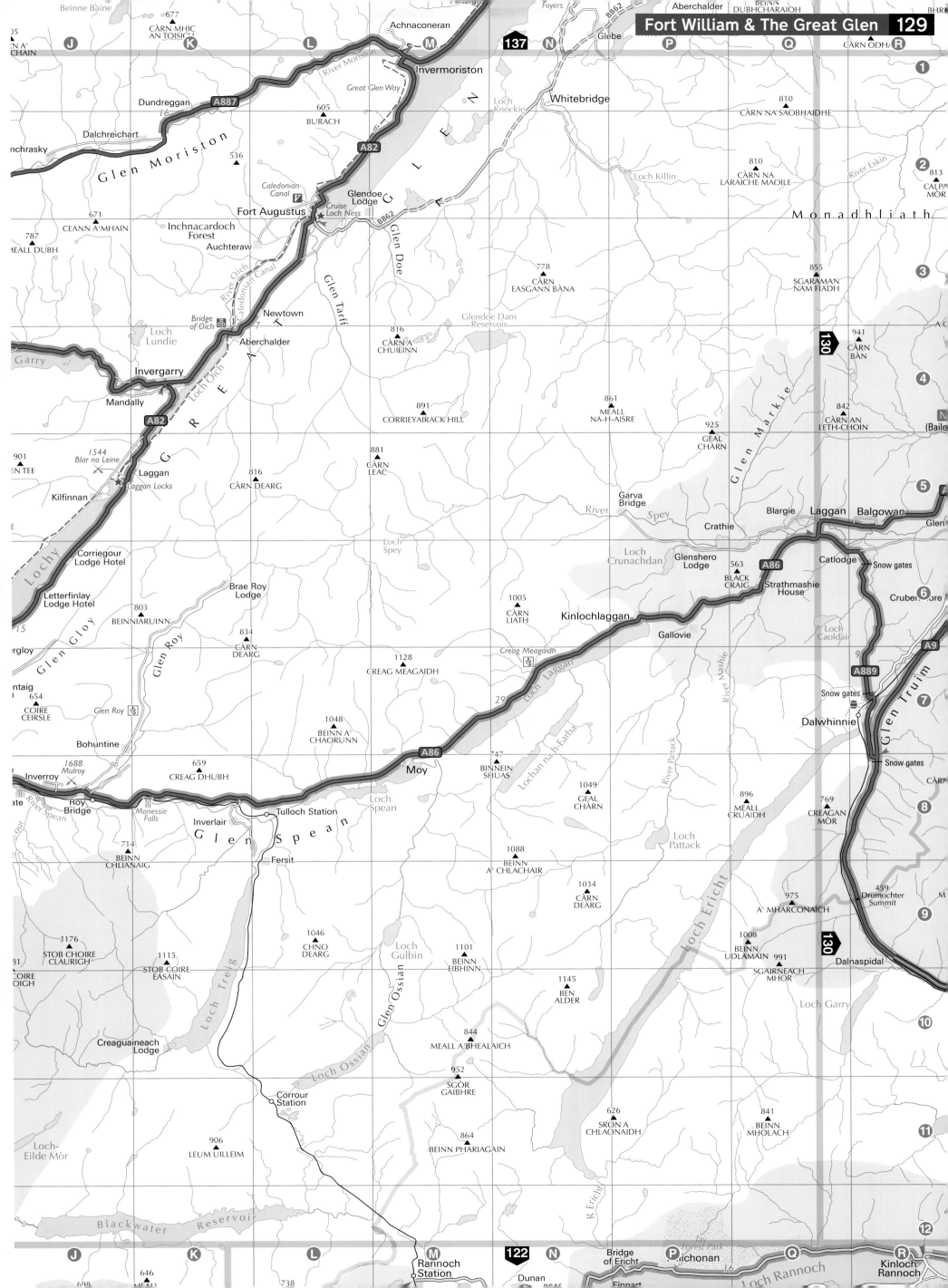

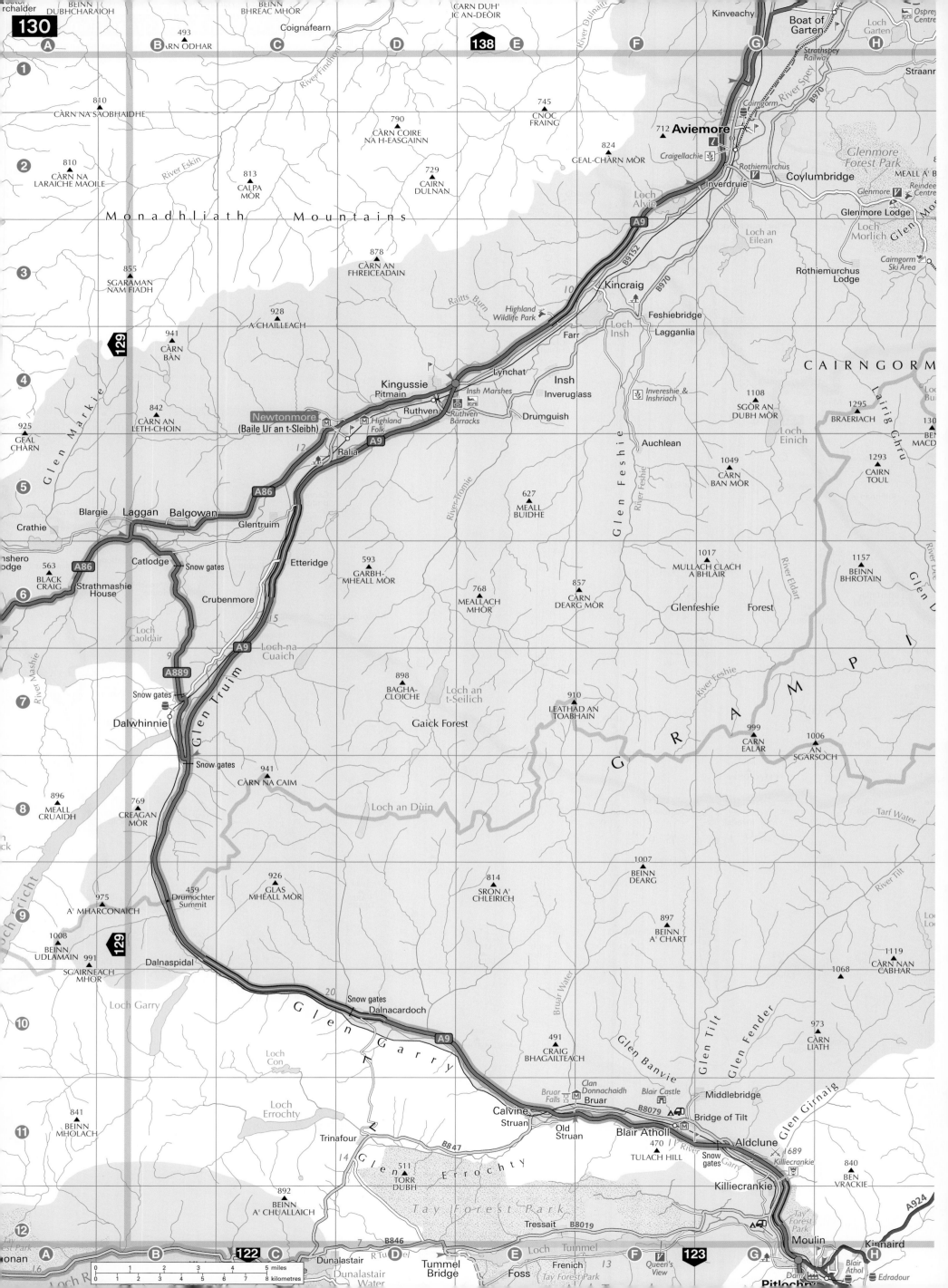

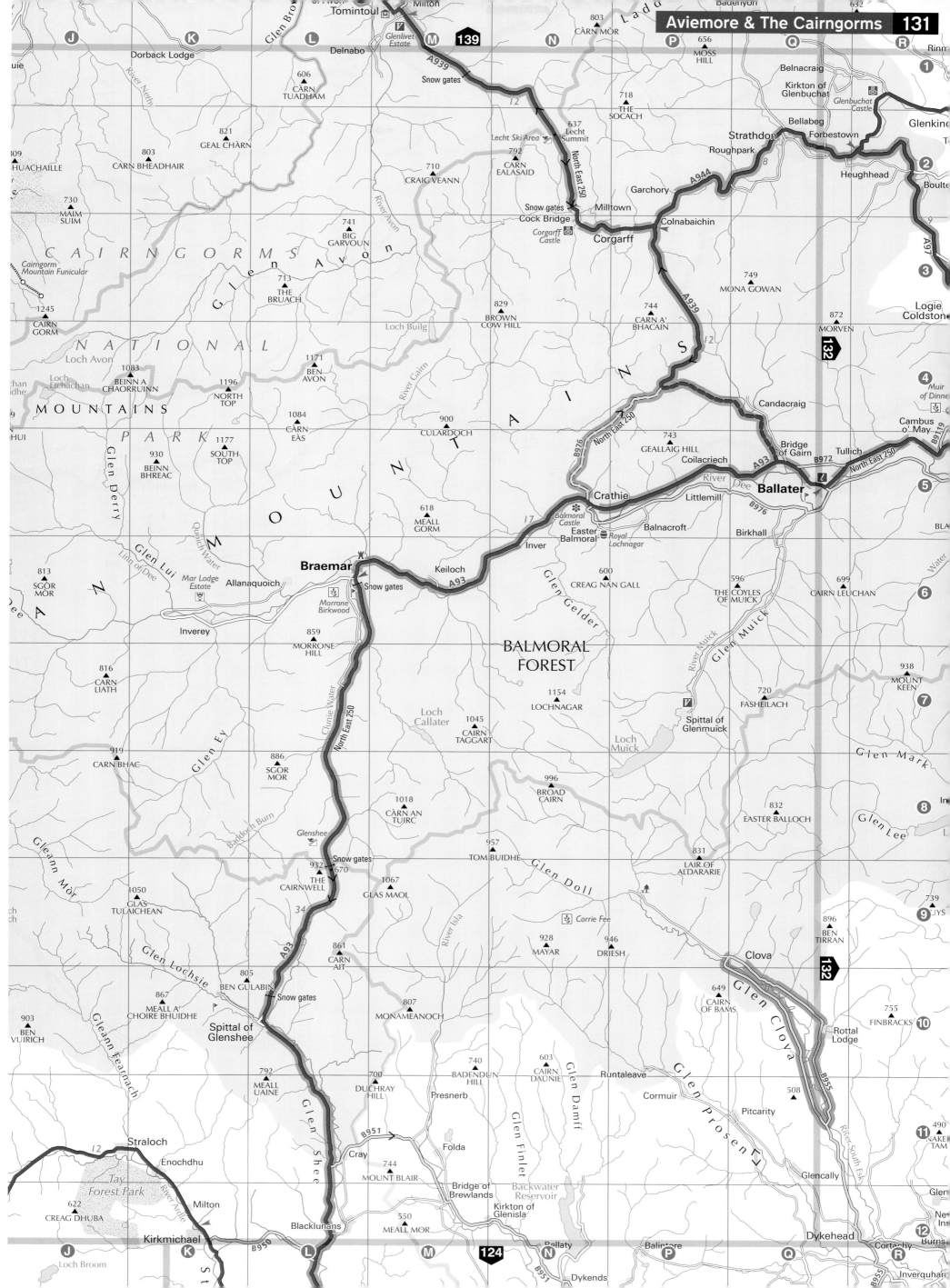

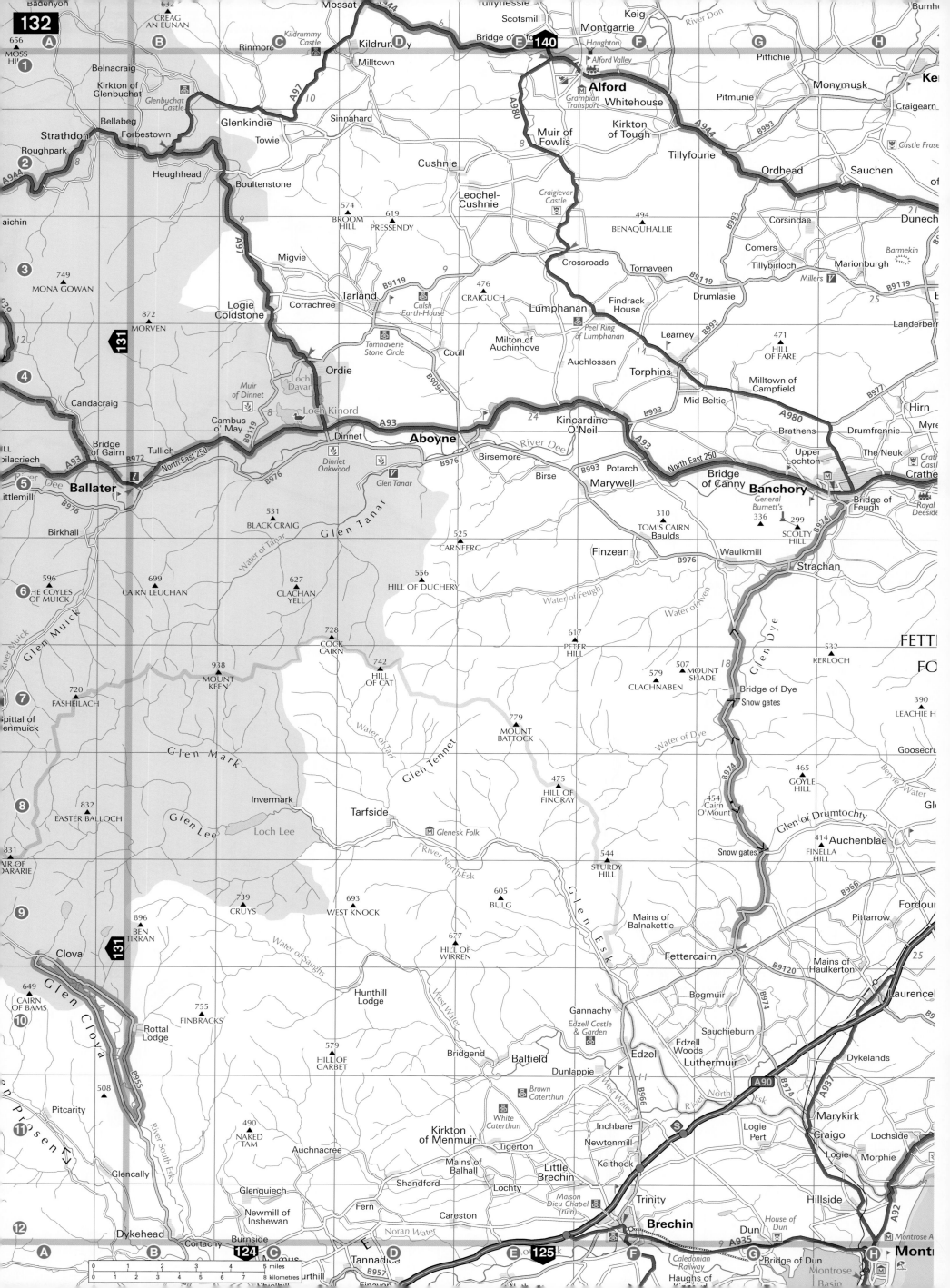

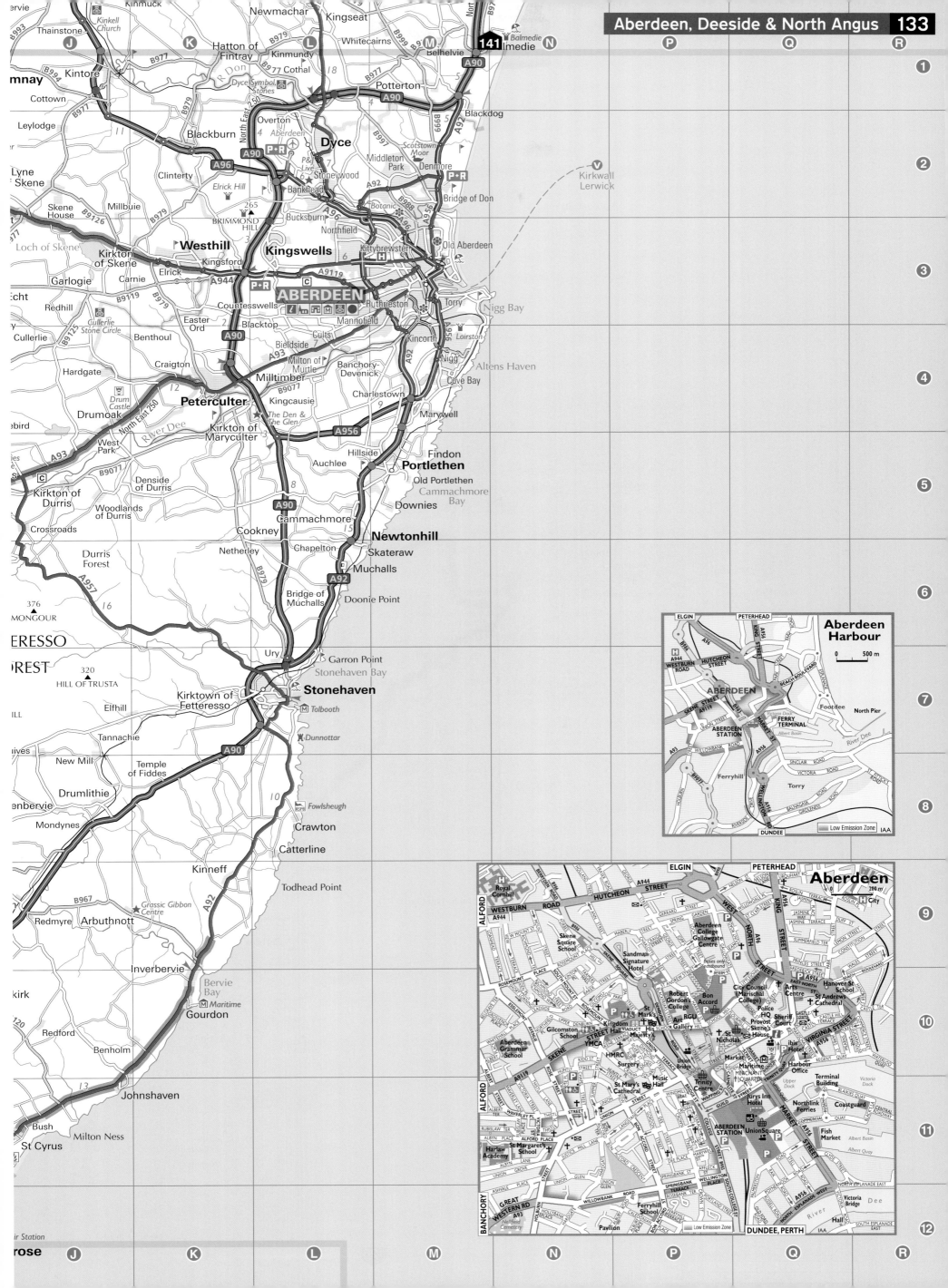

Aberdeen Harbour

ELGIN
PETERHEAD
ABERDEEN
WESTBURN ROAD
HUTCHEON STREET
KING STREET
SKENE STREET
A9119
MARKET ST
BEACH BOULEVARD
FERRY TERMINAL
ABERDEEN STATION
Footdee
North Pier
Victoria Dock
Albert Basin
River Dee
A93
WILLOWBANK ROAD
A956
Ferryhill
Torry
SINCLAIR ROAD
VICTORIA ROAD
WELLINGTON RD
BALNAGASK ROAD
GRANDHOLM
A956
0   500 m
Low Emission Zone
IAA
DUNDEE

Aberdeen

ELGIN
PETERHEAD
ALFORD
A944
WESTBURN ROAD
HUTCHEON STREET
A944
WEST NORTH STREET
KING STREET
A96
City
JASMINE WAY
JASMINE TERRACE
DUFF ST
SUMMERFIELD TER
CONSTITUTION
H Royal Cornhill
Aberdeen College Gallowgate Centre
Sandman Signature Hotel
SPRING GARDEN
GERRARD STREET
MABERLY ST
ROSEMOUNT
Skene Square School
PRINCES STREET
FREDERICK STREET
CASTLE TERRACE
City Council (Marischal College)
Arts Centre
St Andrew's Cathedral
Police HQ
Sheriff Court
Provost Skene's House
CASTLE STREET
ibis Hotel
Hanover St School
HARDGATE
ESSLEMONT AVENUE
UPPER DENBURN
ROSEMOUNT VIADUCT
Robert Gordon's College
Bon Accord
Art Gallery RGU
St Mark's
His Majesty's
St Nicholas
Kingdom
Gilcomston School
YMCA
Skene St
SKENE STREET
Aberdeen Grammar School
HMRC Surgery
Union Bridge
Maritime
Music Hall
St Mary's Cathedral
Trinity Centre
MERCHANT QUARTER
Market
Harbour Office
Terminal Building
Victoria Dock
UNION STREET
WAPPING ST
GUILD
Jurys Inn Hotel
Northlink Ferries
Coastguard
CENTRAL QUAY
ALBYN PLACE
RUBISLAW TER
WAVERLEY PL
ALFORD PLACE
St Margaret's School
ALFORD STREET
SKENE STREET
JUSTICE MILL LANE
Fish Market
ABERDEEN STATION
UnionSquare
Albert Quay
GATE ST
Harlaw Academy
ALBYN GROVE
ALFORD PLACE
BLOOMFIELD ROAD
BON ACCORD
WILLOWBANK ROAD
WELLINGTON PLACE
SOUTH COLLEGE ST
NORTH ESPLANADE EAST
BANCHORY
GREAT WESTERN RD
A93
Nellfield Cemetery
Ferryhill School
HOLBURN STREET
WILLOWBANK ROAD
MARYWELL ST
SPRINGBANK TER
AFFLECK ST
WELLINGTON ROAD
A956
Victoria Bridge
River Dee
NORTH ESPLANADE EAST
SOUTH ESPLANADE EAST
Pavilion
Hall
Low Emission Zone
DUNDEE, PERTH
IAA
0   200 m

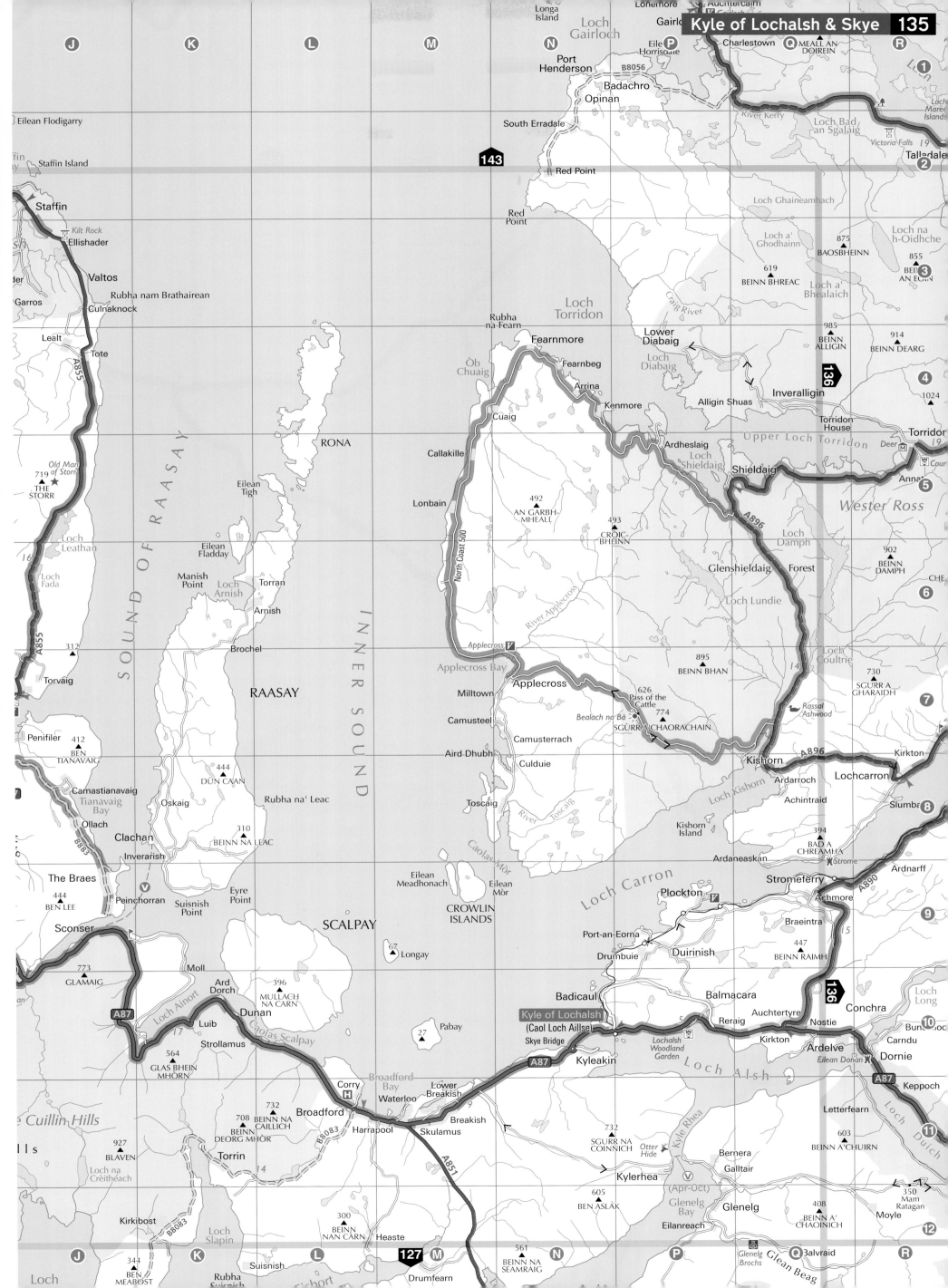

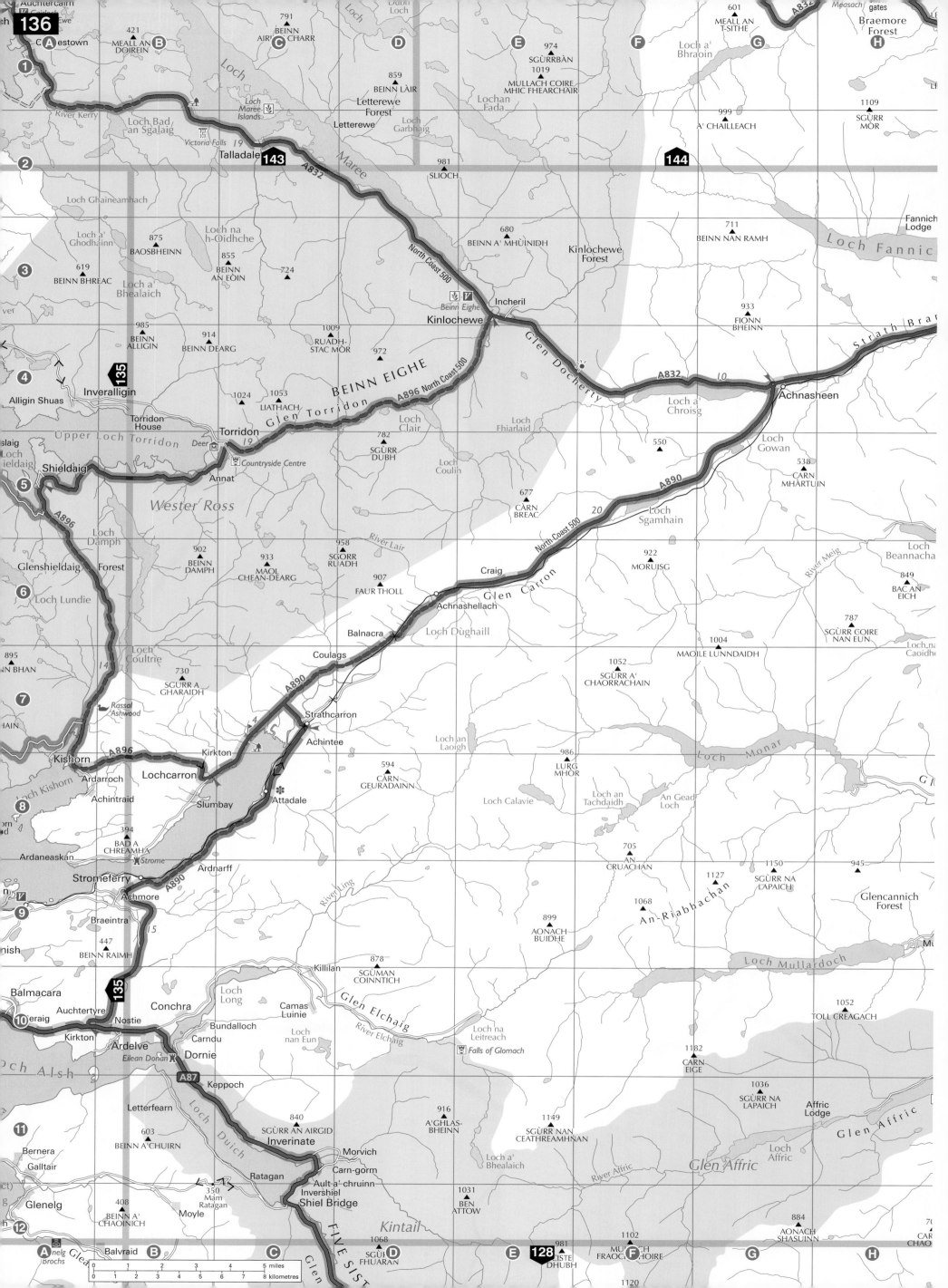

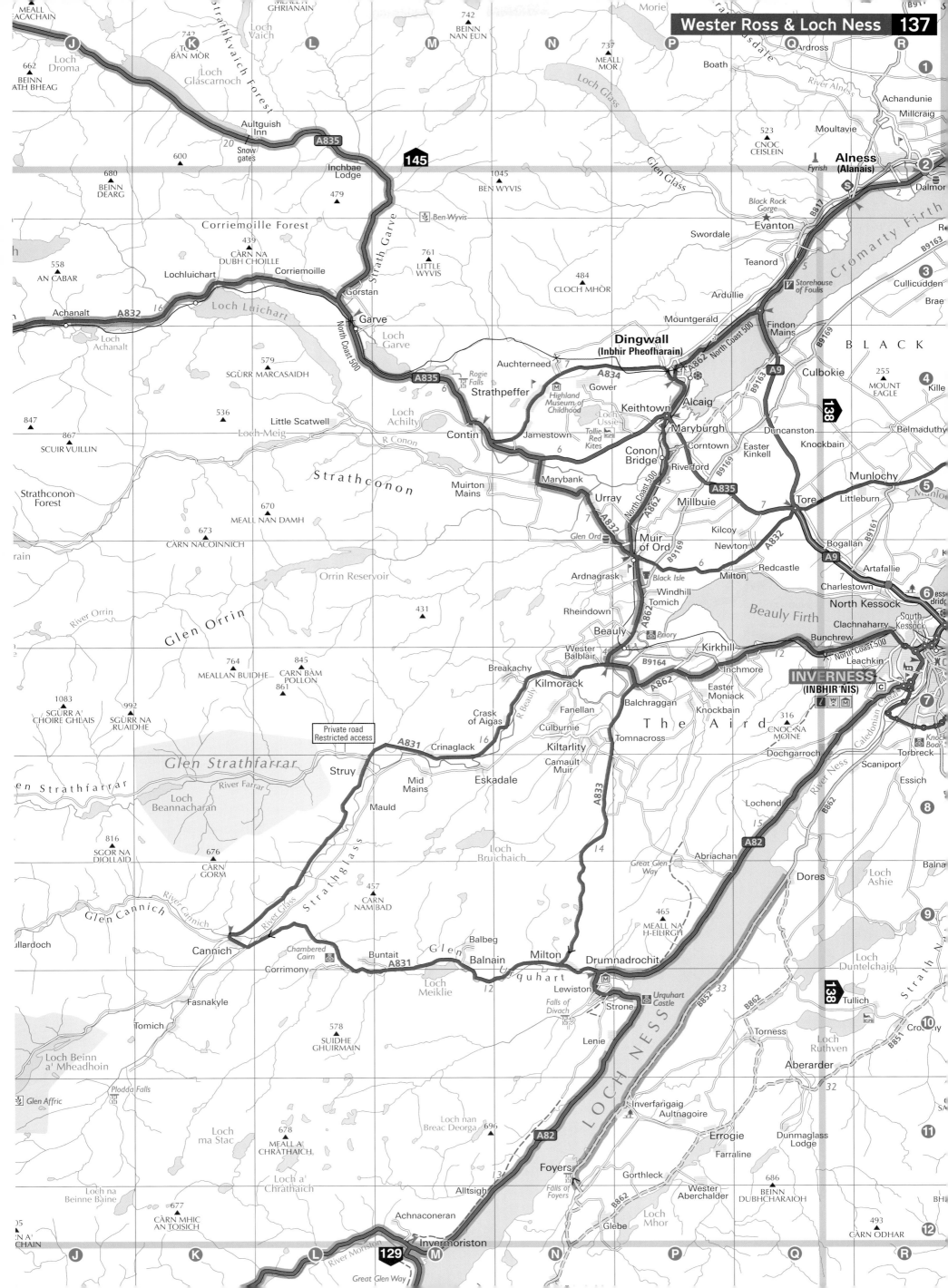

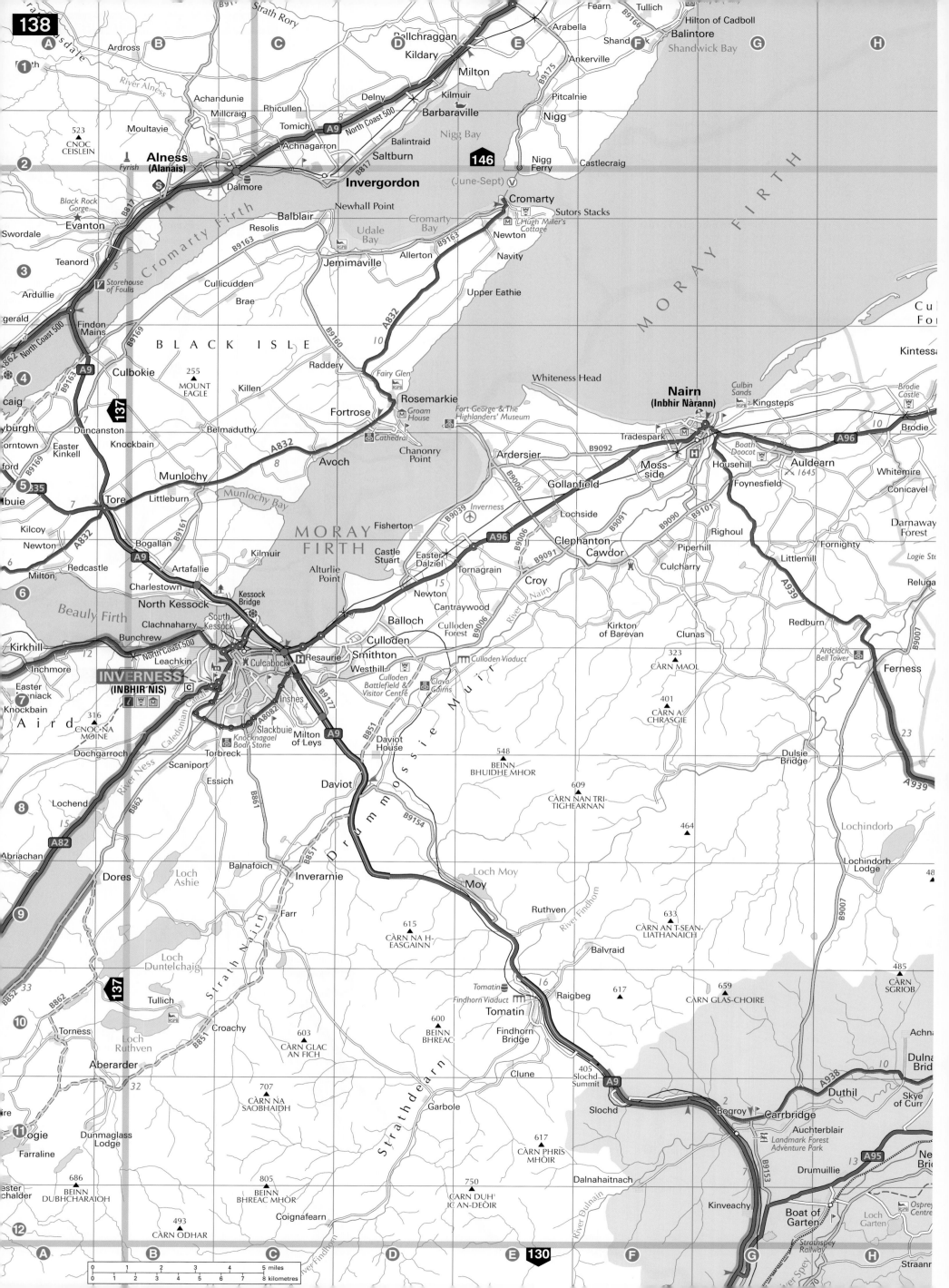

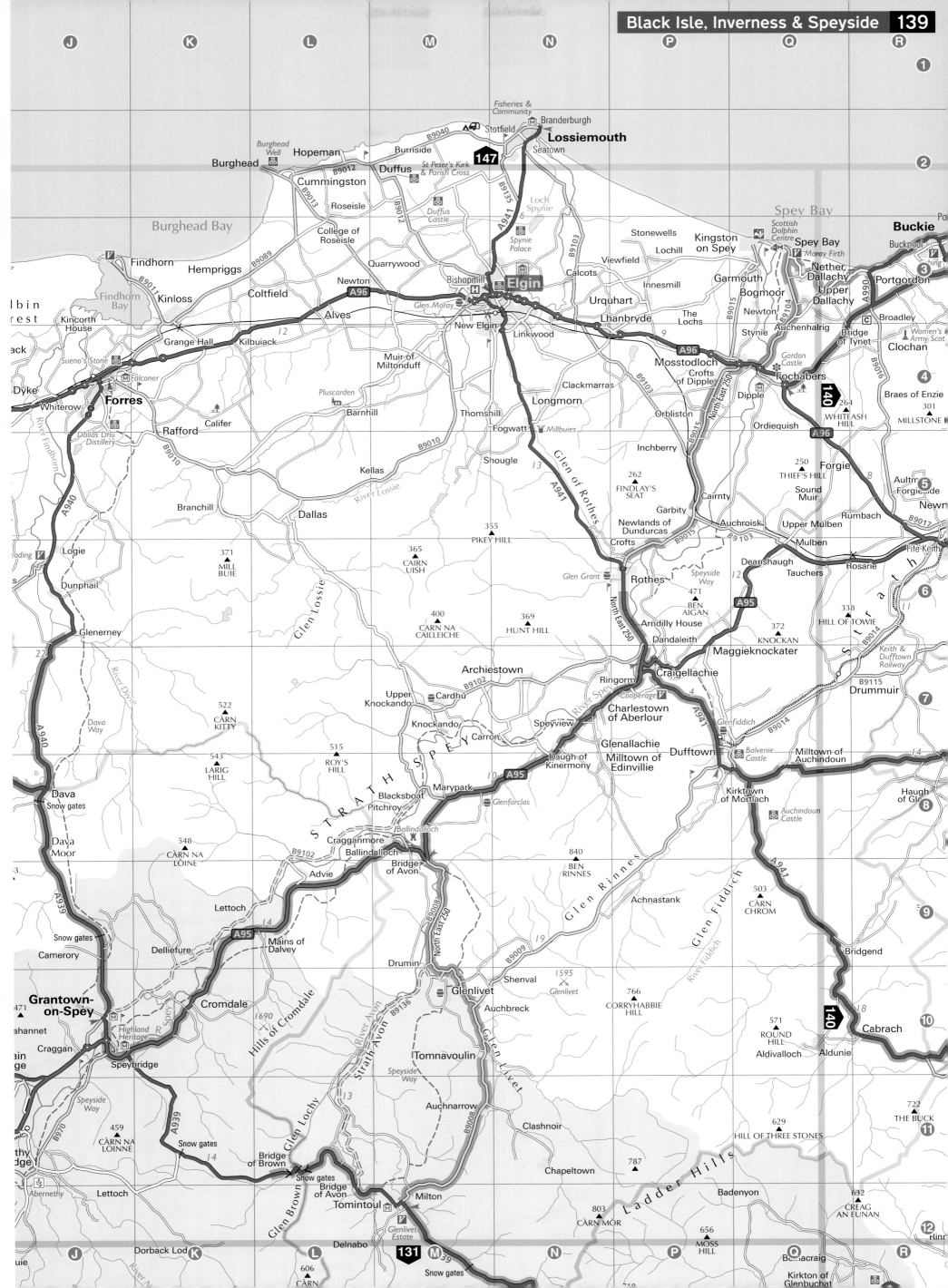

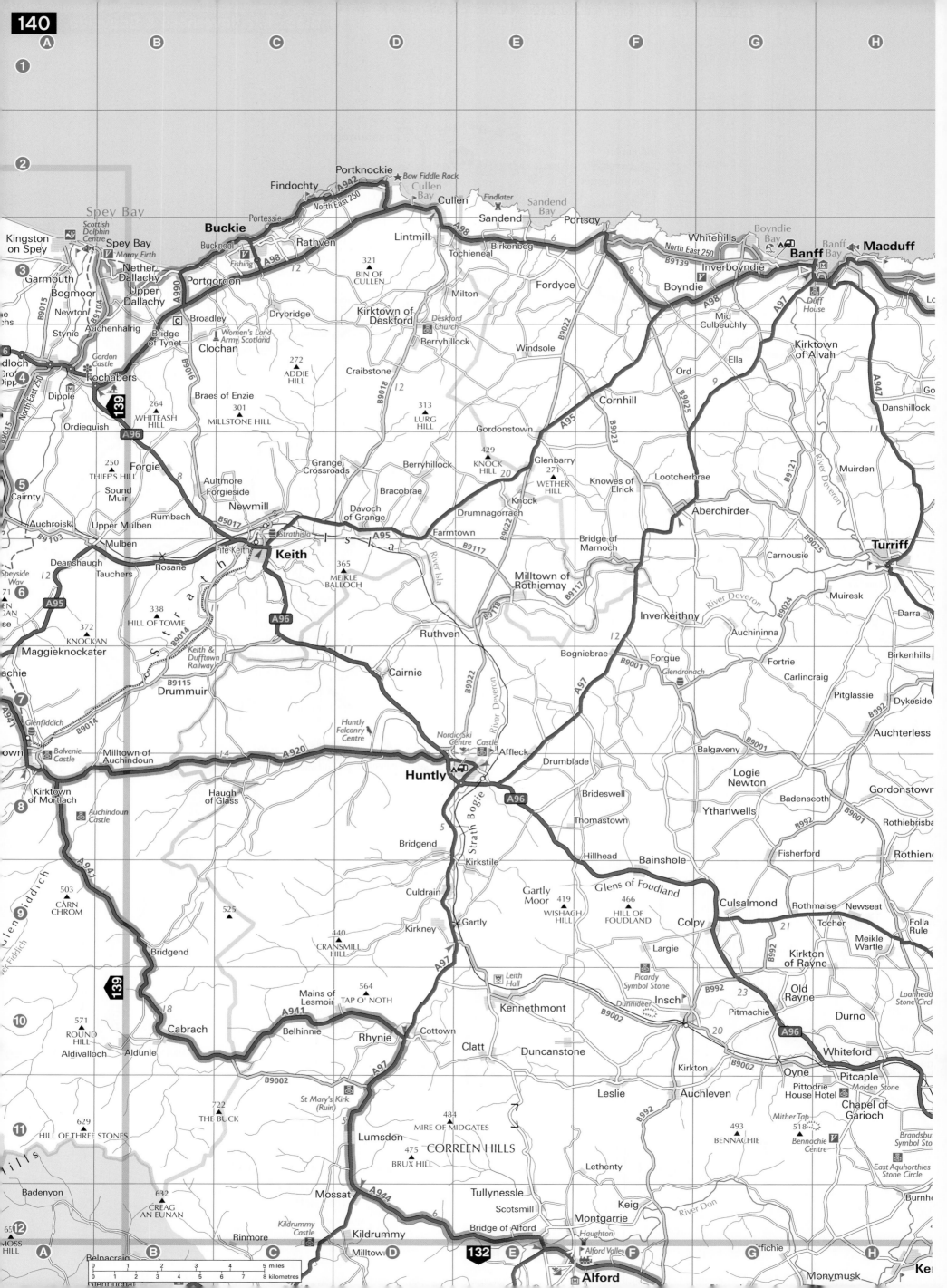

Troup
Head
Cullykhan
Bay
Gamrie Bay
Silverford
Gardenstown
Crovie
Dubford
B9031
Pennan
21
Aberdour Bay
Rosehearty
Pittulie
Sandhaven
Castle, Lighthouse & Museum
Kinnaird Head
Fraserburgh
B9031
Pitsligo
Peathill
Kirktown
Fraserburgh Bay
Maggie's Hoosie
Cairnbulg
Inverallochy
Whitelinks Bay
B9033
longmanhill
Protstonhill
Craigiefold
Percyhorner
Pitblae
A90
B9031
Coburby
Mid Ardlaw
St Combs
B9031
New Aberdour
North East 250
B9032
Boyndlie
Memsie
A98
Clenerty
Tyrie
10
Memsie Cairn
Rathen
Crofts of Savoch
Minnonie
Netherbrae
221
Glasslaw
12
Newburgh
Lonmay
Loch of Strathbeg
Rattray Head
BRACKLAMORE HILL
A981
15
Crudie
A98
B9093
234
WAUGHTON HILL
Strichen
A952
Crimond
Blackhill
North East 250
18
Fintry
New Pitsligo
New Leeds
12
B9105
New Byth
B9093
Leys
Kirktown
St Fergus
Scotstown Head
Garmond
B9027
Bonnykelly
Denhead
Backfolds
A90
Delgatie
Balthangie
Fetterangus
Rora
Cuminestown
A981
A950
Deer Abbey
Dunshillock
13
4
6
B9106
Aden
Mintlaw
Longside
Inverugie
Peterhead
Howe of Teuchar
New Deer
Maud
B9029
Old Deer
A950
Inverquhomery
9
Buchanhaven
Peterhead
B9170
B9029
Railway
Blackhill of Clackriach
Stuartfield
Peterhead
Arbuthnot
B9028
B9170
A948
Drymuir
Bulwark
Millbreck
Nether Kinmundy
Hillhead of Cocklaw
Peterhead Bay
Prison
Invernettie
North Millbrex
Nethermuir
Knaven
B9030
Kinnadie
Clola
Blackhill
Stirling
Boddam
Gourdas
Cottown of Gight
Cairnorrie
Auchnagatt
Kinknockie
Lendrum Terrace
Buchan Ness
A947
Letheny
Brownhill
12
Inkhorn
Ardallie
Longhaven
17
Fyvie Castle
Woodhead
Crofts of Haddo
Coldwells
A952
A90
Auchiries
Bullers of Buchan
Fyvie
Methlick
R Ythan
A948
14
Arthrath
Muirtack
Hatton
North Haven
Barthol Chapel
Earlsford
Haddo House
Ythanbank
Toll of Birness
14
Bogbrae
Chapel Hill
Slains
Cruden Bay
St Katherines
B9005
17
North East 250
A975
Bay of Cruden
Cross of Jackston
Wedderlairs
Auchedly
Birness
Artrochie
Whinnyfold
20
The Skares
Tulloch
Altar Tomb of William Forbes
Kinharrachie
Ellon
P·R
Kirkton of Logie Buchan
Kirktown of Slains
Tarves
Ythsie
Craigdam
Esslemont
Collieston
B999
A920
10
B9005
6
Oldmeldrum
Tolquhon Castle
Pitmedden Garden
Pitmedden
Logierieve
Forvie
Daviot
Glen Garioch
A920
Carnbrogie
Housieside
B9000
A947
Udny Green
B9000
Kirktown of Bourtie
Whiterashes
Woodland
Pettymuk
Udny Station
A90
Newburgh
B9001
Uryside
Tillygreig
Cultercullen
Foveran
A975
Inverurie
B993
Nether Crimond
Straloch
Delfrigs
Garioch
Straloch
Reisque
Causeyend
North East 250
B977
Port Elphinstone
Kinkell Church
Newmachar
Kingseat
Whitecairns
B979
B999
B977
Hatton of Fintray
B979
Kinmundy
B977
Cotha
Balmedie
B993
Thainstone
B977
Dyce Symbol Stones
Balmedie
mnay
B994
Kintore
Don
L
Belhelvie
A90
133
N
Potterton
5

J K L M N P Q R

1 2 3 4 5 6 7 8 9 10 11 12

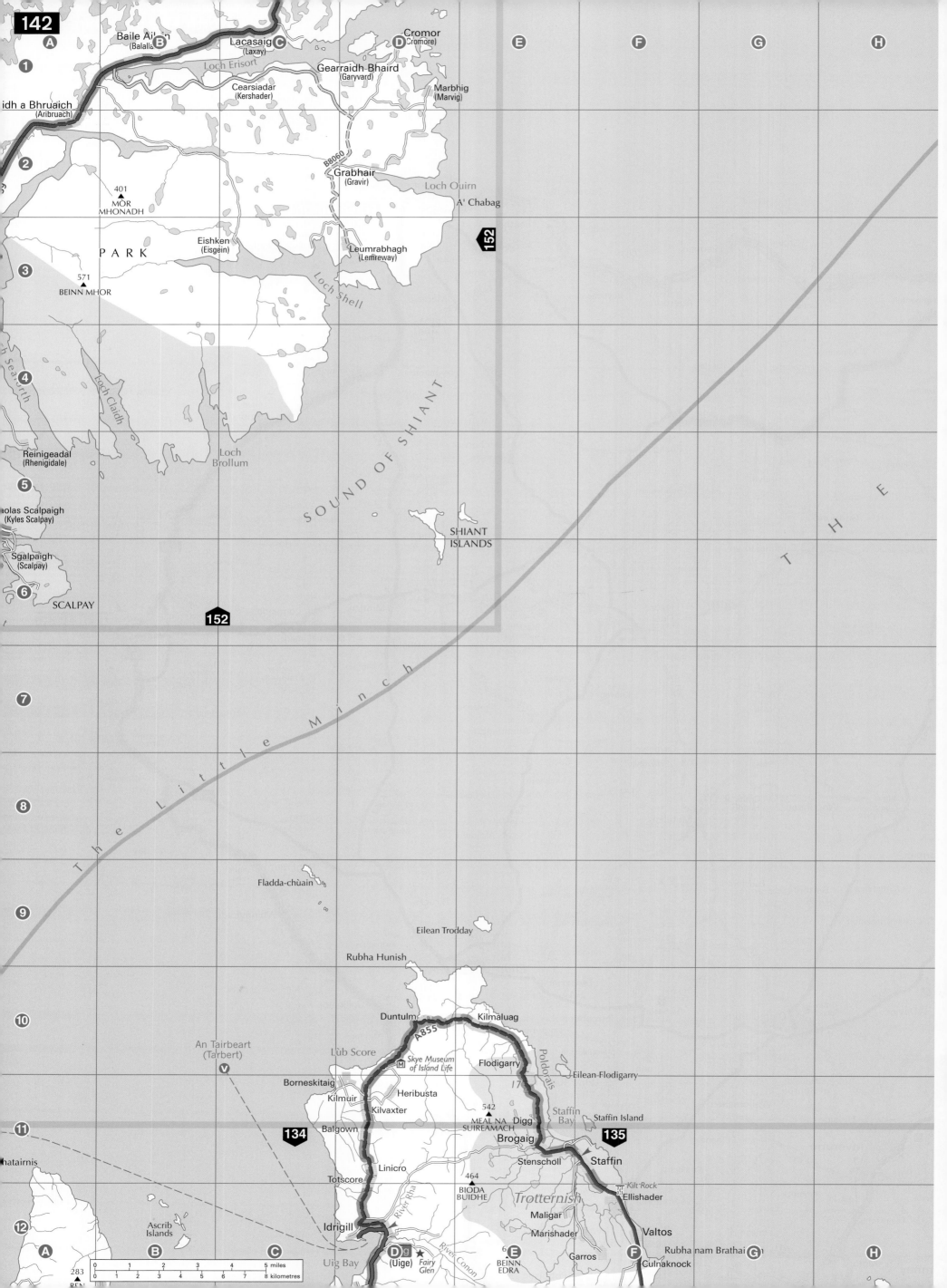

A · B · C · D · E · F · G · H

1

Baile Ailein
(Balallan)
Lacasaig
(Laxay)
Cromor
(Cromore)
Gearraidh Bhaird
(Garyvard)
Loch Erisort
Cearsiadar
(Kershader)
Marbhig
(Marvig)
idh a Bhruaich
(Aribruach)

2
B8060
Grabhair
(Gravir)
Loch Ouirn
401
MOR
MHONADH
A' Chabag
152

3
PARK
Eishken
(Eisgein)
Leumrabhagh
(Lemreway)
571
BEINN MHOR
Loch Shell

4
h Searrth
Loch Claidh
Loch Brollum
SOUND OF SHIANT

5
Reinigeadal
(Rhenigidale)
Loch
Brollum

6
aolas Scalpaigh
(Kyles Scalpay)
Sgalpaigh
(Scalpay)
SCALPAY
SHIANT
ISLANDS
152
T H E

7
The Little Minch

8

9
Fladda-chùain
Eilean Trodday

10
Rubha Hunish
Duntulm
Kilmaluag
An Tairbeart
(Tarbert)
A855
Lùb Score
Skye Museum
of Island Life
Flodigarry
Poldorais
Eilean-Flodigarry

11
Borneskitaig
Kilmuir
Heribusta
Kilvaxter
Balgown
542
MEAL NA
SUIREAMACH
Digg
Brogaig
Stenscholl
Staffin Bay
Staffin Island
Staffin
134
135
hatairnis
Linicro
464
BIODA
BUIDHE
Kilt Rock
Ellishader

12
Totscore
Idrigill
Ascrib
Islands
Uig Bay
(Uige)
Fairy
Glen
River Rha
River Conon
6
BEINN
EDRA
Trotternish
Maligar
Marishader
Garros
Valtos
Rubha nam Brathai
Culnaknock

A · B · C · D g · E · F · G · H

0 1 2 3 4 5 miles
0 1 2 3 4 5 6 7 8 kilometres
283

148

Q

J   K   L   M   N   P   Q   R

Baddidarrach

Inverkirkaig   1

7

Rubha Còigeach

Eilean Mòr   2

Enard Bay

Rubha Mòr

Reiff

Achnahaird

Altandhu   144

Isle Ristol   Polbain   Loch Osgaig   3

Eilean Mullagrach   Badentarbet   Loch Bad a' Ghaill

Glas-leac Mòr   *SUMMER ISLES*   Achiltibuie

Tanera   Beg   Badentarbat Bay   Polglass

Steòrnabhagh V   Tanera Mòr   Ben Mòr Coigach   4

(Stornoway)   Horse Island   Horse Sound   Achduart

Glas-leac Beag   Culnacraig   BEN COI

Eilean Dubh

Priest Island   5

Leac Dhonn   Isle Martin

Annat Bay   R

Greenstone Point   Cailleach Head   6

Scoraig   Ruigh'riabhach

Rubha Beag   635   BEINN GHOBHLACH

Mellon Udrigle   Stattic Point   P   Badluarach   Little Loch Broom

Foura   Achgarve   GRUINARD   A832   Badrallach

Rubha nan Sasan   ISLAND   *Gruinard Bay*   Badcaul   764   North Coast 500   Ardessie   Camus...gaul   7

Rubha Rèidh   Mellon Charles   Laide   Gruinard   SÀIL MHÒR   32

Cove   296   AN CUAIDH   Ormiscaig   Aultbea   70   Gruinard   Lochan Gaineamhaich   Dundonnell

Melvaig   B8057   Loch a'   Little Gruinard River   347   CREAG-MHEAL BEAG   1062   AN TEALLACH   8

Aultgrishin   293   CNOC   ISLE OF EWE   Bhàid-luachraich   Loch Fada   Strathnasheallag Forest

BREAC   Loch Ewe   Inverasdale   681   BEINN A' CHAISGEIN BEAG   Loch na Sealga   9

Naast   250   MEALL NA MEINE   906   BEINN DEARG MHOR

North Erradale   B8021   Inverewe Garden   13   144   Fisherfield Forest   *Wester Ross*

Poolewe   Londubh   Fionn Loch   Dubh Loch   10

Big Sand   A832   791   BEINN AIRIDH CHARR   974   SGÙRRBÀN   1019   MULLACH COIRE MHIC FHEARCHAIR

Smithstown   Strath   Heritage   421   MEALL AN DOIREIN

Longa Island   Lonemore   Auchtercairn   Gairloch & Loch Ewe   Lochan Fada   11

Gairloch   Charlestown   859   BEINN LÀIR   Letterewe Forest   Loch Garbhaig

Loch Gairloch   Eilean Horrisdale   Letterewe   981   SLIOCH

Port Henderson   B8056   River Kerry   Loch Bad an Sgalaig   Loch Maree Islands   Loch Maree

Badachro   Opinan   Victoria Falls   19   A832   12

South Erradale   Talladale   North Coast 500

Red Point   135   136   680   BEINN A' MHÙINIDH   Kinlochewe Forest

Red Point   Loch Ghaineamhach   875   BAOSBHEINN   855   BEINN AN EÒIN   724   Beinn Eighe   Incheril

J   K   L   M   N   P   Q   R

Rubha na Fearn   Loch Torridon   619   BEINN BHREAC   Loch a' Bhealaich   985   Kinlochewe

Loch a' Ghodhainn   Loch na h-Oidhche

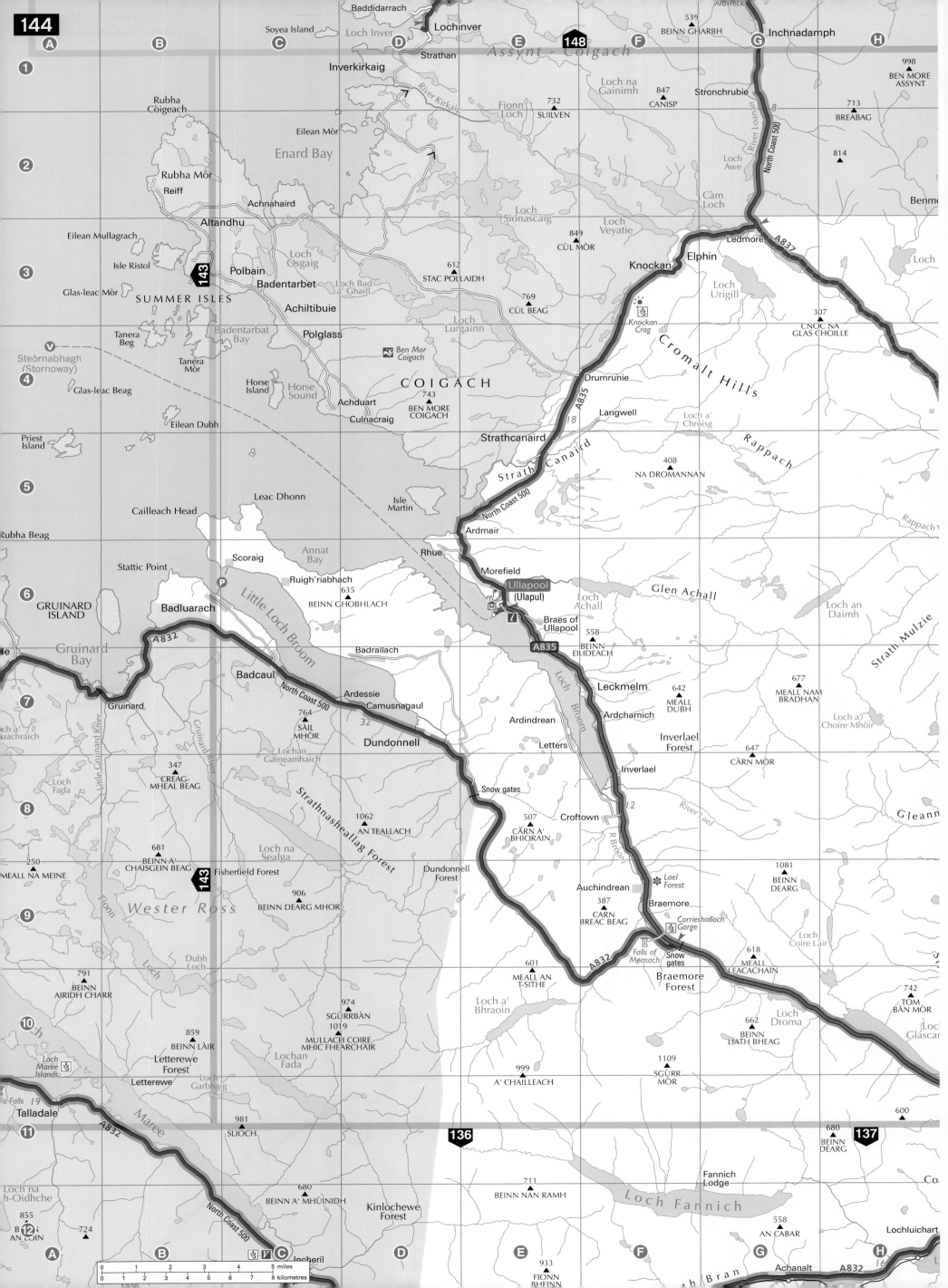

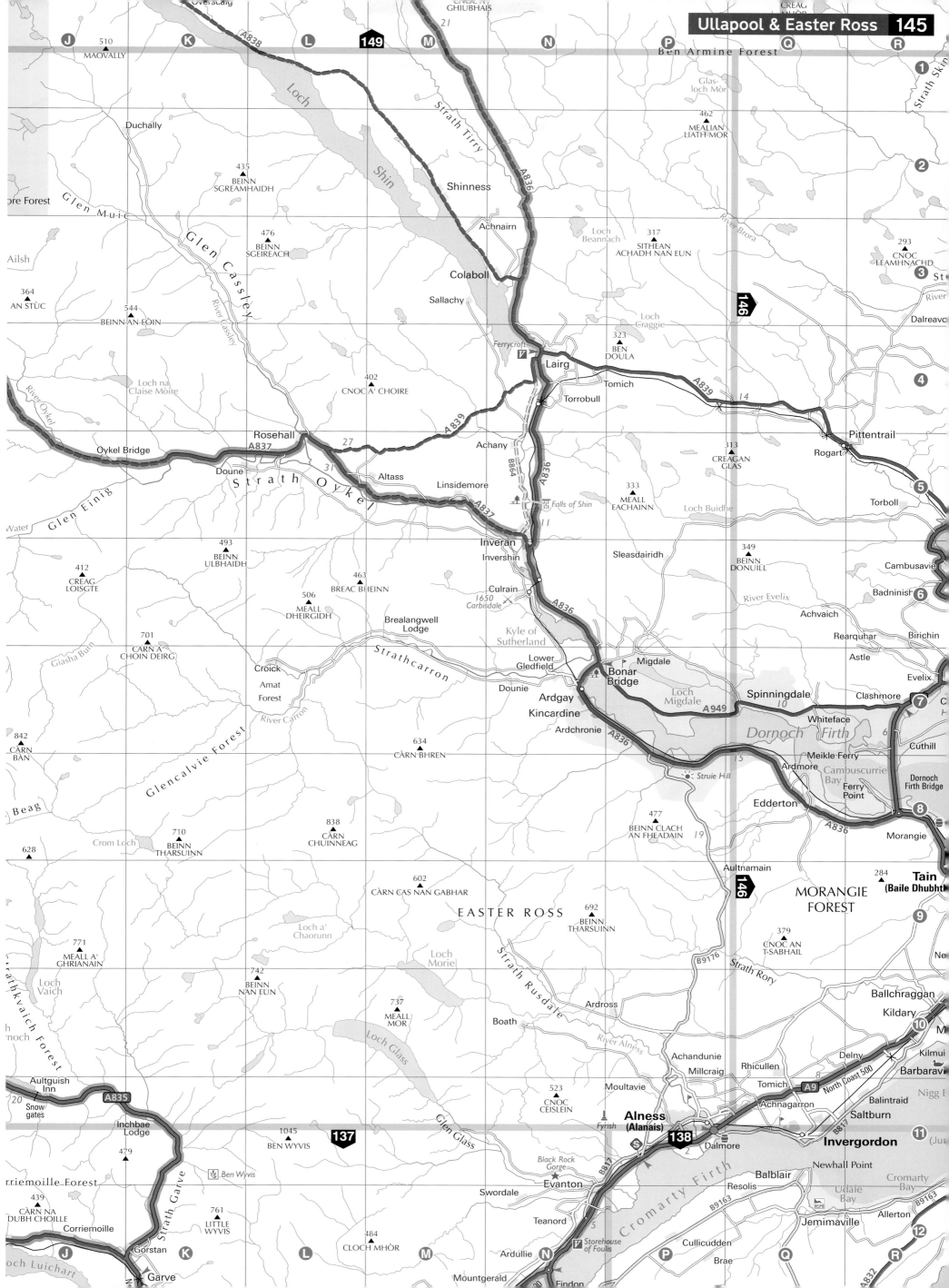

J K L 149 M N P Q R

Ben Armine Forest

510
MAOVALLY

Duchally

Loch Shin

Strath Tirry

Strath Skin

Glas-loch Mòr

462
MEALIAN
LIATH MÒR

Glen Muic

435
BEINN
SGREAMHAIDH

476
BEINN
SGEIREACH

Shinness

Achnairn

Loch
Beannach

317
SITHEAN
ACHADH NAN EUN

River Brora

293
CNOC
LEAMHNACHD

Glen Cassley

Glen Muie

364
AN STÙC

544
BEINN-AN-EÒIN

River Cassley

Loch na
Claise Mòire

402
CNOC A' CHOIRE

Colaboll

Sallachy

Ferrycroft

Lairg

323
BEN
DOULA

Loch
Craggie

146

Dalreavo

River

Ailsh

River Oykel

Oykel Bridge

A837

Rosehall

Doune

27

31

Strath Oykel

Altass

Achany

Torrobull

A839

Linsidemore

B864

A836

A837

Falls of Shin

11

Tomich

A839

14

313
CREAGAN
GLAS

Pittentrail

Rogart

5

Torboll

Glen Einig

Glen Einig

Water

412
CREAG
LOISGTE

493
BEINN
ULBHAIDH

463
BREAC BHEINN

506
MEALL
DHEIRGIDH

1650
Carbisdale

Culrain

Inveran

Invershin

Sleasdairidh

349
BEINN
DONUILL

Cambusavie

Badninish

Achvaich

River Evelix

Rearquhar

Birichin

Astle

6

Giasha Burn

701
CARN A'
CHOIN DEIRG

Brealangwell
Lodge

Strathcarron

Kyle of
Sutherland

Lower
Gledfield

Migdale

Bonar
Bridge

Loch
Migdale

A949

Spinningdale

10

Clashmore

Evelix

7

Glencalvie Forest

Croick

Amat
Forest

River Carron

Dounie

Ardgay

Kincardine

Ardchronie

A836

Whiteface

Dornoch Firth

Meikle Ferry

Cuthill

Beag

842
CÀRN
BÀN

634
CÀRN BHREN

15

Struie Hill

Ardmore

Cambuscurrie
Bay

Dornoch
Firth Bridge

8

628

710
BEINN
THARSUINN

838
CÀRN
CHUINNEAG

477
BEINN CLACH
AN FHEADAIN

19

Edderton

Ferry
Point

Morangie

A836

Cром Loch

602
CÀRN CAS NAN GABHAR

EASTER ROSS

692
BEINN
THARSUINN

Aultnamain

146

MORANGIE
FOREST

284
▲

Tain
(Baile Dhubht

771
MEALL A'
GHRIANAIN

Loch a'
Chaorunn

Loch
Morie

379
CNOC AN
T-SABHAIL

9

rathkvaich Forest

Loch
Vaich

742
BEINN
NAN EUN

737
MEALL
MÒR

Strath Rusdale

Ardross

Boath

River Alness

Strath Rory

B9176

Ballchraggan

Kildary

10

noch Forest

A835

Aultguish
Inn

Snow
gates

Inchbae
Lodge

479

137

1045
BEN WYVIS

Ben Wyvis

523
CNOC
CEISLEIN

Glen Glass

Moultavie

Achandunie

Millcraig

Rhicullen

Fyrish

Alness
(Alanais)

138

Tomich

A9

North Coast 500

Achnagarron

8

Delny

Kilmui

Barbarav

Invergordon

11

riemoille Forest

439
CÀRN NA
DUBH CHOILLE

Strath Garve

761
LITTLE
WYVIS

484
CLOCH MHÒR

Black Rock
Gorge

Swordale

Teanord

Evanton

Storehouse
of Foulis

Dalmore

2

Balblair

B817

Resolis

Newhall Point

B9163

Cromarty
Bay

Udale
Bay

Allerton

Corriemoille

Gorstan

Garve

och Luichart

J K L M Ardullie N Findon Brae Cullicudden P Mountgerald Q Jemimaville R 12

Balintraid

Saltburn

Cromarty Firth

Nigg B

CAPE WRATH

Kearvaig
Bay

Cléit
Dhubh

371
SGRIBHIS-
BHEINN

297
CNOC A'
GHIUBHAIS

300
MAOVALLY

THE PARPH

457
FASHVEN

Loch Àirigh
na Beinne

(May-Sept

P   Ke

Sandwood
Bay

Sandwood
Loch

485
CREAG
RIABHACH

467
AN GRIANAN

464
MEALL
NA MÒINE

331
GHLAS-
BHEINN

Rubh' an Fhir Lèithe

Sheigra

Balchrick   Blairmore

Oldshoremore

355
AN
SOCACH

521
FARRMHEALL

19

773
BEINN
SPIONNAIDH

Kinlochbervie   Badcall

801
CRANSTACKIE

Loch Clash   Achriesgill

B801

North Coast 500

Achlyness

Rhiconich

Loch na
Claise Càrnaich

Rubha Ruadh

Skerricha

Loch Laxford

A838

Strath Dionard

River Dionard

908
FOINAVEN

Fanagmore

Tarbet

Foindle

North-west Sutherland

Loch na Tuadh

HANDA
ISLAND

7

786
ARKLE

Scourie Bay

Scourie

A894

Laxford
Bridge

River Laxford

Loch
Stack

729
SÀBHAL

Scourie More

Upper
Badcall

Lower
Badcall

721
BEN STACK

Badcall
Bay

Loch a'
Mhuilinn

386
BEN
AUSKAIRD

Strath Stack

Achfary

333
BEN
SCREAVIE

800

CÀ
DE

Rubh' a'
Mhucard

North Coast 500

17

A838

Loch More

Point of Stoer

OLDANY
ISLAND

Eddrachillis
Bay

Locha Chàirn Bhàin

419
BEN
STROME

Loch an
Leathaid Bhuain

Kinloch

Old Man
of Stoer

Culkein

Clashnessie
Bay

Culkein
Drumbeg

Kylestrome

Kylesku

Glendhu Forest

Clashmore

Oldany

Drumbeg

B869

Unapool
The Rock Stop

Loch Glendhu

525
BEINN AIRD
DA LOCH

613
MEALL AN FHEUR LO

Achnacarnin

Nedd

Loch
Poll

Glen Leirg

Loch an
Leothaid

776
SAIL
GHORM

Loch
Glencoul

792
BEINN LEOID

Clashnessie

809
QUINAG

Loch na
Gainmhich

Loch Beag

Eas a' Chùal Aluinn

Stoer

B869

North Coast 500

Loch
Beannach

A894

774
GLAS BHEINN

Clachtoll

Rhicarn

11

Bay of Clachtoll

Achmelvich
Bay

A837

Loch Assynt

Achmelvich

Baddidarrach

Lochinver

Ardvreck

539
BEINN GHARBH

Inchnadamph

Soyea Island

Loch Inver

Strathan

Assynt - Coigach

Inverkiri

0   1   2   3   4   5 miles
0   1   2   3   4   5   6   7   8 kilometres

Loch na
Gainimh

847

Stronchrubie

998
BEN MORE
ASSYNT

MAO

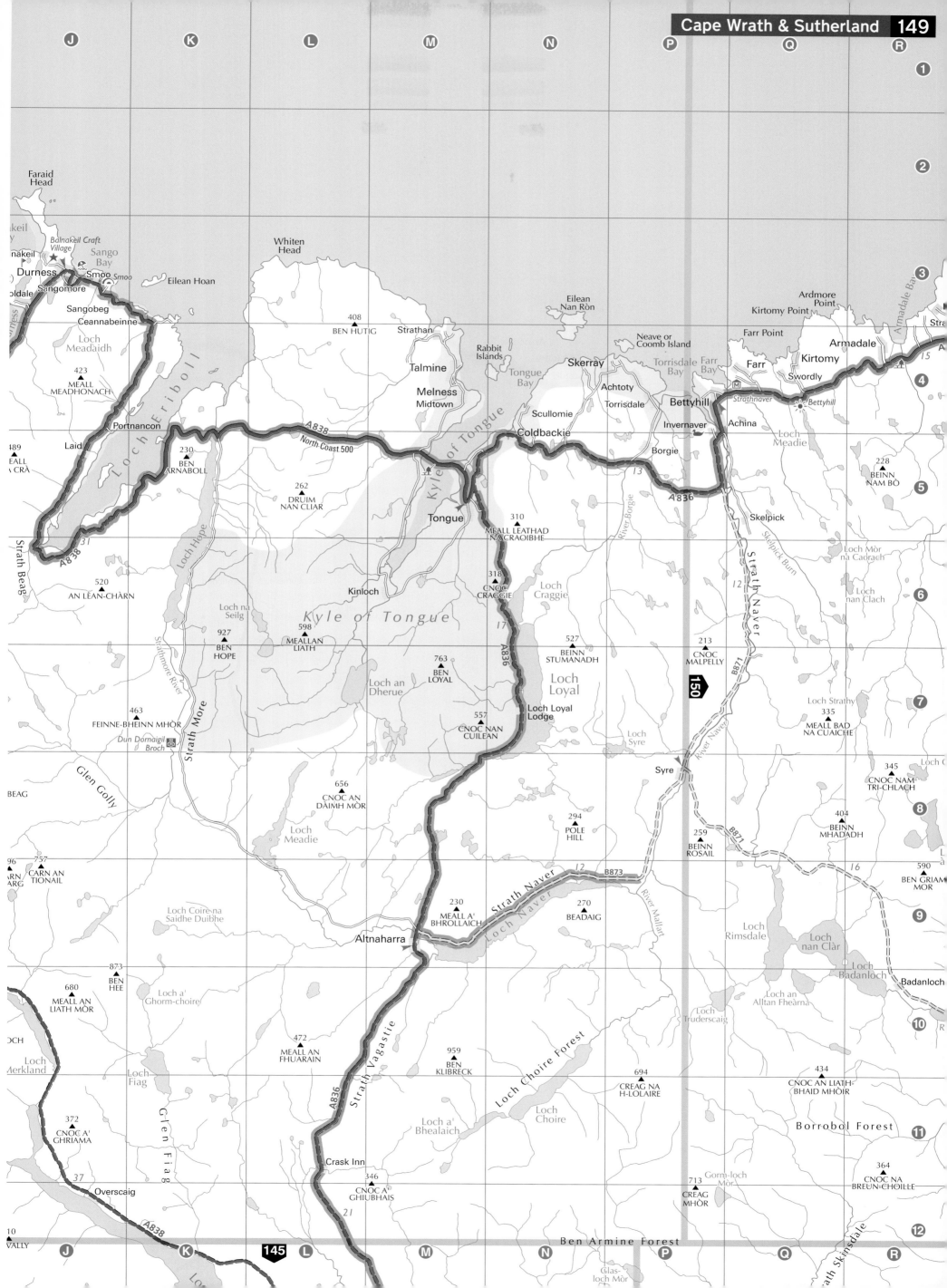

J K L M N P Q R
1
2

Faraid
Head

Balnakeil Craft
Village
Balnakeil   Sango
Bay   Whiten
Head

Durness   Sango
Smoo Smoo   Eilean Hoan
Sangomore
oldale
Sangobeg
Ceannabeinne

Loch
Meadaidh   408   Strathan
BEN HUTIG   Eilean
Nan Ròn
Rabbit   Neave or
Islands   Coomb Island
3
Ardmore
Point
Kirtomy Point
423   Talmine   Skerray   Torrisdale Farr
MEALL   Farr   Bay
MEADHONACH   Melness   Achtoty   Farr   Armadale
Midtown   Tongue   Kirtomy   Stra
Portnancon   Bay   Scullomie   Bettyhill   Swordly
A838   Torrisdale   Strathnaver   Bettyhill   4
489   North Coast 500   Coldbackie   Invernaver   Achina
EALL   Laid   230   13   Borgie   Loch   228
A CRÀ   BEN   A836   Skelpick   Meadie   BEINN   5
ARNABOLL   NAM BÒ
262   310
DRUIM   MEALL LEATHAD   Loch Mòr
NAN CLIAR   NA CRAOIBHE   na Caorach
Tongue
Strath Beag   Kinloch   318   Loch   Loch   6
CNOC   Craggie   nan Clach
A838   520   CRAGGIE   12
AN LEAN-CHÀRN   Kyle of Tongue   17   527   213
598   BEINN   CNOC   Loch Strathy
927   MEALLAN   STUMANADH   MALPELLY   335
BEN   LIATH   763   MEALL BAD   7
HOPE   BEN   Loch   150   NA CUAICHE
LOYAL   Loyal   B871
463   Loch an   Loch
FEINNE-BHEINN MHÒR   Dherue   557   Syre   345
CNOC NAN   Loch Loyal   CNOC NAM
Dun Dòrnaigil   CUILEAN   Lodge   TRI-CHLACH
Broch   8
404
Syre   259   BEINN
656   BEINN   MHADADH
Glen Golly   CNOC AN   ROSAIL   B871
BEAG   DÀIMH MÒR   294   16   590
Loch   POLE   BEN GRIAM
Meadie   HILL   MÒR   9
12   B873
96   757   230   270
RN   CARN AN   MEALL A'   Strath Naver   BEADAIG   Loch
ARG   TIONAIL   BHROLLAICH   Loch Naver   Rimsdale   Loch
Loch Coire na   River Mallart   nan Clàr
Saidhe Duibhe   Altnaharra   Loch
Badanloch   10
873   680   Loch an   Badanloch
BEN   MEALL AN   Loch a'   Alltan Fhearna
HEE   LIATH MÒR   Ghorm-choire   Loch
OCH   Truderscaig
Loch   472   11
Merkland   MEALL AN   959   694
Loch   FHUARAIN   BEN   CREAG NA   CNOC AN LIATH-
Fiag   A836   KLIBRECK   H-LOLAIRE   BHAID MHÒR
Glen Fiag   Strath Vagastie   Loch a'   Loch   Borrobol Forest
372   Bhealaich   Choire
CNOC A'   Loch   11
GHRIAMA   Choire   364
37   Crask Inn   713   CNOC NA
Overscaig   346   Gorm-loch   CREAG   BREUN-CHOILLE
A838   CNOC A'   Mòr   MHÒR
VALLY   GHIUBHAIS   21   Ben Armine Forest   12
10
J   K   145   L   M   N   P   Q   R
Glas-
loch Mòr

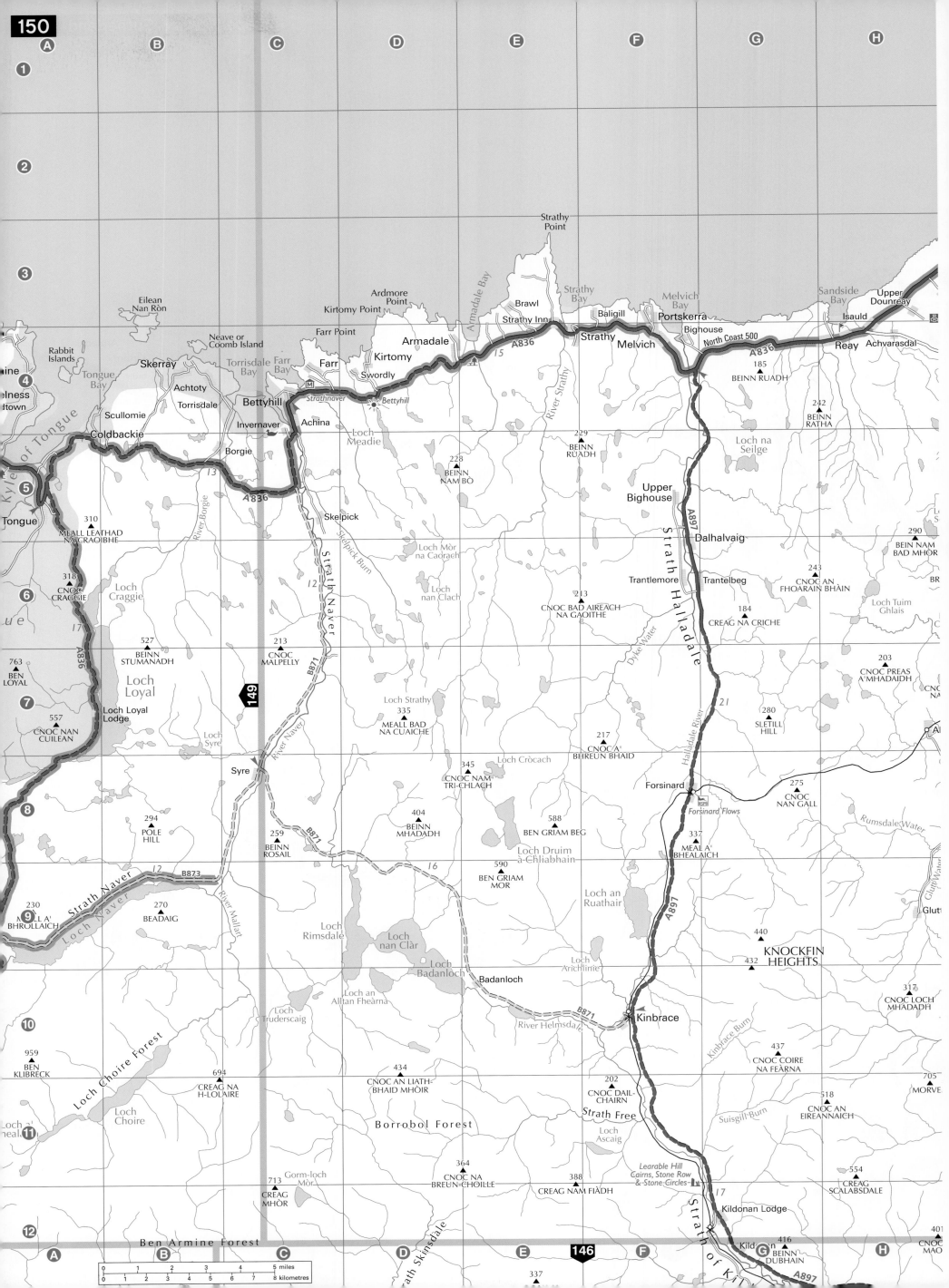

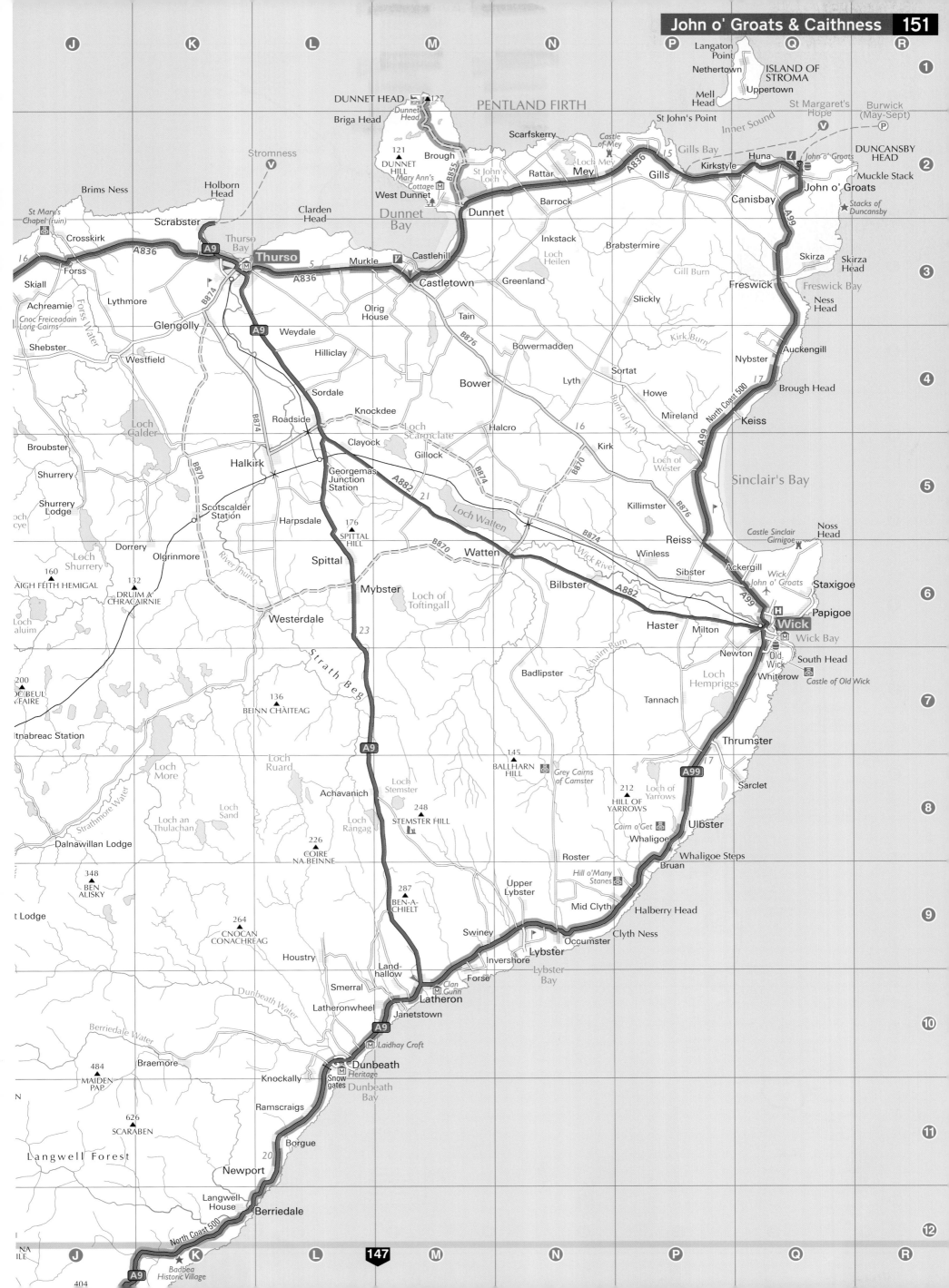

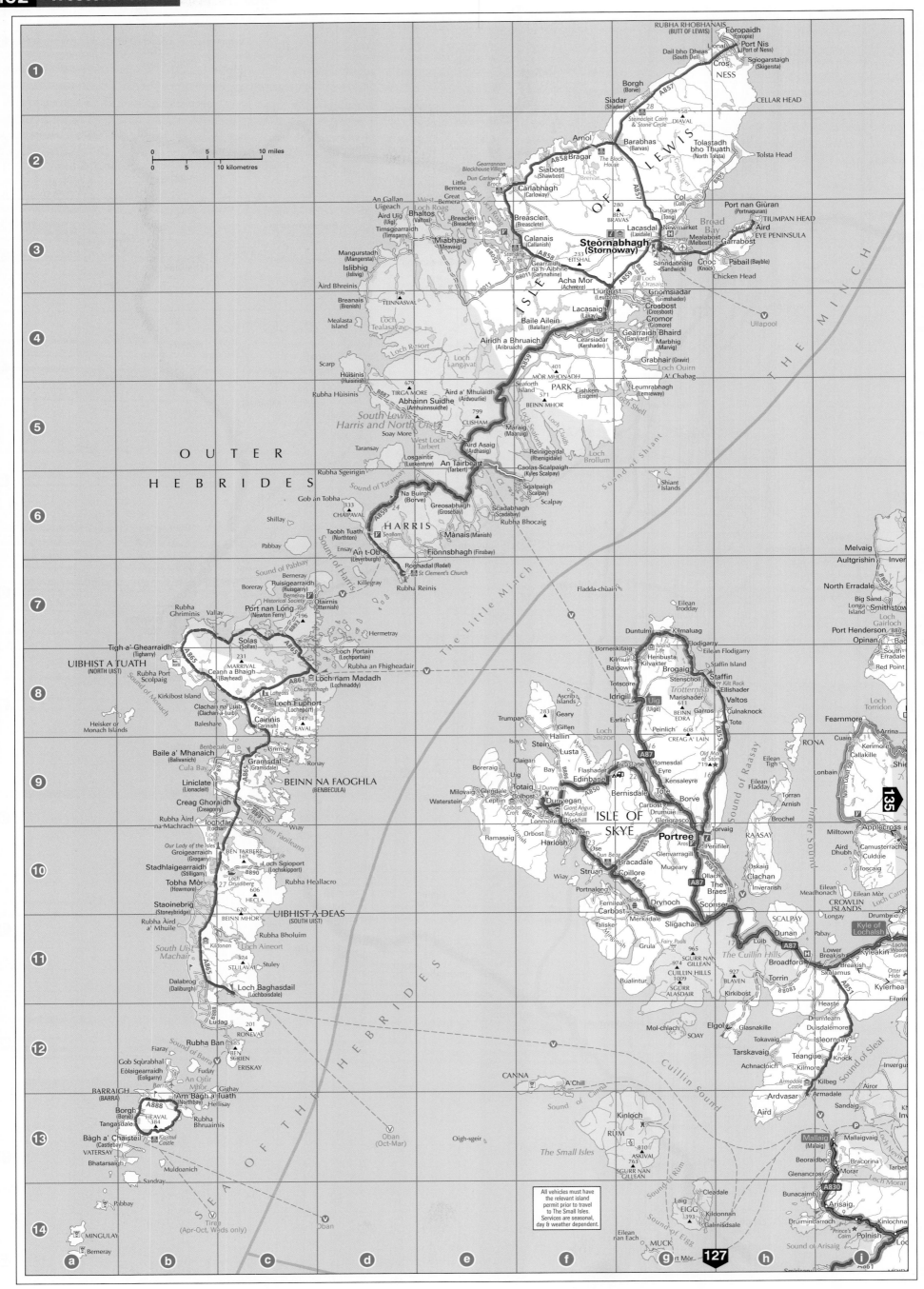

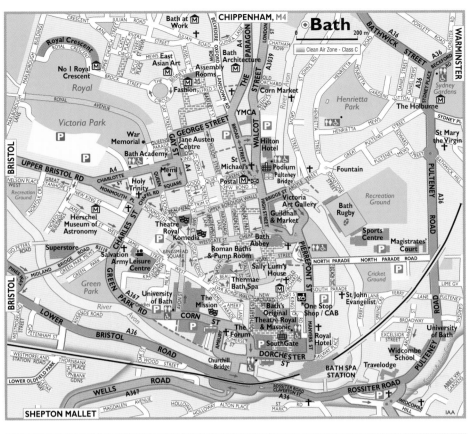

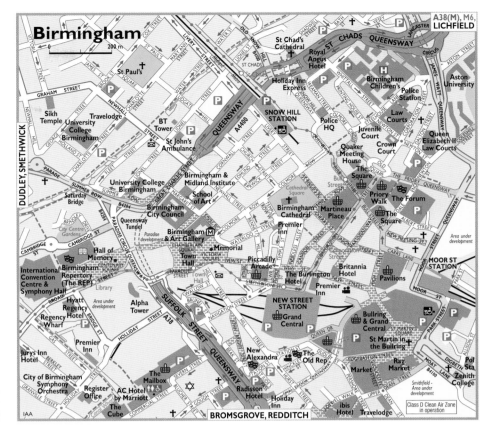

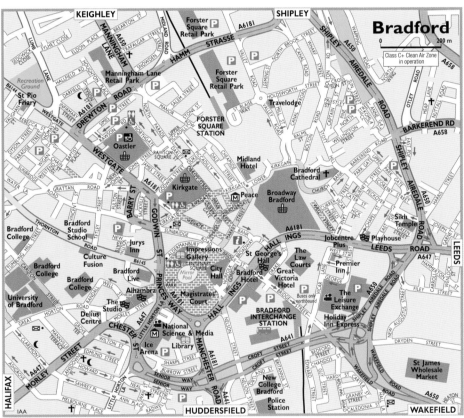

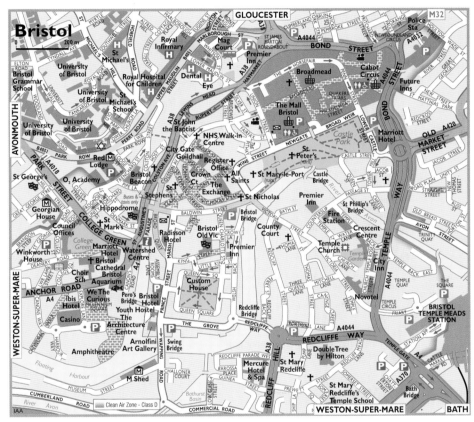

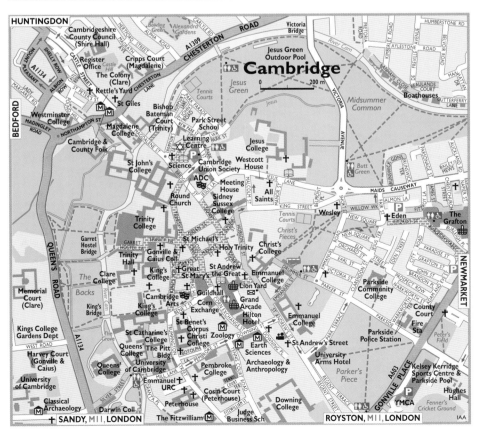

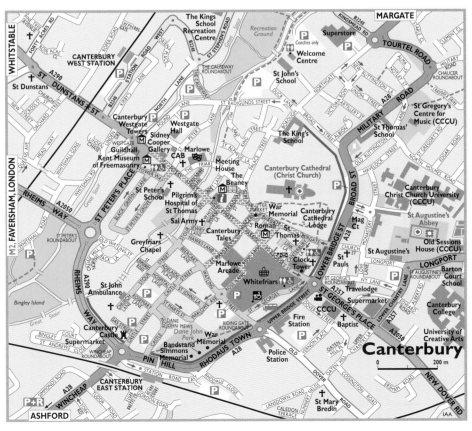

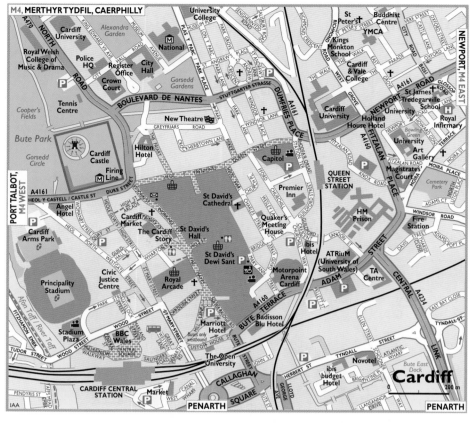

Cardiff

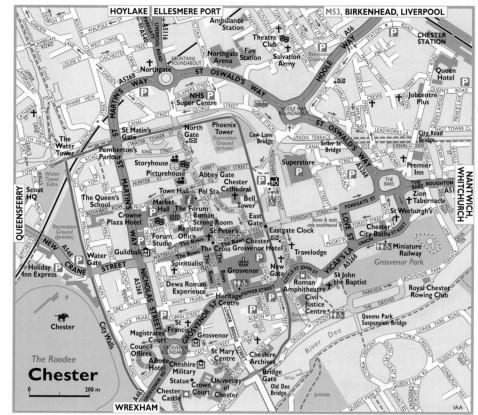

Chester

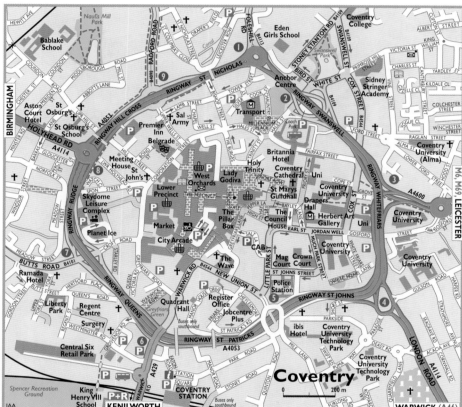

Coventry

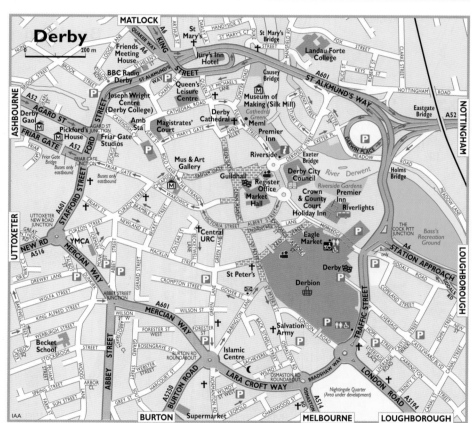

Derby

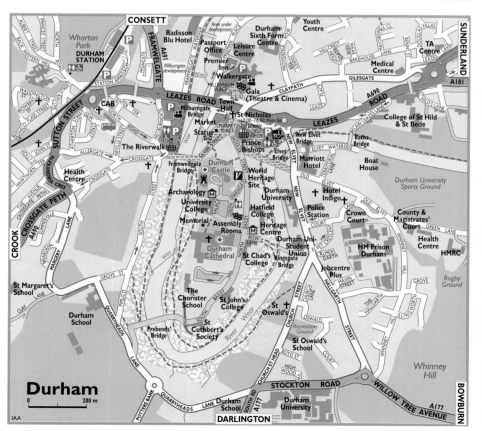

Durham

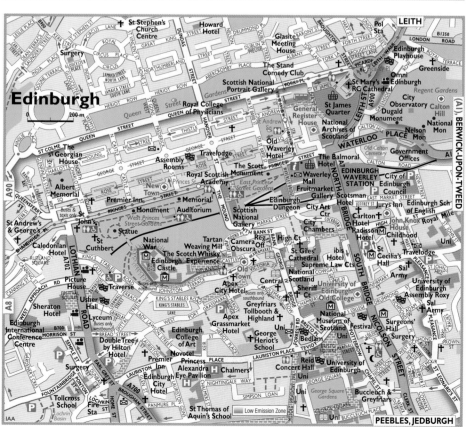

Edinburgh

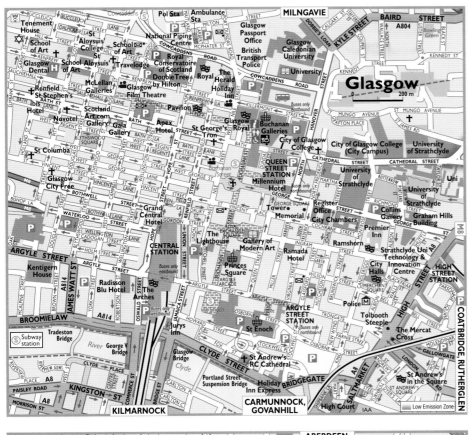

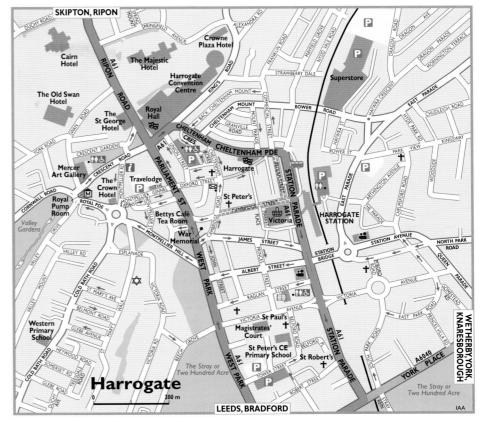

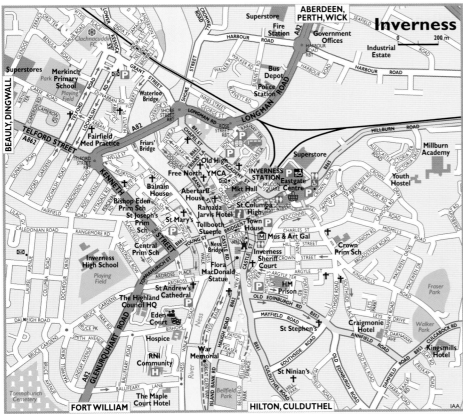

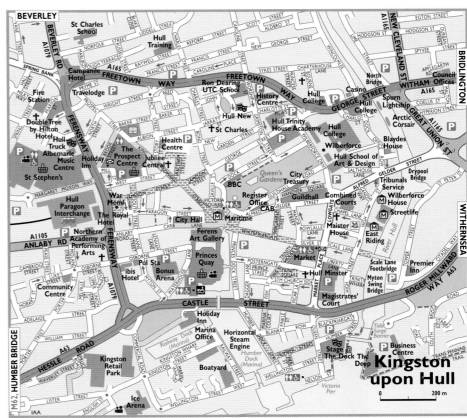

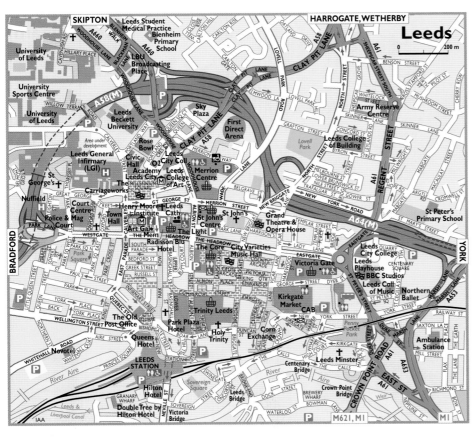

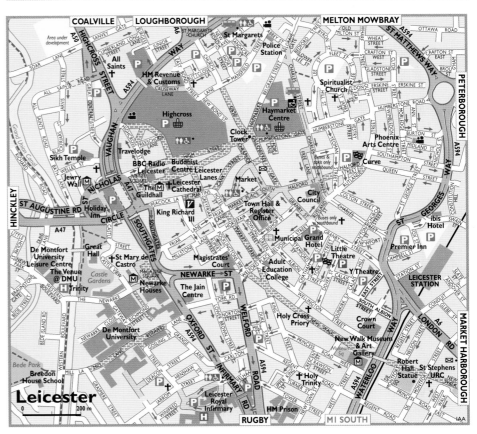

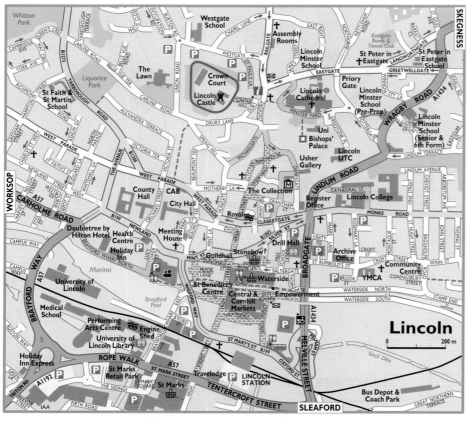

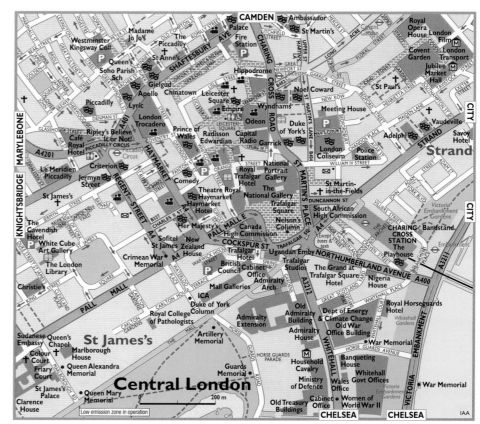

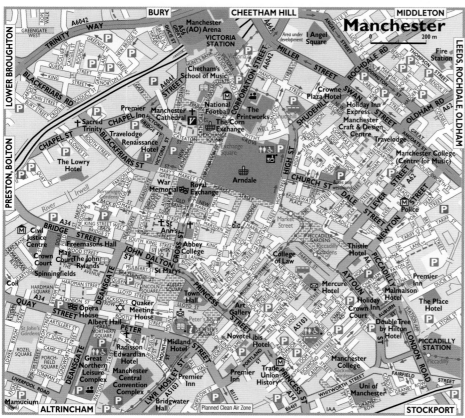

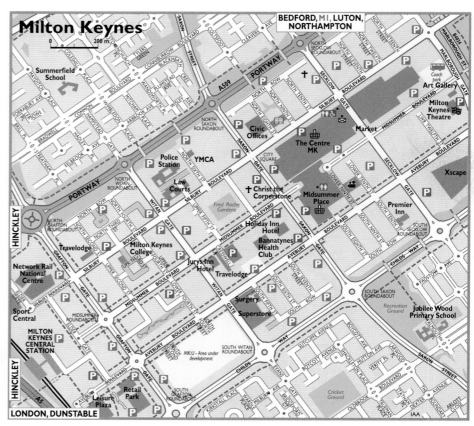

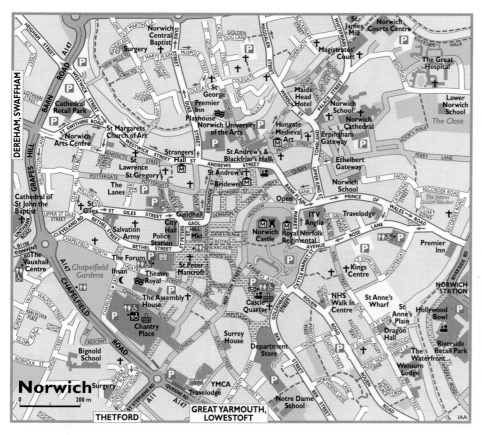

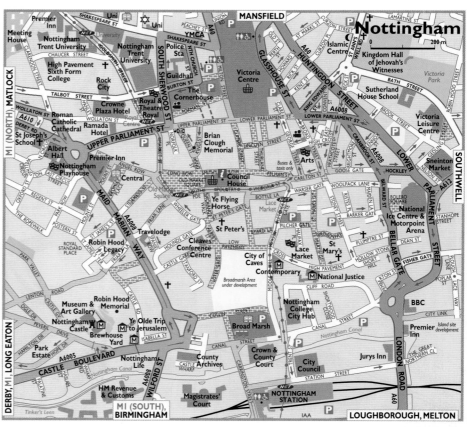

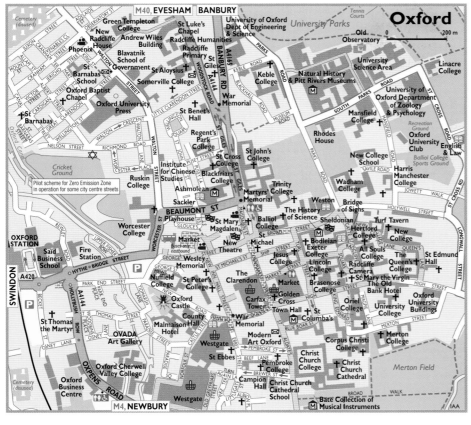

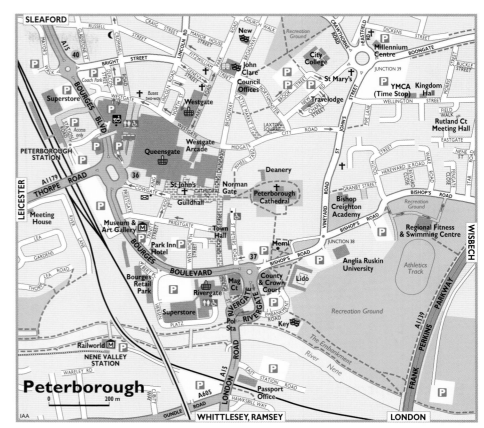

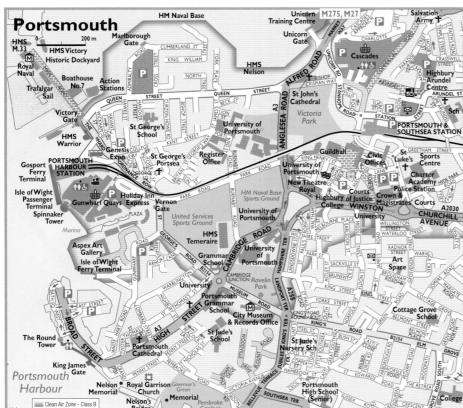

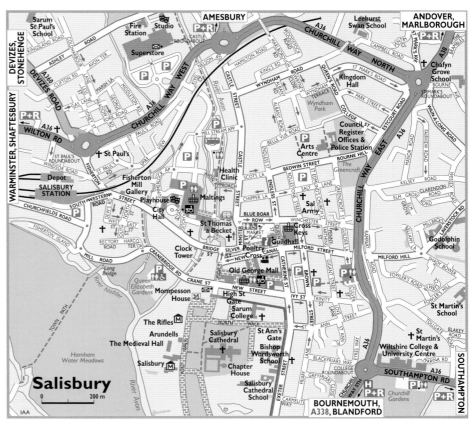

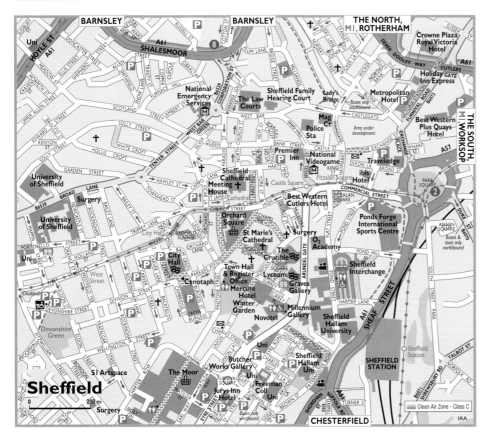

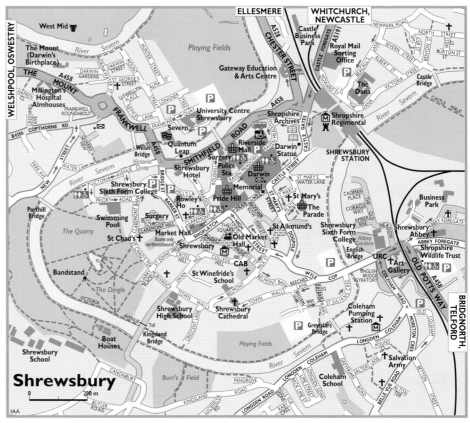

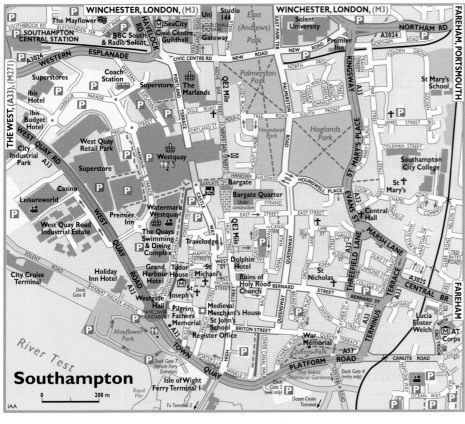

Southampton

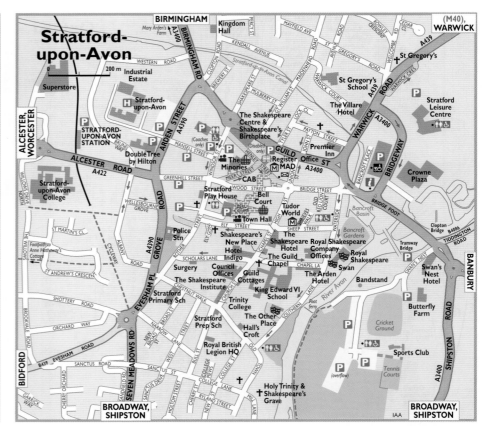

Stratford-upon-Avon

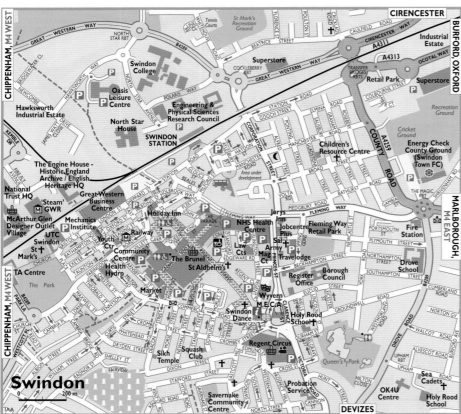

Swindon

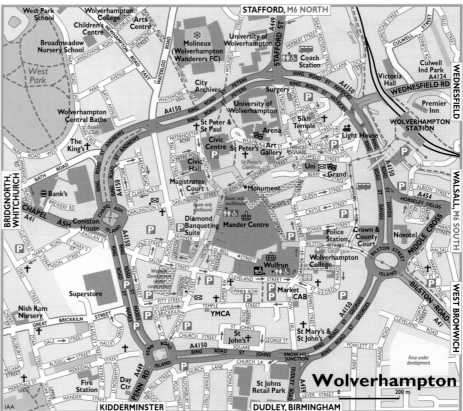

Wolverhampton

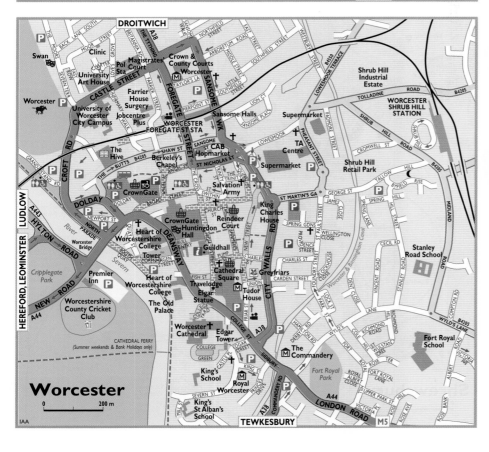

Worcester

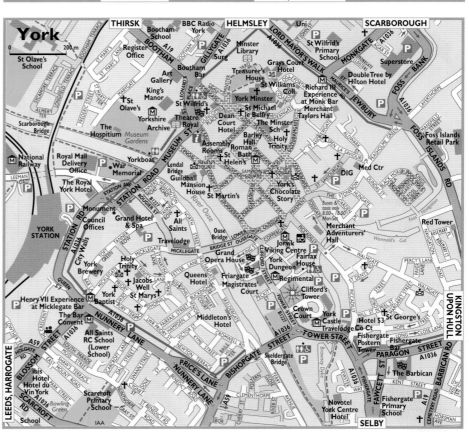

York

ENGLAND

- Acorn Bank Garden CA10 1SP Cumb 89 Q1
- Aldborough Roman Site YO51 9ES N York 82 N2
- Alfriston Clergy House BN26 5TL E Susx 15 P10
- Alton Towers ST10 4DB Staffs 65 K3
- Anglesey Abbey CB25 9EJ Cambs 57 K8
- Anne Hathaway's Cottage CV37 9HH Warwks 53 M9
- Antony House PL11 2QA Cnwll 4 F5
- Appuldurcombe House PO38 3EW IoW 13 J9
- Apsley House W1J 7NT Gt Lon 33 K6
- Arlington Court EX31 4LP Devon 19 M5
- Ascott LU7 0PS Bucks 44 C7
- Ashby-de-la-Zouch Castle LE65 1BR Leics 66 B9
- Athelhampton House & Gardens DT2 7LG Dorset 11 J6
- Attingham Park SY4 4TP Shrops 63 P10
- Audley End House & Gardens CB11 4JF Essex 45 P4
- Avebury SN8 1RD Wilts 30 C8
- Baconsthorpe Castle NR25 6LN Norfk 70 G4
- Baddesley Clinton Hall B93 0DQ Warwks 53 M6
- Bamburgh Castle NE69 7DF Nthumb 109 K3
- Barnard Castle DL12 8PR Dur 90 H3
- Barrington Court TA19 0NQ Somset 21 N9
- Basildon Park RG8 9NR W Berk 31 M7
- Bateman's TN19 7DS E Susx 16 B6
- Battle of Britain Memorial Flight Visitor Centre LN4 4SY Lincs 80 E12
- Beamish - The Living Museum of the North DH9 0RG Dur 100 G7
- Beatrix Potter Gallery LA22 0NS Cumb 89 K7
- Beaulieu (National Motor Museum/Palace House) SO42 7ZN Hants 12 F4
- Belton House NG32 2LS Lincs 67 M4
- Belvoir Castle NG32 1PE Leics 67 K5
- Bembridge Windmill PO35 5SQ IoW 13 L7
- Beningbrough Hall YO30 1DD N York 85 Q3
- Benthall Hall TF12 5RX Shrops 64 C11
- Berkeley Castle GL13 9PJ Gloucs 29 L3
- Berrington Hall HR6 0DW Herefs 51 N8
- Berry Pomeroy Castle TQ9 6LJ Devon 5 P4
- Beth Chatto's Plants & Gardens CO7 7DB Essex 47 J7
- Biddulph Grange Garden ST8 7SD Staffs 76 G11
- Bishop's Waltham Palace SO32 1DH Hants 25 J10
- Blackpool Zoo FY3 8PP Bpool 82 H8
- Blenheim Palace OX20 1PX Oxon 43 J8
- Bletchley Park Museum MK3 6EB M Keyn 44 B5
- Blickling Estate NR11 6NF Norfk 70 H6
- Blue John Cavern S33 8WA Derbys 77 L7
- Bodiam Castle TN32 5UA E Susx 16 D6
- Bolsover Castle S44 6PR Derbys 78 D9
- Boscobel House and The Royal Oak ST19 9AR Staffs 64 F10
- Bowes Castle DL12 9LD Dur 90 G4
- Bradford Industrial Museum BD2 3HP W Yorks 85 J8
- Bradley TQ12 6BN Devon 8 F10
- Bramber Castle BN44 3WW W Susx 14 H8
- Brinkburn Priory NE65 8AR Nthumb 109 J10
- Brockhampton WR6 5TB Herefs 52 C9
- Brough Castle CA17 4EJ Cumb 90 C4
- Buckfast Abbey TQ11 0EE Devon 5 M3
- Buckingham Palace SW1A 1AA Gt Lon 33 K6
- Buckland Abbey PL20 6EY Devon 4 G3
- Buscot Park SN7 8BU Oxon 30 F3
- Byland Abbey YO61 4BD N York 92 B11
- Cadbury World B30 1JR Birm 53 K4
- Calke Abbey DE73 7LE Derbys 66 B7
- Canons Ashby NN11 3SD Nhants 54 F10
- Canterbury Cathedral CT1 2EH Kent 35 L10
- Carisbrooke Castle PO30 1XY IoW 12 H7
- Carlyle's House SW3 5HL Gt Lon 33 K7
- Castle Drogo EX6 6PB Devon 8 D7
- Castle Howard YO60 7DA N York 86 D1
- Castle Rising Castle PE31 6AH Norfk 69 M7
- Charlecote Park CV35 9ER Warwks 53 N9
- Chartwell TN16 1PS Kent 33 N12
- Chastleton GL56 0SU Oxon 42 F6
- Chatsworth DE45 1PP Derbys 77 N9
- Chedworth Roman Villa GL54 3LJ Gloucs 42 B9
- Chessington World of Adventures KT9 2NE Gt Lon 32 H10
- Chester Cathedral CH1 2HU Ches W 75 L10
- Chester Zoo CH2 1EU Ches W 75 L9
- Chesters Roman Fort & Museum NE46 4EU Nthumb 99 P4
- Children's Country House at Sudbury DE6 5HT Derbys 65 M6
- Chiswick House & Gardens W4 2RP Gt Lon 32 H7
- Chysauster Ancient Village TR20 8XA Cnwll 2 D7
- Claremont Landscape Garden KT10 9JG Surrey 32 G9
- Claydon MK18 2EY Bucks 43 P6
- Cleeve Abbey TA23 0PS Somset 20 G5
- Clevedon Court BS21 6QU N Som 28 F8
- Cliveden SL6 0JA Bucks 32 C5
- Clouds Hill BH20 7NQ Dorset 11 K6
- Clumber Park S80 3AZ Notts 78 G8
- Colchester Zoo CO3 0SL Essex 46 G7
- Coleridge Cottage TA5 1NQ Somset 21 K5
- Coleton Fishacre TQ6 0EQ Devon 5 Q6
- Compton Castle TQ3 1TA Devon 5 P4
- Conisbrough Castle DN12 3BU Donc 78 E4
- Corbridge Roman Town NE45 5NT Nthumb 100 C5
- Corfe Castle BH20 5EZ Dorset 11 M8
- Corsham Court SN13 0BZ Wilts 29 P8
- Cotehele PL12 6TA Cnwll 4 F3
- Cotswold Wildlife Park & Gardens OX18 4JP Oxon 42 F10
- Coughton Court B49 5JA Warwks 53 K8
- Courts Garden BA14 6RR Wilts 29 P10
- Cragside NE65 7PX Nthumb 108 H9
- Crealy Theme Park & Resort EX5 1DR Devon 9 J7
- Crich Tramway Village DE4 5DP Derbys 65 Q1
- Croft Castle HR6 9PW Herefs 51 M7
- Croome WR8 9DW Worcs 41 P3
- Deddington Castle OX15 0TE Oxon 43 K5
- Didcot Railway Centre OX11 7NJ Oxon 31 L4
- Dover Castle CT16 1HU Kent 17 P2
- Drayton Manor Resort B78 3SA Staffs 65 M12
- Dudmaston WV15 6QN Shrops 52 D3
- Dunham Massey WA14 4SJ Traffd 76 D6
- Dunstanburgh Castle NE66 3TT Nthumb 109 L5
- Dunster Castle & Watermill TA24 6SL Somset 20 F5
- Durham Cathedral DH1 3EH Dur 100 H10
- Duxford IWM CB22 4QR Cambs 45 N3
- Dyrham Park SN14 8HY S Glos 29 L7
- East Riddlesden Hall BD20 5EL Brad 84 G7
- Eden Project PL24 2SG Cnwll 3 P4
- Eltham Palace & Gardens SE9 5QE Gt Lon 33 M7
- Emmetts Garden TN14 6BA Kent 33 N12
- Exmoor Zoo EX31 4SG Devon 19 M5
- Farleigh Hungerford Castle BA2 7RS Somset 29 N10
- Farnborough Hall OX17 1DU Warwks 54 C10
- Felbrigg Hall Gardens & Estate NR11 8PR Norfk 71 J4
- Fenton House & Garden NW3 6SP Gt Lon 33 J5
- Finch Foundry EX20 2NW Devon 8 C6
- Finchale Priory DH1 5SH Dur 100 H9
- Fishbourne Roman Palace PO19 3QR W Susx 13 P4
- Flamingo Land Resort YO17 6UX N York 92 F10
- Forde Abbey House & Gardens TA20 4LU Somset 9 Q4
- Fountains Abbey & Studley Royal HG4 3DY N York 85 K1
- Gawthorpe Hall BB12 8UA Lancs 84 B8
- Gisborough Priory TS14 6HG R & Cl 92 C3
- Glendurgan Garden TR11 5JZ Cnwll 3 J9
- Goodrich Castle HR9 6HY Herefs 41 J7
- Great Chalfield Manor & Garden SN12 8NH Wilts 29 P9
- Great Coxwell Barn SN7 7LZ Oxon 30 F3
- Greenway TQ5 0ES Devon 5 P6
- Haddon Hall DE45 1LA Derbys 77 N10
- Hailes Abbey GL54 5PB Gloucs 42 B6
- Ham House & Garden TW10 7RS Gt Lon 32 H8
- Hampton Court Palace KT8 9AU Gt Lon 32 H8
- Hanbury Hall WR9 7EA Worcs 52 H8
- Hardwick S44 5QJ Derbys 78 D11
- Hardy's Cottage DT2 8QJ Dorset 10 H6
- Hare Hill SK10 4PY Ches E 76 G8
- Hatchlands Park GU4 7RT Surrey 32 F12
- Heale Garden SP4 6NU Wilts 23 P6
- Helmsley Castle YO62 5AB N York 92 C10
- Hereford Cathedral HR1 2NG Herefs 40 G4
- Hergest Croft Gardens HR5 3EG Herefs 51 J9
- Hever Castle & Gardens TN8 7NG Kent 15 N2
- Hidcote GL55 6LR Gloucs 42 E3
- Hill Top LA22 0LF Cumb 89 K7
- Hinton Ampner SO24 0LA Hants 25 K8
- Holkham Hall NR23 1AB Norfk 70 C4
- Housesteads Roman Fort NE47 6NN Nthumb 99 M4
- Howletts Wild Animal Park CT4 5EL Kent 35 M11
- Hughenden HP14 4LA Bucks 32 B3
- Hurst Castle SO41 0TP Hants 12 E7
- Hylands Estate CM2 8WQ Essex 46 B11
- Ickworth IP29 5QE Suffk 58 B8
- Ightham Mote TN15 0NT Kent 33 Q11
- Ironbridge Gorge Museums TF8 7DQ Wrekin 64 C11
- Kedleston Hall DE22 5JH Derbys 65 P4
- Kenilworth Castle & Elizabethan Garden CV8 1NE Warwks 53 P6
- Kensington Palace W8 4PX Gt Lon 33 J6
- Kenwood NW3 7JR Gt Lon 33 K5
- Killerton EX5 3LE Devon 8 H5
- King John's Hunting Lodge BS26 2AP Somset 21 P2
- Kingston Lacy BH21 4EA Dorset 11 N4
- Kirby Hall NN17 3EN Nhants 55 M2
- Knightshayes EX16 7RQ Devon 20 E10
- Knole TN13 1HU Kent 33 P11
- Knowsley Safari Park L34 4AN Knows 75M5
- Lacock SN15 2LG Wilts 29 Q8
- Lamb House TN31 7ES E Susx 16 G7
- Lanhydrock PL30 5AD Cnwll 3 Q2
- Launceston Castle PL15 7DR Cnwll 7 L8
- Leeds Castle ME17 1PB Kent 34 E11
- Legoland SL4 4AY W & M 32 D7
- Lightwater Valley Family Adventure Park HG4 3HT N York 91 M11
- Lindisfarne Castle TD15 2SH Nthumb 109 J1
- Lindisfarne Priory TD15 2RX Nthumb 109 J1
- Little Moreton Hall CW12 4SD Ches E 76 F11
- Liverpool Cathedral L1 7AZ Lpool 75 K6
- London Zoo ZSL NW1 4RY Gt Lon 33 K6
- Longleat BA12 7NW Wilts 22 H5
- Loseley Park GU3 1HS Surrey 14 D1
- Ludgershall Castle & Cross SP11 9QR Wilts 24 D3
- Lydford Castle & Saxon Town EX20 4BH Devon 7 P8
- Lyme SK12 2NX Ches E 76 H7
- Lytes Cary Manor TA11 7HU Somset 22 C8
- Lyveden PE8 5AT Nhant 55 N4
- Maiden Castle DT2 9PP Dorset 10 G7
- Mapledurham Estate RG4 7TR Oxon 31 N7
- Marble Hill TW1 2NL Gt Lon 32 H7
- Marwell Zoo SO21 1JH Hants 24 H9
- Melford Hall CO10 9AA Suffk 46 F2
- Merseyside Maritime Museum L3 4AQ Lpool 75 K6
- Minster Lovell Hall & Dovecote OX29 0RR Oxon 42 G9
- Mompesson House SP1 2EL Wilts 23 P7
- Monk Bretton Priory S71 5QD Barns 78 B2
- Montacute House TA15 6XP Somset 22 C10
- Morwellham Quay PL19 8JL Devon 4 G3
- Moseley Old Hall WV10 7HY Staffs 64 H11
- Mottisfont SO51 0LP Hants 24 E8
- Mottistone Manor & Garden PO30 4ED IoW 12 G8
- Mount Grace Priory DL6 3JG N York 91 Q7
- Muckleburgh Military Collection NR25 7EH Norfk 70 G3
- National Maritime Museum SE10 9NF Gt Lon 33 M7
- National Memorial Arboretum DE13 7AR Staffs 65 M9
- National Motorcycle Museum B92 0ED Solhll 53 M4
- National Portrait Gallery WC2H 0HE Gt Lon 33 K6
- National Railway Museum YO26 4XJ York 86 B5
- National Space Centre LE4 5NS C Leic 66 F10
- Natural History Museum SW7 5BD Gt Lon 33 K6
- Needles Old Battery & New Battery PO39 0JH IoW 12 E8
- Nene Valley Railway PE8 6LR Cambs 56 C1
- Netley Abbey SO31 5FB Hants 12 G3
- Newark Air Museum NG24 2NY Notts 79 L12
- Newquay Zoo TR7 2NL Cnwll 3 K2
- Newtown National Nature Reserve & Old Town Hall PO30 4PA IoW 12 G6
- North Leigh Roman Villa OX29 6QB Oxon 43 J8
- Norwich Cathedral NR1 4DH Norfk 71 J10
- Nostell WF4 1QE Wakefd 85 N11
- Nunnington Hall YO62 5UY N York 92 D11
- Nymans RH17 6EB W Susx 15 K5
- O2 Arena SE10 0DX Gt Lon 33 M6
- Old Royal Naval College SE10 9NN Gt Lon 33 M7
- Old Sarum SP1 3SD Wilts 23 P7
- Old Wardour Castle SP3 6RR Wilts 23 K8
- Oliver Cromwell's House CB7 4HF Cambs 57 K4
- Orford Castle IP12 2ND Suffk 59 N10
- Ormesby Hall TS3 0SR R & Cl 92 B3
- Osborne PO32 6JX IoW 13 J6
- Osterley Park & House TW7 4RB Gt Lon 32 G7
- Overbeck's Garden at Sharpitor TQ8 8LW Devon 5 M9
- Oxburgh Hall PE33 9PS Norfk 69 P12
- Packwood House B94 6AT Warwks 53 M6
- Paignton Zoo TQ4 7EU Torbay 5 P5
- Paultons Park SO51 6AL Hants 24 E10
- Paycocke's House & Garden CO6 1NS Essex 46 E7
- Peckover House & Garden PE13 1JR Cambs 69 J10
- Pendennis Castle TR11 4LP Cnwll 3 K8
- Petworth House & Park GU28 9LR W Susx 14 D6
- Pevensey Castle BN24 5LE E Susx 16 B10
- Peveril Castle S33 8WQ Derbys 77 L7
- Pleasurewood Hills NR32 5DZ Suffk 59 Q1
- Polesden Lacey RH5 6BD Surrey 32 G11
- Portland Castle DT5 1AZ Dorset 10 G10
- Portsmouth Historic Dockyard PO1 3LJ C Port 13 L5
- Powderham Castle EX6 8JQ Devon 8 H8
- Prior Park Landscape Garden BA2 5AH BaNES 29 M9
- Prudhoe Castle NE42 6NA Nthumb 100 E5
- Quarry Bank Mill & Styal SK9 4HP Ches E 76 F7
- Quebec House TN16 1TD Kent 33 N11
- RAF Museum Cosford TF11 8UP Shrops 64 E11
- RAF Museum London NW9 5LL Gt Lon 33 J4
- Ramsey Abbey Gatehouse PE26 1DH Cambs 56 F4
- Reculver Towers & Roman Fort CT6 6SU Kent 35 M8
- Red House DA6 8JF Gt Lon 33 N7
- Restormel Castle PL22 0EE Cnwll 3 Q2
- RHS Garden Harlow Carr HG3 1QB N York 85 L4
- RHS Garden Wisley GU23 6QB Surrey 32 F10
- Richborough Roman Fort & Amphitheatre CT13 9JW Kent 35 P10
- Richmond Castle DL10 4QW N York 91 K6
- Roche Abbey S66 8NW Rothm 78 E6
- Rochester Castle ME1 1SW Medway 34 C8
- Rockbourne Roman Villa SP6 3PG Hants 23 P10
- Roman Baths, Bath BA1 1LZ BaNES 29 M9
- Royal Botanic Gardens, Kew TW9 3AB Gt Lon 32 H7
- Royal Observatory Greenwich SE10 8XJ Gt Lon 33 M7
- Rufford Abbey NG22 9DF Notts 78 G11
- Rufford Old Hall L40 1SG Lancs 83 L12
- Runnymede & Ankerwycke SL4 2JJ W & M 32 E8
- Rushton Triangular Lodge NN14 1RP Nhants 55 L4
- Rycote Chapel OX9 2PA Oxon 43 P10
- St Leonard's Tower ME19 6PE Kent 34 B11
- St Michael's Mount TR17 0HT Cnwll 2 E8
- St Paul's Cathedral EC4M 8AD Gt Lon 33 L6
- Salisbury Cathedral SP1 2EJ Wilts 23 P7
- Saltram PL7 1UH C Plym 4 H5
- Sandham Memorial Chapel RG20 9JT Hants 31 K10
- Sandringham Estate PE35 6EH Norfk 69 N6
- Saxtead Green Post Mill IP13 9QQ Suffk 59 K8
- Scarborough Castle YO11 1HY N York 93 L9
- Science Museum SW7 2DD Gt Lon 33 K6
- Scotney Castle TN3 8JN Kent 16 B4
- Shaw's Corner AL6 9BX Herts 44 H8
- Sheffield Park & Garden TN22 3QX E Susx 15 M6
- Sherborne Old Castle DT9 3SA Dorset 22 E10
- Sissinghurst Castle Garden TN17 2AB Kent 16 E3
- Sizergh LA8 8AE Cumb 89 M9
- Smallhythe Place TN30 7NG Kent 16 F5
- Snowshill Manor & Garden WR12 7JU Gloucs 42 C5
- Souter Lighthouse & The Leas SR6 7NH S Tyne 101 K5
- Speke Hall L24 1XD Lpool 75 M7
- Spinnaker Tower PO1 3TT C Port 13 L5
- Stokesay Castle SY7 9AH Shrops 51 M4
- Stonehenge SP4 7DE Wilts 23 P5
- Stourhead BA12 6QD Wilts 22 H6
- Stowe MK18 5EQ Bucks 43 P4
- Sulgrave Manor & Garden OX17 2SD Nhants 43 M3
- Sunnycroft TF1 2DR Wrekin 64 C10
- Sutton Hoo IP12 3DJ Suffk 59 K10
- Sutton House & Breaker's Yard E9 6JQ Gt Lon 33 L5
- Tate Britain SW1P 4RG Gt Lon 33 K6
- Tate Liverpool L3 4BB Lpool 75 K6
- Tate Modern SE1 9TG Gt Lon 33 K6
- Tattershall Castle LN4 4LR Lincs 80 D12
- Tatton Park WA16 6QN Ches E 76 D7
- The British Library NW1 2DB Gt Lon 33 K6
- The British Museum WC1B 3DG Gt Lon 33 K6
- The Deep HU1 4DP C KuH 87 L9
- The Lost Gardens of Heligan PL26 6EN Cnwll 3 N5
- The Lowry M50 3AZ Salfd 76 E4
- The National Gallery WC2N 5DN Gt Lon 33 K6
- The Tank Museum BH20 6JG Dorset 11 K7
- The Vyne RG24 9HL Hants 31 N11
- The Weir Garden HR4 7QF Herefs 40 F3
- Thornton Abbey & Gatehouse DN39 6TU N Linc 87 L11
- Thorpe Park Resort KT16 8PN Surrey 32 E8
- Tilbury Fort RM18 7NR Thurr 34 B7
- Tintagel Castle PL34 0HE Cnwll 6 F7
- Tintinhull Garden BA22 8PZ Somset 22 C9
- Totnes Castle TQ9 5NU Devon 5 N4
- Tower of London EC3N 4AB Gt Lon 33 L6
- Townend LA23 1LB Cumb 89 L6
- Treasurer's House YO1 7JL York 86 B5
- Trelissick Garden TR3 6QL Cnwll 3 K6
- Trengwainton Garden TR20 8RZ Cnwll 2 C8
- Trerice TR8 4PG Cnwll 3 L3
- Tropical World Leeds LS8 2ER Leeds 85 L7
- Twycross Zoo CV9 3PX Leics 65 P11
- Ullswater 'Steamers' CA11 0US Cumb 89 L3
- Upnor Castle ME2 4XG Medway 34 D8
- Uppark House & Garden GU31 5QR W Susx 25 N10
- Upton House & Gardens OX15 6HT Warwks 42 H3
- Victoria & Albert Museum SW7 2RL Gt Lon 33 K6
- Waddesdon Manor HP18 0JH Bucks 43 Q8
- Wakehurst RH17 6TN W Susx 15 L4
- Wall Roman Site WS14 0AW Staffs 65 L11
- Wallington NE61 4AR Nthumb 100 C1
- Walmer Castle & Gardens CT14 7LJ Kent 35 Q12
- Warkworth Castle & Hermitage NE65 0UJ Nthumb 109 L8
- Warner Bros. Studio Tour London WD25 7LR Herts 32 F2
- Warwick Castle CV34 4QU Warwks 53 P7
- Washington Old Hall NE38 7LE Sundld 101 J7
- Waterperry Gardens OX33 1LG Oxon 43 N10
- Weeting Castle IP27 0RQ Norfk 57 P3
- Wenlock Priory TF13 6HS Shrops 64 B12
- West Midland Safari Park DY12 1LF Worcs 52 E5
- West Wycombe Park, Village & Hill HP14 3AJ Bucks 32 B3
- Westbury Court Garden GL14 1PD Gloucs 41 L9
- Westminster Abbey SW1P 3PA Gt Lon 33 K6
- Westonbirt, The National Arboretum GL8 8QS Gloucs 29 N4
- Weston Park TF11 8LE Staffs 64 E10
- Westwood Manor BA15 2AF Wilts 29 N10
- Whipsnade Zoo ZSL LU6 2LF C Beds 44 E8
- Whitby Abbey YO22 4JT N York 93 J4
- Wicksteed Park NN15 6NJ Nhants 55 L5
- Wightwick Manor & Gardens WV6 8EE Wolves 52 F1
- Wild Place Project BS10 7TP S Glos 28 H6
- Wimpole Estate SG8 0BW Cambs 56 F10
- Winchester Cathedral SO23 9LS Hants 24 H7
- Winchester City Mill SO23 0EJ Hants 24 H7
- Windermere Jetty Museum LA23 1BN Cumb 89 L7
- Windsor Castle SL4 1NJ W & M 32 D7
- Winkworth Arboretum GU8 4AD Surrey 14 E3
- Woburn Safari Park MK17 9QN C Beds 44 D5
- Wollaton Hall NG8 2AE C Nott 66 E4
- Wookey Hole Caves BA5 1BA Somset 22 C4
- Woolsthorpe Manor NG33 5PD Lincs 67 M7
- Wordsworth House CA13 9RX Cumb 97 M12
- Wrest Park MK45 4HR Beds C 44 F4
- Wroxeter Roman City SY5 6PR Shrops 63 P10
- WWT Arundel Wetland Centre BN18 9PB W Susx 14 E9
- WWT Slimbridge Wetland Centre GL2 7BT Gloucs 41 L10
- Yarmouth Castle PO41 0PB IoW 12 F7
- York Minster YO1 7HH York 86 B5

SCOTLAND

- Aberdour Castle & Gardens KY3 0SL Fife 115 M4
- Alloa Tower FK10 1PP Clacks 114 G3
- Arbroath Abbey DD11 1EG Angus 125 M4
- Arduaine Garden PA34 4XQ Ag & B 120 E10
- Bachelors' Club KA5 5RB S Ayrs 104 H4
- Balmoral Castle & Estate AB35 5TB Abers 131 N5
- Balvenie Castle AB55 4DH Moray 139 P7
- Bannockburn FK7 0LU Stirlg 114 E3
- Blackness Castle EH49 7NH Falk 115 J5
- Blair Castle & Gardens PH18 5TL P & K 130 F11
- Bothwell Castle G71 8BL S Lans 114 C9
- Branklyn Garden PH2 7BB P & K 124 C8
- Brodick Castle, Garden & Country Park KA27 8HY N Ayrs 103 Q2
- Brodie Castle IV36 2TE Moray 138 H4
- Broughton House & Garden DG6 4JX D & G 96 D8
- Burleigh Castle KY13 9GG P & K 124 C11
- Caerlaverock Castle DG1 4RU D & G 97 L5
- Cardoness Castle DG7 2EH D & G 96 C7
- Castle Campbell FK14 7PP Clacks 114 H1
- Castle Fraser, Garden & Estate AB51 7LD Abers 132 H2
- Castle Kennedy Gardens DG9 8SL D & G 94 G6
- Castle Menzies PH15 2JD P & K 123 L3
- Corgarff Castle AB36 8YP Abers 131 N3
- Craigievar Castle AB33 8JF Abers 132 E2
- Craigmillar Castle EH16 4SY C Edin 115 P7
- Crarae Garden PA32 8YA Ag & B 112 E2
- Crathes Castle, Garden & Estate AB31 5QJ Abers 132 H5
- Crichton Castle EH37 5XA Mdloth 115 Q9
- Crossraguel Abbey KA19 8HQ S Ayrs 104 E8
- Culloden IV2 5EU Highld 138 D7
- Culross KY12 8JH Fife 114 H4
- Culzean Castle & Country Park KA19 8LE S Ayrs 104 D8
- Dallas Dhu Distillery IV36 2RR Moray 139 J4
- David Livingstone Birthplace G72 9BY S Lans 114 C9
- Dirleton Castle & Gardens EH39 5ER E Loth 116 C4
- Doune Castle FK16 6EA Stirlg 114 D1
- Drum Castle, Garden & Estate AB31 5EY Abers 133 J4
- Dryburgh Abbey TD6 0RQ Border 107 P3
- Duff House AB45 3SX Abers 140 H3
- Dumbarton Castle G82 1JJ W Duns 113 M6
- Dundrennan Abbey DG6 4QH D & G 96 F9
- Dunnottar Castle AB39 2TL Abers 133 L7
- Dunstaffnage Castle & Chapel PA37 1PZ Ag & B 120 G6
- Dynamic Earth EH8 8AS C Edin 115 N6
- Edinburgh Castle EH1 2NG C Edin 115 N6
- Edinburgh Zoo RZSS EH12 6TS C Edin 115 M6
- Edzell Castle & Garden DD9 7UE Angus 132 F10
- Eilean Donan Castle IV40 8DX Highld 136 B10
- Elgin Cathedral IV30 1HU Moray 139 N3
- Falkirk Wheel FK1 4RS Falk 114 F5
- Falkland Palace & Garden KY15 7BU Fife 124 E11
- Fort George IV2 7TE Highld 138 D4
- Fyvie Castle AB53 8JS Abers 141 J8
- Georgian House EH2 4DR C Edin 115 N6
- Gladstone's Land EH1 2NT C Edin 115 N6
- Glamis Castle DD8 1RJ Angus 124 H3
- Glasgow Botanic Gardens G12 0UE C Glas 113 Q8
- Glasgow Cathedral G4 0QZ C Glas 114 A8
- Glasgow Science Centre G51 1EA C Glas 113 Q8
- Glen Grant Distillery AB38 7BS Moray 139 N6
- Glenluce Abbey DG8 0AF D & G 94 H6
- Greenbank Garden G76 8RB E Rens 113 Q10
- Haddo House AB41 7EQ Abers 141 L9
- Harmony Garden TD6 9LJ Border 107 N3
- Hermitage Castle TD9 0LU Border 107 M10
- Highland Wildlife Park RZSS PH21 1NL Highld 130 E3
- Hill House G84 9AJ Ag & B 113 L4
- Hill of Tarvit Mansion & Garden KY15 5PB Fife 124 H10
- Holmwood G44 3YG C Glas 113 R9
- House of Dun DD10 9LQ Angus 132 G12
- House of the Binns EH49 7NA W Loth 115 J6
- Huntingtower Castle PH1 3JL P & K 124 B8
- Huntly Castle AB54 4SH Abers 140 E7
- Inchmahome Priory FK8 3RA Stirlg 113 Q1
- Inveresk Lodge Garden EH21 7TE E Loth 115 Q7
- Inverewe IV22 2LG Highld 143 M8
- Inverlochy Castle PH33 6SN Highld 128 F9
- Kellie Castle & Garden KY10 2RF Fife 125 K11
- Kildrummy Castle AB33 8RA Abers 132 C1
- Killiecrankie PH16 5LG P & K 130 G11
- Leith Hall Garden AB54 4NQ Abers 140 E10
- Linlithgow Palace EH49 7AL W Loth 115 J6
- Lochleven Castle KY13 8UF P & K 124 C12
- Logan Botanic Garden DG9 9ND D & G 94 F9
- Malleny Garden EH14 7AF C Edin 115 L8
- Melrose Abbey TD6 9LG Border 107 N3
- National Museum of Scotland EH1 1JF C Edin 115 N6
- Newark Castle PA14 5NH Inver 113 L6
- Palace of Holyroodhouse EH8 8DX C Edin 115 N6
- Pitmedden Garden AB41 7PD Abers 141 L10
- Preston Mill & Phantassie Doocot EH40 3DS E Loth 116 E6
- Priorwood Garden TD6 9PX Border 107 N3
- Robert Smail's Printing Works EH44 6HA Border 107 J2
- Rothesay Castle PA20 0DA Ag & B 112 G8
- Royal Botanic Garden Edinburgh EH3 5LR C Edin 115 N6
- Royal Yacht Britannia EH6 6JJ C Edin 115 N6
- St Andrews Aquarium KY16 9AS Fife 125 K9
- St Andrews Botanic Garden KY16 8RT Fife 125 K9
- Scone Palace PH2 6BD P & K 90 H6
- Scottish Seabird Centre EH39 4SS E Loth 116 D4
- Smailholm Tower TD5 7PG Border 107 Q3
- Souter Johnnie's Cottage KA19 8HY S Ayrs 104 D8
- Stirling Castle FK8 1EJ Stirlg 114 E2
- Sweetheart Abbey DG2 8BU D & G 97 K5
- Tantallon Castle EH39 5PN E Loth 116 E4
- The Burrell Collection G43 1AT C Glas 113 Q9
- The Hunterian Museum G12 8QQ C Glas 113 Q8
- The Tenement House G3 6QN C Glas 113 R8
- Threave Castle DG7 1TJ D & G 96 E6
- Threave Garden & Estate DG7 1RX D & G 96 F6
- Tolquhon Castle AB41 7LP Abers 141 L10
- Traquair House EH44 6PW Border 107 J3
- Urquhart Castle IV63 6XJ Highld 137 P10
- Weaver's Cottage PA10 2JG Rens 113 M8
- Whithorn Priory & Museum DG8 8PY D & G 95 N10

WALES

- Aberconwy House LL32 8AY Conwy 73 N8
- Aberdulais Tin Works & Waterfall SA10 8EU Neath 27 J2
- Beaumaris Castle LL58 8AP IoA 73 K8
- Big Pit National Coal Museum NP4 9XP Torfn 40 B10
- Bodnant Garden LL28 5RE Conwy 73 P9
- Caerleon Roman Fortress & Baths NP18 1AE Newpt 28 D4
- Caernarfon Castle LL55 2AY Gwynd 72 H11
- Caldicot Castle & Country Park NP26 4HU Mons 28 G5
- Cardiff Castle CF10 3RB Cardif 28 A7
- Castell Coch CF15 7JS Cardif 27 Q6
- Chirk Castle LL14 5AF Wrexhm 63 J4
- Colby Woodland Garden SA67 8PP Pembks 37 M9
- Conwy Castle LL32 8AY Conwy 73 N8
- Criccieth Castle LL52 0DP Gwynd 60 H5
- Cyfarthfa Castle Museum CF47 8RE Myr Td 39 P10
- Dinefwr SA19 6RT Carmth 38 F7
- Dolaucothi SA19 8US Carmth 38 G4
- Erddig LL13 0YT Wrexhm 63 K2
- Ffestiniog Railway LL49 9NF Gwynd 61 K4
- Harlech Castle LL46 2YH Gwynd 61 K6
- Llanerchaeron SA48 8DG Cerdgn 48 H8
- National Showcaves Centre for Wales SA9 1GJ Powys 39 K8
- Penrhyn Castle & Garden LL57 4HT Gwynd 73 K9
- Plas Newydd House & Garden LL61 6DQ IoA 73 J9
- Plas yn Rhiw LL53 8AB Gwynd 60 C6
- Portmeirion LL48 6ER Gwynd 61 K5
- Powis Castle & Garden SY21 8RF Powys 62 H11
- Raglan Castle NP15 2BT Mons 40 F10
- St Davids Cathedral SA62 6RD Pembks 36 E5
- St Fagans National Museum of History CF5 6XB Cardif 27 Q7
- Sygun Copper Mine LL55 4NE Gwynd 61 K2
- Tintern Abbey NP16 6SE Mons 28 H2
- Tudor Merchant's House SA70 7BX Pembks 37 M10
- Tŷ Mawr Wybrnant LL25 0HJ Conwy 61 N2
- Valle Crucis Abbey LL20 8DD Denbgs 62 H3

Index to place names

This index lists places appearing in the main map section of the atlas in alphabetical order. The reference following each name gives the atlas page number and grid reference of the square in which the place appears. The map shows counties, unitary authorities and administrative areas, together with a list of the abbreviated name forms used in the index.

The top 100 places of tourist interest are indexed in **red**, World Heritage sites in **green**, motorway service areas in **blue**, airports in blue *italic* and National Parks in green *italic*.

Scotland

Abers Aberdeenshire
Ag & B Argyll and Bute
Angus Angus
Border Scottish Borders
C Aber City of Aberdeen
C Dund City of Dundee
C Edin City of Edinburgh
C Glas City of Glasgow
Clacks Clackmannanshire (1)
D & G Dumfries & Galloway
E Ayrs East Ayrshire
E Duns East Dunbartonshire (2)
E Loth East Lothian
E Rens East Renfrewshire (3)
Falk Falkirk
Fife Fife
Highld Highland
Inver Inverclyde (4)
Mdloth Midlothian (5)
Moray Moray
N Ayrs North Ayrshire
N Lans North Lanarkshire (6)
Ork Orkney Islands
P & K Perth & Kinross
Rens Renfrewshire (7)
S Ayrs South Ayrshire
S Lans South Lanarkshire
Shet Shetland Islands
Stirlg Stirling
W Duns West Dunbartonshire (8)
W Isls Western Isles (Na h-Eileanan an Iar)
W Loth West Lothian

Wales

Blae G Blaenau Gwent (9)
Brdgnd Bridgend (10)
Caerph Caerphilly (11)
Cardif Cardiff
Carmth Carmarthenshire
Cerdgn Ceredigion
Conwy Conwy
Denbgs Denbighshire
Flints Flintshire
Gwynd Gwynedd
IoA Isle of Anglesey
Mons Monmouthshire
Myr Td Merthyr Tydfil (12)
Neath Neath Port Talbot (13)
Newpt Newport (14)
Pembks Pembrokeshire
Powys Powys
Rhondd Rhondda Cynon Taf (15)
Swans Swansea
Torfn Torfaen (16)
V Glam Vale of Glamorgan (17)
Wrexhm Wrexham

England

BaNES Bath & N E Somerset (18)
Barns Barnsley (19)
BCP Bournemouth, Christchurch and Poole (20)
Bed Bedford
Birm Birmingham
Bl w D Blackburn with Darwen (21)
Bolton Bolton (22)
Bpool Blackpool
Br & H Brighton & Hove (23)
Br For Bracknell Forest (24)
Bristl City of Bristol
Bucks Buckinghamshire
Bury Bury (25)
C Beds Central Bedfordshire
C Brad City of Bradford
C Derb City of Derby
C KuH City of Kingston upon Hull
C Leic City of Leicester
C Nott City of Nottingham
C Pete City of Peterborough
C Plym City of Plymouth
C Port City of Portsmouth
C Sotn City of Southampton
C Stke City of Stoke-on-Trent
C York City of York
Calder Calderdale (26)
Cambs Cambridgeshire
Ches E Cheshire East
Ches W Cheshire West and Chester
Cnwll Cornwall
Covtry Coventry
Cumb Cumbria
Darltn Darlington (27)
Derbys Derbyshire
Devon Devon
Donc Doncaster (28)
Dorset Dorset
Dudley Dudley (29)
Dur Durham
E R Yk East Riding of Yorkshire
E Susx East Sussex
Essex Essex
Gatesd Gateshead (30)
Gloucs Gloucestershire
Gt Lon Greater London
Halton Halton (31)
Hants Hampshire
Hartpl Hartlepool (32)
Herefs Herefordshire
Herts Hertfordshire
IoS Isles of Scilly
IoW Isle of Wight
Kent Kent
Kirk Kirklees (33)
Knows Knowsley (34)
Lancs Lancashire
Leeds Leeds
Leics Leicestershire
Lincs Lincolnshire
Lpool Liverpool
Luton Luton
M Keyn Milton Keynes
Manch Manchester
Medway Medway
Middsb Middlesbrough
N Linc North Lincolnshire
N Som North Somerset
N Tyne North Tyneside (35)
N u Ty Newcastle upon Tyne
N York North Yorkshire
NE Lin North East Lincolnshire
Nhants Northamptonshire
Norfk Norfolk
Notts Nottinghamshire
Nthumb Northumberland
Oldham Oldham (36)
Oxon Oxfordshire
R & Cl Redcar & Cleveland
Readg Reading
Rochdl Rochdale (37)
Rothm Rotherham (38)
Rutlnd Rutland
S Glos South Gloucestershire (39)
S on T Stockton-on-Tees (40)
S Tyne South Tyneside (41)
Salfd Salford (42)
Sandw Sandwell (43)
Sefton Sefton (44)
Sheff Sheffield
Shrops Shropshire
Slough Slough (45)
Solhll Solihull (46)
Somset Somerset
St Hel St Helens (47)
Staffs Staffordshire
Sthend Southend-on-Sea
Stockp Stockport (48)
Suffk Suffolk
Sundld Sunderland
Surrey Surrey
Swindn Swindon
Tamesd Tameside (49)
Thurr Thurrock (50)
Torbay Torbay
Traffd Trafford (51)
W & M Windsor & Maidenhead (52)
W Berk West Berkshire
W Susx West Sussex
Wakefd Wakefield (53)
Warrtn Warrington (54)
Warwks Warwickshire
Wigan Wigan (55)
Wilts Wiltshire
Wirral Wirral (56)
Wokham Wokingham (57)
Wolves Wolverhampton (58)
Worcs Worcestershire
Wrekin Telford & Wrekin (59)
Wsall Walsall (60)

Channel Islands & Isle of Man

Guern Guernsey
Jersey Jersey
IoM Isle of Man

A

Abbas Combe Somset 22 F9
Abberley Worcs 52 D7
Abberley Common Worcs 52 D7
Abberton Essex 46 H8
Abberton Worcs 53 J10
Abberwick Nthumb 109 J7
Abbess Roding Essex 45 Q9
Abbey Devon 9 M3
Abbeycwmhir Powys 50 E6
Abbeydale Sheff 77 Q7
Abbey Dore Herefs 40 E5
Abbey Green Staffs 76 H12
Abbey Hill Somset 21 L9
Abbey St Bathans Border 116 G9
Abbeystead Lancs 83 M4
Abbeytown Cumb 97 N8
Abbey Village Lancs 83 P10
Abbey Wood Gt Lon 33 N6
Abbotrule Border 107 P7
Abbots Bickington Devon 18 H10
Abbots Bromley Staffs 65 K7
Abbotsbury Dorset 10 E7
Abbot's Chair Derbys 77 J6
Abbots Deuglie P & K 124 C10
Abbotsham Devon 18 H8
Abbotskerswell Devon 5 P3
Abbots Langley Herts 44 F11
Abbotsleigh Devon 5 N7
Abbots Leigh N Som 28 H7
Abbotsley Cambs 56 E9
Abbots Morton Worcs 53 J9
Abbots Ripton Cambs 56 E5
Abbot's Salford Warwks 53 K10
Abbotstone Hants 25 J6
Abbotswood Hants 24 F8
Abbots Worthy Hants 24 H7
Abbotts Ann Hants 24 E5
Abbott Street Dorset 11 N5
Abcott Shrops 51 L5
Abdon Shrops 51 P3
Abenhall Gloucs 41 K8
Aberaeron Cerdgn 48 G8
Aberaman Rhondd 27 N2
Aberangell Gwynd 61 P10
Aber-arad Carmth 37 Q3
Aberarder Highld 138 B10
Aberargie P & K 124 D9
Aberarth Cerdgn 48 H8
Aberavon Neath 26 H4
Aber-banc Cerdgn 38 A3
Aberbargoed Caerph 27 R2
Aberbeeg Blae G 40 B11
Abercanaid Myr Td 39 P11
Abercarn Caerph 28 B3
Abercastle Pembks 36 G4
Abercegir Powys 61 P11
Aberchalder Highld 129 K4
Aberchirder Abers 140 F5
Aber Clydach Powys 39 Q7
Abercorn W Loth 115 K5
Abercraf Powys 39 K9
Abercregan Neath 27 K3
Abercwmboi Rhondd 27 N2
Abercych Pembks 37 P2
Abercynon Rhondd 27 P3
Aberdalgie P & K 124 B9
Aberdare Rhondd 39 N11
Aberdaron Gwynd 60 B7
Aberdeen C Aber 133 M3
Aberdeen Airport C Aber 133 L2
Aberdesach Gwynd 60 G2
Aberdour Fife 115 M4
Aberdulais Neath 27 J2
Aberdyfi Gwynd 49 K1
Aberedw Powys 39 P2
Abereiddy Pembks 36 F4
Abererch Gwynd 60 F5
Aberfan Myr Td 27 P2
Aberfeldy P & K 123 L3
Aberffraw IoA 72 F10
Aberffrwd Cerdgn 49 L5
Aberford Leeds 85 N8
Aberfoyle Stirlg 113 Q1
Abergarw Brdgnd 27 L5
Abergarwed Neath 39 J11
Abergavenny Mons 40 D9
Abergele Conwy 74 C8
Aber-giar Carmth 38 D3
Abergorlech Carmth 38 E5
Abergwesyn Powys 49 Q10
Abergwili Carmth 38 C7
Abergwydol Powys 61 N11
Abergwynfi Neath 27 L3
Abergwyngregyn Gwynd 73 L9
Abergynolwyn Gwynd 61 L10
Aberhafesp Powys 50 E2
Aberhosan Powys 49 P1
Aberkenfig Brdgnd 27 L5
Aberlady E Loth 116 B5
Aberlemno Angus 125 K2
Aberllefenni Gwynd 61 N10
Aberllynfi Powys 40 A4
Aberlour, Charlestown of Moray 139 N7
Abermagwr Cerdgn 49 L6
Aber-meurig Cerdgn 49 J9
Abermorddu Flints 75 J12
Abermule Powys 50 G2
Abernant Carmth 37 R6
Abernant Rhondd 39 N11
Abernethy P & K 124 D9
Abernyte P & K 124 E6
Aberporth Cerdgn 48 D10
Abersoch Gwynd 60 E6
Abersychan Torfn 40 C11
Aberthin V Glam 27 N7
Abertillery Blae G 40 B11
Abertridwr Caerph 27 Q4
Abertridwr Powys 62 E8
Abertysswg Caerph 39 Q10
Aberuthven P & K 123 N9
Aberwheeler Denbgs 74 F10
Aberyscir Powys 39 N6
Aberystwyth Cerdgn 49 K4
Abingdon-on-Thames Oxon 31 K3
Abinger Common Surrey 14 G2
Abinger Hammer Surrey 14 F1
Abington Nhants 55 K8
Abington S Lans 106 B5
Abington Pigotts Cambs 45 K3
Abington Services S Lans 106 B5
Abingworth W Susx 14 G7
Ab Kettleby Leics 67 J7
Ab Lench Worcs 53 J10
Ablington Gloucs 42 C10
Ablington Wilts 23 P4
Abney Derbys 77 M7
Above Church Staffs 65 J2
Aboyne Abers 132 E5
Abhainn Suidhe W Isls 152 d5
Abram Wigan 75 Q3
Abriachan Highld 137 P9
Abridge Essex 33 N3
Abronhill N Lans 114 E6
Abson S Glos 29 L7
Abthorpe Nhants 43 N2
Aby Lincs 80 H8
Acaster Malbis C York 86 A6
Acaster Selby N York 85 R7
Accrington Lancs 84 A9
Acha Ag & B 118 G2
Achahoish Ag & B 112 A6
Achalader P & K 124 C4
Achaleven Ag & B 120 H6
Acha Mor W Isls 152 f3
Achanalt Highld 137 J3
Achandunie Highld 145 P10
Achany Highld 145 N5
Acharacle Highld 127 M10
Acharn Highld 120 D3
Acharn P & K 123 K4
Achavanich Highld 151 M8
Achduart Highld 144 C4
Achfary Highld 148 G8
Achgarve Highld 143 N6
A'Chill Highld 126 E3
Achiltibuie Highld 144 C3
Achina Highld 150 C4
Achinhoan Ag & B 103 K6
Achintee Highld 136 C7
Achintraid Highld 135 Q8
Achlyness Highld 148 F6
Achmelvich Highld 148 C11
Achmore Highld 135 Q9
Achmore W Isls 152 f3
Achnacarnin Highld 148 C10
Achnacarry Highld 128 G7
Achnacloich Highld 127 K3
Achnaconeran Highld 137 M12
Achnacroish Ag & B 120 F4
Achnadrish Ag & B 119 M2
Achnafauld P & K 123 M5
Achnagarron Highld 146 C11
Achnaha Highld 126 H10
Achnahaird Highld 144 C2
Achnahannet Highld 138 H10
Achnairn Highld 145 M3
Achnalea Highld 127 Q12
Achnamara Ag & B 112 A4
Achnasheen Highld 136 G4
Achnashellach Highld 136 D6
Achnastank Moray 139 P9
Achosnich Highld 126 H10
Achranich Highld 120 D3
Achreamie Highld 151 J3
Achriabhach Highld 128 G10
Achriesgill Highld 148 F6
Achtoty Highld 149 P4
Achurch Nhants 55 P4
Achvaich Highld 146 C6
Achvarasdal Highld 150 H4
Ackergill Highld 151 Q6
Acklam Middsb 91 R3
Acklam N York 86 E3
Ackleton Shrops 52 E1
Acklington Nthumb 109 L9
Ackton Wakefd 85 N10
Ackworth Moor Top Wakefd 85 N12
Acle Norfk 71 M10
Acock's Green Birm 53 L4
Acol Kent 35 P9
Acomb C York 85 R5
Acomb Nthumb 99 P5
Acombe Somset 21 K10
Aconbury Herefs 40 G5
Acre Lancs 84 B10
Acrefair Wrexhm 63 J3
Acresford Derbys 65 P9
Acton Ches E 64 B2
Acton Dorset 11 N9
Acton Gt Lon 32 H6
Acton Shrops 51 K4
Acton Staffs 64 F4
Acton Suffk 46 F3
Acton Worcs 52 F7
Acton Wrexhm 63 K2
Acton Beauchamp Herefs 52 C10
Acton Bridge Ches W 75 Q8
Acton Burnell Shrops 63 P11
Acton Green Herefs 52 C10
Acton Pigott Shrops 63 P11
Acton Round Shrops 52 B2
Acton Scott Shrops 51 M3
Acton Trussell Staffs 64 H8
Acton Turville S Glos 29 N6
Adbaston Staffs 64 E6
Adber Dorset 22 D9
Adbolton Notts 66 F4
Adderbury Oxon 43 K4
Adderley Shrops 64 C4
Adderstone Nthumb 109 J4
Addiewell W Loth 114 H8
Addingham C Brad 84 G5
Addington Bucks 43 Q6
Addington Gt Lon 33 L9
Addington Kent 34 B10
Addiscombe Gt Lon 33 L9
Addlestone Surrey 32 F9
Addlestonemoor Surrey 32 F9
Addlethorpe Lincs 81 K10
Adeney Wrekin 64 C8
Adeyfield Herts 44 F10
Adfa Powys 62 E12
Adforton Herefs 51 L6
Adisham Kent 35 M11
Adlestrop Gloucs 42 F6
Adlingfleet E R Yk 86 F11
Adlington Ches E 76 G7
Adlington Lancs 75 Q1
Admaston Staffs 65 K7
Admaston Wrekin 64 B9
Admington Warwks 42 E3
Adpar Cerdgn 37 Q2
Adsborough Somset 21 L7
Adscombe Somset 21 J6
Adstock Bucks 43 Q6
Adstone Nhants 54 F10
Adswood Stockp 76 G6
Adversane W Susx 14 F6
Advie Highld 139 L9
Adwalton Leeds 85 K9
Adwell Oxon 31 P2
Adwick le Street Donc 78 E2
Adwick upon Dearne Donc 78 D3
Ae D & G 106 C12
Ae Bridgend D & G 97 K1
Afan Forest Park Neath 27 K3
Affetside Bury 76 D1
Affleck Abers 140 E8
Affpuddle Dorset 11 K6
Affric Lodge Highld 136 H11
Afon-wen Flints 74 F9
Afon Wen Gwynd 60 G5
Afton Devon 5 P4
Afton IoW 12 F7
Agglethorpe N York 90 H9
Aigburth Lpool 75 L6
Aike E R Yk 87 K6

Aiketgate Cumb 98 F9
Aikhead Cumb 97 P8
Aikton Cumb 98 C7
Ailby Lincs 80 H8
Ailey Herefs 51 K11
Ailsworth C Pete 68 C12
Ainderby Quernhow N York 91 N10
Ainderby Steeple N York 91 N8
Aingers Green Essex 47 K7
Ainsdale Sefton 75 K1
Ainsdale-on-Sea Sefton 75 J1
Ainstable Cumb 98 G9
Ainsworth Bury 76 E2
Ainthorpe N York 92 E5
Aintree Sefton 75 L4
Ainville W Loth 115 K8
Aird Ag & B 111 R1
Aird D & G 94 F6
Aird Highld 127 K4
Aird W Isls 152 h3
Àird a' Mhulaidh W Isls 152 e5
Aird Asaig W Isls 152 e5
Aird Dhubh Highld 135 N8
Airdeny Ag & B 121 J7
Airdrie N Lans 114 D8
Airdriehill N Lans 114 E8
Airds of Kells D & G 96 D4
Àird Uig W Isls 152 d3
Airidh a bhruaich W Isls 152 f4
Airieland D & G 96 F7
Airlie Angus 124 F3
Airmyn E R Yk 86 D10
Airntully P & K 124 C6
Airor Highld 127 N3
Airth Falk 114 G4
Airton N York 84 D3
Aisby Lincs 67 P4
Aisby Lincs 79 L5
Aisgill Cumb 90 C7
Aish Devon 5 L4
Aish Devon 5 P5
Aisholt Somset 21 K6
Aiskew N York 91 M9
Aislaby N York 92 F9
Aislaby N York 92 H5
Aislaby S on T 91 P4
Aisthorpe Lincs 79 N7
Aith Shet 147 i6
Akeld Nthumb 108 F4
Akeley Bucks 43 P4
Akenham Suffk 58 H11
Albaston Cnwll 7 M10
Alberbury Shrops 63 K9
Albourne W Susx 15 J7
Albourne Green W Susx 15 J7
Albrighton Shrops 63 N8
Albrighton Shrops 64 E11
Alburgh Norfk 59 K3
Albury Herts 45 N7
Albury Oxon 43 N10
Albury Surrey 14 F1
Albury End Herts 45 M7
Albury Heath Surrey 14 F2
Alby Hill Norfk 71 J5
Alcaig Highld 137 P4
Alcaston Shrops 51 M3
Alcester Warwks 53 K9
Alciston E Susx 15 P9
Alcombe Somset 20 F4
Alcombe Wilts 29 N8
Alconbury Cambs 56 D5
Alconbury Weald Cambs 56 D5
Alconbury Weston Cambs 56 D5
Aldborough N York 85 N2
Aldborough Norfk 71 J5
Aldbourne Wilts 30 F7
Aldbrough E R Yk 87 N7
Aldbrough St John N York 91 K4
Aldbury Herts 44 D9
Aldcliffe Lancs 83 L3
Aldclune P & K 130 G11
Aldeburgh Suffk 59 P9
Aldeby Norfk 59 N2
Aldenham Herts 32 G3
Alderbury Wilts 24 C8
Aldercar Derbys 66 D3
Alderford Norfk 70 H8
Alderholt Dorset 23 P10
Alderley Gloucs 29 M4
Alderley Edge Ches E 76 F8
Aldermans Green Covtry 54 B4
Aldermaston W Berk 31 M9
Alderminster Warwks 53 N11
Alder Moor Staffs 65 N7
Aldersey Green Ches W 75 M12
Aldershot Hants 25 Q3
Alderton Gloucs 42 B5
Alderton Nhants 43 Q2
Alderton Shrops 63 N7
Alderton Suffk 47 P3
Alderton Wilts 29 N6
Alderwasley Derbys 65 P1
Aldfield N York 85 K1
Aldford Ches W 75 M11
Aldgate RutInd 67 N11
Aldham Essex 46 G6
Aldham Suffk 47 J3
Aldingbourne W Susx 14 D9
Aldingham Cumb 82 G1
Aldington Kent 17 J3
Aldington Worcs 42 C3
Aldington Corner Kent 17 J3
Aldivalloch Moray 139 Q10
Aldochlay Ag & B 113 M3
Aldon Shrops 51 M5
Aldoth Cumb 97 N8
Aldreth Cambs 56 H6
Aldridge Wsall 65 K12
Aldringham Suffk 59 N8
Aldro N York 86 E3
Aldsworth Gloucs 42 D9
Aldsworth W Susx 13 N3
Aldunie Moray 139 Q10
Aldwark Derbys 77 N12
Aldwark N York 85 P3
Aldwick W Susx 14 C11
Aldwincle Nhants 55 P4
Aldworth W Berk 31 L6
Alexandria W Duns 113 M5
Aley Somset 21 J6
Alfardisworthy Devon 7 K2
Alfington Devon 9 L5
Alfold Surrey 14 E4
Alfold Bars W Susx 14 E4
Alfold Crossways Surrey 14 E4
Alford Abers 132 F1
Alford Lincs 81 J8
Alford Somset 22 E7
Alfreton Derbys 66 C1
Alfrick Worcs 52 D10
Alfrick Pound Worcs 52 D10
Alfriston E Susx 15 P10
Algarkirk Lincs 68 F5
Alhampton Somset 22 E6
Alkborough N Linc 86 G11
Alkerton Gloucs 41 M10
Alkerton Oxon 42 H3
Alkham Kent 17 N2
Alkington Shrops 63 P4
Alkmonton Derbys 65 M4
Allaleigh Devon 5 N6
Allanaquoich Abers 131 L6
Allanbank N Lans 114 F9
Allanton Border 117 J10
Allanton N Lans 114 F10
Allanton S Lans 114 D10
Allaston Gloucs 41 K10
Allbrook Hants 24 G9
All Cannings Wilts 30 C10
Allendale Nthumb 99 N7
Allen End Warwks 53 M1
Allenheads Nthumb 99 N9
Allensford Dur 100 D8
Allen's Green Herts 45 N8
Allensmore Herefs 40 G4
Allenton C Derb 66 B6
Aller Devon 19 P8
Aller Somset 21 N7
Allerby Cumb 97 M10
Allercombe Devon 9 K6
Aller Cross Devon 19 N8
Allerford Somset 20 D4
Allerston N York 92 H10
Allerthorpe E R Yk 86 E6
Allerton C Brad 84 H8
Allerton Highld 138 D3
Allerton Lpool 75 L6
Allerton Bywater Leeds 85 N9
Allerton Mauleverer N York 85 N4
Allesley Covtry 53 P4
Allestree C Derb 65 Q4
Allet Cnwll 3 K5
Allexton Leics 67 K12
Allgreave Ches E 76 H10
Allhallows Medway 34 E7
Allhallows-on-Sea Medway 34 E6
Alligin Shuas Highld 135 Q4
Allimore Green Staffs 64 F8
Allington Dorset 10 C6
Allington Kent 34 D10
Allington Lincs 67 L4
Allington Wilts 24 C5
Allington Wilts 29 P7
Allington Wilts 30 C9
Allithwaite Cumb 89 K11
Alloa Clacks 114 F3
Allonby Cumb 97 M9
Allostock Ches W 76 D9
Alloway S Ayrs 104 F6
Allowenshay Somset 21 N10
All Saints South Elmham Suffk 59 L4
Allscott Shrops 52 D1
Allscott Wrekin 63 Q9
All Stretton Shrops 51 M2
Alltami Flints 75 J10
Alltchaorunn Highld 121 M3
Alltmawr Powys 39 P2
Alltsigh Highld 137 M12
Alltwalis Carmth 38 C5
Alltwen Neath 38 H11
Alltyblaca Cerdgn 38 D3
Allwood Green Suffk 58 F6
Almeley Herefs 51 K10
Almeley Wooton Herefs 51 K10
Almer Dorset 11 L5
Almholme Donc 78 F2
Almington Staffs 64 C5
Almodington W Susx 13 P5
Almondbank P & K 123 Q7
Almondbury Kirk 85 J12
Almondsbury S Glos 29 J5
Alne N York 85 P2
Alness Highld 145 P11
Alnham Nthumb 108 F7
Alnmouth Nthumb 109 L7
Alnwick Nthumb 109 K7
Alperton Gt Lon 32 H5
Alphamstone Essex 46 F4
Alpheton Suffk 58 C10
Alphington Devon 8 H7
Alpington Norfk 71 L12
Alport Derbys 77 N10
Alpraham Ches E 75 P11
Alresford Essex 47 J7
Alrewas Staffs 65 M9
Alsager Ches E 64 E1
Alsagers Bank Staffs 64 E3
Alsop en le Dale Derbys 65 M1
Alston Cumb 99 K9
Alston Devon 9 P4
Alstone Gloucs 41 R5
Alstone Somset 21 M4
Alstonefield Staffs 65 L1
Alston Sutton Somset 21 P3
Alswear Devon 19 P9
Alt Oldham 76 H3
Altandhu Highld 143 P3
Altarnun Cnwll 7 J8
Altass Highld 145 M5
Altcreich Ag & B 120 C5
Altgaltraig Ag & B 112 F6
Altham Lancs 84 A8
Althorne Essex 34 G3
Althorpe N Linc 79 L2
Altnabreac Station Highld 150 H7
Altnaharra Highld 149 M9
Altofts Wakefd 85 M10
Alton Derbys 78 B10
Alton Hants 25 M5
Alton Staffs 65 K4
Alton Wilts 23 P4
Alton Barnes Wilts 30 C10
Alton Pancras Dorset 10 H4
Alton Priors Wilts 30 C10
Alton Towers Staffs 65 K4
Altrincham Traffd 76 E6
Altskeith Hotel Stirlg 122 D12
Alva Clacks 114 F2
Alvanley Ches W 75 N9
Alvaston C Derb 66 C5
Alvechurch Worcs 53 J6
Alvecote Warwks 65 N11
Alvediston Wilts 23 L8
Alveley Shrops 52 D4
Alverdiscott Devon 19 K8
Alverstoke Hants 13 K5
Alverstone IoW 13 K7
Alverthorpe Wakefd 85 L11
Alverton Notts 67 K4
Alves Moray 139 L3
Alvescot Oxon 42 F10
Alveston S Glos 29 K5
Alveston Warwks 53 N9
Alvingham Lincs 80 G5
Alvington Gloucs 29 J2
Alwalton C Pete 56 C1
Alweston Dorset 22 F10
Alwinton Nthumb 108 E8
Alwoodley Leeds 85 L7
Alwoodley Gates Leeds 85 L7
Alyth P & K 124 E3
Am Bàgh a Tuath W Isls 152 b13
Ambergate Derbys 65 Q1
Amber Hill Lincs 68 E3
Amberley Gloucs 29 N2
Amberley W Susx 14 E8
Amber Row Derbys 78 C12
Amberstone E Susx 15 Q8
Amble Nthumb 109 L9
Amblecote Dudley 52 G3
Ambler Thorn C Brad 84 G9
Ambleside Cumb 89 K6
Ambleston Pembks 37 K5
Ambrosden Oxon 43 M8
Amcotts N Linc 86 F12
America Cambs 56 H5
Amersham Bucks 32 D3
Amersham Common Bucks 32 D3
Amersham Old Town Bucks 32 D3
Amersham on the Hill Bucks 32 D3
Amerton Staffs 65 J7
Amesbury Wilts 23 P5
Amhuinnsuidhe W Isls 152 d5
Amington Staffs 65 N11
Amisfield D & G 97 K2
Amlwch IoA 72 G5
Ammanford Carmth 38 F9
Amotherby N York 92 F12
Ampfield Hants 24 F8
Ampleforth N York 92 C11
Ampney Crucis Gloucs 42 C11
Ampney St Mary Gloucs 42 C11
Ampney St Peter Gloucs 30 C2
Amport Hants 24 E4
Ampthill C Beds 44 E4
Ampton Suffk 58 C6
Amroth Pembks 37 M9
Amulree P & K 123 M5
Amwell Herts 44 H9
Anaheilt Highld 127 P11
Ancaster Lincs 67 N3
Ancells Farm Hants 25 P2
Anchor Shrops 50 G4
Ancroft Nthumb 117 M12
Ancrum Border 107 Q5
Ancton W Susx 14 D10
Anderby Lincs 81 K8
Anderby Creek Lincs 81 K8
Andersea Somset 21 M6
Andersfield Somset 21 L6
Anderson Dorset 11 L5
Anderton Ches W 76 B8
Anderton Cnwll 4 F6
Andover Hants 24 F4
Andover Down Hants 24 F4
Andoversford Gloucs 42 B8
Andreas IoM 102 e3
Anelog Gwynd 60 B6
Anerley Gt Lon 33 L8
Anfield Lpool 75 L5
Angarrack Cnwll 2 F7
Angarrick Cnwll 3 K7
Angelbank Shrops 51 P5
Angersleigh Somset 21 K9
Angerton Cumb 97 P7
Angle Pembks 36 G10
Anglesey IoA 72 G7
Anglesey Abbey Cambs 57 K8
Angmering W Susx 14 F10
Angram N York 85 Q5
Angram N York 90 E7
Angrouse Cnwll 2 G10
Anick Nthumb 99 Q5
Ankerville Highld 146 E10
Ankle Hill Leics 67 J8
Anlaby E R Yk 87 J9
Anmer Norfk 69 P6
Anmore Hants 13 L2
Annan D & G 97 P5
Annandale Water Services D & G 106 E11
Annaside Cumb 88 E9
Annat Highld 136 B5
Annathill N Lans 114 D7
Anna Valley Hants 24 F4
Annbank S Ayrs 104 G5
Anne Hathaway's Cottage Warwks 53 M9
Annesley Notts 66 E1
Annesley Woodhouse Notts 66 E2
Annfield Plain Dur 100 F8
Anniesland C Glas 113 Q7
Annitsford N Tyne 100 H3
Annscroft Shrops 63 M10
Ansdell Lancs 82 H9
Ansford Somset 22 E7
Ansley Warwks 53 P2
Anslow Staffs 65 N7
Anslow Gate Staffs 65 M7
Anslow Lees Staffs 65 M7
Ansteadbrook Surrey 14 D4
Anstey Hants 25 M5
Anstey Herts 45 M5
Anstey Leics 66 F10
Anstruther Fife 125 L12
Ansty W Susx 15 K6
Ansty Warwks 54 C4
Ansty Wilts 23 L8
Ansty Cross Dorset 11 J4
An Tairbeart W Isls 152 e5
Anthill Common Hants 25 L11
Anthonys Surrey 32 E10
Anthorn Cumb 97 P6
Antingham Norfk 71 K5
An t-Ob W Isls 152 d6
Antonine Wall 114 F5
Anton's Gowt Lincs 68 F3
Antony Cnwll 4 F6
Antrobus Ches W 76 B8
Anvil Corner Devon 7 M4
Anvil Green Kent 35 K12
Anwick Lincs 68 C2
Anwoth D & G 96 C7
Aperfield Gt Lon 33 M10
Apes Dale Worcs 53 J6
Apethorpe Nhants 55 P2
Apeton Staffs 64 F8
Apley Lincs 80 B8
Apperknowle Derbys 78 C8
Apperley Gloucs 41 P6
Apperley Bridge C Brad 85 J7
Apperley Dene Nthumb 100 D6
Appersett N York 90 D8
Appin Ag & B 120 H4
Appleby N Linc 86 H12
Appleby-in-Westmorland Cumb 90 A3
Appleby Magna Leics 65 P10
Appleby Parva Leics 65 P10
Appleby Street Herts 45 L10
Applecross Highld 135 N7
Appledore Devon 19 J7
Appledore Devon 20 G10
Appledore Kent 16 G5
Appledore Heath Kent 16 G5
Appleford Oxon 31 L4
Applegarth Town D & G 97 M1
Applehaigh Wakefd 78 B1
Applemore Hants 12 F3
Appleshaw Hants 24 E4
Applethwaite Cumb 88 H2
Appleton Halton 75 N6
Appleton Oxon 31 J2
Appleton Warrtn 76 B7
Appleton-le-Moors N York 92 E9
Appleton-le-Street N York 92 E12
Appleton Roebuck N York 85 Q7
Appleton Thorn Warrtn 76 B7
Appleton Wiske N York 91 P6
Appletreehall Border 107 N6
Appletreewick N York 84 F3
Appley Somset 20 G9
Appley Bridge Lancs 75 N2
Apse Heath IoW 13 J8
Apsley End C Beds 44 G5
Apuldram W Susx 13 P4
Arabella Highld 146 E10
Arbirlot Angus 125 M5
Arborfield Wokham 31 Q9
Arborfield Cross Wokham 31 Q9
Arborfield Green Wokham 31 Q9
Arbourthorne Sheff 78 B6
Arbroath Angus 125 M5
Arbuthnott Abers 133 J9
Arcadia Kent 16 F3
Archddu Carmth 26 C2
Archdeacon Newton Darltn 91 L3
Archencarroch W Duns 113 N5
Archiestown Moray 139 N7
Archirondel Jersey 13 d2
Arclid Ches E 76 E11
Ardallie Abers 141 N8
Ardanaiseig Hotel Ag & B 121 K8
Ardaneaskan Highld 135 Q9
Ardarroch Highld 135 Q8
Ardbeg Ag & B 111 J12
Ardbeg Ag & B 112 H5
Ardbeg Ag & B 112 G5
Ardcharnich Highld 144 F7
Ardchiavaig Ag & B 119 L9
Ardchonnell Ag & B 121 J10
Ardchronie Highld 145 N7
Ardchullarie More Stirlg 122 F10
Arddarroch Ag & B 113 J2
Arddleen Powys 63 J9
Ard Dorch Highld 135 K10
Ardechive Highld 128 G6
Ardeer N Ayrs 104 E2
Ardeley Herts 45 K6
Ardelve Highld 136 B10
Arden Ag & B 113 M4
Ardens Grafton Warwks 53 L9
Ardentallen Ag & B 120 F8
Ardentinny Ag & B 113 J4
Ardentraive Ag & B 112 F6
Ardeonaig Stirlg 122 H6
Ardersier Highld 138 E5
Ardessie Highld 144 D7
Ardfern Ag & B 120 E12
Ardfernal Ag & B 111 M7
Ardgartan Ag & B 121 P12
Ardgay Highld 145 N7
Ardgour Highld 128 E11
Ardgowan Inver 113 J6
Ardhallow Ag & B 112 H6
Ardhasig W Isls 152 e5
Ardheslaig Highld 135 P5
Ardindrean Highld 144 E7
Ardingly W Susx 15 L5
Ardington Oxon 31 J5
Ardington Wick Oxon 31 J4
Ardlamont Ag & B 112 E8
Ardleigh Essex 47 J6
Ardleigh Heath Essex 47 J5
Ardler P & K 124 F4
Ardley Oxon 43 L6
Ardley End Essex 45 P9
Ardlui Ag & B 121 Q9
Ardlussa Ag & B 111 N4
Ardmair Highld 144 D5
Ardmaleish Ag & B 112 F7
Ardminish Ag & B 111 P11
Ardmolich Highld 127 N10
Ardmore Ag & B 113 L5
Ardmore Highld 146 C8
Ardnadam Ag & B 112 H5
Ardnagrask Highld 137 P6
Ardnamurchan Highld 127 K10
Ardnarff Highld 136 B8
Ardnastang Highld 127 P12
Ardpatrick Ag & B 111 Q9
Ardrishaig Ag & B 112 C4
Ardross Highld 145 P10
Ardrossan N Ayrs 104 D1
Ardsley Barns 78 C3
Ardslignish Highld 127 K12
Ardtalla Ag & B 111 K10
Ardtoe Highld 127 L10
Arduaine Ag & B 120 E10
Ardullie Highld 137 Q3
Ardvasar Highld 127 L4
Ardvorlich P & K 122 G8
Ardvourlie W Isls 152 e5
Ardwell D & G 94 G9
Ardwick Manch 76 F4
Areley Kings Worcs 52 E6
Arevegaig Highld 127 M10
Arford Hants 25 P6
Arglam E R Yk 86 E8
Arglam E R Yk 86 E8
Argoed Caerph 28 A2
Argoed Shrops 63 K8
Argoed Mill Powys 50 D8
Argos Hill E Susx 15 Q5
Argyll Forest Park Ag & B 121 N12
Aribruach W Isls 152 f4
Aridhglas Ag & B 119 K8
Arileod Ag & B 118 G2
Arinagour Ag & B 118 H1
Ariogan Ag & B 120 G7
Arisaig Highld 127 M7
Arisaig House Highld 127 M7
Arkendale N York 85 M3
Arkesden Essex 45 N5
Arkholme Lancs 89 P12
Arkleby Cumb 97 N10
Arkleton D & G 107 K11
Arkle Town N York 90 G6
Arkley Gt Lon 33 J3
Arksey Donc 78 F2
Arkwright Town Derbys 78 C9
Arle Gloucs 41 Q7
Arlecdon Cumb 88 D3
Arlescote Warwks 54 C11
Arlesey C Beds 44 H4
Arleston Wrekin 64 C10
Arley Ches E 76 C7
Arlingham Gloucs 41 L9
Arlington Devon 19 M5
Arlington E Susx 15 P9
Arlington Gloucs 42 C10
Arlington Beccott Devon 19 M5
Armadale Highld 127 L4
Armadale Highld 150 D4
Armadale W Loth 114 G7
Armaside Cumb 88 F1
Armathwaite Cumb 98 G9
Arminghall Norfk 71 K11
Armitage Staffs 65 K9
Armitage Bridge Kirk 77 L1
Armley Leeds 85 L8
Armscote Warwks 42 F3
Armshead Staffs 64 H2
Armston Nhants 55 Q3
Armthorpe Donc 78 G3
Arnabost Ag & B 126 D12
Arnaby Cumb 88 G10
Arncliffe N York 90 F12
Arncliffe Cote N York 84 E1
Arncroach Fife 125 K11
Arndilly House Moray 139 P6
Arne Dorset 11 N7
Arnesby Leics 54 G2
Arngask P & K 124 C10
Arnisdale Highld 127 Q2
Arnish Highld 135 K6
Arniston Mdloth 115 Q9
Arnol W Isls 152 f2
Arnold E R Yk 87 L7
Arnold Notts 66 F3
Arnprior Stirlg 114 B2
Arnside Cumb 89 M11
Aros Ag & B 119 P4
Arowry Wrexhm 63 M4
Arrad Foot Cumb 89 J10
Arram E R Yk 87 K6
Arran N Ayrs 103 P3
Arrathorne N York 91 K8
Arreton IoW 13 J7
Arrina Highld 135 N4
Arrington Cambs 56 F10
Arrochar Ag & B 121 P12
Arrow Warwks 53 K9
Arrowfield Top Worcs 53 J6
Arscott Shrops 63 M10
Artafallie Highld 138 B6
Arthington Leeds 85 K6
Arthingworth Nhants 55 J4
Arthog Gwynd 61 L9
Arthrath Abers 141 M8
Arthursdale Leeds 85 M7
Artrochie Abers 141 N9
Arundel W Susx 14 E9
Asby Cumb 88 E3
Ascog Ag & B 112 G8
Ascot W & M 32 D8
Ascott Warwks 42 G5
Ascott Earl Oxon 42 G8
Ascott-under-Wychwood Oxon 42 G8
Asenby N York 91 P11
Asfordby Leics 66 H8
Asfordby Hill Leics 67 J8
Asgarby Lincs 68 C3
Asgarby Lincs 80 F10
Ash Devon 5 P7
Ash Devon 7 P3
Ash Dorset 11 L3
Ash Kent 33 R9
Ash Kent 35 N10
Ash Somset 21 L9
Ash Somset 21 Q9
Ash Surrey 32 C12
Ashampstead W Berk 31 M7
Ashampstead Green W Berk 31 M7
Ashbocking Suffk 59 J9
Ashbourne Derbys 65 M3
Ashbrittle Somset 20 G9
Ashburnham Place E Susx 16 C8
Ashburton Devon 5 M3
Ashbury Devon 7 P5
Ashbury Oxon 30 F5
Ashby N Linc 79 M2
Ashby by Partney Lincs 80 H10
Ashby cum Fenby NE Lin 80 E4
Ashby de la Launde Lincs 67 P1
Ashby-de-la-Zouch Leics 66 B9
Ashby Folville Leics 66 H9
Ashby Magna Leics 54 F3
Ashby Parva Leics 54 E3
Ashby Puerorum Lincs 80 F9
Ashby St Ledgers Nhants 54 F7
Ashby St Mary Norfk 71 L11
Ashchurch Gloucs 41 Q5
Ashcombe Devon 8 G9
Ashcombe N Som 28 D10
Ashcott Somset 21 P6
Ashdon Essex 45 Q3
Ashdown Forest E Susx 15 N5
Ashe Hants 25 J3
Asheldham Essex 34 H2
Ashen Essex 46 D3
Ashendon Bucks 43 P9
Asheridge Bucks 44 D10
Ashfield Hants 24 F10
Ashfield Herefs 41 J7
Ashfield Stirlg 123 K12
Ashfield cum Thorpe Suffk 59 J8
Ashfield Green Suffk 57 P9
Ashfield Green Suffk 59 K6
Ashfold Crossways W Susx 15 J5
Ashford Devon 5 L7
Ashford Devon 19 K6
Ashford Kent 16 H2
Ashford Surrey 32 F8
Ashford Bowdler Shrops 51 N6
Ashford Carbonell Shrops 51 N6
Ashford Hill Hants 31 L10
Ashford in the Water Derbys 77 M9
Ashgill S Lans 114 E11
Ash Green Surrey 14 C1
Ash Green Warwks 53 Q4
Ashill Devon 9 L2
Ashill Norfk 70 C11
Ashill Somset 21 M10
Ashingdon Essex 34 F4
Ashington BCP 11 N5
Ashington Nthumb 109 L12
Ashington Somset 22 D9
Ashington W Susx 14 G7
Ashkirk Border 107 M5
Ashlett Hants 12 H4
Ashleworth Gloucs 41 N6
Ashleworth Quay Gloucs 41 N6
Ashley Cambs 57 N8
Ashley Ches E 76 E7
Ashley Devon 8 C2
Ashley Dorset 11 Q4
Ashley Gloucs 29 Q3
Ashley Hants 12 D6
Ashley Hants 24 F7
Ashley Kent 17 P1
Ashley Nhants 55 K2
Ashley Staffs 64 E5
Ashley Wilts 29 N8
Ashley Green Bucks 44 D10
Ashleyhay Derbys 65 P2
Ashley Heath Dorset 11 Q4
Ashley Moor Herefs 51 N7
Ash Magna Shrops 63 P4
Ashmansworth Hants 31 J11
Ashmansworthy Devon 18 G9
Ashmead Green Gloucs 29 M2
Ashmill Devon 7 M6
Ash Mill Devon 19 Q8
Ashmore Dorset 23 K10
Ashmore Green W Berk 31 K8
Ashorne Warwks 53 P9
Ashover Derbys 77 Q11
Ashover Hay Derbys 77 Q11
Ashow Warwks 53 P6
Ash Parva Shrops 63 P4
Ashperton Herefs 41 K3
Ashprington Devon 5 N5
Ash Priors Somset 21 J7
Ashreigney Devon 19 M10
Ash Street Suffk 46 H2
Ashtead Surrey 32 H10
Ash Thomas Devon 9 J3
Ashton C Pete 68 B11
Ashton Cnwll 2 F9
Ashton Devon 8 F8
Ashton Hants 25 J9
Ashton Herefs 51 N8
Ashton Inver 113 J6
Ashton Nhants 55 J10
Ashton Nhants 55 Q3
Ashton Somset 21 N3
Ashton Common Wilts 29 P10
Ashton Hayes Ches W 75 N10
Ashton Hill Wilts 29 P10
Ashton-in-Makerfield Wigan 75 P4
Ashton Keynes Wilts 30 B3
Ashton-on-Ribble Lancs 83 L9
Ashton under Hill Worcs 42 A4
Ashton-under-Lyne Tamesd 76 H4
Ashton upon Mersey Traffd 76 E5
Ashton Vale Bristl 28 H8
Ashurst Hants 12 E3
Ashurst Kent 15 P3
Ashurst Lancs 75 N2
Ashurst W Susx 14 H7
Ashurst Wood W Susx 15 M3
Ash Vale Surrey 32 C12
Ashwater Devon 7 M6
Ashwell Herts 45 K4
Ashwell RutInd 67 L9
Ashwell Somset 21 N10
Ashwell End Herts 45 J4
Ashwellthorpe Norfk 58 H1
Ashwick Somset 22 E4
Ashwicken Norfk 69 N8
Ashwood Staffs 52 F3
Askam in Furness Cumb 88 G11
Askern Donc 78 F1
Askerswell Dorset 10 E6
Askett Bucks 44 B10
Askham Cumb 89 N2
Askham Notts 79 J8
Askham Bryan C York 85 Q5
Askham Richard C York 85 Q5
Asknish Ag & B 112 D3
Askrigg N York 90 F8
Askwith N York 85 J5
Aslackby Lincs 68 B6
Aslacton Norfk 58 H2
Aslockton Notts 67 J4
Asney Somset 21 P6
Aspall Suffk 58 H7
Aspatria Cumb 97 N10
Aspenden Herts 45 L6
Aspenshaw Derbys 77 J6
Asperton Lincs 68 E5
Aspley Staffs 64 F5
Aspley Guise C Beds 44 D4
Aspley Heath C Beds 44 D5
Aspley Heath Warwks 53 L6
Aspull Wigan 75 Q2
Aspull Common Wigan 76 B4
Asselby E R Yk 86 D9
Asserby Lincs 81 J8
Asserby Turn Lincs 81 J8
Assington Suffk 46 G4
Assington Green Suffk 57 P10
Astbury Ches E 76 F11
Astcote Nhants 54 H10
Asterby Lincs 80 E8
Asterley Shrops 63 L10
Asterton Shrops 51 L2
Asthall Oxon 42 G9
Asthall Leigh Oxon 42 G9
Astle Highld 146 D7
Astley Shrops 63 N8
Astley Warwks 53 P3
Astley Wigan 76 C3
Astley Worcs 52 E7
Astley Abbots Shrops 52 D1
Astley Bridge Bolton 76 D1
Astley Cross Worcs 52 E7
Astley Green Wigan 76 D4
Aston Birm 53 K3
Aston Ches E 63 Q3
Aston Ches W 75 P8
Aston Derbys 77 M7
Aston Flints 75 J10
Aston Herefs 51 M8
Aston Herts 45 K7
Aston Oxon 42 H11
Aston Rothm 78 D6
Aston Shrops 52 E2
Aston Shrops 63 N6
Aston Staffs 64 D4
Aston Staffs 64 G7
Aston Wokham 31 Q5
Aston Wrekin 63 Q10
Aston Abbotts Bucks 44 B7
Aston Botterell Shrops 52 B4
Aston-by-Stone Staffs 64 G6
Aston Cantlow Warwks 53 L8
Aston Clinton Bucks 44 C9
Aston Crews Herefs 41 K7
Aston Cross Gloucs 41 Q5
Aston End Herts 45 K7
Aston-Eyre Shrops 52 C2
Aston Fields Worcs 52 H7
Aston Flamville Leics 54 D2
Aston Heath Ches W 75 P8
Aston Ingham Herefs 41 K7
Aston juxta Mondrum Ches E 76 C12
Aston le Walls Nhants 54 E10
Aston Magna Gloucs 42 E4
Aston Munslow Shrops 51 N3
Aston-on-Carrant Gloucs 41 Q5
Aston on Clun Shrops 51 L4
Aston Pigott Shrops 63 K11
Aston Rogers Shrops 63 K11
Aston Rowant Oxon 31 P3
Aston Sandford Bucks 43 Q10
Aston Somerville Worcs 42 B4
Aston-sub-Edge Gloucs 42 D3
Aston Tirrold Oxon 31 L5
Aston-upon-Trent Derbys 66 C6
Aston Upthorpe Oxon 31 L5
Astrop Nhants 43 L4
Astrope Herts 44 C8
Astwick C Beds 45 J4
Astwith Derbys 78 D11
Astwood M Keyn 55 N11
Astwood Worcs 52 H7
Astwood Bank Worcs 53 K8
Aswarby Lincs 67 Q4
Aswardby Lincs 80 G9
Atcham Shrops 63 P10
Atch Lench Worcs 53 J10
Athelhampton Dorset 11 J6
Athelington Suffk 59 J6
Athelney Somset 21 M7
Athelstaneford E Loth 116 C6
Atherfield Green IoW 12 H9
Atherington Devon 19 L9
Atherington W Susx 14 E10
Athersley Barns 78 B2
Atherstone Somset 21 N10
Atherstone Warwks 53 P1
Atherstone on Stour Warwks 53 M10
Atherton Wigan 76 C3
Atley Hill N York 91 M6
Atlow Derbys 65 N2
Attadale Highld 136 C8
Attenborough Notts 66 E5
Atterby Lincs 79 N5
Attercliffe Sheff 78 B6
Atterley Shrops 52 B1
Atterton Leics 54 B1
Attingham Park Shrops 63 P10
Attleborough Norfk 58 F2
Attleborough Warwks 54 B2
Attlebridge Norfk 70 H9
Attleton Green Suffk 57 N10
Atwick E R Yk 87 M5
Atworth Wilts 29 P9
Auberrow Herefs 40 G2
Aubourn Lincs 79 M11
Auchbreck Moray 139 M10
Auchedly Abers 141 L9
Auchenblae Abers 132 H8
Auchenbowie Stirlg 114 E4
Auchencairn D & G 96 G8
Auchencairn D & G 97 K1
Auchencairn N Ayrs 103 Q4
Auchencrow Border 117 J9
Auchendinny Mdloth 115 N9
Auchengray S Lans 114 H10
Auchenhalrig Moray 140 B3
Auchenheath S Lans 105 Q1
Auchenhessnane D & G 105 P10
Auchenlochan Ag & B 112 E7
Auchenmade N Ayrs 113 L11
Auchenmalg D & G 95 J8
Auchentiber N Ayrs 113 M11
Auchindrain Ag & B 121 K12
Auchindrean Highld 144 F9
Auchininna Abers 140 G6
Auchinleck E Ayrs 105 K5
Auchinloch N Lans 114 B7
Auchinstarry N Lans 114 C6
Auchintore Highld 128 F10
Auchiries Abers 141 P8
Auchlean Highld 130 F5
Auchlee Abers 133 L5
Auchleven Abers 140 F11
Auchlochan S Lans 105 P2
Auchlossan Abers 132 E4
Auchlyne Stirlg 122 E7
Auchmillan E Ayrs 105 J4
Auchmithie Angus 125 N4
Auchmuirbridge Fife 115 M1
Auchnacree Angus 132 D11
Auchnagatt Abers 141 M7
Auchnarrow Moray 139 M11
Auchnotteroch D & G 94 E6
Auchroisk Moray 139 Q5
Auchterarder P & K 123 N10
Auchteraw Highld 129 L3
Auchterblair Highld 138 G11
Auchtercairn Highld 143 L9
Auchterderran Fife 115 M2
Auchterhouse Angus 124 G5
Auchterless Abers 140 H7
Auchtermuchty Fife 124 E10
Auchterneed Highld 137 N4
Auchtertool Fife 115 M3
Auchtertyre Highld 135 Q10
Auchtubh Stirlg 122 F8
Auckengill Highld 151 Q4
Auckley Donc 78 G3
Audenshaw Tamesd 76 G4
Audlem Ches E 64 C3
Audley Staffs 64 E2
Audley End Essex 45 P4
Audley End Essex 46 E4
Audley End Suffk 58 C10
Audley End House & Gardens Essex 45 P4
Audmore Staffs 64 F8
Audnam Dudley 52 G3
Aughertree Cumb 97 Q10
Aughton E R Yk 86 D7
Aughton Lancs 75 L3
Aughton Lancs 83 M2
Aughton Rothm 78 D6
Aughton Wilts 30 F11
Aughton Park Lancs 75 L2
Auldearn Highld 138 G5
Aulden Herefs 51 M9
Auldgirth D & G 97 J1
Auldhouse S Lans 114 B11
Ault a' chruinn Highld 136 C11
Aultbea Highld 143 M7
Aultgrishin Highld 143 K8
Aultguish Inn Highld 145 J11
Ault Hucknall Derbys 78 D10
Aultmore Moray 140 B5
Aultnagoire Highld 137 P11
Aultnamain Highld 145 P9
Aunby Lincs 67 P9
Aunk Devon 9 K5
Aunsby Lincs 67 P4
Aust S Glos 28 H4
Austendike Lincs 68 F8
Austerfield Donc 78 H5
Austerlands Oldham 76 H3
Austhorpe Leeds 85 M8
Austonley Kirk 77 L2
Austrey Warwks 65 P11
Austwick N York 84 A2
Authorpe Lincs 80 H7
Authorpe Row Lincs 81 K9
Avebury Wilts 30 C8
Avebury Wilts 30 C8
Avebury Trusloe Wilts 30 B8
Aveley Thurr 33 Q6
Avening Gloucs 29 P3
Averham Notts 67 J1
Aveton Gifford Devon 5 L7
Aviemore Highld 130 G2
Avington W Berk 30 H9
Avoch Highld 138 C5
Avon Hants 12 B5
Avonbridge Falk 114 G7
Avon Dassett Warwks 54 C10
Avonmouth Bristl 28 G7
Avonwick Devon 5 L5
Awbridge Hants 24 E8
Awkley S Glos 29 J5
Awliscombe Devon 9 L4
Awre Gloucs 41 L10
Awsworth Notts 66 D3
Axborough Worcs 52 F5
Axbridge Somset 21 P2
Axford Hants 25 K5
Axford Wilts 30 F8
Axmansford Hants 31 M10
Axminster Devon 9 P5
Axmouth Devon 9 P6
Axton Flints 74 F7
Aycliffe Dur 91 M2
Aydon Nthumb 100 C5
Aylburton Gloucs 41 J11
Ayle Nthumb 99 K8
Aylesbeare Devon 9 K6
Aylesbury Bucks 44 B9
Aylesby NE Lin 80 D2
Aylesford Kent 34 C10
Aylesham Kent 35 M11
Aylestone C Leic 66 F12
Aylestone Park C Leic 66 F12
Aylmerton Norfk 71 J4
Aylsham Norfk 71 J7
Aylton Herefs 41 K4
Aylworth Gloucs 42 C7
Aymestrey Herefs 51 M7
Aynho Nhants 43 L5
Ayot Green Herts 45 J9
Ayot St Lawrence Herts 44 H8
Ayot St Peter Herts 45 J8
Ayr S Ayrs 104 F5
Aysgarth N York 90 G9
Ayshford Devon 20 G10
Ayside Cumb 89 L10
Ayston RutInd 67 L12
Aythorpe Roding Essex 45 Q8
Ayton Border 117 K9
Azerley N York 91 L11

B

Babbacombe Torbay 5 Q4
Babbington Notts 66 E3
Babbinswood Shrops 63 K6
Babbs Green Herts 45 M8
Babcary Somset 22 D7
Babel Carmth 39 K4
Babel Green Suffk 57 P11
Babell Flints 74 G9
Babeny Devon 8 C9

Bablock Hythe Oxon 43 J11
Babraham Cambs 57 K10
Babworth Notts 78 H7
Bachau IoA 72 G7
Bache Shrops 51 M4
Bacheldre Powys 50 H2
Bachelor's Bump E Susx 16 E8
Backaland Ork 147 d3
Backbarrow Cumb 89 K10
Backe Carmth 37 P7
Backfolds Abers 141 N5
Backford Ches W 75 L9
Backford Cross Ches W 75 L9
Backies Highld 146 E5
Back of Keppoch Highld 127 M7
Back o' th' Brook Staffs 65 K2
Back Street Suffk 57 P9
Backwell N Som 28 G8
Backworth N Tyne 100 H4
Bacon's End Solhll 53 M3
Baconsthorpe Norfk 70 H5
Bacton Herefs 40 E5
Bacton Norfk 71 L5
Bacton Suffk 58 F7
Bacton Green Suffk 58 F7
Bacup Lancs 84 C10
Badachro Highld 143 L10
Badanloch Highld 150 E10
Badbury Swindn 30 E6
Badby Nhants 54 F9
Badcall Highld 148 F5
Badcaul Highld 144 C7
Baddeley Edge C Stke 64 G2
Baddeley Green C Stke 64 G2
Baddesley Clinton Warwks 53 N6
Baddesley Ensor Warwks 53 P1
Baddidarrach Highld 148 C12
Baddinsgill Border 115 L10
Badenscoth Abers 140 H8
Badentarbet Highld 144 C3
Badenyon Abers 139 Q12
Badersfield Norfk 71 K7
Badgall Cnwll 7 J7
Badgeney Cambs 56 H1
Badger Shrops 64 E12
Badger's Cross Cnwll 2 D8
Badgers Mount Kent 33 P10
Badgeworth Gloucs 41 P8
Badgworth Somset 21 N3
Badharlick Cnwll 7 K7
Badicaul Highld 135 N10
Badingham Suffk 59 L7
Badlesmere Kent 34 H11
Badlieu Border 106 D6
Badlipster Highld 151 N7
Badluarach Highld 144 B6
Badninish Highld 146 D6
Badrallach Highld 144 D7
Badsey Worcs 42 C3
Badshot Lea Surrey 14 B1
Badsworth Wakefd 85 P12
Badwell Ash Suffk 58 E7
Badwell Green Suffk 58 E7
Bagber Dorset 22 G10
Bagby N York 91 Q10
Bag Enderby Lincs 80 G9
Bagendon Gloucs 42 B10
Bagginswood Shrops 52 C4
Baggrow Cumb 97 N10
Bàgh a' Chaisteil W Isls 152 b13
Bagham Kent 35 J11
Bagillt Flints 74 H8
Baginton Warwks 53 Q6
Baglan Neath 26 H4
Bagley Leeds 85 K8
Bagley Shrops 63 L7
Bagley Somset 21 P4
Bagmore Hants 25 L4
Bagnall Staffs 64 H2
Bagnor W Berk 31 K8
Bagshot Surrey 32 C9
Bagshot Wilts 30 G9
Bagstone S Glos 29 L5
Bagthorpe Notts 66 D2
Bagworth Leics 66 D10
Bagwyllydiart Herefs 40 F6
Baildon C Brad 84 H7
Baildon Green C Brad 84 H7
Baile Ailein W Isls 152 f4
Baile a' Mhanaich W Isls 152 c9
Baile Mòr Ag & B 119 J8
Bailey Green Hants 25 L8
Baileyhead Cumb 98 G2
Bailiff Bridge Calder 84 H10
Baillieston C Glas 114 C8
Bailrigg Lancs 83 L4
Bainbridge N York 90 F8
Bainshole Abers 140 F9
Bainton C Pete 68 B11
Bainton E R Yk 86 H5
Bainton Oxon 43 M6
Baintown Fife 124 G12
Bairnkine Border 107 Q6
Baker's End Herts 45 M8
Baker Street Thurr 34 B6
Bakewell Derbys 77 N10
Bala Gwynd 62 C5
Balallan W Isls 152 f4
Balbeg Highld 137 M9
Balbeggie P & K 124 D7
Balblair Highld 138 C3
Balby Donc 78 F3
Balcary D & G 96 G8
Balchraggan Highld 137 P7
Balchrick Highld 148 E5
Balcombe W Susx 15 K5
Balcombe Lane W Susx 15 K4
Balcomie Links Fife 125 M11
Baldersby N York 91 N11
Baldersby St James N York 91 N11
Balderstone Lancs 83 P8
Balderstone Rochdl 76 G2
Balderton Notts 67 K2
Baldhu Cnwll 3 J6
Baldinnie Fife 124 H10
Baldinnies P & K 123 P9
Baldock Herts 45 J5
Baldock Services Herts 45 J4
Baldovie C Dund 125 J6
Baldrine IoM 102 f5
Baldslow E Susx 16 E8
Baldwin IoM 102 d5
Baldwinholme Cumb 98 D8
Baldwin's Gate Staffs 64 E4
Baldwin's Hill W Susx 15 M3
Bale Norfk 70 E5
Baledgarno P & K 124 F7
Balemartine Ag & B 118 D4
Balerno C Edin 115 L8
Balfarg Fife 124 F12
Balfield Angus 132 E10
Balfour Ork 147 c4
Balfron Stirlg 113 Q3
Balgaveny Abers 140 G7
Balgonar Fife 115 J3
Balgowan D & G 94 G9
Balgowan Highld 130 B5
Balgown Highld 134 G2
Balgracie D & G 94 E6
Balgray S Lans 106 A5
Balham Gt Lon 33 K7
Balhary P & K 124 F3
Balholmie P & K 124 C5
Baligill Highld 150 F3
Balintore Angus 124 F1
Balintore Highld 146 F10
Balintraid Highld 146 D11
Balivanich W Isls 152 c9
Balk N York 91 Q10
Balkeerie Angus 124 G4
Balkholme E R Yk 86 E9
Ballabeg IoM 102 c7
Ballachulish Highld 121 K1
Ballafesson IoM 102 b7
Ballajora IoM 102 f4
Ballakilpheric IoM 102 b6
Ballamodha IoM 102 c6
Ballantrae S Ayrs 94 F2
Ballards Gore Essex 34 F4
Ballards Green Warwks 53 P2
Ballasalla IoM 102 c7
Ballater Abers 132 B5
Ballaugh IoM 102 d3
Ballchraggan Highld 146 D10
Ballencrieff E Loth 116 C6
Ballevullin Ag & B 118 C3
Ball Green C Stke 64 G2
Ball Haye Green Staffs 77 J12
Ball Hill Hants 31 J9
Ballianlay Ag & B 112 F9
Ballidon Derbys 65 M1
Balliekine N Ayrs 103 M2
Balliemore Ag & B 112 G1
Balligmorrie S Ayrs 104 D11
Ballimore Stirlg 122 F9
Ballindalloch Moray 139 M8
Ballindean P & K 124 E7
Ballingdon Suffk 46 F3
Ballinger Common Bucks 44 C11
Ballingham Herefs 41 J5
Ballingry Fife 115 M2
Ballinluig P & K 123 N2
Ballinshoe Angus 124 H2
Ballintuim P & K 124 C2
Balloch Highld 138 D6
Balloch N Lans 114 D6
Balloch P & K 123 L9
Balloch S Ayrs 104 F10
Balloch W Duns 113 M5
Balls Cross W Susx 14 E5
Balls Green E Susx 15 P3
Ball's Green Gloucs 29 P2
Ballygown Ag & B 119 M4
Ballygrant Ag & B 111 J8
Ballyhaugh Ag & B 118 G1
Balmacara Highld 135 P10
Balmaclellan D & G 96 D2
Balmae D & G 96 E9
Balmaha Stirlg 113 N3
Balmalcolm Fife 124 G11
Balmangan D & G 96 D9
Balmedie Abers 141 M12
Balmer Heath Shrops 63 M5
Balmerino Fife 124 G8
Balmerlawn Hants 12 E4
Balmichael N Ayrs 103 N3
Balmore E Duns 114 A6
Balmuchy Highld 146 F9
Balmule Fife 115 M4
Balmullo Fife 124 H8
Balnacoil Highld 146 E3
Balnacra Highld 136 D6
Balnacroft Abers 131 P5
Balnafoich Highld 138 C9
Balnaguard P & K 123 N2
Balnahard Ag & B 119 M6
Balnain Highld 137 M9
Balnakeil Highld 149 J3
Balne N York 86 B11
Balquharn P & K 123 P5
Balquhidder Stirlg 122 F8
Balsall Common Solhll 53 N5
Balsall Heath Birm 53 K4
Balsall Street Solhll 53 N5
Balscote Oxon 42 H3
Balsham Cambs 57 L10
Baltasound Shet 147 k2
Balterley Staffs 64 E2
Balterley Green Staffs 64 E2
Balterley Heath Staffs 64 D2
Baltersan D & G 95 M6
Balthangie Abers 141 K5
Baltonsborough Somset 22 C6
Balvicar Ag & B 120 E9
Balvraid Highld 127 Q1
Balvraid Highld 138 F9
Balwest Cnwll 2 F8
Bamber Bridge Lancs 83 M10
Bamber's Green Essex 45 Q7
Bamburgh Nthumb 109 K3
Bamburgh Castle Nthumb 109 K3
Bamford Derbys 77 N7
Bamford Rochdl 76 F1
Bampton Cumb 89 N3
Bampton Devon 20 E9
Bampton Oxon 42 G11
Bampton Grange Cumb 89 N3
Banavie Highld 128 F9
Banbury Oxon 43 K4
Bancffosfelen Carmth 38 D9
Banchory Abers 132 H5
Banchory-Devenick Abers 133 L4
Bancycapel Carmth 38 C8
Bancyfelin Carmth 37 Q7
Banc-y-ffordd Carmth 38 B4
Bandirran P & K 124 D7
Bandrake Head Cumb 89 J9
Banff Abers 140 G3
Bangor Gwynd 73 K9
Bangor-on-Dee Wrexhm 63 L3
Bangors Cnwll 7 J5
Bangor's Green Lancs 75 L2
Bangour Village W Loth 115 J7
Bangrove Suffk 58 D6
Banham Norfk 58 F3
Bank Hants 12 D3
Bankend D & G 97 L4
Bankfoot P & K 124 B6
Bankglen E Ayrs 105 L7
Bank Ground Cumb 89 J7
Bankhead C Aber 133 L2
Bankhead S Lans 114 H12
Bank Newton N York 84 D4
Banknock Falk 114 E5
Banks Cumb 98 H5
Banks Lancs 83 J11
Banks Green Worcs 53 J7
Bankshill D & G 97 P2
Bank Street Worcs 52 B8
Bank Top Calder 84 G10
Bank Top Lancs 75 N2
Banningham Norfk 71 J6
Bannister Green Essex 46 C7
Bannockburn Stirlg 114 E3
Banstead Surrey 33 J10
Bantham Devon 5 L8
Banton N Lans 114 D5
Banwell N Som 28 E10
Bapchild Kent 34 G9
Bapton Wilts 23 L6
Barabhas W Isls 152 g2
Barassie S Ayrs 104 F3
Barbaraville Highld 146 D10
Barber Booth Derbys 77 L7
Barber Green Cumb 89 L10
Barbieston S Ayrs 104 H6
Barbon Cumb 89 Q10
Barbridge Ches E 75 Q12
Barbrook Devon 19 N4
Barby Nhants 54 E6
Barcaldine Ag & B 120 H4
Barcheston Warwks 42 F4
Barclose Cumb 98 F6
Barcombe E Susx 15 M8
Barcombe Cross E Susx 15 M7
Barcroft C Brad 84 F7
Barden N York 91 J8
Barden Park Kent 15 Q2
Bardfield End Green Essex 46 A5
Bardfield Saling Essex 46 B6
Bardney Lincs 80 C10
Bardon Leics 66 D9
Bardon Mill Nthumb 99 M5
Bardowie E Duns 113 R6
Bardown E Susx 16 B5
Bardrainney Inver 113 L6
Bardsea Cumb 89 J11
Bardsey Leeds 85 M6
Bardsey Island Gwynd 60 A8
Bardsley Oldham 76 H3
Bardwell Suffk 58 D6
Bare Lancs 83 K2
Bareppa Cnwll 3 J8
Barfad D & G 95 L5
Barford Norfk 70 G10
Barford Warwks 53 P8
Barford St John Oxon 43 J5
Barford St Martin Wilts 23 N7
Barford St Michael Oxon 43 J5
Barfrestone Kent 35 N12
Bargate Derbys 66 B3
Bargeddie N Lans 114 C8
Bargoed Caerph 27 Q2
Bargrennan D & G 95 L3
Barham Cambs 56 C5
Barham Kent 35 M12
Barham Suffk 58 H10
Barham Suffk 56 G8
Bar Hill Cambs 56 G8
Barholm Lincs 68 B10
Barkby Leics 66 G10
Barkby Thorpe Leics 66 G10
Barkers Green Shrops 63 N6
Barkestone-le-Vale Leics 67 K5
Barkham Wokham 31 Q9
Barking Gt Lon 33 N5
Barking Suffk 58 G10
Barking Riverside Gt Lon 33 N6
Barkingside Gt Lon 33 N4
Barking Tye Suffk 58 F10
Barkisland Calder 84 G11
Barkla Shop Cnwll 3 J4
Barkston Lincs 67 M4
Barkston Ash N York 85 P8
Barkway Herts 45 M4
Barlanark C Glas 114 B8
Barlaston Staffs 64 G4
Barlavington W Susx 14 D7
Barlborough Derbys 78 D8
Barlby N York 86 B8
Barlestone Leics 66 C11
Barley Herts 45 M4
Barley Lancs 84 B7
Barleycroft End Herts 45 N6
Barley Hole Rothm 78 B4
Barleythorpe RutInd 67 L10
Barling Essex 34 G4
Barlings Lincs 79 Q8
Barlochan D & G 96 G7
Barlow Derbys 77 Q9
Barlow Gatesd 100 F6
Barlow N York 86 B9
Barmby Moor E R Yk 86 E5
Barmby on the Marsh E R Yk 86 C9
Barmer Norfk 69 Q5
Barming Heath Kent 34 C11
Barmollack Ag & B 103 L1
Barmouth Gwynd 61 K9
Barmpton Darltn 91 N3
Barmston E R Yk 87 M3
Barnaby Green Suffk 59 P5
Barnacarry Ag & B 112 E2
Barnack C Pete 67 Q11
Barnacle Warwks 54 C4
Barnard Castle Dur 90 H3
Barnard Gate Oxon 43 J9
Barnardiston Suffk 57 N11
Barnbarroch D & G 96 G7
Barnburgh Donc 78 D3
Barnby Suffk 59 P3
Barnby Dun Donc 78 G2
Barnby in the Willows Notts 67 L2
Barnby Moor Notts 78 H7
Barncorkrie D & G 94 F11
Barnehurst Gt Lon 33 P7
Barnes Gt Lon 33 J7
Barnes Street Kent 16 B1
Barnet Gt Lon 33 J3
Barnetby le Wold N Linc 79 Q2
Barnet Gate Gt Lon 33 J3
Barney Norfk 70 E6
Barnham Suffk 58 C5
Barnham W Susx 14 D10
Barnham Broom Norfk 70 G10
Barnhead Angus 125 N1
Barnhill C Dund 125 J6
Barnhill Ches W 63 N1
Barnhill Moray 139 L4
Barnhills D & G 94 E4
Barningham Dur 90 H5
Barningham Suffk 58 E5
Barnoldby le Beck NE Lin 80 E3
Barnoldswick Lancs 84 C6
Barnsdale Bar Donc 78 E1
Barns Green W Susx 14 G5
Barnsley Barns 77 Q2
Barnsley Gloucs 42 C10
Barnsole Kent 35 N11
Barnstaple Devon 19 L7
Barnston Essex 46 B8
Barnston Wirral 75 J7
Barnstone Notts 67 J4
Barnt Green Worcs 53 J6
Barnton C Edin 115 M6
Barnton Ches W 76 B8
Barnwell All Saints Nhants 55 P4
Barnwell St Andrew Nhants 55 P4
Barnwood Gloucs 41 P8
Baron's Cross Herefs 51 N9
Baronwood Cumb 98 G9
Barr S Ayrs 104 E11
Barra W Isls 152 b13
Barra Airport W Isls 152 b12
Barrachan D & G 95 L8
Barraigh W Isls 152 b13
Barrananaoil Ag & B 120 F11
Barrapoll Ag & B 118 C4
Barras Cumb 90 D4
Barrasford Nthumb 99 P4
Barregarrow IoM 102 d4
Barrets Green Ches E 75 Q11
Barrhead E Rens 113 P9
Barrhill S Ayrs 95 J2
Barrington Cambs 56 G10
Barrington Somset 21 N9
Barripper Cnwll 2 G7
Barrmill N Ayrs 113 M11
Barrock Highld 151 N2
Barrow Gloucs 41 P7
Barrow Lancs 83 Q7
Barrow Rutlnd 67 M9
Barrow Shrops 64 C12
Barrow Somset 22 G7
Barrow Suffk 57 P8
Barroway Drove Norfk 69 L11
Barrow Bridge Bolton 76 C1
Barrow Burn Nthumb 108 D7
Barrowby Lincs 67 L5
Barrow Common N Som 28 H9
Barrowden Rutlnd 67 N12
Barrowford Lancs 84 C7
Barrow Gurney N Som 28 H8
Barrow Haven N Linc 87 K10
Barrow Hill Derbys 78 C8
Barrow-in-Furness Cumb 82 F1
Barrow Island Cumb 82 F2
Barrow Nook Lancs 75 M3
Barrow's Green Ches E 76 C12
Barrows Green Cumb 89 N9
Barrow Street Wilts 22 G7
Barrow-upon-Humber N Linc 87 K11
Barrow upon Soar Leics 66 F8
Barrow upon Trent Derbys 66 B6
Barrow Vale BaNES 29 K10
Barry Angus 125 K6
Barry V Glam 27 Q8
Barry Island V Glam 27 Q9
Barsby Leics 66 H10
Barsham Suffk 59 M3
Barston Solhll 53 N5
Bartestree Herefs 40 H4
Barthol Chapel Abers 141 K9
Bartholomew Green Essex 46 C7
Barthomley Ches E 64 E2
Bartley Hants 24 E10
Bartley Green Birm 53 J4
Bartlow Cambs 45 Q3
Barton Cambs 56 H9
Barton Ches W 63 M2
Barton Gloucs 42 C6
Barton Herefs 51 J9
Barton Lancs 75 K2
Barton Lancs 83 L8
Barton N York 91 L5
Barton Oxon 43 L10
Barton Torbay 5 Q3
Barton Warwks 53 L10
Barton Bendish Norfk 69 N11
Barton End Gloucs 29 N3
Barton Green Staffs 65 M8
Barton Hartshorn Bucks 43 N5
Barton Hill N York 86 D2
Barton in Fabis Notts 66 E6
Barton in the Beans Leics 66 C11
Barton-le-Clay C Beds 44 F5
Barton-le-Street N York 92 E12
Barton-le-Willows N York 86 D3
Barton Mills Suffk 57 N6
Barton-on-Sea Hants 12 D6
Barton-on-the-Heath Warwks 42 F5
Barton St David Somset 22 C7
Barton Seagrave Nhants 55 M5
Barton Stacey Hants 24 G5
Barton Town Devon 19 N5
Barton Turf Norfk 71 M7
Barton-under-Needwood Staffs 65 M8
Barton-upon-Humber N Linc 87 J11
Barton upon Irwell Salfd 76 E4
Barton Waterside N Linc 87 J10
Barugh Barns 77 P2
Barugh Green Barns 77 P2
Barvas W Isls 152 g2
Barway Cambs 57 K5
Barwell Leics 54 D1
Barwick Devon 8 E3
Barwick Herts 45 M8
Barwick Somset 22 D10
Barwick in Elmet Leeds 85 N7
Baschurch Shrops 63 M8
Bascote Warwks 54 C8
Bascote Heath Warwks 54 C8
Base Green Suffk 58 F8
Basford Green Staffs 65 J2
Bashall Eaves Lancs 83 Q6
Bashall Town Lancs 83 Q7
Bashley Hants 12 D5
Basildon Essex 34 C4
Basingstoke Hants 25 L3
Baslow Derbys 77 N9
Bason Bridge Somset 21 M4
Bassaleg Newpt 28 C5
Bassendean Border 116 E12
Bassenthwaite Cumb 97 P11
Bassett C Sotn 24 G10
Bassingbourn-cum-Kneesworth Cambs 45 L3
Bassingfield Notts 66 G5
Bassingham Lincs 79 M11
Bassingthorpe Lincs 67 N6
Bassus Green Herts 45 K6
Basted Kent 33 R11
Baston Lincs 68 C9
Bastwick Norfk 71 N8
Batch Somset 28 D10
Batchworth Herts 32 F3
Batchworth Heath Herts 32 E4
Batcombe Dorset 10 F4
Batcombe Somset 22 F6
Bate Heath Ches E 76 C8
Batford Herts 44 G8
Bath BaNES 29 M9
Bath BaNES 29 M9
Bathampton BaNES 29 M9
Bathealton Somset 20 H8
Batheaston BaNES 29 M9
Bathford BaNES 29 M9
Bathgate W Loth 114 H7
Bathley Notts 79 K11
Bathpool Cnwll 7 K9
Bathpool Somset 21 L8
Bath Side Essex 47 N5
Bathville W Loth 114 G8
Bathway Somset 22 D3
Batley Kirk 85 K10
Batsford Gloucs 42 E5
Batson Devon 5 M9
Battersby N York 92 C5
Battersea Gt Lon 33 K7
Battisborough Cross Devon 5 J7
Battisford Suffk 58 F9
Battisford Tye Suffk 58 F10
Battle E Susx 16 D7
Battle Powys 39 N5
Battleborough Somset 21 M3
Battledown Gloucs 41 Q7
Battledykes Angus 125 J2
Battlefield Shrops 63 N9
Battlesbridge Essex 34 D3
Battlesden C Beds 44 D6
Battleton Somset 20 E8
Battlies Green Suffk 58 D8
Battram Leics 66 C10
Battramsley Cross Hants 12 E5
Batt's Corner Hants 25 P5
Baughton Worcs 41 P3
Baughurst Hants 31 M10
Baulds Abers 132 F5
Baulking Oxon 30 G4
Baumber Lincs 80 D9
Baunton Gloucs 42 B10
Baveney Wood Shrops 52 C5
Baverstock Wilts 23 M7
Bawburgh Norfk 70 H10
Bawdeswell Norfk 70 F8
Bawdrip Somset 21 M5
Bawdsey Suffk 47 P4
Bawsey Norfk 69 N8
Bawtry Donc 78 G5
Baxenden Lancs 84 B10
Baxterley Warwks 53 P1
Baxter's Green Suffk 57 P9
Bay Highld 134 E5
Bayble W Isls 152 h3
Baybridge Hants 25 J8
Baybridge Nthumb 99 Q8
Baycliff Cumb 89 J12
Baydon Wilts 30 G7
Bayford Herts 45 K10
Bayford Somset 22 G7
Bayhead W Isls 152 b8
Bay Horse Lancs 83 L5
Bayley's Hill Kent 33 P12
Baylham Suffk 58 G10
Baynard's Green Oxon 43 L6
Baysdale Abbey N York 92 C5
Baysham Herefs 40 H6
Bayston Hill Shrops 63 N10
Baythorne End Essex 46 C3
Bayton Worcs 52 C6
Bayton Common Worcs 52 D6
Bayworth Oxon 31 K2
Beach S Glos 29 L8
Beachampton Bucks 43 Q4
Beachamwell Norfk 69 P11
Beachley Gloucs 28 H4
Beachy Head E Susx 15 Q11
Beacon Devon 9 M4
Beacon End Essex 46 G6
Beacon Hill Kent 16 E4
Beacon Hill Notts 67 K1
Beacon Hill Surrey 14 C3
Beacon's Bottom Bucks 31 R3
Beaconsfield Bucks 32 D4
Beaconsfield Services Bucks 32 D5
Beadlam N York 92 D10
Beadlow C Beds 44 G4
Beadnell Nthumb 109 L4
Beaford Devon 19 L10
Beal N York 85 Q10
Beal Nthumb 108 H1
Bealbury Cnwll 4 E3
Bealsmill Cnwll 7 L9
Beam Hill Staffs 65 N7
Beamhurst Staffs 65 K5
Beaminster Dorset 10 D4
Beamish Dur 100 G7
Beamish - The Living Museum of the North Dur 100 G7
Beamsley N York 84 G5
Bean Kent 33 Q8
Beanacre Wilts 29 P9
Beanley Nthumb 108 H6
Beardon Devon 7 P8
Beardwood Bl w D 83 P9
Beare Devon 9 J4
Beare Green Surrey 14 H2
Bearley Warwks 53 M8
Bearley Cross Warwks 53 M8
Bearpark Dur 100 G9
Bearsden E Duns 113 Q7
Bearsted Kent 34 E11
Bearstone Shrops 64 D4
Bearwood BCP 11 P5
Bearwood Birm 53 J3
Bearwood Herefs 51 L9
Beattock D & G 106 E9
Beauchamp Roding Essex 45 Q9
Beauchief Sheff 77 Q7
Beaudesert Warwks 53 M7
Beaufort Blae G 40 A9
Beaulieu Essex 46 C9
Beaulieu Hants 12 F4
Beaulieu (National Motor Museum/Palace House) Hants 12 F4
Beaulieu Road Station Hants 12 F3
Beauly Highld 137 P6
Beaumaris IoA 73 K8
Beaumaris Castle IoA 73 K8
Beaumont Cumb 98 D6
Beaumont Essex 47 L7
Beaumont Jersey 13 b2
Beaumont Hill Darltn 91 M3
Beaumont Leys C Leic 66 F10
Beausale Warwks 53 N6
Beauworth Hants 25 K8
Beaworthy Devon 7 N5
Beazley End Essex 46 C6
Bebington Wirral 75 K7
Bebside Nthumb 100 H2
Beccles Suffk 59 N3
Becconsall Lancs 83 K10
Beckbury Shrops 64 E11
Beckenham Gt Lon 33 L8
Beckermet Cumb 88 D5
Beckett End Norfk 69 P12
Beckfoot Cumb 88 G6
Beckfoot Cumb 88 F7
Beck Foot Cumb 89 Q7
Beckfoot Cumb 97 M8
Beckford Worcs 41 R4
Beckhampton Wilts 30 C8
Beck Hole N York 92 G6
Beckingham Lincs 67 L1
Beckingham Notts 79 K6
Beckington Somset 22 H3
Beckjay Shrops 51 L5
Beckley E Susx 16 E6
Beckley Hants 12 C5
Beckley Oxon 43 M9
Beck Row Suffk 57 N5
Becks C Brad 84 F6
Beck Side Cumb 88 H10
Beck Side Cumb 89 K10
Beckton Gt Lon 33 M6
Beckwithshaw N York 85 K4
Becontree Gt Lon 33 N5
Becquet Vincent Jersey 13 c2
Bedale N York 91 M9
Bedburn Dur 100 E12
Bedchester Dorset 23 J10
Beddau Rhondd 27 P5
Beddgelert Gwynd 61 K3
Beddingham E Susx 15 N9
Beddington Gt Lon 33 K9
Beddington Corner Gt Lon 33 K9
Bedfield Suffk 59 J7
Bedfield Little Green Suffk 59 J7
Bedford Bed 55 P10
Bedgebury Cross Kent 16 C4
Bedgrove Bucks 44 B9
Bedham W Susx 14 E6
Bedhampton Hants 13 M3
Bedingfield Suffk 58 H7
Bedingfield Green Suffk 58 H7
Bedlam N York 85 K3
Bedlington Nthumb 100 H2
Bedlinog Myr Td 39 Q11
Bedminster Bristl 29 J8
Bedminster Down Bristl 29 J8
Bedmond Herts 44 G11
Bednall Staffs 64 H8
Bedrule Border 107 P6
Bedstone Shrops 51 L5
Bedwas Caerph 28 A4
Bedwellty Caerph 27 R2
Bedworth Warwks 54 B3
Bedworth Woodlands Warwks 53 Q3
Beeby Leics 66 H10
Beech Hants 25 M5
Beech Staffs 64 F4
Beech Hill W Berk 31 P9
Beechingstoke Wilts 30 C10
Beedon W Berk 31 K7
Beedon Hill W Berk 31 K7
Beeford E R Yk 87 L4
Beeley Derbys 77 P10
Beelsby NE Lin 80 D3
Beenham W Berk 31 M8
Beenham's Heath W & M 32 B7
Beeny Cnwll 6 G6
Beer Devon 9 N7
Beer Somset 21 N7
Beercrocombe Somset 21 M9
Beer Hackett Dorset 10 F2
Beesands Devon 5 N8
Beesby Lincs 81 J7
Beeson Devon 5 N8
Beeston C Beds 56 D11
Beeston Ches W 75 P12
Beeston Leeds 85 L9
Beeston Norfk 70 D9
Beeston Notts 66 E5
Beeston Regis Norfk 70 H4
Beeswing D & G 96 H4
Beetham Cumb 89 M11
Beetham Somset 21 L11
Beetley Norfk 70 E8
Began Cardif 28 B6
Begbroke Oxon 43 K9
Begdale Cambs 69 J11
Begelly Pembks 37 M9
Beggarington Hill Leeds 85 L10
Beggar's Bush Powys 51 J8
Beguildy Powys 50 G5
Beighton Norfk 71 M10
Beighton Sheff 78 D7
Beinn Na Faoghla W Isls 152 c9
Beith N Ayrs 113 L10
Bekesbourne Kent 35 M11
Bekesbourne Hill Kent 35 L11
Belaugh Norfk 71 K8
Belbroughton Worcs 52 H5
Belchalwell Dorset 11 J3
Belchalwell Street Dorset 11 J3
Belchamp Otten Essex 46 E3
Belchamp St Paul Essex 46 D3
Belchamp Walter Essex 46 E3
Belchford Lincs 80 F8
Belford Nthumb 109 J3
Belgrave C Leic 66 F10
Belhaven E Loth 116 F5
Belhelvie Abers 141 M12
Belhinnie Abers 140 C10
Bellabeg Abers 131 Q2
Bellamore Herefs 40 E4
Bellanoch Ag & B 112 B3
Bellasize E R Yk 86 F9
Bellaty Angus 124 E1
Bell Bar Herts 45 J10
Bell Busk N York 84 D4
Belleau Lincs 80 H8
Bell End Worcs 52 H5
Bellerby N York 91 J8
Bellever Devon 8 C9
Belle Vue Cumb 98 D7
Belle Vue Wakefd 85 M11
Bellfield S Lans 105 Q3
Bellfields Surrey 32 E12
Bell Heath Worcs 52 H5
Bell Hill Hants 25 M8
Bellingdon Bucks 44 D10
Bellingham Nthumb 99 N2
Belloch Ag & B 103 J2
Bellochantuy Ag & B 103 J3
Bell o' th' Hill Ches W 63 N3
Bellows Cross Dorset 23 N10
Bells Cross Suffk 58 H10
Bellshill N Lans 114 D9
Bellshill Nthumb 109 J4
Bellside N Lans 114 E9
Bellsquarry W Loth 115 J8
Bells Yew Green E Susx 15 R4
Belluton BaNES 29 J9
Belmaduthy Highld 138 B4
Belmesthorpe RutInd 67 P10
Belmont Bl w D 83 P12
Belmont Gt Lon 33 J10
Belmont S Ayrs 104 F6
Belmont Shet 147 j3
Belnacraig Abers 132 B1
Belowda Cnwll 3 N2
Belper Derbys 66 B3
Belper Lane End Derbys 65 Q2
Belph Derbys 78 E8
Belsay Nthumb 100 E2
Belses Border 107 P5
Belsford Devon 5 M5
Belsize Herts 32 E2
Belstead Suffk 47 K3
Belstone Devon 8 B6
Belthorn Bl w D 83 Q10
Beltinge Kent 35 M9
Beltingham Nthumb 99 M5
Beltoft N Linc 79 K2
Belton Leics 66 D8
Belton Lincs 67 M4
Belton N Linc 79 K2
Belton Norfk 71 P11
Belton House Lincs 67 M4
Belton in Rutland RutInd 67 K12
Beltring Kent 16 B1
Belvedere Gt Lon 33 P6
Belvoir Leics 67 K5
Bembridge IoW 13 K7
Bemerton Wilts 23 P7
Bempton E R Yk 93 P12
Benacre Suffk 59 P4
Benbecula W Isls 152 c9
Benbecula Airport W Isls 152 c9
Benbuie D & G 105 N10
Benderloch Ag & B 120 G5
Benenden Kent 16 E4
Benfieldside Dur 100 E7
Benfleet Essex 34 D5
Bengate Norfk 71 L7
Bengeo Herts 45 L9
Bengeworth Worcs 42 B3
Benhall Green Suffk 59 M8
Benhall Street Suffk 59 M8
Benholm Abers 133 K10
Beningbrough N York 85 Q4
Benington Herts 45 K7
Benington Lincs 68 H3
Benington Sea End Lincs 68 H3
Benllech IoA 72 H7
Benmore Ag & B 112 H4
Bennacott Cnwll 7 K6
Bennan N Ayrs 103 Q5
Bennet Head Cumb 89 L2
Bennetland E R Yk 86 F9
Bennett End Bucks 31 Q3
Ben Nevis Highld 128 G10
Benniworth Lincs 80 D7
Benover Kent 16 C1
Ben Rhydding C Brad 84 H6
Benslie N Ayrs 104 F1
Benson Oxon 31 N4
Benthall Green Essex 45 P6
Benthall Shrops 64 C11
Bentham Gloucs 41 P8
Benthoul C Aber 133 J4
Bentlawnt Shrops 63 K12
Bentley Donc 78 F3
Bentley E R Yk 87 J8
Bentley Hants 25 N4
Bentley Suffk 47 K4
Bentley Warwks 53 P2
Bentley Heath Herts 33 J2
Bentley Heath Solhll 53 M5
Benton Devon 19 M6
Bentpath D & G 107 J11
Bentwichen Devon 19 P6
Bentworth Hants 25 L5
Benvie Angus 124 G6
Benville Dorset 10 E4
Benwick Cambs 56 G3
Beoley Worcs 53 K7
Beoraidbeg Highld 127 M5
Bepton W Susx 25 Q9
Berden Essex 45 N6
Berea Pembks 36 F4
Bere Alston Devon 4 G3
Bere Ferrers Devon 4 G4
Berepper Cnwll 2 G10
Bere Regis Dorset 11 K6
Bergh Apton Norfk 71 L12
Berhill Somset 21 P6
Berinsfield Oxon 31 M3
Berkeley Gloucs 29 K2
Berkeley Heath Gloucs 29 L2
Berkeley Road Gloucs 29 L2
Berkhamsted Herts 44 E10
Berkley Somset 22 H3
Berkswell Solhll 53 N5
Bermondsey Gt Lon 33 L6
Bermuda Warwks 54 B3
Bernera Highld 135 P11
Bernisdale Highld 134 G6
Berrick Prior Oxon 31 N3
Berrick Salome Oxon 31 N4
Berriedale Highld 151 K12
Berrier Cumb 98 E12
Berriew Powys 62 G12
Berrington Nthumb 108 G1
Berrington Shrops 63 N10
Berrington Worcs 51 P7
Berrington Green Worcs 51 P7
Berrow Somset 21 L3
Berrow Worcs 41 M5
Berrow Green Worcs 52 D9
Berry Brow Kirk 84 H12
Berry Cross Devon 19 J10
Berry Down Cross Devon 19 L5
Berryfield Wilts 29 P10
Berryfields Bucks 43 R8
Berry Hill Gloucs 40 H9
Berry Hill Pembks 37 L2
Berryhillock Moray 140 D4
Berryhillock Moray 140 D5
Berrynarbor Devon 19 L4
Berry Pomeroy Devon 5 P4
Berry's Green Gt Lon 33 N10
Bersham Wrexhm 63 J2
Bersted W Susx 14 C10
Bertha Park P & K 124 B7
Berthengam Flints 74 F8
Berwick E Susx 15 P9
Berwick Bassett Wilts 30 C7
Berwick Hill Nthumb 100 F3
Berwick St James Wilts 23 N5
Berwick St John Wilts 23 L9
Berwick St Leonard Wilts 23 K7
Berwick Station E Susx 15 P9
Berwick-upon-Tweed Nthumb 117 M10
Bescaby Leics 67 K7
Bescar Lancs 75 L1
Besford Shrops 63 P7
Besford Worcs 41 Q3
Bessacarr Donc 78 G4
Bessels Leigh Oxon 43 K11
Besses o' th' Barn Bury 76 E3
Bessingby E R Yk 87 M2
Bessingham Norfk 70 H5
Bestbeech Hill E Susx 16 A4
Besthorpe Norfk 58 F2
Besthorpe Notts 79 K10
Bestwood Village Notts 66 F3
Beswick E R Yk 87 J5
Betchcott Shrops 51 M1
Betchworth Surrey 33 J12
Bethania Cerdgn 49 K8
Bethania Gwynd 61 K8
Bethel Gwynd 62 D4
Bethel Gwynd 73 J10
Bethel IoA 72 F9
Bethel Powys 62 F8
Bethersden Kent 16 G3
Bethesda Gwynd 73 K10
Bethesda Pembks 37 L7
Bethlehem Carmth 38 G6
Bethnal Green Gt Lon 33 L6
Betley Staffs 64 D2
Betsham Kent 33 R8
Betteshanger Kent 35 P11
Bettiscombe Dorset 10 B5
Bettisfield Wrexhm 63 M5
Betton Shrops 64 C5
Betton Strange Shrops 63 N10
Bettws Brdgnd 27 L5
Bettws Newpt 28 C4
Bettws Cedewain Powys 50 F1
Bettws Ifan Cerdgn 48 E11
Bettws-Newydd Mons 40 E10
Bettyhill Highld 150 C4
Betws Carmth 38 F9
Betws Bledrws Cerdgn 49 K10
Betws Garmon Gwynd 73 J12
Betws Gwerfil Goch Denbgs 62 E3
Betws-y-Coed Conwy 61 N1
Betws-yn-Rhos Conwy 74 B9
Beulah Cerdgn 48 D11
Beulah Powys 50 C10
Bevendean Br & H 15 L9
Bevercotes Notts 78 H9
Beverley E R Yk 87 J7
Beverston Gloucs 29 P3
Bevington Gloucs 29 K3
Bewaldeth Cumb 97 P11
Bewcastle Cumb 98 H3
Bewdley Worcs 52 E5
Bewerley N York 84 H2
Bewholme E R Yk 87 M5
Bewlbridge Kent 16 B4
Bexhill-on-Sea E Susx 16 C9
Bexley Gt Lon 33 P7
Bexleyheath Gt Lon 33 N7
Bexleyhill W Susx 14 C6
Bexon Kent 34 F10
Bexwell Norfk 69 M11
Beyton Suffk 58 D8
Beyton Green Suffk 58 D8
Bhaltos W Isls 152 e3
Bhatarsaigh W Isls 152 b13
Bibstone S Glos 29 L4
Bibury Gloucs 42 D10
Bicester Oxon 43 M7
Bickenhill Solhll 53 M4
Bicker Lincs 68 E5
Bicker Bar Lincs 68 E4
Bicker Gauntlet Lincs 68 D4
Bickershaw Wigan 76 B3
Bickerstaffe Lancs 75 M3
Bickerton Ches E 63 N2

Bickerton Devon 5 N9
Bickerton N York 85 P5
Bickerton Nthumb 108 G9
Bickford Staffs 64 G9
Bickington Devon 8 E10
Bickington Devon 19 K7
Bickleigh Devon 4 H4
Bickleigh Devon 8 H3
Bickleton Devon 19 K7
Bickley Ches W 63 P2
Bickley Gt Lon 33 M8
Bickley N York 93 J8
Bickley Worcs 52 B6
Bickley Moss Ches W 63 P2
Bicknacre Essex 46 D11
Bicknoller Somset 20 H5
Bicknor Kent 34 F10
Bickton Hants 23 P11
Bicton Herefs 51 M8
Bicton Shrops 51 J4
Bicton Shrops 63 M9
Bidborough Kent 15 Q2
Bidden Hants 25 M3
Biddenden Kent 16 E3
Biddenden Green Kent 16 F2
Biddenham Bed 55 P10
Biddestone Wilts 29 P7
Biddisham Somset 21 N3
Biddlesden Bucks 43 N4
Biddlestone Nthumb 108 F8
Biddulph Staffs 76 G12
Biddulph Moor Staffs 76 G12
Bideford Devon 19 J8
Bidford-on-Avon Warwks 53 L10
Bidston Wirral 75 J6
Bielby E R Yk 86 E6
Bieldside C Aber 133 L4
Bierley IoW 12 H9
Bierton Bucks 44 B8
Big Balcraig D & G 95 M9
Bigbury Devon 5 L7
Bigbury-on-Sea Devon 5 K8
Bigby Lincs 79 Q2
Biggar Cumb 82 F2
Biggar S Lans 106 D2
Biggin Derbys 65 N2
Biggin Derbys 77 M11
Biggin N York 85 Q8
Biggin Hill Gt Lon 33 M10
Biggleswade C Beds 44 H3
Bigholms D & G 98 C2
Bighouse Highld 150 F4
Bighton Hants 25 K6
Biglands Cumb 97 Q7
Bignall End Staffs 64 E2
Bignor W Susx 14 D8
Bigrigg Cumb 88 D4
Big Sand Highld 143 K9
Bigton Shet 147 i9
Bilborough C Nott 66 E4
Bilbrook Somset 20 G5
Bilbrook Staffs 64 G11
Bilbrough N York 85 Q6
Bilbster Highld 151 N6
Bildershaw Dur 91 K2
Bildeston Suffk 58 E10
Billacott Cnwll 7 K6
Billericay Essex 34 B3
Billesdon Leics 67 J11
Billesley Warwks 53 L9
Billingborough Lincs 68 C5
Billinge St Hel 75 N4
Billingford Norfk 58 H5
Billingford Norfk 70 F8
Billingham S on T 91 Q2
Billinghay Lincs 68 C1
Billingley Barns 78 D3
Billingshurst W Susx 14 F6
Billingsley Shrops 52 D4
Billington C Beds 44 D7
Billington Lancs 83 Q8
Billington Staffs 64 G8
Billockby Norfk 71 N9
Billy Row Dur 100 F10
Bilsborrow Lancs 83 L7
Bilsby Lincs 81 J8
Bilsham W Susx 14 D10
Bilsington Kent 17 J4
Bilsthorpe Notts 78 G11
Bilsthorpe Moor Notts 78 G11
Bilston Mdloth 115 N8
Bilston Wolves 52 H1
Bilstone Leics 66 B11
Bilting Kent 17 J1
Bilton E R Yk 87 M8
Bilton N York 85 L4
Bilton Nthumb 109 L7
Bilton Warwks 54 D6
Bilton Banks Nthumb 109 K8
Bilton-in-Ainsty N York 85 P5
Binbrook Lincs 80 D5
Binchester Blocks Dur 100 G11
Bincombe Dorset 10 G8
Binegar Somset 22 E3
Bines Green W Susx 14 H7
Binfield Br For 32 B8
Binfield Heath Oxon 31 Q7
Bingfield Nthumb 100 C4
Bingham Notts 66 H4
Bingham's Melcombe Dorset 11 J4
Bingley C Brad 84 G7
Bings Heath Shrops 63 P8
Binham Norfk 70 E4
Binley Covtry 54 C5
Binley Hants 24 G3
Binley Woods Warwks 54 C5
Binnegar Dorset 11 L7
Binniehill Falk 114 F7
Binscombe Surrey 14 D2
Binsey Oxon 43 K10
Binstead IoW 13 K6
Binsted Hants 25 N5
Binsted W Susx 14 D9
Binton Warwks 53 L10
Bintree Norfk 70 F7
Binweston Shrops 63 J11
Birch Essex 46 G7
Birch Rochdl 76 F2
Birchall Staffs 65 J1
Bircham Newton Norfk 69 P5
Bircham Tofts Norfk 69 P6
Birchanger Essex 45 P7
Birchanger Green Services Essex 45 P7
Birch Cross Staffs 65 L6
Birchencliffe Kirk 84 H11
Bircher Herefs 51 N7
Birchett's Green E Susx 16 B4
Birchfield Birm 53 K2
Birch Green Essex 46 G8
Birch Green Herts 45 K9
Birch Green Worcs 41 P3
Birchgrove Cardif 28 A6
Birchgrove Swans 26 H3
Birchgrove W Susx 15 M5
Birch Heath Ches W 75 P11
Birch Hill Ches W 75 N9
Birchington Kent 35 N8
Birchington-on-Sea Kent 35 N8
Birchley Heath Warwks 53 P2
Birchmoor Warwks 65 N11
Birchmoor Green C Beds 44 D5
Birchover Derbys 77 N11
Birch Services Rochdl 76 F2
Birch Vale Derbys 77 J6
Birchwood Lincs 79 M10
Birch Wood Somset 21 K10
Birchwood Warrtn 76 C5
Bircotes Notts 78 G5
Birdbrook Essex 46 C3
Birdforth N York 91 R11
Birdham W Susx 13 P5
Birdingbury Warwks 54 C7
Birdlip Gloucs 41 Q9
Birdoswald Cumb 99 J5
Birdsall N York 86 F2
Birds Edge Kirk 77 M2
Birds Green Essex 45 Q10
Birdsgreen Shrops 52 E4
Birdsmoorgate Dorset 10 B4
Bird Street Suffk 58 E10
Birdwell Barns 77 Q3
Birdwood Gloucs 41 L8
Birgham Border 108 C2
Birichin Highld 146 D6
Birkacre Lancs 83 M12
Birkby N York 91 N6
Birkdale Sefton 82 H12
Birkenbog Abers 140 E3
Birkenhead Wirral 75 K6
Birkenhead (Queensway) Tunnel Lpool 75 K6
Birkenhills Abers 140 H7
Birkenshaw Kirk 85 J9
Birkhall Abers 131 Q5
Birkhill Angus 124 G6
Birkhill D & G 106 G6
Birkholme Lincs 67 N7
Birkin N York 85 Q10
Birks Leeds 85 K10
Birkshaw Nthumb 99 L5
Birley Herefs 51 M10
Birley Carr Sheff 77 Q5
Birling Kent 34 B10
Birling Nthumb 109 L8
Birling Gap E Susx 15 Q11
Birlingham Worcs 41 Q3
Birmingham Birm 53 K3
Birmingham Airport Solhll 53 M4
Birnam P & K 123 Q4
Birness Abers 141 N9
Birse Abers 132 E5
Birsemore Abers 132 E5
Birstall Kirk 85 K10
Birstall Leics 66 F10
Birstwith N York 85 K3
Birthorpe Lincs 68 B5
Birtley Gatesd 100 H7
Birtley Herefs 51 L7
Birtley Nthumb 99 N3
Birts Street Worcs 41 M4
Bisbrooke Rutlnd 67 M12
Biscathorpe Lincs 80 E7
Biscovey Cnwll 3 P4
Bisham W & M 32 B5
Bishampton Worcs 53 J10
Bish Mill Devon 19 P8
Bishop Auckland Dur 91 L1
Bishopbridge Lincs 79 P5
Bishopbriggs E Duns 114 A7
Bishop Burton E R Yk 87 J7
Bishop Middleham Dur 101 J12
Bishopmill Moray 139 N3
Bishop Monkton N York 85 L2
Bishop Norton Lincs 79 N5
Bishopsbourne Kent 35 L11
Bishops Cannings Wilts 30 B9
Bishop's Castle Shrops 51 K3
Bishop's Caundle Dorset 22 F10
Bishop's Cleeve Gloucs 41 Q6
Bishop's Frome Herefs 52 C11
Bishops Gate Surrey 32 D8
Bishop's Green Essex 46 A8
Bishop's Green Hants 31 K9
Bishop's Hull Somset 21 K8
Bishop's Itchington Warwks 54 C9
Bishops Lydeard Somset 21 J7
Bishop's Norton Gloucs 41 N7
Bishop's Nympton Devon 19 P8
Bishop's Offley Staffs 64 E6
Bishop's Stortford Herts 45 N7
Bishop's Sutton Hants 25 K7
Bishop's Tachbrook Warwks 53 P8
Bishop's Tawton Devon 19 L7
Bishopsteignton Devon 8 G10
Bishopstoke Hants 24 H9
Bishopston Swans 26 E4
Bishopstone Bucks 44 A9
Bishopstone E Susx 15 N10
Bishopstone Herefs 40 F3
Bishopstone Kent 35 M8
Bishopstone Swindn 30 F5
Bishopstone Wilts 23 N8
Bishopstrow Wilts 23 K5
Bishop Sutton BaNES 29 J10
Bishop's Waltham Hants 25 J10
Bishopswood Somset 21 L10
Bishop's Wood Staffs 64 F10
Bishopsworth Bristl 28 H8
Bishop Thornton N York 85 K3
Bishopthorpe C York 86 B6
Bishopton Darltn 91 N2
Bishopton Rens 113 N7
Bishopton Warwks 53 M9
Bishop Wilton E R Yk 86 E4
Bishton Newpt 28 E5
Bishton Staffs 65 J8
Bisley Gloucs 41 P10
Bisley Surrey 32 D10
Bisley Camp Surrey 32 D10
Bispham Bpool 82 H7
Bispham Green Lancs 75 N1
Bissoe Cnwll 3 J6
Bisterne Hants 12 B4
Bitchet Green Kent 33 Q11
Bitchfield Lincs 67 N6
Bittadon Devon 19 K5
Bittaford Devon 5 L5
Bittering Norfk 70 D8
Bitterley Shrops 51 P5
Bitterne C Sotn 24 G10
Bitteswell Leics 54 E3
Bitton S Glos 29 K8
Bix Oxon 31 P5
Bixter Shet 147 i6
Blaby Leics 54 F1
Blackadder Border 117 J10
Blackawton Devon 5 N6
Blackbeck Cumb 88 D5
Blackborough Devon 9 L3
Blackborough End Norfk 69 M9
Black Bourton Oxon 42 G10
Blackboys E Susx 15 P6
Blackbrook Derbys 65 Q3
Blackbrook St Hel 75 P4
Blackbrook Staffs 64 E4
Blackbrook Surrey 14 H1
Blackburn Abers 133 K2
Blackburn Bl w D 83 P9
Blackburn Rothm 78 C5
Blackburn W Loth 114 H8
Blackburn with Darwen Services Bl w D 83 Q10
Black Callerton N u Ty 100 F4
Black Carr Norfk 58 G2
Black Corner W Susx 15 K3
Blackcraig E Ayrs 105 L8
Black Crofts Ag & B 120 H6
Black Cross Cnwll 3 M2
Blackden Heath Ches E 76 E9
Blackdog Abers 133 M1
Black Dog Devon 8 E3
Blackdown Devon 7 P9
Blackdown Dorset 10 B4
Blackdyke Cumb 97 N8
Blacker Barns 77 Q2
Blacker Hill Barns 78 B3
Blackfen Gt Lon 33 N7
Blackfield Hants 12 G4
Blackford Cumb 98 E6
Blackford P & K 123 M11
Blackford Somset 21 N4
Blackford Somset 22 F8
Blackfordby Leics 65 Q8
Blackgang IoW 12 H9
Blackhall C Edin 115 M6
Blackhall Colliery Dur 101 L10
Blackhall Mill Gatesd 100 E7
Blackhall Rocks Dur 101 L10
Blackham E Susx 15 P3
Blackhaugh Border 107 L2
Blackheath Essex 46 H7
Blackheath Gt Lon 33 M7
Blackheath Sandw 52 H3
Blackheath Suffk 59 N6
Blackheath Surrey 14 E2
Black Heddon Nthumb 100 D3
Blackhill Abers 141 P5
Blackhill Abers 141 Q7
Blackhill Dur 100 E8
Blackhill of Clackriach Abers 141 M6
Blackjack Lincs 68 E4
Blackland Wilts 30 B8
Black Lane Ends Lancs 84 D6
Blacklaw D & G 106 D8
Blackley Manch 76 F3
Blacklunans P & K 131 L12
Blackmarstone Herefs 40 G4
Blackmill Brdgnd 27 M5
Blackmoor Hants 25 N7
Black Moor Leeds 85 L7
Blackmoor N Som 28 G10
Blackmoorfoot Kirk 77 L1
Blackmoor Gate Devon 19 M5
Blackmore Essex 45 R11
Blackmore End Essex 46 C5
Blackmore End Herts 44 H8
Black Mountains 40 C6
Blackness Falk 115 J5
Blacknest Hants 25 P5
Blacknest W & M 32 D8
Black Notley Essex 46 D7
Blacko Lancs 84 C7
Black Pill Swans 26 F4
Blackpool Bpool 82 H8
Blackpool Devon 5 P7
Blackpool Devon 8 F10
Blackpool Gate Cumb 98 G3
Blackpool Zoo Bpool 82 H8
Blackridge W Loth 114 G8
Blackrock Cnwll 2 G7
Blackrock Mons 40 B9
Blackrod Bolton 75 Q2
Blacksboat Moray 139 M8
Blackshaw D & G 97 L5
Blackshaw Head Calder 84 E9
Blacksmith's Green Suffk 58 H7
Blacksnape Bl w D 83 Q11
Blackstone W Susx 15 J7
Black Street Suffk 59 P3
Black Tar Pembks 37 J8
Blackthorn Oxon 43 N8
Blackthorpe Suffk 58 D8
Blacktoft E R Yk 86 F10
Blacktop C Aber 133 L3
Black Torrington Devon 7 N4
Blackwall Derbys 65 N2
Blackwall Tunnel Gt Lon 33 M6
Blackwater Cnwll 3 J5
Blackwater Hants 32 B10
Blackwater IoW 12 H7
Blackwater Somset 21 L10
Blackwaterfoot N Ayrs 103 N4
Blackwell Cumb 98 E7
Blackwell Darltn 91 M4
Blackwell Derbys 77 L9
Blackwell Derbys 78 D12
Blackwell Warwks 42 F3
Blackwell Worcs 53 J6
Blackwellsend Green Gloucs 41 M6
Blackwood Caerph 28 A3
Blackwood D & G 106 B12
Blackwood S Lans 105 P1
Blackwood Hill Staffs 64 G1
Blacon Ches W 75 L10
Bladbean Kent 17 L1
Bladnoch D & G 95 M7
Bladon Oxon 43 K8
Bladon Somset 21 P9
Blaenannerch Cerdgn 48 D11
Blaenau Ffestiniog Gwynd 61 M3
Blaenau Ffestiniog Gwynd 61 M3
Blaenavon Torfn 40 C10
Blaenavon Industrial Landscape Torfn 40 C10
Blaencwm Rhondd 27 L3
Blaen Dyryn Powys 39 M4
Blaenffos Pembks 37 N3
Blaengarw Brdgnd 27 L4
Blaengeuffordd Cerdgn 49 L4
Blaengwrach Neath 39 K10
Blaengwynfi Neath 27 L3
Blaenllechau Rhondd 27 N3
Blaenpennal Cerdgn 49 K8
Blaenplwyf Cerdgn 49 K5
Blaenporth Cerdgn 48 D11
Blaenrhondda Rhondd 27 M2
Blaenwaun Carmth 37 P5
Blaen-y-coed Carmth 37 R5
Blaen-y-cwm Blae G 39 Q9
Blaenycwm Cerdgn 49 P5
Blagdon N Som 28 G10
Blagdon Somset 21 K9
Blagdon Torbay 5 P4
Blagdon Hill Somset 21 K10
Blagill Cumb 99 L9
Blaguegate Lancs 75 M2
Blaich Highld 128 E9
Blain Highld 127 M10
Blaina Blae G 40 B10
Blair Atholl P & K 130 F11
Blair Drummond Stirlg 114 D2
Blairgowrie P & K 124 D4
Blairhall Fife 114 H3
Blairingone P & K 114 H2
Blairlogie Stirlg 114 E2
Blairmore Ag & B 113 J5
Blairmore Highld 148 E5
Blair's Ferry Ag & B 112 E7
Blaisdon Gloucs 41 L8
Blakebrook Worcs 52 F5
Blakedown Worcs 52 G5
Blake End Essex 46 C7
Blakeley Lane Staffs 64 H3
Blakemere Ches W 75 P9
Blakemere Herefs 40 E3
Blakemore Devon 5 M5
Blakenall Heath Wsall 65 J11
Blakeney Gloucs 41 K10
Blakeney Norfk 70 F3
Blakenhall Ches E 64 D3
Blakenhall Wolves 52 G1
Blakeshall Worcs 52 F4
Blakesley Nhants 54 G10
Blanchland Nthumb 100 B8
Blandford Camp Dorset 11 M3
Blandford Forum Dorset 11 L3
Blandford St Mary Dorset 11 L4
Bland Hill N York 85 J4
Blanefield Stirlg 113 Q5
Blankney Lincs 79 Q11
Blantyre S Lans 114 C9
Blàr a' Chaorainn Highld 128 F11
Blarghour Ag & B 121 J10
Blargie Highld 129 Q5
Blarmachfoldach Highld 128 F10
Blashford Hants 12 B3
Blaston Leics 55 K2
Blatherwycke Nhants 55 N2
Blawith Cumb 89 J9
Blawquhairn D & G 96 C2
Blaxhall Suffk 59 M9
Blaxton Donc 78 H4
Blaydon Gatesd 100 F5
Bleadney Somset 22 B4
Bleadon N Som 28 D11
Bleak Street Somset 22 G7
Blean Kent 35 K10
Bleasby Lincs 80 C7
Bleasby Notts 66 H2
Bleasdale Lancs 83 N6
Bleatarn Cumb 90 B4
Bleathwood Herefs 51 P6
Blebocraigs Fife 124 H10
Bleddfa Powys 50 H7
Bledington Gloucs 42 F7
Bledlow Bucks 43 Q11
Bledlow Ridge Bucks 31 R3
Bleet Wilts 29 P10
Blegbie E Loth 116 C9
Blencarn Cumb 99 J12
Blencogo Cumb 97 P8
Blendworth Hants 25 M10
Blenheim Palace Oxon 43 J8
Blennerhasset Cumb 97 N10
Bletchingdon Oxon 43 K8
Bletchingley Surrey 33 L12
Bletchley M Keyn 44 B5
Bletchley Shrops 64 B5
Bletchley Park Museum M Keyn 44 B5
Bletherston Pembks 37 L6
Bletsoe Bed 55 P9
Blewbury Oxon 31 L5
Blickling Norfk 70 H6
Blidworth Notts 66 F1
Blidworth Bottoms Notts 66 F1
Blindburn Nthumb 108 C7
Blindcrake Cumb 97 N11
Blindley Heath Surrey 15 L2
Blindwells E Loth 115 R6
Blisland Cnwll 6 G10
Blissford Hants 24 B10
Bliss Gate Worcs 52 D6
Blisworth Nhants 55 J10
Blithbury Staffs 65 K8
Blitterlees Cumb 97 M8
Blockley Gloucs 42 D5
Blofield Norfk 71 L10
Blofield Heath Norfk 71 L10
Blo Norton Norfk 58 F5
Bloomfield Border 107 P5
Blore Staffs 64 D5
Blore Staffs 65 L2
Blounce Hants 25 M4
Blounts Green Staffs 65 K6
Blowick Sefton 83 J12
Bloxham Oxon 43 J4
Bloxholm Lincs 67 Q1
Bloxwich Wsall 65 J11
Bloxworth Dorset 11 L6
Blubberhouses N York 85 J4
Blue Anchor Cnwll 3 M3
Blue Anchor Somset 20 G5
Blue Bell Hill Kent 34 D10
Blue John Cavern Derbys 77 L7
Blundellsands Sefton 75 J4
Blundeston Suffk 59 Q1
Blunham C Beds 56 C10
Blunsdon St Andrew Swindn 30 D4
Bluntington Worcs 52 G6
Bluntisham Cambs 56 G6
Blunts Cnwll 4 E4
Blunts Green Warwks 53 L7
Blurton C Stke 64 G4
Blyborough Lincs 79 M5
Blyford Suffk 59 N5
Blymhill Staffs 64 E9
Blymhill Lawn Staffs 64 F10
Blyth Notts 78 G6
Blyth Nthumb 101 J2
Blyth Bridge Border 115 L12
Blythburgh Suffk 59 N5
Blythe Border 116 D11
Blythe Bridge Staffs 64 H4
Blythe End Warwks 53 N2
Blythe Marsh Staffs 64 H4
Blyth Services Notts 78 G6
Blyton Lincs 79 L5
Boarhills Fife 125 L10
Boarhunt Hants 13 K3
Boarley Kent 34 D10
Boarsgreave Lancs 84 C11
Boarshead E Susx 15 P4
Boar's Head Wigan 75 P2
Boars Hill Oxon 43 K11
Boarstall Bucks 43 N9
Boasley Cross Devon 7 P6
Boath Highld 145 N10
Boat of Garten Highld 138 H12
Bobbing Kent 34 F9
Bobbington Staffs 52 E2
Bobbingworth Essex 45 P10
Bocaddon Cnwll 4 B5
Bocking Essex 46 D7
Bocking Churchstreet Essex 46 D6
Bockleton Worcs 51 Q8
Boconnoc Cnwll 4 A4
Boddam Abers 141 Q7
Boddam Shet 147 i9
Boddington Gloucs 41 P6
Bodedern IoA 72 E7
Bodelwyddan Denbgs 74 D8
Bodenham Herefs 51 P10
Bodenham Wilts 23 Q8
Bodenham Moor Herefs 51 P10
Bodewryd IoA 72 F5
Bodfari Denbgs 74 F9
Bodffordd IoA 72 G8
Bodham Norfk 70 H4
Bodiam E Susx 16 D6
Bodicote Oxon 43 K4
Bodieve Cnwll 6 E10
Bodinnick Cnwll 3 R4
Bodle Street Green E Susx 16 B8
Bodmin Cnwll 6 F11
Bodmin Moor Cnwll 6 H9
Bodney Norfk 70 B12
Bodorgan IoA 72 F10
Bodsham Kent 17 K2
Boduan Gwynd 60 E4
Bodwen Cnwll 3 P2
Bodymoor Heath Warwks 53 M1
Bogallan Highld 138 B6
Bogbrae Abers 141 P8
Bogend S Ayrs 104 G3
Boggs Holdings E Loth 116 B7
Boghall Mdloth 115 N8
Boghall W Loth 114 H7
Boghead S Lans 105 P1
Bogmoor Moray 139 Q3
Bogmuir Abers 132 G10
Bogniebrae Abers 140 F7
Bognor Regis W Susx 14 D11
Bogroy Highld 138 G11
Bogue D & G 96 D2
Bohetherick Cnwll 4 F3
Bohortha Cnwll 3 L8
Bohuntine Highld 129 J7
Bojewyan Cnwll 2 C7
Bokiddick Cnwll 3 P2
Bolam Dur 91 K2
Bolam Nthumb 100 E2
Bolberry Devon 5 L9
Bold Heath St Hel 75 P6
Boldmere Birm 53 L2
Boldon Colliery S Tyne 101 J6
Boldre Hants 12 E5
Boldron Dur 90 G4
Bole Notts 79 K6
Bolehill Derbys 65 P1
Bole Hill Derbys 77 Q9
Bolenowe Cnwll 2 G7
Bolham Devon 20 E10
Bolham Water Devon 21 J11
Bolingey Cnwll 3 J4
Bollington Ches E 76 H8
Bollington Cross Ches E 76 G8
Bollow Gloucs 41 M9
Bolney W Susx 15 J6
Bolnhurst Bed 56 B8
Bolnore W Susx 15 L6
Bolshan Angus 125 M2
Bolsover Derbys 78 D9
Bolster Moor Kirk 84 G12
Bolsterstone Sheff 77 P4
Boltby N York 91 R9
Bolter End Bucks 31 R4
Bolton Bolton 76 D2
Bolton Cumb 89 Q2
Bolton E Loth 116 C7
Bolton E R Yk 86 E5
Bolton Nthumb 109 J7
Bolton Abbey N York 84 G4
Bolton Bridge N York 84 G4
Bolton-by-Bowland Lancs 84 B5
Boltonfellend Cumb 98 F4
Boltongate Cumb 97 P10
Bolton-le-Sands Lancs 83 L2
Bolton Low Houses Cumb 97 P9
Bolton New Houses Cumb 97 Q9
Bolton-on-Swale N York 91 L7
Bolton Percy N York 85 Q7
Bolton Town End Lancs 83 L2
Bolton upon Dearne Barns 78 D3
Bolventor Cnwll 6 H9
Bomarsund Nthumb 100 H1
Bomere Heath Shrops 63 M8
Bonar Bridge Highld 145 N7
Bonawe Ag & B 121 J6
Bonby N Linc 87 J12
Boncath Pembks 37 N3
Bonchester Bridge Border 107 P7
Bonchurch IoW 13 K9
Bondleigh Devon 8 C4
Bonds Lancs 83 L6
Bonehill Devon 8 D9
Bonehill Staffs 65 M11
Bo'ness Falk 114 H5
Boney Hay Staffs 65 K10
Bonhill W Duns 113 M5
Boningale Shrops 64 F11
Bonjedward Border 107 Q5
Bonkle N Lans 114 F10
Bonnington Angus 125 L5
Bonnington Kent 17 J4
Bonnybank Fife 124 G12
Bonnybridge Falk 114 E5
Bonnykelly Abers 141 L5
Bonnyrigg Mdloth 115 P8
Bonnyton Angus 124 G5
Bonsall Derbys 77 P12
Bonshaw Tower D & G 97 P4
Bont Mons 40 E8
Bontddu Gwynd 61 L8
Bont-Dolgadfan Powys 62 B12
Bont-goch Cerdgn 49 L3
Bonthorpe Lincs 81 J9
Bontnewydd Cerdgn 49 K7
Bontnewydd Gwynd 72 H11
Bontuchel Denbgs 74 F12
Bonvilston V Glam 27 P7
Bonwm Denbgs 62 F4
Bon-y-maen Swans 26 G3
Boode Devon 19 K6
Booker Bucks 32 B4
Booley Shrops 63 P7
Boon Border 116 D12
Boon Hill Staffs 64 E2
Boorley Green Hants 24 H10
Boosbeck R & Cl 92 D3
Boose's Green Essex 46 E5
Boot Cumb 88 G6
Booth Calder 84 F9
Boothby Graffoe Lincs 79 N11
Boothby Pagnell Lincs 67 N6
Boothferry E R Yk 86 D10
Booth Green Ches E 76 G7
Boothstown Salfd 76 D3
Boothtown Calder 84 G10
Boothville Nhants 55 K8
Bootle Cumb 88 E9
Bootle Sefton 75 K5
Boots Green Ches W 76 D9
Boot Street Suffk 59 J11
Booze N York 90 G6
Boraston Shrops 51 Q6
Bordeaux Guern 12 d1
Borden Kent 34 F9
Borden W Susx 25 P8
Border Cumb 97 N7
Bordesley Worcs 53 K6
Bordley N York 84 E2
Bordon Hants 25 P6
Boreham Essex 46 D9
Boreham Wilts 23 K4
Boreham Street E Susx 16 B8
Borehamwood Herts 32 H3
Boreland D & G 106 F11
Boreraig Highld 134 C5
Boreton Shrops 63 N10
Borgh W Isls 152 b13
Borgh W Isls 152 g1
Borgie Highld 149 P5
Borgue D & G 96 D8
Borgue Highld 151 L11
Borley Essex 46 E3
Borley Green Essex 46 E3
Borley Green Suffk 58 E8
Borneskitaig Highld 142 D11
Borness D & G 96 C9
Boroughbridge N York 85 N2
Borough Green Kent 33 R11
Borras Head Wrexhm 63 L2
Borrowash Derbys 66 C5
Borrowby N York 91 P9
Borrowby N York 92 F4
Borrowdale Cumb 88 H3
Borrowstoun Falk 114 H5
Borstal Medway 34 C9
Borth Cerdgn 49 K3
Borthwick Mdloth 115 Q9
Borthwickbrae Border 107 L7
Borthwickshiels Border 107 L6
Borth-y-Gest Gwynd 61 J5
Borve Highld 134 H6
Borve W Isls 152 b13
Borve W Isls 152 d6
Borve W Isls 152 g1
Borwick Lancs 89 N12
Borwick Lodge Cumb 89 K7
Borwick Rails Cumb 88 G10
Bosavern Cnwll 2 B8
Bosbury Herefs 41 L3
Boscarne Cnwll 6 F11
Boscastle Cnwll 6 G6
Boscombe BCP 11 Q6
Boscombe Wilts 24 C5
Boscoppa Cnwll 3 P4
Bosham W Susx 13 P4
Bosham Hoe W Susx 13 P4
Bosherston Pembks 37 J11
Boskednan Cnwll 2 C7
Boskenna Cnwll 2 C9
Bosley Ches E 76 G10
Bosoughan Cnwll 3 L2
Bossall N York 86 D3
Bossiney Cnwll 6 F7
Bossingham Kent 17 L1
Bossington Somset 20 D4
Bostock Green Ches W 76 C10
Boston Lincs 68 F3
Boston Spa Leeds 85 N6
Boswarthan Cnwll 2 C8
Boswinger Cnwll 3 N6
Botallack Cnwll 2 B8
Botany Bay Gt Lon 33 K3
Botcheston Leics 66 D11
Botesdale Suffk 58 F5
Bothal Nthumb 100 G1
Bothampstead W Berk 31 L7
Bothamsall Notts 78 H9
Bothel Cumb 97 N10
Bothenhampton Dorset 10 D6
Bothwell S Lans 114 C9
Bothwell Services (southbound) S Lans 114 C9
Botley Bucks 44 D11
Botley Hants 24 H10
Botley Oxon 43 K10
Botolph Claydon Bucks 43 Q7
Botolphs W Susx 14 H9
Botolph's Bridge Kent 17 K4
Bottesford Leics 67 K4
Bottesford N Linc 79 M2
Bottisham Cambs 57 K8
Bottomcraig Fife 124 G8
Bottom of Hutton Lancs 83 L9
Bottom o' th' Moor Bolton 76 C1
Bottoms Calder 84 D11
Bottoms Cnwll 2 B9
Botts Green Warwks 53 N2
Botusfleming Cnwll 4 F4
Botwnnog Gwynd 60 D6
Bough Beech Kent 15 P1
Boughrood Powys 39 Q4
Boughspring Gloucs 28 H3
Boughton Nhants 55 J7
Boughton Norfk 69 N11
Boughton Notts 78 H10
Boughton Aluph Kent 17 J1
Boughton End C Beds 44 E4
Boughton Green Kent 34 D12
Boughton Lees Kent 17 J1
Boughton Malherbe Kent 34 F12
Boughton Monchelsea Kent 34 D12
Boughton Street Kent 35 J10
Boulby R & Cl 92 F3
Boulder Clough Calder 84 F10
Bouldnor IoW 12 F7
Bouldon Shrops 51 P4
Boulmer Nthumb 109 L7
Boulston Pembks 37 J8
Boultenstone Abers 132 C2
Boultham Lincs 79 N10
Boundary Staffs 64 H4
Bourn Cambs 56 F9
Bournbrook Birm 53 K4
Bourne Lincs 68 B8
Bournebridge Essex 33 P3
Bourne End Bed 55 P8
Bourne End Bucks 32 C5
Bourne End C Beds 44 D3
Bourne End Herts 44 E10
Bournemouth BCP 11 Q6
Bournemouth Airport BCP 11 Q5
Bournes Green Gloucs 41 Q10
Bournes Green Sthend 34 F5
Bournheath Worcs 52 H6
Bournmoor Dur 100 H8
Bournstream Gloucs 29 M3
Bournville Birm 53 K4
Bourton Dorset 22 G7
Bourton N Som 28 E9
Bourton Oxon 30 F5
Bourton Shrops 51 Q1
Bourton Wilts 30 B9
Bourton on Dunsmore Warwks 54 D6
Bourton-on-the-Hill Gloucs 42 E5
Bourton-on-the-Water Gloucs 42 E7
Bousd Ag & B 126 D11
Boustead Hill Cumb 98 C6
Bouth Cumb 89 J9
Bouthwaite N York 84 H1
Bouts Worcs 53 J9
Boveney Bucks 32 D7
Boveridge Dorset 23 N10
Bovey Tracey Devon 8 F9
Bovingdon Herts 44 E11
Bovingdon Green Bucks 32 B5
Bovinger Essex 45 P10
Bovington Dorset 11 K7
Bovington Camp Dorset 11 K7
Bow Cumb 98 D7
Bow Devon 5 N5
Bow Devon 8 D4
Bow Gt Lon 33 L6
Bow Ork 147 c6
Bowbank Dur 90 F2
Bow Brickhill M Keyn 44 C5
Bowbridge Gloucs 41 P10
Bowburn Dur 100 H10
Bowcombe IoW 12 H7
Bowd Devon 9 L7
Bowden Border 107 N4
Bowden Devon 5 P7
Bowden Hill Wilts 29 Q9
Bowdon Traffd 76 E6
Bower Highld 151 N4
Bowerchalke Wilts 23 M8
Bowerhill Wilts 29 Q10
Bower Hinton Somset 21 P10
Bower House Tye Suffk 46 H3
Bowermadden Highld 151 N4
Bowers Staffs 64 F5
Bowers Gifford Essex 34 D5
Bowershall Fife 115 K3
Bower's Row Leeds 85 N9
Bowes Dur 90 G4
Bowgreave Lancs 83 L6
Bowhouse D & G 97 L5
Bowithick Cnwll 6 H8
Bowker's Green Lancs 75 L3
Bowland Border 107 M2
Bowland Bridge Cumb 89 L9
Bowley Herefs 51 P10
Bowley Town Herefs 51 P10
Bowlhead Green Surrey 14 C3
Bowling C Brad 85 J9
Bowling W Duns 113 N6
Bowling Bank Wrexhm 63 L2
Bowling Green Worcs 52 F10
Bowmanstead Cumb 89 J7
Bowmore Ag & B 110 G9
Bowness-on-Solway Cumb 97 P6
Bowness-on-Windermere Cumb 89 L7
Bow of Fife Fife 124 G10
Bowriefauld Angus 125 K3
Bowscale Cumb 98 D12
Bowsden Nthumb 108 G1
Bowston Cumb 89 M7
Bow Street Cerdgn 49 K4
Bow Street Norfk 58 F1
Bowthorpe Norfk 70 H10
Box Gloucs 29 P2
Box Wilts 29 N8
Boxbush Gloucs 41 K7
Boxbush Gloucs 41 M9
Box End Bed 55 P10
Boxford Suffk 46 G4
Boxford W Berk 31 J8
Boxgrove W Susx 14 C9
Box Hill Surrey 32 H12
Boxley Kent 34 D10
Boxmoor Herts 44 F10
Box's Shop Cnwll 7 J4
Boxted Essex 46 H5
Boxted Suffk 58 B10
Boxted Cross Essex 46 H5
Boxwell Gloucs 29 N4
Boxworth Cambs 56 G8
Boyden End Suffk 57 P9
Boyden Gate Kent 35 M9
Boylestone Derbys 65 M5
Boyndie Abers 140 G3
Boyndlie Abers 141 L3
Boynton E R Yk 87 L2
Boysack Angus 125 M3
Boys Hill Dorset 10 G3
Boythorpe Derbys 78 C9
Boyton Cnwll 7 L6
Boyton Suffk 47 Q2
Boyton Wilts 23 L5
Boyton Cross Essex 46 B10
Boyton End Suffk 46 C3
Bozeat Nhants 55 M9
Braaid IoM 102 d6
Brabling Green Suffk 59 L7
Brabourne Kent 17 K2
Brabourne Lees Kent 17 K3
Brabstermire Highld 151 P3
Bracadale Highld 134 F8
Braceborough Lincs 67 Q9
Bracebridge Heath Lincs 79 N10
Bracebridge Low Fields Lincs 79 N10
Braceby Lincs 67 P5
Bracewell Lancs 84 C5
Brackenfield Derbys 78 B12
Brackenhirst N Lans 114 D7
Brackenthwaite Cumb 98 C9
Brackenthwaite N York 85 L5
Brackla Brdgnd 27 L6
Bracklesham W Susx 13 P5
Brackletter Highld 128 H8
Brackley Nhants 43 M4
Brackley Hatch Nhants 43 N3
Bracknell Br For 32 B8
Braco P & K 123 L11
Bracobrae Moray 140 D5
Bracon Ash Norfk 71 J12
Bracora Highld 127 N6
Bracorina Highld 127 N6
Bradaford Devon 7 M6
Bradbourne Derbys 65 M2
Bradbury Dur 91 N1
Bradden Nhants 54 G11
Braddock Cnwll 4 B4
Bradeley C Stke 64 G2
Bradenham Bucks 32 B3
Bradenstoke Wilts 30 B6
Bradfield Devon 9 K3
Bradfield Essex 47 L5
Bradfield Norfk 71 K5
Bradfield Sheff 77 P5
Bradfield W Berk 31 M8
Bradfield Combust Suffk 58 C9
Bradfield Green Ches E 76 C11
Bradfield Heath Essex 47 L6
Bradfield St Clare Suffk 58 D9
Bradfield St George Suffk 58 D8
Bradfield Southend W Berk 31 M8
Bradford C Brad 84 H8
Bradford Cnwll 6 G9
Bradford Devon 7 M3
Bradford Nthumb 100 D2
Bradford Nthumb 109 J3
Bradford Abbas Dorset 22 D10
Bradford Leigh Wilts 29 N10
Bradford-on-Avon Wilts 29 N10
Bradford-on-Tone Somset 21 J9
Bradford Peverell Dorset 10 G6
Bradiford Devon 19 L6
Brading IoW 13 K7
Bradley Ches W 63 N3
Bradley Derbys 65 N3
Bradley Hants 25 L5
Bradley Kirk 85 J11
Bradley N York 90 G10
Bradley NE Lin 80 E2
Bradley Staffs 64 G8
Bradley Wolves 52 H2
Bradley Worcs 53 J8
Bradley Wrexhm 63 K1
Bradley Green Somset 21 L6
Bradley Green Warwks 65 P12
Bradley Green Worcs 53 J8
Bradley in the Moors Staffs 65 K4
Bradley Stoke S Glos 29 J6
Bradmore Notts 66 F6
Bradney Somset 21 M5
Bradninch Devon 9 J4
Bradninch Devon 19 M7
Bradnop Staffs 65 J1
Bradnor Green Herefs 51 J9
Bradpole Dorset 10 D6
Bradshaw Bolton 76 D1
Bradshaw Calder 84 G9
Bradshaw Kirk 84 G12
Bradstone Devon 7 M8
Bradwall Green Ches E 76 E11
Bradwell Derbys 77 M7
Bradwell Devon 19 K5
Bradwell Essex 46 E7
Bradwell M Keyn 44 B3
Bradwell Norfk 71 P11
Bradwell-on-Sea Essex 46 H10
Bradwell Waterside Essex 46 H10
Bradworthy Devon 18 F10
Brae Highld 138 C3
Brae Shet 147 i5
Braeface Falk 114 E5

Braehead Angus 125 N2
Braehead D & G 95 M8
Braehead S Lans 114 H11
Braeintra Highld 136 B9
Braemar Abers 131 L6
Braemore Highld 144 F9
Braemore Highld 151 K10
Brae Roy Lodge Highld 129 K6
Braeside Inver 113 J6
Braes of Coul Angus 124 F1
Braes of Enzie Moray 140 B4
Braes of Ullapool Highld 144 E6
Braeswick Ork 147 e2
Braevallich Ag & B 120 H11
Braewick Shet 147 h4
Brafferton Darltn 91 M2
Brafferton N York 85 N1
Brafield-on-the-Green Nhants 55 K9
Bragar W Isls 152 f2
Bragbury End Herts 45 K7
Braidwood S Lans 114 F11
Brailsford Derbys 65 N4
Brailsford Green Derbys 65 N4
Brain's Green Gloucs 41 K10
Braintree Essex 46 D7
Braiseworth Suffk 58 H6
Braishfield Hants 24 F8
Braiswick Essex 46 H6
Braithwaite C Brad 84 F7
Braithwaite Cumb 88 H2
Braithwell Donc 78 E5
Braken Hill Wakefd 85 N12
Bramber W Susx 14 H8
Brambridge Hants 24 H9
Bramcote Notts 66 E5
Bramcote Warwks 54 C3
Bramdean Hants 25 K8
Bramerton Norfk 71 L11
Bramfield Herts 45 K8
Bramfield Suffk 59 M6
Bramford Suffk 47 K2
Bramhall Stockp 76 G7
Bramham Leeds 85 N6
Bramhope Leeds 85 K6
Bramley Hants 31 N10
Bramley Leeds 85 K8
Bramley Rothm 78 D5
Bramley Surrey 14 E2
Bramley Corner Hants 31 N10
Bramley Green Hants 31 N10
Bramley Head N York 84 H4
Bramling Kent 35 M11
Brampford Speke Devon 8 H5
Brampton Cambs 56 D6
Brampton Cumb 89 R2
Brampton Cumb 98 G6
Brampton Lincs 79 L8
Brampton Norfk 71 J7
Brampton Rothm 78 C3
Brampton Suffk 59 N4
Brampton Abbotts Herefs 41 J6
Brampton Ash Nhants 55 K3
Brampton Bryan Herefs 51 L6
Brampton-en-le-Morthen Rothm 78 D6
Bramshall Staffs 65 K5
Bramshaw Hants 24 D10
Bramshill Hants 31 Q10
Bramshott Hants 25 P7
Bramwell Somset 21 P7
Branault Highld 127 J10
Brancaster Norfk 69 Q3
Brancaster Staithe Norfk 69 Q3
Brancepeth Dur 100 G10
Branchill Moray 139 K5
Brand End Lincs 68 G3
Branderburgh Moray 147 N11
Brandesburton E R Yk 87 L6
Brandeston Suffk 59 K8
Brand Green Gloucs 41 L6
Brandis Corner Devon 7 M4
Brandiston Norfk 70 H8
Brandon Dur 100 G10
Brandon Lincs 67 M3
Brandon Nthumb 108 G6
Brandon Suffk 57 Q3
Brandon Warwks 54 C5
Brandon Bank Norfk 57 M3
Brandon Creek Norfk 57 L2
Brandon Parva Norfk 70 G10
Brandsby N York 92 C12
Brandy Wharf Lincs 79 P4
Brane Cnwll 2 C9
Bran End Essex 46 B6
Branksome BCP 11 P6
Branksome Park BCP 11 P6
Bransbury Hants 24 G5
Bransby Lincs 79 M8
Branscombe Devon 9 M7
Bransford Worcs 52 E10
Bransgore Hants 12 C5
Bransholme C KuH 87 L8
Bransley Shrops 52 C5
Branson's Cross Worcs 53 K6
Branston Leics 67 K6
Branston Lincs 79 P10
Branston Staffs 65 N8
Branston Booths Lincs 79 Q10
Branstone IoW 13 J8
Brant Broughton Lincs 67 M1
Brantham Suffk 47 K5
Branthwaite Cumb 88 E2
Branthwaite Cumb 98 C10
Brantingham E R Yk 86 H9
Branton Donc 78 G3
Branton Nthumb 108 G6
Branton Green N York 85 N3
Branxton Nthumb 108 E2
Brassey Green Ches W 75 N11
Brasside Dur 100 H9
Brassington Derbys 65 N1
Brasted Kent 33 N11
Brasted Chart Kent 33 N11
Brathens Abers 132 G5
Bratoft Lincs 81 J10
Brattleby Lincs 79 N7
Bratton Somset 20 E4
Bratton Wilts 23 K3
Bratton Wrekin 64 B9
Bratton Clovelly Devon 7 N6
Bratton Fleming Devon 19 M6
Bratton Seymour Somset 22 F7
Braughing Herts 45 M6
Braughing Friars Herts 45 M7
Braunston Nhants 54 E7
Braunston Rutlnd 67 L10
Braunstone Town Leics 66 F11
Braunton Devon 19 J6
Brawby N York 92 E11
Brawl Highld 150 E3
Braworth N York 92 A5
Bray W & M 32 C6
Braybrooke Nhants 55 J4
Braydon Wilts 30 B5
Braydon Brook Wilts 30 A4
Braydon Side Wilts 30 B5
Brayford Devon 19 N6
Bray's Hill E Susx 16 B8
Bray Shop Cnwll 7 L10
Braystones Cumb 88 D5
Braythorn N York 85 J5
Brayton N York 86 B9
Braywick W & M 32 B6
Braywoodside W & M 32 C7
Brazacott Cnwll 7 K6
Breach Kent 17 M1
Breach Kent 34 E9
Breachwood Green Herts 44 G7
Breacleit W Isls 152 e3
Breaclete W Isls 152 e3
Breaden Heath Shrops 63 M5
Breadsall Derbys 66 B4
Breadstone Gloucs 29 L2
Breage Cnwll 2 F9
Breakachy Highld 137 N7
Breakish Highld 135 M11
Brealangwell Lodge Highld 145 M6
Bream Gloucs 41 J10
Breamore Hants 23 P9
Brean Somset 28 D11
Breanais W Isls 152 d4
Brearley Calder 84 F10
Brearton N York 85 L3
Breascleit W Isls 152 f3
Breasclete W Isls 152 f3
Breaston Derbys 66 D5
Brechfa Carmth 38 D6
Brechin Angus 132 F12
Breckles Norfk 58 D2
Brecon Powys 39 P6
Brecon Beacons National Park 39 N7
Bredbury Stockp 76 G5
Brede E Susx 16 E7
Bredenbury Herefs 51 Q9
Bredfield Suffk 59 K10
Bredgar Kent 34 F10
Bredhurst Kent 34 D10
Bredon Worcs 41 Q4
Bredon's Hardwick Worcs 41 P5
Bredon's Norton Worcs 41 Q4
Bredward Herefs 51 J9
Bredwardine Herefs 40 D3
Breedon on the Hill Leics 66 C7
Breich W Loth 114 H9
Breightmet Bolton 76 D2
Breighton E R Yk 86 D8
Breinton Herefs 40 G4
Bremhill Wilts 29 R8
Bremridge Devon 19 N7
Brenchley Kent 16 B2
Brendon Devon 7 L3
Brendon Devon 19 P4
Brendon Hill Somset 20 G6
Brenfield Ag & B 112 B5
Brenish W Isls 152 d4
Brenkley N u Ty 100 G3
Brent Cross Gt Lon 33 J5
Brent Eleigh Suffk 58 D11
Brentford Gt Lon 32 H7
Brentingby Leics 67 K8
Brent Knoll Somset 21 M3
Brent Mill Devon 5 L5
Brent Pelham Herts 45 N5
Brentwood Essex 33 Q4
Brenzett Kent 16 H5
Brenzett Green Kent 16 H5
Brereton Staffs 65 K9
Brereton Green Ches E 76 E10
Brereton Heath Ches E 76 E10
Brereton Hill Staffs 65 K9
Bressay Shet 147 j7
Bressingham Norfk 58 G4
Bressingham Common Norfk 58 G4
Bretby Derbys 65 P7
Bretford Warwks 54 C5
Bretforton Worcs 42 C3
Bretherton Lancs 83 L11
Brettabister Shet 147 i6
Brettenham Norfk 58 D4
Brettenham Suffk 58 E10
Bretton C Pete 68 C12
Bretton Derbys 77 M8
Bretton Flints 75 K11
Brewers End Essex 45 Q7
Brewer Street Surrey 33 L12
Brewood Staffs 64 G10
Briantspuddle Dorset 11 K6
Brick End Essex 45 Q6
Brickendon Herts 45 L10
Bricket Wood Herts 44 G11
Brick Houses Sheff 77 P7
Brickkiln Green Essex 46 C5
Bricklehampton Worcs 41 R3
Bride IoM 102 f2
Bridekirk Cumb 97 M11
Bridell Pembks 37 N2
Bridestowe Devon 7 P7
Brideswell Abers 140 F8
Bridford Devon 8 F7
Bridge Kent 35 L11
Bridge End Cumb 88 G10
Bridge End Cumb 98 D8
Bridge End Devon 5 L7
Bridge End Dur 100 C11
Bridge End Essex 46 B5
Bridge End Lincs 68 C5
Bridgefoot Angus 124 H6
Bridgefoot Cumb 97 L12
Bridge Green Essex 45 N4
Bridgehampton Somset 22 D8
Bridge Hewick N York 85 M1
Bridgehill Dur 100 E8
Bridgehouse Gate N York 84 H2
Bridgemary Hants 13 K4
Bridgemere Ches E 64 D3
Bridgend Abers 140 D8
Bridgend Ag & B 103 L2
Bridgend Ag & B 110 H9
Bridgend Ag & B 112 C3
Bridgend Angus 132 E10
Bridgend Brdgnd 27 L6
Bridgend Cerdgn 48 B11
Bridgend Cumb 89 L4
Bridgend D & G 106 E8
Bridgend Devon 5 J7
Bridgend Fife 124 H10
Bridgend Moray 140 B9
Bridgend P & K 124 C8
Bridgend W Loth 115 J6
Bridgend of Lintrathen Angus 124 F2
Bridge of Alford Abers 140 E12
Bridge of Allan Stirlg 114 E2
Bridge of Avon Moray 139 L12
Bridge of Avon Moray 139 M8
Bridge of Balgie P & K 122 F3
Bridge of Brewlands Angus 131 M12
Bridge of Brown Highld 139 L11
Bridge of Cally P & K 124 C3
Bridge of Canny Abers 132 G5
Bridge of Craigisla Angus 124 E2
Bridge of Dee D & G 96 E6
Bridge of Don C Aber 133 M2
Bridge of Dun Angus 125 N1
Bridge of Dye Abers 132 G7
Bridge of Earn P & K 124 C9
Bridge of Ericht P & K 122 E1
Bridge of Feugh Abers 132 H5
Bridge of Gairn Abers 131 Q5
Bridge of Gaur P & K 122 E1
Bridge of Marnoch Abers 140 F6
Bridge of Muchalls Abers 133 L6
Bridge of Orchy Ag & B 121 P5
Bridge of Tilt P & K 130 F11
Bridge of Tynet Moray 140 B4
Bridge of Walls Shet 147 h6
Bridge of Weir Rens 113 M8
Bridge Reeve Devon 19 M10
Bridgerule Devon 7 K4
Bridges Shrops 51 L1
Bridge Sollers Herefs 40 F3
Bridge Street Suffk 58 C10
Bridgetown Cnwll 7 L7
Bridgetown Somset 20 E7
Bridge Trafford Ches W 75 M9
Bridge Yate S Glos 29 K8
Bridgham Norfk 58 E3
Bridgnorth Shrops 52 D2
Bridgwater Somset 21 L6
Bridgwater Services Somset 21 M6
Bridlington E R Yk 87 M2
Bridport Dorset 10 D6
Bridstow Herefs 41 J7
Brierfield Lancs 84 C8
Brierley Barns 78 C2
Brierley Gloucs 41 J8
Brierley Herefs 51 N9
Brierley Hill Dudley 52 G3
Brierlow Bar Derbys 77 K9
Brierton Hartpl 101 L12
Briery Cumb 89 J2
Brigg N Linc 79 P2
Briggate Norfk 71 L7
Briggswath N York 92 H5
Brigham Cumb 89 J2
Brigham Cumb 97 M12
Brigham E R Yk 87 K4
Brighouse Calder 84 H10
Brighstone IoW 12 G8
Brightgate Derbys 77 P11
Brighthampton Oxon 42 H11
Brightholmlee Sheff 77 P4
Brightley Devon 8 B5
Brightling E Susx 16 B6
Brightlingsea Essex 47 K8
Brighton Br & H 15 K10
Brighton Cnwll 3 M4
Brighton City Airport W Susx 14 H9
Brighton le Sands Sefton 75 K4
Brightons Falk 114 G6
Brightwalton W Berk 31 J6
Brightwalton Green W Berk 31 J6
Brightwalton Holt W Berk 31 J7
Brightwell Suffk 47 N3
Brightwell Baldwin Oxon 31 N3
Brightwell-cum-Sotwell Oxon 31 M4
Brightwell Upperton Oxon 31 N3
Brignall Dur 90 H4
Brig o'Turk Stirlg 122 F11
Brigsley NE Lin 80 E3
Brigsteer Cumb 89 M9
Brigstock Nhants 55 N4
Brill Bucks 43 N9
Brill Cnwll 2 H8
Brilley Herefs 51 J11
Brimfield Herefs 51 N7
Brimfield Cross Herefs 51 P7
Brimington Derbys 78 C9
Brimley Devon 8 E9
Brimpsfield Gloucs 41 Q9
Brimpton W Berk 31 L9
Brimpton Common W Berk 31 M9
Brimscombe Gloucs 41 P11
Brimstage Wirral 75 J7
Brincliffe Sheff 77 Q7
Brind E R Yk 86 D9
Brindham Somset 22 C5
Brindister Shet 147 h6
Brindle Lancs 83 N10
Brindley Ches E 63 Q2
Brineton Staffs 64 E9
Bringhurst Leics 55 L2
Bringsty Common Herefs 52 C9
Brington Cambs 56 B5
Brinian Ork 147 c3
Briningham Norfk 70 F5
Brinkely Notts 66 H2
Brinkhill Lincs 80 G9
Brinkley Cambs 57 M9
Brinklow Warwks 54 D5
Brinkworth Wilts 30 B5
Brinscall Lancs 83 N11
Brinscombe Somset 21 P3
Brinsea N Som 28 F10
Brinsley Notts 66 D2
Brinsop Herefs 40 F3
Brinsworth Rothm 78 C6
Brinton Norfk 70 F5
Brisco Cumb 98 E8
Brisley Norfk 70 D8
Brislington Bristl 29 J8
Brissenden Green Kent 16 G3
Bristol Bristl 29 J8
Bristol Airport N Som 28 G9
Briston Norfk 70 F6
Brisworthy Devon 5 J4
Britannia Lancs 84 C11
Britford Wilts 23 P8
Brithdir Caerph 39 Q11
Brithdir Gwynd 61 N8
British Legion Village Kent 34 C10
Briton Ferry Neath 26 H3
Britwell Salome Oxon 31 N4
Brixham Torbay 5 Q5
Brixton Devon 5 J6
Brixton Gt Lon 33 K7
Brixton Deverill Wilts 23 J5
Brixworth Nhants 55 J6
Brize Norton Oxon 42 G10
Brize Norton Airport Oxon 42 G10
Broad Alley Worcs 52 G7
Broad Blunsdon Swindn 30 D4
Broadbottom Tamesd 77 J5
Broadbridge W Susx 13 P4
Broadbridge Heath W Susx 14 G4
Broad Campden Gloucs 42 D4
Broad Carr Calder 84 G11
Broad Chalke Wilts 23 M8
Broad Clough Lancs 84 C10
Broadclyst Devon 9 J5
Broadfield Inver 113 L6
Broadfield Pembks 37 M9
Broadford Highld 135 L11
Broad Ford Kent 16 C3
Broadford Bridge W Susx 14 G6
Broadgairhill Border 106 G7
Broadgrass Green Suffk 58 E8
Broad Green Cambs 57 N8
Broad Green Essex 46 F7
Broad Green Worcs 52 E9
Broad Green Worcs 53 J6
Broadhaugh Border 117 J10
Broad Haven Pembks 36 G8
Broadheath Traffd 76 E6
Broadhembury Devon 9 L4
Broadhempston Devon 5 N3
Broad Hill Cambs 57 L5
Broad Hinton Wilts 30 C7
Broadholme Lincs 79 M9
Broadland Row E Susx 16 E7
Broadlay Carmth 38 B10
Broad Layings Hants 31 J10
Broadley Essex 45 M10
Broadley Lancs 84 C12
Broadley Moray 140 B3
Broadley Common Essex 45 M10
Broad Marston Worcs 42 D2
Broadmayne Dorset 10 H7
Broad Meadow Staffs 64 F2
Broadmere Hants 25 K4
Broadmoor Gloucs 41 K8
Broadmoor Pembks 37 L9
Broadnymett Devon 8 D4
Broad Oak Carmth 38 E7
Broad Oak Cumb 88 F8
Broadoak Dorset 10 C5
Broad Oak E Susx 16 C6
Broad Oak E Susx 16 E7
Broadoak Gloucs 41 L9
Broad Oak Hants 25 N3
Broad Oak Herefs 40 G7
Broad Oak Kent 35 L10
Broad Oak St Hel 75 P5
Broadoak Wrexhm 75 L12
Broad Road Suffk 59 K5
Broadsands Torbay 5 Q5
Broad's Green Essex 46 C9
Broadstairs Kent 35 Q9
Broadstone BCP 11 N6
Broadstone Mons 40 G11
Broadstone Shrops 51 P3
Broad Street E Susx 16 F7
Broad Street Essex 45 Q8
Broad Street Kent 17 K3
Broad Street Kent 34 E11
Broad Street Medway 34 D8
Broad Street Wilts 30 C10
Broad Street Green Essex 46 F9
Broad Town Wilts 30 C7
Broadwas Worcs 52 D9
Broadwater Herts 45 J7
Broadwater W Susx 14 G10
Broadwaters Worcs 52 F5
Broadway Carmth 37 Q9
Broadway Carmth 38 B10
Broadway Pembks 36 G8
Broadway Somset 21 M10
Broadway Suffk 59 M5
Broadway Worcs 42 C4
Broadwell Gloucs 41 J9
Broadwell Gloucs 42 E6
Broadwell Oxon 42 F10
Broadwell Warwks 54 D7
Broadwey Dorset 10 G8
Broadwindsor Dorset 10 C4
Broadwood Kelly Devon 8 B3
Broadwoodwidger Devon 7 M7
Brobury Herefs 40 D3
Brochel Highld 135 K6
Brochroy Ag & B 121 J6
Brock Lancs 83 L7
Brockamin Worcs 52 E10
Brockbridge Hants 25 K9
Brockdish Norfk 59 J5
Brockencote Worcs 52 G6
Brockenhurst Hants 12 E4
Brocketsbrae S Lans 105 Q2
Brockford Green Suffk 58 G7
Brockford Street Suffk 58 G7
Brockhall Nhants 54 G8
Brockhall Village Lancs 83 Q8
Brockham Surrey 14 H1
Brockhampton Gloucs 41 Q6
Brockhampton Gloucs 42 B7
Brockhampton Hants 13 M3
Brockhampton Herefs 41 J5
Brockhampton Green Dorset 10 H3
Brockholes Kirk 77 M2
Brockhurst Derbys 77 Q10
Brockhurst Warwks 54 D4
Brocklebank Cumb 98 C9
Brocklesby Lincs 80 C1
Brockley N Som 28 G9
Brockley Suffk 58 B6
Brockley Green Suffk 46 C2
Brockley Green Suffk 58 B9
Brockleymoor Cumb 98 F11
Brockmoor Dudley 52 G3
Brockscombe Devon 7 N6
Brock's Green Hants 31 K10
Brockton Shrops 51 K3
Brockton Shrops 51 P2
Brockton Shrops 63 K11
Brockton Shrops 64 D11
Brockton Staffs 64 F6
Brockweir Gloucs 28 H2
Brockwood Park Hants 25 K8
Brockworth Gloucs 41 P8
Brocton Cnwll 6 E11
Brocton Staffs 64 H8
Brodick N Ayrs 103 Q3
Brodie Moray 138 H4
Brodsworth Donc 78 E2
Brogaig Highld 134 H2
Brogborough C Beds 44 D4
Brokenborough Wilts 29 Q4
Broken Cross Ches E 76 G9
Broken Cross Ches W 76 C9
Brokerswood Wilts 23 J3
Bromborough Wirral 75 K7
Brome Suffk 58 H5
Brome Street Suffk 58 H5
Bromeswell Suffk 59 L10
Bromfield Cumb 97 N9
Bromfield Shrops 51 N5
Bromham Bed 55 P10
Bromham Wilts 29 Q9
Bromley Barns 77 Q4
Bromley Dudley 52 G3
Bromley Gt Lon 33 M8
Bromley Shrops 52 D2
Bromley Common Gt Lon 33 M9
Bromley Cross Bolton 76 D1
Bromley Cross Essex 47 J6
Bromley Green Kent 16 H3
Bromlow Shrops 63 K11
Brompton Medway 34 D8
Brompton N York 91 P7
Brompton-by-Sawdon N York 93 J10
Brompton-on-Swale N York 91 L7
Brompton Ralph Somset 20 H7
Brompton Regis Somset 20 E7
Bromsash Herefs 41 K7
Bromsberrow Gloucs 41 L5
Bromsberrow Heath Gloucs 41 L5
Bromsgrove Worcs 52 H6
Bromstead Heath Staffs 64 E8
Bromyard Herefs 52 C9
Bromyard Downs Herefs 52 C9
Bronaber Gwynd 61 M6
Bronant Cerdgn 49 L7
Broncroft Shrops 51 P3
Brongest Cerdgn 48 E11
Bronington Wrexhm 63 M5
Bronllys Powys 39 Q5
Bronwydd Carmth 38 B7
Bronydd Powys 40 B3
Bronygarth Shrops 63 J5
Brook Carmth 37 P8
Brook Hants 24 D10
Brook Hants 24 E7
Brook IoW 12 F8
Brook Kent 17 J2
Brook Surrey 14 D3
Brook Surrey 14 F2
Brooke Norfk 71 K12
Brooke Rutlnd 67 L11
Brookenby Lincs 80 D5
Brook End Bed 55 Q8
Brook End C Beds 56 C11
Brook End Cambs 55 Q6
Brook End M Keyn 44 C3
Brookfield Rens 113 N8
Brookhampton Oxon 31 M3
Brookhampton Somset 22 E8
Brook Hill Hants 24 D10
Brookhouse Denbgs 74 E10
Brookhouse Lancs 83 M2
Brookhouse Rothm 78 E6
Brookhouse Green Ches E 76 E11
Brookhouses Derbys 77 J6
Brookland Kent 16 H5
Brooklands Traffd 76 E5
Brookmans Park Herts 45 J11
Brooks Powys 62 G12
Brooksby Leics 66 H9
Brooks End Kent 35 N9
Brooks Green W Susx 14 G6
Brook Street Essex 33 Q4
Brook Street Kent 16 G4
Brook Street Suffk 58 B11
Brook Street W Susx 15 K5
Brookthorpe Gloucs 41 N9
Brookville Norfk 57 P1
Brookwood Surrey 32 D11
Broom C Beds 44 H3
Broom Rothm 78 D5
Broom Warwks 53 K10
Broombank Worcs 52 C6
Broome Norfk 59 M2
Broome Shrops 51 L4
Broome Worcs 52 G5
Broomedge Warrtn 76 D6
Broome Park Nthumb 109 J7
Broomer's Corner W Susx 14 G6
Broomershill W Susx 14 F7
Broomfield Essex 46 C9
Broomfield Kent 34 E11
Broomfield Kent 35 M9
Broomfield Somset 21 K7
Broomfields Shrops 63 M8
Broomfleet E R Yk 86 G9
Broom Green Norfk 70 E7
Broomhall W & M 32 D9
Broomhaugh Nthumb 100 C6
Broom Hill Barns 78 C3
Broom Hill Dorset 11 P4
Broom Hill Notts 66 E3
Broomhill Nthumb 109 L9
Broom Hill Worcs 52 G5
Broomhill Green Ches E 63 Q3
Broomley Nthumb 100 D6
Broompark Dur 100 G10
Broom's Green Gloucs 41 L5
Broomsthorpe Norfk 70 C6
Broom Street Kent 35 J10
Brora Highld 146 G4
Broseley Shrops 64 C11
Brotherhouse Bar Lincs 68 E9
Brotherlee Dur 99 P10
Brothertoft Lincs 68 E3
Brotherton N York 85 P10
Brotton R & Cl 92 E3
Broubster Highld 151 J5
Brough Cumb 90 C4
Brough Derbys 77 M7
Brough E R Yk 86 H10
Brough Highld 151 M2
Brough Notts 79 L12
Brough Shet 147 j5
Broughall Shrops 63 P4
Brough Lodge Shet 147 k3
Brough Sowerby Cumb 90 C4
Broughton Border 106 E3
Broughton Bucks 44 B9
Broughton Cambs 56 F5
Broughton Flints 75 K11
Broughton Hants 24 E7
Broughton Lancs 83 M8
Broughton M Keyn 44 C4
Broughton N Linc 79 N2
Broughton N York 84 D5
Broughton N York 92 F12
Broughton Nhants 55 L5
Broughton Oxon 43 J4
Broughton Salfd 76 F3
Broughton Staffs 64 E5
Broughton V Glam 27 L8
Broughton Astley Leics 54 E2
Broughton Beck Cumb 89 J10
Broughton Gifford Wilts 29 P9
Broughton Green Worcs 52 H8
Broughton Hackett Worcs 52 G9
Broughton-in-Furness Cumb 88 G9
Broughton Mains D & G 95 N9
Broughton Mills Cumb 88 H8
Broughton Moor Cumb 97 L11
Broughton Poggs Oxon 42 F10
Broughton Tower Cumb 88 G9
Broughty Ferry C Dund 125 J7
Brough with St Giles N York 91 L7
Brow End Cumb 88 H11
Brownber Cumb 90 B5
Brown Candover Hants 25 K5
Brown Edge Lancs 83 J12
Brown Edge Staffs 64 G1
Brown Heath Ches W 75 M10
Brownheath Shrops 63 M6
Brownhill Abers 141 L8
Brownhills Fife 125 K9
Brownhills Wsall 65 K11
Brownieside Nthumb 109 K5
Browninghill Green Hants 31 M10
Brown Knowl Ches W 63 N1
Brown Lees Staffs 76 G12
Brownlow Heath Ches E 76 F11
Brownrigg Cumb 88 D3
Brownrigg Cumb 97 N8
Brownsea Island Dorset 11 N7
Brown's Green Birm 53 K2
Brownsham Devon 18 F8
Browns Hill Gloucs 41 P11
Brownsover Warwks 54 E5
Brownston Devon 5 L6
Brown Street Suffk 58 F8
Browston Green Norfk 71 P11
Broxa N York 93 J8
Broxbourne Herts 45 L10
Broxburn E Loth 116 F6
Broxburn W Loth 115 K7
Broxfield Nthumb 109 K6
Broxted Essex 45 Q6
Broxton Ches W 63 N1
Broyle Side E Susx 15 N8
Bruan Highld 151 P8
Bruar P & K 130 F11
Bruchag Ag & B 112 G9
Bruera Ches W 75 M11
Bruern Abbey Oxon 42 F7
Bruichladdich Ag & B 110 G9
Bruisyard Suffk 59 L7
Bruisyard Street Suffk 59 L7
Brumby N Linc 79 M2
Brund Staffs 77 L11
Brundall Norfk 71 L10
Brundish Suffk 59 K7
Brundish Street Suffk 59 K6
Brunery Highld 127 N10
Brunnion Cnwll 2 E7
Brunslow Shrops 51 L4
Brunswick Village N u Ty 100 G4
Bruntcliffe Leeds 85 K10
Brunthwaite C Brad 84 F6
Bruntingthorpe Leics 54 G3
Brunton Fife 124 G8
Brunton Nthumb 109 K5
Brunton Wilts 30 F11
Brushford Devon 8 C3
Brushford Somset 20 E8
Bruton Somset 22 F6
Bryan's Green Worcs 52 G7
Bryanston Dorset 11 L3
Bryant's Bottom Bucks 32 B2
Brydekirk D & G 97 N4
Bryher IoS 2 b1
Brymbo Wrexhm 63 J1
Brympton Somset 22 C10
Bryn Carmth 26 E2
Bryn Ches W 75 Q9
Bryn Neath 27 J4
Bryn Shrops 51 J4
Bryn Wigan 75 P3
Brynamman Carmth 38 H9
Brynberian Pembks 37 L3
Brynbryddan Neath 27 J4
Bryn Bwbach Gwynd 61 K5
Bryncae Rhondd 27 N6
Bryncethin Brdgnd 27 L5
Bryncir Gwynd 60 H3
Bryn-côch Neath 26 H2
Bryncroes Gwynd 60 C6
Bryncrug Gwynd 61 K11
Bryn Du IoA 72 E9
Bryn-Eden Gwynd 61 M6
Bryneglwys Denbgs 62 G3
Bryneglwys & Abergynolwyn Slate Landscape Gwynd 61 L11
Brynfields Wrexhm 63 K3
Brynford Flints 74 G9
Bryn Gates Wigan 75 Q3
Bryn Golau Rhondd 27 N5
Bryngwran IoA 72 F8
Bryngwyn Mons 40 E10
Bryngwyn Powys 50 G10
Bryn-Henllan Pembks 37 K3
Brynhoffnant Cerdgn 48 E10
Bryning Lancs 83 J9
Brynithel Blae G 28 B2
Brynmawr Blae G 40 B9
Bryn-mawr Gwynd 60 D5
Brynmenyn Brdgnd 27 L5
Brynmill Swans 26 F4
Brynna Rhondd 27 N6
Brynnau Gwynion Rhondd 27 M6
Bryn-penarth Powys 62 F11
Brynrefail Gwynd 73 J11
Brynrefail IoA 72 H6
Brynsadler Rhondd 27 N6
Bryn Saith Marchog Denbgs 62 E2
Brynsiencyn IoA 72 H10
Brynteg IoA 72 H7
Bryn-y-bal Flints 75 J10
Bryn-y-Maen Conwy 73 P8
Bryn-yr-Eos Wrexhm 63 J4
Bualintur Highld 134 G11
Buarth-draw Flints 74 G8
Bubbenhall Warwks 54 B6
Bubwith E R Yk 86 D8
Buccleuch Border 107 J7
Buchanan Smithy Stirlg 113 N3
Buchanhaven Abers 141 Q6
Buchanty P & K 123 N7
Buchany Stirlg 123 J12
Buchlyvie Stirlg 113 Q2
Buckabank Cumb 98 D8
Buckden Cambs 56 D7
Buckden N York 90 F11
Buckenham Norfk 71 M11
Buckerell Devon 9 L5
Buckfast Devon 5 M3
Buckfastleigh Devon 5 M3
Buckhaven Fife 115 Q2
Buckholt Mons 40 G8
Buckhorn Devon 7 M5
Buckhorn Weston Dorset 22 G8
Buckhurst Hill Essex 33 M3
Buckie Moray 140 C3
Buckingham Bucks 43 P5
Buckland Bucks 44 C9
Buckland Devon 5 L8
Buckland Gloucs 42 C4
Buckland Hants 12 E5
Buckland Herts 45 L5
Buckland Kent 17 P2
Buckland Oxon 30 H3
Buckland Surrey 33 J12
Buckland Brewer Devon 18 H9
Buckland Common Bucks 44 C10
Buckland Dinham Somset 22 G3
Buckland Filleigh Devon 7 N3
Buckland in the Moor Devon 8 D10
Buckland Monachorum Devon 4 H3
Buckland Newton Dorset 10 G4
Buckland Ripers Dorset 10 G8
Buckland St Mary Somset 21 L10
Buckland-Tout-Saints Devon 5 M7
Bucklebury W Berk 31 L8
Bucklers Hard Hants 12 G5
Bucklesham Suffk 47 M3
Buckley Flints 75 J11
Buckley Green Warwks 53 M7
Bucklow Hill Ches E 76 D7
Buckminster Leics 67 L7
Bucknall C Stke 64 G3
Bucknall Lincs 80 D10
Bucknell Oxon 43 M6
Bucknell Shrops 51 K6
Buckpool Moray 140 C3
Bucksburn C Aber 133 L2
Buck's Cross Devon 18 G9
Bucks Green W Susx 14 F4
Buckshaw Village Lancs 83 M11
Bucks Hill Herts 32 F2
Bucks Horn Oak Hants 25 P5
Buck's Mills Devon 18 G8
Buckton E R Yk 93 N12
Buckton Herefs 51 L6
Buckton Nthumb 108 H2
Buckworth Cambs 56 C5
Budby Notts 78 G9
Buddileigh Staffs 64 D2
Bude Cnwll 7 J4
Budge's Shop Cnwll 4 E5
Budlake Devon 9 J5
Budle Nthumb 109 J3
Budleigh Salterton Devon 9 K8
Budlett's Common E Susx 15 N6
Budock Water Cnwll 3 J8
Buerton Ches E 64 C4
Bugbrooke Nhants 54 H9
Bugford Devon 5 N6
Buglawton Ches E 76 G11
Bugle Cnwll 3 P3
Bugley Dorset 22 H8
Bugthorpe E R Yk 86 E4
Buildwas Shrops 64 B11
Builth Road Powys 50 D10
Builth Wells Powys 50 E10
Bulbourne Herts 44 D9
Bulbridge Wilts 23 N7
Bulby Lincs 67 Q7
Bulcote Notts 66 G3
Buldoo Highld 150 H3
Bulford Wilts 23 Q5
Bulford Camp Wilts 24 C5
Bulkeley Ches E 63 P1
Bulkington Warwks 54 C3
Bulkington Wilts 29 Q10
Bulkworthy Devon 18 H10
Bullamoor N York 91 P8
Bull Bay IoA 72 G5
Bullbridge Derbys 66 B2
Bullbrook Br For 32 C8
Bullen's Green Herts 45 J10
Bulley Gloucs 41 M8
Bullgill Cumb 97 M10
Bullingham Herefs 40 G4
Bullinghope Herefs 40 G4
Bullington Hants 24 G5
Bullington Lincs 80 B8
Bullockstone Kent 35 L9
Bull's Green Herts 45 K8
Bull's Green Norfk 59 N2
Bulmer Essex 46 E4
Bulmer N York 86 C2
Bulmer Tye Essex 46 E4
Bulphan Thurr 34 B5
Bulstone Devon 9 M7
Bulstrode Herts 44 E11
Bulverhythe E Susx 16 D9
Bulwark Abers 141 M7
Bulwell C Nott 66 E3
Bulwick Nhants 55 N2
Bumble's Green Essex 45 M10
Bunacaimb Highld 127 M6
Bunarkaig Highld 128 H7
Bunbury Ches E 75 P12
Bunbury Heath Ches E 75 P12
Bunchrew Highld 138 B6
Buncton W Susx 14 G8
Bundalloch Highld 136 B10
Bunessan Ag & B 119 L8
Bungay Suffk 59 L3
Bunker's Hill Lincs 68 E1
Bunnahabhain Ag & B 111 J6
Bunny Notts 66 F6
Buntait Highld 137 L9
Buntingford Herts 45 L6
Bunwell Norfk 58 G2
Bunwell Hill Norfk 58 H2
Bupton Derbys 65 N5
Burbage Derbys 77 K9
Burbage Leics 54 D2
Burbage Wilts 30 F10
Burcher Herefs 51 K8
Burchett's Green W & M 32 B6
Burcombe Wilts 23 N7
Burcot Oxon 31 M3
Burcot Worcs 52 H6
Burcote Shrops 52 D2
Burcott Bucks 44 B8
Burcott Bucks 44 C7
Burdale N York 86 G3
Bures Essex 46 F5
Burford Oxon 42 F9
Burford Shrops 51 Q7
Burg Ag & B 119 L4
Burgate Suffk 58 G5
Burgates Hants 25 N7
Burge End Herts 44 G5
Burgess Hill W Susx 15 K7
Burgh Suffk 59 J10
Burgh by Sands Cumb 98 C6
Burgh Castle Norfk 71 P11
Burghclere Hants 31 K10
Burghead Moray 139 L2
Burghfield W Berk 31 N8
Burghfield Common W Berk 31 N9
Burgh Heath Surrey 33 J10
Burgh Hill E Susx 16 C5
Burghill Herefs 40 G3
Burgh Island Devon 5 K8
Burgh le Marsh Lincs 81 J10
Burgh next Aylsham Norfk 71 J7
Burgh on Bain Lincs 80 D6
Burgh St Margaret Norfk 71 N9
Burgh St Peter Norfk 59 P2
Burghwallis Donc 78 E1
Burham Kent 34 C10
Buriton Hants 25 M9
Burland Ches E 63 Q2
Burlawn Cnwll 6 E10
Burleigh Gloucs 41 P11
Burlescombe Devon 20 G10
Burleston Dorset 11 J6
Burlestone Devon 5 N7
Burley Hants 12 C4
Burley Rutlnd 67 L10
Burley Shrops 51 N4
Burleydam Ches E 63 Q4
Burley Gate Herefs 41 J2
Burley in Wharfedale C Brad 84 H6
Burley Lawn Hants 12 C4
Burley Street Hants 12 C4
Burley Wood Head C Brad 84 H6
Burlingham Green Norfk 71 M10
Burlingjobb Powys 51 J9
Burlington Shrops 64 E10
Burlton Shrops 63 M7
Burmarsh Kent 17 K4
Burmington Warwks 42 F4
Burn N York 86 B9
Burnage Manch 76 F5
Burnaston Derbys 65 P6
Burnbanks Cumb 89 N3
Burnbrae N Lans 114 F9
Burn Bridge N York 85 L5
Burnby E R Yk 86 F6
Burn Cross Sheff 77 Q4
Burndell W Susx 14 E10
Burnden Bolton 76 D2
Burnedge Rochdl 76 G2
Burneside Cumb 89 N7
Burneston N York 91 M9
Burnett BaNES 29 K9
Burnfoot Border 107 L7
Burnfoot Border 107 N6
Burnfoot D & G 106 C11
Burnfoot D & G 107 J12
Burnfoot D & G 107 K10
Burnfoot P & K 123 P12
Burnham Bucks 32 D6
Burnham N Linc 87 K11
Burnham Deepdale Norfk 69 Q3
Burnham Green Herts 45 J8
Burnham Market Norfk 70 B4
Burnham Norton Norfk 70 B3
Burnham-on-Crouch Essex 34 G3
Burnham-on-Sea Somset 21 M3
Burnham Overy Norfk 70 B4
Burnham Overy Staithe Norfk 70 C3
Burnham Thorpe Norfk 70 C4
Burnhead D & G 105 Q10
Burnhervie Abers 140 H12
Burnhill Green Staffs 64 E12
Burnhope Dur 100 F8
Burnhouse N Ayrs 113 M11
Burniston N York 93 K8
Burnley Lancs 84 C8
Burnmouth Border 117 L9
Burn Naze Lancs 82 H6
Burn of Cambus Stirlg 123 J12
Burnopfield Dur 100 F7
Burnrigg Cumb 98 F7
Burnsall N York 84 F3
Burnside Angus 124 H1

Burnside Angus 125 K3
Burnside Fife 124 D11
Burnside Moray 147 L11
Burnside W Loth 115 K6
Burnside of Duntrune Angus 125 J6
Burntcommon Surrey 32 E11
Burntheath Derbys 65 N6
Burnt Heath Essex 47 J6
Burnt Hill W Berk 31 M7
Burnthouse Cnwll 3 J7
Burnt Houses Dur 91 J2
Burntisland Fife 115 N4
Burnt Oak E Susx 15 P5
Burnton E Ayrs 105 J8
Burntwood Flints 75 J10
Burntwood Staffs 65 K10
Burntwood Green Staffs 65 K10
Burnt Yates N York 85 K3
Burnworthy Somset 21 K10
Burpham Surrey 32 E12
Burpham W Susx 14 E9
Burradon N Tyne 100 H4
Burradon Nthumb 108 F8
Burrafirth Shet 147 k2
Burras Cnwll 2 H7
Burraton Cnwll 4 F3
Burravoe Shet 147 j4
Burray Village Ork 147 c5
Burrells Cumb 89 R3
Burrelton P & K 124 D5
Burridge Devon 9 Q3
Burridge Devon 19 L6
Burridge Hants 13 J3
Burrill N York 91 L9
Burringham N Linc 79 L2
Burrington Devon 19 M10
Burrington Herefs 51 M6
Burrington N Som 28 G10
Burrough End Cambs 57 M9
Burrough Green Cambs 57 M9
Burrough on the Hill Leics 67 J10
Burrow Lancs 89 Q11
Burrow Somset 20 E5
Burrow Bridge Somset 21 M7
Burrowhill Surrey 32 D9
Burrows Cross Surrey 14 F2
Burry Swans 26 C4
Burry Green Swans 26 C4
Burry Port Carmth 26 C2
Burscough Lancs 75 M1
Burscough Bridge Lancs 75 M1
Bursea E R Yk 86 E8
Burshill E R Yk 87 K5
Bursledon Hants 12 H3
Burslem C Stke 64 F2
Burstall Suffk 47 K3
Burstock Dorset 10 C4
Burston Norfk 58 H4
Burston Staffs 64 H6
Burstow Surrey 15 K3
Burstwick E R Yk 87 N9
Burtersett N York 90 E9
Burtholme Cumb 98 G5
Burthorpe Green Suffk 57 P8
Burthwaite Cumb 98 E8
Burthy Cnwll 3 M3
Burtle Somset 21 N5
Burtle Hill Somset 21 N4
Burtoft Lincs 68 E5
Burton BCP 12 B6
Burton Ches W 75 K9
Burton Ches W 75 N11
Burton Dorset 10 G6
Burton Nthumb 109 K3
Burton Pembks 37 J9
Burton Somset 21 K4
Burton Somset 22 C10
Burton Wilts 22 H7
Burton Wilts 29 N6
Burton Agnes E R Yk 87 L3
Burton Bradstock Dorset 10 D7
Burton-by-Lincoln Lincs 79 N9
Burton Coggles Lincs 67 N7
Burton Dassett Warwks 54 C10
Burton End Essex 45 P7
Burton End Suffk 46 B3
Burton Fleming E R Yk 93 M12
Burton Green Warwks 53 P5
Burton Green Wrexhm 75 K12
Burton Hastings Warwks 54 C3
Burton Hill Wilts 29 Q5
Burton-in-Kendal Cumb 89 N11
Burton-in-Kendal Services Cumb 89 N11
Burton in Lonsdale N York 89 Q12
Burton Joyce Notts 66 G3
Burton Latimer Nhants 55 M6
Burton Lazars Leics 67 J9
Burton Leonard N York 85 L2
Burton on the Wolds Leics 66 F8
Burton Overy Leics 54 H1
Burton Pedwardine Lincs 68 C4
Burton Pidsea E R Yk 87 N9
Burton Salmon N York 85 P9
Burton's Green Essex 46 E6
Burton upon Stather N Linc 86 G11
Burton upon Trent Staffs 65 N7
Burton Waters Lincs 79 M9
Burtonwood Warrtn 75 P5
Burtonwood Services Warrtn 75 P5
Burwardsley Ches W 75 N12
Burwarton Shrops 52 B4
Burwash E Susx 16 B6
Burwash Common E Susx 16 B6
Burwash Weald E Susx 16 B6
Burwell Cambs 57 L7
Burwell Lincs 80 G8
Burwen IoA 72 G5
Burwick Ork 147 c6
Bury Bury 76 E1
Bury Cambs 56 F4
Bury Somset 20 E8
Bury W Susx 14 E8
Bury End C Beds 44 G5
Bury Green Herts 45 N7
Bury St Edmunds Suffk 58 C8
Burythorpe N York 86 E2
Busby E Rens 113 Q10
Busby Stoop N York 91 P10
Buscot Oxon 30 F3
Bush Abers 133 J11
Bush Cnwll 7 J3
Bush Bank Herefs 51 M10
Bushbury Wolves 64 G11
Bushby Leics 66 G11
Bushey Herts 32 G3
Bushey Heath Herts 32 G3
Bush Green Norfk 59 J3
Bush Green Suffk 58 D9
Bush Hill Park Gt Lon 33 L3
Bushley Worcs 41 P5
Bushley Green Worcs 41 P5
Bushmead Bed 56 C8
Bushmoor Shrops 51 M3
Bushton Wilts 30 C7
Busk Cumb 98 H10
Buslingthorpe Lincs 79 Q6
Bussage Gloucs 41 P11
Bussex Somset 21 M6
Butcher's Cross E Susx 15 Q6
Butcombe N Som 28 G10
Bute Ag & B 112 F7
Butleigh Somset 22 C6
Butleigh Wootton Somset 22 C6
Butler's Cross Bucks 44 B10
Butler's Hill Notts 66 E3
Butlers Marston Warwks 53 Q10
Butley Suffk 59 M10
Butley High Corner Suffk 59 M10
Buttercrambe N York 86 D4
Butterdean Border 116 H8
Butterknowle Dur 91 J2
Butterleigh Devon 9 J3
Butterley Derbys 66 C2
Buttermere Cumb 88 G3
Buttermere Wilts 30 H10
Buttershaw C Brad 84 H9
Butterstone P & K 123 Q4
Butterton Staffs 64 F4
Butterton Staffs 77 K12
Butterwick Dur 101 K12
Butterwick Lincs 68 G3
Butterwick N York 87 J1
Butterwick N York 92 E11
Butt Green Ches E 64 C2
Buttington Powys 62 H10
Buttonbridge Shrops 52 D5
Buttonoak Shrops 52 D5
Buttsash Hants 12 G3
Buttsbear Cross Cnwll 7 K4
Butt's Green Essex 46 D11
Buxhall Suffk 58 E9
Buxhall Fen Street Suffk 58 E9
Buxted E Susx 15 P6
Buxton Derbys 77 K9
Buxton Norfk 71 J7
Buxton Heath Norfk 71 J8
Buxworth Derbys 77 J7
Bwlch Powys 39 Q7
Bwlchgwyn Wrexhm 63 J2
Bwlchllan Cerdgn 49 K9
Bwlchnewydd Carmth 38 A7
Bwlchtocyn Gwynd 60 E7
Bwlch-y-cibau Powys 62 G8
Bwlch-y-Ddar Powys 62 G8
Bwlchyfadfa Cerdgn 48 G10
Bwlch-y-ffridd Powys 50 E2
Bwlch-y-groes Pembks 37 P3
Bwlchymyrdd Swans 26 E3
Bwlch-y-sarnau Powys 50 E6
Byermoor Gatesd 100 F7
Byers Green Dur 100 G11
Byfield Nhants 54 E10
Byfleet Surrey 32 F10
Byford Herefs 40 E3
Bygrave Herts 45 K4
Byker N u Ty 100 H5
Byland Abbey N York 92 B11
Bylaugh Norfk 70 F8
Bylchau Conwy 74 D11
Byley Ches W 76 D10
Bynea Carmth 26 E3
Byram N York 85 P10
Byrness Nthumb 108 C9
Bystock Devon 9 J8
Bythorn Cambs 55 Q5
Byton Herefs 51 L8
Bywell Nthumb 100 D6
Byworth W Susx 14 E6

C

Cabbacott Devon 18 H9
Cabourne Lincs 80 C3
Cabrach Ag & B 111 L8
Cabrach Moray 140 B10
Cabus Lancs 83 L5
Cackle Street E Susx 15 N5
Cackle Street E Susx 16 C7
Cackle Street E Susx 16 E7
Cadbury Devon 8 G4
Cadbury Barton Devon 19 N10
Cadbury World Birm 53 K4
Cadder E Duns 114 B7
Caddington C Beds 44 F8
Caddonfoot Border 107 L3
Cadeby Donc 78 E4
Cadeby Leics 66 C11
Cadeleigh Devon 8 H3
Cade Street E Susx 15 R6
Cadgwith Cnwll 2 H11
Cadham Fife 124 F12
Cadishead Salfd 76 D5
Cadle Swans 26 F3
Cadley Lancs 83 M9
Cadley Wilts 24 D3
Cadley Wilts 30 E9
Cadmore End Bucks 31 R4
Cadnam Hants 24 E10
Cadney N Linc 79 P3
Cadole Flints 74 H11
Cadoxton V Glam 27 Q8
Cadoxton Juxta-Neath Neath 26 H3
Cadwst Denbgs 62 E5
Caeathro Gwynd 72 H11
Caehopkin Powys 39 K9
Caenby Lincs 79 P6
Caerau Brdgnd 27 K3
Caerau Cardif 27 Q7
Cae'r-bont Powys 39 J9
Cae'r bryn Carmth 38 F9
Caerdeon Gwynd 61 L8
Caer Farchell Pembks 36 F5
Caergeiliog IoA 72 E8
Caergwrle Flints 75 J12
Caerhun Conwy 73 N9
Caerlanrig Border 107 K9
Caerleon Newpt 28 D4
Caernarfon Gwynd 72 H11
Caernarfon Castle Gwynd 72 H11
Caerphilly Caerph 27 R5
Caersws Powys 50 E2
Caerwedros Cerdgn 48 F9
Caerwent Mons 28 G4
Caerwys Flints 74 F9
Caerynwch Gwynd 61 N8
Caggle Street Mons 40 E8
Caim IoA 73 K7
Caio Carmth 38 G4
Cairinis W Isls 152 c8
Cairnbaan Ag & B 112 B3
Cairnbulg Abers 141 P3
Cairncross Border 117 K8
Cairncurran Inver 113 L7
Cairndow Ag & B 121 M10
Cairneyhill Fife 115 J4
Cairngarroch D & G 94 F8
Cairngorms National Park 131 K4
Cairnie Abers 140 D7
Cairn Lodge Services S Lans 105 Q3
Cairnorrie Abers 141 L7
Cairnryan D & G 94 F4
Cairnty Moray 139 P5
Caister-on-Sea Norfk 71 P9
Caistor Lincs 80 C3
Caistor St Edmund Norfk 71 J11
Cakebole Worcs 52 F6
Cake Street Norfk 58 G2
Calais Street Suffk 46 H4
Calanais W Isls 152 f3
Calbourne IoW 12 G7
Calceby Lincs 80 G8
Calcoed Flints 74 G8
Calcot Gloucs 42 C9
Calcot W Berk 31 N8
Calcot Row W Berk 31 P8
Calcots Moray 139 N3
Calcott Kent 35 L9
Calcott Shrops 63 M9
Calcutt N York 85 M4
Calcutt Wilts 30 C4
Caldbeck Cumb 98 C10
Caldbergh N York 91 J9
Caldecote Cambs 56 C3
Caldecote Cambs 56 G9
Caldecote Herts 45 J4
Caldecote Nhants 54 H10
Caldecott Nhants 55 N7
Caldecott Oxon 31 K3
Caldecott Rutlnd 55 L2
Caldecotte M Keyn 44 C5
Calder Cumb 88 D6
Calderbank N Lans 114 D8
Calder Bridge Cumb 88 D5
Calderbrook Rochdl 84 E11
Caldercruix N Lans 114 E7
Calder Grove Wakefd 85 L11
Caldermill S Lans 105 M1
Caldermore Rochdl 84 D12
Calder Vale Lancs 83 M6
Calderwood S Lans 114 B10
Caldey Island Pembks 37 M11
Caldicot Mons 28 G5
Caldmore Wsall 53 J1
Caldwell N York 91 K4
Caldy Wirral 74 H6
Calenick Cnwll 3 K6
Calf of Man IoM 102 a7
Calford Green Suffk 46 C3
Calfsound Ork 147 d2
Calgary Ag & B 119 L2
Califer Moray 139 K4
California Falk 114 G6
California Norfk 71 P9
California Cross Devon 5 L6
Calke Derbys 66 B8
Calke Abbey Derbys 66 B8
Callakille Highld 135 M5
Callander Stirlg 122 G11
Callanish W Isls 152 f3
Callaughton Shrops 52 B1
Callerton N u Ty 100 F4
Callestick Cnwll 3 J4
Calligarry Highld 127 L4
Callington Cnwll 4 E3
Callingwood Staffs 65 M7
Callow Herefs 40 G5
Callow End Worcs 52 F10
Callow Hill Wilts 30 B5
Callow Hill Worcs 52 D6
Callow Hill Worcs 53 J7
Callows Grave Worcs 51 Q7
Calmore Hants 24 E10
Calmsden Gloucs 42 B10
Calne Wilts 30 A8
Calow Derbys 78 C9
Calshot Hants 12 H4
Calstock Cnwll 4 G3
Calstone Wellington Wilts 30 B8
Calthorpe Norfk 71 J6
Calthorpe Street Norfk 71 M7
Calthwaite Cumb 98 F10
Calton N York 84 D3
Calton Staffs 65 L2
Calveley Ches E 75 Q12
Calver Derbys 77 N9
Calverhall Shrops 63 Q5
Calver Hill Herefs 51 L11
Calverleigh Devon 20 E10
Calverley Leeds 85 J8
Calver Sough Derbys 77 N8
Calvert Bucks 43 P7
Calverton M Keyn 43 R4
Calverton Notts 66 G2
Calvine P & K 130 E11
Calvo Cumb 97 N7
Calzeat Border 106 E3
Cam Gloucs 29 M2
Camasachoirce Highld 127 P12
Camasine Highld 127 N12
Camas Luinie Highld 136 C10
Camastianavaig Highld 135 J8
Camault Muir Highld 137 N8
Camber E Susx 16 G7
Camberley Surrey 32 C10
Camberwell Gt Lon 33 L7
Camblesforth N York 86 C10
Cambo Nthumb 100 C1
Cambois Nthumb 101 J2
Camborne Cnwll 2 G6
Camborne & Redruth Mining District Cnwll 2 G6
Cambourne Cambs 56 F8
Cambridge Cambs 57 J9
Cambridge Gloucs 41 M11
Cambridge Airport Cambs 57 J9
Cambrose Cnwll 2 H5
Cambus Clacks 114 F2
Cambusavie Highld 146 D6
Cambusbarron Stirlg 114 E3
Cambuskenneth Stirlg 114 E2
Cambuslang S Lans 114 B9
Cambus o' May Abers 132 C5
Cambuswallace S Lans 106 D2
Camden Town Gt Lon 33 K5
Cameley BaNES 29 J11
Camelford Cnwll 6 G8
Camelon Falk 114 F5
Camerory Highld 139 J9
Camer's Green Worcs 41 M5
Camerton BaNES 29 K11
Camerton Cumb 97 L12
Camghouran P & K 122 F2
Camieston Border 107 P4
Cammachmore Abers 133 L5
Cammeringham Lincs 79 N7
Camore Highld 146 D7
Campbeltown Ag & B 103 K6
Campbeltown Airport Ag & B 103 J5
Camperdown N Tyne 100 H4
Cample D & G 106 B11
Campmuir P & K 124 E5
Camps W Loth 115 K7
Campsall Donc 78 E1
Campsea Ash Suffk 59 L9
Camps End Cambs 45 R3
Campton C Beds 44 G4
Camptown Border 107 R7
Camrose Pembks 36 H6
Camserney P & K 123 L3
Camusnagaul Highld 128 F9
Camusnagaul Highld 144 D7
Camusteel Highld 135 N7
Camusterrach Highld 135 N7
Canada Hants 24 D9
Canal Foot Cumb 89 J11
Canaston Bridge Pembks 37 L7
Candacraig Abers 131 Q4
Candlesby Lincs 81 J10
Candle Street Suffk 58 F6
Candover Green Shrops 63 N11
Candy Mill Border 106 E1
Cane End Oxon 31 P6
Canewdon Essex 34 F3
Canford Bottom Dorset 11 P5
Canford Cliffs BCP 11 P7
Canford Heath BCP 11 P6
Canford Magna BCP 11 P5
Canhams Green Suffk 58 F7
Canisbay Highld 151 Q2
Canklow Rothm 78 C5
Canley Covtry 53 P5
Cann Dorset 23 J9
Canna Highld 126 D3
Cann Common Dorset 23 K9
Cannich Highld 137 K9
Cannington Somset 21 L5
Canning Town Gt Lon 33 M6
Cannock Staffs 64 H10
Cannock Chase Staffs 65 J8
Cannock Wood Staffs 65 K9
Cannon Bridge Herefs 40 F3
Canonbie D & G 98 E3
Canon Frome Herefs 41 K3
Canon Pyon Herefs 51 M11
Canons Ashby Nhants 54 F10
Canonstown Cnwll 2 E7
Canterbury Kent 35 L10
Canterbury Cathedral Kent 35 L10
Cantley Norfk 71 M11
Cantlop Shrops 63 N11
Canton Cardif 27 R7
Cantraywood Highld 138 E6
Cantsfield Lancs 89 Q12
Canvey Island Essex 34 D6
Canwick Lincs 79 N10
Canworthy Water Cnwll 7 J6
Caol Highld 128 F9
Caolas Scalpaigh W Isls 152 f6
Caoles Ag & B 118 E3
Caonich Highld 128 E6
Capel Kent 16 B2
Capel Surrey 14 H3
Capel Bangor Cerdgn 49 L4
Capel Betws Lleucu Cerdgn 49 K9
Capel Coch IoA 72 G7
Capel Curig Conwy 73 M12
Capel Cynon Cerdgn 48 F10
Capel Dewi Carmth 38 C7
Capel Dewi Cerdgn 38 C3
Capel-Dewi Cerdgn 49 K4
Capel Garmon Conwy 61 P1
Capel Green Suffk 59 M10
Capel Gwyn Carmth 38 C7
Capel Gwyn IoA 72 E8
Capel Gwynfe Carmth 38 H7
Capel Hendre Carmth 38 F9
Capel Isaac Carmth 38 E6
Capel Iwan Carmth 37 Q3
Capel-le-Ferne Kent 17 N3
Capelles Guern 12 c2
Capel Llanilltern Cardif 27 P6
Capel Mawr IoA 72 G9
Capel Parc IoA 72 G6
Capel St Andrew Suffk 59 M11
Capel St Mary Suffk 47 K4
Capel Seion Cerdgn 49 L5
Capel Trisant Cerdgn 49 M5
Capeluchaf Gwynd 60 G2
Capelulo Conwy 73 N8
Capel-y-ffin Powys 40 C5
Capel-y-graig Gwynd 73 J10
Capenhurst Ches W 75 L9
Capernwray Lancs 89 N12
Cape Wrath Highld 148 F2
Capheaton Nthumb 100 D2
Caplaw E Rens 113 N9
Capon's Green Suffk 59 K7
Cappercleuch Border 106 H5
Capstone Medway 34 D9
Capton Devon 5 P6
Capton Somset 20 H5
Caputh P & K 124 B5
Caradon Mining District Cnwll 7 K10
Caradon Town Cnwll 7 K10
Carbeth Stirlg 113 Q5
Carbis Cnwll 3 N3
Carbis Bay Cnwll 2 E7
Carbost Highld 134 G6
Carbost Highld 134 G9
Carbrook Sheff 78 C6
Carbrooke Norfk 70 D11
Carburton Notts 78 G9
Carclaze Cnwll 3 P4
Car Colston Notts 67 J4
Carcroft Donc 78 E2
Cardenden Fife 115 M2
Cardeston Shrops 63 L9
Cardewlees Cumb 98 D8
Cardhu Moray 139 M7
Cardiff Cardif 28 A7
Cardiff Airport V Glam 27 P9
Cardiff Gate Services Cardif 28 B6
Cardiff West Services Cardif 27 P6
Cardigan Cerdgn 48 B11
Cardinal's Green Cambs 46 A2
Cardington Bed 56 B11
Cardington Shrops 51 N2
Cardinham Cnwll 6 G11
Cardrain D & G 94 G12
Cardrona Border 107 J2
Cardross Ag & B 113 L6
Cardryne D & G 94 G11
Cardurnock Cumb 97 N6
Careby Lincs 67 P9
Careston Angus 132 E12
Carew Pembks 37 K9
Carew Cheriton Pembks 37 K10
Carew Newton Pembks 37 K9
Carey Herefs 40 H5
Carfin N Lans 114 E9
Carfraemill Border 116 C10
Cargate Green Norfk 71 M9
Cargenbridge D & G 97 J3
Cargill P & K 124 C5
Cargo Cumb 98 D6
Cargreen Cnwll 4 F4
Cargurrel Cnwll 3 L7
Carham Nthumb 108 C2
Carhampton Somset 20 F5
Carharrack Cnwll 3 J6
Carie P & K 122 G1
Carinish W Isls 152 c8
Carisbrooke IoW 12 H7
Cark Cumb 89 K11
Carkeel Cnwll 4 F5
Càrlabhagh W Isls 152 e2
Carland Cross Cnwll 3 L4
Carlbury Darltn 91 L4
Carlby Lincs 67 P9
Carlcroft Nthumb 108 D7
Carlecotes Barns 77 M3
Carleen Cnwll 2 F8
Carlesmoor N York 91 L12
Carleton Cumb 88 D5
Carleton Cumb 98 E7
Carleton Cumb 98 G12
Carleton Lancs 82 H7
Carleton Wakefd 85 P11
Carleton Forehoe Norfk 70 G11
Carleton-in-Craven N York 84 E5
Carleton Rode Norfk 58 G2
Carleton St Peter Norfk 71 L11
Carlidnack Cnwll 3 J8
Carlincraig Abers 140 G7
Carlingcott BaNES 29 L10
Carlin How R & Cl 92 E3
Carlisle Cumb 98 E7
Carlisle Lake District Airport Cumb 98 F6
Carloggas Cnwll 6 C11
Carlops Border 115 L10
Carloway W Isls 152 e2
Carlton Barns 78 B2
Carlton Bed 55 N9
Carlton Cambs 57 M10
Carlton Leeds 85 M9
Carlton Leics 66 C11
Carlton N York 86 C10
Carlton N York 90 H10
Carlton N York 92 C9
Carlton Notts 66 G4
Carlton S on T 91 P2
Carlton Suffk 59 M8
Carlton Colville Suffk 59 P3
Carlton Curlieu Leics 54 H1
Carlton Green Cambs 57 M10
Carlton Husthwaite N York 92 A11
Carlton-in-Cleveland N York 92 A6
Carlton in Lindrick Notts 78 F7
Carlton-le-Moorland Lincs 79 M12
Carlton Miniott N York 91 P10
Carlton-on-Trent Notts 79 K11
Carlton Scroop Lincs 67 N3
Carluke S Lans 114 F11
Carlyon Bay Cnwll 3 P4
Carmacoup S Lans 105 P4
Carmarthen Carmth 38 B7
Carmel Carmth 38 E8
Carmel Flints 74 G8
Carmel Gwynd 60 H1
Carmichael S Lans 106 B2
Carmunnock C Glas 114 A9
Carmyle C Glas 114 B9
Carmyllie Angus 125 L4
Carnaby E R Yk 87 L2
Carnbee Fife 125 K12
Carnbo P & K 123 Q12
Carn Brea Cnwll 2 H6
Carnbrogie Abers 141 K10
Carndu Highld 136 B10
Carnduff S Lans 114 B12
Carne Cnwll 3 J9
Carne Cnwll 3 M7
Carne Cnwll 3 N3
Carnell E Ayrs 105 J3
Carnewas Cnwll 6 B11
Carnforth Lancs 83 L1
Carn-gorm Highld 136 C11
Carnhedryn Pembks 36 F5
Carnhell Green Cnwll 2 F7
Carnie Abers 133 K3
Carnkie Cnwll 2 H6
Carnkie Cnwll 2 H7
Carnkief Cnwll 3 J4
Carno Powys 50 C1
Carnock Fife 115 J3
Carnon Downs Cnwll 3 K6
Carnousie Abers 140 G6
Carnoustie Angus 125 L6
Carnsmerry Cnwll 3 P3
Carnwath S Lans 114 H12
Carnyorth Cnwll 2 B8
Carol Green Solhll 53 N5
Carpalla Cnwll 3 N4
Carperby N York 90 G9
Carr Rothm 78 E6
Carradale Ag & B 103 L2
Carradale Village Ag & B 103 L2
Carrbridge Highld 138 G11
Carrbrook Tamesd 77 J3
Carrefour Jersey 13 b1
Carreglefn IoA 72 F6
Carr Gate Wakefd 85 L10
Carrhouse N Linc 79 K2
Carrick Ag & B 112 D4
Carrick Castle Ag & B 113 J2
Carriden Falk 115 J5
Carrington Lincs 68 F1
Carrington Mdloth 115 P9
Carrington Traffd 76 D5
Carrog Conwy 61 N3
Carrog Denbgs 62 F3
Carron Falk 114 F5
Carron Moray 139 N7
Carronbridge D & G 105 R10
Carron Bridge Stirlg 114 D4
Carronshore Falk 114 G5
Carrow Hill Mons 28 F4
Carr Shield Nthumb 99 M8
Carrutherstown D & G 97 M4
Carruth House Inver 113 M8
Carr Vale Derbys 78 D9
Carrville Dur 100 H9
Carsaig Ag & B 119 P8
Carseriggan D & G 95 K5
Carsethorn D & G 97 K6
Carshalton Gt Lon 33 K9
Carsington Derbys 65 N1
Carskey Ag & B 103 J8
Carsluith D & G 95 N7
Carsphairn D & G 105 K11
Carstairs S Lans 114 G12
Carstairs Junction S Lans 114 H12
Carswell Marsh Oxon 30 G3
Carter's Clay Hants 24 E8
Carters Green Essex 45 P9
Carterton Oxon 42 G10
Carterway Heads Nthumb 100 D8
Carthew Cnwll 3 N3
Carthorpe N York 91 M10
Cartington Nthumb 108 G9
Cartland S Lans 114 F12
Cartledge Derbys 77 Q8
Cartmel Cumb 89 K11
Cartmel Fell Cumb 89 L9
Carway Carmth 38 C10
Carwinley Cumb 98 E4
Cashe's Green Gloucs 41 N10
Cashmoor Dorset 23 L10
Cassington Oxon 43 K9
Cassop Dur 101 J10
Castallack Cnwll 2 D9
Castel Guern 12 c2
Castell Conwy 73 N10
Castell-y-bwch Torfn 28 C4
Casterton Cumb 89 Q11
Castle Cnwll 3 Q3
Castle Acre Norfk 70 B9
Castle Ashby Nhants 55 L8
Castlebay W Isls 152 b13
Castle Bolton N York 90 G8
Castle Bromwich Solhll 53 L3
Castle Bytham Lincs 67 N8
Castlebythe Pembks 37 K5
Castle Caereinion Powys 62 G11
Castle Camps Cambs 46 A3
Castle Carrock Cumb 98 G7
Castlecary N Lans 114 E5
Castle Cary Somset 22 E7
Castle Combe Wilts 29 N7
Castlecraig Highld 146 E11
Castle Donington Leics 66 D7
Castle Douglas D & G 96 F6
Castle Eaton Swindn 30 D3
Castle Eden Dur 101 K10
Castle End C Pete 68 C10
Castleford Wakefd 85 N10
Castle Frome Herefs 41 K3
Castle Gate Cnwll 2 D7
Castle Green Cumb 89 N8
Castle Green Surrey 32 D10
Castle Gresley Derbys 65 P8
Castle Hedingham Essex 46 D4
Castlehill Border 106 G3
Castlehill Highld 151 M3
Castle Hill Kent 16 C2
Castle Hill Suffk 47 L2
Castlehill W Duns 113 M6
Castle Howard N York 86 D1
Castle Kennedy D & G 94 G6
Castle Lachlan Ag & B 112 E2
Castlemartin Pembks 36 H11
Castlemilk C Glas 114 A9
Castle Morris Pembks 36 H4
Castlemorton Worcs 41 M4
Castlemorton Common Worcs 41 M4
Castle O'er D & G 106 H11
Castle Rising Norfk 69 M7
Castleside Dur 100 D8
Castle Stuart Highld 138 D6
Castlethorpe M Keyn 44 A3
Castlethorpe N Linc 79 N2
Castleton Ag & B 112 C4
Castleton Border 107 N11
Castleton Derbys 77 M7
Castleton N York 92 E5
Castleton Newpt 28 C6
Castleton Rochdl 76 G2
Castletown Ches W 63 M3
Castletown Dorset 10 G10
Castletown Highld 151 M3
Castletown IoM 102 c7
Castletown Sundld 101 J6
Castley N York 85 K6
Caston Norfk 58 E1
Castor C Pete 56 C1
Caswell Bay Swans 26 E5
Catacol N Ayrs 112 D11
Cat and Fiddle Derbys 77 J9
Catbrain S Glos 29 J6
Catbrook Mons 40 G11
Catch Flints 74 H9
Catchall Cnwll 2 C9
Catchem's Corner Solhll 53 N5
Catchgate Dur 100 F8
Catcliffe Rothm 78 C6
Catcomb Wilts 30 B7
Catcott Somset 21 N5
Caterham Surrey 33 L11
Catfield Norfk 71 M8
Catfield Common Norfk 71 M8
Catford Gt Lon 33 L8
Catforth Lancs 83 L8
Cathcart C Glas 113 R9
Cathedine Powys 39 Q6
Catherine-de-Barnes Solhll 53 M5
Catherine Slack C Brad 84 G9
Catherington Hants 25 M10
Catherston Leweston Dorset 10 B6
Catherton Shrops 52 C5
Catisfield Hants 13 J3
Catley Herefs 41 K3
Catley Lane Head Rochdl 84 C12
Catlodge Highld 130 B6
Catlow Lancs 84 C8
Catlowdy Cumb 98 F3
Catmere End Essex 45 P4
Catmore W Berk 31 K6
Caton Devon 8 E10
Caton Lancs 83 M2
Caton Green Lancs 83 M2
Cator Court Devon 8 C9
Catrine E Ayrs 105 K5
Cat's Ash Newpt 28 E4
Catsfield E Susx 16 C8
Catsfield Stream E Susx 16 C8
Catsgore Somset 22 C8
Catsham Somset 22 D6
Catshill Worcs 52 H6
Catstree Shrops 52 D1
Cattadale Ag & B 103 J7
Cattal N York 85 P4
Cattawade Suffk 47 K5
Catterall Lancs 83 L6
Catteralslane Shrops 63 P4
Catterick N York 91 L7
Catterick Bridge N York 91 L7
Catterick Garrison N York 91 K7
Catterlen Cumb 98 F11
Catterline Abers 133 L8
Catterton N York 85 Q6
Catteshall Surrey 14 E2
Catthorpe Leics 54 F5
Cattishall Suffk 58 C7
Cattistock Dorset 10 F5
Catton N York 91 N11
Catton Nthumb 99 M7
Catwick E R Yk 87 L6
Catworth Cambs 56 B6
Caudle Green Gloucs 41 Q9
Caulcott C Beds 44 E3
Caulcott Oxon 43 L7
Cauldcots Angus 125 N3
Cauldhame Stirlg 114 B2
Cauldmill Border 107 N6
Cauldon Staffs 65 K2
Cauldon Lowe Staffs 65 K3
Cauldwell Derbys 65 N9
Caulkerbush D & G 97 J7
Caulside D & G 98 F2
Caundle Marsh Dorset 22 F10
Caunsall Worcs 52 F4
Caunton Notts 79 J11
Causeway Hants 25 N9
Causeway End Cumb 89 M9
Causeway End D & G 95 M6
Causeway End Essex 46 B8
Causewayend S Lans 106 D2
Causewayhead Cumb 97 M7
Causewayhead Stirlg 114 E2
Causeyend Abers 141 M12
Causey Park Nthumb 109 K10
Causey Park Bridge Nthumb 109 K10
Cavendish Suffk 46 E2
Cavenham Suffk 57 P6
Caversfield Oxon 43 M6
Caversham Readg 31 P7
Caverswall Staffs 64 H4
Caverton Mill Border 108 B5
Cavil E R Yk 86 E9
Cawdor Highld 138 F6
Cawkwell Lincs 80 F7
Cawood N York 86 A8
Cawsand Cnwll 4 F6
Cawston Norfk 70 H7
Cawston Warwks 54 D6
Cawthorn N York 92 F9
Cawthorne Barns 77 P2
Cawton N York 92 D11
Caxton Cambs 56 F9
Caxton End Cambs 56 F9
Caxton Gibbet Cambs 56 E8
Caynham Shrops 51 P6
Caythorpe Lincs 67 M2
Caythorpe Notts 66 H3
Cayton N York 93 L10
Ceannabeinne Highld 149 K3
Ceann a Bhaigh W Isls 152 b8
Ceannacroc Lodge Highld 128 H2
Cearsiadar W Isls 152 f4
Ceciliford Mons 40 G11
Cefn Newpt 28 C5
Cefn Berain Conwy 74 D10
Cefn-brîth Conwy 62 C2
Cefn-bryn-brain Carmth 38 H9
Cefn Byrle Powys 39 K9
Cefn Canel Powys 62 H6
Cefn Coch Powys 62 F7
Cefn-coed-y-cymmer Myr Td 39 N10
Cefn Cribwr Brdgnd 27 K6
Cefn Cross Brdgnd 27 K6
Cefn-ddwysarn Gwynd 62 C4
Cefn-Einion Shrops 51 J3
Cefneithin Carmth 38 E9
Cefngorwydd Powys 39 L3
Cefn-mawr Wrexhm 63 J4
Cefnpennar Rhondd 27 N2
Cefn-y-bedd Flints 63 K1
Cefn-y-pant Carmth 37 N5
Ceint IoA 72 H8
Cellan Cerdgn 49 K10
Cellardyke Fife 125 L12
Cellarhead Staffs 64 H3
Celleron Cumb 89 M2
Celynen Caerph 28 B3
Cemaes IoA 72 F5
Cemmaes Powys 61 P11
Cemmaes Road Powys 61 P11
Cenarth Cerdgn 37 P2
Cerbyd Pembks 36 F5
Ceres Fife 124 H10
Cerne Abbas Dorset 10 G4
Cerney Wick Gloucs 30 C3
Cerrigceinwen IoA 72 G9
Cerrigydrudion Conwy 62 C2
Cess Norfk 71 N8
Ceunant Gwynd 73 J11
Chaceley Gloucs 41 P5
Chacewater Cnwll 3 J5
Chackmore Bucks 43 P4
Chacombe Nhants 43 K3
Chadbury Worcs 42 B2
Chadderton Oldham 76 G3
Chadderton Fold Oldham 76 G2
Chaddesden C Derb 66 C5
Chaddesley Corbett Worcs 52 G6
Chaddlehanger Devon 7 N9
Chaddleworth W Berk 31 J7
Chadlington Oxon 42 G7
Chadshunt Warwks 53 Q10
Chadwell Leics 67 K7
Chadwell Shrops 64 E9
Chadwell End Bed 55 Q7
Chadwell Heath Gt Lon 33 N5
Chadwell St Mary Thurr 34 B6
Chadwick Worcs 52 F7
Chadwick End Solhll 53 N6
Chadwick Green St Hel 75 N4
Chaffcombe Somset 9 Q3
Chafford Hundred Thurr 33 R6
Chagford Devon 8 D7
Chailey E Susx 15 M7
Chainbridge Cambs 68 H12
Chainhurst Kent 16 C1
Chalbury Dorset 11 N3
Chalbury Common Dorset 11 P3
Chaldon Surrey 33 K11
Chaldon Herring Dorset 11 J8
Chale IoW 12 H9
Chale Green IoW 12 H9
Chalfont Common Bucks 32 E4
Chalfont St Giles Bucks 32 E4
Chalfont St Peter Bucks 32 E4
Chalford Gloucs 41 P11
Chalford Oxon 31 P2
Chalford Wilts 23 J3
Chalgrave C Beds 44 E6
Chalgrove Oxon 31 N3
Chalk Kent 34 B8
Chalk End Essex 46 A9
Chalkhouse Green Oxon 31 P6
Chalkway Somset 10 B3
Chalkwell Kent 34 F9
Challaborough Devon 5 K8
Challacombe Devon 19 N5
Challoch D & G 95 M5
Challock Kent 34 H12
Chalmington Dorset 10 F4
Chalton C Beds 44 F6
Chalton C Beds 56 C10
Chalton Hants 25 M10
Chalvey Slough 32 D6
Chalvington E Susx 15 P9
Chambers Green Kent 16 G2
Chandler's Cross Herts 32 F3
Chandlers Cross Worcs 41 M4
Chandler's Ford Hants 24 G9
Channel's End Bed 56 B9
Channel Tunnel Terminal Kent 17 L3
Chantry Somset 22 G4
Chantry Suffk 47 L3
Chapel Cumb 97 P12
Chapel Fife 115 N3
Chapel Allerton Leeds 85 L8
Chapel Allerton Somset 21 N3
Chapel Amble Cnwll 6 E9
Chapel Brampton Nhants 55 J7
Chapelbridge Cambs 56 E2
Chapel Chorlton Staffs 64 E5
Chapel Cross E Susx 15 R7
Chapel End Bed 56 B9
Chapel End C Beds 44 F3
Chapel End Cambs 56 C4
Chapel End Warwks 53 Q2
Chapelend Way Essex 46 C4
Chapel-en-le-Frith Derbys 77 K7
Chapel Field Bury 76 E2
Chapelgate Lincs 68 H7
Chapel Green Warwks 53 P4
Chapel Green Warwks 54 D8
Chapel Haddlesey N York 86 A10
Chapelhall N Lans 114 E8
Chapel Hill Abers 141 P9
Chapel Hill Lincs 68 D1
Chapel Hill Mons 28 H2
Chapelhope Border 106 G6
Chapelknowe D & G 98 C4
Chapel Lawn Shrops 51 K5
Chapel-le-Dale N York 90 B11
Chapel Leigh Somset 20 H7
Chapel Milton Derbys 77 K7
Chapel of Garioch Abers 140 H11
Chapel Rossan D & G 94 G9
Chapel Row E Susx 16 B8
Chapel Row Essex 34 D2
Chapel Row W Berk 31 M8
Chapels Cumb 88 H10
Chapel St Leonards Lincs 81 L9
Chapel Stile Cumb 89 J6
Chapelton Abers 133 L6
Chapelton Angus 125 M3
Chapelton Devon 19 L8
Chapelton S Lans 114 C11
Chapeltown Bl w D 83 Q12
Chapel Town Cnwll 3 L3
Chapeltown Moray 139 N11
Chapeltown Sheff 78 B4
Chapmanslade Wilts 23 J4
Chapmans Well Devon 7 L6
Chapmore End Herts 45 L8
Chappel Essex 46 F6
Charaton Cnwll 4 D3
Chard Somset 9 Q3
Chard Junction Somset 9 Q4
Chardleigh Green Somset 9 Q3

Chardstock Devon 9 Q4
Charfield S Glos 29 L4
Chargrove Gloucs 41 Q8
Charing Kent 16 G1
Charing Heath Kent 16 G1
Charing Hill Kent 34 G12
Charingworth Gloucs 42 E4
Charlbury Oxon 42 H7
Charlcombe BaNES 29 M9
Charlcutt Wilts 30 A7
Charlecote Warwks 53 P9
Charlemont Sandw 53 J2
Charles Devon 19 N7
Charleshill Surrey 14 C2
Charleston Angus 124 H4
Charlestown C Aber 133 M4
Charlestown C Brad 84 H7
Charlestown Calder 84 E10
Charlestown Cnwll 3 P4
Charlestown Cnwll 3 P4
Charlestown Derbys 77 J5
Charlestown Dorset 10 G9
Charlestown Fife 115 K4
Charlestown Highld 138 B6
Charlestown Highld 143 L10
Charlestown Salfd 76 E4
Charlestown of Aberlour Moray 139 N7
Charles Tye Suffk 58 F10
Charlesworth Derbys 77 J5
Charlinch Somset 21 K6
Charlottetown Fife 124 F10
Charlton Gt Lon 33 M7
Charlton Hants 24 F4
Charlton Herts 44 H6
Charlton Nhants 43 L4
Charlton Nthumb 99 M1
Charlton Oxon 31 J5
Charlton Somset 21 L8
Charlton Somset 22 E5
Charlton Somset 22 F3
Charlton Surrey 32 F8
Charlton W Susx 14 C8
Charlton Wilts 23 K9
Charlton Wilts 29 Q4
Charlton Worcs 42 B3
Charlton Worcs 52 F6
Charlton Wrekin 63 Q10
Charlton Abbots Gloucs 42 B7
Charlton Adam Somset 22 C7
Charlton All Saints Wilts 24 B8
Charlton Down Dorset 10 G6
Charlton Hill Shrops 63 P10
Charlton Horethorne Somset 22 F8
Charlton Kings Gloucs 41 Q7
Charlton Mackrell Somset 22 C7
Charlton Marshall Dorset 11 L4
Charlton Musgrove Somset 22 G7
Charlton-on-Otmoor Oxon 43 M8
Charlton on the Hill Dorset 11 L4
Charlton St Peter Wilts 30 D11
Charlwood Hants 25 L7
Charlwood Surrey 15 J3
Charminster Dorset 10 G6
Charmouth Dorset 10 B6
Charndon Bucks 43 P7
Charney Bassett Oxon 30 H3
Charnock Green Lancs 83 M11
Charnock Richard Lancs 83 M12
Charnock Richard Services Lancs 83 M12
Charsfield Suffk 59 K9
Chart Corner Kent 34 D12
Charter Alley Hants 31 M10
Charterhall Border 116 H11
Charterhouse Somset 22 C2
Chartershall Stirlg 114 E3
Charterville Allotments Oxon 42 G9
Chartham Kent 35 K11
Chartham Hatch Kent 35 K11
Chart Hill Kent 16 D1
Chartridge Bucks 44 D11
Chart Sutton Kent 16 E1
Chartway Street Kent 34 E12
Charvil Wokham 31 Q7
Charwelton Nhants 54 E9
Chase Cross Gt Lon 33 P4
Chase Terrace Staffs 65 J10
Chasetown Staffs 65 K10
Chastleton Oxon 42 F6
Chasty Devon 7 L4
Chatburn Lancs 84 A6
Chatcull Staffs 64 E5
Chatham Caerph 28 B4
Chatham Medway 34 D9
Chatham Green Essex 46 C8
Chathill Nthumb 109 K4
Chatley Worcs 52 F8
Chatsworth Derbys 77 N9
Chattenden Medway 34 D8
Chatter End Essex 45 N6
Chatteris Cambs 56 H3
Chatterton Lancs 84 B11
Chattisham Suffk 47 K3
Chatto Border 108 C6
Chatton Nthumb 108 H4
Chaul End C Beds 44 F7
Chawleigh Devon 19 N11
Chawley Oxon 43 K10
Chawston Bed 56 C9
Chawton Hants 25 M6
Chaxhill Gloucs 41 L9
Chazey Heath Oxon 31 P7
Cheadle Staffs 65 J3
Cheadle Stockp 76 F6
Cheadle Heath Stockp 76 G6
Cheadle Hulme Stockp 76 G6
Cheam Gt Lon 33 J9
Cheapside W & M 32 D8
Chearsley Bucks 43 P9
Chebsey Staffs 64 F6
Checkendon Oxon 31 N6
Checkley Ches E 64 D3
Checkley Herefs 41 J4
Checkley Staffs 65 J5
Checkley Green Ches E 64 D3
Chedburgh Suffk 57 Q9
Cheddar Somset 21 P3
Cheddington Bucks 44 C8
Cheddleton Staffs 64 H2
Cheddleton Heath Staffs 65 J2
Cheddon Fitzpaine Somset 21 K8
Chedglow Wilts 29 Q4
Chedgrave Norfk 71 M12
Chedington Dorset 10 D4
Chediston Suffk 59 M5
Chediston Green Suffk 59 M5
Chedworth Gloucs 42 B9
Chedzoy Somset 21 M6
Cheeseman's Green Kent 17 J3
Cheetham Hill Manch 76 F3
Cheldon Devon 19 P10
Chelford Ches E 76 F9
Chellaston C Derb 66 B6
Chellington Bed 55 N9
Chelmarsh Shrops 52 D3
Chelmer Village Essex 46 C10
Chelmick Shrops 51 M2
Chelmondiston Suffk 47 M4
Chelmorton Derbys 77 L9
Chelmsford Essex 46 C10
Chelmsley Wood Solhll 53 M3
Chelsea Gt Lon 33 K7
Chelsfield Gt Lon 33 N9
Chelsham Surrey 33 L10
Chelston Somset 21 J9
Chelsworth Suffk 58 E11
Cheltenham Gloucs 41 Q7
Chelveston Nhants 55 N7
Chelvey N Som 28 G8
Chelwood BaNES 29 K10
Chelwood Common E Susx 15 M5
Chelwood Gate E Susx 15 M5
Chelworth Wilts 29 R3
Chelworth Lower Green Wilts 30 C4
Chelworth Upper Green Wilts 30 C4
Cheney Longville Shrops 51 M4
Chenies Bucks 32 E3
Chepstow Mons 28 H4
Chequerbent Bolton 76 C2
Chequers Corner Norfk 69 J10
Cherhill Wilts 30 B8
Cherington Gloucs 29 P3
Cherington Warwks 42 G4
Cheriton Devon 19 P4
Cheriton Hants 25 K7
Cheriton Kent 17 M3
Cheriton Pembks 37 J11
Cheriton Swans 26 C4
Cheriton Bishop Devon 8 E6
Cheriton Fitzpaine Devon 8 G3
Cherrington Wrekin 64 C8
Cherry Burton E R Yk 87 J7
Cherry Hinton Cambs 57 J9
Cherry Orchard Worcs 52 F10
Cherry Willingham Lincs 79 P9
Chertsey Surrey 32 F9
Cherwell Valley Services Oxon 43 L6
Cheselbourne Dorset 11 J5
Chesham Bucks 44 D11
Chesham Bury 76 E1
Chesham Bois Bucks 32 D2
Cheshunt Herts 45 L11
Chesil Beach Dorset 10 F9
Chesley Kent 34 E9
Cheslyn Hay Staffs 64 H10
Chessetts Wood Warwks 53 M6
Chessington Gt Lon 32 H9
Chessington World of Adventures Gt Lon 32 H10
Chester Ches W 75 L10
Chesterblade Somset 22 F5
Chesterfield Derbys 78 C9
Chesterfield Staffs 65 L11
Chesterhill Mdloth 115 Q8
Chester-le-Street Dur 100 H8
Chester Moor Dur 100 H8
Chesters Border 107 P5
Chesters Border 107 Q7
Chester Services Ches W 75 M8
Chesterton Cambs 56 C2
Chesterton Cambs 57 J8
Chesterton Gloucs 30 B2
Chesterton Oxon 43 M7
Chesterton Shrops 52 E1
Chesterton Staffs 64 F2
Chesterton Green Warwks 54 B9
Chesterwood Nthumb 99 M5
Chester Zoo Ches W 75 L9
Chestfield Kent 35 K9
Chestnut Street Kent 34 F9
Cheston Devon 5 L5
Cheswardine Shrops 64 D6
Cheswick Nthumb 117 M12
Cheswick Green Solhll 53 L5
Chetnole Dorset 10 F3
Chettiscombe Devon 20 F10
Chettisham Cambs 57 K4
Chettle Dorset 23 L10
Chetton Shrops 52 C3
Chetwode Bucks 43 N6
Chetwynd Wrekin 64 D8
Chetwynd Aston Wrekin 64 D8
Cheveley Cambs 57 N8
Chevening Kent 33 N10
Cheverton IoW 12 G8
Chevington Suffk 57 Q8
Cheviot Hills 108 B8
Chevithorne Devon 20 F10
Chew Magna BaNES 29 J9
Chew Moor Bolton 76 C2
Chew Stoke BaNES 28 H10
Chewton Keynsham BaNES 29 K9
Chewton Mendip Somset 22 D3
Chichacott Devon 8 B5
Chicheley M Keyn 44 C2
Chichester W Susx 14 B10
Chickerell Dorset 10 G8
Chickering Suffk 59 J5
Chicklade Wilts 23 K6
Chicksands C Beds 44 G4
Chickward Herefs 51 J10
Chidden Hants 25 L10
Chiddingfold Surrey 14 D4
Chiddingly E Susx 15 Q8
Chiddingstone Kent 15 P2
Chiddingstone Causeway Kent 15 P1
Chiddingstone Hoath Kent 15 P2
Chideock Dorset 10 C6
Chidham W Susx 13 N4
Chidswell Kirk 85 K10
Chieveley W Berk 31 K7
Chieveley Services W Berk 31 K8
Chignall St James Essex 46 B9
Chignall Smealy Essex 46 B9
Chigwell Essex 33 N3
Chigwell Row Essex 33 N4
Chilbolton Hants 24 F5
Chilcomb Hants 24 H7
Chilcombe Dorset 10 E6
Chilcompton Somset 22 E3
Chilcote Leics 65 P10
Childer Thornton Ches W 75 L8
Child Okeford Dorset 23 J10
Childrey Oxon 30 H5
Child's Ercall Shrops 64 C7
Childswickham Worcs 42 C4
Childwall Lpool 75 L6
Childwick Bury Herts 44 G9
Childwick Green Herts 44 G9
Chilfrome Dorset 10 F5
Chilgrove W Susx 25 P10
Chilham Kent 35 J11
Chilla Devon 7 N4
Chillaton Devon 7 N8
Chillenden Kent 35 N11
Chillerton IoW 12 H8
Chillesford Suffk 59 M10
Chillingham Nthumb 108 H5
Chillington Devon 5 N8
Chillington Somset 10 B3
Chilmark Wilts 23 L7
Chilmington Green Kent 16 H3
Chilson Oxon 42 G8
Chilsworthy Cnwll 7 M10
Chilsworthy Devon 7 L3
Chiltern Green C Beds 44 G8
Chiltern Hills 31 Q3
Chilthorne Domer Somset 22 C9
Chilton Bucks 43 P9
Chilton Devon 8 G4
Chilton Dur 100 H12
Chilton Kent 17 N2
Chilton Oxon 31 K5
Chilton Suffk 46 F3
Chilton Candover Hants 25 K5
Chilton Cantelo Somset 22 D9
Chilton Foliat Wilts 30 G8
Chilton Polden Somset 21 N5
Chilton Street Suffk 46 D2
Chilton Trinity Somset 21 L5
Chilwell Notts 66 E5
Chilworth Hants 24 G9
Chilworth Surrey 14 E1
Chimney Oxon 30 H2
Chineham Hants 25 L2
Chingford Gt Lon 33 M3
Chinley Derbys 77 K7
Chinnor Oxon 31 Q2
Chipchase Castle Nthumb 99 N3
Chipnall Shrops 64 D6
Chippenham Cambs 57 M6
Chippenham Wilts 29 Q7
Chipperfield Herts 44 F11
Chipping Herts 45 L5
Chipping Lancs 83 N6
Chipping Campden Gloucs 42 D4
Chipping Hill Essex 46 E8
Chipping Norton Oxon 42 G6
Chipping Ongar Essex 45 Q11
Chipping Sodbury S Glos 29 L6
Chipping Warden Nhants 54 E11
Chipshop Devon 7 N9
Chipstable Somset 20 G8
Chipstead Kent 33 P11
Chipstead Surrey 33 K11
Chirbury Shrops 51 J1
Chirk Wrexhm 63 J5
Chirnside Border 117 J10
Chirnsidebridge Border 117 J10
Chirton Wilts 30 C11
Chisbury Wilts 30 F9
Chiselborough Somset 21 P10
Chiseldon Swindn 30 E6
Chiselhampton Oxon 31 M2
Chiserley Calder 84 F9
Chisholme Border 107 L7
Chislehurst Gt Lon 33 N8
Chislet Kent 35 M9
Chiswell Green Herts 44 G10
Chiswick Gt Lon 33 J7
Chiswick End Cambs 45 L3
Chisworth Derbys 77 J5
Chitcombe E Susx 16 E7
Chithurst W Susx 25 P8
Chittering Cambs 57 J7
Chitterne Wilts 23 L5
Chittlehamholt Devon 19 M9
Chittlehampton Devon 19 M8
Chittoe Wilts 29 Q9
Chivelstone Devon 5 N9
Chivenor Devon 19 K6
Chiverton Cross Cnwll 3 J5
Chlenry D & G 94 G6
Chobham Surrey 32 D10
Cholderton Wilts 24 C5
Cholesbury Bucks 44 D10
Chollerford Nthumb 99 P4
Chollerton Nthumb 99 P4
Cholmondeston Ches E 76 B11
Cholsey Oxon 31 M5
Cholstrey Herefs 51 M9
Chop Gate N York 92 B7
Choppington Nthumb 100 H2
Chopwell Gatesd 100 E6
Chorley Ches E 63 P2
Chorley Lancs 83 N11
Chorley Shrops 52 C4
Chorley Staffs 65 K10
Chorleywood Herts 32 E3
Chorleywood West Herts 32 E3
Chorlton Ches E 64 D2
Chorlton-cum-Hardy Manch 76 E5
Chorlton Lane Ches W 63 M3
Choulton Shrops 51 L3
Chowley Ches W 75 N12
Chrishall Essex 45 N4
Chrisswell Inver 113 J6
Christchurch BCP 12 B6
Christchurch Cambs 57 J1
Christchurch Gloucs 40 H9
Christchurch Newpt 28 D4
Christian Malford Wilts 29 Q6
Christleton Ches W 75 M10
Christmas Common Oxon 31 P4
Christmas Pie Surrey 32 C12
Christon N Som 28 E11
Christon Bank Nthumb 109 K5
Christow Devon 8 F8
Christ's Hospital W Susx 14 G5
Chuck Hatch E Susx 15 N4
Chudleigh Devon 8 G9
Chudleigh Knighton Devon 8 F9
Chulmleigh Devon 19 N10
Chunal Derbys 77 J5
Church Lancs 83 R9
Churcham Gloucs 41 M8
Church Aston Wrekin 64 D8
Church Brampton Nhants 55 J7
Church Brough Cumb 90 C4
Church Broughton Derbys 65 M5
Church Cove Cnwll 2 H12
Church Crookham Hants 25 P3
Churchdown Gloucs 41 P7
Church Eaton Staffs 64 F8
Church End Bed 55 P9
Church End Bed 56 B9
Church End Bucks 43 Q10
Church End C Beds 44 D5
Church End C Beds 44 E5
Church End C Beds 44 E7
Church End C Beds 44 E8
Church End C Beds 44 H4
Church End C Beds 56 C10
Church End Cambs 56 B6
Church End Cambs 56 D4
Church End Cambs 56 F5
Churchend Essex 34 H4
Church End Essex 46 A7
Church End Essex 46 B6
Church End Essex 46 C8
Church End Gloucs 41 P4
Church End Gt Lon 33 J4
Church End Herts 44 G9
Church End Herts 45 K6
Church End Herts 45 N7
Church End Lincs 68 E5
Church End Lincs 81 J4
Church End Suffk 47 M4
Church End Warwks 53 N2
Church End Warwks 53 P2
Church Enstone Oxon 42 H6
Church Fenton N York 85 Q8
Churchfield Sandw 53 J2
Churchgate Herts 45 L11
Churchgate Street Essex 45 N9
Church Green Devon 9 M5
Church Gresley Derbys 65 P8
Church Hanborough Oxon 43 J9
Church Hill Staffs 65 J10
Church Houses N York 92 D7
Churchill Devon 9 P4
Churchill Devon 19 L5
Churchill N Som 28 F10
Churchill Oxon 42 G7
Churchill Worcs 52 G10
Churchill Worcs 52 G5
Churchinford Somset 21 K11
Church Knowle Dorset 11 M8
Church Laneham Notts 79 K8
Church Langton Leics 55 J2
Church Lawford Warwks 54 D5
Church Lawton Ches E 64 F1
Church Leigh Staffs 65 J5
Church Lench Worcs 53 J10
Church Mayfield Staffs 65 M3
Church Minshull Ches E 76 C11
Church Norton W Susx 14 B11
Churchover Warwks 54 E4
Church Preen Shrops 51 P1
Church Pulverbatch Shrops 63 M11
Churchstanton Somset 21 K10
Churchstoke Powys 51 J2
Churchstow Devon 5 M7
Church Stowe Nhants 54 G9
Church Street Essex 46 D3
Church Street Kent 34 C7
Church Street Suffk 59 P4
Church Stretton Shrops 51 M2
Churchthorpe Lincs 80 F4
Churchtown Bpool 82 H7
Churchtown Cnwll 6 G9
Churchtown Derbys 77 P11
Churchtown Devon 19 N4
Churchtown IoM 102 f3
Churchtown Lancs 83 L6
Churchtown Sefton 83 J11
Church Town N Linc 79 K2
Church Village Rhondd 27 P5
Church Warsop Notts 78 F10
Church Wilne Derbys 66 D6
Churnsike Lodge Nthumb 99 K3
Churston Ferrers Torbay 5 Q5
Churt Surrey 25 Q6
Churton Ches W 75 M12
Churwell Leeds 85 K9
Chwilog Gwynd 60 G4
Chyandour Cnwll 2 D8
Chyanvounder Cnwll 2 G10
Chyeowling Cnwll 3 K6
Chyvarloe Cnwll 2 G10
Cîl Powys 62 G11
Cilcain Flints 74 G10
Cilcennin Cerdgn 49 J8
Cilcewydd Powys 62 H11
Cilfrew Neath 27 J2
Cilfynydd Rhondd 27 P4
Cilgerran Pembks 37 N2
Cilgwyn Carmth 38 H6
Cilgwyn Gwynd 60 H1
Ciliau-Aeron Cerdgn 48 H9
Cilmaengwyn Neath 38 H10
Cilmery Powys 50 D10
Cilrhedyn Pembks 37 Q3
Cilsan Carmth 38 F7
Ciltalgarth Gwynd 62 B4
Cilycwm Carmth 38 H4
Cimla Neath 27 J3
Cinderford Gloucs 41 K9
Cinder Hill Wolves 52 H2
Cippenham Slough 32 D6
Cirencester Gloucs 30 B2
Citadilla N York 91 L7
City Gt Lon 33 L6
City V Glam 27 N7
City Airport Gt Lon 33 M6
City Dulas IoA 72 H6
Clabhach Ag & B 118 G1
Clachaig Ag & B 112 G5
Clachaig Inn Highld 121 L1
Clachan Ag & B 111 Q10
Clachan Ag & B 112 G1
Clachan Ag & B 120 E9
Clachan Ag & B 120 F4
Clachan Highld 135 K8
Clachan-a-Luib W Isls 152 c8
Clachan Mor Ag & B 118 D3
Clachan na Luib W Isls 152 c8
Clachan of Campsie E Duns 114 A5
Clachan-Seil Ag & B 120 E9
Clachnaharry Highld 138 B6
Clachtoll Highld 148 C11
Clacket Lane Services Surrey 33 M11
Clackmannan Clacks 114 G3
Clackmannanshire Bridge Fife 114 G4
Clackmarras Moray 139 N4
Clacton-on-Sea Essex 47 L8
Cladich Ag & B 121 L8
Cladswell Worcs 53 K9
Claggan Highld 120 D3
Claigan Highld 134 D5
Clandown BaNES 22 F2
Clanfield Hants 25 M10
Clanfield Oxon 42 G11
Clannaborough Devon 8 D4
Clanville Hants 24 E4
Clanville Somset 22 E7
Claonaig Ag & B 112 C10
Clapgate Dorset 11 N4
Clapgate Herts 45 N7
Clapham Bed 55 P10
Clapham Devon 8 G7
Clapham Gt Lon 33 K7
Clapham N York 83 R1
Clapham W Susx 14 G9
Clapham Green Bed 55 P10
Clap Hill Kent 17 J3
Clappersgate Cumb 89 K6
Clapton Somset 10 C3
Clapton Somset 22 E3
Clapton-in-Gordano N Som 28 G7
Clapton-on-the-Hill Gloucs 42 D8
Clapworthy Devon 19 N8
Clarach Cerdgn 49 K4
Claravale Gatesd 100 E5
Clarbeston Pembks 37 K6
Clarbeston Road Pembks 37 K6
Clarborough Notts 79 J7
Clare Suffk 46 D3
Clarebrand D & G 96 F4
Clarencefield D & G 97 M4
Clarewood Nthumb 100 C4
Clarilaw Border 107 N6
Clark's Green Surrey 14 H3
Clarkston E Rens 113 Q9
Clashmore Highld 146 D7
Clashmore Highld 148 C10
Clashnessie Highld 148 C10
Clashnoir Moray 139 N11
Clathy P & K 123 P9
Clathymore P & K 123 P8
Clatt Abers 140 E10
Clatter Powys 50 D2
Clatterford End Essex 46 A9
Clatworthy Somset 20 G7
Claughton Lancs 83 M2
Claughton Lancs 83 M6
Claughton Wirral 75 J6
Clavelshay Somset 21 L7
Claverdon Warwks 53 M7
Claverham N Som 28 F9
Clavering Essex 45 N5
Claverley Shrops 52 E2
Claverton BaNES 29 M9
Claverton Down BaNES 29 M9
Clawdd-coch V Glam 27 P7
Clawdd-newydd Denbgs 62 E2
Clawthorpe Cumb 89 N11
Clawton Devon 7 L5
Claxby Lincs 80 C5
Claxby Lincs 81 J9
Claxton N York 86 C3
Claxton Norfk 71 L11
Claybrooke Magna Leics 54 E3
Clay Common Suffk 59 P4
Clay Coton Nhants 54 F5
Clay Cross Derbys 78 C11
Claydon Oxon 54 D10
Claydon Suffk 58 H10
Clay End Herts 45 K7
Claygate D & G 98 E2
Claygate Kent 16 C2
Claygate Surrey 32 H9
Claygate Cross Kent 33 R11
Clayhall Gt Lon 33 M4
Clayhanger Devon 20 G9
Clayhanger Wsall 65 K11
Clayhidon Devon 21 J10
Clayhill E Susx 16 E6
Clayhill Hants 12 E3
Clayhithe Cambs 57 J8
Clayock Highld 151 L5
Claypit Hill Cambs 56 G9
Claypits Gloucs 41 M10
Claypole Lincs 67 L2
Claythorpe Lincs 80 H8
Clayton C Brad 84 H9
Clayton Donc 78 D2
Clayton W Susx 15 K8
Clayton Green Lancs 83 N10
Clayton-le-Moors Lancs 83 R9
Clayton-le-Woods Lancs 83 M10
Clayton West Kirk 77 N2
Clayworth Notts 79 J6
Cleadale Highld 126 H6
Cleadon S Tyne 101 K6
Cleadon Park S Tyne 101 K5
Clearbrook Devon 4 H4
Clearwell Gloucs 40 H10
Cleasby N York 91 L4
Cleat Ork 147 c6
Cleatlam Dur 91 J3
Cleator Cumb 88 D4
Cleator Moor Cumb 88 D4
Cleckheaton Kirk 85 J10
Cleedownton Shrops 51 P4
Cleehill Shrops 51 Q5
Cleekhimin N Lans 114 D9
Clee St Margaret Shrops 51 P4
Cleestanton Shrops 51 P5
Cleethorpes NE Lin 80 F2
Cleeton St Mary Shrops 51 Q5
Cleeve N Som 28 F9
Cleeve Oxon 31 M6
Cleeve Hill Gloucs 41 R6
Cleeve Prior Worcs 53 K10
Cleghornie E Loth 116 D5
Clehonger Herefs 40 F4
Cleish P & K 115 K2
Cleland N Lans 114 E9
Clement's End C Beds 44 E8
Clement Street Kent 33 P8
Clenamacrie Ag & B 120 H7
Clench Common Wilts 30 E9
Clenchwarton Norfk 69 L8
Clenerty Abers 141 J4
Clent Worcs 52 H5
Cleobury Mortimer Shrops 52 C5
Cleobury North Shrops 52 B3
Cleongart Ag & B 103 J3
Clephanton Highld 138 E6
Clerkhill D & G 106 H10
Cleuch-head D & G 105 Q9
Clevancy Wilts 30 B7
Clevedon N Som 28 F8
Cleveley Oxon 42 H7
Cleveleys Lancs 82 H6
Cleverton Wilts 29 R5
Clewer Somset 21 P3
Cley next the Sea Norfk 70 F3
Cliburn Cumb 89 P2
Cliddesden Hants 25 L3
Cliff Warwks 53 N1
Cliffe Lancs 83 Q8
Cliffe Medway 34 C7
Cliffe N York 86 C9
Cliffe N York 91 L4
Cliff End E Susx 16 F8
Cliffe Woods Medway 34 C7
Clifford Herefs 40 C3
Clifford Leeds 85 N6
Clifford Chambers Warwks 53 M10
Clifford's Mesne Gloucs 41 L7
Cliffsend Kent 35 P9
Clifton Bristl 28 H7
Clifton C Beds 44 H4
Clifton C Nott 66 E5
Clifton C York 86 B5
Clifton Calder 84 H10
Clifton Cumb 89 N1
Clifton Derbys 65 M3
Clifton Devon 19 L5
Clifton Donc 78 E4
Clifton Lancs 83 L9
Clifton N York 85 J5
Clifton Nthumb 100 G2
Clifton Oxon 43 K5
Clifton Salfd 76 E3
Clifton Worcs 41 N2
Clifton Campville Staffs 65 N10
Clifton Hampden Oxon 31 L3
Clifton Reynes M Keyn 55 M10
Clifton upon Dunsmore Warwks 54 E5
Clifton upon Teme Worcs 52 D8
Cliftonville Kent 35 Q8
Climping W Susx 14 E10
Clink Somset 22 H4
Clint N York 85 K3
Clinterty C Aber 133 K2
Clint Green Norfk 70 F10
Clintmains Border 107 P3
Clipiau Gwynd 61 P10
Clippesby Norfk 71 N9
Clipsham Rutlnd 67 N9
Clipston Nhants 54 H4
Clipston Notts 66 G5
Clipstone C Beds 44 D6
Clipstone Notts 78 F11
Clitheroe Lancs 83 R7
Clive Shrops 63 N7
Cliveden Bucks 32 C5
Clixby Lincs 80 B3
Cloatley Wilts 29 R4
Clocaenog Denbgs 62 E1
Clochan Moray 140 B4
Clock Face St Hel 75 N5
Cloddiau Powys 62 H10
Clodock Herefs 40 D6
Cloford Somset 22 G4
Clola Abers 141 N7
Clophill C Beds 44 F4
Clopton Nhants 55 Q5
Clopton Suffk 59 J10
Clopton Corner Suffk 59 J9
Clopton Green Suffk 57 P9
Clopton Green Suffk 58 E8
Clos du Valle Guern 12 d1
Closeburn D & G 106 B11
Closeburnmill D & G 106 B10
Closeclark IoM 102 c6
Closworth Somset 10 E3
Clothall Herts 45 K5
Clotton Ches W 75 N11
Cloudesley Bush Warwks 54 D3
Clouds Herefs 41 J4
Clough Oldham 76 H2
Clough Foot Calder 84 D10
Clough Head Calder 84 G11
Cloughton N York 93 K8
Cloughton Newlands N York 93 K7
Clousta Shet 147 h6
Clova Angus 131 Q9
Clovelly Devon 18 F8
Clovenfords Border 107 L2
Clovulin Highld 128 D11
Clow Bridge Lancs 84 B9
Clowne Derbys 78 D8
Clows Top Worcs 52 D6
Cloy Wrexhm 63 L4
Cluanie Inn Highld 128 F2
Cluanie Lodge Highld 128 F2
Clubworthy Cnwll 7 K6
Clugston D & G 95 L7
Clun Shrops 51 J4
Clunas Highld 138 G6
Clunbury Shrops 51 L4
Clunderwen Carmth 37 M6
Clune Highld 138 E10
Clunes Highld 128 H6
Clungunford Shrops 51 L5
Clunie P & K 124 C4
Clunton Shrops 51 K4
Cluny Fife 115 N2
Clutton BaNES 29 J10
Clutton Ches W 63 M1
Clutton Hill BaNES 29 K10
Clwt Conwy 74 C11
Clwt-y-bont Gwynd 73 K11
Clydach Mons 40 B9
Clydach Swans 26 G2
Clydach Vale Rhondd 27 M4
Clydebank W Duns 113 P7
Clydey Pembks 37 P3
Clyffe Pypard Wilts 30 C7
Clynder Ag & B 113 K4
Clyne Neath 27 L2
Clynnog Fawr Gwynd 60 G2
Clyro Powys 40 B3
Clyst Honiton Devon 9 J6
Clyst Hydon Devon 9 K4
Clyst St George Devon 9 J7
Clyst St Lawrence Devon 9 K5
Clyst St Mary Devon 9 J6
Cnoc W Isls 152 g3
Cnwch Coch Cerdgn 49 L6
Coad's Green Cnwll 7 K9
Coal Aston Derbys 78 B8
Coalbrookvale Blae G 40 B10
Coalburn S Lans 105 Q3
Coalburns Gatesd 100 E6
Coaley Gloucs 41 M11
Coalhill Essex 34 D3
Coalmoor Wrekin 64 C10
Coalpit Heath S Glos 29 K6
Coal Pool Wsall 65 J12
Coalport Wrekin 64 C11
Coalsnaughton Clacks 114 G2
Coal Street Suffk 59 J6
Coaltown of Balgonie Fife 115 P1
Coaltown of Wemyss Fife 115 P2
Coalville Leics 66 C9
Coanwood Nthumb 99 K6
Coat Somset 21 P9
Coatbridge N Lans 114 D8
Coatdyke N Lans 114 D8
Coate Swindn 30 E6
Coate Wilts 30 B10
Coates Cambs 56 F1
Coates Gloucs 29 R2
Coates Lincs 79 M7
Coates Notts 79 K7
Coates W Susx 14 E7
Coatham R & Cl 92 C2
Coatham Mundeville Darltn 91 M3
Cobbaton Devon 19 M8
Coberley Gloucs 41 Q8
Cobhall Common Herefs 40 F5
Cobham Kent 34 B8
Cobham Surrey 32 G10
Cobham Services Surrey 32 G10
Coblers Green Essex 46 C8
Cobley Dorset 23 M9
Cobnash Herefs 51 M8
Cobo Guern 12 c2
Cobridge C Stke 64 G2
Coburby Abers 141 M3
Cock Alley Derbys 78 C9
Cockayne N York 92 C7
Cockayne Hatley C Beds 56 E10
Cock Bank Wrexhm 63 K3
Cock Bevington Warwks 53 K10
Cock Bridge Abers 131 N3
Cockburnspath Border 116 H7
Cock Clarks Essex 46 E11
Cock & End Suffk 57 N10
Cockenzie and Port Seton E Loth 115 R6
Cocker Bar Lancs 83 L10
Cocker Brook Lancs 83 R10
Cockerham Lancs 83 L5
Cockermouth Cumb 97 M12
Cockernhoe Herts 44 G7
Cockersdale Leeds 85 K9
Cockett Swans 26 F3
Cockfield Dur 91 J2
Cockfield Suffk 58 D9
Cockfosters Gt Lon 33 K3
Cock Green Essex 46 C7
Cocking W Susx 14 C7
Cocking Causeway W Susx 14 C7
Cockington Torbay 5 Q4
Cocklake Somset 21 P3
Cockley Beck Cumb 88 H6
Cockley Cley Norfk 69 Q11
Cock Marling E Susx 16 F7
Cockpole Green Wokham 31 R6
Cocks Cnwll 3 J4
Cockshutford Shrops 51 P3
Cockshutt Shrops 63 M6
Cock Street Kent 34 D12
Cockthorpe Norfk 70 E4
Cockwells Cnwll 2 E8
Cockwood Devon 9 J8
Cockwood Somset 21 K5
Cockyard Derbys 77 K7
Cockyard Herefs 40 F5
Coddenham Suffk 58 H9
Coddington Ches W 63 M1
Coddington Herefs 41 L3
Coddington Notts 67 L1
Codford St Mary Wilts 23 L5
Codford St Peter Wilts 23 L5
Codicote Herts 45 J8
Codmore Hill W Susx 14 F7
Codnor Derbys 66 C2
Codrington S Glos 29 L6
Codsall Staffs 64 F11
Codsall Wood Staffs 64 F11
Coed Darcy Neath 26 H3
Coedely Rhondd 27 N5
Coed Hirwaun Neath 27 K5
Coedkernew Newpt 28 C6
Coed Morgan Mons 40 E9
Coedpoeth Wrexhm 63 J2
Coed Talon Flints 75 J11
Coedway Powys 63 K9
Coed-y-Bryn Cerdgn 48 F11
Coed-y-caerau Newpt 28 E4
Coed-y-paen Mons 28 D3
Coed-yr-ynys Powys 39 R7
Coed Ystumgwern Gwynd 61 K7
Coelbren Powys 39 K9
Coffinswell Devon 5 Q3
Coffle End Bed 55 P9
Cofton Devon 8 H8
Cofton Hackett Worcs 53 J5
Cogan V Glam 28 A8
Cogenhoe Nhants 55 L8
Cogges Oxon 42 H9
Coggeshall Essex 46 E7
Coggin's Mill E Susx 15 Q5
Coignafearn Highld 138 C12
Coilacriech Abers 131 P5
Coilantogle Stirlg 122 G11
Coillore Highld 134 F8
Coity Brdgnd 27 L6
Col W Isls 152 g3
Colaboll Highld 145 N3
Colan Cnwll 3 L2
Colaton Raleigh Devon 9 K7
Colbost Highld 134 D6
Colburn N York 91 K7
Colby Cumb 89 Q3
Colby IoM 102 c7
Colby Norfk 71 J6
Colchester Essex 46 H6
Colchester Zoo Essex 46 G7
Cold Ash W Berk 31 L8
Cold Ashby Nhants 54 G5
Cold Ashton S Glos 29 M8
Cold Aston Gloucs 42 D8
Coldbackie Highld 149 N5
Coldbeck Cumb 90 B6
Cold Blow Pembks 37 M8
Cold Brayfield M Keyn 55 M10
Cold Cotes N York 83 Q1
Coldean Br & H 15 L9
Coldeast Devon 8 F10
Colden Calder 84 E9
Colden Common Hants 24 H9
Coldfair Green Suffk 59 N8
Coldham Cambs 68 H11
Cold Hanworth Lincs 79 P7
Coldharbour Cnwll 3 J5
Coldharbour Devon 20 G11
Coldharbour Gloucs 40 H11
Cold Harbour Herts 44 G8
Cold Harbour Oxon 31 N6
Coldharbour Surrey 14 G2
Cold Hatton Wrekin 64 B8
Cold Hatton Heath Wrekin 64 B8
Cold Hesledon Dur 101 K9
Cold Hiendley Wakefd 78 B1
Cold Higham Nhants 54 H10
Coldingham Border 117 K8
Cold Kirby N York 92 B10
Coldmeece Staffs 64 F6
Cold Newton Leics 66 H11
Cold Northcott Cnwll 7 J7
Cold Norton Essex 34 E2
Cold Overton Leics 67 K10
Coldred Kent 17 N1
Coldridge Devon 8 D3
Coldstream Border 108 D2
Coldwaltham W Susx 14 E7
Coldwell Herefs 40 F4
Coldwells Abers 141 M8
Cold Weston Shrops 51 P4
Cole Somset 22 F6
Colebatch Shrops 51 K3
Colebrook C Plym 4 H5
Colebrook Devon 9 J3
Colebrooke Devon 8 E5
Coleby Lincs 79 N11
Coleby N Linc 86 G11
Cole End Warwks 53 M3
Coleford Devon 8 E4
Coleford Gloucs 41 J9
Coleford Somset 22 F4
Coleford Water Somset 20 H6
Colegate End Norfk 59 J3
Cole Green Herts 45 K9
Cole Green Herts 45 M5
Cole Henley Hants 24 H3
Colehill Dorset 11 P4
Coleman Green Herts 44 H9
Coleman's Hatch E Susx 15 N4
Colemere Shrops 63 M6
Colemore Hants 25 M7
Colemore Green Shrops 52 D1
Colenden P & K 124 C7
Coleorton Leics 66 C9
Colerne Wilts 29 N8
Colesbourne Gloucs 42 B9
Cole's Cross Devon 5 N7
Coles Cross Dorset 10 B4
Colesden Bed 56 C9
Coles Green Suffk 47 K3
Coleshill Bucks 32 D3
Coleshill Oxon 30 F4
Coleshill Warwks 53 M3
Colestocks Devon 9 L5
Coley BaNES 22 D2
Colgate W Susx 15 J4
Colinsburgh Fife 125 J12
Colinton C Edin 115 M7
Colintraive Ag & B 112 F6
Colkirk Norfk 70 D7
Coll Ag & B 118 H1
Coll W Isls 152 g3
Collace P & K 124 D6
Collafirth Shet 147 i4
Coll Airport Ag & B 118 G2
Collaton Devon 5 M9
Collaton St Mary Torbay 5 P5
College of Roseisle Moray 139 L3
College Town Br For 32 B10
Collessie Fife 124 F10
Colleton Mills Devon 19 N10
Collier Row Gt Lon 33 P4
Collier's End Herts 45 L7
Collier's Green E Susx 16 D6
Colliers Green Kent 16 D3
Collier Street Kent 16 C2
Colliery Row Sundld 101 J8
Collieston Abers 141 P10
Collin D & G 97 L3
Collingbourne Ducis Wilts 24 D3
Collingbourne Kingston Wilts 24 D2
Collingham Leeds 85 N6
Collingham Notts 79 L11
Collington Herefs 52 C8
Collingtree Nhants 55 J9
Collins Green Warrtn 75 P5
Collins Green Worcs 52 D9
Colliston Angus 125 M4
Colliton Devon 9 L4
Collyweston Nhants 67 N11
Colmonell S Ayrs 94 G1

Colmworth Bed 56 B9
Colnabaichin Abers 131 P3
Colnbrook Slough 32 E7
Colne Cambs 56 G5
Colne Lancs 84 D7
Colne Bridge Kirk 85 J11
Colne Edge Lancs 84 D7
Colne Engaine Essex 46 E5
Colney Norfk 70 H10
Colney Heath Herts 44 H10
Colney Street Herts 44 H11
Coln Rogers Gloucs 42 C9
Coln St Aldwyns Gloucs 42 D10
Coln St Dennis Gloucs 42 C9
Colonsay Ag & B 111 J2
Colonsay Airport Ag & B 110 H3
Colpy Abers 140 G9
Colquhar Border 107 J1
Colquite Cnwll 6 C9
Colscott Devon 18 G10
Colsterdale N York 91 J10
Colsterworth Lincs 67 M7
Colston Bassett Notts 66 H5
Coltfield Moray 139 L3
Colt Hill Hants 25 N3
Coltishall Norfk 71 K8
Colton Cumb 89 J9
Colton Leeds 85 M8
Colton N York 85 Q6
Colton Norfk 70 G10
Colton Staffs 65 K8
Colt's Hill Kent 16 B2
Columbjohn Devon 8 H4
Colva Powys 50 H10
Colvend D & G 96 H7
Colwall Herefs 41 M3
Colwell Nthumb 99 Q3
Colwich Staffs 65 J8
Colwick Notts 66 G4
Colwinston V Glam 27 M7
Colworth W Susx 14 C10
Colwyn Bay Conwy 73 P8
Colyford Devon 9 N6
Colyton Devon 9 N6
Combe Devon 5 M9
Combe Herefs 51 K8
Combe Oxon 43 J8
Combe W Berk 30 H10
Combe Almer Dorset 11 M5
Combe Common Surrey 14 D4
Combe Down BaNES 29 M10
Combe Fishacre Devon 5 P4
Combe Florey Somset 21 J7
Combe Hay BaNES 29 L10
Combeinteignhead Devon 8 G10
Combe Martin Devon 19 L4
Combe Raleigh Devon 9 M4
Comberbach Ches W 76 B8
Comberford Staffs 65 M10
Comberton Cambs 56 G9
Comberton Herefs 51 N7
Combe St Nicholas Somset 9 P2
Combpyne Devon 9 N6
Combridge Staffs 65 K5
Combrook Warwks 53 P10
Combs Derbys 77 K8
Combs Suffk 58 F9
Combs Ford Suffk 58 F9
Comers Abers 132 G3
Cometrowe Somset 21 K8
Comhampton Worcs 52 F7
Commercial End Cambs 57 K8
Commins Coch Powys 61 N1
Commondale N York 92 D5
Common Edge Bpool 82 H8
Common End Cumb 88 D2
Common Moor Cnwll 4 G7
Common Platt Wilts 30 C5
Commonside Ches W 75 P9
Commonside Derbys 65 N4
Common Side Derbys 77 Q8
Commonwood Shrops 63 N6
Commonwood Wrexhm 63 L1
Compass Somset 21 L6
Compstall Stockp 76 H5
Compstonend D & G 96 D7
Compton Devon 5 P4
Compton Hants 24 F7
Compton Hants 24 H8
Compton Staffs 52 F4
Compton Surrey 14 D1
Compton W Berk 31 L6
Compton W Susx 25 N10
Compton Wilts 23 P3
Compton Abbas Dorset 23 J9
Compton Abdale Gloucs 42 C8
Compton Bassett Wilts 30 B8
Compton Beauchamp Oxon 30 F5
Compton Bishop Somset 21 N2
Compton Chamberlayne Wilts 23 M7
Compton Dando BaNES 29 K9
Compton Dundon Somset 22 C7
Compton Durville Somset 21 P10
Compton Greenfield S Glos 28 H6
Compton Martin BaNES 28 H11
Compton Pauncefoot Somset 22 E8
Compton Valence Dorset 10 F6
Comrie Fife 115 J3
Comrie P & K 123 K8
Conaglen House Highld 128 E10
Conchra Highld 136 B10
Concraigie P & K 124 C4
Conder Green Lancs 83 K4
Conderton Worcs 41 Q4
Condicote Gloucs 42 D6
Condorrat N Lans 114 D6
Condover Shrops 63 N11
Coney Hill Gloucs 41 N8
Coneyhurst W Susx 14 G6
Coneysthorpe N York 86 B4
Coneythorpe N York 85 N3
Coney Weston Suffk 58 E5
Conford Hants 25 N7
Congdon's Shop Cnwll 4 G5
Congerstone Leics 66 B11
Congham Norfk 69 N8
Congleton Ches E 76 F11
Congl-y-wal Gwynd 61 M3
Congresbury N Som 28 F9
Congreve Staffs 64 G9
Conheath D & G 97 K4
Conicavel Moray 138 H5
Coningsby Lincs 80 D12
Conington Cambs 56 F7
Conington Cambs 56 F7
Conisbrough Donc 78 G4
Conisholme Lincs 80 H4
Coniston Cumb 89 J7
Coniston E R Yk 87 M8
Coniston Cold N York 84 D4
Conistone N York 84 D1
Connah's Quay Flints 75 J9
Connel Ag & B 120 G6
Connel Park E Ayrs 105 L7
Connor Downs Cnwll 2 F8
Conon Bridge Highld 137 P5
Cononley N York 84 E5
Consall Staffs 64 H2
Consett Dur 100 E6
Constable Burton N York 91 K8

Constable Lee Lancs 84 B10
Constantine Cnwll 3 J8
Constantine Bay Cnwll 6 C10
Contin Highld 137 N4
Conwy Conwy 73 N8
Conwy Castle Conwy 73 N8
Conyer Kent 34 G9
Conyer's Green Suffk 58 C7
Cooden E Susx 16 C9
Cookbury Devon 7 M3
Cookbury Wick Devon 7 M4
Cookham W & M 32 C5
Cookham Dean W & M 32 C5
Cookham Rise W & M 32 C5
Cookhill Worcs 53 K9
Cookley Suffk 59 L5
Cookley Worcs 52 F5
Cookley Green Oxon 31 P4
Cookney Abers 133 L6
Cooksbridge E Susx 15 M8
Cooksey Green Worcs 52 G7
Cook's Green Essex 47 L8
Cooks Green Suffk 58 E10
Cooksland Cnwll 6 F11
Cooksmill Green Essex 46 B10
Cookson Green Ches W 75 P9
Coolham W Susx 14 G6
Cooling Medway 34 D7
Cooling Street Medway 34 D7
Coombe Cnwll 2 G6
Coombe Cnwll 3 K6
Coombe Cnwll 3 M4
Coombe Devon 8 F8
Coombe Devon 9 L6
Coombe Gloucs 29 M3
Coombe Wilts 25 L9
Coombe Wilts 23 P3
Coombe Bissett Wilts 23 P8
Coombe Cellars Devon 8 G10
Coombe Cross Hants 25 L9
Coombe Hill Gloucs 41 P6
Coombe Keynes Dorset 11 K8
Coombes W Susx 14 H9
Coombes-Moor Herefs 51 L8
Coombe Street Somset 22 G7
Coombeswood Dudley 52 H3
Coopersale Common Essex 45 N11
Coopersale Street Essex 45 N11
Cooper's Corner Kent 33 P12
Coopers Green E Susx 15 N6
Coopers Green Herts 44 H9
Cooper Street Kent 35 P10
Cooper Turning Bolton 76 B2
Cootham W Susx 14 F8
Copdock Suffk 47 K3
Copford Essex 46 G7
Copford Green Essex 46 G7
Copgrove N York 85 M3
Copister Shet 147 J4
Cople Bed 56 B11
Copley Calder 84 G10
Copley Dur 90 H2
Copley Tamesd 76 H4
Coplow Dale Derbys 77 M8
Copmanthorpe C York 85 R6
Compere End Staffs 64 E6
Copp Lancs 83 K7
Coppathorne Cnwll 7 J5
Coppenhall Staffs 64 G8
Coppenhall Moss Ches W 76 D12
Copperhouse Cnwll 2 F7
Coppicegate Shrops 52 D5
Coppingford Cambs 56 C5
Coppins Corner Kent 16 G1
Copplestone Devon 8 E4
Coppull Lancs 83 M12
Coppull Moor Lancs 75 P1
Copsale W Susx 14 H6
Copster Green Lancs 83 P8
Copston Magna Warwks 54 D3
Cop Street Kent 35 N10
Copthall Green Essex 33 M2
Copt Heath Solhll 53 M5
Copt Hewick N York 85 M1
Copthorne Cnwll 7 K6
Copthorne W Susx 15 K3
Copt Oak Leics 66 D9
Copy's Green Norfk 70 D4
Copythorne Hants 24 E10
Coram Street Suffk 46 H3
Corbets Tey Gt Lon 33 Q5
Corbière Jersey 13 a3
Corbridge Nthumb 100 C5
Corby Nhants 55 M3
Corby Glen Lincs 67 P7
Corby Hill Cumb 98 F7
Cordon N Ayrs 103 Q3
Cordwell Derbys 77 P8
Coreley Shrops 52 B6
Cores End Bucks 32 C5
Corfe Somset 21 K9
Corfe Castle Dorset 11 L8
Corfe Mullen Dorset 11 N5
Corfton Shrops 51 N4
Corgarff Abers 131 P3
Corhampton Hants 25 K9
Corks Pond Kent 16 B3
Corlae D & G 105 M10
Corley Warwks 53 P4
Corley Ash Warwks 53 P4
Corley Moor Warwks 53 P4
Corley Services Warwks 53 P3
Cormuir Angus 131 P11
Cornard Tye Suffk 46 F3
Corndon Devon 8 C7
Corner Row Lancs 83 K8
Corney Cumb 88 F8
Cornforth Dur 101 J11
Cornhill Abers 140 F4
Cornhill-on-Tweed Nthumb 108 D2
Cornholme Calder 84 D10
Cornish Hall End Essex 46 B4
Cornoigmore Ag & B 118 D3
Cornriggs Dur 99 N10
Cornsay Dur 100 F9
Cornsay Colliery Dur 100 F9
Corntown Highld 137 P5
Corntown V Glam 27 L7
Cornwall Airport Newquay Cnwll 3 L2
Cornwell Oxon 42 F6
Cornwood Devon 5 K5
Cornworthy Devon 5 P5
Corpach Highld 128 F9
Corpusty Norfk 70 G6
Corrachree Abers 132 D3
Corran Highld 127 Q2
Corran Highld 128 f1
Corrany IoM 102 f4
Corrie N Ayrs 103 Q2
Corriecravie N Ayrs 103 P4
Corriegills N Ayrs 103 Q3
Corriegour Lodge Hotel Highld 129 J6
Corriemoille Highld 137 L5
Corrimony Highld 137 L10
Corringham Lincs 79 L5
Corringham Thurr 34 C5
Corris Gwynd 61 N10
Corris Uchaf Gwynd 61 N10
Corrow Ag & B 113 J1

Corry Highld 135 L11
Corscombe Devon 8 B5
Corscombe Dorset 10 D4
Corse Gloucs 41 M6
Corse Lawn Gloucs 41 N5
Corsham Wilts 29 P8
Corsindae Abers 132 G3
Corsley Wilts 23 J4
Corsley Heath Wilts 22 H4
Corsock D & G 96 F3
Corston BaNES 29 L9
Corston Wilts 29 Q5
Corstorphine C Edin 115 M7
Cors-y-Gedol Gwynd 61 K7
Cortachy Angus 132 B12
Corton Suffk 59 Q1
Corton Wilts 23 K5
Corton Denham Somset 22 E9
Coruanan Highld 128 E10
Corwen Denbgs 62 E3
Coryates Dorset 10 F7
Coryton Devon 7 N8
Coryton Thurr 34 C6
Cosby Leics 54 F2
Coseley Dudley 52 H2
Cosford Shrops 64 E11
Cosgrove Nhants 43 R3
Cosham C Port 13 L4
Coshieville P & K 123 K3
Cossall Notts 66 D4
Cossall Marsh Notts 66 D4
Cossington Leics 66 G9
Cossington Somset 21 M5
Costessey Norfk 70 H9
Costock Notts 66 F7
Coston Leics 67 L8
Coston Norfk 70 F11
Cote Oxon 42 H11
Cote Somset 21 M4
Cotebrook Ches W 75 P10
Cotehill Cumb 98 F8
Cotes Cumb 89 M9
Cotes Leics 66 F8
Cotes Staffs 64 E6
Cotesbach Leics 54 E4
Cotes Heath Staffs 64 E5
Cotford St Luke Somset 21 J8
Cotgrave Notts 66 G5
Cothal Abers 133 L1
Cotham Notts 67 K3
Cothelstone Somset 21 J7
Cotherstone Dur 90 H3
Cothill Oxon 31 L2
Cotleigh Devon 9 N4
Cotmanhay Derbys 66 D3
Coton Cambs 56 H9
Coton Nhants 54 H6
Coton Shrops 63 P5
Coton Staffs 64 E8
Coton Staffs 65 J8
Coton Staffs 65 M11
Coton Clanford Staffs 64 F7
Coton Hayes Staffs 64 J5
Coton Hill Shrops 63 N9
Coton in the Clay Staffs 65 M6
Coton in the Elms Derbys 65 N9
Coton Park Derbys 65 P8
Cotswold Airport Wilts 29 Q3
Cotswolds 42 A10
Cotswold Wildlife Park & Gardens Oxon 42 F10
Cott Devon 5 N4
Cottam E R Yk 87 J2
Cottam Lancs 83 L8
Cottam Notts 79 K8
Cottenham Cambs 57 J7
Cotterdale N York 90 D8
Cottered Herts 45 K6
Cotteridge Birm 53 K5
Cotterstock Nhants 55 P3
Cottesbrooke Nhants 54 H6
Cottesmore Rutlnd 67 N9
Cottingham E R Yk 87 K8
Cottingham Nhants 55 L3
Cottingley C Brad 84 H8
Cottisford Oxon 43 M5
Cotton Suffk 58 G7
Cotton End Bed 44 F3
Cotton Tree Lancs 84 D7
Cottown Abers 133 J1
Cottown Abers 140 D10
Cottown of Gight Abers 141 K8
Cotts Devon 4 H4
Cotwall Wrekin 63 Q8
Cotwalton Staffs 64 H5
Couch's Mill Cnwll 4 C5
Coughton Herefs 41 J7
Coughton Warwks 53 K8
Coulaghailtro Ag & B 111 Q8
Coulags Highld 136 D7
Coulby Newham Middsb 92 A4
Coulderton Cumb 88 C5
Coull Abers 132 E4
Coulport Ag & B 113 M4
Coulsdon Gt Lon 33 K10
Coulston Wilts 23 L3
Coulter S Lans 106 D3
Coultershaw Bridge W Susx 14 D7
Coultings Somset 21 K5
Coulton N York 92 D12
Coultra Fife 124 G8
Cound Shrops 63 P11
Coundlane Shrops 63 P11
Coundon Dur 100 G12
Coundon Grange Dur 91 L1
Countersett N York 90 H9
Countess Wilts 23 P5
Countess Cross Essex 46 F5
Countess Wear Devon 8 H7
Countesswells C Aber 133 L3
Countesthorpe Leics 54 F2
Countisbury Devon 19 Q3
Coupar Angus P & K 124 E5
Coup Green Lancs 83 N9
Coupland Cumb 89 Q3
Coupland Nthumb 108 F4
Cour Ag & B 112 B11
Court-at-Street Kent 17 K4
Courteachan Highld 127 M5
Courteenhall Nhants 55 J10
Court Henry Carmth 38 E7
Courtsend Essex 35 J4
Courtway Somset 21 K6
Cousland Mdloth 115 Q7
Cousley Wood E Susx 16 B4
Cove Ag & B 113 L4
Cove Border 116 H7
Cove Devon 20 E9
Cove Hants 25 Q2
Cove Highld 143 L4
Cove Bay C Aber 133 M4
Cove Bottom Suffk 59 M5
Covehithe Suffk 59 Q4
Coven Staffs 64 G11
Coveney Cambs 57 J4
Covenham St Bartholomew Lincs 80 G5
Covenham St Mary Lincs 80 G5
Coven Heath Staffs 64 G11
Coventry Covtry 53 Q5
Coverack Cnwll 3 J11
Coverack Bridges Cnwll 2 G8
Coverham N York 91 J9
Covington Cambs 55 P6
Covington S Lans 106 C2

Cowan Bridge Lancs 89 Q11
Cowbeech E Susx 16 A8
Cowbit Lincs 68 E9
Cowbridge V Glam 27 N7
Cowdale Derbys 77 K9
Cowden Kent 15 N2
Cowdenbeath Fife 115 L3
Cowden Pound Kent 15 N2
Cowden Station Kent 15 N2
Cowers Lane Derbys 65 Q3
Cowes IoW 12 H5
Cowesby N York 91 R9
Cowesfield Green Wilts 24 D8
Cowfold W Susx 15 J6
Cowgill Cumb 90 C9
Cow Green Suffk 58 F7
Cowhill S Glos 29 J4
Cowie Abers 133 L7
Cowie Stirlg 114 F3
Cowley Devon 8 H5
Cowley Gloucs 41 Q8
Cowley Gt Lon 32 E5
Cowley Oxon 43 L11
Cowling Lancs 83 N11
Cowling N York 84 F6
Cowling N York 91 L9
Cowlinge Suffk 57 N10
Cowmes Kirk 85 J12
Cowpe Lancs 84 C11
Cowpen Nthumb 100 H3
Cowpen Bewley S on T 91 M3
Cowplain Hants 13 M3
Cowshill Dur 99 N9
Cowslip Green N Som 28 G10
Cowthorpe N York 85 N5
Coxall Herefs 51 L6
Coxbank Ches E 64 C4
Coxbench Derbys 66 B3
Coxbridge Somset 22 C6
Cox Common Suffk 59 M4
Coxford Cnwll 6 H5
Coxford Norfk 70 C6
Coxgreen Staffs 52 E3
Cox Green Surrey 14 H4
Coxheath Kent 34 C12
Coxhoe Dur 101 J11
Coxley Somset 22 C5
Coxley Wakefd 85 K11
Coxley Wick Somset 22 C4
Coxtie Green Essex 33 Q3
Coxwold N York 92 B11
Coychurch Brdgnd 27 M6
Coylton S Ayrs 104 H6
Coylumbridge Highld 130 G6
Coytrahen Brdgnd 27 L5
Crabbs Cross Worcs 53 K7
Crab Orchard Dorset 11 N3
Crabtree W Susx 15 J6
Crabtree Green Wrexhm 63 K3
Crackenthorpe Cumb 89 Q2
Crackington Haven Cnwll 6 G4
Crackley Staffs 64 F2
Crackley Warwks 53 P6
Crackleybank Shrops 64 E10
Crackpot N York 90 H7
Cracoe N York 84 E2
Craddock Devon 20 H11
Cradle End Herts 45 N7
Cradley Dudley 52 H4
Cradley Herefs 41 L2
Cradley Heath Sandw 52 H3
Cradoc Powys 39 N5
Crafthole Cnwll 4 G6
Crafton Bucks 44 C8
Crag Foot Lancs 89 M12
Craggan Highld 139 J2
Cragganmore Moray 139 M8
Cragg Hill Leeds 85 J7
Cragg Vale Calder 84 F10
Craghead Dur 100 G8
Crai Powys 39 J7
Craibstone Moray 140 D4
Craichie Angus 125 J3
Craig Angus 125 N2
Craig Highld 136 H6
Craigbank E Ayrs 105 L7
Craig-cefn-parc Swans 38 G11
Craigcleuch D & G 107 K12
Craigdam Abers 141 K10
Craigdarroch D & G 105 Q10
Craigdhu Ag & B 120 F11
Craigearn Abers 132 H2
Craigellachie Moray 139 P7
Craigend P & K 124 C6
Craigendoran Ag & B 113 N4
Craigends Rens 113 N6
Craighat Stirlg 113 P4
Craighlaw D & G 95 K6
Craighouse Ag & B 111 J8
Craigie P & K 124 C3
Craigie P & K 124 F4
Craigie S Ayrs 104 H3
Craigiefold Abers 141 M3
Craiglockhart C Edin 115 M7
Craigmillar C Edin 115 P7
Craignant Shrops 63 J5
Craigneston D & G 105 K12
Craigneuk N Lans 114 D10
Craigneuk N Lans 114 D8
Craignure Ag & B 120 D5
Craigo Angus 132 H11
Craigrothie Fife 124 H10
Craigruie Stirlg 122 H4
Craig's End Essex 46 C4
Craigton Angus 125 J5
Craigton C Aber 133 K4
Craigton E Rens 113 P8
Craigton of Airlie Angus 124 G3
Craig-y-Duke Neath 38 H11
Craig-y-nos Powys 39 J9
Craik Border 107 J7
Crail Fife 125 M11
Crailing Border 107 R5
Crailinghall Border 114 ?
Craiselound N Linc 79 J4
Crakehall N York 91 L9
Crakehill N York 91 Q12
Crakemarsh Staffs 65 K5
Crambe N York 86 B2
Crambeck N York 86 C2
Cramlington Nthumb 100 H3
Cramond C Edin 115 M6
Cramond Bridge C Edin 115 M6
Crampmoor Hants 24 F9
Cranage Ches E 76 D10
Cranberry Staffs 64 F5
Cranborne Dorset 23 N10
Cranbourne Br For 32 C8
Cranbrook Kent 16 D4
Cranbrook Common Kent 16 D3
Crane Moor Barns 77 P4
Crane's Corner Norfk 70 D9
Cranfield C Beds 44 D3
Cranford Devon 18 G9
Cranford Gt Lon 32 G7
Cranford St Andrew Nhants 55 M5
Cranford St John Nhants 55 M5
Cranham Gloucs 41 P9
Cranham Gt Lon 33 Q5
Cranhill Warwks 53 L10
Crank St Hel 75 N3
Cranleigh Surrey 14 F3

Cranmer Green Suffk 58 F6
Cranmore IoW 12 F7
Cranmore Somset 22 F5
Cranoe Leics 55 J2
Cransford Suffk 59 L7
Cranshaws Border 116 F9
Cranstal IoM 102 f2
Cranswick E R Yk 87 J3
Crantock Cnwll 3 K2
Cranwell Lincs 67 P2
Cranwich Norfk 57 P2
Cranworth Norfk 70 E11
Craobh Haven Ag & B 120 E11
Crapstone Devon 4 H3
Crarae Ag & B 112 E2
Crask Inn Highld 149 L11
Crask of Aigas Highld 137 N7
Craster Nthumb 109 L6
Craswall Herefs 40 E3
Crateford Staffs 64 G10
Cratfield Suffk 59 L5
Crathes Abers 133 J5
Crathie Abers 131 N5
Crathie Highld 129 N5
Crathorne N York 91 Q5
Craven Arms Shrops 51 M4
Crawcrook Gatesd 100 E5
Crawford Lancs 75 N3
Crawford S Lans 106 C5
Crawfordjohn S Lans 106 A5
Crawley Hants 24 G6
Crawley Oxon 42 H9
Crawley W Susx 15 K3
Crawley Down W Susx 15 L3
Crawleyside Dur 100 C10
Crawshawbooth Lancs 84 B10
Crawton Abers 133 L8
Craxe's Green Essex 46 G8
Cray N York 90 F11
Cray P & K 131 L11
Crayford Gt Lon 33 P7
Crayke N York 85 R1
Craymere Beck Norfk 70 F6
Crays Hill Essex 34 C4
Cray's Pond Oxon 31 N6
Craythorne Staffs 65 N7
Craze Lowman Devon 20 F10
Crazies Hill Wokham 31 N6
Creacombe Devon 20 C9
Creagan Ag & B 121 J4
Creag Ghoraidh W Isls 152 c9
Creaguaineach Lodge Highld 129 K10
Creamore Bank Shrops 63 N6
Creaton Nhants 54 H6
Creca D & G 97 P4
Credenhill Herefs 40 F3
Crediton Devon 8 F4
Creebank D & G 95 L3
Creebridge D & G 95 M5
Creech Dorset 11 M8
Creech Heathfield Somset 21 L8
Creech St Michael Somset 21 L8
Creed Cnwll 3 N5
Creekmoor BCP 11 N6
Creekmouth Gt Lon 33 N6
Creeksea Essex 34 G4
Creeting St Mary Suffk 58 G9
Creeting St Peter Suffk 58 G9
Creeton Lincs 67 P8
Creetown D & G 95 N6
Cregneash IoM 102 b7
Creg ny Baa IoM 102 e5
Cregrina Powys 50 F10
Creich Fife 124 G8
Creigiau Cardif 27 P6
Cremyll Cnwll 4 H7
Cressage Shrops 63 Q11
Cressbrook Derbys 77 M9
Cresselly Pembks 37 L9
Cressex Bucks 32 B4
Cressing Essex 46 D7
Cresswell Nthumb 109 M11
Cresswell Pembks 37 K9
Cresswell Staffs 64 H4
Creswell Green Staffs 65 K10
Cretingham Suffk 59 J8
Cretshengan Ag & B 111 Q8
Crewe Ches E 64 D1
Crewe-by-Farndon Ches E 63 M2
Crewe Green Ches E 64 D1
Crew Green Powys 63 K9
Crewkerne Somset 10 C3
Crews Hill Gt Lon 33 K2
Crewton C Derb 66 B5
Crianlarich Stirlg 122 C8
Cribyn Cerdgn 49 J10
Criccieth Gwynd 60 H4
Crich Derbys 65 Q1
Crichton Mdloth 115 Q8
Crick Nhants 54 E6
Crick Mons 28 G4
Crickadarn Powys 39 P3
Cricket St Thomas Somset 10 B3
Crickheath Shrops 63 J8
Crickhowell Powys 40 B7
Cricklade Wilts 30 D3
Cricklewood Gt Lon 33 J4
Cridling Stubbs N York 85 Q11
Crieff P & K 123 L8
Criggan Cnwll 3 P2
Criggion Powys 63 J9
Crigglestone Wakefd 85 L12
Crimble Rochdl 76 F1
Crimond Abers 141 P4
Crimplesham Norfk 69 M11
Crimscote Warwks 42 G2
Crinaglack Highld 137 M8
Crinan Ag & B 112 A2
Crindledyke N Lans 114 E10
Cringleford Norfk 71 J11
Cringles C Brad 84 F6
Crinow Pembks 37 M7
Cripplesease Cnwll 2 E7
Cripplestyle Dorset 23 N11
Cripp's Corner E Susx 16 D6
Croachy Highld 138 B10
Crockenhill Kent 33 P9
Crocker End Oxon 31 P5
Crockerhill W Susx 14 C10
Crockernwell Devon 8 D6
Crockerton Wilts 23 J5
Crocketford D & G 96 H3
Crockey Hill C York 86 B6
Crockham Hill Kent 33 N11
Crockhurst Street Kent 16 B2
Crockleford Heath Essex 47 J6
Crock Street Somset 21 M11
Croeserw Neath 27 K3
Croes-goch Pembks 36 F4
Croes-lan Cerdgn 38 B3
Croesor Gwynd 61 L3
Croespenmaen Caerph 28 B2
Croesyceiliog Carmth 38 D8
Croesyceiliog Torfn 28 C3
Croes-y-mwyalch Torfn 28 C4
Croes-y-pant Mons 40 D10
Croft Leics 54 E2
Croft Lincs 81 K11

Croft Warrtn 76 B5
Croftamie Stirlg 113 P4
Croft Mitchell Cnwll 2 G7
Crofton Cumb 98 C8
Crofton Wakefd 85 M11
Crofton Wilts 30 F9
Croft-on-Tees N York 91 M5
Croftown Highld 144 F8
Crofts Moray 139 P6
Crofts Bank Traffd 76 E4
Crofts of Dipple Moray 139 P4
Crofts of Haddo Abers 141 K8
Crofts of Savoch Abers 141 P4
Crofty Swans 26 C3
Crogen Gwynd 62 D5
Croggan Ag & B 120 D7
Croglin Cumb 98 H9
Croick Highld 145 L7
Cromarty Highld 138 E2
Crombie Fife 115 J4
Cromdale Highld 139 K10
Cromer Herts 45 K6
Cromer Norfk 71 J4
Cromford Derbys 77 P12
Cromhall S Glos 29 J4
Cromhall Common S Glos 29 L4
Cromor W Isls 152 g4
Cromra Highld 129 N5
Crompton Fold Oldham 76 H2
Cromwell Notts 79 K11
Cronberry E Ayrs 105 L5
Crondall Hants 25 N4
Cronkbourne IoM 102 e6
Cronk-y-Voddy IoM 102 d4
Cronton Knows 75 N6
Crook Cumb 89 M7
Crook Dur 100 F11
Crookdake Cumb 97 P9
Crooke Wigan 75 P2
Crooked End Gloucs 41 J8
Crookedholm E Ayrs 104 H3
Crooked Soley Wilts 30 G8
Crookes Sheff 77 Q6
Crookhall Dur 100 E8
Crookham Nthumb 108 E2
Crookham W Berk 31 L9
Crookham Village Hants 25 N3
Crook Inn Border 106 E4
Crooklands Cumb 89 N10
Crook of Devon P & K 115 J1
Cropper Derbys 65 N5
Cropredy Oxon 43 K2
Cropston Leics 66 F10
Cropthorne Worcs 42 A3
Cropton N York 92 F9
Cropwell Bishop Notts 66 H5
Cropwell Butler Notts 66 H5
Cros W Isls 152 h1
Crosbost W Isls 152 g4
Crosby Cumb 97 M10
Crosby IoM 102 d5
Crosby N Linc 79 M1
Crosby Sefton 75 K4
Crosby Garret Cumb 90 B5
Crosby Ravensworth Cumb 89 Q4
Crosby Villa Cumb 97 M10
Croscombe Somset 22 D4
Crosemere Shrops 63 M6
Crosland Edge Kirk 77 L1
Crosland Hill Kirk 84 H12
Cross Somset 21 N2
Crossaig Ag & B 112 B11
Crossapol Ag & B 118 B4
Cross Ash Mons 40 F8
Cross-at-Hand Kent 16 D2
Crossbush W Susx 14 E9
Crosscanonby Cumb 97 L10
Cross Coombe Cnwll 2 H4
Crossdale Street Norfk 71 J4
Cross End Bed 55 Q9
Cross End Essex 46 F5
Crossens Sefton 83 J11
Cross Flatts C Brad 84 G7
Crossford Fife 115 J4
Crossford S Lans 114 E12
Crossgate Cnwll 7 L6
Crossgate Lincs 68 E7
Crossgate Staffs 64 H5
Crossgatehall E Loth 115 Q7
Crossgates E Ayrs 113 M12
Crossgates Fife 115 K4
Crossgates N York 93 L11
Cross Gates Leeds 85 M8
Crossgates Powys 50 F7
Crossgill Lancs 83 M3
Cross Green Devon 7 M7
Cross Green Leeds 85 L9
Cross Green Staffs 64 G11
Cross Green Suffk 58 B10
Cross Green Suffk 58 D10
Cross Green Suffk 58 E10
Crosshands Carmth 38 D7
Crosshands E Ayrs 104 H4
Cross Hands Pembks 37 L8
Cross Hill Derbys 66 C2
Crosshill Fife 115 M2
Cross Hills N York 84 F6
Crosshill S Ayrs 104 F6
Crosshouse E Ayrs 104 G2
Cross Houses Shrops 63 P11
Cross in Hand E Susx 15 Q6
Cross Inn Cerdgn 48 F10
Cross Inn Cerdgn 49 J8
Cross Inn Rhondd 27 P6
Cross Keys Ag & B 113 L4
Crosskeys Caerph 28 B3
Crosskirk Highld 151 J3
Crosslands Cumb 89 L8
Cross Lane IoW 12 H7
Cross Lane Head Shrops 52 D1
Cross Lanes Cnwll 2 H10
Cross Lanes N York 85 Q3
Cross Lanes Shrops 63 K8
Cross Lanes Wrexhm 63 L2
Crosslee Rens 113 N8
Crossmichael D & G 96 E5
Cross Oak Powys 39 Q6
Cross of Jackston Abers 141 J9
Crossroads Abers 133 E3
Cross Roads C Brad 84 F7
Crossroads E Ayrs 104 H3
Cross Street Suffk 59 J5
Crosston Angus 125 J2
Crossway Mons 40 E8
Crossway Powys 50 F9
Crossway Green Mons 29 J6
Crossway Green Worcs 52 F7
Crossways Dorset 11 J7
Crosswell Pembks 37 L3
Crosswood Cerdgn 49 M5
Crosthwaite Cumb 89 L8
Croston Lancs 83 L12
Crostwick Norfk 71 K9
Crostwight Norfk 71 L7
Crouch Kent 34 A11
Crouch End Gt Lon 33 K5

Croucheston Wilts 23 N8
Crouch Hill Dorset 10 H3
Crough House Green Kent 15 N2
Croughton Nhants 43 L5
Crovie Abers 141 K3
Crow Hants 12 B4
Crowan Cnwll 2 G7
Crowborough E Susx 15 P4
Crowborough Warren E Susx 15 P5
Crowcombe Somset 21 J6
Crowdecote Derbys 77 L10
Crowden Derbys 77 K4
Crowden Devon 7 P5
Crowdhill Hants 24 H9
Crowdleham Kent 33 Q10
Crow Edge Barns 77 M3
Crowell Oxon 31 Q2
Crow End Cambs 56 F9
Crowfield Nhants 43 M3
Crowfield Suffk 58 H9
Crowfield Green Suffk 58 H9
Crowgate Street Norfk 71 L8
Crow Green Essex 33 Q3
Crowhill E Loth 116 G6
Crow Hill Herefs 41 K6
Crowhole Derbys 77 Q8
Crowhurst E Susx 16 C8
Crowhurst Surrey 15 M1
Crowhurst Lane End Surrey 15 M1
Crowland Lincs 68 E10
Crowland Suffk 58 F6
Crowlas Cnwll 2 E8
Crowle N Linc 79 J1
Crowle Worcs 52 G9
Crowle Green Worcs 52 G9
Crowmarsh Gifford Oxon 31 N4
Crown Corner Suffk 59 K6
Crownhill C Plym 4 G5
Crownpits Surrey 14 D2
Crownthorpe Norfk 70 G11
Crowntown Cnwll 2 G8
Crows-an-Wra Cnwll 2 C9
Crow's Green Essex 46 C6
Crowshill Norfk 70 D11
Crow's Nest Cnwll 4 C3
Crowsnest Shrops 63 L11
Crowthorne Wokham 32 B9
Crowton Ches W 75 P9
Croxall Staffs 65 M9
Croxby Lincs 80 D4
Croxdale Dur 100 H11
Croxden Staffs 65 K4
Croxley Green Herts 32 F3
Croxteth Lpool 75 L4
Croxton Cambs 56 E8
Croxton N Linc 80 E1
Croxton Norfk 58 C3
Croxton Norfk 70 C6
Croxton Staffs 64 E6
Croxtonbank Staffs 64 E6
Croxton Green Ches E 63 P2
Croxton Kerrial Leics 67 L6
Croy Highld 138 E6
Croy N Lans 114 E6
Croyde Devon 19 J5
Croyde Bay Devon 18 H5
Croydon Cambs 56 F10
Croydon Gt Lon 33 K8
Cruckmeole Shrops 63 M10
Cruckton Shrops 63 M10
Cruden Bay Abers 141 Q8
Crudgington Wrekin 64 B8
Crudie Abers 141 J4
Crudwell Wilts 29 Q4
Cruft Devon 7 P5
Crûg Powys 50 G6
Crugmeer Cnwll 6 C9
Crugybar Carmth 38 G4
Crug-y-byddar Powys 50 G4
Crumlin Caerph 28 B3
Crumplehorn Cnwll 4 B6
Crumpsall Manch 76 F3
Crundale Kent 17 J1
Crundale Pembks 37 J7
Crunwere Farm Pembks 37 N8
Cruwys Morchard Devon 20 D11
Crux Easton Hants 31 J11
Cruxton Dorset 10 F5
Crwbin Carmth 38 C7
Cryers Hill Bucks 32 C3
Crymych Pembks 37 M4
Crynant Neath 39 J10
Crystal Palace Gt Lon 33 L8
Cuaig Highld 135 N4
Cuan Ag & B 120 E10
Cubbington Warwks 53 Q7
Cubert Cnwll 3 J3
Cubley Barns 77 N3
Cublington Bucks 44 B7
Cublington Herefs 40 E4
Cuckfield W Susx 15 K6
Cucklington Somset 22 G9
Cuckney Notts 78 F9
Cuckoo Bridge Lincs 68 D8
Cuckoo's Corner Hants 25 N5
Cuckoo's Nest Ches W 75 L11
Cuddesdon Oxon 43 M11
Cuddington Bucks 43 Q9
Cuddington Ches W 75 Q9
Cuddington Heath Ches W 63 M3
Cuddy Hill Lancs 83 L8
Cudham Gt Lon 33 N10
Cudliptown Devon 7 P9
Cudnell BCP 11 P5
Cudworth Barns 78 C2
Cudworth Somset 10 B2
Cuerdley Cross Warrtn 75 P6
Cufaude Hants 31 N11
Cuffley Herts 45 L11
Cuil Highld 120 G2
Culbokie Highld 137 Q4
Culbone Somset 20 C4
Culburnie Highld 137 N7
Culcabock Highld 138 C7
Culcharry Highld 138 F6
Culcheth Warrtn 76 B4
Culdrain Abers 140 D9
Culduie Highld 135 N8
Culford Suffk 58 B6
Culgaith Cumb 99 J12
Culham Oxon 31 M3
Culkein Highld 148 C10
Culkein Drumbeg Highld 148 D10
Culkerton Gloucs 29 Q3
Cullen Moray 140 D2
Cullercoats N Tyne 101 J4
Cullerlie Abers 133 J4
Cullicudden Highld 138 B3
Cullingworth C Brad 84 G8
Cuillin Hills Highld 135 J11
Cullipool Ag & B 120 D10
Cullivoe Shet 147 J2
Culloden Highld 138 E6
Cullompton Devon 9 J3
Cullompton Services Devon 9 J3
Culm Davy Devon 20 H10
Culmington Shrops 51 N4
Culmstock Devon 20 H10
Culnacraig Highld 144 D4
Culnaightrie D & G 96 D8
Culnaknock Highld 135 J3

Culpho Suffk 59 J10
Culrain Highld 145 N6
Culross Fife 114 H4
Culroy S Ayrs 104 F7
Culsalmond Abers 140 G9
Culscadden D & G 95 N8
Culshabbin D & G 95 K8
Culswick Shet 147 h7
Cultercullen Abers 141 M11
Cults C Aber 133 L4
Culverstone Green Kent 34 B9
Culverthorpe Lincs 67 P4
Culworth Nhants 43 L2
Culzean Castle & Country Park S Ayrs 104 D8
Cumbernauld N Lans 114 D6
Cumbernauld Village N Lans 114 D6
Cumberworth Lincs 81 K9
Cumdivock Cumb 98 D8
Cuminestown Abers 141 K6
Cumledge Border 116 H10
Cummersdale Cumb 98 E7
Cummertrees D & G 97 N5
Cummingston Moray 139 L2
Cumnock E Ayrs 105 K6
Cumnor Oxon 43 K11
Cumrew Cumb 98 G8
Cumrue D & G 97 L1
Cumwhinton Cumb 98 F7
Cumwhitton Cumb 98 G8
Cundall N York 91 P12
Cunninghamhead N Ayrs 104 G1
Cunningsburgh Shet 147 i8
Cupar Fife 124 G10
Cupar Muir Fife 124 G10
Curbar Derbys 77 N9
Curbridge Hants 13 J2
Curbridge Oxon 42 G10
Curdridge Hants 25 J10
Curdworth Warwks 53 M2
Curland Somset 21 L10
Curridge W Berk 31 K8
Currie C Edin 115 M8
Curry Mallet Somset 21 M9
Curry Rivel Somset 21 N8
Curteis Corner Kent 16 E3
Curtisden Green Kent 16 C3
Curtisknowle Devon 5 M6
Cury Cnwll 2 H10
Cushnie Abers 132 D2
Cushuish Somset 21 K7
Cusop Herefs 40 C3
Cusworth Donc 78 F3
Cutcloy D & G 95 N11
Cutcombe Somset 20 E5
Cutgate Rochdl 84 C12
Cuthill Highld 146 D7
Cutiau Gwynd 61 L8
Cutler's Green Essex 45 Q5
Cutmadoc Cnwll 3 Q2
Cutmere Cnwll 4 E4
Cutnall Green Worcs 52 G7
Cutsdean Gloucs 42 C6
Cutthorpe Derbys 77 Q9
Cuttivett Cnwll 4 E4
Cuxham Oxon 31 N3
Cuxton Medway 34 C9
Cuxwold Lincs 80 D3
Cwm Blae G 40 B10
Cwm Denbgs 74 E8
Cwmafan Neath 27 J4
Cwmaman Rhondd 27 N2
Cwmann Carmth 38 E2
Cwmavon Torfn 40 C10
Cwmbach Carmth 37 P5
Cwmbach Carmth 38 D11
Cwmbâch Powys 40 A4
Cwmbach Rhondd 39 N11
Cwmbach Llechrhyd Powys 50 E10
Cwmbelan Powys 50 C4
Cwmbran Torfn 28 C3
Cwmbrwyno Cerdgn 49 M4
Cwm Capel Carmth 38 C11
Cwmcarn Caerph 28 B4
Cwmcarvan Mons 40 G10
Cwm-celyn Blae G 40 B10
Cwm-Cewydd Gwynd 61 Q9
Cwm-cou Cerdgn 37 Q2
Cwm Crawnon Powys 39 Q7
Cwmdare Rhondd 39 N11
Cwmdu Carmth 38 F6
Cwmdu Powys 40 A7
Cwmdu Swans 26 F3
Cwmduad Carmth 38 B5
Cwm Dulais Swans 38 F11
Cwmdwr Carmth 38 H5
Cwmfelin Brdgnd 27 K4
Cwmfelin Myr Td 27 P2
Cwmfelin Boeth Carmth 37 N7
Cwmfelinfach Caerph 28 B4
Cwmfelin Mynach Carmth 37 P5
Cwmffrwd Carmth 38 B8
Cwmgiedd Powys 39 J9
Cwmgorse Carmth 38 G9
Cwm Gwaun Pembks 37 K4
Cwmgwili Carmth 38 E9
Cwmgwrach Neath 39 K10
Cwmhiraeth Carmth 37 R3
Cwmifor Carmth 38 G6
Cwm Irfon Powys 49 Q10
Cwmisfael Carmth 38 D8
Cwm Llinau Powys 61 P10
Cwmllynfell Neath 38 H9
Cwmmawr Carmth 38 D9
Cwm Morgan Carmth 37 Q3
Cwmparc Rhondd 27 M3
Cwmpengraig Carmth 37 R3
Cwm Penmachno Conwy 61 N3
Cwmpennar Rhondd 27 N2
Cwmrhos Powys 40 B7
Cwmrhydyceirw Swans 26 G2
Cwmsychbant Cerdgn 38 C2
Cwmtillery Blae G 40 B10
Cwm-twrch Isaf Powys 39 J9
Cwm-twrch Uchaf Powys 38 H9
Cwm-y-glo Carmth 38 E9
Cwm-y-glo Gwynd 73 J11
Cwmyoy Mons 40 D7
Cwmystwyth Cerdgn 49 N6
Cwrt Gwynd 61 M12
Cwrtnewydd Cerdgn 48 H11
Cwrt-y-gollen Powys 40 B8
Cyfarthfa Castle Museum Myr Td 39 P10
Cyffylliog Denbgs 74 E12
Cyfronydd Powys 62 G10
Cylibebyll Neath 38 H11
Cymau Flints 63 J1
Cymmer Neath 27 K3
Cymmer Rhondd 27 N4
Cyncoed Cardif 28 B6
Cynghordy Carmth 39 J4
Cynheidre Carmth 38 D10
Cynonville Neath 27 K3
Cynwyd Denbgs 62 E4
Cynwyl Elfed Carmth 38 B6

D

Daccombe Devon 5 Q3
Dacre Cumb 89 M1
Dacre N York 85 J3
Dacre Banks N York 85 J3
Daddry Shield Dur 99 P10
Dadford Bucks 43 N4
Dadlington Leics 54 C1
Dafen Carmth 26 D2
Daffy Green Norfk 70 E10
Dagenham Gt Lon 33 P5
Daglingworth Gloucs 42 A10
Dagnall Bucks 44 E8
Dagworth Suffk 58 F8
Dail bho Dheas W Isls 152 g1
Dailly S Ayrs 104 E9
Dainton Devon 5 P3
Dairsie Fife 124 H9
Daisy Hill Bolton 76 C3
Daisy Hill Leeds 85 K9
Dalabrog W Isls 152 b11
Dalavich Ag & B 120 H10
Dalbeattie D & G 96 G6
Dalbury Derbys 65 N5
Dalby IoM 102 b5
Dalby Lincs 80 H9
Dalby N York 86 B1
Dalcapon P & K 123 N2
Dalchalm Highld 146 G4
Dalchreichart Highld 129 J2
Dalchruin P & K 123 J9
Dalcrue P & K 123 P7
Dalderby Lincs 80 E10
Dalditch Devon 9 K8
Dale Cumb 98 G9
Dale Pembks 36 F9
Dale Abbey Derbys 66 C4
Dale Bottom Cumb 89 J2
Dale End Derbys 77 N11
Dale End N York 84 E6
Dale Hill E Susx 16 C5
Dalehouse N York 92 F3
Dalelia Highld 127 N10
Dalgarven N Ayrs 113 K12
Dalgety Bay Fife 115 L4
Dalgig E Ayrs 105 K7
Dalginross P & K 123 K8
Dalguise P & K 123 P3
Dalhalvaig Highld 150 F6
Dalham Suffk 57 N8
Daliburgh W Isls 152 b11
Dalkeith Mdloth 115 Q8
Dallas Moray 139 L5
Dallinghoo Suffk 59 K9
Dallington E Susx 16 B7
Dallington Nhants 55 J8
Dallow N York 91 K12
Dalmally Ag & B 121 M7
Dalmary Stirlg 113 P2
Dalmellington E Ayrs 105 J8
Dalmeny C Edin 115 L6
Dalmore Highld 138 C2
Dalmuir W Duns 113 P7
Dalnabreck Highld 127 M10
Dalnacardoch P & K 130 D10
Dalnahaitnach Highld 138 F11
Dalnaspidal P & K 130 B9
Dalnawillan Lodge Highld 151 J8
Dalness Highld 121 M3
Dalqueich P & K 124 B12
Dalquhairn S Ayrs 104 F10
Dalreavoch Highld 146 D3
Dalry N Ayrs 113 K11
Dalrymple E Ayrs 104 F7
Dalserf S Lans 114 E11
Dalsmeran Ag & B 102 H7
Dalston Cumb 98 D8
Dalston Gt Lon 33 L5
Dalswinton D & G 97 J1
Dalton Cumb 89 N11
Dalton D & G 97 M3
Dalton Lancs 75 N2
Dalton N York 91 J5
Dalton N York 91 Q11
Dalton Nthumb 100 E4
Dalton Rothm 78 D5
Dalton-in-Furness Cumb 88 H12
Dalton-le-Dale Dur 101 K8
Dalton Magna Rothm 78 D5
Dalton-on-Tees N York 91 M5
Dalton Parva Rothm 78 D5
Dalton Piercy Hartpl 101 L12
Dalveich Stirlg 122 G8
Dalwhinnie Highld 130 B7
Dalwood Devon 9 N5
Damask Green Herts 45 J6
Damerham Hants 23 N10
Damgate Norfk 71 M10
Dam Green Norfk 58 F4
Damnaglaur D & G 94 G11
Danaway Kent 34 F9
Danbury Essex 46 D10
Danby N York 92 E5
Danby Bottom N York 92 E6
Danby Wiske N York 91 N7
Dandaleith Moray 139 P6
Danderhall Mdloth 115 P7
Danebridge Ches E 76 H10
Dane End Herts 45 L7
Danegate E Susx 15 Q4
Danehill E Susx 15 M5
Dane Hills C Leic 66 F11
Danemoor Green Norfk 70 F11
Danesford Shrops 52 D2
Danesmoor Derbys 78 C11
Dane Street Kent 35 J11
Daniel's Water Kent 16 G3
Danshillock Abers 140 H4
Danskine E Loth 116 D8
Danthorpe E R Yk 87 N8
Danzey Green Warwks 53 L7
Dapple Heath Staffs 65 K7
Darby Green Hants 32 B10
Darcy Lever Bolton 76 D2
Dardy Powys 40 B8
Darenth Kent 33 Q8
Daresbury Halton 75 P7
Darfield Barns 78 C3
Darfoulds Notts 78 F8
Dargate Kent 35 K10
Dargavel Rens 113 N7
Darite Cnwll 4 C3
Darland Medway 34 D9
Darland Wrexhm 75 L12
Darlaston Wsall 52 H1
Darlaston Green Wsall 52 H1
Darley N York 85 J3
Darley Abbey C Derb 66 B4
Darley Bridge Derbys 77 P11
Darley Dale Derbys 77 P11
Darley Green Solhll 53 M6
Darleyhall Herts 44 G7
Darley Head N York 85 J3
Darlingscott Warwks 42 F3
Darlington Darltn 91 M4
Darliston Shrops 63 P5
Darlton Notts 79 K9
Darnford Staffs 65 L10
Darnick Border 107 N3
Darowen Powys 61 P11
Darra Abers 140 H6
Darracott Devon 18 E9
Darracott Devon 19 J5
Darras Hall Nthumb 100 F4
Darrington Wakefd 85 P11
Darsham Suffk 59 N6
Darshill Somset 22 E4
Dartford Kent 33 Q7
Dartford Crossing Kent 33 Q7
Dartington Devon 5 N4
Dartmeet Devon 8 C10
Dartmoor National Park Devon 8 D9
Dartmouth Devon 5 P6
Darton Barns 77 P2
Darvel E Ayrs 105 K2
Darwell Hole E Susx 16 C7
Darwen Bl w D 83 Q10
Datchet W & M 32 E7
Datchworth Herts 45 K8
Datchworth Green Herts 45 K8
Daubhill Bolton 76 C2
Daugh of Kinermony Moray 139 N7
Dauntsey Wilts 30 A6
Dava Highld 139 J8
Davenham Ches W 76 C9
Davenport Stockp 76 G6
Davenport Green Ches E 76 F8
Davenport Green Traffd 76 E6
Daventry Nhants 54 F8
Davidson's Mains C Edin 115 M6
Davidstow Cnwll 6 H7
David Street Kent 34 B9
Davington D & G 106 H9
Davington Kent 34 H10
Daviot Abers 141 J10
Daviot Highld 138 D8
Daviot House Highld 138 D7
Davis's Town E Susx 15 P7
Davoch of Grange Moray 140 D5
Davyhulme Traffd 76 D4
Daw End Wsall 65 J12
Dawesgreen Surrey 15 J1
Dawley Wrekin 64 C10
Dawlish Devon 8 H9
Dawlish Warren Devon 9 J9
Dawn Conwy 73 Q9
Daws Green Somset 21 K9
Daws Heath Essex 34 E5
Daw's House Cnwll 7 L8
Dawsmere Lincs 68 H6
Daybrook Notts 66 F3
Day Green Ches E 76 E12
Dayhills Staffs 64 H5
Dayhouse Bank Worcs 52 H5
Daylesford Gloucs 42 F6
Ddol Flints 74 G9
Ddol-Cownwy Powys 62 D8
Deal Kent 35 Q12
Dean Cumb 88 E2
Dean Devon 5 M4
Dean Devon 19 N4
Dean Devon 19 M4
Dean Dorset 23 L10
Dean Hants 24 G7
Dean Hants 25 J10
Dean Lancs 84 C10
Dean Oxon 42 H7
Dean Somset 22 F5
Dean Bottom Kent 33 Q8
Deanburnhaugh Border 107 K7
Deancombe Devon 5 M3
Dean Court Oxon 43 K10
Deane Bolton 76 C3
Deane Hants 25 J3
Dean End Dorset 23 L10
Dean Head Barns 77 P4
Deanhead Kirk 84 F12
Deanland Dorset 23 M9
Deanlane End W Susx 25 N11
Dean Prior Devon 5 M4
Deanraw Nthumb 99 M6
Dean Row Ches E 76 G7
Deans W Loth 115 J7
Deanscales Cumb 88 E1
Deanshanger Nhants 43 Q4
Deanshaugh Moray 139 Q6
Deanston Stirlg 114 C1
Dean Street Kent 34 C11
Dearham Cumb 97 L11
Dearnley Rochdl 84 D12
Debach Suffk 59 K10
Debden Essex 33 N3
Debden Essex 45 Q5
Debden Green Essex 45 Q5
Debenham Suffk 58 H8
Deblin's Green Worcs 52 E11
Dechmont W Loth 115 J7
Deddington Oxon 43 K5
Dedham Essex 47 J5
Dedham Heath Essex 47 J5
Dedworth W & M 32 D7
Deene Nhants 55 N2
Deenethorpe Nhants 55 N2
Deepcar Sheff 77 P4
Deepcut Surrey 32 C11
Deepdale Cumb 90 B9
Deepdale N York 90 E10
Deeping Gate C Pete 68 C10
Deeping St James Lincs 68 C10
Deeping St Nicholas Lincs 68 D9
Deerhurst Gloucs 41 P6
Deerhurst Walton Gloucs 41 P6
Deerton Street Kent 34 H9
Defford Worcs 41 Q3
Defynnog Powys 39 L6
Deganwy Conwy 73 N8
Degnish Ag & B 120 E10
Deighton C York 86 B6
Deighton N York 91 P6
Deiniolen Gwynd 73 K11
Delabole Cnwll 6 F8
Delamere Ches W 75 P10
Delamere Park Ches W 75 Q9
Delfrigs Abers 141 M11
Delliefure Highld 139 K9
Dell Quay W Susx 13 P4
Delly End Oxon 43 J8
Delnabo Moray 139 L12
Delny Highld 146 D10
Delph Oldham 77 J2
Delves Dur 100 E8
Delvin End Essex 46 D5
Dembleby Lincs 67 P5
Demelza Cnwll 3 N2
Denaby Donc 78 D4
Denaby Main Donc 78 E4
Denbies Surrey 32 G12
Denbigh Denbgs 74 E10
Denbrae Fife 124 H9
Denbury Devon 5 N4
Denby Derbys 66 C3
Denby Bottles Derbys 66 C3
Denby Dale Kirk 77 N2
Denchworth Oxon 30 H4
Dendron Cumb 82 G1
Denel End C Beds 44 E4
Denfield P & K 123 N9
Denford Nhants 55 N5
Dengie Essex 46 H11
Denham Bucks 32 F5
Denham Suffk 57 P8
Denham Suffk 58 H6
Denham End Suffk 57 P8
Denham Green Bucks 32 F5
Denham Green Suffk 59 J6
Denhead Abers 141 N5
Denhead Fife 125 J10
Denhead of Gray C Dund 124 G6
Denholm Border 107 P6
Denholme C Brad 84 G8
Denholme Clough C Brad 84 G8
Denio Gwynd 60 F5
Denmead Hants 25 L11
Denmore C Aber 133 M2
Denne Park W Susx 14 H5
Dennington Suffk 59 K7
Denny Falk 114 E5
Dennyloanhead Falk 114 E5
Den of Lindores Fife 124 E9
Denshaw Oldham 76 H2
Denside of Durris Abers 133 K5
Densole Kent 17 M2
Denston Suffk 57 P10
Denstone Staffs 65 L4
Denstroude Kent 35 K10
Dent Cumb 90 B9
Denton Cambs 56 C3
Denton Darltn 91 L3
Denton E Susx 15 N10
Denton Kent 17 M1
Denton Kent 34 B7
Denton Lincs 67 L6
Denton N York 84 H5
Denton Nhants 55 L9
Denton Norfk 59 K3
Denton Oxon 43 M11
Denton Tamesd 76 G5
Denver Norfk 69 L11
Denwick Nthumb 109 K7
Deopham Norfk 70 F12
Deopham Green Norfk 70 F12
Depden Suffk 57 P9
Depden Green Suffk 57 P9
Deptford Gt Lon 33 L7
Deptford Wilts 23 N6
Derby C Derb 66 B5
Derby Devon 19 L6
Derbyhaven IoM 102 c7
Derculich P & K 123 M2
Dereham Norfk 70 E9
Deri Caerph 27 Q2
Derril Devon 7 K4
Derringstone Kent 35 M12
Derrington Staffs 64 G7
Derriton Devon 7 L4
Derry Hill Wilts 29 Q8
Derrythorpe N Linc 79 K2
Dersingham Norfk 69 N6
Dervaig Ag & B 119 M2
Derwen Denbgs 62 E2
Derwenlas Powys 61 M12
Derwent Valley Mills Derbys 65 P1
Derwent Water Cumb 88 H3
Derwydd Carmth 38 F8
Desborough Nhants 55 K4
Desford Leics 66 D11
Detchant Nthumb 108 H2
Detling Kent 34 D10
Deuxhill Shrops 52 C3
Devauden Mons 28 G3
Devil's Bridge Cerdgn 49 M5
Devitts Green Warwks 53 P3
Devizes Wilts 30 B10
Devonport C Plym 4 G6
Devonside Clacks 114 G2
Devoran Cnwll 3 K7
Devoran & Perran Cnwll 3 K7
Dewarton Mdloth 115 Q8
Dewlish Dorset 11 J5
Dewsbury Kirk 85 K10
Dewsbury Moor Kirk 85 K10
Deytheur Powys 62 H8
Dial N Som 28 H9
Dial Green W Susx 14 C5
Dial Post W Susx 14 H7
Dibberford Dorset 10 D4
Dibden Hants 12 G3
Dibden Purlieu Hants 12 G3
Dickens Heath Solhll 53 L5
Dickleburgh Norfk 58 H4
Didbrook Gloucs 42 B5
Didcot Oxon 31 L4
Diddington Cambs 56 D7
Diddlebury Shrops 51 N3
Didley Herefs 40 F5
Didling W Susx 25 P9
Didmarton Gloucs 29 N5
Didsbury Manch 76 F5
Didworthy Devon 5 L4
Digby Lincs 67 Q1
Digg Highld 134 H2
Diggle Oldham 77 J2
Digmoor Lancs 75 N3
Digswell Herts 45 J8
Digswell Water Herts 45 J8
Dihewyd Cerdgn 48 H9
Dilham Norfk 71 L7
Dilhorne Staffs 64 H3
Dill Hall Lancs 83 R9
Dillington Cambs 56 C7
Dilston Nthumb 100 C5
Dilton Wilts 23 J4
Dilton Marsh Wilts 23 J3
Dilwyn Herefs 51 L9
Dimple Bolton 83 Q12
Dimple Derbys 77 P11
Dinas Carmth 37 P4
Dinas Cnwll 6 C10
Dinas Gwynd 60 D5
Dinas Gwynd 72 H12
Dinas Rhondd 27 N4
Dinas Cross Pembks 37 K3
Dinas Dinlle Gwynd 72 G12
Dinas-Mawddwy Gwynd 61 Q9
Dinas Powys V Glam 27 R8
Dinder Somset 22 D4
Dinedor Herefs 40 H4
Dingestow Mons 40 F9
Dingle Lpool 75 L6
Dingleden Kent 16 E5
Dingley Nhants 55 K3
Dingwall Highld 137 P4
Dinmael Conwy 62 D3
Dinnet Abers 132 C5
Dinnington N u Ty 100 G4
Dinnington Rothm 78 E6
Dinnington Somset 21 N11
Dinorwig Gwynd 73 K11
Dinorwig Slate Landscape Gwynd 73 K11
Dinton Bucks 43 Q9
Dinton Wilts 23 M7
Dinwoodie D & G 106 E11
Dinworthy Devon 18 F10
Dipford Somset 21 K9
Dipley Hants 31 Q11
Dippen Ag & B 103 L2
Dippenhall Surrey 25 P4
Dippermill Devon 7 N3
Dippertown Devon 7 N8
Dippin N Ayrs 103 Q5
Dipple Moray 139 Q4
Dipple S Ayrs 104 D9
Diptford Devon 5 M5
Dipton Dur 100 F7
Diptonmill Nthumb 99 P6
Dirleton E Loth 116 C4
Dirt Pot Nthumb 99 N9
Discoed Powys 51 J7
Diseworth Leics 66 D7
Dishforth N York 91 P12
Disley Ches E 76 H7
Diss Norfk 58 G4
Disserth Powys 50 E9
Distington Cumb 88 D2
Ditchampton Wilts 23 N7
Ditcheat Somset 22 E6
Ditchingham Norfk 59 L2
Ditchling E Susx 15 L8
Ditherington Shrops 63 N9
Ditteridge Wilts 29 N8
Dittisham Devon 5 P6
Ditton Kent 34 C10
Ditton Green Cambs 57 M9
Ditton Priors Shrops 51 Q3
Dixton Gloucs 41 R5
Dixton Mons 40 G9
Dizzard Cnwll 6 H5
Dobcross Oldham 77 J2
Dobwalls Cnwll 4 C4
Doccombe Devon 8 E7
Dochgarroch Highld 138 B7
Dockenfield Surrey 25 P5
Docker Lancs 89 P11
Docking Norfk 69 P5
Docklow Herefs 51 P9
Dockray Cumb 89 L2
Dockray Cumb 98 B8
Dodbrooke Devon 5 M8
Doddinghurst Essex 33 Q2
Doddington Cambs 56 H3
Doddington Kent 34 G11
Doddington Lincs 79 M9
Doddington Nthumb 108 G3
Doddington Shrops 52 B5
Doddiscombsleigh Devon 8 F7
Dodd's Green Ches E 63 Q4
Doddshill Norfk 69 N6
Doddy Cross Cnwll 4 D4
Dodford Nhants 54 G8
Dodford Worcs 52 H6
Dodington S Glos 29 M6
Dodington Somset 21 J5
Dodleston Ches W 75 K11
Dodscott Devon 19 K9
Dodside E Rens 113 P10
Dod's Leigh Staffs 65 J5
Dodworth Barns 77 P3
Dodworth Bottom Barns 77 Q3
Dodworth Green Barns 77 P3
Doe Bank Birm 53 L1
Doe Lea Derbys 78 D10
Dogdyke Lincs 68 D1
Dogley Lane Kirk 85 J12
Dogmersfield Hants 25 N3
Dogridge Wilts 30 C5
Dogsthorpe C Pete 68 D12
Dog Village Devon 9 J5
Dolanog Powys 62 E9
Dolau Powys 50 G7
Dolaucothi Carmth 38 G3
Dolbenmaen Gwynd 60 H4
Doley Staffs 64 D6
Dolfach Powys 62 B11
Dolfor Powys 50 F3
Dol-för Powys 61 P11
Dolgarrog Conwy 73 N10
Dolgellau Gwynd 61 M8
Dolgoch Gwynd 61 L11
Dol-gran Carmth 38 C5
Doll Highld 146 F4
Dollar Clacks 114 H2
Dollarfield Clacks 114 H2
Dolley Green Powys 51 J7
Dollwen Cerdgn 49 M4
Dolphin Flints 74 H9
Dolphinholme Lancs 83 M4
Dolphinton S Lans 115 K12
Dolton Devon 19 L11
Dolwen Conwy 73 Q9
Dolwyddelan Conwy 61 M2
Dolybont Cerdgn 49 K3
Dolyhir Powys 50 H9
Domgay Powys 63 J8
Donaldson's Lodge Nthumb 108 D1
Doncaster Donc 78 F3
Doncaster Carr Donc 78 F3
Doncaster North Services Donc 78 H1
Doncaster Sheffield Airport Donc 78 G4
Donhead St Andrew Wilts 23 K8
Donhead St Mary Wilts 23 K8
Donibristle Fife 115 L3
Doniford Somset 20 H5
Donington Lincs 68 D5
Donington on Bain Lincs 80 E7
Donington Park Services Leics 66 D7
Donington Southing Lincs 68 D5
Donisthorpe Leics 65 P9
Donkey Street Kent 17 K4
Donkey Town Surrey 32 D10
Donnington Gloucs 42 E6
Donnington Herefs 41 L5
Donnington Shrops 63 P10
Donnington W Berk 31 K8
Donnington W Susx 13 Q4
Donnington Wrekin 64 D9
Donnington Wood Wrekin 64 D9
Donyatt Somset 21 M10
Doomsday Green W Susx 14 H5
Doonfoot S Ayrs 104 F6
Dora's Green Hants 25 P4
Dorback Lodge Highld 131 K1
Dorchester Dorset 10 H6
Dorchester-on-Thames Oxon 31 M3
Dordon Warwks 65 N12
Dore Sheff 77 Q7
Dores Highld 137 Q9
Dorking Surrey 14 H1
Dorking Tye Suffk 46 G4
Dormansland Surrey 15 M2
Dormans Park Surrey 15 M3
Dormington Herefs 41 J4
Dormston Worcs 53 J9
Dorn Gloucs 42 E5
Dorney Bucks 32 D6
Dorney Reach Bucks 32 C6
Dornie Highld 136 B10
Dornoch Highld 146 E7
Dornock D & G 97 P5
Dorrery Highld 151 K6
Dorridge Solhll 53 M6
Dorrington Lincs 67 Q2
Dorrington Shrops 63 N11
Dorrington Shrops 64 D4
Dorsington Warwks 53 L10
Dorstone Herefs 40 D3
Dorton Bucks 43 P9
Dosthill Staffs 65 N12
Dothan IoA 72 F9
Dottery Dorset 10 C6
Doublebois Cnwll 4 B4
Doughton Gloucs 29 P4
Douglas IoM 102 e6
Douglas S Lans 105 Q4
Douglas and Angus C Dund 124 H6
Douglas Pier Ag & B 113 J1
Douglastown Angus 124 H3
Douglas Water S Lans 105 R3
Douglas West S Lans 105 Q3
Doulting Somset 22 E5
Dounby Ork 147 b4
Doune Highld 145 L5
Doune Stirlg 114 D1
Dounepark S Ayrs 104 C10
Dounie Highld 145 N7
Dousland Devon 4 H3
Dovaston Shrops 63 K8
Dove Dale Derbys 65 L2
Dove Green Notts 66 D2
Dove Holes Derbys 77 K8
Dovenby Cumb 97 M11
Dover Kent 17 P2
Dover Wigan 75 Q4
Dover Castle Kent 17 P2
Dovercourt Essex 47 N5
Doverdale Worcs 52 F7
Doveridge Derbys 65 L5
Doversgreen Surrey 15 J1
Dowally P & K 123 P3
Dowbridge Lancs 83 K9
Dowdeswell Gloucs 42 B7
Dowlais Myr Td 39 P10
Dowland Devon 7 Q3
Dowlish Ford Somset 21 M10
Dowlish Wake Somset 21 N10
Down Ampney Gloucs 30 C3
Downderry Cnwll 4 D6
Downe Gt Lon 33 M10
Downend Gloucs 29 N3
Downend IoW 13 J7
Downend S Glos 29 K7
Downend W Berk 31 K7
Downfield C Dund 124 H6
Downgate Cnwll 7 K10
Downgate Cnwll 7 L10
Downham Essex 34 C3
Downham Gt Lon 33 M8
Downham Lancs 84 B6
Downham Market Norfk 69 L11
Down Hatherley Gloucs 41 P7
Downhead Somset 22 D8
Downhead Somset 22 F4
Downhill Cnwll 6 B11
Downhill P & K 124 C7
Downholland Cross Lancs 75 L2
Downholme N York 91 J7
Downicarey Devon 7 M7
Downies Abers 133 M5
Downing Flints 74 G8
Downley Bucks 32 B3
Down St Mary Devon 8 D4
Downside Somset 22 E3
Downside Somset 22 E4
Downside Surrey 32 G10
Down Thomas Devon 4 H7
Downton Hants 12 D6
Downton Wilts 24 C9
Dowsby Lincs 68 C6
Dowsdale Lincs 68 F10
Doxey Staffs 64 G7
Doxford Nthumb 109 K5
Doynton S Glos 29 L7
Draethen Caerph 28 B5
Draffan S Lans 114 E12
Dragonby N Linc 79 M1
Dragons Green W Susx 14 G6
Drakeholes Notts 78 H5
Drakelow Worcs 52 F4
Drakemyre N Ayrs 113 K11
Drakes Broughton Worcs 52 H11
Drakewalls Cnwll 7 N10
Draughton N York 84 F5
Draughton Nhants 55 J5
Drax N York 86 C10
Drax Hales N York 86 C10
Draycote Warwks 54 D6
Draycot Foliat Swindn 30 E7
Draycott Derbys 66 D5
Draycott Gloucs 42 E4
Draycott Shrops 52 E2
Draycott Somset 21 Q3
Draycott Somset 22 D9
Draycott Worcs 52 F11
Draycott in the Clay Staffs 65 M6
Draycott in the Moors Staffs 64 H4
Drayford Devon 19 Q10
Drayton C Port 13 L4
Drayton Leics 55 L2
Drayton Lincs 68 E4
Drayton Norfk 71 J9
Drayton Oxon 31 K3
Drayton Oxon 43 J3
Drayton Somset 21 N8
Drayton Somset 21 P10
Drayton Worcs 52 G5
Drayton Bassett Staffs 65 M12
Drayton Beauchamp Bucks 44 C9
Drayton Manor Resort Staffs 65 M12
Drayton Parslow Bucks 44 B6
Drayton St Leonard Oxon 31 M3
Drebley N York 84 F3
Dreemskerry IoM 102 f4
Dreen Hill Pembks 36 H7
Drefach Carmth 38 A4
Drefach Carmth 38 D9
Drefach Cerdgn 38 D3
Drefelin Carmth 38 A4
Dreghorn N Ayrs 104 F2
Drellingore Kent 17 M3
Drem E Loth 116 C5
Dresden C Stke 64 G4
Drewsteignton Devon 8 D6
Driby Lincs 80 G9
Driffield E R Yk 87 J4
Driffield Gloucs 30 C2
Driffield Cross Roads Gloucs 30 C3
Drift Cnwll 2 C9
Drigg Cumb 88 E7
Drighlington Leeds 85 K9
Drimnin Highld 119 P2
Drimpton Dorset 10 C4
Drimsallie Highld 128 D8
Dringhouses C York 86 A5
Drinkstone Suffk 58 E8
Drinkstone Green Suffk 58 E8
Drive End Dorset 10 F3
Driver's End Herts 45 J7
Drointon Staffs 65 J7
Droitwich Spa Worcs 52 G8
Dron P & K 124 C9
Dronfield Derbys 78 B8
Dronfield Woodhouse Derbys 77 Q8
Drongan E Ayrs 104 H6
Dronley Angus 124 G6
Droop Dorset 11 J3
Dropping Well Rothm 78 C5
Droxford Hants 25 K10
Droylsden Tamesd 76 G4
Druid Denbgs 62 E3
Druidston Pembks 36 G7
Druimarbin Highld 128 F10
Druimavuic Ag & B 121 J4
Druimdrishaig Ag & B 111 Q7
Druimindarroch Highld 127 M7
Drum Ag & B 112 D6
Drum P & K 115 J1
Drumalbin S Lans 106 B2
Drumbeg Highld 148 D10
Drumblade Abers 140 F8
Drumbreddon D & G 94 F9
Drumbuie Highld 135 P9
Drumburgh Cumb 98 B6
Drumburn D & G 97 K6
Drumburn D & G 97 K7
Drumchapel C Glas 113 Q7
Drumchastle P & K 122 H1
Drumclog S Lans 105 M2
Drumeldrie Fife 125 J12
Drumelzier Border 106 F3
Drumfearn Highld 127 M1
Drumfrennie Abers 132 H5
Drumgley Angus 124 H3
Drumguish Highld 130 E4
Drumin Moray 139 M10
Drumjohn D & G 105 J10
Drumlamford S Ayrs 95 K3
Drumlasie Abers 132 G3
Drumleaning Cumb 98 B8
Drumlemble Ag & B 103 J6
Drumlithie Abers 133 J8
Drummoddie D & G 95 M9
Drummore D & G 94 G11
Drummuir Moray 140 B7
Drumnadrochit Highld 137 N10
Drumnagorrach Moray 140 E5
Drumoak Abers 133 J4
Drumpark D & G 96 H2
Drumrunie Highld 144 F4
Drumshang S Ayrs 104 E7
Drumuie Highld 134 H6
Drumuillie Highld 138 H11
Drumvaich Stirlg 122 H12
Drunzie P & K 124 C11
Druridge Nthumb 109 M10
Drury Flints 75 J10
Drws-y-coed Gwynd 61 J1
Drybeck Cumb 89 Q4
Drybridge Moray 140 C3
Drybridge N Ayrs 104 G2
Drybrook Gloucs 41 K8
Dryburgh Border 107 P3
Dry Doddington Lincs 67 L3
Dry Drayton Cambs 56 G8
Dryhill Kent 33 P11
Drymen Stirlg 113 P3
Drymuir Abers 141 L6
Drynoch Highld 134 G9
Dry Sandford Oxon 31 K2
Dryslwyn Carmth 38 E7
Dry Street Essex 34 B5
Dryton Shrops 63 P11
Dubford Abers 141 J3
Dublin Suffk 58 H7
Duchally Highld 145 J2
Duck End Bed 44 F3
Duck End Cambs 56 E8
Duck End Essex 46 B5
Duck End Essex 46 B6
Duckend Green Essex 46 C7
Duckington Ches W 63 N2
Ducklington Oxon 42 H10
Duck's Cross Bed 56 B9
Duddenhoe End Essex 45 N4
Duddingston C Edin 115 P7
Duddington Nhants 67 N12
Duddlestone Somset 21 K9
Duddleswell E Susx 15 N5
Duddlewick Shrops 52 C4
Duddo Nthumb 108 F1
Duddon Ches W 75 N10
Duddon Bridge Cumb 88 G9
Duddon Common Ches W 75 N10
Dudleston Shrops 63 K4
Dudleston Heath Shrops 63 L5
Dudley Dudley 52 H3
Dudley N Tyne 100 H3
Dudley Hill C Brad 85 J9
Dudley Port Sandw 52 H2
Dudnill Shrops 52 C6
Dudsbury Dorset 11 P5
Dudswell Herts 44 D9
Duffield Derbys 65 Q3
Duffryn Neath 27 K3
Dufftown Moray 139 P8
Duffus Moray 139 M2
Dufton Cumb 90 A2
Duggleby N York 86 G2
Duirinish Highld 135 P9
Duisdalemore Highld 127 M2
Duisky Highld 128 D9
Dukestown Blae G 39 Q9
Duke Street Suffk 47 J3
Dukinfield Tamesd 76 H4
Dulas IoA 72 H6
Dulcote Somset 22 D4
Dulford Devon 9 L3
Dull P & K 123 K3
Dullatur N Lans 114 D6
Dullingham Cambs 57 M9
Dullingham Ley Cambs 57 M9
Dulnain Bridge Highld 139 J11
Duloe Bed 56 C8
Duloe Cnwll 4 C5
Dulsie Bridge Highld 138 G7
Dulverton Somset 20 E8
Dulwich Gt Lon 33 L7
Dumbarton W Duns 113 M6
Dumbleton Gloucs 42 B4
Dumfries D & G 97 K3
Dumgoyne Stirlg 113 Q5
Dummer Hants 25 K4
Dumpton Kent 35 Q9
Dun Angus 132 G12
Dunalastair P & K 123 J1
Dunan Highld 135 K10
Dunan P & K 122 D1
Dunaverty Ag & B 103 J8
Dunball Somset 21 M5
Dunbar E Loth 116 F5
Dunbeath Highld 151 L11
Dunbeg Ag & B 120 G6
Dunblane Stirlg 114 E1
Dunbog Fife 124 F9
Dunbridge Hants 24 E8
Duncanston Highld 137 Q4
Duncanstone Abers 140 E10
Dunchideock Devon 8 G7
Dunchurch Warwks 54 D6
Duncote Nhants 54 H10
Duncow D & G 97 K2
Duncrievie P & K 124 C11
Duncton W Susx 14 D7
Dundee C Dund 124 H7
Dundee Airport C Dund 124 H7
Dundon Somset 22 B7
Dundonald S Ayrs 104 G3
Dundonnell Highld 144 E8
Dundraw Cumb 97 P8
Dundreggan Highld 129 K1
Dundrennan D & G 96 F9
Dundry N Som 28 H9
Dunecht Abers 133 J2
Dunfermline Fife 115 K4
Dunfield Gloucs 30 D3
Dunford Bridge Barns 77 M3
Dungate Kent 34 G10
Dungavel S Lans 105 M2
Dunge Wilts 23 K3
Dungeness Kent 17 K7
Dungworth Sheff 77 P6
Dunham Massey Traffd 76 D6
Dunham-on-the-Hill Ches W 75 M9
Dunham-on-Trent Notts 79 K9
Dunhampstead Worcs 52 G8
Dunhampton Worcs 52 F7
Dunham Town Traffd 76 D6
Dunham Woodhouses Traffd 76 D6
Dunholme Lincs 79 P8
Dunino Fife 125 K10
Dunipace Falk 114 E4
Dunkeld P & K 123 P4
Dunkerton BaNES 29 L10
Dunkeswell Devon 9 M3
Dunkeswick N York 85 L6

Dunkirk Ches W 75 L9
Dunkirk Kent 35 J10
Dunkirk S Glos 29 M5
Dunkirk Wilts 30 A10
Dunk's Green Kent 33 R11
Dunlappie Angus 132 F10
Dunley Hants 24 G3
Dunley Worcs 52 E7
Dunlop E Ayrs 113 M11
Dunmaglass Highld 137 Q11
Dunmere Cnwll 6 F11
Dunmore Falk 114 G3
Dunnet Highld 151 M2
Dunnichen Angus 125 K3
Dunning P & K 123 P10
Dunnington C York 86 C5
Dunnington E R Yk 87 M5
Dunnington Warwks 53 K10
Dunnockshaw Lancs 84 B9
Dunn Street Kent 34 D10
Dunoon Ag & B 112 H6
Dunphail Moray 139 J6
Dunragit D & G 94 H7
Duns Border 116 H10
Dunsa Derbys 77 N9
Dunsby Lincs 68 B7
Dunscar Bolton 76 D1
Dunscore D & G 96 H1
Dunscroft Donc 78 G2
Dunsdale R & Cl 92 C3
Dunsden Green Oxon 31 Q7
Dunsdon Devon 7 K3
Dunsfold Surrey 14 E4
Dunsford Devon 8 F7
Dunshalt Fife 124 E10
Dunshillock Abers 141 N6
Dunsill Notts 78 D11
Dunsley N York 92 H4
Dunsley Staffs 52 F4
Dunsmore Bucks 44 B10
Dunsop Bridge Lancs 83 P5
Dunstable C Beds 44 E7
Dunstall Staffs 65 M8
Dunstall Common Worcs 41 P3
Dunstall Green Suffk 57 P8
Dunstan Nthumb 109 L6
Dunstan Steads Nthumb 109 L5
Dunster Somset 20 F5
Duns Tew Oxon 43 K6
Dunston Gatesd 100 G6
Dunston Lincs 79 Q11
Dunston Norfk 71 J11
Dunston Staffs 64 H8
Dunstone Devon 5 J6
Dunstone Devon 8 D9
Dunston Heath Staffs 64 G8
Dunsville Donc 78 G2
Dunswell E R Yk 87 K8
Dunsyre S Lans 115 K11
Dunterton Devon 7 M9
Dunthrop Oxon 42 H6
Duntisbourne Abbots Gloucs 42 R10
Duntisbourne Leer Gloucs 41 R10
Duntisbourne Rouse Gloucs 42 A10
Duntish Dorset 10 H3
Duntocher W Duns 113 P7
Dunton Bucks 44 B7
Dunton C Beds 45 J3
Dunton Norfk 70 C6
Dunton Bassett Leics 54 E3
Dunton Green Kent 33 P11
Dunton Wayletts Essex 34 B4
Duntulm Highld 142 D10
Dunure S Ayrs 104 E7
Dunvant Swans 26 F4
Dunvegan Highld 134 D6
Dunwich Suffk 59 P6
Dunwood Staffs 64 H1
Durdar Cumb 98 E8
Durgan Cnwll 3 J9
Durgates E Susx 16 B4
Durham Dur 100 H9
Durham Cathedral Dur 100 H10
Durham Services Dur 100 H11
Durisdeer D & G 106 A9
Durisdeermill D & G 106 A9
Durkar Wakefd 85 L11
Durleigh Somset 21 L6
Durley Hants 24 J10
Durley Wilts 30 F9
Durley Street Hants 25 J10
Durlock Kent 35 N10
Durlock Kent 35 P9
Durlow Common Herefs 41 K4
Durn Rochdl 84 E12
Durness Highld 149 J3
Durno Abers 140 H10
Duror Highld 121 J2
Durran Ag & B 120 H11
Durrington W Susx 14 G9
Durrington Wilts 23 P4
Dursley Gloucs 29 M3
Dursley Cross Gloucs 41 L7
Durston Somset 21 L7
Durweston Dorset 11 L3
Duston Nhants 55 J8
Duthil Highld 138 H11
Dutlas Powys 50 H5
Duton Hill Essex 45 R6
Dutson Cnwll 7 L7
Dutton Ches W 75 P8
Duxford Cambs 45 N2
Duxford Oxon 30 H2
Duxford IWM Cambs 45 N3
Dwygyfylchi Conwy 73 M8
Dwyran IoA 72 G10
Dyce C Aber 133 L2
Dyer's End Essex 46 C4
Dyfatty Carmth 26 C2
Dyffrydan Gwynd 61 M9
Dyffryn Brdgnd 27 K3
Dyffryn Myr Td 39 P11
Dyffryn V Glam 27 P8
Dyffryn Ardudwy Gwynd 61 K7
Dyffryn Castell Cerdgn 49 N4
Dyffryn Cellwen Neath 39 K9
Dyke Lincs 68 B7
Dyke Moray 138 H4
Dykehead Angus 124 E2
Dykehead Angus 132 B12
Dykehead N Lans 114 F9
Dykehead Stirlg 114 A2
Dykelands Abers 132 H10
Dykends Angus 124 E1
Dykeside Abers 140 H7
Dykes of Gray C Dund 124 G6
Dylife Powys 49 Q2
Dymchurch Kent 17 K5
Dymock Gloucs 41 L5
Dynamic Earth C Edin 115 N6
Dyrham S Glos 29 L7
Dysart Fife 115 P3
Dyserth Denbgs 74 E8

E

Eachway Worcs 53 J5
Eachwick Nthumb 100 E4
Eagland Hill Lancs 83 K6
Eagle Lincs 79 L10
Eagle Barnsdale Lincs 79 L10
Eagle Moor Lincs 79 M10
Eaglescliffe S on T 91 P4
Eaglesfield Cumb 88 E1
Eaglesfield D & G 97 P3
Eaglesham E Rens 113 Q11
Eagley Bolton 76 D1
Eairy IoM 102 d6
Eakring Notts 78 H11
Ealand N Linc 79 K1
Ealing Gt Lon 32 H6
Eals Nthumb 99 K7
Eamont Bridge Cumb 89 N1
Earby Lancs 84 D6
Earcroft Bl w D 83 P10
Eardington Shrops 52 D2
Eardisland Herefs 51 L9
Eardisley Herefs 51 K11
Eardiston Shrops 63 L7
Eardiston Worcs 52 C7
Earith Cambs 56 G6
Earle Nthumb 108 F4
Earlestown St Hel 75 P5
Earley Wokham 31 Q8
Earlham Norfk 71 J10
Earlish Highld 134 G4
Earls Barton Nhants 55 L8
Earls Colne Essex 46 F6
Earls Common Worcs 52 H9
Earl's Croome Worcs 41 P3
Earlsditton Shrops 52 B5
Earlsdon Covtry 53 Q5
Earl's Down E Susx 16 B7
Earlsferry Fife 116 C1
Earlsfield Gt Lon 33 J8
Earlsford Abers 141 K9
Earl's Green Suffk 58 F7
Earlsheaton Kirk 85 K11
Earl Shilton Leics 54 D1
Earl Soham Suffk 59 J8
Earl Sterndale Derbys 77 K10
Earlston Border 107 P2
Earlston E Ayrs 104 G3
Earl Stonham Suffk 58 G9
Earlswood Surrey 15 K1
Earlswood Warwks 53 L6
Earlswood Common Mons 28 F3
Earnley W Susx 13 P5
Earnshaw Bridge Lancs 83 M10
Earsdon N Tyne 101 J4
Earsdon Nthumb 109 K11
Earsham Norfk 59 L3
Earswick C York 86 B4
Eartham W Susx 14 D9
Earthcott S Glos 29 K5
Easby N York 92 C5
Easdale Ag & B 120 D9
Easebourne W Susx 14 C6
Easenhall Warwks 54 D5
Eashing Surrey 14 D2
Easington Bucks 43 P9
Easington Dur 101 K9
Easington E R Yk 87 R11
Easington Nthumb 109 J3
Easington Oxon 31 N3
Easington R & Cl 92 F3
Easington Colliery Dur 101 L9
Easington Lane Sundld 101 K9
Easingwold N York 85 Q1
Easole Street Kent 35 N12
Eassie and Nevay Angus 124 G4
East Aberthaw V Glam 27 N9
East Allington Devon 5 N7
East Anstey Devon 20 D8
East Anton Hants 24 F4
East Appleton N York 91 L7
East Ardsley Leeds 85 L10
East Ashey IoW 13 K7
East Ashling W Susx 13 P3
East Aston Hants 24 G4
East Ayton N York 93 K9
East Balsdon Cnwll 7 K5
East Bank Blae G 40 B10
East Barkwith Lincs 80 D7
East Barming Kent 34 C11
East Barnby N York 92 G4
East Barnet Gt Lon 33 K3
East Barns E Loth 116 G6
East Barsham Norfk 70 D5
East Beckham Norfk 70 H4
East Bedfont Gt Lon 32 F7
East Bergholt Suffk 47 J5
East Bierley Kirk 85 J9
East Bilney Norfk 70 D8
East Blatchington E Susx 15 N10
East Bloxworth Dorset 11 L6
East Boldon S Tyne 101 K6
East Boldre Hants 12 F5
East Bolton Nthumb 109 J6
Eastbourne Darltn 91 M4
Eastbourne E Susx 16 A11
East Bower Somset 21 M6
East Bradenham Norfk 70 D10
East Brent Somset 21 M3
Eastbridge Suffk 59 N7
East Bridgford Notts 66 H3
East Briscoe Dur 90 F3
Eastbrook V Glam 27 R8
East Buckland Devon 19 N7
East Budleigh Devon 9 K8
Eastburn C Brad 84 F6
Eastburn E R Yk 87 J4
East Burnham Bucks 32 D5
East Burton Dorset 11 K7
Eastbury W Berk 30 H7
East Butsfield Dur 100 E9
East Butterwick N Linc 79 L2
Eastby N York 84 F4
East Calder W Loth 115 K7
East Carleton Norfk 70 H11
East Carlton Leeds 85 J6
East Carlton Nhants 55 L3
East Chaldon Dorset 11 J8
East Challow Oxon 30 H5
East Charleton Devon 5 M8
East Chelborough Dorset 10 E4
East Chiltington E Susx 15 L8
East Chinnock Somset 22 C10
East Chisenbury Wilts 23 P3
East Cholderton Hants 24 E4
Eastchurch Kent 34 H8
East Clandon Surrey 32 F12
East Claydon Bucks 43 Q6
East Clevedon N Som 28 F8
East Coker Somset 22 C11
Eastcombe Gloucs 41 P10
Eastcombe Somset 21 J7
East Compton Somset 22 E5
East Cornworthy Devon 5 P6
East Cote Cumb 97 M7
Eastcote Gt Lon 32 G5
Eastcote Nhants 54 H10
Eastcote Solhll 53 M5
Eastcott Cnwll 18 E10
Eastcott Wilts 23 L2
East Cottingwith E R Yk 86 D7
Eastcourt Wilts 29 R4
Eastcourt Wilts 30 F10
East Cowes IoW 12 H5
East Cowick E R Yk 86 C11
East Cowton N York 91 N6
East Cramlington Nthumb 100 H3
East Cranmore Somset 22 F5
East Creech Dorset 11 M8
East Curthwaite Cumb 98 D8
East Dean E Susx 15 Q11
East Dean Gloucs 41 K7
East Dean Hants 24 D8
East Dean W Susx 14 C8
Eastdown Devon 5 P7
East Down Devon 19 L5
East Drayton Notts 79 K8
East Dulwich Gt Lon 33 L7
East Dundry N Som 28 H9
East Ella C KuH 87 K9
East End Bed 56 B9
East End C Beds 44 D3
East End E R Yk 87 M9
East End E R Yk 87 P9
Eastend Essex 34 G4
East End Essex 45 M9
East End Hants 12 F5
East End Hants 31 J10
East End Herts 45 N6
East End Kent 16 E4
East End Kent 34 H7
East End M Keyn 44 D3
East End Oxon 43 J8
East End Somset 22 F4
East End Suffk 47 K5
Easter Balmoral Abers 131 N5
Easter Compton S Glos 28 H6
Easter Dalziel Highld 138 D6
Eastergate W Susx 14 D10
Easterhouse C Glas 114 C8
Easter Howgate Mdloth 115 N8
Easter Kinkell Highld 137 Q5
Easter Moniack Highld 137 P7
Eastern Green Covtry 53 P5
Easter Ord Abers 133 K3
Easter Pitkierie Fife 125 L11
Easter Skeld Shet 147 h7
Easter Softlaw Border 108 B3
Easterton Wilts 23 M2
Eastertown Somset 21 M2
East Everleigh Wilts 24 C3
East Farleigh Kent 34 C11
East Farndon Nhants 55 J4
East Ferry Lincs 79 K4
Eastfield N Lans 114 G8
Eastfield N York 93 L10
East Firsby Lincs 79 P6
East Fortune E Loth 116 D5
East Garforth Leeds 85 N8
East Garston W Berk 30 H7
Eastgate Dur 99 Q10
Eastgate Lincs 68 B8
Eastgate Norfk 70 H7
East Ginge Oxon 31 J5
East Goscote Leics 66 G9
East Grafton Wilts 30 F10
East Green Suffk 59 M7
East Grimstead Wilts 24 C8
East Grinstead W Susx 15 M3
East Guldeford E Susx 16 G6
East Haddon Nhants 54 H7
East Hagbourne Oxon 31 L5
East Halton N Linc 87 L11
East Ham Gt Lon 33 M5
Eastham Wirral 75 K7
Eastham Ferry Wirral 75 L7
Easthampton Herefs 51 L8
East Hanney Oxon 31 J4
East Hanningfield Essex 34 D2
East Hardwick Wakefd 85 P11
East Harling Norfk 58 E3
East Harlsey N York 91 P7
East Harnham Wilts 23 P7
East Harptree BaNES 28 H11
East Hartford Nthumb 100 H2
East Harting W Susx 25 P9
East Hatch Wilts 23 K7
East Hatley Cambs 56 F10
East Hauxwell N York 91 K8
East Haven Angus 125 L5
Eastheath Wokham 31 R9
East Heckington Lincs 68 D3
East Hedleyhope Dur 100 F10
East Helmsdale Highld 147 J2
East Hendred Oxon 31 K5
East Heslerton N York 93 J11
East Hewish N Som 28 E9
East Hoathly E Susx 15 P7
East Holme Dorset 11 L7
East Hope Dur 90 H5
Easthope Shrops 51 P2
Easthorpe Essex 46 G7
Easthorpe Notts 66 H1
East Horrington Somset 22 D4
East Horsley Surrey 32 F11
East Horton Nthumb 108 G4
East Howe BCP 11 P6
East Huntspill Somset 21 M4
East Hyde C Beds 44 G8
East Ilkerton Devon 19 N4
East Ilsley W Berk 31 K6
Eastington Devon 8 D3
Eastington Gloucs 41 M10
Eastington Gloucs 42 D9
East Keal Lincs 80 G11
East Kennett Wilts 30 D9
East Keswick Leeds 85 M6
East Kilbride S Lans 114 B10
East Kimber Devon 7 P5
East Kirkby Lincs 80 F11
East Knighton Dorset 11 K7
East Knowstone Devon 20 C8
East Knoyle Wilts 23 K7
East Lambrook Somset 21 P9
Eastlands D & G 96 G4
East Langdon Kent 17 P2
East Langton Leics 55 J2
East Lavant W Susx 13 Q3
East Lavington W Susx 14 D7
East Layton N York 91 K5
Eastleach Martin Gloucs 42 E10
Eastleach Turville Gloucs 42 E10
East Leake Notts 66 F7
East Learmouth Nthumb 108 D2
East Leigh Devon 5 L6
East Leigh Devon 5 M5
East Leigh Devon 8 D4
Eastleigh Devon 19 J8
Eastleigh Hants 24 G9
East Lexham Norfk 70 C8
Eastling Kent 34 G11
East Linton E Loth 116 D6
East Liss Hants 25 N8
East Lockinge Oxon 31 J5
East Lound N Linc 79 K4
East Lulworth Dorset 11 L8
East Lutton N York 86 H1
East Lydeard Somset 21 J7
East Lydford Somset 22 D7
East Malling Kent 34 C11
East Malling Heath Kent 34 C11
East Marden W Susx 25 P10
East Markham Notts 79 J9
East Martin Hants 23 N9
East Marton N York 84 D5
East Meon Hants 25 L9
East Mere Devon 20 F10
East Mersea Essex 47 J9
East Midlands Airport Leics 66 D7
East Molesey Surrey 32 G9
Eastmoor Norfk 69 P11
East Morden Dorset 11 M6
East Morton C Brad 84 G7
East Morton D & G 106 A9
East Ness N York 92 E11
East Newton E R Yk 87 P7
Eastney C Port 13 L5
Eastnor Herefs 41 L4
East Norton Leics 67 K12
Eastoft N Linc 86 E12
East Ogwell Devon 5 P3
Easton Cambs 56 C6
Easton Cumb 98 C6
Easton Devon 8 D7
Easton Dorset 10 H10
Easton Hants 24 H7
Easton Lincs 67 M7
Easton Norfk 70 H10
Easton Somset 22 C4
Easton Suffk 59 K9
Easton Wilts 29 P8
Easton Grey Wilts 29 P5
Easton-in-Gordano N Som 28 G7
Easton Maudit Nhants 55 M9
Easton-on-the-Hill Nhants 67 P11
Easton Royal Wilts 30 E10
East Orchard Dorset 23 J10
East Ord Nthumb 117 L11
East Panson Devon 7 L6
East Parley BCP 11 Q5
East Peckham Kent 16 B1
East Pennard Somset 22 D6
East Portlemouth Devon 5 M9
East Prawle Devon 5 N9
East Preston W Susx 14 F10
East Pulham Dorset 10 H3
East Putford Devon 18 G10
East Quantoxhead Somset 21 J5
East Rainham Medway 34 E9
East Rainton Sundld 101 J8
East Ravendale NE Lin 80 E4
East Raynham Norfk 70 C7
Eastrea Cambs 56 F1
Eastriggs D & G 97 Q5
East Rigton Leeds 85 M6
Eastrington E R Yk 86 E9
East Rolstone N Som 28 E10
Eastrop Swindn 30 E4
East Rounton N York 91 P6
East Rudham Norfk 70 B6
East Runton Norfk 71 J4
East Ruston Norfk 71 L6
Eastry Kent 35 P11
East Saltoun E Loth 116 B8
Eastshaw W Susx 14 C6
East Sheen Gt Lon 32 H7
East Shefford W Berk 30 H7
East Sleekburn Nthumb 100 H2
East Somerton Norfk 71 P8
East Stockwith Lincs 79 K5
East Stoke Dorset 11 L7
East Stoke Notts 67 J2
East Stour Dorset 22 H9
East Stour Common Dorset 22 H8
East Stourmouth Kent 35 N10
East Stowford Devon 19 M8
East Stratton Hants 25 J5
East Studdal Kent 17 P1
East Sutton Kent 16 E1
East Taphouse Cnwll 4 B4
East-the-Water Devon 19 J8
East Thirston Nthumb 109 K9
East Tilbury Thurr 34 B6
East Tilbury Village Thurr 34 B7
East Tisted Hants 25 M7
East Torrington Lincs 80 C7
East Tuddenham Norfk 70 G10
East Tytherley Hants 24 E7
East Tytherton Wilts 29 Q7
East Village Devon 8 F4
Eastville Bristl 29 J7
Eastville Lincs 80 H12
East Wall Shrops 51 N2
East Walton Norfk 69 P9
East Water Somset 22 C3
East Week Devon 8 C6
Eastwell Leics 67 K6
East Wellow Hants 24 E9
East Wemyss Fife 115 Q2
East Whitburn W Loth 114 H8
Eastwick Herts 45 N9
East Wickham Gt Lon 33 N7
East Williamston Pembks 37 L9
East Winch Norfk 69 N9
East Winterslow Wilts 24 D6
East Wittering W Susx 13 N5
East Witton N York 91 J9
Eastwood Notts 66 D3
Eastwood Sthend 34 E5
East Woodburn Nthumb 99 P1
Eastwood End Cambs 56 H2
East Woodhay Hants 31 J10
East Woodlands Somset 22 H4
East Worldham Hants 25 N6
East Worthing W Susx 14 H10
East Wretham Norfk 58 D3
East Youlstone Devon 18 F10
Eathorpe Warwks 54 C7
Eaton Ches E 76 F10
Eaton Ches W 75 P11
Eaton Leics 67 K6
Eaton Norfk 71 J11
Eaton Notts 78 H8
Eaton Oxon 43 J11
Eaton Shrops 51 L3
Eaton Shrops 51 N3
Eaton Bishop Herefs 40 F4
Eaton Bray C Beds 44 D7
Eaton Constantine Shrops 63 Q11
Eaton Ford Cambs 56 D8
Eaton Green C Beds 44 D7
Eaton Hastings Oxon 30 F3
Eaton Mascott Shrops 63 P11
Eaton Socon Cambs 56 D9
Eaton upon Tern Shrops 64 C7
Eaves Brow Warrtn 76 B5
Eaves Green Solhll 53 N4
Ebberston N York 92 H10
Ebbesborne Wake Wilts 23 L8
Ebbsfleet Kent 33 R8
Ebbw Vale Blae G 39 R9
Ebchester Dur 100 E7
Ebdon N Som 28 E9
Ebernoe W Susx 14 D5
Ebford Devon 9 J7
Ebley Gloucs 41 N10
Ebnal Ches W 63 N2
Ebnall Herefs 51 M9
Ebrington Gloucs 42 E4
Ebsworthy Devon 7 P6
Ecchinswell Hants 31 K10
Ecclaw Border 116 G7
Ecclefechan D & G 97 P3
Eccles Border 108 B2
Eccles Kent 34 C10
Eccles Salfd 76 E4
Ecclesall Sheff 77 Q7
Ecclesfield Sheff 78 B5
Eccles Green Herefs 51 L11
Eccleshall Staffs 64 F6
Eccleshill C Brad 85 J8
Ecclesmachan W Loth 115 K6
Eccles on Sea Norfk 71 N6
Eccles Road Norfk 58 F3
Eccleston Ches W 75 L11
Eccleston Lancs 83 M11
Eccleston St Hel 75 N4
Eccleston Green Lancs 83 M12
Echt Abers 132 H3
Eckford Border 108 A4
Eckington Derbys 78 C8
Eckington Worcs 41 Q3
Ecton Nhants 55 L8
Ecton Staffs 77 L12
Edale Derbys 77 L6
Eday Ork 147 d3
Eday Airport Ork 147 d2
Edburton W Susx 15 J8
Edderside Cumb 97 M9
Edderton Highld 146 C8
Eddington Cambs 56 H8
Eddington Kent 35 L9
Eddleston Border 115 N11
Eddlewood S Lans 114 C10
Edenbridge Kent 15 N2
Edenfield Lancs 84 B11
Edenhall Cumb 98 H11
Edenham Lincs 67 Q8
Eden Mount Cumb 89 L11
Eden Park Gt Lon 33 L9
Eden Project Cnwll 3 P4
Edensor Derbys 77 N9
Edentaggart Ag & B 113 L3
Edenthorpe Donc 78 G2
Edern Gwynd 60 D4
Edgarley Somset 22 C6
Edgbaston Birm 53 K4
Edgcott Bucks 43 P7
Edgcott Somset 20 C5
Edgcumbe Cnwll 2 H8
Edge Gloucs 41 N9
Edge Shrops 63 L10
Edgebolton Shrops 63 P8
Edge End Gloucs 41 J9
Edgefield Norfk 70 G5
Edgefield Green Norfk 70 G5
Edgefold Bolton 76 C3
Edge Green Ches W 63 N2
Edgehill Warwks 42 H2
Edgerley Shrops 63 L8
Edgerton Kirk 84 H11
Edgeside Lancs 84 C10
Edgeworth Gloucs 41 Q10
Edgeworthy Devon 20 C10
Edginswell Torbay 5 Q3
Edgiock Worcs 53 K8
Edgmond Wrekin 64 D8
Edgmond Marsh Wrekin 64 D8
Edgton Shrops 51 L3
Edgware Gt Lon 32 H4
Edgworth Bl w D 83 R11
Edinbane Highld 134 F6
Edinburgh C Edin 115 N6
Edinburgh Airport C Edin 115 L6
Edinburgh Castle C Edin 115 N6
Edinburgh Old & New Town C Edin 115 N6
Edinburgh Zoo RZSS C Edin 115 M6
Edingale Staffs 65 N9
Edingham D & G 96 G6
Edingley Notts 66 H1
Edingthorpe Norfk 71 L6
Edingthorpe Green Norfk 71 L6
Edington Border 117 K10
Edington Nthumb 100 F2
Edington Somset 21 N5
Edington Wilts 23 K3
Edingworth Somset 21 N3
Edistone Devon 18 E9
Edithmead Somset 21 M3
Edith Weston RutInd 67 M11
Edlesborough Bucks 44 D8
Edlingham Nthumb 109 J8
Edlington Lincs 80 E9
Edmond Castle Cumb 98 G6
Edmondsham Dorset 11 P2
Edmondsley Dur 100 G8
Edmondstown Rhondd 27 N4
Edmondthorpe Leics 67 L8
Edmonton Cnwll 6 D10
Edmonton Gt Lon 33 L4
Edmundbyers Dur 100 C8
Ednam Border 108 B2
Ednaston Derbys 65 N4
Edney Common Essex 46 B10
Edradynate P & K 123 M2
Edrom Border 117 J10
Edstaston Shrops 63 N5
Edstone Warwks 53 M8
Edvin Loach Herefs 52 C9
Edwalton Notts 66 F5
Edwardstone Suffk 46 G3
Edwardsville Myr Td 27 P3
Edwinsford Carmth 38 G5
Edwinstowe Notts 78 G10
Edworth C Beds 45 J3
Edwyn Ralph Herefs 52 B9
Edzell Angus 132 F10
Edzell Woods Abers 132 F10
Efail-fach Neath 27 J4
Efail Isaf Rhondd 27 P5
Efailnewydd Gwynd 60 F5
Efail-Rhyd Powys 62 G7
Efailwen Carmth 37 M5
Efenechtyd Denbgs 62 F1
Effgill D & G 107 J11
Effingham Surrey 32 G11
Effingham Junction Surrey 32 G11
Efflinch Staffs 65 M9
Efford Devon 8 F4
Egbury Hants 24 G3
Egdean W Susx 14 E7
Egerton Bolton 83 Q12
Egerton Kent 16 F1
Egerton Forstal Kent 16 F2
Eggborough N York 85 R10
Eggbuckland C Plym 4 H5
Eggesford Devon 8 B3
Eggington C Beds 44 D6
Egginton Derbys 65 P6
Egglescliffe S on T 91 P4
Eggleston Dur 90 G2
Egham Surrey 32 E8
Egham Wick Surrey 32 D8
Egleton RutInd 67 L10
Eglingham Nthumb 109 J6
Egloshayle Cnwll 6 E10
Egloskerry Cnwll 7 K7
Eglwysbach Conwy 73 P9
Eglwys-Brewis V Glam 27 P8
Eglwys Cross Wrexhm 63 M4
Eglwys Fach Cerdgn 49 M1
Eglwyswrw Pembks 37 M3
Egmanton Notts 79 J10
Egremont Cumb 88 D5
Egremont Wirral 75 K5
Egton N York 92 G5
Egton Bridge N York 92 G6
Egypt Bucks 32 D5
Egypt Hants 24 H5
Eigg Highld 126 H7
Eight Ash Green Essex 46 G6
Eilanreach Highld 135 P12
Eilean Donan Castle Highld 136 B10
Eisgein W Isls 152 f5
Eishken W Isls 152 f5
Eisteddfa Gurig Cerdgn 49 N4
Elan Valley Powys 50 B7
Elan Village Powys 50 C7
Elberton S Glos 29 J5
Elbridge W Susx 14 C10
Elburton C Plym 4 H6
Elcombe Swindn 30 D6
Elcot W Berk 31 J8
Eldernell Cambs 68 F12
Eldersfield Worcs 41 M5
Elderslie Rens 113 N8
Elder Street Essex 45 Q5
Eldon Dur 91 L1
Eldwick C Brad 84 H7
Elerch Cerdgn 49 L3
Elfhill Abers 133 J7
Elford Nthumb 109 K3
Elford Staffs 65 M10
Elgin Moray 139 N3
Elgol Highld 127 J2
Elham Kent 17 L2
Elie Fife 116 C1
Elilaw Nthumb 108 F8
Elim IoA 72 F7
Eling Hants 24 F11
Elkesley Notts 78 H8
Elkstone Gloucs 41 R9
Ella Abers 140 G4
Ellacombe Torbay 5 Q4
Elland Calder 84 H11
Elland Lower Edge Calder 84 H11
Ellary Ag & B 111 Q6
Ellastone Staffs 65 L3
Ellel Lancs 83 L4
Ellemford Border 116 G9
Ellenabeich Ag & B 120 D9
Ellenborough Cumb 97 L11
Ellenbrook Salfd 76 D3
Ellenhall Staffs 64 F7
Ellen's Green Surrey 14 G4
Ellerbeck N York 91 Q7
Ellerby N York 92 G4
Ellerdine Heath Wrekin 64 B7
Ellerhayes Devon 9 J4
Elleric Ag & B 121 K3
Ellerker E R Yk 86 G9
Ellers N York 84 F6
Ellerton E R Yk 86 D7
Ellerton N York 91 L7
Ellerton Shrops 64 D7
Ellesborough Bucks 44 B10
Ellesmere Shrops 63 L5
Ellesmere Port Ches W 75 L8
Ellicombe Somset 20 F4
Ellingham Hants 12 B3
Ellingham Norfk 59 M2
Ellingham Nthumb 109 K5
Ellingstring N York 91 K10
Ellington Cambs 56 C6
Ellington Nthumb 109 M11
Ellington Thorpe Cambs 56 C6
Elliots Green Somset 22 H4
Ellisfield Hants 25 L4
Ellishader Highld 135 J3
Ellistown Leics 66 C10
Ellon Abers 141 M9
Ellonby Cumb 98 E11
Ellough Suffk 59 N3
Elloughton E R Yk 86 H9
Ellwood Gloucs 41 J10
Elm Cambs 69 J10
Elmbridge Worcs 52 G7
Elmdon Essex 45 N4
Elmdon Solhll 53 M4
Elmdon Heath Solhll 53 M4
Elmer W Susx 14 E10
Elmers End Gt Lon 33 L8
Elmer's Green Lancs 75 N2
Elmesthorpe Leics 54 D1
Elm Green Essex 46 D10
Elmhurst Staffs 65 L9
Elmington Nhants 55 Q3
Elmley Castle Worcs 41 R3
Elmley Lovett Worcs 52 G7
Elmore Gloucs 41 M8
Elmore Back Gloucs 41 M8
Elm Park Gt Lon 33 P5
Elmscott Devon 18 E9
Elmsett Suffk 47 J2
Elms Green Worcs 52 D7
Elmstead Heath Essex 47 J7
Elmstead Market Essex 47 J7
Elmstead Row Essex 47 J7
Elmsted Kent 17 K2
Elmstone Kent 35 N10
Elmstone Hardwicke Gloucs 41 Q6
Elmswell E R Yk 87 J3
Elmswell Suffk 58 E8
Elmton Derbys 78 E9
Elphin Highld 144 F3
Elphinstone E Loth 115 R7
Elrick Abers 133 K3
Elrig D & G 95 L8
Elrington Nthumb 99 N5
Elsdon Nthumb 108 E11
Elsecar Barns 78 C4
Elsenham Essex 45 P6
Elsfield Oxon 43 L9
Elsham N Linc 79 P1
Elsing Norfk 70 F9
Elslack N York 84 D5
Elson Hants 13 K4
Elson Shrops 63 L5
Elsrickle S Lans 106 D1
Elstead Surrey 14 C2
Elsted W Susx 25 P9
Elsted Marsh W Susx 25 P9
Elsthorpe Lincs 67 Q7
Elstob Dur 91 N2
Elston Lancs 83 N8
Elston Notts 67 J3
Elston Wilts 23 N5
Elstone Devon 19 N10
Elstow Bed 44 F2
Elstree Herts 32 H3
Elstronwick E R Yk 87 N9
Elswick Lancs 83 K7
Elswick N u Ty 100 G5
Elsworth Cambs 56 F8
Elterwater Cumb 89 J6
Eltham Gt Lon 33 M7
Eltisley Cambs 56 E8
Elton Bury 76 E1
Elton Cambs 56 B2
Elton Ches W 75 M8
Elton Derbys 77 N11
Elton Gloucs 41 L9
Elton Herefs 51 M6
Elton S on T 91 P3
Elton Green Ches W 75 M8
Elton-on-the-Hill Notts 67 J4
Eltringham Nthumb 100 D6
Elvanfoot S Lans 106 C6
Elvaston Derbys 66 C6
Elveden Suffk 58 B5
Elvetham Heath Hants 25 P2
Elvingston E Loth 116 B6
Elvington C York 86 C6
Elvington Kent 35 N12
Elwell Devon 19 M7
Elwick Hartpl 101 L11
Elwick Nthumb 109 J2
Elworth Ches E 76 D11
Elworthy Somset 20 H6
Ely Cambs 57 K4
Ely Cardif 27 Q7
Emberton M Keyn 55 M10
Embleton Cumb 97 N12
Embleton Dur 101 K12
Embleton Nthumb 109 L5
Embo Highld 146 E6
Emborough Somset 22 E3
Embo Street Highld 146 E7
Embsay N York 84 F4
Emery Down Hants 12 D3
Emley Kirk 77 N1
Emley Moor Kirk 77 N1
Emmbrook Wokham 32 A8
Emmer Green Readg 31 P7
Emmett Carr Derbys 78 D8
Emmington Oxon 43 Q11
Emneth Norfk 69 J10
Emneth Hungate Norfk 69 K10
Empingham RutInd 67 N10
Empshott Hants 25 N7
Empshott Green Hants 25 N7
Emsworth Hants 13 N3
Enborne W Berk 31 J9
Enborne Row W Berk 31 J9
Enchmarsh Shrops 51 N1
Enderby Leics 66 E12
Endmoor Cumb 89 N10
Endon Staffs 64 G2
Endon Bank Staffs 64 G1
Enfield Gt Lon 33 L3
Enfield Lock Gt Lon 33 L3
Enfield Wash Gt Lon 33 L3
Enford Wilts 23 P3
Engine Common S Glos 29 L5
England's Gate Herefs 51 P10
Englefield W Berk 31 N8
Englefield Green Surrey 32 E8
Engleseabrook Ches E 64 D2
English Bicknor Gloucs 41 J8
Englishcombe BaNES 29 L9
English Frankton Shrops 63 M6
Engollan Cnwll 6 B10
Enham Alamein Hants 24 F3
Enmore Somset 21 K6
Enmore Green Dorset 23 J8
Ennerdale Bridge Cumb 88 E3
Enniscaven Cnwll 3 N3
Enochdhu P & K 131 K11
Ensay Ag & B 119 K3
Ensbury BCP 11 Q5
Ensdon Shrops 63 L9
Ensis Devon 19 L8
Enson Staffs 64 H6
Enstone Oxon 42 H7
Enterkinfoot D & G 105 Q9
Enterpen N York 91 Q5
Enville Staffs 52 F3
Eochar W Isls 152 b9
Eòlaigearraidh W Isls 152 b12
Eoligarry W Isls 152 b12
Eòropaidh W Isls 152 h1
Eoropie W Isls 152 h1
Epney Gloucs 41 M9
Epperstone Notts 66 G2
Epping Essex 45 N11
Epping Green Essex 45 N10
Epping Green Herts 45 K10
Epping Upland Essex 45 N10
Eppleby N York 91 K4
Eppleworth E R Yk 87 J9
Epsom Surrey 33 J10
Epwell Oxon 42 H4
Epworth N Linc 79 K3
Epworth Turbary N Linc 79 J3
Erbistock Wrexhm 63 K4
Erdington Birm 53 L2
Eridge Green E Susx 15 Q4
Eridge Station E Susx 15 P4
Erines Ag & B 112 C6
Eriska Ag & B 120 G4
Eriswell Suffk 57 N5
Erith Gt Lon 33 P7
Erlestoke Wilts 23 L3
Ermington Devon 5 K6
Ernesettle C Plym 4 G5
Erpingham Norfk 71 J6
Erriottwood Kent 34 G10
Errogie Highld 137 P11
Errol P & K 124 E8
Erskine Rens 113 P7
Erskine Bridge Rens 113 N7
Ervie D & G 94 E5
Erwarton Suffk 47 M5
Erwood Powys 39 Q3
Eryholme N York 91 N5
Eryrys Denbgs 74 H12
Escalls Cnwll 2 B9
Escomb Dur 100 F12
Escott Somset 20 H6
Escrick N York 86 B6
Esgair Carmth 38 B6
Esgair Cerdgn 49 K7
Esgairgeiliog Powys 61 N11
Esgerdawe Carmth 38 F3
Esgyryn Conwy 73 P8
Esh Dur 100 F9
Esher Surrey 32 G9
Esholt C Brad 85 J7
Eshott Nthumb 109 K10
Eshton N York 84 D4
Esh Winning Dur 100 G10
Eskadale Highld 137 M8
Eskbank Mdloth 115 P8
Eskdale Green Cumb 88 F6
Eskdalemuir D & G 106 H10
Eske E R Yk 87 K6
Eskham Lincs 80 G4
Eskholme Donc 86 B11
Esperley Lane Ends Dur 91 J2
Esprick Lancs 83 K8
Essendine RutInd 67 P9
Essendon Herts 45 K10
Essich Highld 138 B8
Essington Staffs 64 H11
Esslemont Abers 141 M10
Eston R & Cl 92 B3
Etal Nthumb 108 E2
Etchilhampton Wilts 30 B10
Etchingham E Susx 16 C5
Etchinghill Kent 17 L3
Etchinghill Staffs 65 J8
Etchingwood E Susx 15 P6
Etling Green Norfk 70 F9
Etloe Gloucs 41 K10
Eton W & M 32 D7
Eton Wick W & M 32 D6
Etruria C Stke 64 F3
Etteridge Highld 130 C6
Ettersgill Dur 99 N12
Ettiley Heath Ches E 76 D11
Ettingshall Wolves 52 H1
Ettington Warwks 53 P11
Etton C Pete 68 C11
Etton E R Yk 86 H6
Ettrick Border 106 H7
Ettrickbridge Border 107 K5
Ettrickhill Border 106 H7
Etwall Derbys 65 P6
Eudon George Shrops 52 C3
Euston Suffk 58 C5
Euximoor Drove Cambs 57 J1
Euxton Lancs 83 M11
Evancoyd Powys 51 J8
Evanton Highld 137 Q3
Evedon Lincs 68 B3
Evelith Shrops 64 D11
Evelix Highld 146 D7
Evenjobb Powys 51 J8
Evenley Nhants 43 M5
Evenlode Gloucs 42 E6
Evenwood Dur 91 K2
Evenwood Gate Dur 91 K2
Evercreech Somset 22 E5
Everingham E R Yk 86 F7
Everleigh Wilts 24 C3

Everley N York....93 K9
Eversholt C Beds....44 E5
Evershot Dorset....10 E4
Eversley Hants....31 Q10
Eversley Cross Hants....31 R10
Everthorpe E R Yk....86 G9
Everton C Beds....56 D10
Everton Hants....12 D6
Everton Lpool....75 K5
Everton Notts....78 H5
Evertown D & G....98 D3
Evesbatch Herefs....52 C11
Evesham Worcs....42 B3
Evington C Leic....66 G11
Ewden Village Sheff....77 M4
Ewell Surrey....33 J9
Ewell Minnis Kent....17 N2
Ewelme Oxon....31 N4
Ewen Gloucs....30 B3
Ewenny V Glam....27 L7
Ewerby Lincs....68 C3
Ewerby Thorpe Lincs....68 C3
Ewhurst Surrey....14 F3
Ewhurst Green E Susx....16 D6
Ewhurst Green Surrey....14 F3
Ewloe Flints....75 J10
Ewloe Green Flints....75 J10
Ewood Bl w D....83 P10
Ewood Bridge Lancs....84 B11
Eworthy Devon....7 N6
Ewshot Hants....25 P3
Ewyas Harold Herefs....40 E6
Exbourne Devon....8 B4
Exbury Hants....12 G5
Exceat E Susx....15 P11
Exebridge Somset....20 E8
Exelby N York....91 M9
Exeter Devon....8 H6
Exeter Airport Devon....9 J6
Exeter Services Devon....8 H6
Exford Somset....20 D6
Exfordsgreen Shrops....63 M11
Exhall Warwks....53 L9
Exhall Warwks....54 B3
Exlade Street Oxon....31 N6
Exley Head C Brad....84 F7
Exminster Devon....8 H7
Exmoor National Park....20 D5
Exmouth Devon....9 J8
Exning Suffk....57 M7
Exted Kent....17 L2
Exton Devon....9 J7
Exton Hants....25 K9
Exton Rutlnd....67 M10
Exton Somset....20 E6
Exwick Devon....8 G6
Eyam Derbys....77 N8
Eydon Nhants....54 E10
Eye C Pete....68 E11
Eye Herefs....51 N8
Eye Suffk....58 H6
Eye Green C Pete....68 E11
Eyemouth Border....117 L8
Eyeworth C Beds....45 J3
Eyhorne Street Kent....34 E11
Eyke Suffk....59 L10
Eynesbury Cambs....56 D9
Eynsford Kent....33 P9
Eynsham Oxon....43 J10
Eype Dorset....10 C6
Eyre Highld....134 G5
Eythorne Kent....17 N1
Eyton Herefs....51 N8
Eyton Shrops....51 L3
Eyton Shrops....63 L9
Eyton Shrops....63 M7
Eyton Wrexhm....63 K3
Eyton on Severn Shrops....63 P11
Eyton upon the Weald
   Moors Wrekin....64 C9

F

Faccombe Hants....30 H10
Faceby N York....91 R6
Fachwen Powys....62 E9
Facit Lancs....84 D11
Fackley Notts....78 D11
Faddiley Ches E....63 P2
Fadmoor N York....92 D9
Faerdre Swans....26 G2
Faifley W Duns....113 Q6
Failand N Som....28 G8
Failford S Ayrs....104 H4
Failsworth Oldham....76 G3
Fairbourn Gwynd....61 K9
Fairburn N York....85 P9
Fairfield Derbys....77 K9
Fairfield Kent....16 G5
Fairfield Worcs....52 H5
Fairfield Park Herts....44 H5
Fairford Gloucs....30 D2
Fairford Park Gloucs....30 D2
Fairgirth D & G....96 H7
Fair Green Norfk....69 M8
Fairhaven Lancs....82 H9
Fair Isle Shet....147 h10
Fair Isle Airport Shet....147 h10
Fairlands Surrey....32 D11
Fairlie N Ayrs....113 J10
Fairlight E Susx....16 F8
Fairlight Cove E Susx....16 F8
Fairmile Devon....9 L5
Fairmile Surrey....32 G10
Fairmilehead C Edin....115 N7
Fairmilee Border....107 M3
Fair Oak Hants....24 H9
Fairoak Staffs....64 E5
Fair Oak Green Hants....31 N10
Fairseat Kent....34 A10
Fairstead Essex....46 D8
Fairstead Norfk....69 M8
Fairwarp E Susx....15 N5
Fairwater Cardif....27 Q7
Fairy Cross Devon....18 H8
Fakenham Norfk....70 D6
Fakenham Magna Suffk....58 D5
Fala Mdloth....116 B9
Fala Dam Mdloth....116 B9
Falcut Nhants....43 M3
Faldingworth Lincs....79 Q7
Faldouet Jersey....13 c2
Falfield S Glos....29 K4
Falkenham Suffk....47 N4
Falkirk Falk....114 F5
Falkirk Wheel Falk....114 F5
Falkland Fife....124 E11
Fallburn S Lans....106 C2
Fallgate Derbys....78 B11
Fallin Stirlg....114 E3
Fallodon Nthumb....109 K5
Fallowfield Manch....76 F5
Fallowfield Nthumb....99 P4
Falmer E Susx....15 L9
Falmouth Cnwll....3 K8
Falnash Border....107 K8
Falsgrave N York....93 L9
Falstone Nthumb....108 B12
Fanagmore Highld....148 E6
Fancott C Beds....44 E6
Fanellan Highld....137 N7
Fangdale Beck N York....92 B8
Fangfoss E R Yk....86 E4
Fanmore Ag & B....119 L4

Fannich Lodge Highld....136 H3
Fans Border....107 P2
Far Bletchley M Keyn....44 B5
Farcet Cambs....56 D2
Far Cotton Nhants....54 H9
Farden Shrops....51 P5
Fareham Hants....13 J3
Farewell Staffs....65 K10
Far Forest Worcs....52 D6
Farforth Lincs....80 F8
Faringdon Oxon....30 G3
Farington Lancs....83 M10
Farlam Cumb....99 H6
Farleigh N Som....28 G8
Farleigh Surrey....33 L10
Farleigh Hungerford
   Somset....29 N11
Farleigh Wallop Hants....25 K4
Farlesthorpe Lincs....81 J9
Farleton Cumb....89 N10
Farleton Lancs....83 N2
Farley Derbys....77 P11
Farley Staffs....65 K3
Farley Wilts....24 C7
Farley Green Suffk....57 P10
Farley Green Surrey....14 F2
Farley Hill Wokham....31 Q9
Farleys End Gloucs....41 M8
Farlington C Port....13 M4
Farlington N York....86 B2
Farlow Shrops....52 B4
Farmborough BaNES....29 K10
Farmbridge End Essex....46 A9
Farmcote Gloucs....42 C6
Farmcote Shrops....52 E2
Farmington Gloucs....42 D8
Farmoor Oxon....43 K10
Farms Common Cnwll....2 H7
Farmtown Moray....140 D5
Farnah Green Derbys....65 Q3
Farnborough Gt Lon....33 N9
Farnborough Hants....32 C11
Farnborough W Berk....31 J6
Farnborough Warwks....54 C10
Farnborough Park Hants....32 C11
Farncombe Surrey....14 D2
Farndish Bed....55 M8
Farndon Ches W....63 L1
Farndon Notts....67 N2
Farne Islands Nthumb....109 L2
Farnell Angus....125 M2
Farnham Dorset....23 L10
Farnham Essex....45 N7
Farnham N York....85 M8
Farnham Suffk....59 M8
Farnham Surrey....25 P4
Farnham Common Bucks....32 D5
Farnham Green Essex....45 N6
Farnham Royal Bucks....32 D6
Farnley Kent....85 K8
Farnley Leeds....85 K8
Farnley N York....85 J5
Farnley Tyas Kirk....77 M1
Farnsfield Notts....78 G12
Farnworth Bolton....76 D2
Farnworth Halton....75 N6
Far Oakridge Gloucs....41 Q11
Farr Highld....130 F4
Farr Highld....138 C9
Farr Highld....150 C4
Farraline Highld....137 P11
Farringdon Devon....9 J6
Farrington Gurney BaNES....29 K10
Far Sawrey Cumb....89 K7
Farsley Leeds....85 J8
Farther Howegreen
   Essex....34 G2
Farthing Green Kent....16 E2
Farthinghoe Nhants....43 L4
Farthingloe Kent....17 N3
Farthingstone Nhants....54 G9
Farthing Street Gt Lon....33 N9
Fartown Kirk....84 H11
Farway Devon....9 M6
Fasnacloich Ag & B....121 J3
Fasnakyle Highld....137 K10
Fassfern Highld....128 E8
Fatfield Sundld....100 H7
Faugh Cumb....98 G7
Fauld Staffs....65 M6
Fauldhouse W Loth....114 H9
Faulkbourne Essex....46 D8
Faulkland Somset....22 G2
Fauls Shrops....63 Q6
Faversham Kent....34 H10
Fawdington N York....91 Q12
Fawdon N u Ty....100 G6
Fawdon Nthumb....108 G6
Fawfieldhead Staffs....77 K11
Fawkham Green Kent....33 Q9
Fawler Oxon....42 H8
Fawley Bucks....31 Q5
Fawley Hants....12 G5
Fawley W Berk....30 H6
Fawley Chapel Herefs....41 J6
Fawnog Flints....74 H10
Fawsley Nhants....54 F9
Faxfleet E R Yk....86 F10
Faygate W Susx....15 J4
Fazakerley Lpool....75 L4
Fazeley Staffs....65 M11
Fearby N York....91 K10
Fearn Highld....146 F9
Fearnan P & K....123 J4
Fearnbeg Highld....135 N4
Fearnhead Warrtn....76 B5
Fearnmore Highld....135 M4
Fearnoch Ag & B....112 D5
Featherstone Staffs....64 H11
Featherstone Wakefd....85 N11
Feckenham Worcs....53 J8
Feering Essex....46 F7
Feetham N York....90 H7
Feizor N York....84 B2
Felbridge Surrey....15 L3
Felbrigg Norfk....71 J4
Felcourt Surrey....15 M3
Felden Herts....44 F10
Felindre Carmth....38 A4
Felindre Carmth....38 C1
Felindre Carmth....38 H6
Felindre Powys....40 A7
Felindre Powys....50 E4
Felindre Swans....26 G4
Felindre Farchog Pembks....37 L3
Felinfach Cerdgn....49 K4
Felinfach Powys....39 P5
Felinfoel Carmth....26 D3
Felingwmisaf Carmth....38 D7
Felingwmuchaf Carmth....38 D7
Felin-newydd Powys....39 Q4
Felixkirk N York....91 Q10
Felixstowe Suffk....47 N5
Felixstowe Ferry Suffk....47 N5
Felkington Nthumb....117 L12
Felkirk Wakefd....78 C1
Felling Gatesd....100 H6
Fell Lane C Brad....84 F7
Fell Side Cumb....98 C10
Felmersham Bed....55 M9
Felmingham Norfk....71 K6
Felpham W Susx....14 C11
Felsham Suffk....58 D9

Felsted Essex....46 B7
Feltham Gt Lon....32 G8
Felthamhill Surrey....32 G8
Felthorpe Norfk....70 H8
Felton Herefs....51 P11
Felton N Som....28 H9
Felton Nthumb....109 K9
Felton Butler Shrops....63 L9
Feltwell Norfk....57 N2
Fenay Bridge Kirk....85 J12
Fence Lancs....84 B8
Fence Rothm....78 D6
Fence Houses Sundld....101 J8
Fendike Corner Lincs....81 J11
Fen Ditton Cambs....57 J8
Fen Drayton Cambs....56 G7
Fen End Lincs....68 E8
Fen End Solhll....53 N6
Fenham Nthumb....108 H2
Feniscliffe Bl w D....83 P10
Feniscowles Bl w D....83 P10
Feniton Devon....9 L5
Feniton Court Devon....9 L5
Fenn Green Shrops....52 E4
Fenn Street Medway....34 D7
Fenny Bentley Derbys....65 M2
Fenny Bridges Devon....9 L5
Fenny Compton Warwks....54 C10
Fenny Drayton Leics....54 C5
Fenny Stratford M Keyn....44 C5
Fenrother Nthumb....109 K11
Fenstanton Cambs....56 F7
Fenstead End Suffk....57 Q10
Fen Street Norfk....58 E2
Fen Street Suffk....58 F6
Fenton C Stke....64 G3
Fenton Cambs....56 F5
Fenton Cumb....98 G7
Fenton Lincs....67 L2
Fenton Lincs....79 L8
Fenton Notts....78 H5
Fenton Nthumb....108 F3
Fenton Barns E Loth....116 C5
Fenwick Donc....86 B12
Fenwick E Ayrs....104 H1
Fenwick Nthumb....100 D4
Fenwick Nthumb....108 H2
Feock Cnwll....3 K7
Feolin Ferry Ag & B....111 K7
Fergushill N Ayrs....104 F1
Feriniquarrie Highld....134 C6
Fermain Bay Guern....12 c3
Fern Angus....132 D12
Ferndale Rhondd....27 N3
Ferndown Dorset....11 P4
Ferness Highld....138 H7
Fernham Oxon....30 G4
Fernhill Heath Worcs....52 G9
Fernhurst W Susx....14 C5
Fernie Fife....124 F9
Ferniegair S Lans....114 D10
Fernilea Highld....134 F9
Fernilee Derbys....77 J8
Ferrensby N York....85 M6
Ferring W Susx....14 F10
Ferrybridge Services
   Wakefd....85 P10
Ferryden Angus....125 P2
Ferryhill Dur....100 H11
Ferryhill Station Dur....100 H12
Ferry Point Highld....146 D8
Ferryside Carmth....38 A9
Fersfield Norfk....58 F4
Fersit Highld....129 L8
Feshiebridge Highld....130 F3
Fetcham Surrey....32 G11
Fetlar Shet....147 k3
Fetterangus Abers....141 N6
Fettercairn Abers....132 G9
Fewcott Oxon....43 L6
Fewston N York....85 J4
Ffairfach Carmth....38 F7
Ffair Rhos Cerdgn....49 M7
Ffald-y-Brenin Carmth....38 E3
Ffarmers Carmth....38 G3
Ffawyddog Powys....40 A8
Ffestiniog Gwynd....61 K4
Ffestiniog Railway Gwynd....61 K4
Ffordd-las Denbgs....74 F10
Fforest Carmth....38 E10
Fforest Gôch Neath....26 H2
Ffostrasol Cerdgn....48 F11
Ffrith Flints....63 J1
Ffynnonddewi Cerdgn....48 F10
Ffynnongroyw Flints....74 F7
Ffynnon-oer Cerdgn....49 J10
Fickleshole Surrey....33 M10
Fiddington Somset....21 J5
Fiddington Somset....21 K5
Fiddleford Dorset....22 H10
Fiddlers Green Cnwll....3 K3
Fiddlers Hamlet Essex....33 N3
Field Staffs....65 J5
Field Broughton Cumb....89 L10
Field Dalling Norfk....70 E4
Fieldhead Cumb....98 F10
Field Head Leics....66 E10
Fifehead Magdalen
   Dorset....22 H9
Fifehead Neville Dorset....11 J3
Fifehead St Quintin
   Dorset....11 J3
Fife Keith Moray....140 C6
Fifield Oxon....42 F8
Fifield W & M....32 C7
Fifield Wilts....23 P3
Figheldean Wilts....23 P4
Filands Wilts....29 Q5
Filby Norfk....71 P9
Filey N York....93 M10
Filgrave M Keyn....55 L11
Filkins Oxon....42 F10
Filleigh Devon....19 N8
Fillingham Lincs....79 N6
Fillongley Warwks....53 P5
Filmore Hill Hants....25 L6
Filton S Glos....29 J6
Fimber E R Yk....86 G3
Finavon Angus....125 K1
Finberry Kent....17 J3
Fincham Norfk....69 N10
Finchampstead Wokham....31 R9
Finchdean Hants....25 M10
Finchingfield Essex....46 B5
Finchley Gt Lon....33 K4
Findern Derbys....65 P6
Findhorn Moray....139 J3
Findhorn Bridge Highld....138 H10
Findochty Moray....140 C2
Findo Gask P & K....123 P9
Findon Abers....133 M5
Findon W Susx....14 G9
Findon Mains Highld....137 Q4
Findrack House Abers....132 F3
Finedon Nhants....55 M6
Fingal Street Suffk....59 J6
Fingask P & K....124 D9
Fingest Bucks....31 Q4
Finghall N York....91 K9
Fingland Cumb....97 Q7
Fingland D & G....105 P6
Finglesham Kent....35 P11
Fingringhoe Essex....47 J7
Finkle Green Essex....46 C4
Finkle Street Barns....77 P4
Finlake Devon....8 F8
Finlarig Stirlg....122 F6
Finmere Oxon....43 N5
Finnart P & K....122 E1
Finningham Suffk....58 F7
Finningley Donc....78 H4
Finsbay W Isls....152 e6
Finstall Worcs....52 H6
Finsthwaite Cumb....89 K9
Finstock Oxon....42 H8
Finstown Ork....147 c4
Fintry Abers....141 J5
Fintry Stirlg....114 B4
Finzean Abers....132 F6
Fionnphort Ag & B....119 J8
Fionnsbhagh W Isls....152 e6
Firbank Cumb....89 N8
Firbeck Rothm....78 F6
Firby N York....86 D2
Firby N York....91 M9
Firgrove Rochdl....76 G1
Firle E Susx....15 N9
Firsby Lincs....81 J11
Firsdown Wilts....24 C7
Fir Tree Dur....100 F11
Fishbourne IoW....13 J7
Fishbourne W Susx....13 P4
Fishbourne Roman
   Palace W Susx....13 P4
Fishburn Dur....101 K11
Fishcross Clacks....114 G2
Fisher W Susx....14 B10
Fisherford Abers....140 G8
Fisherrow E Loth....115 Q7
Fisher's Pond Hants....24 H9
Fisher's Row Lancs....83 K5
Fisherstreet W Susx....14 D4
Fisherton Highld....138 D5
Fisherton S Ayrs....104 E7
Fisherton de la Mere
   Wilts....23 M6
Fisherwick Staffs....65 M10
Fishery W & M....32 C7
Fishguard Pembks....37 J3
Fishlake Donc....78 G1
Fishleigh Devon....8 C6
Fishmere End Lincs....68 E5
Fishnish Pier Ag & B....120 C4
Fishpond Bottom Dorset....10 B5
Fishponds Bristl....29 J7
Fishtoft Lincs....68 G4
Fishtoft Drove Lincs....68 F2
Fishwick Lancs....83 M9
Fiskavaig Highld....134 F9
Fiskerton Lincs....79 P9
Fiskerton Notts....67 J2
Fitling E R Yk....87 N8
Fittleton Wilts....23 P3
Fittleworth W Susx....14 E7
Fitton End Cambs....68 H9
Fitz Shrops....63 M9
Fitzhead Somset....20 H7
Fitzroy Somset....21 K8
Fitzwilliam Wakefd....85 N12
Five Ash Down E Susx....15 N6
Five Ashes E Susx....15 Q6
Five Bells Somset....20 G5
Five Bridges Herefs....41 K2
Fivecrosses Ches W....75 N8
Fivehead Somset....21 M9
Five Lanes Mons....28 F4
Five Oak Green Kent....16 B2
Five Oaks Jersey....13 c2
Five Oaks W Susx....14 G5
Five Roads Carmth....38 D10
Flack's Green Essex....34 D1
Flackwell Heath Bucks....32 C4
Fladbury Worcs....42 A2
Fladdabister Shet....147 i8
Flagg Derbys....77 L10
Flamborough E R Yk....87 N1
Flamborough Head
   E R Yk....87 N1
Flamingo Land Resort
   N York....92 F10
Flamstead Herts....44 F8
Flamstead End Herts....45 L11
Flansham W Susx....14 D10
Flanshaw Wakefd....85 L11
Flappit Spring C Brad....84 F8
Flasby N York....84 E4
Flash Staffs....77 J10
Flashader Highld....134 F5
Flaunden Herts....32 E2
Flawborough Notts....67 K4
Flawith N York....85 P2
Flax Bourton N Som....28 H8
Flaxby N York....85 M5
Flaxley Gloucs....41 K8
Flaxmere Ches W....75 P9
Flaxpool Somset....21 J6
Flaxton N York....86 C3
Fleckney Leics....54 G2
Flecknoe Warwks....54 E8
Fledborough Notts....79 K9
Fleet Dorset....10 G8
Fleet Hants....13 M4
Fleet Hants....25 P3
Fleet Lincs....68 H7
Fleetend Hants....13 J3
Fleet Hargate Lincs....68 H7
Fleet Services Hants....25 P3
Fleetwood Lancs....82 H5
Fleggburgh Norfk....71 N8
Flemingston V Glam....27 N8
Flemington S Lans....114 B9
Flempton Suffk....57 Q7
Fletcher's Green Kent....33 P12
Fletchertown Cumb....97 P9
Fletching E Susx....15 M6
Fleur-de-lis Caerph....27 R3
Flexbury Cnwll....7 J4
Flexford Surrey....32 C12
Flimby Cumb....97 L11
Flimwell E Susx....16 C4
Flint Flints....74 H9
Flint Mountain Flints....74 H9
Flinton E R Yk....87 N8
Flint's Green Solhll....53 P6
Flishinghurst Kent....16 D3
Flitcham Norfk....69 P7
Flitton C Beds....44 F4
Flitwick C Beds....44 F4
Flixborough N Linc....79 L2
Flixborough Stather
   N Linc....86 G12
Flixton N York....93 L11
Flixton Suffk....59 L3
Flixton Traffd....76 D3
Flockton Kirk....85 K12
Flockton Green Kirk....85 L12
Flodden Nthumb....108 E3
Flodigarry Highld....142 F4
Flookburgh Cumb....89 K11
Flordon Norfk....58 H2
Flore Nhants....54 F8
Flotterton Nthumb....108 G8

Flowers Green E Susx....16 B8
Flowton Suffk....47 K1
Flushdyke Wakefd....85 L11
Flushing Cnwll....3 K8
Fluxton Devon....9 L6
Flyford Flavell Worcs....52 H9
Fobbing Thurr....34 C5
Fochabers Moray....139 Q4
Fochriw Caerph....39 Q10
Fockerby N Linc....86 F11
Foddington Somset....22 D7
Foel Powys....62 D10
Foelgastell Carmth....38 E8
Foel y Dyffryn Brdgnd....27 K5
Foggathorpe E R Yk....86 D7
Fogo Border....116 H11
Fogwatt Moray....139 N4
Foindle Highld....148 E7
Folda Angus....131 M11
Fole Staffs....65 K5
Foleshill Covtry....54 B4
Folke Dorset....22 F10
Folkestone Kent....17 M4
Folkestone Services Kent....17 K3
Folkingham Lincs....67 Q5
Folkington E Susx....15 Q10
Folksworth Cambs....56 C3
Folkton N York....93 L10
Folla Rule Abers....140 H9
Follifoot N York....85 M5
Folly Gate Devon....8 C5
Folly Hill Surrey....25 P4
Fonmon V Glam....27 P9
Fonthill Bishop Wilts....23 L7
Fonthill Gifford Wilts....23 K7
Fontmell Magna Dorset....23 J10
Fontmell Parva Dorset....23 J10
Fontwell W Susx....14 D9
Foolow Derbys....77 M8
Foots Cray Gt Lon....33 N8
Forbestown Abers....131 Q2
Forcett N York....91 K4
Ford Ag & B....120 G2
Ford Bucks....43 Q10
Ford Derbys....78 C7
Ford Devon....5 K6
Ford Devon....6 H8
Ford Gloucs....42 C6
Ford Nthumb....108 E2
Ford Shrops....63 L9
Ford Somset....20 F7
Ford Somset....22 D3
Ford Staffs....65 K2
Ford W Susx....14 E10
Ford Wilts....29 N7
Forda Devon....7 P6
Fordcombe Kent....15 P3
Fordell Fife....115 K4
Forden Powys....62 H12
Ford End Essex....46 B8
Forder Green Devon....5 N3
Ford Green Lancs....83 L6
Fordham Cambs....57 L6
Fordham Essex....46 G6
Fordham Norfk....69 M12
Fordham Heath Essex....46 G6
Ford Heath Shrops....63 L9
Fordingbridge Hants....23 P10
Fordon E R Yk....93 L11
Fordoun Abers....133 J9
Ford's Green Suffk....58 F7
Fordstreet Essex....46 G6
Ford Street Somset....21 J10
Fordton Devon....8 G5
Fordwells Oxon....42 G9
Fordwich Kent....35 L10
Fordyce Abers....140 E3
Forebridge Staffs....64 H7
Foremark Derbys....66 B7
Forest Guern....12 c3
Forest N York....91 M6
Forest Becks Lancs....84 B5
Forestburn Gate Nthumb....108 H9
Forest Chapel Ches E....76 H9
Forest Coal Pit Mons....40 C7
Forest Gate Gt Lon....33 M5
Forest Green Surrey....14 G2
Forest Hall N Tyne....100 H4
Forest Hill Gt Lon....33 L8
Forest Hill Oxon....43 M10
Forest-in-Teesdale Dur....99 N12
Forest Lane Head N York....85 M4
Forest Mill Clacks....114 H2
Forest of Bowland Lancs....83 P4
Forest of Dean Gloucs....41 K9
Forest Row E Susx....15 M4
Forest Side IoW....12 H7
Forestside W Susx....25 M11
Forest Town Notts....78 F11
Forfar Angus....125 J3
Forgandenny P & K....124 F9
Forge Powys....61 N12
Forge Hammer Torfn....28 C3
Forge Side Torfn....40 C10
Forgie Moray....140 B5
Forgieside Moray....140 B5
Forgue Abers....140 F7
Forhill Worcs....53 K5
Formby Sefton....75 J2
Forncett End Norfk....58 H2
Forncett St Mary Norfk....58 H2
Forncett St Peter Norfk....58 H2
Fornham All Saints Suffk....58 B7
Fornham St Martin Suffk....58 C7
Fornham St Genevieve
   Suffk....58 C7
Fornighty Highld....138 H6
Forres Moray....139 J4
Forsbrook Staffs....64 H4
Forse Highld....151 N9
Forshaw Heath Warwks....53 K6
Forsinard Highld....150 G8
Forss Highld....151 J3
Forston Dorset....10 G5
Fort Augustus Highld....129 L2
Forteviot P & K....123 R9
Forth S Lans....114 G10
Forthampton Gloucs....41 P5
Fort Hommet Guern....12 b2
Fortingall P & K....123 J4
Fort Rail Bridge C Edin....115 L5
Forth Road Bridge Fife....115 L5
Forton Hants....25 J4
Forton Lancs....83 L5
Forton Shrops....63 L9
Forton Somset....10 B4
Forton Staffs....64 E8
Fortrie Abers....140 G6
Fort Richmond Guern....12 b2
Fortrose Highld....138 D5
Fortuneswell Dorset....10 G10
Forty Green Bucks....32 D4
Forty Hill Gt Lon....33 L3
Forward Green Suffk....58 F8
Fosbury Wilts....24 D3
Foscot Oxon....42 F7
Foscote Nhants....43 N3
Fosdyke Lincs....68 F6
Fosdyke Bridge Lincs....68 F6
Foss P & K....123 J2
Foss-y-ffin Cerdgn....48 G8
Foston Derbys....65 M6
Foston Leics....54 G2
Foston Lincs....67 L4
Foston N York....86 C2
Foston on the Wolds
   E R Yk....87 L4
Fotherby Lincs....80 F5
Fothergill Cumb....97 L11
Fotheringhay Nhants....55 Q2
Foula Shet....147 h8
Foula Airport Shet....147 h8
Foul Anchor Cambs....69 J8
Foulbridge Cumb....98 E8
Foulby Wakefd....85 N11
Foulden Border....117 L10
Foulden Norfk....69 P12
Foul End Warwks....53 N2
Foul Mile E Susx....16 A8
Foulridge Lancs....84 D7
Foulsham Norfk....70 F7
Fountainhall Border....116 B11
Four Ashes Solhll....53 M6
Four Ashes Staffs....52 E3
Four Ashes Staffs....64 G10
Four Ashes Suffk....58 E6
Four Cabots Guern....12 c2
Four Crosses Powys....63 J8
Four Crosses Powys....62 G10
Four Elms Kent....15 N1
Four Foot Somset....22 D6
Four Forks Somset....21 K6
Four Gates Bolton....76 B2
Four Lane End Barns....77 P3
Four Lane Ends Ches W....75 P11
Four Lanes Cnwll....2 H7
Fourlanes End Ches E....76 E12
Four Marks Hants....25 L6
Four Mile Bridge IoA....72 D8
Four Oaks Birm....53 L1
Four Oaks E Susx....16 F6
Four Oaks Gloucs....41 L6
Four Oaks Solhll....53 N4
Fourpenny Highld....146 F6
Four Points W Berk....31 L6
Four Roads Carmth....38 C10
Four Shire Stone Warwks....42 F5
Fourstones Nthumb....99 N5
Four Throws Kent....16 D5
Four Wents Kent....34 A12
Fovant Wilts....23 M7
Foveran Abers....141 N11
Fowey Cnwll....4 R4
Fowley Common Warrtn....76 C4
Fowlhall Kent....16 C2
Fowlis Angus....124 F6
Fowlis Wester P & K....123 P8
Fowlmere Cambs....45 M2
Fownhope Herefs....41 J5
Foxbar Rens....113 P7
Foxcombe Devon....5 N3
Foxcote Gloucs....42 B8
Foxcote Somset....22 G2
Foxdale IoM....102 c5
Foxearth Essex....46 E4
Foxendown Kent....34 B9
Foxfield Cumb....88 H9
Foxham Wilts....29 R7
Fox Hatch Essex....33 Q3
Foxhole Cnwll....3 N4
Foxholes N York....93 K12
Foxhunt Green E Susx....15 P7
Foxley Nhants....54 G10
Foxley Norfk....70 F7
Foxlydiate Worcs....53 J7
Fox Street Essex....47 J6
Foxt Staffs....65 K3
Foxton Cambs....56 H11
Foxton Dur....91 P2
Foxton Leics....54 H3
Foxton N York....91 P7
Foxup N York....90 E11
Foxwist Green Ches W....76 B10
Foxwood Shrops....52 B5
Foy Herefs....41 J6
Foyers Highld....137 N11
Foynesfield Highld....138 G5
Fraddam Cnwll....2 F7
Fraddon Cnwll....3 M3
Fradley Staffs....65 M9
Fradswell Staffs....65 J5
Fraisthorpe E R Yk....87 M3
Framfield E Susx....15 N6
Framingham Earl Norfk....71 K11
Framingham Pigot Norfk....71 K11
Framlingham Suffk....59 K8
Frampton Dorset....10 G6
Frampton Lincs....68 F5
Frampton Cotterell
   S Glos....29 K6
Frampton Mansell Gloucs....41 Q11
Frampton-on-Severn
   Gloucs....41 M10
Frampton West End Lincs....68 E4
Framsden Suffk....59 J8
Framwellgate Moor Dur....100 H10
Franche Worcs....52 F5
Frandley Ches W....76 B8
Frankaborough Devon....7 M6
Frankby Wirral....75 J6
Frankfort Norfk....71 L7
Franklands Gate Herefs....40 H2
Frankley Worcs....52 H4
Frankley Services Worcs....53 J4
Franksbridge Powys....50 F9
Frankton Warwks....54 C6
Frant E Susx....15 Q4
Fraserburgh Abers....141 N2
Frating Essex....47 J7
Frating Green Essex....47 K7
Freathy Cnwll....4 F6
Freckenham Suffk....57 M6
Freckleton Lancs....83 K9
Freebirch Derbys....77 P10
Freeby Leics....67 K8
Freefolk Hants....25 J3
Freehay Staffs....65 K4
Freeland Oxon....43 J9
Freethorpe Norfk....71 N11
Freethorpe Common
   Norfk....71 N11
Freiston Lincs....68 G4
Fremington Devon....17 K5
Fremington N York....91 J7
Frenchay S Glos....29 J7
Frenchbeer Devon....8 C7
French Street Kent....33 N11
Frenich P & K....123 L1
Frensham Surrey....25 P5
Frenze Norfk....58 G4
Fresgoe Highld....150 H3
Freshfield Sefton....75 J2
Freshford Wilts....29 N10
Freshwater IoW....12 F7
Freshwater Bay IoW....12 F7
Freshwater East Pembks....37 K11
Fressingfield Suffk....59 K5
Freston Suffk....47 L4
Freswick Highld....151 Q3
Fretherne Gloucs....41 M9
Frettenham Norfk....71 K8
Freuchie Fife....124 F11

Freystrop Pembks....37 J8
Friar Park Sandw....53 J2
Friar's Gate E Susx....15 N4
Friars' Hill N York....92 F9
Friar Waddon Dorset....10 G7
Friday Bridge Cambs....69 J11
Friday Street Suffk....59 K8
Friday Street Suffk....59 L10
Friday Street Suffk....59 M8
Friday Street Surrey....14 G2
Fridaythorpe E R Yk....86 G3
Friden Derbys....77 M11
Friendly Calder....84 F10
Friern Barnet Gt Lon....33 K4
Friesthorpe Lincs....79 P7
Frieston Lincs....67 M3
Frieth Bucks....31 R4
Friezeland Notts....66 D2
Frilford Oxon....31 L8
Frilsham W Berk....31 L8
Frimley Surrey....32 C11
Frimley Green Surrey....32 C11
Frindsbury Medway....34 C8
Fring Norfk....69 P5
Fringford Oxon....43 M6
Frinsted Kent....34 F11
Frinton-on-Sea Essex....47 M7
Friockheim Angus....125 K3
Friog Gwynd....61 K9
Frisby on the Wreake
   Leics....66 H8
Friskney Lincs....81 J11
Friskney Eaudike Lincs....69 J1
Friston E Susx....15 Q11
Friston Suffk....59 N8
Fritchley Derbys....66 B2
Frith Bank Lincs....68 F3
Frith Common Worcs....52 C7
Fritham Hants....24 C10
Frithelstock Devon....19 J9
Frithelstock Stone Devon....19 J9
Frithend Hants....25 P5
Frithsden Herts....44 E9
Frithville Lincs....68 F2
Frittenden Kent....16 E3
Frittiscombe Devon....5 N8
Fritton Norfk....59 J2
Fritton Norfk....71 P12
Fritwell Oxon....43 L6
Frizinghall C Brad....84 H8
Frizington Cumb....88 D3
Frocester Gloucs....41 M11
Frodesley Shrops....63 N12
Frodsham Ches W....75 N8
Frog End Cambs....45 M2
Frog End Cambs....45 K9
Froggatt Derbys....77 N8
Froghall Staffs....65 K3
Frogham Hants....23 Q10
Frogham Kent....35 N11
Frogmore Devon....5 N8
Frognall Lincs....68 C10
Frogpool Cnwll....3 K6
Frog Pool Worcs....52 E7
Frogwell Cnwll....4 E3
Frolesworth Leics....54 E2
Frome Somset....22 H4
Frome St Quintin Dorset....10 F4
Fromes Hill Herefs....41 K2
Fron Gwynd....60 F4
Fron Gwynd....60 H3
Fron Powys....50 G1
Fron Powys....62 H11
Froncysyllte Wrexhm....63 J4
Fron-goch Gwynd....62 B4
Fron Isaf Wrexhm....63 J4
Frostenden Suffk....59 P4
Frosterley Dur....100 C11
Froxfield C Beds....44 D5
Froxfield Wilts....30 G8
Froxfield Green Hants....25 M8
Fryern Hill Hants....24 H9
Fryerning Essex....34 B2
Fryton N York....92 E11
Fuinary Highld....120 B3
Fulbeck Lincs....67 M2
Fulbourn Cambs....57 K9
Fulbrook Oxon....42 F9
Fulflood Hants....24 H7
Fulford C York....86 B5
Fulford Somset....21 K7
Fulford Staffs....64 H5
Fulham Gt Lon....33 J7
Fulking W Susx....15 J8
Fullaford Devon....19 N6
Fullarton N Ayrs....104 F2
Fuller's End Essex....45 P6
Fuller's Moor Ches W....63 N1
Fuller Street Essex....46 D8
Fullerton Hants....24 G6
Fulletby Lincs....80 F9
Fullready Warwks....42 G2
Full Sutton E R Yk....86 D4
Fullwood E Ayrs....113 N11
Fulmer Bucks....32 E5
Fulmodeston Norfk....70 E6
Fulnetby Lincs....80 B8
Fulney Lincs....68 E8
Fulstone Kirk....77 M2
Fulstow Lincs....80 F4
Fulwell Oxon....42 H7
Fulwell Sundld....101 K6
Fulwood Lancs....83 M9
Fulwood Notts....78 D12
Fulwood Sheff....77 P7
Fulwood Somset....21 K9
Fundenhall Norfk....58 H2
Funtington W Susx....13 P3
Funtley Hants....13 J3
Funtullich P & K....123 J7
Furley Devon....9 P4
Furnace Ag & B....112 F1
Furnace Carmth....26 B2
Furnace Cerdgn....49 L2
Furnace End Warwks....53 N3
Furner's Green E Susx....15 M5
Furness Vale Derbys....77 J7
Furneux Pelham Herts....45 M6
Further Quarter Kent....16 F3
Furtho Nhants....43 Q3
Furzehill Devon....19 N4
Furzehill Dorset....11 N4
Furzehills Lincs....80 E9
Furzeley Corner Hants....13 L3
Furze Platt W & M....32 C6
Furzley Hants....24 C10
Fyfett Somset....21 K10
Fyfield Essex....45 Q10
Fyfield Hants....24 E4
Fyfield Oxon....31 J3
Fyfield Wilts....30 D8
Fyfield Wilts....30 D9
Fyfield Bavant Wilts....23 M8
Fylingthorpe N York....93 J6
Fyning W Susx....25 P8
Fyvie Abers....141 J9

G

Gabroc Hill E Ayrs....113 N11
Gaddesby Leics....66 H9
Gaddesden Row Herts....44 F8
Gadfa IoA....72 G6

Gadgirth S Ayrs 104 G5
Gadlas Shrops 63 L5
Gaer Powys 40 A7
Gaerllwyd Mons 28 F3
Gaerwen IoA 72 H9
Gagingwell Oxon 43 J6
Gailes N Ayrs 104 F3
Gailey Staffs 64 G10
Gainford Dur 91 K3
Gainsborough Lincs 79 K6
Gainsborough Suffk 47 L3
Gainsford End Essex 46 C4
Gairloch Highld 143 L9
Gairlochy Highld 128 G7
Gairneybridge P & K 115 L2
Gaisgill Cumb 89 Q6
Gaitsgill Cumb 98 E9
Galashiels Border 107 M3
Galgate Lancs 83 L4
Galhampton Somset 22 E7
Gallanachbeg Ag & B 120 F7
Gallanachmore Ag & B 120 F7
Gallantry Bank Ches E 63 N1
Gallatown Fife 115 P2
Galley Common Warwks 53 P2
Galleywood Essex 46 C11
Gallovie Highld 129 P6
Galloway Forest Park 95 N1
Gallowfauld Angus 125 J4
Gallowhill P & K 124 D5
Gallows Green Essex 46 G6
Gallows Green Worcs 52 H8
Gallowstree Common
Oxon 31 P6
Galltair Highld 135 P11
Gallt-y-foel Gwynd 73 K11
Gallypot Street E Susx 15 N4
Galmisdale Highld 127 J7
Galmpton Devon 5 L8
Galmpton Torbay 5 Q5
Galphay N York 91 L12
Galston E Ayrs 105 J2
Gamballs Green Staffs 77 J10
Gamblesby Cumb 99 J10
Gambles Green Essex 46 D8
Gamelsby Cumb 97 Q8
Gamesley Derbys 77 J5
Gamlingay Cambs 56 E10
Gamlingay Cinques
Cambs 56 E10
Gamlingay Great Heath
Cambs 56 D10
Gammersgill N York 90 H10
Gamrie Abers 141 J3
Gamston Notts 66 F5
Gamston Notts 78 H8
Ganarew Herefs 40 H8
Ganavan Bay Ag & B 120 F6
Gang Cnwll 4 D3
Ganllwyd Gwynd 61 M7
Gannachy Angus 132 F10
Ganstead E R Yk 87 L8
Ganthorpe N York 86 C1
Ganton N York 93 K11
Ganwick Corner Herts 33 J2
Gappah Devon 8 G9
Garbity Moray 139 P5
Garboldisham Norfk 58 E4
Garbole Highld 138 D11
Garchory Abers 131 P2
Garden City Flints 75 K10
Gardeners Green Wokham 32 B9
Gardenstown Abers 141 J3
Garden Village Sheff 77 N4
Garderhouse Shet 147 i7
Gardham E R Yk 86 H7
Gare Hill Somset 22 H5
Garelochhead Ag & B 113 J3
Garford Oxon 31 J3
Garforth Leeds 85 N8
Gargrave N York 84 D4
Gargunnock Stirlg 114 C2
Garlic Street Norfk 59 J4
Garlieston D & G 95 N9
Garlinge Kent 35 P8
Garlinge Green Kent 35 K11
Garlogie Abers 133 J3
Garmond Abers 141 K5
Garmouth Moray 139 Q3
Garmston Shrops 63 Q11
Garnant Carmth 38 G9
Garndolbenmaen Gwynd 60 H3
Garnett Bridge Cumb 89 N7
Garnfadryn Gwynd 60 D5
Garnlydan Blae G 39 R9
Garnswllt Swans 38 F9
Garn-yr-erw Torfn 40 B9
Garrabost W Isls 152 h3
Garrallan E Ayrs 105 K6
Garras Cnwll 2 H9
Garreg Gwynd 61 K4
Garrigill Cumb 99 L10
Garriston N York 91 K8
Garroch D & G 96 C2
Garrochtrie D & G 94 G10
Garrochty Ag & B 112 G10
Garros Highld 135 J3
Garsdale Cumb 90 B9
Garsdale Head Cumb 90 C8
Garsdon Wilts 29 Q5
Garshall Green Staffs 64 H5
Garsington Oxon 43 M11
Garstang Lancs 83 L6
Garston Herts 32 G2
Garston Lpool 75 L7
Garswood St Hel 75 P4
Gartachossan Ag & B 110 H9
Gartcosh N Lans 114 C7
Garth Brdgnd 27 K4
Garth Mons 28 D4
Garth Powys 50 C10
Garth Powys 51 J6
Garth Wrexhm 63 J4
Garthamlock C Glas 114 B8
Garthbrengy Powys 39 P5
Gartheli Cerdgn 49 K9
Garthmyl Powys 62 G12
Garthorpe Leics 67 L8
Garthorpe N Linc 86 F11
Garth Row Cumb 89 N7
Garths Cumb 89 N9
Gartly Abers 140 E9
Gartmore Stirlg 113 Q2
Gartness N Lans 114 E8
Gartness Stirlg 113 P4
Gartocharn W Duns 113 N4
Garton E R Yk 87 P8
Garton-on-the-Wolds
E R Yk 86 H3
Gartymore Highld 147 J2
Garva Bridge Highld 129 P5
Garvald Border 115 K11
Garvald E Loth 116 D7
Garvan Highld 128 D9
Garvard Ag & B 111 J3
Garve Highld 137 L3
Garvellachs Ag & B 120 C10
Garvestone Norfk 70 F10
Garvock Inver 113 K7
Garway Herefs 40 F7
Garway Common Herefs 40 G7
Garway Hill Herefs 40 F6
Garynahine W Isls 152 f3
Garyvard W Isls 152 g4
Gasper Wilts 22 G7
Gastard Wilts 29 P8
Gasthorpe Norfk 58 E4
Gaston Green Essex 45 P8
Gatcombe IoW 12 H8
Gateacre Lpool 75 M6
Gatebeck Cumb 89 N9
Gate Burton Lincs 79 L7
Gateford Notts 78 F7
Gateforth N York 85 R9
Gatehead E Ayrs 104 G2
Gate Helmsley N York 86 C4
Gatehouse Nthumb 108 C12
Gatehouse of Fleet D & G 96 C7
Gateley Norfk 70 E7
Gatenby N York 91 N9
Gatesgarth Cumb 88 G4
Gateshaw Border 108 C5
Gateshead Gatesd 100 G6
Gates Heath Ches W 75 M11
Gateside Angus 125 J4
Gateside E Rens 113 P9
Gateside Fife 124 D11
Gateside N Ayrs 113 M10
Gateslack D & G 106 A9
Gathurst Wigan 75 P2
Gatley Stockp 76 F6
Gatton Surrey 33 K11
Gattonside Border 107 N3
Gatwick Airport W Susx 15 K3
Gaufron Powys 50 D7
Gaulby Leics 66 H12
Gauldry Fife 124 H8
Gauldswell P & K 124 E3
Gaulkthorn Lancs 83 R10
Gaultree Norfk 69 J10
Gaunton's Bank Ches E 63 P3
Gaunt's Common Dorset 11 N4
Gaunt's End Essex 45 Q6
Gautby Lincs 80 D9
Gavinton Border 116 H11
Gawber Barns 77 Q2
Gawcott Bucks 43 P5
Gawsworth Ches E 76 G9
Gawthorpe Wakefd 85 K11
Gawthrop Cumb 90 A9
Gawthwaite Cumb 88 H9
Gay Bowers Essex 46 D10
Gaydon Warwks 54 B10
Gayhurst M Keyn 44 B2
Gayle N York 90 D9
Gayles N York 91 J5
Gay Street W Susx 14 F7
Gayton Nhants 54 H9
Gayton Norfk 69 N8
Gayton Staffs 64 H6
Gayton Wirral 75 J7
Gayton le Marsh Lincs 80 H7
Gayton Thorpe Norfk 69 P8
Gaywood Norfk 69 M8
Gazeley Suffk 57 N8
Gear Cnwll 2 H9
Gearraidh Bhaird W Isls 152 g4
Gearraidh na h-Aibhne
W Isls 152 f3
Geary Highld 134 E3
Gedding Suffk 58 D9
Geddington Nhants 55 M4
Gedling Notts 66 G4
Gedney Lincs 68 H7
Gedney Broadgate Lincs 68 H7
Gedney Drove End Lincs 69 J6
Gedney Dyke Lincs 68 H7
Gedney Hill Lincs 68 G10
Gee Cross Tamesd 76 H5
Geeston Rutlnd 67 N11
Geirinis W Isls 152 c10
Geldeston Norfk 59 M2
Gelli Rhondd 27 M3
Gelli Torfn 28 C4
Gellideg Myr Td 39 N10
Gellifor Denbgs 74 F11
Gelligaer Caerph 27 Q3
Gelligroes Caerph 28 A3
Gelligron Neath 38 H10
Gellilydan Gwynd 61 L4
Gellinudd Neath 38 H11
Gelly Pembks 37 L6
Gellyburn P & K 124 C5
Gellywen Carmth 37 P6
Gelston D & G 96 F6
Gelston Lincs 67 M3
Gembling E R Yk 87 L4
Gentleshaw Staffs 65 K10
Georgefield D & G 107 J11
George Green Bucks 32 E6
Georgeham Devon 19 J5
Georgemas Junction
Station Highld 151 L5
George Nympton Devon 19 N8
Georgetown Blae G 39 Q10
Georgia Cnwll 2 D7
Georth Ork 147 c3
Gerinish W Isls 152 c10
Gerlan Gwynd 73 L10
Germansweek Devon 7 N6
Germoe Cnwll 2 F8
Gerrans Cnwll 3 L7
Gerrards Cross Bucks 32 E5
Gerrick R & Cl 92 E4
Gestingthorpe Essex 46 E4
Gethsemane Pembks 37 L2
Geuffordd Powys 62 H9
Gib Hill Ches W 76 B8
Gibraltar Lincs 81 K12
Gibsmere Notts 67 J2
Giddeahall Wilts 29 P7
Giddy Green Dorset 11 K7
Gidea Park Gt Lon 33 P4
Gidleigh Devon 8 C7
Giffnock E Rens 113 Q9
Gifford E Loth 116 C7
Giffordtown Fife 124 F10
Giggleswick N York 84 B2
Gigha Ag & B 111 N11
Gilberdyke E R Yk 86 F9
Gilbert's End Worcs 41 N3
Gilbert Street Hants 25 L7
Gilchriston E Loth 116 C8
Gilcrux Cumb 97 M10
Gildersome Leeds 85 K9
Gildingwells Rothm 78 F6
Gilesgate Moor Dur 100 H9
Gileston V Glam 27 N9
Gilfach Caerph 27 R3
Gilfach Goch Brdgnd 27 M4
Gilfachrheda Cerdgn 48 G9
Gilgarran Cumb 88 D2
Gill Cumb 98 F12
Gillamoor N York 92 D8
Gillan Cnwll 3 J9
Gillen Highld 134 E4
Gillesbie D & G 106 F11
Gilling East N York 92 C11
Gillingham Dorset 22 H8
Gillingham Medway 34 D8
Gillingham Norfk 59 N2
Gilling West N York 91 K6
Gillock Highld 151 M5
Gillow Heath Staffs 76 G12
Gills Highld 151 P2
Gill's Green Kent 16 D4
Gilmanscleuch Border 107 J5
Gilmerton C Edin 115 P7
Gilmerton P & K 123 M8
Gilmonby Dur 90 G4
Gilmorton Leics 54 F3
Gilsland Nthumb 99 J5
Gilson Warwks 53 M3
Gilstead C Brad 84 H7
Gilston Border 116 B10
Gilston Herts 45 N9
Gilston Park Herts 45 N9
Giltbrook Notts 66 D3
Gilwern Mons 40 C9
Gimingham Norfk 71 K5
Ginclough Ches E 76 H8
Gingers Green E Susx 16 A8
Gipping Suffk 58 G8
Gipsey Bridge Lincs 68 F2
Girdle Toll N Ayrs 104 F2
Girlington C Brad 84 H8
Girlsta Shet 147 i7
Girsby N York 91 N5
Girtford C Beds 56 C10
Girthon D & G 96 C7
Girton Cambs 56 H8
Girton Notts 79 K10
Girvan S Ayrs 104 C10
Gisburn Lancs 84 B5
Gisleham Suffk 59 P3
Gislingham Suffk 58 G6
Gissing Norfk 58 H3
Gittisham Devon 9 L5
Givons Grove Surrey 32 H11
Gladestry Powys 50 H9
Gladsmuir E Loth 116 B6
Glais Swans 26 G2
Glaisdale N York 92 F5
Glamis Angus 124 H3
Glanaber Gwynd 61 L2
Glanaman Carmth 38 G9
Glandford Norfk 70 F4
Glan-Duar Carmth 38 D3
Glandwr Pembks 37 N5
Glan-Dwyfach Gwynd 60 H3
Glandy Cross Carmth 37 M5
Glandyfi Cerdgn 49 M1
Glangrwyney Powys 40 C8
Glanllynfi Brdgnd 27 K4
Glanmule Powys 50 G3
Glanrhyd Pembks 37 M2
Glan-rhyd Powys 39 J10
Glanton Nthumb 108 H7
Glanton Pike Nthumb 108 H7
Glanvilles Wootton
Dorset 10 G3
Glan-y-don Flints 74 G8
Glan-y-llyn Cardif 27 Q5
Glan-y-nant Powys 50 C4
Glan-yr-afon Gwynd 62 B4
Glan-yr-afon Gwynd 62 D4
Glan-yr-afon IoA 73 K7
Glan-yr-afon Swans 38 F10
Glan-y-wern Gwynd 61 K5
Glapthorn Nhants 55 P3
Glapwell Derbys 78 D10
Glasbury Powys 40 A4
Glascoed Denbgs 74 D9
Glascoed Mons 40 D11
Glascote Staffs 65 N11
Glascwm Powys 50 G10
Glasfryn Conwy 62 C2
Glasgow C Glas 113 R8
Glasgow Airport Rens 113 P8
Glasgow Prestwick
Airport S Ayrs 104 G4
Glasgow Science Centre
C Glas 113 Q8
Glasinfryn Gwynd 73 K10
Glasnacardoch Bay
Highld 127 M5
Glasnakille Highld 127 K2
Glasphein Highld 134 C6
Glaspwll Powys 49 M1
Glassenbury Kent 16 D3
Glassford S Lans 114 D12
Glasshoughton Wakefd 85 N10
Glasshouse Gloucs 41 L7
Glasshouse Hill Gloucs 41 L7
Glasshouses N York 85 J2
Glasslaw Abers 141 K4
Glasson Cumb 97 Q6
Glassonby Cumb 98 H10
Glasson Dock Lancs 83 K4
Glasterlaw Angus 125 L3
Glaston Rutlnd 67 M12
Glastonbury Somset 22 C5
Glatton Cambs 56 C3
Glazebrook Warrtn 76 C5
Glazebury Warrtn 76 C4
Glazeley Shrops 52 D3
Gleadless Sheff 78 B7
Gleadsmoss Ches E 76 F10
Gleaston Cumb 82 G1
Glebe Highld 137 N12
Gledhow Leeds 85 L8
Gledpark D & G 96 C8
Gledrid Shrops 63 J5
Glemsford Suffk 58 B11
Glen Achulish Highld 121 K1
Glenallachie Moray 139 N7
Glenancross Highld 127 M6
Glenaros House Ag & B 119 P4
Glen Auldyn IoM 102 f3
Glenbarr Ag & B 103 J2
Glenbarry Abers 140 E5
Glenbeg Highld 127 K11
Glenbervie Abers 133 J8
Glenboig N Lans 114 C7
Glenborrodale Highld 127 L12
Glenbranter Ag & B 112 G2
Glenbreck Border 106 D5
Glenbrittle Highld 134 G11
Glenbuck E Ayrs 105 N4
Glencally Angus 131 Q11
Glencaple D & G 97 K4
Glencarse P & K 124 D8
Glencoe Highld 121 L1
Glencothe Border 106 E4
Glencraig Fife 115 M2
Glencrosh D & G 105 P12
Glendale Highld 134 C6
Glendaruel Ag & B 112 E4
Glendevon P & K 123 P12
Glendoe Lodge Highld 129 L2
Glendoick P & K 124 E8
Glenduckie Fife 124 F9
Glenegedale Ag & B 110 H11
Glenelg Highld 135 P12
Glenerney Moray 139 J6
Glenfarg P & K 124 C10
Glenfield Leics 66 E11
Glenfinnan Highld 128 B8
Glenfintaig Lodge Highld 128 H7
Glenfoot P & K 124 D9
Glenfyne Lodge Ag & B 121 N9
Glengarnock N Ayrs 113 L10
Glengolly Highld 151 K3
Glengorm Castle Ag & B 119 M1
Glengrasco Highld 134 H7
Glenholm Border 106 E3
Glenhoul D & G 105 L12
Glenkin Ag & B 112 H5
Glenkindie Abers 132 C2
Glenlivet Moray 139 M10
Glenlochar D & G 96 E5
Glenlomond P & K 124 D12
Glenluce D & G 94 H7
Glenmassen Ag & B 112 G4
Glenmavis N Lans 114 D8
Glen Maye IoM 102 c5
Glen Mona IoM 102 f4
Glenmore Highld 134 H8
Glenmore Lodge Highld 130 H2
Glen Nevis House Highld 128 G10
Glenochil Clacks 114 F2
Glen Parva Leics 66 F12
Glenquiech Angus 132 C12
Glenralloch Ag & B 112 C7
Glenridding Cumb 89 K3
Glenrothes Fife 115 N1
Glenshero Lodge Highld 129 P6
Glenstriven Ag & B 112 G5
Glentham Lincs 79 P6
Glentrool D & G 95 L3
Glen Trool Lodge D & G 95 M2
Glentruim Highld 130 C5
Glentworth Lincs 79 N6
Glenuig Highld 127 M9
Glenvarragill Highld 134 H8
Glen Vine IoM 102 d5
Glenwhilly D & G 94 H4
Glespin S Lans 105 Q4
Glewstone Herefs 40 H7
Glinton C Pete 68 C11
Glooston Leics 55 J2
Glossop Derbys 77 J5
Gloster Hill Nthumb 109 L9
Gloucester Gloucs 41 N8
Gloucester Services
Gloucs 41 N9
Gloucestershire Airport
Gloucs 41 P7
Glusburn N York 84 F6
Glutt Lodge Highld 150 H9
Gluvian Cnwll 3 M2
Glympton Oxon 43 J7
Glynarthen Cerdgn 48 E11
Glyn Ceiriog Wrexhm 62 H4
Glyncoch Rhondd 27 P4
Glyncorrwg Neath 27 L3
Glynde E Susx 15 N9
Glyndebourne E Susx 15 N8
Glyndyfrdwy Denbgs 62 G4
Glynneath Neath 39 L10
Glynogwr Brdgnd 27 M5
Glyntaff Rhondd 27 P4
Glyntawe Powys 39 K8
Glynteg Carmth 38 A4
Gnosall Staffs 64 F8
Gnosall Heath Staffs 64 F8
Goadby Leics 67 J12
Goadby Marwood Leics 67 K7
Goatacre Wilts 30 B7
Goatham Green E Susx 16 E7
Goathill Dorset 22 F10
Goathland N York 92 G6
Goathurst Somset 21 L6
Goathurst Common Kent 33 P12
Goat Lees Kent 16 H2
Gobowen Shrops 63 J5
Godalming Surrey 14 D2
Goddard's Corner Suffk 59 K7
Goddard's Green Kent 16 E4
Goddards Green W Susx 15 K7
Godden Green Kent 33 Q11
Godford Cross Devon 9 L4
Godington Oxon 43 N6
Godley Tamesd 76 H5
Godmanchester Cambs 56 E6
Godmanstone Dorset 10 G5
Godmersham Kent 35 J12
Godney Somset 22 B5
Godolphin Cross Cnwll 2 F8
Godre'r-graig Neath 38 H10
Godshill Hants 24 B10
Godshill IoW 13 J8
Godstone Staffs 65 J5
Godstone Surrey 33 L12
Godsworthy Devon 7 P9
Godwinscroft Hants 12 C5
Goetre Mons 40 D10
Goff's Oak Herts 45 L11
Gogar C Edin 115 L7
Goginan Cerdgn 49 M4
Golan Gwynd 61 J4
Golant Cnwll 3 R4
Golberdon Cnwll 7 L10
Golborne Wigan 75 Q4
Golcar Kirk 84 G12
Goldcliff Newpt 28 E6
Golden Cross E Susx 15 P8
Golden Green Kent 16 B1
Golden Grove Carmth 38 E8
Goldenhill C Stke 64 F2
Golden Hill Pembks 37 J10
Golden Pot Hants 25 M5
Golden Valley Derbys 66 C2
Golders Green Gt Lon 33 J5
Goldfinch Bottom W Berk 31 L9
Goldhanger Essex 46 F10
Gold Hill Cambs 57 K2
Gold Hill Dorset 23 J10
Golding Shrops 63 P11
Goldington Bed 55 Q10
Goldsborough N York 85 M4
Goldsborough N York 92 G4
Goldsithney Cnwll 2 E8
Goldstone Kent 35 N10
Goldstone Shrops 64 D6
Goldthorpe Barns 78 D3
Goldworthy Devon 18 H9
Golford Kent 16 D3
Golford Green Kent 16 D4
Gollanfield Highld 138 E5
Gollinglith Foot N York 91 K10
Golly Wrexhm 75 K12
Golsoncott Somset 20 G5
Golspie Highld 146 E5
Gomeldon Wilts 24 C6
Gomersal Kirk 85 J10
Gomshall Surrey 14 F1
Gonalston Notts 66 H3
Gonerby Hill Foot Lincs 67 M5
Gonerby Moor Lincs 67 M4
Gonfirth Shet 147 i6
Goodameavy Devon 4 H4
Good Easter Essex 46 A9
Gooderstone Norfk 69 P11
Goodleigh Devon 19 L6
Goodmanham E R Yk 86 G6
Goodmayes Gt Lon 33 N5
Goodnestone Kent 35 J10
Goodnestone Kent 35 N11
Goodrich Herefs 40 H8
Goodrington Torbay 5 Q5
Goodshaw Lancs 84 B10
Goodshaw Fold Lancs 84 B10
Goodstone Devon 8 E10
Goodwick Pembks 37 J3
Goodwood W Susx 14 C9
Goodworth Clatford
Hants 24 F5
Goodyers End Warwks 53 Q3
Goole E R Yk 86 D10
Goole Fields E R Yk 86 E11
Goom's Hill Worcs 53 J9
Goonbell Cnwll 2 H4
Goonhavern Cnwll 3 K4
Goonvrea Cnwll 2 H4
Goosecruives Abers 133 J7
Gooseford Devon 8 C6
Goose Green Essex 47 L6
Goose Green Kent 16 E3
Goose Green Kent 34 B12
Goose Green S Glos 29 K7
Goose Green W Susx 14 G7
Goose Green Wigan 75 P3
Gooseham Cnwll 18 E10
Gooseham Mill Cnwll 18 E10
Goosehill Green Worcs 52 H8
Goose Pool Herefs 40 G4
Goosey Oxon 30 H4
Goosnargh Lancs 83 M8
Goostrey Ches E 76 E9
Gordano Services N Som 28 G7
Gorddinog Conwy 73 L9
Gordon Border 107 Q1
Gordon Arms Hotel
Border 107 J5
Gordonstown Abers 140 E5
Gordonstown Abers 140 H8
Gore Powys 51 J9
Gorebridge Mdloth 115 Q9
Gorefield Cambs 68 H9
Gore Pit Essex 46 F8
Gores Wilts 30 C10
Gore Street Kent 35 N9
Gorey Jersey 13 d2
Goring Oxon 31 M6
Goring-by-Sea W Susx 14 G10
Goring Heath Oxon 31 N6
Gorleston-on-Sea Norfk 71 Q11
Gorrachie Abers 140 H4
Gorran Churchtown
Cnwll 3 N6
Gorran Haven Cnwll 3 P6
Gorran High Lanes Cnwll 3 N6
Gorrig Cerdgn 38 B3
Gors Cerdgn 49 K5
Gorsedd Flints 74 G8
Gorseddau Slate
Landscape Gwynd 61 J3
Gorse Hill Swindn 30 D5
Gorseinon Swans 26 F3
Gorseybank Derbys 65 P2
Gorsgoch Cerdgn 48 H10
Gorslas Carmth 38 E9
Gorsley Gloucs 41 K6
Gorsley Common Herefs 41 K6
Gorstage Ches W 75 Q9
Gorstan Highld 137 L3
Gorstella Ches W 75 K11
Gorsten Ag & B 120 D6
Gorst Hill Worcs 52 D6
Gorsty Hill Staffs 65 L6
Gorthleck Highld 137 P11
Gorton Manch 76 G4
Gosbeck Suffk 58 H9
Gosberton Lincs 68 E6
Gosberton Clough Lincs 68 D6
Gosfield Essex 46 D6
Gosford Devon 9 L5
Gosford Oxon 43 K9
Gosforth Cumb 88 E6
Gosforth N u Ty 100 G4
Gosling Street Somset 22 C7
Gosmore Herts 44 H6
Gospel End Staffs 52 G2
Gospel Green W Susx 14 D4
Gosport Hants 13 K5
Gossard's Green C Beds 44 D3
Gossington Gloucs 41 L11
Goswick Nthumb 117 N12
Gotham Notts 66 E6
Gotherington Gloucs 41 Q6
Gotton Somset 21 L7
Goudhurst Kent 16 C3
Goulceby Lincs 80 E8
Gourdas Abers 141 J7
Gourdie C Dund 124 G6
Gourdon Abers 133 K10
Gourock Inver 113 K6
Govan C Glas 113 Q8
Goveton Devon 5 M7
Govilon Mons 40 C9
Gowdall E R Yk 86 B10
Gower Highld 137 N4
Gower Swans 26 D4
Gowerton Swans 26 E3
Gowkhall Fife 115 J3
Gowthorpe E R Yk 86 E4
Goxhill E R Yk 87 M6
Goxhill N Linc 87 L11
Goytre Neath 27 J4
Grabhair W Isls 152 g4
Graby Lincs 68 B6
Grade Cnwll 2 H11
Gradeley Green Ches E 63 Q2
Graffham W Susx 14 C7
Grafham Cambs 56 C7
Grafham Surrey 14 E2
Grafton Herefs 40 G4
Grafton Oxon 30 F2
Grafton Shrops 63 M8
Grafton Worcs 42 A4
Grafton Worcs 51 P8
Grafton Flyford Worcs 52 H9
Grafton Regis Nhants 43 Q2
Grafton Underwood
Nhants 55 M5
Grafty Green Kent 16 F1
Graianrhyd Denbgs 74 H12
Graig Conwy 73 P9
Graig Denbgs 74 F9
Graigfechan Denbgs 62 G1
Grain Medway 34 F7
Grains Bar Oldham 76 H2
Grainsby Lincs 80 E4
Grainthorpe Lincs 80 G4
Grampound Cnwll 3 M5
Grampound Road Cnwll 3 M4
Gramsdal W Isls 152 c9
Gramsdale W Isls 152 c9
Granborough Bucks 43 Q7
Granby Notts 67 J5
Grandborough Warwks 54 E7
Grand Chemins Jersey 13 c2
Grandes Rocques Guern 12 c1
Grandtully P & K 123 M2
Grange Cumb 88 H3
Grange Medway 34 D8
Grange P & K 124 F8
Grange Wirral 74 H6
Grange Crossroads
Moray 140 D5
Grange Hall Moray 139 K4
Grangehall S Lans 106 C1
Grange Hill Essex 33 N4
Grangemill Derbys 77 N12
Grange Moor Kirk 85 J12
Grangemouth Falk 114 G5
Grange of Lindores Fife 124 E9
Grange-over-Sands
Cumb 89 L11
Grangepans Falk 115 J5
Grange Park Nhants 55 J9
Grangetown R & Cl 92 B3
Grangetown Sundld 101 K7
Grange Villa Dur 100 G8
Gransmoor E R Yk 87 L3
Gransmore Green Essex 46 C7
Granston Pembks 36 H4
Grantchester Cambs 56 H9
Grantham Lincs 67 M5
Granton C Edin 115 N6
Grantown-on-Spey
Highld 139 J10
Grantsfield Herefs 51 N8
Grantshouse Border 116 H8
Grappenhall Warrtn 76 B6
Grasby Lincs 80 B3
Grasmere Cumb 89 K5
Grasscroft Oldham 76 H3
Grassendale Lpool 75 L6
Grassgarth Cumb 98 D9
Grass Green Essex 46 C4
Grassington N York 84 F2
Grassmoor Derbys 78 C10
Grassthorpe Notts 79 K10
Grateley Hants 24 D5
Gratwich Staffs 65 J6
Graveley Cambs 56 E8
Graveley Herts 45 J6
Gravelly Hill Birm 53 L3
Gravelsbank Shrops 63 K12
Graveney Kent 35 J9
Gravesend Kent 34 B7
Gravir W Isls 152 g4
Grayingham Lincs 79 M4
Grayrigg Cumb 89 P7
Grays Thurr 34 A7
Grayshott Hants 14 C4
Grayson Green Cumb 88 D2
Grayswood Surrey 14 C4
Graythorpe Hartpl 92 B1
Grazeley Wokham 31 P9
Greasbrough Rothm 78 C4
Greasby Wirral 75 J6
Greasley Notts 66 D3
Great Abington Cambs 57 K11
Great Addington Nhants 55 N5
Great Alne Warwks 53 L8
Great Altcar Lancs 75 K2
Great Amwell Herts 45 L9
Great Asby Cumb 89 R4
Great Ashfield Suffk 58 E7
Great Ayton N York 92 B4
Great Baddow Essex 46 C10
Great Badminton S Glos 29 N6
Great Bardfield Essex 46 B5
Great Barford Bed 56 C10
Great Barr Sandw 53 K2
Great Barrington Gloucs 42 E9
Great Barrow Ches W 75 M10
Great Barton Suffk 58 C7
Great Barugh N York 92 F11
Great Bavington Nthumb 100 C2
Great Bealings Suffk 59 J11
Great Bedwyn Wilts 30 F9
Great Bentley Essex 47 K7
Great Billing Nhants 55 K8
Great Bircham Norfk 69 P6
Great Blakenham Suffk 58 G10
Great Blencow Cumb 98 F11
Great Bolas Wrekin 64 B8
Great Bookham Surrey 32 G11
Great Bosullow Cnwll 2 C8
Great Bourton Oxon 43 K3
Great Bowden Leics 55 J3
Great Bradley Suffk 57 N10
Great Braxted Essex 46 F9
Great Bricett Suffk 58 F10
Great Brickhill Bucks 44 C5
Great Bridge Sandw 52 H2
Great Bridgeford Staffs 64 G7
Great Brington Nhants 54 H7
Great Bromley Essex 47 K6
Great Broughton Cumb 97 L12
Great Broughton N York 92 B5
Great Budworth Ches W 76 C8
Great Burdon Darltn 91 N3
Great Burstead Essex 34 B4
Great Busby N York 92 B5
Great Canfield Essex 45 Q8
Great Carlton Lincs 80 H6
Great Casterton Rutlnd 67 P10
Great Chalfield Wilts 29 P9
Great Chart Kent 16 H2
Great Chatwell Staffs 64 E9
Great Chell C Stke 64 F2
Great Chesterford Essex 45 P3
Great Cheverell Wilts 23 L2
Great Chishill Cambs 45 M4
Great Clacton Essex 47 L8
Great Cliff Wakefd 85 L12
Great Clifton Cumb 97 L12
Great Coates NE Lin 80 E2
Great Comberton Worcs 41 Q3
Great Comp Kent 34 A11
Great Corby Cumb 98 F7
Great Cornard Suffk 46 F4
Great Cowden E R Yk 87 N7
Great Coxwell Oxon 30 F4
Great Cransley Nhants 55 L5
Great Cressingham Norfk 70 C11
Great Crosthwaite Cumb 88 H2
Great Cubley Derbys 65 M4
Great Cumbrae Island
N Ayrs 112 H10
Great Dalby Leics 67 J9
Great Denham Bed 55 P11
Great Doddington Nhants 55 M7
Great Doward Herefs 40 H8
Great Dunham Norfk 70 C9
Great Dunmow Essex 46 A7
Great Durnford Wilts 23 P6
Great Easton Essex 45 R6
Great Easton Leics 55 L2
Great Eccleston Lancs 83 K7
Great Edstone N York 92 E10
Great Ellingham Norfk 58 F1
Great Elm Somset 22 G3
Great Everdon Nhants 54 F9
Great Eversden Cambs 56 G10
Great Fencote N York 91 M8
Greatfield Wilts 30 C5
Great Finborough Suffk 58 F9
Greatford Lincs 68 B10
Great Fransham Norfk 70 C9
Great Gaddesden Herts 44 E9
Greatgate Staffs 65 K4
Great Gidding Cambs 56 C4
Great Givendale E R Yk 86 E4
Great Glemham Suffk 59 L8
Great Glen Leics 54 G1
Great Gonerby Lincs 67 M4
Great Gransden Cambs 56 E9
Great Green Cambs 45 K3
Great Green Norfk 59 K3
Great Green Suffk 58 D7
Great Green Suffk 58 D9
Great Habton N York 92 F11
Great Hale Lincs 68 C4
Great Hallingbury Essex 45 P8
Greatham Hants 25 N7
Greatham Hartpl 91 R1
Greatham W Susx 14 F7
Great Hampden Bucks 32 B2
Great Harrowden Nhants 55 L6
Great Harwood Lancs 83 Q8
Great Haseley Oxon 43 N11
Great Hatfield E R Yk 87 M6
Great Haywood Staffs 65 J7
Great Heck N York 86 B11
Great Henny Essex 46 F4
Great Hinton Wilts 29 P10
Great Hockham Norfk 58 D2
Great Holland Essex 47 M8
Great Hollands Br For 32 B9
Great Horkesley Essex 46 H5
Great Hormead Herts 45 M6
Great Horton C Brad 84 H9
Great Horwood Bucks 43 Q5
Great Houghton Barns 78 C2
Great Houghton Nhants 55 K9
Great Hucklow Derbys 77 M8
Great Kelk E R Yk 87 L3
Great Kimble Bucks 44 B10
Great Kingshill Bucks 32 C3
Great Langdale Cumb 89 J5
Great Langton N York 91 M7
Great Leighs Essex 46 C8
Great Limber Lincs 80 C2
Great Linford M Keyn 44 B3
Great Livermere Suffk 58 C6
Great Longstone Derbys 77 M9
Great Lumley Dur 100 H8
Great Lyth Shrops 63 M10
Great Malvern Worcs 41 M3
Great Maplestead Essex 46 E5
Great Marton Bpool 82 H8
Great Massingham Norfk 69 Q7
Great Melton Norfk 70 H10
Great Meols Wirral 74 H5
Great Milton Oxon 43 N11
Great Missenden Bucks 32 C2
Great Mitton Lancs 83 Q7
Great Mongeham Kent 35 P12
Great Moulton Norfk 58 H3
Great Munden Herts 45 L7
Great Musgrave Cumb 90 C4
Great Ness Shrops 63 L8
Great Notley Essex 46 D7
Great Oak Mons 40 E9
Great Oakley Essex 47 M6
Great Oakley Nhants 55 L3
Great Offley Herts 44 G6
Great Ormside Cumb 90 B3
Great Orton Cumb 98 D7
Great Ouseburn N York 85 P3
Great Oxendon Nhants 55 J4
Great Oxney Green Essex 46 B10
Great Palgrave Norfk 70 B9
Great Parndon Essex 45 N10
Great Pattenden Kent 16 C2
Great Paxton Cambs 56 D8
Great Plumpton Lancs 83 J8
Great Plumstead Norfk 71 L10
Great Ponton Lincs 67 M6
Great Potheridge Devon 19 K10
Great Preston Leeds 85 N9
Great Purston Nhants 43 L4
Great Raveley Cambs 56 E4
Great Rissington Gloucs 42 E8
Great Rollright Oxon 42 G5
Great Ryburgh Norfk 70 E7
Great Ryle Nthumb 108 G7
Great Ryton Shrops 63 N11
Great Saling Essex 46 C6
Great Salkeld Cumb 98 G11
Great Sampford Essex 46 B4
Great Saredon Staffs 64 H10
Great Saughall Ches W 75 K9
Great Saxham Suffk 57 Q8
Great Shefford W Berk 30 H7
Great Shelford Cambs 57 J10
Great Smeaton N York 91 N6
Great Snoring Norfk 70 D5
Great Somerford Wilts 29 Q6
Great Soudley Shrops 64 D6
Great Stainton Darltn 91 N2
Great Stambridge Essex 34 F4
Great Staughton Cambs 56 C7
Great Steeping Lincs 80 H10
Great Stonar Kent 35 P10
Greatstone-on-Sea Kent 17 K6
Great Strickland Cumb 89 P2
Great Stukeley Cambs 56 E6
Great Sturton Lincs 80 D8
Great Sutton Ches W 75 L8
Great Sutton Shrops 51 N4
Great Swinburne Nthumb 99 P3
Great Tew Oxon 43 J6
Great Tey Essex 46 F6
Great Thurlow Suffk 57 N10
Great Torrington Devon 19 J9
Great Tosson Nthumb 108 G9
Great Totham Essex 46 F9
Great Totham Essex 46 F9
Great Tows Lincs 80 E5
Great Urswick Cumb 88 H11
Great Wakering Essex 34 G5
Great Waldingfield Suffk 46 F3
Great Walsingham Norfk 70 D5
Great Waltham Essex 46 C9
Great Warford Ches E 76 E8
Great Warley Essex 33 Q4
Great Washbourne
Gloucs 42 A5
Great Weeke Devon 8 D7
Great Welnetham Suffk 58 C9
Great Wenham Suffk 47 J4
Great Whittington
Nthumb 100 C4
Great Wigborough Essex 46 G8
Great Wilbraham Cambs 57 K9
Great Wilne Derbys 66 D6
Great Wishford Wilts 23 N6
Great Witchingham Norfk 70 G8
Great Witcombe Gloucs 41 Q8
Great Witley Worcs 52 D7
Great Wolford Warwks 42 F5
Greatworth Nhants 43 L3
Great Wratting Suffk 57 N11
Great Wymondley Herts 45 J6
Great Wyrley Staffs 65 J10
Great Wytheford Shrops 63 P8
Great Yarmouth Norfk 71 Q10
Great Yeldham Essex 46 D4
Grebby Lincs 80 H10
Greeba IoM 102 d5
Green Denbgs 74 E10
Green Bank Cumb 89 K10
Greenbottom Cnwll 3 J5
Greenburn W Loth 114 G9
Greencroft Hall Dur 100 F8
Green Cross Surrey 14 B3
Green Down Somset 22 D3
Green End Bed 55 P11
Green End Bed 55 Q7
Green End Bed 56 B8
Green End Bed 56 C10
Green End Cambs 56 C4
Green End Cambs 56 E6
Green End Cambs 56 G9
Green End Cambs 57 J7
Green End Cambs 57 J8
Green End Herts 45 J5
Green End Herts 45 L5
Green End Herts 45 L7
Greenend Oxon 42 G7
Green End Warwks 53 N3
Greenfield Ag & B 113 K3
Greenfield C Beds 44 F5
Greenfield Flints 74 H8
Greenfield Highld 128 H4
Greenfield Oldham 77 J3
Greenfield Oxon 31 P4
Greenford Gt Lon 32 G6
Greengairs N Lans 114 E7
Greengates C Brad 85 J8
Greengill Cumb 97 M10
Greenhalgh Lancs 83 J8
Greenham Somset 20 H9
Greenham W Berk 31 K9
Green Hammerton N York 85 P4
Greenhaugh Nthumb 108 C12
Green Head Cumb 98 D8
Greenhead Nthumb 99 J5
Green Heath Staffs 65 J9
Greenheys Salfd 76 D3
Greenhill D & G 97 M2
Greenhill Falk 114 E5
Greenhill Herefs 52 D11
Greenhill Kent 35 L9
Greenhill Leics 66 D9
Greenhill S Lans 106 B3
Green Hill Wilts 30 C5
Greenhillocks Derbys 66 C2
Greenhills S Lans 114 B10
Greenhithe Kent 33 Q7
Greenholm E Ayrs 105 K2
Greenholme Cumb 89 P5

Greenhouse Border 107 N5
Greenhow Hill N York 84 H2
Greenland Highld 151 N3
Greenland Sheff 78 C6
Greenlands Bucks 31 Q5
Green Lane Devon 8 E9
Green Lane Worcs 53 K7
Greenlaw Border 116 G12
Greenlea D & G 97 L3
Greenloaning P & K 123 L11
Green Moor Barns 77 P4
Greenmount Bury 84 B12
Green Oak E R Yk 86 E9
Greenock Inver 113 K6
Greenodd Cumb 89 J10
Green Ore Somset 22 D3
Green Park Readg 31 P8
Green Quarter Cumb 89 M6
Greensgate Norfk 70 G9
Greenshields S Lans 106 D1
Greenside Gatesd 100 E6
Greenside Kirk 85 J12
Greens Norton Nhants 54 H10
Greenstead Green Essex 46 E6
Greensted Essex 45 P11
Green Street E Susx 16 D8
Green Street Gloucs 41 P8
Green Street Herts 32 H3
Green Street Herts 45 N7
Green Street Worcs 52 G11
Green Street Green Gt Lon 33 N9
Green Street Green Kent 33 Q8
Greenstreet Green Suffk 58 F10
Green Tye Herts 45 N8
Greenway Gloucs 41 L5
Greenway Somset 21 M8
Greenway V Glam 27 P7
Greenway Worcs 52 C6
Greenwich Gt Lon 33 M7
Greenwich Maritime Gt Lon 33 M7
Greet Gloucs 42 B6
Greete Shrops 51 P6
Greetham Lincs 80 F9
Greetham Rutlnd 67 M9
Greetland Calder 84 G11
Gregson Lane Lancs 83 N10
Greinton Somset 21 N6
Grenaby IoM 102 c6
Grendon Nhants 55 L8
Grendon Warwks 65 P12
Grendon Green Herefs 51 Q9
Grendon Underwood Bucks 43 P7
Grenofen Devon 7 N10
Grenoside Sheff 77 Q5
Greosabhagh W Isls 152 e6
Gresford Wrexhm 63 K1
Gresham Norfk 70 H4
Greshornish Highld 134 F5
Gressenhall Norfk 70 E9
Gressenhall Green Norfk 70 E9
Gressingham Lancs 83 M1
Gresty Green Ches E 64 D1
Greta Bridge Dur 90 H4
Gretna D & G 98 C5
Gretna Green D & G 98 C5
Gretna Services D & G 98 C4
Gretton Gloucs 42 B5
Gretton Nhants 55 M2
Gretton Shrops 51 N1
Grewelthorpe N York 91 L11
Grey Friars Suffk 59 P6
Greygarth N York 91 K12
Grey Green N Linc 79 K2
Greylake Somset 21 N6
Greylees Lincs 67 P3
Greyrigg D & G 106 E12
Greys Green Oxon 31 P6
Greysouthen Cumb 97 L12
Greystoke Cumb 98 F12
Greystone Angus 125 K4
Greywell Hants 25 M3
Gribb Dorset 10 B4
Gribthorpe E R Yk 86 E8
Griff Warwks 54 B3
Griffithstown Torfn 28 C3
Griffydam Leics 66 C8
Griggs Green Hants 25 P7
Grimeford Village Lancs 76 B1
Grimesthorpe Sheff 78 B6
Grimethorpe Barns 78 C2
Grimister Shet 147 j3
Grimley Worcs 52 F8
Grimmet S Ayrs 104 F7
Grimoldby Lincs 80 G6
Grimpo Shrops 63 L7
Grimsargh Lancs 83 N8
Grimsby NE Lin 80 E2
Grimscote Nhants 54 G10
Grimscott Cnwll 7 K3
Grimshader W Isls 152 g4
Grimshaw Bl w D 83 Q10
Grimshaw Green Lancs 75 N1
Grimsthorpe Lincs 67 P7
Grimston E R Yk 87 P8
Grimston Leics 66 H8
Grimston Norfk 69 N7
Grimstone Dorset 10 G6
Grimstone End Suffk 58 D7
Grinacombe Moor Devon 7 M6
Grindale E R Yk 87 L1
Grindle Shrops 64 D11
Grindleford Derbys 77 N8
Grindleton Lancs 84 A6
Grindley Brook Shrops 63 N4
Grindlow Derbys 77 M8
Grindon Nthumb 117 K12
Grindon S on T 91 P2
Grindon Staffs 65 K1
Grindon Hill Nthumb 99 M5
Grindonrigg Nthumb 108 E1
Gringley on the Hill Notts 79 J5
Grinsdale Cumb 98 D6
Grinshill Shrops 63 P7
Grinton N York 90 H7
Griomsiadar W Isls 152 g4
Grishipoll Ag & B 118 G1
Grisling Common E Susx 15 N6
Gristhorpe N York 93 M10
Griston Norfk 70 D12
Gritley Ork 147 d5
Grittenham Wilts 30 B6
Grittleton Wilts 29 P6
Grizebeck Cumb 88 H9
Grizedale Cumb 89 K8
Groby Leics 66 E10
Groes Conwy 74 D10
Groes-faen Rhondd 27 P6
Groesffordd Gwynd 60 D4
Groesffordd Powys 39 P6
Groesffordd Marli Denbgs 74 E9
Groeslon Gwynd 60 H1
Groeslon Gwynd 73 J11
Groes-lwyd Powys 62 H10
Groes-Wen Caerph 27 Q5
Grogarry W Isls 152 c10
Grogport Ag & B 112 B12
Groigearraidh W Isls 152 c10
Gromford Suffk 59 M9
Gronant Flints 74 F7
Groombridge E Susx 15 P3
Grosebay W Isls 152 e6
Grosmont Mons 40 E7
Grosmont N York 92 G6
Groton Suffk 46 G3
Grotton Oldham 76 H3
Grouville Jersey 13 d3
Grove Bucks 44 C7
Grove Dorset 10 H10
Grove Kent 35 M10
Grove Notts 79 J8
Grove Oxon 31 J4
Grove Pembks 37 J10
Grove Green Kent 34 D11
Grovenhurst Kent 16 C3
Grove Park Gt Lon 33 M8
Grovesend S Glos 29 K4
Grovesend Swans 26 E2
Grubb Street Kent 33 Q8
Gruinard Highld 143 P7
Gruinart Ag & B 110 G8
Grula Highld 134 G10
Gruline Ag & B 119 P5
Grumbla Cnwll 2 C8
Grundisburgh Suffk 59 J10
Gruting Shet 147 h7
Grutness Shet 147 i10
Gualachulain Highld 121 L4
Guanockgate Lincs 68 G10
Guardbridge Fife 125 J9
Guarlford Worcs 41 N3
Guay P & K 123 P3
Guernsey Guern 12 c2
Guernsey Airport Guern 12 b3
Guestling Green E Susx 16 E8
Guestling Thorn E Susx 16 E7
Guestwick Norfk 70 F7
Guide Bridge Tamesd 76 G4
Guide Post Nthumb 100 H1
Guilden Morden Cambs 45 K3
Guilden Sutton Ches W 75 M10
Guildford Surrey 14 E1
Guildstead Kent 34 E10
Guildtown P & K 124 C6
Guilsborough Nhants 54 H6
Guilsfield Powys 62 H10
Guilton Kent 35 N10
Guiltreehill S Ayrs 104 G7
Guineaford Devon 19 K6
Guisborough R & Cl 92 C4
Guiseley Leeds 85 J7
Guist Norfk 70 E7
Guiting Power Gloucs 42 C7
Gullane E Loth 116 C5
Gulling Green Suffk 58 B9
Gulval Cnwll 2 D8
Gulworthy Devon 7 N10
Gumfreston Pembks 37 L10
Gumley Leics 54 H3
Gummow's Shop Cnwll 3 L3
Gunby E R Yk 86 D8
Gunby Lincs 67 M8
Gundleton Hants 25 K7
Gun Green Kent 16 D4
Gun Hill E Susx 15 Q8
Gun Hill Warwks 53 P3
Gunn Devon 19 M7
Gunnerside N York 90 F7
Gunnerton Nthumb 99 P3
Gunness N Linc 79 L1
Gunnislake Cnwll 7 N10
Gunnista Shet 147 j7
Gunthorpe C Pete 68 D11
Gunthorpe N Linc 79 K4
Gunthorpe Norfk 70 F5
Gunthorpe Notts 66 H3
Gunton Suffk 59 Q2
Gunwalloe Cnwll 2 G10
Gupworthy Somset 20 F6
Gurnard IoW 12 H6
Gurnett Ches E 76 G9
Gurney Slade Somset 22 E3
Gurnos Powys 39 J10
Gushmere Kent 35 J11
Gussage All Saints Dorset 11 N3
Gussage St Andrew Dorset 23 L10
Gussage St Michael Dorset 11 N2
Guston Kent 17 P2
Gutcher Shet 147 j3
Guthrie Angus 125 L3
Guyhirn Cambs 68 H11
Guyhirn Gull Cambs 68 G11
Guy's Marsh Dorset 23 J9
Guyzance Nthumb 109 K9
Gwaenysgor Flints 74 E7
Gwalchmai IoA 72 F8
Gwastadnant Gwynd 73 K12
Gwaun-Cae-Gurwen Carmth 38 G9
Gwbert on Sea Cerdgn 48 B10
Gwealavellan Cnwll 2 F6
Gweek Cnwll 2 H9
Gwehelog Mons 40 E10
Gwenddwr Powys 39 P3
Gwennap Cnwll 3 J6
Gwennap Mining District Cnwll 3 J6
Gwenter Cnwll 3 J11
Gwernaffield Flints 74 H10
Gwernesney Mons 40 F11
Gwernogle Carmth 38 D5
Gwernymynydd Flints 74 H11
Gwersyllt Wrexhm 63 K2
Gwespyr Flints 74 F7
Gwindra Cnwll 3 M4
Gwinear Cnwll 2 F7
Gwithian Cnwll 2 F6
Gwredog IoA 72 G6
Gwrhay Caerph 28 B3
Gwyddelwern Denbgs 62 E3
Gwyddgrug Carmth 38 C4
Gwynfryn Wrexhm 63 J2
Gwystre Powys 50 E7
Gwytherin Conwy 73 Q11
Gyfelia Wrexhm 63 K3
Gyrn Goch Gwynd 60 F2

H

Habberley Shrops 63 L11
Habberley Worcs 52 E5
Habergham Lancs 84 B8
Habertoft Lincs 81 J10
Habin W Susx 25 P9
Habrough NE Lin 80 C1
Hacconby Lincs 68 B7
Haceby Lincs 67 P5
Hacheston Suffk 59 L9
Hackbridge Gt Lon 33 K9
Hackenthorpe Sheff 78 C7
Hackford Norfk 70 F11
Hackforth N York 91 L8
Hack Green Ches E 64 C3
Hackland Ork 147 c4
Hackleton Nhants 55 K9
Hacklinge Kent 35 P11
Hackman's Gate Worcs 52 G5
Hackness N York 93 K8
Hackness Somset 21 M4
Hackney Gt Lon 33 L5
Hackthorn Lincs 79 N7
Hackthorpe Cumb 89 N2
Hacton Gt Lon 33 Q5
Hadden Border 108 C3
Haddenham Bucks 43 Q10
Haddenham Cambs 57 J5
Haddington E Loth 116 C6
Haddington Lincs 79 M11
Haddiscoe Norfk 59 N1
Haddon Cambs 56 C2
Hade Edge Kirk 77 L3
Hadfield Derbys 77 J4
Hadham Cross Herts 45 M8
Hadham Ford Herts 45 N7
Hadleigh Essex 34 E5
Hadleigh Suffk 47 J3
Hadleigh Heath Suffk 46 H3
Hadley Worcs 52 F8
Hadley Wrekin 64 C10
Hadley End Staffs 65 L8
Hadley Wood Gt Lon 33 J3
Hadlow Kent 34 B12
Hadlow Down E Susx 15 P6
Hadnall Shrops 63 N8
Hadrian's Wall 100 B4
Hadstock Essex 45 Q3
Hadston Nthumb 109 L9
Hadzor Worcs 52 G8
Haffenden Quarter Kent 16 F3
Hafodunos Conwy 73 Q10
Hafod-y-bwch Wrexhm 63 K3
Hafod-y-coed Blae G 28 B2
Hafodyrynys Caerph 28 B3
Haggate Lancs 84 C8
Haggbeck Cumb 98 F3
Haggersta Shet 147 i7
Haggerston Nthumb 108 G1
Haggington Hill Devon 19 L4
Haggs Falk 114 E5
Hagley Herefs 40 H3
Hagley Worcs 52 G4
Hagmore Green Suffk 46 G4
Hagnaby Lincs 80 G11
Hagnaby Lincs 81 J7
Hagworthingham Lincs 80 G10
Haigh Wigan 75 Q2
Haighton Green Lancs 83 M8
Haile Cumb 88 D5
Hailes Gloucs 42 B6
Hailey Herts 45 L9
Hailey Oxon 31 N5
Hailey Oxon 42 H9
Hailsham E Susx 15 Q9
Hail Weston Cambs 56 C8
Hainault Gt Lon 33 N4
Haine Kent 35 P9
Hainford Norfk 71 J8
Hainton Lincs 80 D7
Hainworth C Brad 84 G7
Haisthorpe E R Yk 87 L2
Hakin Pembks 36 H9
Halam Notts 66 H1
Halbeath Fife 115 L3
Halberton Devon 20 F10
Halcro Highld 151 M4
Hale Cumb 89 N11
Hale Halton 75 M7
Hale Hants 24 C9
Hale Somset 22 G8
Hale Surrey 25 P4
Hale Traffd 76 E6
Hale Bank Halton 75 N7
Hale Barns Traffd 76 E6
Hale Green E Susx 15 Q8
Hale Nook Lancs 83 J6
Hales Norfk 59 M1
Hales Staffs 64 D5
Halesgate Lincs 68 F7
Hales Green Derbys 65 M4
Halesowen Dudley 52 H4
Hales Place Kent 35 L10
Hale Street Kent 16 B1
Halesville Essex 34 F4
Halesworth Suffk 59 M5
Halewood Knows 75 M6
Halford Devon 8 F10
Halford Shrops 51 M4
Halford Warwks 42 F3
Halfpenny Cumb 89 N9
Halfpenny Green Staffs 52 F2
Halfpenny Houses N York 91 L10
Halfway Carmth 38 F5
Halfway Carmth 39 K5
Halfway Sheff 78 C7
Halfway W Berk 31 J8
Halfway Bridge W Susx 14 D6
Halfway House Shrops 63 K10
Halfway Houses Kent 34 G8
Halifax Calder 84 G10
Halket E Ayrs 113 N10
Halkirk Highld 151 L5
Halkyn Flints 74 H9
Hall E Rens 113 N10
Hallam Fields Derbys 66 D4
Halland E Susx 15 P7
Hallaton Leics 55 K1
Hallatrow BaNES 29 K11
Hallbankgate Cumb 98 H6
Hallbeck Cumb 89 Q9
Hall Cliffe Wakefd 85 L11
Hall Cross Lancs 83 K9
Hall Dunnerdale Cumb 88 G7
Hallen S Glos 28 H6
Hall End Bed 44 E3
Hall End C Beds 44 F4
Hallfield Gate Derbys 78 C12
Hallgarth Dur 101 J9
Hallglen Falk 114 G5
Hall Green Birm 53 L4
Hallin Highld 134 D4
Halling Medway 34 C9
Hallington Lincs 80 F6
Hallington Nthumb 100 C3
Halliwell Bolton 76 C2
Halloughton Notts 66 H2
Hallow Worcs 52 F9
Hallow Heath Worcs 52 F9
Hallsands Devon 5 N9
Hall's Green Essex 45 M10
Hall's Green Herts 45 K6
Hallthwaites Cumb 88 G9
Hallworthy Cnwll 6 H7
Hallyne Border 106 G2
Halmer End Staffs 64 E2
Halmond's Frome Herefs 52 C11
Halmore Gloucs 41 L11
Halnaker W Susx 14 C9
Halsall Lancs 75 L2
Halse Nhants 43 M4
Halse Somset 21 J8
Halsetown Cnwll 2 D7
Halsham E R Yk 87 P9
Halsinger Devon 19 K5
Halstead Essex 46 E5
Halstead Kent 33 N10
Halstead Leics 67 J11
Halstock Dorset 10 E3
Halsway Somset 20 H6
Haltcliff Bridge Cumb 98 D11
Haltham Lincs 80 E11
Haltoft End Lincs 68 G3
Halton Bucks 44 C9
Halton Halton 75 P7
Halton Lancs 83 L2
Halton Leeds 85 M8
Halton Nthumb 100 C5
Halton Wrexhm 63 J4
Halton East N York 84 F4
Halton Fenside Lincs 80 H11
Halton Gill N York 90 E11
Halton Green Lancs 83 L2
Halton Holegate Lincs 80 H10
Halton Lea Gate Nthumb 99 J6
Halton Quay Cnwll 4 F4
Halton Shields Nthumb 100 C4
Halton West N York 84 C4
Haltwhistle Nthumb 99 K5
Halvana Cnwll 7 J9
Halvergate Norfk 71 N10
Halwell Devon 5 N6
Halwill Devon 7 N5
Halwill Junction Devon 7 N5
Ham Devon 9 N4
Ham Gloucs 29 K3
Ham Gloucs 41 R7
Ham Gt Lon 32 H8
Ham Kent 35 P11
Ham Somset 21 L8
Ham Somset 22 F4
Ham Wilts 30 G9
Hambleden Bucks 31 R5
Hambledon Hants 25 L10
Hambledon Surrey 14 D3
Hamble-le-Rice Hants 12 H3
Hambleton Lancs 83 J7
Hambleton N York 85 Q9
Hambleton Moss Side Lancs 83 J7
Hambridge Somset 21 N9
Hambrook S Glos 29 K6
Hambrook W Susx 13 N3
Ham Common Dorset 22 H8
Hameringham Lincs 80 F10
Hamerton Cambs 56 C5
Ham Green Herefs 41 M3
Ham Green Kent 16 F5
Ham Green Kent 34 E8
Ham Green N Som 28 H7
Ham Green Worcs 53 J8
Ham Hill Kent 34 C10
Hamilton S Lans 114 D10
Hamilton Services (northbound) S Lans 114 C10
Hamlet Dorset 10 F3
Hammer W Susx 14 C4
Hammerpot W Susx 14 F9
Hammersmith Gt Lon 33 J6
Hammer Vale Hants 14 B4
Hammerwich Staffs 65 K10
Hammerwood E Susx 15 M3
Hammond Street Herts 45 L10
Hammoon Dorset 22 H10
Hamnavoe Shet 147 i8
Hampden Park E Susx 15 R10
Hamperden End Essex 45 Q5
Hampnett Gloucs 42 C8
Hampole Donc 78 E2
Hampreston Dorset 11 P5
Hampsfield Cumb 89 L10
Hampson Green Lancs 83 L4
Hampstead Gt Lon 33 J5
Hampstead Norreys W Berk 31 L7
Hampsthwaite N York 85 K3
Hampton Devon 9 P5
Hampton Gt Lon 32 G8
Hampton Kent 35 L8
Hampton Shrops 52 D3
Hampton Swindn 30 E4
Hampton Worcs 42 B3
Hampton Bishop Herefs 40 H4
Hampton Court Palace Gt Lon 32 H8
Hampton Fields Gloucs 29 P2
Hampton Green Ches W 63 N2
Hampton Hargate C Pete 56 D2
Hampton Heath Ches W 63 N2
Hampton-in-Arden Solhll 53 M4
Hampton Loade Shrops 52 D3
Hampton Lovett Worcs 52 G7
Hampton Lucy Warwks 53 N9
Hampton Magna Warwks 53 N7
Hampton on the Hill Warwks 53 N8
Hampton Park Wilts 23 P7
Hampton Poyle Oxon 43 L8
Hampton Vale C Pete 56 C2
Hampton Wick Gt Lon 32 H8
Hamptworth Wilts 24 D9
Hamrow Norfk 70 D7
Hamsey E Susx 15 M8
Hamsey Green Surrey 33 L10
Hamstall Ridware Staffs 65 L8
Hamstead Birm 53 K2
Hamstead IoW 12 F6
Hamstead Marshall W Berk 31 J9
Hamsterley Dur 100 E12
Hamsterley Dur 100 E7
Hamsterley Mill Dur 100 E7
Hamstreet Kent 16 H4
Ham Street Somset 22 D6
Hamwood N Som 28 E11
Hamworthy BCP 11 N6
Hanbury Staffs 65 M6
Hanbury Worcs 52 H7
Hanby Lincs 67 P6
Hanchet End Suffk 46 B2
Hanchurch Staffs 64 F4
Handa Island Highld 148 D7
Handale R & Cl 92 E4
Hand and Pen Devon 9 K5
Handbridge Ches W 75 L10
Handcross W Susx 15 J5
Handforth Ches E 76 F7
Hand Green Ches W 75 P11
Handley Ches W 75 M12
Handley Derbys 78 B11
Handley Green Essex 46 B11
Handsacre Staffs 65 K9
Handsworth Birm 53 K2
Handsworth Sheff 78 C6
Handy Cross Bucks 32 B4
Hanford C Stke 64 F4
Hanford Dorset 11 K3
Hanging Heaton Kirk 85 K10
Hanging Houghton Nhants 55 J6
Hanging Langford Wilts 23 M6
Hangleton Br & H 15 K9
Hangleton W Susx 14 F10
Hanham S Glos 29 K8
Hankelow Ches E 64 C3
Hankerton Wilts 29 R4
Hankham E Susx 16 A9
Hanley C Stke 64 G3
Hanley Broadheath Worcs 52 C7
Hanley Castle Worcs 41 N3
Hanley Child Worcs 52 C8
Hanley Swan Worcs 41 N3
Hanley William Worcs 52 C7
Hanlith N York 84 D3
Hanmer Wrexhm 63 M4
Hannaford Devon 19 L7
Hannah Lincs 81 J8
Hannington Hants 25 J2
Hannington Nhants 55 K6
Hannington Swindn 30 E4
Hannington Wick Swindn 30 E3
Hanscombe End C Beds 44 G5
Hanslope M Keyn 44 A2
Hanthorpe Lincs 68 B7
Hanwell Gt Lon 32 H6
Hanwell Oxon 43 J3
Hanwood Shrops 63 M10
Hanworth Gt Lon 32 G8
Hanworth Norfk 71 J5
Happendon S Lans 105 Q3
Happisburgh Norfk 71 M6
Happisburgh Common Norfk 71 M6
Hapsford Ches W 75 M9
Hapton Lancs 84 B9
Hapton Norfk 58 H1
Harberton Devon 5 N5
Harbertonford Devon 5 N5
Harbledown Kent 35 K10
Harborne Birm 53 J4
Harborough Magna Warwks 54 D5
Harbottle Nthumb 108 E9
Harbourneford Devon 5 M4
Harbours Hill Worcs 52 H7
Harbridge Hants 12 B3
Harbridge Green Hants 12 B3
Harburn W Loth 115 J9
Harbury Warwks 54 B8
Harby Leics 67 J6
Harby Notts 79 L9
Harcombe Devon 9 J8
Harcombe Devon 9 M7
Harcombe Bottom Devon 9 Q5
Harden C Brad 84 G7
Harden Wsall 65 J12
Hardendale Cumb 89 P4
Hardenhuish Wilts 29 P7
Hardgate Abers 133 J4
Hardgate D & G 96 G5
Hardgate N York 85 K3
Hardgate W Duns 113 P7
Hardham W Susx 14 E7
Hardhorn Lancs 83 J8
Hardingham Norfk 70 F11
Hardingstone Nhants 55 J9
Hardington Somset 22 G3
Hardington Mandeville Somset 10 D2
Hardington Marsh Somset 10 D3
Hardington Moor Somset 22 C11
Hardisworthy Devon 18 E9
Hardley Hants 12 G4
Hardley Street Norfk 71 M12
Hardmead M Keyn 55 M11
Hardraw N York 90 D8
Hardsough Lancs 84 B11
Hardstoft Derbys 78 D11
Hardway Hants 13 K4
Hardway Somset 22 G6
Hardwick Bucks 44 A8
Hardwick Cambs 56 G9
Hardwick Derbys 78 D11
Hardwick Nhants 55 L7
Hardwick Norfk 59 J3
Hardwick Oxon 42 H10
Hardwick Oxon 43 M6
Hardwick Rothm 78 D6
Hardwick Wsall 65 L4
Hardwicke Gloucs 41 M9
Hardwicke Gloucs 41 P6
Hardwick Village Notts 78 G8
Hardy's Green Essex 46 G7
Harebeating E Susx 15 Q8
Hareby Lincs 80 G10
Hare Croft C Brad 84 G8
Harefield Gt Lon 32 F4
Hare Green Essex 47 K6
Hare Hatch Wokham 32 A7
Harehill Derbys 65 M5
Harehills Leeds 85 L8
Harehope Nthumb 108 H6
Harelaw Border 107 N5
Harelaw D & G 98 E3
Harelaw Dur 100 F7
Hareplain Kent 16 E3
Haresceugh Cumb 99 J9
Harescombe Gloucs 41 N9
Haresfield Gloucs 41 N9
Harestock Hants 24 H7
Hare Street Essex 33 P2
Hare Street Essex 45 M9
Hare Street Herts 45 M6
Harewood Leeds 85 L6
Harewood End Herefs 40 H6
Harford Devon 5 L5
Hargate Norfk 58 G2
Hargatewall Derbys 77 L8
Hargrave Ches W 75 N11
Hargrave Nhants 55 P6
Hargrave Suffk 57 P8
Harker Cumb 98 E6
Harkstead Suffk 47 L5
Harlaston Staffs 65 N10
Harlaxton Lincs 67 L6
Harlech Gwynd 61 K6
Harlech Castle Gwynd 61 K6
Harlescott Shrops 63 N9
Harlesden Gt Lon 33 J6
Harlesthorpe Derbys 78 E8
Harleston Devon 5 N7
Harleston Norfk 59 K4
Harleston Suffk 58 F8
Harlestone Nhants 54 H8
Harle Syke Lancs 84 C8
Harley Rothm 78 B4
Harley Shrops 63 Q11
Harling Road Norfk 58 E3
Harlington C Beds 44 E5
Harlington Donc 78 D3
Harlington Gt Lon 32 F7
Harlosh Highld 134 E7
Harlow Essex 45 N9
Harlow Hill Nthumb 100 D4
Harlthorpe E R Yk 86 D8
Harlton Cambs 56 G10
Harlyn Cnwll 6 C9
Harman's Cross Dorset 11 N8
Harmby N York 91 J9
Harmer Green Herts 45 J8
Harmer Hill Shrops 63 N8
Harmondsworth Gt Lon 32 F7
Harmston Lincs 79 N11
Harnage Shrops 63 P11
Harnham Nthumb 100 D2
Harnhill Gloucs 30 C2
Harold Hill Gt Lon 33 P4
Haroldston West Pembks 36 G7
Haroldswick Shet 147 k2
Harold Wood Gt Lon 33 Q4
Harome N York 92 D10
Harpenden Herts 44 G9
Harpford Devon 9 L7
Harpham E R Yk 87 K3
Harpley Norfk 69 Q7
Harpley Worcs 52 C8
Harpole Nhants 54 H8
Harpsdale Highld 151 L5
Harpsden Oxon 31 Q6
Harpswell Lincs 79 M6
Harpurhey Manch 76 F3
Harpur Hill Derbys 77 K9
Harraby Cumb 98 E7
Harracott Devon 19 L8
Harrapool Highld 135 M11
Harras Cumb 88 C3
Harrietfield P & K 123 P7
Harrietsham Kent 34 F11
Harringay Gt Lon 33 K5
Harrington Cumb 88 C1
Harrington Lincs 80 G9
Harrington Nhants 55 J4
Harringworth Nhants 55 M1
Harris W Isls 152 e6
Harriseahead Staffs 64 F1
Harriston Cumb 97 N10
Harrogate N York 85 L4
Harrold Bed 55 N9
Harrop Dale Oldham 77 J2
Harrow Gt Lon 32 H5
Harrowbarrow Cnwll 7 M10
Harrowden Bed 44 F2
Harrowgate Village Darltn 91 M3
Harrow Green Suffk 58 C9
Harrow Hill Gloucs 41 K8
Harrow on the Hill Gt Lon 32 H5
Harrow Weald Gt Lon 32 H4
Harston Cambs 56 H10
Harston Leics 67 L6
Harswell E R Yk 86 F7
Hart Hartpl 101 L11
Hartburn Nthumb 100 E1
Hartburn S on T 91 P3
Hartest Suffk 58 B10
Hartfield E Susx 15 N4
Hartford Cambs 56 E6
Hartford Ches W 76 B9
Hartford Somset 20 E7
Hartfordbridge Hants 31 Q10
Hartford End Essex 46 B8
Hartforth N York 91 K5
Hartgrove Dorset 23 J9
Harthill Ches W 63 N1
Harthill N Lans 114 G8
Harthill Rothm 78 E7
Harthope D & G 106 D7
Hartington Derbys 77 L11
Hartington Nthumb 108 G12
Hartland Devon 18 E8
Hartland Quay Devon 18 E8
Hartlebury Worcs 52 F6
Hartlepool Hartpl 101 M11
Hartley Cumb 90 C5
Hartley Kent 16 D4
Hartley Kent 33 R9
Hartley Nthumb 101 J3
Hartley Green Kent 33 R9
Hartley Green Staffs 64 H6
Hartley Wespall Hants 31 P10
Hartley Wintney Hants 31 Q11
Hartlip Kent 34 E9
Hartoft End N York 92 F8
Harton N York 86 D3
Harton S Tyne 101 K5
Harton Shrops 51 N3
Hartpury Gloucs 41 M7
Hartshead Kirk 85 J10
Hartshead Moor Services Calder 85 J10
Hartshead Moor Top Kirk 85 J10
Hartshill C Stke 64 F3
Hartshill Warwks 53 Q2
Hartshorne Derbys 65 Q8
Hartside Nthumb 108 F6
Hartsop Cumb 89 L4
Hart Station Hartpl 101 M11
Hartswell Somset 20 H8
Hartwell Nhants 55 K10
Hartwith N York 85 J3
Hartwood N Lans 114 F9
Hartwoodmyres Border 107 L5
Harvel Kent 34 B9
Harvington Worcs 52 G6
Harvington Worcs 53 K10
Harwell Notts 78 H5
Harwell Oxon 31 K4
Harwich Essex 47 N5
Harwood Bolton 76 D2
Harwood Dur 99 M11
Harwood Nthumb 108 G11
Harwood Dale N York 93 K7
Harwood Lee Bolton 76 D1
Harworth Notts 78 G5
Hasbury Dudley 52 H4
Hascombe Surrey 14 E3
Haselbech Nhants 54 H5
Haselbury Plucknett Somset 10 D3
Haseley Warwks 53 N7
Haseley Green Warwks 53 N7
Haseley Knob Warwks 53 N6
Haselor Warwks 53 L9
Hasfield Gloucs 41 N6
Hasguard Pembks 36 G8
Hasholme E R Yk 86 F8
Haskayne Lancs 75 K2
Hasketon Suffk 59 K10
Hasland Derbys 78 C9
Haslemere Surrey 14 C4
Haslingden Lancs 84 B10
Haslingfield Cambs 56 H10
Haslington Ches E 64 D1
Hassall Ches E 76 E12
Hassall Green Ches E 76 E12
Hassell Street Kent 17 K2
Hassingham Norfk 71 M11
Hassness Cumb 88 G3
Hassocks W Susx 15 K7
Hassop Derbys 77 N9
Haste Hill Surrey 14 C4
Haster Highld 151 P6
Hasthorpe Lincs 81 J9
Hastingleigh Kent 17 K2
Hastings E Susx 16 E9
Hastings Somset 21 M10
Hastingwood Essex 45 N10
Hastoe Herts 44 C9
Haswell Dur 101 K9
Haswell Plough Dur 101 K10
Hatch C Beds 56 C11
Hatch Beauchamp Somset 21 M9
Hatch End Bed 55 Q8
Hatch End Gt Lon 32 G4
Hatchet Gate Hants 12 F4
Hatching Green Herts 44 G9
Hatchmere Ches W 75 P9
Hatch Warren Hants 25 K4
Hatcliffe NE Lin 80 D4
Hatfield Donc 78 H2
Hatfield Herefs 51 Q8
Hatfield Herts 45 J10
Hatfield Worcs 52 G10
Hatfield Broad Oak Essex 45 Q8
Hatfield Heath Essex 45 P8
Hatfield Peverel Essex 46 D9
Hatfield Woodhouse Donc 78 H2
Hatford Oxon 30 H3
Hatherden Hants 24 E3
Hatherleigh Devon 7 Q4
Hathern Leics 66 E8
Hatherop Gloucs 42 D10
Hathersage Derbys 77 N7
Hathersage Booths Derbys 77 N7
Hatherton Ches E 64 C3
Hatherton Staffs 64 H10
Hatley St George Cambs 56 E10
Hatt Cnwll 4 F4
Hattersley Tamesd 77 J5
Hattingley Hants 25 L6
Hatton Abers 141 P8
Hatton Angus 125 J4
Hatton Derbys 65 N6
Hatton Gt Lon 32 G7
Hatton Lincs 80 D8
Hatton Shrops 51 N2
Hatton Warrtn 75 Q7
Hatton Warwks 53 N7
Hatton Heath Ches W 75 M11
Hatton of Fintray Abers 133 K1
Hatton Park Warwks 53 N7
Haugh E Ayrs 105 J5
Haugh Lincs 80 H8
Haugh Rochdl 76 H1
Haugham Lincs 80 G7
Haughhead E Duns 114 A5
Haugh Head Nthumb 108 G4
Haughley Suffk 58 F8
Haughley Green Suffk 58 F8
Haugh of Glass Moray 140 C8
Haugh of Urr D & G 96 G5
Haughs of Kinnaird Angus 125 M1
Haughton Ches E 75 P12
Haughton Notts 78 H9
Haughton Powys 63 J8
Haughton Shrops 52 C1
Haughton Shrops 63 L7
Haughton Shrops 63 P9
Haughton Shrops 64 D10
Haughton Staffs 64 F8
Haughton Green Tamesd 76 H5
Haughton le Skerne Darltn 91 M3
Haultwick Herts 45 L7
Haunton Staffs 65 N10
Hautes Croix Jersey 13 c1
Hauxton Cambs 56 H10
Havannah Ches E 76 F10
Havant Hants 13 M3
Haven Herefs 51 L10
Haven Bank Lincs 68 E2
Haven Side E R Yk 87 M9
Havenstreet IoW 13 J6
Havercroft Wakefd 78 C1
Haverfordwest Pembks 37 J7
Haverhill Suffk 46 B3
Haverigg Cumb 88 F11
Havering-atte-Bower Gt Lon 33 P4
Haversham M Keyn 44 B3
Haverthwaite Cumb 89 K10
Haverton Hill S on T 91 R2
Havyatt N Som 28 G10
Havyatt Somset 22 C6
Hawarden Flints 75 K10
Hawbridge Worcs 52 G10
Hawbush Green Essex 46 D7
Hawcoat Cumb 88 G12
Hawen Cerdgn 48 E11
Hawes N York 90 E9
Hawe's Green Norfk 71 K12
Hawford Worcs 52 F8
Hawick Border 107 M7
Hawkchurch Devon 9 Q5
Hawkedon Suffk 57 Q10
Hawkenbury Kent 16 E2
Hawkeridge Wilts 23 J3
Hawkerland Devon 9 K7
Hawker's Cove Cnwll 6 C9
Hawkesbury S Glos 29 M5
Hawkesbury Warwks 54 B4
Hawkesbury Upton S Glos 29 M5
Hawkes End Covtry 53 P4
Hawk Green Stockp 76 H6
Hawkhead Rens 113 P9
Hawkhill Nthumb 109 L7
Hawkhurst Kent 16 D5
Hawkhurst Common E Susx 15 P7
Hawkinge Kent 17 M3
Hawkley Hants 25 N7
Hawkley Wigan 75 P3
Hawkridge Somset 20 D7
Hawksdale Cumb 98 D8
Hawkshaw Bury 84 A12
Hawkshead Cumb 89 K7
Hawkshead Hill Cumb 89 K7
Hawksland S Lans 105 Q2
Hawkspur Green Essex 46 B5
Hawkstone Shrops 63 P6
Hawkswick N York 84 E1
Hawksworth Leeds 85 J7
Hawksworth Notts 67 J3
Hawkwell Essex 34 E4
Hawkwell Nthumb 100 D4
Hawley Hants 32 B10
Hawley Kent 33 Q8
Hawling Gloucs 42 C7
Hawnby N York 92 B9
Haworth C Brad 84 F8
Hawridge Bucks 44 D10
Hawstead Suffk 58 C9
Hawstead Green Suffk 58 C9
Hawthorn Dur 101 K9
Hawthorn Hants 25 L6
Hawthorn Rhondd 27 Q5
Hawthorn Hill Br For 32 B7
Hawthorn Hill Lincs 68 D1
Hawthorpe Lincs 67 P7
Hawton Notts 67 K2
Haxby C York 86 B4
Haxby Gates C York 86 B4
Haxey N Linc 79 K4
Haxey Carr N Linc 79 J3
Haxted Surrey 15 M2
Haxton Wilts 23 P3
Hay Cnwll 3 N4
Hay Cnwll 6 E10
Haydock St Hel 75 P4
Haydon BaNES 22 F3
Haydon Dorset 22 F10
Haydon Somset 21 L8
Haydon Bridge Nthumb 99 N5
Haydon Wick Swindn 30 D5
Haye Cnwll 4 E3
Hayes Gt Lon 32 G6
Hayes Gt Lon 33 M9
Hayes End Gt Lon 32 F6
Hayfield Ag & B 121 K8
Hayfield Derbys 77 J6
Hayfield Green Donc 78 G4
Haygate Wrekin 64 B10
Hay Green Norfk 69 K8
Hayhillock Angus 125 K4
Hayle Cnwll 2 E7
Hayle Port Cnwll 2 E7
Hayley Green Dudley 52 H4
Hayling Island Hants 13 M4
Haymoor Green Ches E 64 C2
Hayne Devon 8 E7
Hayne Devon 20 E10
Haynes C Beds 44 G3
Haynes Church End C Beds 44 F3
Haynes West End C Beds 44 F4
Hay-on-Wye Powys 40 B3
Hayscastle Pembks 36 H5
Hayscastle Cross Pembks 36 H5
Hay Street Herts 45 M6
Hayton Cumb 97 M10
Hayton Cumb 98 G7
Hayton E R Yk 86 F6
Hayton Notts 79 J7
Hayton's Bent Shrops 51 N4
Haytor Vale Devon 8 E9
Haytown Devon 18 G10
Haywards Heath W Susx 15 L6
Haywood Donc 78 F1
Haywood Herefs 40 G5
Haywood Oaks Notts 66 G1
Hazards Green E Susx 16 C8
Hazelbank S Lans 114 F12
Hazelbury Bryan Dorset 10 H3
Hazeleigh Essex 46 E11
Hazeley Hants 31 Q10
Hazelford Notts 67 J2
Hazel Grove Stockp 76 G6

Hazelhurst Tamesd 76 H4
Hazelslade Staffs.............65 J9
Hazel Street Kent...........16 C3
Hazel Stub Suff.............46 B3
Hazelton Walls Fife 124 G8
Hazelwood Derbys 65 Q3
Hazlemere Bucks.............32 C3
Hazlerigg N u Ty...........100 C4
Hazles Staffs..................65 J3
Hazleton Gloucs 42 C8
Heacham Norfk...............69 N5
Headbourne Worthy
    Devon.....................24 H7
Headbrook Herefs..........51 J9
Headcorn Kent..............16 E2
Headingley Leeds..........85 L8
Headington Oxon 43 L10
Headlam Dur 91 K3
Headless Cross Worcs.....53 J7
Headley Hants................25 P6
Headley Hants................31 L10
Headley Surrey..............32 K11
Headley Down Hants......25 P6
Headley Heath Worcs.....53 K5
Headon Devon 7 L4
Headon Notts.................79 J8
Heads Nook Cumb...........98 G2
Heage Derbys.................66 B2
Healaugh N York............85 P6
Healaugh N York............90 G7
Heald Green Stockp.......76 F6
Heale Devon 19 M4
Heale Somset 21 K9
Heale Somset 21 N8
Healey N York................91 K10
Healey Nthumb............100 C6
Healey Rochdl...............84 D12
Healey Wakefd...............85 K11
Healeyfield Dur.............100 D8
Healing NE Lin...............80 D2
Heamoor Cnwll 2 D8
Heanor Derbys...............66 C3
Heanton Punchardon
    Devon.....................19 K6
Heapham Lincs...............79 L6
Hearn Hants..................25 P6
Heart of Scotland
    Services N Lans.......114 G8
Hearts Delight Kent.......34 F10
Heasley Mill Devon 19 P7
Heaste Highld..............135 L12
Heath Derbys 78 D10
Heath Wakefd................85 M11
Heath and Reach C Beds...44 C6
Heath Common W Susx...14 G8
Heathcote Derbys...........77 L11
Heathcote Shrops...........64 C6
Heath End Bucks 32 C3
Heath End Hants............31 J10
Heath End Leics.............66 B8
Heath End Warwks.........53 N8
Heather Leics................66 C10
Heathfield Cambs...........45 N2
Heathfield Devon 8 C5
Heathfield E Susx 15 Q6
Heathfield N York..........84 H2
Heathfield Somset...........18 F8
Heathfield Village Oxon...43 L8
Heath Green Worcs.........53 K6
Heath Hall D & G 97 K2
Heath Hayes &
    Wimblebury Staffs....65 J10
Heath Hill Shrops..........64 E9
Heath House Somset......21 P4
Heathrow Airport Gt Lon...32 F7
Heathstock Devon 9 K4
Heathton Shrops............52 E2
Heath Town Wolves........64 H12
Heathwaite N York.........91 N6
Heatley Staffs................65 K7
Heatley Warrtn 76 C6
Heaton Bolton................84 H8
Heaton C Brad...............84 H8
Heaton Lancs.................83 K3
Heaton N u Ty..............100 H5
Heaton Staffs.................76 H11
Heaton Chapel Stockp....76 G5
Heaton Mersey Stockp....76 F5
Heaton Norris Stockp.....76 G5
Heaton's Bridge Lancs....75 L1
Heaverham Kent............33 Q10
Heaviley Stockp.............76 G6
Heavitree Devon 8 H6
Hebburn S Tyne...........101 J5
Hebden N York...............84 F3
Hebden Bridge Calder....84 E9
Hebden Green Ches W....76 B10
Hebing End Herts...........45 K7
Hebron Carmth..............42 G7
Hebron Nthumb............109 K11
Heckfield Hants.............31 P10
Heckfield Green Suffk....58 G5
Heckfordbridge Essex....46 G7
Heckington Lincs............68 C4
Heckmondwike Kirk.......85 J10
Heddington Wilts...........30 A9
Heddon-on-the-Wall
    Nthumb..................100 D6
Hedenham Norfk...........59 L2
Hedge End Hants...........24 H10
Hedgerley Bucks...........32 D5
Hedgerley Green Bucks...32 D5
Hedging Somset.............21 L7
Hedley on the Hill
    Nthumb..................100 D6
Hednesford Staffs..........65 J9
Hedon E R Yk................87 M9
Hedsor Bucks.................32 C5
Heeley Sheff..................78 D7
Hegdon Hill Herefs........51 Q10
Heglibister Shet...........147 i6
Heighington Darltn........91 L2
Heighington Lincs.........79 P10
Heightington Worcs........52 E6
Heiton Border...............108 D3
Hele Devon 5 M3
Hele Devon 8 C2
Hele Devon 19 K4
Hele Somset 21 J8
Helebridge Cnwll 7 J4
Hele Lane Devon 9 J4
Helensburgh Ag & B.....113 K5
Helenton S Ayrs............104 G4
Helford Cnwll 3 J9
Helford Passage Cnwll 3 J9
Helhoughton Norfk........70 C7
Helions Bumpstead
    Essex.....................46 B3
Hellaby Rothm................78 E5
Helland Cnwll 6 F10
Hellandbridge Cnwll.......6 F10
Hell Corner W Berk........30 H9
Hellescott Cnwll...............7 K7
Hellesdon Norfk.............71 J9
Hellesveor Cnwll 2 D6
Hellidon Nhants.............54 C4
Hellifield N York............84 C4
Hellingly E Susx............15 Q10
Hellington Norfk............71 L11
Helm Nthumb................109 K10
Helmdon Nhants............43 M3
Helme Kirk....................77 L1
Helmingham Suffk.........59 J4
Helmington Row Dur.....100 F11
Helmsdale Highld.........147 J2

Helmshore Lancs............84 B11
Helmsley N York............92 C10
Helperby N York.............85 N1
Helperthorpe N York......86 H1
Helpringham Lincs..........68 C4
Helpston C Pete..............68 C11
Helsby Ches W...............75 N8
Helsey Lincs...................81 K9
Helston Cnwll 2 G9
Helstone Cnwll 6 F8
Helton Cumb..................89 N2
Helwith N York...............90 H6
Helwith Bridge N York....84 B1
Hemblington Norfk.........71 L10
Hembridge Somset..........22 D6
Hemel Hempstead Herts...44 F10
Hemerdon Devon..............5 J7
Hemingbrough N York.....86 C9
Hemingby Lincs...............80 E9
Hemingfield Barns..........78 C3
Hemingford Abbots
    Cambs....................56 F6
Hemingford Grey Cambs...56 F6
Hemingstone Suffk.........58 H10
Hemington Leics.............66 D6
Hemington Nhants..........56 B4
Hemington Somset..........22 G3
Hemley Suffk..................47 N3
Hemlington Middsb.........92 A4
Hempholme E R Yk.........87 K5
Hempnall Norfk..............59 K2
Hempnall Green Norfk....59 K2
Hempriggs Moray.........139 K3
Hempstead Essex............46 B4
Hempstead Medway........34 D9
Hempstead Norfk...........70 G5
Hempstead Norfk...........71 N6
Hempsted Gloucs............41 N8
Hempton Norfk..............70 D6
Hempton Oxon...............43 J5
Hemsby Norfk................71 P8
Hemswell Lincs..............79 M5
Hemswell Cliff Lincs.......79 N6
Hemsworth Wakefd........78 C1
Hemyock Devon 21 J10
Henbury Bristl................28 H6
Henbury Ches E.............76 G9
Hendham Devon...............5 M6
Hendomen Powys............50 H1
Hendon Gt Lon..............33 J4
Hendon Sundld.............101 K7
Hendra Cnwll 2 H7
Hendra Cnwll 6 E9
Hendre Brdgnd...............27 M6
Hendre Flints.................74 G10
Hendredenny Caerph.....27 Q5
Hendy Carmth................38 E11
Heneglwys IoA...............72 G8
Henfield W Susx.............15 J7
Henford Devon.................7 M6
Henfynyw Cerdgn...........48 G8
Henghurst Kent..............16 G3
Hengoed Caerph............27 R3
Hengoed Powys..............50 H10
Hengrave Suffk..............58 B7
Henham Essex................45 Q6
Heniarth Powys..............62 F10
Henlade Somset..............21 L8
Henley Dorset................10 H4
Henley Gloucs................41 P8
Henley Shrops................51 M3
Henley Shrops................51 P5
Henley Somset...............21 P7
Henley Suffk..................58 H10
Henley W Susx...............14 C6
Henley Green Covtry......54 B4
Henley-in-Arden Warwks...53 M7
Henley-on-Thames Oxon...31 Q6
Henley Park Surrey.........32 D11
Henley's Down E Susx...16 C8
Henley Street Kent.........34 B9
Henllan Cerdgn..............48 B8
Henllan Denbgs.............74 D10
Henllan Amgoed Carmth...37 N6
Henllys Torfn.................28 C4
Henlow C Beds...............44 H4
Henlow Camp C Beds.....44 H5
Hennock Devon................8 C8
Henny Street Essex........46 F4
Henryd Conwy.................73 N9
Henry's Moat (Castell
    Hendre) Pembks........37 K5
Hensall N York...............86 B10
Henshaw Nthumb............99 L5
Hensingham Cumb.........88 C3
Henstead Suffk...............59 P3
Hensting Hants...............24 H9
Henstridge Somset..........22 G9
Henstridge Ash Somset...22 G9
Henstridge Marsh
    Somset....................22 G9
Henton Oxon..................43 Q11
Henton Somset...............22 C4
Henwick Worcs...............52 F9
Henwood Cnwll 7 K10
Henwood Oxon...............43 K11
Heolgerrig Myr Td..........39 N10
Heol-las Swans...............26 G3
Heol Senni Powys...........39 L7
Heol-y-Cyw Brdgnd........27 M5
Hepburn Nthumb...........108 H5
Hepple Nthumb.............108 H5
Hepscott Nthumb..........100 G1
Heptonstall Calder.........84 E9
Hepworth Kirk................77 M2
Hepworth Suffk..............58 E6
Herbrandston Pembks....36 G9
Hereford Herefs.............40 C3
Hereson Kent.................35 Q9
Heribusta Highld..........142 D11
Heriot C Edin................115 M7
Hermiston C Edin..........115 M7
Hermitage Border..........107 M13
Hermitage Dorset...........10 G3
Hermitage W Berk..........31 L8
Hermitage W Susx.........13 M4
Hermit Hill Barns...........77 Q3
Hermon Carmth.............38 A5
Hermon IoA....................72 F10
Hermon Pembks.............37 N4
Herne Kent....................35 L9
Herne Bay Kent..............35 L9
Herne Common Kent.....35 L9
Herne Hill Gt Lon...........33 L7
Herne Pound Kent..........34 B11
Herner Devon.................19 L8
Hernhill Kent.................35 J10
Herodsfoot Cnwll.............4 H4
Heronden Kent...............35 N11
Herongate Essex............34 A4
Heronsford S Ayrs..........94 E2
Heronsgate Herts...........32 E3
Herriard Hants...............25 L4
Herringfleet Suffk..........59 P1
Herring's Green Bed.......44 F3
Herringswell Suffk.........57 N6
Herringthorpe Rothm.....78 D5
Hersden Kent.................35 M10
Hersham Cnwll.................7 K3
Hersham Surrey..............32 G9
Herstmonceux E Susx....16 B8
Herston Dorset...............11 N9
Herston Ork..................147 c6
Hertford Herts...............45 L9
Hertford Heath Herts.....45 L9

Hertingfordbury Herts.....45 K9
Hesketh Bank Lancs.......83 K10
Hesketh Lane Lancs........83 N7
Hesket Newmarket Cumb...98 D10
Heskin Green Lancs........83 M12
Hesleden Dur 101 L10
Hesleden N York.............90 E11
Hesley Donc...................78 G5
Hesleyside Nthumb.........99 M2
Heslington C York...........86 B5
Hessay C York................85 Q4
Hessenford Cnwll.............4 D5
Hessett Suffk.................58 D8
Hessle E R Yk................87 J10
Hessle Wakefd...............85 N11
Hest Bank Lancs.............83 L2
Hestley Green Suffk.........58 H7
Heston Gt Lon................32 G7
Heston Services Gt Lon...32 G7
Hestwall Ork.................147 b4
Heswall Wirral................75 J7
Hethe Oxon...................43 M6
Hethersett Norfk............70 H11
Hethersgill Cumb............98 F5
Hetherside Cumb............98 E5
Hetherson Green
    Ches W...................63 N2
Hethpool Nthumb..........108 E4
Hett Dur.....................100 H11
Hetton N York................84 E3
Hetton-le-Hole Sundld...101 J8
Hetton Steads Nthumb...108 G3
Heugh Nthumb.............100 E4
Heughhead Abers.........132 B2
Heugh Head Border.......117 K9
Hever Kent....................15 N2
Heversham Cumb...........89 M10
Hevingham Norfk............71 J8
Hewas Water Cnwll..........3 N4
Hewelsfield Gloucs.........40 H11
Hewenden C Brad..........84 G8
Hewish N Som................28 E9
Hewish Somset...............10 C3
Hewood Dorset................9 Q4
Hexham Nthumb..............99 P5
Hextable Kent................33 P8
Hexthorpe Donc.............78 F3
Hexton Herts..................44 H5
Hexworthy Cnwll..............7 L8
Hexworthy Devon.............8 C10
Hey Lancs.....................84 C6
Heybridge Essex............34 B3
Heybridge Essex............46 E10
Heybridge Basin Essex....46 F10
Heybrook Bay Devon........4 H7
Heydon Cambs...............45 N4
Heydon Norfk.................70 G7
Heydour Lincs................67 P4
Hey Houses Lancs...........82 H9
Heylipoll Ag & B...........118 C3
Heylor Shet...................147 h4
Heyrod Tamesd..............76 H4
Heysham Lancs...............83 K3
Heyshott W Susx............14 C7
Heyside Oldham..............76 H2
Heytesbury Wilts............23 K5
Heythrop Oxon...............42 H6
Heywood Rochdl.............76 F2
Heywood Wilts...............23 J3
Hibaldstow N Linc...........79 N3
Hickleton Donc...............78 D3
Hickling Norfk................71 N7
Hickling Notts................66 H6
Hickling Green Norfk.......71 N7
Hickling Heath Norfk......71 M7
Hickmans Green Kent.....35 J10
Hicks Forstal Kent..........35 L9
Hickstead W Susx...........15 K7
Hidcote Bartrim Gloucs...42 E3
Hidcote Boyce Gloucs.....42 E3
High Ackworth Wakefd....85 N11
Higham Barns.................77 P2
Higham Derbys...............78 C12
Higham Kent..................15 R1
Higham Kent..................34 C8
Higham Lancs.................84 B8
Higham Suffk.................47 J4
Higham Suffk.................57 P7
Higham Dykes Nthumb....100 E3
Higham Ferrers Nhants....55 N7
Higham Gobion C Beds...44 G5
Higham Hill Gt Lon.........33 L4
Higham on the Hill Leics...54 C2
Highampton Devon...........7 M4
Highams Park Gt Lon......33 M4
Highampton Derbys........110 E1
High Ardwell D & G.........94 F9
High Auldgirth D & G....106 B12
High Bankhill Cumb.........98 H10
High Barnet Gt Lon.........33 J3
High Beach Essex............33 M3
High Bentham N York......83 P1
High Bewaldeth Cumb.....97 P11
High Bickington Devon....19 L9
High Biggins Cumb.........89 P11
High Birkwith N York......90 C11
High Blantyre S Lans.....114 C10
High Bonnybridge Falk...114 E5
High Borrans Cumb.........89 L6
High Bradley N York........84 F5
High Bray Devon.............19 N6
Highbridge Hants...........24 H9
Highbridge Somset..........21 M4
Highbrook W Susx...........15 L5
High Brooms Kent...........15 Q2
High Bullen Devon...........19 K9
Highburton Kirk.............77 M1
Highbury Gt Lon.............33 K5
Highbury Somset.............22 F4
High Buston Nthumb.....109 L8
High Callerton Nthumb...100 F4
High Casterton Cumb......89 Q11
High Catton E R Yk.........86 D4
Highclere Hants..............31 J10
Highcliffe BCP................12 C6
High Close Dur...............91 K4
High Cogges Oxon..........42 H10
High Common Norfk.......70 E11
High Coniscliffe Darltn...91 L4
High Crosby Cumb...........98 F6
High Cross Cnwll 3 J8
High Cross E Susx.........113 M12
High Cross Hants............25 M8
High Cross Herts............45 L8
Highcross Lancs..............82 H7
High Cross W Susx.........15 J7
High Cross Warwks.........53 J7
High Drummore D & G....94 G11
High Dubmire Sundld.....101 J8
High Easter Essex..........46 A8
High Eggborough N York...86 A11
High Ellington N York.....91 K10
Higher Alham Somset......22 F5
Higher Ansty Dorset.......11 J4
Higher Ballam Lancs.......83 J9
Higher Bartle Lancs........83 L8
Higher Berry End C Beds...44 D5
Higher Bockhampton
    Dorset....................10 H6
Higher Brixham Torbay....5 Q6
Higher Burrowton Devon...9 J5
Higher Burwardsley
    Ches W...................75 N12
High Ercall Wrekin..........63 Q8

Higher Chillington
    Somset....................10 B3
Higher Clovelly Devon 18 F8
Higher Coombe Dorset....10 D3
Highercombe Somset......20 D7
Higher Disley Ches E.......76 H7
Higher Folds Wigan........76 C4
Higherford Lancs............84 C7
Higher Gabwell Devon......5 Q3
Higher Halstock Leigh
    Dorset....................10 D3
Higher Harpers Lancs......84 B7
Higher Heysham Lancs....83 K3
Higher Hurdsfield Ches E...76 H8
Higher Irlam Salfd..........76 D5
Higher Kingcombe
    Dorset....................10 E5
Higher Kinnerton Flints...75 K11
Higher Marston Ches W...76 C8
Higher Muddiford Devon...19 L6
Higher Nyland Dorset......22 G9
Higher Ogden Rochdl......76 H1
Higher Pentire Cnwll........2 G9
Higher Penwortham
    Lancs.....................83 L9
Higher Prestacott Devon...7 M5
Higher Studfold N York....84 B1
Higher Town Cnwll 3 N1
Higher Town Cnwll 3 N7
Higher Town IoS..............2 b1
Higher Tregantle Cnwll 4 F6
Higher Walton Lancs.......83 N9
Higher Walton Warrtn.....75 Q6
Higher Wambrook
    Somset....................9 P3
Higher Waterston Dorset...10 H5
Higher Whatcombe
    Dorset....................11 K4
Higher Wheelton Lancs...83 N10
Higher Whitley Ches W....76 B7
Higher Wincham Ches W...76 C8
Higher Wraxhall Dorset...10 E4
Higher Wych Ches W.......63 N3
High Etherley Dur...........91 K1
High Ferry Lincs.............68 G2
Highfield E R Yk.............86 D8
Highfield Gatesd...........100 F6
Highfield N Ayrs...........113 L11
Highfields Caldecote
    Cambs....................56 G9
High Flats Kirk...............77 N2
High Garrett Essex.........46 D6
Highgate E Susx.............16 M4
Highgate Gt Lon.............33 K5
Highgate Kent................15 D5
Highgate Kent................16 H3
High Grange Dur...........100 F12
High Grantley N York......85 K1
High Green Cumb............89 L6
High Green Norfk............58 J12
High Green Norfk............58 H3
High Green Norfk............70 H11
High Green Sheff............77 Q4
High Green Shrops..........52 C4
High Green Suffk.............58 C8
High Green Worcs...........41 P3
Highgreen Manor
    Nthumb..................108 C11
High Halden Kent............16 F3
High Halstow Medway......34 D7
High Ham Somset............21 P7
High Harrington Cumb....88 D2
High Harrogate N York....85 L4
High Haswell Dur...........101 K9
High Hatton Shrops........63 Q7
High Hauxley Nthumb....109 M9
High Hawsker N York......93 J5
High Hesket Cumb..........98 F9
High Hoyland Barns........77 P2
High Hunsley E R Yk.......86 H8
High Hurstwood E Susx...15 P5
High Hutton N York.........86 D2
High Ireby Cumb.............97 P10
High Kelling Norfk...........70 G4
High Kilburn N York........92 B10
High Killerby N York........93 L10
High Knipe Cumb............89 N3
High Lands Dur...............91 J2
Highlane Ches E.............76 H7
Highlane Derbys..............78 C7
High Lane Stockp............76 H6
High Lanes Cnwll 2 F7
High Laver Essex............45 P10
Highlaws Cumb...............97 N8
Highleadon Gloucs.........41 M7
High Legh Ches E............76 C6
Highleigh W Susx...........13 P5
High Leven S on T...........91 U4
Highley Shrops...............52 D4
High Littleton BaNES.......29 K10
High Lorton Cumb..........88 F2
High Marishes N York......92 G11
High Marnham Notts.......79 K9
High Melton Donc...........78 D3
High Mickley Nthumb......100 D6
Highmoor Cumb..............98 B8
Highmoor Oxon...............31 P5
Highmoor Cross Oxon......31 P5
Highmoor Hill Mons.........28 F4
High Moorsley Sundld.....101 J8
Highnam Gloucs..............41 M7
High Newport Sundld......101 K7
High Newton Cumb.........89 L10
High Newton-by-the-
    Sea Nthumb............109 L5
High Nibthwaite Cumb....89 J9
High Offley Staffs............64 E7
High Ongar Essex...........45 Q11
High Onn Staffs..............64 F9
High Park Corner Essex...47 J7
High Pennyvenie E Ayrs...105 J4
High Pittington Dur.......101 J9
High Post Wilts...............23 N4
Highridge N Som.............28 H9
High Roding Essex..........45 R8
High Row Cumb...............89 K2
High Row Cumb...............98 D10
High Salter Lancs............83 N1
High Salvington W Susx....14 G9
High Scales Cumb............97 N9
High Seaton Cumb...........97 L11
High Shaw N York............90 H8
High Side Cumb...............97 P12
High Spen Gatesd..........100 E6
Highstead Kent................35 M9
Highsted Kent.................34 F9
High Stoop Dur..............100 E10
High Street Cnwll 3 N4
High Street Kent..............16 D5
High Street Suffk.............59 L5
High Street Suffk.............59 N4
High Street Suffk.............59 P6
Hightae D & G................97 L3
Highstreet Green Essex...46 D4
Highstreet Green Surrey....14 D4
Hightae D & G................97 L3
Higher's Heath Birm.......53 K5
High Throston Hartpl.....101 M11
Hightown Ches E............76 H11
Hightown Hants.............12 B4
Hightown Sefton.............75 J3
High Town Staffs.............65 J9
Hightown Green Suffk.....58 E9
High Toynton Lincs.........80 E9
High Trewhitt Nthumb....109 J10
High Urpeth Dur............100 G2
High Valleyfield Fife......114 H6

High Warden Nthumb......99 P5
Highway Herefs...............51 N10
Highway Wilts.................30 B7
Highweek Devon...............8 F10
High Westwood Dur.......100 E7
Highwood Essex...............46 B11
Highwood Staffs..............65 L6
Highwood Hill Gt Lon......33 J4
Highwoods Essex.............34 H5
High Woolaston Gloucs....28 G4
High Worsall N York........91 P5
Highworth Swindn..........30 E4
High Wray Cumb.............89 K7
High Wych Herts.............45 P8
High Wycombe Bucks......32 B4
Hilborough Norfk............70 B12
Hilcote Derbys................78 D12
Hilcott Wilts...................30 C10
Hildenborough Kent.......15 Q1
Hilden Park Kent.............15 Q1
Hildersham Cambs..........57 K11
Hilderstone Staffs...........64 H4
Hilderthorpe E R Yk........87 M2
Hilfield Dorset................10 G4
Hilgay Norfk...................57 P11
Hill S Glos.....................29 K3
Hill Warwks...................54 D7
Hillam N York.................85 Q9
Hillbeck Cumb................90 C2
Hillborough Kent............35 M8
Hill Brow Hants..............25 N4
Hill Chorlton Staffs.........64 E4
Hillclifflane Derbys.........65 P3
Hill Common Norfk.........71 N7
Hill Common Somset......21 J8
Hill Deverill Wilts...........23 J5
Hilldyke Lincs.................68 G3
Hill End Dur..................100 C11
Hill End Fife..................115 J1
Hill End Gloucs...............41 P4
Hillend Mdloth..............115 N8
Hillend N Lans...............114 F5
Hillend Swans................26 B4
Hillersland Gloucs...........40 H9
Hillerton Devon................8 D5
Hillesden Bucks..............43 N6
Hillesley Gloucs..............29 M4
Hillfarrance Somset........21 J8
Hill Green Kent...............34 E10
Hillgrove W Susx............14 D5
Hillhampton Herefs.........41 J2
Hillhead Abers..............140 F8
Hillhead Devon................5 Q6
Hill Head Hants..............13 J4
Hillhead S Lans.............106 C2
Hillhead of Cocklaw
    Abers.....................141 Q7
Hilliard's Cross Staffs......65 M10
Hilliclay Highld.............151 L4
Hillingdon Gt Lon...........32 F6
Hillington C Glas...........113 P8
Hillington Norfk..............69 N7
Hillis Corner IoW............12 G6
Hillmorton Warwks........54 E6
Hill of Beath Fife...........115 L3
Hill of Fearn Highld......146 E9
Hillowton D & G.............96 F5
Hillpool Worcs................52 G5
Hillpound Hants.............25 K10
Hill Ridware Staffs..........65 K8
Hillside Abers...............133 M5
Hillside Angus..............132 H12
Hillside Devon..................5 L4
Hill Side Kirk................85 J11
Hill Side Worcs...............52 D8
Hillstreet Hants.............24 E9
Hillswick Shet...............147 h4
Hill Top Dur...................90 F4
Hill Top Hants................12 F4
Hill Top N York...............78 C1
Hill Top Rothm................78 C5
Hill Top Sandw...............53 J2
Hill Top Wakefd..............85 M12
Hillwell Shet.................147 i9
Hilmarton Wilts..............30 B7
Hilperton Wilts...............29 P10
Hilperton Marsh Wilts.....29 P10
Hilsea C Port..................13 J4
Hilston E R Yk................87 P8
Hiltingbury Hants............24 G9
Hilton Border................117 K11
Hilton Cambs.................56 F7
Hilton Cumb...................90 B3
Hilton Derbys.................65 N6
Hilton Dorset.................11 J4
Hilton Dur.....................91 K2
Hilton S on T.................91 Q4
Hilton Shrops.................52 E2
Hilton of Cadboll Highld...146 F10
Hilton Park Services
    Staffs.....................64 H11
Himbleton Worcs.............52 H9
Himley Staffs..................52 F2
Hincaster Cumb.............89 N10
Hinchley Wood Surrey....32 H9
Hinckley Leics................54 C2
Hinderclay Suffk.............58 F5
Hinderwell N York...........92 H3
Hindford Shrops.............63 K5
Hindhead Surrey.............14 C4
Hindle Fold Lancs...........83 Q8
Hindley Nthumb............100 B6
Hindley Wigan.................76 B3
Hindley Green Wigan......76 B3
Hindlip Worcs.................52 G9
Hindolveston Norfk.........70 F7
Hindon Wilts...................23 K7
Hindringham Norfk.........70 E5
Hingham Norfk...............70 F11
Hinksford Staffs.............52 F3
Hinksey North Oxon.........75 N10
Hinstock Shrops.............64 C7
Hintlesham Suffk...........47 J3
Hinton Gloucs................41 K11
Hinton Hants..................12 C5
Hinton Herefs.................40 B6
Hinton Nhants................54 E10
Hinton S Glos.................29 L6
Hinton Shrops.................52 C4
Hinton Admiral Hants.....12 C5
Hinton Ampner Hants.....25 K8
Hinton Blewett BaNES....29 J11
Hinton Charterhouse
    BaNES....................29 M10
Hinton Cross Worcs.........42 B4
Hinton-in-the-Hedges
    Nhants....................43 M4
Hinton Marsh Hants........25 K8
Hinton Martell Dorset......11 N3
Hinton on the Green
    Worcs.....................42 B4
Hinton Parva Dorset........30 F6
Hinton St George Somset...21 P11
Hinton St Mary Dorset....22 H10
Hinton Waldrist Oxon......30 H3
Hints Shrops..................52 C5
Hints Staffs....................65 M11
Hinwick Bed..................55 M8
Hinxhill Kent..................17 J2
Hinxton Cambs...............45 J4
Hinxworth Herts.............45 J4

Hipperholme Calder........84 H10
Hipsburn Nthumb.........109 L7
Hipswell N York..............91 K7
Hirn Abers...................132 H4
Hirnant Powys................62 E7
Hirst Nthumb................109 M12
Hirwaun Denbgs.............74 F11
Hirwaun Rhondd.............39 M10
Hiscott Devon.................19 L8
Histon Cambs.................56 H7
Hitcham Suffk................58 E10
Hitcham Causeway Suffk...58 E10
Hitcham Street Suffk.......58 E10
Hitchin Herts.................44 H6
Hither Green Gt Lon........33 M7
Hittisleigh Devon.............8 D5
Hive E R Yk....................86 F9
Hixon Staffs...................65 J7
Hoaden Kent..................35 N10
Hoar Cross Staffs............65 L8
Hoarwithy Herefs...........40 H6
Hoath Kent....................35 M9
Hoathly Kent..................16 B3
Hobarris Shrops..............51 K5
Hobbles Green Suffk.......57 N10
Hobbs Cross Essex.........33 N2
Hobbs Cross Essex.........45 P9
Hobkirk Border..............107 P7
Hobland Hall Norfk.........71 P11
Hobsick Notts.................66 D2
Hobson Dur..................100 F7
Hoby Leics.....................66 H8
Hoccombe Somset...........20 H7
Hockering Norfk...............70 G9
Hockerton Notts..............79 J12
Hockley Ches E...............76 H7
Hockley Covtry................53 P5
Hockley Essex................34 E4
Hockley Staffs................65 N12
Hockley Heath Solhll......53 M6
Hockliffe C Beds.............44 D6
Hockwold cum Wilton
    Norfk.....................57 P3
Hockworthy Devon..........20 G9
Hoddesdon Herts...........45 L10
Hoddlesden Bl w D.........83 Q10
Hoddom Cross D & G......97 N3
Hoddom Mains D & G......97 N4
Hodgehill Ches E............76 F9
Hodgeston Pembks.........37 K10
Hodnet Shrops................63 Q6
Hodsock Notts................78 G6
Hodsoll Street Kent.........34 A9
Hodson Swindn...............30 D4
Hodthorpe Derbys..........78 E8
Hoe Hants......................25 J10
Hoe Norfk......................70 E9
Hoe Gate Hants..............25 K10
Hoff Cumb.....................89 N3
Hogben's Hill Kent..........35 J11
Hoggards Green Suffk.....58 C9
Hoggeston Bucks............43 N7
Hoggrill's End Warwks....53 N2
Hog Hill E Susx...............16 F7
Hoghton Lancs...............83 N9
Hognaston Derbys...........65 N2
Hogsthorpe Lincs............81 K9
Holbeach Lincs...............68 H7
Holbeach Bank Lincs.......68 G7
Holbeach Clough Lincs....68 G7
Holbeach Drove Lincs......68 F9
Holbeach Hurn Lincs.......68 G7
Holbeach St Johns Lincs...68 F8
Holbeach St Mark's Lincs...68 G6
Holbeach St Matthew
    Lincs.....................68 H6
Holbeck Notts................78 E9
Holberrow Green Worcs...53 J8
Holbeton Devon...............5 K6
Holborn Gt Lon...............33 L6
Holborough Kent.............34 C10
Holbrook Derbys.............66 B3
Holbrook Sheff................78 D7
Holbrook Suffk................47 L4
Holbrook Moor Derbys....66 B3
Holbrooks Covtry.............53 Q4
Holburn Nthumb............108 G3
Holbury Hants.................12 G5
Holcombe Devon..............8 H9
Holcombe Somset...........22 F3
Holcombe Rogus Devon...20 G9
Holcot Nhants.................55 K7
Holden Lancs..................84 A6
Holdenby Nhants............54 H7
Holder's Green Essex......46 B6
Holdgate Shrops.............51 P3
Holdingham Lincs...........67 Q3
Holditch Dorset...............9 Q4
Holdsworth Calder..........84 G9
Holehouse Derbys...........77 J6
Hole-in-the-Wall Herefs...41 J6
Holemoor Devon...............7 M4
Hole Street W Susx.........14 G8
Holford Somset..............21 J4
Holgate C York................86 A5
Holker Cumb..................89 K11
Holkham Norfk................70 C4
Hollacombe Devon............7 M4
Holland Fen Lincs...........68 E2
Holland Lees Lancs.........75 N2
Holland-on-Sea Essex....47 M8
Hollandstoun Ork..........147 f1
Hollee D & G..................98 B4
Hollesley Suffk...............47 P3
Hollicombe Torbay...........5 Q4
Hollingbourne Kent.........34 E11
Hollingdon Bucks...........44 C6
Hollingrove E Susx.........16 C6
Hollingthorpe Leeds.......85 M9
Hollington Derbys...........65 N4
Hollington Staffs.............65 K4
Hollingworth Tamesd......77 J5
Hollins Bury...................76 E2
Hollins Derbys................77 P9
Hollins Staffs.................65 J3
Hollinsclough Staffs.......77 J9
Hollins End Sheff............78 C7
Hollins Green Warrtn......76 C5
Hollins Lane Lancs..........83 L5
Hollinswood Wrekin........64 C10
Hollinwood Shrops.........63 N5
Hollocombe Devon...........19 M10
Holloway Derbys.............77 P12
Holloway Gt Lon.............33 K5
Holloway Wilts...............23 J7
Hollowell Nhants............54 H6
Hollowmoor Heath
    Ches W...................75 N10
Hollows D & G................98 F2
Hollybush Caerph...........39 R11
Hollybush E Ayrs..........104 G5
Hollybush Herefs............41 M4
Holly End Norfk..............57 L9
Holly Green Worcs..........41 P3
Hollyhurst Ches E...........63 P4
Hollym E R Yk................87 Q10
Hollywood Worcs............53 K5
Holmacott Devon............19 K8
Holman Clavel Somset....21 J10
Holmbridge Kirk.............77 L2
Holmbury St Mary Surrey...14 G2

Holmbush Cnwll 3 P4
Holmcroft Staffs.............64 G7
Holme Cambs.................56 D3
Holme Cumb..................89 N11
Holme Kirk....................77 L2
Holme N Linc.................79 M2
Holme Notts...................79 K11
Holme Chapel Lancs.......84 C9
Holme Green N York........85 Q7
Holme Hale Norfk...........70 C10
Holme Lacy Herefs..........40 H5
Holme Marsh Herefs.......51 K9
Holme next the Sea
    Norfk.....................69 N3
Holme on the Wolds
    E R Yk....................86 H6
Holme Pierrepont Notts...66 G4
Holmer Herefs................40 G3
Holmer Green Bucks.......32 C3
Holme St Cuthbert Cumb...97 M9
Holmes Chapel Ches E....76 E10
Holmesfield Derbys.........77 Q8
Holmes Hill E Susx.........15 P8
Holmeswood Lancs..........83 K12
Holmethorpe Surrey.......33 K12
Holme upon Spalding
    Moor E R Yk............86 E7
Holmewood Derbys.........78 C10
Holmfield Calder.............84 G9
Holmfirth Kirk................77 L2
Holmgate Derbys............78 C11
Holmhead E Ayrs...........105 K6
Holmpton E R Yk............87 Q10
Holmrook Cumb..............88 E7
Holmshurst E Susx.........16 B6
Holmside Dur................100 G8
Holmwrangle Cumb........98 G8
Holne Devon....................5 L3
Holnest Dorset...............10 G3
Holnicote Somset............20 E4
Holsworthy Devon.............7 L4
Holsworthy Beacon
    Devon.....................7 L3
Holt Dorset....................11 P4
Holt Norfk......................70 G4
Holt Wilts......................29 P10
Holt Worcs.....................52 F8
Holt Wrexhm..................63 L11
Holtby C York.................86 C4
Holt End Worcs...............53 K7
Holt Fleet Worcs.............52 F8
Holt Green Lancs............75 L3
Holt Heath Dorset...........11 P4
Holt Heath Worcs............52 F8
Holton Oxon...................43 M10
Holton Somset................22 F8
Holton Suffk...................59 M5
Holton cum Beckering
    Lincs.....................80 C7
Holton Heath Dorset.......11 M6
Holton le Clay Lincs........80 E3
Holton le Moor Lincs.......79 Q4
Holton St Mary Suffk......47 J4
Holt Street Kent..............35 N12
Holtye E Susx..................15 N3
Holway Flints..................74 G8
Holwell Dorset................10 H2
Holwell Herts.................44 H5
Holwell Leics.................67 J7
Holwell Oxon..................42 F10
Holwick Dur...................90 E1
Holworth Dorset.............11 J8
Holybourne Hants...........25 M5
Holy Cross Worcs............52 G5
Holyfield Essex...............45 M11
Holyhead IoA..................72 D7
Holy Island IoA...............72 D9
Holy Island Nthumb.......109 J1
Holy Island Nthumb.......109 J1
Holymoorside Derbys......77 Q10
Holyport W & M..............32 C7
Holystone Nthumb........108 H9
Holytown N Lans...........114 D9
Holywell C Beds..............44 E8
Holywell Cambs..............56 G6
Holywell Cnwll 3 J3
Holywell Dorset..............10 F4
Holywell Flints................74 G8
Holywell Nthumb...........101 J3
Holywell Warwks............53 M7
Holywell Green Calder....84 G11
Holywell Lake Somset.....20 H8
Holywell Row Suffk.........57 N5
Holywood D & G..............97 J2
Holywood Village D & G...64 J22
Homer Shrops..................52 C2
Homer Green Sefton........75 K3
Homersfield Suffk...........59 K3
Homescales Cumb...........89 N9
Hom Green Herefs...........41 J7
Homington Wilts.............23 P8
Honeyborough Pembks....37 J9
Honeybourne Worcs........42 D3
Honeychurch Devon..........8 B4
Honey Hill Kent..............35 K10
Honeystreet Wilts...........30 C10
Honey Tye Suffk..............46 G4
Honiley Warwks..............53 N6
Honing Norfk..................71 L6
Honingham Norfk............70 G10
Honington Lincs..............67 N3
Honington Suffk.............58 D6
Honington Warwks.........42 H3
Honiton Devon..................9 M5
Honley Kirk....................77 L1
Honnington Wrekin.........64 D9
Hoo Kent.......................35 N9
Hoobrook Worcs.............52 F6
Hood Green Barns...........77 P3
Hood Hill Rothm..............78 B4
Hooe C Plym...................4 H6
Hooe E Susx....................16 C8
Hoo End Herts................44 H7
Hoo Green Ches E...........76 D7
Hoohill Bpool.................82 H7
Hook Cambs...................56 H2
Hook Devon 9 J4
Hook E R Yk...................86 E10
Hook Gt Lon...................32 H9
Hook Hants....................12 H4
Hook Hants....................25 M3
Hook Pembks..................37 J8
Hook Wilts.....................30 C5
Hook-a-Gate Shrops........63 N11
Hook Bank Worcs............41 N3
Hooke Dorset..................10 E5
Hooker Gate Gatesd........100 E7
Hookgate Staffs..............64 E5
Hook Green Kent.............16 B4
Hook Green Kent.............33 Q8
Hook Norton Oxon..........42 H5
Hook Street Gloucs..........29 K2
Hook Street Wilts............30 C5
Hookway Devon................8 G5
Hookwood Surrey............15 J2
Hooley Surrey.................33 J11
Hooley Bridge Rochdl......76 F1
Hoo Meavy Devon.............4 H3
Hoo St Werburgh
    Medway..................34 D8
Hooton Ches W...............75 L8
Hooton Levitt Rothm.......78 E5
Hooton Pagnell Donc......78 D2
Hooton Roberts Rothm....78 D4
Hopcrofts Holt Oxon.......43 K7

Hope Derbys 77 M7
Hope Devon 5 L8
Hope Flints 75 K12
Hope Powys 63 J10
Hope Shrops 63 K12
Hope Staffs 65 L1
Hope Bagot Shrops 51 Q6
Hope Bowdler Shrops 51 N2
Hope End Green Essex 45 Q7
Hopehouse Border 107 J6
Hopeman Moray 147 L11
Hope Mansell Herefs 41 J8
Hopesay Shrops 51 L4
Hopetown Wakefd 85 N10
Hope under Dinmore Herefs 51 N10
Hopgrove C York 86 B4
Hopperton N York 85 N4
Hop Pole Lincs 68 D9
Hopsford Warwks 54 C4
Hopstone Shrops 52 E2
Hopton Derbys 65 N2
Hopton Shrops 63 L8
Hopton Staffs 64 H7
Hopton Suffk 58 E5
Hopton Cangeford Shrops 51 P4
Hopton Castle Shrops 51 L5
Hoptonheath Shrops 51 L5
Hopton on Sea Norfk 71 Q12
Hopton Wafers Shrops 52 B5
Hopwas Staffs 65 M11
Hopwood Rochdl 76 F2
Hopwood Worcs 53 J5
Hopwood Park Services Worcs 53 J6
Horam E Susx 15 Q7
Horbling Lincs 68 C5
Horbury Wakefd 85 L11
Horcott Gloucs 30 D2
Horden Dur 101 L10
Horderley Shrops 51 L3
Hordle Hants 12 D6
Hordley Shrops 63 L6
Horeb Carmth 38 D10
Horeb Cerdgn 38 B3
Horfield Bristl 29 J7
Horham Suffk 59 J6
Horkesley Heath Essex 46 H6
Horkstow N Linc 87 J11
Horley Oxon 43 J3
Horley Surrey 15 K2
Hornblotton Green Somset 22 D6
Hornby Lancs 83 N2
Hornby N York 91 L8
Hornby N York 91 N5
Horncastle Lincs 80 E10
Hornchurch Gt Lon 33 P5
Horncliffe Nthumb 117 K11
Horndean Border 117 K11
Horndean Hants 25 M10
Horndon Devon 7 P8
Horndon on the Hill Thurr 34 B6
Horne Surrey 15 L2
Horner Somset 20 D4
Horne Row Essex 46 D10
Horners Green Suffk 46 G3
Horney Common E Susx 15 N6
Horn Hill Bucks 32 E4
Horning Norfk 71 L8
Horninghold Leics 55 K1
Horninglow Staffs 65 N7
Horningsea Cambs 57 J8
Horningsham Wilts 22 H5
Horningtoft Norfk 70 D7
Horningtops Cnwll 4 D4
Hornsbury Somset 9 Q3
Hornsby Cumb 98 G8
Hornsbygate Cumb 98 G8
Horns Cross Devon 18 H8
Horns Cross E Susx 16 E6
Hornsea E R Yk 87 M6
Hornsey Gt Lon 33 K4
Horn's Green Gt Lon 33 N10
Horn Street Kent 17 L4
Hornton Oxon 42 H3
Horpit Swindn 30 E5
Horrabridge Devon 4 H3
Horringer Suffk 58 B8
Horringford IoW 13 J7
Horrocks Fold Bolton 76 C1
Horrocksford Lancs 83 R6
Horsacott Devon 19 K7
Horsebridge Devon 7 M9
Horsebridge E Susx 15 Q8
Horsebridge Hants 24 E7
Horsebridge Shrops 63 L11
Horsebridge Staffs 64 H1
Horsebrook Staffs 64 G10
Horsecastle N Som 28 F9
Horsedown Cnwll 2 F7
Horsehay Wrekin 64 C10
Horseheath Cambs 45 R2
Horsehouse N York 90 H10
Horsell Surrey 32 E10
Horseman's Green Wrexhm 63 M4
Horsenden Bucks 43 R11
Horsey Norfk 71 P7
Horsey Somset 21 M5
Horsey Corner Norfk 71 N7
Horsford Norfk 71 J9
Horsforth Leeds 85 K7
Horsham W Susx 14 H5
Horsham Worcs 52 D9
Horsham St Faith Norfk 71 J9
Horsington Lincs 80 D10
Horsington Somset 22 F8
Horsley Derbys 66 B3
Horsley Gloucs 29 N3
Horsley Nthumb 100 E5
Horsley Nthumb 108 D10
Horsley Cross Essex 47 K6
Horsleycross Street Essex 47 K6
Horsley-Gate Derbys 77 P8
Horsleyhill Border 107 N6
Horsley's Green Bucks 31 R3
Horsley Woodhouse Derbys 66 C3
Horsmonden Kent 16 C3
Horspath Oxon 43 M10
Horstead Norfk 71 K8
Horsted Keynes W Susx 15 M5
Horton Bucks 44 C8
Horton Dorset 11 P3
Horton Lancs 84 C5
Horton Nhants 55 K9
Horton S Glos 29 M5
Horton Shrops 63 N6
Horton Somset 21 M10
Horton Staffs 76 H12
Horton Surrey 32 H10
Horton Swans 26 C5
Horton W & M 32 E7
Horton Wilts 30 B9
Horton Wrekin 64 C9
Horton Cross Somset 21 M10
Horton-cum-Studley Oxon 43 M9
Horton Green Ches W 63 M2
Horton Heath Hants 24 H10
Horton-in-Ribblesdale N York 90 C12
Horton Kirby Kent 33 Q8
Horwich Bolton 76 B1
Horwich End Derbys 77 J7
Horwood Devon 19 K8
Hoscar Lancs 75 M1
Hoscote Border 107 K7
Hose Leics 67 J6
Hosey Hill Kent 33 N11
Hosh P & K 123 L8
Hoswick Shet 147 i9
Hotham E R Yk 86 G8
Hothfield Kent 16 G2
Hoton Leics 66 F7
Hott Nthumb 99 L1
Hough Ches E 64 D2
Hough Ches E 76 F8
Hougham Lincs 67 M3
Hough End Leeds 85 K8
Hough Green Halton 75 N6
Hough-on-the-Hill Lincs 67 M3
Houghton Cambs 56 F6
Houghton Cumb 98 E6
Houghton Hants 24 E7
Houghton Nthumb 100 E5
Houghton Pembks 37 J9
Houghton W Susx 14 E8
Houghton Conquest C Beds 44 F3
Houghton Gate Dur 100 H8
Houghton Green E Susx 16 G6
Houghton Green Warrtn 76 B5
Houghton le Side Darltn 91 L2
Houghton-le-Spring Sundld 101 J8
Houghton on the Hill Leics 66 H11
Houghton Regis C Beds 44 E7
Houghton St Giles Norfk 70 D5
Houlton Warwks 54 F6
Hound Green Hants 31 Q10
Houndslow Border 116 E11
Houndsmoor Somset 20 H8
Houndwood Border 117 J8
Hounslow Gt Lon 32 G7
Househill Highld 138 G5
Houses Hill Kirk 85 J11
Housieside Abers 141 L10
Houston Rens 113 M8
Houstry Highld 151 L9
Houton Ork 147 b5
Hove Br & H 15 K10
Hove Edge Calder 84 H10
Hoveringham Notts 66 H3
Hoveton Norfk 71 L8
Hovingham N York 92 D11
Howbrook Barns 77 Q4
How Caple Herefs 41 J6
Howden E R Yk 86 D9
Howden-le-Wear Dur 100 F11
Howe Highld 151 P4
Howe IoM 102 b7
Howe N York 91 N10
Howe Norfk 71 K12
Howe Bridge Wigan 76 C3
Howegreen Essex 34 E2
Howe Green Essex 46 D11
Howell Lincs 68 C3
How End C Beds 44 E3
Howe of Teuchar Abers 141 J6
Howes D & G 97 P5
Howe Street Essex 46 C5
Howe Street Essex 46 C8
Howey Powys 50 E9
Howgate Cumb 88 C2
Howgate Mdloth 115 N9
Howgill Lancs 84 B6
Howick Nthumb 109 L6
Howle Wrekin 64 C7
Howle Hill Herefs 41 J7
Howlett End Essex 45 Q5
Howley Somset 9 P3
How Mill Cumb 98 G7
Howmore W Isls 152 b10
Hownam Border 108 C6
Howrigg Cumb 98 D8
Howsham N Linc 79 P3
Howsham N York 86 D3
Howtel Nthumb 108 E3
Howt Green Kent 34 F9
Howton Herefs 40 F6
Howtown Cumb 89 L3
How Wood Herts 44 G11
Howwood Rens 113 M9
Hoxa Ork 147 c6
Hoxne Suffk 58 H5
Hoy Ork 147 b5
Hoylake Wirral 74 H6
Hoyland Barns 78 B4
Hoyland Common Barns 78 B4
Hoylandswaine Barns 77 N3
Hoyle W Susx 14 C7
Hoyle Mill Barns 78 B2
Hubberholme N York 90 F11
Hubberston Pembks 36 H9
Hubbert's Bridge Lincs 68 E3
Huby N York 85 K6
Huby N York 85 R2
Huccaby Devon 8 C10
Hucclecote Gloucs 41 P8
Hucking Kent 34 E10
Hucknall Notts 66 E2
Huddersfield Kirk 84 H12
Huddington Worcs 52 H9
Hudnall Herts 44 E9
Hudswell N York 91 K7
Huggate E R Yk 86 G4
Hugglescote Leics 66 C9
Hughenden Valley Bucks 32 B3
Hughley Shrops 51 P1
Hugh Town IoS 2 b2
Huish Devon 7 P2
Huish Wilts 30 D9
Huish Champflower Somset 20 G7
Huish Episcopi Somset 21 P8
Hùisinis W Isls 152 d5
Huisinish W Isls 152 d5
Hulcote C Beds 44 D4
Hulcote Nhants 54 H10
Hulcott Bucks 44 B8
Hulham Devon 9 J8
Hulland Derbys 65 N3
Hulland Ward Derbys 65 N3
Hullavington Wilts 29 P6
Hull Bridge E R Yk 87 K7
Hullbridge Essex 34 E3
Hull, Kingston upon C KuH 87 K9
Hulme Manch 76 F4
Hulme Staffs 64 H3
Hulme Warrtn 75 Q5
Hulme End Staffs 77 L11
Hulme Walfield Ches E 76 F10
Hulse Heath Ches E 76 D7
Hulton Lane Ends Bolton 76 C3
Hulverstone IoW 12 F8
Hulver Street Norfk 70 D10
Hulver Street Suffk 59 P3
Humber Devon 8 G9
Humber Herefs 51 P9
Humber Bridge N Linc 87 J10
Humberside Airport N Linc 80 B2
Humberston NE Lin 80 F3
Humberstone C Leic 66 G11
Humberton N York 85 N1
Humbie E Loth 116 B9
Humbleton E R Yk 87 N8
Humbleton Nthumb 108 F4
Humby Lincs 67 P5
Hume Border 108 A1
Humshaugh Nthumb 99 P4
Huna Highld 151 Q2
Huncoat Lancs 84 B9
Huncote Leics 54 E1
Hundalee Border 107 Q6
Hundall Derbys 78 C8
Hunderthwaite Dur 90 G2
Hundleby Lincs 80 G10
Hundle Houses Lincs 68 E1
Hundleton Pembks 37 J10
Hundon Suffk 57 P11
Hundred End Lancs 83 K10
Hundred House Powys 50 F10
Hungarton Leics 66 H10
Hungerford Hants 23 Q11
Hungerford Somset 20 G5
Hungerford W Berk 30 H8
Hungerford Newtown W Berk 30 H8
Hunger Hill Bolton 76 C2
Hunger Hill Lancs 75 P1
Hungerstone Herefs 40 F5
Hungerton Lincs 67 L6
Hungryhatton Shrops 64 C7
Hunmanby N York 93 M11
Hunningham Warwks 54 B7
Hunnington Worcs 52 H4
Hunsbury Hill Nhants 55 J9
Hunsdon Herts 45 M9
Hunsdonbury Herts 45 M9
Hunsingore N York 85 N4
Hunslet Leeds 85 L9
Hunsonby Cumb 98 H11
Hunstanton Norfk 69 N4
Hunstanworth Dur 99 Q8
Hunsterson Ches E 64 C3
Hunston Suffk 58 E7
Hunston W Susx 13 Q4
Hunston Green Suffk 58 E7
Hunstrete BaNES 29 K10
Hunsworth Kirk 85 J9
Hunt End Worcs 53 J8
Hunter's Inn Devon 19 M4
Hunter's Quay Ag & B 112 H5
Huntham Somset 21 M8
Hunthill Lodge Angus 132 D10
Huntingdon Cambs 56 E6
Huntingfield Suffk 59 L6
Huntingford Dorset 22 H7
Huntington C York 86 B4
Huntington Ches W 75 M10
Huntington E Loth 116 C6
Huntington Herefs 40 G3
Huntington Herefs 51 J10
Huntington Staffs 64 H9
Huntingtowerfield P & K 124 B7
Huntley Gloucs 41 L8
Huntly Abers 140 E8
Hunton Hants 24 H5
Hunton Kent 16 C1
Hunton N York 91 K8
Hunton Bridge Herts 32 F2
Hunt's Corner Norfk 58 F3
Huntscott Somset 20 E4
Hunt's Cross Lpool 75 M7
Hunts Green Bucks 44 C11
Hunts Green Warwks 53 M1
Huntsham Devon 20 F9
Huntshaw Devon 19 K9
Huntshaw Cross Devon 19 K9
Huntspill Somset 21 M4
Huntstile Somset 21 L6
Huntworth Somset 21 M6
Hunwick Dur 100 F11
Hunworth Norfk 70 F5
Hurcott Somset 21 N10
Hurdcott Wilts 23 Q6
Hurdsfield Ches E 76 H9
Hurley W & M 32 B5
Hurley Warwks 53 N1
Hurley Bottom W & M 32 B6
Hurley Common Warwks 53 N1
Hurlford E Ayrs 104 H2
Hurlston Green Lancs 75 L1
Hurn BCP 11 Q5
Hurn's End Lincs 68 H2
Hursley Hants 24 G8
Hurst Dorset 11 J7
Hurst N York 90 H6
Hurst Somset 21 P9
Hurst Wokham 31 R8
Hurstbourne Priors Hants 24 G4
Hurstbourne Tarrant Hants 24 F3
Hurst Green E Susx 16 C5
Hurst Green Essex 47 K8
Hurst Green Lancs 83 Q7
Hurst Green Surrey 33 M12
Hurst Hill Dudley 52 H2
Hurstley Herefs 51 K11
Hurstpierpoint W Susx 15 K7
Hurst Wickham W Susx 15 K7
Hurstwood Lancs 84 C9
Hurtiso Ork 147 d5
Hurtmore Surrey 14 D2
Hurworth Burn Dur 101 K11
Hurworth-on-Tees Darltn 91 M5
Hurworth Place Darltn 91 M5
Hury Dur 90 F3
Husbands Bosworth Leics 54 G4
Husborne Crawley C Beds 44 D4
Husthwaite N York 92 B11
Hutcherleigh Devon 5 N6
Hut Green N York 85 R10
Huthwaite Notts 78 D11
Huttoft Lincs 81 K8
Hutton Border 117 K10
Hutton Cumb 89 L1
Hutton E R Yk 87 J4
Hutton Essex 34 B3
Hutton Lancs 83 L10
Hutton N Som 28 D10
Hutton Bonville N York 91 N7
Hutton Buscel N York 93 K10
Hutton Conyers N York 91 N12
Hutton Cranswick E R Yk 87 J5
Hutton End Cumb 98 F10
Hutton Hang N York 91 K9
Hutton Henry Dur 101 L11
Hutton-le-Hole N York 92 E8
Hutton Lowcross R & Cl 92 C4
Hutton Magna Dur 91 J4
Hutton Mulgrave N York 92 G5
Hutton Roof Cumb 89 P11
Hutton Roof Cumb 98 D11
Hutton Rudby N York 91 Q5
Hutton Sessay N York 91 Q11
Hutton Wandesley N York 85 Q5
Huxham Devon 8 H5
Huxham Green Somset 22 D6
Huxley Ches W 75 N11
Huyton Knows 75 M5
Hycemoor Cumb 88 E9
Hyde Gloucs 41 P11
Hyde Hants 23 Q10
Hyde Tamesd 76 H5
Hyde Heath Bucks 32 D2
Hyde Lea Staffs 64 G8
Hydestile Surrey 14 D3
Hykeham Moor Lincs 79 M10
Hylands Estate Essex 46 B11
Hyndford Bridge S Lans 106 B1
Hynish Ag & B 118 D5
Hyssington Powys 51 K2
Hystfield Gloucs 29 K3
Hythe Essex 46 H7
Hythe Hants 12 G3
Hythe Kent 17 L4
Hythe Somset 21 P3
Hythe End W & M 32 E8
Hyton Cumb 88 E9

I

Ibberton Dorset 11 J3
Ible Derbys 77 N12
Ibsley Hants 12 B3
Ibstock Leics 66 C10
Ibstone Bucks 31 Q4
Ibthorpe Hants 24 F3
Iburndale N York 92 H5
Ibworth Hants 25 J2
Icelton N Som 28 E9
Ichrachan Ag & B 121 J6
Ickburgh Norfk 57 Q2
Ickenham Gt Lon 32 F5
Ickford Bucks 43 N10
Ickham Kent 35 M10
Ickleford Herts 44 H5
Icklesham E Susx 16 F7
Ickleton Cambs 45 P3
Icklingham Suffk 57 P6
Ickornshaw N York 84 E6
Ickwell Green C Beds 44 G3
Icomb Gloucs 42 E7
Idbury Oxon 42 F8
Iddesleigh Devon 7 Q3
Ide Devon 8 G6
Ideford Devon 8 G9
Ide Hill Kent 33 N12
Iden E Susx 16 G6
Iden Green Kent 16 D3
Iden Green Kent 16 E4
Idle C Brad 85 J7
Idless Cnwll 3 K5
Idlicote Warwks 42 G3
Idmiston Wilts 24 C6
Idole Carmth 38 B8
Idridgehay Derbys 65 P2
Idrigill Highld 134 G3
Idstone Oxon 30 F5
Iffley Oxon 43 L11
Ifield W Susx 15 J3
Ifold W Susx 14 E4
Iford BCP 12 B6
Iford E Susx 15 M9
Ifton Mons 28 G5
Ifton Heath Shrops 63 K5
Ightfield Shrops 63 Q4
Ightham Kent 33 Q11
Iken Suffk 59 N9
Ilam Staffs 65 L2
Ilchester Somset 22 C9
Ilderton Nthumb 108 G5
Ilford Gt Lon 33 N5
Ilford Somset 21 N10
Ilfracombe Devon 19 K4
Ilkeston Derbys 66 D4
Ilketshall St Andrew Suffk 59 M3
Ilketshall St John Suffk 59 M3
Ilketshall St Lawrence Suffk 59 M4
Ilketshall St Margaret Suffk 59 L4
Ilkley C Brad 84 H6
Illand Cnwll 7 K9
Illey Dudley 52 H4
Illidge Green Ches E 76 E11
Illingworth Calder 84 G9
Illogan Cnwll 2 G6
Illston on the Hill Leics 66 H12
Ilmer Bucks 43 Q10
Ilmington Warwks 42 E3
Ilminster Somset 21 N10
Ilsington Devon 8 E9
Ilsington Dorset 11 J6
Ilston Swans 26 E4
Ilton N York 91 K11
Ilton Somset 21 M10
Imachar N Ayrs 103 M2
Immingham NE Lin 87 M12
Immingham Dock NE Lin 87 M12
Impington Cambs 56 H8
Ince Ches W 75 M8
Ince Blundell Sefton 75 K3
Ince-in-Makerfield Wigan 75 Q3
Inchbae Lodge Highld 145 K11
Inchbare Angus 132 F11
Inchberry Moray 139 P5
Incheril Highld 136 E3
Inchinnan Rens 113 P7
Inchlaggan Highld 128 G4
Inchmichael P & K 124 E8
Inchmore Highld 137 P7
Inchnadamph Highld 148 F12
Inchture P & K 124 F7
Inchyra P & K 124 D8
Indian Queens Cnwll 3 M3
Ingatestone Essex 34 B2
Ingbirchworth Barns 77 N3
Ingerthorpe N York 85 L2
Ingestre Staffs 64 H7
Ingham Lincs 79 N7
Ingham Norfk 71 M7
Ingham Suffk 58 C6
Ingham Corner Norfk 71 M7
Ingleborough Norfk 69 J9
Ingleby Derbys 65 Q7
Ingleby Arncliffe N York 91 Q6
Ingleby Barwick S on T 91 Q4
Ingleby Cross N York 91 Q6
Ingleby Greenhow N York 92 C5
Ingleigh Green Devon 8 B3
Inglesbatch BaNES 29 L10
Inglesham Swindn 30 E3
Ingleston D & G 97 K5
Ingleton Dur 91 K3
Ingleton N York 90 A12
Inglewhite Lancs 83 M7
Ingmanthorpe N York 85 N5
Ingoe Nthumb 100 D3
Ingol Lancs 83 L9
Ingoldisthorpe Norfk 69 N5
Ingoldmells Lincs 81 K10
Ingoldsby Lincs 67 P6
Ingram Nthumb 108 G6
Ingrave Essex 34 A4
Ingrow C Brad 84 F7
Ings Cumb 89 M7
Ingst S Glos 29 J5
Ingthorpe Rutlnd 67 N10
Ingworth Norfk 71 J6
Inkberrow Worcs 53 J9
Inkerman Dur 100 E10
Inkersall Green Derbys 78 C9
Inkhorn Abers 141 M8
Inkpen W Berk 30 H9
Inkstack Highld 151 N3
Inmarsh Wilts 29 Q10
Innellan Ag & B 112 H7
Innerleithen Border 107 J2
Innerleven Fife 115 Q1
Innermessan D & G 94 F6
Innerwick E Loth 116 G6
Innesmill Moray 139 P3
Innsworth Gloucs 41 P7
Insch Abers 140 F10
Insh Highld 130 E4
Inshes Highld 138 C7
Inskip Lancs 83 L7
Inskip Moss Side Lancs 83 K7
Instow Devon 19 J7
Insworke Cnwll 4 F6
Intake Sheff 78 C7
Inver Abers 131 N6
Inver Highld 146 F8
Inver P & K 123 P4
Inverailort Highld 127 P8
Inveralligin Highld 135 Q4
Inverallochy Abers 141 P3
Inveran Highld 145 N5
Inveraray Ag & B 121 L11
Inverarish Highld 135 K8
Inverarity Angus 125 J4
Inverarnan Stirlg 121 Q9
Inverarnie Highld 138 C9
Inverasdale Highld 143 L8
Inverbeg Ag & B 113 L2
Inverbervie Abers 133 K10
Inverboyndie Abers 140 G3
Invercreran Lodge Ag & B 121 J3
Inverdruie Highld 130 G2
Inveresk E Loth 115 Q7
Inveresragan Ag & B 121 J6
Inverey Abers 131 K6
Inverfarigaig Highld 137 P11
Inverfolla Ag & B 120 H4
Invergarry Highld 129 K4
Invergeldie P & K 123 J7
Invergloy Highld 128 H6
Invergordon Highld 138 C2
Invergowrie P & K 124 G7
Inverguseran Highld 127 N3
Inverhadden P & K 122 H1
Inverie Highld 127 P4
Inverinan Ag & B 121 J9
Inverinate Highld 136 C11
Inverkeilor Angus 125 N3
Inverkeithing Fife 115 L5
Inverkeithny Abers 140 F6
Inverkip Inver 113 J7
Inverkirkaig Highld 144 D1
Inverlael Highld 144 F8
Inverlair Highld 129 K8
Inverliever Lodge Ag & B 120 G11
Inverlochy Ag & B 121 M7
Invermark Angus 132 C8
Invermoriston Highld 129 M1
Invernaver Highld 150 C4
Inverneill Ag & B 112 B5
Inverness Highld 138 C7
Inverness Airport Highld 138 E5
Invernettie Abers 141 Q7
Invernoaden Ag & B 112 G2
Inveroran Hotel Ag & B 121 P4
Inverquharity Angus 124 H1
Inverquhomery Abers 141 N6
Inverroy Highld 129 J8
Inversanda Highld 128 C12
Invershiel Highld 136 C12
Invershin Highld 145 N6
Invershore Highld 151 N9
Inversnaid Hotel Stirlg 122 B11
Inverugie Abers 141 Q6
Inveruglas Ag & B 121 Q11
Inveruglass Highld 130 E4
Inverurie Abers 141 J11
Inwardleigh Devon 7 Q5
Inworth Essex 46 F8
Iochdar W Isls 152 b9
Iona Ag & B 119 J8
Iping W Susx 25 P9
iPort Logistics Park Donc 78 F4
Ipplepen Devon 5 P3
Ipsden Oxon 31 N5
Ipstones Staffs 65 J2
Ipswich Suffk 47 L3
Irby Wirral 75 J7
Irby in the Marsh Lincs 81 J11
Irby upon Humber NE Lin 80 D3
Irchester Nhants 55 M7
Ireby Cumb 97 P10
Ireby Lancs 89 Q11
Ireland C Beds 44 G3
Ireleth Cumb 88 H11
Ireshopeburn Dur 99 N10
Ireton Wood Derbys 65 P3
Irlam Salfd 76 D5
Irnham Lincs 67 P7
Iron Acton S Glos 29 K5
Iron Bridge Cambs 57 J1
Ironbridge Wrekin 64 C11
Ironbridge Gorge Wrekin 64 C11
Iron Cross Warwks 53 K10
Ironmacannie D & G 96 D3
Irons Bottom Surrey 15 J2
Ironville Derbys 66 C2
Irstead Norfk 71 M8
Irthington Cumb 98 G6
Irthlingborough Nhants 55 N6
Irton N York 93 K10
Irvine N Ayrs 104 F2
Isauld Highld 150 H4
Isbister Shet 147 i3
Isbister Shet 147 k5
Isfield E Susx 15 N7
Isham Nhants 55 M6
Isington Hants 25 N5
Islandpool Worcs 52 F4
Islay Ag & B 111 J10
Islay Airport Ag & B 110 H11
Isle Abbotts Somset 21 M9
Isle Brewers Somset 21 N9
Isleham Cambs 57 M6
Isle of Dogs Gt Lon 33 M6
Isle of Grain Medway 34 F7
Isle of Lewis W Isls 152 f3
Isle of Man IoM 102 e4
Isle of Man Ronaldsway Airport IoM 102 c7
Isle of Mull Ag & B 119 Q6
Isle of Purbeck Dorset 11 N8
Isle of Sheppey Kent 34 H8
Isle of Skye Highld 134 G8
Isle of Thanet Kent 35 P9
Isle of Walney Cumb 82 F2
Isle of Whithorn D & G 95 N11
Isle of Wight IoW 13 J7
Isleornsay Highld 127 M2
Isles of Scilly IoS 2 b2
Isles of Scilly St Mary's Airport IoS 2 b2
Islesteps D & G 97 K4
Islet Village Guern 12 c1
Isleworth Gt Lon 32 H7
Isley Walton Leics 66 C7
Islibhig W Isls 152 d3
Islington Gt Lon 33 K5
Islip Nhants 55 N5
Islip Oxon 43 L9
Islivig W Isls 152 d3
Isombridge Wrekin 63 Q9
Istead Rise Kent 34 B8
Itchen Abbas Hants 25 J7
Itchen Stoke Hants 25 J7
Itchingfield W Susx 14 G5
Itchington S Glos 29 K5
Itteringham Norfk 70 H6
Itton Devon 8 C5
Itton Mons 28 G3
Itton Common Mons 28 G3
Ivegill Cumb 98 E9
Ivelet N York 90 F7
Iver Bucks 32 E6
Iver Heath Bucks 32 E6
Iveston Dur 100 E8
Ivinghoe Bucks 44 D8
Ivinghoe Aston Bucks 44 D8
Ivington Herefs 51 N9
Ivington Green Herefs 51 M9
Ivybridge Devon 5 K5
Ivychurch Kent 17 J5
Ivy Cross Dorset 23 J8
Ivy Hatch Kent 33 Q11
Ivy Todd Norfk 70 C10
Iwade Kent 34 F9
Iwerne Courtney Dorset 23 J10
Iwerne Minster Dorset 23 J10
Ixworth Suffk 58 D6
Ixworth Thorpe Suffk 58 D6

J

Jack Green Lancs 83 N10
Jack Hill N York 85 J5
Jack-in-the-Green Devon 9 J6
Jack's Bush Hants 24 D6
Jacksdale Notts 66 D2
Jackson Bridge Kirk 77 M2
Jackton S Lans 113 R10
Jacobstow Cnwll 6 H5
Jacobstowe Devon 8 B4
Jacobs Well Surrey 32 E11
Jameston Pembks 37 L10
Jamestown Highld 137 N4
Jamestown W Duns 113 M5
Janetstown Highld 151 M10
Jardine Hall D & G 106 E12
Jarrow S Tyne 101 J5
Jarvis Brook E Susx 15 P5
Jasper's Green Essex 46 C6
Jawcraig Falk 114 F6
Jaywick Essex 47 L9
Jealott's Hill Br For 32 B7
Jeater Houses N York 91 Q8
Jedburgh Border 107 Q6
Jeffreyston Pembks 37 L9
Jemimaville Highld 138 D3
Jerbourg Guern 12 c3
Jersey Jersey 13 c2
Jersey Airport Jersey 13 b2
Jersey Marine Neath 26 H3
Jerusalem Lincs 79 M9
Jesmond N u Ty 100 H5
Jevington E Susx 15 Q10
Jingle Street Mons 40 G9
Jockey End Herts 44 F9
Jodrell Bank Ches E 76 E9
Jodrell Bank Ches E 76 E9
Johnby Cumb 98 E11
John Lennon Airport Lpool 75 M7
John o' Groats Highld 151 Q2
Johns Cross E Susx 16 D6
Johnshaven Abers 133 J11
Johnson Street Norfk 71 M8
Johnston Pembks 36 H8
Johnstone D & G 106 H9
Johnstone Rens 113 N8
Johnstonebridge D & G 106 E11
Johnstown Carmth 38 B8
Johnstown Wrexhm 63 J3
Joppa C Edin 115 P6
Joppa Cerdgn 49 J7
Joppa S Ayrs 104 G6
Jordans Bucks 32 D4
Jordanston Pembks 36 H4
Jordanthorpe Sheff 78 B7
Joyden's Wood Kent 33 P8
Jubilee Corner Kent 16 E1
Jump Barns 78 C3
Jumper's Town E Susx 15 N4
Juniper Nthumb 99 P6
Juniper Green C Edin 115 M7
Jura Ag & B 111 L4
Jurassic Coast Devon 9 Q7
Jurby IoM 102 e3
Jurston Devon 8 D8

K

Kaber Cumb 90 C4
Kaimend S Lans 114 H12
Kames Ag & B 112 E7
Kames E Ayrs 105 M4
Kea Cnwll 3 K6
Keadby N Linc 79 L1
Keal Cotes Lincs 80 G11
Kearby Town End N York 85 M6
Kearsley Bolton 76 D3
Kearsley Nthumb 100 D3
Kearsney Kent 17 N2
Kearstwick Cumb 89 P10
Kearton N York 90 G7
Keasden N York 83 Q2
Keaton Devon 5 K6
Keckwick Halton 75 P7
Keddington Lincs 80 G6
Keddington Corner Lincs 80 G6
Kedington Suffk 46 C2
Kedleston Derbys 65 P4
Keelby Lincs 80 C2
Keele Staffs 64 E3
Keele Services Staffs 64 E3
Keele University Staffs 64 F3
Keeley Green Bed 44 E2
Keelham C Brad 84 G8
Keeres Green Essex 45 Q9
Keeston Pembks 36 H6
Keevil Wilts 29 Q10
Kegworth Leics 66 D7
Kehelland Cnwll 2 G6
Keig Abers 140 F12
Keighley C Brad 84 G7
Keilarsbrae Clacks 114 G2
Keillour P & K 123 N7
Keiloch Abers 131 M6
Keils Ag & B 111 L7
Keinton Mandeville Somset 22 D7
Keir Mill D & G 105 Q11
Keirsleywell Row Nthumb 99 L8
Keisby Lincs 67 P6
Keisley Cumb 90 B2
Keiss Highld 151 Q4
Keith Moray 140 C6
Keithick P & K 124 D5
Keithock Angus 132 F11
Keithtown Highld 137 P4
Kelbrook Lancs 84 D6
Kelby Lincs 67 P4
Keld Cumb 89 N4
Keld N York 90 E6
Keld Head N York 92 F10
Keldholme N York 92 E9
Kelfield N Linc 79 K3
Kelfield N York 86 B7
Kelham Notts 67 K1
Kelhead D & G 97 N4
Kellacott Devon 7 M7
Kellamergh Lancs 83 J9
Kellas Angus 125 J6
Kellas Moray 139 M5
Kellaton Devon 5 N9
Kelleth Cumb 89 Q6
Kelling Norfk 70 G4
Kellingley N York 85 Q10
Kellington N York 85 Q10
Kelloe Dur 101 J11
Kelloholm D & G 105 N7
Kells Cumb 88 C3
Kelly Devon 7 M8
Kelly Bray Cnwll 7 L10
Kelmarsh Nhants 55 J5
Kelmscott Oxon 30 F2
Kelsale Suffk 59 M7
Kelsall Ches W 75 N10
Kelshall Herts 45 L4
Kelsick Cumb 97 P8
Kelso Border 108 B3
Kelstedge Derbys 77 Q11
Kelstern Lincs 80 E6
Kelsterton Flints 75 J9
Kelston BaNES 29 L9
Keltneyburn P & K 123 K3
Kelton D & G 97 K4
Kelty Fife 115 L2
Kelvedon Essex 46 F8
Kelvedon Hatch Essex 33 Q3
Kelvinhead N Lans 114 D5
Kelynack Cnwll 2 B8
Kemacott Devon 19 M4
Kemback Fife 124 H10
Kemberton Shrops 64 D11
Kemble Gloucs 30 A3
Kemble Wick Gloucs 29 R3
Kemerton Worcs 41 Q4
Kemeys Commander Mons 40 D10
Kemnay Abers 132 H1
Kempe's Corner Kent 17 J2
Kempley Gloucs 41 K6
Kempley Green Gloucs 41 K6
Kempsey Worcs 52 F10
Kempsford Gloucs 30 D3
Kemps Green Warwks 53 L6
Kempshott Hants 25 K3
Kempston Bed 55 P11
Kempston Hardwick Bed 44 E3
Kempton Shrops 51 K4
Kemp Town Br & H 15 L10
Kemsing Kent 33 Q10
Kemsley Kent 34 F9
Kemsley Street Kent 34 E10
Kenardington Kent 16 H4
Kenchester Herefs 40 F3
Kencot Oxon 42 F10
Kendal Cumb 89 N8
Kenderchurch Herefs 40 E6
Kendleshire S Glos 29 K6
Kenfig Brdgnd 27 J6
Kenfig Hill Brdgnd 27 K6
Kenilworth Warwks 53 P6
Kenley Gt Lon 33 L10
Kenley Shrops 63 P12
Kenmore Highld 135 N4
Kenmore P & K 123 K4
Kenn Devon 8 H7
Kenn N Som 28 F8
Kennacraig Ag & B 112 B8
Kennall Vale Cnwll 3 J7
Kennards House Cnwll 7 K8
Kenneggy Cnwll 2 F9
Kennerleigh Devon 8 F3
Kennet Clacks 114 G3
Kennethmont Abers 140 E10
Kennett Cambs 57 N7
Kennford Devon 8 G7
Kenninghall Norfk 58 F3
Kennington Kent 17 J2
Kennington Oxon 43 L11
Kennington Lees Kent 16 H2
Kennoway Fife 124 G12
Kenny Somset 21 M9
Kenny Hill Suffk 57 M5
Kennythorpe N York 86 E2
Kenovay Ag & B 118 D4
Kensaleyre Highld 134 G5
Kensington Gt Lon 33 J6
Kensington Palace Gt Lon 33 J6
Kensworth Common C Beds 44 E8
Kentallen Highld 121 J1
Kentchurch Herefs 40 F6
Kentford Suffk 57 N7
Kent Green Ches E 76 F12
Kentisbeare Devon 9 K3
Kentisbury Devon 19 M4
Kentisbury Ford Devon 19 M5
Kentish Town Gt Lon 33 K5
Kentmere Cumb 89 M6
Kenton Devon 8 H8
Kenton Gt Lon 32 H5
Kenton N u Ty 100 G5
Kenton Suffk 59 J7
Kenton Bankfoot N u Ty 100 G4
Kentra Highld 127 M10
Kents Bank Cumb 89 L11
Kentsboro Hants 24 E5
Kent's Green Gloucs 41 L7
Kent's Oak Hants 24 E8
Kent Street E Susx 16 D7
Kent Street Kent 34 B11
Kenwick Shrops 63 M6
Kenwyn Cnwll 3 K5
Kenyon Warrtn 76 B5
Keoldale Highld 149 J3
Keppoch Highld 136 B11
Kepwick N York 91 Q8
Keresley Covtry 53 Q4
Kermincham Ches E 76 E10
Kernborough Devon 5 N8
Kerne Bridge Herefs 41 J8
Kerrera Ag & B 120 F7
Kerridge Ches E 76 H8
Kerridge-end Ches E 76 H8
Kerris Cnwll 2 C9
Kerry Powys 50 G3
Kerrycroy Ag & B 112 G9
Kersall Notts 78 H11
Kersbrook Devon 9 K8
Kerscott Devon 19 M7
Kersey Suffk 46 H3
Kersey Tye Suffk 46 H3
Kersey Upland Suffk 46 H3
Kershader W Isls 152 f4
Kershopefoot Cumb 98 F2
Kersoe Worcs 42 A4
Kerswell Devon 9 K3
Kerswell Green Worcs 41 P2
Kerthen Wood Cnwll 2 F8
Kesgrave Suffk 47 M3
Kessingland Suffk 59 Q3
Kessingland Beach Suffk 59 Q3
Kestle Cnwll 3 N5
Kestle Mill Cnwll 3 L3
Keston Gt Lon 33 M9
Keswick Cumb 88 H2
Keswick Norfk 71 J11
Ketsby Lincs 80 G8
Kettering Nhants 55 L5
Ketteringham Norfk 70 H11
Kettins P & K 124 E5
Kettlebaston Suffk 58 E10
Kettlebridge Fife 124 F11
Kettlebrook Staffs 65 N11
Kettleburgh Suffk 59 K8
Kettle Green Herts 45 M8
Kettleholm D & G 97 N3
Kettleness N York 92 G4
Kettleshulme Ches E 77 J8

Kettlesing N York.....85 J4
Kettlesing Bottom N York..85 K4
Kettlestone Norfk.....70 E6
Kettlethorpe Lincs.....79 L8
Kettletoft Ork.....147 e2
Kettlewell N York.....90 F12
Ketton Rutlnd.....67 N11
Kew Gt Lon.....32 H7
Kew Royal Botanic
Gardens Gt Lon.....32 G7
Kewstoke N Som.....28 D9
Kexbrough Barns.....77 P2
Kexby C York.....86 C5
Kexby Lincs.....79 L6
Key Green Ches E.....76 G11
Key Green N York.....92 G6
Keyham Leics.....66 H11
Keyhaven Hants.....12 K6
Keyingham E R Yk.....87 N10
Keymer W Susx.....15 K8
Keynsham BaNES.....29 K8
Keysoe Bed.....55 Q8
Keysoe Row Bed.....56 B8
Keyston Cambs.....55 P5
Key Street Kent.....34 F9
Keyworth Notts.....66 G6
Kibbear Somset.....21 K9
Kibblesworth Gatesd.....100 G7
Kibworth Beauchamp
Leics.....54 H2
Kibworth Harcourt Leics..54 H2
Kidbrooke Gt Lon.....33 M7
Kidburngill Cumb.....88 E2
Kiddemore Green Staffs..64 F10
Kidderminster Worcs.....52 F5
Kiddington Oxon.....43 J7
Kidd's Moor Norfk.....70 G11
Kidlington Oxon.....43 K9
Kidmore End Oxon.....31 P6
Kidsdale D & G.....95 N11
Kidsgrove Staffs.....64 F1
Kidstones N York.....90 F10
Kidwelly Carmth.....38 B10
Kiel Crofts Ag & B.....120 G5
Kielder Nthumb.....107 Q11
Kielder Forest.....107 P12
Kiells Ag & B.....111 J7
Kilbarchan Rens.....113 N8
Kilbeg Highld.....127 M3
Kilberry Ag & B.....111 Q8
Kilbirnie N Ayrs.....113 L10
Kilbride Ag & B.....111 Q5
Kilbride Ag & B.....120 F5
Kilbuiack Moray.....139 K4
Kilburn Derbys.....66 C3
Kilburn Gt Lon.....33 J6
Kilburn N York.....92 A11
Kilby Leics.....54 G2
Kilchamaig Ag & B.....112 B9
Kilchattan Ag & B.....111 J2
Kilchattan Ag & B.....112 G10
Kilcheran Ag & B.....120 F5
Kilchoan Highld.....127 J11
Kilchoman Ag & B.....110 F8
Kilchrenan Ag & B.....121 K8
Kilconquhar Fife.....125 K12
Kilcot Gloucs.....41 L6
Kilcoy Highld.....137 Q5
Kilcreggan Ag & B.....113 K5
Kildale N York.....92 E8
Kildalloig Ag & B.....103 K6
Kildary Highld.....146 E10
Kildavaig Ag & B.....112 E8
Kildavanan Ag & B.....112 F8
Kildonan Highld.....146 G1
Kildonan N Ayrs.....103 Q5
Kildonan Lodge Highld...150 G12
Kildonnan Highld.....127 J2
Kildrochet House D & G..94 F7
Kildrummy Abers.....140 D12
Kildwick N York.....84 F6
Kilfinan Ag & B.....112 D5
Kilfinnan Highld.....129 J5
Kilford Denbgs.....74 E10
Kilgetty Pembks.....37 M9
Kilgrammie S Ayrs.....104 E9
Kilgwrrwg Common
Mons.....28 G3
Kilham E R Yk.....87 K2
Kilham Nthumb.....108 E3
Kilkenneth Ag & B.....118 C4
Kilkenzie Ag & B.....103 J5
Kilkerran Ag & B.....103 K6
Kilkhampton Cnwll.....7 J2
Killamarsh Derbys.....78 D7
Killay Swans.....26 H4
Killean Stirlg.....113 Q4
Killen Highld.....138 C4
Killerby Darltn.....91 K3
Killerton Devon.....9 J5
Killichonan P & K.....122 F1
Killiechonate Highld.....129 J8
Killiechronan Ag & B.....119 P4
Killiecrankie P & K.....130 G11
Killilan Highld.....136 C10
Killimster Highld.....151 P5
Killin Stirlg.....122 F6
Killinghall N York.....85 L3
Killington Cumb.....89 Q9
Killington Devon.....19 N4
Killington Lake Services
Cumb.....89 Q9
Killingworth N Tyne.....100 H4
Killiow Cnwll.....3 L6
Killochyett Border.....116 B12
Kilmacolm Inver.....113 M7
Kilmahog Stirlg.....122 G11
Kilmahumaig Ag & B.....112 A3
Kilmaluag Highld.....142 E10
Kilmany Fife.....124 H8
Kilmarnock E Ayrs.....104 H2
Kilmartin Ag & B.....112 B2
Kilmaurs E Ayrs.....104 G2
Kilmelford Ag & B.....120 F10
Kilmersdon Somset.....22 F3
Kilmeston Hants.....25 K8
Kilmichael Ag & B.....103 J5
Kilmichael Glassary
Ag & B.....112 C3
Kilmichael of Inverlussa
Ag & B.....112 A4
Kilmington Devon.....9 P5
Kilmington Wilts.....22 H6
Kilmington Common
Wilts.....22 H6
Kilmington Street Wilts..22 H6
Kilmorack Highld.....137 N7
Kilmore Ag & B.....120 G8
Kilmore Highld.....127 M3
Kilmory Ag & B.....111 P6
Kilmory Highld.....127 K3
Kilmory N Ayrs.....103 P5
Kilmory Highld.....134 D8
Kilmuir Highld.....138 C6
Kilmuir Highld.....142 D11
Kilmuir Highld.....146 D10
Kilmun Ag & B.....112 H5
Kilnave Ag & B.....110 C9
Kilncadzow S Lans.....114 F11
Kilndown Kent.....16 D4
Kiln Green Wokham.....32 A6
Kilnhill Cumb.....97 P11
Kilnhurst Rothm.....78 D4
Kilninian Ag & B.....119 K4
Kilninver Ag & B.....120 F9
Kiln Pit Hill Nthumb.....100 D7
Kilnsea E R Yk.....87 R12
Kilnsey N York.....84 E1

Kilnwick E R Yk.....87 J5
Kilnwick Percy E R Yk.....86 F5
Kilnwood Vale W Susx.....15 J4
Kiloran Ag & B.....111 J2
Kilpatrick N Ayrs.....103 N4
Kilpeck Herefs.....40 F5
Kilpin E R Yk.....86 E10
Kilpin Pike E R Yk.....86 E10
Kilrenny Fife.....125 L11
Kilsby Nhants.....54 F6
Kilspindie P & K.....124 E7
Kilstay D & G.....94 G10
Kilsyth N Lans.....114 C6
Kiltarlity Highld.....137 N7
Kilton R & Cl.....92 E3
Kilton Somset.....21 J4
Kilton Thorpe R & Cl.....92 E3
Kilve Somset.....21 J4
Kilvington Notts.....67 K4
Kilwinning N Ayrs.....104 E1
Kimberley Norfk.....70 G11
Kimberley Notts.....66 E3
Kimberworth Rothm.....78 C5
Kimblesworth Dur.....100 H9
Kimble Wick Bucks.....44 A10
Kimbolton Cambs.....56 B7
Kimbolton Herefs.....51 N8
Kimcote Leics.....54 F3
Kimmeridge Dorset.....11 M9
Kimmerston Nthumb.....108 F3
Kimpton Hants.....24 D4
Kimpton Herts.....44 H8
Kimworthy Devon.....18 F10
Kinbrace Highld.....150 F10
Kinbuck Stirlg.....123 K11
Kincaple Fife.....125 J9
Kincardine Fife.....114 G4
Kincardine Highld.....145 N7
Kincardine Bridge Fife..114 G4
Kincardine O'Neil Abers..132 F4
Kinclaven P & K.....124 C5
Kincorth C Aber.....133 M4
Kincorth House Moray...139 J3
Kincraig Highld.....130 F3
Kincraigie P & K.....123 P3
Kindallachan P & K.....123 P3
Kinerarach Ag & B.....111 P10
Kineton Gloucs.....42 C6
Kineton Warwks.....53 Q10
Kinfauns P & K.....124 D8
Kingarth Ag & B.....112 G10
Kingcausie Abers.....133 L4
Kingcoed Mons.....40 F11
Kingerby Lincs.....79 Q5
Kingford Devon.....7 K3
Kingham Oxon.....42 F7
Kinghorn Fife.....115 N4
Kinglassie Fife.....115 N2
Kingoodie P & K.....124 G7
King's Acre Herefs.....40 G3
Kingsand Cnwll.....4 G6
Kingsash Bucks.....44 C10
Kingsbarns Fife.....125 L10
Kingsbridge Devon.....5 M8
Kingsbridge Somset.....20 F6
King's Bromley Staffs.....65 L9
Kingsbrook Bucks.....44 B9
Kingsburgh Highld.....134 G5
Kingsbury Gt Lon.....32 H5
Kingsbury Warwks.....53 N1
Kingsbury Episcopi
Somset.....21 P9
King's Caple Herefs.....40 H4
Kingsclere Hants.....31 L10
King's Cliffe Nhants.....55 P1
Kings Clipstone Notts.....78 G10
Kingscote Gloucs.....29 N3
Kingscott Devon.....19 K9
King's Coughton Warwks..53 K9
Kingscross N Ayrs.....103 R4
Kingsdon Somset.....22 C8
Kingsdown Kent.....17 Q1
Kingsdown Swindn.....30 D6
Kingsdown Wilts.....29 N9
Kingseat Abers.....141 L12
Kingseat Fife.....115 L3
Kingsey Bucks.....43 Q10
Kingsfold W Susx.....14 H4
Kingsford C Aber.....133 K3
Kingsford E Ayrs.....113 N11
Kingsford Worcs.....52 F4
Kingsgate Kent.....35 Q8
Kings Green Gloucs.....41 M5
Kingshall Street Suffk.....58 D8
Kingsheanton Devon.....19 L6
King's Heath Birm.....53 K4
Kings Hill Kent.....34 B11
King's Hill Wsall.....52 H1
Kings House Hotel Highld.121 P4
Kingshurst Solhll.....53 M3
Kingskerswell Devon.....5 P3
Kingskettle Fife.....124 F11
Kingsland Dorset.....10 C5
Kingsland Herefs.....51 M8
Kingsland IoA.....72 D7
Kings Langley Herts.....44 F11
Kingsley Ches W.....75 P9
Kingsley Hants.....25 N6
Kingsley Staffs.....65 J3
Kingsley Green W Susx.....14 C5
Kingsley Holt Staffs.....65 J3
Kingsley Park Nhants.....55 J8
Kingslow Shrops.....52 E1
King's Lynn Norfk.....69 M8
Kings Meaburn Cumb.....89 Q2
Kingsmead Hants.....25 K10
King's Mills Guern.....12 b2
King's Moss St Hel.....75 N3
Kingsmuir Angus.....125 J3
Kings Muir Border.....106 C2
King's Newnham Warwks..54 D5
King's Newton Derbys.....66 C7
Kingsnorth Kent.....16 H3
King's Norton Birm.....53 K5
King's Norton Leics.....66 H12
King's Nympton Devon.....19 N9
King's Pyon Herefs.....51 M10
Kings Ripton Cambs.....56 E5
King's Somborne Hants..24 F7
King's Stag Dorset.....10 H3
King's Stanley Gloucs.....41 N11
King's Sutton Nhants.....43 K4
Kingstanding Birm.....53 K2
Kingsteignton Devon.....8 G10
Kingsteps Highld.....138 G6
King Sterndale Derbys.....77 K9
Kingsthorne Herefs.....40 G5
Kingsthorpe Nhants.....55 J8
Kingston Cambs.....56 G9
Kingston Cnwll.....7 J5
Kingston Devon.....5 K7
Kingston Devon.....9 N4
Kingston Dorset.....10 H5
Kingston Dorset.....11 M9
Kingston E Loth.....116 D5
Kingston Hants.....12 H4
Kingston IoW.....12 H8
Kingston Kent.....35 L11
Kingston W Susx.....14 F10
Kingston Bagpuize Oxon..31 J3
Kingston Blount Oxon.....31 Q2

Kingston by Sea W Susx..15 J9
Kingston Deverill Wilts.....23 J6
Kingstone Herefs.....40 F5
Kingstone Somset.....21 N10
Kingstone Staffs.....65 K6
Kingstone Winslow Oxon..30 F5
Kingston Lacy Dorset.....11 M4
Kingston Lisle Oxon.....30 G5
Kingston near Lewes
E Susx.....15 M9
Kingston on Soar Notts...66 E6
Kingston on Spey Moray.139 Q3
Kingston Russell Dorset...10 F6
Kingston St Mary Somset.21 J7
Kingston Seymour N Som..28 E9
Kingston Stert Oxon.....31 Q2
Kingston upon Hull
C KuH.....87 K9
Kingston upon Thames
Gt Lon.....32 H8
Kingstown Cumb.....98 E6
King's Walden Herts.....44 H7
Kingswear Devon.....5 Q5
Kingswells C Aber.....133 L3
Kings Weston Bristl.....28 H7
Kingswinford Dudley.....52 G3
Kingswood Bucks.....43 P8
Kingswood C KuH.....87 K8
Kingswood Gloucs.....29 M4
Kingswood Kent.....34 E12
Kingswood Powys.....62 H11
Kingswood S Glos.....29 K7
Kingswood Somset.....20 H6
Kingswood Surrey.....33 J11
Kingswood Warwks.....53 M6
Kingswood Brook
Warwks.....53 M6
Kingswood Common
Herefs.....51 J10
Kingswood Common
Staffs.....64 F11
Kings Worthy Hants.....24 H7
Kingthorpe Lincs.....80 C8
Kington Herefs.....51 J9
Kington S Glos.....29 J4
Kington Worcs.....53 J9
Kington Langley Wilts.....29 Q7
Kington Magna Dorset...22 G9
Kington St Michael Wilts..29 P7
Kingussie Highld.....130 D4
Kingweston Somset.....22 C7
Kinharrachie Abers.....141 M9
Kinharvie D & G.....97 J5
Kinkell Bridge P & K.....123 N9
Kinknockie Abers.....141 N7
Kinleith C Edin.....115 M8
Kinlet Shrops.....52 D4
Kinloch Fife.....124 G10
Kinloch Highld.....126 G4
Kinloch Highld.....148 H9
Kinloch Highld.....149 M6
Kinloch P & K.....124 B5
Kinlochard Stirlg.....122 D12
Kinlochbervie Highld.....148 F5
Kinlocheil Highld.....128 D8
Kinlochewe Highld.....136 B3
Kinloch Hourn Highld.....128 C3
Kinlochlaggan Highld.....129 P6
Kinlochleven Highld.....128 H12
Kinlochmoidart Highld...127 M9
Kinlochnanuagh Highld..127 N7
Kinloch Rannoch P & K...122 H1
Kinloss Moray.....139 K3
Kinmel Bay Conwy.....74 D7
Kinmuck Abers.....141 K12
Kinmundy Abers.....133 L1
Kinnabus Ag & B.....102 B3
Kinnadie Abers.....141 N7
Kinnaird P & K.....123 N1
Kinneff Abers.....133 K9
Kinnelhead D & G.....106 D9
Kinnell Angus.....125 M3
Kinnerley Shrops.....63 K8
Kinnersley Herefs.....51 K10
Kinnersley Worcs.....41 P3
Kinnerton Powys.....51 J8
Kinnerton Shrops.....51 L1
Kinnerton Green Flints...75 K11
Kinnesswood P & K.....124 D12
Kinninvie Dur.....90 H2
Kinnordy Angus.....124 G2
Kinoulton Notts.....66 H6
Kinross P & K.....124 C12
Kinrossie P & K.....124 D6
Kinross Services P & K....124 C12
Kinsbourne Green Herts..44 G8
Kinsey Heath Ches E.....64 C4
Kinsham Herefs.....51 K7
Kinsham Worcs.....41 Q4
Kinsley Wakefd.....85 M12
Kinson BCP.....11 P5
Kintail Highld.....136 D12
Kintbury W Berk.....30 H9
Kintessack Moray.....139 J4
Kintillo P & K.....124 C9
Kinton Herefs.....51 M6
Kinton Shrops.....63 L8
Kintore Abers.....133 J1
Kintour Ag & B.....111 K11
Kintra Ag & B.....110 H11
Kintra Ag & B.....119 K8
Kintraw Ag & B.....120 F11
Kintyre Ag & B.....103 K2
Kinveachy Highld.....138 G12
Kinver Staffs.....52 F4
Kiplin N York.....91 M7
Kippax Leeds.....85 N9
Kippen Stirlg.....114 B2
Kippford D & G.....96 G7
Kipping's Cross Kent.....16 B3
Kirbister Ork.....147 c5
Kirby Bedon Norfk.....71 K11
Kirby Bellars Leics.....67 J8
Kirby Cane Norfk.....59 M2
Kirby Corner Covtry.....53 P5
Kirby Cross Essex.....47 M7
Kirby Fields Leics.....66 E12
Kirby Green Norfk.....59 M2
Kirby Grindalythe N York..86 G2
Kirby Hill N York.....85 N2
Kirby Hill N York.....91 M6
Kirby Knowle N York.....91 Q10
Kirby-le-Soken Essex.....47 M7
Kirby Misperton N York....92 F12
Kirby Muxloe Leics.....66 E11
Kirby Sigston N York.....91 Q9
Kirby Underdale E R Yk....86 F3
Kirby Wiske N York.....91 P11
Kirdford W Susx.....14 E5
Kirk Highld.....151 N5
Kirkabister Shet.....147 i7
Kirkandrews D & G.....96 C8
Kirkandrews upon Eden
Cumb.....98 D6
Kirkbampton Cumb.....98 C6
Kirkbean D & G.....97 J6
Kirk Bramwith Donc.....78 H2
Kirkbride Cumb.....97 P7
Kirkbridge N York.....91 L9
Kirkbuddo Angus.....125 J4
Kirkburn E R Yk.....86 H4
Kirkburton Kirk.....77 N2
Kirkby Knows.....75 N4
Kirkby Lincs.....79 Q5
Kirkby N York.....92 B8
Kirkby Fleetham N York....91 M9
Kirkby Green Lincs.....80 D12

Kirkby-in-Ashfield Notts..78 E12
Kirkby-in-Furness Cumb..88 H10
Kirkby la Thorpe Lincs.....68 B3
Kirkby Lonsdale Cumb.....89 P11
Kirkby Malham N York.....84 D3
Kirkby Mallory Leics.....66 D12
Kirkby Malzeard N York...91 L11
Kirkbymoorside N York...92 E9
Kirkby on Bain Lincs.....80 E11
Kirkby Overblow N York...85 L6
Kirkby Stephen Cumb.....90 C5
Kirkby Thore Cumb.....89 Q2
Kirkby Underwood Lincs..67 Q7
Kirkby Wharf N York.....85 N7
Kirkby Woodhouse Notts..66 E1
Kirkcaldy Fife.....115 P3
Kirkcambeck Cumb.....98 H5
Kirkchrist D & G.....96 D8
Kirkcolm D & G.....94 E4
Kirkconnel D & G.....105 N7
Kirkconnell D & G.....97 K5
Kirkcowan D & G.....95 L6
Kirkcudbright D & G.....96 D8
Kirkdale Lpool.....75 K5
Kirk Deighton N York.....85 N5
Kirk Ella E R Yk.....87 J9
Kirkfieldbank S Lans.....105 R1
Kirkgunzeon D & G.....96 H5
Kirk Hallam Derbys.....66 D4
Kirkham Lancs.....83 K9
Kirkham N York.....86 D2
Kirkhamgate Wakefd.....85 M9
Kirk Hammerton N York...85 N4
Kirkharle Nthumb.....100 C12
Kirkhaugh Nthumb.....99 K8
Kirkheaton Kirk.....85 J11
Kirkheaton Nthumb.....100 C3
Kirkhill Highld.....137 N7
Kirkhope S Lans.....106 C6
Kirkhouse Cumb.....98 H6
Kirkibost Highld.....135 K12
Kirkinch P & K.....124 F3
Kirkinner D & G.....95 M7
Kirkintilloch E Duns.....114 B6
Kirk Ireton Derbys.....65 P2
Kirkland Cumb.....88 D3
Kirkland Cumb.....99 J11
Kirkland D & G.....97 L3
Kirkland D & G.....105 Q11
Kirkland D & G.....105 N7
Kirkland Guards Cumb....97 N10
Kirk Langley Derbys.....65 P4
Kirkleatham R & Cl.....92 C2
Kirklevington S on T.....91 Q5
Kirkley Suffk.....59 Q2
Kirklington N York.....91 N10
Kirklington Notts.....78 G11
Kirklinton Cumb.....98 E5
Kirkliston C Edin.....115 L6
Kirkmabreck D & G.....95 N7
Kirkmaiden D & G.....94 E9
Kirk Merrington Dur.....100 H12
Kirkmichael P & K.....124 F2
Kirkmichael S Ayrs.....104 F8
Kirkmuirhill S Lans.....105 P1
Kirknewton Nthumb.....108 E4
Kirknewton W Loth.....115 L8
Kirkney Abers.....140 D9
Kirk of Shotts N Lans.....114 F8
Kirkoswald Cumb.....98 H10
Kirkoswald S Ayrs.....104 E8
Kirkpatrick D & G.....106 B11
Kirkpatrick Durham
D & G.....96 F4
Kirkpatrick-Fleming
D & G.....98 C4
Kirk Sandall Donc.....78 G2
Kirksanton Cumb.....88 F10
Kirk Smeaton N York.....85 Q12
Kirkstall Leeds.....85 K8
Kirkstead Lincs.....80 D11
Kirkstile Abers.....140 E9
Kirkstone Pass Inn Cumb..89 L5
Kirkstyle Highld.....151 P2
Kirkthorpe Wakefd.....85 M11
Kirkton Abers.....140 G10
Kirkton D & G.....97 K2
Kirkton Fife.....124 G8
Kirkton Highld.....136 C6
Kirkton Highld.....136 C7
Kirkton P & K.....123 N9
Kirkton Manor Border....106 C3
Kirkton of
Auchterhouse Angus..124 G5
Kirkton of Barevan
Highld.....138 F8
Kirkton of Collace P & K..124 D6
Kirkton of Durris Abers...133 J5
Kirkton of Glenbuchat
Abers.....132 B1
Kirkton of Glenisla
Angus.....131 N12
Kirkton of Kingoldrum
Angus.....124 G2
Kirkton of Lethendy
P & K.....124 C5
Kirkton of Logie Buchan
Abers.....141 N10
Kirkton of Maryculter
Abers.....133 K4
Kirkton of Menmuir
Angus.....132 E12
Kirkton of Monikie
Angus.....125 K5
Kirkton of Rayne Abers..140 H10
Kirkton of Skene Abers...133 K3
Kirkton of Tealing Angus.124 H5
Kirkton of Tough Abers...132 F2
Kirktown Abers.....141 N5
Kirktown Abers.....141 Q5
Kirktown of Alvah Abers..140 G4
Kirktown of Bourtie
Abers.....141 K10
Kirktown of Deskford
Moray.....140 D4
Kirktown of Fetteresso
Abers.....133 K7
Kirktown of Mortlach
Moray.....139 P8
Kirktown of Slains
Abers.....141 P10
Kirkurd Border.....105 M1
Kirkwall Ork.....147 c4
Kirkwall Airport Ork.....147 d5
Kirkwhelpington Nthumb.100 D2
Kirk Yetholm Border.....108 E4
Kirmington N Linc.....80 H3
Kirmond le Mire Lincs.....80 C6
Kirn Ag & B.....112 H6
Kirriemuir Angus.....124 G2
Kirstead Green Norfk.....59 L1
Kirtlebridge D & G.....97 Q4
Kirtling Cambs.....57 N9
Kirtling Green Cambs.....57 N9
Kirtlington Oxon.....43 K8
Kirtomy Highld.....150 G3
Kirton Lincs.....68 G4
Kirton Notts.....78 H10
Kirton Suffk.....47 N4
Kirton End Lincs.....68 F3
Kirtonhill W Duns.....113 M6
Kirton Holme Lincs.....68 F4

Kirton in Lindsey N Linc..79 M4
Kirwaugh D & G.....95 M7
Kishorn Highld.....135 Q8
Kislingbury Nhants.....54 H9
Kitebrook Warwks.....42 F5
Kite Green Warwks.....53 M7
Kites Hardwick Warwks...54 D7
Kitleigh Cnwll.....7 J3
Kitt Green Wigan.....75 P3
Kittisford Somset.....20 H9
Kittle Swans.....26 E4
Kitt's Green Birm.....53 M3
Kittybrewster C Aber.....133 M3
Kitwood Hants.....25 L8
Kivernoll Herefs.....40 G5
Kiveton Park Rothm.....78 E7
Knaith Lincs.....79 L6
Knaith Park Lincs.....79 L6
Knap Corner Dorset.....22 H8
Knaphill Surrey.....32 D10
Knapp Hill Hants.....24 G8
Knapthorpe Notts.....79 J12
Knapton C York.....85 R5
Knapton N York.....92 H11
Knapton Norfk.....71 L5
Knapton Green Herefs....51 M10
Knapwell Cambs.....56 F8
Knaresborough N York....85 M4
Knarsdale Nthumb.....99 K7
Knaven Abers.....141 L7
Knayton N York.....91 Q9
Knebworth Herts.....45 J8
Knedlington E R Yk.....86 D9
Kneesall Notts.....78 H11
Kneesworth Cambs.....45 L3
Knelston Swans.....26 C4
Knenhall Staffs.....64 H5
Knettishall Suffk.....58 E4
Knightacott Devon.....19 N5
Knightcote Warwks.....54 C9
Knightley Staffs.....64 F7
Knightley Dale Staffs.....64 F7
Knighton BCP.....11 P5
Knighton C Leic.....66 G12
Knighton Devon.....5 K7
Knighton Dorset.....10 H2
Knighton Powys.....51 J6
Knighton Somset.....21 K4
Knighton Staffs.....64 D7
Knighton Staffs.....64 D4
Knighton on Teme Worcs..52 B6
Knightsbridge Gloucs.....41 P6
Knightsmill Cnwll.....6 H4
Knightwick Worcs.....52 D9
Knill Herefs.....51 J8
Knipoch Ag & B.....120 F8
Knipton Leics.....67 L5
Knitsley Dur.....100 E8
Kniveton Derbys.....65 N3
Knock Cumb.....89 R1
Knock Highld.....127 M4
Knock Moray.....140 E5
Knock W Isls.....152 g3
Knockally Highld.....151 L10
Knockan Highld.....144 F3
Knockando Moray.....139 M7
Knockbain Highld.....137 P7
Knockbain Highld.....138 B5
Knockbreck Highld.....134 C5
Knockbrex D & G.....96 B9
Knock Castle N Ayrs.....113 J8
Knockdee Highld.....151 L4
Knockdow Ag & B.....112 G7
Knockdown Wilts.....29 N5
Knockeen S Ayrs.....104 F10
Knockenkelly N Ayrs.....103 Q4
Knockentiber E Ayrs.....104 G2
Knockhall Kent.....33 Q7
Knockholt Kent.....33 N10
Knockholt Pound Kent....33 N10
Knockin Shrops.....63 K7
Knockinlaw E Ayrs.....104 H2
Knocknain D & G.....94 C4
Knockrome Ag & B.....111 M7
Knocksharry IoM.....102 c4
Knocksheen D & G.....96 C2
Knockvennie Smithy
D & G.....96 F4
Knodishall Suffk.....59 N8
Knodishall Common
Suffk.....59 N8
Knole Somset.....21 P8
Knole Park S Glos.....29 J6
Knolls Green Ches E.....76 F8
Knolton Wrexhm.....63 L4
Knook Wilts.....23 J5
Knossington Leics.....67 K10
Knott End-on-Sea Lancs..82 H5
Knotting Bed.....55 P8
Knotting Green Bed.....55 P8
Knottingley Wakefd.....85 Q10
Knotty Ash Lpool.....75 L5
Knotty Green Bucks.....32 C3
Knowbury Shrops.....51 P6
Knowe D & G.....95 K5
Knowehead D & G.....105 L11
Knoweside S Ayrs.....104 E7
Knowes of Elrick Abers...140 F5
Knowle Bristl.....29 J7
Knowle Devon.....8 C8
Knowle Devon.....9 J7
Knowle Devon.....9 K8
Knowle Devon.....19 J6
Knowle Shrops.....51 Q6
Knowle Solhll.....53 M5
Knowle Somset.....20 D6
Knowle Cross Devon.....9 K6
Knowlefield Cumb.....98 E7
Knowle Green Lancs.....83 M8
Knowle Hill Surrey.....32 D9
Knowle St Giles Somset...21 N10
Knowle Village Hants.....13 J3
Knowl Green Essex.....46 D4
Knowl Hill W & M.....32 B7
Knowlton Kent.....35 N11
Knowsley Knows.....75 M4
Knowsley Safari Knows...75 M5
Knowstone Devon.....20 C9
Knox N York.....85 L4
Knox Bridge Kent.....16 E3
Knoydart Highld.....127 P4
Knucklas Powys.....51 J6
Knuston Nhants.....55 M7
Knutsford Ches E.....76 D8
Knutsford Services
Ches E.....76 D8
Knutton Staffs.....64 F3
Krumlin Calder.....84 G11
Kuggar Cnwll.....2 H11
Kyleakin Highld.....135 P11
Kyle of Lochalsh
Highld.....135 N10
Kylerhea Highld.....127 N2
Kylesku Highld.....148 E9
Kylesmorar Highld.....127 P6
Kyles Scalpay W Isls.....152 f5
Kylestrome Highld.....148 E9
Kynaston Herefs.....41 J5
Kynaston Shrops.....63 K8
Kynnersley Wrekin.....64 C9
Kyre Green Worcs.....52 B8
Kyre Park Worcs.....52 B8
Kyrewood Worcs.....52 B7
Kyrle Somset.....20 D9

L

La Bellieuse Guern.....12 c3
Lacasaigh W Isls.....152 f4
Lacasdal W Isls.....152 g3
Laceby NE Lin.....80 D2
Lacey Green Bucks.....32 B2
Lach Dennis Ches W.....76 D9
Lackenby R & Cl.....92 C2
Lackford Suffk.....57 Q6
Lackford Green Suffk.....57 Q6
Lacock Wilts.....29 Q8
Ladbroke Warwks.....54 C9
Ladderedge Staffs.....64 H1
Laddingford Kent.....16 C1
Lade Bank Lincs.....68 H2
Ladock Cnwll.....3 L4
Lady Ork.....147 e2
Ladybank Fife.....124 F11
Ladycross Cnwll.....7 L7
Ladygill S Lans.....106 B4
Lady Hall Cumb.....88 G9
Ladykirk Border.....117 K11
Ladyridge Herefs.....41 L5
Lady's Green Suffk.....57 P9
Ladywood Birm.....53 K3
Ladywood Worcs.....52 F8
La Fontenelle Guern.....12 c1
La Fosse Guern.....12 c3
Lag D & G.....96 H1
Lagavulin Ag & B.....111 J12
Lagg N Ayrs.....103 P5
Laggan Highld.....129 K5
Laggan Highld.....130 B5
Lagganlia Highld.....130 F4
La Grève de Lecq Jersey..13 a1
La Hougue Bie Jersey.....13 b2
La Houguette Guern.....12 b2
Laid Highld.....149 J5
Laide Highld.....143 N7
Laig Highld.....126 H7
Laigh Clunch E Ayrs.....113 N11
Laigh Fenwick E Ayrs.....104 H1
Laigh Glenmuir E Ayrs...105 L6
Laighstonehall S Lans....114 C10
Laindon Essex.....34 B4
Lairg Highld.....145 N4
Laisterdyke C Brad.....85 J8
Laithes Cumb.....98 F11
Lake Devon.....7 L7
Lake Devon.....19 L7
Lake IoW.....13 K8
Lake Wilts.....23 P5
Lake District Cumb.....88 H4
Lake District National
Park Cumb.....88 H4
Lakenham Norfk.....71 J10
Lakenheath Suffk.....57 N4
Laker's Green Surrey.....14 E4
Lakes End Norfk.....57 K1
Lakeside Cumb.....89 K9
Laleham Surrey.....32 F8
Laleston Brdgnd.....27 L6
Lamanva Cnwll.....3 J8
Lamarsh Essex.....46 F4
Lamas Norfk.....71 J7
Lamb Roe Lancs.....83 Q7
Lambden Border.....108 B3
Lamberhurst Kent.....16 B4
Lamberhurst Down Kent..16 B4
Lamberton Border.....117 L9
Lambeth Gt Lon.....33 K6
Lambfair Green Suffk.....57 N10
Lambley Notts.....66 G3
Lambley Nthumb.....99 K6
Lambourn End Essex.....33 N3
Lambourn Woodlands
W Berk.....30 G7
Lambs Green W Susx.....15 J3
Lambston Pembks.....36 H7
Lamellion Cnwll.....4 C4
Lamerton Devon.....7 Q7
Lamesley Gatesd.....100 G6
Lamington S Lans.....106 C4
Lamlash N Ayrs.....103 Q4
Lamloch D & G.....105 K10
Lamonby Cumb.....98 E11
Lamorick Cnwll.....3 P2
Lamorna Cnwll.....2 C9
Lamorran Cnwll.....3 L5
Lampen Cnwll.....4 B3
Lampeter Cerdgn.....49 K11
Lampeter Velfrey Pembks.37 M7
Lamphey Pembks.....37 K10
Lamplugh Cumb.....88 E3
Lamport Nhants.....55 K6
Lamyatt Somset.....22 F6
Lana Devon.....7 K5
Lana Devon.....7 L5
Lanark S Lans.....106 A1
Lancaster Lancs.....83 L3
Lancaster Services Lancs..83 L3
Lancaut Gloucs.....28 H3
Lanchester Dur.....100 F9
Lancing W Susx.....14 H9
Landbeach Cambs.....57 J8
Landcross Devon.....19 J8
Landerberry Abers.....133 J3
Landford Wilts.....24 D9
Land-hallow Highld.....151 M10
Landimore Swans.....26 C4
Landkey Devon.....19 L7
Landore Swans.....26 G4
Landrake Cnwll.....4 F5
Landscove Devon.....5 N3
Land's End Airport Cnwll...2 B8
Landshipping Pembks.....37 K8
Landue Cnwll.....7 L9
Landulph Cnwll.....4 G4
Landwade Suffk.....57 M7
Lane Cnwll.....3 K2
Laneast Cnwll.....7 J7
Lane Bottom Lancs.....84 C8
Lane End Bucks.....32 B4
Lane End Cnwll.....6 F11
Lane End Hants.....25 J7
Lane End Kent.....33 Q8
Lane End Lancs.....84 C7
Lane End Warrtn.....76 C6
Lane End Wilts.....23 J4
Lane Ends Derbys.....65 N5
Lane Ends Lancs.....83 Q9
Lane Ends N York.....84 E6
Lane Green Staffs.....64 F11
Lane Head Dur.....91 J4
Lanehead Dur.....99 N10
Lanehead Nthumb.....99 M11
Lane Head Wigan.....76 B4
Lane Head Wsall.....64 H12
Lane Heads Lancs.....83 J8
Lanercost Cumb.....98 H5
Laneshaw Bridge Lancs...84 C7
Lane Side Lancs.....84 B10
Langaford Devon.....7 M5
Langal Highld.....127 M10
Langaller Somset.....21 K8
Langar Notts.....67 J5
Langbank Rens.....113 M6
Langbar N York.....84 G5
Langbaurgh N York.....92 D7
Langcliffe N York.....84 B2

Langdale End N York.....93 J8
Langdon Cnwll.....7 K7
Langdon Beck Dur.....99 N12
Langdon Hills Essex.....34 B5
Langdown Hants.....12 G3
Langdyke Fife.....124 G11
Langenhoe Essex.....46 H8
Langford C Beds.....44 H3
Langford Devon.....9 J4
Langford Essex.....46 E10
Langford Notts.....79 K12
Langford Oxon.....42 F11
Langford Budville Somset.20 H9
Langham Dorset.....22 H8
Langham Essex.....46 H5
Langham Norfk.....70 F3
Langham Rutlnd.....67 K9
Langham Suffk.....58 E6
Langho Lancs.....83 P8
Langholm D & G.....98 D1
Langland Swans.....26 F6
Langlee Border.....107 M3
Langley Ches E.....76 H9
Langley Derbys.....66 D3
Langley Gloucs.....42 B6
Langley Hants.....12 G4
Langley Herts.....45 J7
Langley Kent.....34 E12
Langley Nthumb.....99 M6
Langley Oxon.....42 G8
Langley Rochdl.....76 F2
Langley Slough.....32 E6
Langley W Susx.....25 P9
Langley Warwks.....53 M8
Langley Burrell Wilts.....29 Q7
Langley Castle Nthumb...99 N6
Langley Common Derbys..65 P4
Langley Green Derbys.....65 P4
Langley Green Essex.....46 F7
Langley Green Warwks....53 M8
Langley Heath Kent.....34 E12
Langley Lower Green
Essex.....45 N5
Langley Marsh Somset.....20 G9
Langley Mill Derbys.....66 D3
Langley Moor Dur.....100 G10
Langley Park Dur.....100 G9
Langley Street Norfk.....71 M11
Langley Upper Green
Essex.....45 N5
Langley Vale Surrey.....33 J10
Langney E Susx.....16 C9
Langold Notts.....78 F6
Langore Cnwll.....7 K7
Langport Somset.....21 P8
Langrick Lincs.....68 F3
Langridge BaNES.....29 L8
Langridgeford Devon.....19 L9
Langrigg Cumb.....97 N9
Langrish Hants.....25 M8
Langsett Barns.....77 N4
Langside P & K.....123 K10
Langstone Hants.....13 M4
Langstone Newpt.....28 E4
Langthorne N York.....91 L8
Langthorpe N York.....85 M2
Langthwaite N York.....90 G6
Langtoft E R Yk.....87 J2
Langtoft Lincs.....68 C8
Langton Dur.....91 K3
Langton Lincs.....80 E10
Langton Lincs.....80 G9
Langton by Wragby Lincs..80 C8
Langton Green Kent.....15 Q2
Langton Green Suffk.....58 H6
Langton Herring Dorset...10 F8
Langton Long Blandford
Dorset.....11 L4
Langton Matravers
Dorset.....11 N9
Langtree Devon.....19 J10
Langtree Week Devon.....19 J10
Langwathby Cumb.....98 H11
Langwell Highld.....144 H4
Langwell House Highld...151 K12
Langwith Derbys.....78 E10
Langwith Junction
Derbys.....78 E10
Langworth Lincs.....79 Q9
Lanhydrock Cnwll.....3 Q2
Lanivet Cnwll.....3 P2
Lanjeth Cnwll.....3 N4
Lank Cnwll.....6 H7
Lanlivery Cnwll.....3 Q3
Lanner Cnwll.....2 H7
Lanoy Cnwll.....7 K9
Lanreath Cnwll.....4 C5
Lansallos Cnwll.....4 B6
Lanteglos Highway Cnwll..4 B6
Lanton Border.....107 P5
Lanton Nthumb.....108 E3
La Passee Guern.....12 c1
Lapford Devon.....8 B3
Laphroaig Ag & B.....111 J12
Lapley Staffs.....64 G9
La Pulente Jersey.....13 a2
Lapworth Warwks.....53 M6
Larachbeg Highld.....120 D1
Larbert Falk.....114 F5
Larbreck Lancs.....83 K7
Largie Abers.....140 F9
Largiemore Ag & B.....112 D4
Largoward Fife.....125 J11
Largs N Ayrs.....113 J6
Largybeg N Ayrs.....103 Q5
Largymore N Ayrs.....103 Q5
Larkbeare Devon.....9 K5
Larkfield Inver.....113 K6
Larkfield Kent.....34 C10
Larkhall S Lans.....114 D11
Larkhill Wilts.....23 P4
Larling Norfk.....58 E3
La Rocque Jersey.....13 c3
Lartington Dur.....90 H3
Lasborough Gloucs.....29 N5
Lasham Hants.....25 M3
Lashbrook Devon.....7 M3
Lashbrook Devon.....19 N4
Lashenden Kent.....16 E3
Lask Edge Staffs.....76 G12
Lasswade Mdloth.....115 P8
Lastingham N York.....92 H8
Latcham Somset.....21 P4
Latchford Herts.....45 M7
Latchford Oxon.....31 N2
Lately Common Warrtn....76 C4
Lathbury M Keyn.....55 L10
Latheron Highld.....151 M10
Latheronwheel Highld....151 M10
Lathom Lancs.....75 M2
Lathones Fife.....125 J11
Latimer Bucks.....32 E3
Latteridge S Gloucs.....29 K5
Lattiford Somset.....22 F8
Latton Wilts.....30 C4
Lauder Border.....116 C11
Laugharne Carmth.....37 N8
Laughterton Lincs.....79 L8

Laughton E Susx 15 P8
Laughton Leics 54 H3
Laughton Lincs 67 Q6
Laughton Lincs 79 L4
Laughton Common Rothm 78 E6
Laughton-en-le-Morthen Rothm 78 E6
Launcells Cnwll 7 J4
Launcells Cross Cnwll 7 K4
Launceston Cnwll 7 L8
Launton Oxon 43 M7
Laurencekirk Abers 132 H10
Laurieston D & G 96 D5
Laurieston Falk 114 G5
Lavendon M Keyn 55 M10
Lavenham Suffk 58 D10
Lavernock V Glam 28 A8
Laversdale Cumb 98 F6
Laverstock Wilts 23 P7
Laverstoke Hants 24 H4
Laverton Gloucs 42 C4
Laverton N York 91 L12
Laverton Somset 22 H3
La Villette Guern 12 c3
Lavister Wrexhm 75 L12
Law S Lans 114 E10
Lawers P & K 122 H5
Lawford Essex 47 K5
Lawford Somset 21 J6
Law Hill S Lans 114 E11
Lawhitton Cnwll 7 L8
Lawkland N York 84 A2
Lawkland Green N York 84 B2
Lawley Wrekin 64 C10
Lawnhead Staffs 64 F7
Lawrence Weston Bristl 28 H6
Lawrenny Pembks 37 K9
Lawrenny Quay Pembks 37 K9
Lawshall Suffk 58 C10
Lawshall Green Suffk 58 C10
Lawton Herefs 51 M9
Laxay W Isls 152 f4
Laxdale W Isls 152 g3
Laxey IoM 102 f5
Laxfield Suffk 59 L6
Laxford Bridge Highld 148 F7
Laxo Shet 147 j5
Laxton E R Yk 86 E10
Laxton Nhants 55 N1
Laxton Notts 79 J10
Laycock C Brad 84 F7
Layer Breton Essex 46 G8
Layer-de-la-Haye Essex 46 G7
Layer Marney Essex 46 G8
Layham Suffk 47 J4
Laymore Dorset 10 B4
Layter's Green Bucks 32 E4
Laytham E R Yk 86 D7
Laythes Cumb 97 P7
Lazenby R & Cl 92 C3
Lazonby Cumb 98 G10
Lea Derbys 77 Q12
Lea Herefs 41 K7
Lea Lincs 79 L6
Lea Shrops 51 K3
Lea Shrops 63 L10
Lea Wilts 29 Q5
Leachkin Highld 138 B7
Leadburn Border 115 N10
Leadenham Lincs 67 N2
Leaden Roding Essex 45 Q9
Leadgate Cumb 99 K9
Leadgate Dur 100 E8
Leadgate Nthumb 100 E6
Leadhills S Lans 106 A7
Leadingcross Green Kent 34 F12
Leadmill Derbys 77 N7
Leafield Oxon 42 G8
Leagrave Luton 44 F7
Leahead Ches W 76 C10
Lea Heath Staffs 65 J7
Leake N York 91 Q8
Leake Common Side Lincs 68 H2
Lealholm N York 92 F5
Lealholm Side N York 92 F5
Lealt Highld 135 J4
Leam Derbys 77 N8
Lea Marston Warwks 53 M2
Leamington Hastings Warwks 54 D7
Leamington Spa Warwks 53 Q7
Leamside Dur 101 J9
Leap Cross E Susx 15 Q9
Learney Abers 132 F4
Leasgill Cumb 89 M10
Leasingham Lincs 67 Q2
Leasingthorne Dur 100 H12
Leatherhead Surrey 32 H11
Leathley N York 85 K6
Leaton Shrops 63 M8
Leaton Wrekin 63 Q10
Lea Town Lancs 83 L9
Leaveland Kent 34 H11
Leavenheath Suffk 46 G4
Leavening N York 86 E3
Leaves Green Gt Lon 33 M10
Lea Yeat Cumb 90 C9
Lebberston N York 93 M10
Le Bigard Guern 12 b3
Le Bourg Guern 12 c3
Le Bourg Jersey 13 d3
Lechlade on Thames Gloucs 30 E2
Lecht Gruinart Ag & B 110 G7
Leck Lancs 89 Q11
Leckbuie P & K 123 J5
Leckford Hants 24 F6
Leckhampstead Bucks 43 P4
Leckhampstead W Berk 31 J7
Leckhampstead Thicket W Berk 31 J7
Leckhampton Gloucs 41 Q8
Leckmelm Highld 144 F7
Leckwith V Glam 27 R7
Leconfield E R Yk 87 J6
Ledaig Ag & B 120 G5
Ledburn Bucks 44 C7
Ledbury Herefs 41 L4
Leddington Gloucs 41 L5
Ledgemoor Herefs 51 L10
Ledicot Herefs 51 L8
Ledmore Highld 144 G3
Ledsham Ches W 75 K9
Ledsham Leeds 85 P9
Ledston Leeds 85 N9
Ledstone Devon 5 M7
Ledston Luck Leeds 85 N9
Ledwell Oxon 43 J6
Lee Devon 19 J4
Lee Gt Lon 33 M7
Lee Hants 24 F9
Lee Shrops 63 L6
Leebotwood Shrops 51 N1
Lee Brockhurst Shrops 63 P7
Leece Cumb 82 G1
Lee Chapel Essex 34 C5
Lee Clump Bucks 44 C10
Lee Common Bucks 44 C11
Leeds Kent 34 E11
Leeds Leeds 85 L8
Leeds Bradford Airport Leeds 85 K7
Leeds Castle Kent 34 E11
Leeds Skelton Lake Services Leeds 85 M9
Leedstown Cnwll 2 F7
Lee Green Ches E 76 C11
Leek Staffs 77 J12
Leek Wootton Warwks 53 P7
Lee Mill Devon 5 J5
Leeming C Brad 84 F8
Leeming N York 91 M9
Leeming Bar N York 91 M8
Leeming Bar Rest Area N York 91 M9
Lee Moor Devon 5 J4
Lee-on-the-Solent Hants 13 J5
Lees C Brad 84 F7
Lees Derbys 65 N5
Lees Oldham 76 H3
Lees Green Derbys 65 N5
Leesthorpe Leics 67 K9
Leeswood Flints 75 J11
Leetown P & K 124 E8
Leftwich Ches W 76 C9
Legar Powys 40 B8
Legbourne Lincs 80 G7
Legburthwaite Cumb 89 J3
Legerwood Border 107 P1
Legoland W & M 32 D7
Le Gron Guern 12 b3
Legsby Lincs 80 C6
Le Haguais Jersey 13 c3
Le Hocq Jersey 13 d3
Leicester C Leic 66 F11
Leicester Forest East Leics 66 E11
Leicester Forest East Services Leics 66 E11
Leigh Devon 19 P11
Leigh Dorset 10 F3
Leigh Gloucs 41 P6
Leigh Kent 15 Q2
Leigh Shrops 63 K11
Leigh Surrey 15 J1
Leigh Wigan 76 C4
Leigh Wilts 30 C4
Leigh Worcs 52 E10
Leigh Beck Essex 34 E6
Leigh Delamere Wilts 29 P6
Leigh Delamere Services Wilts 29 P6
Leigh Green Kent 16 F4
Leigh Knoweglass S Lans 114 B11
Leighland Chapel Somset 20 G6
Leigh-on-Sea Sthend 34 E5
Leigh Park Dorset 11 P5
Leigh Park Hants 13 M3
Leigh Sinton Worcs 52 E10
Leighswood Wsall 65 K12
Leighterton Gloucs 29 N4
Leighton N York 91 K11
Leighton Powys 62 H11
Leighton Shrops 63 Q11
Leighton Somset 22 F4
Leighton Bromswold Cambs 56 C5
Leighton Buzzard C Beds 44 C6
Leigh upon Mendip Somset 22 F4
Leigh Woods N Som 28 H8
Leinthall Earls Herefs 51 M7
Leinthall Starkes Herefs 51 M7
Leintwardine Herefs 51 L6
Leire Leics 54 E3
Leiston Suffk 59 N8
Leith C Edin 115 N6
Leitholm Border 108 C1
Lelant Cnwll 2 E7
Lelley E R Yk 87 N8
Lem Hill Worcs 52 D5
Lempitlaw Border 108 C3
Lemreway W Isls 152 g5
Lemsford Herts 45 J9
Lenchwick Worcs 42 B2
Lendalfoot S Ayrs 104 C11
Lendrick Stirlg 122 F11
Lendrum Terrace Abers 141 Q7
Lenham Kent 34 F12
Lenham Heath Kent 34 G12
Lenie Highld 137 N10
Lennel Border 108 D2
Lennox Plunton D & G 96 C8
Lennoxtown E Duns 114 B6
Lent Bucks 32 D6
Lenton C Nott 66 F4
Lenton Lincs 67 P6
Lenwade Norfk 70 G8
Lenzie E Duns 114 B7
Leochel-Cushnie Abers 132 E2
Leomansley Staffs 65 L10
Leominster Herefs 51 N9
Leonard Stanley Gloucs 41 N11
Leoville Jersey 13 a1
Lepe Hants 12 G5
Lephin Highld 134 C6
Leppington N York 86 E3
Lepton Kirk 85 J12
Lerags Ag & B 120 F7
L'Erée Guern 12 b2
Lerryn Cnwll 4 A5
Lerwick Shet 147 j7
Les Arquêts Guern 12 b3
Lesbury Nthumb 109 L7
Les Hubits Guern 12 c3
Leslie Abers 140 F11
Leslie Fife 115 N1
Les Lohiers Guern 12 b2
Lesmahagow S Lans 105 Q2
Les Murchez Guern 12 b3
Lesnewth Cnwll 6 G6
Les Nicolles Guern 12 c3
Les Quartiers Guern 12 c2
Les Quennevais Jersey 13 a2
Les Sages Guern 12 b3
Lessingham Norfk 71 M6
Lessonhall Cumb 97 P8
Lestowder Cnwll 3 K9
Les Villets Guern 12 b3
Leswalt D & G 94 E5
L'Etacq Jersey 13 a1
Letchmore Heath Herts 32 G3
Letchworth Garden City Herts 45 J5
Letcombe Bassett Oxon 30 H5
Letcombe Regis Oxon 30 H5
Letham Angus 125 K3
Letham Border 107 Q8
Letham Falk 114 G4
Letham Fife 124 F10
Letham Grange Angus 125 M4
Lethenty Abers 140 F11
Lethenty Abers 141 K8
Letheringham Suffk 59 K9
Letheringsett Norfk 70 F4
Lettaford Devon 8 D8
Letterewe Highld 143 P11
Letterfearn Highld 136 B11
Letterfinlay Lodge Hotel Highld 129 J6
Letters Highld 144 E7
Lettershaw S Lans 106 B6
Letterston Pembks 36 H4
Lettoch Highld 139 J12
Lettoch Highld 139 K9
Letton Herefs 40 D2
Letton Herefs 51 L6
Lett's Green Kent 33 N10
Letty Green Herts 45 K9
Letwell Rothm 78 F6
Leuchars Fife 125 J8
Leumrabhagh W Isls 152 g5
Leurbost W Isls 152 g4
Levalsa Meor Cnwll 3 N5
Levan Inver 113 J6
Levedale Staffs 64 G9
Level's Green Essex 45 N7
Leven E R Yk 87 L6
Leven Fife 115 Q1
Levens Cumb 89 M9
Levens Green Herts 45 L7
Levenshulme Manch 76 G5
Levenwick Shet 147 i9
Leverburgh W Isls 152 d6
Leverington Cambs 68 H10
Leverstock Green Herts 44 F10
Leverton Lincs 68 H3
Le Villocq Guern 12 c2
Levington Suffk 47 M4
Levisham N York 92 G8
Lew Oxon 42 G10
Lewannick Cnwll 7 K8
Lewdown Devon 7 N7
Lewes E Susx 15 M9
Leweston Pembks 36 H6
Lewisham Gt Lon 33 M7
Lewiston Highld 137 N10
Lewistown Brdgnd 27 M5
Lewis Wych Herefs 51 K9
Lewknor Oxon 31 P3
Leworthy Devon 7 L4
Leworthy Devon 19 N6
Lewson Street Kent 34 G10
Lewth Lancs 83 L8
Lewtrenchard Devon 7 N7
Lexden Essex 46 G6
Lexworthy Somset 21 L6
Ley Cnwll 4 B3
Leybourne Kent 34 B10
Leyburn N York 91 J8
Leycett Staffs 64 E3
Leygreen Herts 44 H7
Ley Hill Bucks 44 E11
Leyland Lancs 83 M10
Leyland Green St Hel 75 P4
Leylodge Abers 133 J2
Leys Abers 141 N5
Leys P & K 124 E5
Leysdown-on-Sea Kent 35 J8
Leysmill Angus 125 M3
Leys of Cossans Angus 124 H3
Leysters Herefs 51 P8
Leyton Gt Lon 33 M5
Leytonstone Gt Lon 33 M5
Lezant Cnwll 7 L9
Lezerea Cnwll 2 H8
Leziate Norfk 69 N8
Lhanbryde Moray 139 P4
Libanus Powys 39 N6
Libberton S Lans 106 C1
Libbery Worcs 52 H9
Liberton C Edin 115 N7
Lichfield Staffs 65 L10
Lickey Worcs 53 J6
Lickey End Worcs 52 H6
Lickey Rock Worcs 52 H6
Lickfold W Susx 14 C5
Liddaton Green Devon 7 N8
Liddesdale Highld 127 P12
Liddington Swindn 30 E6
Lidgate Derbys 77 P8
Lidgate Suffk 57 N9
Lidget Donc 78 G4
Lidgett Notts 78 G10
Lidham Hill E Susx 16 E7
Lidlington C Beds 44 E4
Lidsey W Susx 14 D10
Lidsing Kent 34 D10
Liff Angus 124 G6
Lifford Birm 53 K5
Lifton Devon 7 M8
Liftondown Devon 7 L7
Lighthorne Warwks 53 Q9
Lighthorne Heath Warwks 54 B9
Lightwater Surrey 32 D10
Lightwater Valley Family Adventure Park N York 91 M11
Lightwood C Stke 64 G4
Lightwood Green Ches E 64 B4
Lightwood Green Wrexhm 63 L4
Lilbourne Nhants 54 F5
Lilburn Tower Nthumb 108 G5
Lilford Nhants 55 P4
Lilleshall Wrekin 64 D9
Lilley Herts 44 G6
Lilley W Berk 31 J6
Lilliesleaf Border 107 N5
Lillingstone Dayrell Bucks 43 P4
Lillingstone Lovell Bucks 43 P4
Lillington Dorset 22 E11
Lilliput BCP 11 P7
Lilstock Somset 21 J4
Lilyhurst Shrops 64 D9
Limbrick Lancs 83 N12
Limbury Luton 44 F7
Limebrook Herefs 51 L7
Limefield Bury 76 E1
Limekilnburn S Lans 114 C11
Limekilns Fife 115 K5
Limerigg Falk 114 F7
Limerstone IoW 12 G8
Limestone Brae Nthumb 99 M8
Lime Street Worcs 41 N5
Limington Somset 22 C9
Limmerhaugh E Ayrs 105 L4
Limpenhoe Norfk 71 M11
Limpley Stoke Wilts 29 M10
Limpsfield Surrey 33 M11
Limpsfield Chart Surrey 33 M12
Linby Notts 66 E2
Linchmere W Susx 14 B5
Lincluden D & G 97 K3
Lincoln Lincs 79 N9
Lincomb Worcs 52 F7
Lincombe Devon 5 M8
Lincombe Devon 19 K4
Lindale Cumb 89 L10
Lindal in Furness Cumb 88 H11
Lindfield W Susx 15 L6
Lindford Hants 25 P6
Lindley Kirk 84 H11
Lindley N York 85 K5
Lindores Fife 124 F9
Lindow End Ches E 76 F8
Lindridge Worcs 52 C7
Lindsell Essex 46 B6
Lindsey Suffk 46 H3
Lindsey Tye Suffk 46 H3
Liney Somset 21 N6
Linford Hants 12 C3
Linford Thurr 34 B6
Lingbob C Brad 84 G8
Lingdale R & Cl 92 D3
Lingen Herefs 51 L7
Lingfield Surrey 15 M2
Lingfield Common Surrey 15 M2
Lingwood Norfk 71 M10
Liniclate W Isls 152 c9
Linicro Highld 134 G2
Linkend Worcs 41 N5
Linkenholt Hants 30 H10
Linkhill Kent 16 E5
Linkinhorne Cnwll 7 L10
Linktown Fife 115 N3
Linkwood Moray 139 N4
Linley Shrops 51 K2
Linley Green Herefs 52 C10
Linleygreen Shrops 52 C1
Linlithgow W Loth 114 H6
Linshiels Nthumb 108 E8
Linsidemore Highld 145 M5
Linslade C Beds 44 C7
Linstead Parva Suffk 59 L5
Linstock Cumb 98 E6
Linthurst Worcs 53 J6
Linthwaite Kirk 84 G12
Lintlaw Border 117 J9
Lintmill Moray 140 D3
Linton Border 108 C4
Linton Cambs 45 Q2
Linton Derbys 65 P9
Linton Herefs 41 K6
Linton Kent 34 D12
Linton Leeds 85 N6
Linton N York 84 E3
Linton Nthumb 109 L11
Linton Heath Derbys 65 P9
Linton Hill Herefs 41 K7
Linton-on-Ouse N York 85 P3
Linwood Hants 12 C3
Linwood Lincs 80 B6
Linwood Rens 113 N8
Lionacleit W Isls 152 c9
Lìonal W Isls 152 h1
Lions Green E Susx 15 Q7
Liphook Hants 25 P7
Lipley Shrops 64 D6
Liscard Wirral 75 J5
Liscombe Somset 20 D7
Liskeard Cnwll 4 C4
Lismore Ag & B 120 F4
Liss Hants 25 N8
Lissett E R Yk 87 L4
Liss Forest Hants 25 N7
Lissington Lincs 80 B7
Liston Essex 46 E3
Lisvane Cardif 28 B6
Liswerry Newpt 28 D5
Litcham Norfk 70 C8
Litchborough Nhants 54 G10
Litchfield Hants 24 H3
Litherland Sefton 75 K4
Litlington Cambs 45 K3
Litlington E Susx 15 P10
Little Abington Cambs 57 K10
Little Addington Nhants 55 N6
Little Airies D & G 95 M8
Little Almshoe Herts 44 H6
Little Alne Warwks 53 L8
Little Altcar Sefton 75 J2
Little Amwell Herts 45 L9
Little Asby Cumb 90 A5
Little Aston Staffs 65 K12
Little Atherfield IoW 12 H9
Little Ayton N York 92 B5
Little Baddow Essex 46 D10
Little Badminton S Glos 29 N5
Little Bampton Cumb 98 B7
Little Bardfield Essex 46 B5
Little Barford Bed 56 D9
Little Barningham Norfk 70 H5
Little Barrington Gloucs 42 E9
Little Barrow Ches W 75 M9
Little Barugh N York 92 F10
Little Bavington Nthumb 100 C3
Little Bealings Suffk 59 J11
Littlebeck N York 92 H6
Little Bedwyn Wilts 30 G9
Little Bentley Essex 47 K6
Little Berkhamsted Herts 45 K10
Little Billing Nhants 55 K8
Little Billington C Beds 44 D7
Little Birch Herefs 40 G5
Little Bispham Bpool 82 H7
Little Blakenham Suffk 58 G11
Little Blencow Cumb 98 F11
Little Bloxwich Wsall 65 J11
Little Bognor W Susx 14 E7
Little Bolehill Derbys 65 P1
Little Bollington Ches E 76 D6
Little Bookham Surrey 32 G11
Littleborough Devon 8 F3
Littleborough Notts 79 K7
Littleborough Rochdl 84 D12
Littlebourne Kent 35 M10
Little Bourton Oxon 43 K3
Little Bowden Leics 55 J3
Little Bradley Suffk 57 N10
Little Brampton Herefs 51 J8
Little Brampton Shrops 51 L4
Little Braxted Essex 46 E8
Little Brechin Angus 132 F11
Littlebredy Dorset 10 F7
Little Brickhill M Keyn 44 C5
Little Bridgeford Staffs 64 G7
Little Brington Nhants 54 H8
Little Bromley Essex 47 K6
Little Broughton Cumb 97 M11
Little Budworth Ches W 75 Q10
Littleburn Highld 138 B5
Little Burstead Essex 34 B4
Littlebury Essex 45 P4
Littlebury Green Essex 45 P4
Little Bytham Lincs 67 P8
Little Canfield Essex 45 Q7
Little Carlton Lincs 80 H6
Little Carlton Notts 79 K12
Little Casterton Rutlnd 67 P10
Little Catwick E R Yk 87 L6
Little Catworth Cambs 56 B6
Little Cawthorpe Lincs 80 G7
Little Chalfont Bucks 32 E3
Little Chart Kent 16 G2
Little Chesterford Essex 45 P3
Little Cheveney Kent 16 C2
Little Cheverell Wilts 23 L3
Little Chishill Cambs 45 M4
Little Clacton Essex 47 L8
Little Clanfield Oxon 30 F2
Little Clifton Cumb 88 E1
Little Coates NE Lin 80 E2
Little Comberton Worcs 41 Q3
Little Common E Susx 16 C9
Little Comp Kent 34 B11
Little Compton Warwks 42 F6
Little Corby Cumb 98 F7
Little Cornard Suffk 46 F4
Littlecott Wilts 23 P3
Little Cowarne Herefs 51 Q10
Little Coxwell Oxon 30 G4
Little Crakehall N York 91 L8
Little Cransley Nhants 55 L5
Little Cressingham Norfk 70 C12
Little Crosby Sefton 75 K3
Little Crosthwaite Cumb 88 H1
Little Cubley Derbys 65 M5
Little Dalby Leics 67 K9
Littledean Gloucs 41 K9
Little Dewchurch Herefs 40 H5
Little Ditton Cambs 57 M9
Little Doward Herefs 40 H8
Littledown Hants 30 H10
Little Downham Cambs 57 K4
Little Driffield E R Yk 87 J4
Little Dunham Norfk 70 C9
Little Dunkeld P & K 123 P4
Little Dunmow Essex 46 B7
Little Durnford Wilts 23 P6
Little Easton Essex 45 R7
Little Eaton Derbys 66 B4
Little Ellingham Norfk 70 E12
Little Elm Somset 22 F4
Little Everdon Nhants 54 F9
Little Eversden Cambs 56 G10
Little Faringdon Oxon 30 F2
Little Fencote N York 91 M8
Little Fenton N York 85 Q8
Littleferry Highld 146 E6
Little Fransham Norfk 70 D9
Little Gaddesden Herts 44 E9
Little Garway Herefs 40 F7
Little Gidding Cambs 56 C4
Little Glemham Suffk 59 L9
Little Gorsley Herefs 41 L7
Little Gransden Cambs 56 E9
Little Green Notts 67 J3
Little Green Somset 22 G4
Little Grimsby Lincs 80 F5
Little Gringley Notts 79 J7
Little Habton N York 92 F11
Little Hadham Herts 45 N7
Little Hale Lincs 68 C4
Little Hallam Derbys 66 D4
Little Hallingbury Essex 45 P8
Littleham Devon 9 K8
Littleham Devon 18 H8
Little Hampden Bucks 44 B11
Littlehampton W Susx 14 E10
Little Hanford Dorset 11 K2
Little Harrowden Nhants 55 L6
Little Haseley Oxon 31 N2
Little Hatfield E R Yk 87 M6
Little Hautbois Norfk 71 K8
Little Haven Pembks 36 G8
Littlehaven W Susx 14 H4
Little Hay Staffs 65 L11
Little Hayfield Derbys 77 J6
Little Haywood Staffs 65 J8
Little Heath Staffs 64 G8
Little Heath W Berk 31 N7
Littlehempston Devon 5 N4
Little Hereford Herefs 51 P7
Little Horkesley Essex 46 G5
Little Hormead Herts 45 M6
Little Horsted E Susx 15 N7
Little Horton C Brad 84 H9
Little Horton Wilts 30 B10
Little Horwood Bucks 43 R5
Little Houghton Barns 78 C2
Little Houghton Nhants 55 K8
Littlehoughton Nthumb 109 L6
Little Hucklow Derbys 77 M8
Little Hulton Salfd 76 D3
Little Hungerford W Berk 31 L7
Little Hutton N York 91 Q11
Little Irchester Nhants 55 M7
Little Kelk E R Yk 87 L3
Little Keyford Somset 22 H4
Little Kimble Bucks 44 B10
Little Kineton Warwks 53 Q10
Little Kingshill Bucks 32 C3
Little Knox D & G 96 G6
Little Langdale Cumb 89 J6
Little Langford Wilts 23 N6
Little Laver Essex 45 Q9
Little Leigh Ches W 76 B8
Little Leighs Essex 46 C8
Little Lever Bolton 76 D2
Little Linford M Keyn 44 B3
Little Load Somset 21 P8
Little London Bucks 43 N9
Little London Cambs 56 H1
Little London E Susx 15 Q7
Little London Essex 45 N6
Little London Essex 46 B5
Little London Gloucs 41 L8
Little London Hants 24 F3
Little London Hants 31 N10
Little London Leeds 85 J7
Little London Lincs 68 E8
Little London Lincs 68 H7
Little London Lincs 80 F8
Little London Norfk 69 L8
Little London Powys 50 E3
Little Longstone Derbys 77 M9
Little Madeley Staffs 64 E3
Little Malvern Worcs 41 M4
Little Mancot Flints 75 K10
Little Maplestead Essex 46 E5
Little Marcle Herefs 41 K4
Little Marland Devon 19 K11
Little Marlow Bucks 32 C5
Little Massingham Norfk 69 Q7
Little Melton Norfk 70 H10
Littlemill Abers 131 P5
Littlemill Highld 138 G6
Little Mill Mons 40 D11
Little Milton Oxon 31 N2
Little Missenden Bucks 32 C3
Little Mongeham Kent 35 P12
Littlemoor Derbys 78 B11
Little Moor Somset 21 M7
Littlemore Oxon 43 L11
Little Musgrave Cumb 90 C4
Little Ness Shrops 63 L8
Little Neston Ches W 75 J8
Little Newcastle Pembks 37 J5
Little Newsham Dur 91 J3
Little Norton Somset 21 Q10
Little Oakley Essex 47 M6
Little Oakley Nhants 55 M3
Little Odell Bed 55 N9
Little Offley Herts 44 G6
Little Ormside Cumb 90 B3
Little Orton Cumb 98 D7
Little Ouse Cambs 57 M3
Little Ouseburn N York 85 P3
Littleover C Derb 65 Q5
Little Oxendon Nhants 55 J4
Little Packington Warwks 53 N4
Little Pattenden Kent 16 C2
Little Paxton Cambs 56 D8
Little Petherick Cnwll 6 C10
Little Plumpton Lancs 83 J8
Little Plumstead Norfk 71 L9
Little Ponton Lincs 67 M6
Littleport Cambs 57 L3
Littleport Bridge Cambs 57 L3
Little Posbrook Hants 13 J4
Little Potheridge Devon 19 K10
Little Preston Leeds 85 M9
Little Preston Nhants 54 F10
Littler Ches W 76 B10
Little Raveley Cambs 56 E5
Little Reedness E R Yk 86 E10
Little Ribston N York 85 M4
Little Rissington Gloucs 42 E7
Little Rollright Oxon 42 G6
Little Rowsley Derbys 77 N10
Little Ryburgh Norfk 70 E6
Little Ryle Nthumb 108 G7
Little Ryton Shrops 63 N11
Little Salkeld Cumb 98 H11
Little Sampford Essex 46 B5
Little Sandhurst Br For 32 B10
Little Saredon Staffs 64 H10
Little Saughall Ches W 75 L10
Little Saxham Suffk 57 Q8
Little Scatwell Highld 137 L4
Little Shelford Cambs 57 J10
Little Shrewley Warwks 53 N7
Little Silver Devon 8 G3
Little Singleton Lancs 83 J7
Little Skipwith N York 86 C7
Little Smeaton N York 85 Q11
Little Snoring Norfk 70 D6
Little Sodbury S Glos 29 M6
Little Sodbury End S Glos 29 M5
Little Somborne Hants 24 F7
Little Somerford Wilts 29 Q5
Little Soudley Shrops 64 D6
Little Stainforth N York 84 B2
Little Stainton Darltn 91 N3
Little Stanion Nhants 55 M3
Little Stanney Ches W 75 L9
Little Staughton Bed 56 B8
Little Steeping Lincs 80 H11
Little Stoke Staffs 64 G5
Littlestone-on-Sea Kent 17 K6
Little Stonham Suffk 58 G8
Little Stretton Leics 66 H12
Little Stretton Shrops 51 M2
Little Strickland Cumb 89 P3
Little Stukeley Cambs 56 D5
Little Sugnall Staffs 64 E6
Little Sutton Ches W 75 L8
Little Sutton Shrops 51 N4
Little Swinburne Nthumb 99 Q3
Little Sypland D & G 96 E7
Little Tew Oxon 42 H6
Little Tey Essex 46 F7
Little Thetford Cambs 57 K5
Little Thirkleby N York 91 Q11
Little Thornage Norfk 70 F4
Little Thornton Lancs 83 J7
Little Thorpe Dur 101 L9
Littlethorpe Leics 54 E1
Littlethorpe N York 85 L1
Little Thurlow Suffk 57 N10
Little Thurlow Green Suffk 57 N10
Little Thurrock Thurr 34 A7
Littleton BaNES 28 H9
Littleton Ches W 75 M10
Littleton D & G 96 D7
Littleton Dorset 11 L4
Littleton Hants 24 G7
Littleton Somset 22 C7
Littleton Surrey 14 D1
Littleton Surrey 32 F8
Littleton Drew Wilts 29 N6
Littleton of Airlie Angus 124 G3
Littleton-on-Severn S Glos 29 J4
Littleton Panell Wilts 23 M2
Little Torrington Devon 19 J10
Little Totham Essex 46 F9
Little Town Cumb 88 H3
Littletown Dur 101 J9
Little Town Lancs 83 P8
Little Town Warrtn 76 B5
Little Twycross Leics 65 Q11
Little Urswick Cumb 88 H12
Little Wakering Essex 34 G5
Little Walden Essex 45 Q3
Little Waldingfield Suffk 46 G3
Little Walsingham Norfk 70 D5
Little Waltham Essex 46 C9
Little Warley Essex 33 R4
Little Washbourne Gloucs 42 A5
Little Weighton E R Yk 87 J8
Little Welnetham Suffk 58 C8
Little Welton Lincs 80 F6
Little Wenham Suffk 47 K4
Little Wenlock Wrekin 64 C10
Little Weston Somset 22 E8
Little Whitefield IoW 13 K7
Little Whittingham Green Suffk 59 K5
Little Whittington Nthumb 100 C4
Littlewick Green W & M 32 B6
Little Wilbraham Cambs 57 K9
Littlewindsor Dorset 10 C4
Little Witcombe Gloucs 41 P8
Little Witley Worcs 52 E8
Little Wittenham Oxon 31 M4
Little Wolford Warwks 42 F5
Littlewood Staffs 64 H10
Little Woodcote Gt Lon 33 K10
Littleworth Bucks 44 C7
Littleworth Oxon 30 G3
Littleworth Staffs 64 H7
Littleworth Staffs 65 J10
Littleworth W Susx 14 H7
Littleworth Worcs 52 G10
Littleworth Worcs 53 J8
Littleworth Common Bucks 32 D5
Little Wratting Suffk 46 C2
Little Wymington Bed 55 N7
Little Wymondley Herts 45 J6
Little Wyrley Staffs 65 J11
Little Wytheford Shrops 63 P8
Little Yeldham Essex 46 D4
Littley Green Essex 46 C8
Litton Derbys 77 M8
Litton N York 90 E12
Litton Somset 22 D2
Litton Cheney Dorset 10 E6
Liurbost W Isls 152 g4
Liverpool Lpool 75 K5
Liversedge Kirk 85 J10
Liverton Devon 8 E9
Liverton R & Cl 92 E4
Liverton Mines R & Cl 92 E3
Liverton Street Kent 34 F12
Livingston W Loth 115 K7
Livingston Village W Loth 115 J8
Lixwm Flints 74 G9
Lizard Cnwll 2 H12
Llaingoch IoA 72 C7
Llaithddu Powys 50 E5
Llan Powys 61 Q12
Llanaber Gwynd 61 K8
Llanaelhaearn Gwynd 60 F3
Llanafan Cerdgn 49 M6
Llanafan-Fawr Powys 50 C9
Llanallgo IoA 72 H6
Llanarmon Gwynd 60 G4
Llanarmon Dyffryn Ceiriog Wrexhm 62 G6
Llanarmon-yn-Ial Denbgs 74 G12
Llanarth Cerdgn 48 G9
Llanarth Mons 40 E9
Llanarthne Carmth 38 D7
Llanasa Flints 74 F7
Llanbabo IoA 72 F6
Llanbadarn Fawr Cerdgn 49 K4
Llanbadarn Fynydd Powys 50 F5
Llanbadarn-y-garreg Powys 50 F11
Llanbadoc Mons 28 E2
Llanbadrig IoA 72 F5
Llanbeder Newpt 28 E4
Llanbedr Gwynd 61 K7
Llanbedr Powys 39 Q2
Llanbedr Powys 40 B7
Llanbedr-Dyffryn-Clwyd Denbgs 74 G11
Llanbedrgoch IoA 72 H7
Llanbedrog Gwynd 60 E6
Llanbedr-y-Cennin Conwy 73 N10
Llanberis Gwynd 73 K11
Llanbethêry V Glam 27 N8
Llanbister Powys 50 F6
Llanblethian V Glam 27 N7
Llanboidy Carmth 37 N6
Llanbradach Caerph 27 Q4
Llanbrynmair Powys 62 B11
Llancadle V Glam 27 N8
Llancarfan V Glam 27 P8
Llancayo Mons 40 E11
Llancloudy Herefs 40 G7
Llancynfelyn Cerdgn 49 L2
Llandaff Cardif 27 R7
Llandanwg Gwynd 61 J6
Llandarcy Neath 26 H3
Llandawke Carmth 37 Q8
Llanddaniel Fab IoA 72 H9
Llanddarog Carmth 38 D8
Llanddeiniol Cerdgn 49 J6
Llanddeiniolen Gwynd 73 J10
Llandderfel Gwynd 62 D5
Llanddeusant Carmth 39 J7
Llanddeusant IoA 72 E6
Llanddew Powys 39 P5
Llanddewi Swans 26 C4
Llanddewi Brefi Cerdgn 49 L9
Llanddewi'r Cwm Powys 50 E11
Llanddewi Rhydderch Mons 40 D9
Llanddewi Velfrey Pembks 37 M7
Llanddewi Ystradenni Powys 50 F7
Llanddoged Conwy 73 P11
Llanddona IoA 73 J8
Llanddowror Carmth 37 P7
Llanddulas Conwy 74 B8
Llanddwywe Gwynd 61 K8
Llanddyfnan IoA 72 H8
Llandecwyn Gwynd 61 K5
Llandefaelog Powys 39 N5
Llandefaelog-Tre'r-Graig Powys 39 Q6
Llandefalle Powys 39 Q4
Llandegfan IoA 73 J9
Llandegla Denbgs 62 H2
Llandegley Powys 50 G8
Llandegveth Mons 28 D3
Llandegwning Gwynd 60 D6
Llandeilo Carmth 38 F7
Llandeilo Graban Powys 39 P3
Llandeilo'r Fan Powys 39 L5
Llandeloy Pembks 36 G5
Llandenny Mons 40 F11
Llandevaud Newpt 28 E4
Llandevenny Mons 28 F5
Llandinabo Herefs 40 G6
Llandinam Powys 50 E3
Llandissilio Pembks 37 M6
Llandogo Mons 40 H11
Llandough V Glam 27 N8
Llandough V Glam 27 R8
Llandovery Carmth 39 J5
Llandow V Glam 27 M7
Llandre Carmth 38 G3
Llandre Cerdgn 49 K3
Llandre Isaf Pembks 37 M5
Llandrillo Denbgs 62 E5
Llandrillo-yn-Rhôs Conwy 73 P7
Llandrindod Wells Powys 50 E8
Llandrinio Powys 63 J8
Llandudno Conwy 73 N7
Llandudno Junction Conwy 73 N8
Llandulas Powys 39 L3
Llandwrog Gwynd 60 G1
Llandybie Carmth 38 F8
Llandyfaelog Carmth 38 B9
Llandyfan Carmth 38 F8
Llandyfriog Cerdgn 37 Q2
Llandyfrydog IoA 72 G6
Llandygai Gwynd 73 K9
Llandygwydd Cerdgn 37 P2
Llandynan Denbgs 62 G3
Llandyrnog Denbgs 74 F10
Llandyssil Powys 50 H2
Llandysul Cerdgn 38 B3
Llanedeyrn Cardif 28 B6
Llanedi Carmth 38 E10
Llaneglwys Powys 39 P4
Llanegryn Gwynd 61 K11
Llanegwad Carmth 38 D7
Llaneilian IoA 72 H5
Llanelian-yn-Rhôs Conwy 73 Q8
Llanelidan Denbgs 62 F2
Llanelieu Powys 40 A5
Llanellen Mons 40 D9
Llanelli Carmth 26 D2
Llanelltyd Gwynd 61 M8
Llanelly Mons 40 B8
Llanelly Hill Mons 40 B9
Llanelwedd Powys 50 E10
Llanenddwyn Gwynd 61 K7
Llanengan Gwynd 60 E7
Llanerch Gwynd 62 B9
Llanerch Powys 51 J2
Llanerchymedd IoA 72 G7
Llanerfyl Powys 62 E10
Llanfabon Caerph 27 Q4
Llanfachraeth IoA 72 E7
Llanfachreth Gwynd 61 N7
Llanfaelog IoA 72 E9
Llanfaelrhys Gwynd 60 C7
Llanfaenor Mons 40 F8
Llanfaes IoA 73 K8
Llanfaes Powys 39 N6
Llanfaethlu IoA 72 E6
Llanfair Gwynd 61 K6
Llanfair Caereinion Powys 62 F11
Llanfair Clydogau Cerdgn 49 K10
Llanfair Dyffryn Clwyd Denbgs 62 F1
Llanfairfechan Conwy 73 L9
Llanfair Kilgeddin Mons 40 D10
Llanfair-Nant-Gwyn Pembks 37 M3
Llanfairpwllgwyngyll IoA 73 J9
Llanfair Talhaiarn Conwy 74 C9
Llanfair Waterdine Shrops 50 H5
Llanfairynghornwy IoA 72 E5
Llanfair-yn-Neubwll IoA 72 E8
Llanfallteg Carmth 37 M6
Llanfallteg West Carmth 37 M6
Llanfarian Cerdgn 49 K5
Llanfechain Powys 62 G8
Llanfechan Powys 50 D10
Llanfechell IoA 72 F5
Llanferres Denbgs 74 G11
Llan Ffestiniog Gwynd 61 M4
Llanfflewyn IoA 72 F6
Llanfigael IoA 72 E7
Llanfihangel-ar-arth Carmth 38 C4
Llanfihangel Glyn Myfyr Conwy 62 D2
Llanfihangel Nant Bran Powys 39 M5
Llanfihangel-nant-Melan Powys 50 G9
Llanfihangel Rhydithon Powys 50 G7
Llanfihangel Rogiet Mons 28 F5
Llanfihangel Tal-y-llyn Powys 39 Q6
Llanfihangel-uwch-Gwili Carmth 38 D7
Llanfihangel-y-Creuddyn Cerdgn 49 L5
Llanfihangel-yng-Ngwynfa Powys 62 E9
Llanfihangel yn Nhowyn IoA 72 E8
Llanfihangel-y-pennant Gwynd 61 J3

Llanfihangel-y-pennant Gwynd 61 L10
Llanfilo Powys 39 Q5
Llanfoist Mons 40 C9
Llanfor Gwynd 62 C5
Llanfrechfa Torfn 28 D4
Llanfrothen Gwynd 61 K4
Llanfrynach Powys 39 P6
Llanfwrog Denbgs 74 F12
Llanfwrog IoA 72 E7
Llanfyllin Powys 62 G8
Llanfynydd Carmth 38 E6
Llanfynydd Flints 75 J12
Llanfyrnach Pembks 37 P4
Llangadfan Powys 62 D10
Llangadog Carmth 38 B10
Llangadog Carmth 38 H6
Llangadwaladr IoA 72 F10
Llangadwaladr Powys 62 G6
Llangaffo IoA 72 G10
Llangain Carmth 38 B8
Llangammarch Wells Powys 39 M2
Llangan V Glam 27 M7
Llangarron Herefs 40 H7
Llangasty-Talyllyn Powys 39 Q6
Llangathen Carmth 38 F7
Llangattock Powys 40 B8
Llangattock Lingoed Mons 40 E7
Llangattock-Vibon-Avel Mons 40 F8
Llangedwyn Powys 62 G7
Llangefni IoA 72 G8
Llangeinor Brdgnd 27 L5
Llangeitho Cerdgn 49 K8
Llangeler Carmth 38 B4
Llangelynin Gwynd 61 K10
Llangennech Carmth 26 E2
Llangennith Swans 26 C4
Llangenny Powys 40 C8
Llangernyw Conwy 73 Q10
Llangian Gwynd 60 E6
Llangiwg Neath 38 H10
Llangloffan Pembks 36 H4
Llanglydwen Carmth 37 N5
Llangoed IoA 73 K8
Llangoedmor Cerdgn 48 C11
Llangollen Denbgs 62 H4
Llangolman Pembks 37 M5
Llangors Powys 39 Q6
Llangorwen Cerdgn 49 K4
Llangovan Mons 40 F10
Llangower Gwynd 62 B6
Llangrannog Cerdgn 48 E10
Llangristiolus IoA 72 G9
Llangrove Herefs 40 H8
Llangua Mons 40 E6
Llangunllo Powys 50 H6
Llangunnor Carmth 38 C7
Llangurig Powys 50 B5
Llangwm Conwy 62 C3
Llangwm Mons 28 F2
Llangwm Pembks 37 J8
Llangwnnadl Gwynd 60 C5
Llangwyfan Denbgs 74 F10
Llangwyllog IoA 72 G8
Llangwyryfon Cerdgn 49 K6
Llangybi Cerdgn 49 K10
Llangybi Gwynd 60 G4
Llangybi Mons 28 E3
Llangyfelach Swans 26 F3
Llangyndeyrn Carmth 38 C9
Llangynhafal Denbgs 74 F11
Llangynidr Powys 39 R8
Llangynin Carmth 37 P6
Llangynllo Cerdgn 37 R2
Llangynog Carmth 37 R7
Llangynog Powys 62 E7
Llangynwyd Brdgnd 27 K5
Llanhamlach Powys 39 P6
Llanharan Rhondd 27 N6
Llanharry Rhondd 27 N6
Llanhennock Mons 28 E4
Llanhilleth Blae G 28 B2
Llanidan IoA 72 H10
Llanidloes Powys 50 C4
Llaniestyn Gwynd 60 D5
Llanigon Powys 40 B4
Llanilar Cerdgn 49 K6
Llanilid Rhondd 27 M6
Llanina Cerdgn 48 F8
Llanio Cerdgn 49 L9
Llanishen Cardif 28 A6
Llanishen Mons 40 G11
Llanllechid Gwynd 73 K10
Llanlleonfel Powys 50 C10
Llanllowell Mons 28 E3
Llanllugan Powys 62 E11
Llanllwch Carmth 38 B8
Llanllwchaiarn Powys 50 F2
Llanllwni Carmth 38 D4
Llanllyfni Gwynd 60 H2
Llanmadoc Swans 26 C4
Llanmaes V Glam 27 M8
Llanmartin Newpt 28 E4
Llanmerewig Powys 50 G2
Llanmihangel V Glam 27 M8
Llanmiloe Carmth 37 P9
Llanmorlais Swans 26 D3
Llannefydd Conwy 74 D9
Llannon Carmth 38 E10
Llannor Gwynd 60 F5
Llanon Cerdgn 48 H7
Llanover Mons 40 D10
Llanpumsaint Carmth 38 B6
Llanrhaeadr-ym-Mochnant Powys 62 F7
Llanrhian Pembks 36 F4
Llanrhidian Swans 26 D4
Llanrhos Conwy 73 N7
Llanrhychwyn Conwy 73 N11
Llanrhyddlad IoA 72 E6
Llanrhystud Cerdgn 49 J7
Llanrothal Herefs 40 G8
Llanrug Gwynd 73 J11
Llanrumney Cardif 28 B6
Llanrwst Conwy 73 P11
Llansadurnen Carmth 37 Q8
Llansadwrn Carmth 38 G5
Llansadwrn IoA 73 J8
Llansaint Carmth 38 B10
Llansamlet Swans 26 G3
Llansanffraid Glan Conwy Conwy 73 P8
Llansannan Conwy 74 C10
Llansannor V Glam 27 N7
Llansantffraed Powys 39 Q7
Llansantffraed-Cwmdeuddwr Powys 50 C7
Llansantffraed-in-Elvel Powys 50 F9
Llansantffraid Cerdgn 49 J7
Llansantffraid-ym-Mechain Powys 62 H8
Llansawel Carmth 38 F4
Llansilin Powys 62 H6
Llansoy Mons 40 F11
Llanspyddid Powys 39 N6
Llanstadwell Pembks 37 J9
Llansteffan Carmth 37 R8
Llanstephan Powys 39 Q3
Llantarnam Torfn 28 D4
Llanteg Pembks 37 N8
Llanthewy Skirrid Mons 40 D8
Llanthony Mons 40 C6
Llantilio-Crossenny Mons 40 E8
Llantilio Pertholey Mons 40 D8
Llantood Pembks 37 M2
Llantrisant IoA 72 F7
Llantrisant Mons 28 E3
Llantrisant Rhondd 27 P6
Llantrithyd V Glam 27 P8
Llantwit Fardre Rhondd 27 P5
Llantwit Major V Glam 27 M8
Llantysilio Denbgs 62 H3
Llanuwchllyn Gwynd 61 Q6
Llanvaches Newpt 28 F4
Llanvair Discoed Mons 28 F4
Llanvapley Mons 40 E9
Llanvetherine Mons 40 E8
Llanveynoe Herefs 40 D5
Llanvihangel Crucorney Mons 40 D7
Llanvihangel Gobion Mons 40 D9
Llanvihangel-Ystern-Llewern Mons 40 F9
Llanwarne Herefs 40 G6
Llanwddyn Powys 62 D8
Llanwenarth Mons 40 C8
Llanwenog Cerdgn 38 D3
Llanwern Newpt 28 E5
Llanwinio Carmth 37 P5
Llanwnda Gwynd 72 H12
Llanwnda Pembks 36 H3
Llanwnnen Cerdgn 38 D2
Llanwnog Powys 50 D2
Llanwonno Rhondd 27 N3
Llanwrda Carmth 38 H5
Llanwrin Powys 61 N11
Llanwrthwl Powys 50 D8
Llanwrtyd Powys 49 Q11
Llanwrtyd Wells Powys 39 L2
Llanwyddelan Powys 62 E12
Llanyblodwel Shrops 62 H7
Llanybri Carmth 37 R8
Llanybydder Carmth 38 D3
Llanycefn Pembks 37 L6
Llanychaer Pembks 37 J3
Llanycil Gwynd 62 B5
Llanycrwys Carmth 38 F3
Llanymawddwy Gwynd 62 B8
Llanymynech Powys 63 J8
Llanynghenedl IoA 72 E7
Llanynys Denbgs 74 F11
Llan-y-pwll Wrexhm 63 L2
Llanyre Powys 50 E8
Llanystumdwy Gwynd 60 H4
Llanywern Powys 39 Q6
Llawhaden Pembks 37 L7
Llawryglyn Powys 50 C2
Llay Wrexhm 63 K1
Llechcynfarwy IoA 72 F7
Llechfaen Powys 39 P6
Llechryd Caerph 39 Q10
Llechryd Cerdgn 37 N2
Llechylched IoA 72 E8
Lledrod Cerdgn 49 L6
Llidiardau Gwynd 61 Q4
Llidiartnenog Carmth 38 E4
Llidiart-y-parc Denbgs 62 F3
Llithfaen Gwynd 60 F4
Lloc Flints 74 G8
Llowes Powys 40 B3
Llwydcoed Rhondd 39 N10
Llwydiarth Powys 62 E9
Llwyn Denbgs 74 E10
Llwyncelyn Cerdgn 48 G8
Llwyndafydd Cerdgn 48 F9
Llwynderw Powys 62 H11
Llwyn-drain Pembks 37 P4
Llwyn-du Mons 40 C8
Llwyndyrys Gwynd 60 F4
Llwyngwril Gwynd 61 K10
Llwynhendy Carmth 26 E2
Llwynmawr Wrexhm 62 H5
Llwyn-on Myr Td 39 N9
Llwyn-y-brain Carmth 37 N7
Llwyn-y-groes Cerdgn 49 K9
Llwynypia Rhondd 27 N4
Llynclys Shrops 63 J7
Llynfaes IoA 72 G8
Llŷn Peninsula Gwynd 60 E5
Llyn-y-pandy Flints 74 H10
Llysfaen Conwy 74 B8
Llyswen Cerdgn 48 G8
Llyswen Powys 39 Q4
Llysworney V Glam 27 M7
Llys-y-frân Pembks 37 K6
Llywel Powys 39 K6
Load Brook Sheff 77 P6
Loan Falk 114 H6
Loanend Nthumb 117 L11
Loanhead Mdloth 115 P8
Loaningfoot D & G 97 J7
Loans S Ayrs 104 F3
Lobb Devon 19 J6
Lobhillcross Devon 8 N7
Lochailort Highld 127 P8
Lochaline Highld 120 C4
Lochans D & G 94 F7
Locharbriggs D & G 97 K2
Lochavich Ag & B 120 H9
Lochawe Ag & B 121 L7
Loch Baghasdail W Isls 152 c11
Lochboisdale W Isls 152 c11
Lochbuie Ag & B 119 Q8
Lochcarron Highld 136 B8
Lochdon Ag & B 120 D6
Lochdonhead Ag & B 120 D6
Lochead Ag & B 111 R6
Lochearnhead Stirlg 122 G8
Lochee C Dund 124 H6
Loch Eil Highld 128 E8
Locheilside Station Highld 128 D8
Lochend Highld 137 Q8
Locheport W Isls 152 c8
Loch Euphort W Isls 152 c8
Lochfoot D & G 96 H3
Lochgair Ag & B 112 D3
Lochgelly Fife 115 M3
Lochgilphead Ag & B 112 C4
Lochgoilhead Ag & B 113 J3
Lochieheads Fife 124 E10
Lochill Moray 139 P3
Lochindorb Lodge Highld 138 H9
Lochinver Highld 148 C12
Loch Lomond and The Trossachs National Park 122 D10
Loch Loyal Lodge Highld 149 N7
Lochluichart Highld 137 K3
Lochmaben D & G 97 M2
Lochmaddy W Isls 152 d8
Loch nam Madadh W Isls 152 d8
Loch Ness Highld 137 P10
Lochore Fife 115 M2
Loch Portain W Isls 152 d8
Lochportain W Isls 152 d8
Lochranza N Ayrs 112 D11
Loch Sgioport W Isls 152 c10
Lochside Abers 132 H11
Lochside D & G 97 J3
Lochside Highld 138 E5
Lochskipport W Isls 152 c10
Lochslin Highld 146 F9
Lochton S Ayrs 95 J2
Lochty Angus 132 E11
Lochty Fife 125 K11
Lochuisge Highld 120 E2
Lochwinnoch Rens 113 L9
Lochwood D & G 106 E10
Lockengate Cnwll 3 P2
Lockerbie D & G 97 N2
Lockeridge Wilts 30 D9
Lockerley Hants 24 E8
Locking N Som 28 E10
Locking Stumps Warrtn 76 B5
Lockington E R Yk 87 J6
Lockington Leics 66 D6
Lockleywood Shrops 64 C6
Locksbottom Gt Lon 33 M9
Locksgreen IoW 12 G6
Locks Heath Hants 12 H3
Lockton N York 92 G9
Loddington Leics 67 K11
Loddington Nhants 55 K5
Loddiswell Devon 5 M7
Loddon Norfk 71 M12
Lode Cambs 57 K8
Lode Heath Solhll 53 M4
Loders Dorset 10 D6
Lodsworth W Susx 14 D6
Lofthouse Leeds 85 L10
Lofthouse N York 91 J12
Lofthouse Gate Wakefd 85 L10
Loftus R & Cl 92 E3
Logan E Ayrs 105 L6
Loganbeck Cumb 88 G8
Loganlea W Loth 114 H9
Loggerheads Staffs 64 D5
Logie Angus 132 H11
Logie Fife 124 H8
Logie Moray 139 J6
Logie Coldstone Abers 132 C3
Logie Newton Abers 140 G8
Logie Pert Angus 132 G11
Logierait P & K 123 N2
Logierieve Abers 141 M10
Login Carmth 37 M6
Lolworth Cambs 56 G8
Lonbain Highld 135 M5
Londesborough E R Yk 86 F6
London Gt Lon 33 L6
London Apprentice Cnwll 3 N4
London Ashford Airport Kent 17 J6
London Beach Kent 16 F3
London City Airport Gt Lon 33 M6
London Colney Herts 44 H11
Londonderry N York 91 M9
London Gateway Services Gt Lon 32 H3
London Gatwick Airport W Susx 15 K3
London Heathrow Airport Gt Lon 32 F7
London Luton Airport Luton 44 G7
London Oxford Airport Oxon 43 K8
London Southend Airport Essex 34 F4
London Stansted Airport Essex 45 Q7
Londonthorpe Lincs 67 N4
London Zoo ZSL Gt Lon 33 K6
Londubh Highld 143 M9
Lonemore Highld 143 L9
Long Ashton N Som 28 H8
Long Bank Worcs 52 E6
Long Bennington Lincs 67 L3
Longbenton N Tyne 100 H4
Longborough Gloucs 42 E6
Long Bredy Dorset 10 E7
Longbridge Birm 53 J5
Longbridge Warwks 53 P8
Longbridge Deverill Wilts 23 J5
Long Buckby Nhants 54 G7
Longburgh Cumb 98 C6
Longburton Dorset 22 E10
Long Cause Devon 5 N4
Long Clawson Leics 67 J7
Longcliffe Derbys 65 N1
Longcombe Devon 5 P5
Long Common Hants 24 H10
Long Compton Staffs 64 F7
Long Compton Warwks 42 G5
Longcot Oxon 30 F4
Long Crendon Bucks 43 P10
Long Crichel Dorset 11 N3
Longcroft Cumb 97 P6
Longcross Surrey 32 E9
Longden Shrops 63 M11
Longden Common Shrops 63 M11
Long Ditton Surrey 32 H9
Longdon Staffs 65 K9
Longdon Worcs 41 N4
Longdon Green Staffs 65 K9
Longdon Heath Worcs 41 N4
Longdon upon Tern Wrekin 63 Q9
Longdown Devon 8 F6
Longdowns Cnwll 3 J7
Long Drax N York 86 C9
Long Duckmanton Derbys 78 D9
Long Eaton Derbys 66 D5
Longfield Kent 33 R8
Longford Covtry 54 B4
Longford Derbys 65 N5
Longford Gloucs 41 N7
Longford Gt Lon 32 F7
Longford Kent 33 P11
Longford Shrops 64 B5
Longford Wrekin 64 D8
Longforgan P & K 124 F7
Longformacus Border 116 F10
Longframlington Nthumb 109 J9
Long Green Ches W 75 N9
Long Green Worcs 41 N5
Longham Dorset 11 P5
Longham Norfk 70 D9
Long Hanborough Oxon 43 J9
Longhaven Abers 141 Q8
Long Hedges Lincs 68 G3
Longhirst Nthumb 109 L12
Longhope Gloucs 41 L8
Longhope Ork 147 b6
Longhorsley Nthumb 109 J11
Longhoughton Nthumb 109 L7
Long Itchington Warwks 54 C7
Longlands Cumb 98 B11
Longlane Derbys 65 N4
Long Lawford Warwks 54 D5
Longleat Wilts 22 H4
Longlevens Gloucs 41 N8
Longley Calder 84 G10
Longley Kirk 77 L2
Longley Green Worcs 52 D10
Longleys P & K 124 F4
Long Load Somset 21 P8
Longmanhill Abers 140 H3
Long Marston Herts 44 C8
Long Marston N York 85 Q5
Long Marston Warwks 53 M11
Long Marton Cumb 89 Q2
Long Meadowend Shrops 51 L4
Long Melford Suffk 46 F3
Longmoor Camp Hants 25 N7
Longmorn Moray 139 N4
Longmoss Ches E 76 G9
Long Newnton Gloucs 29 P4
Longnewton Border 107 P4
Long Newton E Loth 116 C8
Longnewton S on T 91 P3
Longney Gloucs 41 M9
Longniddry E Loth 116 B6
Longnor Shrops 63 N12
Longnor Staffs 77 K10
Longparish Hants 24 G4
Longpark Cumb 98 E6
Long Preston N York 84 C4
Longridge Lancs 83 N8
Longridge Staffs 64 G9
Longridge W Loth 114 H9
Longriggend N Lans 114 E7
Long Riston E R Yk 87 L7
Longrock Cnwll 2 D8
Longsdon Staffs 64 H1
Longshaw Wigan 75 P3
Longside Abers 141 P6
Long Sight Oldham 76 G2
Longslow Shrops 64 C5
Longstanton Cambs 56 H7
Longstock Hants 24 F6
Longstone Pembks 37 M8
Longstowe Cambs 56 F9
Long Stratton Norfk 59 J2
Long Street M Keyn 55 K11
Longstreet Wilts 23 P3
Long Sutton Hants 25 M4
Long Sutton Lincs 68 H7
Long Sutton Somset 21 P8
Longthorpe C Pete 56 C1
Long Thurlow Suffk 58 E7
Longthwaite Cumb 89 L2
Longton C Stke 64 G3
Longton Lancs 83 L10
Longtown Cumb 98 E4
Longtown Herefs 40 D6
Longueville Jersey 13 c3
Longville in the Dale Shrops 51 P2
Long Waste Wrekin 64 B9
Long Whatton Leics 66 D7
Longwick Bucks 43 R10
Long Wittenham Oxon 31 L4
Longwitton Nthumb 108 H12
Longwood D & G 96 E6
Longwood Shrops 63 Q10
Longworth Oxon 30 H2
Longyester E Loth 116 D8
Lôn-las Swans 26 H3
Lonmay Abers 141 N4
Lonmore Highld 134 E6
Looe Cnwll 4 C6
Loose Kent 34 D12
Loosebeare Devon 8 D4
Loosegate Lincs 68 F7
Loosley Row Bucks 32 B2
Lootcherbrae Abers 140 F5
Lopcombe Corner Wilts 24 D6
Lopen Somset 21 P10
Loppington Shrops 63 M6
Lorbottle Nthumb 108 G8
Lordington W Susx 13 N3
Lordsbridge Norfk 69 L9
Lordshill C Sotn 24 F10
Lords Wood Medway 34 D10
Lornty P & K 124 D4
Loscoe Derbys 66 C3
Loscombe Dorset 10 D5
Losgaintir W Isls 152 e5
Lossiemouth Moray 147 N11
Lostford Shrops 64 B6
Lostock Gralam Ches W 76 C8
Lostock Green Ches W 76 C9
Lostock Hall Lancs 83 M10
Lostock Hall Fold Bolton 76 C2
Lostock Junction Bolton 76 C2
Lostwithiel Cnwll 3 Q3
Lothbeg Highld 146 G3
Lothersdale N York 84 E6
Lothmore Highld 146 H3
Loudwater Bucks 32 C4
Loudwater Herts 32 F3
Loughborough Leics 66 E8
Loughor Swans 26 E3
Loughton Essex 33 M3
Loughton M Keyn 44 B4
Loughton Shrops 52 B4
Lound Lincs 67 Q8
Lound Notts 78 H6
Lound Suffk 71 Q12
Lounston Devon 8 E9
Lount Leics 66 C8
Louth Lincs 80 F6
Loveclough Lancs 84 B9
Lovedean Hants 25 L10
Lover Wilts 24 C9
Loversall Donc 78 F4
Loves Green Essex 46 B10
Lovesome Hill N York 91 N7
Loveston Pembks 37 L9
Lovington Somset 22 D7
Low Ackworth Wakefd 85 P11
Low Angerton Nthumb 100 E1
Lowbands Gloucs 41 M5
Low Barbeth D & G 94 E5
Low Barlings Lincs 80 B9
Low Bell End N York 92 E7
Low Bentham N York 83 P1
Low Biggins Cumb 89 P11
Low Borrowbridge Cumb 89 P6
Low Bradfield Sheff 77 N5
Low Bradley N York 84 F5
Low Braithwaite Cumb 98 E10
Low Burnham N Linc 79 K3
Low Buston Nthumb 109 L8
Lowca Cumb 88 C2
Low Catton E R Yk 86 D4
Low Coniscliffe Darltn 91 L4
Low Crosby Cumb 98 F6
Lowdham Notts 66 H3
Low Dinsdale Darltn 91 N4
Lowe Shrops 63 N6
Lowe Hill Staffs 65 J1
Low Ellington N York 91 L10
Lower Aisholt Somset 21 K6
Lower Ansty Dorset 11 J4
Lower Apperley Gloucs 41 P6
Lower Arboll Highld 146 F9
Lower Arncott Oxon 43 M8
Lower Ashton Devon 8 F8
Lower Assendon Oxon 31 Q5
Lower Badcall Highld 148 E8
Lower Ballam Lancs 83 J9
Lower Bartle Lancs 83 L8
Lower Basildon W Berk 31 M6
Lower Bearwood Herefs 51 L9
Lower Beeding W Susx 15 J5
Lower Benefield Nhants 55 N3
Lower Bentley Worcs 53 J7
Lower Beobridge Shrops 52 E2
Lower Birchwood Derbys 66 C1
Lower Boddington Nhants 54 D10
Lower Boscaswell Cnwll 2 B7
Lower Bourne Surrey 25 P4
Lower Brailes Warwks 42 G4
Lower Breakish Highld 135 M11
Lower Bredbury Stockp 76 G5
Lower Broadheath Worcs 52 E9
Lower Broxwood Herefs 51 L9
Lower Buckenhill Herefs 41 J5
Lower Bullingham Herefs 40 G4
Lower Burgate Hants 23 P10
Lower Burrowton Devon 9 J5
Lower Burton Herefs 51 M9
Lower Caldecote C Beds 44 H2
Lower Cam Gloucs 29 M2
Lower Canada N Som 28 E10
Lower Catesby Nhants 54 E9
Lower Chapel Powys 39 N4
Lower Chicksgrove Wilts 23 L7
Lower Chute Wilts 24 E3
Lower Clapton Gt Lon 33 L5
Lower Clent Worcs 52 G5
Lower Common Hants 31 Q10
Lower Compton Wilts 30 B8
Lower Creedy Devon 8 F4
Lower Crossings Derbys 77 K7
Lower Cumberworth Kirk 77 N2
Lower Darwen Bl w D 83 Q10
Lower Dean Bed 55 Q7
Lower Denby Kirk 77 N2
Lower Diabaig Highld 135 P4
Lower Dicker E Susx 15 Q8
Lower Dinchope Shrops 51 N4
Lower Down Shrops 51 K4
Lower Dunsforth N York 85 N2
Lower Egleton Herefs 41 J3
Lower Elkstone Staffs 77 K12
Lower Ellastone Staffs 65 L4
Lower End Bucks 43 P10
Lower End M Keyn 44 D4
Lower End Nhants 55 K9
Lower End Nhants 55 L8
Lower Everleigh Wilts 24 C2
Lower Exbury Hants 12 G5
Lower Eythorne Kent 35 N12
Lower Failand N Som 28 G7
Lower Farringdon Hants 25 M6
Lower Feltham Gt Lon 32 F8
Lower Fittleworth W Susx 14 F7
Lower Foxdale IoM 102 c5
Lower Frankton Shrops 63 L6
Lower Freystrop Pembks 37 J8
Lower Froyle Hants 25 N4
Lower Gabwell Devon 5 Q3
Lower Gledfield Highld 145 N7
Lower Godney Somset 21 Q5
Lower Gornal Dudley 52 G2
Lower Gravenhurst C Beds 44 G5
Lower Green Herts 44 H5
Lower Green Herts 45 M5
Lower Green Kent 15 Q3
Lower Green Kent 16 A2
Lower Green Norfk 70 E5
Lower Green Staffs 64 G10
Lower Green Suffk 57 P7
Lower Hacheston Suffk 59 L9
Lower Halstock Leigh Dorset 10 E3
Lower Halstow Kent 34 F9
Lower Hamworthy BCP 11 N6
Lower Hardres Kent 35 L11
Lower Harpton Herefs 51 J8
Lower Hartlip Kent 34 E9
Lower Hartshay Derbys 66 C2
Lower Hartwell Bucks 43 R9
Lower Hatton Staffs 64 F5
Lower Hawthwaite Cumb 88 G9
Lower Haysden Kent 15 Q2
Lower Hergest Herefs 51 J9
Lower Heyford Oxon 43 K7
Lower Heysham Lancs 83 K3
Lower Higham Kent 34 C8
Lower Holbrook Suffk 47 L5
Lower Hordley Shrops 63 L6
Lower Horncroft W Susx 14 E7
Lowerhouse Lancs 84 B8
Lower Houses Kirk 84 H12
Lower Howsell Worcs 52 E11
Lower Irlam Salfd 76 D5
Lower Kilburn Derbys 66 B3
Lower Kilcott Gloucs 29 M4
Lower Killeyan Ag & B 102 B1
Lower Kingcombe Dorset 10 E5
Lower Kingswood Surrey 33 J11
Lower Kinnerton Ches W 75 K11
Lower Langford N Som 28 F10
Lower Largo Fife 124 H12
Lower Leigh Staffs 65 J5
Lower Lemington Gloucs 42 E5
Lower Llanfadog Powys 50 C7
Lower Lovacott Devon 19 K8
Lower Loxhore Devon 19 M6
Lower Lydbrook Gloucs 41 J8
Lower Lye Herefs 51 L7
Lower Machen Newpt 28 B5
Lower Maes-coed Herefs 40 D5
Lower Mannington Dorset 11 P4
Lower Marston Somset 22 G4
Lower Meend Gloucs 40 H10
Lower Merridge Somset 21 K6
Lower Middleton Cheney Nhants 43 L3
Lower Milton Somset 22 C4
Lower Moor Worcs 41 R2
Lower Morton S Glos 29 K4
Lower Nazeing Essex 45 M10
Lower Norton Warwks 53 M8
Lower Nyland Dorset 22 G9
Lower Oddington Gloucs 42 F6
Lower Penarth V Glam 28 A8
Lower Penn Staffs 52 G1
Lower Pennington Hants 12 E6
Lower Penwortham Lancs 83 M10
Lower Peover Ches E 76 D9
Lower Place Rochdl 76 G1
Lower Pollicott Bucks 43 P9
Lower Quinton Warwks 42 E2
Lower Rainham Medway 34 E9
Lower Raydon Suffk 47 J4
Lower Roadwater Somset 20 G5
Lower Salter Lancs 83 N3
Lower Seagry Wilts 29 Q6
Lower Sheering Essex 45 P9
Lower Shelton C Beds 44 E3
Lower Shiplake Oxon 31 Q6
Lower Shuckburgh Warwks 54 D8
Lower Slaughter Gloucs 42 D7
Lower Soothill Kirk 85 K10
Lower Soudley Gloucs 41 K9
Lower Standen Kent 17 M3
Lower Stanton St Quintin Wilts 29 Q6
Lower Stoke Medway 34 E7
Lower Stondon C Beds 44 H5
Lower Stone Gloucs 29 L3
Lower Stonnall Staffs 65 K11
Lower Stow Bedon Norfk 58 E2
Lower Street Dorset 11 K5
Lower Street E Susx 16 C8
Lower Street Norfk 71 K5
Lower Street Suffk 57 Q10
Lower Street Suffk 58 G10
Lower Stretton Warrtn 76 B7
Lower Stroud Dorset 10 C5
Lower Sundon C Beds 44 F6
Lower Swanwick Hants 12 H3
Lower Swell Gloucs 42 E6
Lower Tadmarton Oxon 43 J4
Lower Tale Devon 9 K4
Lower Tasburgh Norfk 59 J1
Lower Tean Staffs 65 J4
Lower Thurlton Norfk 71 N12
Lower Town Cnwll 2 G8
Lower Town Devon 8 D10
Lower Town Herefs 41 K3
Lower Town IoS 2 b1
Lower Town Pembks 37 J3
Lower Trebullett Cnwll 7 L9
Lower Treluswell Cnwll 3 J7
Lower Tysoe Warwks 42 H3
Lower Ufford Suffk 59 L10
Lower Upcott Devon 8 G8
Lower Upham Hants 25 J9
Lower Upnor Medway 34 D8
Lower Vexford Somset 20 H6
Lower Walton Warrtn 75 Q6
Lower Waterston Dorset 10 H6
Lower Weare Somset 21 N3
Lower Weedon Nhants 54 G9
Lower Welson Herefs 51 J10
Lower Westmancote Worcs 41 Q4
Lower Whatcombe Dorset 11 K4
Lower Whatley Somset 22 G4
Lower Whitley Ches W 75 Q8
Lower Wick Gloucs 29 L3
Lower Wick Worcs 52 F10
Lower Wield Hants 25 L5
Lower Willingdon E Susx 15 Q10
Lower Withington Ches E 76 E9
Lower Woodend Bucks 32 B5
Lower Woodford Wilts 23 P6
Lower Wraxhall Dorset 10 F4
Lower Wyche Worcs 41 M3
Lower Wyke C Brad 84 H10
Lowesby Leics 67 J10
Lowestoft Suffk 59 Q2
Loweswater Cumb 88 F3
Low Etherley Dur 91 K1
Low Fell Gatesd 100 H6
Lowfield Heath W Susx 15 K3
Low Gartachorrans Stirlg 113 P4
Low Gate Nthumb 99 P5
Low Gettbridge Cumb 98 G6
Lowgill Cumb 89 Q7
Lowgill Lancs 83 P2
Low Grantley N York 85 K1
Low Green N York 85 J4
Low Habberley Worcs 52 E5
Low Ham Somset 21 P7
Low Harrogate N York 85 L4
Low Hawsker N York 93 J5
Low Hesket Cumb 98 F9
Low Hutton N York 86 E2
Lowick Cumb 89 J9
Lowick Nhants 55 N4
Lowick Nthumb 108 G2
Lowick Bridge Cumb 89 J9
Lowick Green Cumb 89 J9
Low Knipe Cumb 89 N3
Low Laithe N York 85 J3
Lowlands Dur 91 J2
Lowlands Torfn 28 C3
Low Langton Lincs 80 C8
Low Leighton Derbys 77 J6
Low Lorton Cumb 88 F2
Low Marishes N York 92 G11
Low Marnham Notts 79 K10
Low Middleton Nthumb 109 J3
Low Mill N York 92 D7
Low Moor C Brad 84 H9
Low Moorsley Sundld 101 J9
Low Moresby Cumb 88 D3
Low Newton Cumb 89 L10
Low Newton-by-the-Sea Nthumb 109 L5
Lownie Moor Angus 125 J3
Low Pittington Dur 101 J9
Low Row Cumb 97 P9
Low Row Cumb 98 D11
Low Row Cumb 99 J5
Low Row N York 90 G7
Low Salchrie D & G 94 E5
Low Santon N Linc 79 N1
Lowsonford Warwks 53 M7
Low Street Norfk 71 L7
Low Street Thurr 34 B7
Low Tharston Norfk 59 J2
Lowther Cumb 89 N2
Lowthorpe E R Yk 87 K3
Lowton Devon 8 C4
Lowton Somset 21 K9
Lowton Wigan 76 B4
Lowton Common Wigan 76 B4
Lowton St Mary's Wigan 76 B4
Low Torry Fife 115 J4
Low Toynton Lincs 80 E9
Low Valley Barns 78 C3
Low Wood Cumb 89 K10
Low Worsall N York 91 P5
Low Wray Cumb 89 K6
Loxbeare Devon 20 E10
Loxhill Surrey 14 E4
Loxhore Devon 19 M5
Loxhore Cott Devon 19 M6
Loxley Warwks 53 N10
Loxley Green Staffs 65 K6
Loxter Herefs 41 L3
Loxton N Som 21 N2
Loxwood W Susx 14 E4
Lubenham Leics 54 H3
Lucasgate Lincs 68 H3
Lucas Green Surrey 32 D10
Luccombe Somset 20 E4
Luccombe Village IoW 13 K9
Lucker Nthumb 109 J4
Luckett Cnwll 7 M10
Lucking Street Essex 46 E5
Luckington Wilts 29 N5
Lucklawhill Fife 124 H8
Lucknam Wilts 29 N8
Luckwell Bridge Somset 20 D5
Lucton Herefs 51 M8
Lucy Cross N York 91 L4
Ludag W Isls 152 c12
Ludborough Lincs 80 F4
Ludbrook Devon 5 L6
Ludchurch Pembks 37 M8
Luddenden Calder 84 F10
Luddenden Foot Calder 84 F10
Luddenham Court Kent 34 H9
Luddesdown Kent 34 B9
Luddington N Linc 86 F12
Luddington Warwks 53 M10
Luddington in the Brook Nhants 56 B4
Ludford Lincs 80 D6
Ludford Shrops 51 N6
Ludgershall Bucks 43 N8
Ludgershall Wilts 24 D3
Ludgvan Cnwll 2 D8
Ludham Norfk 71 M8
Ludlow Shrops 51 N5
Ludney Somset 10 B2
Ludwell Wilts 23 K9
Ludworth Dur 101 J10
Luffenhall Herts 45 K6
Luffincott Devon 7 L6
Luffness E Loth 116 B5
Lugar E Ayrs 105 L5
Luggate Burn E Loth 116 E6
Lugg Green Herefs 51 M8
Luggiebank N Lans 114 D7
Lugton E Ayrs 113 N10
Lugwardine Herefs 40 H3
Luib Highld 135 K10
Luing Ag & B 120 D10
Lulham Herefs 40 F3
Lullington Derbys 65 N9
Lullington E Susx 15 P10
Lullington Somset 22 H3
Lulsgate Bottom N Som 28 G9
Lulsley Worcs 52 D9
Lulworth Camp Dorset 11 K8
Lumb Calder 84 F11
Lumb Lancs 84 C10
Lumbutts Calder 84 E10
Lumby N York 85 P9
Lumphanan Abers 132 F3
Lumphinnans Fife 115 M3
Lumsden Abers 140 D11
Lunan Angus 125 N2
Lunanhead Angus 125 J2
Luncarty P & K 124 C7
Lund E R Yk 86 H5
Lund N York 86 C8
Lundie Angus 124 F5
Lundin Links Fife 124 H12
Lundin Mill Fife 124 H12
Lundy Devon 18 C4
Lundy Green Norfk 59 K2
Lunga Ag & B 120 D11
Lunna Shet 147 j5
Lunsford Kent 34 C10
Lunsford's Cross E Susx 16 C8
Lunt Sefton 75 K3
Luntley Herefs 51 L9
Luppitt Devon 9 M3
Lupridge Devon 5 M6
Lupset Wakefd 85 L11
Lupton Cumb 89 N10
Lurgashall W Susx 14 D5
Lurley Devon 20 E10
Lusby Lincs 80 G10
Luscombe Devon 5 N5
Luskentyre W Isls 152 e5
Luson Devon 5 J7
Luss Ag & B 113 M3
Lussagiven Ag & B 111 N4
Lusta Highld 134 E4
Lustleigh Devon 8 E8
Luston Herefs 51 N8
Luthermuir Abers 132 G10
Luthrie Fife 124 G9
Lutley Dudley 52 H4
Luton Devon 8 G9
Luton Devon 9 K4
Luton Luton 44 F7
Luton Medway 34 D9
Luton Airport Luton 44 G7
Lutterworth Leics 54 E4
Lutton Devon 5 J5
Lutton Devon 5 L4
Lutton Lincs 68 H7
Lutton Nhants 56 C3
Luxborough Somset 20 F6
Luxulyan Cnwll 3 P3
Luxulyan Valley Cnwll 3 P3
Luzley Tamesd 76 H3
Lybster Highld 151 N9
Lydbury North Shrops 51 K3
Lydcott Devon 19 N6
Lydd Kent 17 J6
Lydd Airport Kent 17 J6
Lydden Kent 17 N2
Lydden Kent 35 P9
Lyddington RutInd 55 L1
Lydd-on-Sea Kent 17 K7
Lydeard St Lawrence Somset 20 H7
Lyde Green Hants 31 P11
Lyde Green S Glos 29 K7
Lydford Devon 7 P8
Lydford on Fosse Somset 22 D7
Lydgate Calder 84 D10
Lydgate Rochdl 84 E12
Lydham Shrops 51 K2
Lydiard Green Wilts 30 C5
Lydiard Millicent Wilts 30 C5
Lydiard Tregoze Swindn 30 C5
Lydiate Sefton 75 L3
Lydiate Ash Worcs 52 H5
Lydlinch Dorset 22 G10
Lydney Gloucs 41 K11
Lydstep Pembks 37 L11
Lye Dudley 52 G4
Lye Cross N Som 28 G10
Lye Green Bucks 44 D11
Lye Green E Susx 15 P4
Lye Green Warwks 53 M7
Lye Head Worcs 52 D6
Lye's Green Wilts 22 H4
Lyford Oxon 30 H3
Lymbridge Green Kent 17 K2
Lyme Regis Dorset 9 Q6
Lyminge Kent 17 L3
Lymington Hants 12 E5
Lyminster W Susx 14 E10
Lymm Warrtn 76 C6
Lymm Services Warrtn 76 C7
Lympne Kent 17 K4
Lympsham Somset 21 M2
Lympstone Devon 9 J8
Lynbridge Devon 19 N4
Lynchat Highld 130 E4
Lynch Green Norfk 70 H11
Lyndhurst Hants 12 E3
Lyndon RutInd 67 M11
Lyndon Green Birm 53 L4
Lyne Border 106 G2
Lyne Surrey 32 E9
Lyneal Shrops 63 M5
Lyne Down Herefs 41 K5
Lyneham Oxon 42 F7
Lyneham Wilts 30 B6
Lyneholmford Cumb 98 G4
Lynemouth Nthumb 109 M11
Lyne of Skene Abers 133 J2
Lynesack Dur 90 H2
Lyness Ork 147 b6
Lyng Norfk 70 F8
Lyng Somset 21 M7
Lynmouth Devon 19 P3
Lynn Staffs 65 K11
Lynn Wrekin 64 E9
Lynsted Kent 34 G10
Lynstone Cnwll 7 J4
Lynton Devon 19 N3
Lynton Cross Devon 19 K5
Lyon's Gate Dorset 10 G4
Lyonshall Herefs 51 K9
Lytchett Matravers Dorset 11 M6
Lytchett Minster Dorset 11 M6
Lyth Highld 151 N4
Lytham Lancs 83 J9
Lytham St Annes Lancs 82 H9
Lythbank Shrops 63 M10
Lythe N York 92 G4
Lythmore Highld 151 J3

M

Maaruig W Isls 152 e5
Mabe Burnthouse Cnwll 3 J7
Mablethorpe Lincs 81 K7
Macclesfield Ches E 76 G9
Macduff Abers 140 H3
Macharioch Ag & B 103 K8
Machen Caerph 28 B4
Machrie N Ayrs 103 N3
Machrihanish Ag & B 102 H5
Machrins Ag & B 111 J3
Machroes Gwynd 60 E7
Machynlleth Powys 61 N12
Machynys Carmth 26 D3
Mackworth Derbys 65 P5
Macmerry E Loth 116 B7
Maddaford Devon 7 Q6

Madderty P & K 123 N8
Maddington Wilts 23 N4
Maddiston Falk 114 G6
Madehurst W Susx 14 E8
Madeley Staffs 64 E3
Madeley Wrekin 64 C11
Madeley Heath Staffs 64 E3
Madeley Park Wood Staffs 64 E4
Madford Devon 9 M3
Madingley Cambs 56 H8
Madley Herefs 40 F4
Madresfield Worcs 52 E11
Madron Cnwll 2 D8
Maenaddwyn IoA 72 G7
Maenan Conwy 73 N10
Maenclochog Pembks 37 L5
Maendy V Glam 27 N7
Maenporth Cnwll 3 K8
Maentwrog Gwynd 61 L4
Maen-y-groes Cerdgn 48 F9
Maer Cnwll 7 J3
Maer Staffs 64 E4
Maerdy Carmth 38 G6
Maerdy Conwy 62 D3
Maerdy Rhondd 27 M3
Maesbrook Shrops 63 J8
Maesbury Shrops 63 J7
Maesbury Marsh Shrops 63 K7
Maes-glas Newpt 28 D5
Maesgwynne Carmth 37 N6
Maeshafn Denbgs 74 H11
Maesllyn Cerdgn 38 A3
Maesmynis Powys 39 N2
Maesmynis Powys 50 E10
Maesteg Brdgnd 27 K4
Maesybont Carmth 38 E8
Maesycwmmer Caerph 27 R3
Magdalen Laver Essex 45 P10
Maggieknockater Moray 139 P7
Maggots End Essex 45 N6
Magham Down E Susx 15 R8
Maghull Sefton 75 L3
Magna Park Leics 54 E4
Magor Mons 28 F5
Magor Services Mons 28 F5
Maidenbower W Susx 15 K4
Maiden Bradley Wilts 22 H5
Maidencombe Torbay 5 Q3
Maidenhayne Devon 9 P6
Maiden Head N Som 28 H9
Maidenhead W & M 32 C6
Maiden Law Dur 100 F8
Maiden Newton Dorset 10 F5
Maidens S Ayrs 104 D8
Maiden's Green Br For 32 C8
Maidenwell Lincs 80 F8
Maiden Wells Pembks 37 J10
Maidford Nhants 54 G10
Maids Moreton Bucks 43 P4
Maidstone Kent 34 D11
Maidstone Services Kent 34 E11
Maidwell Nhants 55 J5
Mail Shet 147 j7
Maindee Newpt 28 D5
Mainland Ork 147 c4
Mainland Shet 147 i6
Mainsforth Dur 101 J12
Mains of Balhall Angus 132 D11
Mains of Balnakettle Abers 132 F9
Mains of Dalvey Highld 139 L9
Mains of Haulkerton Abers 132 H9
Mains of Lesmoir Abers 140 D10
Mains of Melgunds Angus 125 L2
Mainsriddle D & G 97 J7
Mainstone Shrops 51 J3
Maisemore Gloucs 41 N7
Major's Green Worcs 53 L5
Makeney Derbys 66 B3
Malborough Devon 5 L8
Malcoff Derbys 77 K7
Malden Rushett Gt Lon 32 H10
Maldon Essex 46 E10
Malham N York 84 D3
Maligar Highld 134 H3
Mallaig Highld 127 M5
Mallaigvaig Highld 127 M5
Malleny Mills C Edin 115 L8
Mallows Green Essex 45 N6
Malltraeth IoA 72 G10
Mallwyd Gwynd 61 Q9
Malmesbury Wilts 29 Q5
Malmsmead Devon 20 B4
Malpas Ches W 63 N3
Malpas Cnwll 3 K6
Malpas Newpt 28 D4
Malshanger Hants 25 J3
Malswick Gloucs 41 L7
Maltby Lincs 80 F7
Maltby Rothm 78 E5
Maltby S on T 91 Q4
Maltby le Marsh Lincs 81 J7
Malting Green Essex 46 H7
Maltman's Hill Kent 16 F2
Malton N York 92 F12
Malvern Worcs 41 M2
Malvern Hills 41 M3
Malvern Link Worcs 52 E11
Malvern Wells Worcs 41 M3
Mamble Worcs 52 C6
Mamhilad Mons 40 D11
Manaccan Cnwll 3 J9
Manafon Powys 62 F11
Mànais W Isls 152 e6
Manaton Devon 8 E8
Manby Lincs 80 H6
Mancetter Warwks 53 Q1
Manchester Manch 76 F4
Manchester Airport Manch 76 F7
Mancot Flints 75 K10
Mandally Highld 129 K4
Manea Cambs 57 J3
Maney Birm 53 L2
Manfield N York 91 L4
Mangersta W Isls 152 d3
Mangerton Dorset 10 D5
Mangotsfield S Glos 29 K7
Mangrove Green Herts 44 G7
Mangurstadh W Isls 152 d3
Manhay Cnwll 2 H8
Manish W Isls 152 e6
Mankinholes Calder 84 E10
Manley Ches W 75 N9
Manmoel Caerph 40 A11
Mannal Ag & B 118 D5
Manningford Bohune Wilts 30 D10
Manningford Bruce Wilts 30 D10
Manningham C Brad 84 H8
Mannings Heath W Susx 14 H5
Mannington Dorset 11 P4
Manningtree Essex 47 K5
Mannofield C Aber 133 M3
Manorbier Pembks 37 L11
Manorbier Newton Pembks 37 K10
Manordeilo Carmth 38 G6
Manorhill Border 107 Q3
Manorowen Pembks 36 H3
Manor Park Gt Lon 33 M5
Mansell Gamage Herefs 40 E3
Mansell Lacy Herefs 40 F3
Mansergh Cumb 89 P10
Mansfield E Ayrs 105 L7
Mansfield Notts 78 E11
Mansfield Woodhouse Notts 78 E11
Mansriggs Cumb 89 J10
Manston Dorset 22 H10
Manston Kent 35 P9
Manston Leeds 85 M8
Manswood Dorset 11 N3
Manthorpe Lincs 67 M5
Manthorpe Lincs 67 Q9
Manton N Linc 79 M3
Manton Notts 78 G8
Manton Rutlnd 67 L11
Manton Wilts 30 E8
Manuden Essex 45 P6
Manwood Green Essex 45 Q9
Maperton Somset 22 F8
Maplebeck Notts 78 H11
Maple Cross Herts 32 E4
Mapledurham Oxon 31 N7
Mapledurwell Hants 25 M3
Maplehurst W Susx 14 H6
Maplescombe Kent 33 Q9
Mapleton Derbys 65 M3
Mapleton Kent 15 N1
Mapperley Derbys 66 C4
Mapperley Park C Nott 66 F4
Mapperton Dorset 10 D5
Mappleborough Green Warwks 53 K7
Mappleton E R Yk 87 N6
Mapplewell Barns 77 Q2
Mappowder Dorset 10 H3
Màraig W Isls 152 e5
Marazanvose Cnwll 3 K4
Marazion Cnwll 2 E8
Marbhig W Isls 152 g4
Marbury Ches E 63 P3
March Cambs 56 H1
March S Lans 106 C7
Marcham Oxon 31 K3
Marchamley Shrops 63 Q6
Marchamley Wood Shrops 63 Q6
Marchington Staffs 65 L6
Marchington Woodlands Staffs 65 L6
Marchwiel Wrexhm 63 K3
Marchwood Hants 12 F3
Marcross V Glam 27 L8
Marden Herefs 40 H2
Marden Kent 16 D2
Marden Wilts 30 C10
Marden Ash Essex 45 Q11
Marden Beech Kent 16 C2
Marden's Hill E Susx 15 P4
Marden Thorn Kent 16 D2
Mardlebury Herts 45 K8
Mardy Mons 40 D8
Marefield Leics 67 J10
Mareham le Fen Lincs 80 E11
Mareham on the Hill Lincs 80 F10
Marehay Derbys 66 C3
Marehill W Susx 14 F7
Maresfield E Susx 15 N6
Marfleet C KuH 87 L9
Marford Wrexhm 75 K12
Margam Neath 27 J5
Margaret Marsh Dorset 22 H9
Margaret Roding Essex 45 Q9
Margaretting Essex 34 B2
Margaretting Tye Essex 34 B2
Margate Kent 35 P8
Margnaheglish N Ayrs 103 Q3
Margrie D & G 96 C8
Margrove Park R & Cl 92 D4
Marham Norfk 69 N10
Marhamchurch Cnwll 7 J4
Marham Park Suffk 58 B7
Marholm C Pete 68 C11
Marian-glas IoA 72 H7
Mariansleigh Devon 19 P9
Marine Town Kent 34 G7
Marionburgh Abers 132 H3
Marishader Highld 135 J3
Maristow Devon 4 G4
Marjoriebanks D & G 97 M2
Mark Somset 21 N4
Markbeech Kent 15 N2
Markby Lincs 81 J8
Mark Causeway Somset 21 N4
Mark Cross E Susx 15 Q4
Markeaton C Derb 65 Q5
Market Bosworth Leics 66 C11
Market Deeping Lincs 68 C10
Market Drayton Shrops 64 C5
Market Harborough Leics 55 J3
Market Lavington Wilts 23 M3
Market Overton Rutlnd 67 M9
Market Rasen Lincs 80 B6
Market Stainton Lincs 80 E7
Market Warsop Notts 78 F10
Market Weighton E R Yk 86 G7
Market Weston Suffk 58 E5
Markfield Leics 66 D10
Markham Caerph 28 A2
Markham Moor Notts 79 J9
Markinch Fife 115 P1
Markington N York 85 L2
Markle E Loth 116 D6
Marksbury BaNES 29 K10
Mark's Corner IoW 12 H6
Marks Tey Essex 46 F7
Markwell Cnwll 4 E5
Markyate Herts 44 F8
Marlborough Wilts 30 E8
Marlbrook Herefs 51 N9
Marlbrook Worcs 52 H6
Marlcliff Warwks 53 L10
Marldon Devon 5 P4
Marle Green E Susx 15 Q7
Marlesford Suffk 59 L9
Marley Kent 35 L12
Marley Kent 35 P11
Marley Green Ches E 63 P3
Marley Hill Gatesd 100 G6
Marlingford Norfk 70 H10
Marloes Pembks 36 F9
Marlow Bucks 32 B5
Marlow Herefs 51 L5
Marlow Bottom Bucks 32 B5
Marlpit Hill Kent 15 N1
Marlpits E Susx 15 N5
Marlpits E Susx 16 C8
Marlpool Derbys 66 D3
Marnhull Dorset 22 H9
Marple Stockp 76 H6
Marple Bridge Stockp 76 H6
Marr Donc 78 E3
Marrick N York 90 H7
Marros Carmth 37 N9
Marsden Kirk 77 K1
Marsden S Tyne 101 K5
Marsden Height Lancs 84 C8
Marsett N York 90 E9
Marsh Bucks 44 A10
Marsh C Brad 84 F8
Marsh Devon 9 P3
Marshall's Heath Herts 44 H8
Marshalswick Herts 44 H10
Marsham Norfk 71 J7
Marsh Baldon Oxon 31 M3
Marsh Benham W Berk 31 J9
Marshborough Kent 35 P11
Marshbrook Shrops 51 M3
Marshchapel Lincs 80 G4
Marsh Farm Luton 44 F6
Marshfield Newpt 28 C6
Marshfield S Glos 29 M7
Marshgate Cnwll 6 H6
Marsh Gibbon Bucks 43 N7
Marsh Green Devon 9 K6
Marsh Green Kent 15 N2
Marsh Green Wrekin 63 Q9
Marshland St James Norfk 69 K10
Marsh Lane Derbys 78 C8
Marsh Lane Gloucs 41 J10
Marshside Sefton 83 J11
Marsh Street Somset 20 F4
Marshwood Dorset 10 B5
Marske N York 91 J6
Marske-by-the-Sea R & Cl 92 D2
Marsland Green Wigan 76 C4
Marston Ches W 76 C8
Marston Herefs 51 L9
Marston Lincs 67 M3
Marston Oxon 43 L10
Marston Staffs 64 F9
Marston Staffs 64 G7
Marston Warwks 53 N2
Marston Wilts 29 Q11
Marston Green Solhll 53 M4
Marston Jabbet Warwks 54 B3
Marston Magna Somset 22 D9
Marston Meysey Wilts 30 D3
Marston Montgomery Derbys 65 L5
Marston Moretaine C Beds 44 E3
Marston on Dove Derbys 65 N6
Marston St Lawrence Nhants 43 L3
Marston Stannett Herefs 51 P9
Marston Trussell Nhants 54 H3
Marstow Herefs 40 H8
Marsworth Bucks 44 C8
Marten Wilts 30 G10
Marthall Ches E 76 E8
Martham Norfk 71 N8
Martin Hants 23 N9
Martin Kent 17 P1
Martin Lincs 80 C11
Martin Lincs 80 E10
Martindale Cumb 89 L3
Martin Dales Lincs 80 D11
Martin Drove End Hants 23 N9
Martinhoe Devon 19 N4
Martin Hussingtree Worcs 52 G8
Martinscroft Warrtn 76 C6
Martinstown Dorset 10 G7
Martlesham Suffk 47 N2
Martlesham Heath Suffk 47 M3
Martletwy Pembks 37 K8
Martley Worcs 52 D8
Martock Somset 21 P9
Marton Ches E 76 F10
Marton Ches W 76 B10
Marton Cumb 88 H11
Marton E R Yk 87 M1
Marton E R Yk 87 M7
Marton Lincs 79 L7
Marton Middsb 92 B3
Marton N York 92 E10
Marton Shrops 63 J11
Marton Warwks 54 C7
Marton-cum-Grafton N York 85 N3
Marton-le-Moor N York 85 M1
Martyr's Green Surrey 32 F11
Martyr Worthy Hants 24 H7
Marvig W Isls 152 g4
Marwell Zoo Hants 24 H9
Marwick Ork 147 b3
Marwood Devon 19 K6
Marybank Highld 137 N5
Maryburgh Highld 137 P4
Marygold Border 116 H9
Maryhill C Glas 113 Q7
Marykirk Abers 132 G11
Maryland Mons 40 G10
Marylebone Gt Lon 33 K6
Marylebone Wigan 75 P2
Marypark Moray 139 M8
Maryport Cumb 97 L11
Maryport D & G 94 G11
Marystow Devon 7 N8
Mary Tavy Devon 7 P9
Maryton Angus 124 H2
Maryton Angus 125 N2
Marywell Abers 132 F5
Marywell Abers 133 M4
Marywell Angus 125 M4
Masham N York 91 L10
Mashbury Essex 46 B9
Masongill N York 89 Q11
Mastin Moor Derbys 78 D8
Matching Essex 45 P9
Matching Green Essex 45 P9
Matching Tye Essex 45 P9
Matfen Nthumb 100 D4
Matfield Kent 16 B2
Mathern Mons 28 H4
Mathon Herefs 41 L2
Mathry Pembks 36 G4
Matlask Norfk 70 H5
Matlock Derbys 77 P11
Matlock Bank Derbys 77 P11
Matlock Bath Derbys 77 P12
Matlock Dale Derbys 77 P12
Matson Gloucs 41 N8
Matterdale End Cumb 89 L2
Mattersey Notts 78 H6
Mattersey Thorpe Notts 78 H6
Mattingley Hants 31 Q10
Mattishall Norfk 70 F10
Mattishall Burgh Norfk 70 F9
Mauchline E Ayrs 105 J4
Maud Abers 141 M6
Maufant Jersey 13 d2
Maugersbury Gloucs 42 E7
Maughold IoM 102 g4
Mauld Highld 137 L8
Maulden C Beds 44 F4
Maulds Meaburn Cumb 89 Q3
Maunby N York 91 N9
Maund Bryan Herefs 51 P10
Maundown Somset 20 G7
Mautby Norfk 71 P9
Mavesyn Ridware Staffs 65 K9
Mavis Enderby Lincs 80 G10
Mawbray Cumb 97 M9
Mawdesley Lancs 83 L12
Mawdlam Brdgnd 27 J6
Mawgan Cnwll 2 H9
Mawgan Porth Cnwll 6 B11
Maw Green Ches E 76 D12
Mawla Cnwll 2 H5
Mawnan Cnwll 3 K9
Mawnan Smith Cnwll 3 J9
Mawsley Nhants 55 K5
Mawthorpe Lincs 81 J9
Maxey C Pete 68 C10
Maxstoke Warwks 53 N3
Maxted Street Kent 17 K2
Maxton Border 107 P4
Maxton Kent 17 N3
Maxwelltown D & G 97 J3
Maxworthy Cnwll 7 J6
Mayals Swans 26 F4
May Bank Staffs 64 F3
Maybole S Ayrs 104 E8
Maybury Surrey 32 E10
Mayes Green Surrey 14 G3
Mayfield E Susx 15 Q5
Mayfield Mdloth 115 Q8
Mayfield Staffs 65 M3
Mayford Surrey 32 E11
May Hill Gloucs 41 L7
Mayland Essex 46 G11
Maylandsea Essex 46 F11
Maynard's Green E Susx 15 Q7
Maypole Birm 53 K5
Maypole Kent 35 M9
Maypole Mons 40 G8
Maypole Green Norfk 59 N2
Maypole Green Suffk 58 D9
Maypole Green Suffk 59 K7
May's Green Oxon 31 Q6
May's Green Surrey 32 F11
Mead Devon 18 E9
Meadgate BaNES 29 K10
Meadle Bucks 44 A10
Meadowfield Dur 100 G10
Meadowtown Shrops 63 K12
Meadwell Devon 7 M8
Meaford Staffs 64 G5
Mealabost W Isls 152 g3
Meal Bank Cumb 89 N7
Mealrigg Cumb 97 N9
Mealsgate Cumb 97 P10
Meanwood Leeds 85 L8
Mearbeck N York 84 B3
Meare Somset 21 P5
Meare Green Somset 21 L9
Meare Green Somset 21 M8
Mearns E Rens 113 Q10
Mears Ashby Nhants 55 L7
Measham Leics 65 Q9
Meath Green Surrey 15 K2
Meathop Cumb 89 L10
Meaux E R Yk 87 L7
Meavaig W Isls 152 e3
Meavy Devon 4 H3
Medbourne Leics 55 K2
Medburn Nthumb 100 E4
Meddon Devon 18 F10
Meden Vale Notts 78 F9
Medlam Lincs 68 F1
Medlar Lancs 83 K8
Medmenham Bucks 32 A5
Medomsley Dur 100 E7
Medstead Hants 25 L6
Medway Services Medway 34 E9
Meerbrook Staffs 77 J11
Meer Common Herefs 51 K10
Meesden Herts 45 M5
Meeson Wrekin 64 C8
Meeth Devon 7 Q3
Meeting Green Suffk 57 P9
Meeting House Hill Norfk 71 L6
Meidrim Carmth 37 Q6
Meifod Powys 62 G9
Meigle P & K 124 F4
Meikle Carco D & G 105 P7
Meikle Earnock S Lans 114 C10
Meikle Ferry Highld 146 D7
Meikle Kilmory Ag & B 112 F9
Meikle Obney P & K 123 Q5
Meikleour P & K 124 D5
Meikle Wartle Abers 140 H9
Meinciau Carmth 38 C9
Meir C Stke 64 H4
Meir Heath Staffs 64 H4
Melbost W Isls 152 g3
Melbourn Cambs 45 M3
Melbourne Derbys 66 C7
Melbourne E R Yk 86 D6
Melbourne Essex 46 C10
Melbur Cnwll 3 M3
Melbury Devon 18 G9
Melbury Abbas Dorset 23 K9
Melbury Bubb Dorset 10 F3
Melbury Osmond Dorset 10 E3
Melbury Sampford Dorset 10 E4
Melchbourne Bed 55 P7
Melcombe Bingham Dorset 11 J4
Meldon Devon 7 Q6
Meldon Nthumb 100 E1
Meldon Park Nthumb 100 E1
Meldreth Cambs 45 M2
Meldrum Stirlg 114 C1
Melfort Ag & B 120 F10
Meliden Denbgs 74 E7
Melinau Pembks 37 N8
Melin-byrhedyn Powys 61 P12
Melincourt Neath 39 K11
Melin-y-coed Conwy 73 P11
Melin-y-ddol Powys 62 F10
Melin-y-wîg Denbgs 62 E2
Melkinthorpe Cumb 89 P2
Melkridge Nthumb 99 L5
Melksham Wilts 29 P9
Mellangoose Cnwll 2 H9
Mell Green W Berk 31 K7
Mellguards Cumb 98 F9
Melling Lancs 83 N1
Melling Sefton 75 L4
Melling Mount Sefton 75 L3
Mellis Suffk 58 G6
Mellon Charles Highld 143 M7
Mellon Udrigle Highld 143 N6
Mellor Lancs 83 P9
Mellor Stockp 77 J6
Mellor Brook Lancs 83 P9
Mells Somset 22 G4
Mells Suffk 59 M5
Melmerby Cumb 99 J10
Melmerby N York 90 H9
Melmerby N York 91 N11
Melness Highld 149 M4
Melon Green Suffk 58 C9
Melplash Dorset 10 D5
Melrose Border 107 N3
Melsetter Ork 147 b6
Melsonby N York 91 K5
Meltham Kirk 77 L2
Meltham Mills Kirk 77 L2
Melton E R Yk 86 H10
Melton Suffk 59 K10
Meltonby E R Yk 86 E5
Melton Constable Norfk 70 F5
Melton Mowbray Leics 67 J8
Melton Ross N Linc 79 Q2
Melvaig Highld 143 K8
Melverley Shrops 63 K9
Melverley Green Shrops 63 K8
Melvich Highld 150 F4
Membury Devon 9 P4
Membury Services W Berk 30 G7
Memsie Abers 141 N3
Memus Angus 124 H1
Menabilly Cnwll 3 Q4
Menagissey Cnwll 2 H5
Menai Bridge IoA 73 J9
Mendham Suffk 59 K4
Mendip Hills 22 C3
Mendlesham Suffk 58 G7
Mendlesham Green Suffk 58 G8
Menheniot Cnwll 4 D4
Menithwood Worcs 52 D7
Menna Cnwll 3 M4
Mennock D & G 105 Q8
Menston C Brad 85 J6
Menstrie Clacks 114 F2
Menthorpe N York 86 C8
Mentmore Bucks 44 C8
Meoble Highld 127 P7
Meole Brace Shrops 63 N10
Meonstoke Hants 25 K9
Meon Vale Warwks 42 D2
Meopham Kent 34 B9
Meopham Green Kent 34 B9
Meopham Station Kent 34 B9
Mepal Cambs 56 H4
Meppershall C Beds 44 G4
Merbach Herefs 40 D3
Mere Ches E 76 D7
Mere Wilts 22 H7
Mere Brow Lancs 83 K11
Mereclough Lancs 84 C9
Mere Green Birm 65 L12
Mere Green Worcs 52 H8
Mere Heath Ches W 76 C9
Meresborough Medway 34 E9
Mereworth Kent 34 B11
Meriden Solhll 53 N4
Merkadale Highld 134 G9
Merley BCP 11 N5
Merlin's Bridge Pembks 37 J7
Merrington Shrops 63 M8
Merrion Pembks 36 H11
Merriott Somset 21 P11
Merrivale Devon 7 Q9
Merrow Surrey 32 E12
Merry Field Hill Dorset 11 N4
Merry Hill Herts 32 G3
Merryhill Wolves 52 G1
Merry Lees Leics 66 D11
Merrymeet Cnwll 4 D3
Mersea Island Essex 47 J8
Mersey Gateway Bridge Halton 75 N7
Mersham Kent 17 J3
Merstham Surrey 33 K11
Merston W Susx 14 C10
Merstone IoW 13 J8
Merther Cnwll 3 L5
Merthyr Carmth 38 A7
Merthyr Cynog Powys 39 N4
Merthyr Dyfan V Glam 27 Q8
Merthyr Mawr Brdgnd 27 L7
Merthyr Tydfil Myr Td 39 P10
Merthyr Vale Myr Td 27 P2
Merton Devon 19 K11
Merton Gt Lon 33 J8
Merton Norfk 70 D12
Merton Oxon 43 M8
Meshaw Devon 19 P9
Messing Essex 46 F8
Messingham N Linc 79 M3
Metal Bridge Dur 100 H11
Metfield Suffk 59 L4
Metherell Cnwll 4 F3
Metheringham Lincs 79 Q11
Methil Fife 115 Q1
Methilhill Fife 115 Q1
Methley Leeds 85 M10
Methley Junction Leeds 85 N10
Methlick Abers 141 K8
Methven P & K 123 P7
Methwold Norfk 57 P2
Methwold Hythe Norfk 57 N2
Mettingham Suffk 59 M3
Metton Norfk 71 J5
Mevagissey Cnwll 3 P5
Mexborough Donc 78 D4
Mey Highld 151 N2
Meysey Hampton Gloucs 30 D2
Miabhaig W Isls 152 e3
Michaelchurch Herefs 40 H6
Michaelchurch Escley Herefs 40 D5
Michaelchurch-on-Arrow Powys 50 H10
Michaelstone-y-Fedw Newpt 28 C5
Michaelston-le-Pit V Glam 27 Q8
Michaelstow Cnwll 6 F9
Michaelwood Services Gloucs 29 L3
Michelcombe Devon 5 L3
Micheldever Hants 24 H5
Micheldever Station Hants 24 H5
Michelmersh Hants 24 F8
Mickfield Suffk 58 H8
Micklebring Donc 78 E5
Mickleby N York 92 G4
Micklefield Leeds 85 N8
Micklefield Green Herts 32 F3
Mickleham Surrey 32 H11
Mickleover C Derb 65 P5
Micklethwaite C Brad 84 G7
Micklethwaite Cumb 98 C8
Mickleton Dur 90 F2
Mickleton Gloucs 42 D3
Mickletown Leeds 85 N9
Mickle Trafford Ches W 75 M9
Mickley Derbys 77 Q8
Mickley N York 91 L11
Mickley Green Suffk 58 B9
Mickley Square Nthumb 100 D6
Mid Ardlaw Abers 141 M3
Midbea Ork 147 c2
Mid Beltie Abers 132 F4
Mid Bockhampton BCP 12 B5
Mid Calder W Loth 115 K8
Mid Clyth Highld 151 P9
Mid Culbeuchly Abers 140 G3
Middle Assendon Oxon 31 Q5
Middle Aston Oxon 43 K6
Middle Barton Oxon 43 J6
Middlebie D & G 97 P3
Middlebridge P & K 130 G11
Middle Chinnock Somset 21 Q10
Middle Claydon Bucks 43 P6
Middlecliffe Barns 78 C3
Middlecott Devon 8 D7
Middlecroft Derbys 78 C9
Middle Duntisbourne Gloucs 41 R10
Middleham N York 91 J9
Middle Handley Derbys 78 C8
Middle Harling Norfk 58 E3
Middlehill Cnwll 4 D3
Middlehill Wilts 29 N8
Middlehope Shrops 51 N3
Middle Kames Ag & B 112 D3
Middle Littleton Worcs 42 C2
Middle Madeley Staffs 64 E3
Middle Maes-coed Herefs 40 D5
Middlemarsh Dorset 10 G3
Middle Mayfield Staffs 65 L3
Middle Mill Pembks 36 F5
Middlemoor Devon 7 P10
Middle Quarter Kent 16 F3
Middle Rasen Lincs 80 B6
Middle Rocombe Devon 5 Q3
Middle Salter Lancs 83 N3
Middlesbrough Middsb 92 A3
Middlesceugh Cumb 98 E10
Middleshaw Cumb 89 N9
Middlesmoor N York 91 J12
Middle Stoford Somset 21 J9
Middle Stoke Medway 34 E7
Middlestone Dur 100 H12
Middlestone Moor Dur 100 G11
Middle Stoughton Somset 21 P3
Middlestown Wakefd 85 K11
Middle Street Gloucs 41 M10
Middle Taphouse Cnwll 4 B4
Middlethird Border 107 R1
Middleton Ag & B 118 C4
Middleton Cumb 89 Q9
Middleton Derbys 65 P1
Middleton Derbys 77 M11
Middleton Essex 46 F4
Middleton Hants 24 G4
Middleton Herefs 51 P7
Middleton Lancs 83 K3
Middleton Leeds 85 L9
Middleton N York 84 H5
Middleton N York 92 F9
Middleton Nhants 55 L3
Middleton Norfk 69 M9
Middleton Nthumb 100 D1
Middleton Nthumb 108 H3
Middleton P & K 124 C11
Middleton Rochdl 76 F3
Middleton Shrops 51 P5
Middleton Shrops 63 K6
Middleton Suffk 59 N7
Middleton Swans 26 B5
Middleton Warwks 65 M12
Middleton Cheney Nhants 43 K3
Middleton Green Staffs 65 J5
Middleton Hall Nthumb 108 F5
Middleton-in-Teesdale Dur 90 F2
Middleton Moor Suffk 59 N7
Middleton One Row Darltn 91 N4
Middleton-on-Leven N York 91 Q5
Middleton-on-Sea W Susx 14 D10
Middleton on the Hill Herefs 51 P7
Middleton on the Wolds E R Yk 86 H5
Middleton Park C Aber 133 M2
Middleton Priors Shrops 52 B3
Middleton Quernhow N York 91 N11
Middleton St George Darltn 91 N4
Middleton Scriven Shrops 52 C3
Middleton Stoney Oxon 43 L7
Middleton Tyas N York 91 L5
Middletown Cumb 88 C5
Middle Town IoS 2 b3
Middletown N Som 28 F8
Middletown Powys 63 K9
Middle Tysoe Warwks 42 H3
Middle Wallop Hants 24 E6
Middlewich Ches E 76 C10
Middle Winterslow Wilts 24 D7
Middlewood Cnwll 7 K9
Middlewood Herefs 40 C3
Middle Woodford Wilts 23 P6
Middlewood Green Suffk 58 G8
Middle Yard Gloucs 41 N11
Middlezoy Somset 21 N7
Middridge Dur 91 L2
Midford BaNES 29 M10
Midge Hall Lancs 83 L10
Midgeholme Cumb 99 J6
Midgham W Berk 31 L9
Midgley Calder 84 F10
Midgley Wakefd 85 K12
Mid Holmwood Surrey 14 H2
Midhopestones Sheff 77 N4
Midhurst W Susx 14 C6
Mid Lavant W Susx 13 Q3
Midlem Border 107 N4
Mid Mains Highld 137 M8
Midney Somset 22 C8
Midpark Ag & B 112 F9
Midsomer Norton BaNES 22 F3
Midtown Highld 149 M4
Midville Lincs 80 G12
Midway Ches E 76 G7
Mid Yell Shet 147 j3
Migdale Highld 145 P7
Migvie Abers 132 C3
Milborne Port Somset 22 F9
Milborne St Andrew Dorset 11 K5
Milborne Wick Somset 22 F9
Milbourne Nthumb 100 E3
Milbourne Wilts 29 Q5
Milburn Cumb 99 J12
Milbury Heath S Glos 29 K4
Milby N York 85 N2
Milcombe Oxon 43 J5
Milden Suffk 46 G2
Mildenhall Suffk 57 N6
Mildenhall Wilts 30 E8
Milebrook Powys 51 K6
Milebush Kent 16 D2
Mile Elm Wilts 30 A8
Mile End Gloucs 41 J9
Mile End Suffk 59 L3
Mileham Norfk 70 D8
Mile Oak Br & H 15 J9
Mile Oak Kent 16 B2
Mile Oak Staffs 65 M11
Miles Green Staffs 64 E2
Miles Hope Herefs 51 P7
Milesmark Fife 115 K4
Miles Platting Manch 76 F4
Mile Town Kent 34 G7
Milfield Nthumb 108 E3
Milford Derbys 66 B3
Milford Devon 18 E9
Milford Powys 50 F2
Milford Staffs 64 H8
Milford Surrey 14 D2
Milford Haven Pembks 36 H9
Milford on Sea Hants 12 D6
Milkwall Gloucs 41 J10
Millais Jersey 13 a1
Milland W Susx 25 P8
Milland Marsh W Susx 25 P8
Mill Bank Calder 84 F11
Millbeck Cumb 88 H2
Millbreck Abers 141 N7
Millbridge Surrey 25 P5
Millbrook C Beds 44 E4
Millbrook C Sotn 24 F10
Millbrook Cnwll 4 F6
Millbrook Jersey 13 b2
Millbrook Tamesd 76 H4
Mill Brow Stockp 76 H6
Millbuie Abers 133 J2
Millbuie Highld 137 P5
Millcombe Devon 5 N7
Mill Common Norfk 71 L11
Mill Common Suffk 59 N4
Millcorner E Susx 16 E6
Millcraig Highld 145 P11
Mill Cross Devon 5 M4
Milldale Staffs 65 L1
Mill End Bucks 31 R5
Millend Gloucs 29 M3
Mill End Herts 45 L5
Millerhill Mdloth 115 P7
Miller's Dale Derbys 77 L9
Millers Green Derbys 65 P2
Miller's Green Essex 45 Q10
Millerston C Glas 114 B8
Millgate Lancs 84 D11
Mill Green Cambs 46 A3
Mill Green Essex 34 B2
Mill Green Herts 45 J9
Mill Green Lincs 68 E7
Mill Green Norfk 58 H4
Millgreen Shrops 64 C6
Mill Green Staffs 65 K12
Mill Green Staffs 65 K8
Mill Green Suffk 46 G3
Mill Green Suffk 58 E9
Mill Green Suffk 58 H8
Mill Green Suffk 59 L8
Millhalf Herefs 51 J11
Millhayes Devon 9 N4
Millhead Lancs 83 L1
Millheugh S Lans 114 D11
Mill Hill E Susx 16 A9
Mill Hill Gt Lon 33 J4
Millhouse Ag & B 112 D7
Millhouse Cumb 98 D10
Millhousebridge D & G 97 M1
Millhouse Green Barns 77 N3
Millhouses Barns 78 C3
Millhouses Sheff 77 Q7
Milliken Park Rens 113 N9
Millin Cross Pembks 37 J7
Millington E R Yk 86 F5
Mill Lane Hants 25 N3
Millmeece Staffs 64 F5
Millness Cumb 89 N10
Mill of Drummond P & K 123 L9
Mill of Haldane W Duns 113 M5
Millom Cumb 88 G10
Millook Cnwll 6 H5
Millpool Cnwll 2 F8
Millpool Cnwll 6 G10
Millport N Ayrs 112 H10
Mill Side Cumb 89 M10
Mill Street Kent 34 C11
Mill Street Norfk 70 F8
Mill Street Suffk 58 F6
Millthorpe Derbys 77 P8
Millthrop Cumb 89 Q8
Milltimber C Aber 133 L4
Milltown Abers 131 N2
Milltown Abers 132 D1
Milltown Cnwll 3 Q3
Milltown D & G 98 D3
Milltown Derbys 78 B11
Milltown Devon 19 L5
Milltown Highld 135 N7
Milltown of Auchindoun Moray 139 Q8
Milltown of Campfield Abers 132 G4
Milltown of Edinvillie Moray 139 N8
Milltown of Rothiemay Moray 140 E6
Milnathort P & K 124 C11
Milngavie E Duns 113 Q6
Milnrow Rochdl 76 G1
Milnthorpe Cumb 89 M10
Milnthorpe Wakefd 85 M11
Milovaig Highld 134 C6
Milson Shrops 52 B6
Milstead Kent 34 F10
Milston Wilts 23 Q4
Milthorpe Lincs 68 C6
Milthorpe Nhants 43 M2
Milton C Stke 64 G2
Milton Cambs 57 J8
Milton Cumb 98 H6
Milton D & G 95 J7
Milton D & G 96 G4
Milton Derbys 65 P7
Milton Highld 137 N9
Milton Highld 137 Q6
Milton Highld 146 D10
Milton Highld 151 P6
Milton Inver 113 L7
Milton Kent 34 B7
Milton Moray 139 M12
Milton Moray 140 D3
Milton N Som 28 D10
Milton Newpt 28 E5
Milton Notts 78 H9
Milton Oxon 31 K4
Milton Oxon 43 K5
Milton P & K 131 K12
Milton Pembks 37 K10
Milton Somset 21 P9
Milton Stirlg 113 P1
Milton W Duns 113 N6
Milton Abbas Dorset 11 K4
Milton Abbot Devon 7 M9
Milton Bridge Mdloth 115 N8
Milton Bryan C Beds 44 D6
Milton Clevedon Somset 22 F6
Milton Combe Devon 4 G3
Milton Common Oxon 43 N11
Milton Damerel Devon 7 M3
Milton End Gloucs 30 D2
Milton End Gloucs 41 L9
Milton Ernest Bed 55 P9
Milton Green Ches W 75 M12
Milton Hill Oxon 31 K4
Milton Keynes M Keyn 44 B4
Milton Lilbourne Wilts 30 E10
Milton Malsor Nhants 55 J9
Milton Morenish P & K 122 G5
Milton of Auchinhove Abers 132 E4
Milton of Balgonie Fife 115 P1
Milton of Buchanan Stirlg 113 N3
Milton of Campsie E Duns 114 B6
Milton of Finavon Angus 125 K1
Milton of Leys Highld 138 C7
Milton of Murtle C Aber 133 L4
Milton on Stour Dorset 22 H7
Milton Regis Kent 34 F9
Milton Street E Susx 15 P10
Milton-under-Wychwood Oxon 42 F8
Milverton Somset 20 H8
Milverton Warwks 53 P7
Milwich Staffs 64 H6
Milwr Flints 74 G8
Minard Ag & B 112 E2
Minchington Dorset 23 L10
Minchinhampton Gloucs 29 P2
Mindenhurst Surrey 32 C10
Mindrum Nthumb 108 D3
Minehead Somset 20 F4
Minera Wrexhm 63 J2
Minety Wilts 30 B4
Minffordd Gwynd 61 K4
Mingarrypark Highld 127 M10
Miningsby Lincs 80 F11
Minions Cnwll 7 K10
Minishant S Ayrs 104 F7
Minllyn Gwynd 61 Q9
Minnigaff D & G 95 M5
Minnonie Abers 141 J4
Minshull Vernon Ches E 76 C11
Minskip N York 85 M2
Minstead Hants 12 D3
Minsted W Susx 25 Q9
Minster Kent 35 P9
Minsterley Shrops 63 L11
Minster Lovell Oxon 42 G9
Minster-on-Sea Kent 34 G8
Minsterworth Gloucs 41 M8
Minterne Magna Dorset 10 G4
Minterne Parva Dorset 10 G4

Minting Lincs 80 D9
Mintlaw Abers 141 N6
Minto Border 107 N6
Minton Shrops 51 M2
Minwear Pembks 37 K8
Minworth Birm 53 M2
Mirehouse Cumb 88 C4
Mireland Highld 151 P4
Mirfield Kirk 85 J11
Miserden Gloucs 41 Q10
Miskin Rhondd 27 P3
Miskin Rhondd 27 P6
Misson Notts 78 H5
Misterton Leics 54 F4
Misterton Notts 79 J5
Misterton Somset 10 C3
Mistley Essex 47 K5
Mistley Heath Essex 47 K5
Mitcham Gt Lon 33 K8
Mitcheldean Gloucs 41 K8
Mitchell Cnwll 3 L4
Mitchellslacks D & G 106 C10
Mitchel Troy Mons 40 G9
Mitford Nthumb 100 F1
Mithian Cnwll 3 J4
Mitton Staffs 64 G9
Mixbury Oxon 43 M5
Mixenden Calder 84 G9
Moats Tye Suffk 58 F9
Mobberley Ches E 76 E8
Mobberley Staffs 65 J4
Moccas Herefs 40 E3
Mochdre Conwy 73 P8
Mochdre Powys 50 E3
Mochrum D & G 95 L9
Mockbeggar Hants 12 B3
Mockbeggar Kent 16 C1
Mockerkin Cumb 88 E2
Modbury Devon 5 L6
Moddershall Staffs 64 G5
Moelfre IoA 72 H6
Moelfre Powys 62 G6
Moel Tryfan Gwynd 60 H1
Moffat D & G 106 E8
Mogador Surrey 33 J11
Moggerhanger C Beds 56 C10
Moira Leics 65 P9
Molash Kent 35 J12
Mol-chlach Highld 126 H2
Mold Flints 74 H11
Moldgreen Kirk 84 H12
Molehill Green Essex 45 Q7
Molehill Green Essex 46 C7
Molescroft E R Yk 87 J7
Molesden Nthumb 100 F1
Molesworth Cambs 55 Q5
Moll Highld 135 K9
Molland Devon 20 C7
Mollington Ches W 75 L9
Mollington Oxon 54 D11
Mollinsburn N Lans 114 C7
Monachty Cerdgn 48 H8
Mondynes Abers 133 J8
Monewden Suffk 59 K9
Moneydie P & K 124 B7
Moneyrow Green W & M 32 C7
Moniaive D & G 105 P11
Monifieth Angus 125 K6
Monikie Angus 125 K5
Monimail Fife 124 F10
Monington Pembks 37 M2
Monk Bretton Barns 78 B2
Monken Hadley Gt Lon 33 J3
Monk Fryston N York 85 Q9
Monkhide Herefs 41 J3
Monkhill Cumb 98 D6
Monkhopton Shrops 52 B2
Monkland Herefs 51 M9
Monkleigh Devon 19 J9
Monknash V Glam 27 L8
Monkokehampton Devon 7 Q4
Monkseaton N Tyne 101 J4
Monks Eleigh Suffk 58 E11
Monk's Gate W Susx 14 H5
Monks Heath Ches E 76 F9
Monk Sherborne Hants 31 M11
Monks Horton Kent 17 K3
Monksilver Somset 20 G6
Monks Kirby Warwks 54 D4
Monk Soham Suffk 59 J7
Monkspath Solhll 53 L5
Monks Risborough Bucks 44 A10
Monksthorpe Lincs 80 H10
Monk Street Essex 45 R6
Monkswood Mons 40 D11
Monkton Devon 9 M4
Monkton Kent 35 N9
Monkton S Ayrs 104 F4
Monkton S Tyne 101 J5
Monkton V Glam 27 M8
Monkton Combe BaNES 29 M10
Monkton Deverill Wilts 23 J6
Monkton Farleigh Wilts 29 N9
Monkton Heathfield Somset 21 L8
Monkton Up Wimborne Dorset 23 M10
Monkton Wyld Dorset 9 Q5
Monkwearmouth Sundld 101 K6
Monkwood Hants 25 L7
Monmore Green Wolves 52 H1
Monmouth Mons 40 G9
Monnington on Wye Herefs 40 E3
Monreith D & G 95 L10
Montacute Somset 22 C10
Montcliffe Bolton 76 C1
Montford Shrops 63 L9
Montford Bridge Shrops 63 M9
Montgarrie Abers 140 E12
Montgomery Powys 50 H1
Monton Salfd 76 E4
Montrose Angus 125 P1
Mont Saint Guern 12 b2
Monxton Hants 24 E4
Monyash Derbys 77 L10
Monymusk Abers 132 G1
Monzie P & K 123 M8
Moodiesburn N Lans 114 C7
Moonzie Fife 124 G9
Moor Allerton Leeds 85 L7
Moorbath Dorset 10 C6
Moorby Lincs 80 F11
Moorcot Herefs 51 K9
Moor Crichel Dorset 11 N3
Moordown BCP 11 Q6
Moore Halton 75 P7
Moor End C Beds 44 D7
Moor End Calder 84 F9
Moor End Devon 8 C3
Moorend Gloucs 41 L11
Moor End Lancs 83 J6
Moor End N York 86 B7
Moorends Donc 86 C12
Moorgreen Hants 24 H10
Moor Green Herts 45 L6
Moorgreen Notts 66 D3
Moorhall Derbys 77 P8
Moorhampton Herefs 40 E3
Moorhead C Brad 84 H8
Moor Head Leeds 85 K9
Moorhouse Cumb 98 B6
Moorhouse Cumb 98 D7
Moorhouse Donc 78 D2
Moorhouse Notts 79 J10
Moorhouse Bank Surrey 33 M11
Moorland Somset 21 M7
Moorlinch Somset 21 N6
Moor Monkton N York 85 Q4
Moor Row Cumb 88 D4
Moor Row Cumb 97 P8
Moorsholm R & Cl 92 E4
Moorside Dorset 22 H9
Moorside Dur 100 E8
Moor Side Lancs 83 K8
Moor Side Lancs 83 L8
Moorside Leeds 85 K8
Moor Side Lincs 80 E12
Moorside Oldham 76 H2
Moorstock Kent 17 K3
Moor Street Medway 34 E9
Moorswater Cnwll 4 C4
Moorthorpe Wakefd 78 D2
Moortown Devon 7 P10
Moortown Hants 12 B4
Moortown IoW 12 G8
Moortown Leeds 85 L7
Moortown Lincs 79 Q4
Moortown Wrekin 63 Q8
Morangie Highld 146 D8
Morar Highld 127 M6
Morborne Cambs 56 C2
Morchard Bishop Devon 8 E3
Morchard Road Devon 8 E4
Morcombelake Dorset 10 B6
Morcott Rutlnd 67 M12
Morda Shrops 63 J6
Morden Dorset 11 M5
Morden Gt Lon 33 J8
Mordiford Herefs 40 H4
Mordon Dur 91 N1
More Shrops 51 K2
Morebath Devon 20 E8
Morebattle Border 108 C5
Morecambe Lancs 83 K2
Moredon Swindn 30 D5
Morefield Highld 144 E6
Morehall Kent 17 M3
Moreleigh Devon 5 M6
Morenish P & K 122 G6
Moresby Parks Cumb 88 D3
Morestead Hants 24 H8
Moreton Dorset 11 K7
Moreton Essex 45 P10
Moreton Herefs 51 N8
Moreton Oxon 43 P10
Moreton Staffs 64 E8
Moreton Staffs 65 L6
Moreton Wirral 75 J6
Moreton Corbet Shrops 63 P7
Moreton Hall Suffk 58 C8
Moretonhampstead Devon 8 E7
Moreton-in-Marsh Gloucs 42 E5
Moreton Jeffries Herefs 51 Q11
Moretonmill Shrops 63 P7
Moreton Morrell Warwks 53 P9
Moreton on Lugg Herefs 40 G3
Moreton Paddox Warwks 53 P9
Moreton Pinkney Nhants 54 F11
Moreton Say Shrops 64 B5
Moreton Valence Gloucs 41 M9
Morfa Cerdgn 48 E10
Morfa Bychan Gwynd 61 J5
Morfa Dinlle Gwynd 72 G12
Morfa Glas Neath 39 K10
Morfa Nefyn Gwynd 60 D4
Morganstown Cardif 27 Q6
Morgan's Vale Wilts 24 C9
Morham E Loth 116 D7
Moriah Cerdgn 49 K5
Morland Cumb 89 P2
Morley Ches E 76 F7
Morley Derbys 66 C4
Morley Dur 91 J1
Morley Leeds 85 K9
Morley Green Ches E 76 F7
Morley St Botolph Norfk 70 G12
Mornick Cnwll 7 L10
Morningside C Edin 115 N7
Morningside N Lans 114 E10
Morningthorpe Norfk 59 J2
Morpeth Nthumb 100 G1
Morphie Abers 132 H11
Morrey Staffs 65 L8
Morridge Side Staffs 65 J1
Morriston Swans 26 G3
Morston Norfk 70 E3
Mortehoe Devon 19 J4
Morthen Rothm 78 D6
Mortimer W Berk 31 N9
Mortimer Common W Berk 31 N9
Mortimer's Cross Herefs 51 M8
Mortimer West End Hants 31 N9
Mortlake Gt Lon 32 H7
Morton Cumb 98 E7
Morton Cumb 98 F10
Morton Derbys 78 C11
Morton IoW 13 K7
Morton Lincs 68 B7
Morton Lincs 79 K5
Morton Lincs 79 M11
Morton Notts 67 J2
Morton Shrops 63 J7
Morton-on-Swale N York 91 N8
Morton on the Hill Norfk 70 G9
Morton Tinmouth Dur 91 K2
Morvah Cnwll 2 C7
Morval Cnwll 4 C5
Morvich Highld 136 D11
Morville Shrops 52 C2
Morville Heath Shrops 52 C2
Morwenstow Cnwll 18 D10
Mosborough Sheff 78 C7
Moscow E Ayrs 105 J2
Mose Shrops 52 D3
Mosedale Cumb 98 D11
Moseley Birm 53 K4
Moseley Wolves 52 H1
Moseley Worcs 52 E8
Moses Gate Bolton 76 D2
Moss Ag & B 118 C4
Moss Donc 86 B12
Moss Wrexhm 63 J2
Mossat Abers 140 D12
Mossbank Shet 147 j5
Moss Bank St Hel 75 N4
Mossbay Cumb 88 C1
Mossblown S Ayrs 104 G5
Mossbrow Traffd 76 D6
Mossburnford Border 107 Q6
Mossdale D & G 96 D4
Mossdale E Ayrs 105 J9
Moss Edge Lancs 83 K6
Moss End Ches E 76 C8
Mossend N Lans 114 D9
Mosser Mains Cumb 88 F2
Mossley Ches E 76 G11
Mossley Tamesd 76 H3
Mosspaul Inn Border 107 L10
Moss Side Cumb 97 P8
Moss-side Highld 138 F5
Moss Side Lancs 83 J9
Moss Side Sefton 75 L3
Mosstodloch Moray 139 Q4
Mossyard D & G 95 Q8
Mossy Lea Lancs 75 P1
Mosterton Dorset 10 C4
Moston Manch 76 G3
Moston Shrops 63 P7
Moston Green Ches E 76 D11
Mostyn Flints 74 G7
Motcombe Dorset 23 J8
Mothecombe Devon 5 K7
Motherby Cumb 98 E12
Motherwell N Lans 114 D10
Motspur Park Gt Lon 33 J9
Mottingham Gt Lon 33 M8
Mottisfont Hants 24 E8
Mottisfont Hants 24 E8
Mottistone IoW 12 G8
Mottram in Longdendale Tamesd 77 J5
Mottram St Andrew Ches E 76 G8
Mouilpied Guern 12 c3
Mouldsworth Ches W 75 N9
Moulin P & K 123 N1
Moulsecoomb Br & H 15 L9
Moulsford Oxon 31 M5
Moulsoe M Keyn 44 C3
Moultavie Highld 145 P11
Moulton Ches W 76 C9
Moulton Lincs 68 F7
Moulton N York 91 L6
Moulton Nhants 55 K7
Moulton Suffk 57 N8
Moulton V Glam 27 P8
Moulton Chapel Lincs 68 F8
Moulton St Mary Norfk 71 M10
Moulton Seas End Lincs 68 F6
Mount Cnwll 3 J3
Mount Cnwll 4 A3
Mount Kirk 84 G11
Mountain C Brad 84 G9
Mountain Ash Rhondd 27 P3
Mountain Cross Border 115 L12
Mountain Street Kent 35 J11
Mount Ambrose Cnwll 2 H6
Mount Bures Essex 46 F5
Mountfield E Susx 16 C7
Mountgerald Highld 137 P3
Mount Hawke Cnwll 2 H5
Mount Hermon Cnwll 2 H11
Mountjoy Cnwll 3 L2
Mount Lothian Mdloth 115 N10
Mountnessing Essex 34 A3
Mounton Mons 28 G4
Mount Pleasant Ches E 76 F12
Mount Pleasant Derbys 65 P8
Mount Pleasant Derbys 65 Q2
Mount Pleasant Dur 100 H11
Mount Pleasant E R Yk 87 N7
Mount Pleasant E Susx 15 M7
Mount Pleasant Norfk 58 E2
Mount Pleasant Suffk 57 P11
Mount Pleasant Sundld 101 J7
Mount Pleasant Worcs 53 J7
Mountsorrel Leics 66 F9
Mount Sorrel Wilts 23 M8
Mount Tabor Calder 84 G9
Mousehole Cnwll 2 D9
Mouswald D & G 97 L4
Mow Cop Ches E 76 F12
Mowhaugh Border 108 C5
Mowmacre Hill C Leic 66 F10
Mowsley Leics 54 G3
Moy Highld 129 M8
Moy Highld 138 E9
Moyle Highld 136 B12
Moylegrove Pembks 48 A11
Muasdale Ag & B 103 J2
Muchalls Abers 133 L6
Much Birch Herefs 40 G5
Much Cowarne Herefs 41 J2
Much Dewchurch Herefs 40 G5
Muchelney Somset 21 P8
Muchelney Ham Somset 21 P8
Much Hadham Herts 45 M8
Much Hoole Lancs 83 L10
Much Hoole Town Lancs 83 L10
Muchlarnick Cnwll 4 C5
Much Marcle Herefs 41 K5
Much Wenlock Shrops 64 B12
Muck Highld 126 G8
Mucking Thurr 34 B6
Muckleburgh Military Collection Norfk 70 G3
Muckleford Dorset 10 G6
Mucklestone Staffs 64 D5
Muckley Shrops 52 B2
Muckton Lincs 80 G7
Muddiford Devon 19 L6
Muddles Green E Susx 15 Q8
Mudeford BCP 12 C6
Mudford Somset 22 D9
Mudford Sock Somset 22 D9
Mudgley Somset 21 P4
Mud Row Kent 34 H8
Mugdock Stirlg 113 Q6
Mugeary Highld 134 H8
Mugginton Derbys 65 P4
Muggintonlane End Derbys 65 P3
Muggleswick Dur 100 D8
Muirden Abers 140 H5
Muirdrum Angus 125 L5
Muiresk Abers 140 H6
Muirhead Angus 124 G6
Muirhead Fife 124 F11
Muirhead N Lans 114 C7
Muirhouses Falk 115 J5
Muirkirk E Ayrs 105 N4
Muirmill Stirlg 114 D4
Muir of Fowlis Abers 132 E2
Muir of Miltonduff Moray 139 M4
Muir of Ord Highld 137 P6
Muirshearlich Highld 128 G8
Muirtack Abers 141 N8
Muirton P & K 123 N10
Muirton Mains Highld 137 M5
Muirton of Ardblair P & K 124 D4
Muker N York 90 E7
Mulbarton Norfk 71 J12
Mulben Moray 139 Q6
Mulfra Cnwll 2 D7
Mull Ag & B 119 Q6
Mullacott Cross Devon 19 K4
Mullardoch Highld 136 H9
Mullion Cnwll 2 H10
Mullion Cove Cnwll 2 G11
Mumby Lincs 81 K9
Munderfield Row Herefs 52 C10
Munderfield Stocks Herefs 52 C10
Mundesley Norfk 71 L5
Mundford Norfk 57 Q2
Mundham Norfk 59 L1
Mundon Essex 46 F11
Mundy Bois Kent 16 F2
Mungrisdale Cumb 98 D12
Munlochy Highld 138 B5
Munnoch N Ayrs 113 K11
Munsley Herefs 41 K3
Munslow Shrops 51 N3
Murchington Devon 8 C7
Murcot Worcs 42 C4
Murcott Oxon 43 M8
Murcott Wilts 29 Q4
Murkle Highld 151 L3
Murlaggan Highld 128 D6
Murrell Green Hants 25 N2
Murroes Angus 125 J6
Murrow Cambs 68 G10
Mursley Bucks 44 B6
Murston Kent 34 G9
Murthill Angus 125 J1
Murthly P & K 124 C5
Murton C York 86 C5
Murton Cumb 90 B2
Murton Dur 101 K9
Murton N Tyne 101 J4
Murton Nthumb 117 L11
Murton Swans 26 E4
Musbury Devon 9 P6
Muscoates N York 92 E10
Musselburgh E Loth 115 Q7
Muston Leics 67 K5
Muston N York 93 M10
Mustow Green Worcs 52 F6
Muswell Hill Gt Lon 33 K4
Mutehill D & G 96 E8
Mutford Suffk 59 P3
Muthill P & K 123 M9
Mutterton Devon 9 J4
Muxton Wrekin 64 D9
Mybster Highld 151 L6
Myddfai Carmth 39 J5
Myddle Shrops 63 M7
Mydroilyn Cerdgn 48 G9
Myerscough Lancs 83 L7
Mylor Cnwll 3 K7
Mylor Bridge Cnwll 3 K7
Mynachlog ddu Pembks 37 M4
Myndd-llan Flints 74 G9
Myndtown Shrops 51 L3
Mynydd Bach Cerdgn 49 M5
Mynydd-bach Mons 28 G3
Mynydd-Bach Swans 26 G3
Mynyddgarreg Carmth 38 C10
Mynydd Isa Flints 75 J11
Mynydd Llandygai Gwynd 73 K10
Mynydd Mechell IoA 72 F6
Mynytho Gwynd 60 E6
Myrebird Abers 132 H4
Myredykes Border 107 P10
Mytchett Surrey 32 C11
Mytholm Calder 84 E9
Mytholmroyd Calder 84 F10
Mythop Lancs 83 J8
Myton-on-Swale N York 85 N2

N

Naast Highld 143 M8
Nab's Head Lancs 83 N9
Na Buirgh W Isls 152 d6
Naburn C York 86 B6
Naccolt Kent 17 J2
Nackington Kent 35 L11
Nacton Suffk 47 M4
Nafferton E R Yk 87 K3
Nag's Head Gloucs 29 P3
Nailbridge Gloucs 41 K8
Nailsbourne Somset 21 K7
Nailsea N Som 28 G8
Nailstone Leics 66 C10
Nailsworth Gloucs 29 N2
Nairn Highld 138 G5
Nalderswood Surrey 15 J2
Nancegollan Cnwll 2 G8
Nancledra Cnwll 2 D7
Nanhoron Gwynd 60 D6
Nannerch Flints 74 G9
Nanpantan Leics 66 E8
Nanpean Cnwll 3 N3
Nanquidno Cnwll 2 B8
Nanstallon Cnwll 6 F11
Nant-ddu Powys 39 N8
Nanternis Cerdgn 48 F9
Nantgaredig Carmth 38 D7
Nantgarw Rhondd 27 Q5
Nant-glas Powys 50 D7
Nantglyn Denbgs 74 D11
Nantgwyn Powys 50 D5
Nant Gwynant Gwynd 61 L2
Nantlle Gwynd 60 H2
Nantlle Valley Slate Landscape Gwynd 60 H1
Nantmawr Shrops 63 J7
Nantmel Powys 50 E7
Nantmor Gwynd 61 K3
Nant Peris Gwynd 73 K12
Nantwich Ches E 64 C2
Nant-y-Bwch Blae G 39 Q9
Nantycaws Carmth 38 C8
Nant-y-derry Mons 40 D10
Nant-y-ffin Carmth 38 E5
Nantyffyllon Brdgnd 27 K4
Nantyglo Blae G 40 B9
Nant-y-gollen Shrops 62 H6
Nant-y-moel Brdgnd 27 M4
Nant-y-pandy Conwy 73 M9
Naphill Bucks 32 B3
Napleton Worcs 52 F11
Nappa N York 84 C4
Napton on the Hill Warwks 54 D8
Narberth Pembks 37 L7
Narborough Leics 54 E1
Narborough Norfk 69 P9
Narkurs Cnwll 4 E5
Nasareth Gwynd 60 H2
Naseby Nhants 54 H5
Nash Bucks 43 Q5
Nash Gt Lon 33 M9
Nash Herefs 51 K8
Nash Newpt 28 D5
Nash Shrops 51 Q6
Nash End Worcs 52 E4
Nashes Green Hants 25 L4
Nash Lee Bucks 44 B10
Nash Street Kent 34 B8
Nassington Nhants 55 Q1
Nastend Gloucs 41 M10
Nasty Herts 45 L7
Nateby Cumb 90 C5
Nateby Lancs 83 L6
National Memorial Arboretum Staffs 65 M9
National Space Centre C Leic 66 F10
Natland Cumb 89 N9
Naughton Suffk 58 F10
Naunton Gloucs 42 D7
Naunton Worcs 41 P4
Naunton Beauchamp Worcs 52 H10
Navenby Lincs 79 N12
Navestock Essex 33 P3
Navestock Side Essex 33 Q3
Navidale Highld 147 J2
Navity Highld 138 E3
Nawton N York 92 D9
Nayland Suffk 46 H5
Nazeing Essex 45 M10
Nazeing Gate Essex 45 M10
Neacroft Hants 12 C5
Neal's Green Warwks 53 Q4
Neap Shet 147 j6
Near Cotton Staffs 65 K3
Near Sawrey Cumb 89 K7
Neasden Gt Lon 33 J5
Neasham Darltn 91 N5
Neath Neath 26 H3
Neatham Hants 25 M5
Neatishead Norfk 71 L8
Nebo Cerdgn 49 J7
Nebo Conwy 61 P1
Nebo Gwynd 60 H2
Nebo IoA 72 H5
Necton Norfk 70 C10
Nedd Highld 148 D10
Nedderton Nthumb 100 G2
Nedging Suffk 58 E11
Nedging Tye Suffk 58 F10
Needham Norfk 59 J4
Needham Market Suffk 58 G9
Needham Street Suffk 57 N7
Needingworth Cambs 56 G6
Neen Savage Shrops 52 C5
Neen Sollars Shrops 52 C6
Neenton Shrops 52 B3
Nefyn Gwynd 60 E4
Neilston E Rens 113 P10
Nelson Caerph 27 Q3
Nelson Lancs 84 C7
Nemphlar S Lans 105 Q1
Nempnett Thrubwell BaNES 28 H10
Nenthall Cumb 99 L9
Nenthead Cumb 99 M9
Nenthorn Border 107 R2
Neopardy Devon 8 E5
Nep Town W Susx 15 J8
Nerabus Ag & B 110 F10
Nercwys Flints 74 H11
Nerston S Lans 114 B10
Nesbit Nthumb 108 G3
Nesfield N York 84 G5
Ness Ches W 75 J8
Nesscliffe Shrops 63 L8
Neston Ches W 75 J8
Neston Wilts 29 P8
Netchwood Shrops 52 B2
Nether Abington S Lans 106 B5
Nether Alderley Ches E 76 F8
Netheravon Wilts 23 P4
Nether Blainslie Border 107 N1
Netherbrae Abers 141 J4
Nether Broughton Leics 66 H7
Netherburn S Lans 114 E11
Netherbury Dorset 10 D5
Netherby Cumb 98 E4
Netherby N York 85 M6
Nether Cerne Dorset 10 G5
Nethercleuch D & G 97 M1
Nether Compton Dorset 22 D10
Nethercote Warwks 54 E8
Nethercott Devon 7 L5
Nethercott Devon 19 J5
Nether Crimond Abers 141 K11
Nether Dallachy Moray 139 Q3
Netherend Gloucs 29 J2
Nether Exe Devon 8 H5
Netherfield E Susx 16 C7
Netherfield Leics 66 G9
Netherfield Notts 66 G4
Nether Fingland S Lans 106 B7
Nethergate N Linc 79 J4
Nethergate Norfk 70 F6
Netherhampton Wilts 23 P7
Nether Handley Derbys 78 C8
Nether Handwick Angus 124 G4
Nether Haugh Rothm 78 C4
Netherhay Dorset 10 C4
Nether Headon Notts 79 J8
Nether Heage Derbys 66 B2
Nether Heyford Nhants 54 H9
Nether Kellet Lancs 83 L2
Nether Kinmundy Abers 141 P7
Netherland Green Staffs 65 L6
Nether Langwith Notts 78 E9
Netherley Abers 133 K6
Netherley Lpool 75 M6
Nethermill D & G 106 D12
Nethermuir Abers 141 L7
Netherne-on-the-Hill Surrey 33 K11
Netheroyd Hill Kirk 84 H11
Nether Padley Derbys 77 N8
Nether Poppleton C York 85 R4
Nether Row Cumb 98 C10
Netherseal Derbys 65 P9
Nether Silton N York 91 Q8
Nether Skyborry Shrops 51 J6
Nether Stowey Somset 21 K5
Nether Street Essex 45 Q9
Netherstreet Wilts 29 R9
Netherthird E Ayrs 105 K6
Netherthong Kirk 77 L2
Netherthorpe Derbys 78 D8
Netherton Angus 125 L1
Netherton Devon 8 G10
Netherton Dudley 52 H3
Netherton Hants 30 H10
Netherton Herefs 40 H6
Netherton Kirk 77 L1
Netherton N Lans 114 E10
Netherton Nthumb 108 F8
Netherton Oxon 31 J2
Netherton P & K 124 C2
Netherton Sefton 75 K4
Netherton Shrops 52 D4
Netherton Stirlg 113 Q5
Netherton Wakefd 85 L11
Netherton Worcs 42 A3
Nethertown Cumb 88 C5
Nethertown Highld 151 Q1
Nethertown Lancs 83 Q8
Nethertown Staffs 65 L8
Netherurd Border 115 K12
Nether Wallop Hants 24 E6
Nether Wasdale Cumb 88 F6
Nether Welton Cumb 98 D9
Nether Westcote Gloucs 42 F7
Nether Whitacre Warwks 53 N2
Nether Whitecleuch S Lans 105 Q6
Nether Winchendon Bucks 43 Q9
Netherwitton Nthumb 108 H11
Nethy Bridge Highld 139 J11
Netley Hants 12 G3
Netley Marsh Hants 24 E10
Nettlebed Oxon 31 P5
Nettlebridge Somset 22 E4
Nettlecombe Dorset 10 D6
Nettlecombe IoW 13 J9
Nettleden Herts 44 E9
Nettleham Lincs 79 P8
Nettlestead Kent 34 B12
Nettlestead Green Kent 34 B12
Nettlestone IoW 13 K6
Nettlesworth Dur 100 H8
Nettleton Lincs 80 B4
Nettleton Wilts 29 N6
Nettleton Shrub Wilts 29 N7
Netton Devon 5 J7
Netton Wilts 23 P6
Neuadd Carmth 39 J8
Neuadd-ddu Powys 50 C5
Nevendon Essex 34 D4
Nevern Pembks 37 L3
Nevill Holt Leics 55 K2
New Abbey D & G 97 K5
New Aberdour Abers 141 L3
New Addington Gt Lon 33 M9
Newall Leeds 85 J5
New Alresford Hants 25 K7
New Alyth P & K 124 E3
Newark C Pete 68 D12
Newark Ork 147 e2
Newark-on-Trent Notts 67 K1
New Arley Warwks 53 P3
New Arram E R Yk 87 J6
Newarthill N Lans 114 E9
New Ash Green Kent 33 R8
New Balderton Notts 67 K2
Newbarn Kent 17 L3
New Barn Kent 34 A8
New Barnet Gt Lon 33 K3
New Barnetby N Linc 79 Q2
New Barton Nhants 55 L8
Newbattle Mdloth 115 P8
New Bewick Nthumb 108 H6
Newbie D & G 97 N5
Newbiggin Cumb 82 G1
Newbiggin Cumb 88 E8
Newbiggin Cumb 89 Q1
Newbiggin Cumb 98 F12
Newbiggin Cumb 98 H8
Newbiggin Dur 90 E1
Newbiggin Dur 100 F8
Newbiggin N York 90 F8
Newbiggin N York 90 G9
Newbiggin-by-the-Sea Nthumb 109 M12
Newbigging Angus 124 F4
Newbigging Angus 124 H5
Newbigging Angus 125 K5
Newbigging S Lans 115 J12
Newbiggin-on-Lune Cumb 90 B6
New Bilton Warwks 54 D5
Newbold Derbys 78 B9
Newbold Leics 66 C8
Newbold on Avon Warwks 54 D5
Newbold on Stour Warwks 42 F2
Newbold Pacey Warwks 53 P9
Newbold Revel Warwks 54 D4
Newbold Verdon Leics 66 D11
New Bolingbroke Lincs 80 F12
Newborough C Pete 68 D11
Newborough IoA 72 G10
Newborough Staffs 65 L7
Newbottle Nhants 43 L4
Newbottle Sundld 101 J8
New Boultham Lincs 79 N9
Newbourne Suffk 47 N3
New Bradwell M Keyn 44 B3
New Brampton Derbys 78 B9
New Brancepeth Dur 100 G10
Newbridge C Edin 115 L7
Newbridge Caerph 28 B3
Newbridge Cerdgn 48 H9
Newbridge Cnwll 2 C8
Newbridge Cnwll 3 K6
Newbridge D & G 97 J2
Newbridge Hants 24 E10
Newbridge IoW 12 G7
New Bridge N York 92 F9
Newbridge Oxon 31 J2
Newbridge Wrexhm 63 J4
Newbridge Green Worcs 41 N4
Newbridge-on-Usk Mons 28 E3
Newbridge-on-Wye Powys 50 D9
New Brighton Flints 75 J10
New Brighton Wirral 75 K5
New Brinsley Notts 66 D2
Newbrough Nthumb 99 N5
New Broughton Wrexhm 63 K2
New Buckenham Norfk 58 G3
Newbuildings Devon 8 E4
Newburgh Abers 141 M4
Newburgh Abers 141 N10
Newburgh Fife 124 E9
Newburgh Lancs 75 N2
Newburn N u Ty 100 F5
New Bury Bolton 76 D3
Newbury Somset 22 F3
Newbury W Berk 31 K9
Newbury Wilts 22 H5
Newbury Park Gt Lon 33 N5
Newby Cumb 89 P2
Newby Lancs 84 B6
Newby N York 83 Q1
Newby N York 92 A4
Newby N York 93 K8
Newby Bridge Cumb 89 K9
Newby Cross Cumb 98 D7
Newby East Cumb 98 F6
Newby Head Cumb 89 P2
New Byth Abers 141 K5
Newby West Cumb 98 D7
Newby Wiske N York 91 N9
Newcastle Mons 40 F8
Newcastle Shrops 50 H4
Newcastle Airport Nthumb 100 F4
Newcastle Emlyn Carmth 37 Q2
Newcastle Great Park N u Ty 100 G4
Newcastleton Border 107 M12
Newcastle-under-Lyme Staffs 64 F3
Newcastle upon Tyne N u Ty 100 G5
Newchapel Pembks 37 P3
Newchapel Staffs 64 F1
Newchapel Surrey 15 L2
Newchurch Blae G 40 A9
Newchurch Herefs 51 L10
Newchurch IoW 13 J7
Newchurch Kent 17 J4
Newchurch Mons 28 F3
Newchurch Powys 50 H10
Newchurch Staffs 65 L7
Newchurch in Pendle Lancs 84 B7
New Costessey Norfk 71 J10
New Cowper Cumb 97 M9
Newcraighall C Edin 115 P7
New Crofton Wakefd 85 M11
New Cross Cerdgn 49 L5
New Cross Gt Lon 33 L7
New Cross Somset 21 P9
New Cumnock E Ayrs 105 L7
New Cut E Susx 16 E7
New Deer Abers 141 L6
New Delaval Nthumb 100 H2
New Delph Oldham 77 J2
New Denham Bucks 32 F5
Newdigate Surrey 14 H2
New Duston Nhants 55 J8
New Earswick C York 86 B4
New Eastwood Notts 66 D3
New Edlington Donc 78 E4
New Elgin Moray 139 N3
New Ellerby E R Yk 87 M7
Newell Green Br For 32 C8
New Eltham Gt Lon 33 N8
New End Worcs 53 K8
Newenden Kent 16 E5
New England C Pete 68 D12
New England Essex 46 C3
Newent Gloucs 41 L6
New Farnley Leeds 85 K9
New Ferry Wirral 75 K6
Newfield Dur 100 G11
Newfield Dur 100 G8
Newfield Highld 146 D9
New Fletton C Pete 56 D1
New Forest National Park 12 D3
Newfound Hants 25 K3
New Fryston Wakefd 85 P10
Newgale Pembks 36 G6
New Galloway D & G 96 D3
Newgate Norfk 70 F4
Newgate Street Herts 45 K10
New Gilston Fife 125 J11
New Grimsby IoS 2 b1
Newhall Ches E 63 Q3
Newhall Derbys 65 P8
Newham Nthumb 109 K4
New Hartley Nthumb 100 H3
Newhaven C Edin 115 N6
Newhaven Derbys 77 M11
Newhaven E Susx 15 N10
New Haw Surrey 32 F9
New Hedges Pembks 37 M10
New Herrington Sundld 101 J7
Newhey Rochdl 76 H1
New Holkham Norfk 70 C4
New Holland N Linc 87 K10
Newholm N York 92 H5
New Houghton Derbys 78 E10
New Houghton Norfk 69 Q6
Newhouse N Lans 114 E9
New Houses N York 90 C12
New Hutton Cumb 89 P8
New Hythe Kent 34 C10
Newick E Susx 15 M6
Newingreen Kent 17 K4
Newington Kent 17 L3
Newington Kent 34 F9
Newington Oxon 31 M3
Newington Shrops 51 M4
Newington Bagpath Gloucs 29 N3
New Inn Carmth 38 C4
New Inn Pembks 37 L4
New Inn Torfn 28 D2
New Invention Shrops 51 J5
New Lanark S Lans 106 A1
New Lanark Village S Lans 106 A1
Newland C KuH 87 K9
Newland Cumb 89 J10
Newland E R Yk 86 E9
Newland Gloucs 40 H9
Newland N York 86 C10
Newland Oxon 42 H9
Newland Somset 20 C6
Newland Worcs 52 E11
Newlandrig Mdloth 115 Q9
Newlands Border 107 M11
Newlands Cumb 98 D10
Newlands Nthumb 100 E7
Newlands of Dundurcas Moray 139 P6
New Lane Lancs 75 M1
New Lane End Warrtn 76 B5
New Langholm D & G 98 D1
New Leake Lincs 80 H12
New Leeds Abers 141 N5
New Lodge Barns 78 B2
New Longton Lancs 83 L10
New Luce D & G 94 H5
Newlyn Cnwll 2 D9
Newmachar Abers 141 L12
Newmains N Lans 114 E10
New Malden Gt Lon 33 J8
Newman's End Essex 45 P9
Newman's Green Suffk 46 F3
Newmarket Suffk 57 M8
Newmarket W Isls 152 g3
New Marske R & Cl 92 C2
New Marston Oxon 43 L10
New Marton Shrops 63 K5
New Mill Abers 133 J7
Newmill Border 107 L7
New Mill Cnwll 2 D7
New Mill Herts 44 C9
New Mill Kirk 77 M2
Newmill Moray 140 C5
Newmillerdam Wakefd 85 L12
Newmill of Inshewan Angus 132 C12
Newmills C Edin 115 L8
New Mills Cnwll 3 L4
New Mills Derbys 77 J6
Newmills Fife 115 J4
Newmills Mons 40 G10
New Mills Powys 62 F12
Newmiln P & K 124 C7
Newmilns E Ayrs 105 K2
New Milton Hants 12 D6
New Mistley Essex 47 K5
New Moat Pembks 37 L5
Newnes Shrops 63 L5
Newney Green Essex 46 B10
Newnham Hants 25 M3
Newnham Herts 45 J4
Newnham Kent 34 G11
Newnham Nhants 54 F9
Newnham Bridge Worcs 52 B7
Newnham on Severn Gloucs 41 L9
New Ollerton Notts 78 H10
New Oscott Birm 53 L2
New Pitsligo Abers 141 L5
New Polzeath Cnwll 6 D9
Newport Cnwll 7 L7
Newport Dorset 11 L6
Newport E R Yk 86 F9
Newport Essex 45 P5
Newport Gloucs 29 L3
Newport Highld 151 L11
Newport IoW 12 H7
Newport Newpt 28 D5
Newport Norfk 71 P8
Newport Pembks 37 L3
Newport Wrekin 64 D8
Newport-on-Tay Fife 124 H7
Newport Pagnell M Keyn 44 B3
Newport Pagnell Services M Keyn 44 B3
Newpound Common W Susx 14 F5
New Prestwick S Ayrs 104 F5
New Quay Cerdgn 48 F8
Newquay Cnwll 3 K2
New Quay Essex 46 H7
Newquay Zoo Cnwll 3 K2
New Rackheath Norfk 71 K9
New Radnor Powys 50 H8
New Rent Cumb 98 F11
New Ridley Nthumb 100 D6
New Road Side N York 84 E6
New Romney Kent 17 J6
New Rossington Donc 78 G4
New Row Cerdgn 49 M6
New Row Lancs 83 P7
New Sauchie Clacks 114 G2
Newsbank Ches E 76 F10
Newseat Abers 140 H9
Newsham Lancs 83 L8
Newsham N York 91 J5
Newsham N York 91 P10
Newsham Nthumb 100 H2
New Sharlston Wakefd 85 M11
Newsholme E R Yk 86 D9
Newsholme Lancs 84 C5
New Shoreston Nthumb 109 K3
New Silksworth Sundld 101 K7
New Skelton R & Cl 92 D3
Newsome Kirk 84 H12
New Somerby Lincs 67 M5
New Springs Wigan 75 Q2
Newstead Border 107 N3
Newstead Notts 66 E2
Newstead Nthumb 109 J4
New Stevenston N Lans 114 D9
New Street Herefs 51 K9
New Swanage Dorset 11 P8
New Swannington Leics 66 C9
Newthorpe N York 85 P8
Newthorpe Notts 66 D3

New Thundersley Essex 34 D4
Newtimber W Susx 15 K8
Newtoft Lincs 79 P6
Newton Ag & B 112 F2
Newton Border 107 P5
Newton Brgnd 27 K7
Newton C Beds 45 J3
Newton Cambs 56 H10
Newton Cambs 68 H9
Newton Cardif 28 B6
Newton Ches W 75 L10
Newton Ches W 75 N11
Newton Ches W 75 N8
Newton Cumb 88 H12
Newton Derbys 78 D11
Newton Herefs 40 D5
Newton Herefs 51 L7
Newton Herefs 51 N10
Newton Highld 137 Q6
Newton Highld 138 D3
Newton Highld 138 E3
Newton Highld 151 Q6
Newton Lancs 82 H8
Newton Lancs 89 P11
Newton Lincs 67 P5
Newton Mdloth 115 P7
Newton Moray 139 M3
Newton Moray 139 Q3
Newton N York 92 H12
Newton Nhants 55 L4
Newton Norfk 70 B9
Newton Notts 66 H4
Newton Nthumb 100 D5
Newton Nthumb 108 F8
Newton S Lans 106 B3
Newton S Lans 114 C9
Newton Sandw 53 J2
Newton Shrops 63 M5
Newton Somset 20 H6
Newton Staffs 65 J7
Newton S Loth 46 G3
Newton W Loth 115 M6
Newton Warwks 54 E5
Newton Wilts 24 C9
Newton Abbot Devon 8 F10
Newton Arlosh Cumb 97 P7
Newton Aycliffe Dur 91 M2
Newton Bewley Hartpl 91 Q1
Newton Blossomville M Keyn 55 M10
Newton Bromswold Nhants 55 P7
Newton Burgoland Leics 66 B10
Newton by Toft Lincs 79 P6
Newton Ferrers Devon 5 J7
Newton Ferry W Isls 152 c7
Newton Flotman Norfk 59 J1
Newtongrange Mdloth 115 P8
Newton Green Mons 28 G4
Newton Harcourt Leics 54 G1
Newton Heath Manch 76 G4
Newtonhill Abers 133 L5
Newton Hill Wakefd 85 L10
Newton-in-Bowland Lancs 83 Q5
Newton Kyme N York 85 P6
Newton-le-Willows N York 91 L9
Newton-le-Willows St Hel 75 Q4
Newtonloan Mdloth 115 P8
Newton Longville Bucks 44 B5
Newton Mearns E Rens 113 Q10
Newtonmill Angus 132 F11
Newtonmore Highld 130 C4
Newton Morrell N York 91 L5
Newton Mountain Pembks 37 J9
Newton Mulgrave N York 92 F4
Newton of Balcanquhal P & K 124 D10
Newton of Balcormo Fife 125 K12
Newton of Belltrees Rens 113 M9
Newton-on-Ayr S Ayrs 104 F5
Newton-on-Ouse N York 85 Q3
Newton-on-Rawcliffe N York 92 G8
Newton on the Hill Shrops 63 N7
Newton-on-the-Moor Nthumb 109 K8
Newton on Trent Lincs 79 L9
Newton Poppleford Devon 9 L7
Newton Purcell Oxon 43 N5
Newton Regis Warwks 65 P10
Newton Reigny Cumb 101 N4
Newton St Cyres Devon 8 G5
Newton St Faith Norfk 71 J8
Newton St Loe BaNES 29 L9
Newton St Petrock Devon 18 H11
Newton Solney Derbys 65 P7
Newton Stacey Hants 24 G5
Newton Stewart D & G 95 M5
Newton Tony Wilts 24 C5
Newton Tracey Devon 19 K8
Newton under Roseberry R & Cl 92 B4
Newton Underwood Nthumb 100 F1
Newton upon Derwent E R Yk 86 D5
Newton Valence Hants 25 M7
Newton Wamphray D & G 106 E10
Newton with Scales Lancs 83 K9
Newtown BCP 11 P6
Newtown Blae G 40 A9
Newtown Ches W 75 N8
Newtown Cnwll 2 H9
Newtown Cnwll 7 K9
Newtown Cumb 89 N2
Newtown Cumb 97 M8
Newtown Cumb 98 E6
Newtown Cumb 98 G6
Newtown D & G 105 P8
Newtown Derbys 77 J7
Newtown Devon 9 N5
Newtown Devon 19 P8
Newtown Dorset 10 D4
Newtown Dorset 11 N3
New Town E Susx 25 L10
New Town E Susx 23 L10
New Town Somset 20 H7
New Town E Susx 15 N7
Newtown Gloucs 41 K11
Newtown Hants 12 D3
Newtown Hants 25 K10
Newtown Hants 31 K9
Newtown Herefs 40 H5
Newtown Herefs 41 J3
Newtown Herefs 51 N9
Newtown Highld 129 P11
Newtown IoW 12 G6
Newtown Nthumb 108 F3
Newtown Nthumb 108 G3
Newtown Nthumb 108 G9
Newtown Powys 50 F2
Newtown Rhondd 27 P3
Newtown Shrops 63 N6
Newtown Shrops 63 N6
Newtown Somset 21 L10
Newtown Staffs 76 G11
Newtown Staffs 77 P3
Newtown Wigan 75 P3
Newtown Wilts 23 K7
Newtown Worcs 52 G9

Newtown Worcs 52 H5
Newtown-in-St Martin Cnwll 3 J10
Newtown Linford Leics 66 E10
Newtown St Boswells Border 107 P3
Newtown Unthank Leics 66 E11
New Tredegar Caerph 39 Q1
New Trows S Lans 105 Q2
New Tupton Derbys 78 C10
Newtyle Angus 124 F5
New Walsoken Cambs 69 J10
New Waltham NE Lin 80 F3
New Whittington Derbys 78 C8
New Winton E Loth 116 B7
New Yatt Oxon 42 H9
Newyears Green Gt Lon 32 F5
Newyork Ag & B 120 H10
New York Lincs 68 E1
New York N Tyne 101 J4
New York N York 85 J3
New Zealand Wilts 30 B7
Nextend Herefs 51 K9
Neyland Pembks 37 J9
Niarbyl IoM 102 b6
Nibley Gloucs 41 K10
Nibley S Glos 29 L6
Nibley Green Gloucs 29 L3
Nicholashayne Devon 20 H10
Nicholaston Swans 26 D5
Nickies Hill Cumb 98 G5
Nidd N York 85 L3
Nigg C Aber 133 M4
Nigg Highld 146 E10
Nigg Ferry Highld 146 E11
Nimlet BaNES 29 M8
Ninebanks Nthumb 99 M7
Nine Elms Swindn 30 C5
Nine Wells Pembks 36 F5
Ninfield E Susx 16 C8
Ningwood IoW 12 F7
Nisbet Border 107 Q5
Nisbet Hill Border 116 H11
Niton IoW 12 H9
Nitshill C Glas 113 P9
Noah's Ark Kent 33 Q10
Noak Bridge Essex 34 C4
Noak Hill Gt Lon 33 P3
Noblethorpe Barns 77 P3
Nobold Shrops 63 M10
Nobottle Nhants 54 H8
Nocton Lincs 79 Q11
Nogdam End Norfk 71 M12
Noke Oxon 43 L9
Nolton Pembks 36 G7
Nolton Haven Pembks 36 G7
No Man's Heath Ches W 63 N3
No Man's Heath Warwks 65 P10
No Man's Land Cnwll 4 D5
Nomansland Devon 20 D10
Nomansland Wilts 24 D10
Noneley Shrops 63 N6
Nonington Kent 35 N11
Nook Cumb 89 N10
Nook Cumb 98 F2
Norbiton Gt Lon 32 H8
Norbreck Bpool 82 H7
Norbridge Herefs 41 L3
Norbury Ches E 63 P3
Norbury Derbys 65 M4
Norbury Gt Lon 33 K8
Norbury Shrops 51 L2
Norbury Staffs 64 E7
Norbury Common Ches E 63 P2
Norbury Junction Staffs 64 E7
Norchard Worcs 52 F7
Norcott Brook Ches W 75 Q7
Norcross Lancs 82 H7
Nordelph Norfk 69 K12
Norden Rochdl 84 C12
Nordley Shrops 52 C1
Norfolk Broads Norfk 71 P10
Norham Nthumb 117 K11
Norland Calder 84 G10
Norley Ches W 75 P9
Norleywood Hants 12 F5
Norlington E Susx 15 N8
Normanby Lincs 79 P6
Normanby N Linc 86 G12
Normanby N York 92 H10
Normanby R & Cl 92 B3
Normanby le Wold Lincs 80 C5
Norman Cross Cambs 56 C2
Normandy Surrey 32 D12
Normans Bay E Susx 16 B9
Norman's Green Devon 9 K4
Normanton C Derb 65 Q5
Normanton Leics 67 K4
Normanton Notts 66 H1
Normanton Rutlnd 67 M11
Normanton Wakefd 85 M10
Normanton Wilts 23 P5
Normanton le Heath Leics 66 B9
Normanton on Cliffe Lincs 67 N3
Normanton on Soar Notts 66 E7
Normanton on the Wolds Notts 66 G6
Normanton on Trent Notts 79 K10
Normoss Lancs 82 H7
Norney Surrey 14 D2
Norrington Common Wilts 29 P9
Norris Green Cnwll 4 F3
Norris Green Lpool 75 L5
Norris Hill Leics 65 Q9
Norristhorpe Kirk 85 J10
Northacre Norfk 58 E1
Northall Bucks 44 D7
Northallerton N York 91 N8
Northall Green Norfk 70 E9
Northam C Soton 24 G11
Northam Devon 19 J7
Northampton Nhants 55 J8
Northampton Worcs 52 F7
Northampton Services Nhants 55 J9
North Anston Rothm 78 E7
North Ascot Br For 32 C8
North Aston Oxon 43 K6
Northaw Herts 45 K11
Northay Somset 9 P3
North Baddesley Hants 24 F9
North Ballachulish Highld 128 L12
North Barrow Somset 22 E7
North Barsham Norfk 70 D5
Northbay W Isls 152 b13
North Benfleet Essex 34 D4
North Berwick E Loth 116 D4
North Bitchburn Dur 100 F11
North Blyth Nthumb 101 J2
North Boarhunt Hants 13 K3
North Bockhampton BCP 12 B5
Northborough C Pete 68 C10
Northbourne Kent 35 P12
North Bovey Devon 8 D8
North Bradley Wilts 23 K7
North Brentor Devon 7 N6
North Brewham Somset 22 E6
North Bridge Surrey 14 D3
Northbridge Street E Susx 16 C6
Northbrook Hants 25 K7
Northbrook Oxon 43 K7

North Brook End Cambs 45 K3
North Buckland Devon 19 J5
North Burlingham Norfk 71 M10
North Cadbury Somset 22 E8
North Carlton Lincs 79 N8
North Carlton Notts 78 F7
North Cave E R Yk 86 G8
North Cerney Gloucs 42 B10
Northchapel W Susx 14 D5
North Charford Hants 24 C9
North Charlton Nthumb 109 K5
North Cheam Gt Lon 33 J9
North Cheriton Somset 22 F8
North Chideock Dorset 10 C6
Northchurch Herts 44 D10
North Cliffe E R Yk 86 G8
North Clifton Notts 79 K9
North Close Dur 100 H11
North Cockerington Lincs 80 G5
North Connel Ag & B 120 G6
North Cornelly Brdgnd 27 K6
North Corner Cnwll 3 J10
North Cotes Lincs 80 G4
Northcott Devon 7 L6
Northcott Devon 9 L3
Northcott Devon 20 H10
North Country Cnwll 2 H6
Northcourt Oxon 31 K3
North Cove Suffk 59 P3
North Cowton N York 91 M6
North Crawley M Keyn 44 C3
North Cray Gt Lon 33 N8
North Creake Norfk 70 C4
North Curry Somset 21 M8
North Dalton E R Yk 86 H5
North Deighton N York 85 N5
Northdown Kent 35 Q8
North Downs 8 G11
North Duffield N York 86 C8
Northedge Derbys 78 B10
North Elham Kent 17 L2
North Elkington Lincs 80 F5
North Elmham Norfk 70 E8
North Elmsall Wakefd 78 D1
Northend Bucks 31 Q4
North End C Port 13 J4
North End Cumb 98 C6
North End Dorset 22 J8
North End E R Yk 87 M7
North End E R Yk 87 P9
North End Essex 46 B8
North End Hants 23 N10
North End Hants 25 K7
North End Leics 66 F9
North End Lincs 68 E4
North End Lincs 79 P4
North End Lincs 80 F3
North End Lincs 80 H6
North End N Linc 86 G10
North End N Som 28 F9
North End Nhants 55 N7
North End Norfk 58 E2
North End Nthumb 109 J9
North End N York 85 J6
North End Sefton 75 J3
North End W Susx 14 D10
North End W Susx 14 G9
North End W Susx 14 G9
Northend Warwks 54 C10
Northenden Manch 76 F6
Northend Woods Bucks 32 C4
North Erradale Highld 143 K6
North Evington C Leic 66 G11
North Fambridge Essex 34 E3
North Featherstone Wakefd 85 N11
North Ferriby E R Yk 87 J10
Northfield Birm 53 J5
Northfield C Aber 133 L3
Northfield E R Yk 87 J10
Northfields Lincs 67 Q10
Northfleet Kent 34 B7
North Frodingham E R Yk 87 L5
Northgate Lincs 68 D7
North Gorley Hants 12 B2
North Green Suffk 59 J3
North Green Suffk 59 L8
North Green Suffk 59 M5
North Greetwell Lincs 79 P9
North Grimston N York 86 F2
North Halling Medway 34 C9
North Hayling Hants 13 M4
North Hazelrigg Nthumb 108 H3
North Heasley Devon 19 P7
North Heath W Susx 14 F6
North Hele Devon 20 G8
North Hill Cnwll 7 K9
North Hillingdon Gt Lon 32 F5
North Hinksey Village Oxon 43 K10
North Holmwood Surrey 14 H1
North Huish Devon 5 L5
North Hykeham Lincs 79 N10
Northiam E Susx 16 E6
Northill C Beds 44 H2
Northington Gloucs 41 L10
Northington Hants 25 J6
North Kelsey Lincs 79 P3
North Kessock Highld 138 B6
North Killingholme N Linc 87 L11
North Kilvington N York 91 N9
North Kilworth Leics 54 G4
North Kingston Hants 12 B4
North Kyme Lincs 68 C2
North Lancing W Susx 14 H9
North Landing E R Yk 93 P12
Northlands Lincs 68 G12
Northleach Gloucs 42 D9
North Lee Bucks 44 B10
North Lees N York 91 M12
Northleigh Devon 9 M5
Northleigh Devon 19 L6
North Leigh Kent 17 K1
North Leigh Oxon 42 H9
North Leverton with Habblesthorpe Notts 79 K7
Northlew Devon 7 P3
North Littleton Worcs 53 K11
Northload Bridge Somset 22 C5
North Lopham Norfk 58 F4
North Luffenham Rutlnd 67 M11
North Marden W Susx 25 P10
North Marston Bucks 43 Q6
North Middleton Mdloth 115 Q8
North Middleton Nthumb 108 H5
North Millbrex Abers 141 K6
North Milmain D & G 94 F7
North Molton Devon 19 P7
Northmoor Oxon 43 J10
North Moreton Oxon 31 M4
Northmuir Angus 124 H2
North Mundham W Susx 14 C10
North Muskham Notts 79 K12
North Newbald E R Yk 86 H8
North Newington Oxon 43 J4
North Newnton Wilts 30 D11
North Newton Somset 21 M5
Northney Hants 13 M4
North Nibley Gloucs 29 L4
North Oakley Hants 25 J2
North Ockendon Gt Lon 33 Q5
Northolt Gt Lon 32 G5
Northolt Airport Gt Lon 32 G5
Northop Flints 74 H10
Northop Hall Flints 75 J10
North Ormesby Middsb 92 A3
North Ormsby Lincs 80 E5

Northorpe Kirk 85 J11
Northorpe Lincs 68 B5
Northorpe Lincs 68 D5
North Otterington N York 91 N9
Northover Somset 22 B4
Northover Somset 22 C8
North Owersby Lincs 79 N5
North Perrott Somset 21 L7
North Petherton Somset 21 L7
North Petherwin Cnwll 7 K7
North Pickenham Norfk 70 C10
North Piddle Worcs 52 H9
North Poorton Dorset 10 D5
Northport Dorset 11 M7
North Poulner Hants 12 B3
North Queensferry Fife 115 J5
North Radworthy Devon 19 P6
North Rauceby Lincs 67 P3
Northrepps Norfk 71 K4
North Reston Lincs 80 F7
North Rigton N York 85 L5
North Ripley Hants 12 B5
North Rode Ches E 76 G10
North Ronaldsay Ork 147 f1
North Ronaldsay Airport Ork 147 f1
North Row Cumb 97 P11
North Runcton Norfk 69 M9
North Scale Cumb 82 F7
North Scarle Lincs 79 L10
North Seaton Nthumb 100 H1
North Seaton Colliery Nthumb 100 H1
North Shian Ag & B 120 H4
North Shields N Tyne 101 J5
North Shoebury Sthend 34 G5
North Shore Bpool 82 H8
North Side C Pete 68 E12
North Skelton R & Cl 92 D3
North Somercotes Lincs 80 H4
North Stainley N York 91 M11
North Stainmore Cumb 90 H4
North Stifford Thurr 33 Q6
North Stoke BaNES 29 L8
North Stoke Oxon 31 M5
North Stoke W Susx 14 F8
Northstowe Cambs 57 J7
North Street Cambs 57 L7
North Street Hants 25 L7
North Street Kent 34 H11
North Street Medway 34 E7
North Street W Berk 31 N8
North Sunderland Nthumb 109 L3
North Tamerton Cnwll 7 K5
North Tawton Devon 8 D3
North Third Stirlg 114 D3
North Thoresby Lincs 80 F4
North Togston Nthumb 109 L9
North Tolsta W Isls 152 h2
Northton W Isls 152 d6
North Town Devon 19 M8
North Town Somset 22 D5
North Town Somset 22 F5
North Town W & M 32 C6
North Tuddenham Norfk 70 F9
North Uist W Isls 152 c6
Northumberland National Park Nthumb 99 M2
North Walbottle N u Ty 100 F5
North Walsham Norfk 71 K6
North Waltham Hants 25 J4
North Warnborough Hants 25 M3
Northway Somset 21 J7
North Weald Bassett Essex 45 P11
North Wheatley Notts 79 J6
North Whilborough Devon 5 P3
Northwich Ches W 76 C9
North Wick BaNES 28 H9
Northwick S Glos 28 H5
Northwick Worcs 52 F9
North Widcombe BaNES 28 H10
North Willingham Lincs 80 C6
North Wingfield Derbys 78 C10
North Witham Lincs 67 M8
Northwold Norfk 57 N1
Northwood C Stke 64 F3
Northwood Derbys 77 P10
Northwood Gt Lon 32 F4
Northwood IoW 12 H6
Northwood Shrops 63 M5
Northwood Worcs 52 E6
Northwood Green Gloucs 41 L8
North Wootton Dorset 22 E10
North Wootton Norfk 69 M7
North Wootton Somset 22 D5
North Wraxall Wilts 29 N6
North Wroughton Swindn 30 D6
North York Moors National Park 92 H6
Norton Donc 85 Q12
Norton E Susx 15 N10
Norton Gloucs 41 P7
Norton Halton 75 N5
Norton Hants 24 H5
Norton Herts 45 J5
Norton IoW 12 F7
Norton Mons 28 G4
Norton N Som 28 D9
Norton Nhants 54 F8
Norton Notts 78 F9
Norton Powys 51 J7
Norton S on T 91 Q2
Norton Sheff 78 B7
Norton Shrops 51 M4
Norton Shrops 52 D1
Norton Shrops 63 P10
Norton Suffk 58 D7
Norton Suffk 58 D7
Norton Swans 26 F6
Norton W Susx 14 C9
Norton W Susx 14 C10
Norton Wilts 29 P6
Norton Worcs 52 F10
Norton Worcs 53 L11
Norton Bavant Wilts 23 K5
Norton Bridge Staffs 64 F6
Norton Canes Staffs 65 Q9
Norton Canon Herefs 40 E2
Norton Corner Norfk 70 G7
Norton Disney Lincs 79 M11
Norton Ferris Wilts 22 F6
Norton Fitzwarren Somset 21 K8
Norton Green IoW 12 F7
Norton Hawkfield BaNES 29 J9
Norton Heath Essex 45 R10
Norton in Hales Shrops 64 C5
Norton-Juxta-Twycross Leics 65 Q10
Norton-le-Clay N York 85 N1
Norton-le-Moors C Stke 76 G2
Norton Lindsey Warwks 53 N8
Norton Little Green Suffk 58 E7
Norton Malreward BaNES 29 J9
Norton Mandeville Essex 45 Q10
Norton-on-Derwent N York 86 E1

Norton St Philip Somset 22 H2
Norton Subcourse Norfk 59 N1
Norton sub Hamdon Somset 21 P10
Norton Wood Herefs 51 L11
Norwell Notts 79 K11
Norwell Woodhouse Notts 79 J11
Norwich Norfk 71 J10
Norwich Airport Norfk 71 J9
Norwick Shet 147 k2
Norwood Clacks 114 F3
Norwood Derbys 78 D7
Norwood Kent 17 J5
Norwood Green Calder 84 H10
Norwood Green Gt Lon 32 G6
Norwood Hill Surrey 15 J2
Norwoodside Cambs 56 H1
Noseley Leics 55 J1
Noss Mayo Devon 5 J7
Nosterfield N York 91 M10
Nosterfield End Cambs 46 B3
Nostie Highld 135 Q10
Notgrove Gloucs 42 C7
Nottage Brgnd 27 K7
Notter Cnwll 4 F4
Nottingham C Nott 66 F4
Nottington Dorset 10 G8
Notton Wakefd 77 Q1
Notton Wilts 29 P8
Nounsley Essex 52 E7
Noutard's Green Worcs 52 E7
Nox Shrops 63 L10
Nuffield Oxon 31 N5
Nunburnholme E R Yk 86 F6
Nuncargate Notts 66 E1
Nunclose Cumb 98 F9
Nuneaton Warwks 54 B2
Nuneham Courtenay Oxon 31 L2
Nunhead Gt Lon 33 L7
Nunkeeling E R Yk 87 L5
Nun Monkton N York 85 Q4
Nunney Somset 22 G4
Nunney Catch Somset 22 G4
Nunnington Herefs 40 H3
Nunnington N York 92 D11
Nunsthorpe NE Lin 80 E2
Nunthorpe Middsb 92 B4
Nunthorpe Village Middsb 92 B4
Nunton Wilts 23 P8
Nunwick N York 91 N11
Nunwick Nthumb 99 N3
Nupdown S Glos 29 J3
Nup End Bucks 44 B8
Nupend Gloucs 41 M10
Nuptown Br For 32 C7
Nursling Hants 24 F10
Nursted Hants 25 N9
Nursteed Wilts 30 B10
Nurton Staffs 64 F12
Nutbourne W Susx 13 M3
Nutbourne W Susx 14 F7
Nutfield Surrey 33 K12
Nuthall Notts 66 E4
Nuthampstead Herts 45 M5
Nuthurst W Susx 14 H6
Nutley E Susx 15 N5
Nutley Hants 25 K4
Nuttall Bury 84 B12
Nutwell Donc 78 G3
Nybster Highld 151 Q4
Nyetimber W Susx 14 C11
Nyewood W Susx 25 P9
Nymans W Susx 15 K5
Nymet Rowland Devon 8 D3
Nymet Tracey Devon 8 E4
Nympsfield Gloucs 29 N2
Nynehead Somset 21 J9
Nythe Somset 21 P6
Nyton W Susx 14 D9

Oadby Leics 66 G12
Oad Street Kent 34 F10
Oakall Green Worcs 52 E8
Oakamoor Staffs 65 K3
Oakbank W Loth 115 K8
Oak Cross Devon 7 P3
Oakdale Caerph 28 B3
Oake Somset 21 J8
Oaken Staffs 64 F11
Oakenclough Lancs 83 M6
Oakengates Wrekin 64 C10
Oakenholt Flints 75 J9
Oakenshaw Dur 100 F10
Oakenshaw Kirk 85 J9
Oakerthorpe Derbys 66 C1
Oakford Cerdgn 48 G9
Oakford Devon 20 E9
Oakfordbridge Devon 20 E9
Oakgrove Ches E 76 G10
Oakham Rutlnd 67 L10
Oakhanger Ches E 64 D2
Oakhanger Hants 25 N6
Oakhill Somset 22 E4
Oakhurst Kent 33 Q12
Oakington Cambs 56 H8
Oaklands Herts 45 J8
Oaklands Powys 50 G10
Oakle Street Gloucs 41 M8
Oakley BCP 11 N5
Oakley Bed 55 P10
Oakley Bucks 43 Q9
Oakley Fife 115 J3
Oakley Hants 25 J3
Oakley Oxon 31 Q2
Oakley Suffk 58 H5
Oakley Green W & M 32 D7
Oakley Park Powys 50 D3
Oakridge Lynch Gloucs 41 Q10
Oaks Lancs 83 P8
Oaks Shrops 63 L11
Oaksey Wilts 30 A4
Oaks Green Derbys 65 M5
Oakshaw Ford Cumb 98 G3
Oakthorpe Leics 65 Q9
Oak Tree Darltn 91 N4
Oakwood C Derb 66 B4
Oakwood Nthumb 99 P5
Oakworth C Brad 84 F7
Oare Kent 34 H9
Oare Somset 20 B4
Oare W Berk 31 K7
Oare Wilts 30 D10
Oasby Lincs 67 P4
Oath Somset 21 N7
Oathlaw Angus 125 J2
Oatlands Park Surrey 32 F9
Oban Ag & B 120 F6
Oban Airport Ag & B 120 G6
Obley Shrops 51 K5
Obney P & K 123 P7
Oborne Dorset 22 E9
Obthorpe Lincs 68 B9
Occold Suffk 58 H6
Occumster Highld 151 N8
Ochiltree E Ayrs 105 K4
Ockbrook Derbys 66 C5
Ocker Hill Sandw 52 H2
Ockeridge Worcs 52 E8

Oldways End Somset 20 D8
Old Weston Cambs 56 B5
Old Wick Highld 151 Q7
Old Windsor W & M 32 D7
Old Wives Lees Kent 35 J11
Old Woking Surrey 32 E11
Old Wolverton M Keyn 44 A3
Old Woodhall Lincs 80 D10
Old Woods Shrops 63 M8
Oliver's Battery Hants 24 G8
Ollaberry Shet 147 i4
Ollach Highld 135 J8
Ollerton Ches E 76 E8
Ollerton Notts 78 G10
Ollerton Shrops 64 C7
Olmarch Cerdgn 49 K9
Olmstead Green Cambs 46 A3
Olney M Keyn 55 M10
Olrig House Highld 151 M3
Olton Solhll 53 L4
Olveston S Glos 29 J5
Ombersley Worcs 52 F8
Ompton Notts 78 H10
Once Brewed Nthumb 99 L5
Onchan IoM 102 e5
Onecote Staffs 65 J1
Onehouse Suffk 58 F9
Onen Mons 40 F9
Ongar Street Herefs 51 L7
Onibury Shrops 51 M5
Onich Highld 128 E2
Onllwyn Neath 39 K9
Onneley Staffs 64 D4
Onslow Green Essex 46 B8
Onslow Village Surrey 14 D1
Onston Ches W 75 Q9
Openwoodgate Derbys 66 B3
Opinan Highld 143 K10
Orbliston Moray 139 P4
Orbost Highld 134 D7
Orby Lincs 81 J10
Orchard Portman Somset 21 K9
Orcheston Wilts 23 N4
Orcop Herefs 40 G6
Orcop Hill Herefs 40 G6
Ord Abers 140 F4
Ordhead Abers 132 G2
Ordie Abers 132 C4
Ordiequish Moray 139 Q4
Ordley Nthumb 99 P6
Ordsall Notts 78 H8
Ore E Susx 16 E8
Oreleton Common Herefs 51 N7
Oreton Shrops 52 C4
Orford Suffk 59 N11
Orford Warrtn 75 Q5
Organford Dorset 11 M6
Orgreave Staffs 65 L9
Orkney Islands Ork 147 c4
Orkney Neolithic Ork 147 b6
Orlestone Kent 16 H4
Orleton Herefs 51 M7
Orleton Worcs 52 C7
Orlingbury Nhants 55 L6
Ormathwaite Cumb 88 H2
Ormesby R & Cl 92 B3
Ormesby St Margaret Norfk 71 P9
Ormesby St Michael Norfk 71 P9
Ormiscaig Highld 143 K6
Ormiston E Loth 116 A7
Ormsaigmore Highld 126 H11
Ormsary Ag & B 111 Q2
Ormskirk Lancs 75 L2
Ornsby Hill Dur 100 F8
Oronsay Ag & B 110 H3
Orphir Ork 147 b5
Orpington Gt Lon 33 N9
Orrell Lancs 75 N3
Orrell Wigan 75 P3
Orrell Post Wigan 75 P3
Orrisdale IoM 102 d3
Orroland D & G 96 F9
Orsett Thurr 34 B6
Orsett Heath Thurr 34 B6
Orslow Staffs 64 F9
Orston Notts 67 J3
Orthwaite Cumb 97 Q11
Ortner Lancs 83 M4
Orton Cumb 89 Q5
Orton Nhants 55 M5
Orton Staffs 52 F2
Orton Longueville C Pete 56 D7
Orton-on-the-Hill Leics 65 P11
Orton Rigg Cumb 98 D8
Orton Waterville C Pete 56 C1
Orwell Cambs 56 G10
Osbaldeston Lancs 83 N8
Osbaldeston Green Lancs 83 N8
Osbaldwick C York 86 B5
Osbaston Leics 66 C11
Osbaston Shrops 63 K8
Osbaston Mons 40 G9
Osborne IoW 13 J5
Osbournby Lincs 67 Q4
Oscroft Ches W 75 N10
Ose Highld 134 F7
Osgathorpe Leics 66 C8
Osgodby Lincs 79 Q5
Osgodby N York 86 B8
Osgodby N York 93 L10
Oskaig Highld 135 K8
Oskamull Ag & B 119 M5
Osmaston Derbys 65 M3
Osmington Dorset 10 H8
Osmington Mills Dorset 10 H8
Osmondthorpe Leeds 85 L8
Osmotherley N York 91 Q7
Osney Oxon 43 K10
Ospringe Kent 34 H10
Ossett Wakefd 85 K11
Ossington Notts 79 J10
Ostend Essex 34 G3
Osterley Gt Lon 32 H7
Oswaldkirk N York 92 C11
Oswaldtwistle Lancs 83 Q9
Oswestry Shrops 63 J6
Otairnis W Isls 152 c12
Otford Kent 33 P10
Otham Kent 34 D11
Otham Hole Kent 34 E11
Othery Somset 21 N7
Otley Leeds 85 J5
Otley Suffk 59 J9
Otley Green Suffk 59 J9
Otterburn N York 84 C4
Otterburn Nthumb 108 E11
Otter Ferry Ag & B 112 D4
Otterham Cnwll 6 H5
Otterhampton Somset 21 K5
Otterham Quay Kent 34 E9
Ottershaw Surrey 32 E9
Otterswick Shet 147 j4
Otterton Devon 9 L7
Otterwood Hants 12 G4
Ottery St Mary Devon 9 L6
Ottinge Kent 17 L2
Ottringham E R Yk 87 N10
Oughterby Cumb 98 C7

Oughtershaw N York 90 E10
Oughterside Cumb 97 M10
Oughtibridge Sheff 77 P5
Oughtrington Warrtn 76 C6
Oulston N York 92 B12
Oulton Cumb 97 Q8
Oulton Leeds 85 M9
Oulton Norfk 70 H6
Oulton Staffs 64 E7
Oulton Staffs 64 G5
Oulton Suffk 59 Q2
Oulton Broad Suffk 59 Q2
Oulton Street Norfk 70 H7
Oundle Nhants 55 P3
Ounsdale Staffs 52 F2
Ousby Cumb 99 J11
Ousden Suffk 57 P8
Ousefleet E R Yk 86 F10
Ouston Dur 100 H7
Outchester Nthumb 109 J3
Out Elmstead Kent 35 M12
Outgate Cumb 89 K7
Outhgill Cumb 90 C6
Outhill Warwks 53 L7
Outlands Staffs 64 E6
Outlane Kirk 84 G11
Out Newton E R Yk 87 R11
Out Rawcliffe Lancs 83 J7
Out Skerries Shet 147 k5
Outwell Norfk 69 K11
Outwick Hants 23 P10
Outwood Surrey 15 K2
Outwood Wakefd 85 L10
Outwood Gate Bury 76 E2
Outwoods Leics 66 C8
Outwoods Staffs 64 E8
Ouzlewell Green Leeds 85 M10
Ovenden Calder 84 G10
Over Cambs 56 G6
Over Ches W 76 B10
Over Gloucs 41 N8
Over S Glos 29 J6
Over Burrows Derbys 65 N4
Overbury Worcs 41 Q4
Overcombe Dorset 10 H8
Over Compton Dorset 22 D10
Over End Cambs 56 B2
Overgreen Derbys 77 Q9
Over Green Warwks 53 M2
Over Haddon Derbys 77 M10
Over Hulton Bolton 76 C3
Over Kellet Lancs 83 M1
Over Kiddington Oxon 43 J7
Overleigh Somset 22 B6
Overley Staffs 65 M9
Over Monnow Mons 40 G9
Over Norton Oxon 42 G6
Over Peover Ches E 76 E9
Overpool Ches W 75 L8
Overscaig Highld 149 J12
Overseal Derbys 65 P9
Over Silton N York 91 Q8
Oversland Kent 35 J11
Oversley Green Warwks 53 L9
Overstone Nhants 55 K7
Over Stowey Somset 21 J6
Overstrand Norfk 71 K4
Over Stratton Somset 21 P10
Overstreet Wilts 23 N6
Over Tabley Ches E 76 D7
Overthorpe Nhants 43 K4
Overton C Aber 133 L2
Overton Ches W 75 N8
Overton Hants 24 H3
Overton Lancs 83 K4
Overton N York 85 Q4
Overton Shrops 51 N6
Overton Swans 26 C5
Overton Wakefd 85 K12
Overton Wrexhm 63 L4
Overton Bridge Wrexhm 63 K4
Overton Green Ches E 76 E11
Overtown Lancs 84 C9
Overtown Lancs 89 Q11
Overtown N Lans 114 E10
Overtown Swindn 30 D6
Overtown Wakefd 85 M12
Over Wallop Hants 24 D6
Over Whitacre Warwks 53 N2
Over Woodhouse Derbys 78 D9
Over Worton Oxon 43 J6
Overy Oxon 31 M3
Oving Bucks 43 Q7
Oving W Susx 14 C10
Ovingdean Br & H 15 L10
Ovingham Nthumb 100 E5
Ovington Dur 91 J4
Ovington Essex 46 D3
Ovington Hants 25 J7
Ovington Norfk 70 D11
Ovington Nthumb 100 D5
Ower Hants 12 H4
Ower Hants 24 E10
Owermoigne Dorset 11 J7
Owlbury Shrops 51 K2
Owlerton Sheff 77 Q6
Owlpen Gloucs 29 M3
Owl's Green Suffk 59 K7
Owlsmoor Br For 32 B10
Owlswick Bucks 43 R10
Owmby Lincs 79 P6
Owmby Lincs 79 Q3
Owslebury Hants 24 H8
Owston Donc 78 F1
Owston Leics 67 K10
Owston Ferry N Linc 79 K4
Owstwick E R Yk 87 P8
Owthorne E R Yk 87 Q9
Owthorpe Notts 66 H6
Owton Manor Hartpl 101 M12
Oxborough Norfk 69 P11
Oxbridge Dorset 10 D6
Oxcombe Lincs 80 F8
Oxcroft Derbys 78 D9
Oxen End Essex 46 B6
Oxenholme Cumb 89 N9
Oxenhope C Brad 84 F8
Oxen Park Cumb 89 J9
Oxenpill Somset 21 P5
Oxenton Gloucs 41 Q5
Oxenwood Wilts 30 G10
Oxford Oxon 43 L10
Oxford Airport Oxon 43 K8
Oxford Services Oxon 43 N10
Oxgangs C Edin 115 N7
Oxhey Herts 32 G3
Oxhill Dur 100 F8
Oxhill Warwks 42 G2
Oxley Wolves 64 G11
Oxley Green Essex 46 F9
Oxley's Green E Susx 16 C6
Oxlode Cambs 57 J3
Oxnam Border 108 A6
Oxnead Norfk 71 J7
Oxshott Surrey 32 G10
Oxshott Heath Surrey 32 G10
Oxspring Barns 77 P3
Oxted Surrey 33 M11
Oxton Border 116 C10
Oxton N York 85 Q6
Oxton Notts 66 G2
Oxton Wirral 75 J6
Oxwich Swans 26 D5
Oxwich Green Swans 26 D5
Oxwick Norfk 70 D7
Oykel Bridge Highld 145 J5
Oyne Abers 140 G10
Oystermouth Swans 26 F5
Ozleworth Gloucs 29 M4

P

Pabail W Isls 152 h3
Packers Hill Dorset 10 H3
Packington Leics 66 B9
Packmoor C Stke 64 F1
Packmores Warwks 53 P7
Padanaram Angus 124 H2
Padbury Bucks 43 P5
Paddington Gt Lon 33 K6
Paddington Warrtn 76 B6
Paddlesworth Kent 17 M3
Paddlesworth Kent 34 B10
Paddock Wood Kent 16 B2
Paddolgreen Shrops 63 N6
Padfield Derbys 77 J4
Padgate Warrtn 76 B6
Padhams Green Essex 34 B3
Padiham Lancs 84 B8
Padside N York 84 H3
Padstow Cnwll 6 C9
Padworth W Berk 31 M9
Page Bank Dur 100 G11
Pagham W Susx 14 C11
Paglesham Essex 34 G4
Paignton Torbay 5 Q4
Pailton Warwks 54 D4
Paine's Cross E Susx 16 A6
Painleyhill Staffs 65 J5
Painscastle Powys 40 A2
Painshawfield Nthumb 100 D6
Painsthorpe E R Yk 86 F4
Painswick Gloucs 41 P9
Painter's Forstal Kent 34 H10
Paisley Rens 113 P8
Pakefield Suffk 59 Q3
Pakenham Suffk 58 D7
Pale Gwynd 62 C4
Pale Green Essex 46 B3
Palestine Hants 24 D5
Paley Street W & M 32 B7
Palfrey Wsall 53 J1
Palgrave Suffk 58 G5
Pallington Dorset 11 J6
Palmarsh Kent 17 L4
Palmers Green Gt Lon 33 K4
Palmerston E Ayrs 105 J6
Palmerstown V Glam 27 Q8
Palnackie D & G 96 G7
Palnure D & G 95 N5
Palterton Derbys 78 D10
Pamber End Hants 31 M10
Pamber Green Hants 31 M10
Pamber Heath Hants 31 M10
Pamington Gloucs 41 Q5
Pamphill Dorset 11 N5
Pampisford Cambs 57 J11
Panborough Somset 21 Q4
Panbride Angus 125 L6
Pancrasweek Devon 7 K4
Pancross V Glam 27 P8
Pandy Gwynd 61 K11
Pandy Gwynd 62 A6
Pandy Mons 40 D7
Pandy Powys 62 B11
Pandy Wrexhm 62 H5
Pandy Wrexhm 63 K2
Pandy'r Capel Denbgs 62 F2
Pandy Tudur Conwy 73 Q11
Panfield Essex 46 C6
Pangbourne W Berk 31 N7
Pangdean W Susx 15 K8
Panks Bridge Herefs 52 B11
Pannal N York 85 L5
Pannal Ash N York 85 K5
Pant Shrops 63 J8
Pantasaph Flints 74 G8
Panteg Pembks 36 H4
Pantersbridge Cnwll 4 B3
Pant-ffrwyth Brdgnd 27 M5
Pant Glas Gwynd 60 H3
Pantglas Powys 61 N12
Pant-Gwyn Carmth 38 E6
Pant-lasau Swans 26 G2
Pant Mawr Powys 49 P4
Panton Lincs 80 D8
Pant-pastynog Denbgs 74 E11
Pantperthog Gwynd 61 N11
Pantside Caerph 28 B3
Pant-y-caws Carmth 37 M5
Pant-y-dwr Powys 50 D6
Pant-y-ffridd Powys 62 G11
Pantyffynnon Carmth 38 F9
Pantygaseg Torfn 28 C2
Pantygelli Mons 40 D8
Pant-y-gog Brdgnd 27 L4
Pantymwyn Flints 74 H10
Panxworth Norfk 71 M9
Papa Stour Shet 147 g6
Papa Stour Airport Shet 147 g6
Papa Westray Ork 147 d1
Papa Westray Airport Ork 147 d1
Papcastle Cumb 97 M12
Papigoe Highld 151 Q6
Papple E Loth 116 D7
Papplewick Notts 66 F2
Papworth Everard Cambs 56 F8
Papworth St Agnes Cambs 56 E8
Par Cnwll 3 Q4
Paramour Street Kent 35 N10
Parbold Lancs 75 N2
Parbrook Somset 22 D6
Parbrook W Susx 14 F6
Parc Gwynd 62 A6
Parcllyn Cerdgn 48 D10
Parc Seymour Newpt 28 F4
Pardown Hants 25 K4
Pardshaw Cumb 88 E2
Parham Suffk 59 L8
Park D & G 106 B11
Park Nthumb 99 K6
Park Bottom Cnwll 2 G6
Park Bridge Tamesd 76 H3
Park Corner E Susx 15 P4
Park Corner Oxon 31 P5
Park Corner W & M 32 B6
Park End Bed 55 N10
Parkend Gloucs 41 J10
Park End Nthumb 99 N3
Parker's Green Kent 15 R1
Parkeston Essex 47 M5
Parkeston Quay Essex 47 M5
Park Farm Kent 16 H3
Parkgate Ches W 75 J8
Parkgate Cumb 97 P9
Parkgate D & G 106 D12
Parkgate E Susx 16 C8
Parkgate Essex 46 B6
Park Gate Hants 13 J3
Parkgate Kent 16 E4
Parkgate Kent 33 P9
Park Gate Leeds 85 J7
Parkgate Surrey 15 J2
Park Gate Worcs 52 H6
Park Green Essex 45 N6
Park Green Suffk 58 H8
Parkhall W Duns 113 P7
Parkham Devon 18 H9
Parkham Ash Devon 18 G9
Park Head Derbys 66 B1
Parkhill Dur 101 J11
Park Hill Gloucs 28 H2
Parkhouse Mons 40 G11
Parkmill Swans 26 E4
Park Royal Gt Lon 32 H6
Parkside Dur 101 L8
Parkside N Lans 114 E9
Parkside Wrexhm 63 L1
Parkstone BCP 11 P6
Park Street Herts 44 G11
Park Street W Susx 14 G4
Parkway Herefs 41 L4
Parley Green BCP 11 Q5
Parmoor Bucks 31 R4
Parracombe Devon 19 N4
Parrog Pembks 37 K3
Parsonby Cumb 97 N10
Parson Cross Sheff 77 Q5
Parson Drove Cambs 68 G10
Parson's Heath Essex 46 H6
Parson's Hill Derbys 65 P7
Partick C Glas 113 Q8
Partington Traffd 76 D5
Partney Lincs 80 H10
Parton Cumb 88 C3
Partridge Green W Susx 14 H7
Partrishow Powys 40 C7
Parwich Derbys 65 M1
Paslow Wood Common Essex 45 Q11
Passenham Nhants 43 Q4
Passfield Hants 25 P6
Passingford Bridge Essex 33 P3
Paston C Pete 68 D11
Paston Norfk 71 L5
Pasturefields Staffs 65 J7
Patchacott Devon 7 N5
Patcham Br & H 15 K9
Patchetts Green Herts 32 G3
Patching W Susx 14 F9
Patchole Devon 19 M5
Patchway S Glos 29 J6
Pateley Bridge N York 84 H2
Paternoster Heath Essex 46 G8
Pathe Somset 21 N7
Pathhead Fife 115 P3
Pathhead Mdloth 115 R8
Pathlow Warwks 53 M9
Path of Condie P & K 124 B10
Patmore Heath Herts 45 N6
Patna E Ayrs 104 H7
Patney Wilts 30 C10
Patrick IoM 102 c5
Patrick Brompton N York 91 L8
Patricroft Salfd 76 D4
Patrington E R Yk 87 P10
Patrington Haven E R Yk 87 P11
Patrixbourne Kent 35 L11
Patterdale Cumb 89 L4
Pattingham Staffs 64 F12
Pattishall Nhants 54 H10
Pattiswick Green Essex 46 E7
Patton Shrops 51 P2
Patton Bridge Cumb 89 P7
Paul Cnwll 2 D9
Paulerspury Nhants 43 P3
Paull E R Yk 87 M10
Paulton BaNES 29 K11
Paultons Park Hants 24 E10
Paunton Herefs 52 C10
Pauperhaugh Nthumb 108 H10
Pave Lane Wrekin 64 E9
Pavenham Bed 55 N9
Pawlett Somset 21 L5
Pawston Nthumb 108 D3
Paxford Gloucs 42 E4
Paxton Border 117 L10
Payden Street Kent 34 G11
Payhembury Devon 9 L4
Paynter's Lane End Cnwll 2 G6
Paythorne Lancs 84 B5
Paytoe Herefs 51 L6
Peacehaven E Susx 15 M10
Peak Dale Derbys 77 K8
Peak District National Park 77 M5
Peak Forest Derbys 77 L8
Peak Hill Lincs 68 E9
Peakirk C Pete 68 C11
Pearson's Green Kent 16 C2
Peartree Green Herefs 41 J5
Peasedown St John BaNES 29 L11
Peasehill Derbys 66 C2
Peaseland Green Norfk 70 F9
Peasemore W Berk 31 K7
Peasenhall Suffk 59 M7
Pease Pottage W Susx 15 J4
Pease Pottage Services W Susx 15 J4
Peaslake Surrey 14 F2
Peasley Cross St Hel 75 N5
Peasmarsh E Susx 16 F6
Peasmarsh Somset 21 M11
Peasmarsh Surrey 14 E2
Peathill Abers 141 M3
Peat Inn Fife 125 J11
Peatling Magna Leics 54 F2
Peatling Parva Leics 54 F3
Peaton Shrops 51 P4
Pebmarsh Essex 46 E5
Pebsham E Susx 16 D9
Pebworth Worcs 42 D2
Pecket Well Calder 84 E9
Peckforton Ches E 75 P12
Peckham Gt Lon 33 L7
Peckleton Leics 66 D12
Pedairffordd Powys 62 F7
Pedlinge Kent 17 L4
Pedmore Dudley 52 G4
Pedwell Somset 21 P6
Peebles Border 106 H2
Peel IoM 102 c5
Peel Lancs 83 J9
Peel Common Hants 13 K4
Peene Kent 17 L3
Peening Quarter Kent 16 F5
Peggs Green Leics 66 C8
Pegsdon C Beds 44 G5
Pegswood Nthumb 109 L12
Pegwell Kent 35 Q9
Peinchorran Highld 135 J9
Peinlich Highld 134 G4
Pelcomb Pembks 36 H7
Pelcomb Bridge Pembks 36 H7
Pelcomb Cross Pembks 36 H7
Peldon Essex 46 H8
Pell Green E Susx 16 B4
Pelsall Wsall 65 J11
Pelsall Wood Wsall 65 J11
Pelton Dur 100 G7
Pelton Fell Dur 100 H8
Pelutho Cumb 97 M8
Pelynt Cnwll 4 B6
Pemberton Carmth 26 D2
Pemberton Wigan 75 P3
Pembles Cross Kent 16 F1
Pembrey Carmth 26 C2
Pembridge Herefs 51 L9
Pembroke Pembks 37 J10
Pembroke Dock Pembks 37 J10
Pembrokeshire Coast National Park Pembks 36 G6
Pembury Kent 16 A3
Pen-allt Herefs 40 H6
Penallt Mons 40 H9
Penally Pembks 37 M10
Penare Cnwll 3 N6
Penarth V Glam 28 B8
Penblewin Pembks 37 M7
Pen-bont Rhydybeddau Cerdgn 49 L4
Penbryn Cerdgn 48 E10
Pencader Carmth 38 C4
Pencaenewydd Gwynd 60 G4
Pencaitland E Loth 116 B7
Pencarnisiog IoA 72 F9
Pencarreg Carmth 38 E3
Pencarrow Cnwll 6 G8
Pencelli Powys 39 P7
Penclawdd Swans 26 E3
Pencoed Brdgnd 27 M6
Pencombe Herefs 51 Q10
Pencoyd Herefs 40 G6
Pencraig Herefs 40 H7
Pencraig Powys 62 E7
Pendeen Cnwll 2 B7
Penderyn Rhondd 39 M10
Pendine Carmth 37 P9
Pendlebury Salfd 76 E3
Pendleton Lancs 84 A7
Pendock Worcs 41 M5
Pendoggett Cnwll 6 E9
Pendomer Somset 10 E3
Pendoylan V Glam 27 P7
Penegoes Powys 61 N12
Penelewey Cnwll 3 K6
Pen-ffordd Pembks 37 L6
Pengam Caerph 27 R3
Pengam Cardif 28 B7
Penge Gt Lon 33 L8
Pengelly Cnwll 6 F8
Pengenffordd Powys 40 A6
Pengorffwysfa IoA 72 H5
Pengover Green Cnwll 4 D4
Pen-groes-oped Mons 40 D10
Pengwern Denbgs 74 D8
Penhale Cnwll 2 H10
Penhale Cnwll 3 M3
Penhale Cnwll 3 Q2
Penhale Cnwll 4 F6
Penhallow Cnwll 3 J4
Penhalurick Cnwll 2 H7
Penhalvean Cnwll 2 H7
Penhill Swindn 30 D5
Penhow Newpt 28 F4
Penhurst E Susx 16 C7
Peniarth Gwynd 61 K11
Penicuik Mdloth 115 N9
Peniel Carmth 38 C7
Peniel Denbgs 74 E11
Penifiler Highld 135 J7
Peninver Ag & B 103 K5
Penisarwaun Gwynd 73 J11
Penistone Barns 77 N3
Penjerrick Cnwll 3 J8
Penketh Warrtn 75 P6
Penkill S Ayrs 104 D10
Penkridge Staffs 64 H9
Penlean Cnwll 7 J5
Penleigh Wilts 23 J3
Penley Wrexhm 63 L4
Penllergaer Swans 26 F3
Pen-llyn IoA 72 F7
Pen-lôn IoA 72 G10
Penmachno Conwy 61 N2
Penmaen Caerph 28 A3
Penmaen Swans 26 D5
Penmaenan Conwy 73 M8
Penmaenmawr Conwy 73 M8
Penmaenpool Gwynd 61 M8
Penmark V Glam 27 P8
Penmon IoA 73 K7
Penmorfa Gwynd 61 J4
Penmynydd IoA 72 H9
Penn Bucks 32 C4
Penn Wolves 52 G2
Pennal Gwynd 61 M12
Pennan Abers 141 K3
Pennant Cerdgn 48 H8
Pennant Denbgs 62 E5
Pennant Powys 49 Q1
Pennant-Melangell Powys 62 D7
Pennar Pembks 37 J10
Pennard Swans 26 E5
Pennerley Shrops 63 K12
Pennicott Devon 8 G4
Pennines 84 E8
Pennington Cumb 88 H11
Pennington Hants 12 E6
Pennington Green Wigan 76 B2
Pennorth Powys 39 Q6
Penn Street Bucks 32 C3
Pennsylvania S Glos 29 M7
Penny Bridge Cumb 89 J10
Pennycross Ag & B 119 N7
Pennygate Norfk 71 L7
Pennyghael Ag & B 119 N7
Pennyglen S Ayrs 104 E7
Penny Green Derbys 78 E8
Penny Hill Lincs 68 G7
Pennymoor Devon 8 G3
Pennywell Sundld 101 J7
Penparc Cerdgn 48 C11
Penparcau Cerdgn 49 K4
Penpedairheol Caerph 27 Q3
Penpedairheol Mons 40 D11
Penpergwm Mons 40 D9
Penperlleni Mons 40 D10
Penpethy Cnwll 6 F7
Penpillick Cnwll 3 Q3
Penpol Cnwll 3 K7
Penpoll Cnwll 4 A6
Penponds Cnwll 2 G7
Penpont Cnwll 6 F10
Penpont D & G 105 Q11
Penpont Powys 39 M6
Penquit Devon 5 K6
Penrest Cnwll 7 L9
Penrherber Carmth 37 Q3
Pen-rhiw Pembks 37 P2
Penrhiwceiber Rhondd 27 P3
Pen Rhiwfawr Neath 38 H9
Penrhiwgoch Carmth 38 E8
Penrhiwllan Cerdgn 38 B3
Penrhiwpal Cerdgn 48 E11
Penrhos Gwynd 60 E5
Penrhos IoA 72 D7
Penrhos Mons 40 F9
Penrhos Powys 39 J9
Penrhos garnedd Gwynd 73 J9
Penrhyn Bay Conwy 73 P7
Penrhyn-coch Cerdgn 49 L4
Penrhyndeudraeth Gwynd 61 K4
Penrhyn-side Conwy 73 P7
Penrhyn Slate Landscape Gwynd 73 K10
Penrhys Rhondd 27 N3
Penrice Swans 26 D5
Penrioch N Ayrs 112 C12
Penrith Cumb 98 G12
Penrose Cnwll 6 C10
Penruddock Cumb 89 L1
Penryn Cnwll 3 J7
Pensarn Conwy 74 C8
Pensax Worcs 52 D7
Pensby Wirral 75 J7
Penselwood Somset 22 G7
Pensford BaNES 29 J9
Pensham Worcs 41 Q3
Penshaw Sundld 101 J7
Penshurst Kent 15 P2
Penshurst Station Kent 15 P2
Pensilva Cnwll 4 D3
Pensnett Dudley 52 G3
Penstone Devon 8 E5
Penstrowed Powys 50 E2
Pentewan Cnwll 3 Q5
Pentir Gwynd 73 J10
Pentire Cnwll 3 K2
Pentlepoir Pembks 37 M9
Pentlow Essex 46 E3
Pentlow Street Essex 46 E3
Pentney Norfk 69 N9
Pentonbridge Cumb 98 F3
Penton Grafton Hants 24 E4
Penton Mewsey Hants 24 E4
Pentraeth IoA 73 J8
Pentre Denbgs 74 F11
Pentre Flints 75 K10
Pentre Mons 28 E2
Pentre Mons 40 D10
Pentre Powys 50 E3
Pentre Powys 50 G3
Pentre Powys 51 J2
Pentre Rhondd 27 M3
Pentre Shrops 63 L8
Pentre Wrexhm 63 J4
Pentre-bâch Cerdgn 38 E3
Pentre Bach Flints 74 H8
Pentrebach Myr Td 39 P11
Pentre-bach Powys 39 L5
Pentrebeirdd Powys 62 G9
Pentre Berw IoA 72 H9
Pentre-bont Conwy 61 M2
Pentre-cagel Carmth 37 R2
Pentrecelyn Denbgs 62 G2
Pentre-celyn Powys 62 B11
Pentre-chwyth Swans 26 G3
Pentre-clawdd Shrops 63 J6
Pentre-cwrt Carmth 38 B4
Pentredwr Denbgs 62 H3
Pentrefelin Gwynd 61 J4
Pentrefelin IoA 72 G5
Pentre Ffwrndan Flints 75 J9
Pentrefoelas Conwy 61 Q2
Pentregalar Pembks 37 N4
Pentregat Cerdgn 48 F10
Pentre-Gwenlais Carmth 38 F8
Pentre Gwynfryn Gwynd 61 K7
Pentre Halkyn Flints 74 H9
Pentre Hodrey Shrops 51 K5
Pentre Isaf Conwy 74 D9
Pentre Llanrhaeadr Denbgs 74 E11
Pentre Llifior Powys 50 G1
Pentre-llwyn-llwyd Powys 50 C9
Pentre-llyn Cerdgn 49 K6
Pentre-llyn-cymmer Conwy 62 D2
Pentre-Maw Powys 62 B11
Pentre Meyrick V Glam 27 M7
Pentre-piod Torfn 40 C11
Pentre-poeth Newpt 28 C5
Pentre'rbryn Cerdgn 48 F9
Pentre'r-felin Cerdgn 49 K11
Pentre'r Felin Conwy 73 P10
Pentre'r-felin Powys 39 L5
Pentre Saron Denbgs 74 E11
Pentre-tafarn-y-fedw Conwy 73 P11
Pentre ty gwyn Carmth 39 K4
Pentrich Derbys 66 C2
Pentridge Dorset 23 M10
Pen-twyn Caerph 28 B2
Pentwyn Cardif 28 B6
Pen-twyn Mons 40 H10
Pen-twyn Torfn 40 C11
Pentwynmaur Caerph 28 A3
Pentyrch Cardif 27 Q6
Penwithick Cnwll 3 P3
Penwood Hants 31 J10
Penwyllt Powys 39 K8
Penybanc Carmth 38 F7
Penybont Powys 50 F8
Pen-y-bont Powys 62 H7
Penybontfawr Powys 62 E7
Pen-y-bryn Pembks 37 N2
Pen-y-cae Powys 39 K9
Penycae Wrexhm 63 J3
Pen-y-cae-mawr Mons 28 F3
Penycaerau Gwynd 60 C6
Pen-y-cefn Flints 74 G8
Pen-y-clawdd Mons 40 F10
Pen-y-coedcae Rhondd 27 P5
Penycwn Pembks 36 G6
Pen-y-fai Brdgnd 27 L6
Pen-y-felin Flints 74 G9
Penyffordd Flints 75 K11
Penyffridd Gwynd 72 H12
Pen-y-garn Cerdgn 49 K3
Pen-y-Garnedd Powys 62 F7
Pen-y-graig Gwynd 60 C5
Penygraig Rhondd 27 N4
Penygroes Carmth 38 E9
Penygroes Gwynd 60 H2
Penygroeslon Gwynd 60 D5
Pen-y-Gwryd Gwynd 61 L1
Pen-y-lan V Glam 27 N7
Pen-y-Mynydd Carmth 38 C11
Penymynydd Flints 75 J11
Pen-y-pass Gwynd 61 L1
Pen-yr-Heol Mons 40 F9
Penysarn IoA 72 G5
Pen-y-stryt Denbgs 62 H2
Penywaun Rhondd 39 M10
Penzance Cnwll 2 D8
Peopleton Worcs 52 H10
Peover Heath Ches E 76 E9
Peper Harow Surrey 14 D2
Peplow Shrops 64 B7
Pepper's Green Essex 46 A9
Pepperstock C Beds 44 F8
Perceton N Ayrs 104 F2
Percyhorner Abers 141 M3
Perelle Guern 12 b2
Perham Down Wilts 24 D4
Periton Somset 20 E4
Perivale Gt Lon 32 H6
Perkins Village Devon 9 J6
Perkinsville Dur 100 H7
Perlethorpe Notts 78 G9
Perranarworthal Cnwll 3 J7
Perranporth Cnwll 3 J4
Perranuthnoe Cnwll 2 E8
Perranwell Cnwll 3 J6
Perranwell Cnwll 3 J7
Perran Wharf Cnwll 3 J7
Perranzabuloe Cnwll 3 J4
Perrott's Brook Gloucs 42 B10
Perry Birm 53 K2
Perry Cambs 56 C7
Perry Barr Birm 53 K2
Perry Green Essex 46 E7
Perry Green Herts 45 N8
Perry Green Wilts 29 R4
Perrystone Hill Herefs 41 K6
Perry Street Somset 9 Q4
Pershall Staffs 64 E6
Pershore Worcs 41 Q2
Pertenhall Bed 56 B7
Perth P & K 124 C8
Perthy Shrops 63 L5
Perton Herefs 41 J4
Perton Staffs 64 F12
Pertwood Wilts 23 K6
Peterborough C Pete 68 D12
Peterborough Services Cambs 56 C2
Peterchurch Herefs 40 D4
Peterculter C Aber 133 K4
Peterhead Abers 141 Q6
Peterlee Dur 101 L10
Petersfield Hants 25 N8
Peter's Green Herts 44 G8
Petersham Gt Lon 32 H7
Peters Marland Devon 19 J10
Peterstone Wentlooge Newpt 28 C6
Peterston-super-Ely V Glam 27 P7
Peterstow Herefs 40 H7
Peters Village Kent 34 C9
Peter Tavy Devon 7 P9
Petham Kent 35 K12
Petherwin Gate Cnwll 7 K7
Petrockstow Devon 7 P3
Petsoe End M Keyn 55 M10
Pet Street Kent 17 K1
Pett E Susx 16 F8
Pettaugh Suffk 58 H8
Pett Bottom Kent 35 L12
Petterden Angus 124 H5
Pettinain S Lans 106 C1
Pettistree Suffk 59 L9
Petton Devon 20 F8
Petton Shrops 63 M7
Petts Wood Gt Lon 33 N9
Pettycur Fife 115 N4
Petty France S Glos 29 M5
Pettymuk Abers 141 L11
Petworth W Susx 14 D6
Pevensey E Susx 16 B10
Pevensey Bay E Susx 16 B10
Pewsey Wilts 30 D10
Pewsham Wilts 29 Q8
Pheasant's Hill Bucks 31 R5
Phepson Worcs 52 H8
Philadelphia Sundld 101 J8
Philham Devon 18 E9
Philiphaugh Border 107 L4
Phillack Cnwll 2 F7
Philleigh Cnwll 3 L6
Philpot End Essex 45 R8
Philpstoun W Loth 115 K6
Phocle Green Herefs 41 K6
Phoenix Green Hants 25 N2
Pibsbury Somset 21 N8
Pica Cumb 88 D2
Piccadilly Warwks 53 N1
Piccotts End Herts 44 F9
Pickburn Donc 78 E2
Pickering N York 92 F10
Picket Piece Hants 24 F4
Picket Post Hants 12 C3
Picket Twenty Hants 24 F4
Pickford Covtry 53 P4
Pickford Green Covtry 53 P4
Pickhill N York 91 N10
Picklescott Shrops 63 M12
Pickmere Ches E 76 C8
Pickney Somset 21 K7
Pickstock Wrekin 64 D7
Pickup Bank Bl w D 83 Q10
Pickwell Devon 19 J5
Pickwell Leics 67 K10
Pickwick Wilts 29 P8
Pickworth Lincs 67 P5
Pickworth Rutlnd 67 N10
Picton Ches W 75 M9
Picton Flints 74 F7
Picton N York 91 P5
Piddinghoe E Susx 15 N10
Piddington Bucks 32 A3
Piddington Nhants 55 K9
Piddington Oxon 43 N8
Piddlehinton Dorset 10 H5
Piddletrenthide Dorset 10 H5
Pidley Cambs 56 F5
Piercebridge Darltn 91 L4
Pierowall Ork 147 c1
Piff's Elm Gloucs 41 P6
Pigdon Nthumb 109 J12
Pigeon Green Warwks 53 N8
Pig Oak Dorset 11 N4
Pig Street Herefs 51 L11
Pikehall Derbys 77 M12
Pilford Dorset 11 P4
Pilgrims Hatch Essex 33 Q3
Pilham Lincs 79 L5
Pill N Som 28 H7
Pillaton Cnwll 4 E4
Pillatonmill Cnwll 4 E4
Pillerton Hersey Warwks 53 P11
Pillerton Priors Warwks 53 P11
Pilleth Powys 51 J7
Pilley Barns 77 Q4
Pilley Hants 12 E5
Pilley Bailey Hants 12 E5
Pillgwenlly Newpt 28 D5
Pillhead Devon 19 J8
Pilling Lancs 83 J5
Pilling Lane Lancs 83 J6
Pilning S Glos 28 H5
Pilot Inn Kent 17 K7
Pilsbury Derbys 77 L11
Pilsdon Dorset 10 C5
Pilsgate C Pete 67 Q11
Pilsley Derbys 77 N9
Pilsley Derbys 78 C11
Pilson Green Norfk 71 M9
Piltdown E Susx 15 N6
Pilton Devon 19 L6
Pilton Nhants 55 P4
Pilton Rutlnd 67 M11
Pilton Somset 22 D5
Pilton Green Swans 26 C5
Pimbo Lancs 75 N3
Pimlico Herts 44 F10
Pimlico Lancs 83 Q7
Pimlico Nhants 43 N3
Pimperne Dorset 11 L3
Pinchbeck Lincs 68 E7
Pinchbeck Bars Lincs 68 D7
Pincheon Green Donc 86 C11
Pinchinthorpe R & Cl 92 C4
Pincock Lancs 83 M11
Pinfold Lancs 75 L1
Pinford End Suffk 58 C8
Pinged Carmth 38 B11
Pingewood W Berk 31 P8
Pin Green Herts 45 J6
Pinhoe Devon 8 H6
Pinkett's Booth Covtry 53 P4
Pinkney Wilts 29 P5
Pinkneys Green W & M 32 B6
Pinley Covtry 53 Q5
Pinley Green Warwks 53 N7
Pin Mill Suffk 47 M4
Pinminnoch S Ayrs 104 C11
Pinmore S Ayrs 104 D11
Pinn Devon 9 L7
Pinner Gt Lon 32 G4
Pinner Green Gt Lon 32 G4
Pinsley Green Ches E 63 P3
Pinvin Worcs 52 H11
Pinwherry S Ayrs 104 D12
Pinxton Derbys 66 D1
Pipe and Lyde Herefs 40 G3
Pipe Aston Herefs 51 M6
Pipe Gate Shrops 64 D4
Pipehill Staffs 65 K10
Piperdam Angus 124 F6
Piperhill Highld 138 F6
Pipers Pool Cnwll 7 J8
Pipewell Nhants 55 L3
Pippacott Devon 19 K6
Pippin Street Lancs 83 N10
Pipton Powys 39 R4
Pirbright Surrey 32 D11
Pirbright Camp Surrey 32 D11
Pirnie Border 107 Q4
Pirnmill N Ayrs 112 C12
Pirton Herts 44 G5
Pirton Worcs 52 G11
Pisgah Cerdgn 49 L5
Pishill Oxon 31 P4
Pistyll Gwynd 60 E4
Pitblae Abers 141 N3
Pitcairngreen P & K 123 Q7
Pitcalnie Highld 146 E10
Pitcaple Abers 140 H10
Pitcarity Angus 131 Q11
Pitchcombe Gloucs 41 N10
Pitchcott Bucks 43 Q7
Pitcher Row Lincs 68 F5
Pitchford Shrops 63 P11
Pitch Green Bucks 43 Q11
Pitch Place Surrey 14 C3
Pitch Place Surrey 32 D11
Pitchroy Moray 139 M8
Pitcombe Somset 22 F7
Pitcot V Glam 27 L7
Pitcox E Loth 116 E6
Pitfichie Abers 132 G1
Pitglassie Abers 140 H7
Pitgrudy Highld 146 E7
Pitlessie Fife 124 G11
Pitlochry P & K 123 N1
Pitmachie Abers 140 G10
Pitmain Highld 130 D4
Pitmedden Abers 141 L10
Pitmedden Garden Abers 141 L10
Pitminster Somset 21 K9
Pitmuies Angus 125 L3
Pitmunie Abers 132 G1
Pitney Somset 21 P7
Pitroddie P & K 124 E8
Pitscottie Fife 124 H10
Pitsea Essex 34 C5
Pitses Oldham 76 H3
Pitsford Nhants 55 J7
Pitstone Bucks 44 D8
Pitt Devon 20 G10
Pitt Hants 24 G8
Pittarrow Abers 132 H9
Pitt Court Gloucs 29 M3
Pittentrail Highld 146 C5
Pittenweem Fife 125 L12
Pitteuchar Fife 115 P1
Pittodrie House Hotel Abers 140 H11
Pitton Wilts 24 C7
Pitt's Wood Kent 33 R12
Pittulie Abers 141 M2
Pityme Cnwll 6 D9
Pity Me Dur 100 H9
Pivington Kent 16 G2
Pixey Green Suffk 59 K5
Pixham Surrey 32 H12
Plains N Lans 114 E8
Plain Street Cnwll 6 E9
Plaish Shrops 51 N1
Plaistow Gt Lon 33 M6
Plaistow W Susx 14 E5
Plaitford Hants 24 D9
Plank Lane Wigan 76 B4
Plas Cymyran IoA 72 E8
Plastow Green Hants 31 L10
Platt Bridge Wigan 75 Q3
Platt Lane Shrops 63 N5
Platts Heath Kent 34 F12
Plawsworth Dur 100 H8
Plaxtol Kent 33 R11
Playden E Susx 16 G6
Playford Suffk 59 J11
Play Hatch Oxon 31 Q7
Playing Place Cnwll 3 K6
Playley Green Gloucs 41 M5
Plealey Shrops 63 M10
Plean Stirlg 114 F4
Pleasance Fife 124 E10
Pleasington Bl w D 83 P10
Pleasley Derbys 78 E10
Pleasleyhill Notts 78 E11
Pleasurewood Hills Suffk 59 Q1
Pleck Dorset 10 H3
Pledgdon Green Essex 45 Q6
Pledwick Wakefd 85 M12
Pleinheaume Guern 12 c1
Plemont Jersey 13 a1
Plemstall Ches W 75 M9
Plenmeller Nthumb 99 K6
Pleshey Essex 46 B9
Plockton Highld 135 P9
Plowden Shrops 51 L3
Plox Green Shrops 63 L11
Pluckley Kent 16 G2
Pluckley Station Kent 16 G2
Pluckley Thorne Kent 16 G2
Plucks Gutter Kent 35 N9
Plumbland Cumb 97 N10
Plumgarths Cumb 89 M8
Plumley Ches E 76 D8
Plump Hill Gloucs 41 K8
Plumpton Cumb 89 J11
Plumpton Cumb 98 G11
Plumpton E Susx 15 L8
Plumpton Nhants 54 F11
Plumpton End Nhants 43 P3
Plumpton Green E Susx 15 L7
Plumpton Head Cumb 98 G11
Plumstead Gt Lon 33 N6
Plumstead Norfk 70 H5
Plumstead Green Norfk 70 H5
Plumtree Notts 66 G5
Plumtree Green Kent 16 E2
Plungar Leics 67 J5
Plurenden Kent 16 G3
Plush Dorset 10 H4
Plusha Cnwll 7 J8
Plushabridge Cnwll 7 K10
Plwmp Cerdgn 48 F10
Plymouth C Plym 4 G6
Plympton C Plym 4 H5
Plymstock C Plym 4 H6
Plymtree Devon 9 K4
Pockley N York 92 D9
Pocklington E R Yk 86 E5
Pode Hole Lincs 68 D8
Podimore Somset 22 C8
Podington Bed 55 N8
Podmore Staffs 64 E5
Point Clear Essex 47 K8
Pointon Lincs 68 C6
Pokesdown BCP 11 Q6
Polbain Highld 144 C3
Polbathic Cnwll 4 E5
Polbeth W Loth 115 J8
Polbrock Cnwll 6 E11
Poldark Mine Cnwll 2 H8
Polebrook Nhants 55 Q3
Pole Elm Worcs 52 F10
Polegate E Susx 15 Q10
Pole Moor Kirk 84 G12
Polesden Lacey Surrey 32 G12
Polesworth Warwks 65 N11
Polglass Highld 144 C4

Polgooth Cnwll 3 N4
Polgown D & G 105 N9
Poling W Susx 14 F10
Poling Corner W Susx 14 F9
Polkerris Cnwll 3 Q4
Pollard Street Norfk 71 L5
Pollington E R Yk 86 B11
Polloch Highld 127 P10
Pollok C Glas 113 Q9
Pollokshaws C Glas 113 Q9
Pollokshields C Glas 113 Q8
Polmassick Cnwll 3 N5
Polmear Cnwll 3 Q4
Polmont Falk 114 G6
Polnish Highld 127 N8
Polperro Cnwll 4 B6
Polruan Cnwll 3 R4
Polsham Somset 22 C5
Polstead Suffk 46 H4
Polstead Heath Suffk 46 H4
Poltalloch Ag & B 112 B2
Poltescoe Cnwll 2 H11
Poltimore Devon 8 H5
Polton Mdloth 115 P8
Polwarth Border 116 G11
Polyphant Cnwll 7 K8
Polzeath Cnwll 6 D9
Pomathorn Mdloth 115 N9
Pomeroy Derbys 77 L10
Ponde Powys 39 Q4
Pondersbridge Cambs 56 E2
Ponders End Gt Lon 33 L3
Ponsanooth Cnwll 3 J7
Ponsonby Cumb 88 E5
Ponsongath Cnwll 3 J11
Ponsworthy Devon 8 D10
Pont Abraham Services
Carmth 38 E10
Pontac Jersey 13 d3
Pontamman Carmth 38 F9
Pontantwn Carmth 38 C9
Pontardawe Neath 38 H11
Pontarddulais Swans 38 E11
Pont-ar-gothi Carmth 38 D7
Pont-ar-Hydfer Powys 39 K6
Pont-ar-llechau Carmth 38 H7
Pontarsais Carmth 38 C6
Pontblyddyn Flints 75 J11
Pont Cyfyng Conwy 73 M12
Pontcysyllte Aqueduct
Wrexhm 63 J4
Pont Dolgarrog Conwy 73 N10
Pontdolgoch Powys 50 D2
Pont-Ebbw Newpt 28 C5
Pontefract Wakefd 85 P11
Ponteland Nthumb 100 F4
Ponterwyd Cerdgn 49 N4
Pontesbury Shrops 63 L11
Pontesbury Hill Shrops 63 L11
Pontesford Shrops 63 L11
Pontfadog Wrexhm 62 H4
Pontfaen Pembks 37 K4
Pont-faen Powys 39 N5
Pontgarreg Cerdgn 48 E10
Pontgarreg Pembks 37 M2
Pont Henri Carmth 38 C10
Ponthir Torfn 28 D4
Ponthirwaun Cerdgn 48 D11
Pontllanfraith Caerph 28 A3
Pontlliw Swans 26 F2
Pontllyfni Gwynd 60 G2
Pontlottyn Caerph 39 Q10
Pont Morlais Carmth 38 E10
Pontnêddféchan Neath 39 L10
Pontnewydd Torfn 28 C3
Pontnewynydd Torfn 28 C2
Pont Pen-y-benglog
Gwynd 73 L11
Pontrhydfendigaid
Cerdgn 49 M7
Pont Rhyd-sarn Gwynd 61 Q6
Pont Rhyd-y-cyff Brdgnd 27 K4
Pontrhydyfen Neath 27 J3
Pont-rhyd-y-groes
Cerdgn 49 M6
Pontrhydyrun Torfn 28 D3
Pontrilas Herefs 40 E6
Pont Robert Powys 62 F9
Pont-rug Gwynd 72 H11
Ponts Green E Susx 16 B7
Pontshill Herefs 41 K7
Pontsian Cerdgn 38 C2
Pontsticill Myr Td 39 P9
Pont Walby Neath 39 L10
Pontwelly Carmth 38 B4
Pontyates Carmth 38 C10
Pontyberem Carmth 38 D9
Pont-y-blew Wrexhm 63 K4
Pontybodkin Flints 75 J11
Pontyclun Rhondd 27 N6
Pontycymer Brdgnd 27 L4
Pontyglasier Pembks 37 M3
Pontygwaith Rhondd 27 N3
Pontygynon Pembks 37 M3
Pontymister Caerph 28 C4
Pont-y-pant Conwy 61 N1
Pontypool Torfn 28 C2
Pontypridd Rhondd 27 P4
Pont-yr-hafod Pembks 36 H5
Pont-yr-Rhyl Brdgnd 27 L4
Pontywaun Caerph 28 B4
Pool Cnwll 2 G6
Poole BCP 11 N7
Poole Keynes Gloucs 30 A3
Poolewe Highld 143 M9
Pooley Bridge Cumb 89 M2
Pooley Street Norfk 58 F4
Poolfold Staffs 76 G11
Pool Head Herefs 51 P10
Poolhill Gloucs 41 L6
Pool in Wharfedale
Leeds 85 K6
Pool of Muckhart Clacks 114 H1
Pool Quay Powys 63 J10
Pool Street Essex 46 D4
Pootings Kent 15 N1
Popes Hill Gloucs 41 L9
Popham Hants 25 J4
Poplar Gt Lon 33 L6
Poplar Street Suffk 59 N7
Porchfield IoW 12 G6
Poringland Norfk 71 K11
Porkellis Cnwll 2 H8
Porlock Somset 20 D4
Porlock Weir Somset 20 D4
Portachoillan Ag & B 111 Q9
Port-an-Eorna Highld 135 P9
Port Appin Ag & B 120 G4
Port Askaig Ag & B 111 K7
Portavadie Ag & B 112 D7
Port Bannatyne Ag & B 112 G8
Portbury N Som 28 G7
Port Carlisle Cumb 97 P6
Port Charlotte Ag & B 110 F9
Portchester Hants 13 K4
Port Clarence S on T 91 R2
Port Driseach Ag & B 112 E6
Port Ellen Ag & B 110 H12
Port Elphinstone Abers 141 J11
Portencalzie D & G 94 E4
Portencross N Ayrs 112 H11
Port Erin IoM 102 b7
Portesham Dorset 10 F7
Portessie Moray 140 C3
Port e Vullen IoM 102 f3
Port Eynon Swans 26 C5
Portfield Gate Pembks 36 H7
Portgate Devon 7 M7
Port Gaverne Cnwll 6 E8
Port Glasgow Inver 113 L6
Portgordon Moray 140 B3
Portgower Highld 146 H2
Porth Cnwll 3 K2
Porth Rhondd 27 N4
Porthallow Cnwll 3 K10
Porthallow Cnwll 4 C6
Porthcawl Brdgnd 27 K7
Porthcothan Cnwll 6 B10
Porthcurno Cnwll 2 B10
Porthdinllaen Gwynd 60 D4
Port Henderson Highld 143 K10
Porthgain Pembks 36 F4
Porthgwarra Cnwll 2 B10
Porthill Staffs 64 F2
Porthkea Cnwll 3 K6
Porthkerry V Glam 27 P9
Porthleven Cnwll 2 G9
Porthmadog Gwynd 61 J4
Porthmadog Gwynd 61 J4
Porthmeor Cnwll 2 C7
Porth Navas Cnwll 3 J9
Portholland Cnwll 3 N6
Porthoustock Cnwll 3 K10
Porthpean Cnwll 3 P4
Porthtowan Cnwll 2 H5
Porthwgan Wrexhm 63 L3
Porthyrhyd Carmth 38 D8
Porth-y-Waen Shrops 63 J7
Portincaple Ag & B 113 J3
Portinfer Jersey 13 a1
Portington E R Yk 86 E9
Portinnisherrich Ag & B 121 J10
Portinscale Cumb 88 H2
Port Isaac Cnwll 6 E8
Portishead N Som 28 G7
Portknockie Moray 140 D2
Portland Dorset 10 G10
Portlethen Abers 133 M5
Portling D & G 96 H7
Portloe Cnwll 3 M6
Port Logan D & G 94 G10
Portlooe Cnwll 4 C6
Portmahomack Highld 146 G8
Port Mary D & G 96 F9
Portmeirion Gwynd 61 K5
Portmellon Cnwll 3 P6
Port Mòr Highld 126 G8
Portmore Hants 12 E5
Port Mulgrave N York 92 G3
Portnacroish Ag & B 120 H3
Portnaguran W Isls 152 h3
Portnahaven Ag & B 110 E10
Portnalong Highld 134 F9
Portnancon Highld 149 J5
Port nan Giùran W Isls 152 h3
Port nan Long W Isls 152 c7
Port Nis W Isls 152 h1
Portobello C Edin 115 P6
Portobello Gatesd 100 H7
Portobello Wolves 52 H1
Port of Menteith Stirlg 113 R1
Port of Ness W Isls 152 h1
Porton Wilts 24 C6
Portontown Devon 7 M9
Portpatrick D & G 94 E7
Port Quin Cnwll 6 D8
Port Ramsay Ag & B 120 G4
Portreath Cnwll 2 G5
Portreath Harbour Cnwll 2 G5
Portree Highld 134 H7
Port Righ Ag & B 103 L2
Port St Mary IoM 102 b7
Portscatho Cnwll 3 L7
Portsea C Port 13 L5
Portskerra Highld 150 F3
Portskewett Mons 28 G5
Portslade Br & H 15 J9
Portslade-by-Sea Br & H 15 J10
Portslogan D & G 94 E6
Portsmouth C Port 13 L5
Portsmouth Calder 84 D10
Portsmouth Arms Devon 19 M9
Portsmouth Historic
Dockyard C Port 13 K4
Port Soderick IoM 102 d6
Port Solent C Port 13 L4
Portsonachan Hotel
Ag & B 121 K8
Portsoy Abers 140 F3
Port Sunlight Wirral 75 K7
Portswood C Sotn 24 G10
Port Talbot Neath 27 J4
Port Tennant Swans 26 G4
Portuairk Highld 126 H10
Portway Herefs 40 G3
Portway Herefs 40 G5
Portway Sandw 52 H3
Portway Worcs 53 K6
Port Wemyss Ag & B 110 E11
Port William D & G 95 L9
Portwrinkle Cnwll 4 E6
Portyerrock D & G 95 N10
Posbury Devon 8 F5
Posenhall Shrops 64 C11
Poslingford Suffk 57 P11
Posso Border 106 G3
Postbridge Devon 8 C9
Postcombe Oxon 31 P2
Post Green Dorset 11 M6
Postling Kent 17 L3
Postwick Norfk 71 L10
Potarch Abers 132 F5
Potsgrove C Beds 44 D6
Potten End Herts 44 E10
Potten Street Kent 35 N9
Potter Brompton N York 93 K11
Pottergate Street Norfk 58 H2
Potterhanworth Lincs 79 Q10
Potterhanworth Booths
Lincs 79 Q10
Potter Heigham Norfk 71 N8
Potterne Wilts 30 A10
Potterne Wick Wilts 30 A10
Potter Row Bucks 44 C11
Potters Bar Herts 33 J2
Potters Brook Lancs 83 L5
Potters Corner Kent 16 H2
Potter's Cross Staffs 52 F4
Potters Crouch Herts 44 G10
Potter's Forstal Kent 16 F2
Potters Green Covtry 54 B4
Potter's Green E Susx 15 P6
Potter's Green Herts 45 L7
Pottersheath Herts 45 J8
Potters Marston Leics 54 E1
Potter Somersal Derbys 65 L5
Potterspury Nhants 43 Q3
Potter Street Essex 45 N10
Potterton Abers 133 M1
Potterton Leeds 85 N7
Potthorpe Norfk 70 D7
Pottle Street Wilts 22 H5
Potto N York 91 Q6
Potton C Beds 56 D10
Pott Row Norfk 69 N8
Pott's Green Essex 46 F7
Pott Shrigley Ches E 76 H8
Poughill Cnwll 7 J3
Poughill Devon 8 F3
Poulner Hants 12 B3
Poulshot Wilts 29 R10
Poulton Gloucs 30 C2
Poulton Wirral 75 J5
Poulton-le-Fylde Lancs 82 H7
Poulton Priory Gloucs 30 C2
Pound Bank Worcs 52 D6
Poundbury Dorset 10 G7
Poundffald Swans 26 E3
Poundgate E Susx 15 P5
Pound Green E Susx 15 P6
Pound Green Suffk 57 N10
Pound Green Worcs 52 D5
Pound Hill W Susx 15 K3
Poundon Bucks 43 N6
Poundsbridge Kent 15 P2
Poundsgate Devon 8 D10
Poundstock Cnwll 7 J5
Pound Street Hants 31 K10
Pounsley E Susx 15 P6
Pouton D & G 95 N9
Pouy Street Suffk 59 M6
Povey Cross Surrey 15 K2
Powburn Nthumb 108 H6
Powderham Devon 8 H8
Powerstock Dorset 10 D5
Powfoot D & G 97 N5
Pow Green Herefs 41 L3
Powhill Cumb 97 P7
Powick Worcs 52 F10
Powmill P & K 115 J2
Poxwell Dorset 10 H8
Poyle Slough 32 E7
Poynings W Susx 15 J8
Poyntington Dorset 22 E9
Poynton Ches E 76 G7
Poynton Wrekin 63 P8
Poynton Green Wrekin 63 P8
Poyston Cross Pembks 37 J6
Poystreet Green Suffk 58 E9
Praa Sands Cnwll 2 F9
Pratt's Bottom Gt Lon 33 N10
Praze-an-Beeble Cnwll 2 G7
Predannack Wollas Cnwll 2 G11
Prees Shrops 63 P5
Preesall Lancs 83 J6
Prees Green Shrops 63 P6
Preesgweene Shrops 63 J5
Prees Heath Shrops 63 P4
Prees Higher Heath
Shrops 63 P5
Prees Lower Heath
Shrops 63 P5
Prendwick Nthumb 108 G7
Pren-gwyn Cerdgn 38 C3
Prenteg Gwynd 61 K4
Prenton Wirral 75 J6
Prescot Knows 75 M5
Prescott Devon 20 H10
Prescott Shrops 52 C4
Prescott Shrops 63 M8
Presnerb Angus 131 M11
Pressen Nthumb 108 D3
Prestatyn Denbgs 74 E7
Prestbury Ches E 76 G8
Prestbury Gloucs 41 R7
Presteigne Powys 51 K8
Prestleigh Somset 22 E5
Prestolee Bolton 76 D3
Preston Border 116 H10
Preston Br & H 15 K9
Preston Devon 8 F10
Preston Dorset 10 H8
Preston E R Yk 87 M9
Preston Gloucs 30 B2
Preston Herts 44 H7
Preston Kent 34 H10
Preston Kent 35 N10
Preston Lancs 83 M9
Preston Nthumb 109 K5
Preston Rutlnd 67 L11
Preston Shrops 63 N9
Preston Somset 20 H6
Preston Torbay 5 Q4
Preston Wilts 30 B7
Preston Wilts 30 F7
Preston Bagot Warwks 53 M7
Preston Bissett Bucks 43 N6
Preston Bowyer Somset 21 J8
Preston Brockhurst
Shrops 63 P7
Preston Brook Halton 75 P7
Preston Candover Hants 25 K5
Preston Capes Nhants 54 F9
Preston Crowmarsh Oxon 31 M4
Preston Deanery Nhants 55 K9
Preston Green Warwks 53 M7
Preston Gubbals Shrops 63 N8
Preston Montford Shrops 63 M9
Preston on Stour Warwks 53 M10
Preston on Tees S on T 91 Q3
Preston on the Hill
Halton 75 P7
Preston on Wye Herefs 40 E3
Prestonpans E Loth 115 Q6
Preston Patrick Cumb 89 N10
Preston Plucknett
Somset 22 C10
Preston St Mary Suffk 58 D10
Preston Street Kent 35 N10
Preston-under-Scar
N York 90 H8
Preston upon the Weald
Moors Wrekin 64 C9
Preston Wynne Herefs 40 H2
Prestwich Bury 76 F3
Prestwick Nthumb 100 F4
Prestwick S Ayrs 104 F5
Prestwick Airport S Ayrs 104 G4
Prestwood Bucks 32 C2
Prestwood Staffs 52 F3
Price Town Brdgnd 27 M4
Prickwillow Cambs 57 L4
Priddy Somset 22 C3
Priestacott Devon 7 N3
Priestcliffe Derbys 77 L9
Priestcliffe Ditch Derbys 77 L9
Priest Hutton Lancs 89 N12
Priestland E Ayrs 105 K2
Priestley Green Calder 84 H10
Priest Weston Shrops 51 J1
Priestwood Green Kent 34 B9
Primethorpe Leics 54 E2
Primrose Green Norfk 70 G9
Primrosehill Border 116 H9
Primrose Hill Cambs 56 G3
Primrose Hill Derbys 78 C12
Primrose Hill Dudley 52 H3
Primrose Hill Lancs 75 L2
Primsidemill Border 108 C4
Prince of Wales Bridge
Mons 28 G5
Princes Gate Pembks 37 M8
Princes Risborough
Bucks 44 A11
Princethorpe Warwks 54 C6
Princetown Devon 8 B10
Prinsted W Susx 13 N4
Prion Denbgs 74 E11
Prior Rigg Cumb 98 F4
Priors Halton Shrops 51 N5
Priors Hardwick Warwks 54 D9
Priorslee Wrekin 64 D10
Priors Marston Warwks 54 E9
Priors Norton Gloucs 41 P7
Priors Park Gloucs 41 P5
Priory Wood Herefs 40 C3
Prisk V Glam 27 N7
Priston BaNES 29 L10
Pristow Green Norfk 58 H3
Prittlewell Sthend 34 F5
Privett Hants 25 L8
Prixford Devon 19 K6
Probus Cnwll 3 M5
Prora E Loth 116 C5
Prospect Cumb 97 M10
Prospidnick Cnwll 2 G8
Protstonhill Abers 141 K3
Prudhoe Nthumb 100 E6
Prussia Cove Cnwll 2 E9
Pubil P & K 122 D4
Publow BaNES 29 J9
Puckeridge Herts 45 M7
Puckington Somset 21 N9
Pucklechurch S Glos 29 L7
Puckrup Gloucs 41 P4
Puddinglake Ches W 76 D9
Puddington Ches W 75 K9
Puddington Devon 8 F3
Puddledock Norfk 58 F2
Puddletown Dorset 11 J6
Pudleston Herefs 51 P8
Pudsey Leeds 85 K8
Pulborough W Susx 14 F7
Puleston Wrekin 64 D7
Pulford Ches W 75 L12
Pulham Dorset 10 H3
Pulham Market Norfk 59 J3
Pulham St Mary Norfk 59 J4
Pullens Green S Glos 29 J4
Pulloxhill C Beds 44 F5
Pulverbatch Shrops 63 M11
Pumpherston W Loth 115 K7
Pumsaint Carmth 38 G4
Puncheston Pembks 37 K4
Puncknowle Dorset 10 E7
Punnett's Town E Susx 16 A7
Purbrook Hants 13 L3
Purfleet-on-Thames
Thurr 33 Q7
Puriton Somset 21 M5
Purleigh Essex 46 E11
Purley Gt Lon 33 K10
Purley on Thames W Berk 31 N7
Purlogue Shrops 51 J5
Purlpit Wilts 29 P9
Purls Bridge Cambs 57 J3
Purse Caundle Dorset 22 F10
Purshull Green Worcs 52 G6
Purslow Shrops 51 K4
Purston Jaglin Wakefd 85 N11
Purtington Somset 10 B3
Purton Gloucs 41 K10
Purton Gloucs 41 L11
Purton Wilts 30 C5
Purton Stoke Wilts 30 C4
Pury End Nhants 43 P3
Pusey Oxon 30 H3
Putley Herefs 41 K4
Putley Green Herefs 41 K4
Putloe Gloucs 41 M9
Putney Gt Lon 33 J7
Putsborough Devon 19 J5
Puttenham Herts 44 C8
Puttenham Surrey 14 D1
Puttock End Essex 46 E4
Putton Dorset 10 G8
Putts Corner Devon 9 M5
Puxley Nhants 43 Q3
Puxton N Som 28 E9
Pwll Carmth 26 D2
Pwllcrochan Pembks 36 H10
Pwll-du Mons 40 C9
Pwll-glâs Denbgs 62 F1
Pwllgloyw Powys 39 N5
Pwllheli Gwynd 60 F5
Pwllmeyric Mons 28 H4
Pwll-trap Carmth 37 P7
Pwll-y-glaw Neath 27 J4
Pydew Conwy 73 P8
Pye Bridge Derbys 66 D2
Pyecombe W Susx 15 K8
Pye Corner Newpt 28 D5
Pye Green Staffs 65 J9
Pyle Brdgnd 27 K6
Pyleigh Somset 20 H7
Pylle Somset 22 E6
Pymoor Cambs 57 J3
Pymore Dorset 10 D6
Pyrford Surrey 32 E10
Pyrton Oxon 31 P3
Pytchley Nhants 55 L6
Pyworthy Devon 7 K4

Q

Quabbs Shrops 50 H4
Quadring Lincs 68 E5
Quadring Eaudike Lincs 68 E5
Quainton Bucks 43 Q7
Quaker's Yard Myr Td 27 P3
Quaking Houses Dur 100 F8
Quantock Hills Somset 21 J6
Quarff Shet 147 i8
Quarley Hants 24 D5
Quarndon Derbys 65 Q4
Quarr Hill IoW 13 J6
Quarrier's Village Inver 113 M8
Quarrington Lincs 67 Q3
Quarrington Hill Dur 101 J10
Quarrybank Ches W 75 P10
Quarry Bank Dudley 52 H3
Quarrywood Moray 139 M3
Quarter N Ayrs 113 J9
Quarter S Lans 114 D11
Quatford Shrops 52 D2
Quatt Shrops 52 D3
Quebec Dur 100 F9
Quedgeley Gloucs 41 N9
Queen Adelaide Cambs 57 L4
Queenborough Kent 34 F8
Queen Camel Somset 22 D8
Queen Charlton BaNES 29 K9
Queen Dart Devon 20 C10
Queen Elizabeth Forest
Park Stirlg 122 E11
Queen Elizabeth II
Bridge Thurr 33 Q7
Queenhill Worcs 41 P4
Queen Oak Dorset 22 H7
Queen's Bower IoW 13 J8
Queensbury C Brad 84 G9
Queensferry Flints 75 K10
Queensferry Crossing
Fife 115 L5
Queen's Head Shrops 63 K7
Queen's Hills Norfk 70 H9
Queenslie C Glas 114 B8
Queen's Park Bed 55 P10
Queen's Park Essex 34 B3
Queen's Park Nhants 55 J8
Queen Street Kent 16 B2
Queen Street Wilts 30 B5
Queenzieburn N Lans 114 C6
Quendon Essex 45 P6
Queniborough Leics 66 G9
Quenington Gloucs 42 D11
Quernmore Lancs 83 M3
Queslett Birm 53 K2
Quethiock Cnwll 4 D4
Quick's Green W Berk 31 M7
Quidenham Norfk 58 F3
Quidhampton Hants 25 J3
Quidhampton Wilts 23 P7
Quina Brook Shrops 63 N5
Quinbury End Nhants 54 G10
Quinton Dudley 53 J4
Quinton Nhants 55 K10
Quinton Green Nhants 55 K10
Quintrell Downs Cnwll 3 L2
Quixhall Staffs 65 L4
Quixwood Border 116 H8
Quoditch Devon 7 M5
Quoig P & K 123 L8
Quorn Leics 66 F9
Quothquan S Lans 106 C2
Quoyburray Ork 147 d5
Quoyloo Ork 147 b4

R

Raasay Highld 135 K7
Rabbit's Cross Kent 16 D1
Rableyheath Herts 45 J8
Raby Cumb 97 P8
Raby Wirral 75 K8
Rachan Mill Border 106 E3
Rachub Gwynd 73 K10
Rackenford Devon 20 C9
Rackham W Susx 14 F8
Rackheath Norfk 71 K9
Racks D & G 97 L3
Rackwick Ork 147 a5
Radbourne Derbys 65 P5
Radcliffe Bury 76 E2
Radcliffe Nthumb 109 L9
Radcliffe on Trent Notts 66 G4
Radclive Bucks 43 P5
Radcot Oxon 30 G2
Raddery Highld 138 C4
Raddington Somset 20 F8
Radernie Fife 125 J11
Radford Covtry 53 Q4
Radford Semele Warwks 53 Q8
Radlet Somset 21 K6
Radlett Herts 32 H2
Radley Devon 19 P8
Radley Oxon 31 L3
Radley W Berk 30 H8
Radley Green Essex 46 A10
Radmore Green Ches E 63 Q1
Radnage Bucks 31 R3
Radstock BaNES 22 F2
Radstone Nhants 43 M4
Radway Warwks 54 B11
Radwell Bed 55 P9
Radwell Herts 45 J4
Radwinter Essex 45 R4
Radwinter End Essex 45 R4
Radyr Cardif 27 Q6
RAF College (Cranwell)
Lincs 67 P2
Rafford Moray 139 K4
RAF Museum Cosford
Shrops 64 E11
RAF Museum London
Gt Lon 33 J4
Ragdale Leics 66 H8
Ragdon Shrops 51 M2
Raginnis Cnwll 2 D9
Raglan Mons 40 F10
Ragnall Notts 79 K9
Raigbeg Highld 138 E10
Rainbow Hill Worcs 52 F9
Rainford St Hel 75 N3
Rainford Junction St Hel 75 N3
Rainham Gt Lon 33 P6
Rainham Medway 34 E9
Rainhill St Hel 75 N5
Rainhill Stoops St Hel 75 N6
Rainow Ches E 76 H8
Rainsough Bury 76 E3
Rainton N York 91 N11
Rainworth Notts 78 F12
Raisbeck Cumb 89 Q5
Raise Cumb 99 K9
Raisthorpe N York 86 F3
Rait P & K 124 E7
Raithby Lincs 80 F7
Raithby Lincs 80 G10
Raithwaite N York 92 H4
Rake Hants 25 P8
Rakewood Rochdl 84 E12
Ralia Highld 130 C5
Ram Carmth 38 E2
Ramasaig Highld 134 C7
Rame Cnwll 2 H8
Rame Cnwll 4 F7
Ram Hill S Glos 29 K6
Ram Lane Kent 16 H2
Rampisham Dorset 10 E4
Rampside Cumb 82 G2
Rampton Cambs 56 H7
Rampton Notts 79 K8
Ramsbottom Bury 84 B11
Ramsbury Wilts 30 F8
Ramscraigs Highld 151 L11
Ramsdean Hants 25 M9
Ramsdell Hants 31 M10
Ramsden Oxon 42 H8
Ramsden Worcs 41 Q2
Ramsden Bellhouse
Essex 34 C3
Ramsden Heath Essex 34 C3
Ramsey Cambs 56 F4
Ramsey Essex 47 M5
Ramsey IoM 102 f3
Ramsey Forty Foot
Cambs 56 F3
Ramsey Heights Cambs 56 E4
Ramsey Island Pembks 36 D6
Ramsey Mereside Cambs 56 F3
Ramsey St Mary's Cambs 56 E3
Ramsgate Kent 35 Q9
Ramsgill N York 84 H1
Ramshaw Dur 91 K2
Ramshaw Dur 99 Q9
Ramsholt Suffk 47 P3
Ramshope Nthumb 108 B9
Ramshorn Staffs 65 K3
Ramsley Devon 8 C6
Ramsnest Common
Surrey 14 D4
Ranby Lincs 80 E8
Ranby Notts 78 G7
Rand Lincs 80 B8
Randwick Gloucs 41 N10
Ranfurly Rens 113 M8
Rangemore Staffs 65 M7
Rangeworthy S Glos 29 L5
Rankinston E Ayrs 104 H7
Ranksborough Rutlnd 67 L10
Rank's Green Essex 46 D8
Rannoch Station P & K 122 D1
Ranscombe Somset 20 E5
Ranskill Notts 78 G6
Ranton Staffs 64 F7
Ranton Green Staffs 64 F7
Ranworth Norfk 71 M9
Raploch Stirlg 114 E2
Rapness Ork 147 d2
Rapps Somset 21 M10
Rascarrel D & G 96 G8
Rashfield Ag & B 112 H5
Rashwood Worcs 52 G7
Raskelf N York 85 P1
Rassau Blae G 39 R9
Rastrick Calder 84 H10
Ratagan Highld 136 C11
Ratby Leics 66 E11
Ratcliffe Culey Leics 65 Q12
Ratcliffe on Soar Notts 66 E6
Ratcliffe on the Wreake
Leics 66 G9
Rathen Abers 141 N4
Rathillet Fife 124 G8
Rathmell N York 84 B3
Ratho C Edin 115 L7
Ratho Station C Edin 115 L7
Rathven Moray 140 C3
Ratlake Hants 24 G8
Ratley Warwks 42 H2
Ratling Kent 35 M11
Ratlinghope Shrops 51 L1
Rattar Highld 151 N2
Ratten Row Cumb 98 C10
Ratten Row Cumb 98 E8
Ratten Row Lancs 83 K7
Rattery Devon 5 M4
Rattlesden Suffk 58 E9
Ratton Village E Susx 15 Q10
Rattray P & K 124 D4
Raughton Cumb 98 E8
Raughton Head Cumb 98 D9
Raunds Nhants 55 P6
Ravenfield Rothm 78 D5
Ravenglass Cumb 88 E7
Ravenhills Green Worcs 52 D9
Raveningham Norfk 59 M1
Ravenscar N York 93 K6
Ravenscraig N Lans 114 D10
Ravensdale IoM 102 d4
Ravensden Bed 55 Q10
Ravenseat N York 90 D6
Ravenshead Notts 66 F1
Ravensmoor Ches E 64 B2
Ravensthorpe Kirk 85 K11
Ravensthorpe Nhants 54 H6
Ravenstone Leics 66 C9
Ravenstone M Keyn 55 L10
Ravenstonedale Cumb 90 B6
Ravenstruther S Lans 114 G12
Ravensworth N York 91 J5
Raw N York 93 J5
Rawcliffe C York 86 A4
Rawcliffe E R Yk 86 C10
Rawcliffe Bridge E R Yk 86 C11
Rawdon Leeds 85 J7
Rawling Street Kent 34 F10
Rawmarsh Rothm 78 D4
Rawnsley Staffs 65 J9
Rawreth Essex 34 D4
Rawridge Devon 9 N3
Rawtenstall Lancs 84 B10
Raydon Suffk 47 J4
Raylees Nthumb 108 E11
Rayleigh Essex 34 E4
Raymond's Hill Devon 9 Q5
Rayne Essex 46 C7
Raynes Park Gt Lon 33 J8
Reach Cambs 57 L7
Read Lancs 84 A8
Reading Readg 31 P7
Reading Services W Berk 31 P8
Reading Street Kent 16 G5
Reading Street Kent 35 Q8
Reagill Cumb 89 P3
Rearquhar Highld 146 D6
Rearsby Leics 66 G9
Rease Heath Ches E 64 B1
Reawla Cnwll 2 F7
Reay Highld 150 H4
Reculver Kent 35 M8
Red Ball Devon 20 H10
Redberth Pembks 37 L9
Redbourn Herts 44 G9
Redbourne N Linc 79 N4
Redbrook Gloucs 40 H9
Redbrook Wrexhm 63 N4
Redbrook Street Kent 16 G4
Redburn Highld 138 H6
Redburn Nthumb 99 L5
Redcar R & Cl 92 C2
Redcastle D & G 96 G5
Redcastle Highld 137 Q6
Red Dial Cumb 97 Q9
Redding Falk 114 G5
Reddingmuirhead Falk 114 G6
Reddish Stockp 76 G5
Redditch Worcs 53 K7
Rede Suffk 57 Q9
Redenhall Norfk 59 K4
Redenham Hants 24 E3
Redesmouth Nthumb 99 N2
Redford Abers 133 J10
Redford Angus 125 L4
Redford W Susx 25 Q8
Redfordgreen Border 107 K6
Redgate Rhondd 27 N5
Redgorton P & K 124 B7
Redgrave Suffk 58 F5
Redhill Abers 133 J3
Red Hill BCP 11 Q5
Redhill Herts 45 K5
Redhill N Som 28 G9
Redhill Surrey 33 K12
Red Hill Warwks 53 L9
Redisham Suffk 59 N4
Redland Bristl 29 J7
Redland Ork 147 c3
Redlingfield Suffk 59 J6
Redlingfield Green Suffk 59 J6
Red Lodge Suffk 57 N6
Red Lumb Rochdl 84 C12
Redlynch Somset 22 F6
Redlynch Wilts 24 C9
Redmain Cumb 97 N11
Redmarley Worcs 52 E7
Redmarley D'Abitot
Gloucs 41 M5
Redmarshall S on T 91 P3
Redmile Leics 67 K5
Redmire N York 90 H8
Redmyre Abers 133 J9
Rednal Birm 53 J5
Rednal Shrops 63 L6
Redpath Border 107 P3
Red Point Highld 135 N2
Red Post Cnwll 7 K4
Red Rice Hants 24 E5
Red Rock Wigan 75 P2
Red Roses Carmth 37 N8
Red Row Nthumb 109 L10
Redruth Cnwll 2 H6
Redstocks Wilts 29 Q9
Redstone P & K 124 D6
Redstone Cross Pembks 37 L7
Red Street Staffs 64 F2
Redvales Bury 76 E2
Red Wharf Bay IoA 73 J7
Redwick Newpt 28 F5
Redwick S Glos 28 H5
Redworth Darltn 91 L2
Reed Herts 45 L4
Reedham Norfk 71 N11
Reedness E R Yk 86 E10
Reeds Beck Lincs 80 D10
Reeds Holme Lancs 84 B10
Reepham Lincs 79 P9
Reepham Norfk 70 G7
Reeth N York 90 H7
Reeves Green Solhll 53 N5
Regaby IoM 102 f3
Regil N Som 28 H9
Reiff Highld 143 P2
Reigate Surrey 33 J12
Reighton N York 93 N11
Reinigeadal W Isls 152 f5
Reisque Abers 141 L11
Reiss Highld 151 P6
Rejerrah Cnwll 3 K3
Releath Cnwll 2 G8
Relubbus Cnwll 2 F8
Relugas Moray 139 J6
Remenham Wokham 31 Q5
Remenham Hill Wokham 31 Q6
Rempstone Notts 66 F7
Rendcomb Gloucs 42 B9
Rendham Suffk 59 L8
Rendlesham Suffk 59 L10
Renfrew Rens 113 P8
Renhold Bed 56 B10
Renishaw Derbys 78 D8
Rennington Nthumb 109 K6
Renton W Duns 113 M6
Renwick Cumb 98 H9
Repps Norfk 71 N9
Repton Derbys 65 P7
Reraig Highld 135 P10
Resaurie Highld 138 C7
Rescassa Cnwll 3 N6
Rescorla Cnwll 3 N5
Resipole Burn Highld 127 N11
Reskadinnick Cnwll 2 G6
Resolis Highld 138 C3
Resolven Neath 39 K11
Rest and be thankful
Ag & B 121 N11
Reston Border 117 K9
Restronguet Cnwll 3 K7
Reswallie Angus 125 K3
Reterth Cnwll 3 M2
Retford Notts 78 H7
Retire Cnwll 3 N2
Rettendon Common
Essex 34 D3
Rettendon Village Essex 34 D3
Retyn Cnwll 3 L3
Revesby Lincs 80 F11
Rew Devon 5 M9
Rew Devon 8 E10
Rewe Devon 8 H5
Rew Street IoW 12 H6
Rexon Devon 7 M7
Reydon Suffk 59 P5
Reymerston Norfk 70 F11
Reynalton Pembks 37 L9
Reynoldston Swans 26 D4
Rezare Cnwll 7 L9
Rhadyr Mons 40 E11
Rhandirmwyn Carmth 39 J3
Rhayader Powys 50 D7
Rheindown Highld 137 P6
Rhenigidale W Isls 152 f5
Rhes-y-cae Flints 74 G9
Rhewl Denbgs 62 G3
Rhewl Denbgs 74 F11
Rhewl Mostyn Flints 74 G7
Rhicarn Highld 148 C11
Rhiconich Highld 148 F6
Rhicullen Highld 146 C10
Rhigos Rhondd 39 L10
Rhives Highld 146 E5
Rhiwbina Cardif 27 R6
Rhiwbryfdir Gwynd 61 M3
Rhiwderyn Newpt 28 C5
Rhiwen Gwynd 73 J11
Rhiwinder Rhondd 27 N5
Rhiwlas Gwynd 62 C5
Rhiwlas Gwynd 73 K10
Rhiwlas Powys 62 H6
Rhiwsaeson Rhondd 27 P6
Rhode Somset 21 L6
Rhoden Green Kent 16 B2
Rhodesia Notts 78 F7
Rhodes Minnis Kent 17 L2
Rhodiad-y-brenin
Pembks 36 E5
Rhonehouse D & G 96 F6
Rhoose V Glam 27 P9
Rhos Carmth 38 B5
Rhos Denbgs 74 F11
Rhos Neath 38 H11
Rhosaman Carmth 38 H9
Rhosbeirio IoA 72 F5
Rhoscefnhir IoA 73 J8
Rhoscolyn IoA 72 D8
Rhoscrowther Pembks 36 H10
Rhosesmor Flints 74 H10
Rhos-fawr Gwynd 60 F4
Rhosgadfan Gwynd 72 H12
Rhosgoch IoA 72 G6
Rhosgoch Powys 50 G11
Rhos Haminiog Cerdgn 49 J8
Rhoshill Pembks 37 N2
Rhoshirwaun Gwynd 60 C6
Rhoslan Gwynd 60 H4
Rhoslefain Gwynd 61 K11
Rhosllanerchrugog
Wrexhm 63 J3
Rhôs Lligwy IoA 72 H6
Rhosmaen Carmth 38 F7
Rhosmeirch IoA 72 H8
Rhosneigr IoA 72 E9
Rhosnesni Wrexhm 63 K2
Rhôs-on-Sea Conwy 73 P7
Rhosrobin Wrexhm 63 K2
Rhossili Swans 26 B5
Rhostrehwfa IoA 72 G8
Rhostryfan Gwynd 72 H12
Rhostyllen Wrexhm 63 K2
Rhosybol IoA 72 G6
Rhos-y-brithdir Powys 62 F7
Rhosygadfa Shrops 63 K5
Rhos-y-garth Cerdgn 49 L6
Rhos-y-gwaliau Gwynd 62 C5
Rhos-y-llan Gwynd 60 D5
Rhosymedre Wrexhm 63 J4
Rhos-y-meirch Powys 51 J7
RHS Garden Harlow
Carr N York 85 L4
RHS Garden Wisley
Surrey 32 F10
Rhu Ag & B 113 K4
Rhuallt Denbgs 74 E8
Rhubodach Ag & B 112 F6
Rhuddall Heath Ches W 75 P11
Rhuddlan Cerdgn 38 D3
Rhuddlan Denbgs 74 D8
Rhue Highld 144 D6
Rhulen Powys 50 F10
Rhunahaorine Ag & B 111 Q11
Rhyd Gwynd 61 L4
Rhydargaeau Carmth 38 C6
Rhydcymerau Carmth 38 E4
Rhydd Worcs 41 N3
Rhyd-Ddu Gwynd 61 J2
Rhydding Neath 26 H3
Rhydgaled Conwy 74 D10
Rhydlanfair Conwy 61 P2
Rhydlewis Cerdgn 48 E11
Rhydlios Gwynd 60 C6
Rhydlydan Conwy 62 B2
Rhydowen Cerdgn 38 C3
Rhydroser Cerdgn 49 J7
Rhydspence Herefs 40 C2
Rhydtalog Flints 62 H1
Rhyd-uchaf Gwynd 62 B5
Rhyd-y-clafdy Gwynd 60 E5
Rhydycroesau Shrops 62 H6
Rhydyfelin Cerdgn 49 K5
Rhydyfelin Rhondd 27 P5
Rhyd-y-foel Conwy 74 B8
Rhydyfro Neath 38 H10
Rhyd-y-groes Gwynd 73 K10
Rhydymain Gwynd 61 P8

Rhyd-y-meirch Mons 40 D10
Rhydymwyn Flints 74 H10
Rhyd-y-pennau Cerdgn 49 L3
Rhyd-yr-onnen Gwynd 61 K11
Rhyd-y-sarn Gwynd 61 M4
Rhyl Denbgs 74 D7
Rhymney Caerph 39 Q10
Rhynd P & K 124 D9
Rhynie Abers 140 D10
Rhynie Highld 146 F9
Ribbesford Worcs 52 E6
Ribbleton Lancs 83 M9
Ribby Lancs 83 J9
Ribchester Lancs 83 P8
Riber Derbys 77 P11
Riby Lincs 80 D2
Riccall N York 86 B7
Riccarton Border 107 N10
Riccarton E Ayrs 104 H3
Richards Castle Herefs 51 N7
Richings Park Bucks 32 E6
Richmond Gt Lon 32 H7
Richmond N York 91 K6
Richmond Sheff 78 C7
Rich's Holford Somset 21 J6
Rickerscote Staffs 64 G8
Rickford N Som 28 G10
Rickham Devon 5 M9
Rickinghall Suffk 58 F5
Rickling Essex 45 P5
Rickling Green Essex 45 P6
Rickmansworth Herts 32 F3
Riddell Border 107 N5
Riddings Derbys 66 C2
Riddlecombe Devon 19 M10
Riddlesden C Brad 84 G6
Ridge BaNES 28 H11
Ridge Dorset 11 M7
Ridge Herts 33 J2
Ridge Wilts 23 L7
Ridgebourne Powys 50 E8
Ridge Green Surrey 15 K1
Ridge Lane Warwks 53 P2
Ridge Row Kent 17 M2
Ridgeway Derbys 78 C7
Ridgeway Worcs 53 K8
Ridgeway Cross Herefs 41 L2
Ridgewell Essex 46 C3
Ridgewood E Susx 15 N7
Ridgmont C Beds 44 D4
Riding Mill Nthumb 100 C6
Ridley Kent 34 A9
Ridley Nthumb 99 M5
Ridley Green Ches E 63 P1
Ridlington Norfk 71 L6
Ridlington Rutlnd 67 L11
Ridlington Street Norfk 71 L6
Ridsdale Nthumb 99 P1
Rievaulx N York 92 C9
Rigg D & G 98 C5
Riggend N Lans 114 D7
Righoul Highld 138 G5
Rigmadon Park Cumb 89 P9
Rigsby Lincs 80 H8
Rigside S Lans 105 R3
Riley Green Lancs 83 N10
Rileyhill Staffs 65 L9
Rilla Mill Cnwll 7 K10
Rillaton Cnwll 7 K10
Rillington N York 92 H11
Rimington Lancs 84 B6
Rimpton Somset 22 E9
Rimswell E R Yk 87 P9
Rinaston Pembks 37 J5
Rindleford Shrops 52 D2
Ringford D & G 96 E7
Ringinglow Sheff 77 P7
Ringland Norfk 70 H9
Ringles Cross E Susx 15 N6
Ringlestone Kent 34 F11
Ringley Bolton 76 E3
Ringmer E Susx 15 N8
Ringmore Devon 5 K7
Ringmore Devon 8 H10
Ringorm Moray 139 N7
Ring's End Cambs 68 H11
Ringsfield Suffk 59 M3
Ringsfield Corner Suffk 59 N3
Ringshall Herts 44 E9
Ringshall Suffk 58 F10
Ringshall Stocks Suffk 58 F10
Ringstead Nhants 55 N5
Ringstead Norfk 69 N4
Ringwood Hants 12 B4
Ringwould Kent 17 P1
Rinmore Abers 132 C1
Rinsey Cnwll 2 F9
Rinsey Croft Cnwll 2 F9
Ripe E Susx 15 P9
Ripley Derbys 66 C2
Ripley Hants 12 B5
Ripley N York 85 L3
Ripley Surrey 32 F11
Riplingham E R Yk 86 H9
Riplington Hants 25 L8
Ripon N York 85 L1
Rippingale Lincs 68 B6
Ripple Kent 35 P12
Ripple Worcs 41 P4
Ripponden Calder 84 F11
Risabus Ag & B 102 B1
Risbury Herefs 51 P9
Risby N Linc 86 G12
Risby Suffk 57 Q7
Risca Caerph 28 B4
Rise E R Yk 87 M7
Riseden E Susx 16 A5
Riseden Kent 16 C4
Risegate Lincs 68 D6
Riseholme Lincs 79 N8
Risehow Cumb 97 L11
Riseley Bed 55 P8
Riseley Wokham 31 P9
Rishangles Suffk 58 H7
Rishton Lancs 83 Q9
Rishworth Calder 84 F11
Rising Bridge Lancs 84 B10
Risley Derbys 66 D5
Risley Warrtn 76 C5
Risplith N York 85 K1
Rivar Wilts 30 G10
Rivenhall End Essex 46 E8
River Kent 17 N2
River W Susx 14 D6
River Bank Cambs 57 K7
Riverford Highld 137 P5
Riverhead Kent 33 P11
Rivers Corner Dorset 22 H10
Rivington Lancs 83 N12
Rivington Services Lancs 76 B1
Roachill Devon 20 C9
Roade Nhants 55 J10
Road Green Norfk 59 K2
Roadhead Cumb 98 G3
Roadmeetings S Lans 114 F11
Roadside E Ayrs 105 K6
Roadside Highld 151 L4
Roadwater Somset 20 G6
Roag Highld 134 E7
Roa Island Cumb 82 F2
Roan of Craigoch S Ayrs 104 E9
Roast Green Essex 45 N5
Roath Cardif 28 B7
Roberton Border 107 L7
Roberton S Lans 106 B4
Robertsbridge E Susx 16 C6
Roberttown Kirk 85 J10
Robeston Wathen Pembks 37 L7
Robgill Tower D & G 97 Q4
Robin Hill Staffs 76 G12
Robin Hood Lancs 75 N1
Robin Hood Leeds 85 L9
Robinhood End Essex 46 C4
Robin Hood's Bay N York 93 J6
Roborough Devon 4 H4
Roborough Devon 19 L10
Robroyston C Glas 114 B7
Roby Knows 75 M5
Roby Mill Lancs 75 N2
Rocester Staffs 65 L4
Roch Pembks 36 G6
Rochdale Rochdl 76 G1
Roche Cnwll 3 N2
Rochester Medway 34 D8
Rochester Nthumb 108 D10
Rochford Essex 34 F4
Rochford Worcs 52 B7
Roch Gate Pembks 36 G6
Rock Cnwll 6 D9
Rock Neath 27 J4
Rock Nthumb 109 K6
Rock W Susx 14 G8
Rock Worcs 52 D6
Rockbeare Devon 9 J6
Rockbourne Hants 23 P9
Rockcliffe Cumb 98 D6
Rockcliffe D & G 96 G7
Rockcliffe Cross Cumb 98 D6
Rock End Staffs 76 G12
Rockend Torbay 5 Q4
Rock Ferry Wirral 75 K6
Rockfield Highld 146 G8
Rockfield Mons 40 G8
Rockford Devon 19 P4
Rockford Hants 12 B3
Rockgreen Shrops 51 N5
Rockhampton S Glos 29 K4
Rockhead Cnwll 6 F8
Rockhill Shrops 51 J5
Rock Hill Worcs 52 H7
Rockingham Nhants 55 L2
Rockland All Saints Norfk 58 E1
Rockland St Mary Norfk 71 L11
Rockland St Peter Norfk 58 E1
Rockley Notts 78 H8
Rockley Wilts 30 D8
Rockliffe Lancs 84 C10
Rockville Ag & B 113 J3
Rockwell End Bucks 31 R5
Rockwell Green Somset 20 H9
Rodborough Gloucs 41 N10
Rodbourne Swindn 30 D5
Rodbourne Wilts 29 Q6
Rodd Herefs 51 K8
Roddam Nthumb 108 G6
Rodden Dorset 10 F8
Roddymoor Dur 100 F11
Rode Somset 22 H3
Rode Heath Ches E 76 E12
Rode Heath Ches E 76 G10
Rodel W Isls 152 d7
Roden Wrekin 63 P9
Rodhuish Somset 20 F5
Rodington Wrekin 63 Q9
Rodington Heath Wrekin 63 P9
Rodley Gloucs 41 M9
Rodley Leeds 85 K8
Rodmarton Gloucs 29 Q3
Rodmell E Susx 15 M9
Rodmersham Kent 34 G10
Rodmersham Green Kent 34 G10
Rodney Stoke Somset 22 B3
Rodsley Derbys 65 M4
Rodway Somset 21 L5
Roecliffe N York 85 M2
Roe Cross Tamesd 77 J4
Roe Green Herts 45 J10
Roe Green Herts 45 K5
Roe Green Salfd 76 D3
Roehampton Gt Lon 33 J7
Roffey W Susx 14 H4
Rogart Highld 146 C5
Rogate W Susx 25 P8
Roger Ground Cumb 89 K7
Rogerstone Newpt 28 C5
Roghadal W Isls 152 d7
Rogiet Mons 28 F5
Roke Oxon 31 N4
Roker Sundld 101 K6
Rollesby Norfk 71 N9
Rolleston Leics 67 J12
Rolleston Notts 67 J2
Rollestone Wilts 23 N4
Rolleston on Dove Staffs 65 N6
Rolston E R Yk 87 N6
Rolstone N Som 28 E10
Rolvenden Kent 16 E4
Rolvenden Layne Kent 16 E5
Romaldkirk Dur 90 G2
Romanby N York 91 N8
Romanno Bridge Border 115 L11
Romansleigh Devon 19 P9
Romden Castle Kent 16 F2
Romesdal Highld 134 G5
Romford Dorset 11 P3
Romford Gt Lon 33 P4
Romiley Stockp 76 H5
Romney Street Kent 33 Q10
Romsey Cambs 57 J9
Romsey Hants 24 F9
Romsley Shrops 52 E4
Romsley Worcs 52 H5
Rona Highld 135 L4
Ronachan Ag & B 111 Q10
Rood Ashton Wilts 29 P11
Rookhope Dur 99 P9
Rookley IoW 12 H8
Rookley Green IoW 12 H8
Rooks Bridge Somset 21 N3
Rooks Nest Somset 20 H7
Rookwith N York 91 L9
Roos E R Yk 87 P9
Roose Cumb 82 F1
Roosebeck Cumb 82 G2
Roothams Green Bed 56 B9
Ropley Hants 25 L7
Ropley Dean Hants 25 L7
Ropley Soke Hants 25 L6
Ropsley Lincs 67 N5
Rora Abers 141 P6
Rorrington Shrops 63 J12
Rosarie Moray 140 B6
Rose Cnwll 3 J4
Roseacre Lancs 83 K8
Rose Ash Devon 20 B10
Rosebank S Lans 114 E11
Rosebush Pembks 37 L5
Rosecare Cnwll 6 H5
Rosecliston Cnwll 3 K3
Rosedale Abbey N York 92 E7
Rose Green Essex 46 F6
Rose Green Suffk 46 G4
Rose Green Suffk 46 H3
Rose Green W Susx 14 C11
Rosehall Highld 145 L5
Rosehearty Abers 141 M2
Rose Hill E Susx 15 N7
Rose Hill Lancs 84 B9
Rosehill Shrops 63 M9
Roseisle Moray 139 L2
Roselands E Susx 16 A10
Rosemarket Pembks 37 J9
Rosemarkie Highld 138 D4
Rosemary Lane Devon 21 J10
Rosemount P & K 124 D4
Rosenannon Cnwll 6 D11
Rosenithon Cnwll 3 K10
Roser's Cross E Susx 15 Q7
Rosevean Cnwll 3 P3
Rosevine Cnwll 3 L7
Rosewarne Cnwll 2 F7
Rosewell Mdloth 115 P9
Roseworth S on T 91 P2
Roseworthy Cnwll 2 F6
Rosgill Cumb 89 N3
Roskestal Cnwll 2 B10
Roskhill Highld 134 E7
Roskorwell Cnwll 3 K9
Rosley Cumb 98 C9
Roslin Mdloth 115 N8
Rosliston Derbys 65 N9
Rosneath Ag & B 113 K5
Ross D & G 96 D9
Ross Nthumb 109 J2
Rossett Wrexhm 75 L12
Rossett Green N York 85 L5
Rossington Donc 78 G4
Ross-on-Wye Herefs 41 J7
Roster Highld 151 N8
Rostherne Ches E 76 D7
Rosthwaite Cumb 88 H4
Roston Derbys 65 L4
Rosudgeon Cnwll 2 E8
Rosyth Fife 115 L4
Rothbury Nthumb 108 H9
Rotherby Leics 66 H9
Rotherfield E Susx 15 Q5
Rotherfield Greys Oxon 31 P6
Rotherfield Peppard Oxon 31 P6
Rotherham Rothm 78 C5
Rothersthorpe Nhants 55 J9
Rotherwick Hants 31 P11
Rothes Moray 139 P6
Rothesay Ag & B 112 G8
Rothiebrisbane Abers 141 J8
Rothiemurchus Lodge Highld 130 H3
Rothienorman Abers 140 H8
Rothley Leics 66 F9
Rothley Nthumb 108 G12
Rothmaise Abers 140 G9
Rothwell Leeds 85 M9
Rothwell Lincs 80 C4
Rothwell Nhants 55 K4
Rotsea E R Yk 87 K5
Rottal Lodge Angus 132 B10
Rottingdean Br & H 15 L10
Rottington Cumb 88 C4
Roucan D & G 97 L3
Roud IoW 12 H8
Rougham Norfk 70 B8
Rougham Suffk 58 D8
Rough Close Staffs 64 G4
Rough Common Kent 35 K10
Roughlee Lancs 84 C7
Roughpark Abers 131 Q2
Roughton Lincs 80 E10
Roughton Norfk 71 J5
Roughton Shrops 52 D2
Roughway Kent 34 A11
Roundbush Essex 34 F2
Round Bush Herts 32 G3
Roundbush Green Essex 45 Q8
Round Green Luton 44 G7
Roundham Somset 10 C3
Roundhay Leeds 85 M8
Rounds Green Sandw 52 H3
Round Street Kent 34 B8
Roundstreet Common W Susx 14 F5
Roundswell Devon 19 K7
Roundway Wilts 30 B9
Roundyhill Angus 124 H3
Rousay Ork 147 c3
Rousdon Devon 9 P6
Rousham Oxon 43 K7
Rous Lench Worcs 53 J10
Routenburn N Ayrs 113 J9
Routh E R Yk 87 K7
Rout's Green Bucks 31 R3
Row Cnwll 6 G9
Row Cumb 89 M9
Row Cumb 99 J11
Rowanburn D & G 98 E3
Rowardennan Stirlg 113 M2
Rowarth Derbys 77 J6
Row Ash Hants 25 J10
Rowberrow Somset 28 F10
Rowborough IoW 12 H8
Rowde Wilts 29 R10
Rowden Devon 8 C5
Rowen Conwy 73 N9
Rowfield Derbys 65 M2
Rowfoot Nthumb 99 K6
Rowford Somset 21 K8
Row Green Essex 46 D7
Rowhedge Essex 47 J7
Rowhook W Susx 14 G4
Rowington Warwks 53 M7
Rowland Derbys 77 N9
Rowland's Castle Hants 13 M3
Rowlands Gill Gatesd 100 F6
Rowledge Surrey 25 P5
Rowley Dur 100 E8
Rowley E R Yk 86 H9
Rowley Shrops 63 J11
Rowley Hill Kirk 85 J12
Rowley Regis Sandw 52 H3
Rowlstone Herefs 40 E6
Rowly Surrey 14 F3
Rowner Hants 13 K4
Rowney Green Worcs 53 J6
Rownhams Hants 24 F10
Rownhams Services Hants 24 F9
Rowrah Cumb 88 E3
Rowsham Bucks 44 B8
Rowsley Derbys 77 N10
Rowstock Oxon 31 K5
Rowston Lincs 80 B12
Rowthorne Derbys 78 D10
Rowton Ches W 75 M11
Rowton Shrops 51 L4
Rowton Shrops 63 L9
Rowton Wrekin 63 Q8
Row Town Surrey 32 E9
Roxburgh Border 108 A4
Roxby N Linc 86 G11
Roxby N York 92 F3
Roxton Bed 56 C9
Roxwell Essex 46 B10
Royal Botanic Garden Edinburgh C Edin 115 N6
Royal Leamington Spa Warwks 53 Q7
Royal Oak Darltn 91 L2
Royal Oak Lancs 75 L3
Royal's Green Ches E 64 B4
Royal Sutton Coldfield Birm 53 L1
Royal Tunbridge Wells Kent 15 Q3
Royal Wootton Bassett Wilts 30 C6
Royal Yacht Britannia C Edin 115 N6
Roy Bridge Highld 129 J8
Roydhouse Kirk 77 N1
Roydon Essex 45 M9
Roydon Norfk 58 G4
Roydon Norfk 69 N7
Roydon Hamlet Essex 45 M10
Royston Barns 78 B1
Royston Herts 45 L3
Royton Oldham 76 G2
Rozel Jersey 13 d1
Ruabon Wrexhm 63 J3
Ruaig Ag & B 118 E3
Ruan High Lanes Cnwll 3 M6
Ruan Lanihorne Cnwll 3 L6
Ruan Major Cnwll 2 H11
Ruan Minor Cnwll 2 H11
Ruardean Gloucs 41 J8
Ruardean Hill Gloucs 41 K8
Ruardean Woodside Gloucs 41 J8
Rubery Birm 53 J5
Rubha Ban W Isls 152 c12
Ruckcroft Cumb 98 G9
Ruckhall Herefs 40 F4
Ruckinge Kent 17 J4
Ruckland Lincs 80 F8
Ruckley Shrops 63 P12
Rudbaxton Pembks 37 J6
Rudby N York 91 Q5
Rudchester Nthumb 100 E5
Ruddington Notts 66 F5
Ruddle Gloucs 41 K9
Ruddlemoor Cnwll 3 N3
Rudford Gloucs 41 M7
Rudge Somset 23 J3
Rudgeway S Glos 29 J5
Rudgwick W Susx 14 F4
Rudhall Herefs 41 J6
Rudheath Ches W 76 C9
Rudheath Woods Ches E 76 D9
Rudley Green Essex 46 E11
Rudloe Wilts 29 N8
Rudry Caerph 28 B5
Rudston E R Yk 87 L2
Rudyard Staffs 76 H12
Ruecastle Border 107 P6
Rufford Lancs 83 K12
Rufford Abbey Notts 78 G11
Rufforth C York 85 Q5
Rug Denbgs 62 E3
Rugby Warwks 54 E5
Rugby Services Warwks 54 E5
Rugeley Staffs 65 K8
Ruigh'riabhach Highld 144 C6
Ruisgarry W Isls 152 d7
Ruishton Somset 21 L8
Ruisigearraidh W Isls 152 d7
Ruislip Gt Lon 32 F5
Rùm Highld 126 F6
Rumbach Moray 140 B5
Rumbling Bridge P & K 115 J1
Rumburgh Suffk 59 L4
Rumby Hill Dur 100 F11
Rumford Cnwll 6 C10
Rumford Falk 114 G6
Rumney Cardif 28 B6
Rumwell Somset 21 K8
Runcorn Halton 75 N7
Runcton W Susx 14 C10
Runcton Holme Norfk 69 M10
Runfold Surrey 14 B1
Runhall Norfk 70 F10
Runham Norfk 71 P10
Runham Norfk 71 Q10
Runnington Somset 20 H9
Runsell Green Essex 46 D10
Runshaw Moor Lancs 83 M11
Runswick N York 92 G3
Runtaleave Angus 131 P10
Runwell Essex 34 D3
Ruscombe Wokham 31 R7
Rushall Herefs 41 K5
Rushall Norfk 59 J4
Rushall Wilts 23 P2
Rushall Wsall 65 J11
Rushbrooke Suffk 58 C8
Rushbury Shrops 51 N2
Rushden Herts 45 K5
Rushden Nhants 55 N7
Rushenden Kent 34 F8
Rusher's Cross E Susx 15 R5
Rushford Devon 7 N9
Rushford Norfk 58 D4
Rush Green Essex 47 L8
Rush Green Gt Lon 33 P5
Rush Green Herts 45 J7
Rush Green Warrtn 76 C6
Rushlake Green E Susx 16 A7
Rushmere Suffk 59 P3
Rushmere St Andrew Suffk 47 M2
Rushmoor Surrey 14 B3
Rushock Herefs 51 K9
Rushock Worcs 52 G6
Rusholme Manch 76 F5
Rushton Ches W 75 P11
Rushton Nhants 55 L4
Rushton Shrops 63 Q10
Rushton Spencer Staffs 76 H11
Rushwick Worcs 52 F10
Rushyford Dur 91 M1
Ruskie Stirlg 114 B1
Ruskington Lincs 68 B2
Rusland Cross Cumb 89 K9
Rusper W Susx 14 H3
Ruspidge Gloucs 41 K9
Russell Green Essex 46 D9
Russell's Water Oxon 31 P4
Russel's Green Suffk 59 K6
Russ Hill Surrey 15 J3
Rusthall Kent 15 Q3
Rustington W Susx 14 F10
Ruston N York 93 J10
Ruston Parva E R Yk 87 K3
Ruswarp N York 92 H5
Ruthall Shrops 51 Q3
Rutherford Border 107 Q4
Rutherglen S Lans 114 B9
Ruthernbridge Cnwll 6 E11
Ruthin Denbgs 74 F12
Ruthrieston C Aber 133 M3
Ruthven Abers 140 D6
Ruthven Angus 124 F3
Ruthven Highld 130 D4
Ruthven Highld 138 E9
Ruthvoes Cnwll 3 M2
Ruthwaite Cumb 97 P11
Ruthwell D & G 97 M5
Ruxley Gt Lon 33 N8
Ruxton Green Herefs 40 H8
Ruyton-XI-Towns Shrops 63 L8
Ryal Nthumb 100 C3
Ryall Dorset 10 B6
Ryall Worcs 41 P3
Ryarsh Kent 34 B10
Rycote Oxon 43 P10
Rydal Cumb 89 K5
Ryde IoW 13 K6
Rye E Susx 16 G7
Ryebank Shrops 63 N6
Ryeford Herefs 41 K7
Rye Foreign E Susx 16 F6
Rye Harbour E Susx 16 G7
Ryehill E R Yk 87 N10
Ryeish Green Wokham 31 P9
Rye Street Worcs 41 M4
Ryhall Rutlnd 67 P10
Ryhill Wakefd 85 M12
Ryhope Sundld 101 K7
Rylah Derbys 78 D10
Ryland Lincs 79 P8
Rylands Notts 66 E5
Rylstone N York 84 E3
Ryme Intrinseca Dorset 10 F3
Ryther N York 85 Q7
Ryton Gatesd 100 F5
Ryton N York 92 F11
Ryton Shrops 64 E11
Ryton Warwks 54 C3
Ryton-on-Dunsmore Warwks 54 C6
Ryton Woodside Gatesd 100 F6
RZSS Edinburgh Zoo C Edin 115 M6

S

Sabden Lancs 84 B7
Sabine's Green Essex 33 Q3
Sacombe Herts 45 L8
Sacombe Green Herts 45 L8
Sacriston Dur 100 G9
Sadberge Darltn 91 N3
Saddell Ag & B 103 L3
Saddington Leics 54 H2
Saddlebow Norfk 69 L9
Saddlescombe W Susx 15 K8
Sadgill Cumb 89 M6
Saffron Walden Essex 45 P4
Sageston Pembks 37 L10
Saham Hills Norfk 70 D11
Saham Toney Norfk 70 C11
Saighton Ches W 75 M11
St Abbs Border 117 K8
St Agnes Border 116 F8
St Agnes Cnwll 2 H4
St Agnes IoS 2 b3
St Agnes Mining District Cnwll 2 H4
St Albans Herts 44 G10
St Allen Cnwll 3 K4
St Andrew Guern 12 c2
St Andrews Fife 125 K9
St Andrews Botanic Garden Fife 125 K9
St Andrews Major V Glam 27 Q8
St Andrews Well Dorset 10 D6
St Anne's Lancs 82 H9
St Ann's D & G 106 E11
St Ann's Chapel Cnwll 7 M10
St Ann's Chapel Devon 5 L7
St Anthony-in-Meneage Cnwll 3 J9
St Anthony's Hill E Susx 16 A10
St Arvans Mons 28 H3
St Asaph Denbgs 74 E9
St Athan V Glam 27 N9
St Aubin Jersey 13 b2
St Austell Cnwll 3 P4
St Bees Cumb 88 C4
St Blazey Cnwll 3 Q4
St Blazey Gate Cnwll 3 P4
St Boswells Border 107 P4
St Brelade Jersey 13 a2
St Brelade's Bay Jersey 13 a2
St Breock Cnwll 6 E10
St Breward Cnwll 6 G9
St Briavels Gloucs 40 H10
St Brides Pembks 36 F8
St Brides Major V Glam 27 L7
St Brides Netherwent Mons 28 F4
St Brides-super-Ely V Glam 27 P7
St Brides Wentlooge Newpt 28 C6
St Budeaux C Plym 4 G5
Saintbury Gloucs 42 D4
St Buryan Cnwll 2 C9
St Catherine BaNES 29 M8
St Catherines Ag & B 121 L11
St Chloe Gloucs 41 N11
St Clears Carmth 37 Q7
St Cleer Cnwll 4 C3
St Clement Cnwll 3 L6
St Clement Jersey 13 d3
St Clether Cnwll 7 J8
St Colmac Ag & B 112 F8
St Columb Major Cnwll 3 M2
St Columb Minor Cnwll 3 K2
St Columb Road Cnwll 3 M3
St Combs Abers 141 P3
St Cross South Elmham Suffk 59 L4
St Cyrus Abers 133 J11
St David's P & K 123 N9
St Davids Pembks 36 E5
St Davids Cathedral Pembks 36 E5
St Day Cnwll 2 H6
St Decumans Somset 20 G5
St Dennis Cnwll 3 M3
St Devereux Herefs 40 F5
St Dogmaels Pembks 48 B11
St Dogwells Pembks 37 J5
St Dominick Cnwll 4 F3
St Donats V Glam 27 M8
St Edith's Marsh Wilts 29 R9
St Endellion Cnwll 6 E9
St Enoder Cnwll 3 L3
St Erme Cnwll 3 L4
St Erney Cnwll 4 E5
St Erth Cnwll 2 E7
St Erth Praze Cnwll 2 F7
St Ervan Cnwll 6 C10
St Eval Cnwll 6 C11
St Ewe Cnwll 3 N5
St Fagans Cardif 27 Q7
St Fagans National Museum of History Cardif 27 Q7
St Fergus Abers 141 Q5
St Fillans P & K 122 H8
St Florence Pembks 37 L10
St Gennys Cnwll 6 H5
St George Conwy 74 D8
St Georges N Som 28 E9
St George's V Glam 27 Q7
St George's Hill Surrey 32 F10
St Germans Cnwll 4 E5
St Giles in the Wood Devon 19 K9
St Giles-on-the-Heath Devon 7 L7
St Gluvia's Cnwll 3 K7
St Harmon Powys 50 D6
St Helen Auckland Dur 91 K1
St Helens Cumb 97 L11
St Helen's E Susx 16 E8
St Helens IoW 13 K7
St Helens St Hel 75 N5
St Helier Gt Lon 33 J9
St Helier Jersey 13 c2
St Hilary Cnwll 2 E8
St Hilary V Glam 27 N8
Saint Hill Devon 9 L3
Saint Hill W Susx 15 M4
St Illtyd Blae G 40 B11
St Ippolyts Herts 44 H6
St Ishmael's Pembks 36 G9
St Issey Cnwll 6 D10
St Ive Cnwll 4 D3
St Ive Cross Cnwll 4 D3
St Ives Cambs 56 F6
St Ives Cnwll 2 E6
St Ives Dorset 11 Q4
St James Norfk 71 K8
St James's End Nhants 55 J8
St James South Elmham Suffk 59 L4
St Jidgey Cnwll 6 D10
St John Cnwll 4 F6
St John Jersey 13 b1
St Johns Dur 100 D11
St John's E Susx 15 P4
St John's IoM 102 c5
St John's Kent 33 P11
St Johns Surrey 32 E10
St Johns Worcs 52 F10
St John's Chapel Devon 19 K7
St John's Chapel Dur 99 N10
St John's Fen End Norfk 69 K9
St John's Highway Norfk 69 K9
St John's Kirk S Lans 106 C3
St John's Town of Dalry D & G 96 C2
St John's Wood Gt Lon 33 K6
St Judes IoM 102 e3
St Just Cnwll 2 B8
St Just-in-Roseland Cnwll 3 L7
St Just Mining District Cnwll 2 B8
St Katherines Abers 141 J9
St Keverne Cnwll 3 K10
St Kew Cnwll 6 E9
St Kew Highway Cnwll 6 F9
St Keyne Cnwll 4 C4
St Lawrence Cnwll 6 F11
St Lawrence Essex 46 G11
St Lawrence IoW 13 J9
St Lawrence Jersey 13 b2
St Lawrence Kent 35 Q9
St Lawrence Bay Essex 46 G10
St Leonards Bucks 44 C10
St Leonards Dorset 11 Q4
St Leonards E Susx 16 E9
St Leonard's Street Kent 34 B11
St Levan Cnwll 2 B10
St Luke's Park Essex 34 D3
St Lythans V Glam 27 Q8
St Mabyn Cnwll 6 F10
St Madoes P & K 124 D8
St Margarets Herefs 40 E5
St Margarets Herts 45 M9
St Margaret's at Cliffe Kent 17 P2
St Margaret's Hope Ork 147 c6
St Margaret South Elmham Suffk 59 L4
St Marks IoM 102 d6
St Martin Cnwll 3 J9
St Martin Cnwll 4 C6
St Martin Guern 12 c3
St Martin Jersey 13 d2
St Martin's IoS 2 c1
St Martin's P & K 124 D7
St Martin's Shrops 63 K5
St Martin's Moor Shrops 63 K5
St Mary Jersey 13 b1
St Mary Bourne Hants 24 G3
St Marychurch Torbay 5 Q3
St Mary Church V Glam 27 N8
St Mary Cray Gt Lon 33 N8
St Mary Hill V Glam 27 M7
St Mary in the Marsh Kent 17 J5
St Mary's IoS 2 b2
St Mary's Ork 147 c5
St Mary's Bay Kent 17 K5
St Mary's Hoo Medway 34 E7
St Mary's Platt Kent 34 A11
St Maughans Mons 40 F8
St Maughans Green Mons 40 G8
St Mawes Cnwll 3 L8
St Mawgan Cnwll 6 C11
St Mellion Cnwll 4 F4
St Mellons Cardif 28 B6
St Merryn Cnwll 6 C10
St Mewan Cnwll 3 N4
St Michael Caerhays Cnwll 3 N6
St Michael Church Somset 21 M7
St Michael Penkevil Cnwll 3 L6
St Michaels Kent 16 F4
St Michaels Worcs 51 P7
St Michael's Mount Cnwll 2 E8
St Michael's on Wyre Lancs 83 K7
St Michael South Elmham Suffk 59 L4
St Minver Cnwll 6 D9
St Monans Fife 116 C1
St Neot Cnwll 4 B3
St Neots Cambs 56 D8
St Newlyn East Cnwll 3 K3
St Nicholas Pembks 36 H3
St Nicholas V Glam 27 P7
St Nicholas-at-Wade Kent 35 N9
St Ninians Stirlg 114 E3
St Olaves Norfk 71 N12
St Osyth Essex 47 K8
St Ouen Jersey 13 a1
St Owen's Cross Herefs 40 H7
St Paul's Cray Gt Lon 33 N8
St Paul's Walden Herts 44 H7
St Peter Jersey 13 b2
St Peter Port Guern 12 c2
St Peter's Guern 12 b3
St Peter's Kent 35 Q8
St Peter's Hill Cambs 56 E6
St Petrox Pembks 37 J11
St Pinnock Cnwll 4 B4
St Quivox S Ayrs 104 G5
St Ruan Cnwll 2 H11
St Sampson Guern 12 d1
St Saviour Guern 12 b2
St Saviour Jersey 13 c2
St Stephen Cnwll 3 M4
St Stephens Cnwll 4 F5
St Stephens Cnwll 7 L7
St Teath Cnwll 6 F8
St Thomas Devon 8 G6
St Margaret's Bay Kent 17 Q2
St Tudy Cnwll 6 F9
St Twynnells Pembks 37 J11
St Veep Cnwll 4 A6
St Vigeans Angus 125 M4
St Wenn Cnwll 6 D11
St Weonards Herefs 40 G7
St Winnow Cnwll 3 Q3
St y-Nyll V Glam 27 Q7
Salcombe Devon 5 M9
Salcombe Regis Devon 9 M7
Salcott-cum-Virley Essex 46 G9
Sale Traffd 76 E5
Saleby Lincs 81 J8
Sale Green Worcs 52 H9
Salehurst E Susx 16 D6
Salem Carmth 38 F6
Salem Cerdgn 61 L9
Salen Ag & B 119 P4
Salen Highld 127 M11
Salesbury Lancs 83 P8
Salford C Beds 44 D4
Salford Oxon 42 G6
Salford Salfd 76 E4
Salford Priors Warwks 53 K10
Salfords Surrey 15 K2
Salhouse Norfk 71 L9
Saline Fife 115 J3
Salisbury Wilts 23 P7
Salisbury Plain Wilts 23 N4
Salkeld Dykes Cumb 98 G10
Sallachy Highld 145 M3
Salle Norfk 70 G7
Salmonby Lincs 80 F9
Salperton Gloucs 42 C7
Salph End Bed 55 Q10
Salsburgh N Lans 114 E8
Salt Staffs 64 H6
Salta Cumb 97 M9
Saltaire C Brad 84 H7
Saltaire C Brad 84 H7
Saltash Cnwll 4 F5
Saltburn Highld 146 C11
Saltburn-by-the-Sea R & Cl 92 D3
Saltby Leics 67 L7
Salt Coates Cumb 97 P7
Saltcoats Cumb 88 E7
Saltcoats N Ayrs 104 D2
Saltcotes Lancs 83 J9
Saltdean Br & H 15 M10
Salterbeck Cumb 88 C1
Salterforth Lancs 84 D6
Salterswall Ches W 76 B10
Salterton Wilts 23 P6
Saltfleet Lincs 81 J5
Saltfleetby All Saints Lincs 81 J5
Saltfleetby St Clement Lincs 81 J5
Saltfleetby St Peter Lincs 80 H6
Saltford BaNES 29 K9
Salthouse Norfk 70 G3
Saltley Birm 53 L3
Saltmarsh Newpt 28 D6
Saltmarshe E R Yk 86 E10
Saltney Flints 75 L10
Salton N York 92 E10
Saltrens Devon 19 J9
Saltwick Nthumb 100 F2
Saltwood Kent 17 L4
Salvington W Susx 14 G9
Salwarpe Worcs 52 G8
Salway Ash Dorset 10 C5
Sambourne Warwks 53 K8
Sambrook Wrekin 64 D7
Samlesbury Lancs 83 N9
Samlesbury Bottoms Lancs 83 N9
Sampford Arundel Somset 20 H9
Sampford Brett Somset 20 H5
Sampford Courtenay Devon 8 B4
Sampford Moor Somset 20 H9
Sampford Peverell Devon 20 G10
Sampford Spiney Devon 7 P10
Samsonlane Ork 147 e3
Samson's Corner Essex 47 K8
Samuelston E Loth 116 B7
Sanaigmore Ag & B 110 F7
Sancreed Cnwll 2 C8
Sancton E R Yk 86 G7
Sand Somset 21 P4
Sandaig Highld 127 N4
Sandale Cumb 97 Q10
Sandal Magna Wakefd 85 M11
Sanday Ork 147 e2
Sanday Airport Ork 147 e2
Sandbach Ches E 76 D11
Sandbach Services Ches E 76 E11
Sandbank Ag & B 112 H5
Sandbanks BCP 11 P7
Sandend Abers 140 E3
Sanderstead Gt Lon 33 L10
Sandford Cumb 90 B3
Sandford Devon 8 F4
Sandford Dorset 11 M7
Sandford Hants 12 B4
Sandford IoW 13 J8
Sandford N Som 28 F10
Sandford S Lans 105 N1
Sandford Shrops 63 K7
Sandford Shrops 63 P5
Sandford-on-Thames Oxon 43 L11
Sandford Orcas Dorset 22 E9
Sandford St Martin Oxon 43 J6
Sandgate Kent 17 M4
Sandhaven Abers 141 M2
Sandhead D & G 94 G8
Sandhill Rothm 78 D4
Sandhills Dorset 10 F5
Sandhills Dorset 10 G3
Sand Hills Leeds 85 M7
Sandhills Oxon 43 L10
Sandhills Surrey 14 D3
Sandhoe Nthumb 100 B5
Sandhole Ag & B 112 E2
Sand Hole E R Yk 86 E8
Sandholme E R Yk 86 F9
Sandholme Lincs 68 G5
Sandhurst Br For 32 B10
Sandhurst Gloucs 41 N7
Sandhurst Kent 16 D5
Sandhurst Cross Kent 16 D5
Sand Hutton N York 86 C3
Sandhutton N York 91 P10
Sandiacre Derbys 66 D5
Sandilands Lincs 81 K7
Sandiway Ches W 75 Q9
Sandleheath Hants 23 P10
Sandleigh Oxon 31 K2
Sandley Dorset 22 H8
Sandling Kent 34 D10
Sandlow Green Ches E 76 E10
Sandness Shet 147 h6
Sandon Essex 46 C10
Sandon Herts 45 L5
Sandon Staffs 64 H6
Sandon Bank Staffs 64 H6
Sandown IoW 13 K8
Sandplace Cnwll 4 C5
Sandridge Herts 44 H9
Sandridge Wilts 29 Q9
Sandringham Norfk 69 N6
Sands Bucks 32 B4
Sandsend N York 92 H4
Sand Side Cumb 88 H10
Sandside Cumb 89 M10
Sandtoft N Linc 79 J2
Sandway Kent 34 F12
Sandwich Kent 35 P10
Sandwich Bay Kent 35 Q11
Sandwick Cumb 89 L3
Sandwick Shet 147 i9
Sandwick W Isls 152 g3
Sandwith Cumb 88 C4
Sandwith Newtown Cumb 88 C4
Sandy C Beds 56 D10
Sandy Bank Lincs 68 E1
Sandycroft Flints 75 K10
Sandy Cross E Susx 15 Q7
Sandy Cross Herefs 52 C9
Sandyford D & G 106 G11
Sandygate Devon 8 G9
Sandygate IoM 102 e3
Sandy Haven Pembks 36 G9
Sandyhills D & G 96 H7
Sandylands Lancs 83 K3

Sandy Lane C Brad 84 H8
Sandylane Staffs 64 D5
Sandylane Swans 26 E4
Sandy Lane Wilts 29 Q8
Sandy Lane Wrexhm 63 L4
Sandy Park Devon 8 D7
Sandysike Cumb 98 E5
Sandyway Herefs 40 G6
Sangobeg Highld 149 J3
Sangomore Highld 149 J3
Sankey Bridges Warrtn 75 P6
Sankyn's Green Worcs 52 E7
Sanna Highld 126 H10
Sanndabhaig W Isls 152 g3
Sannox N Ayrs 112 E12
Sanquhar D & G 105 P8
Santon Cumb 88 E6
Santon IoM 102 d6
Santon Bridge Cumb 88 F6
Santon Downham Suffk 58 B3
Sapcote Leics 54 D2
Sapey Common Herefs 52 C8
Sapiston Suffk 58 D5
Sapley Cambs 56 E6
Sapperton Derbys 65 M5
Sapperton Gloucs 41 Q11
Sapperton Lincs 67 P5
Saracen's Head Lincs 68 G7
Sarclet Highld 151 Q8
Sarisbury Hants 12 H3
Sarn Brdgnd 27 L6
Sarn Powys 50 H2
Sarnau Carmth 37 Q7
Sarnau Cerdgn 48 E10
Sarnau Gwynd 62 C4
Sarnau Powys 39 N5
Sarnau Powys 62 H9
Sarn Bach Gwynd 60 E7
Sarnesfield Herefs 51 L10
Sarn Mellteyrn Gwynd 60 D6
Sarn Park Services Brdgnd 27 L6
Sarn-wen Powys 63 J8
Saron Carmth 38 B4
Saron Carmth 38 F9
Saron Gwynd 72 H12
Saron Gwynd 73 J10
Sarratt Herts 32 F2
Sarre Kent 35 N9
Sarsden Oxon 42 G7
Sarson Hants 24 E4
Satley Dur 100 E9
Satmar Kent 17 N3
Satron N York 90 F7
Satterleigh Devon 19 N9
Satterthwaite Cumb 89 K8
Satwell Oxon 31 P6
Sauchen Abers 132 H2
Saucher P & K 124 D6
Sauchieburn Abers 132 G10
Saul Gloucs 41 M10
Saundby Notts 79 K6
Saundersfoot Pembks 37 M9
Saunderton Bucks 44 A11
Saunderton Station Bucks 32 A3
Saunton Devon 19 J6
Sausthorpe Lincs 80 G10
Saverley Green Staffs 64 H4
Savile Town Kirk 85 K11
Sawbridge Warwks 54 E7
Sawbridgeworth Herts 45 N8
Sawdon N York 93 J9
Sawley Derbys 66 D6
Sawley Lancs 84 B6
Sawley N York 85 K2
Sawston Cambs 57 J11
Sawtry Cambs 56 C4
Saxby Leics 67 K8
Saxby Lincs 79 P6
Saxby All Saints N Linc 87 J12
Saxelbye Leics 66 H8
Saxham Street Suffk 58 G8
Saxilby Lincs 79 M8
Saxlingham Norfk 70 F4
Saxlingham Green Norfk 59 K1
Saxlingham Nethergate Norfk 59 J1
Saxlingham Thorpe Norfk 59 J1
Saxmundham Suffk 59 M8
Saxondale Notts 66 H4
Saxon Street Cambs 57 N9
Saxtead Suffk 59 K7
Saxtead Green Suffk 59 K8
Saxtead Little Green Suffk 59 K7
Saxthorpe Norfk 70 G6
Saxton N York 85 P8
Sayers Common W Susx 15 K7
Scackleton N York 92 D12
Scadabay W Isls 152 e6
Scadabhagh W Isls 152 e6
Scafell Pike Cumb 88 G5
Scaftworth Notts 78 H5
Scagglethorpe N York 92 G12
Scalasaig Ag & B 111 J2
Scalby E R Yk 86 F9
Scalby N York 93 K8
Scald End Bed 55 P9
Scaldwell Nhants 55 J6
Scaleby Cumb 98 F5
Scalebyhill Cumb 98 F5
Scale Houses Cumb 98 H9
Scales Cumb 88 H12
Scales Cumb 89 K1
Scalesceugh Cumb 98 F8
Scalford Leics 67 J7
Scaling N York 92 F4
Scaling Dam R & Cl 92 F4
Scalloway Shet 147 i7
Scalpay Highld 135 L9
Scalpay W Isls 152 f6
Scamblesby Lincs 80 E8
Scammonden Kirk 84 F12
Scamodale Highld 127 Q9
Scampston N York 92 H11
Scampton Lincs 79 N8
Scaniport Highld 138 B8
Scapegoat Hill Kirk 84 G12
Scarba Ag & B 120 D12
Scarborough N York 93 L9
Scarcewater Cnwll 3 M4
Scarcliffe Derbys 78 E10
Scarcroft Leeds 85 M7
Scarfskerry Highld 151 N2
Scargill Dur 90 H4
Scarinish Ag & B 118 E4
Scarisbrick Lancs 75 L1
Scarness Cumb 97 P12
Scarning Norfk 70 D9
Scarrington Notts 67 J4
Scarth Hill Lancs 75 M2
Scarthingwell N York 85 P8
Scartho NE Lin 80 E2
Scatsta Airport Shet 147 i5
Scaur D & G 96 G7
Scawby N Linc 79 N3
Scawsby Donc 78 E3
Scawthorpe Donc 78 F2
Scawton N York 92 B10
Scayne's Hill W Susx 15 L6
Scethrog Powys 39 Q6
Scholar Green Ches E 76 F12
Scholes Kirk 77 M2
Scholes Kirk 85 J10
Scholes Leeds 85 M8
Scholes Rothm 78 C5
Scholes Wigan 75 Q3
School Aycliffe Dur 91 L2
School Green C Brad 84 H8
School Green Ches W 76 B11
Schoolgreen Wokham 31 Q9
School House Dorset 10 B4
Scissett Kirk 77 N2
Scleddau Pembks 36 H4
Scofton Notts 78 G7
Scole Norfk 58 H5
Scone P & K 124 C7
Sconser Highld 135 J9
Scoonie Fife 115 Q1
Scopwick Lincs 79 Q12
Scoraig Highld 144 C6
Scorborough E R Yk 87 J6
Scorrier Cnwll 2 H6
Scorriton Devon 5 L3
Scorton Lancs 83 L5
Scorton N York 91 L7
Sco Ruston Norfk 71 K8
Scotby Cumb 98 F7
Scotch Corner N York 91 L6
Scotch Corner Rest Area N York 91 L6
Scotforth Lancs 83 L3
Scot Hay Staffs 64 E3
Scothern Lincs 79 P8
Scotland Lincs 67 P6
Scotland Gate Nthumb 100 H1
Scotlandwell P & K 115 M1
Scot Lane End Bolton 76 B2
Scotscalder Station Highld 151 K5
Scotsdike Cumb 98 E4
Scot's Gap Nthumb 100 D1
Scotsmill Abers 140 E12
Scotstoun C Glas 113 Q8
Scotswood N u Ty 100 G5
Scotter Lincs 79 L4
Scotterthorpe Lincs 79 L3
Scottish Seabird Centre E Loth 116 D4
Scottlethorpe Lincs 67 Q8
Scotton Lincs 79 M4
Scotton N York 85 L3
Scotton N York 91 K7
Scottow Norfk 71 K7
Scott Willoughby Lincs 67 Q5
Scoulton Norfk 70 E12
Scounslow Green Staffs 65 K6
Scourie Highld 148 E7
Scourie More Highld 148 D8
Scousburgh Shet 147 i9
Scouthead Oldham 76 H3
Scrabster Highld 151 K3
Scraesburgh Border 107 Q6
Scrafield Lincs 80 F10
Scrainwood Nthumb 108 F8
Scrane End Lincs 68 G4
Scraptoft Leics 66 G11
Scratby Norfk 71 P9
Scrayingham N York 86 D3
Scrays E Susx 16 D7
Scredington Lincs 68 B4
Scremby Lincs 80 H10
Scremerston Nthumb 117 M11
Screveton Notts 67 J3
Scrivelsby Lincs 80 E10
Scriven N York 85 M3
Scrooby Notts 78 G5
Scropton Derbys 65 M6
Scrub Hill Lincs 68 E1
Scruton N York 91 M8
Scuggate Cumb 98 F3
Scullomie Highld 149 N4
Sculthorpe Norfk 70 C6
Scunthorpe N Linc 79 M2
Scurlage Swans 26 C5
Sea Somset 21 M10
Seaborough Dorset 10 C3
Seabridge Staffs 64 F3
Seabrook Kent 17 L4
Seaburn Sundld 101 K6
Seacombe Wirral 75 K5
Seacroft Leeds 85 M8
Seacroft Lincs 81 L11
Seadyke Lincs 68 F5
Seafield W Loth 115 J8
Seaford E Susx 15 N11
Seaforth Sefton 75 K4
Seagrave Leics 66 G8
Seagry Heath Wilts 29 Q6
Seaham Dur 101 K8
Seahouses Nthumb 109 L3
Seal Kent 33 Q11
Sealand Flints 75 K10
Seale Surrey 14 C1
Seamer N York 91 R5
Seamer N York 93 K10
Seamill N Ayrs 113 J12
Sea Palling Norfk 71 N7
Searby Lincs 79 Q3
Seasalter Kent 35 K9
Seascale Cumb 88 D6
Seathwaite Cumb 88 H4
Seathwaite Cumb 88 H7
Seatle Cumb 89 K10
Seatoller Cumb 88 H4
Seaton Cnwll 4 D6
Seaton Cumb 97 K12
Seaton Devon 9 N6
Seaton Dur 101 K8
Seaton E R Yk 87 M6
Seaton Kent 35 M10
Seaton Nthumb 101 J3
Seaton Rutlnd 55 M1
Seaton Burn N Tyne 100 G3
Seaton Carew Hartpl 101 M12
Seaton Delaval Nthumb 100 H3
Seaton Ross E R Yk 86 E7
Seaton Sluice Nthumb 101 J3
Seatown Dorset 10 C6
Seatown Moray 147 M11
Seave Green N York 92 B7
Seaview IoW 13 K6
Seaville Cumb 97 N7
Seavington St Mary Somset 21 N10
Seavington St Michael Somset 21 N10
Sebastopol Torfn 28 C3
Sebergham Cumb 98 D10
Seckington Warwks 65 N10
Second Severn Crossing Mons 28 G5
Sedbergh Cumb 89 Q8
Sedbury Gloucs 28 H4
Sedbusk N York 90 E8
Sedgeberrow Worcs 42 B4
Sedgebrook Lincs 67 L4
Sedge Fen Suffk 57 M4
Sedgefield Dur 91 N1
Sedgeford Norfk 69 N5
Sedgehill Wilts 23 J8
Sedgemoor Services Somset 21 N3
Sedgley Dudley 52 G2
Sedgley Park Bury 76 F3
Sedgwick Cumb 89 N9
Sedlescombe E Susx 16 D7
Sedrup Bucks 44 A9
Seed Kent 34 G11
Seend Wilts 29 Q10
Seend Cleeve Wilts 29 Q10
Seer Green Bucks 32 D4
Seething Norfk 59 L1
Sefton Sefton 75 K3
Seghill Nthumb 100 H3
Seighford Staffs 64 G7
Seion Gwynd 73 J10
Seisdon Staffs 52 F2
Selattyn Shrops 63 J5
Selborne Hants 25 N6
Selby N York 86 B9
Selham W Susx 14 D7
Selhurst Gt Lon 33 L9
Selkirk Border 107 M4
Sellack Herefs 40 H6
Sellafield Station Cumb 88 D6
Sellafirth Shet 147 j3
Sellan Cnwll 2 C8
Sellick's Green Somset 21 K9
Sellindge Kent 17 K3
Selling Kent 35 J11
Sells Green Wilts 29 Q10
Selly Oak Birm 53 K4
Selmeston E Susx 15 P9
Selsdon Gt Lon 33 L10
Selsey W Susx 13 Q6
Selsfield Common W Susx 15 L4
Selside Cumb 89 N7
Selside N York 90 C11
Selsley Gloucs 41 N11
Selsted Kent 17 M2
Selston Notts 66 D2
Selworthy Somset 20 E4
Semer Suffk 46 H2
Semington Wilts 29 P10
Semley Wilts 23 K8
Sempringham Lincs 68 C5
Send Surrey 32 E11
Send Marsh Surrey 32 E11
Senghenydd Caerph 27 Q4
Sennen Cnwll 2 B9
Sennen Cove Cnwll 2 B9
Sennybridge Powys 39 L6
Serlby Notts 78 G6
Sessay N York 91 Q11
Setchey Norfk 69 M9
Setley Hants 12 E5
Seton Mains E Loth 116 B6
Settle N York 84 B2
Settrington N York 86 F1
Seven Ash Somset 21 J7
Sevenhampton Gloucs 42 B7
Sevenhampton Swindn 30 E4
Seven Kings Gt Lon 33 N5
Sevenoaks Kent 33 P11
Sevenoaks Weald Kent 33 P12
Seven Sisters Neath 39 K10
Seven Springs Gloucs 41 Q8
Seven Star Green Essex 46 G6
Severn Beach S Glos 28 H5
Severn Bridge S Glos 28 H4
Severn Stoke Worcs 41 P3
Severn View Services S Glos 28 H4
Sevick End Bed 56 B10
Sevington Kent 17 J3
Sewards End Essex 45 Q4
Sewardstonebury Essex 33 M3
Sewell C Beds 44 E7
Sewerby E R Yk 87 M2
Seworgan Cnwll 2 H8
Sewstern Leics 67 M8
Sexhow N York 91 Q5
Sgalpaigh W Isls 152 f6
Sgiogarstaigh W Isls 152 h1
Shabbington Bucks 43 N10
Shackerley Shrops 64 F11
Shackerstone Leics 66 B10
Shacklecross Derbys 66 C5
Shackleford Surrey 14 D2
Shade Calder 84 D10
Shader W Isls 152 g1
Shadforth Dur 101 J10
Shadingfield Suffk 59 N4
Shadoxhurst Kent 16 H3
Shadwell Leeds 85 M7
Shadwell Norfk 58 D4
Shaftenhoe End Herts 45 M4
Shaftesbury Dorset 23 J9
Shaftholme Donc 78 F2
Shafton Barns 78 C2
Shafton Two Gates Barns 78 C2
Shakerley Wigan 76 C3
Shalbourne Wilts 30 G9
Shalcombe IoW 12 F7
Shalden Hants 25 M5
Shalden Green Hants 25 M5
Shaldon Devon 8 H10
Shalfleet IoW 12 G7
Shalford Essex 46 C6
Shalford Surrey 14 E1
Shalford Green Essex 46 C6
Shallowford Staffs 64 G6
Shalmsford Street Kent 35 K11
Shalstone Bucks 43 N4
Shamley Green Surrey 14 E2
Shandford Angus 132 D11
Shandon Ag & B 113 K4
Shandwick Highld 146 F10
Shangton Leics 55 J1
Shankhouse Nthumb 100 H3
Shanklin IoW 13 K8
Shantron Ag & B 113 L4
Shap Cumb 89 P4
Shapinsay Ork 147 d4
Shapwick Dorset 11 M4
Shapwick Somset 21 P6
Shard End Birm 53 M3
Shardlow Derbys 66 C6
Shareshill Staffs 64 H11
Sharlston Wakefd 85 N11
Sharlston Common Wakefd 85 N11
Sharmans Cross Solhll 53 L5
Sharnal Street Medway 34 D7
Sharnbrook Bed 55 N8
Sharneyford Lancs 84 C10
Sharnford Leics 54 D2
Sharnhill Green Dorset 10 H4
Sharoe Green Lancs 83 M8
Sharow N York 91 N12
Sharpenhoe C Beds 44 F5
Sharperton Nthumb 108 F9
Sharp Green Norfk 71 M8
Sharpness Gloucs 41 K11
Sharpthorne W Susx 15 L4
Sharptor Cnwll 7 K10
Sharpway Gate Worcs 52 H7
Sharrington Norfk 70 F5
Shatterford Worcs 52 E4
Shatterling Kent 35 N10
Shatton Derbys 77 M7
Shaugh Prior Devon 4 H4
Shave Cross Dorset 10 C5
Shavington Ches E 64 C2
Shaw C Brad 84 F8
Shaw Oldham 76 H2
Shaw Swindn 30 D5
Shaw W Berk 31 K8
Shaw Wilts 29 P9
Shawbirch Wrekin 64 B9
Shawbost W Isls 152 f2
Shawbury Shrops 63 P8
Shawclough Rochdl 84 D12
Shaw Common Gloucs 41 L6
Shawdon Hill Nthumb 108 H7
Shawell Leics 54 E5
Shawford Hants 24 H8
Shawforth Lancs 84 D11
Shaw Green Herts 45 K5
Shaw Green Lancs 83 M11
Shaw Green N York 85 K5
Shawhead D & G 96 H3
Shaw Mills N York 85 K3
Shawsburn S Lans 114 E11
Shear Cross Wilts 23 J5
Shearington D & G 97 L5
Shearsby Leics 54 G2
Shearston Somset 21 L7
Shebbear Devon 7 N3
Shebdon Staffs 64 E7
Shebster Highld 151 J4
Shedfield Hants 25 J10
Sheen Staffs 77 L11
Sheepbridge Derbys 78 B9
Sheep Hill Dur 100 F7
Sheepridge Kirk 84 H11
Sheepscar Leeds 85 L8
Sheepscombe Gloucs 41 P9
Sheepstor Devon 5 J3
Sheepwash Devon 7 P3
Sheepwash Nthumb 100 H1
Sheepway N Som 28 G7
Sheepy Magna Leics 65 Q12
Sheepy Parva Leics 65 Q11
Sheering Essex 45 P9
Sheerness Kent 34 G7
Sheerwater Surrey 32 E10
Sheet Hants 25 N8
Sheffield Cnwll 2 D9
Sheffield Sheff 78 B6
Sheffield Bottom W Berk 31 N8
Sheffield Green E Susx 15 M6
Sheffield Park & Garden E Susx 15 M6
Shefford C Beds 44 G4
Shefford Woodlands W Berk 30 H8
Sheigra Highld 148 E4
Sheinton Shrops 63 Q11
Shelderton Shrops 51 L5
Sheldon Birm 53 L4
Sheldon Derbys 77 M10
Sheldon Devon 9 L3
Sheldwich Kent 34 H11
Sheldwich Lees Kent 34 H11
Shelf Calder 84 H9
Shelfanger Norfk 58 G4
Shelfield Warwks 53 L8
Shelfield Wsall 65 J11
Shelfield Green Warwks 53 L8
Shelford Notts 66 H4
Shelford Warwks 54 C3
Shellacres Nthumb 108 E1
Shelley Essex 45 Q10
Shelley Kirk 77 M2
Shelley Suffk 47 J4
Shelley Far Bank Kirk 77 M2
Shellingford Oxon 30 G4
Shellow Bowells Essex 45 R10
Shelsley Beauchamp Worcs 52 D8
Shelsley Walsh Worcs 52 D8
Shelton Bed 55 P7
Shelton Norfk 59 J2
Shelton Notts 67 K3
Shelton Shrops 63 M9
Shelton Green Norfk 59 J3
Shelton Lock C Derb 66 B6
Shelton Under Harley Staffs 64 F4
Shelve Shrops 63 K12
Shelwick Herefs 40 H3
Shenfield Essex 33 R3
Shenington Oxon 42 H3
Shenley Herts 32 H2
Shenley Brook End M Keyn 44 B5
Shenleybury Herts 44 H11
Shenley Church End M Keyn 44 B4
Shenmore Herefs 40 E4
Shennanton D & G 95 L5
Shenstone Staffs 65 L11
Shenstone Worcs 52 F6
Shenstone Woodend Staffs 65 L12
Shenton Leics 66 C12
Shenval Moray 139 N10
Shepeau Stow Lincs 68 F9
Shephall Herts 45 J7
Shepherd's Bush Gt Lon 33 J6
Shepherd's Green Oxon 31 P6
Shepherds Patch Gloucs 41 L10
Shepherdswell Kent 17 N1
Shepley Kirk 77 M2
Shepperdine S Glos 29 J3
Shepperton Surrey 32 F9
Shepperton Green Surrey 32 F9
Shepreth Cambs 56 H11
Shepshed Leics 66 D8
Shepton Beauchamp Somset 21 N10
Shepton Mallet Somset 22 E5
Shepton Montague Somset 22 F7
Shepway Kent 34 D11
Sheraton Dur 101 L11
Sherborne Dorset 22 E10
Sherborne Gloucs 42 E8
Sherborne Somset 22 D2
Sherborne St John Hants 25 K2
Sherbourne Warwks 53 N8
Sherburn Dur 101 J10
Sherburn N York 93 J11
Sherburn Hill Dur 101 J10
Sherburn in Elmet N York 85 P8
Shere Surrey 14 F1
Shereford Norfk 70 C6
Sherfield English Hants 24 D9
Sherfield on Loddon Hants 31 P10
Sherfin Lancs 84 B10
Sherford Devon 4 H6
Sherford Devon 5 N8
Sherford Dorset 11 M6
Sheriffhales Shrops 64 D9
Sheriff Hutton N York 86 C2
Sheringham Norfk 70 H3
Sherington M Keyn 44 C2
Shermanbury W Susx 14 H7
Shernborne Norfk 69 N6
Sherrington Wilts 23 L5
Sherston Wilts 29 N5
Sherwood C Nott 66 F3
Sherwood Forest Notts 78 G11
Shetland Islands Shet 147 i6
Shettleston C Glas 114 B8
Shevington Wigan 75 P2
Shevington Moor Wigan 75 P2
Shevington Vale Wigan 75 N2
Sheviock Cnwll 4 E6
Shibden Head C Brad 84 G9
Shide IoW 12 H7
Shidlaw Nthumb 108 C2
Shiel Bridge Highld 136 C12
Shieldaig Highld 135 P5
Shieldhill D & G 97 L1
Shieldhill Falk 114 G6
Shieldhill House Hotel S Lans 106 C2
Shields N Lans 114 D10
Shielfoot Highld 127 M10
Shielhill Angus 124 H1
Shielhill Inver 113 K7
Shifford Oxon 42 H11
Shifnal Shrops 64 D10
Shilbottle Nthumb 109 K8
Shildon Dur 91 L1
Shillford E Rens 113 N10
Shillingford Devon 20 F8
Shillingford Oxon 31 M4
Shillingford Abbot Devon 8 G7
Shillingford St George Devon 8 G7
Shillingstone Dorset 11 K2
Shillington C Beds 44 G5
Shillmoor Nthumb 108 E8
Shilton Oxon 42 F10
Shilton Warwks 54 C4
Shimpling Norfk 58 H4
Shimpling Suffk 58 C10
Shimpling Street Suffk 58 C10
Shincliffe Dur 100 H10
Shiney Row Sundld 101 J8
Shinfield Wokham 31 Q8
Shingay Cambs 45 K2
Shingle Street Suffk 47 Q3
Shinnersbridge Devon 5 N4
Shinness Highld 145 M2
Shipbourne Kent 33 Q12
Shipdham Norfk 70 E10
Shipham Somset 28 F11
Shiphay Torbay 5 Q4
Shiplake Oxon 31 Q7
Shiplake Row Oxon 31 Q6
Shiplate N Som 28 E11
Shipley C Brad 84 H8
Shipley Derbys 66 D3
Shipley Shrops 52 E1
Shipley W Susx 14 G6
Shipley Bridge Surrey 15 K3
Shipley Hatch Kent 16 H3
Shipmeadow Suffk 59 M3
Shippea Hill Station Cambs 57 M4
Shippon Oxon 31 K3
Shipston-on-Stour Warwks 42 F4
Shipton Bucks 43 Q6
Shipton Gloucs 42 B8
Shipton N York 85 Q3
Shipton Shrops 51 P2
Shipton Bellinger Hants 24 C4
Shipton Gorge Dorset 10 D6
Shipton Green W Susx 13 P5
Shipton Moyne Gloucs 29 P4
Shipton-on-Cherwell Oxon 43 K8
Shiptonthorpe E R Yk 86 F6
Shipton-under-Wychwood Oxon 42 G8
Shirburn Oxon 31 P3
Shirdley Hill Lancs 75 K1
Shire Cumb 99 J11
Shirebrook Derbys 78 E10
Shiregreen Sheff 78 B5
Shirehampton Bristl 28 H7
Shiremoor N Tyne 101 J4
Shirenewton Mons 28 G4
Shire Oak Wsall 65 K11
Shireoaks Notts 78 F7
Shirkoak Kent 16 G4
Shirland Derbys 78 C12
Shirlett Shrops 52 C1
Shirley C Sotn 24 F10
Shirley Derbys 65 N4
Shirley Gt Lon 33 L9
Shirley Solhll 53 L5
Shirl Heath Herefs 51 M8
Shirrell Heath Hants 25 J10
Shirwell Devon 19 L6
Shiskine N Ayrs 103 N4
Shittlehope Dur 100 C10
Shobdon Herefs 51 L8
Shobley Hants 12 C3
Shobrooke Devon 8 G4
Shoby Leics 66 H8
Shocklach Ches W 63 M2
Shocklach Green Ches W 63 M2
Shoeburyness Sthend 34 G5
Sholden Kent 35 P12
Sholing C Sotn 12 G2
Shoot Hill Shrops 63 L9
Shop Cnwll 6 C10
Shop Cnwll 18 E10
Shopwyke W Susx 14 C9
Shore Rochdl 84 D11
Shoreditch Gt Lon 33 L6
Shoreditch Somset 21 K9
Shoreham Kent 33 P10
Shoreham-by-Sea W Susx 15 J10
Shoreswood Nthumb 117 L12
Shorley Hants 25 K8
Shorncote Gloucs 30 B3
Shorne Kent 34 C8
Shortacross Cnwll 4 D5
Shortbridge E Susx 15 N6
Shortfield Common Surrey 25 P5
Shortgate E Susx 15 P8
Short Heath Birm 53 L2
Shortheath Hants 25 N6
Short Heath Wsall 64 H12
Shortlanesend Cnwll 3 K5
Shortlees E Ayrs 104 H3
Shortstown Bed 44 F2
Shorwell IoW 12 G8
Shoscombe BaNES 29 L11
Shotesham Norfk 71 K12
Shotgate Essex 34 D4
Shotley Suffk 47 M5
Shotley Bridge Dur 100 E7
Shotleyfield Nthumb 100 D7
Shotley Gate Suffk 47 M5
Shottenden Kent 35 J11
Shottermill Surrey 14 C4
Shottery Warwks 53 M9
Shotteswell Warwks 43 J3
Shottisham Suffk 47 P3
Shottle Derbys 65 P2
Shottlegate Derbys 65 Q3
Shotton Dur 91 N2
Shotton Dur 101 K10
Shotton Flints 75 K10
Shotton Nthumb 100 G3
Shotton Nthumb 108 D4
Shotton Colliery Dur 101 K10
Shotts N Lans 114 F9
Shotwick Ches W 75 K9
Shougle Moray 139 M5
Shouldham Norfk 69 N10
Shouldham Thorpe Norfk 69 M10
Shoulton Worcs 52 E9
Shover's Green E Susx 16 B5
Shraleybrook Staffs 64 E2
Shrawardine Shrops 63 L9
Shrawley Worcs 52 E7
Shreding Green Bucks 32 E6
Shrewley Warwks 53 N7
Shrewsbury Shrops 63 N9
Shrewton Wilts 23 N5
Shripney W Susx 14 D10
Shrivenham Oxon 30 F4
Shropham Norfk 58 E2
Shroton Dorset 23 J10
Shrub End Essex 46 H7
Shucknall Herefs 41 J3
Shudy Camps Cambs 46 A3
Shuna Ag & B 120 E11
Shurdington Gloucs 41 Q8
Shurlock Row W & M 32 B7
Shurnock Worcs 53 J8
Shurrery Highld 151 J5
Shurrery Lodge Highld 151 J5
Shurton Somset 21 K4
Shustoke Warwks 53 N3
Shute Devon 8 G5
Shute Devon 9 N5
Shutford Oxon 42 H4
Shut Heath Staffs 64 F8
Shuthonger Gloucs 41 P5
Shutlanger Nhants 55 J10
Shutterton Devon 8 H9
Shutt Green Staffs 64 G10
Shuttington Warwks 65 N11
Shuttlewood Derbys 78 D9
Shuttleworth Bury 84 B11
Siabost W Isls 152 f2
Siadar W Isls 152 g1
Sibbertoft Nhants 54 H4
Sibdon Carwood Shrops 51 L4
Sibford Ferris Oxon 42 H4
Sibford Gower Oxon 42 H4
Sible Hedingham Essex 46 D5
Sibley's Green Essex 46 A6
Siblyback Cnwll 7 J10
Sibsey Lincs 68 G2
Sibsey Fenside Lincs 68 G2
Sibson Cambs 56 B1
Sibson Leics 66 B12
Sibster Highld 151 P6
Sibthorpe Notts 67 J3
Sibthorpe Notts 79 J9
Sibton Suffk 59 M7
Sicklesmere Suffk 58 C8
Sicklinghall N York 85 M5
Sidbrook Somset 21 L8
Sidbury Devon 9 L6
Sidbury Shrops 52 C3
Sid Cop Barns 78 C2
Sidcot N Som 28 F11
Sidcup Gt Lon 33 N8
Siddick Cumb 97 K12
Siddington Ches E 76 F9
Siddington Gloucs 30 B2
Sidemoor Worcs 52 H6
Sidestrand Norfk 71 K4
Sidford Devon 9 L7
Sidlesham W Susx 13 Q5
Sidlesham Common W Susx 13 P5
Sidley E Susx 16 C9
Sidmouth Devon 9 L7
Siefton Shrops 51 N4
Sigford Devon 8 E10
Sigglesthorne E R Yk 87 M6
Sigingstone V Glam 27 M8
Signet Oxon 42 F9
Silchester Hants 31 N10
Sileby Leics 66 G9
Silecroft Cumb 88 F10
Silfield Norfk 70 G12
Silian Cerdgn 49 J10
Silkstead Hants 24 G8
Silkstone Barns 77 P3
Silkstone Common Barns 77 P3
Silk Willoughby Lincs 67 Q4
Silloth Cumb 97 M7
Silpho N York 93 K8
Silsden C Brad 84 F6
Silsoe C Beds 44 F4
Silton Dorset 22 H7
Silverburn Mdloth 115 M9
Silverdale Lancs 89 M11
Silverdale Staffs 64 E3
Silver End Essex 46 E8
Silverford Abers 141 J3
Silvergate Norfk 70 H6
Silver Jubilee Bridge Halton 75 N7
Silverlace Green Suffk 59 L8
Silverley's Green Suffk 59 L5
Silverstone Nhants 43 N3
Silver Street Kent 34 F10
Silver Street Somset 22 C7
Silverton Devon 8 H4
Silverwell Cnwll 3 J5
Silvington Shrops 52 B5
Simister Bury 76 F2
Simmondley Derbys 77 J5
Simonburn Nthumb 99 N3
Simonsbath Somset 19 P5
Simonsburrow Devon 21 J10
Simonstone Lancs 84 B8
Simonstone N York 90 E8
Simprim Border 117 J12
Simpson M Keyn 44 C4
Simpson Cross Pembks 36 H6
Sinclair's Hill Border 116 H11
Sinclairston E Ayrs 105 J6
Sinderby N York 91 N10
Sinderhope Nthumb 99 N8
Sinderland Green Traffd 76 D6
Sindlesham Wokham 31 Q8
Sinfin C Derb 65 Q6
Singleborough Bucks 43 Q5
Single Street Gt Lon 33 N10
Singleton Kent 16 H3
Singleton Lancs 83 J7
Singleton W Susx 14 C8
Singlewell Kent 34 B8
Sinkhurst Green Kent 16 E2
Sinnahard Abers 132 D2
Sinnington N York 92 F9
Sinope Leics 66 C9
Sinton Worcs 52 F8
Sinton Worcs 52 F8
Sinton Green Worcs 52 E8
Sipson Gt Lon 32 F7
Sirhowy Blae G 39 Q9
Sissinghurst Kent 16 D3
Siston S Glos 29 L7
Sitcott Devon 7 L6
Sithney Cnwll 2 G8
Sithney Common Cnwll 2 G9
Sithney Green Cnwll 2 G8
Sittingbourne Kent 34 F9
Six Ashes Shrops 52 E3
Six Bells Blae G 40 B11
Six Hills Leics 66 G8
Sixhills Lincs 80 D6
Six Mile Bottom Cambs 57 L9
Sixmile Cottages Kent 17 K2
Sixpenny Handley Dorset 23 M10
Six Rues Jersey 13 b1
Sizewell Suffk 59 P8
Skaill Ork 147 d5
Skara Brae Ork 147 b4
Skares E Ayrs 105 K6
Skateraw Abers 133 L6
Skateraw E Loth 116 G6
Skeabost Highld 134 G6
Skeeby N York 91 K6
Skeffington Leics 67 J11
Skeffling E R Yk 87 Q11
Skegby Notts 78 D11
Skegby Notts 79 K9
Skegness Lincs 81 L11
Skelbo Highld 146 E6
Skelbo Street Highld 146 E6
Skelbrooke Donc 78 E1
Skeldyke Lincs 68 G5
Skellingthorpe Lincs 79 M9
Skellorn Green Ches E 76 G7
Skellow Donc 78 E2
Skelmanthorpe Kirk 77 N2
Skelmersdale Lancs 75 M2
Skelmorlie N Ayrs 113 J8
Skelpick Highld 150 C5
Skelston D & G 96 G1
Skelton C York 85 R4
Skelton Cumb 98 E11
Skelton E R Yk 86 E10
Skelton N York 91 J6
Skelton R & Cl 92 D3
Skelton on Ure N York 85 M2
Skelwith Bridge Cumb 89 K6
Skendleby Lincs 80 H9
Skene House Abers 133 J2
Skenfrith Mons 40 F7
Skerne E R Yk 87 K4
Skerray Highld 149 P4
Skerricha Highld 148 F6
Skerton Lancs 83 L3
Sketchley Leics 54 C2
Sketty Swans 26 F4
Skewen Neath 26 H3
Skewsby N York 86 B1
Skeyton Norfk 71 K7
Skeyton Corner Norfk 71 K7
Skiall Highld 151 J3
Skidbrooke Lincs 80 H5
Skidbrooke North End Lincs 80 H5
Skidby E R Yk 87 J8
Skigersta W Isls 152 h1
Skilgate Somset 20 F8
Skillington Lincs 67 M7
Skinburness Cumb 97 M7
Skinflats Falk 114 G5
Skinidin Highld 134 D6
Skinners Green W Berk 31 K9
Skinningrove R & Cl 92 E3
Skipness Ag & B 112 C9
Skipper's Bridge D & G 98 D2
Skiprigg Cumb 98 E9
Skipsea E R Yk 87 M4
Skipsea Brough E R Yk 87 M4
Skipton N York 84 E5
Skipton-on-Swale N York 91 N10
Skipwith N York 86 C7
Skirbeck Lincs 68 G3
Skirlaugh E R Yk 87 L7
Skirling Border 106 E2
Skirmett Bucks 31 Q4
Skirpenbeck E R Yk 86 D4
Skirwith Cumb 99 J11
Skirwith N York 90 B12
Skirza Highld 151 Q3
Skitby Cumb 98 F5
Skittle Green Bucks 43 Q11
Skokholm Island Pembks 36 E9
Skomer Island Pembks 36 E8
Skulamus Highld 135 M11
Skyborry Green Shrops 51 J6
Skye Green Essex 46 F7
Skye of Curr Highld 138 H11
Skyreholme N York 84 G3
Slack Calder 84 E9
Slackbuie Highld 138 C7
Slackcote Oldham 76 H2
Slack Head Cumb 89 M11
Slackholme End Lincs 81 K9
Slacks of Cairnbanno Abers 141 K7
Slad Gloucs 41 P10
Slade Devon 9 L3
Slade Devon 19 K4
Slade Devon 20 C8
Slade End Oxon 31 M4
Slade Green Gt Lon 33 P7
Slade Heath Staffs 64 G11
Slade Hooton Rothm 78 E6
Sladesbridge Cnwll 6 E10
Slades Green Worcs 41 N5
Slaggyford Nthumb 99 K8
Slaidburn Lancs 83 Q5
Slaithwaite Kirk 84 G12
Slaley Derbys 77 P12
Slaley Nthumb 100 B7
Slamannan Falk 114 F7
Slapton Bucks 44 D7
Slapton Devon 5 N7
Slapton Nhants 43 N2
Slattocks Rochdl 76 G2
Slaugham W Susx 15 J5
Slaughterford Wilts 29 N7
Slawston Leics 55 K2
Sleaford Hants 25 P6
Sleaford Lincs 67 Q3
Sleagill Cumb 89 P3
Sleap Shrops 63 N7
Sleapford Wrekin 64 B9
Sleapshyde Herts 44 H10
Sleasdairidh Highld 145 P6
Slebech Pembks 37 K7
Sledge Green Worcs 41 N5
Sledmere E R Yk 86 H2
Sleetbeck Cumb 98 G3
Sleight Dorset 11 N5
Sleightholme Dur 90 F5
Sleights N York 92 H5
Slepe Dorset 11 M6
Slickly Highld 151 P3
Sliddery N Ayrs 103 N5
Sligachan Highld 135 J10
Sligrachan Ag & B 112 H3
Slimbridge Gloucs 41 L11
Slindon Staffs 64 F6
Slindon W Susx 14 D9
Slinfold W Susx 14 G4
Sling Gloucs 41 J10
Sling Gwynd 73 K10
Slingsby N York 92 E11
Slip End C Beds 44 F8
Slip End Herts 45 K4
Slipton Nhants 55 N5
Slitting Mill Staffs 65 J8
Slochd Highld 138 F11
Slockavullin Ag & B 112 B2
Sloley Norfk 71 K7
Sloncombe Devon 8 D7
Sloothby Lincs 81 J9
Slough Slough 32 D6
Slough Green Somset 21 L9
Slough Green W Susx 15 K5
Slumbay Highld 136 B8
Slyfield Surrey 32 E12
Slyne Lancs 83 L2
Smailholm Border 107 Q2
Smallbridge Rochdl 84 D12
Smallbrook Devon 8 G5
Smallbrook Gloucs 29 J2
Smallburgh Norfk 71 L7
Smallburn E Ayrs 105 M4
Smalldale Derbys 77 L8
Smalldale Derbys 77 M7
Small Dole W Susx 15 J8
Smalley Derbys 66 C3
Smalley Common Derbys 66 C4
Smalley Green Derbys 66 C3
Smallfield Surrey 15 K2
Smallford Herts 44 H10
Small Heath Birm 53 L3
Small Hythe Kent 16 F5
Smallridge Devon 9 P4
Smallthorne C Stke 64 G2
Smallways N York 91 J4
Smallwood Ches E 76 E11
Small Wood Hey Lancs 83 J5
Smallworth Norfk 58 E4
Smannell Hants 24 F4
Smardale Cumb 90 B5
Smarden Kent 16 F2
Smarden Bell Kent 16 F2

Smart's Hill Kent 15 P2
Smeafield Nthumb 108 H2
Smeatharpe Devon 9 M3
Smeeth Kent 17 J3
Smeeton Westerby Leics 54 H2
Smelthouses N York 85 J2
Smerral Highld 151 L10
Smestow Staffs 52 F2
Smethwick Sandw 53 J3
Smethwick Green Ches E 76 E11
Smirisary Highld 127 L9
Smisby Derbys 65 Q8
Smith End Green Worcs 52 E10
Smithfield Cumb 98 F5
Smith Green Lancs 83 L4
Smithies Barns 77 Q2
Smithincott Devon 9 K2
Smith's End Herts 45 M4
Smith's Green Essex 45 Q7
Smith's Green Essex 46 B4
Smithstown Highld 143 L9
Smithton Highld 138 D7
Smithy Bridge Rochdl 84 D12
Smithy Green Ches E 76 D9
Smithy Green Stockp 76 G6
Smithy Houses Derbys 66 C3
Smockington Leics 54 D3
Smoo Highld 149 J3
Smythe's Green Essex 46 G8
Snade D & G 96 G1
Snailbeach Shrops 63 L11
Snailwell Cambs 57 M7
Snainton N York 93 J10
Snaith E R Yk 86 B10
Snake Pass Inn Derbys 77 L5
Snape N York 91 M10
Snape Suffk 59 M9
Snape Green Lancs 83 J12
Snape Street Suffk 59 M9
Snaresbrook Gt Lon 33 M4
Snarestone Leics 65 Q10
Snarford Lincs 79 P7
Snargate Kent 16 H5
Snave Kent 16 H5
Sneachill Worcs 52 G10
Snead Powys 51 K2
Sneath Common Norfk 58 H3
Sneaton N York 92 H5
Sneatonthorpe N York 92 H5
Snelland Lincs 79 Q7
Snelson Ches E 76 E8
Snelston Derbys 65 L3
Snetterton Norfk 58 E2
Snettisham Norfk 69 N5
Snibston Leics 66 C9
Snig's End Gloucs 41 M6
Snitter Nthumb 108 G9
Snitterby Lincs 79 N5
Snitterfield Warwks 53 N8
Snitterton Derbys 77 P11
Snitton Shrops 51 P5
Snoadhill Kent 16 G2
Snodhill Herefs 40 D4
Snodland Kent 34 C10
Snoll Hatch Kent 16 B1
Snowden Hill Barns 77 N4
Snowdon Gwynd 61 K1
Snowdon Kent 35 N12
Snowdonia National Park 61 P6
Snow End Herts 45 M5
Snowshill Gloucs 42 C5
Snow Street Norfk 58 G4
Soake Hants 13 L2
Soar Cardif 27 P6
Soar Devon 5 L9
Soar Powys 39 M5
Soay Highld 126 H2
Soberton Hants 25 K10
Soberton Heath Hants 25 K10
Sockbridge Cumb 89 M1
Sockburn Darltn 91 N5
Sodom Denbgs 74 F9
Sodylt Bank Shrops 63 K4
Soham Cambs 57 L6
Soham Cotes Cambs 57 L6
Solas W Isls 152 c7
Solbury Pembks 36 H8
Soldon Devon 7 L3
Soldon Cross Devon 7 L3
Soldridge Hants 25 L6
Sole Street Kent 17 K1
Sole Street Kent 34 B9
Solihull Solhll 53 M5
Sollas W Isls 152 c7
Sollers Dilwyn Herefs 51 M9
Sollers Hope Herefs 41 J5
Sollom Lancs 83 K11
Solva Pembks 36 F6
Solwaybank D & G 98 C3
Somerby Leics 67 K10
Somerby Lincs 79 Q2
Somercotes Derbys 66 C1
Somerford BCP 12 B6
Somerford Keynes Gloucs 30 B3
Somerley W Susx 13 P5
Somerleyton Suffk 59 P1
Somersal Herbert Derbys 65 L5
Somersby Lincs 80 G9
Somersham Cambs 56 G5
Somersham Suffk 58 G11
Somerton Oxon 43 K6
Somerton Somset 22 C7
Somerton Suffk 57 Q10
Somerwood Shrops 63 P9
Sompting W Susx 14 H10
Sompting Abbotts W Susx 14 H9
Sonning Wokham 31 Q7
Sonning Common Oxon 31 P6
Sonning Eye Oxon 31 Q7
Sontley Wrexhm 63 K3
Sopley Hants 12 B5
Sopwell Herts 44 H10
Sopworth Wilts 29 N5
Sorbie D & G 95 N9
Sordale Highld 151 L4
Sorisdale Ag & B 126 E11
Sorn E Ayrs 105 K4
Sornhill E Ayrs 105 J3
Sortat Highld 151 N4
Sotby Lincs 80 D8
Sots Hole Lincs 80 C11
Sotterley Suffk 59 N4
Soughton Flints 74 H10
Soulbury Bucks 44 C6
Soulby Cumb 89 M2
Soulby Cumb 90 B4
Souldern Oxon 43 L5
Souldrop Bed 55 N8
Sound Ches E 64 B3
Sound Muir Moray 140 B5
Soundwell S Glos 29 K7
Sourton Devon 7 P6
Soutergate Cumb 88 H10
South Acre Norfk 69 Q9
South Alkham Kent 17 N2
Southall Gt Lon 32 G6
South Allington Devon 5 N9
South Alloa Falk 114 F3
Southam Gloucs 41 R6
Southam Warwks 54 C8
South Ambersham W Susx 14 C7
Southampton C Sotn 24 G11
Southampton Airport Hants 24 G10
South Anston Rothm 78 E7
South Ascot W & M 32 C8
South Ashford Kent 16 H2
South Baddesley Hants 12 F5
South Bank C York 86 B5
South Bank R & Cl 92 B3
South Barrow Somset 22 E8
South Beddington Gt Lon 33 K9
South Beer Cnwll 7 K6
South Benfleet Essex 34 D5
South Bockhampton BCP 12 B5
Southborough Gt Lon 33 M9
Southborough Kent 15 Q2
Southbourne BCP 12 B6
Southbourne W Susx 13 N4
South Bowood Dorset 10 C5
South Bramwith Donc 78 G1
South Brent Devon 5 L5
South Brewham Somset 22 G6
South Broomhill Nthumb 109 L10
Southburgh Norfk 70 E11
South Burlingham Norfk 71 M10
Southburn E R Yk 87 J4
South Cadbury Somset 22 E8
South Carlton Lincs 79 N8
South Carlton Notts 78 F7
South Cave E R Yk 86 G9
South Cerney Gloucs 30 B3
South Chailey E Susx 15 M7
South Chard Somset 10 B3
South Charlton Nthumb 109 K6
South Cheriton Somset 22 F8
South Church Dur 91 L1
Southchurch Sthend 34 F5
South Cleatlam Dur 91 J3
South Cliffe E R Yk 86 G8
South Clifton Notts 79 K9
South Cockerington Lincs 80 G6
South Cornelly Brdgnd 27 K6
Southcott Cnwll 6 H6
Southcott Devon 7 Q6
Southcott Devon 8 E8
Southcott Devon 19 J10
Southcott Wilts 30 E10
Southcourt Bucks 44 A9
South Cove Suffk 59 P4
South Creake Norfk 70 C5
South Crosland Kirk 77 L1
South Croxton Leics 66 H10
South Dalton E R Yk 86 H6
South Darenth Kent 33 Q8
South Dell W Isls 152 g1
South Downs National Park 15 L9
South Duffield N York 86 C8
South Earlswood Surrey 15 K1
Southease E Susx 15 M10
South Elkington Lincs 80 F6
South Elmsall Wakefd 78 D1
Southend Ag & B 103 J8
South End E R Yk 87 R11
South End Hants 23 N10
South End Herefs 41 L3
South End N Linc 87 L11
South End Norfk 58 E3
Southend Wilts 30 E7
Southend Airport Essex 34 F4
Southend-on-Sea Sthend 34 F5
Southerby Cumb 98 D10
Southernden Kent 16 F2
Southerndown V Glam 27 L7
Southerness D & G 97 K7
South Erradale Highld 143 K11
Southerton Devon 9 K6
Southery Norfk 57 M2
South Fambridge Essex 34 F3
South Fawley W Berk 30 H6
South Ferriby N Linc 87 J11
South Field E R Yk 87 J10
Southfield Falk 114 F7
Southfleet Kent 33 R8
Southford IoW 13 J9
Southgate Gt Lon 33 K3
Southgate Norfk 69 N5
Southgate Norfk 70 C5
Southgate Norfk 70 H7
Southgate Swans 26 E5
South Godstone Surrey 15 L1
South Gorley Hants 12 B3
South Gosforth N u Ty 100 G5
South Green Essex 34 B4
South Green Essex 47 J8
South Green Kent 34 E10
South Green Norfk 70 F10
South Green Suffk 58 H5
South Gyle C Edin 115 M7
South Hanningfield Essex 34 C3
South Harting W Susx 25 N9
South Hayling Hants 13 M5
South Hazelrigg Nthumb 108 H5
South Heath Bucks 44 C11
South Heighton E Susx 15 N10
South Hetton Dur 101 K9
South Hiendley Wakefd 78 C1
South Hill Cnwll 7 L10
South Hill Somset 21 Q8
South Hinksey Oxon 43 L11
South Hole Devon 18 E9
South Holmwood Surrey 14 H2
South Hornchurch Gt Lon 33 P5
South Horrington Somset 22 D4
South Huish Devon 5 L8
South Hykeham Lincs 79 M10
South Hylton Sundld 101 J7
Southill C Beds 44 H3
Southington Hants 24 H3
South Kelsey Lincs 79 P4
South Kessock Highld 138 C6
South Killingholme N Linc 87 L12
South Kilvington N York 91 P10
South Kilworth Leics 54 G4
South Kirkby Wakefd 78 D2
South Knighton Devon 8 F10
South Kyme Lincs 68 D2
Southleigh Devon 9 N6
South Leigh Oxon 43 J10
South Leverton Notts 79 K7
South Littleton Worcs 42 C2
South Lopham Norfk 58 F4
South Luffenham Rutlnd 67 M11
South Lynn Norfk 69 M8
South Malling E Susx 15 N8
South Marston Swindn 30 E5
South Merstham Surrey 33 K12
South Middleton Nthumb 108 G5
South Milford N York 85 P9
South Milton Devon 5 L8
South Mimms Herts 33 J2
South Mimms Services Herts 33 J2
Southminster Essex 34 G2
South Molton Devon 19 N8
South Moor Dur 100 F8
Southmoor Oxon 31 J3
South Moreton Oxon 31 M5
Southmuir Angus 124 H2
South Mundham W Susx 14 C10
South Muskham Notts 79 K12
South Newbald E R Yk 86 G8
South Newington Oxon 43 J5
South Newsham Nthumb 100 H2
South Newton Wilts 23 N6
South Nitshill C Glas 113 P9
South Normanton Derbys 78 D12
South Norwood Gt Lon 33 L8
South Nutfield Surrey 15 K1
South Ockendon Thurr 33 Q6
Southoe Cambs 56 D8
Southolt Suffk 59 J7
South Ormsby Lincs 80 G8
Southorpe C Pete 67 Q11
South Ossett Wakefd 85 L11
South Otterington N York 91 N9
Southover Dorset 10 F6
Southover E Susx 16 B6
South Owersby Lincs 79 Q5
Southowram Calder 84 H10
South Park Surrey 15 J1
South Perrott Dorset 10 D3
South Petherton Somset 21 P10
South Petherwin Cnwll 7 K8
South Pickenham Norfk 70 C11
South Pill Cnwll 4 F5
South Pool Devon 5 N8
South Poorton Dorset 10 E5
Southport Sefton 82 H11
South Queensferry C Edin 115 L6
South Radworthy Devon 19 P7
South Rauceby Lincs 67 P3
South Raynham Norfk 70 C7
South Reddish Stockp 76 G5
Southrepps Norfk 71 K5
South Reston Lincs 80 H7
Southrey Lincs 80 C10
South Ronaldsay Ork 147 c6
Southrop Gloucs 42 E11
Southrope Hants 25 L4
South Runcton Norfk 69 M10
South Scarle Notts 79 L11
Southsea C Port 13 L5
Southsea Wrexhm 63 J2
South Shian Ag & B 120 G4
South Shields S Tyne 101 K5
South Shore Bpool 82 H8
Southside Dur 91 J1
South Somercotes Lincs 80 H5
South Stainley N York 85 L3
South Stifford Thurr 33 Q7
South Stoke BaNES 29 M10
South Stoke Oxon 31 M5
South Stoke W Susx 14 E9
South Stour Kent 17 J3
South Street Kent 34 B9
South Street Kent 35 J10
South Street Kent 35 K9
South Tarbrax S Lans 115 J10
South Tawton Devon 8 C6
South Tehidy Cnwll 2 G6
South Thoresby Lincs 80 H8
South Thorpe Dur 91 J4
South Town Hants 25 L6
Southtown Norfk 71 Q11
Southtown Somset 21 M10
South Uist W Isls 152 c10
Southwaite Cumb 98 F9
Southwaite Services Cumb 98 F9
South Walsham Norfk 71 M9
Southwark Gt Lon 33 L6
South Warnborough Hants 25 M4
Southwater W Susx 14 H5
Southwater Street W Susx 14 H5
Southway C Plym 4 G4
Southway Somset 22 C5
South Weald Essex 33 Q4
Southwell Dorset 10 G10
Southwell Notts 66 H1
South Weston Oxon 31 P3
South Wheatley Cnwll 7 J6
South Wheatley Notts 79 J6
Southwick Hants 13 K3
Southwick Nhants 55 P2
Southwick Somset 21 N4
Southwick Sundld 101 K6
Southwick W Susx 15 J10
Southwick Wilts 23 J2
South Widcombe BaNES 29 J11
South Wigston Leics 54 F1
South Willingham Lincs 80 D7
South Wingate Dur 101 K11
South Wingfield Derbys 66 B1
South Witham Lincs 67 M8
Southwold Suffk 59 Q5
South Wonston Hants 24 H6
Southwood Norfk 71 M11
Southwood Somset 22 D7
South Woodham Ferrers Essex 34 E3
South Wootton Norfk 69 M7
South Wraxall Wilts 29 N10
South Zeal Devon 8 C6
Sovereign Harbour E Susx 16 B10
Sowerby Calder 84 F10
Sowerby N York 91 Q10
Sowerby Bridge Calder 84 G10
Sowerby Row Cumb 98 D10
Sower Carr Lancs 83 J6
Sowerhill Somset 20 D8
Sowhill Torfn 28 C2
Sowley Green Suffk 57 N10
Sowood Calder 84 G11
Sowton Devon 4 H4
Sowton Devon 9 J6
Soyland Town Calder 84 F11
Spa Common Norfk 71 L6
Spain's End Essex 46 B4
Spalding Lincs 68 E7
Spaldington E R Yk 86 D8
Spaldwick Cambs 56 C6
Spalford Notts 79 L10
Spanby Lincs 68 B4
Spanish Green Hants 31 P10
Sparham Norfk 70 G8
Sparhamill Norfk 70 G8
Spark Bridge Cumb 89 J10
Sparket Cumb 89 L2
Sparkford Somset 22 E8
Sparkhill Birm 53 L4
Sparkwell Devon 5 J5
Sparrow Green Norfk 70 D9
Sparrowpit Derbys 77 K7
Sparrows Green E Susx 16 B4
Sparsholt Hants 24 G7
Sparsholt Oxon 30 H5
Spartylea Nthumb 99 N8
Spath Staffs 65 K5
Spaunton N York 92 F9
Spaxton Somset 21 K6
Spean Bridge Highld 128 H8
Spear Hill W Susx 14 G7
Spearywell Hants 24 E8
Speen Bucks 32 B2
Speen W Berk 31 K8
Speeton N York 93 N11
Speke Lpool 75 M7
Speldhurst Kent 15 Q2
Spellbrook Herts 45 N8
Spelmonden Kent 16 C3
Spelsbury Oxon 42 H7
Spen Kirk 85 J10
Spencers Wood Wokham 31 P9
Spen Green Ches E 76 F11
Spennithorne N York 91 J9
Spennymoor Dur 100 H11
Spernall Warwks 53 K8
Spetchley Worcs 52 G10
Spetisbury Dorset 11 M4
Spexhall Suffk 59 M5
Spey Bay Moray 139 Q3
Speybridge Highld 139 J10
Speyview Moray 139 N7
Spilsby Lincs 80 H10
Spindlestone Nthumb 109 J3
Spinkhill Derbys 78 D8
Spinningdale Highld 146 B7
Spion Kop Notts 78 F10
Spirthill Wilts 30 A7
Spital Wirral 75 K7
Spital Hill Donc 78 G5
Spital in the Street Lincs 79 N6
Spithurst E Susx 15 M7
Spittal E Loth 116 B6
Spittal E R Yk 86 E5
Spittal Highld 151 L6
Spittal Nthumb 117 M11
Spittal Pembks 37 J6
Spittalfield P & K 124 C5
Spittal of Glenmuick Abers 131 P7
Spittal of Glenshee P & K 131 L10
Spittal-on-Rule Border 107 P6
Spixworth Norfk 71 K9
Splatt Cnwll 6 D9
Splatt Cnwll 7 J7
Splatt Devon 8 B4
Splayne's Green E Susx 15 M6
Splott Cardif 28 B7
Spofforth N York 85 M5
Spondon C Derb 66 C5
Spon Green Flints 75 J11
Spooner Row Norfk 58 G1
Sporle Norfk 70 C10
Spott E Loth 116 F6
Spottiswoode Border 116 E11
Spratton Nhants 55 J6
Spreakley Surrey 25 P5
Spreyton Devon 8 D5
Spriddlestone Devon 4 H6
Spridlington Lincs 79 P7
Springburn C Glas 114 A7
Springfield D & G 98 C4
Springfield Essex 46 C10
Springfield Fife 124 G10
Springhill Staffs 64 H11
Springhill Staffs 65 K11
Springholm D & G 96 G4
Springside N Ayrs 104 G2
Springthorpe Lincs 79 L6
Spring Vale Barns 77 N3
Springwell Sundld 100 H6
Sproatley E R Yk 87 M8
Sproston Green Ches W 76 D10
Sprotbrough Donc 78 E3
Sproughton Suffk 47 K3
Sprouston Border 108 B3
Sprowston Norfk 71 K9
Sproxton Leics 67 L7
Sproxton N York 92 C10
Spunhill Shrops 63 L5
Spurstow Ches E 75 P12
Spyway Dorset 10 E6
Square and Compass Pembks 36 G4
Stableford Shrops 52 D1
Stableford Staffs 64 E4
Stacey Bank Sheff 77 P5
Stackhouse N York 84 B2
Stackpole Pembks 37 J11
Stackpole Elidor Pembks 37 J11
Stacksford Norfk 58 F3
Stacksteads Lancs 84 C11
Staddiscombe C Plym 4 H6
Staddlethorpe E R Yk 86 F9
Staden Derbys 77 K9
Stadhampton Oxon 31 M3
Stadhlaigearraidh W Isls 152 b10
Staffield Cumb 98 G9
Staffin Highld 135 J2
Stafford Staffs 64 G7
Stafford Services (northbound) Staffs 64 G6
Stafford Services (southbound) Staffs 64 G6
Stagsden Bed 55 N11
Stainborough Barns 77 Q3
Stainburn Cumb 88 D1
Stainburn N York 85 K5
Stainby Lincs 67 M7
Staincross Barns 77 Q2
Staindrop Dur 91 J2
Staines-upon-Thames Surrey 32 E8
Stainfield Lincs 67 Q7
Stainfield Lincs 80 C9
Stainforth Donc 78 G2
Stainforth N York 84 B2
Staining Lancs 82 H8
Stainland Calder 84 G11
Stainsacre N York 93 J5
Stainsby Derbys 78 D10
Stainton Cumb 89 M1
Stainton Cumb 89 N9
Stainton Cumb 98 D7
Stainton Donc 78 F5
Stainton Dur 90 H3
Stainton Middsb 91 Q4
Stainton N York 91 J7
Stainton by Langworth Lincs 79 Q8
Staintondale N York 93 K7
Stainton Grove Dur 90 H3
Stainton le Vale Lincs 80 C5
Stainton with Adgarley Cumb 88 H12
Stair Cumb 88 H2
Stair E Ayrs 104 H5
Stairfoot Barns 78 B3
Stairhaven D & G 95 K8
Staithes N York 92 F3
Stakeford Nthumb 100 H1
Stake Pool Lancs 83 K5
Stakes Hants 13 M3
Stalbridge Dorset 22 G10
Stalbridge Weston Dorset 22 G10
Stalham Norfk 71 M7
Stalham Green Norfk 71 M7
Stalisfield Green Kent 34 G11
Stalland Common Norfk 58 F1
Stallen Dorset 22 E10
Stallingborough NE Lin 80 D1
Stalling Busk N York 90 E9
Stallington Staffs 64 H4
Stalmine Lancs 83 J6
Stalmine Moss Side Lancs 83 J6
Stalybridge Tamesd 76 H4
Stambourne Essex 46 C4
Stambourne Green Essex 46 C4
Stamford Lincs 67 P10
Stamford Nthumb 109 L6
Stamford Bridge Ches W 75 M10
Stamford Bridge E R Yk 86 D4
Stamfordham Nthumb 100 D4
Stamford Hill Gt Lon 33 L5
Stanah Lancs 83 J6
Stanborough Herts 45 J9
Stanbridge C Beds 44 D7
Stanbridge Dorset 11 N4
Stanbury C Brad 84 F8
Stand N Lans 114 D7
Standburn Falk 114 G7
Standeford Staffs 64 G10
Standen Kent 16 F3
Standen Street Kent 16 E5
Standerwick Somset 22 H3
Standford Hants 25 P6
Standingstone Cumb 97 L11
Standish Gloucs 41 M10
Standish Wigan 75 P2
Standish Lower Ground Wigan 75 P2
Standlake Oxon 43 J11
Standon Hants 24 G8
Standon Herts 45 M7
Standon Staffs 64 E5
Standon Green End Herts 45 L7
Standwell Green Suffk 58 H6
Stane N Lans 114 F9
Stanfield Norfk 70 D8
Stanford C Beds 44 H3
Stanford Kent 17 K3
Stanford Shrops 63 K9
Stanford Bishop Herefs 52 C10
Stanford Bridge Worcs 52 D7
Stanford Bridge Wrekin 64 D7
Stanford Dingley W Berk 31 M8
Stanford in the Vale Oxon 30 H4
Stanford le Hope Thurr 34 B6
Stanford on Avon Nhants 54 F5
Stanford on Soar Notts 66 E8
Stanford on Teme Worcs 52 D7
Stanford Rivers Essex 33 P2
Stanfree Derbys 78 D9
Stanghow R & Cl 92 D4
Stanground C Pete 56 D1
Stanhill Lancs 83 Q9
Stanhoe Norfk 69 Q5
Stanhope Border 106 F4
Stanhope Dur 100 C10
Stanhope Kent 16 H3
Stanhope Bretby Derbys 65 P8
Stanion Nhants 55 N3
Stanklin Worcs 52 F6
Stanley Derbys 66 C4
Stanley Dur 100 F7
Stanley Notts 78 D11
Stanley P & K 124 C6
Stanley Shrops 52 D4
Stanley Staffs 64 H2
Stanley Wakefd 85 M10
Stanley Common Derbys 66 C4
Stanley Crook Dur 100 F10
Stanley Ferry Wakefd 85 M10
Stanley Gate Lancs 75 M3
Stanley Moor Staffs 64 G2
Stanley Pontlarge Gloucs 42 B5
Stanmer Br & H 15 L9
Stanmore Gt Lon 32 H4
Stanmore Hants 24 H7
Stanmore W Berk 31 K6
Stannersburn Nthumb 99 L1
Stanningfield Suffk 58 C9
Stanningley Leeds 85 K8
Stannington Nthumb 100 G2
Stannington Sheff 77 P6
Stannington Station Nthumb 100 G2
Stansbatch Herefs 51 K8
Stansfield Suffk 57 P10
Stanshope Staffs 65 L1
Stanstead Suffk 58 B11
Stanstead Abbotts Herts 45 M9
Stansted Kent 33 R10
Stansted Airport Essex 45 Q7
Stansted Mountfitchet Essex 45 P6
Stanton Derbys 65 P8
Stanton Gloucs 42 C5
Stanton Mons 40 D7
Stanton Nthumb 109 J11
Stanton Staffs 65 L3
Stanton Suffk 58 E6
Stanton by Bridge Derbys 66 B7
Stanton by Dale Derbys 66 D4
Stanton Cross Nhants 55 M7
Stanton Drew BaNES 29 J9
Stanton Fitzwarren Swindn 30 E4
Stanton Harcourt Oxon 43 J10
Stanton Hill Notts 78 D11
Stanton in Peak Derbys 77 N11
Stanton Lacy Shrops 51 N5
Stanton Lees Derbys 77 P11
Stanton Long Shrops 51 P2
Stanton-on-the-Wolds Notts 66 G6
Stanton Prior BaNES 29 K10
Stanton St Bernard Wilts 30 C10
Stanton St John Oxon 43 M10
Stanton St Quintin Wilts 29 P6
Stanton Street Suffk 58 D7
Stanton under Bardon Leics 66 D10
Stanton upon Hine Heath Shrops 63 P7
Stanton Wick BaNES 29 J10
Stantway Gloucs 41 L9
Stanwardine in the Field Shrops 63 L7
Stanwardine in the Wood Shrops 63 M6
Stanway Essex 46 G7
Stanway Gloucs 42 C5
Stanway Green Essex 46 G7
Stanway Green Suffk 59 K6
Stanwell Surrey 32 F7
Stanwell Moor Surrey 32 F7
Stanwick Nhants 55 N6
Stanwick St John N York 91 K4
Stanwix Cumb 98 E7
Staoinebrig W Isls 152 b10
Stape N York 92 G8
Stapehill Dorset 11 P5
Stapeley Ches E 64 C3
Stapenhill Staffs 65 N8
Staple Kent 35 N11
Staple Cross Devon 20 G9
Staplecross E Susx 16 D6
Staplefield W Susx 15 K5
Staple Fitzpaine Somset 21 L9
Stapleford Cambs 57 J10
Stapleford Herts 45 K8
Stapleford Leics 67 K8
Stapleford Lincs 79 L12
Stapleford Notts 66 D5
Stapleford Wilts 23 N6
Stapleford Abbotts Essex 33 P3
Stapleford Tawney Essex 33 P3
Staplegrove Somset 21 K8
Staplehay Somset 21 K9
Staple Hill Worcs 53 J6
Staplehurst Kent 16 D2
Staplers IoW 12 H7
Staplestreet Kent 35 J10
Stapleton Cumb 98 G4
Stapleton Herefs 51 K7
Stapleton Leics 54 C1
Stapleton N York 91 M4
Stapleton Shrops 63 M11
Stapleton Somset 21 P9
Stapley Somset 21 K10
Staploe Bed 56 C8
Staplow Herefs 41 L3
Star Fife 124 F12
Star IoA 72 H9
Star Pembks 37 P3
Star Somset 28 F10
Starbeck N York 85 L4
Starbotton N York 90 F11
Starcross Devon 9 J8
Stareton Warwks 53 Q6
Starkholmes Derbys 77 P12
Starlings Green Essex 45 N5
Starr's Green E Susx 16 D8
Starston Norfk 59 J4
Start Devon 5 N8
Startforth Dur 90 H3
Startley Wilts 29 Q6
Statenborough Kent 35 P11
Statham Warrtn 76 C6
Stathe Somset 21 N7
Stathern Leics 67 K6
Station Town Dur 101 K11
Staughton Green Cambs 56 C7
Staughton Highway Cambs 56 C8
Staunton Gloucs 40 H9
Staunton Gloucs 41 M6
Staunton in the Vale Notts 67 K3
Staunton on Arrow Herefs 51 L8
Staunton on Wye Herefs 40 E3
Staveley Cumb 89 M7
Staveley Derbys 78 C8
Staveley N York 85 M3
Staveley-in-Cartmel Cumb 89 K9
Staverton Devon 5 N4
Staverton Gloucs 41 P7
Staverton Nhants 54 E8
Staverton Wilts 29 N10
Staverton Bridge Gloucs 41 P7
Stawell Somset 21 N6
Stawley Somset 20 G9
Staxigoe Highld 151 Q6
Staxton N York 93 K11
Staylittle Cerdgn 49 L3
Staylittle Powys 50 B2
Staynall Lancs 83 J6
Staythorpe Notts 67 J1
Stead C Brad 84 H6
Stean N York 90 H12
Stearsby N York 86 B1
Steart Somset 21 L4
Stebbing Essex 46 B7
Stebbing Green Essex 46 C7
Stechford Birm 53 L3
Stede Quarter Kent 16 F3
Stedham W Susx 14 B6
Steel Nthumb 99 P6
Steel Cross E Susx 15 P4
Steelend Fife 115 J3
Steele Road Border 107 N11
Steel Green Cumb 88 G11
Steel Heath Shrops 63 P5
Steen's Bridge Herefs 51 P9
Steep Hants 25 N8
Steephill IoW 13 J9
Steep Lane Calder 84 F10
Steeple Dorset 11 L8
Steeple Essex 46 G11
Steeple Ashton Wilts 29 P11
Steeple Aston Oxon 43 K6
Steeple Barton Oxon 43 K7
Steeple Bumpstead Essex 46 B3
Steeple Claydon Bucks 43 P6
Steeple Gidding Cambs 56 C4
Steeple Langford Wilts 23 M6
Steeple Morden Cambs 45 K3
Steep Marsh Hants 25 N8
Steeton C Brad 84 F6
Stein Highld 134 E4
Stella Gatesd 100 F5
Stelling Minnis Kent 17 L1
Stembridge Somset 21 P9
Stenalees Cnwll 3 P3
Stenhouse D & G 105 P11
Stenhousemuir Falk 114 F5
Stenigot Lincs 80 E7
Stenness Ork 147 b4
Stenscholl Highld 134 H2
Stenson Fields Derbys 65 Q6
Stenton E Loth 116 E6
Steòrnabhagh W Isls 152 g3
Stepaside Pembks 37 M9
Stepford D & G 96 H2
Stepney Gt Lon 33 L6
Stepping Hill Stockp 76 G6
Steppingley C Beds 44 E4
Stepps N Lans 114 B7
Sternfield Suffk 59 M8
Stert Wilts 30 B10
Stetchworth Cambs 57 M9
Stevenage Herts 45 J6
Steven's Crouch E Susx 16 C8
Stevenston N Ayrs 104 E1
Steventon Hants 25 J4
Steventon Oxon 31 K4
Steventon End Essex 45 Q3
Stevington Bed 55 N10
Stewartby Bed 44 E3
Stewartfield S Lans 114 B10
Stewarton Ag & B 103 J6
Stewarton E Ayrs 113 N12
Stewkley Bucks 44 B6
Stewley Somset 21 M9
Stewton Lincs 80 G6
Steyne Cross IoW 13 L7
Steyning W Susx 14 H8
Steynton Pembks 36 H9
Stibb Cnwll 7 J3
Stibbard Norfk 70 E6
Stibb Cross Devon 18 H10
Stibb Green Wilts 30 F10
Stibbington Cambs 56 B1
Stichill Border 108 B2
Sticker Cnwll 3 N4
Stickford Lincs 80 G11
Sticklepath Devon 8 C6
Sticklepath Somset 20 G6
Stickling Green Essex 45 N5
Stickney Lincs 80 G12
Stiffkey Norfk 70 E4
Stifford Clays Thurr 34 A6
Stifford's Bridge Herefs 52 D11
Stiff Street Kent 34 F10
Stile Bridge Kent 16 D1
Stileway Somset 21 P5
Stilligarry W Isls 152 b10
Stillingfleet N York 86 B7
Stillington N York 86 A2
Stillington S on T 91 P2
Stilton Cambs 56 C3
Stinchcombe Gloucs 29 L3
Stinsford Dorset 10 H6
Stiperstones Shrops 63 L12
Stirchley Birm 53 K4
Stirchley Wrekin 64 C10
Stirling Abers 141 Q7
Stirling Stirlg 114 E3
Stirling Castle Stirlg 114 E2
Stirling Services Stirlg 114 E3
Stirtloe Cambs 56 D7
Stirton N York 84 E5
Stisted Essex 46 D7
Stitchcombe Wilts 30 F8
Stithians Cnwll 3 J7
Stivichall Covtry 53 Q5
Stixwould Lincs 80 D10
St Michaels Fife 125 J8
Stoak Ches W 75 M9
Stobo Border 106 G2
Stoborough Dorset 11 M7
Stoborough Green Dorset 11 M7
Stobs Castle Border 107 M8
Stobswood Nthumb 109 L10
Stock Essex 34 C3
Stock N Som 28 F10
Stockbridge Hants 24 F6
Stockbridge W Susx 13 Q4
Stockbriggs S Lans 105 P2
Stockbury Kent 34 E10
Stockcross W Berk 31 J8
Stockdalewath Cumb 98 E9
Stocker's Head Kent 34 G12
Stockerston Leics 55 L1
Stock Green Worcs 53 J9
Stocking Herefs 41 J5
Stockingford Warwks 53 Q2
Stocking Pelham Herts 45 N6
Stockland Devon 9 N4
Stockland Bristol Somset 21 K4
Stockland Green Kent 15 Q2
Stockleigh English Devon 8 F3
Stockleigh Pomeroy Devon 8 G4
Stockley Wilts 30 A9
Stockley Hill Herefs 40 E4
Stocklinch Somset 21 N10
Stockmoor Herefs 51 L9
Stockport Stockp 76 G5
Stocksbridge Sheff 77 P4
Stocksfield Nthumb 100 D6
Stocksmoor Kirk 77 M2
Stockton Herefs 51 N8
Stockton Norfk 59 M2
Stockton Shrops 63 J12
Stockton Shrops 64 D12
Stockton Warwks 54 D8
Stockton Wilts 23 L6
Stockton Wrekin 64 E9
Stockton Brook Staffs 64 G2
Stockton Heath Warrtn 75 Q6
Stockton-on-Tees S on T 91 Q3
Stockton on Teme Worcs 52 D7
Stockton on the Forest C York 86 C4
Stockwell Gloucs 41 Q9
Stockwell End Wolves 64 G12
Stockwell Heath Staffs 65 K8
Stockwood Bristl 29 J8
Stockwood Dorset 10 F3
Stock Wood Worcs 53 J9
Stodday Lancs 83 L3
Stodmarsh Kent 35 M10
Stody Norfk 70 F5
Stoer Highld 148 B11
Stoford Somset 22 D10
Stoford Wilts 23 N6
Stogumber Somset 20 H6
Stogursey Somset 21 K5
Stoke Covtry 54 B5
Stoke Devon 18 E8
Stoke Hants 13 M4
Stoke Hants 24 F3
Stoke Medway 34 E7
Stoke Abbott Dorset 10 C5
Stoke Albany Nhants 55 K3
Stoke Ash Suffk 58 G6
Stoke Bardolph Notts 66 G4
Stoke Bliss Worcs 52 C8
Stoke Bruerne Nhants 55 J10
Stoke-by-Clare Suffk 46 C3
Stoke-by-Nayland Suffk 46 H4
Stoke Canon Devon 8 H5
Stoke Charity Hants 24 H5
Stoke Climsland Cnwll 7 L10
Stoke Cross Herefs 52 B10
Stoke D'Abernon Surrey 32 G10
Stoke Doyle Nhants 55 P3
Stoke Dry Rutlnd 55 L1
Stoke Edith Herefs 41 J3
Stoke End Warwks 53 M1
Stoke Farthing Wilts 23 N8
Stoke Ferry Norfk 69 N12
Stoke Fleming Devon 5 P7
Stokeford Dorset 11 L7
Stoke Gabriel Devon 5 P5
Stoke Gifford S Glos 29 J6
Stoke Golding Leics 54 C1
Stoke Goldington M Keyn 55 L11
Stoke Green Bucks 32 D6
Stokeham Notts 79 K8
Stoke Hammond Bucks 44 C6
Stoke Heath Shrops 64 C6
Stoke Heath Worcs 52 H7
Stoke Holy Cross Norfk 71 J11
Stokeinteignhead Devon 8 G10
Stoke Lacy Herefs 52 B10
Stoke Lyne Oxon 43 M6
Stoke Mandeville Bucks 44 B9
Stokenchurch Bucks 31 Q3
Stoke Newington Gt Lon 33 L5
Stokenham Devon 5 N8
Stoke-on-Trent C Stke 64 G3
Stoke Orchard Gloucs 41 Q6
Stoke Poges Bucks 32 D6
Stoke Pound Worcs 52 H7
Stoke Prior Herefs 51 N9
Stoke Prior Worcs 52 H7
Stoke Rivers Devon 19 M6
Stoke Rochford Lincs 67 M7
Stoke Row Oxon 31 P5
Stoke St Gregory Somset 21 M8
Stoke St Mary Somset 21 L9
Stoke St Michael Somset 22 F4
Stoke St Milborough Shrops 51 P4
Stokesay Shrops 51 M4
Stokesby Norfk 71 N10
Stokesley N York 92 B5
Stoke sub Hamdon Somset 21 Q10
Stoke Talmage Oxon 31 P2
Stoke Trister Somset 22 G7
Stoke upon Tern Shrops 64 B6
Stoke-upon-Trent C Stke 64 G3
Stoke Wake Dorset 11 J3
Stoke Wharf Worcs 52 H7
Stolford Somset 21 K4
Stondon Massey Essex 33 Q2
Stone Bucks 43 R9
Stone Gloucs 29 K3
Stone Kent 33 Q7
Stone Rothm 78 F6
Stone Somset 22 D6
Stone Staffs 64 G5
Stone Worcs 52 F5
Stonea Cambs 57 J2
Stone Allerton Somset 21 N3
Ston Easton Somset 22 E3
Stonebridge N Som 28 E10
Stonebridge Norfk 58 D2
Stonebridge Warwks 53 N4
Stone Bridge Corner C Pete 68 E12
Stonebroom Derbys 78 C11
Stone Chair Calder 84 H9
Stone Cross E Susx 15 P5
Stone Cross E Susx 15 R10
Stone Cross E Susx 16 B4
Stone Cross Kent 15 P3
Stone Cross Kent 17 J3
Stone Cross Kent 35 P11
Stonecross Green Suffk 58 B9
Stonecrouch Kent 16 C4
Stone-edge-Batch N Som 28 G8
Stoneferry C KuH 87 L9
Stonefield Castle Hotel Ag & B 112 C7
Stonegate E Susx 16 B5
Stonegate N York 92 F5

Stonegrave N York 92 D11
Stonehall Worcs 52 G11
Stonehaugh Nthumb 99 M3
Stonehaven Abers 133 L7
Stonehenge Wilts 23 P5
Stone Hill Donc 78 H2
Stonehouse C Plym 4 G6
Stone House Cumb 90 C9
Stonehouse Gloucs 41 N10
Stonehouse Nthumb 99 K6
Stonehouse S Lans 114 D12
Stone in Oxney Kent 16 G5
Stoneleigh Warwks 53 Q6
Stoneley Green Ches E 63 Q2
Stonely Cambs 56 B7
Stoner Hill Hants 25 M8
Stonesby Leics 67 K7
Stonesfield Oxon 43 J8
Stones Green Essex 47 L6
Stone Street Kent 33 Q11
Stone Street Suffk 46 G4
Stone Street Suffk 46 H3
Stone Street Suffk 59 M4
Stonestreet Green Kent 17 J3
Stonethwaite Cumb 88 H4
Stonewells Moray 139 P3
Stonewood Kent 33 Q8
Stoneybridge W Isls 152 b10
Stoneybridge Worcs 52 H5
Stoneyburn W Loth 114 H8
Stoney Cross Hants 12 D2
Stoneygate C Leic 66 G11
Stoneyhills Essex 34 G3
Stoneykirk D & G 94 F7
Stoney Middleton Derbys 77 N8
Stoney Stanton Leics 54 D2
Stoney Stoke Somset 22 F7
Stoney Stratton Somset 22 F6
Stoney Stretton Shrops 63 L10
Stoneywood C Aber 133 L2
Stoneywood Falk 114 E5
Stonham Aspal Suffk 58 H8
Stonnall Staffs 65 K11
Stonor Oxon 31 Q5
Stonton Wyville Leics 55 J2
Stonybreck Shet 147 h10
Stony Cross Herefs 51 P7
Stony Cross Herefs 52 D11
Stonyford Hants 24 E10
Stony Houghton Derbys 78 E10
Stony Stratford M Keyn 43 R4
Stonywell Staffs 65 K9
Stoodleigh Devon 19 M7
Stoodleigh Devon 20 E9
Stopham W Susx 14 E7
Stopsley Luton 44 G7
Stoptide Cnwll 6 D9
Storeton Wirral 75 J7
Storeyard Green Herefs 41 L3
Storey Arms Powys 39 M7
Stornoway W Isls 152 g3
Stornoway Airport W Isls 152 g3
Storridge Herefs 52 D11
Storrington W Susx 14 F8
Storth Cumb 89 M10
Storwood E R Yk 86 D6
Stotfield Moray 147 M11
Stotfold C Beds 45 J4
Stottesdon Shrops 52 C4
Stoughton Leics 66 G11
Stoughton Surrey 32 D12
Stoughton W Susx 13 P2
Stoulton Worcs 52 G10
Stourbridge Dudley 52 G4
Stourhead Wilts 22 H6
Stourpaine Dorset 11 L3
Stourport-on-Severn
Worcs 52 E6
Stour Provost Dorset 22 H9
Stour Row Dorset 22 H9
Stourton Leeds 85 L9
Stourton Staffs 52 F4
Stourton Warwks 42 G4
Stourton Wilts 22 H6
Stourton Caundle Dorset 22 G10
Stout Somset 21 P7
Stove Shet 147 i9
Stoven Suffk 59 N4
Stow Border 116 B12
Stow Lincs 79 L7
Stow Bardolph Norfk 69 M11
Stow Bedon Norfk 58 E1
Stowbridge Norfk 69 L10
Stow-cum-Quy Cambs 57 K8
Stowe Gloucs 40 H10
Stowe Shrops 51 K6
Stowe-by-Chartley Staffs 65 J7
Stowehill Nhants 54 G9
Stowell Somset 22 F9
Stowey BaNES 29 J10
Stowford Devon 7 N5
Stowford Devon 7 N7
Stowford Devon 9 L7
Stowford Devon 19 M5
Stowlangtoft Suffk 58 E7
Stow Longa Cambs 56 B6
Stow Maries Essex 34 E2
Stowmarket Suffk 58 F9
Stow-on-the-Wold
Gloucs 42 E6
Stowting Kent 17 K2
Stowting Common Kent 17 K2
Stowupland Suffk 58 G8
Straad Ag & B 112 F9
Straanruie Highld 131 J1
Strachan Abers 132 G6
Strachur Ag & B 112 G1
Stradbroke Suffk 59 J6
Stradbrook Wilts 23 K3
Stradishall Suffk 57 P10
Stradsett Norfk 69 M11
Stragglethorpe Lincs 67 M2
Stragglethorpe Notts 66 G5
Straight Soley Wilts 30 G8
Straiton Mdloth 115 N8
Straiton S Ayrs 104 G9
Straloch Abers 141 L11
Straloch P & K 131 J11
Stramshall Staffs 65 K5
Strang IoM 102 e5
Strangeways Salfd 76 F4
Strangford Herefs 41 J6
Stranraer D & G 94 F6
Strata Florida Cerdgn 49 N7
Stratfield Mortimer
W Berk 31 N9
Stratfield Saye Hants 31 P10
Stratfield Turgis Hants 31 P10
Stratford C Beds 56 D11
Stratford Gt Lon 33 M5
Stratford St Andrew
Suffk 59 M8
Stratford St Mary Suffk 47 J5
Stratford sub Castle
Wilts 23 P7
Stratford Tony Wilts 23 N8
Stratford-upon-Avon
Warwks 53 M9
Strath Highld 143 L9
Strathan Highld 144 D11
Strathan Highld 149 M4
Strathaven S Lans 114 C12
Strathblane Stirlg 113 Q5
Strathcanaird Highld 144 E5
Strathcarron Highld 136 C7
Strathcoil Ag & B 120 C7
Strathdon Abers 131 Q2
Strathkinness Fife 125 J9
Strathloanhead W Loth 114 G7
Strathmashie House
Highld 129 Q6
Strathmiglo Fife 124 E11
Strathpeffer Highld 137 N4
Strathtay P & K 123 M2
Strathwhillan N Ayrs 103 Q3
Strathy Highld 150 E4
Strathy Inn Highld 150 E3
Strathyre Stirlg 122 F9
Stratton Cnwll 7 J3
Stratton Dorset 10 G6
Stratton Gloucs 42 B11
Stratton Audley Oxon 43 M6
Stratton-on-the-Fosse
Somset 22 F3
Stratton St Margaret
Swindn 30 E5
Stratton St Michael
Norfk 59 J2
Stratton Strawless Norfk 71 J8
Stream Somset 20 G5
Streat E Susx 15 L8
Streatham Gt Lon 33 K8
Streatley C Beds 44 F6
Streatley W Berk 31 M6
Street Devon 9 M7
Street Lancs 83 M5
Street N York 92 E6
Street Somset 22 B6
Street Ashton Warwks 54 D4
Street Dinas Shrops 63 K4
Street End E Susx 15 R6
Street End Kent 35 L11
Street End W Susx 13 P5
Street Gate Gatesd 100 G6
Streethay Staffs 65 L10
Street Houses N York 85 Q6
Streetlam N York 91 M7
Street Lane Derbys 66 C3
Streetly Wsall 53 K1
Streetly End Cambs 57 L11
Street on the Fosse
Somset 22 E5
Strefford Shrops 51 M3
Strelitz P & K 124 D5
Strelley Notts 66 E4
Strensall C York 86 B3
Strensham Worcs 41 Q4
Strensham Services
(northbound) Worcs 41 P3
Strensham Services
(southbound) Worcs 41 P4
Stretcholt Somset 21 L4
Strete Devon 5 P7
Stretford Herefs 51 M9
Stretford Herefs 51 N9
Stretford Traffd 76 E5
Strethall Essex 45 N4
Stretham Cambs 57 K6
Strettington W Susx 14 C9
Stretton Ches W 63 M2
Stretton Derbys 78 C11
Stretton Rutlnd 67 N9
Stretton Staffs 64 G10
Stretton Staffs 65 N7
Stretton Warrtn 76 B7
Stretton en le Field Leics 65 P10
Stretton Grandison
Herefs 41 K3
Stretton-on-Dunsmore
Warwks 54 C6
Stretton on Fosse
Warwks 42 E4
Stretton Sugwas Herefs 40 G3
Stretton under Fosse
Warwks 54 D4
Stretton Westwood
Shrops 51 Q1
Strichen Abers 141 M5
Strines Stockp 76 H6
Stringston Somset 21 J5
Strixton Nhants 55 M8
Stroat Gloucs 28 H3
Strollamus Highld 135 K10
Stroma Highld 151 Q1
Stromeferry Highld 136 B9
Stromness Ork 147 b4
Stronaba Highld 128 H7
Stronachlachar Stirlg 122 C10
Stronafian Ag & B 112 F5
Stronchrubie Highld 144 G1
Strone Ag & B 113 J5
Strone Highld 128 G8
Strone Highld 137 P10
Stronmilchan Ag & B 121 M7
Stronsay Ork 147 e3
Stronsay Airport Ork 147 e3
Strontian Highld 127 P12
Strood Kent 16 E4
Strood Medway 34 C8
Strood Green Surrey 14 H1
Strood Green W Susx 14 E6
Stroud Gloucs 41 N10
Stroud Hants 25 M8
Stroude Surrey 32 E8
Stroud Green Essex 34 F4
Stroud Green Gloucs 41 N10
Stroxton Lincs 67 M6
Struan Highld 134 F8
Struan P & K 130 E11
Strubby Lincs 81 J7
Strumpshaw Norfk 71 M10
Strutherhill S Lans 114 D11
Struthers Fife 124 H11
Struy Highld 137 L8
Stryd-y-Facsen IoA 72 E7
Stuartfield Abers 141 N7
Stubbers Green Wsall 65 K11
Stubbington Hants 13 J4
Stubbins Lancs 84 B11
Stubbs Cross Kent 16 H3
Stubbs Green Norfk 59 K1
Stubhampton Dorset 23 K10
Stubley Derbys 77 Q8
Stubshaw Cross Wigan 75 Q4
Stubton Lincs 67 L2
Stuckton Hants 23 Q10
Studfold N York 84 B1
Stud Green W & M 32 C7
Studham C Beds 44 E8
Studholme Cumb 98 B7
Studland Dorset 11 P8
Studlands Park Suffk 57 M7
Studley Warwks 53 K8
Studley Wilts 29 Q8
Studley Common Warwks 53 K8
Studley Roger N York 85 L1
Studley Royal N York 85 K1
Studley Royal Park & Fountains Abbey
N York 85 K2
Stuntney Cambs 57 K5
Stunts Green E Susx 16 A8
Sturbridge Staffs 64 F6
Sturgate Lincs 79 L6
Sturmer Essex 46 C3
Sturminster Common
Dorset 22 H11
Sturminster Marshall
Dorset 11 M5
Sturminster Newton
Dorset 22 H10
Sturry Kent 35 L10
Sturton N Linc 79 N3
Sturton by Stow Lincs 79 M7
Sturton le Steeple Notts 79 K7
Stuston Suffk 58 H5
Stutton N York 85 P7
Stutton Suffk 47 L5
Styal Ches E 76 F7
Stydd Lancs 83 P8
Stynie Moray 139 Q4
Styrrup Notts 78 G5
Succoth Ag & B 121 P11
Suckley Worcs 52 D10
Suckley Green Worcs 52 D10
Sudborough Nhants 55 N4
Sudbourne Suffk 59 N10
Sudbrook Lincs 67 N3
Sudbrook Mons 28 G5
Sudbrooke Lincs 79 P8
Sudbury Derbys 65 M6
Sudbury Gt Lon 32 H5
Sudbury Suffk 46 F3
Sudden Rochdl 76 G1
Sudgrove Gloucs 41 Q10
Suffield N York 93 K8
Suffield Norfk 71 J5
Sugdon Wrekin 63 Q9
Sugnall Staffs 64 E6
Sugwas Pool Herefs 40 F3
Suisnish Highld 127 K1
Sulby IoM 102 e3
Sulgrave Nhants 43 L3
Sulham W Berk 31 N7
Sulhamstead W Berk 31 N8
Sulhamstead Abbots
W Berk 31 N9
Sulhamstead Bannister
W Berk 31 N8
Sullington W Susx 14 G8
Sullom Shet 147 i5
Sullom Voe Shet 147 i5
Sully V Glam 27 Q8
Sumburgh Airport Shet 147 i10
Summerbridge N York 85 J3
Summercourt Cnwll 3 L3
Summerfield Norfk 69 P4
Summerfield Worcs 52 F6
Summer Heath Bucks 31 Q4
Summerhill Pembks 37 M9
Summerhill Staffs 65 K11
Summer Hill Wrexhm 63 K1
Summerhouse Darltn 91 K3
Summerlands Cumb 89 N9
Summerley Derbys 78 B8
Summersdale W Susx 14 B9
Summerseat Bury 84 B12
Summertown Oxon 43 L10
Summit Oldham 76 G2
Summit Rochdl 84 E11
Sunbiggin Cumb 89 Q5
Sunbury-on-Thames
Surrey 32 G8
Sundaywell D & G 96 G1
Sunderland Ag & B 110 F8
Sunderland Cumb 97 N11
Sunderland Lancs 83 K4
Sunderland Sundld 101 K7
Sunderland Bridge Dur 100 H10
Sundhope Border 107 J5
Sundon Park Luton 44 F6
Sundridge Kent 33 N11
Sunk Island E R Yk 87 P11
Sunningdale W & M 32 D9
Sunninghill W & M 32 D9
Sunningwell Oxon 31 K2
Sunniside Dur 100 F10
Sunniside Gatesd 100 G6
Sunny Brow Dur 100 F11
Sunnyhill C Derb 65 Q6
Sunnyhurst Bl w D 83 P10
Sunnylaw Stirlg 114 E2
Sunnymead Oxon 43 L9
Sunton Wilts 24 D2
Surbiton Gt Lon 32 H9
Surfleet Lincs 68 E6
Surfleet Seas End Lincs 68 E6
Surlingham Norfk 71 L11
Surrex Essex 46 F7
Sustead Norfk 71 J5
Susworth Lincs 79 L3
Sutcombe Devon 7 L2
Sutcombemill Devon 7 L2
Suton Norfk 70 G12
Sutterby Lincs 80 G9
Sutterton Lincs 68 F5
Sutton C Beds 45 J2
Sutton C Pete 68 B12
Sutton Cambs 56 H5
Sutton Devon 5 L8
Sutton Devon 8 D4
Sutton Donc 78 F1
Sutton E Susx 15 P11
Sutton Gt Lon 33 J9
Sutton Kent 35 P12
Sutton N York 85 P10
Sutton Norfk 71 M7
Sutton Notts 67 J5
Sutton Oxon 43 J10
Sutton Pembks 36 H7
Sutton Shrops 52 D3
Sutton Shrops 63 K7
Sutton Shrops 63 N10
Sutton Shrops 64 C6
Sutton St Hel 75 P5
Sutton Staffs 64 E8
Sutton Suffk 47 P2
Sutton W Susx 14 D8
Sutton Abinger Surrey 14 G2
Sutton-at-Hone Kent 33 Q8
Sutton Bassett Nhants 55 J3
Sutton Benger Wilts 29 Q6
Sutton Bingham Somset 10 E3
Sutton Bonington Notts 66 E7
Sutton Bridge Lincs 69 J8
Sutton Cheney Leics 66 C12
Sutton Coldfield Birm 53 L1
Sutton Courtenay Oxon 31 L3
Sutton Crosses Lincs 68 H8
Sutton cum Lound Notts 78 H7
Sutton Fields Notts 66 E7
Sutton Green Surrey 32 E11
Sutton Green Wrexhm 63 L3
Sutton Heath Suffk 59 L11
Sutton Howgrave N York 91 M11
Sutton-in-Ashfield Notts 78 D12
Sutton-in-Craven N York 84 F6
Sutton in the Elms Leics 54 E2
Sutton Lane Ends Ches E 76 H9
Sutton Maddock Shrops 64 D12
Sutton Mallet Somset 21 N6
Sutton Mandeville Wilts 23 L7
Sutton Manor St Hel 75 N5
Sutton Marsh Herefs 40 H3
Sutton Montis Somset 22 E8
Sutton-on-Hull C KuH 87 L8
Sutton on Sea Lincs 81 K7
Sutton-on-the-Forest
N York 86 A2
Sutton on the Hill
Derbys 65 N5
Sutton on Trent Notts 79 K10
Sutton Poyntz Dorset 10 H8
Sutton St Edmund Lincs 68 G9
Sutton St James Lincs 68 H8
Sutton St Nicholas
Herefs 40 H3
Sutton Scotney Hants 24 H5
Sutton Street Kent 34 E11
Sutton-under-Brailes
Warwks 42 G4
Sutton-under-Whitestonecliffe
N York 91 Q10
Sutton upon Derwent
E R Yk 86 D6
Sutton Valence Kent 16 E1
Sutton Veny Wilts 23 K5
Sutton Waldron Dorset 23 J10
Sutton Weaver Ches W 75 P8
Sutton Wick BaNES 29 J10
Sutton Wick Oxon 31 K3
Swaby Lincs 80 G8
Swadlincote Derbys 65 P8
Swaffham Norfk 70 B10
Swaffham Bulbeck
Cambs 57 K8
Swaffham Prior Cambs 57 L8
Swafield Norfk 71 K6
Swainby N York 91 Q6
Swainshill Herefs 40 G3
Swainsthorpe Norfk 71 J12
Swainswick BaNES 29 M8
Swalcliffe Oxon 42 H4
Swalecliffe Kent 35 K9
Swallow Lincs 80 D3
Swallow Beck Lincs 79 N10
Swallowcliffe Wilts 23 L8
Swallowfield Wokham 31 P9
Swallownest Rothm 78 D6
Swallows Cross Essex 33 R3
Swampton Hants 24 G3
Swanage Dorset 11 P9
Swanbourne Bucks 44 A6
Swanbridge V Glam 27 R9
Swancote Shrops 52 D2
Swan Green Ches W 76 D9
Swanland E R Yk 87 J9
Swanley Kent 33 P8
Swanley Village Kent 33 P8
Swanmore Hants 25 J10
Swannington Leics 66 C9
Swannington Norfk 70 H8
Swanpool Lincs 79 N10
Swanscombe Kent 33 R7
Swansea Swans 26 G4
Swansea Airport Swans 26 E4
Swansea West Services
Swans 26 F2
Swan Street Essex 46 F6
Swanton Abbot Norfk 71 K7
Swanton Morley Norfk 70 F8
Swanton Novers Norfk 70 F6
Swanton Street Kent 34 F10
Swan Valley Nhants 55 J9
Swan Village Sandw 53 J2
Swanwick Derbys 66 C2
Swanwick Hants 12 H3
Swarby Lincs 67 P4
Swardeston Norfk 71 J11
Swarkestone Derbys 66 B6
Swarland Nthumb 109 K9
Swarraton Hants 25 J6
Swartha C Brad 84 F6
Swarthmoor Cumb 88 H11
Swaton Lincs 68 C5
Swavesey Cambs 56 G7
Sway Hants 12 D5
Swayfield Lincs 67 N7
Swaythling C Sotn 24 G10
Sweet Green Worcs 52 C8
Sweetham Devon 8 G5
Sweethaws E Susx 15 P5
Sweetlands Corner Kent 16 D2
Sweets Cnwll 6 H5
Sweetshouse Cnwll 3 Q2
Swefling Suffk 59 L8
Swepstone Leics 66 B10
Swerford Oxon 42 H5
Swettenham Ches E 76 E10
Swffryd Blae G 28 B3
Swift's Green Kent 16 F2
Swilland Suffk 59 J10
Swillbrook Lancs 83 L8
Swillington Leeds 85 M9
Swimbridge Devon 19 M7
Swimbridge Newland
Devon 19 L7
Swinbrook Oxon 42 G9
Swincliffe Kirk 85 J9
Swincliffe N York 85 K4
Swincombe Devon 19 N5
Swindale Cumb 89 N4
Swinden N York 84 C4
Swinderby Lincs 79 L11
Swindon Gloucs 41 Q7
Swindon Nthumb 108 F10
Swindon Staffs 52 F3
Swindon Swindn 30 D5
Swine E R Yk 87 L8
Swinefleet E R Yk 86 E10
Swineford S Glos 29 L8
Swineshead Bed 55 Q7
Swineshead Lincs 68 E4
Swineshead Bridge Lincs 68 D4
Swiney Highld 151 M9
Swinford Leics 54 F5
Swinford Oxon 43 J10
Swingate Notts 66 E3
Swingfield Minnis Kent 17 M2
Swingfield Street Kent 17 N2
Swingleton Green Suffk 46 G2
Swinhoe Nthumb 109 K4
Swinhope Lincs 80 D4
Swinithwaite N York 90 H9
Swinmore Common
Herefs 41 K3
Swinscoe Staffs 65 L3
Swinside Cumb 88 H2
Swinstead Lincs 67 P7
Swinthorpe Lincs 79 Q7
Swinton Border 117 J11
Swinton N York 91 L10
Swinton N York 92 F12
Swinton Rothm 78 D4
Swinton Salfd 76 E3
Swiss Valley Carmth 38 D11
Swithland Leics 66 F9
Swordale Highld 137 Q3
Swordland Highld 127 P6
Swordly Highld 150 D4
Sworton Heath Ches E 76 C7
Swyddffynnon Cerdgn 49 M7
Swyncombe Oxon 31 P4
Swynnerton Staffs 64 F5
Swyre Dorset 10 E7
Sycharth Powys 62 H7
Sychnant Powys 50 D5
Sychtyn Powys 62 D10
Sydallt Wrexhm 63 K1
Syde Gloucs 41 Q9
Sydenham Gt Lon 33 L8
Sydenham Oxon 43 Q11
Sydenham Damerel
Devon 7 M9
Sydenhurst Surrey 14 D4
Syderstone Norfk 70 B6
Sydling St Nicholas
Dorset 10 F5
Sydmonton Hants 31 K10
Sydnal Lane Shrops 64 E11
Syerston Notts 67 J3
Syke Rochdl 84 D12
Sykehouse Donc 86 B11
Syleham Suffk 59 J5
Sylen Carmth 38 D10
Symbister Shet 147 j6
Symington S Ayrs 104 G3
Symington S Lans 106 C3
Symondsbury Dorset 10 C6
Symonds Yat (East)
Herefs 40 H8
Symonds Yat (West)
Herefs 40 H8
Sympson Green C Brad 85 J7
Synderford Dorset 10 B4
Synod Inn Cerdgn 48 F9
Syre Highld 149 P8
Syreford Gloucs 42 B7
Syresham Nhants 43 N3
Syston Leics 66 G10
Syston Lincs 67 M4
Sytchampton Worcs 52 F7
Sywell Nhants 55 K7

T

Tabley Hill Ches E 76 D8
Tackley Oxon 43 K7
Tacolneston Norfk 58 H2
Tadcaster N York 85 P6
Taddington Derbys 77 L9
Taddington Gloucs 42 C5
Taddiport Devon 19 J9
Tadley Hants 31 M10
Tadlow Cambs 56 F11
Tadmarton Oxon 42 H4
Tadpole Swindn 30 D4
Tadwick BaNES 29 L8
Tadworth Surrey 33 J11
Tafarnaubach Blae G 39 Q9
Tafarn-y-bwlch Pembks 37 L4
Tafarn-y-Gelyn Denbgs 74 G11
Taff's Well Cardif 27 Q6
Tafolwern Powys 62 B11
Taibach Neath 27 J5
Tain Highld 146 D8
Tain Highld 151 M3
Tai'n Lôn Gwynd 60 G2
Tai'r Bull Powys 39 N6
Tairgwaith Neath 38 H9
Takeley Essex 45 Q7
Takeley Street Essex 45 Q7
Talachddu Powys 39 P5
Talacre Flints 74 F7
Talaton Devon 9 K5
Talbenny Pembks 36 G8
Talbot Green Rhondd 27 N6
Talbot Village BCP 11 P6
Taleford Devon 9 L5
Talerddig Powys 62 C12
Talgarreg Cerdgn 48 G10
Talgarth Powys 39 R5
Talisker Highld 134 F10
Talke Staffs 64 F2
Talke Pits Staffs 64 F2
Talkin Cumb 98 G7
Talladale Highld 143 N11
Talla Linnfoots Border 106 F6
Tallaminnock S Ayrs 104 G10
Tallarn Green Wrexhm 63 M3
Tallentire Cumb 97 M11
Talley Carmth 38 F5
Tallington Lincs 68 B10
Talmine Highld 149 M4
Talog Carmth 37 Q5
Talsarn Cerdgn 49 J9
Talsarnau Gwynd 61 K5
Talskiddy Cnwll 6 C11
Talwrn IoA 72 H8
Talwrn Wrexhm 63 L3
Tal-y-bont Cerdgn 49 L3
Tal-y-Bont Conwy 73 N10
Talybont Gwynd 61 K8
Tal-y-bont Gwynd 73 K9
Talybont-on-Usk Powys 39 Q7
Tal-y-Cafn Conwy 73 N9
Tal-y-coed Mons 40 F8
Tal-y-garn Rhondd 27 N6
Tal-y-llyn Gwynd 61 M10
Talysarn Gwynd 60 H2
Tal-y-Waun Torfn 40 C10
Talywern Powys 61 P12
Tamar Valley Mining District Devon 4 F3
Tamer Lane End Wigan 76 B3
Tamerton Foliot C Plym 4 G4
Tamworth Staffs 65 N11
Tamworth Green Lincs 68 G4
Tamworth Services
Warwks 65 N12
Tancred N York 85 P3
Tancredston Pembks 36 G5
Tandridge Surrey 33 L12
Tanfield Dur 100 F7
Tanfield Lea Dur 100 F7
Tangasdale W Isls 152 b13
Tangiers Pembks 37 J7
Tangley Hants 24 E3
Tangmere W Susx 14 C9
Tan Hill N York 90 E5
Tankerness Ork 147 d4
Tankersley Barns 77 Q4
Tankerton Kent 35 K9
Tannach Highld 151 P7
Tannachie Abers 133 J7
Tannadice Angus 125 J1
Tanner's Green Worcs 53 K6
Tannington Suffk 59 K7
Tannochside N Lans 114 C9
Tansley Derbys 77 Q11
Tansor Nhants 55 Q2
Tantobie Dur 100 F7
Tanton N York 92 B5
Tanwood Worcs 52 G6
Tanworth in Arden
Warwks 53 L6
Tan-y-Bwlch Gwynd 61 L4
Tan-y-fron Conwy 74 C11
Tan-y-fron Wrexhm 63 J2
Tan-y-grisiau Gwynd 61 M3
Tan-y-groes Cerdgn 48 D10
Taobh Tuath W Isls 152 d6
Taplow Bucks 32 C6
Tarbert Ag & B 111 P11
Tarbert Ag & B 112 C7
Tarbert W Isls 152 e5
Tarbet Ag & B 121 Q12
Tarbet Highld 127 P6
Tarbet Highld 148 E7
Tarbock Green Knows 75 M6
Tarbolton S Ayrs 104 H4
Tarbrax S Lans 115 J10
Tardebigge Worcs 53 J7
Tarfside Angus 132 D8
Tarland Abers 132 D4
Tarleton Lancs 83 K11
Tarlscough Lancs 83 K12
Tarlton Gloucs 29 Q2
Tarnock Somset 21 N3
Tarns Cumb 97 M8
Tarnside Cumb 89 L8
Tarporley Ches W 75 P11
Tarr Somset 20 D7
Tarrant Crawford Dorset 11 N4
Tarrant Gunville Dorset 23 K10
Tarrant Hinton Dorset 11 M2
Tarrant Keyneston Dorset 11 M4
Tarrant Launceston
Dorset 11 M3
Tarrant Monkton Dorset 11 M3
Tarrant Rawston Dorset 11 M3
Tarrant Rushton Dorset 11 M4
Tarring Neville E Susx 15 N10
Tarrington Herefs 41 J4
Tarskavaig Highld 127 K2
Tarves Abers 141 L9
Tarvin Ches W 75 N10
Tarvin Sands Ches W 75 N10
Tasburgh Norfk 59 J2
Tasley Shrops 52 C2
Taston Oxon 42 H7
Tatenhill Staffs 65 M8
Tathall End M Keyn 44 B2
Tatham Lancs 83 N1
Tathwell Lincs 80 F7
Tatsfield Surrey 33 M11
Tattenhall Ches W 75 N12
Tatterford Norfk 70 C6
Tattersett Norfk 70 C6
Tattershall Lincs 80 D12
Tattershall Bridge Lincs 68 D1
Tattershall Thorpe Lincs 80 D11
Tattingstone Suffk 47 K4
Tattingstone White Horse Suffk 47 L4
Tatton Park Ches E 76 D7
Tatworth Somset 9 Q4
Tauchers Moray 140 B6
Taunton Somset 21 K8
Taunton Deane Services
Somset 21 K9
Taverham Norfk 70 H9
Taverners Green Essex 45 Q8
Tavernspite Pembks 37 N8
Tavistock Devon 7 N10
Tavistock Devon 7 N10
Taw Green Devon 8 C5
Tawstock Devon 19 L7
Taxal Derbys 77 J8
Tay Bridge C Dund 124 H7
Taychreggan Hotel
Ag & B 121 K8
Tay Forest Park P & K 130 E12
Tayinloan Ag & B 111 P12
Taynton Gloucs 41 L7
Taynton Oxon 42 F9
Taynuilt Ag & B 121 J6
Tayport Fife 125 J7
Tayvallich Ag & B 111 Q4
Tealby Lincs 80 C5
Tealing Angus 124 H5
Team Valley Gatesd 100 G6
Teangue Highld 127 M2
Teanord Highld 137 Q3
Tebay Cumb 89 Q6
Tebay Services Cumb 89 P5
Tebworth C Beds 44 E6
Tedburn St Mary Devon 8 F6
Teddington Gloucs 41 Q5
Teddington Gt Lon 32 H8
Tedstone Delamere
Herefs 52 C9
Tedstone Wafer Herefs 52 C9
Teesport R & Cl 92 B2
Teesside International Airport S on T 91 P4
Teesside Park S on T 91 Q3
Teeton Nhants 54 H6
Teffont Evias Wilts 23 L7
Teffont Magna Wilts 23 L7
Tegryn Pembks 37 P4
Teigh Rutlnd 67 L9
Teigncombe Devon 8 C7
Teigngrace Devon 8 F10
Teignmouth Devon 8 H10
Teindside Border 107 L8
Telford Wrekin 64 C10
Telford Services Shrops 64 D10
Telham E Susx 16 D8
Tellisford Somset 22 H2
Telscombe E Susx 15 M10
Telscombe Cliffs E Susx 15 M10
Tempar P & K 122 H1
Templand D & G 97 M1
Temple Cnwll 6 H10
Temple Mdloth 115 P9
Temple Balsall Solhll 53 N5
Temple Bar Cerdgn 49 J10
Temple Cloud BaNES 29 J10
Templecombe Somset 22 F9
Temple End Suffk 57 M10
Temple Ewell Kent 17 N2
Temple Grafton Warwks 53 L9
Temple Guiting Gloucs 42 C6
Temple Herdewyke
Warwks 54 C10
Temple Hirst N York 86 B10
Temple Normanton
Derbys 78 C10
Temple of Fiddes Abers 133 K8
Temple Sowerby Cumb 89 Q1
Templeton Devon 20 D10
Templeton Pembks 37 M8
Templetown Dur 100 E8
Tempsford C Beds 56 D10
Tenbury Wells Worcs 51 Q7
Tenby Pembks 37 M10
Tendring Essex 47 L7
Tendring Green Essex 47 L6
Tendring Heath Essex 47 L6
Ten Mile Bank Norfk 57 L1
Tenpenny Heath Essex 47 K7
Tenterden Kent 16 F4
Terling Essex 46 D8
Tern Wrekin 64 B9
Ternhill Shrops 64 B6
Terregles D & G 97 J3
Terrington N York 86 C1
Terrington St Clement
Norfk 69 K8
Terrington St John Norfk 69 K9
Terry's Green Warwks 53 L6
Teston Kent 34 C11
Testwood Hants 24 F10
Tetbury Gloucs 29 P4
Tetbury Upton Gloucs 29 P3
Tetchill Shrops 63 L5
Tetcott Devon 7 L5
Tetford Lincs 80 F9
Tetney Lincs 80 F3
Tetney Lock Lincs 80 G3
Tetsworth Oxon 43 P11
Tettenhall Wolves 64 G12
Tettenhall Wood Wolves 64 G12
Teversal Notts 78 D11
Teversham Cambs 57 J9
Teviothead Border 107 L8
Tewin Herts 45 K8
Tewin Wood Herts 45 K8
Tewkesbury Gloucs 41 P5
Teynham Kent 34 G10
Thackley C Brad 85 J7
Thackthwaite Cumb 88 F2
Thackthwaite Cumb 89 L1
Thainstone Abers 141 J12
Thakeham W Susx 14 G7
Thame Oxon 43 P10
Thames Ditton Surrey 32 H9
Thamesmead Gt Lon 33 N6
Thamesport Medway 34 F7
Thanington Kent 35 L11
Thankerton S Lans 106 C2
Tharston Norfk 59 J2
Thatcham W Berk 31 L9
Thatto Heath St Hel 75 N5
Thaxted Essex 45 R5
Theakston N York 91 M9
Thealby N Linc 86 G11
Theale Somset 21 P4
Theale W Berk 31 N8
Thearne E R Yk 87 K8
The Bank Ches E 76 F12
The Beeches Gloucs 42 B11
Theberton Suffk 59 N7
The Blythe Staffs 65 K6
The Bog Shrops 51 K1
The Bourne Worcs 52 H9
The Braes Highld 135 J9
The Bratch Staffs 52 F2
The Bridge Kent 33 Q7
The Broad Herefs 51 N8
The Broads 71 P10
The Brunt E Loth 116 F6
The Bryn Mons 40 D9
The Bungalow IoM 102 e4
The Burf Worcs 52 E7
The Camp Gloucs 41 Q9
The Chequer Wrexhm 63 N4
The City Bed 56 B9
The City Bucks 31 R3
The Common Oxon 42 G6
The Common Wilts 24 D7
The Common Wilts 30 B5
The Corner Kent 16 C2
The Cronk IoM 102 d3
Theddingworth Leics 54 H3
Theddlethorpe All Saints Lincs 81 J6
Theddlethorpe St Helen
Lincs 81 J6
The Deep C KuH 87 L9
The Den N Ayrs 113 L11
The Forge Herefs 51 K9
The Forstal Kent 17 J3
The Fouralls Shrops 64 C6
The Green Cumb 88 G10
The Green Essex 46 D8
The Green N York 92 F5
The Green Wilts 23 J7
The Grove Dur 100 E8
The Grove Worcs 41 P3
The Haven W Susx 14 F5
The Haw Gloucs 41 N6
The Hendre Mons 40 F9
The Hill Cumb 88 G10
The Holt Wokham 32 A7
The Hundred Herefs 51 N8
Thelbridge Cross Devon 8 E2
The Leacon Kent 16 H4
The Lee Bucks 44 C11
The Lhen IoM 102 e2
Thelnetham Suffk 58 F5
The Lochs Moray 139 P3
Thelveton Norfk 58 H4
Thelwall Warrtn 76 C6
The Marsh Powys 51 K1
Themelthorpe Norfk 70 F7
The Middles Dur 100 G8
The Moor Kent 16 D5
The Mumbles Swans 26 F5
The Murray S Lans 114 B10
The Mythe Gloucs 41 P5
The Narth Mons 40 H10
The Neuk Abers 132 H5
Thenford Nhants 43 L3
Theobald's Green Wilts 30 B8
The Quarry Gloucs 29 L2
The Quarter Kent 16 F2
The Reddings Gloucs 41 P7
Therfield Herts 45 L4
The Rhôs Powys 40 A5
The Ross P & K 123 K8
The Sands Surrey 14 C2
The Shoe Wilts 29 N7
The Smithies Shrops 52 C1
The Spring Warwks 53 P6
The Square Torfn 28 C3
The Stair Kent 15 R1
The Stocks Kent 16 G5
The Straits Hants 25 N5
The Strand Wilts 29 Q10
Thetford Norfk 58 C4
Thetford Forest Park 57 Q3
Thethwaite Cumb 98 D9
The Towans Cnwll 2 F7
The Town IoS 2 b1
The Vauld Herefs 51 P10
The Wyke Shrops 64 D10
Theydon Bois Essex 33 N2
Theydon Mount Essex 33 P2
Thicket Priory N York 86 C6
Thickwood Wilts 29 N8
Thimbleby Lincs 80 E9
Thimbleby N York 91 Q7
Thingwall Wirral 75 J7
Thirkleby N York 91 Q11
Thirlby N York 91 R10
Thirlestane Border 116 D11
Thirn N York 91 L9
Thirsk N York 91 Q10
Thirtleby E R Yk 87 M8
Thistleton Lancs 83 K7
Thistleton Rutlnd 67 M8
Thistley Green Suffk 57 M5
Thixendale N York 86 F3
Thockrington Nthumb 99 Q2
Tholomas Drove Cambs 68 H11
Tholthorpe N York 85 P2
Thomas Chapel Pembks 37 L8
Thomas Close Cumb 98 E10
Thomastown Abers 140 E8
Thompson Norfk 58 D1
Thomshill Moray 139 M4
Thong Kent 34 B8
Thongsbridge Kirk 77 M2
Thoralby N York 90 G9
Thoresby Notts 78 G9
Thoresthorpe Lincs 81 J8
Thoresway Lincs 80 D4
Thorganby Lincs 80 D4
Thorganby N York 86 C7
Thorgill N York 92 E7
Thorington Suffk 59 N6
Thorington Street Suffk 46 H4
Thorlby N York 84 E5
Thorley Herts 45 N8
Thorley IoW 12 F7
Thorley Houses Herts 45 N7
Thorley Street IoW 12 F7
Thormanby N York 91 R11
Thornaby-on-Tees S on T 91 Q4
Thornage Norfk 70 F5
Thornborough Bucks 43 Q5
Thornborough N York 91 M10
Thornbury C Brad 85 J8
Thornbury Devon 7 M3
Thornbury Herefs 52 B8
Thornbury S Glos 29 K4
Thornby Cumb 98 C8
Thornby Nhants 54 H5
Thorncliff Staffs 77 J12
Thorncombe Dorset 10 B4
Thorncombe Street
Surrey 14 E2
Thorncott Green C Beds 56 C11
Thorncross IoW 12 G8
Thorndon Suffk 58 H7
Thorndon Cross Devon 7 P6
Thorne Donc 78 H1
Thorne Coffin Somset 22 C10
Thornecroft Devon 5 N3
Thornehillhead Devon 18 H10
Thorner Leeds 85 M7
Thornes Staffs 65 K11
Thornes Wakefd 85 L11

Thorne St Margaret Somset 20 H9
Thorney Bucks 32 F6
Thorney C Pete 68 F11
Thorney Notts 79 L9
Thorney Somset 21 P8
Thorney Hill Hants 12 C5
Thorney Island W Susx 13 N4
Thorney Toll Cambs 68 G11
Thornfalcon Somset 21 L8
Thornford Dorset 22 E10
Thorngrafton Nthumb 99 M5
Thorngrove Somset 21 N7
Thorngumbald E R Yk 87 N10
Thornham Norfk 69 P3
Thornham Magna Suffk 58 G6
Thornham Parva Suffk 58 G6
Thornhaugh C Pete 67 Q12
Thornhill C Sotn 24 H10
Thornhill Caerph 27 R5
Thornhill Cumb 88 D5
Thornhill D & G 105 R10
Thornhill Derbys 77 M7
Thornhill Kirk 85 K11
Thornhill Stirlg 114 B1
Thornhill Lees Kirk 85 K11
Thornhills Calder 84 H10
Thornholme E R Yk 87 L2
Thornicombe Dorset 11 L4
Thornington Nthumb 108 E3
Thornley Dur 100 E10
Thornley Dur 101 J10
Thornley Gate Nthumb 99 M7
Thornliebank E Rens 113 Q9
Thorns Suffk 57 P9
Thornsett Derbys 77 J6
Thorns Green Ches E 76 E7
Thornthwaite Cumb 88 H2
Thornthwaite N York 85 J3
Thornton Angus 124 H3
Thornton Bucks 43 Q4
Thornton C Brad 84 G8
Thornton E R Yk 86 E6
Thornton Fife 115 P2
Thornton Lancs 82 H7
Thornton Leics 66 D10
Thornton Lincs 80 E10
Thornton Middsb 91 Q4
Thornton Nthumb 117 L11
Thornton Pembks 36 H9
Thornton Sefton 75 K3
Thornton Curtis N Linc 87 K11
Thorntonhall S Lans 113 R10
Thornton Heath Gt Lon 33 K8
Thornton Hough Wirral 75 J7
Thornton-in-Craven N York 84 D5
Thornton in Lonsdale N York 89 R12
Thornton-le-Beans N York 91 P8
Thornton-le-Clay N York 86 C2
Thornton-le-Dale N York 92 G10
Thornton le Moor Lincs 79 P4
Thornton-le-Moor N York 91 P9
Thornton-le-Moors Ches W 75 M9
Thornton-le-Street N York 91 P9
Thorntonloch E Loth 116 G6
Thornton Rust N York 90 F9
Thornton Steward N York 91 K9
Thornton Watlass N York 91 L9
Thornwood Common Essex 45 N10
Thornydykes Border 116 E11
Thornythwaite Cumb 89 L2
Thoroton Notts 67 J4
Thorp Arch Leeds 85 N6
Thorpe Derbys 65 M2
Thorpe E R Yk 87 J6
Thorpe Lincs 81 J7
Thorpe N York 84 F3
Thorpe Norfk 59 N1
Thorpe Notts 67 J2
Thorpe Surrey 32 E8
Thorpe Abbotts Norfk 59 J5
Thorpe Acre Leics 66 E8
Thorpe Arnold Leics 67 K8
Thorpe Audlin Wakefd 85 P12
Thorpe Bassett N York 92 H12
Thorpe Bay Sthend 34 G5
Thorpe by Water Rutlnd 55 M1
Thorpe Common Rothm 78 C5
Thorpe Constantine Staffs 65 N10
Thorpe End Norfk 71 K10
Thorpe Green Essex 47 L7
Thorpe Green Lancs 83 N10
Thorpe Green Suffk 58 D9
Thorpe Hesley Rothm 78 B4
Thorpe in Balne Donc 78 F2
Thorpe Langton Leics 55 J2
Thorpe Larches Dur 91 P2
Thorpe Lea Surrey 32 E8
Thorpe le Fallows Lincs 79 M7
Thorpe-le-Soken Essex 47 L7
Thorpe le Street E R Yk 86 F6
Thorpe Malsor Nhants 55 L5
Thorpe Mandeville Nhants 43 L3
Thorpe Market Norfk 71 K5
Thorpe Marriot Norfk 70 H9
Thorpe Morieux Suffk 58 D10
Thorpeness Suffk 59 P8
Thorpe on the Hill Leeds 85 L10
Thorpe on the Hill Lincs 79 M10
Thorpe Park Resort Surrey 32 E8
Thorpe St Andrew Norfk 71 K10
Thorpe St Peter Lincs 81 J11
Thorpe Salvin Rothm 78 E7
Thorpe Satchville Leics 67 J10
Thorpe Thewles S on T 91 P2
Thorpe Tilney Lincs 80 C12
Thorpe Underwood N York 85 P3
Thorpe Underwood Nhants 55 K4
Thorpe Waterville Nhants 55 P4
Thorpe Willoughby N York 86 A9
Thorpland Norfk 69 M10
Thorrington Essex 47 K7
Thorverton Devon 8 H4
Thrales End C Beds 44 G8
Thrandeston Suffk 58 G5
Thrapston Nhants 55 P5
Threapland Cumb 97 N10
Threapland N York 84 E3
Threapwood Ches W 63 M3
Threapwood Staffs 65 J4
Threapwood Head Staffs 65 J4
Threave S Ayrs 104 F8
Three Ashes Herefs 40 G7
Three Bridges W Susx 15 K3
Three Burrows Cnwll 3 J5
Three Chimneys Kent 16 E3
Three Cocks Powys 40 A4
Three Crosses Swans 26 E3
Three Cups Corner E Susx 16 B7
Three Gates Worcs 52 C8
Threehammer Common Norfk 71 L8
Three Hammers Cnwll 7 J7
Three Holes Norfk 69 K12
Threekingham Lincs 68 B5
Three Leg Cross E Susx 16 B4
Three Legged Cross Dorset 11 Q4
Three Mile Cross Wokham 31 P9
Threemilestone Cnwll 3 J5
Threemiletown W Loth 115 K6
Three Oaks E Susx 16 E8
Threlkeld Cumb 89 J2
Threshers Bush Essex 45 P10
Threshfield N York 84 E2
Thrigby Norfk 71 P9
Thringarth Dur 90 F2
Thringstone Leics 66 C8
Thrintoft N York 91 N8
Thriplow Cambs 45 N2
Throapham Rothm 78 E6
Throckenhalt Lincs 68 G10
Throcking Herts 45 L6
Throckley N u Ty 100 F5
Throckmorton Worcs 52 H10
Throop BCP 11 Q6
Throop Dorset 11 K6
Throphill Nthumb 100 E1
Thropton Nthumb 108 G9
Throsk Stirlg 114 F3
Througham Gloucs 41 Q10
Throughgate D & G 96 H1
Throwleigh Devon 8 C6
Throwley Kent 34 H11
Throwley Forstal Kent 34 H11
Thrumpton Notts 66 E6
Thrumpton Notts 78 H7
Thrumster Highld 151 P7
Thrunscoe NE Lin 80 F2
Thrunton Nthumb 108 H7
Thrup Oxon 30 G3
Thrupp Gloucs 41 P11
Thrupp Oxon 43 K8
Thrushelton Devon 7 N7
Thrussington Leics 66 G9
Thruxton Hants 24 D4
Thruxton Herefs 40 F5
Thrybergh Rothm 78 D5
Thulston Derbys 66 C6
Thundersley Essex 34 D5
Thurcaston Leics 66 F10
Thurcroft Rothm 78 E6
Thurdon Cnwll 7 K3
Thurgarton Norfk 71 J5
Thurgarton Notts 66 H2
Thurgoland Barns 77 P3
Thurlaston Leics 66 E12
Thurlaston Warwks 54 D6
Thurlbear Somset 21 L9
Thurlby Lincs 68 B9
Thurlby Lincs 79 M11
Thurlby Lincs 81 J8
Thurleigh Bed 55 Q9
Thurlestone Devon 5 L8
Thurloxton Somset 21 L7
Thurlstone Barns 77 N3
Thurlton Norfk 59 N1
Thurlwood Ches E 76 E12
Thurmaston Leics 66 G10
Thurnby Leics 66 G11
Thurne Norfk 71 M9
Thurnham Kent 34 E10
Thurning Nhants 56 B4
Thurning Norfk 70 G6
Thurnscoe Barns 78 D3
Thurrock Services Thurr 33 Q6
Thursby Cumb 98 C8
Thursden Lancs 84 D8
Thursford Norfk 70 E5
Thursley Surrey 14 C3
Thurso Highld 151 K3
Thurstaston Wirral 74 H7
Thurston Suffk 58 D7
Thurston Clough Oldham 76 H2
Thurstonfield Cumb 98 C7
Thurstonland Kirk 77 M2
Thurston Planche Suffk 58 D8
Thurton Norfk 71 L12
Thurvaston Derbys 65 N5
Thuxton Norfk 70 F10
Thwaite N York 90 E7
Thwaite Suffk 58 G7
Thwaite Head Cumb 89 K8
Thwaites C Brad 84 G7
Thwaite St Mary Norfk 59 L2
Thwaites Brow C Brad 84 G7
Thwing E R Yk 87 K1
Tibbermore P & K 123 Q8
Tibbers D & G 105 Q10
Tibberton Gloucs 41 M7
Tibberton Worcs 52 G9
Tibberton Wrekin 64 C8
Tibenham Norfk 58 H3
Tibshelf Derbys 78 D11
Tibshelf Services Derbys 78 D11
Tibthorpe E R Yk 86 H4
Ticehurst E Susx 16 C5
Tichborne Hants 25 J7
Tickencote Rutlnd 67 N10
Tickenham N Som 28 F8
Tickford End M Keyn 44 C3
Tickhill Donc 78 F5
Ticklerton Shrops 51 N2
Ticknall Derbys 66 B7
Tickton E R Yk 87 K7
Tidbury Green Solhll 53 L5
Tidcombe Wilts 30 G10
Tiddington Oxon 43 N10
Tiddington Warwks 53 N9
Tiddleywink Wilts 29 P7
Tidebrook E Susx 15 R5
Tideford Cnwll 4 E5
Tideford Cross Cnwll 4 E4
Tidenham Gloucs 28 H3
Tideswell Derbys 77 M8
Tidmarsh W Berk 31 N7
Tidmington Warwks 42 F4
Tidpit Hants 23 N9
Tidworth Wilts 24 D4
Tiers Cross Pembks 36 H8
Tiffield Nhants 54 H10
Tigerton Angus 132 E11
Tigh a' Ghearraidh W Isls 152 b8
Tigharry W Isls 152 b8
Tighnabruaich Ag & B 112 E7
Tigley Devon 5 M4
Tilbrook Cambs 55 Q7
Tilbury Thurr 34 B7
Tilbury Dock Thurr 34 B7
Tilbury Green Essex 46 D3
Tilbury Juxta Clare Essex 46 D4
Tile Cross Birm 53 M3
Tile Hill Covtry 53 P5
Tilehouse Green Solhll 53 M5
Tilehurst Readg 31 N7
Tilford Surrey 14 B2
Tilgate W Susx 15 K4
Tilgate Forest Row W Susx 15 J4
Tilham Street Somset 22 D6
Tillers Green Gloucs 41 L5
Tilley Shrops 63 N6
Tillicoultry Clacks 114 G2
Tillietudlem S Lans 114 E12
Tillingham Essex 46 H11
Tillington Herefs 40 G3
Tillington W Susx 14 D6
Tillington Common Herefs 40 F3
Tillybirloch Abers 132 G3
Tillyfourie Abers 132 G2
Tillygreig Abers 141 L11
Tillyrie P & K 124 C11
Tilmanstone Kent 35 N12
Tilney All Saints Norfk 69 L8
Tilney High End Norfk 69 L8
Tilney St Lawrence Norfk 69 K9
Tilshead Wilts 23 M4
Tilstock Shrops 63 P5
Tilston Ches W 63 M2
Tilstone Bank Ches W 75 P11
Tilstone Fearnall Ches W 75 P11
Tilsworth C Beds 44 D7
Tilton on the Hill Leics 67 J11
Tiltups End Gloucs 29 N3
Tilty Essex 45 Q6
Timberland Lincs 80 C12
Timbersbrook Ches E 76 G11
Timberscombe Somset 20 E5
Timble N York 85 J4
Timewell Devon 20 E8
Timpanheck D & G 98 C3
Timperley Traffd 76 E6
Timsbury BaNES 29 K10
Timsbury Hants 24 E8
Timsgarry W Isls 152 d3
Timsgearraidh W Isls 152 d3
Timworth Suffk 58 C7
Timworth Green Suffk 58 C7
Tincleton Dorset 11 J6
Tindale Cumb 99 J6
Tingewick Bucks 43 N5
Tingley Leeds 85 L10
Tingrith C Beds 44 E5
Tingwall Airport Shet 147 i7
Tingwell Ork 147 c3
Tinhay Devon 7 M7
Tinker's Hill Hants 24 F4
Tinkersley Derbys 77 P10
Tinsley Sheff 78 C5
Tinsley Green W Susx 15 K3
Tintagel Cnwll 6 F7
Tintern Mons 28 H2
Tintinhull Somset 22 C9
Tintwistle Derbys 77 J4
Tinwald D & G 97 K2
Tinwell Rutlnd 67 P11
Tippacott Devon 19 P4
Tipp's End Norfk 57 K2
Tiptoe Hants 12 D5
Tipton Sandw 52 H2
Tipton Green Sandw 52 H2
Tipton St John Devon 9 L6
Tiptree Essex 46 F8
Tiptree Heath Essex 46 F8
Tirabad Powys 39 L3
Tircoed Swans 26 F2
Tiree Ag & B 118 E4
Tiree Airport Ag & B 118 D4
Tiretigan Ag & B 111 Q9
Tirley Gloucs 41 N6
Tiroran Ag & B 119 N7
Tirphil Caerph 39 Q11
Tirril Cumb 89 N1
Tir-y-fron Flints 75 J11
Tisbury Wilts 23 L7
Tisman's Common W Susx 14 F4
Tissington Derbys 65 M2
Titchberry Devon 18 E8
Titchfield Hants 13 J4
Titchfield Common Hants 13 J3
Titchmarsh Nhants 55 P5
Titchwell Norfk 69 P3
Tithby Notts 66 H5
Tithebarn Devon 9 J6
Titley Herefs 51 K8
Titmore Green Herts 45 J6
Titsey Surrey 33 M11
Titson Cnwll 7 J4
Tittensor Staffs 64 G4
Tittleshall Norfk 70 C8
Titton Worcs 52 F6
Tiverton Ches W 75 P11
Tiverton Devon 20 E10
Tivetshall St Margaret Norfk 58 H3
Tivetshall St Mary Norfk 58 H3
Tivington Somset 20 E4
Tivy Dale Barns 77 P2
Tixall Staffs 64 H7
Tixover Rutlnd 67 N12
Toab Shet 147 i10
Toadhole Derbys 78 C12
Toadmoor Derbys 65 Q2
Tobermory Ag & B 119 N2
Toberonochy Ag & B 120 D11
Tobha Mòr W Isls 152 b10
Tocher Abers 140 H9
Tochieneal Moray 140 D3
Tockenham Wilts 30 B6
Tockenham Wick Wilts 30 B6
Tocketts R & Cl 92 C3
Tockholes Bl w D 83 P10
Tockington S Glos 29 J5
Tockwith N York 85 P5
Todber Dorset 22 H9
Todburn Nthumb 109 J10
Toddington C Beds 44 E6
Toddington Gloucs 42 B5
Toddington Services C Beds 44 E6
Todds Green Herts 45 J6
Todenham Gloucs 42 F4
Todhills Angus 124 H5
Todhills Cumb 98 D6
Todhills Dur 100 G11
Todhills Rest Area Cumb 98 D6
Todmorden Calder 84 D10
Todwick Rothm 78 E7
Toft Cambs 56 G9
Toft Ches E 76 E8
Toft Lincs 67 Q8
Toft Shet 147 i5
Toft Warwks 54 D6
Toft Hill Dur 91 K1
Toft Hill Lincs 80 E11
Toft Monks Norfk 59 N2
Toft next Newton Lincs 79 P6
Toftrees Norfk 70 C6
Toftwood Norfk 70 E10
Togston Nthumb 109 L9
Tokavaig Highld 127 L2
Tokers Green Oxon 31 P7
Tolastadh bho Thuath W Isls 152 h2
Toldish Cnwll 3 M3
Tolland Somset 20 H7
Tollard Farnham Dorset 23 L10
Tollard Royal Wilts 23 L10
Toll Bar Donc 78 F2
Tollbar End Covtry 54 B5
Toller Fratrum Dorset 10 F5
Toller Porcorum Dorset 10 E5
Tollerton N York 85 Q2
Tollerton Notts 66 G5
Toller Whelme Dorset 10 D4
Tollesbury Essex 46 G9
Tolleshunt D'Arcy Essex 46 G9
Tolleshunt Knights Essex 46 G8
Tolleshunt Major Essex 46 F9
Tollingham E R Yk 86 F8
Toll of Birness Abers 141 N9
Tolpuddle Dorset 11 J6
Tolworth Gt Lon 32 H9
Tomatin Highld 138 E10
Tomchrasky Highld 129 J2
Tomdoun Highld 128 G4
Tomich Highld 137 K10
Tomich Highld 137 P6
Tomich Highld 145 N4
Tomich Highld 146 C11
Tomintoul Moray 139 M12
Tomlow Warwks 54 D8
Tomnacross Highld 137 N7
Tomnavoulin Moray 139 M10
Tompkin Staffs 64 H2
Ton Mons 28 D2
Ton Mons 28 E3
Tonbridge Kent 15 Q2
Tondu Brdgnd 27 L5
Tonedale Somset 20 H9
Tonfanau Gwynd 61 J11
Tong C Brad 85 J9
Tong Kent 34 G11
Tong Shrops 64 E10
Tong W Isls 152 g3
Tonge Leics 66 C7
Tong Green Kent 34 H11
Tongham Surrey 14 C1
Tongland D & G 96 E7
Tong Norton Shrops 64 E10
Tongue Highld 149 M5
Tongue End Lincs 68 C8
Tongwynlais Cardif 27 Q6
Tonmawr Neath 27 J3
Tonna Neath 27 J3
Ton-teg Rhondd 27 P5
Tonwell Herts 45 L8
Tonypandy Rhondd 27 N4
Tonyrefail Rhondd 27 N5
Toot Baldon Oxon 31 M2
Toot Hill Essex 45 P11
Toothill Hants 24 F9
Toothill Swindn 30 D6
Tooting Gt Lon 33 K8
Tooting Bec Gt Lon 33 K8
Topcliffe N York 91 P11
Topcroft Norfk 59 K2
Topcroft Street Norfk 59 K2
Top End Bed 55 P8
Topham Donc 86 B11
Top of Hebers Rochdl 76 F2
Toppesfield Essex 46 C4
Toprow Norfk 58 H1
Topsham Devon 8 H7
Top-y-rhos Flints 75 J12
Torbeg N Ayrs 103 N4
Torboll Highld 146 D5
Torbreck Highld 138 B7
Torbryan Devon 5 N3
Torcastle Highld 128 G8
Torcross Devon 5 N8
Tore Highld 137 Q5
Torfrey Cnwll 3 Q4
Torinturk Ag & B 112 B8
Torksey Lincs 79 L8
Torlundy Highld 128 G9
Tormarton S Glos 29 M6
Tormore N Ayrs 103 N3
Tornagrain Highld 138 E6
Tornaveen Abers 132 F3
Torness Highld 137 Q10
Toronto Dur 100 G12
Torpenhow Cumb 97 P10
Torphichen W Loth 114 H7
Torphins Abers 132 F4
Torpoint Cnwll 4 G6
Torquay Torbay 5 Q4
Torquhan Border 116 B11
Torr Devon 5 J6
Torran Highld 135 K6
Torrance E Duns 114 B6
Torranyard N Ayrs 104 F1
Torre Somset 20 G5
Torridon Highld 136 C5
Torridon House Highld 136 B4
Torrin Highld 135 K11
Torrisdale Ag & B 103 L3
Torrisdale Highld 149 P4
Torrish Highld 146 H1
Torrisholme Lancs 83 K2
Torrobull Highld 145 N4
Torry C Aber 133 M3
Torryburn Fife 115 J4
Torteval Guern 12 b3
Torthorwald D & G 97 L3
Tortington W Susx 14 E10
Torton Worcs 52 F6
Tortworth S Glos 29 L4
Torvaig Highld 135 J7
Torver Cumb 89 J8
Torwood Falk 114 F4
Torwoodlee Border 107 M2
Torworth Notts 78 G6
Tosberry Devon 18 E9
Toscaig Highld 135 N8
Toseland Cambs 56 E8
Tosside Lancs 84 A4
Tostock Suffk 58 D8
Totaig Highld 134 C6
Tote Highld 134 G6
Tote Highld 135 J4
Tote Hill W Susx 14 B6
Totford Hants 25 J6
Tothill Lincs 80 H7
Totland IoW 12 E7
Totley Sheff 77 P8
Totley Brook Sheff 77 P7
Totnes Devon 5 N5
Toton Notts 66 E5
Totronald Ag & B 118 G2
Totscore Highld 134 G3
Tottenham Gt Lon 33 L4
Tottenhill Norfk 69 M10
Totteridge Gt Lon 33 J3
Totternhoe C Beds 44 D7
Tottington Bury 76 E1
Tottleworth Lancs 83 Q9
Totton Hants 24 F10
Touchen End W & M 32 C7
Toulston N York 85 P6
Toulton Somset 21 K7
Toulvaddie Highld 146 F9
Tovil Kent 34 D11
Towan Cnwll 3 P5
Towan Cnwll 6 C10
Toward Ag & B 112 H7
Toward Quay Ag & B 112 G7
Towcester Nhants 54 H11
Towednack Cnwll 2 D7
Tower of London Gt Lon 33 L6
Towersey Oxon 43 Q10
Towie Abers 132 C2
Tow Law Dur 100 E10
Town End Cambs 56 H2
Town End Cumb 89 K5
Town End Cumb 89 L10
Town End Cumb 89 Q2
Townend W Duns 113 M6
Towngate Cumb 98 G9
Towngate Lincs 68 C10
Town Green Lancs 75 L3
Town Green Norfk 71 M9
Townhead Barns 77 M3
Town Head Cumb 89 L6
Townhead Cumb 97 M11
Townhead Cumb 99 J11
Townhead D & G 106 C12
Town Head N York 84 B3
Townhead of Greenlaw D & G 96 F5
Townhill Fife 115 K3
Town Kelloe Dur 101 J11
Townlake Devon 7 M9
Town Lane Wigan 76 C4
Town Littleworth E Susx 15 M7
Town of Lowton Wigan 75 Q4
Town Row E Susx 15 Q5
Towns End Hants 31 M10
Townsend Somset 21 N10
Townshend Cnwll 2 F8
Town Street Suffk 57 P3
Townwell S Glos 29 L4
Town Yetholm Border 108 C4
Towthorpe C York 86 B3
Towthorpe E R Yk 86 G3
Towton N York 85 P7
Towyn Conwy 74 D8
Toxteth Lpool 75 K6
Toynton All Saints Lincs 80 H11
Toynton Fen Side Lincs 80 H11
Toynton St Peter Lincs 80 H11
Toy's Hill Kent 33 N12
Trabboch E Ayrs 104 H5
Trabbochburn E Ayrs 104 H5
Traboe Cnwll 3 J10
Tracebridge Somset 20 G9
Tradespark Highld 138 F5
Trafford Park Traffd 76 E4
Trallong Powys 39 M6
Tranent E Loth 115 R7
Tranmere Wirral 75 K6
Trantelbeg Highld 150 F6
Trantlemore Highld 150 F6
Tranwell Nthumb 100 F2
Trap Carmth 38 G8
Traprain E Loth 116 D6
Trap's Green Warwks 53 L7
Trapshill W Berk 30 H9
Traquair Border 107 J3
Trash Green W Berk 31 N8
Trawden Lancs 84 D7
Trawscoed Cerdgn 49 L6
Trawsfynydd Gwynd 61 M5
Trealaw Rhondd 27 N4
Treales Lancs 83 K8
Trearddur Bay IoA 72 D8
Treator Cnwll 6 C9
Tre Aubrey V Glam 27 N8
Trebanog Rhondd 27 N4
Trebanos Neath 38 H11
Trebartha Cnwll 7 K9
Trebarwith Cnwll 6 F7
Trebeath Cnwll 7 J7
Trebetherick Cnwll 6 D9
Treborough Somset 20 F6
Trebudannon Cnwll 3 L2
Trebullett Cnwll 7 L9
Treburgett Cnwll 6 F9
Treburley Cnwll 7 L9
Treburrick Cnwll 6 B10
Trebyan Cnwll 3 Q2
Trecastle Powys 39 L6
Trecogo Cnwll 7 K8
Trecott Devon 8 C5
Trecwn Pembks 37 J4
Trecynon Rhondd 39 N11
Tredaule Cnwll 7 J8
Tredavoe Cnwll 2 D9
Tredegar Blae G 39 Q10
Tredethy Cnwll 6 F10
Tredington Gloucs 41 P6
Tredington Warwks 42 F3
Tredinnick Cnwll 3 P3
Tredinnick Cnwll 4 B3
Tredinnick Cnwll 4 C5
Tredinnick Cnwll 4 D5
Tredinnick Cnwll 6 D10
Tredomen Powys 39 Q5
Tredrizzick Cnwll 6 D9
Tredunnock Mons 28 E3
Tredustan Powys 39 Q5
Treen Cnwll 2 B10
Treen Cnwll 2 C7
Treesmill Cnwll 3 Q3
Treeton Rothm 78 C6
Trefasser Pembks 36 H3
Trefdraeth IoA 72 G9
Trefecca Powys 39 Q5
Trefechan Myr Td 39 N10
Trefeglwys Powys 50 C3
Trefenter Cerdgn 49 K7
Treffgarne Pembks 37 J6
Treffgarne Owen Pembks 36 G5
Treffynnon Pembks 36 G5
Trefil Blae G 39 Q9
Trefilan Cerdgn 49 J9
Trefin Pembks 36 G4
Treflach Shrops 63 J7
Trefnannau Powys 62 H9
Trefnant Denbgs 74 E9
Trefonen Shrops 63 J7
Trefor Gwynd 60 F3
Trefor IoA 72 F7
Treforest Rhondd 27 P4
Trefrew Cnwll 6 G8
Trefriw Conwy 73 N11
Tregadillett Cnwll 7 K8
Tre-gagle Mons 40 H10
Tregaian IoA 72 G7
Tregare Mons 40 F9
Tregarne Cnwll 3 J10
Tregaron Cerdgn 49 L8
Tregarth Gwynd 73 K10
Tregaswith Cnwll 3 L2
Tregatta Cnwll 6 F7
Tregawne Cnwll 6 E11
Tregeare Cnwll 7 J7
Tregeiriog Wrexhm 62 G5
Tregele IoA 72 F5
Tregellist Cnwll 6 E9
Tregenna Cnwll 3 L6
Tregeseal Cnwll 2 B8
Tregew Cnwll 3 K7
Tre-Gibbon Rhondd 39 N10
Tregidden Cnwll 3 J10
Tregiskey Cnwll 3 P5
Treglemais Pembks 36 F5
Tregole Cnwll 6 H5
Tregolls Cnwll 3 J7
Tregonce Cnwll 6 D10
Tregonetha Cnwll 3 N2
Tregonning & Gwinear Mining District Cnwll 2 F8
Tregony Cnwll 3 M5
Tregoodwell Cnwll 6 G8
Tregorrick Cnwll 3 P4
Tregoss Cnwll 3 N2
Tregoyd Powys 40 B4
Tregrehan Mills Cnwll 3 P4
Tre-groes Cerdgn 38 B3
Tregullon Cnwll 3 P2
Tregunna Cnwll 6 D10
Tregunnon Cnwll 7 J8
Tregurrian Cnwll 6 B11
Tregynon Powys 50 F1
Tre-gynwr Carmth 38 B8
Trehafod Rhondd 27 P4
Trehan Cnwll 4 F5
Treharris Myr Td 27 P3
Treharrock Cnwll 6 E9
Trehemborne Cnwll 6 C10
Treherbert Carmth 38 E2
Treherbert Rhondd 27 M3
Trehunist Cnwll 4 D4
Trekenner Cnwll 7 L9
Treknow Cnwll 6 F7
Trelan Cnwll 3 J10
Trelash Cnwll 6 H7
Trelassick Cnwll 3 L4
Trelawne Cnwll 4 C6
Trelawnyd Flints 74 F8
Treleague Cnwll 3 K10
Treleaver Cnwll 3 J11
Trelech Carmth 37 Q4
Trelech a'r Betws Carmth 37 Q5
Treleddyd-fawr Pembks 36 E5
Trelew Cnwll 3 K7
Trelewis Myr Td 27 Q3
Treligga Cnwll 6 F8
Trelights Cnwll 6 E9
Trelill Cnwll 6 F9
Trelinnoe Cnwll 7 K8
Trelion Cnwll 3 M4
Trelissick Cnwll 3 K6
Trellech Mons 40 G10
Trelleck Grange Mons 28 G2
Trelogan Flints 74 F7
Trelow Cnwll 6 D10
Trelowarren Cnwll 2 H9
Trelowia Cnwll 4 D5
Treluggan Cnwll 3 L7
Trelystan Powys 63 J11
Tremadog Gwynd 61 J4
Tremail Cnwll 6 H7
Tremain Cerdgn 48 C11
Tremaine Cnwll 7 J7
Tremar Cnwll 4 C3
Trematon Cnwll 4 F5
Trembraze Cnwll 4 C4
Tremeirchion Denbgs 74 F9
Tremethick Cross Cnwll 2 C8
Tremore Cnwll 6 E11
Tre-Mostyn Flints 74 G8
Trenance Cnwll 3 K10
Trenance Cnwll 6 B11
Trenance Cnwll 6 D10
Trenarren Cnwll 3 P5
Trench Wrekin 64 C9
Trench Green Oxon 31 P7
Trendeal Cnwll 3 L4
Trendrine Cnwll 2 D6
Treneague Cnwll 6 E10
Trenear Cnwll 2 H8
Treneglos Cnwll 7 J7
Trenerth Cnwll 2 F7
Trenewan Cnwll 4 B6
Trenewth Cnwll 6 F9
Trengune Cnwll 6 H6
Treninnick Cnwll 3 K2
Trenowah Cnwll 3 K3
Trenoweth Cnwll 3 J8
Trent Dorset 22 D9
Trentham C Stke 64 G4
Trentishoe Devon 19 M4
Trentlock Derbys 66 D6
Trent Port Lincs 79 L7
Trent Vale C Stke 64 F3
Trenwheal Cnwll 2 G8
Treoes V Glam 27 M7
Treorchy Rhondd 27 M3
Trequite Cnwll 6 E9
Tre'r-ddol Cerdgn 49 L2
Trerhyngyll V Glam 27 N7
Trerulefoot Cnwll 4 E5
Tresaith Cerdgn 48 D10
Tresawle Cnwll 3 L5
Tresco IoS 2 b1
Trescott Staffs 52 F1
Trescowe Cnwll 2 F8
Tresean Cnwll 3 J3
Tresham Gloucs 29 M4
Treshnish Isles Ag & B 118 H5
Tresillian Cnwll 3 L5
Tresinney Cnwll 6 G8
Treskinnick Cross Cnwll 7 J5
Tresmeer Cnwll 7 J7
Tresparrett Cnwll 6 G6
Tressait P & K 130 E12
Tresta Shet 147 i6
Tresta Shet 147 k3
Treswell Notts 79 K8
Treswithian Cnwll 2 G6
Tre Taliesin Cerdgn 49 L2
Trethevey Cnwll 6 F7
Trethewey Cnwll 2 B9
Trethomas Caerph 28 A4
Trethosa Cnwll 3 M4
Trethurgy Cnwll 3 P3
Tretio Pembks 36 F5
Tretire Herefs 40 G7
Tretower Powys 40 B7
Treuddyn Flints 75 J12
Trevadlock Cnwll 7 K9
Trevalga Cnwll 6 F7
Trevalyn Wrexhm 75 L12
Trevanger Cnwll 6 D9
Trevanson Cnwll 6 E10
Trevarrack Cnwll 2 D8
Trevarren Cnwll 3 M2
Trevarrian Cnwll 6 B11
Trevarrick Cnwll 3 N6
Trevarth Cnwll 2 H6
Trevaughan Carmth 37 N7
Tre-vaughan Carmth 38 B7
Treveal Cnwll 2 D6
Treveal Cnwll 3 J3
Treveighan Cnwll 6 F9
Trevellas Downs Cnwll 3 J4
Trevelmond Cnwll 4 B4
Trevemper Cnwll 3 K3
Treveor Cnwll 3 N6
Treverbyn Cnwll 3 L5
Treverbyn Cnwll 3 P3
Treverva Cnwll 3 J8
Trevescan Cnwll 2 B9
Trevethin Torfn 40 C11
Trevia Cnwll 6 G8
Trevigro Cnwll 4 E3
Trevilla Cnwll 3 K7
Trevilson Cnwll 3 L3
Treviscoe Cnwll 3 M3
Treviskey Cnwll 3 M6
Trevithick Cnwll 3 L2
Trevithick Cnwll 3 N5
Trevoll Cnwll 3 K3
Trevone Cnwll 6 C9
Trevor Wrexhm 63 J4
Trevorgans Cnwll 2 C9
Trevorrick Cnwll 6 D10
Trevose Cnwll 6 B9
Trew Cnwll 2 F8
Trewalder Cnwll 6 F8
Trewalkin Powys 39 R5
Trewarmett Cnwll 6 F7
Trewassa Cnwll 6 H7
Trewavas Cnwll 2 F9
Trewavas Mining District Cnwll 2 F9
Treween Cnwll 7 J8
Trewellard Cnwll 2 B8
Trewen Cnwll 7 J8
Trewennack Cnwll 2 H9
Trewent Pembks 37 K11
Trewern Powys 63 J10
Trewetha Cnwll 6 E8
Trewethern Cnwll 6 E9
Trewidland Cnwll 4 C5
Trewillis Cnwll 3 J11
Trewint Cnwll 4 D4
Trewint Cnwll 7 J8
Trewithian Cnwll 3 L7
Trewoodloe Cnwll 7 L10
Trewoon Cnwll 2 H10
Trewoon Cnwll 3 N4
Treworga Cnwll 3 L6
Treworgan Cnwll 3 K4
Treworlas Cnwll 3 L7
Treworld Cnwll 6 G6
Treworthal Cnwll 3 L7
Tre-wyn Mons 40 D7
Treyarnon Cnwll 6 B10
Treyford W Susx 25 P9
Trickett's Cross Dorset 11 Q4
Triermain Cumb 98 H5
Triffleton Pembks 37 J6
Trillacott Cnwll 7 K7
Trimdon Dur 101 K11
Trimdon Colliery Dur 101 K11
Trimdon Grange Dur 101 K11
Trimdon Station Dur 101 K11
Trimingham Norfk 71 K4
Trimley Lower Street Suffk 47 N4
Trimley St Martin Suffk 47 N4
Trimley St Mary Suffk 47 N4
Trimpley Worcs 52 E5
Trimsaran Carmth 38 C10
Trims Green Herts 45 N8
Trimstone Devon 19 K5
Trinafour P & K 130 D11
Trinant Caerph 28 B2
Tring Herts 44 C9
Tringford Herts 44 C9
Tring Wharf Herts 44 C9
Trinity Angus 132 F12
Trinity Jersey 13 c1
Trinity Gask P & K 123 N9
Triscombe Somset 21 J6
Trislaig Highld 128 F9
Trispen Cnwll 3 K4
Tritlington Nthumb 109 K11
Troan Cnwll 3 L3
Trochry P & K 123 P5
Troedrhiwfuwch Caerph 39 Q10
Troedyraur Cerdgn 48 E11
Troedyrhiw Myr Td 39 P11
Trofarth Conwy 73 Q9
Trois Bois Jersey 13 b2
Troon Cnwll 2 G7
Troon S Ayrs 104 F4
Tropical World Leeds Leeds 85 L7
Trossachs Stirlg 122 E11
Trossachs Pier Stirlg 122 E11
Troston Suffk 58 C6
Troswell Cnwll 7 J6
Trotshill Worcs 52 G9
Trottiscliffe Kent 34 B10
Trotton W Susx 25 P9
Troughend Nthumb 108 D11
Trough Gate Lancs 84 D11
Troutbeck Cumb 89 L1
Troutbeck Cumb 89 L6
Troutbeck Bridge Cumb 89 L7
Troway Derbys 78 C8
Trowbridge Wilts 29 P10
Trowell Notts 66 D4
Trowell Services Notts 66 E4
Trowle Common Wilts 29 N10
Trowley Bottom Herts 44 F9
Trowse Newton Norfk 71 K10
Troy Leeds 85 K7
Trudoxhill Somset 22 G5
Trull Somset 21 K9
Trumfleet Donc 78 F1
Trumpan Highld 134 D4
Trumpet Herefs 41 K4
Trumpington Cambs 56 H9
Trumpsgreen Surrey 32 E9
Trunch Norfk 71 K5
Trunnah Lancs 82 H6
Truro Cnwll 3 K5
Truscott Cnwll 7 K7
Trusham Devon 8 F8
Trusley Derbys 65 N5
Trusthorpe Lincs 81 K7
Trysull Staffs 52 F2
Tubney Oxon 31 J3
Tuckenhay Devon 5 N5
Tuckhill Shrops 52 E3
Tuckingmill Cnwll 2 G6
Tuckingmill Wilts 23 L7
Tuckton BCP 12 B6
Tucoyse Cnwll 3 N5
Tuddenham Suffk 57 P6
Tuddenham St Martin Suffk 59 J11
Tudeley Kent 16 A2
Tudhoe Dur 100 H11
Tudorville Herefs 41 J7
Tudweiliog Gwynd 60 D5
Tuesley Surrey 14 D2
Tuffley Gloucs 41 N8
Tufton Hants 24 G4
Tufton Pembks 37 K5
Tugby Leics 67 J12
Tugford Shrops 51 P3
Tughall Nthumb 109 K4
Tullibody Clacks 114 F2
Tullich Abers 132 B5
Tullich Highld 138 B10
Tullich Highld 146 F10
Tulliemet P & K 123 P2
Tulloch Abers 141 J9
Tullochgorm Ag & B 112 E2
Tulloch Station Highld 129 L8
Tullymurdoch P & K 124 D2
Tullynessle Abers 140 E12
Tulse Hill Gt Lon 33 K8
Tumble Carmth 38 E9
Tumbler's Green Essex 46 E6
Tumby Lincs 80 E11
Tumby Woodside Lincs 80 E12
Tummel Bridge P & K 123 K1
Tunbridge Wells Kent 15 Q3
Tundergarth D & G 97 N2
Tunga W Isls 152 g3
Tungate Norfk 71 K6
Tunley BaNES 29 L10
Tunstall C Stke 64 F2
Tunstall E R Yk 87 P9
Tunstall Kent 34 F10
Tunstall Lancs 89 P12
Tunstall N York 91 L7
Tunstall Norfk 71 N10
Tunstall Staffs 64 E6
Tunstall Suffk 59 M9
Tunstall Sundld 101 K7
Tunstead Derbys 77 L8
Tunstead Norfk 71 L8
Tunstead Milton Derbys 77 J7
Tunworth Hants 25 L4
Tupsley Herefs 40 H4
Turgis Green Hants 31 P10
Turkdean Gloucs 42 C8
Tur Langton Leics 54 H2
Turleigh Wilts 29 N10
Turleygreen Shrops 52 E4
Turn Lancs 84 B11
Turnastone Herefs 40 E4
Turnberry S Ayrs 104 D8
Turnchapel C Plym 4 H6
Turnditch Derbys 65 P3
Turner Green Lancs 83 N9
Turner's Green E Susx 16 B7
Turner's Green Warwks 53 M7
Turners Hill W Susx 15 L4
Turners Puddle Dorset 11 K6
Turnford Herts 45 L10
Turnhouse C Edin 115 L6
Turnworth Dorset 11 K3
Turriff Abers 140 H6
Turton Bottoms Bl w D 83 Q12

Turves Cambs 56 G1
Turvey Bed 55 N10
Turville Bucks 31 Q4
Turville Heath Bucks 31 Q4
Turweston Bucks 43 M4
Tushielaw Inn Border 107 J6
Tutbury Staffs 65 N6
Tutnall Worcs 53 J6
Tutshill Gloucs 28 H3
Tuttington Norfk 71 J7
Tutts Clump W Berk 31 M8
Tutwell Cnwll 7 M9
Tuxford Notts 79 J9
Twatt Ork 147 b3
Twatt Shet 147 i6
Twechar E Duns 114 C6
Tweedbank Border 107 N3
Tweedmouth Nthumb 117 M10
Tweedsmuir Border 106 E5
Twelveheads Cnwll 3 J6
Twelve Oaks E Susx 16 C7
Twemlow Green Ches E 76 E10
Twenty Lincs 68 C8
Twerton BaNES 29 L9
Twickenham Gt Lon 32 H7
Twigworth Gloucs 41 N7
Twineham W Susx 15 J7
Twineham Green W Susx 15 J7
Twinhoe BaNES 29 M10
Twinstead Essex 46 F4
Twitchen Devon 20 B7
Twitchen Shrops 51 L5
Twitham Kent 35 N11
Two Bridges Devon 8 B9
Two Dales Derbys 77 P11
Two Gates Staffs 65 N12
Two Mile Ash W Susx 14 G5
Two Mile Oak Cross Devon 5 P3
Two Pots Devon 19 K4
Two Waters Herts 44 F10
Twycross Leics 65 Q11
Twycross Zoo Leics 65 P11
Twyford Bucks 43 N6
Twyford Hants 24 H8
Twyford Leics 67 J10
Twyford Lincs 67 M7
Twyford Norfk 70 F7
Twyford Wokham 31 R7
Twyford Common Herefs 40 G5
Twyn-carno Caerph 39 Q10
Twynholm D & G 96 D7
Twyning Gloucs 41 P4
Twynllanan Carmth 38 H7
Twyn-yr-Odyn V Glam 27 Q7
Twyn-y-Sheriff Mons 40 F10
Twywell Nhants 55 N5
Tyberton Herefs 40 E4
Tyburn Birm 53 L2
Tycroes Carmth 38 F9
Ty Croes IoA 72 E9
Tycrwyn Powys 62 F8
Tydd Gote Lincs 69 J8
Tydd St Giles Cambs 68 H9
Tydd St Mary Lincs 68 H8
Tye Hants 13 M4
Tye Green Essex 45 P7
Tye Green Essex 45 Q4
Tye Green Essex 46 D7
Tyersal C Brad 85 J8
Tyldesley Wigan 76 C3
Tyler Hill Kent 35 L10
Tylers Green Bucks 32 C3
Tyler's Green Essex 45 P10
Tylers Green Surrey 33 L12
Tylorstown Rhondd 27 N3
Tylwch Powys 50 D5
Ty-nant Conwy 62 D3
Ty-nant Gwynd 62 B7
Tyncelyn Cerdgn 49 L8
Tyndrum Stirlg 121 Q6
Ty'n-dwr Denbgs 62 H4
Tyneham Dorset 11 L8
Tynemouth N Tyne 101 K4
Tyne Tunnel S Tyne 101 J5
Tynewydd Rhondd 27 M3
Tyninghame E Loth 116 E5
Tynron D & G 105 P11
Ty'n-y-bryn Rhondd 27 N5
Ty'n-y-coedcae Caerph 28 B5
Tynygongl IoA 72 H7
Tynygraig Cerdgn 49 M7
Ty'n-y-Groes Conwy 73 N9
Tyn-y-nant Rhondd 27 P5
Tyrie Abers 141 M3
Tyringham M Keyn 44 B2
Tyseley Birm 53 L4
Tythegston Brdgnd 27 K6
Tytherington Ches E 76 G8
Tytherington S Glos 29 K5
Tytherington Somset 22 H4
Tytherington Wilts 23 K5
Tytherleigh Devon 9 Q4
Tytherton Lucas Wilts 29 Q7
Tyttenhanger Herts 44 H10
Tywardreath Cnwll 3 Q4
Tywardreath Highway Cnwll 3 Q3
Tywyn Conwy 73 N8
Tywyn Gwynd 61 K12

U

Ubbeston Green Suffk 59 L6
Ubley BaNES 28 H10
Uckerby N York 91 L6
Uckfield E Susx 15 N6
Uckinghall Worcs 41 P4
Uckington Gloucs 41 Q7
Uckington Shrops 63 P10
Uddingston S Lans 114 C9
Uddington S Lans 105 Q3
Udimore E Susx 16 F7
Udny Green Abers 141 L10
Udny Station Abers 141 L11
Uffcott Wilts 30 D7
Uffculme Devon 20 G10
Uffington Lincs 67 Q10
Uffington Oxon 30 G4
Uffington Shrops 63 N9
Ufford C Pete 68 B11
Ufford Suffk 59 L10
Ufton Warwks 54 C8
Ufton Nervet W Berk 31 N9
Ugadale Ag & B 103 L4
Ugborough Devon 5 L5
Uggeshall Suffk 59 N5
Ugglebarnby N York 92 H5
Ughill Sheff 77 N5
Ugley Essex 45 P6
Ugley Green Essex 45 P6
Ugthorpe N York 92 G4
Uibhist A Deas W Isls 152 c10
Uibhist A Tuath W Isls 152 b8
Uig Ag & B 118 G2
Uig Highld 134 C5
Uig Highld 134 G3
Uig W Isls 152 d3
Uigshader Highld 134 H6
Uisken Ag & B 119 L9
Ulbster Highld 151 P8
Ulcat Row Cumb 89 L2
Ulceby Lincs 80 H9
Ulceby N Linc 87 L12
Ulceby Skitter N Linc 87 L12
Ulcombe Kent 16 E1
Uldale Cumb 97 Q10
Uley Gloucs 29 M3
Ulgham Nthumb 109 L11
Ullapool Highld 144 E6
Ullenhall Warwks 53 L7
Ullenwood Gloucs 41 Q8
Ulleskelf N York 85 Q7
Ullesthorpe Leics 54 E3
Ulley Rothm 78 D6
Ullingswick Herefs 51 Q10
Ullock Cumb 88 E2
Ullswater Cumb 89 L3
Ullswater 'Steamers' Cumb 89 L3
Ulnes Walton Lancs 83 L11
Ulpha Cumb 88 G8
Ulpha Cumb 89 M10
Ulrome E R Yk 87 M4
Ulsta Shet 147 j4
Ulting Wick Essex 46 E10
Ulva Ag & B 119 L5
Ulverley Green Solhll 53 L4
Ulverston Cumb 89 J11
Ulwell Dorset 11 N8
Ulzieside D & G 105 P8
Umberleigh Devon 19 M8
Unapool Highld 148 F10
Underbarrow Cumb 89 M8
Under Burnmouth Border 98 F2
Undercliffe C Brad 85 J8
Underdale Shrops 63 N9
Underling Green Kent 16 D2
Underriver Kent 33 Q12
Underwood Newpt 28 E5
Underwood Notts 66 D2
Undley Suffk 57 N4
Undy Mons 28 F5
Union Mills IoM 102 d6
Union Street E Susx 16 C4
Unst Shet 147 k2
Unstone Derbys 78 B8
Unstone Green Derbys 78 B8
Unthank Cumb 98 E8
Unthank Cumb 98 F11
Unthank Cumb 98 H10
Unthank Derbys 77 P8
Unthank Nthumb 117 M11
Upavon Wilts 23 P2
Up Cerne Dorset 10 G4
Upchurch Kent 34 E9
Upcott Devon 19 P7
Upcott Herefs 51 K10
Upend Cambs 57 N9
Up Exe Devon 8 H4
Upgate Norfk 70 H8
Upgate Street Norfk 58 G2
Upgate Street Norfk 59 K2
Uphall Dorset 10 E4
Uphall W Loth 115 K7
Upham Devon 8 G3
Upham Hants 25 J9
Uphampton Herefs 51 L8
Uphampton Worcs 52 F7
Uphill N Som 28 D10
Up Holland Lancs 75 N3
Uplawmoor E Rens 113 N10
Upleadon Gloucs 41 M6
Upleatham R & Cl 92 D3
Uplees Kent 34 H9
Uploders Dorset 10 D6
Uplowman Devon 20 F10
Uplyme Devon 9 Q6
Up Marden W Susx 25 N10
Upminster Gt Lon 33 Q5
Up Mudford Somset 22 D9
Up Nately Hants 25 M3
Upottery Devon 9 N3
Upper Affcot Shrops 51 M3
Upper Arley Worcs 52 E4
Upper Arncott Oxon 43 M8
Upper Astrop Nhants 43 L4
Upper Badcall Highld 148 E8
Upper Basildon W Berk 31 M7
Upper Batley Kirk 85 K10
Upper Beeding W Susx 14 H8
Upper Benefield Nhants 55 N3
Upper Bentley Worcs 53 J7
Upper Bighouse Highld 150 F5
Upper Birchwood Derbys 66 D1
Upper Boat Rhondd 27 Q5
Upper Boddington Nhants 54 D10
Upper Borth Cerdgn 49 K3
Upper Brailes Warwks 42 G4
Upper Breinton Herefs 40 G4
Upper Broadheath Worcs 52 E9
Upper Broughton Notts 66 H7
Upper Bucklebury W Berk 31 L8
Upper Burgate Hants 23 P10
Upper Bush Medway 34 C9
Upperby Cumb 98 E7
Upper Caldecote C Beds 44 H2
Upper Canada N Som 28 E10
Upper Canterton Hants 24 D10
Upper Catesby Nhants 54 E9
Upper Catshill Worcs 52 H6
Upper Chapel Powys 39 N4
Upper Cheddon Somset 21 K7
Upper Chicksgrove Wilts 23 L7
Upper Chute Wilts 24 E3
Upper Clapton Gt Lon 33 L5
Upper Clatford Hants 24 F5
Upper Coberley Gloucs 41 R8
Upper Cotton Staffs 65 K3
Upper Cound Shrops 63 P11
Upper Cudworth Barns 78 C2
Upper Cumberworth Kirk 77 N2
Upper Dallachy Moray 139 Q3
Upper Deal Kent 35 Q12
Upper Dean Bed 55 P7
Upper Denby Kirk 77 N2
Upper Denton Cumb 99 J5
Upper Dicker E Susx 15 Q9
Upper Dinchope Shrops 51 M4
Upper Dounreay Highld 150 H3
Upper Dovercourt Essex 47 M5
Upper Drumbane Stirlg 122 H11
Upper Dunsforth N York 85 N3
Upper Eashing Surrey 14 D2
Upper Eathie Highld 138 E3
Upper Egleton Herefs 41 K3
Upper Elkstone Staffs 77 K12
Upper Ellastone Staffs 65 L3
Upper End Derbys 77 K8
Upper Enham Hants 24 F3
Upper Farmcote Shrops 52 E2
Upper Farringdon Hants 25 M6
Upper Framilode Gloucs 41 M9
Upper Froyle Hants 25 N5
Upperglen Highld 134 F5
Upper Godney Somset 22 B5
Upper Gravenhurst C Beds 44 G4
Upper Green Mons 40 E8
Upper Green Suffk 57 P7
Upper Green W Berk 30 H9
Upper Grove Common Herefs 40 H6
Upper Hackney Derbys 77 P11
Upper Hale Surrey 25 P3
Upper Halliford Surrey 32 F8
Upper Halling Medway 34 C9
Upper Hambleton Rutlnd 67 M10
Upper Harbledown Kent 35 K10
Upper Hardres Court Kent 35 L12
Upper Hardwick Herefs 51 L9
Upper Hartfield E Susx 15 N4
Upper Hartshay Derbys 66 C2
Upper Hatherley Gloucs 41 Q7
Upper Hatton Staffs 64 F5
Upper Haugh Rothm 78 C4
Upper Hayton Shrops 51 N4
Upper Heaton Kirk 85 J11
Upper Helmsley N York 86 C4
Upper Hergest Herefs 51 J9
Upper Heyford Nhants 54 H8
Upper Heyford Oxon 43 K6
Upper Hill Herefs 51 M10
Upper Hockenden Kent 33 P8
Upper Hopton Kirk 85 J11
Upper Howsell Worcs 52 E11
Upper Hulme Staffs 77 J11
Upper Ifold Surrey 14 E4
Upper Inglesham Swindn 30 E3
Upper Kilcott Gloucs 29 M5
Upper Killay Swans 26 E4
Upper Kinchrackine Ag & B 121 M7
Upper Knockando Moray 139 M7
Upper Lambourn W Berk 30 G6
Upper Landywood Staffs 64 H11
Upper Langford N Som 28 F10
Upper Langwith Derbys 78 E9
Upper Largo Fife 124 H12
Upper Layham Suffk 47 J3
Upper Leigh Staffs 65 J5
Upper Littleton N Som 28 H9
Upper Lochton Abers 132 H5
Upper Longdon Staffs 65 K9
Upper Ludstone Shrops 52 E2
Upper Lybster Highld 151 N9
Upper Lydbrook Gloucs 41 J8
Upper Lyde Herefs 40 G3
Upper Lye Herefs 51 L7
Upper Maes-coed Herefs 40 D5
Upper Marham Norfk 69 N10
Upper Midhope Sheff 77 N4
Uppermill Oldham 77 J3
Upper Milton Worcs 52 E6
Upper Minety Wilts 30 B4
Upper Moor Worcs 52 H11
Upper Moor Side Leeds 85 K9
Upper Mulben Moray 139 Q5
Upper Netchwood Shrops 51 Q2
Upper Nobut Staffs 65 K5
Upper Norwood W Susx 14 D7
Upper Oddington Gloucs 42 E6
Upper Padley Derbys 77 N8
Upper Pennington Hants 12 E5
Upper Pollicott Bucks 43 P9
Upper Poppleton C York 85 Q4
Upper Quinton Warwks 42 E2
Upper Ratley Hants 24 E8
Upper Rissington Gloucs 42 E7
Upper Rochford Worcs 52 B7
Upper Ruscoe D & G 96 B6
Upper Sapey Herefs 52 C8
Upper Saxondale Notts 66 H4
Upper Seagry Wilts 29 Q6
Upper Shelton C Beds 44 E3
Upper Sheringham Norfk 70 H4
Upper Skelmorlie N Ayrs 113 J8
Upper Slaughter Gloucs 42 D7
Upper Soudley Gloucs 41 K9
Upper Spond Herefs 51 K10
Upper Standen Kent 17 M3
Upper Staploe Bed 56 C8
Upper Stoke Norfk 71 K11
Upper Stondon C Beds 44 G4
Upper Stowe Nhants 54 G9
Upper Street Hants 23 P9
Upper Street Norfk 58 H5
Upper Street Norfk 71 L8
Upper Street Norfk 71 M9
Upper Street Suffk 47 L5
Upper Street Suffk 57 P10
Upper Street Suffk 58 G10
Upper Strensham Worcs 41 P4
Upper Sundon C Beds 44 F6
Upper Swell Gloucs 42 E6
Upper Tankersley Barns 77 Q4
Upper Tean Staffs 65 J4
Upperthong Kirk 77 L2
Upperthorpe Derbys 78 D7
Upperthorpe N Linc 79 J4
Upper Threapwood Ches W 63 M3
Upperton W Susx 14 D6
Upper Town Derbys 65 N2
Uppertown Derbys 77 Q10
Upper Town Dur 100 D10
Upper Town Herefs 51 P11
Uppertown Highld 151 Q1
Upper Town N Som 28 H9
Upper Town Suffk 58 D7
Upper Tumble Carmth 38 E9
Upper Tysoe Warwks 42 H3
Upper Ufford Suffk 59 K10
Upperup Gloucs 30 B3
Upper Upham Wilts 30 F7
Upper Upnor Medway 34 D8
Upper Victoria Angus 125 K5
Upper Vobster Somset 22 F3
Upper Wardington Oxon 43 K3
Upper Weald M Keyn 44 A4
Upper Weedon Nhants 54 G9
Upper Welland Worcs 41 M3
Upper Wellingham E Susx 15 N8
Upper Weston BaNES 29 L9
Upper Weybread Suffk 59 J5
Upper Wick Worcs 52 F10
Upper Wield Hants 25 K5
Upper Winchendon Bucks 43 Q9
Upperwood Derbys 77 P12
Upper Woodford Wilts 23 P6
Upper Woolhampton W Berk 31 M8
Upper Wootton Hants 25 K2
Upper Wraxall Wilts 29 N7
Upper Wyche Worcs 41 M3
Uppincott Devon 8 G3
Uppingham Rutlnd 67 L12
Uppington Dorset 11 N3
Uppington Shrops 63 Q10
Upsall N York 91 Q9
Upsettlington Border 117 K12
Upshire Essex 33 M2
Up Somborne Hants 24 F7
Upstreet Kent 35 M9
Up Sydling Dorset 10 F4
Upthorpe Suffk 58 E6
Upton Bucks 43 Q9
Upton C Pete 68 B12
Upton Cambs 56 D5
Upton Ches W 75 L10
Upton Cnwll 7 J4
Upton Cnwll 7 K10
Upton Cumb 98 C10
Upton Devon 5 L8
Upton Devon 9 L4
Upton Dorset 10 H8
Upton Dorset 11 N6
Upton E R Yk 87 L4
Upton Halton 75 N6
Upton Hants 24 F10
Upton Hants 24 F2
Upton Leics 66 B12
Upton Lincs 79 L6
Upton Nhants 55 J8
Upton Norfk 71 M9
Upton Notts 67 J1
Upton Notts 79 J8
Upton Oxon 31 L5
Upton Oxon 42 F9
Upton Pembks 37 K9
Upton R & Cl 92 F3
Upton Slough 32 D6
Upton Somset 20 F7
Upton Somset 21 P8
Upton Wakefd 78 D1
Upton Warwks 53 L9
Upton Wilts 23 J7
Upton Wirral 75 J6
Upton Bishop Herefs 41 K6
Upton Cheyney S Glos 29 L8
Upton Cressett Shrops 52 C2
Upton Crews Herefs 41 K6
Upton Cross Cnwll 7 K10
Upton End C Beds 44 G5
Upton Grey Hants 25 M4
Upton Heath Ches W 75 L9
Upton Hellions Devon 8 F4
Upton Lovell Wilts 23 L5
Upton Magna Shrops 63 P9
Upton Noble Somset 22 G5
Upton Pyne Devon 8 G5
Upton St Leonards Gloucs 41 P8
Upton Scudamore Wilts 23 J4
Upton Snodsbury Worcs 52 H9
Upton Towans Cnwll 2 F6
Upton-upon-Severn Worcs 41 N4
Upton Warren Worcs 52 H7
Upwaltham W Susx 14 D8
Upware Cambs 57 K6
Upwell Norfk 69 J11
Upwey Dorset 10 G7
Upwick Green Herts 45 N7
Upwood Cambs 56 E4
Urchfont Wilts 30 B11
Urdimarsh Herefs 51 N11
Ure Bank N York 91 N12
Urlay Nook S on T 91 P4
Urmston Traffd 76 E5
Urpeth Dur 100 G7
Urquhart Moray 139 P3
Urquhart Castle Highld 137 P10
Urra N York 92 B6
Urray Highld 137 N5
Ury Abers 133 L7
Uryside Abers 141 J11
Usan Angus 125 P2
Ushaw Moor Dur 100 G9
Usk Mons 28 E2
Usselby Lincs 80 B5
Usworth Sundld 100 H7
Utkinton Ches W 75 P10
Utley C Brad 84 F6
Uton Devon 8 F5
Utterby Lincs 80 F5
Uttoxeter Staffs 65 K5
Uwchmynydd Gwynd 60 B7
Uxbridge Gt Lon 32 F5
Uyeasound Shet 147 k3
Uzmaston Pembks 37 J7

V

Vale Guern 12 c1
Valley IoA 72 D8
Valley End Surrey 32 D9
Valley Truckle Cnwll 6 G8
Valtos Highld 135 J3
Valtos W Isls 152 e3
Vange Essex 34 C5
Varteg Torfn 40 C10
Vatsetter Shet 147 j3
Vatten Highld 134 E7
Vaynor Myr Td 39 P9
Vazon Bay Guern 12 b2
Veensgarth Shet 147 i7
Velindre Powys 40 B4
Vellow Somset 20 H5
Velly Devon 18 F8
Venngreen Devon 7 M2
Vennington Shrops 63 K10
Venn Ottery Devon 9 K6
Venny Tedburn Devon 8 F5
Venterdon Cnwll 7 L10
Ventnor IoW 13 J9
Venton Devon 5 J5
Vernham Dean Hants 30 H11
Vernham Street Hants 30 H11
Vernolds Common Shrops 51 N4
Verwood Dorset 11 Q3
Veryan Cnwll 3 M6
Veryan Green Cnwll 3 M6
Vicarage Devon 9 N7
Vickerstown Cumb 82 F1
Victoria Barns 77 M3
Victoria Blae G 40 A10
Victoria Cnwll 3 N2
Vidlin Shet 147 j5
Viewfield Moray 139 P3
Viewpark N Lans 114 C9
Vigo Kent 34 B10
Village de Putron Guern 12 c3
Ville la Bas Jersey 13 a1
Villiaze Guern 12 b3
Vinehall Street E Susx 16 D7
Vines Cross E Susx 15 Q7
Virginia Water Surrey 32 E9
Virginstow Devon 7 M6
Vobster Somset 22 F4
Voe Shet 147 i6
Vowchurch Herefs 40 E4
Vulcan Village St Hel 75 P5

W

Waberthwaite Cumb 88 E8
Wackerfield Dur 91 K2
Wacton Norfk 58 H2
Wadborough Worcs 52 G11
Waddesdon Bucks 43 Q8
Waddesdon Manor Bucks 43 Q8
Waddeton Devon 5 P5
Waddicar Sefton 75 L4
Waddingham Lincs 79 N4
Waddington Lancs 83 Q6
Waddington Lincs 79 N11
Waddon Devon 8 G9
Waddon Dorset 10 F7
Waddon Gt Lon 33 K9
Wadebridge Cnwll 6 E10
Wadeford Somset 9 Q3
Wadenhoe Nhants 55 P4
Wadesmill Herts 45 L8
Wadhurst E Susx 16 B4
Wadshelf Derbys 77 P9
Wadswick Wilts 29 N9
Wadworth Donc 78 F4
Waen Denbgs 74 D11
Waen Denbgs 74 F10
Waen Powys 62 H8
Waen Fach Powys 62 H8
Waen-pentir Gwynd 73 K10
Waen-wen Gwynd 73 K10
Wagbeach Shrops 63 L11
Wainfelin Torfn 28 C2
Wainfleet All Saints Lincs 81 J12
Wainfleet Bank Lincs 81 J11
Wainfleet St Mary Lincs 81 J12
Wainford Norfk 59 L3
Wainhouse Corner Cnwll 6 H6
Wainscott Medway 34 D8
Wain's Hill N Som 28 E8
Wainstalls Calder 84 F9
Waitby Cumb 90 B5
Waithe Lincs 80 F4
Wakefield Wakefd 85 M11
Wake Green Birm 53 K4
Wakehurst W Susx 15 L5
Wakerley Nhants 67 N12
Wakes Colne Essex 46 F6
Walberswick Suffk 59 P6
Walberton W Susx 14 D9
Walbottle N u Ty 100 F5
Walbutt D & G 96 F4
Walby Cumb 98 F6
Walcombe Somset 22 D4
Walcot Lincs 67 Q5
Walcot N Linc 86 G11
Walcot Shrops 51 K4
Walcot Shrops 63 Q9
Walcot Swindn 30 D5
Walcote Leics 54 F4
Walcote Warwks 53 L9
Walcot Green Norfk 58 H4
Walcott Lincs 80 C12
Walcott Norfk 71 M6
Walden N York 90 G10
Walden Head N York 90 G10
Walden Stubbs N York 85 Q11
Walderslade Medway 34 D9
Walderton W Susx 13 N3
Walditch Dorset 10 D6
Waldley Derbys 65 L5
Waldridge Dur 100 G8
Waldringfield Suffk 47 N3
Waldron E Susx 15 Q7
Wales Rothm 78 D7
Wales Somset 22 D8
Walesby Lincs 80 C5
Walesby Notts 78 H9
Walford Herefs 41 J7
Walford Herefs 51 L6
Walford Shrops 63 M8
Walford Staffs 64 F5
Walford Heath Shrops 63 M8
Walgherton Ches E 64 C2
Walgrave Nhants 55 K6
Walhampton Hants 12 E5
Walkden Salfd 76 D3
Walker N u Ty 100 H5
Walkerburn Border 107 K2
Walker Fold Lancs 83 P7
Walkeringham Notts 79 J5
Walkerith Lincs 79 K5
Walkern Herts 45 K6
Walker's Green Herefs 51 N11
Walker's Heath Birm 53 K5
Walkerton Fife 115 N1
Walkford BCP 12 C6
Walkhampton Devon 4 H3
Walkington E R Yk 87 J8
Walkley Sheff 77 Q6
Walk Mill Lancs 84 C9
Walkwood Worcs 53 J7
Wall Nthumb 99 P4
Wall Staffs 65 L11
Wallacetown S Ayrs 104 E9
Wallacetown S Ayrs 104 F5
Wallands Park E Susx 15 M8
Wallasey Wirral 75 J5
Wallasey (Kingsway) Tunnel Wirral 75 K5
Wall End Cumb 88 H10
Wall End Herefs 51 M9
Wallend Medway 34 F7
Waller's Green Herefs 41 K4
Wallhead Cumb 98 F6
Wall Heath Dudley 52 G3
Wall Houses Nthumb 100 D4
Wallingford Oxon 31 M4
Wallington Gt Lon 33 K9
Wallington Hants 13 K3
Wallington Herts 45 K5
Wallington Heath Wsall 65 J11
Wallis Pembks 37 K5
Wallisdown BCP 11 P6
Walliswood Surrey 14 G3
Walls Shet 147 h7
Wallsend N Tyne 100 H5
Wallthwaite Cumb 89 K1
Wall under Haywood Shrops 51 N2
Wallyford E Loth 115 Q7
Walmer Kent 35 Q12
Walmer Bridge Lancs 83 L10
Walmersley Bury 76 E1
Walmestone Kent 35 N10
Walmley Birm 53 L2
Walmley Ash Birm 53 L2
Walmsgate Lincs 80 G8
Walney Cumb 82 E2
Walpole Somset 21 M5
Walpole Suffk 59 M6
Walpole Cross Keys Norfk 69 K8
Walpole Highway Norfk 69 K9
Walpole St Andrew Norfk 69 J8
Walpole St Peter Norfk 69 J9
Walrow Somset 21 M4
Walsall Wsall 53 J1
Walsall Wood Wsall 65 K11
Walsden Calder 84 D11
Walsgrave on Sowe Covtry 54 C4
Walsham le Willows Suffk 58 E6
Walshaw Bury 76 E1
Walshford N York 85 N4
Walsoken Norfk 69 J10
Walston S Lans 115 K12
Walsworth Herts 44 H5
Walter's Ash Bucks 32 B3
Walters Green Kent 15 P3
Walterston V Glam 27 P8
Walterstone Herefs 40 D6
Waltham Kent 17 K1
Waltham NE Lin 80 E3
Waltham Abbey Essex 33 M2
Waltham Chase Hants 25 J10
Waltham Cross Herts 33 L2
Waltham on the Wolds Leics 67 K7
Waltham St Lawrence W & M 32 B7
Waltham's Cross Essex 46 C5
Walthamstow Gt Lon 33 L4
Walton C Pete 68 D11
Walton Cumb 98 G5
Walton Derbys 78 B10
Walton Leeds 85 N6
Walton Leics 54 F3
Walton M Keyn 44 C4
Walton Powys 51 J8
Walton Shrops 51 M5
Walton Somset 21 P6
Walton Staffs 64 F6
Walton Staffs 64 G5
Walton Suffk 47 N4
Walton W Susx 13 P4
Walton Wakefd 85 M11
Walton Warwks 53 P10
Walton Wrekin 63 P8
Walton Cardiff Gloucs 41 P5
Walton East Pembks 37 K6
Walton Elm Dorset 22 H9
Walton Grounds Nhants 43 L5
Walton Highway Norfk 69 J9
Walton-in-Gordano N Som 28 F7
Walton-le-Dale Lancs 83 M9
Walton-on-Thames Surrey 32 G9
Walton-on-the-Hill Staffs 64 H8
Walton-on-the-Hill Surrey 33 J11
Walton-on-the-Naze Essex 47 N7
Walton on the Wolds Leics 66 F8
Walton-on-Trent Derbys 65 N8
Walton Park N Som 28 F8
Walton West Pembks 36 G8
Walwen Flints 74 F8
Walwen Flints 74 G9
Walwen Flints 74 H8
Walwick Nthumb 99 P4
Walworth Darltn 91 L3
Walworth Gt Lon 33 L7
Walworth Gate Darltn 91 L3
Walwyn's Castle Pembks 36 G8
Wambrook Somset 9 P3
Wampool Cumb 97 P7
Wanborough Surrey 14 D1
Wanborough Swindn 30 E6
Wandon End Herts 44 G7
Wandsworth Gt Lon 33 J7
Wangford Suffk 59 P5
Wanlip Leics 66 F10
Wanlockhead D & G 105 R7
Wannock E Susx 15 Q10
Wansford C Pete 67 Q12
Wansford E R Yk 87 K4
Wanshurst Green Kent 16 D2
Wanstead Gt Lon 33 M5
Wanstrow Somset 22 G5
Wanswell Gloucs 29 K2
Wantage Oxon 31 J5
Wants Green Worcs 52 D9
Wapley S Glos 29 L6
Wappenbury Warwks 54 B7
Wappenham Nhants 43 N3
Warbleton E Susx 15 R7
Warborough Oxon 31 M4
Warboys Cambs 56 F5
Warbreck Bpool 82 H7
Warbstow Cnwll 7 J6
Warburton Traffd 76 C6
Warcop Cumb 90 B4
Warden Kent 35 J8
Warden Nthumb 99 P5
Ward End Birm 53 L3
Warden Street C Beds 44 G3
Ward Green Suffk 58 F8
Ward Green Cross Lancs 83 P8
Wardhedges C Beds 44 F4
Wardington Oxon 43 K2
Wardle Ches E 75 Q12
Wardle Rochdl 84 D11
Wardley Gatesd 100 H6
Wardley Rutlnd 67 L12
Wardley Salfd 76 E3
Wardlow Derbys 77 M8
Wardsend Ches E 76 H7
Wardy Hill Cambs 57 J4
Ware Herts 45 L9
Wareham Dorset 11 M7
Warehorne Kent 16 H4
Warenford Nthumb 109 J4
Waren Mill Nthumb 109 J3
Warenton Nthumb 109 J4
Wareside Herts 45 M8
Waresley Cambs 56 E9
Waresley Worcs 52 F6
Ware Street Kent 34 D11
Warfield Br For 32 C8
Warfleet Devon 5 P7
Wargate Lincs 68 E6
Wargrave Wokham 31 R6
Warham Herefs 40 G4
Warham Norfk 70 D4
Wark Nthumb 99 N3
Wark Nthumb 108 D2
Warkleigh Devon 19 M9
Warkton Nhants 55 M5
Warkworth Nhants 43 K4
Warkworth Nthumb 109 L8
Warlaby N York 91 N8
Warland Calder 84 E11
Warleggan Cnwll 4 B3
Warleigh BaNES 29 M9
Warley Town Calder 84 G10
Warlingham Surrey 33 L10
Warmbrook Derbys 65 P1
Warmfield Wakefd 85 M11
Warmingham Ches E 76 D11
Warmington Nhants 55 Q2
Warmington Warwks 54 C11
Warminster Wilts 23 J4
Warmley S Glos 29 K7
Warmsworth Donc 78 E4
Warmwell Dorset 11 J7
Warndon Worcs 52 G9
Warner Bros. Studio Tour London Herts 32 F2
Warnford Hants 25 K8
Warnham W Susx 14 G4
Warningcamp W Susx 14 E9
Warninglid W Susx 15 J5
Warren Ches E 76 G9
Warren Pembks 36 H11
Warrenby R & Cl 92 C2
Warrenhill S Lans 106 B2
Warren Row W & M 32 A6
Warren's Green Herts 45 K6
Warren Street Kent 34 G11
Warrington M Keyn 55 M10
Warrington Warrtn 75 Q6
Warriston C Edin 115 N6
Warsash Hants 12 H3
Warslow Staffs 77 K12
Warsop Vale Notts 78 E10
Warter E R Yk 86 G5
Warthermaske N York 91 L11
Warthill N York 86 C4
Wartling E Susx 16 B9
Wartnaby Leics 66 H7
Warton Lancs 83 K9
Warton Lancs 89 M12
Warton Nthumb 108 G9
Warton Warwks 65 P11
Warwick Warwks 53 P7
Warwick Bridge Cumb 98 F7
Warwick Castle Warwks 53 P7
Warwick-on-Eden Cumb 98 F7
Warwick Services Warwks 53 Q9
Warwicksland Cumb 98 F3
Wasbister Ork 147 c3
Wasdale Head Cumb 88 G5
Wash Derbys 77 K7
Washall Green Herts 45 N6
Washaway Cnwll 6 F10
Washbourne Devon 5 N6
Washbrook Somset 21 P3
Washbrook Suffk 47 K3
Washfield Devon 20 E10
Washfold N York 90 H6
Washford Somset 20 G5
Washford Pyne Devon 8 F2
Washingborough Lincs 79 P9
Washington Sundld 101 J7
Washington W Susx 14 G8
Washington Services Gatesd 100 H7
Washwood Heath Birm 53 L3
Wasing W Berk 31 M9
Waskerley Dur 100 D9
Wasperton Warwks 53 P9
Wasps Nest Lincs 79 Q10
Wass N York 92 B11
Wast Water Cumb 88 F5
Watchet Somset 20 G5
Watchfield Oxon 30 F4
Watchfield Somset 21 M4
Watchgate Cumb 89 N7
Watchill Cumb 97 N9
Watcombe Torbay 5 Q3
Watendlath Cumb 89 J3
Water Devon 8 E8
Water Lancs 84 C10
Waterbeach Cambs 57 J7
Waterbeach W Susx 14 C9
Waterbeck D & G 97 Q3
Waterden Norfk 70 C5
Water Eaton Oxon 43 L9
Water Eaton Staffs 64 G10
Water End Bed 56 B10
Water End Bed 56 B11
Water End C Beds 44 F4
Waterend Cumb 88 F2
Water End E R Yk 86 E7
Water End Essex 45 Q4
Water End Herts 44 E9
Water End Herts 45 J10
Waterfall Staffs 65 K2
Waterfoot Ag & B 103 L2
Waterfoot E Rens 113 Q10
Waterfoot Lancs 84 C11
Waterford Herts 45 K8
Water Fryston Wakefd 85 P10
Watergate Cnwll 6 G8
Waterhead Cumb 89 K6
Waterheads Border 115 N11
Waterhouses Dur 100 F10
Waterhouses Staffs 65 K2
Wateringbury Kent 34 C11
Waterlane Gloucs 41 Q10
Waterloo Cnwll 6 G10
Waterloo Derbys 78 C11
Waterloo Herefs 51 K11
Waterloo Highld 135 M11
Waterloo N Lans 114 E10
Waterloo Norfk 71 J8
Waterloo P & K 123 Q5
Waterloo Pembks 37 J10
Waterloo Sefton 75 K4
Waterloo Cross Devon 20 G10
Waterloo Port Gwynd 72 H11
Waterlooville Hants 13 L3
Watermead Bucks 44 B8
Watermillock Cumb 89 M2
Water Newton Cambs 56 B1
Water Orton Warwks 53 M2
Waterperry Oxon 43 N10
Waterrow Somset 20 G8
Watersfield W Susx 14 E7
Waterside Bl w D 83 Q10
Waterside Bucks 32 D2
Waterside Cumb 97 P9
Waterside Donc 86 C12
Waterside E Ayrs 104 H8
Waterside E Ayrs 105 J1
Waterside E Duns 114 C6
Water's Nook Bolton 76 C3
Waterstein Highld 134 B6
Waterstock Oxon 43 N10
Waterston Pembks 36 H9
Water Stratford Bucks 43 N5
Water Street Neath 27 J6
Waters Upton Wrekin 64 B8
Water Yeat Cumb 89 J9
Watford Herts 32 G3
Watford Nhants 54 G7
Watford Gap Services Nhants 54 F7
Wath N York 84 H2
Wath N York 91 N11
Wath upon Dearne Rothm 78 C3
Watlington Norfk 69 M10
Watlington Oxon 31 P3
Watnall Notts 66 E3
Watten Highld 151 N6
Wattisfield Suffk 58 E6
Wattisham Suffk 58 E10
Watton Dorset 10 C6
Watton E R Yk 87 J5
Watton Norfk 70 D12
Watton-at-Stone Herts 45 K8
Watton Green Norfk 70 D12
Wattons Green Essex 33 P3
Wattston N Lans 114 D7
Wattstown Rhondd 27 N4
Wattsville Caerph 28 B4
Wauldby E R Yk 86 H9
Waulkmill Abers 132 G6
Waunarlwydd Swans 26 F3
Waun Fach Powys 40 B6
Waunfawr Cerdgn 49 K4
Waunfawr Gwynd 73 J11
Waungron Swans 38 E11
Waunlwyd Blae G 40 A10
Wavendon M Keyn 44 C4
Waverbridge Cumb 97 P8
Waverley Rothm 78 C6
Waverton Ches W 75 M11
Waverton Cumb 97 P9
Wawne E R Yk 87 K8
Waxham Norfk 71 N7
Waxholme E R Yk 87 Q9
Way Kent 35 P9
Waye Devon 8 E10
Wayford Somset 10 B3
Waytown Dorset 10 D5
Way Village Devon 8 G3
Way Wick N Som 28 E10
Weacombe Somset 20 H5
Weald Oxon 42 G11
Wealdstone Gt Lon 32 H4
Weardley Leeds 85 L6
Weare Somset 21 N3
Weare Giffard Devon 19 J9
Wearhead Dur 99 N10
Wearne Somset 21 P8
Weasdale Cumb 90 A6
Weasenham All Saints Norfk 70 C8
Weasenham St Peter Norfk 70 C7
Weaste Salfd 76 E4
Weatheroak Hill Worcs 53 K6
Weaverham Ches W 75 Q9
Weaverslake Staffs 65 L8
Weaverthorpe N York 86 H1
Webbington Somset 21 N2
Webb's Heath S Glos 29 K7
Webheath Worcs 53 J7
Webton Herefs 40 F4
Wedderlairs Abers 141 K9
Wedding Hall Fold N York 84 E6
Weddington Kent 35 N10
Weddington Warwks 54 B2
Wedhampton Wilts 30 C11
Wedmore Somset 21 P4
Wednesbury Sandw 53 J2
Wednesfield Wolves 64 H12
Weecar Notts 79 L10
Weedon Bucks 44 A8

Weedon Bec Nhants 54 G9
Weedon Lois Nhants 43 M2
Weeford Staffs 65 L11
Week Devon 5 N4
Week Devon 19 L8
Week Devon 19 P10
Weeke Devon 8 E3
Weeke Hants 24 H7
Weekley Nhants 55 M4
Week St Mary Cnwll 7 J5
Weel E R Yk 87 K7
Weeley Essex 47 L7
Weeley Heath Essex 47 L7
Weem P & K 123 L3
Weeping Cross Staffs 64 H8
Weethley Warwks 53 K9
Weeting Norfk 57 P3
Weeton E R Yk 87 Q11
Weeton Lancs 83 J8
Weeton N York 85 L6
Weetwood Leeds 85 K7
Weir Lancs 84 C10
Weirbrook Shrops 63 K7
Weir Quay Devon 4 F4
Weisdale Shet 147 i6
Welborne Norfk 70 F10
Welbourn Lincs 67 N1
Welburn N York 86 D2
Welbury N York 91 P6
Welby Lincs 67 N4
Welches Dam Cambs 57 J3
Welcombe Devon 18 E9
Weldon Nhants 55 M3
Weldon Bridge Nthumb 109 J10
Welford Nhants 54 G5
Welford W Berk 31 J8
Welford-on-Avon Warwks 53 L10
Welham Leics 55 J2
Welham Notts 79 J7
Welham Bridge E R Yk 86 E8
Welham Green Herts 45 J10
Well Hants 25 N4
Well Lincs 80 H9
Well N York 91 M10
Welland Worcs 41 M4
Wellbank Angus 125 J5
Well End Bucks 32 C5
Well End Herts 32 H3
Wellesbourne Warwks 53 P9
Wellesbourne Mountford Warwks 53 P9
Well Head Herts 44 H6
Well Hill Kent 33 P9
Wellhouse W Berk 31 L8
Welling Gt Lon 33 N7
Wellingborough Nhants 55 M7
Wellingham Norfk 70 C8
Wellingore Lincs 79 N12
Wellington Cumb 88 E6
Wellington Herefs 51 N11
Wellington Somset 21 J9
Wellington Wrekin 64 C10
Wellington Heath Herefs 41 L4
Wellington Marsh Herefs 40 G2
Wellow BaNES 29 L10
Wellow IoW 12 F7
Wellow Notts 78 H10
Wellpond Green Herts 45 M7
Wells Somset 22 D4
Wellsborough Leics 66 B11
Wells Green Ches E 64 C1
Wells Head C Brad 84 G8
Wells-next-the-Sea Norfk 70 D3
Wellstye Green Essex 46 B8
Well Town Devon 8 G3
Welltree P & K 123 N8
Wellwood Fife 115 K3
Welney Norfk 57 K2
Welshampton Shrops 63 M5
Welsh Bicknor Herefs 41 J8
Welsh End Shrops 63 N5
Welsh Frankton Shrops 63 K5
Welsh Hook Pembks 36 H5
Welsh Newton Herefs 40 G8
Welshpool Powys 62 H10
Welsh St Donats V Glam 27 N7
Welton Cumb 98 D9
Welton E R Yk 86 H9
Welton Lincs 79 P8
Welton Nhants 54 F7
Welton le Marsh Lincs 81 J10
Welton le Wold Lincs 80 E6
Welwick E R Yk 87 Q11
Welwyn Herts 45 J8
Welwyn Garden City Herts 45 J9
Wem Shrops 63 N6
Wembdon Somset 21 L6
Wembley Gt Lon 32 H5
Wembury Devon 4 H7
Wembworthy Devon 8 C3
Wemyss Bay Inver 113 J7
Wenallt Cerdgn 49 L6
Wendens Ambo Essex 45 P4
Wendlebury Oxon 43 M8
Wendling Norfk 70 D9
Wendover Bucks 44 B10
Wendron Cnwll 2 H8
Wendron Mining District Cnwll 2 H8
Wendy Cambs 56 F11
Wenfordbridge Cnwll 6 F9
Wenhaston Suffk 59 N5
Wennington Cambs 56 E5
Wennington Gt Lon 33 P6
Wennington Lancs 83 N1
Wensley Derbys 77 N11
Wensley N York 90 H9
Wentbridge Wakefd 85 P11
Wentnor Shrops 51 L2
Wentworth Cambs 57 J5
Wentworth Rothm 78 C4
Wenvoe V Glam 27 Q8
Weobley Herefs 51 L10
Weobley Marsh Herefs 51 L10
Wepham W Susx 14 F9
Wereham Norfk 69 N11
Wergs Wolves 64 F12
Wern Gwynd 61 J4
Wern Powys 39 Q8
Wern Powys 63 J9
Wern Shrops 63 J5
Werneth Low Tamesd 76 H5
Wernffrwd Swans 26 D3
Wern-Gifford Mons 40 D7
Wern-y-gaer Flints 74 H10
Werrington C Pete 68 C11
Werrington Cnwll 7 L7
Werrington Staffs 64 H3
Wervin Ches W 75 M9
Wesham Lancs 83 K8
Wessington Derbys 78 B12
West Aberthaw V Glam 27 N9
West Acre Norfk 69 P9
West Allerdean Nthumb 117 L12
West Alvington Devon 5 M8
West Amesbury Wilts 23 P5
West Anstey Devon 20 C8
West Appleton N York 91 L8
West Ashby Lincs 80 E9
West Ashling W Susx 13 P3
West Ashton Wilts 23 J2
West Auckland Dur 91 K2
West Ayton N York 93 K9
West Bagborough Somset 21 J6
West Bank Blae G 40 B10
West Bank Halton 75 N7
West Barkwith Lincs 80 C7
West Barnby N York 92 G4
West Barns E Loth 116 F6
West Barsham Norfk 70 D5
West Bay Dorset 10 C6
West Beckham Norfk 70 H4
West Bedfont Surrey 32 F7
Westbere Kent 35 M10
West Bergholt Essex 46 G6
West Bexington Dorset 10 E7
West Bilney Norfk 69 N9
West Blatchington Br & H 15 K9
West Boldon S Tyne 101 J6
Westborough Lincs 67 L3
Westbourne BCP 11 P6
Westbourne W Susx 13 N3
West Bourton Dorset 22 G7
West Bowling C Brad 85 J9
West Brabourne Kent 17 K2
West Bradenham Norfk 70 D10
West Bradford Lancs 83 R6
West Bradley Somset 22 D6
West Bretton Wakefd 77 P1
West Bridgford Notts 66 F5
West Briscoe Dur 90 F3
West Bromwich Sandw 53 J2
Westbrook Kent 35 P8
Westbrook W Berk 31 J8
Westbrook Wilts 29 Q9
West Buckland Devon 19 M7
West Buckland Somset 21 J9
West Burrafirth Shet 147 h6
West Burton N York 90 G9
West Burton W Susx 14 E8
Westbury Bucks 43 N4
Westbury Shrops 63 K10
Westbury Wilts 23 J3
Westbury Leigh Wilts 23 J3
Westbury-on-Severn Gloucs 41 L9
Westbury-on-Trym Bristl 28 H7
Westbury-sub-Mendip Somset 22 C3
West Butsfield Dur 100 E9
West Butterwick N Linc 79 L3
Westby Lancs 83 J9
West Byfleet Surrey 32 F10
West Cairngaan D & G 94 G12
West Caister Norfk 71 P10
West Calder W Loth 115 J8
West Camel Somset 22 D8
West Chaldon Dorset 11 J8
West Challow Oxon 30 H5
West Charleton Devon 5 M8
West Chelborough Dorset 10 E4
West Chevington Nthumb 109 L10
West Chiltington W Susx 14 F7
West Chinnock Somset 21 P10
West Chisenbury Wilts 23 P3
West Clandon Surrey 32 F11
West Cliffe Kent 17 P2
Westcliff-on-Sea Sthend 34 F5
West Clyst Devon 8 H6
West Coker Somset 22 C10
West Combe Devon 5 M4
Westcombe Somset 22 F5
West Compton Somset 22 D5
West Compton Abbas Dorset 10 E6
Westcote Gloucs 42 E7
Westcote Barton Oxon 43 J6
Westcott Bucks 43 P8
Westcott Devon 9 J4
Westcott Surrey 14 G1
West Cottingwith N York 86 C7
Westcourt Wilts 30 E10
West Cowick E R Yk 86 C11
West Cross Swans 26 F4
West Curry Cnwll 7 K6
West Curthwaite Cumb 98 C8
Westdean E Susx 15 P11
West Dean W Susx 14 B8
West Dean Wilts 24 D8
West Deeping Lincs 68 B10
West Derby Lpool 75 L5
West Dereham Norfk 69 M12
West Ditchburn Nthumb 109 J5
West Down Devon 19 K5
Westdown Camp Wilts 23 M4
Westdowns Cnwll 6 F8
West Drayton Gt Lon 32 F6
West Drayton Notts 78 H8
West Dunnet Highld 151 M2
Wested Kent 33 P9
West Ella E R Yk 87 J9
West End Bed 55 N10
West End Br For 32 B8
West End Caerph 28 B3
West End Cumb 98 C6
West End E R Yk 86 G9
West End E R Yk 87 M9
West End E R Yk 87 P9
Westend Gloucs 41 M10
West End Hants 24 H10
West End Hants 25 L6
West End Herts 45 J10
West End Herts 45 L10
West End Lancs 83 Q9
West End Leeds 85 K7
West End Lincs 80 G4
West End N Som 28 F8
West End N York 85 Q7
West End Norfk 70 D10
West End Norfk 71 P10
West End Oxon 31 M5
West End S Glos 29 L5
West End Somset 22 F6
West End Surrey 32 D10
West End Surrey 32 G9
West End W & M 32 B7
West End W Susx 14 H7
West End Wilts 23 K8
West End Wilts 23 L8
West End Wilts 29 R7
West End Green Hants 31 N10
Westend Town Nthumb 99 M5
Westenhanger Kent 17 K3
Wester Aberchalder Highld 137 P11
Wester Balblair Highld 137 N7
Westerdale Highld 151 L6
Westerdale N York 92 D5
Westerfield Suffk 58 H11
Westergate W Susx 14 D10
Wester Hailes C Edin 115 M7
Westerham Kent 33 N11
Westerhope N u Ty 100 F5
Westerland Devon 5 P4
Westerleigh S Glos 29 L6
Western Isles W Isls 152 e6
Wester Ochiltree W Loth 115 J6
Wester Pitkierie Fife 125 L11
Wester Ross Highld 143 P9
Westerton W Susx 14 C9
Westerton of Rossie Angus 125 N2
Westerwick Shet 147 h7
West Ewell Surrey 32 H9
West Farleigh Kent 34 C11
West Farndon Nhants 54 E10
West Felton Shrops 63 K7
Westfield BaNES 22 F3
Westfield Cumb 88 C1
Westfield E Susx 16 E8
Westfield Highld 151 J4
Westfield N Lans 114 D6
Westfield Norfk 70 E10
Westfield Surrey 32 E11
Westfield W Loth 114 G7
Westfields Dorset 10 H3
Westfields Herefs 40 G3
Westfields of Rattray P & K 124 D3
Westfield Sole Kent 34 D10
West Flotmanby N York 93 M11
Westford Somset 20 H9
Westgate Dur 99 P10
Westgate N Linc 79 K2
Westgate Norfk 70 E4
Westgate Hill C Brad 85 J9
Westgate-on-Sea Kent 35 P8
Westgate Street Norfk 71 J8
West Ginge Oxon 31 J5
West Grafton Wilts 30 F10
West Green Hants 31 Q11
West Grimstead Wilts 24 C8
West Grinstead W Susx 14 H6
West Haddlesey N York 85 R10
West Haddon Nhants 54 G6
West Hagbourne Oxon 31 L5
West Hagley Worcs 52 G4
Westhall Suffk 59 N4
West Hallam Derbys 66 C4
West Hallam Common Derbys 66 C4
West Halton N Linc 86 G11
Westham Dorset 10 G9
Westham E Susx 16 B10
West Ham Gt Lon 33 M5
Westham Somset 21 N4
Westhampnett W Susx 14 C9
West Handley Derbys 78 C8
West Hanney Oxon 31 J4
West Hanningfield Essex 34 C2
West Harnham Wilts 23 P7
West Harptree BaNES 28 H11
West Harting W Susx 25 N9
West Hatch Somset 21 L9
West Hatch Wilts 23 K8
West Haven Angus 125 L6
Westhay Somset 21 P5
Westhead Lancs 75 M2
West Head Norfk 69 L11
West Heath Birm 53 J5
West Heath Hants 31 M10
West Helmsdale Highld 147 J2
West Hendred Oxon 31 J5
West Heslerton N York 93 J11
West Hewish N Som 28 E9
Westhide Herefs 41 J3
Westhill Abers 133 K3
West Hill Devon 9 K6
Westhill Highld 138 D7
West Hoathly W Susx 15 L4
West Holme Dorset 11 L7
Westholme Somset 22 D5
Westhope Herefs 51 M10
Westhope Shrops 51 M3
West Horndon Essex 34 A5
Westhorp Nhants 54 E10
Westhorpe Lincs 68 D6
Westhorpe Suffk 58 F7
West Horrington Somset 22 D4
West Horsley Surrey 32 F11
West Horton Nthumb 108 G4
West Hougham Kent 17 N3
Westhoughton Bolton 76 B3
Westhouse N York 89 R12
Westhouses Derbys 78 C12
West Howe BCP 11 P5
West Howetown Somset 20 E6
Westhumble Surrey 32 H12
West Huntingtower P & K 124 B8
West Huntspill Somset 21 M4
West Hyde C Beds 44 G8
West Hyde Herts 32 E4
West Hythe Kent 17 K4
West Ilkerton Devon 19 N4
West Ilsley W Berk 31 K6
West Itchenor W Susx 13 P4
West Keal Lincs 80 G11
West Kennett Wilts 30 C8
West Kilbride N Ayrs 113 J11
West Kingsdown Kent 33 Q9
West Kington Wilts 29 N7
West Kirby Wirral 74 H6
West Knapton N York 92 H11
West Knighton Dorset 10 H7
West Knoyle Wilts 23 J7
West Kyloe Nthumb 108 H2
Westlake Devon 5 K6
West Lambrook Somset 21 P9
Westland Green Herts 45 M7
West Langdon Kent 17 P1
West Lavington W Susx 14 C7
West Lavington Wilts 23 M3
West Layton N York 91 J5
West Leake Notts 66 E7
West Learmouth Nthumb 108 D2
West Lees N York 91 Q6
West Leigh Devon 8 C4
Westleigh Devon 19 J7
Westleigh Devon 20 G10
West Leigh Somset 20 H7
Westleton Suffk 59 N7
West Lexham Norfk 70 C9
Westley Shrops 63 K10
Westley Suffk 58 B8
Westley Waterless Cambs 57 M9
West Lilling N York 86 C2
Westlington Bucks 43 Q9
West Linton Border 115 L11
Westlinton Cumb 98 E5
West Littleton S Glos 29 M7
West Lockinge Oxon 31 J5
West Lulworth Dorset 11 K8
West Lutton N York 86 H1
West Lydford Somset 22 D7
West Lyn Devon 19 P4
West Lyng Somset 21 M7
West Lynn Norfk 69 L8
West Malling Kent 34 B10
West Malvern Worcs 41 M2
West Marden W Susx 25 N10
West Markham Notts 79 J9
Westmarsh Kent 35 N10
West Marsh NE Lin 80 E2
West Marton N York 84 D5
West Melbury Dorset 23 J9
West Melton Rothm 78 C3
West Meon Hants 25 L8
West Meon Hut Hants 25 L8
West Meon Woodlands Hants 25 L8
West Mersea Essex 46 H9
Westmeston E Susx 15 L8
West Mickley Nthumb 100 D6
West Midland Safari Park Worcs 52 E5
Westmill Herts 45 L6
Westmill Herts 45 L6
West Milton Dorset 10 D5
Westminster Gt Lon 33 K6
Westminster Abbey & Palace Gt Lon 33 K6
West Molesey Surrey 32 G8
West Monkton Somset 21 L7
West Moors Dorset 11 P4
West Morden Dorset 11 M6
West Morriston Border 107 P2
West Morton C Brad 84 G6
West Mudford Somset 22 D9
Westmuir Angus 124 G2
West Ness N York 92 E11
West Newbiggin Darltn 91 N3
Westnewton Cumb 97 N9
West Newton E R Yk 87 M7
West Newton Norfk 69 N6
West Newton Somset 21 L7
West Norwood Gt Lon 33 K8
Westoe S Tyne 101 K5
West Ogwell Devon 5 N3
Weston BaNES 29 L9
Weston Ches E 64 D2
Weston Devon 9 M5
Weston Devon 9 M7
Weston Dorset 10 G10
Weston Halton 75 N7
Weston Hants 25 M9
Weston Herefs 51 L9
Weston Herts 45 J5
Weston Lincs 68 F7
Weston N York 85 J6
Weston Nhants 43 M2
Weston Notts 79 K10
Weston Shrops 51 K6
Weston Shrops 51 Q2
Weston Shrops 63 J6
Weston Staffs 64 H7
Weston Suffk 59 N3
Weston W Berk 31 J7
Weston Beggard Herefs 41 J3
Westonbirt Gloucs 29 P4
Weston by Welland Nhants 55 K2
Weston Colley Hants 24 H5
Weston Colville Cambs 57 L10
Weston Corbett Hants 25 M4
Weston Coyney C Stke 64 H4
Weston Favell Nhants 55 K8
Weston Green Cambs 57 M10
Weston Heath Shrops 64 E9
Weston Hills Lincs 68 E8
Weston in Arden Warwks 54 C3
Westoning C Beds 44 E5
Weston-in-Gordano N Som 28 F7
Westoning Woodend C Beds 44 E5
Weston Jones Staffs 64 E8
Weston Longville Norfk 70 G9
Weston Lullingfields Shrops 63 M7
Weston-on-Avon Warwks 53 M10
Weston-on-the-Green Oxon 43 L8
Weston Park Staffs 64 E10
Weston Patrick Hants 25 M4
Weston Rhyn Shrops 63 J5
Weston-sub-Edge Gloucs 42 D3
Weston-super-Mare N Som 28 D10
Weston Turville Bucks 44 B9
Weston-under-Lizard Staffs 64 E10
Weston under Penyard Herefs 41 K7
Weston-under-Redcastle Shrops 63 P6
Weston under Wetherley Warwks 54 B7
Weston Underwood Derbys 65 P4
Weston Underwood M Keyn 55 M10
Weston-upon-Trent Derbys 66 C6
Westonzoyland Somset 21 M6
West Orchard Dorset 22 H10
West Overton Wilts 30 D9
Westow N York 86 D2
West Panson Devon 7 L6
West Park Abers 133 J5
West Parley Dorset 11 Q5
West Peckham Kent 34 B11
West Peeke Devon 7 L6
West Pelton Dur 100 G7
West Pennard Somset 22 D5
West Pentire Cnwll 3 J2
West Pinchbeck Lincs 68 D7
West Porlock Somset 20 D4
Westport Somset 21 N9
West Pulham Dorset 10 H3
West Putford Devon 18 G10
West Quantoxhead Somset 20 H5
Westquarter Falk 114 G5
Westra V Glam 27 Q8
West Raddon Devon 8 G4
West Rainton Dur 101 J9
West Rasen Lincs 79 Q6
West Ravendale NE Lin 80 E4
Westray Ork 147 c2
Westray Airport Ork 147 c1
West Raynham Norfk 70 C7
West Retford Notts 78 H7
Westridge Green W Berk 31 M6
Westrigg W Loth 114 G8
Westrop Swindn 30 E4
West Rounton N York 91 P6
West Row Suffk 57 N5
West Rudham Norfk 70 B6
West Runton Norfk 71 J4
Westruther Border 116 E11
Westry Cambs 56 H1
West Saltoun E Loth 116 B8
West Sandford Devon 8 F4
West Sandwick Shet 147 j4
West Scrafton N York 90 H10
West Sleekburn Nthumb 100 H1
West Somerton Norfk 71 P8
West Stafford Dorset 10 H7
West Stockwith Notts 79 K5
West Stoke W Susx 13 P3
West Stonesdale N York 90 E6
West Stoughton Somset 21 P4
West Stour Dorset 22 H9
West Stourmouth Kent 35 N9
West Stow Suffk 57 Q6
West Stowell Wilts 30 D10
West Stratton Hants 25 J5
West Street Kent 34 F11
West Street Kent 35 P11
West Street Medway 34 C7
West Street Suffk 58 E6
West Tanfield N York 91 M11
West Taphouse Cnwll 4 A4
West Tarbert Ag & B 112 C8
West Tarring W Susx 14 G10
West Thirston Nthumb 109 K10
West Thorney W Susx 13 N4
Westthorpe Derbys 78 D8
West Thorpe Notts 66 G7
West Thurrock Thurr 33 Q7
West Tilbury Thurr 34 B7
West Tisted Hants 25 L7
West Torrington Lincs 80 C7
West Town BaNES 28 G10
West Town Hants 13 M5
West Town Herefs 51 M8
West Town N Som 28 G8
West Town Somset 22 C6
West Town Somset 22 F5
West Tytherley Hants 24 D7
West Walton Norfk 69 J9
Westward Cumb 98 C9
Westward Ho! Devon 18 H7
Westwell Kent 16 H1
Westwell Oxon 42 E9
Westwell Leacon Kent 16 G1
West Wellow Hants 24 D9
West Wembury Devon 4 H7
West Wemyss Fife 115 P2
Westwick Cambs 56 H7
Westwick Dur 90 H4
West Wick N Som 28 E10
Westwick Norfk 71 K7
West Wickham Cambs 57 L10
West Wickham Gt Lon 33 M9
West Williamston Pembks 37 K9
West Winch Norfk 69 M9
West Winterslow Wilts 24 C7
West Wittering W Susx 13 N5
West Witton N York 90 H9
Westwood Devon 9 J5
Westwood Kent 33 R8
Westwood Kent 35 Q9
Westwood Notts 66 D2
Westwood Nthumb 99 L5
Westwood Wilts 29 N10
West Woodburn Nthumb 108 E12
West Woodhay W Berk 31 J9
Westwood Heath Covtry 53 P5
West Woodlands Somset 22 H4
Westwoodside N Linc 79 J4
West Worldham Hants 25 M6
West Worthing W Susx 14 G10
West Wratting Cambs 57 L10
West Wycombe Bucks 32 B3
West Wylam Nthumb 100 F5
West Yatton Wilts 29 P7
West Yoke Kent 33 Q9
West Youlstone Cnwll 18 E10
Wetham Green Kent 34 E8
Wetheral Cumb 98 F7
Wetherby Leeds 85 N5
Wetherby Services N York 85 N5
Wetherden Suffk 58 E8
Wetheringsett Suffk 58 H7
Wethersfield Essex 46 C5
Wetherup Street Suffk 58 H8
Wetley Rocks Staffs 64 H2
Wettenhall Ches E 76 B11
Wetton Staffs 65 L1
Wetwang E R Yk 86 H3
Wetwood Staffs 64 E5
Wexcombe Wilts 30 F10
Wexham Slough 32 E6
Wexham Street Bucks 32 E6
Weybourne Norfk 70 G4
Weybourne Surrey 25 P4
Weybread Suffk 59 K4
Weybread Street Suffk 59 K5
Weybridge Surrey 32 F9
Weycroft Devon 9 P4
Weydale Highld 151 L4
Weyhill Hants 24 E4
Weymouth Dorset 10 G9
Whaddon Bucks 44 A5
Whaddon Cambs 45 L2
Whaddon Gloucs 41 N9
Whaddon Wilts 24 C8
Whaddon Wilts 29 P10
Whale Cumb 89 N2
Whaley Derbys 78 E9
Whaley Bridge Derbys 77 J7
Whaley Thorns Derbys 78 E9
Whaligoe Highld 151 P8
Whalley Lancs 83 Q8
Whalley Banks Lancs 83 Q8
Whalsay Shet 147 k5
Whalton Nthumb 100 E2
Whaplode Lincs 68 F7
Whaplode Drove Lincs 68 F9
Wharf Warwks 54 C10
Wharfe N York 84 B1
Wharles Lancs 83 K8
Wharley End C Beds 44 D3
Wharncliffe Side Sheff 77 P5
Wharram-le-Street N York 86 F2
Wharton Ches W 76 C10
Wharton Herefs 51 N9
Whashton N York 91 K5
Whasset Cumb 89 N10
Whatcote Warwks 42 G3
Whateley Warwks 65 N12
Whatfield Suffk 47 J2
Whatley Somset 21 N9
Whatley Somset 22 G4
Whatley's End S Glos 29 K6
Whatlington E Susx 16 D7
Whatsole Street Kent 17 K2
Whatstandwell Derbys 65 Q1
Whatton-in-the-Vale Notts 67 J4
Whauphill D & G 95 M8
Whaw N York 90 G6
Wheal Peevor Cnwll 2 H5
Wheal Rose Cnwll 2 H5
Wheatacre Norfk 59 P2
Wheatfield Oxon 31 P2
Wheathampstead Herts 44 H9
Wheathill Shrops 52 B4
Wheathill Somset 22 D7
Wheatley Hants 25 N5
Wheatley Oxon 43 M10
Wheatley Hill Dur 101 K10
Wheatley Hills Donc 78 F3
Wheatley Lane Lancs 84 C7
Wheaton Aston Staffs 64 F9
Wheddon Cross Somset 20 E5
Wheelbarrow Town Kent 17 L2
Wheeler End Bucks 32 A4
Wheeler's Green Wokham 31 Q8
Wheelerstreet Surrey 14 D3
Wheelock Ches E 76 D12
Wheelock Heath Ches E 76 D12
Wheelton Lancs 83 N10
Wheldale Wakefd 85 P10
Wheldrake C York 86 C6
Whelford Gloucs 30 D3
Whelpley Hill Bucks 44 E10
Whelpo Cumb 98 C10
Whelston Flints 74 H8
Whempstead Herts 45 K7
Whenby N York 86 B1
Whepstead Suffk 58 B9
Wherstead Suffk 47 L3
Wherwell Hants 24 F5
Wheston Derbys 77 L8
Whetsted Kent 16 B2
Whetstone Gt Lon 33 J4
Whetstone Leics 54 F1
Wheyrigg Cumb 97 P8
Whicham Cumb 88 F10
Whichford Warwks 42 G5
Whickham Gatesd 100 G6
Whiddon Devon 7 N5
Whiddon Down Devon 8 D6
Whigstreet Angus 125 J4
Whilton Nhants 54 G8
Whimble Devon 7 L4
Whimple Devon 9 K5
Whimpwell Green Norfk 71 M6
Whinburgh Norfk 70 E10
Whin Lane End Lancs 83 J7
Whinnieliggate D & G 96 E8
Whinnow Cumb 98 C8
Whinnyfold Abers 141 P9
Whinny Hill S on T 91 P3
Whippingham IoW 12 H6
Whipsnade C Beds 44 E8
Whipsnade Zoo ZSL C Beds 44 E8
Whipton Devon 8 H6
Whirlow Sheff 77 P7
Whisby Lincs 79 M10
Whissendine Rutlnd 67 K9
Whissonsett Norfk 70 D7
Whistlefield Ag & B 113 J3
Whistlefield Inn Ag & B 112 H3
Whistley Green Wokham 31 R7
Whiston Knows 75 N5
Whiston Nhants 55 L8
Whiston Rothm 78 D6
Whiston Staffs 64 G9
Whiston Staffs 65 J3
Whiston Cross Shrops 64 E11
Whiston Eaves Staffs 65 K3
Whitacre Fields Warwks 53 N2
Whitbeck Cumb 88 F10
Whitbourne Herefs 52 D9
Whitburn S Tyne 101 K6
Whitburn W Loth 114 H8
Whitby Ches W 75 L8
Whitby N York 92 H4
Whitbyheath Ches W 75 L9
Whitchester Border 116 G9
Whitchurch BaNES 29 J9
Whitchurch Bucks 44 A7
Whitchurch Cardif 27 R6
Whitchurch Devon 7 P10
Whitchurch Hants 24 H4
Whitchurch Herefs 40 H8
Whitchurch Oxon 31 N7
Whitchurch Pembks 36 F5
Whitchurch Shrops 63 P4
Whitchurch Canonicorum Dorset 10 B6
Whitchurch Hill Oxon 31 N6
Whitcombe Dorset 10 H7
Whitcot Shrops 51 L2
Whitcott Keysett Shrops 51 J4
Whiteacre Kent 17 K1
Whiteacre Heath Warwks 53 N2
Whiteash Green Essex 46 D5
White Ball Somset 20 H9
Whitebridge Highld 129 N1
Whitebrook Mons 40 H10
Whitebushes Surrey 15 K1
Whitecairns Abers 141 M12
Whitechapel Gt Lon 33 L6
White Chapel Lancs 83 M7
Whitechurch Pembks 37 M3
Whitecliff Gloucs 40 H9
White Colne Essex 46 F6
White Coppice Lancs 83 N11
Whitecraig E Loth 115 Q7
Whitecroft Gloucs 41 J10
Whitecrook D & G 94 H7
Whitecross Cnwll 2 E7
White Cross Cnwll 2 H10
Whitecross Cnwll 6 D10
Whitecross Falk 114 H6
White End Worcs 41 M5
Whiteface Highld 146 C7
Whitefarland N Ayrs 103 M1
Whitefaulds S Ayrs 104 E8
Whitefield Bury 76 E2
Whitefield Devon 19 N6
Whitefield Somset 20 G7
Whitefield Lane End Knows 75 M6
Whiteford Abers 140 H10
Whitegate Ches W 76 B10
Whitehall Hants 25 N3
Whitehall Ork 147 e3
Whitehall W Susx 14 G6
Whitehaven Cumb 88 C3
Whitehill Hants 25 N6
Whitehill Kent 34 H10
Whitehill Leics 66 C10
Whitehills Abers 140 G3
Whitehouse Abers 132 F1
Whitehouse Ag & B 112 B9
Whitehouse Common Birm 53 L1
Whitekirk E Loth 116 E5
White Kirkley Dur 100 C11
White Lackington Dorset 10 H5
Whitelackington Somset 21 N10
White Ladies Aston Worcs 52 G10
Whiteleaf Bucks 44 B10
White-le-Head Dur 100 F7
Whiteley Hants 13 J3
Whiteley Bank IoW 13 J8
Whiteley Green Ches E 76 G8
Whiteley Village Surrey 32 F10
Whitemans Green W Susx 15 K6
White Mill Carmth 38 C7
Whitemire Moray 138 H5
Whitemoor C Nott 66 E4
Whitemoor Cnwll 3 N3
Whitemoor Derbys 66 B3
Whitemoor Staffs 76 G11
Whiteness Shet 147 i7
White Notley Essex 46 D8
Whiteoak Green Oxon 42 H9
White Ox Mead BaNES 29 L10
Whiteparish Wilts 24 D8
White Pit Lincs 80 G8
Whiterashes Abers 141 K11
White Roding Essex 45 Q9
Whiterow Highld 151 Q7
Whiterow Moray 139 J4
Whiteshill Gloucs 41 N10
Whitesmith E Susx 15 P8
White Stake Lancs 83 M10
Whitestaunton Somset 9 P3
Whitestone Devon 8 G6
White Stone Herefs 40 H3
Whitestone Warwks 54 C3
Whitestone Cross Devon 8 G6
Whitestreet Green Suffk 46 H4
Whitewall Corner N York 86 E1
White Waltham W & M 32 B7
Whiteway BaNES 29 L9
Whiteway Gloucs 41 Q9
Whitewell Lancs 83 P6
Whiteworks Devon 8 B10
Whitfield C Dund 125 J6
Whitfield Kent 17 N2
Whitfield Nhants 43 M4
Whitfield Nthumb 99 M7
Whitfield S Glos 29 K4
Whitfield Hall Nthumb 99 M7
Whitford Devon 9 P5
Whitford Flints 74 G8
Whitgift E R Yk 86 E10
Whitgreave Staffs 64 G6
Whithorn D & G 95 N10
Whiting Bay N Ayrs 103 Q4
Whitkirk Leeds 85 M8
Whitland Carmth 37 N7
Whitlaw Border 107 M7
Whitletts S Ayrs 104 G5
Whitley N York 85 R11
Whitley Readg 31 P8
Whitley Sheff 77 Q5
Whitley Wilts 29 P9
Whitley Bay N Tyne 101 J4
Whitley Chapel Nthumb 99 P7
Whitley Heath Staffs 64 F7
Whitley Lower Kirk 85 J11
Whitley Row Kent 33 P11
Whitlock's End Solhll 53 L5
Whitminster Gloucs 41 M10
Whitmore Dorset 11 P3
Whitmore Staffs 64 E4
Whitnage Devon 20 G10
Whitnash Warwks 53 Q8
Whitney-on-Wye Herefs 40 C2
Whitrigg Cumb 97 P10
Whitrigg Cumb 97 P6
Whitrigglees Cumb 97 P7
Whitsbury Hants 23 P9
Whitsome Border 117 J11
Whitson Newpt 28 E6
Whitstable Kent 35 K9
Whitstone Cnwll 7 K5
Whittingham Nthumb 108 H7
Whittingslow Shrops 51 M3
Whittington Derbys 78 C8
Whittington Gloucs 42 B7
Whittington Lancs 89 P11
Whittington Norfk 69 N12
Whittington Shrops 63 K6
Whittington Staffs 52 F4
Whittington Staffs 65 M10
Whittington Warwks 65 P12
Whittington Worcs 52 G10
Whittington Moor Derbys 78 B9
Whittlebury Nhants 43 P3
Whittle-le-Woods Lancs 83 N11
Whittlesey Cambs 56 E1
Whittlesford Cambs 57 J11
Whittlestone Head Bl w D 83 Q11
Whitton N Linc 86 G10
Whitton Nthumb 108 H9
Whitton Powys 51 J7
Whitton S on T 91 P2
Whitton Shrops 51 P6
Whitton Suffk 58 H11
Whittonditch Wilts 30 G8
Whittonstall Nthumb 100 D7
Whitway Hants 31 K10
Whitwell Derbys 78 E8
Whitwell Herts 44 H7
Whitwell IoW 13 J9
Whitwell N York 91 M7
Whitwell Rutlnd 67 M10
Whitwell-on-the-Hill N York 86 D2
Whitwell Street Norfk 70 H8
Whitwick Leics 66 D9
Whitwood Wakefd 85 N10
Whitworth Lancs 84 D11
Whixall Shrops 63 N5
Whixley N York 85 N4
Whorlton Dur 91 J4
Whorlton N York 91 Q6
Whyle Herefs 51 P8
Whyteleafe Surrey 33 L10
Wibdon Gloucs 28 H3
Wibsey C Brad 84 H9
Wibtoft Warwks 54 D3
Wichelstowe Swindn 30 D6
Wichenford Worcs 52 E8
Wichling Kent 34 G11
Wick BCP 12 B6
Wick Devon 9 M4
Wick Highld 151 Q6
Wick S Glos 29 L8
Wick Somset 21 K4
Wick Somset 21 N8
Wick V Glam 27 L8
Wick W Susx 14 E10
Wick Wilts 23 Q9
Wick Worcs 41 Q3
Wicken Cambs 57 L6
Wicken Nhants 43 Q4
Wicken Bonhunt Essex 45 P5
Wickenby Lincs 80 B7
Wick End Bed 55 N10
Wicken Green Village Norfk 70 B6
Wickersley Rothm 78 D5
Wicker Street Green Suffk 46 H3
Wickford Essex 34 D4
Wickham Hants 13 K2
Wickham W Berk 31 J8
Wickham Bishops Essex 46 E9
Wickhambreaux Kent 35 M10
Wickhambrook Suffk 57 P9
Wickhamford Worcs 42 C3
Wickham Green Suffk 58 G7
Wickham Green W Berk 31 J8
Wickham Heath W Berk 31 J8
Wickham Market Suffk 59 L9
Wickhampton Norfk 71 N11
Wickham St Paul Essex 46 E4
Wickham Skeith Suffk 58 G7
Wickham Street Suffk 57 P10
Wickham Street Suffk 58 G7
Wickhurst Green W Susx 14 G5
Wick John o' Groats Airport Highld 151 Q6
Wicklewood Norfk 70 G11
Wickmere Norfk 70 H5
Wick St Lawrence N Som 28 E9
Wicksteed Park Nhants 55 L5
Wickstreet E Susx 15 P9
Wickwar S Glos 29 L5
Widdington Essex 45 P5
Widdop Calder 84 D8
Widdrington Nthumb 109 L10
Widdrington Station Nthumb 109 L11
Widecombe in the Moor Devon 8 D9
Widegates Cnwll 4 D5
Widemouth Bay Cnwll 7 J4
Wideopen N Tyne 100 G4
Widford Essex 46 C10
Widford Herts 45 M8
Widham Wilts 30 C5
Widley Hants 13 L3
Widmer End Bucks 32 C3
Widmerpool Notts 66 G6
Widmore Gt Lon 33 M8
Widnes Halton 75 N6
Widworthy Devon 9 N5
Wigan Wigan 75 P3
Wigborough Somset 21 P10
Wiggaton Devon 9 L6
Wiggenhall St Germans Norfk 69 L9
Wiggenhall St Mary Magdalen Norfk 69 L10
Wiggenhall St Mary the Virgin Norfk 69 L9
Wiggenhall St Peter Norfk 69 L9
Wiggens Green Essex 46 B3
Wiggenstall Staffs 77 K11
Wiggington Shrops 63 K5
Wigginton C York 86 B3
Wigginton Herts 44 D9
Wigginton Oxon 42 H5
Wigginton Staffs 65 N11
Wigginton Bottom Herts 44 D10
Wigglesworth N York 84 B4
Wiggonby Cumb 98 C7
Wiggonholt W Susx 14 F7
Wighill N York 85 P6
Wighton Norfk 70 D4
Wightwick Wolves 52 F1
Wigley Derbys 77 P9
Wigley Hants 24 E10
Wigmore Herefs 51 L7
Wigmore Medway 34 D9
Wigsley Notts 79 L9
Wigsthorpe Nhants 55 P4
Wigston Leics 54 G1
Wigston Fields Leics 66 F12
Wigston Parva Leics 54 D3
Wigthorpe Notts 78 F7

Wigtoft Lincs 68 E5
Wigton Cumb 97 Q8
Wigtown D & G 95 N7
Wigtwizzle Sheff 77 N4
Wike Leeds 85 M7
Wilbarston Nhants 55 K3
Wilberfoss E R Yk 86 D5
Wilburton Cambs 57 J6
Wilby Nhants 55 L7
Wilby Norfk 58 F3
Wilby Suffk 59 K6
Wilcot Wilts 30 D10
Wilcott Shrops 63 L8
Wilcove Cnwll 4 F5
Wilcrick Newpt 28 F5
Wilday Green Derbys 77 Q9
Wildboarclough Ches E 76 H10
Wilden Bed 56 B9
Wilden Worcs 52 F6
Wilde Street Suffk 57 N5
Wildern Hants 24 F3
Wildhill Herts 45 J10
Wildmanbridge S Lans 114 E10
Wildmill Brdgnd 27 L6
Wildmoor Hants 25 L2
Wildmoor Worcs 52 H5
Wildsworth Lincs 79 K4
Wilford C Nott 66 F5
Wilkesley Ches E 64 B4
Wilkhaven Highld 146 G8
Wilkieston W Loth 115 L7
Wilkin's Green Herts 44 H10
Wilksby Lincs 80 F11
Willand Devon 9 K3
Willards Hill E Susx 16 C6
Willaston Ches E 64 C2
Willaston Ches W 75 K8
Willen M Keyn 44 C3
Willenhall Covtry 54 B5
Willenhall Wsall 52 H1
Willerby E R Yk 87 J9
Willerby N York 93 K11
Willersey Gloucs 42 C4
Willersley Herefs 40 D2
Willesborough Kent 17 J2
Willesborough Lees Kent 17 J2
Willesden Gt Lon 33 J5
Willesleigh Devon 19 L7
Willesley Wilts 29 N5
Willett Somset 20 H6
Willey Shrops 64 C12
Willey Warwks 54 E4
Willey Green Surrey 32 D12
Williamscot Oxon 43 K3
Williamstown Rhondd 27 N4
Willian Herts 45 J5
Willicote Warwks 42 G3
Willingale Essex 45 Q10
Willingdon E Susx 15 Q10
Willingham Cambs 56 H6
Willingham by Stow Lincs 79 L7
Willingham Green Cambs 57 M10
Willingham St Mary Suffk 59 N4
Willington Bed 56 C10
Willington Derbys 65 P6
Willington Dur 100 G11
Willington Kent 34 D11
Willington N Tyne 101 J4
Willington Warwks 42 F4
Willington Corner Ches W 75 N10
Willitoft E R Yk 86 D8
Williton Somset 20 G5
Willoughby Lincs 81 J9
Willoughby Warwks 54 E7
Willoughby Hills Lincs 68 G3
Willoughby-on-the-Wolds Notts 66 G7
Willoughby Waterleys Leics 54 F2
Willoughton Lincs 79 M5
Willow Green Ches W 75 Q8
Willows Green Essex 46 C8
Willsbridge S Glos 29 K8
Willsworthy Devon 7 P8
Willtown Somset 21 N8
Wilmcote Warwks 53 M9
Wilmington BaNES 29 L10
Wilmington Devon 9 N5
Wilmington E Susx 15 Q10
Wilmington Kent 33 P8
Wilminstone Devon 8 B9
Wilmslow Ches E 76 F7
Wilnecote Staffs 65 N12
Wilpshire Lancs 83 Q8
Wilsden C Brad 84 G8
Wilsford Lincs 67 P4
Wilsford Wilts 23 P5
Wilsford Wilts 30 C11
Wilsham Devon 19 P4
Wilshaw Kirk 77 L2
Wilsill N York 85 J2
Wilsley Green Kent 16 D3
Wilsley Pound Kent 16 D3
Wilson Herefs 40 H7
Wilson Leics 66 C7
Wilsontown S Lans 114 H10
Wilstead Bed 44 F3
Wilsthorpe Lincs 68 B9
Wilstone Herts 44 C9
Wilstone Green Herts 44 C9
Wilton Cumb 88 D4
Wilton Herefs 41 J7
Wilton N York 92 H10
Wilton R & Cl 92 C3
Wilton Wilts 23 N5
Wilton Wilts 30 F10
Wilton Dean Border 107 M4
Wimbish Essex 45 Q4
Wimbish Green Essex 45 R5
Wimbledon Gt Lon 33 J8
Wimblington Cambs 56 H2
Wimboldsley Ches W 76 C11
Wimborne Minster Dorset 11 N5
Wimborne St Giles Dorset 11 P2
Wimbotsham Norfk 69 M11
Wimpole Cambs 56 G11
Wimpstone Warwks 53 N11
Wincanton Somset 22 D7
Winceby Lincs 80 F10
Wincham Ches W 76 C8
Winchburgh W Loth 115 K6
Winchcombe Gloucs 42 B6
Winchelsea E Susx 16 F7
Winchelsea Beach E Susx 16 F7
Winchester Hants 24 H7
Winchester Services Hants 25 J6
Winchet Hill Kent 16 C3
Winchfield Hants 25 N2
Winchmore Hill Bucks 32 D3
Winchmore Hill Gt Lon 33 K3
Wincle Ches E 76 H10
Wincobank Sheff 78 C5
Winder Cumb 88 D3
Windermere Cumb 89 L7
Windermere Jetty Museum Cumb 89 L7
Winderton Warwks 42 G3
Windhill Highld 137 P6
Windlehurst Stockp 76 H6
Windlesham Surrey 32 D10
Windmill Cnwll 6 C9
Windmill Derbys 77 M8
Windmill Hill E Susx 16 C8

Windmill Hill Somset 21 M10
Windrush Gloucs 42 E9
Windsole Abers 140 E4
Windsor W & M 32 D7
Windsor Castle W & M 32 D7
Windsoredge Gloucs 29 N2
Windsor Green Suffk 58 C9
Windygates Fife 115 J7
Windyharbour Ches E 76 F9
Windy Hill Wrexhm 63 J1
Wineham W Susx 15 J7
Winestead E R Yk 87 P10
Winewall Lancs 84 D7
Winfarthing Norfk 58 G4
Winford IoW 13 J8
Winford N Som 28 H9
Winforton Herefs 40 C2
Winfrith Newburgh Dorset 11 K8
Wing Bucks 44 C7
Wing Rutlnd 67 M11
Wingate Dur 101 K11
Wingates Bolton 76 C2
Wingates Nthumb 108 H10
Wingerworth Derbys 78 C10
Wingfield C Beds 44 E6
Wingfield Suffk 59 J5
Wingfield Wilts 29 N11
Wingfield Green Suffk 59 J5
Wingham Kent 35 M11
Wingland Lincs 69 J7
Wingmore Kent 17 L2
Wingrave Bucks 44 B8
Winkburn Notts 78 H12
Winkfield Br For 32 C8
Winkfield Row Br For 32 C8
Winkhill Staffs 65 K2
Winkhurst Green Kent 15 P1
Winkleigh Devon 8 B3
Winksley N York 85 K1
Winkton BCP 12 B5
Winlaton Gatesd 100 F6
Winlaton Mill Gatesd 100 F6
Winless Highld 151 P6
Winllan Powys 62 H8
Winmarleigh Lancs 83 L6
Winnall Hants 24 H7
Winnersh Wokham 31 Q8
Winnington Ches W 76 B9
Winscales Cumb 88 D2
Winscombe N Som 28 F11
Winsford Ches W 76 C10
Winsford Somset 20 D6
Winsham Devon 19 K5
Winsham Somset 10 B3
Winshill Staffs 65 P7
Winshwen Swans 26 G3
Winskill Cumb 98 H11
Winslade Hants 25 L4
Winsley Wilts 29 M10
Winslow Bucks 43 Q6
Winson Gloucs 42 C10
Winsor Hants 24 E10
Winstanley Wigan 75 P3
Winster Cumb 89 L8
Winster Derbys 77 N11
Winston Dur 91 J3
Winston Suffk 58 H8
Winstone Gloucs 41 Q9
Winston Green Suffk 58 H8
Winswell Devon 19 J10
Winterborne Came Dorset 10 H7
Winterborne Clenston Dorset 11 K4
Winterborne Herringston Dorset 10 H7
Winterborne Houghton Dorset 11 K4
Winterborne Kingston Dorset 11 L5
Winterborne Monkton Dorset 10 G7
Winterborne Stickland Dorset 11 K4
Winterborne Tomson Dorset 11 L5
Winterborne Whitechurch Dorset 11 K5
Winterborne Zelston Dorset 11 L5
Winterbourne S Glos 29 K6
Winterbourne W Berk 31 K8
Winterbourne Abbas Dorset 10 F6
Winterbourne Bassett Wilts 30 C7
Winterbourne Dauntsey Wilts 24 B6
Winterbourne Earls Wilts 24 B6
Winterbourne Gunner Wilts 24 B6
Winterbourne Monkton Wilts 30 C8
Winterbourne Steepleton Dorset 10 F7
Winterbourne Stoke Wilts 23 N5
Winterbrook Oxon 31 M5
Winterburn N York 84 D3
Winteringham N Linc 86 H10
Winterley Ches E 76 D12
Wintersett Wakefd 85 M12
Winterslow Wilts 24 C7
Winterton N Linc 86 H11
Winterton-on-Sea Norfk 71 P8
Winthorpe Lincs 81 L10
Winthorpe Notts 79 K12
Winton BCP 11 Q6
Winton Cumb 90 C5
Winton E Susx 15 P10
Winton N York 91 P7
Wintringham Cambs 56 D8
Wintringham N York 92 H12
Winwick Cambs 56 B4
Winwick Nhants 54 G6
Winwick Warrtn 76 B4
Wirksworth Derbys 65 P1
Wirral 75 J6
Wirswall Ches E 63 P3
Wisbech Cambs 69 J10
Wisbech St Mary Cambs 68 H10
Wisborough Green W Susx 14 F5
Wiseman's Bridge Pembks 37 M9
Wiseton Notts 79 J6
Wishanger Gloucs 41 Q9
Wishaw N Lans 114 H10
Wishaw Warwks 53 M2
Wisley Surrey 32 F10
Wispington Lincs 80 D9
Wissenden Kent 16 H3
Wissett Suffk 59 M5
Wistanstow Shrops 51 M4
Wistanswick Shrops 64 C8
Wistaston Ches E 64 C1
Wistaston Green Ches E 64 C1
Wisterfield Ches E 76 F9
Wiston Pembks 37 K7
Wiston S Lans 106 C3
Wiston W Susx 14 G8
Wistow Cambs 56 E4
Wistow Leics 54 H2
Wistow N York 86 B8

Wiswell Lancs 83 R7
Witcham Cambs 57 J5
Witchampton Dorset 11 N3
Witchford Cambs 57 J5
Witcombe Somset 21 Q9
Witham Essex 46 E9
Witham Friary Somset 22 G5
Witham on the Hill Lincs 67 P9
Witham St Hughs Lincs 79 M11
Withcall Lincs 80 F7
Withdean Br & H 15 K9
Witherenden Hill E Susx 16 B5
Witheridge Devon 8 C10
Witherley Leics 53 Q1
Withern Lincs 80 H7
Withernsea E R Yk 87 Q9
Withernwick E R Yk 87 M7
Withersdale Street Suffk 59 K4
Withersfield Suffk 57 M11
Witherslack Cumb 89 L10
Withiel Cnwll 6 E11
Withiel Florey Somset 20 F7
Withielgoose Cnwll 6 E11
Withington Gloucs 42 B8
Withington Herefs 40 H3
Withington Manch 76 F5
Withington Shrops 63 P9
Withington Staffs 65 J5
Withington Green Ches E 76 E9
Withington Marsh Herefs 40 H3
Withleigh Devon 20 D10
Withnell Lancs 83 P10
Withnell Fold Lancs 83 N10
Withybed Green Worcs 53 J6
Withybrook Warwks 54 D4
Withycombe Somset 20 F5
Withyham E Susx 15 P4
Withy Mills BaNES 29 K11
Withypool Somset 19 Q6
Withywood Bristl 28 H9
Witley Surrey 14 D3
Witnesham Suffk 58 H10
Witney Oxon 42 H9
Wittering C Pete 67 Q11
Wittersham Kent 16 F5
Witton Birm 53 K2
Witton Norfk 71 L10
Witton Norfk 71 L6
Witton Gilbert Dur 100 G9
Witton Green Norfk 71 N11
Witton le Wear Dur 100 F12
Witton Park Dur 100 F12
Wivelscombe Somset 20 H8
Wivelsfield E Susx 15 L6
Wivelsfield Green E Susx 15 L7
Wivelsfield Station W Susx 15 L7
Wivenhoe Essex 47 J7
Wivenhoe Cross Essex 47 J7
Wiveton Norfk 70 F4
Wix Essex 47 L6
Wixams Beds 44 F3
Wixford Warwks 53 K9
Wix Green Essex 47 L6
Wixhill Shrops 63 P6
Wixoe Suffk 46 C3
Woburn C Beds 44 D5
Woburn Safari Park C Beds 44 D5
Woburn Sands M Keyn 44 D5
Wokefield Park W Berk 31 N9
Woking Surrey 32 E10
Wokingham Wokham 32 A8
Wolborough Devon 8 F10
Woldingham Surrey 33 L11
Wold Newton E R Yk 93 L12
Wold Newton NE Lin 80 E4
Wolfclyde S Lans 106 D3
Wolferlow Herefs 52 C8
Wolferton Norfk 69 M6
Wolfhampcote Warwks 54 E7
Wolfhill P & K 124 D6
Wolf Hills Nthumb 99 L6
Wolf's Castle Pembks 37 J5
Wolfsdale Pembks 36 H6
Wollaston Dudley 52 G4
Wollaston Nhants 55 M8
Wollaston Shrops 63 K9
Wollaton C Nott 66 E4
Wollaton Hall C Nott 66 E4
Wolleigh Devon 8 F8
Wollerton Shrops 64 B6
Wollescote Dudley 52 H4
Wolseley Bridge Staffs 65 J8
Wolsingham Dur 100 E10
Wolstanton Staffs 64 F3
Wolstenholme Rochdl 84 C12
Wolston Warwks 54 C5
Wolsty Cumb 97 M8
Wolvercote Oxon 43 K9
Wolverhampton Wolves 64 G12
Wolverhampton Halfpenny Green Airport Staffs 52 F2
Wolverley Shrops 63 N6
Wolverley Worcs 52 F5
Wolverton Hants 31 L10
Wolverton Kent 17 N2
Wolverton M Keyn 44 B3
Wolverton Warwks 53 N8
Wolverton Wilts 22 H7
Wolverton Common Hants 31 M10
Wolvesnewton Mons 28 F2
Wolvey Warwks 54 C3
Wolvey Heath Warwks 54 D3
Wolviston S on T 91 Q2
Wombleton N York 92 D10
Wombourne Staffs 52 G2
Wombwell Barns 78 C3
Womenswold Kent 35 M12
Womersley N York 85 Q11
Wonastow Mons 40 H3
Wonersh Surrey 14 E2
Wonford Devon 8 H6
Wonson Devon 8 C7
Wonston Dorset 10 H3
Wonston Hants 24 H5
Wooburn Bucks 32 C5
Wooburn Green Bucks 32 C5
Wooburn Moor Bucks 32 C4
Woodacott Devon 7 M3
Woodale N York 90 G11
Woodall Rothm 78 D6
Woodall Services Rothm 78 D7
Woodbank Ches W 75 K9
Woodbastwick Norfk 71 L9
Woodbeck Notts 79 K8
Wood Bevington Warwks 53 K10
Woodborough Notts 66 G3
Woodborough Wilts 30 C10
Woodbridge Devon 9 M6
Woodbridge Suffk 59 K11
Wood Burcote Nhants 43 P2
Woodbury Devon 9 J7
Woodbury Salterton Devon 9 J7
Woodchester Gloucs 41 N11
Woodchurch Kent 16 H4
Woodchurch Wirral 75 J6
Woodcombe Somset 20 C4
Woodcote Gt Lon 33 K10
Woodcote Oxon 31 N6
Woodcote Wrekin 64 E9
Woodcote Green Worcs 52 H6

Woodcott Hants 24 G2
Woodcroft Gloucs 28 H3
Woodcutts Dorset 23 L10
Wood Dalling Norfk 70 G8
Woodditton Cambs 57 M9
Woodeaton Oxon 43 L9
Wood Eaton Staffs 64 F8
Wood End Bed 44 E2
Wood End Bed 56 B7
Wood End C Beds 44 D3
Wood End Gt Lon 32 G6
Wood End Herts 45 L6
Woodend Highld 127 P12
Woodend Nhants 54 G11
Woodend Staffs 65 M7
Woodend W Susx 13 M5
Wood End W Loth 114 H2
Wood End Warwks 53 L6
Wood End Warwks 53 N3
Wood End Wolves 65 J3
Wood Enderby Lincs 80 E11
Woodfalls Wilts 24 C9
Woodford Cnwll 18 G10
Woodford Devon 5 N6
Woodford Gloucs 29 J3
Woodford Gt Lon 33 M4
Woodford Nhants 55 N6
Woodford Stockp 76 G7
Woodford Bridge Gt Lon 33 M4
Woodford Green Gt Lon 33 M4
Woodford Halse Nhants 54 E10
Woodford Wells Gt Lon 33 M4
Woodgate Birm 53 J4
Woodgate Devon 20 H10
Woodgate Norfk 70 C9
Woodgate Norfk 70 F9
Woodgate W Susx 14 D10
Woodgate Worcs 52 H7
Wood Green Gt Lon 33 L3
Woodgreen Hants 24 B10
Woodgreen Oxon 42 H7
Woodhall N York 90 F8
Woodhall Hill Leeds 85 J8
Woodhall Spa Lincs 80 D11
Woodham Bucks 43 P8
Woodham Surrey 32 F10
Woodham Ferrers Essex 34 D2
Woodham Mortimer Essex 46 E10
Woodham Walter Essex 46 E10
Wood Hayes Wolves 64 H11
Woodhead Abers 141 J8
Woodhill Shrops 52 D4
Woodhill Somset 21 M8
Woodhorn Nthumb 109 M12
Woodhorn Demesne Nthumb 109 M12
Woodhouse Leeds 85 L8
Woodhouse Leics 66 E9
Woodhouse Sheff 78 C7
Woodhouse Wakefd 85 M11
Woodhouse Eaves Leics 66 E9
Woodhouse Green Staffs 76 G11
Woodhouselee Mdloth 115 N8
Woodhouselees D & G 98 E3
Woodhouse Mill Sheff 78 C6
Woodhouses Cumb 98 C8
Woodhouses Oldham 76 G3
Woodhouses Staffs 65 K10
Woodhouses Staffs 65 M8
Woodhuish Devon 5 Q6
Woodhurst Cambs 56 F5
Woodingdean Br & H 15 L9
Woodkirk Leeds 85 K10
Woodland Abers 141 L11
Woodland Devon 5 K5
Woodland Devon 5 N7
Woodland Dur 90 H1
Woodland Kent 17 L3
Woodland S Ayrs 104 C10
Woodland Head Devon 8 E7
Woodlands Donc 78 E2
Woodlands Dorset 11 P3
Woodlands Hants 12 E2
Woodlands Kent 33 Q10
Woodlands N York 85 L4
Woodlands Somset 21 J5
Woodlands of Durris Abers 133 J3
Woodlands Park W & M 32 B6
Woodlands St Mary W Berk 30 G7
Woodland Street Somset 21 Q6
Woodland View Sheff 77 Q6
Wood Lane Shrops 63 L5
Wood Lane Staffs 64 E2
Woodleigh Devon 5 L8
Woodlesford Leeds 85 M9
Woodley Stockp 76 H5
Woodley Wokham 31 Q7
Woodmancote Gloucs 29 M3
Woodmancote Gloucs 42 B10
Woodmancote Gloucs 42 B9
Woodmancote W Susx 15 M8
Woodmancote W Susx 14 B9
Woodmancote W Susx 14 B9
Woodmancott Hants 25 J5
Woodmansey E R Yk 87 K7
Woodmansgreen W Susx 25 N10
Woodmansterne Surrey 33 K10
Woodmanton Devon 9 J7
Woodmarsh Wilts 22 H3
Woodmill Staffs 65 L8
Woodminton Wilts 23 M8
Woodnesborough Kent 35 P11
Woodnewton Nhants 55 P2
Woodnook Notts 66 D2
Woodplumpton Lancs 83 L8
Woodrising Norfk 70 E11
Wood Row Leeds 85 M9
Woodrow Worcs 52 G6
Wood's Corner E Susx 16 B7
Woods Eaves Herefs 51 J11
Woodseaves Shrops 64 C6
Woodseaves Staffs 64 E7
Woodsend Wilts 30 E7
Woodsetts Rothm 78 E7
Woodsford Dorset 11 J6
Wood's Green E Susx 16 B4
Woodside Cumb 97 D8
Woodside Fife 124 H11
Woodside Gt Lon 33 L9
Woodside Hants 12 E6
Woodside Herts 45 J10
Woodside P & K 124 D5
Wood Stanway Gloucs 42 B5
Woodstock Oxon 43 K8
Woodstock Pembks 37 J5
Woodston C Pete 56 D1
Wood Street Norfk 71 M8
Wood Street Village Surrey 32 D12
Woodthorpe Derbys 78 D9
Woodthorpe Leics 66 E9
Woodthorpe Lincs 80 H7
Woodton Norfk 59 M2
Woodtown Devon 18 H8
Woodvale Sefton 75 K2

Woodville Derbys 65 P8
Woodwall Green Staffs 64 D7
Wood Walton Cambs 56 D4
Woodyates Dorset 23 M9
Woody Bay Devon 19 N4
Woofferton Shrops 51 N7
Wookey Somset 22 C4
Wookey Hole Somset 22 C4
Wool Dorset 11 K7
Woolacombe Devon 19 J5
Woolage Green Kent 17 M1
Woolage Village Kent 35 M12
Woolaston Gloucs 29 J2
Woolaston Common Gloucs 28 H2
Woolavington Somset 21 M5
Woolbeding W Susx 14 C6
Woolbrook Devon 9 L7
Woolcotts Somset 20 E7
Wooldale Kirk 77 M2
Wooler Nthumb 108 E3
Woolfardisworthy Devon 8 F3
Woolfardisworthy Devon 18 G9
Woolfold Bury 76 E1
Woolfords S Lans 115 J10
Woolhampton W Berk 31 M9
Woolhope Herefs 41 J4
Woolland Dorset 11 J3
Woollard BaNES 29 K9
Woollensbrook Herts 45 L9
Woolley BaNES 29 M8
Woolley Cambs 56 E5
Woolley Cnwll 18 E10
Woolley Derbys 78 B11
Woolley Wakefd 77 Q1
Woolley Bridge Derbys 77 J4
Woolley Edge Services Wakefd 85 L12
Woolley Green W & M 32 B6
Woolmere Green Worcs 52 H8
Woolmer Green Herts 45 J8
Woolmerston Somset 21 L6
Woolminstone Somset 10 C3
Woolpack Kent 16 E3
Woolpit Suffk 58 E8
Woolpit Green Suffk 58 E8
Woolscott Warwks 54 E7
Woolsgrove Devon 8 E4
Woolsington N u Ty 100 F4
Woolstaston Shrops 51 M1
Woolsthorpe by Belvoir Lincs 67 L5
Woolsthorpe-by-Colsterworth Lincs 67 M7
Woolston C Sotn 12 G3
Woolston Devon 5 M6
Woolston Devon 5 N7
Woolston Shrops 51 M3
Woolston Shrops 51 M8
Woolston Somset 20 H5
Woolston Somset 22 C6
Woolston Warrtn 76 C6
Woolstone Gloucs 41 Q5
Woolstone M Keyn 44 C4
Woolstone Oxon 30 G3
Woolston Green Devon 5 N3
Woolton Lpool 75 M6
Woolton Hill Hants 31 J9
Woolverstone Suffk 47 L4
Woolverton Somset 22 G3
Woolwich Gt Lon 33 N6
Woonton Herefs 51 N11
Woonton Herefs 51 P8
Wooperton Nthumb 108 G6
Woore Shrops 64 D4
Wootten Green Suffk 59 J6
Wootton Bed 44 E3
Wootton Hants 12 D5
Wootton Herefs 51 K10
Wootton IoW 13 J6
Wootton Kent 17 M2
Wootton N Linc 87 L12
Wootton Nhants 55 J9
Wootton Oxon 43 J3
Wootton Oxon 43 K11
Wootton Shrops 63 K5
Wootton Shrops 51 L5
Wootton Staffs 65 K4
Wootton Staffs 65 L3
Wootton Bassett Wilts 30 C6
Wootton Bridge IoW 13 J6
Wootton Broadmead Bed 44 E3
Wootton Common IoW 13 J6
Wootton Courtenay Somset 20 E5
Wootton Fitzpaine Dorset 10 B6
Wootton Rivers Wilts 30 E9
Wootton St Lawrence Hants 25 K3
Wootton Wawen Warwks 53 M8
Worcester Worcs 52 F9
Worcester Park Gt Lon 33 J9
Wordsley Dudley 52 G3
Worfield Shrops 52 D1
Workhouse End Bed 56 B10
Workhouse Green Suffk 46 H5
Workington Cumb 88 D1
Worksop Notts 78 F8
Worlaby Lincs 80 G8
Worlaby N Linc 80 E4
Worlds End Bucks 44 B10
World's End W Berk 31 K7
World's End W Susx 15 L6
Worle N Som 28 E9
Worleston Ches E 76 C12
Worlingham Suffk 59 N3
Worlington Devon 8 E2
Worlington Suffk 57 N5
Worlingworth Suffk 59 J7
Wormald Green N York 85 K2
Wormbridge Herefs 40 F5
Wormegay Norfk 69 M10
Wormelow Tump Herefs 40 G5
Wormhill Derbys 77 L9
Wormhill Herefs 40 F5
Wormingford Essex 46 G6
Worminghall Bucks 43 N10
Wormington Gloucs 42 B5
Worminster Somset 22 D5
Wormit Fife 124 H2
Wormleighton Warwks 54 D10
Wormley Herts 45 L9
Wormley Surrey 14 D3
Wormleybury Herts 45 L9
Wormley Hill Donc 86 C12
Wormshill Kent 34 E11
Wormsley Herefs 51 M11
Worplesdon Surrey 32 E12
Worrall Sheff 77 P5
Worsbrough Barns 78 B3
Worsbrough Bridge Barns 78 B3
Worsbrough Dale Barns 78 B3
Worsley Salfd 76 E3
Worstead Norfk 71 L7
Worsthorne Lancs 84 C8
Worston Devon 5 J6
Worston Lancs 84 A7
Worth Kent 35 P11
Worth Somset 22 C3
Worth W Susx 15 K4
Wortham Suffk 58 G5
Worthen Shrops 63 K11
Worthenbury Wrexhm 63 M3
Worthing Norfk 70 E9

Worthing W Susx 14 G10
Worthington Leics 66 C8
Worth Matravers Dorset 11 N9
Worthybrook Mons 40 G9
Worting Hants 25 K3
Wortley Barns 77 P4
Wortley Gloucs 29 M4
Wortley Leeds 85 K8
Worton N York 90 F8
Worton Wilts 29 R10
Wortwell Norfk 59 K4
Wotherton Shrops 63 J12
Wothorpe C Pete 67 P11
Wotter Devon 5 J4
Wotton Surrey 14 G1
Wotton-under-Edge Gloucs 29 M4
Wotton Underwood Bucks 43 P8
Woughton on the Green M Keyn 44 C4
Wouldham Kent 34 C9
Woundale Shrops 52 E2
Wrabness Essex 47 L5
Wrafton Devon 19 J6
Wragby Lincs 80 C8
Wragby Wakefd 85 N11
Wramplingham Norfk 70 G11
Wrangaton Devon 5 L5
Wrangbrook Wakefd 78 H2
Wrangle Lincs 68 H2
Wrangle Common Lincs 68 H2
Wrangle Lowgate Lincs 68 H2
Wrangway Somset 20 H9
Wrantage Somset 21 M9
Wrawby N Linc 79 P2
Wraxall N Som 28 G8
Wraxall Somset 22 D6
Wraxall Somset 22 D6
Wray Lancs 83 N2
Wraysbury W & M 32 E7
Wrayton Lancs 89 P12
Wrea Green Lancs 83 J9
Wreakes End Cumb 88 H9
Wreay Cumb 98 E9
Wreay Cumb 98 E11
Wrecclesham Surrey 25 P4
Wrekenton Gatesd 100 H6
Wrelton N York 92 F9
Wrenbury Ches E 64 B4
Wrench Green N York 93 K9
Wreningham Norfk 70 H12
Wrentham Suffk 59 P4
Wrenthorpe Wakefd 85 L10
Wrentnall Shrops 63 M11
Wressle E R Yk 86 D9
Wressle N Linc 79 N2
Wrestlingworth C Beds 56 E11
Wretton N Linc 69 N12
Wrexham Wrexhm 63 K2
Wrexham Industrial Estate Wrexhm 63 L2
Wribbenhall Worcs 52 E5
Wrickton Shrops 52 B3
Wrightington Bar Lancs 75 P1
Wright's Green Essex 45 P7
Wrinehill Staffs 64 D3
Wrington N Som 28 G9
Writhlington BaNES 22 F2
Writtle Essex 46 B10
Wrockwardine Wrekin 64 B9
Wroot N Linc 78 H3
Wrose C Brad 85 J8
Wrotham Kent 33 R10
Wrotham Heath Kent 34 B10
Wrottesley Staffs 64 F12
Wroughton Swindn 30 D6
Wroxall IoW 13 J9
Wroxall Warwks 53 N6
Wroxeter Shrops 63 P10
Wroxham Norfk 71 L8
Wroxton Oxon 43 J3
Wyaston Derbys 65 M4
Wyatt's Green Essex 33 Q2
Wyberton Lincs 68 F4
Wyboston Bed 56 C9
Wybunbury Ches E 64 C2
Wychbold Worcs 52 G7
Wych Cross E Susx 15 M4
Wychnor Staffs 65 M9
Wychwood Ches E 64 C2
Wyck Hants 25 N5
Wyck Rissington Gloucs 42 D7
Wycliffe Dur 91 J4
Wycoller Lancs 84 D7
Wycomb Leics 67 K7
Wycombe Marsh Bucks 32 C4
Wyddial Herts 45 L5
Wye Kent 17 J1
Wyesham Mons 40 H9
Wyfordby Leics 67 K8
Wyke Devon 8 H5
Wyke Dorset 22 F8
Wyke Shrops 64 C11
Wyke Surrey 32 C12
Wyke Champflower Somset 22 F6
Wykeham N York 93 K10
Wyken Covtry 54 B4
Wyken Shrops 52 E2
Wyke Regis Dorset 10 G9
Wykey Shrops 63 L7
Wykin Leics 54 C2
Wylam Nthumb 100 E5
Wylde Green Birm 53 L2
Wylye Wilts 23 M6
Wymeswold Leics 66 G7
Wymington Bed 55 N8
Wymondham Leics 67 L8
Wymondham Norfk 70 G12
Wyndham Brdgnd 27 M4
Wynford Eagle Dorset 10 F5
Wynyard Park S on T 91 Q2
Wynyard Village S on T 91 P1
Wyre Piddle Worcs 52 H11
Wysall Notts 66 G7
Wyson Herefs 51 N7
Wythall Worcs 53 K6
Wythall Green Worcs 53 K6
Wythburn Cumb 89 H10
Wythenshawe Manch 76 F6
Wythop Mill Cumb 97 N12
Wyton Cambs 56 F6
Wyton E R Yk 87 M8
Wyton on the Hill Cambs 56 F6
Wyverstone Suffk 58 F7
Wyverstone Street Suffk 58 F7
Wyville Lincs 67 L6

Y

Yaddlethorpe N Linc 79 M2
Yafford IoW 12 G8
Yafforth N York 91 N9
Yalberton Torbay 5 P5
Yalding Kent 34 C12
Yanwath Cumb 89 N3
Yanworth Gloucs 42 C9
Yapham E R Yk 86 E5
Yapton W Susx 14 D10
Yarborough N Som 28 E10
Yarbridge IoW 13 K7
Yarburgh Lincs 80 H5

Yarcombe Devon 9 N3
Yard Devon 19 P9
Yardley Birm 53 L3
Yardley Gobion Nhants 43 Q3
Yardley Hastings Nhants 55 L9
Yardley Wood Birm 53 L5
Yardro Powys 50 H9
Yarford Somset 21 K7
Yarkhill Herefs 41 J3
Yarley Somset 22 C4
Yarlington Somset 22 E7
Yarm S on T 91 P4
Yarmouth IoW 12 F7
Yarnacott Devon 19 M7
Yarnbrook Wilts 23 J2
Yarner Devon 8 F8
Yarnfield Staffs 64 F6
Yarnscombe Devon 19 L8
Yarnton Oxon 43 K9
Yarpole Herefs 51 N7
Yarrow Border 107 K4
Yarrow Somset 21 M4
Yarrow Feus Border 107 J5
Yarrowford Border 107 L4
Yarsop Herefs 40 F2
Yarwell Nhants 55 Q1
Yate S Glos 29 L6
Yateley Hants 32 B9
Yatesbury Wilts 30 C8
Yattendon W Berk 31 L7
Yatton Herefs 51 M7
Yatton N Som 28 F9
Yatton Keynell Wilts 29 N7
Yaverland IoW 13 K7
Yawl Devon 9 Q6
Yawthorpe Lincs 79 M5
Yaxham Norfk 70 E10
Yaxley Cambs 56 D2
Yaxley Suffk 58 G6
Yazor Herefs 40 E2
Yeading Gt Lon 32 G6
Yeadon Leeds 85 J7
Yealand Conyers Lancs 89 N11
Yealand Redmayne Lancs 89 N11
Yealand Storrs Lancs 89 M11
Yealmbridge Devon 5 J6
Yealmpton Devon 5 J6
Yearby R & Cl 92 C2
Yearngill Cumb 97 N9
Yearsley N York 92 C11
Yeaton Shrops 63 M8
Yeaveley Derbys 65 M4
Yeavering Nthumb 108 E4
Yedingham N York 92 H11
Yelford Oxon 42 H10
Yell Shet 147 J4
Yelland Devon 19 J7
Yelling Cambs 56 E8
Yelvertoft Nhants 54 F6
Yelverton Devon 5 J4
Yelverton Norfk 71 L11
Yenston Somset 22 G9
Yeoford Devon 8 E6
Yeolmbridge Cnwll 7 L6
Yeo Mill Devon 20 C7
Yeo Vale Devon 18 H8
Yeovil Somset 22 D10
Yeovil Marsh Somset 22 D9
Yeovilton Somset 22 D8
Yerbeston Pembks 37 L8
Yesnaby Ork 147 B4
Yetlington Nthumb 108 G8
Yetminster Dorset 10 F3
Yetson Devon 5 N5
Yettington Devon 9 K7
Yetts o'Muckhart Clacks 115 J12
Yews Green C Brad 84 G9
Yew Tree Sandw 53 J2
Y Felinheli Gwynd 73 J12
Y Ferwig Cerdgn 48 C10
Y Fôr Gwynd 60 F7
Yielden Bed 55 P7
Yieldingtree Worcs 52 G5
Yieldshields S Lans 114 F11
Y Nant Wrexhm 63 J3
Ynys Gwynd 61 K5
Ynysboeth Rhondd 27 P3
Ynysddu Caerph 28 A4
Ynysforgan Swans 26 G2
Ynyshir Rhondd 27 N4
Ynyslas Cerdgn 49 K2
Ynysmaerdy Rhondd 27 N5
Ynysmeudwy Neath 38 H10
Ynystawe Swans 26 G2
Ynyswen Powys 39 K9
Ynyswen Rhondd 27 M3
Ynysybwl Rhondd 27 P3
Ynysymaengwyn Gwynd 61 K11
Yockenthwaite N York 90 E11
Yockleton Shrops 63 L9
Yokefleet E R Yk 86 F10
Yoker C Glas 113 P7
York York 86 B5
York Lancs 83 Q8
Yorkletts Kent 35 K9
Yorkley Gloucs 41 K9
Yorkshire Dales National Park 90 E11
York Town Surrey 32 B10
Yorton Heath Shrops 63 N7
Youlgreave Derbys 77 N11
Youlthorpe E R Yk 86 E4
Youlton N York 85 P3
Youngsbury Herts 45 L9
Young's End Essex 46 C8
Yoxall Staffs 65 L9
Yoxford Suffk 59 N7
Y Rhiw Gwynd 60 C8
Ysbyty Cynfyn Cerdgn 49 N5
Ysbyty Ifan Conwy 61 P2
Ysbyty Ystwyth Cerdgn 49 M6
Ysceifiog Flints 74 G9
Ysgubor-y-Coed Cerdgn 49 L2
Ystalyfera Neath 39 J10
Ystrad Rhondd 27 M3
Ystrad Aeron Cerdgn 49 J3
Ystradfellte Powys 39 J2
Ystrad Ffin Carmth 49 P3
Ystradgynlais Powys 39 J9
Ystrad Meurig Cerdgn 49 M7
Ystrad Mynach Caerph 27 P5
Ystradowen Carmth 38 H9
Ystradowen V Glam 27 N7
Ystumtuen Cerdgn 49 M5
Ythanbank Abers 141 M11
Ythanwells Abers 140 G8
Ythsie Abers 141 M9

Z

Zeal Monachorum Devon 8 D4
Zeals Wilts 22 H7
Zelah Cnwll 3 K4
Zennor Cnwll 2 C7
Zoar Cnwll 3 J10
Zouch Notts 66 E7
ZSL London Zoo Gt Lon 33 K5
ZSL Whipsnade Zoo C Beds 44 E8